EARTH LAW

EMERGING ECOCENTRIC LAW—A GUIDE FOR PRACTITIONERS

Aspen Coursebook Series

EARTH LAW

EMERGING ECOCENTRIC LAW—A GUIDE FOR PRACTITIONERS

Anthony R. Zelle, Grant Wilson, Rachelle Adam, Herman F. Greene

editors

Wolters Kluwer

Published by Wolters Kluwer in New York.

Wolters Kluwer Legal & Regulatory U.S. serves customers worldwide with CCH, Aspen Publishers, and Kluwer Law International products. (www.WKLegaledu.com)

Cover Image: Fiorella Ikeue.

To contact Customer Service, e-mail customer.service@wolterskluwer.com, call 1-800-234-1660, fax 1-800-901-9075, or mail correspondence to:

Wolters Kluwer
Attn: Order Department
PO Box 990
Frederick, MD 21705

Printed in the United States of America.

2 3 4 5 6 7 8 9 0

ISBN 978-1-5438-2068-3

Library of Congress Cataloging-in-Publication Data
Names: Zelle, Anthony R., editor. | Wilson, Grant, 1957- editor. | Adam, Rachelle, 1951- editor. | Greene, Herman F., editor.
Title: Earth law : emerging ecocentric law : a guide for practitioners / Anthony R. Zelle, Grant Wilson, Rachelle Adam, Herman F. Greene, editors.
Description: New York : Wolters Kluwer, [2021] | Series: Aspen coursebook series | Includes bibliographical references and index. | Summary: "This book is a collaborative effort by more than twenty law school professors and thought leaders across the globe. In addition to providing a text for a semester-long classroom curriculum, the book will include a compendium of ecocentric law that will serve as a comprehensive reference for practitioners"— Provided by publisher.
Identifiers: LCCN 2020030468 (print) | LCCN 2020030469 (ebook) | ISBN 9781543820683 (paperback) | ISBN 9781543820690 (ebook)
Subjects: LCSH: Environmental law | Natural resources—Law and legislation | Environmental law—United States. | Environmental law—Latin America. | Environmental law, International.
Classification: LCC K3585 .E24 2021 (print) | LCC K3585 (ebook) | DDC 344.04/6—dc23
LC record available at https://lccn.loc.gov/2020030468
LC ebook record available at https://lccn.loc.gov/2020030469

About Wolters Kluwer Legal & Regulatory U.S.

Wolters Kluwer Legal & Regulatory U.S. delivers expert content and solutions in the areas of law, corporate compliance, health compliance, reimbursement, and legal education. Its practical solutions help customers successfully navigate the demands of a changing environment to drive their daily activities, enhance decision quality and inspire confident outcomes.

Serving customers worldwide, its legal and regulatory portfolio includes products under the Aspen Publishers, CCH Incorporated, Kluwer Law International, ftwilliam.com and MediRegs names. They are regarded as exceptional and trusted resources for general legal and practice-specific knowledge, compliance and risk management, dynamic workflow solutions, and expert commentary.

To the Earth, in gratitude for the home you provide for us, the sustenance you give us, the magnificent beauty with which you surround us, and for your wondrous diversity of life and life supporting systems.
We are dedicated to protect you.

SUMMARY OF CONTENTS

CONTENTS

Chapter 5: Standing 123

SECTION FIVE

A GLOBAL SURVEY OF EARTH LAW

ACKNOWLEDGMENTS

This book is the work of many lawyers, teachers, thought leaders, researchers, and proponents of the developing body of Earth law. Wolters Kluwer offered the opportunity to write this book to the Earth Law Center ("ELC") and this is the opportunity for ELC to express its gratitude, beginning with our colleagues from Wolters Kluwer, David Herzig, Betsy Farrell, and Jordan Jepsen.

Next, ELC acknowledges its board and staff who brought this project to life, nurtured it, and gifted it to the legal community: Grant Wilson, our Executive and Legal Director, Michelle Bender, our Ocean Rights Manager, and my fellow board members, Darlene Lee, Elise Garcia, Rellie Seville, Herman Greene, and Rachelle Adam. My depth of appreciation for my fellow editors, Herman, Rachelle, and Grant, is unfathomable.

ELC is particularly grateful as well for the contribution of Peter Heap, who through his determined copy editing of the entire book was no less than essential to its completion. We are also grateful for Jordan Michelson, who was instrumental at the outset in developing the topical structure for this book.

We express our gratitude as well for the cover art, by Fiorella Ikeue, which so expressively depicts nature's place in the courtroom.

The insight, expertise, and vision of the authors is remarkable, and they will surely continue to develop Earth law, in practice as well as in theory. ELC thanks:

- Rachelle Adam, Faculty of Law, Hebrew University, Jerusalem (Chapters 10 & 22)
- Yann Aguila, a partner at Bredin Prat, Paris, and chair of the Environmental Law Commission of the Club des Juristes (Chapter 15)
- Camila Bustos, J.D. candidate at Yale Law School (Chapter 18)
- Roger Chennells, founding partner of Chennells Albertyn Attorneys, Stellenbosch, South Africa (Chapter 24)
- *Taita* Hernando Chindoy, an indigenous traditional authority of the Inga People of Colombia, and a university expert on indigenous issues, Universidad Carlos III, Madrid, 2013 (Chapter 25)
- Andrew Cliburn, legal volunteer, Earth Law Center (Chapter 2)
- Cormac Cullinan, director of the Wild Law Institute, chief executive officer of EnAct International, an environmental governance consultancy, and director of Cullinan & Associates Cape Town (Afterword)
- Elizabeth Dunne, attorney at Dunne Law, Honolulu (Chapter 9)
- Earth Law Center, a US-based organization that works to transform the law to recognize and protect nature's inherent rights to exist, thrive, and evolve (Chapters 1 & 20)

- Hugo Echeverria, professor of law at the University of San Francisco, Quito, and a rights of nature attorney in Ecuador (Chapter 17)
- Bedirhan Erdem, Ph.D. candidate and research assistant of criminal law and criminal procedure law at the I.D. Bilkent University Faculty of Law, Ankara, Turkey (Chapter 12)
- The Gaia Foundation, a UK-based organization that works to revive bio-cultural diversity, to regenerate healthy ecosystems and to strengthen community self-governance for climate change resilience in Africa, South America, Asia, and Europe (Chapter 24)
- Shehana Gomez, associate lecturer at the Open University, London, and co-convener of the UK Environmental Law Association's wild law special interest group (Chapter 15)
- Herman Greene, president of the Center for Ecozoic Studies (Chapters 1, 2, 3 & 16)
- Noah Hall, professor of law at Wayne State University Law School (Chapter 7)
- Ted Hamilton, attorney and co-founder of Climate Defense Project (Chapters 4 & 13)
- Craig M. Kauffman, Ph.D., associate professor of Political Science at the University of Oregon (Chapter 6)
- Zachary Klein, law fellow at the National Sea Grant Law Center (Chapters 4 & 13)
- Reed Loder, professor of law at Vermont Law School (Chapter 14)
- Lance N. Long, professor of law at Stetson University College of Law (Chapter 13)
- Catherine Iorns Magallanes, BA, LL.B. (Hons) Well, LL.M. Yale; professor of law at Victoria University of Wellington, New Zealand (Chapter 22)
- Michelle Maloney, co-founder and national convenor of the Australian Earth Laws Alliance (Chapter 2)
- Julio Prieto Méndez, lawyer for the Union of the people affected by Texaco (UDAPT) (Chapter 17)
- Uur Orhan, Ph.D. candidate and research assistant of criminal law and criminal procedure law at the I.D. Bilkent University Faculty of Law, Ankara (Chapter 12)
- Dalit Paradis, Earth law associate, Earth Law Center (Chapter 2)
- Raúl Gutiérrez Patiño, professor of law at the Universidad Iberoamericana, Mexico City (Chapter 19)
- Alessandro Pelizzon, senior lecturer at Southern Cross University School of Law and Justice (Chapter 3)
- Nikoletta Pikramenou, a human rights and gender expert and political participation monitoring coordinator at Make Every Woman Count (Chapter 19)
- Valentijn Punt, pro bono attorney, Earth Law Center (Chapter 23)
- Whitney Richardson, a social science researcher who focuses on human rights and environmental politics (Chapter 18)
- Iván Darío Vargas Roncancio, M.Sc., and Ph.D. candidate in natural resource sciences and fellow of the Leadership for the Ecozoic Program at McGill University, Toronto (Chapter 25)
- Stacy Jane Schaefer, associate director of land conservation at the Maryland Department of Natural Resources (Chapter 8)

- Kevin R. Schneider executive director of the Nonhuman Rights Project (Chapter 11)
- Lindsey Schromen-Wawrin, attorney at Shearwater Law PLLC and member of the city council, Port Angeles, Washington (Chapter 9)
- Margaret R. Stewart, director of the Center of Earth Jurisprudence at Barry University Dwayne O. Andreas School of Law (Chapter 1)
- Grant Wilson, executive director and directing attorney, Earth Law Center (Chapter 2)
- Mary Christina Wood, Philip H. Knight professor of law and faculty director, Environmental and Natural Resources Law Center, University of Oregon School of Law (Foreword)

ELC also thanks the following for granting permission to excerpt their work:

- Berry, Thomas. Ten principles for the Revision of Jurisprudence, from Evening Thoughts: Reflecting on Earth as Sacred Community. Counterpoint Press (2006).
- Carter, Keala & "Coyote" Alberto Ruz Buenfil, Towards a New Jurisprudence of the Earth, ESPERANZA PROJECT (Feb. 23, 2017).
- Earth Law Center, Fighting for Our Shared Future, Protecting Human Rights and Nature's Rights (2015), https://www.earthlawcenter.org/co-violations-of-rights.
- Global Witness, At What Cost? Irresponsible Business and the Murder of Land and Environmental Defenders in 2017, 12 (2018).
- Global Alliance for The Rights of Nature, Peoples' Sustainability Treaty on Rights of Mother Earth, https://sustainabilitytreaties.org/draft-treaties/rights-of-mother-earth. (637) (Global Alliance for The Rights of Nature).
- Houck, Oliver A., Why Do We Protect Endangered Species, And What Does That Say About Whether Restrictions on Private Property To Protect Them Constitute "Takings", 80 Iowa Law Review 297. Reprinted with permission of Iowa Law Review via CCC (1995).
- Ikerd, John, Deep Sustainability; Rediscovering Our Connectedness, ABOUT PLACE JOURNAL, https://aboutplacejournal.org/issues/voices/section-1/john-ikerd.
- Phelan, Joseph, *Purvi & Chuck: Community Lawyering*, ORGANIZING UPGRADE (June 1, 2010), archive.organizingupgrade.com/index.php/modules-menu/community-organizing/item/71-purvi-amp-chuck-community-lawyering [perma.cc/4UK4-57WU].
- Singer, Joseph William, Sovereignty and Property, 86 NW. U.L. Rev. 1, 18-10-50-51. Northwest University Law Review (1990-1992).
- Stone, Christopher, Should Trees Have Standing—Toward Legal Rights for Natural Objects, 45 S. Cal. L. Rev., 450 (1972).
- United Nations, Sustainable Development Goals Report 2019, United Nations, https://unstats.un.org/sdgs/report/2019.
- Wood, Mary, Nature's Trust. Cambridge University Press (2014).

- Thelmadatter, Leigh, Voicing the Concerns of Mexico's Indigenous People, In their Own Language, MEXICO DAILY NEWS (Mar. 4, 2020).
- Rachelle Adam, Finding Safe Passage through a Wave of Extinctions: Israel's Endangered Mountain Gazelle, 19 J. OF INTL. WILDLIFE L. & POLY. 136-158, 136, 137, 147, 148, 149, 150-151, 157 (2016).

Beyond the direct contributors to the book, we acknowledge two extraordinarily important sources of this casebook's materials. First, we acknowledge Indigenous peoples around the world, who have lived in harmony with nature since time immemorial. Their understanding that nature is alive, is the creator of the human species, and must be respected as such, is foundational to the concepts explored in this casebook. Second, we acknowledge Thomas Berry, whose development of Earth jurisprudence has inspired the work of a new generation of lawyers. This coursebook will help put his vision into practice.

Beyond humans, we acknowledge Earth and all its wondrous life and life systems. It is our hope that this coursebook will help promote the development of law that has as its primary concern the restoration of Earth's health and well-being in all its vast and rich diversity.

Finally, dozens of other individuals worked as volunteers to make this book a success. Here are only a few:

Epiphany Alexander	Joyce Bennett	Hannah Borowski
Carlotta Byrne	Jyoti Chaudhari	Clint Cogburn
Consolata Enobakhare	Consolata Enobakhare	Elizabeth Farrell
Constanza Prieto Figelist	Odaria Finemore	David Herzig
Oliver Houck	Mumta Ito	Myra L. Jackson
Devon Kearney	Jan Laitos	Lok Leung
Victoria Lichet	Thomas Lopez	Addison Luck
Christopher Marchesano	Liane McCory	Marsha Moutrie
Alex Pelizzon	Falisha Pierre	Whitney Richardson
Sumangali Rudrakumar	Patricia Siemen	Camelia Stanciu
Sarah Stoughton	Nikita Tanwar	Yasmeen Taylor
Falisha Walcott	Ruihan (Yvette) Wang	Allec Willis

With the utmost respect and gratitude,

Anthony R. Zelle

Editor-in-Chief
President, Earth Law Center

FOREWORD

Mary Christina Wood[1]

We have thrown the planet we inhabit violently out of balance. Humanity's disregard for nature's laws glares through razed forests, vanished species, acidified oceans, polluted rivers, and cascading climate catastrophes. The annihilatory trajectory of industrial civilization over the last seventy years threatens to trigger Earth's sixth mass extinction — the kind that has not occurred since the death of the dinosaurs 65 million years ago. Should the assaults persist even for a few more years, future humanity and other species for untold generations will face a hellish struggle to survive while pummeled by floods, hurricanes, heat waves, fires, disease, crop losses, food shortages, drought, and sea level rise. In *The Bridge at the Edge of the World,* Gus Speth puts it simply: "[W]e're headed toward a ruined planet."[2] And time is not on our side to reverse course. With greenhouse gases flooding the planet's atmosphere, we face an urgency in which to act before crossing climate tripwires poised to send the planet into a state of runaway heating.

So, here we are. We are the granules of sand falling through a minute glass between two worlds — our past world in which nature supported life in infinite ways, and a potential hellish world ahead filled with global chaos and devastation leading to humanity's own self-destruction. One may reasonably ask: Where is environmental law in this apocalyptic picture?

Environmental law helped deliver this ecological emergency to our planet's doorstep.

The Failure of Environmental Law

In the United States, statutes passed five decades ago were supposed to reverse the arc of destruction that was obvious even then. The U.S. Congress passed the Clean Water Act, the Clean Air Act, the Endangered Species Act, the Toxic Substances Control Act, and a multitude of other laws to prohibit environmental harm. This legal model was considered so promising that countries throughout the world emulated it in their legal systems. A burgeoning set of bureaucracies gained authority and funding to carry

[1] Philip H. Knight Professor of Law and Faculty Director, Environmental and Natural Resources Law Center, University of Oregon School of Law, and author of NATURE'S TRUST: ENVIRONMENTAL LAW FOR A NEW ECOLOGICAL AGE (2013). Footnote citations herein are minimal, referring to the work or case as a whole and not to referenced page numbers.

[2] JAMES GUSTAVE SPETH, THE BRIDGE AT THE EDGE OF THE WORLD: CAPITALISM, THE ENVIRONMENT, AND CROSSING FROM CRISIS TO SUSTAINABILITY x (2008).

out the laws. Yet, as agencies became captured by politically powerful interests, the system as a whole degenerated into a monumental failure. The dysfunction now operates on a dangerous, systemic, global level.

Statutes characteristically vest agencies with breathtaking authority and discretion to issue permits allowing the very harms that the laws were designed to prevent. If the agencies were intent on protecting ecosystems and the public in carrying out the laws, they would use their authority to prevent damage. But instead, with few exceptions, agencies operate in alliance with politically powerful corporations and profiteers, using the permit system to legalize massive destruction in the form of oil and gas drilling, coal mining, toxic water pollution, forest clearcutting, habitat eradication, and other injuries too numerous to inventory. Today, rather than organizing an emergency response to an existential climate threat, environmental agencies push the destruction even more, bringing the world to the edge of the climate precipice. Elizabeth Kolbert says, "It may seem impossible to imagine that a technologically advanced society could choose, in essence, to destroy itself, but that is what we are now in the process of doing."[3] Environmental law now serves as the cane on which humanity leans as it walks the plank toward its own destruction.

The Judicial Role in Climate Emergency

In the United States, the President holds power never contemplated by the Founders — the power to push America, other countries, and a vast part of the natural creation over the climate cliff. In this time of extreme climate danger — when the Secretary-General of the United Nations implores nations to slash carbon emissions 45% by 2030 to avert *runaway* planetary heating[4] that would leave Earth largely uninhabitable[5]— President Trump uses his agencies' statutory authority under environmental laws to promote massive domestic fossil fuel development, consumption, and exportation. The United States has expanded oil and gas production four times faster than any other nation and now leads the world in both.[6] Environmental law is affirmatively legalizing these actions.

In 2009, President Obama's science advisor warned that the climate situation was like being "in a car with bad brakes driving towards a cliff in the fog."[7] President Trump, showing frenzied intent, now floors the accelerator with the world's children,

[3] Elizabeth Kolbert, Field Notes from a Catastrophe: Man, Nature, and Climate Change 189 (2006).

[4] Carolyn Beeler, *Why 2020 is a Key Year for Climate Action*, PRI (Sept. 17, 2019), https://www.pri.org/stories/2019-09-17/why-2020-key-year-climate-action.

[5] *See generally* David Wallace-Wells The Uninhabitable Earth: Life After Warming (2019).

[6] The United States surpassed Russia in 2011 to become the world's largest producer of natural gas and surpassed Saudi Arabia in 2018 to become the world's largest producer of petroleum. U.S. Energy Information Administration, *The U.S. Leads Global Petroleum and Natural Gas Production with Record Growth in 2018* (August 20, 2019), https://www.eia.gov/todayinenergy/detail.php?id=40973.

[7] *Obama to Look at Climate Engineering*, The Wall Street Journal (April 8, 2009), https://www.wsj.com/articles/SB123920773503201665.

future generations, and other species on Earth trapped in the back seat. The 16-year old climate revolutionary Greta Thunberg implores, "Pull the emergency brake."[8]

Courts have authority to do just that through their powers of injunctive and declaratory relief. As the third constitutional branch of government, the core duty of the judiciary is to protect fundamental rights. In the landmark case, *Juliana v. United States,*[9] 21 American youth ask the courts to step into the climate emergency before it is too late to save their prospects of future survival and well-being. Challenging the entire system of federal fossil fuel policy as violating their Constitutional rights to life, liberty and property under the Due Process Clause and the venerable Public Trust Principle,[10] the young plaintiffs seek a court-supervised federal plan to shrink the nation's carbon footprint at a rate necessary to stave off disastrous levels of climate change. The youth won a landmark victory in the District Court of Oregon in 2016 when Judge Ann Aiken ruled that plaintiffs had a constitutional right to a "climate system capable of sustaining human life."[11] But an ensuing appellate opinion bears the marks of environmental law's Dark Ages.

On review, two judges of a three-judge Ninth Circuit panel acknowledged that the U.S. government's fossil fuel policies present a threat capable of destroying the nation, but said that courts can do nothing about it.[12] Quoting the song, "Eve of Destruction," Judge Andrew Hurwitz (writing for himself and Judge Mary Murguia) decided that the courts have no role in stopping the government from hastening an "environmental apocalypse" — one capable of burying cities, unleashing life-threatening disasters, and jeopardizing crucial food and water sources. Judges Hurwitz and Murguia did not refute that the young plaintiffs hold constitutional rights to a stable climate system. They observed that atmospheric carbon levels have "skyrocketed to levels not seen for almost three million years," and emphasized the crisis is "approaching the 'point of no return.'" They recognized that the growth of U.S. fossil fuel development "shows no signs of abating" in spite of government's longstanding knowledge that carbon dioxide emissions can cause "catastrophic climate change." Yet, in face of these surreal prospects, Judges Hurwitz and Murguia "reluctantly" concluded that courts have no role in putting brakes on the federal government's fossil fuel scheme. They said that climate policy is a matter for the legislative and executive branches—the same

[8] *Greta Thurnberg's Speech to the World*, Geneva Business News, December 21, 2018, https://www.gbnews.ch/greta-thunbergs-speech-to-the-world/ (providing transcript of Thurnberg's address to the UN COP24 climate talks in Poland in 2018).

[9] For court filings and orders in the case, see Our Children's Trust, https://www.ourchildrenstrust.org/court-orders-and-pleadings.

[10] Under this principle, the sovereign in some manner holds in trust the natural resources of its jurisdiction for the benefit of present and future generations of the public regardless of private ownership.

[11] Juliana v. United States, 217 F. Supp. 3d 1224 (D. Or. 2016), https://static1.squarespace.com/static/571d109b04426270152febe0/t/5824e85e6a49638292ddd1c9/1478813795912/Order+MTD.Aiken.pdf, reversed 947F.3d 1159 (9th Cir. 2020), petition en banc filed March 2, 2020).

[12] Juliana v. United States, 947 F.3d 1159 (9th Cir. 2020), available at https://static1.squarespace.com/static/571d109b04426270152febe0/t/5e22101b7a850a06acdff1bc/1579290663460/2020.01.17+JULIANA+OPINION.pdf, petition en banc filed March 2, 2020. *See* Michael C. Blumm and Mary Christina Wood, *The Dramatic Dismissal of a Landmark Youth Climate Lawsuit Might Not Close the Book on that Case*, The Conversation (Jan. 23, 2020), http://theconversation.com/the-dramatic-dismissal-of-a-landmark-youth-climate-lawsuit-might-not-close-the-book-on-that-case-130162.

branches that created this climate cataclysm. The young plaintiffs have appealed to the full Ninth Circuit asking for *en banc* review by the full panel of 11 judges.

When a fundamental right has no remedy, there is no justice. The majority's *Juliana* opinion embraces a judicial approach that Professor Douglas Kysar and James Weaver call judicial "nihilism"—rejecting their extensive power, the courts "cower before catastrophe."[13] This judicial timorousness has been the pattern over the past few decades as judges have repeatedly analyzed ecological harms through the narrow lens of statutory claims and have reflexively deferred to the agencies on the grounds that they alone hold the expertise necessary to carry out the public interest. As obeisance to the political branches grew, the courts, which had sometimes courageously acted in areas of civil rights, abdicated their constitutional role as the guardian of fundamental rights with respect to the environment despite acknowledging clear and present danger of a climate apocalypse.

Still brave voices stir in the judicial branch. In a scholarly and poignant dissent to the majority's *Juliana* opinion, Judge Josephine Staton countered: "It is as if an asteroid were barreling toward Earth and the government decided to shut down our only defenses. [T]he government bluntly insists that it has the absolute and unreviewable power to destroy the Nation. My colleagues throw up their hands, concluding that this case presents nothing fit for the Judiciary." Delving deeply into the purpose and structure of the U.S. Constitution, she found an embedded "perpetuity principle" obliging courts to prevent the other branches from bringing the nation to its demise. In face of "an existential crisis to the country's perpetuity," Judge Staton's opinion forcefully challenges judges in the United States and elsewhere to choose a side of history: "When the seas envelop our coastal cities, fires and droughts haunt our interiors, and storms ravage everything between, those remaining will ask: Why did so many do so little?"

The Paradigm Shift

Law mediates the struggle between power unjustly wielded and moral truth. It is a system that defines reasonable outcomes. The searing reality of our moment will cause judges around the world to redefine their roles. As they do, one thing is clear: legal reform cannot tinker around the edges of the failed regime of statutory environmental law and practice. That regime lacks ideas truly calibrated to the magnitude of the problem and the roaring pace of change. At this late date, tweaking the law becomes a fool's errand by throwing out a rescue rope that is too short. Even if there were time to accomplish massive regulatory reform, the system as a whole is dysfunctional. The entire paradigm of ecological responsibility must change, and the power of governance must recalibrate before environmental tyranny takes permanent hold. Courts remain

[13] R. Henry Weaver & Douglas A. Kysar, *Courting Disaster: Climate Change and the Adjudication of Catastrophe*, 93 NOTRE DAME L. REV. 295 (2017), http://ndlawreview.org/wp-content/uploads/2017/11/7.-Weaver-Kysar.pdf.

singularly positioned, through their constitutionally vested authority, to rein in government actors and redirect them to protect fundamental rights.

A new legal paradigm must be articulated, examined, rigorously critiqued, and proposed. Then, positioned at the edges of the old destructive regime, it must impart the inspiration needed to animate key moments of transformation, drawing law into the epochal task of restoring vital ecology.

Earth Law: Emerging Ecocentric Law—A Guide for Practitioners (Earth Law) pulls together the most promising jurisprudential and legal approaches world-wide aimed at harmonizing human existence with the natural world. It is a must-read for judges, lawyers, and students who not only want to understand, but also respond meaningfully to the central challenge of their fleeting moment in history. As is often said, we are the first generation to understand the impending cataclysmic consequences of our mode of development, and we are the last generation that will be able to do anything about it. Lawyers, through their advocacy, skill, and position in society, hold unparalleled potential to build new governance structures and operating rules. New ideas remain paramount to this epic endeavor. We need, as Gus Speth says, a "fresh conceptualization and a new way of thinking. . . ."[14] Ecological paradigms will present a vision of co-responsibility and reciprocity among nations, societies, corporations, and nature, and robust and practical legal footholds by which citizens can hold government officials and members of society accountable. New values will power a global assertion of rights and duties in defense of humanity, fellow species, and all future generations of life on Earth.

This book gathers, distills, and analyzes pioneering approaches in law — for the Earth and for our time. It is an assemblage of approaches, not a system. *Earth Law* takes the reader around the world, from the Colombia Supreme Court which recognized bio-cultural constitutional rights of Atrato Basin communities in their battle against toxic mining; to India's Supreme Court which announced a right of glaciers to exist; to the Federal District Court of Oregon (presiding over *Juliana v. United States*) where Judge Ann Aiken declared for the first time in U.S. history an American environmental constitutional right to a "climate system capable of sustaining human life;" and to the Washington Court of Appeals in the United States where a panel of judges found that Ken Ward has a constitutional right to assert the "necessity defense" to justify his peaceful climate civil disobedience when he illegally entered a Kinder Morgan pipeline facility and shut down tar sands oil entering the United States. Compiling a multitude of other cases as well as recent statutes, *Earth Law* anchors these innovative approaches in the shared human experience and transcendental ecological reality of our times. This is a textbook about ideas and what is possible; it cannot help but inspire and guide present and future practitioners.

If there is hope that law will respond to the environmental crisis, it is a hope lodged in a diversity of ideas, realizing that one singular solution does not hold all of the answers. All over the world, judges, legislators, lawyers, and citizens are pioneering new concepts and tools adapted to vastly different bioregions, cultures, and societies.

[14] Speth, *supra* note 2, at xiv.

The widely varying approaches presented in this book share four unifying themes that provide common ground for a truly global legal revolution.

Nature's Supreme Laws

All of the approaches recognize the need for recalibrating industrialized laws to the laws of nature. Indigenous leaders have taught since time immemorial that Nature's own laws rank supreme over human laws. Oren Lyons puts it this way: "The thing you have to understand about nature and natural law is, there's no mercy . . . There's only law. . . ."[15] In one fundamental respect, the most basic task of environmental law is to bring society into compliance with these laws of nature. But industrialized environmental law legalizes the rampant violation of these supreme laws not only at the level of individual species and ecosystems, but also at the level of atmospheric function, ocean health, and biodiversity — a truly planetary level. As Thomas Berry wrote,

> Only a self-destructive arrogance would enable a society to assume the rights to devastate what nature could bring into being but which no power in heaven or on Earth, not even nature herself, could remedy once destruction had taken place. . . .
>
> . . . We need legal structures and political establishments that will know that our way into the future is not through relentless industrial development but through the living forces that brought us into being and are the only forces that can sustain us in the coming centuries.[16]

Fundamental Rights

Earth law, as it continues to develop, will redefine and reorient environmental law as a realm of fundamental rights. These include human rights, civil rights, rights of dignity, biocultural rights of communities, rights to assert the necessity defense in climate civil disobedience cases, rights of nature (such as those increasingly accorded to rivers and wildlife), animal and non-human rights, and rights of present and future generations under the public trust principle to force government protection of the crucial resources supporting all life on Earth. Underlying all of these approaches is a basic reframing of environmental law to pull it out of the narrow confinements of current statutory provisions and connect it to a deeper and more legally forceful set of rights engrained (implicitly or explicitly) in constitutional frameworks.

This necessarily involves reformulation of legal assumptions that drive the law—above all those concerning property concepts. An entire body of Western law has developed around the assumption that nature belongs to humans and they are entitled to exploit, subjugate, and destroy its gifts and vitality. As Thomas Berry wrote, "This

[15] Wood, *supra* note 1, at 3 (quoting Oren Lyons).

[16] Thomas Berry, *Foreword to* Cormac Cullinan, Wild Law, A Manifesto for Earth Justice, at 19 & 21 (2d ed., 2011).

mechanistic world controlled by humans, for human advantage, saw the surrounding world as a vast assembly of natural resources put there for human use, not as manifestation of the sacred and sublime to be experienced in the wonder of its mountains and oceans, in the beauty of its meadows and birds and woodland creatures, in its healing of the loneliness of the human soul and the ills of the human body."[17] *Earth Law* brings to the forefront leading cases, such as the Colombia Supreme Court's *Atrato River* decision, which recognizes and invokes, after centuries of suppression, indigenous conceptions and instructions regarding nature. *Earth Law* also reports on "ecocide," which reverses the notion that nature is here for human use, even to the point of destruction, by criminalizing the eradication of nature.

Recalibrating Governance

Earth Law illuminates ways of recalibrating governance. Judicial authority is needed to break the power held by fortune and corruption, exercised with the support of legislative and executive branches through statutory laws permitting the devastation of air, oceans, forests, fisheries, wildlife, rivers, aquifers, lands, and countless human communities — or by statutory omission and permissive nonenforcement of laws that would prevent such devastation. The Netherlands Supreme Court is leading the way by ordering its government to reduce CO_2 emissions by 25% as compared with 1990 levels by the end of 2020.[18] In Pakistan, the High Court of Lahore created a climate commission. In Colombia, the court created a system of guardianship, supported by advisory commissions and expert panels, to protect the Atrato River.

When courts fail to create meaningful remedies to protect fundament rights, their passivity implicates them by omission in violations of rights they could prevent. As Douglas Kysar and Jim Weaver emphasize, "inaction can inflict a symmetric violence."[19] Judges must not allow the other branches of government to manipulate their constitutional and statutory powers to become environmental despots and bring the world to the "eve of destruction"... and beyond. Further, the public and conscientious legislators and administrators must not allow this. *Earth Law* provides examples of where constructive action is being taken and proposes ideas and principles in furtherance of ecocentric environmental governance.

Inspiring Transformation

Earth Law positions the law in the broader context of society, philosophy, and history, which it must do to provide any true reform. Law is a powerful organizing force in human society for better or worse. As Oliver Wendell Holmes famously wrote: "The law is the witness and external deposit of our moral life. Its history is the history of

[17] *Id.* at 17.
[18] Isabella Kaminski, *Dutch Supreme Court Upholds Landmark Ruling Demanding Climate Action,* THE GUARDIAN (Dec. 20, 2019), https://www.theguardian.com/world/2019/dec/20/dutch-supreme-court-upholds-landmark-ruling-demanding-climate-action.
[19] Weaver & Kysar, *supra* note 13, at 301.

the moral development of the race."[20] When the law feels untrue to our deepest sense of justice, it stings our collective soul and presses us towards reform.

As sentinels of the legal system, lawyers, judges, and lawmakers must take care to not quash the righteous sense of the citizens, but instead continually inspire and empower them to pursue justice. If these sentinels fail to attend to that spark of justice, they imperil democracy by dispensing despair, defeatism, and disempowerment—the breeding grounds of oppression and tyranny. The judicial system in the United States teeters precariously close to that point, such as in the *Juliana* Ninth Circuit majority's opinion in which two judges found there was no conceivable judicial remedy in face of an apocalyptic future directly propelled by the young plaintiffs' own government. As the dissenting Judge Staton wrote, "Where is the hope in today's decision? Plaintiffs' claims are based on science, specifically, an impending point of no return. If plaintiffs' fears, backed by the government's own studies prove true, history will not judge us kindly." By presenting cases in which courageous judges worldwide are developing jurisprudence to steer the world to safety and justice, *Earth Law* kindles the democratic impulse needed to bring new paradigms to fruition.

Earth Law throughout its pages invites practitioners and students as future practitioners to co-create this field using the resources it offers. It calls out to those resolute judges, lawyers, lawmakers, students, and citizens across the planet who refuse to relinquish their collective moment in time. This book will guide us all—as Earth's citizens —inclaiming this moment to stop the onslaught on Mother Earth and work with her to preserve a habitable planet for present and future generations of all species.

Earth Law comes to the world not a moment too soon.

[20] Oliver Wendell Holmes, Jr., *The Path of the Law*, 10 Harv. L. Rev. (1897), *reprinted in* 110 Harv. L. Rev. 991, 992 (1997).

INTRODUCTION

The Emergence of Ecocentric Law and Ideas for the Future of Environmental Law

Earth law is the body of law for protecting, restoring, and stabilizing the functional interdependency of Earth's life and life-support systems at the local, bioregional, national, and global levels. Earth law may be expressed in constitutional, statutory, common law, and customary law, as well as in treaties and other agreements both public and private.

The year 2020, the date of the first publication of this coursebook, is the 50th anniversary of the modern environmental movement. On April 22, 1970, 20 million people participated in the first Earth Day, and in that same year the U.S. Environmental Protection Agency came into being and the U.S. Clean Air Act was enacted. There followed myriad environmental laws and environmental protection agencies in countries around the world, as well as international environmental agreements. These developments were meant to halt the decline of the global environment. Yet, in 2008, James Gustave ("Gus") Speth, cofounder of the National Resources Defense Council and a leading advocate for the international environmental movement, sadly concluded:

> The environmental movement has grown in strength and sophistication, but the environment has continued to deteriorate. . . . How serious is the threat . . . ? [A]ll we have to do to destroy the planet's climate and biota and leave a ruined world to our children and grandchildren is to keep doing exactly what we are doing today. . . . But, of course, human activities are not holding at current levels—they are accelerating, dramatically."[1]

The situation has only grown worse since he penned these words.

This is a book for students and practicing lawyers who seek to preserve a habitable planet and question whether current environmental law is enough for the task. It is for students and lawyers who want to move beyond "exactly what we are doing

[1] JAMES GUSTAVE SPETH, THE BRIDGE AT THE EDGE OF THE WORLD x (2008).

today." They know nature and human environmental rights need to have seats at the table of law—in courts, legislatures, and administrative bodies.

Earth law is the emerging field of ecocentric environmental law that puts nature front and center. As described in this book, there are recently developed laws that do this and there will be more such laws because nature is putting herself front and center through climate change, dying coral reefs, sea level rise, stronger storms, forest fires, plastic and other pollution, water shortages, extinction of species, and many other ways. Humans are increasingly realizing nature counts, her bounty is not inexhaustible, and humans have duties to protect and restore her and develop sustainable, mutually enhancing relations with her.

It takes imagination and spirit to be an Earth lawyer. Can you imagine a world where a gorilla can sue a zoo? Where whales can sue for lack of krill? Where children can claim the right to a habitable planet? Where rivers are given legal personhood? Where all ecosystems have legal guardians? Where constitutions recognize and protect the rights of nature? Where governments maintain the resource base of society as a fundamental obligation? Where humans have legal obligations to maintain the health of soil? Where there are ecological courts? Where care for the health of the Earth community is a primary objective of law?

EARTH LAW WILL BE DEVELOPED IN PRACTICE

The subtitle of this book is "a guide for practitioners." As much as an educational foundation, this book is intended to serve as a guide for lawyers who, through their practices, will develop Earth law. Representing the Earth's interests doesn't fit the legal system as we know it. This book intends to give students some basic understanding of issues they will face in trying to pound a round peg into a square hole. Part of Earth law concerns pedagogy. Earth lawyers will not only be advocates; they will be teachers. This is not unusual in the practice of law. Educating judges, juries, legislators, and administrative decision-makers is a critical aspect of client representation. The educational burden is greater for Earth lawyers because there is little precedent for representing the interests of nature in the ways that will be needed in the next 50 years.

The material presented in this book is intended to enable lawyers to practice Earth law with realism and creativity. Many issues raised by the study of Earth law will not have readily apparent answers. Judges, lawmakers, policymakers, and others will find themselves engaged in a balancing of interests that may seem impossible. There are innumerable factors, interconnections, interrelations, and dynamics, many of which are unknown, that will challenge the generally accepted linear mode of legal thinking. While Earth lawyers must be constructive and work with their clients to obtain results within the law, at times they may find it beneficial to advocate legal positions for which there is no precedent when this yields opportunities to ask more questions and critique more deeply the issues at hand. An entire chapter of this book is devoted to conceptual frameworks to consider in the practice of Earth law. It alerts Earth lawyers to issues they may face and provides guidance for dealing with them.

Earth law is a developing body of both substantive and procedural law reflecting new understandings of the Earth systems' interdependencies and dynamics. In the past 50 years, environmental law has addressed the negative consequences of industrial development, including the destruction of nature and natural systems, generation of toxic waste, and adverse human health effects. While addressing the side effects, a primary objective of environmental law, akin to occupational safety law, has been to promote conventional industrial and commercial development by making it safer for humans. Earth law seeks to make human endeavor safe for nature as well as humans and for future generations of all species.

Since the inception of modern environmental law, new understandings have been gained that require a reevaluation of legal and social norms, including the following:

- The extent of human impact on Earth is orders of magnitude greater than anticipated;
- The scope and scale of issues considered to be environmental issues have vastly increased;
- Knowledge of ecology, biology, geology, evolutionary dynamics, and Earth systems is broader and deeper;
- Perspectives on the nature–culture divide have changed with greater awareness of how the human species is both a part of and the exceptional agent in relation to nonhuman nature;
- Understanding of sentience and consciousness in nonhuman animals has grown;[2]
- Scientific awareness of ecological limits, tipping points, and the potential for irreversible decline and catastrophic state shifts in Earth's functioning has increased;
- Climate change has emerged as a primary environmental concern; and
- Issues of North–South relations and global inequities have come to the fore.
- The Anthropocene Working Group of the International Commission of Stratigraphy has voted favorably on the question of whether the term "Anthropocene" should be treated as a formal chronostratigraphic unit (a strata of rock established to serve as the material reference for other sediment).[3]

People have come to understand that nature is not merely something humans live with or live from. Nature is something humans live within, and the human species is but one of many interrelated and interdependent components, all of which serve a purpose in the balance of biological life. A global movement has arisen to address sustainability and care for the Earth. It challenges the existing globalized system of economic development on which people depend for water, food, clothing, shelter,

[2] This awareness is reflected in law. See the cases discussed in the Chapter 11 on "Nonhuman Rights." See also *Gradually, Nervously, Courts Are Granting Rights to Animals*, The Economist (Dec. 22, 2018), https://www.economist.com/international/2018/12/22/gradually-nervously-courts-are-granting-rights-to-animals.
[3] Anthropocene Working Group of the International Commission on Stratigraphy, Results of Binding Vote (May 21, 2019), http://quaternary.stratigraphy.org/working-groups/anthropocene/.

energy, transportation, and jobs.[4] Current environmental law and practice have been unable to halt the degradation of Earth's life-support systems. Bringing Earth law into being will require transformational changes in the law and social norms, and its application will reflect and reinforce the increasingly urgent quests for human sustainability and a healthy Earth community.

EARTH LAW TAKES AN ECOCENTRIC APPROACH TO ENVIRONMENTAL LAW

Practicing Earth law will involve working with new ideas and ways of thinking that are not currently recognized in the legal system. This book will consider various proposals for making environmental law ecocentric. For example, Earth law may expand the legal community by giving nature juridical personhood and standing as a basis for adjudicating nature's rights and human obligations. Practicing Earth law will also require a strong application of the precautionary principle.[5] More broadly, Earth law necessitates reexamining entire areas of the law, such as property law, which currently treats all that is nonhuman as human property. It may be as challenging to change this perspective as it was for abolitionists to change laws treating slaves as property. Representing nature in courts, administrative proceedings, legislative hearings, and other lawmaking processes will present novel opportunities and obstacles. A nearly blank slate exists for determining when and how nature should be represented, who should represent nature, and how nature's competing interests should be weighed. The roles of science, social dynamics, tradition, human psychology, and ethics will present strategic and tactical issues for Earth lawyers to consider.

Rights of nature, while only one approach to Earth law, is presently prominent in the field. New legal rights may be legislatively created when those seeking the rights challenge a social norm as, for example, with the legislation of civil rights in the United States in the 1960s. New legal rights may also be recognized by judicial declaration when it is perceived to be necessary to better reflect the intent of laws as applied to changing circumstances. Rights of nature will be examined in this context and will be compared and contrasted with human rights. The examination of rights will include basic questions about what a legal right is, the balancing of legally recognized rights, the origin and evolution of property rights, and a critical review of the achievements and setbacks from rights of nature litigation.

The legal corollary of rights—duties and responsibilities—will also be examined. Despite humans' dependency on the Earth's ability to support them, the law does not

[4] Thomas Berry observes that human dependency on this system has become so endemic that an alternative way of life seems more a dream than a possibility. THOMAS BERRY, THE SACRED UNIVERSE, EARTH, SPIRITUALITY, AND RELIGION IN THE TWENTY-FIRST CENTURY 163 (2009).

[5] The precautionary principle has four main components: "taking preventive action in the face of uncertainty; shifting the burden of proof to the proponents of an activity; exploring a wide range of alternatives to possibly harmful actions; and increasing public participation in decision making." David Kriebel et al., *The Precautionary Principle in Environmental Science*, 109 ENVTL. HEALTH PERSP. 871 (2001).

provide a structure to limit human behavior in a manner that conforms to planetary boundaries.[6] Where there is a right to human life, there is a responsibility to act in a way that will support it. Earth lawyers will define and enforce laws that establish human responsibilities for the Earth community.

Earth law will develop within the current global economy. Along with the promotion of ecological well-being, Earth law will encourage and enforce limits on economic growth. Laws developed to sustain a habitable planet will consider factors such as population growth, resource use, the allocation of greenhouse gas sources and sinks, and aggregate limits on production and consumption. In this context, the concept of equity will be considered both in a fundamental sense, ensuring sufficiency for the poor, and in a relative sense, providing for fair distribution of wealth and income among all people.

Applying Earth law will involve new systems of governance at all levels. Effective enforcement of Earth law will depend on a widely held sense of responsibility for the welfare of the planet and future generations, and the acceptance of an obligation of care by all members of society. Since many of the issues of Earth law cross national boundaries or apply to areas of Earth such as oceans that are beyond national control, there will be a need for new global institutions and conventions, and these new formations will need support from nation-states and, within those states, from the executive, legislative, and judicial branches.

Practicing Earth law involves working with new ideas and ways of thinking that are not currently recognized in the legal system. This will involve a new philosophical base, or jurisprudence, for law. Earth jurisprudence posits that the welfare of humans, as members of the Earth community, is dependent on the welfare of Earth as a whole and that the viability of human society depends on its ability to regulate its members and its systems in a way that is consistent with the physical, chemical, and biological functioning of Earth.[7] In addition, Earth lawyers will need to understand Earth systems and reciprocity. Reciprocity is inherent in the way Earth works. It occurs at many scales, ranging from interactions among individual organisms to the Earth system's stabilizing feedback mechanisms among land, ocean, biosphere, and atmosphere.

The ultimate goal of Earth law is to provide the laws and legal structures needed for humans to live within planetary boundaries, prospectively care for ecosystems, restore damaged ecosystems, and justly share the burdens of mitigating and adapting to climate change and other environmental stresses. Success will be measured, *inter alia*, by the effectiveness of strategies to expand the protected legal community to include nonhuman nature and future generations.

[6] A team of researchers developed scientifically measurable planetary boundaries that, if crossed, "increase[s] the risk of generating large-scale abrupt or irreversible environmental changes." The nine planetary boundaries are climate change, ocean acidification, stratospheric ozone depletion, interference with the global phosphorus and nitrogen cycle, rate of biodiversity loss, global freshwater use, land-system change, aerosol loading, and chemical pollution. Johan Rockström et al., *Planetary Boundaries: Exploring the Safe Operating Space for Humanity*, 12(2) ECOLOGY AND SOC'Y 472-75 (2009).

[7] *See generally* "Ten Principles for the Revision of Jurisprudence" in THOMAS BERRY, EVENING THOUGHTS 149-150 (2006).

OVERVIEW OF THIS COURSEBOOK

This coursebook has been developed by the efforts of the Earth Law Center. To produce the first coursebook on this subject, many academics, practicing lawyers, law students, and others participated in researching, writing, editing, cite-checking, and reviewing scores of ecocentric legal materials. Many of the contributors are leaders in the field of Earth law and their contributions reflect lessons learned through practice.

This coursebook has introductory material followed by five major sections: Section I on "The Emergence of Earth Law," Section II on "Addressing Threshold Challenges," Section III on "Litigation Strategies," Section IV on "Transforming the Law," and Section V, "A Global Survey of Earth Law Developments." Each of these is summarized below. The coursebook ends with an Afterword.

Section I: The Emergence of Earth Law

Earth law is more a response to a common set of environmental challenges than it is a common body of law. Each response involves developing a legal theory that goes beyond conventional environmental law. Chapter 1 gives a brief history of conventional environmental law and a general critique of why it is unable to respond to the current environmental challenges. Chapter 2 gives a history of the emergence of the diverse approaches to Earth law. As well as being a response to a common set of environmental challenges, the different approaches to Earth law are tied together by a relatively common set of ideas. Chapter 3 deals with "The Conceptual Frameworks of Earth Law." These concepts are not only important to the history of Earth law but also to its future development.

Section II: Addressing Threshold Challenges

In anthropocentric environmental law, human needs are given priority. Ecocentric environmental law also gives a high priority to human needs but considers thinking that human needs and the needs of nature can be separated is a fallacy. Ecocentric law is holistic and organic. Thinking of nature only as being composed of parts (including the human parts) is, for ecocentric law, like considering whether the heart or the brain is the most important organ in the human organism. Each aspect of the body and the interdependencies and dynamics of the body need to be considered. In terms of health, each has "standing," or a recognized position or status. The threshold challenges for Earth law involve how the various aspects and dynamics of nature gain standing or are taken into account in the human legal system. The first issue deals with the idea that nature belongs to the owner of the property that the nature occupies. This is addressed in Chapter 4. Another issue concerns the way the concept of legal standing operates to prevent nature from being represented in law in its own right. This is addressed in Chapter 5. The final threshold challenge is who speaks for, or who represents, nature in the legal system and who ensures or guards its rights. This is addressed in Chapter 6.

Section III: Litigation Strategies

Litigation is an important tool for extending the reach of the law, and this is what Earth law is about: extending the reach of the law to grant protections to nature. In Section III, various legal strategies for extending the law to protect nature are given: Chapter 7—"The Public Trust Doctrine"; "Chapter 8—"The Rights of Future Generations"; Chapter 9—"The Rights of Nature in the United States"; Chapter 10—"Co-Violations: Human Rights and the Rights of Nature"; Chapter 11—"Nonhuman Rights"; Chapter 12—"Ecocide"; and Chapter 13—"The Climate Necessity Defense."

Section IV: Transforming the Law

The reach of law may also be extended by changing the laws themselves, the procedures for litigating disputes, and the ethics and modes of legal practice. An idea advanced in this book is that the current practice in Western law of adversarial representation of a client's interest is narrowly defined by the legal system as well as by the adversaries and is often principally defined (in economic terms). Treating anything that is not "against the law" as acceptable, such as pollution allowed by government permit, is unsuitable for Earth law. Transforming the law for Earth law purposes means inculcating in the legal system, and also in the larger society, richer senses of the commons, of rights, and of duties. Earth law begins with the propositions that *we are all in this together and we share a global commons,* so *we must work together in mutually beneficial ways for the sake of present and future generations.* Section IV covers transforming the law from three vantage points: Chapter 14—"Through the Eyes of a Bear: Integrating Ethics into Wildlife Law"; Chapter 15—"The United Nations Sustainable Development Initiatives"; and Chapter 16—"Ecocentric Environmental Governance."

Section V: A Global Survey of Earth Law Developments

Chapters 17 through 25 cover developments in Earth law in different jurisdictions around the world. The exception is Chapter 25 on "Indigenous Legalities," which deals with groups of people in various nations who have continuous traditions and lifeways that predate the time of the West's colonial expansion. Indigenous laws and belief systems that have existed for millennia are a major source of guidance for Earth law. Many believe that turning to Indigenous wisdom is one of the most important sources for developing Earth law.

AFTERWORD: THE FUTURE OF EARTH LAW

Earth law, or ecocentric environmental law, is a new field. What exists now is just a beginning. Earth law is coming into being and will always be coming into being because it needs to be as dynamic and responsive as nature herself.

Students and practitioners who study this coursebook will create and enforce Earth law through their practices.

Let's get started.

—*Anthony R. Zelle, Grant Wilson, Rachelle Adam, Herman F. Greene*
Editors

SECTION ONE

THE EMERGENCE OF EARTH LAW

Section I begins the journey into Earth law by reviewing its emergence in the United States, its global origins, and its key elements and concepts. It also defines "Earth law" and introduces basic concepts of ecocentric law that are discussed throughout the book.

Chapter 1, "Modern Environmental Law," reviews current U.S. environmental laws as well as key judicial decisions. Environmental laws developed in relation to the older common law system that provided remedies only after the damage was done. They measure social and economic benefits against environmental damage and calculate injury based on the property value of the land, water, and air as judicially or administratively established. While the current legal system has failed abysmally in stopping and reversing ecological devastation, its gains in warding off specific threats, such as polluted air and water, the extinction of species, and the release of toxins into the environment, should not be discounted. Understanding the successes and shortcomings of U.S. environmental law informs the emergence of Earth law.

Chapter 2, "The Origins of Earth Law," describes how Earth law is both a departure from environmental law and a new context for its extension. It also summarizes how the legal system evolved from localized customary laws to the modern Western legal system based on separation of humans from the rest of nature. The chapter then highlights the global ecological crisis and how Earth law emerges as an ecocentric jurisprudence for protecting life on Earth based on concepts of interdependence, entanglement, and mutuality. Many of these concepts have been practiced by Indigenous peoples since time immemorial and are engrained in their cultures and belief systems. The chapter then introduces various Earth law approaches that are discussed throughout the book—the public trust doctrine, rights-based movements, ecocide, Indigenous legalities, ecocentric governances, and other approaches as applied at international, national, regional, and local levels.

Chapter 3, "Conceptual Frameworks of Earth Law," discusses the framework that Earth law provides for living within planetary boundaries while sustaining ecosystems and biodiversity for the health and well-being of the entire community of life. The chapter explores distinctive concepts and elements of Earth law, such as the transition from the Holocene epoch to the current Anthropocene epoch; Earth law's rejection of anthropocentrism and its adoption of ecocentrism as its approach to the role of humans within the Earth community; rights, responsibilities, and reciprocity in the context of rights of nature; and the core issue of individual rights and property rights versus communal rights and the commons. Protecting the commons through an ecocentric approach will certainly impact current property rights as well as national sovereignty, but it can be done in an equitable and science-based manner and is essential to upholding the integrity of nature.

The ecological crisis that confronts us all demonstrates the limits of the current legal system, which focuses on remediating the symptoms of the ecological crisis rather addressing its causes, among which is the anthropocentric, individualistic, property-based approach to law.

Environmental laws will not be abandoned as alternative concepts of Earth law are developed. Rather, they will co-exist or merge with Earth law and continue to address particular incidents of environmental harm. Earth law signals the birth of a new generation of laws to guide and regulate human behavior in the Anthropocene epoch, with the urgent and immediate goal of avoiding tipping points by protecting, restoring, and stabilizing the functional interdependency of Earth's life and life-support systems.

CHAPTER 1

Modern Environmental Law[1]

"Only within the moment of time represented by the present century has one species–man–acquired significant power to alter the nature of his world."

Rachel Carson, *Silent Spring*, 1962[2]

I. INTRODUCTION

Throughout history there have been environmental laws. What are considered modern-day problems, such as deforestation, water scarcity and quality, toxic pollution, waste disposal, soil erosion and degradation, and exploitation of animals, are discussed in some of history's oldest written works. Environmental regulation has been a part of human experience for a long time, both for the protection of human health and well-being and for the preservation of the natural world as a value in itself.

The brief discussion of modern environmental law presented in this chapter is intended to provide an understanding of the legal background of Earth law. Earth law is both a departure from modern environmental law and a new context for its extension.

II. HISTORY OF MODERN ENVIRONMENTAL LAW

Current environmental law is a product of the modern period, which, for this purpose, began in the sixteenth century as the West moved out of the medieval or feudal period to the modern world. In the feudal period, only a few lords owned land, vassals held land by tenure on the condition of homage and military service, and serfs were forced to work the land. The church held authority over what people could do and what they could know. Even kings were subject to the authority of the church. This was a time of obligation and duty. The Black Plague had a role in ending the medieval period. It peaked between 1347 and 1351, a period in which half of the population of Europe

[1] This chapter was authored by Margaret R. Stewart, Director of the Center of Earth Jurisprudence at Barry University Dwayne O. Andreas School of Law in Orlando, Florida, with contributions from Earth Law Center.
[2] Rachel Carson, Silent Spring 5 (1962).

died, and there were recurrences of the plague throughout the remainder of the fourteenth century to the seventeenth century. This catastrophe raised questions about the ministrations of the church. Greater attention was given to life on Earth than to spirituality and the afterlife. With the decline in population, the value of the working class increased, and commoners were given more freedom. Land and food prices dropped and there was a large turnover of property by inheritance from dead relatives.

The Renaissance, which began in Italy and then spread throughout Europe, gave attention to the humanities and the unique qualities of humans. The invention of the printing press by Gutenberg in 1440 and the spread of the presses was equivalent in its day to the birth of the Internet in ours. Access to the Bible and other information became widely available. The Protestant Reformation began in 1517 when Martin Luther broke with the medieval authority of the church. The scientific revolution brought about by Copernicus, Galileo, Bacon, Newton, and others gave the prospect of the mastery and control of nature for human uses. Cities and towns grew, and power moved from the feudal lords to the bourgeoisie—those who live in the borough—the merchants and craftsmen.

Liberty, individual human rights, and material progress drove the modernists. The nation-state developed and, along with it, new institutions of private property (real, personal, and intangible) that were not primarily controlled by nobility and obligation but rather by labor and free exchange of money. Ownership of private property, which was denied in the medieval period, became a hallmark of freedom in modernity. So began a centuries' long struggle between the state representing oppression, obligation, and necessity, and private property representing freedom and opportunity, as well as status, power, and well-being.

A person had a right to do with their property as they wanted, so long as their usage did not unduly affect others in adjoining property. The legal doctrine that restricted actions unduly affecting others was "nuisance." Prior to modern environmental law, nuisance was the primary way of protecting the environment. Private nuisance was an activity or condition, without actual trespass, harmful to an owner of adjoining property that gave rise to a legal cause of action. Aldred's case of 1610[3] was the first case where an ordinary person was given a right of action for environmental harm against his immediate neighbor. In that case, William Aldred claimed that his neighbor maintained a pigsty too close to Aldred's house, making occupancy unbearable. A right of action also came into being for public nuisance when a person's actions unduly affected the health or welfare of a class of the public.

Nuisance proved to be inadequate to address the mounting environmental problems that followed in the wake of the industrial revolution. For example, during the "Great Stink" of 1858 in London, the odors of sewage released in the Thames River became oppressive and Parliament passed a law to build the London sewerage system. Coal-burning factories released toxic smog into the air causing harm to humans and other species in many places. The chemical industry developed and, with it, novel compounds were released into air, water, and soil; in particular, as plastics developed,

[3] *Aldred's Case* (1610) 9 Co Rep 57b, 58-58b.

plastic waste mounted. Industrial agriculture led to many problems including overgrazing and desertification, aquifer depletion, soil erosion, and the release of chemical fertilizers and pesticides into soil and water and the creation of dead zones in waterways. Mining for petroleum and other minerals increased globally, resulting in high environmental costs.

As problems mounted, only triggering events were needed to bring into being modern environmental law. One triggering event occurred in 1952 with the "Great Smog" in London, which killed thousands and caused illness in tens of thousands of people. This led the United Kingdom Parliament to pass the Clean Air Act of 1956.

A second triggering event occurred in 1956 in Minamata, Japan. People and animals were diagnosed as suffering from mercury poisoning as a result of eating shellfish and fish from Minamata Bay that had ingested methylmercury released by Chisso Corporation in factory wastewater. The mercury poisoning caused ataxia (inability to control muscle movements, gait abnormality, and abnormality in eye movements), muscle weakness, numbness in hands and feet, damage to hearing and speech, and in extreme cases insanity, paralysis, coma, and death. It took twelve years before the government of Japan in 1968 officially recognized the disease and even longer for the victims to be compensated. Photo essays on the people in Minamata who suffered from the disease brought worldwide attention to the effects toxic chemicals could have on humans, animals, plants, and the environment generally.

A third triggering event occurred with the publication in 1962 of Rachel Carson's book, *Silent Spring*, which documented the environmental effects of the indiscriminate use of pesticides, especially DDT. Carson wrote that these chemicals should be called "biocides" rather than pesticides because their effects went far beyond the target species. The book showed the powerful negative effects humans could have on the natural world. It is often credited as having started the modern environmental movement and, with that movement, modern environmental law.

A fourth triggering event occurred in June 1969, when an oil slick on the Cuyahoga River in Cleveland, Ohio, caught fire, damaging two railroad bridges. While it was not the first time the river had caught fire, dramatic photos in *Time* magazine showing flames leaping up from the river caught the public's attention.

A fifth triggering event occurred when a large algal bloom in 1970 created a dead zone in Lake Erie and thousands of dead fish washed up on the shoreline. The lake was already suffering from a toxic mix of pollutants and sewage that had been dumped into the lake. A popular saying arose that "Lake Erie is dead."

By this time, there was widespread alarm about the environment. On April 22, 1970, 20 million Americans gathered on the first Earth Day to express their concern. In 1972, the first global UN summit on the environment occurred in Stockholm, Sweden. And from 1970 onward, many national environmental laws were passed—especially in the 1970s in the United States—and many international environmental treaties came into effect.

Notwithstanding all these laws and treaties, the global environment has deteriorated over the last 50 years. Given that the overwhelming objective of policymakers during this period was economic growth, the environmental laws that came into being arguably were the best that were politically possible. Even now economic growth remains the priority of policymakers. There are reasons for this: It is difficult for nations to compete in the globalized economy and being competitive is deemed necessary for the livelihoods and lives of citizens. Powerful vested interests support the continued focus on growth and wealth accumulation. There is, however, a growing awareness that business as usual is not sustainable. People are presently suffering from the consequences of climate change and other environmental degradation — these consequences are costly and are increasingly difficult to disregard as externalities. The values of modernity are being questioned in two ways: sometimes with a move into reactionary fundamentalism, and sometimes with the search for a new, less materialistic way forward — one that is regenerative, organic, and fit for the planet Earth. This book is an expression of the latter type of movement.

Earth law will not replace contemporary environmental law. The functions of modern environmental law will be needed with no end in sight. Earth law will broaden the context of environmental law, extend its reach, and change its dynamics from a competitive zero-sum struggle between private and public interests to shared responsibility, mutual endeavor, and mutual benefit for the entire community of life.

This book is devoted to legal doctrines that go beyond contemporary environmental law. Before proceeding to an examination of those doctrines, a brief review of how contemporary environmental law works in practice is in order.

III. A BRIEF REVIEW OF CONTEMPORARY ENVIRONMENTAL LAW IN PRACTICE

A number of environmental laws were passed in the United States prior to 1970, including:

- 1899 — Rivers and Harbors Act (Pub. L. 55-425);
- 1916 — National Park Service Organic Act created the National Park Service (Pub. L. 64-235);
- 1948 — Federal Water Pollution Control Act (P.L. 80-845, totally revised by later amendments);
- 1955 — Air Pollution Control Act (Pub. L. 84-159);
- 1963 — Clean Air Act (Pub. L. 84-159, totally revised by later amendments);
- 1964 — Wilderness Act (Pub. L. 88-577);
- 1965 — Motor Vehicle Air Pollution Control Act (Pub. L. 89-272);
- 1965 — Solid Waste Disposal Act (Pub. L. 89-272, later amended and superseded); and
- 1969 — Federal Coal Mine Health and Safety Act (pub. L. 91-173).

The year 1970, however, was the watershed date. That was the year of the enactment of the National Environmental Policy Act and the formation of the U.S. Environmental Protection Agency (EPA). Following 1970, the major environmental legislation in the United States and other countries, and international treaties and other agreements, which collectively constitute contemporary environmental law, came into being.

A. National Environmental Policy Act (1970)

In response to Carson's depiction of the damage to the environment from pesticide use in her book *Silent Spring*, the United States enacted the first of many statutes to better regulate human use and exploitation of the natural world. The National Environmental Policy Act, or NEPA, 42 U.S.C. §§ 4321-47, was signed into law in 1970. This statute required agencies to consider environmental impacts in a way not expected before. The purposes of NEPA are given as:

> (1) To declare a national policy which will encourage productive and enjoyable harmony between man and his environment;
> (2) to promote efforts which will prevent or eliminate damage to the environment and biosphere and stimulate the health and welfare of man;
> (3) to enrich the understanding of the ecological systems and natural resources important to the Nation; and
> (4) and to establish a Council on Environmental Quality.[4]

While NEPA technically requires each federal agency to ensure that its activities are carried out in accordance with the Act, the establishment of the Council on Environmental Quality (CEQ) created a central agency that develops guidelines and promulgates rules for other agencies to follow.

The main tool to fulfill the purposes of the Act is the requirement in 42 U.S.C. § 4332(C) that federal agencies must:

> include in every recommendation or report on proposals for legislation and other major Federal actions significantly affecting the quality of the human environment, a *detailed statement* by the responsible official on
>
> (i) the environmental impact of the proposed action,
> (ii) any adverse environmental effects which cannot be avoided should the proposal be implemented,
> (iii) alternatives to the proposed action,
> (iv) the relationship between local short-term uses of man's environment and the maintenance and enhancement of long-term productivity, and
> (v) any irreversible and irretrievable commitments of resources which would be involved in the proposed action should it be implemented. (Emphasis added.)

[4] 42 U.S.C. § 4321 (numbering added).

These "detailed statements" are known as "Environmental Impact Statements."

The brevity of NEPA can be misleading. Its requirements have been the most litigated of any of the modern environmental law statutes discussed in this chapter. This is interesting when one considers that NEPA is essentially nothing more than the requirement for informed decision-making by governmental agencies.[5] However, this requirement can be quite time-consuming and costly, hence there has been significant pushback.

Calvert Cliffs represented the first significant decision that interpreted what this new federal regulatory landscape would mean in practice.

Calvert Cliffs Coordinating Committee v. United States Atomic Energy Commission

449 F.2d 1109 (D.C. Cir. 1971)[6]

J. SKELLY WRIGHT, Circuit Judge:

These cases are only the beginning of what promises to become a flood of new litigation–litigation seeking judicial assistance in protecting our natural environment. Several recently enacted statutes attest to the commitment of the Government to control, at long last, the destructive engine of material "progress." But it remains to be seen whether the promise of this legislation will become a reality. Therein lies the judicial role. In these cases, we must for the first time interpret the broadest and perhaps most important of the recent statutes: The National Environmental Policy Act of 1969 (NEPA). We must assess claims that one of the agencies charged with its administration has failed to live up to the congressional mandate. Our duty, in short, is to see that important legislative purposes, heralded in the halls of Congress, are not lost or misdirected in the vast hallways of the federal bureaucracy.

NEPA, like so much other reform legislation of the last 40 years, is cast in terms of a general mandate and broad delegation of authority to new and old administrative agencies. It takes the major step of requiring all federal agencies to consider values of environmental preservation in their spheres of activity, and it prescribes certain procedural measures to ensure that those values are in fact fully respected. Petitioners argue that rules recently adopted by the Atomic Energy Commission to govern consideration of environmental matters fail to satisfy the rigor demanded by NEPA. The Commission, on the other hand, contends that the vagueness of the NEPA mandate and delegation leaves much room for discretion and that the rules challenged by petitioners fall well within the broad scope of the Act. We find the policies embodied in NEPA to be a good deal clearer and more demanding than does

[5] *See, e.g., Vermont Yankee Nuclear Power Corp. v. NRDC*, 435 U.S. 519, 558 (1978).

[6] Footnotes omitted from extract.

the Commission. We conclude that the Commission's procedural rules do not comply with the congressional policy. Hence we remand these cases for further rule making.

We begin our analysis with an examination of NEPA's structure and approach and of the Atomic Energy Commission rules which are said to conflict with the requirements of the Act. The relevant portion of NEPA is Title I, consisting of five sections. Section 101 sets forth the Act's basic substantive policy: that the federal government "use all practicable means and measures" to protect environmental values. Congress did not establish environmental protection as an exclusive goal; rather, it desired a reordering of priorities, so that environmental costs and benefits will assume their proper place along with other considerations. In Section 101(b), imposing an explicit duty on federal officials, the Act provides that "it is the continuing responsibility of the Federal Government to use all practicable means, consistent with other essential considerations of national policy," to avoid environmental degradation, preserve "historic, cultural, and natural" resources, and promote "the widest range of beneficial uses of the environment without undesirable and unintended consequences." . . .

NEPA, first of all, makes environmental protection a part of the mandate of every federal agency and department. The Atomic Energy Commission, for example, had continually asserted, prior to NEPA, that it had no statutory authority to concern itself with the adverse environmental effects of its actions. Now, however, its hands are no longer tied. It is not only permitted, but compelled, to take environmental values into account. Perhaps the greatest importance of NEPA is to require the Atomic Energy Commission and other agencies to *consider* environmental issues just as they consider other matters within their mandates. This compulsion is most plainly stated in Section 102. There, "Congress authorizes and directs that, to the fullest extent possible: (1) the policies, regulations, and public laws of the United States shall be interpreted and administered in accordance with the policies set forth in this Act." Congress also "authorizes and directs" that "(2) all agencies of the Federal Government shall" follow certain rigorous procedures in considering environmental values. Senator Jackson, NEPA's principal sponsor, stated that "[n]o agency will [now] be able to maintain that it has no mandate or no requirement to consider the environmental consequences of its actions." He characterized the requirements of Section 102 as "action-forcing" and stated that "[o]therwise, these lofty declarations [in Section 101] are nothing more than that."

The sort of consideration of environmental values which NEPA compels is clarified in Section 102(2)(A) and (B). In general, all agencies must use a "systematic, interdisciplinary approach" to environmental planning and evaluation "in decisionmaking which may have an impact on man's environment." In order to include all possible environmental factors in the decisional equation, agencies must "identify and develop methods and procedures which will insure that presently unquantified environmental amenities and values may be given appropriate consideration in decisionmaking along with economic and technical considerations." "Environmental amenities" will often be in conflict with "economic and technical considerations." To "consider" the former "along with" the latter must involve a balancing process. In some instances environmental costs may outweigh economic and technical benefits and in other instances they may not. But NEPA mandates a rather finely tuned and "systematic" balancing analysis in each instance.

To ensure that the balancing analysis is carried out and given full effect, Section 102(2)(C) requires that responsible officials of all agencies prepare a "detailed statement" covering the impact of particular actions on the environment, the environmental costs which might be avoided, and alternative measures which might alter the cost/benefit equation. The apparent purpose of the "detailed statement" is to aid in the agencies' own decisionmaking process and to advise other interested agencies and the public of the environmental consequences of planned federal action. Beyond the "detailed statement," Section 102(2)(D) requires all agencies specifically to "study, develop, and describe appropriate alternatives to recommended courses of action in any proposal which involves unresolved conflicts concerning alternative uses of available resources." This requirement, like the "detailed statement" requirement, seeks to ensure that each agency decision maker has before him and takes into proper account all possible approaches to a particular project (including total abandonment of the project) which would alter the environmental impact and the cost-benefit balance....

We conclude, then, that Section 102 of NEPA mandates a particular sort of careful and informed decisionmaking process and creates judicially enforceable duties. The reviewing courts probably cannot reverse a substantive decision on its merits, under Section 101, unless it be shown that the actual balance of costs and benefits that was struck was arbitrary or clearly gave insufficient weight to environmental values. But if the decision was reached procedurally without individualized consideration and balancing of environmental factors—conducted fully and in good faith—it is the responsibility of the courts to reverse. As one District Court has said of Section 102 requirements: "It is hard to imagine a clearer or stronger mandate to the Courts."

In the cases before us now, we do not have to review a particular decision by the Atomic Energy Commission granting a construction permit or an operating license. Rather, we must review the Commission's recently promulgated rules which govern consideration of environmental values in all such individual decisions. The rules were devised strictly in order to comply with the NEPA procedural requirements–but petitioners argue that they fall far short of the congressional mandate....

II

NEPA makes only one specific reference to consideration of environmental values in agency review processes. Section 102(2)(C) provides that copies of the staff's "detailed statement" and comments thereon "shall accompany the proposal through the existing agency review processes." The Atomic Energy Commission's rules may seem in technical compliance with the letter of that provision. They state:

> If any party to a proceeding raises any [environmental] issue the Applicant's Environmental Report and the Detailed Statement will be offered in evidence. The atomic safety and licensing board will make findings of fact on, and resolve, the matters in controversy among the parties with regard to those issues. Depending on the resolution of those issues, the permit or license may be granted, denied, or appropriately conditioned to protect environmental values." When no party to a proceeding raises any [environmental] issue such issues will not be considered by the atomic safety and licensing board. Under such circumstances, although the Applicant's Environmental Report, comments thereon, and the Detailed Statement will accompany the application through the Commission's review processes, they will not be received in evidence, and the Commission's responsibilities under the National Environmental Policy Act of 1969 will be carried out in toto outside the hearing process.

The question here is whether the Commission is correct in thinking that its NEPA responsibilities may "be carried out in toto outside the hearing process"–whether it is enough that environmental data and evaluations merely "accompany" an application through the review process, but receive no consideration whatever from the hearing board. . . . We believe that the Commission's crabbed interpretation of NEPA makes a mockery of the Act. . . .

Again, the Commission's approach to statutory interpretation is strange indeed—so strange that it seems to reveal a rather thoroughgoing reluctance to meet the NEPA procedural obligations in the agency review process, the stage at which deliberation is most open to public examination and subject to the participation of public intervenors. The Act, it is true, lacks an "inflexible timetable" for its implementation. But it does have a clear effective date, consistently enforced by reviewing courts up to now. Every federal court having faced the issues has held that the procedural requirements of NEPA must be met in order to uphold federal action taken after January 1, 1970. The absence of a "timetable" for compliance has never been held sufficient, in itself, to put off the date on which a congressional mandate takes effect. The absence of a "timetable," rather, indicates that compliance is required forthwith. . . .

The sweep of NEPA is extraordinarily broad, compelling consideration of any and all types of environmental impact of federal action. However, the Atomic Energy Commission's rules specifically exclude from full consideration a wide variety of environmental issues. First, they provide that no party may raise and the Commission may not independently examine any problem of water quality—perhaps the most significant impact of nuclear power plants.

Rather, the Commission indicates that it will defer totally to water quality standards devised and administered by state agencies and approved by the federal government under the Federal Water Pollution Control Act. Secondly, the rules provide for similar abdication of NEPA authority to the standards of other agencies:

> With respect to those aspects of environmental quality for which environmental quality standards and requirements have been established by authorized Federal, State, and regional agencies, proof that the applicant is equipped to observe and agrees to observe such standards and requirements will be considered a satisfactory showing that there will not be a significant, adverse effect on the environment. Certification by the appropriate agency that there is reasonable assurance that the applicant for the permit or license will observe such standards and requirements will be considered dispositive for this purpose.

The most the Commission will do is include a condition in all construction permits and operating licenses requiring compliance with the water quality or other standards set by such agencies. The upshot is that the NEPA procedures, viewed by the Commission as superfluous, will wither away in disuse, applied only to those environmental issues wholly unregulated by any other federal, state or regional body.

We believe the Commission's rule is in fundamental conflict with the basic purpose of the Act. NEPA mandates a case-by-case balancing judgment on the part of federal agencies. In each individual case, the particular economic and technical benefits of planned action must be assessed and then weighed against the environmental costs; alternatives must be considered which would affect the balance of values....

We hold that . . . the Commission must revise its rules governing consideration of environmental issues. We do not impose a harsh burden on the Commission. For we require only an exercise of substantive discretion which will protect the environment "to the fullest extent possible." No less is required if the grand congressional purposes underlying NEPA are to become a reality.

Remanded for proceedings consistent with this opinion.

The holding in *Calvert Cliffs* assured that environmental considerations be taken into account during agency decision-making. It also set standards for challenges to the assessments made in the environmental impact statements. In construing the statute in this context, the court clarified the congressional intent by reading the statutory requirements more broadly than the agency did. Later holdings by the Supreme Court have tended to narrow the reach of environmental statutes.

B. Clean Air Act (1970)

"It is a fair and reasonable demand on the part of a sovereign that the air over its territory should not be polluted on a great scale by sulphurous acid gas, that the forests on its mountains . . . should not be further destroyed or threatened by the act of persons beyond its control, that the crops and orchards on its hills should not be endangered."

Georgia v. Tennessee Copper Co. and Ducktown Sulphur, Copper & Iron Co.[7]

Assuring the quality of the air we breathe is an obvious reason for environmental protection. Air knows no state or national boundaries. The common law approach of remedying noxious pollution through the tort of nuisance and earlier federal clean air acts[8] became obsolete as production and transportation methods began emitting more and more air pollution.

Identifying the need for a more uniform, comprehensive approach, in 1970 Congress passed the Clean Air Act (CAA)[9] in an effort "to protect and enhance the quality of the Nation's air resources so as to promote the public health and welfare and the productive capacity of its population."[10] The overall goal was to ensure that each level of government, regardless of diverse priorities, was taking action to reduce and prevent air pollution.

To achieve this reduction and prevention, The CAA requires the EPA to identify certain "criteria air pollutants" and issue National Ambient Air Quality Standards (NAAQS) for them.[11] Then by means of cooperative federalism, after these national standards are set, the states are each required to establish a State Implementation Plan (SIP). This plan establishes how the state will implement, maintain, and enforce the NAAQS. If a state fails to submit a SIP, the EPA establishes a Federal Implementation Plan (FIP). This is the basic process of the CAA to ensure that there are uniform standards for air quality throughout the United States.

The case discussed below, *Michigan v. EPA*, demonstrates the disconnect that can occur under contemporary environmental law. In this case, the Supreme Court ruled the EPA *must* consider the cost of compliance before deciding that a CAA regulation is appropriate and necessary. The EPA had promulgated Mercury and Air Toxics Standards (MATS) that would have saved upward of 17,000 lives per year in the

[7] *Georgia v. Tennessee Copper Co. et al.*, 206 U.S. 230 (1907).

[8] Earlier federal air quality control acts were: (1) the 1955 Air Pollution Control Act, (2) the 1963 Clean Air Act, (3) the 1965 Motor Vehicle Air Pollution Control Act, and (4) the Air Quality Act of 1967.

[9] The Act was amended by: (1) the Clean Air Act Amendment of 1977 and (2) the Clean Air Act Amendments of 1990.

[10] 42 U.S.C. § 7401(b)(1). The full purpose of the Clean Air Act found at 42 U.S.C. § 7401(b)(1)-(4) states: The purposes of this subchapter are (1) to protect and enhance the quality of the Nation's air resources so as to promote the public health and welfare and the productive capacity of its population; (2) to initiate and accelerate a national research and development program to achieve the prevention and control of air pollution; (3) to provide technical and financial assistance to State and local governments in connection with the development and execution of their air pollution prevention and control programs; and (4) to encourage and assist the development and operation of regional air pollution prevention and control programs.

[11] Current criteria pollutants include ground-level ozone, particulate matter, carbon monoxide, nitrogen dioxide, sulfur dioxide, and lead.

United States according to its own projections. Since going into effect, the rules had reduced mercury emissions from power plants by 81 percent. However, the Supreme Court struck down the rules because the EPA did not weigh costs to the industry against the benefits to society before formulating the rules. The following excerpt is from the case's syllabus, or "headnote,"[12] which provides a summary of the ruling.

Michigan v. Environmental Protection Agency

576 U.S. ___, 135 S. Ct. 2699 (2015)
Syllabus

Justice SCALIA delivered the opinion of the Court:

The Clean Air Act directs the Environmental Protection Agency to regulate emissions of hazardous air pollutants from certain stationary sources (such as refineries and factories). 42 U.S.C. § 7412. The Agency may regulate power plants under this program only if it concludes that "regulation is appropriate and necessary" after studying hazards to public health posed by power-plant emissions. § 7412(n)(1)(A). Here, EPA found power-plant regulation "appropriate" because the plants' emissions pose risks to public health and the environment and because controls capable of reducing these emissions were available. It found regulation "necessary" because the imposition of other Clean Air Act requirements did not eliminate those risks. The Agency refused to consider cost when making its decision. It estimated, however, that the cost of its regulations to power plants would be $9.6 billion a year, but the quantifiable benefits from the resulting reduction in hazardous-air-pollutant emissions would be $4 to $6 million a year. Petitioners (including 23 States) sought review of EPA's rule in the D.C. Circuit, which upheld the Agency's refusal to consider costs in its decision to regulate.

Held: EPA interpreted § 7412(n)(1)(A) unreasonably when it deemed cost irrelevant to the decision to regulate power plants. Pp. 5-15.

(a) Agency action is unlawful if it does not rest "on a consideration of the relevant factors." *Motor Vehicle Mfrs. Assn. of United States, Inc. v. State Farm Mut. Automobile Ins. Co.*, 463 U.S. 29, 43. Even under the deferential standard of *Chevron U.S.A. Inc. v. Natural Resources Defense Council, Inc.*, 467 U.S. 837, which directs courts to accept an agency's reasonable resolution of an ambiguity in a statute that the agency administers, *id.*, at 842-843, EPA strayed well beyond the bounds of reasonable interpretation in concluding that cost is not a factor relevant to the appropriateness of regulating power plants. Pp. 5-6.

(b) "Appropriate and necessary" is a capacious phrase. Read naturally against the backdrop of established administrative law, this phrase plainly

[12] A headnote is frequently also called a syllabus. In the United States Supreme Court, the syllabus is prepared by the court's reporter. Current practice is for each syllabus to be preceded by the following: "NOTE: Where it is feasible, a syllabus (headnote) will be released, as is being done in connection with this case, at the time the opinion is issued. The syllabus constitutes no part of the opinion of the Court but has been prepared by the Reporter of Decisions for the convenience of the reader." *See United States v. Detroit Timber & Lumber Co.,* 200 U. S. 321, 337 (1906).

encompasses cost. It is not rational, never mind "appropriate," to impose billions of dollars in economic costs in return for a few dollars in health or environmental benefits. Statutory context supports this reading. Section 7412(n)(1) required the EPA to conduct three studies, including one that reflects concern about cost, see § 7412(n)(1)(B); and the Agency agrees that the term "appropriate and necessary" must be interpreted in light of all three studies. Pp. 6-9.

(c) EPA's counterarguments are unpersuasive. That other Clean Air Act provisions expressly mention cost only shows that § 7412(n)(1)(A)'s broad reference to appropriateness encompasses multiple relevant factors, one of which is cost. Similarly, the modest principle of *Whitman v. American Trucking Assns., Inc.*, 531 U.S. 457—when the Clean Air Act expressly directs EPA to regulate on the basis of a discrete factor that does not include cost, the Act should not be read as implicitly allowing consideration of cost anyway—has no bearing on this case. Furthermore, the possibility of considering cost at a later stage, when deciding how much to regulate power plants, does not establish its irrelevance at this stage. And although the Clean Air Act makes cost irrelevant to the initial decision to regulate sources other than power plants, the whole point of having a separate provision for power plants was to treat power plants differently. Pp. 9-12.

(d) EPA must consider cost—including cost of compliance—before deciding whether regulation is appropriate and necessary. It will be up to the Agency to decide (as always, within the limits of reasonable interpretation) how to account for cost. Pp. 12-15. 748 F.3d 1222, reversed and remanded.

* * *

The cost and benefit of environmental regulation continues to be highly contested in all three branches of government. For example, the present Trump administration has taken a far dimmer view of the benefits of environmental regulation than the past Obama administration and has taken steps to repeal or weaken many environmental rules or laws—over 100 as of early 2020[13]—based on the present administration's understanding of economic efficiency and growth.

C. Federal Water Pollution Control Act (Clean Water Act) (1972)

"When the well's dry, we know the worth of water."

Benjamin Franklin

Like the Clean Air Act, the Clean Water Act of 1972 (CWA)[14] was passed to provide for more comprehensive and uniform water quality regulation in the United States.[15] The

[13] Coral Davenport, *Trump Removes Pollution Controls on Streams and Wetlands*, N.Y. Times (Jan. 23, 2020).

[14] The act has been amended by: (1) the Clean Water Act of 1977, and (2) the Water Quality Act of 1987.

[15] Earlier water quality control acts were: (1) the 1899 Rivers and Harbors Act, (2) the 1948 Water Quality Act, and (3) the 1956 Federal Water Pollution Control Act.

laws and regulations under the Act are primarily administered by the EPA in coordination with state governments, though some of its provisions, such as those involving filling and dredging, are administered by the U.S. Army Corps of Engineers.

What does water protection look like under a comprehensive, regulatory approach? The CWA was intended to "restore and maintain the chemical, physical, and biological integrity of the Nation's waters."[16] Like the CAA, the CWA set ambitious goals: The CWA was to "provide for the protection and propagation of fish, shellfish, and wildlife" and for "recreation in and on the water" by 1983, and eliminate all discharges of pollutants into the nation's waterways by 1985."[17]

It sought to ensure all waters be "fishable and swimmable" and provided the EPA and states with the authority to set and implement the standards necessary to achieve these goals. Generally, states set water quality targets and standards that define specific cleanup measures or limit the amount of pollution that can be discharged into bodies of water; the EPA then reviews and approves these targets and standards. The Clean Water Act also established a number of different programs aimed at protecting wetlands, coastal waters, estuaries, and large ecosystems.

How has it done? In 1972, a third of waters were fishable and swimmable according to CWA standards. As of this writing, about half of waters are fishable and swimmable. This is improvement, but many rivers, streams, and other waterways remain unhealthy. One reason for this shortcoming is that some water pollutant sources are underregulated, such as pollution from nonpoint sources (e.g., agricultural runoff), which do not require a permit since it is not a "discharge." Additionally, the CWA chronically underregulates physical impacts to waterways, such as channelization and the dewatering of rivers and streams.[18]

Another major shortcoming of the CWA is that it tasks agencies to protect "navigable waters," a standard that arose from the law's emphasis on protecting waters that are used in commerce. The next case demonstrates how a narrow application of the CWA can exclude large portions of watersheds from protection.

Rapanos v. United States

547 U.S. 715 (2006)

Justice Scalia delivered the opinion of the Court.

In April 1989, petitioner John A. Rapanos backfilled wetlands on a parcel of land in Michigan that he owned and sought to develop. This parcel included 54 acres of land with sometimes-saturated soil conditions.

[16] 33 U.S.C. § 1251(a) (1972).

[17] James Salzman & Barton Thompson, Jr., Environmental Law and Policy 180 (2019) (quoting National Water Commission, Final Report: Water Policies for the Future 70 (1973)).

[18] *See* Earth Law Center, Flow-Impairment Toolkit, https://www.earthlawcenter.org/california-waterways (last visited Mar. 8, 2020).

The nearest body of navigable water was 11 to 20 miles away. 339 F.3d 447, 449 (CA6 2003) *(Rapanos I)*. Regulators had informed Mr. Rapanos that his saturated fields were "waters of the United States," 33 U.S.C. § 1362(7), that could not be filled without a permit. Twelve years of criminal and civil litigation ensued.

The burden of federal regulation on those who would deposit fill material in locations denominated "waters of the United States" is not trivial. In deciding whether to grant or deny a permit, the U.S. Army Corps of Engineers (Corps) exercises the discretion of an enlightened despot, relying on such factors as "economics," "aesthetics," "recreation," and "in general, the needs and welfare of the people," 33 CFR § 320.4(a) (2004). The average applicant for an individual permit spends 788 days and $271,596 in completing the process, and the average applicant for a nationwide permit spends 313 days and $28,915—not counting costs of mitigation or design changes. Sunding & Zilberman, The Economics of Environmental Regulation by Licensing: An Assessment of Recent Changes to the Wetland Permitting Process, 42 Natural Resources J. 59, 74-76 (2002). "[O]ver $1.7 billion is spent each year by the private and public sectors obtaining wetlands permits." *Id.*, at 81. These costs cannot be avoided, because the Clean Water Act "impose[s] criminal liability," as well as steep civil fines, "on a broad range of ordinary industrial and commercial activities." *Hanousek v. United States*, 528 U.S. 1102, 1103 (2000) (Thomas, J., dissenting from denial of certiorari). In this litigation, for example, for backfilling his own wet fields, Mr. Rapanos faced 63 months in prison and hundreds of thousands of dollars in criminal and civil fines. See *United States v. Rapanos*, 235 F.3d 256, 260 (CA6 2000).

The enforcement proceedings against Mr. Rapanos are a small part of the immense expansion of federal regulation of land use that has occurred under the Clean Water Act—without any change in the governing statute—during the past five Presidential administrations. In the last three decades, the Corps and the Environmental Protection Agency (EPA) have interpreted their jurisdiction over "the waters of the United States" to cover 270-to-300 million acres of swampy lands in the United States—including half of Alaska and an area the size of California in the lower 48 States. And that was just the beginning. The Corps has also asserted jurisdiction over virtually any parcel of land containing a channel or conduit—whether man-made or natural, broad or narrow, permanent or ephemeral—through which rainwater or drainage may occasionally or intermittently flow. On this view, the federally regulated "waters of the United States" include storm drains, roadside ditches, ripples of sand in the desert that may contain water once a year, and lands that are covered by floodwaters once every 100 years. Because they include the land containing storm sewers and desert washes, the statutory "waters of the United States" engulf entire cities and immense arid wastelands. In fact, the entire land area of the United States lies in some drainage basin, and an endless network of visible channels furrows the entire surface, containing water ephemerally wherever the rain falls. Any plot of land containing such a channel may potentially be regulated as a "water of the United States."

I

Congress passed the Clean Water Act (CWA or Act) in 1972. The Act's stated objective is "to restore and maintain the chemical, physical, and biological integrity of the Nation's waters." 86 Stat. 816, 33 U.S.C. § 1251(a). The Act also states that "[i]t is the policy of Congress to recognize, preserve, and protect the primary responsibilities and rights of States to prevent, reduce, and eliminate pollution, to plan the development and use (including restoration, preservation, and enhancement) of land and water resources, and to consult with the Administrator in the exercise of his authority under this chapter." § 1251(b).

One of the statute's principal provisions is 33 U.S.C. § 1311(a), which provides that "the discharge of any pollutant by any person shall be unlawful." "The discharge of a pollutant" is defined broadly to include "any addition of any pollutant to navigable waters from any point source," § 1362(12), and "pollutant" is defined broadly to include not only traditional contaminants but also solids such as "dredged spoil, . . . rock, sand, [and] cellar dirt," § 1362(6). And, most relevant here, the CWA defines "navigable waters" as "the waters of the United States, including the territorial seas." § 1362(7).

The Act also provides certain exceptions to its prohibition of "the discharge of any pollutant by any person." § 1311(a). Section 1342(a) authorizes the Administrator of the EPA to "issue a permit for the discharge of any pollutant, . . . notwithstanding section 1311(a) of this title." Section 1344 authorizes the Secretary of the Army, acting through the Corps, to "issue permits . . . for the discharge of dredged or fill material into the navigable waters at specified disposal sites." § 1344(a), (d). It is the discharge of "dredged or fill material"—which, unlike traditional water pollutants, are solids that do not readily wash downstream—that we consider today. . . .

The Corps' current regulations interpret "the waters of the United States" to include, in addition to traditional interstate navigable waters, 33 CFR § 328.3(a)(1) (2004), "[a]ll interstate waters including interstate wetlands," § 328.3(a)(2); "[a]ll other waters such as intrastate lakes, rivers, streams (including intermittent streams), mudflats, sandflats, wetlands, sloughs, prairie potholes, wet meadows, playa lakes, or natural ponds, the use, degradation or destruction of which could affect interstate or foreign commerce," § 328.3(a)(3); "[t]ributaries of [such] waters," § 328.3(a)(5); and "[w]etlands adjacent to [such] waters [and tributaries] (other than waters that are themselves wetlands)," § 328.3(a)(7). The regulation defines "adjacent" wetlands as those "bordering, contiguous [to], or neighboring" waters of the United States. § 328.3(c). It specifically provides that "[w]etlands separated from other waters of the United States by man-made dikes or barriers, natural river berms, beach dunes and the like are 'adjacent wetlands.'" *Ibid.* . . .

In sum, on its only plausible interpretation, the phrase "the waters of the United States" includes only those relatively permanent, standing or continuously flowing bodies of water "forming geographic features" that are described in ordinary parlance as "streams[,] . . . oceans, rivers, [and] lakes." See Webster's Second 2882. The phrase does not include channels through which water flows intermittently or ephemerally, or channels that periodically provide drainage for rainfall. The Corps' expansive interpretation of the "the waters of the United States" is thus not "based on a permissible construction of the statute." *Chevron U.S.A. Inc. v. Natural Resources Defense Council, Inc.*, 467 U.S. 837, 843 (1984)....

Therefore, *only* those wetlands with a continuous surface connection to bodies that are "waters of the United States" in their own right, so that there is no clear demarcation between "waters" and wetlands, are "adjacent to" such waters and covered by the Act. Wetlands with only an intermittent, physically remote hydrologic connection to "waters of the United States" do not implicate the boundary-drawing problem of *Riverside Bayview*, and thus lack the necessary connection to covered waters that we described as a "significant nexus" in *SWANCC*. 531 U.S., at 167. Thus, establishing that wetlands such as those at the Rapanos and Carabell sites are covered by the Act requires two findings: First, that the adjacent channel contains a "wate[r] of the United States," (*i.e.*, a relatively permanent body of water connected to traditional interstate navigable waters); and second, that the wetland has a continuous surface connection with that water, making it difficult to determine where the "water" ends and the "wetland" begins....

Finally, respondents and many *amici* admonish that narrowing the definition of "the waters of the United States" will hamper federal efforts to preserve the Nation's wetlands. It is not clear that the state and local conservation efforts that the CWA explicitly calls for, see 33 U.S.C. § 1251(b), are in any way inadequate for the goal of preservation. In any event, a Comprehensive National Wetlands Protection Act is not before us, and the "wis[dom]" of such a statute, *post*, at 19 (opinion of Stevens, J.), is beyond our ken. What is clear, however, is that Congress did not enact one when it granted the Corps jurisdiction over only "the *waters* of the United States."

VI

In an opinion long on praise of environmental protection and notably short on analysis of the statutory text and structure, the dissent would hold that "the waters of the United States" include any wetlands "adjacent" (no matter how broadly defined) to "tributaries" (again, no matter how broadly defined) of traditional navigable waters. For legal support of its policy-laden conclusion, the dissent relies exclusively on two sources: "[o]ur unanimous opinion in *Riverside Bayview*," *post*, at 6; and "Congress' deliberate acquiescence in the Corps' regulations in 1977," *post*, at 11. Each of these is demonstrably inadequate to support the apparently limitless scope that the dissent would permit the Corps to give to the Act....

We vacate the judgments of the Sixth Circuit in both No. 04-1034 and No. 04-1384, and remand both cases for further proceedings.

Rapanos highlights a major problem in contemporary environmental law, the "silo problem." The case deals with what is considered an "adjacent wetland" for purposes of Section 404 of the CWA. The case is decided based on a technical analysis of whether certain waters touch each other without taking into account the ecosystem that relies on the watershed of a river and whether its sources are touching or not. This case is only one of many cases dealing with just how far federal jurisdiction under the CWA can be extended to ensure fulfillment of its purpose of restoring and maintaining the chemical, physical, and biological integrity of the nation's waters. And it is one of many cases that resolves the issue by a highly technical reading of the statute as opposed to discerning congressional intent.

D. Endangered Species Act of 1973

When considering the overall success rate of the multiple environmental statutes enacted in the 1970s, the Endangered Species Act (ESA) is considered one of the most effective.[19] The Act includes three main elements: (1) Preventing listed species from being killed or harmed, (2) protecting habitat essential to these species' survival, and (3) creating plans to restore healthy populations. The ESA was passed in recognition that, as well as humans, nonhuman species in the Earth community require attention and protection and that human activity has significantly affected their ability to not only thrive, but survive.[20] The overall purposes of the ESA are "to provide a means whereby the ecosystems upon which endangered species and threatened species

[19] According to the Center for Biological Diversity:

> The Endangered Species Act is the strongest law for protecting biodiversity passed by any nation. Its purpose is to prevent the extinction of our most at-risk plants and animals, increase their numbers and effect their full recovery—and eventually their removal from the endangered list.
>
> Currently the Act protects more than 1,600 plant and animal species in the United States and its territories, many of which are successfully recovering.
>
> Over the past four-plus decades, the Endangered Species Act has repeatedly demonstrated that—when used to the full extent of the law—it *works.* The Act has been more than 99 percent successful at preventing extinction. Were it not for the Act, scientists have estimated, at least 227 species would have likely gone extinct since the law's passage in 1973.

Center for Biological Diversity, *The Endangered Species Act: A Wild Success,* https://www.biologicaldiversity.org/campaigns/esa_wild_success (last visited Mar. 7, 2020). Further 233 million acres have been protected as critical habitat. *Id.* A lower measure of success of 41 percent was given by the Congressional Research Service in 2016. Salvador Rizzo, *Has the Endangered Species Act Saved "Very Few" Plants and Animals?* Washington Post (Aug.16, 2019).

[20] The Congress finds and declares that (1) various species of fish, wildlife, and plants in the United States have been rendered extinct as a consequence of economic growth and development untempered by adequate concern and conservation; (2) other species of fish, wildlife, and plants have been so depleted in numbers that they are in danger of or threatened with extinction; (3) these species of fish, wildlife, and plants are of esthetic, ecological, educational, historical, recreational, and scientific value to the Nation and its people; (4) the United States has pledged itself as a sovereign state in the international community to conserve to the extent practicable the various species of fish or wildlife and plants facing extinction, pursuant to (A) migratory bird treaties with Canada and Mexico; (B) the Migratory and Endangered Bird Treaty with Japan; (C) the Convention on Nature Protection and Wildlife Preservation in the Western Hemisphere; (D) the International Convention for the Northwest Atlantic Fisheries; (E) the International Convention for the High Seas Fisheries of the North Pacific Ocean; (F) the Convention on International Trade in Endangered Species of Wild Fauna and Flora; and (G) other international agreements; and (5) encouraging the States and other interested parties, through Federal financial assistance and a system of incentives, to develop and maintain conservation programs which meet national and international standards is a key to meeting the Nation's international commitments and to better safeguarding, for the benefit of all citizens, the Nation's heritage in fish, wildlife, and plants. (16 U.S.C. § 1531(a)(1)-(5) (1973).)

depend may be conserved, to provide a program for the conservation of such endangered species and threatened species, and to take such steps as may be appropriate to achieve the purposes of the treaties and conventions set forth in subsection (a) of this section."[21] The ESA is administered by the National Marine Fisheries Service within the Department of Commerce, which has jurisdiction over marine species, and the U.S. Fish and Wildlife Service within the Department of Interior, which has jurisdiction over freshwater fish and all other species.

Below are two cases decided by the Supreme Court in different periods. In the first, the snail darter was protected at tremendous cost to the parties interested in building the Tellico Dam on the Little Tennessee River. In the second, involving the dusky gopher frog, the unanimous decision paid greater attention to costs as well as to agency discretion in remanding the case for further consideration.

Tennessee Valley Authority v. Hiram G. Hill, Jr.

437 U.S. 153 (1978)

CHIEF JUSTICE BURGER delivered the opinion of the Court.

The Endangered Species Act of 1973 (Act) authorizes the Secretary of the Interior (Secretary) in § 4 to declare a species of life "endangered." Section 7 specifies that all "federal departments and agencies shall, . . . with the assistance of the Secretary, utilize their authorities in furtherance of the purposes of [the] Act by carrying out programs for the conservation of endangered species . . . and by taking such action necessary to insure that actions authorized, funded, or carried out by them do not jeopardize the continued existence of such endangered species and threatened species or result in the destruction or modification of habitat of such species which is determined by the Secretary . . . to be critical." Shortly after the Act's passage the Secretary was petitioned to list a small fish popularly known as the snail darter as an endangered species under the Act. Thereafter the Secretary made the designation. Having determined that the snail darter apparently lives only in that portion of the Little Tennessee River that would be completely inundated by the impoundment of the reservoir created as a consequence of the completion of the Tellico Dam, he declared that area as the snail darter's "critical habitat." Notwithstanding the near completion of the multimillion-dollar dam, the Secretary issued a regulation, in which it was declared that, pursuant to § 7, "all Federal agencies must take such action as is necessary to ensure that actions authorized, funded, or carried out by them do not result in the destruction or modification of this critical habitat area." Respondents brought this suit to enjoin completion of the dam and impoundment of the reservoir, claiming that those actions would violate the Act by causing the snail darter's extinction. The District Court after trial denied relief and dismissed the

[21] *Id.* at § 1531(b).

complaint. Though finding that the impoundment of the reservoir would probably jeopardize the snail darter's continued existence, the court noted that Congress, though fully aware of the snail darter problem, had continued Tellico's appropriations, and concluded that "[a]t some point in time a federal project becomes so near completion and so incapable of modification that a court of equity should not apply a statute enacted long after inception of the project produce an unreasonable result. . . ." The Court of Appeals reversed and ordered the District Court permanently to enjoin completion of the project "until Congress, by appropriate legislation, exempts Tellico from compliance with the Act or the snail darter has been deleted from the list of endangered species or its critical habitat materially redefined." The court held that the record revealed a prima facie violation of § 7 in that the Tennessee Valley Authority had failed to take necessary action to avoid jeopardizing the snail darter's critical habitat by its "actions." The court thus rejected the contention that the word "actions" as used in § 7 was not intended by Congress to encompass the terminal phases of ongoing projects. At various times before, during, and after the foregoing judicial proceedings, TVA represented to congressional Appropriations Committees that the Act did not prohibit completion of the Tellico Project and described its efforts to transplant the snail darter. The Committees consistently recommended appropriations for the dam, sometimes stating their views that the Act did not prohibit completion of the dam at its advanced stage, and Congress each time approved TVA's general budget, which contained funds for the dam's continued construction. Held:

1. The Endangered Species Act prohibits impoundment of the Little Tennessee River by the Tellico Dam. Pp. 172-193.

(a) The language of § 7 is plain and makes no exception such as that urged by petitioner whereby the Act would not apply to a project like Tellico that was well under way when Congress passed the Act. Pp. 172-174.

(b) It is clear from the Act's legislative history that Congress intended to halt and reverse the trend toward species extinction—whatever the cost. The pointed omission of the type of qualified language previously included in endangered species legislation reveals a conscious congressional design to give endangered species priority over the "primary missions" of federal agencies. Congress, moreover, foresaw that § 7 would on occasion require agencies to alter ongoing projects in order to fulfill the Act's goals. Pp. 174-187.

(c) None of the limited "hardship exemptions" provided in the Act would even remotely apply to the Tellico Project. P. 188. . . .

2. The Court of Appeals did not err in ordering that completion of the Tellico Dam which would have violated the Act be enjoined. Congress has spoken in the plainest words, making it clear that endangered species are to be accorded the highest priorities. Since that legislative power has been exercised, it is up to the Executive Branch to administer the law and for the Judiciary to enforce it when, as here, enforcement has been sought. Pp. 193-194.

* * *

Weyerhaeuser Co. v. U.S. Fish and Wildlife Service

586 U.S. ___ (2018)

CHIEF JUSTICE ROBERTS delivered the opinion of the Court.

The Endangered Species Act directs the Secretary of the Interior, upon listing a species as endangered, to also designate the "critical habitat" of the species. A group of landowners whose property was designated as critical habitat for an endangered frog challenged the designation. The landowners urge that their land cannot be *critical* habitat because it is not *habitat*, which they contend refers only to areas where the frog could currently survive. The court below ruled that the Act imposed no such limitation on the scope of critical habitat.

The Act also authorizes the Secretary to exclude an area that would otherwise be included as critical habitat, if the benefits of exclusion outweigh the benefits of designation. The landowners challenged the decision of the Secretary not to exclude their property, but the court below held that the Secretary's action was not subject to judicial review.

We granted certiorari to review both rulings.

I

A

The amphibian *Rana sevosa* is popularly known as the "dusky gopher frog"—"dusky" because of its dark coloring and "gopher" because it lives underground. The dusky gopher frog is about three inches long, with a large head, plump body, and short legs. Warts dot its back, and dark spots cover its entire body. Final Rule to List the Mississippi Gopher Frog Distinct Population Segment of Dusky Gopher Frog as Endangered, 66 Fed. Reg. 62993 (2001) (Final Listing). It is noted for covering its eyes with its front legs when it feels threatened, peeking out periodically until danger passes. *Markle Interests, LLC v. United States Fish and Wildlife Serv.*, 827 F.3d 452, 458, n. 2 (CA5 2016). Less endearingly, it also secretes a bitter, milky substance to deter would-be diners. Brief for Intervenor-Respondents 6, n. 1.

The frog spends most of its time in burrows and stump holes located in upland longleaf pine forests. In such forests, frequent fires help maintain an open canopy, which in turn allows vegetation to grow on the forest floor. The vegetation supports the small insects that the frog eats and provides a place for the frog's eggs to attach when it breeds. The frog breeds in "ephemeral" ponds that are dry for part of the year. Such ponds are safe for tadpoles because predatory fish cannot live in them. Designation of Critical Habitat for Dusky Gopher Frog, 77 Fed. Reg. 35129-35131 (2012) (Designation).

The dusky gopher frog once lived throughout coastal Alabama, Louisiana, and Mississippi, in the longleaf pine forests that used to cover the southeast.

But more than 98% of those forests have been removed to make way for urban development, agriculture, and timber plantations. The timber plantations consist of fast-growing loblolly pines planted as close together as possible, resulting in a closed-canopy forest inhospitable to the frog. The near eradication of the frog's habitat sent the species into severe decline. By 2001, the known wild population of the dusky gopher frog had dwindled to a group of 100 at a single pond in southern Mississippi. That year, the Fish and Wildlife Service, which administers the Endangered Species Act of 1973 on behalf of the Secretary of the Interior, listed the dusky gopher frog as an endangered species. Final Listing 62993–62995; see 87 Stat. 886, 16 U.S.C. § 1533(a)(1).

B

When the Secretary lists a species as endangered, he must also designate the critical habitat of that species. § 1533(a)(3)(A)(i). The ESA defines "critical habitat" as:

> "(i) the specific areas within the geographical area occupied by the species . . . on which are found those physical or biological features (I) essential to the conservation of the species and (II) which may require special management considerations or protection; and
>
> "(ii) specific areas outside the geographical area occupied by the species . . . upon a determination by the Secretary that such areas are essential for the conservation of the species." § 1532(5)(A).

Before the Secretary may designate an area as critical habitat, the ESA requires him to "tak[e] into consideration the economic impact" and other relevant impacts of the designation. § 1533(b)(2). The statute goes on to authorize him to "exclude any area from critical habitat if he determines that the benefits of such exclusion outweigh the benefits of [designation]," unless exclusion would result in extinction of the species. *Ibid.* . . .

Due to resource constraints, the Service did not designate the frog's critical habitat in 2001, when it listed the frog as endangered. Designation, at 35118-35119. In the following years, the Service discovered two additional naturally occurring populations and established another population through translocation. The first population nonetheless remains the only stable one and by far the largest. Dept. of Interior, U.S. Fish and Wildlife Serv., Dusky Gopher Frog (*Rana sevosa*) Recovery Plan iv, 6-7 (2015).

In 2010, in response to litigation by the Center for Biological Diversity, the Service published a proposed critical-habitat designation. Designation, at 35119. The Service proposed to designate as occupied critical habitat all four areas with existing dusky gopher frog populations. The Service found that each of those areas possessed the three features that the Service considered "essential to the conservation" of the frog and that required special protection: ephemeral ponds; upland open-canopy forest containing the holes and burrows in which the frog could live; and open-canopy forest connecting the two. But the Service also determined that designating only those four sites would not adequately ensure the frog's conservation. Because the existing dusky gopher frog populations were all located in two adjacent counties on the Gulf Coast of Mississippi, local events such as extreme weather or an outbreak of an infectious disease could jeopardize the entire species. Designation of Critical Habitat for Mississippi Gopher Frog, 75 Fed. Reg. 31394 (2010) (proposed 50 CFR Part 17).

To protect against that risk, the Service proposed to designate as *unoccupied* critical habitat a 1,544-acre site in St. Tammany Parish, Louisiana. The site, dubbed "Unit 1" by the Service, had been home to the last known population of dusky gopher frogs outside of Mississippi. The frog had not been seen in Unit 1 since 1965, and a closed-canopy timber plantation occupied much of the site. But the Service found that the site retained five ephemeral ponds "of remarkable quality," and determined that an open-canopy forest could be restored on the surrounding uplands "with reasonable effort." Although the uplands in Unit 1 lacked the open-canopy forests (and, of course, the frogs) necessary for designation as occupied critical habitat, the Service concluded that the site met the statutory definition of unoccupied critical habitat because its rare, high-quality breeding ponds and its distance from existing frog populations made it essential for the conservation of the species. Designation, at 35118, 35124, 35133, 35135.

After issuing its proposal, the Service commissioned a report on the probable economic impact of designating each area, including Unit 1, as critical habitat for the dusky gopher frog. See 16 U.S.C. § 1533(b)(2); App. 63. Petitioner Weyerhaeuser Company, a timber company, owns part of Unit 1 and leases the remainder from a group of family landowners. Brief for Petitioner 16. While the critical-habitat designation has no direct effect on the timber operations, St. Tammany Parish is a fast-growing part of the New Orleans metropolitan area, and the landowners have already invested in plans to more profitably develop the site. App. 80-83. The report recognized that anyone developing the area may need to obtain Clean Water Act permits from the Army Corps of Engineers before filling any wetlands on Unit 1. 33 U.S.C. § 1344(a). Because Unit 1 is designated as critical habitat, Section 7 of the ESA would require the Corps to consult with the Service before issuing any permits....

C

Weyerhaeuser and the family landowners sought to vacate the designation in Federal District Court. They contended that Unit 1 could not be critical habitat for the dusky gopher frog because the frog could not survive there: Survival would require replacing the closed-canopy timber plantation encircling the ponds with an open-canopy longleaf pine forest. The District Court nonetheless upheld the designation. *Markle Interests, LLC v. United States Fish and Wildlife Serv.*, 40 F. Supp. 3d 744 (ED La. 2014). The court determined that Unit 1 satisfied the statutory definition of unoccupied critical habitat, which requires only that the Service deem the land "essential for the conservation [of] the species." *Id.*, at 760.

Weyerhaeuser also challenged the Service's decision not to exclude Unit 1 from the dusky gopher frog's critical habitat, arguing that the Service had failed to adequately weigh the benefits of designating Unit 1 against the economic impact. In addition, Weyerhaeuser argued that the Service had used an unreasonable methodology for estimating economic impact and, regardless of methodology, had failed to consider several categories of costs. *Id.*, at 759. The court approved the Service's methodology and declined to consider Weyerhaeuser's challenge to the decision not to exclude. See *id.*, at 763-767, and n. 29.

The Fifth Circuit affirmed. 827 F.3d 452. The Court of Appeals rejected the suggestion that the definition of critical habitat contains any "habitability requirement." *Id.*, at 468. The court also concluded that the Service's decision not to exclude Unit 1 was committed to agency discretion by law and was therefore unreviewable. *Id.*, at 473-475. Judge Owen dissented. She wrote that Unit 1 could not be "essential for the conservation of the species" because it lacked the open-canopy forest that the Service itself had determined was "essential to the conservation" of the frog. *Id.*, at 480-481.

The Fifth Circuit denied rehearing en banc. *Markle Interests, LLC v. United States Fish and Wildlife Serv.*, 848 F.3d 635 (2017). Judge Jones dissented, joined by Judges Jolly, Smith, Clement, Owen, and Elrod. They reasoned that critical habitat must first be habitat, and Unit 1 in its present state could not be habitat for the dusky gopher frog. *Id.*, at 641. The dissenting judges also concluded that the Service's decision not to exclude Unit 1 was reviewable for abuse of discretion. *Id.*, at 654, and n. 21.

We granted certiorari to consider two questions: (1) whether "critical habitat" under the ESA must also be habitat; and (2) whether a federal court may review an agency decision not to exclude a certain area from critical habitat because of the economic impact of such a designation. 583 U.S. ___ (2018)....

Section 4(b)(2) states that the Secretary

> "shall designate critical habitat . . . after taking into consideration the economic impact, the impact on national security, and any other relevant impact, of specifying any particular area as critical habitat. The Secretary may exclude any area from critical habitat if he determines that the benefits of such exclusion outweigh the benefits of specifying such area . . . unless he determines . . . that the failure to designate such area as critical habitat will result in the extinction of the species concerned." 16 U.S C. § 1533(b)(2).

Although the text meanders a bit, we recognized in *Bennett v. Spear*, 520 U.S. 154 (1997), that the provision describes a unified process for weighing the impact of designating an area as critical habitat. The first sentence of Section 4(b)(2) imposes a "categorical requirement" that the Secretary "tak[-e] into consideration" economic and other impacts before such a designation. *Id.*, at 172 (emphasis deleted). The second sentence authorizes the Secretary to act on his consideration by providing that he may exclude an area from critical habitat if he determines that the benefits of exclusion outweigh the benefits of designation. The Service followed that procedure here (albeit in a flawed manner, according to Weyerhaeuser). It commissioned a report to estimate the costs of designating the proposed critical habitat, concluded that those costs were not "disproportionate" to the benefits of designation, and "[c]onsequently" declined to "exercis[e] [its] discretion to exclude any areas from [the] designation of critical habitat." App. 190.

Bennett explained that the Secretary's "ultimate decision" to designate or exclude, which he "arriv[es] at" after considering economic and other impacts, is reviewable "for abuse of discretion." 520 U.S., at 172. The Service dismisses that language as a "passing reference . . . not necessarily inconsistent with the Service's understanding," which is that the Secretary's decision not to exclude an area is wholly discretionary and therefore unreviewable. Brief for Federal Respondents 50. The Service bases its understanding on the second sentence of Section 4(b)(2), which states that the Secretary "*may* exclude [an] area from critical habitat if he determines that the benefits of such exclusion outweigh the benefits of [designation]."

The use of the word "may" certainly confers discretion on the Secretary. That does not, however, segregate his discretionary decision not to exclude from the procedure mandated by Section 4(b)(2), which directs the Secretary to consider the economic and other impacts of designation when making his exclusion decisions. . . .

Because it determined that the Service's decisions not to exclude were committed to agency discretion and therefore unreviewable, the Court of Appeals did not consider whether the Service's assessment of the costs and benefits of designation was flawed in a way that rendered the resulting decision not to exclude Unit 1 arbitrary, capricious, or an abuse of discretion. Accordingly, we remand to the Court of Appeals to consider that question, if necessary, in the first instance.

The judgment of the Court of Appeals for the Fifth Circuit is vacated, and the case is remanded for further proceedings consistent with this opinion.

The ESA is unusual in that, as discussed in *TVA v. Hiram* above, once an endangered species and its critical habitat are identified, the law requires an immediate ban on taking the species and on economic development or exploitation of the species' critical habitat regardless of the cost. Yet, as seen in the later *Weyerhaeuser v. U.S. Fish and Wildlife Service* decision, less discretion is now given to responsible agencies in making these determinations and cost-benefit analysis is required in doing so.

While the ESA is considered one of the strongest environmental laws, some of its weaknesses are that

- *It protects species on a one-by-one basis and doesn't apply until a species is nearly extinct.* The ESA protects only plants and animals that have been officially listed as "endangered" or "threatened." The procedures for listing a species are in § 4 of the ESA, 16 U.S.C. § 1533, and the regulations in 50 C.F.R. Part 424. The actual lists are in 50 C.F.R. Part 17. An "endangered" species is one that is "in danger of extinction" throughout all or a significant portion of its range. 16 U.S.C. § 1532(6). A "threatened" species is one that is "likely to become endangered" within the foreseeable future. 16 U.S.C. § 1532(20).

- *The protections for plant species are weaker.* The prohibition against "taking" covers fish and wildlife but not plants. *Cf.* 16 U.S.C. § 1532(8) and § 1532(14). It is, however, illegal to remove an endangered plant from federal land and reduce it to possession, and federal law also federalizes state law prohibitions on the taking of plants.
- *It has limited effect on privately owned habitat.* "Habitat loss is the primary threat to endangered species in the United States. At present, most endangered and threatened species habitat is privately owned."[22] Designations of critical habitat on private land have limited legal import as private use is usually permitted except where this would clearly be detrimental to the protected species. Further, because of the potential impact of the designation of species and their critical habitat, owners of land and others may sue or threaten suit to prevent or remove designation. This restrains designations, holds them up, and in some cases removes them.
- *The Trump Administration in 2019 significantly weakened regulations under the Act.* Under new rules adopted by the EPA, it is easier to remove an endangered species from the list[23] and protection for threatened species are weakened. The rules shorten the timescale of harm to species in the "foreseeable future," making it more difficult to factor in the effects of climate. The new rules also remove longstanding language that prevents the consideration of economic effects in designating a species as threatened or endangered.[24]

E. Comprehensive Environmental Response, Compensation, and Liability Act of 1980 (CERCLA)

Underlying all cases of environmental degradation is the question: Who is responsible for cleaning up this mess? Despite the numerous statutes and regulations passed from 1970 onward, this question was somehow left unanswered until congress passed the Comprehensive Environmental Response, Compensation, and Liability Act of 1980 (CERCLA).

Both nationally and internationally, the principle of "polluter pays" is generally considered acceptable and equitable.[25] This concept is fairly simple when allocating

[22] JONATHAN ADLER, REBUILDING THE ARK: NEW PERSPECTIVES ON ENDANGERED SPECIES ACT REFORM 7 & 11(2011).
[23] Lisa Friedman, U.S. Significantly Weakens Endangered Species Act, N.Y. TIMES (Aug. 16, 2019), https://www.nytimes.com/2019/08/12/climate/endangered-species-act-changes.html.
[24] *Id.*
[25] "National authorities should endeavour to promote the internalization of environmental costs and the use of economic instruments, taking into account the approach that the polluter should, in principle, bear the cost of pollution, with due regard to the public interest and without distorting international trade and investment." Principle 16 of the Rio Declaration, UN Conference on Environment and Development, Principle 16, UN Doc. A/CONF. 151/5/Rev. 1, *reprinted in* 31 I.L.M. 874 (1992).

responsibility. For example, Corporation A dumps toxic sludge in GreenField. Who is responsible? Corporation A.

However, as our industrial and production methods have become more complex, liability allocation has as well. CERCLA[26] was passed in 1980 in the wake of the Love Canal tragedy, a major environmental disaster in New York in which toxic waste seeped out of a landfill, poisoning local ecosystems and communities. Adopting common law concepts of strict liability into substantive federal law, CERCLA holds four classes of persons potentially liable for the cleanup of environmental disasters:

> (1) the owner and operator of a vessel or a facility,
> (2) any person who at the time of disposal of any hazardous substance owned or operated any facility at which such hazardous substances were disposed of,
> (3) any person who by contract, agreement, or otherwise arranged for disposal or treatment, or arranged with a transporter for transport for disposal or treatment, of hazardous substances owned or possessed by such person, by any other party or entity, at any facility or incineration vessel owned or operated by another party or entity and containing such hazardous substances, and
> (4) any person who accepts or accepted any hazardous substances for transport to disposal or treatment facilities, incineration vessels or sites selected by such person, from which there is a release, or a threatened release which causes the incurrence of response costs, of a hazardous substance....[27]

In *State of New York v. Shore Realty*,[28] Judge Oakes provided a concise overview of CERCLA:

> CERCLA was designed "to bring order to the array of partly redundant, partly inadequate federal hazardous substances cleanup and compensation laws." It applies "primarily to the cleanup of leaking inactive or abandoned sites and to emergency responses to spills." And it distinguishes between two kinds of response: remedial actions—generally long-term or permanent containment or disposal programs—and removal efforts—typically short-term cleanup arrangements.
>
> CERCLA authorizes the federal government to respond in several ways. EPA can use Superfund resources to clean up hazardous waste sites and spills. 42 U.S.C. § 9611. The National Contingency Plan ("NCP"), prepared by EPA pursuant to CERCLA, governs cleanup efforts by "establish[ing] procedures and standards for responding to releases of hazardous substances." At the same time, EPA can sue for reimbursement of cleanup costs from any responsible parties it can locate, allowing the federal government to respond immediately while later trying to shift financial responsibility to others. Thus, Superfund covers cleanup costs if the site has been abandoned, if the responsible parties elude detection, or if private resources are inadequate. In addition, CERCLA authorizes EPA to seek an injunction in federal district court to force a responsible party to clean

[26] Comprehensive Environmental Response, Compensation, and Liability Act, 42 U.S.C. § 9601 (1980).
[27] *Id.* at § 9607.
[28] *State of New York v. Shore Realty*, 759 F.2d 1032 (2d Cir. 1985). Footnotes and some citations omitted.

> up any site or spill that presents an imminent and substantial danger to public health or welfare or the environment. 42 U.S.C. § 9606(a).
>
> In sum, CERCLA is not a regulatory standard-setting statute such as the Clean Air Act. Rather, the government generally undertakes pollution abatement, and polluters pay for such abatement through tax and reimbursement liability. Congress clearly did not intend, however, to leave clean up under CERCLA solely in the hands of the federal government. A state or political subdivision may enter into a contract or cooperative agreement with EPA, whereby both may take action on a cost-sharing basis. And states, like EPA, can sue responsible parties for remedial and removal costs if such efforts are "not inconsistent with" the NCP. While CERCLA expressly does not preempt state law, it precludes "recovering compensation for the same removal costs or damages or claims" under both CERCLA and state or other federal laws, and prohibits states from requiring contributions to any fund "the purpose of which is to pay compensation for claims . . . which may be compensated under" CERCLA, Moreover, "any . . . person" who is acting consistently with the requirements of the NCP may recover "necessary costs of response." Finally, responsible parties are liable for "damages for injury to, destruction of, or loss of natural resources, including the reasonable costs of assessing such injury, destruction, or loss resulting from such a release." 42 U.S.C. § 9607(a)(4)(C).
>
> Congress intended that responsible parties be held strictly liable, even though an explicit provision for strict liability was not included in the compromise. Section 9601(32) provides that "liability" under CERCLA "shall be construed to be the standard of liability" under section 311 of the Clean Water Act, 33 U.S.C. § 1321, which courts have held to be strict liability, and which Congress understood to impose such liability. Moreover, the sponsors of the compromise expressly stated that section 9607 provides for strict liability. Strict liability under CERCLA, however, is not absolute; there are defenses for causation solely by an act of God, an act of war, or acts or omissions of a third party other than an employee or agent of the defendant or one whose act or omission occurs in connection with a contractual relationship with the defendant. 42 U.S.C. § 9607(b).

In some ways, CERCLA has been effective. The joint, strict, and several liability of "potentially responsible parties" puts industry on the hook for cleaning up major environmental contamination. As a result, CERCLA has resulted in the cleanup of some of the nation's most polluted sites.

However, CERLA has major shortcomings, as well. Given the severity of pollution, cleanup can be slow, requiring hundreds of years for some sites. CERCLA also does not do enough to prevent industry from polluting in the first place, which should be an overarching goal of environmental laws. For example, there are over 30,000 report of oil and hazardous substance releases each year that current environmental laws fail to prevent.[29] Finally, case law has also developed that creates loopholes for parties to avoid the "strict liability standard."[30]

[29] National Response System, 2017 Outreach Presentation, https://nrt.org/sites/2/files/NRT-NRS_Outreach_Presentation_2017%20v4.2_31July2018.pdf.
[30] *See United States v. Chem-Dyne Corp.*, 572 F. Supp. 802 (S.D. Ohio 1983).

F. Conclusion

"Two things are needed to guide our judgment . . . for the challenges ahead: A certain alarm at what is happening at present and a fascination with the future available to us only if we respond creatively to the urgencies of the present."

Thomas Berry[31]

While Earth law is being developed to bring about fundamental changes in environmental law, the laws of the past should not be thoughtlessly cast aside. They have worked after a fashion. In the United States, rivers are no longer afire, our air is cleaner, skies are clearer, species that would have otherwise gone extinct are still part of the Earth community, and there are federally uniform standards by which all states are bound to ensure that these improvements continue. However, much like the common law system that preceded it, the current regulatory approach is now showing that more is needed.

For contemporary environmental law to be a functional component of the broader field of Earth law, specific issues need to be addressed and overcome.

- Contemporary environmental law is still part of the modernist project—the modernist project focuses on economic growth, industrial development, and individual human rights without due regard for the health of the Earth community.
- It is part of a legal system that regards nature as property—the logic of nuisance dominates environmental regulation and enforcement; an owner of property owns the nature on their property and can do with that nature as they want, provided that their act doesn't harm adjacent human beings. It treats nature as having primarily, if not only, instrumental value for human benefit and does not consider nature as having intrinsic value.
- It relies on restriction and manipulation of property rights to protect well-being and health—regulation is for the benefit of human health and well-being and is accomplished through restrictions on what owners can do with their property.
- It is a maze of siloed laws, treaties, regulations, and overlapping jurisdictions—environmental laws are a raft of laws and regulations enforceable by diverse agencies, frustrating both regulators and regulated; enforcement is weak and even the capacity to enforce these laws is weak.
- It is weakened by regulatory capture—the industries and people who are regulated through money, political influence, and lobbying gain inordinate influence over the agencies that regulate them.
- It is subject to cost-benefit analysis—policymakers, regulatory agencies, and courts assign a monetary value to nature and weigh that amount against the monetary cost to industries and people subject to regulation and enforcement;

[31] Thomas Berry, *Evening Thoughts* 17 (2006).

this is a too-easily manipulated process and fails to take into account the intrinsic value of nature.
- It is ineffective at protecting against climate change and global environmental degradation — nature is addressed piecemeal; improvements are realized (such as cleaner air in the United States) while generalized global warming and environmental degradation advance.

The current system focuses on the symptoms of environmental degradation and not the causes. As the history of contemporary environmental law presented in this chapter demonstrates, the need for large-scale, comprehensive legal regulation remains. But the foundation of the present regulatory system needs to change. The current system is property-based and anthropocentric. The present system was designed to deal with the negative side effects of economic development. Now society is facing greater environmental risks and risks of different types than those contemplated in the implementation of contemporary environmental law.

To meet these risks, as stated earlier, Earth law is a departure from contemporary environmental law and an extension of it in a new context.

STUDY QUESTIONS

(1) How well have NEPA, the CWA, the CAA and the ESA worked to protect the environment?

(2) What aspects of NEPA, the CWA, the CAA and the ESA might provide opportunities to develop Earth law? What aspects undermine the development of Earth law?

(3) What are the challenges that will be faced in efforts to develop an ecoentric perspective within the state and federal agencies that review and approve permits to discharge pollutants into the air, water, and land? How might judges and justices come to understand the meaning and value of an ecocentric perspective?

(4) In Managing The Environment, Managing Ourselves: A History Of American Environmental Policy, Third Ed. (2020), Richard N.L. Andrews observed: "The most revolutionary element of this new [in the 1970s] public consciousness [which led to the enactment of environmental laws in the U.S.] was a powerful new awareness of the environment as a living system—a 'web of life,' or ecosystem—rather than just a storehouse of commodities to be extracted or a physical or chemical machine to be manipulated." Consider how this "powerful new awareness of the environment as a living system" has ebbed over the ensuing five decades. What factors contributed to the diminution of this awareness? What factors might lead to increased awareness by policymakers in the U.S.? How can this awareness be increased in the general population? What are the obstacles to increasing the awareness?

(5) To what extent has the regulation of conduct that damages the environment, which is codified by NEPA, the CAA, the CWA and other environmental regulatory frameworks, "encourage[d] productive and enjoyable harmony between man and his environment," "promote[d] efforts . . . [to] prevent or eliminate damage to the environment and biosphere and stimulate the health and welfare of man," and "enrich[ed] the understanding of the ecological systems and natural resources important to the Nation"? To what extent has it failed to meet the "national policy" declared in NEPA? What legal developments (as opposed to political developments) might be important to achieving the national policy goals established by NEPA?

(6) Environmental regulation in the United States is a comprehensive yet siloed approach to mitigating and preventing environmental degradation. Other important environmental statutes include, but are not limited to, the Federal Insecticide, Fungicide, and Rodenticide Act (FIFRA), the Marine Protection, Research, and Sanctuaries Act, the Safe Drinking Water Act, the Toxic Substances Contract Act of 1976, and the Resources Conservation and Recovery Act of 1976. Each of these laws represents another piece of the puzzle that should result in environmental protection. How might the approach of regulating each element of the environment separately work when ecosystems function as an interrelated whole? What kind of environmental framework might better protect the overarching health of ecosystems? How might a sustainability model of weighing people, planet, and profits fare in a world in which a viable human economy is perceived as the greatest necessity?

CHAPTER 2

The Origins of Earth Law[1]

I. INTRODUCTION

This chapter continues the history of environmental law given in Chapter 1 by discussing the origins of Earth law. Before beginning, it might be helpful to restate the working definition of Earth law given in the introduction to this book:

> Earth law is the emerging body of law for protecting, restoring, and stabilizing the functional interdependency of Earth's life and life-support systems at the local, bioregional, national, and global levels. Earth law may be expressed in constitutional, statutory, common law, and customary law, as well as in treaties and other agreements both public and private.

It is also useful to restate that Earth law is both *a departure from* environmental law and *a new context for* its extension. Earth law is a departure from environmental law in that it covers matters simply not covered in environmental law. Earth law's philosophical presuppositions and approach are so different that it can be thought of as a new body of law. Earth law is a new context for the extension of environmental law in that many functions of environmental law—such as conserving wild areas, penalizing polluters, containing or restoring damaged ecosystems, and granting permits for projects and activities—will continue, yet, in the Earth law context, the way these functions will be carried out will change. As the transformation occurs, Earth law and environmental law will *not* proceed along parallel paths. Rather, transformed environmental law will become a part of Earth law, though perhaps maintaining its identity as a subset of functions within the larger category of Earth law.

Building on the foregoing, there are two things to understand about the origins of Earth law: (1) the *new context* that is common to Earth law and transformed environmental law; and (2) the *departure* from environmental law, which consists of transitioning to Earth law approaches that diverge from contemporary environmental law.

[1] This chapter was authored by, Grant Wilson, Herman Greene, Dalit Paradis, Andrew Cliburn, & Michelle Maloney.

a. Grant Wilson is Executive Director and Directing Attorney of Earth Law Center.

b. Michelle Maloney is Co-Founder and National Convenor of the Australian Earth Laws Alliance.

c. Dalit Paradis is an Earth Law Associate at Earth Law Center.

d. Andrew Cliburn is a Legal Volunteer at Earth Law Center.

e. Herman Greene is President of the Center for Ecozoic Studies.

This chapter begins with the new context by discussing the movement from a legal system based on separation between the human species and the rest of the world to one based on interdependence, entanglement, and mutuality. Then the chapter discusses the emerging approaches to Earth law covered in this book, namely: (a) the public trust doctrine and atmospheric trust litigation, (b) the rights of future generations, (c) the rights of nature, (d) co-violations: human environmental rights and the rights of nature, (e) nonhuman rights, (g) ecocide, (f) Indigenous legalities, (g) ecocentric environmental governance, and (h) other approaches global and local.

II. THE NEW CONTEXT: FROM AN ORIENTATION OF SEPARATION TO AN ORIENTATION OF CONNECTION[2]

A. Why Environmental Law Falls Short

Although regulation of human relationships with their environments is an enduring feature of history, "environmental law" is a definable set of laws that came into being in the latter half of the twentieth century to remediate urgent problems around the globe involving localized pollution of air, water, and land. By the beginning of the twenty-first century, there was a broad awareness that environmental threats went far beyond localized pollution, and that they extended to the ways that human activities negatively affect the biosphere as a whole through climate change, desertification, deforestation, ocean acidification, habitat fragmentation, species extinctions, and many other ways. Environmental policymakers at the national level failed to respond to the systemic changes that were occurring and instead focused on still more localized responses while taking care not to disadvantage business activity in the increasingly competitive globalized economy. There was environmental policymaking at the international level, as well, but it also failed to respond to these systemic changes.[3] What stands out from this experience is that while environmental law has expanded, the large-scale environmental problems facing the planet have grown worse.

The inability of environmental law to solve the problems is not because these problems are unsolvable or intractable. Environmental law has failed because it relies on a flawed orientation. Most environmental law wrongly, and strangely, presumes that *separation* is the key to effective environmentalism. Environmental law will succeed, and environmental problems will be solved, only when this separation-based orientation is replaced with one based on connection, entanglement, and mutuality—in other words, an orientation of interdependence. The movement to the orientation of interdependence is at the heart of Earth law.

[2] Many of the ideas in this section are taken from an article by Professor Jan G. Laitos entitled *Replacing the Algorithm for Environmental Law.*

[3] More than 3,500 multilateral and bilateral environmental agreements came into being. Ronald Mitchell et al., *What We Know (and Could Know) About International Environmental Agreements*, 20 GLOBAL ENVIRONMENTAL POLITICS (No.1) 103, 105 (Feb. 2020), https://doi.org/10.1162/glep_a_00544. A database of these agreements—called, among other things, "treaties," "conventions," and "protocols,"—is maintained by the International Environmental Agreements (IEA) Database Project, https://iea.uoregon.edu.

B. The Orientation of Separation

Both the harm that humans have done to the environment and the efforts to remedy or control those harms have been grounded in the presumption that humans are separate from nature. This illusion of separation developed over a long period of time. It began around 11,000 years ago at the end of the last ice age and the beginning of the Holocene epoch. The climate became favorable for agriculture involving crops and domesticated animals, and agriculture-based societies emerged in various parts of the world. This has been called the beginning of civilization—the first culture in civilization was agriculture, and agriculture continued to be at the base of all societies until the Industrial Revolution began about 250 years ago.

In agriculture-based societies, food became more abundant and reliable. There were even food surpluses, meaning that not everyone needed to be involved in food production. People could now live in villages, and later larger communities, and divide labor. Writing began around 3,000 BCE. While there were oral histories before this time, the beginning of writing has been considered the beginning of history, because written records could be kept. This was also the time classical civilizations began in the Middle East, Egypt, the Indus Valley, and later, China and Latin America. Each of these developments took humans further from the wild nature by which they had been surrounded as hunter-gatherers. The human drama focused on the relationship with nature. Increasingly, the drama shifted to relations with other humans and building civilization and even empires. Nature could not be taken for granted—there were droughts and floods and volcanic eruptions and plagues—but the steadfast endurance of nature with all of its vicissitudes began to be taken for granted by many.

In a period beginning around 800 BCE and ending around 300 BCE, the Hebrew prophets, Socrates, Plato, Aristotle, Gautama Buddha, the Hindu mystics, Confucius, Mencius, and Lao Tzu gave birth to the wisdom traditions that undergirded the classical civilizations.[4] The Jewish and Christian religious traditions that followed this period included the idea of a deity that entered into human history, bestowed special favor on humans, and granted them dominion over nature. Only humans were made in the image of God. This was another step in the separation of humans and nature.

Separation of a different kind and degree occurred in modernity beginning in the sixteenth century. The science of Francis Bacon (1561–1626), Galileo Galilei (1564–1642), and Isaac Newton (1643–1727) came to understand nature as mechanisms. The philosophy of René Descartes (1596–1650) separated the minds/souls of humans—which are unique to humans—from their bodies and all of the rest of nature, which could be understood as mechanisms.

The latter part of the eighteenth century brought the Industrial Revolution, modern economics, democracy, and a burst of human freedoms and rights. Modern science and the technologies of the Industrial Revolution gave humans almost god-like

[4] The German philosopher Karl Jaspers called this the "Axial Age" because the history of civilization turned upon it. For a thorough treatment of this period and its significance, *see* Karen Armstrong, The Great Transformation: The Beginnings of Our Religious Traditions (2006).

powers. Over time, nature became a resource for industrial development. Industrial development became the secular religion and the prime obligation of Western nations.

Economics supplied the discourse of development with a focus on individual initiative and accumulation of goods and capital. It explained that in the economic marketplace, individuals make choices to maximize their own personal welfare,[5] not for the good of society or nature.[6] When humans engaged in resource-use decisions, they ignored social and environmental values if the social consequences did not promote individual utility.[7] This behavior was not only seen as characteristic, but as normatively good, and something to be harnessed for economic growth and efficient allocation of goods and services.

Democracy and human rights also focused on individual initiative. Individual choice, regardless of morality, was to determine the direction of society. It was assumed that the good—largely defined as economic progress and an increase in human welfare—would be the result of free expression of ideas and preferences. Nature was to be the servant of humans, and now it was increasingly under apparent human mastery and control. Nature in this sense became a collection of objects to be used.

The post-World War II world produced yet another stage of separation, an explosion in economic growth and technology, along with the globalization of the economy and a Westernized materialistic culture. This period is called the "Great Acceleration."[8] Since 1945:

- The number of motor vehicles (cars, trucks, buses) worldwide increased from 40 million to more than 1.3 billion;[9]
- The human population more than tripled and currently stands at about 7.7 billion. The number of people living in cities increased from 700 million to more than 4 billion (more than 54 percent of the total);[10]
- Plastic production increased from 2.3 million tons in 1950 to 448 million tons in 2015. Half the plastic ever produced has been produced in the last 15 years and production is still increasing;[11]

[5] Standard economic theory relies on a model of human behavior based on rational choice theory, which still underscores much environmental policy. Rational choice assumes that humans act rationally to maximize marginal utility when making choices to maximize personal advantage. *See* Jon Elster, Nuts and Bolts for the Social Sciences 29 (1989); *see generally* Binyamin Appelbaum, The Economists' Hour: False Prophets, Free Markets, and the Fracture of Society (2019).

[6] Another standard economic model of human behavior is the *homo economicus* model. Consistent with this model, humans base their choices on their own individual "utility functions," while ignoring social values that might not provide individual utility. Daniel Cohen, Homo Economicus: The (Lost) Prophet of Modern Times 12 (2014). *See also* Gary Becker, The Economic Approach to Human Behavior 3-6 (1976).

[7] Terry L. Anderson o. Donald R. Leal, Free Market Environmentalism 5 (1991).

[8] *See generally* Will Steffen et al., *The Trajectory of the Anthropocene: The Great Acceleration*, 2 The Anthropocene Review, No. 1, 81-98 (2015), https://doi.org/10.1177/2053019614564785.

[9] Sarah Petit, *World Vehicle Population Rose 4.6% in 2016*, Wards Intelligence (Oct. 17, 2017), https://wardsintelligence.informa.com/WI058630/World-Vehicle-Population-Rose-46-in-2016.

[10] Hannah Ritchie and Max Roser, *Urbanization*, Our World in Data, https://ourworldindata.org/urbanization (last visited Mar. 13, 2020).

[11] Laura Parker, *Plastics*, National Geographic, at 40, 59 (June 2018).

- Synthetic nitrogen production (mostly for fertilizer) rose from 4 million tons annually to 85 million tons;[12] and
- 75 percent of human-loading of the atmosphere with greenhouse gases occurred—half in the last 30 years.[13] Atmospheric CO2 concentrations went from around 310 parts per million (ppm) to around 410 at the beginning of 2020.[14]

Connections with nature for most of the world's people has become more and more tenuous.

C. The Orientation of Separation's Effect on Environmental Law

The orientation of separation led to numerous errors in perception and thinking that carried over into environmental law. There was, for example, the mythology of human exceptionalism—the belief that humans were separate from nature and superior to it, and that nature existed for the benefit of humans. There were also the mythologies of boundless resources[15] and of inexhaustible sinks.[16] Until recently, people thought there could be localized shortages of resources and sinks and localized pollution, but that on the large scale of Earth as a whole, there were unlimited resources and sinks and human pollution could only have minor effects. During the Industrial Revolution and especially during the Great Acceleration, humans reached out to tap Earth's bounty on ever-larger scales.

There was also the mythology that Earth, which was understood as an inorganic physical and material reality, provided the sustenance for life. This is true to an extent, but complex life is dependent on other life, and not just for food. The interactions of living organisms create the conditions for the existence of complex life of which humans are a part. James Lovelock and Lynn Margulis pioneered the idea that Earth's inorganic and organic components have evolved together as, and are, a single living system. This theory, first called the Gaia theory and now called Earth systems science,

> suggests that this living system has automatically controlled global temperature, atmospheric content, ocean salinity, and other factors that maintain its own habitability. In

[12] J. R. McNeill & Peter Engelke, The Great Acceleration: Environmental History of the Anthropocene Since 1945 4 (2014)

[13] *Id.*; Peter Frumhoff, *Global Warming Fact: More than Half of All Industrial CO2 Pollution Has Been Emitted Since 1988*, Union of Concerned Scientists (Dec. 15, 2014), https://blog.ucsusa.org/peter-frumhoff/global-warming-fact-co2-emissions-since-1988-764.

[14] Mauna Loa Observatory *Monthly Average Carbon Dioxide Concentration*, Scripps CI2 Program, https://scrippsco2.ucsd.edu/data/atmospheric_co2/primary_mlo_co2_record.html (last visited Mar. 17, 2020).

[15] Resource is the term used by economists and others to describe components of the natural environment. As noted several times throughout this book, the editors believe that using the term "natural resources" or "resources" unfairly defines nature as being a mere human resource or a cog in the wheel of our larger economic system. While we hope this language evolves over time, we use it in the book for the sake of clarity.

[16] The main natural carbon sinks are plants, the ocean, and soil. *See generally* Alice Outwater, Wild at Heart: America's Turbulent Relationship with Nature, From Exploitation to Redemption (2019); Lenard Zobler, *An Economic-Historical View of Natural Resources Use and Conservation*, 38 Econ. Geography 189, 191 (1962).

> a phrase, "life maintains conditions suitable for its own survival." In this respect, the living system of Earth can be thought of analogous to the workings of any individual organism that regulates body temperature, blood salinity, etc. So, for instance, even though the luminosity of the sun—the Earth's heat source—has increased by about 30 percent since life began almost four billion years ago, the living system has reacted as a whole to maintain temperatures at levels suitable for life.[17]

There are many other examples of how Earth as a living system adjusts itself to maintain a dynamic homeostasis—i.e., to self-regulate. One example is that life has maintained oxygen levels in the atmosphere at around 20 percent for millennia.

A twist on the foregoing myth is that this living system, with the exception of the human part of it, works autonomously to sustain itself. Therefore, changes in the human part of it alone will restore the planetary conditions conducive to complex life, including humans. This conclusion is not warranted. The planetary system is interdependent and entangled. To restore Earth means not only changing human activity, but also restoring all the many plants, animals, and their life support systems that have operated mutually to create the conditions in which human civilization has flourished.

These errors in thinking and perception carried over into environmental policy and enforcement by separating what we humans now know—through science—from what we do. This has led to environmental law based on an orientation of separation that has not succeeded. Earth law has arisen from the need to place environmental law on a new foundation—the orientation of connection.

1. Separating what we know through science from what we do

The Industrial Revolution and its culmination in the Great Acceleration are a triumph of science and technology. Science and technology, however, should be distinguished. Science yields knowledge and theories of a wide scope, and technology draws on parts of scientific knowledge that can be turned into useful products, many of which give humans the ability to control large aspects of the natural conditions in which they live. Environmental law has taken a largely technological approach to the control of the environment.

Science from the sixteenth century to the late eighteenth century was reductionistic and mechanistic. While such science continues today and gives rise to new technology, a different, more connected and dynamic science arose beginning in the late nineteenth century. This science encompasses fields such as evolution, thermodynamics, electromagnetism, relativity, quantum mechanics, physical cosmology, systems theory, chaos, complexity, genetic coding, ecology, non-equilibrium dynamics, digital technology, information science, and Earth systems science. Through science, we have come to better know the beauty and elegance of the natural world, even of the universe beyond Earth, and we have a deeper understanding of what it takes for humans to live sustainably in the world.

[17] *Overview*, Gaia Theory: Model and Metaphor for the 21st Century, http://www.gaiatheory.org/overview/ (Last visited Mar. 14, 2020).

Science has been restricted in the role it could play in policymaking.[18] Science assesses how human alteration of nature affects human health and welfare, then turns the data over to lawmakers who determine how that information should be incorporated into a legal standard that is binding on humans.[19] Science is then used in calculating whether these standards have been met and what the consequences of not meeting standards might be.[20]

There is much more that science can do. Science—through such fields as biology, ecology, and Earth systems science—can inform a dynamic, holistic approach to protecting the biosphere as applied through our legal and economic systems. Environmental law typically supports pollutive activities where the economic benefits outweigh the perceived ecological costs through a traditional cost-benefit analysis (CBA). A dam project producing $20 million in annual revenue might receive a permit if that financial benefit is perceived to outweigh the degradation of a river ecosystem. By contrast, a science-based approach to policymaking favors activities that promote ecological systems (of which humans are a part), and disfavors those that do not. The same dam project might not receive a permit due to its negative impact to functioning river systems and the ecosystems and species that rely upon that system.

In the United States, in 2020 (the time of this writing), there has been growing resistance to the use of science in environmental policy. Science that provides economic benefit is readily accepted, but when science identifies costs from such things as climate change, biodiversity loss, and exposure to toxic substances it is not.[21] Notably, scientists working through the Intergovernmental Panel on Climate Change (IPCC) have determined that if the present trajectory of CO2 emissions continues, the global mean surface temperature will rise by 3.7 °C by the end of this century over the mean average temperature for 1986–2005.[22] The IPCC has specified targets that must be met to avoid this result, yet there are no environmental policies in place at the national level in the United States to meet these targets. Thus, localized issues of pollution are addressed in environmental policy while the greatest threat to the global environment is not.

2. Separating our communal and ecological selves from what we do

Humans know the world in part through science. In the West, the world known by science, i.e., nature, is thought of as "out there"—it is something waiting to be "discovered." Even when science studies human bodies, it studies them as objects. This idea

[18] John Holmes and Rebecca Clark, *Enhancing the Use of Science in Environmental Policy-Making and Regulation*, 11 Env. Sci. and Policy 702, 705-06, 709 (2008).

[19] Oliver Houck, *Tales from a Troubled Marriage: Science and Law in Environmental Policy*, 17 Tulane Envtl. L.J. 163, 165 (2003).

[20] Mary Jane Angelo, *Harnessing the Power of Science in Environmental Law: Why We Should, Why We Don't, and How We Can*, 86 Tex. L. Rev. 1527, 1529 (2008).

[21] Steve Cohen, *The Use of Science in Environmental Decision Making*, State of the Planet (Mar 11, 2020).

[22] Intergovernmental Panel on Climate Change, *Representative Concentration Pathway 8.5, Table 2, in* Summary for Policymakers—Climate Change: The Physical Science Basis 23 (2013). The range given for temperature rise by 2100 is 2.6°C to 4.8°C with a mean of 3.7°C.

of the world being composed of separate parts extends throughout Western thought beyond science into economics, politics, and the humanities, and into Western law as well. In the modern period, the idea of a shared commons given by a creator God. . . .

> was replaced by a humanist emphasis on the individual and human reason, which resulted in a mechanistic legal vision. . . .
>
> [There was] a transformation from commons-based folk legal institutions into legally formalized, concentrated private property and eventually into capital. Private ownership—individual dominion over land—became the most important legal concept, dividing the whole into individualistic components. The mechanism governing the relationship between these parts was found in what became the sovereign state.[23]

Thus, the concept of the "rule of law" arose. Owners' rights were to be protected by "due process of law." The law became proficient at protecting individual rights but not collective rights. Customary law based on local practices and customs gave way to "professionalized, common, and potentially scientific" law.[24] This orientation is reflected in the work of Francis Bacon, the father of the scientific method, who was also Lord Chancellor in England and contributed to rules of evidence and other changes in civil procedure to make law more scientific.

These changes were a marked improvement, but they also had the effect of furthering the separation of law from life. As discussed further in Chapter 25, "Indigenous Legalities," natural law for Indigenous people meant laws derived from observation of the natural world. These laws are based on how Earth maintains herself and help humans understand their role in the world. These laws also pertain to relationships, describing how all beings are connected to each other and must be respected for their roles.

Western law in the modern period developed from natural law in a different sense. Western natural law was understood as a body of unchanging moral principles existing independently of human understanding and positive law, yet discernible to humans through reason. Modernity was understood in the West as scientific, as Enlightenment, as the Age of Reason, and, thus, law was reformed accordingly. As top-down legal order developed, the idea of a single legal order within a jurisdiction took hold, and power became centralized in the sovereign. Mechanical jurisprudence took hold—law was to be applied with little interpretation.[25]

Gradually, Western jurisprudence moved away from its moorings in Western natural law (with a notable exception in the area of human rights) to legal positivism, which means the legal justification for a law is simply its adoption in written form by the state. The law is what it says, and there is not necessarily a connection between law and morality (or, in terms of Earth law, ecology). Rather, the law is determined through a process of political preferences and power relationships.

[23] Fritjof Capra & Ugo Mattei, The Ecology of Law: Toward a Legal System in Tune with Nature and Community 45 (2015).
[24] *Id.* at 60.
[25] *Id.* at 103.

Western society's embrace of this mechanistic approach to law is due in large part to its service to the needs of capitalism, which transformed nature and the commons to human property for the production of profit. The following essential protections thus arose in Western law: (i) ownership as the right to enjoy and dispose of property; (ii) contractual agreements to legally bind parties as law; (iii) transfer of ownership regulated by consent of the parties; (iv) the fault concept in tort law, which shields entrepreneurs from liability for harm caused without fault; and (v) juridical personhood for legal entities, which among other things shields investors from loss by making the entities liable rather than the investors.[26] The need for a mechanical, rule-based legal system led to a highly complex system of law interpreted by private and public legal professionals and inaccessible to others.

Thus, "just as taste, scent, color, and beauty [were] banned from scientific inquiry [in modernity], so too were customs, ethics, values, justice, morals, manners, and sentiments—everything that gives life to the law."[27]

No doubt, this absence of life is one reason that aboriginal sensitivities are being recovered in Western thought and, in particular, in Earth law. Contrast the mechanistic, individualistic, ownership-based vision of community in modernity with this account of the aboriginal vision in Australia:

> So why didn't aboriginal people parcel up their land? The answer has been well rehearsed. It is that they saw, they see, the world very differently. In Aboriginal cosmology this isn't a volume or a surface with features, or a space to be occupied by people. Instead it is a process of creation and re-creation. The world, including people, but also what Europeans would think of as topographical features, plants, animals, ritual sites, and ancestral beings, are all necessary participants in a process of continuing creation. And if this doesn't happen then the world starts to hollow itself out. It stops existing.[28]

D. Environmental Law Based on the Orientation of Separation Has Not Succeeded

Those who brought into being environmental law presumed, in accord with the understandings of their time (one not so long in the past), that with the use of utilitarian science, environmental laws could be fashioned that would alter human behavior and environmental conditions to benefit near-term human interests. Within this legal framework, humans could both continue to exploit nature and "protect" the environment. They believed that environmental law would give humans both the legal and natural power to transform their natural surroundings within some limits to suit themselves.[29]

These environmental laws enacted to "protect the environment" have, in reality, created a perverse dependence. People, believing in the efficacy of the laws, have

[26] *Id.* at 101-02.
[27] *Id.* at 61.
[28] John Law, *What's Wrong with a One-World World?*, http://www.heterogeneities.net/publications/Law2011WhatsWrongWithAOneWorldWorld.pdf.
[29] Cormac Cullinan, *Do Humans Have Standing to Deny Trees Rights?* 11 Barry L. Rev. 11, 15 (2008).

relied on them to address the problems. Corporations, so long as they obeyed the laws, were thought to be compliant with "environmental protection." Science described the risks, policymakers wrote the laws based on these assessments, and governments applied a top-down command-and-control approach to modify human behavior. People did not rely on themselves to take needed action; they relied on the law to protect them.

Environmental law based on the orientation of separation has not succeeded.

E. The New Context: The Orientation of Connection

For environmental law to succeed, it needs to operate out of the orientation of connection, which is more fully stated as the orientation of connection, entanglement, and mutuality. Doing so gives rise to Earth law, which, as stated above, includes new bodies of law not presently covered by environmental law, and a reformed environmental law, the functioning of which is transformed by this new context. Some of these bodies of law are discussed in the subsequent section and then explored in detail throughout this book.

III. EMERGING APPROACHES TO EARTH LAW

Earth law is an emerging body of law. The editors of this coursebook have pulled together accounts of various approaches that offer promise in developing Earth law further. While each of the approaches differs, they all arise from the following understandings:

- Earth is precious, for all intents and purposes, and it is the only home for the humans and other living beings that inhabit it;
- Earth is composed of interdependently functioning systems and living and nonliving beings—it has an organic unity and cannot survive in parts;
- Earth as a living planet exists contingently, and it is subject to irreversible damage in its life-sustaining capacities;
- Earth is in a human-caused ecological crisis resulting in unnecessary suffering by both humans and nonhuman beings;
- Conventional Western law, including environmental law, is contributing to this crisis and is in need of reform; and
- Reform of law must be based on an ecocentric approach.

The approaches to Earth law presented in this book are not all new. For example, the public trust doctrine goes back at least to ancient Roman law. Indigenous legalities go back further. What is new is that the approaches are prominent in their expression of ecocentric law and each has been shaped or newly shaped by the awarenesses listed above.

For purposes of discussing the origins of these approaches, they are grouped as follows:

(a) Public trust doctrine (including atmospheric trust litigation);
(b) Rights-based approaches, which can be subdivided as follows:
   i. Rights of nature;
   ii. Rights of future generations;
   iii. Human environmental rights and the rights of nature (co-violations);
   iv. Animal rights (nonhuman rights approach);
(c) Ecocide;
(d) Indigenous legalities;
(e) International Earth law developments; and
(f) Other approaches, both global and local.

A. Public Trust Doctrine

The public trust doctrine has antecedents in law dating back to the Roman *Institutes of Justinian* and the Magna Carta.[30] The public trust means "that the public owns in common certain property interests in natural resources and land within the territory, and that the government is the people's designated trustee with the obligation to protect such property on behalf of the citizens."[31] Traditionally, the doctrine applied to the protection of large watercourses and their banks for navigation, fishing, drinking water, and other uses by the public. According to Joseph Sax, there are three types of restrictions imposed on the government by this doctrine: "[F]irst, the property subject to the trust must not only be used for a public purpose, but it must be held available for use by the general public; second, the property may not be sold, even for a fair cash equivalent; and third, the property must be maintained for particular types of uses."[32] The lodestar public trust case in the United States is *Illinois Central Railroad. v. Illinois*, 146 U.S. 387, 455 (1892), which is discussed in detail in Chapter 7, "Public Trust Doctrine."

The use of the public trust doctrine in litigation has been contentious as it pits claims of private owners against claims of the general public for protection of natural resources for various public interests, including economic, recreational, and aesthetic interests. Joseph Sax's 1970 article on *The Public Trust Doctrine in Natural Resources Law: Effective Judicial Intervention*,[33] and the work of other scholars, spurred the use of the public trust doctrine by environmental advocates and policymakers.[34] It has been

[30] Charles F. Wilkinson, *The Headwaters of the Public Trust: Some Thoughts on the Source and Scope of the Traditional Doctrine*, 19 ENVTL. L. 425, 429 (1989).
[31] Mary Christina Wood, *Advancing the Sovereign Trust of Government to Safeguard the Environment for Present and Future Generations (Part I): Ecological Realism and the Need for a Paradigm Shift*, 39 ENVT'L L. 43, 66 (2009).
[32] Joseph Sax, *The Public Trust Doctrine in Natural Resources Law: Effective Judicial Intervention*, 68 MICH. L. REV. 471, 477 (1970)
[33] *Id.* at 471-566.
[34] *See* Richard Frank, *The Public Trust Doctrine: Assessing Its Recent Past & Charting Its Future*, 45 UNIV. CAL, DAVIS L. REV. 665 (2012).

successfully used in courts in support of various environmental interests, such as to protect recreational use of coastal beaches, bar the filling of privately owned wetlands, extinguish a legislative grant of tidelands in the San Francisco Bay, protect Lake Tahoe, and protect flowing waters and water rights.[35]

In the twenty-first century, a radical extension of the public trust doctrine has been pioneered by Mary Christina Wood in her 2009 two-part law review article, *Advancing the Sovereign Trust of Government to Safeguard the Environment for Present and Future Generations: Ecological Realism and the Need for a Paradigm Shift*,[36] and in her 2014 book, *Nature's Trust: Environmental Law for a New Ecological Age.*[37] Wood's argument went far beyond prior ones. It was not that the public trust doctrine could augment environmental law, it was that environmental law was failing, notably on climate change, but on other aspects of environmental degradation as well. The failure of environmental law fell on the legislative and executive branches of government, and Wood saw that under the public trust doctrine courts could use their authority to impose fiduciary obligations on governments to protect and restore the environment.

Her work on the public trust doctrine became widely-known when young persons in Oregon filed a lawsuit alleging that the U.S. government had, with knowledge of its effects, enabled fossil fuel production and thereby increased climate change, which deprived plaintiffs of their constitutional rights to life, liberty, and property and violated the government's obligations under the federal public trust doctrine.[38] This litigation became the most well-known of many "atmospheric trust" or "climate" lawsuits. As of December 20, 2019, there had been a reported 1,442 atmospheric trust lawsuits worldwide. In the most far-reaching decision related to this litigation, the Supreme Court of the Netherlands ordered the Dutch government to reduce greenhouse gas emissions by 25 percent from 1990 levels by 2020. *The State of the Netherlands v. Urgenda Foundation (Urgenda),* is examined in Chapter 23.

This book covers the public trust doctrine and atmospheric trust litigation in Chapter 7.

B. Rights-Based Approaches

Numerous rights-based movements—for nature, specific animals, and future generations of humans—also play a central role in the development of Earth law. Previous rights-based movements for humans can serve as a blueprint for how these may develop.

[35] *See id.* at 667-70.

[36] Wood, *supra* note 31, and Mary Christina Wood, *Advancing the Sovereign Trust of Government to Safeguard the Environment for Present and Future Generations (Part II): Ecological Realism and the Need for a Paradigm Shift*, 39 Envt'l L. 91 (2009).

[37] Mary Christina Wood, Nature's Trust, Environmental Law for a New Ecological Age (2013).

[38] For a complete account of the proceedings in this case *see* Our Children's Trust, *Juliana v. United States*, https://www.ourchildrenstrust.org/juliana-v-us (last visited Mar. 16, 2020).

1. Inspiration from previous rights-based movements

In the aftermath of the horrors of World War II, international humanitarian law[39] and international human rights law[40] emerged in the Western legal system as part of a concerted effort to ensure future generations would be protected from such atrocities. A number of international human rights instruments came into being in this post-war period, including the modern Geneva Conventions, the Universal Declaration of Human Rights, and the International Covenant on Civil and Political Rights (or ICCPR). Though humanitarian law and human rights law has had a mix of success and failure since the late 1940s,[41] the expansion of these rights has made the lives of millions of people safer and more dignified.

Looking specifically to the United States, other rights-based movements demonstrate how the legal system has evolved to correct injustice and expand rights. Less than 200 years ago, "the United States Supreme Court could straight-facedly tell us in *Dred Scott* that [African Americans] had been denied the rights of citizenship 'as a subordinate and inferior class of beings'. . . ."[42] In the United States, women,[43] Jews, and Chinese people likewise were denied the full legal status and voting rights that for decades had been given to white men.[44]

The work of a rights activist seems extreme in the beginning as is illustrated by this account of the effort to abolish slavery:

> Abolitionists in the United States were called radical and extreme, they saw their businesses burned, their printing presses destroyed, and were subject to mob violence. Over a century later, seeking to have the rights driven into the U.S. Constitution by the Abolitionists finally and fully implemented and enforced, members of the Civil Rights Movement similarly saw their houses burn, their property destroyed, and faced violence from those seeking to preserve the status quo which systematically subordinated blacks in America. . . .
>
> [W]e find those who took to the written word, perhaps instead of the spoken, have often been essential to the origins of a movement. Those who write bear witness to the immorality and illegitimacy of the current state of affairs, and are often calling for change. People like the prolific American Abolitionist William Lloyd Garrison, who in the early days of that movement began writing his newspaper, the *Liberator*, which he published for over thirty years advocating for the urgent end of slavery while blasphemously calling the U.S. Constitution—which codified slavery—a "covenant with death, an agreement with hell." Incidentally, Garrison, who not only wrote widely but also publicly spoke about the need for abolition, would burn the constitution at rallies, which to those in attendance provided perhaps the clearest indication of how tightly the problem of

[39] International humanitarian law is a set of rules that applies during armed conflicts.

[40] International human rights law requires governments to uphold basic human rights and applies both during peace and at war.

[41] *See generally* Melissa Eli, *The Limits of International Humanitarian Law*, Human Rights & Human Welfare (2009).

[42] Christopher D. Stone, *Should Trees Have Standing?: Toward Legal Rights for Natural Objects*, S.C. L. Rev. 453 (1972); *see also Scott v. Sandford*, 60 U.S. 393, 404-405 (1856).

[43] *See Obergefell v. Hodges*, 135 S. Ct. 2584 (2015).

[44] Stone, *supra* note 43, at 450, 453-455.

slavery was woven into the American framework, and thus how deeply the work of the Abolitionists needed to go.[45]

When rights activists succeed, denial of the rights for which they worked seems unthinkable. People in the rights of nature movement acknowledge the debt they owe to slavery abolitionists, suffragettes, and civil rights activists for expanding rights to different peoples throughout history. These efforts established the foundations that have inspired and informed many of the social movements now advocating for the rights of nature.

As Christopher D. Stone, a pioneer in the rights of nature movement, wrote: "[u]ntil the rightless thing receives its rights, we cannot see it as anything but a *thing* for the use of 'us'—those who are holding rights at the time."[46] Rights-based law is ever-changing and, based on historical precedent, moving toward expansion.

2. Rights of nature

One of the scholarly underpinnings of the modern Earth law movement in the United States came in a U.S. Supreme Court case. In *Sierra Club v. Morton*, 405 U.S. 727 (1972), discussed in detail in Chapter 5, "Standing," the Court considered standing requirements for the Sierra Club to bring suit for violation of environmental regulations related to the development of a ski resort in the Sequoia National forest. The issue arose because the Sierra Club did not suffer personal injury from the development. While the Court ruled against the plaintiffs due to lack of standing, Justice William O. Douglas wrote a dissent[47] that foreshadowed the rights of nature movement. He asserted that nature itself should be treated as the central legal party in a case involving environmental law violations.

Justice Douglas's recognition of nature as a rights holder has received significant support from the legal community.[48] From Stone, whose law review article, *Should Trees Have Standing?: Toward Legal Rights for Natural Objects*, inspired Justice Douglas,[49] to Cormac Cullinan, author of the influential book *Wild Law: A Manifesto for Earth Justice*,[50] to David Boyd, author of *The Rights of Nature: A Legal Revolution That Could Save the World*,[51] legal minds have been advocating for and cultivating this field for decades. *Sierra Club v. Morton* and a growing body of subsequent scholarship have elucidated

[45] Mari Margil, *Building an International Movement for the Rights of Nature, in* WILD LAW IN PRACTICE (Peter Burdon & Michelle Maloney eds., 2014) (internal citations omitted).
[46] *Id.* at 455.
[47] Justices Brennan and Blackmun also dissented in this case. Justices Powell and Rehnquist took no part in the decision.
[48] *See, e.g.*, Bryan Norton, *Which Morals Matter? Freeing Moral Reasoning from Ideology*, 37 U.C. DAVIS L. REV. 81 (2003); *see also* Alyson C. Flournoy, *In Search of an Environmental Ethic*, 28 COLUM. J. ENVTL. L. 63 (2003).
[49] Christopher D. Stone, *Should Trees Have Standing?: Toward Legal Rights for Natural Objects*, S.C. L. Rev. 450, 453-455, (1972).
[50] CORMAC CULLINAN, WILD LAW: A MANIFESTO FOR EARTH JUSTICE (1st ed., 2002; 2d ed., 2011).
[51] DAVID BOYD, THE RIGHTS OF NATURE: A LEGAL REVOLUTION THAT COULD SAVE THE WORLD (2017).

the legal workability of the rights of nature and its critical role in forestalling the ecological crisis.[52]

Chapter 9 of this book covers the rights of nature in the United States.

3. The rights of future generations and human environmental rights (co-violations)

At least 155 national governments have recognized that humans possess a right to a healthy environment.[53] Recently, the Inter-American Court of Human Rights also "recognized a fundamental right to a healthy environment."[54] In researching this precedent, David R. Boyd, now the Special Rapporteur on human rights and the environment for the United Nations, argues that the human right to a healthy environment has led to environmental laws as well as court decisions supporting stronger environmental protections.[55] Moreover, as indicated in the 2015 and 2016 Earth Law Center co-violations reports (*see* Chapter 10, "Human Rights and the Rights of Nature"), violations of human rights are also oftentimes violations of nature's rights.

A related rights-based movement has focused on the rights of future generations since the existential threat of climate change mandates a consideration of the rights of those not yet born.[56] Advocates argue that today's population owes a legal obligation to future generations who should therefore be granted standing in court.[57]

The human right to a healthy environment, the rights of future generations, and the rights of the Amazon rainforest were all recognized and supported in a seminal 2018 decision by the Supreme Court of Colombia, which found:

> [I]t can be preached that the fundamental rights of life, health, minimum subsistence, freedom, and human dignity are substantially linked and determined by the environment and the ecosystem. Without a healthy environment, subjects of law, and sentient beings in general, will not be able to survive, much less protect those rights, for our children or for future generations. Neither can the existence of the family, society, or the State itself be guaranteed.[58]

[52] Christopher D. Stone, *Ethics in International Environmental Law*, OXFORD HANDBOOK OF INTL. ENV. L. (2006); *see also* Edith Brown Weiss, *Our Rights and Obligations to Future Generations for the Environment*, 84 AM. J. INT'L L. 198 (1990); *see also* Peter Manus, *The Blackbird Whistling—The Silence Just After Evaluating the Environmental Legacy of Justice Blackmun*, 85 IOWA L. REV. 429 (2000); James May & Daly Erin, *New Directions in Earth Rights, Environmental Rights and Human Rights: Six Facets of Constitutionally Embedded Environmental Rights Worldwide*, 1 IUCN ACAD. OF ENVTL. L.J. 13 (2011); and Nicholas A. Robinson, *Fundamental Principles of Law for the Anthropocene?*, ENV. POLICY & L. 44 (2014).

[53] John H. Knox & Ramin Pejan, *Introduction to The Human Right to a Healthy Environment* 78, *in* THE HUMAN RIGHT TO A HEALTHY ENVIRONMENT (John H. Knox ed., 2018).

[54] Ucilia Wang, *International Court Ruling: A Safe Climate Is a Human Right*, CLIMATE LIABILITY NEWS (Feb. 13, 2018), https://www.climateliabilitynews.org/2018/02/13/inter-american-climate-rights-colombia.

[55] *Id.*, referencing the research of David Boyd.

[56] *See, e.g.*, Charlotte Unruh, *Present Rights for Future Generations*, 30 KRITERION–J. OF PHIL. 77 (2016).

[57] *See* Rachel Johnston, *Lacking Rights and Justice in a Burning World: The Case for Granting Standing to Future Generations in Climate Change Litigation*, 21TILBURG L. REV. 31 (2016).

[58] *Republicà de Colombia*, Corte Suprema de Justicia (Apr. 5, 2018) STC 4360-2018.

Chapter 8 of this book covers the rights of future generations and Chapter 10 covers human environmental rights and the rights of nature (co-violations).

4. Nonhuman rights approach

There is a growing movement to recognize the rights of nonhuman animals in law. An Argentinian court recently held that Cecilia, a chimpanzee long caged in a zoo, had juridical rights and should be released into a Brazilian sanctuary.[59] Likewise, in 2018 in India, the High Court of Uttarakhand held that horse cruelty was illegal because "[e]very species has an inherent right to live and are required to be protected by law."[60] The "Nonhuman Rights Project" has likewise pushed U.S. courts to recognize these rights.[61] The push for rights for animals differs from traditional animal welfare efforts as illustrated by the following objectives of the Nonhuman Rights Project:

1. To change the common law status of great apes, elephants, dolphins, and whales from mere "things," which lack the capacity to possess any legal right, to "legal persons," who possess such fundamental rights as bodily liberty and bodily integrity.
2. To draw on the common law and evolving standards of morality, scientific discovery, and human experience to consider other qualities that may be sufficient for recognition of nonhuman animals' legal personhood and fundamental rights.
3. To develop local, national, and global issue-oriented grassroots and legislative campaigns to promote recognition of nonhuman animals as beings worthy of moral and legal consideration and with their own inherent interests in freedom from captivity, participation in a community of other members of their species, and the protection of their natural habitats.
4. To build a broad-based coalition of organizations and individuals to secure legally recognized fundamental rights for nonhuman animals.
5. To foster understanding of the social, historical, political, and legal justice of our [nonhuman rights] arguments and the scientific discovery of other species' cognitive and emotional complexity that informs them.[62]

Chapter 9 of this book covers nonhuman rights.

[59] Gabriel Samuels, *Chimpanzees Have Rights, Says Argentinian Judge as She Orders Cecilia to Be Released from Jail*, INDEPENDENT (Nov. 7, 2016), https://www.independent.co.uk/news/world/americas/argentina-judge-says-chimpanzee-poor-conditions-has-rights-and-should-be-freed-from-zoo-a7402606.html.

[60] CELDF, *India Court Declares Legal Rights of "Entire Animal Kingdom"* (Jul. 6, 2018), https://celdf.org/2018/07 /press-release-india-court-declares-legal-rights-of-entire-animal-kingdom.

[61] *See generally* Nonhuman Rights Project, *Litigation*, https://www.nonhumanrights.org/litigation (last visited Aug. 25, 2019).

[62] Nonhuman Rights Project, *Our Objectives*, https://www.nonhumanrights.org/who-we-are/ (last visited Mar. 16, 2020).

C. Ecocide

Ecocide refers to the destruction of ecosystems and the species they support on a massive level. Like atmospheric trust litigation, ecocide is a theory used by Earth lawyers to address the environmental crisis in a way that matches its scale. A significant difference from other approaches presented in this book is that ecocide is a criminal law approach.

The term ecocide was first used to describe the massive harm caused by the spraying of Agent Orange by the U.S. Army in the Vietnam War. The chemical was used to defoliate forests so that guerillas could not live or hide in them. In "Operation Ranch Hand," 20 million gallons of Agent Orange and other chemicals were sprayed over an area the size of the state of Massachusetts.[63] This chemical warfare against nature was not prohibited by international conventions as it would have if it had been against humans.

Subsequent to that war, in 2002, the Rome Statute of the International Criminal Court came into being. Without using the term ecocide, the statute makes it an international crime to intentionally launch an attack with the knowledge that the attack will cause "widespread, long-term and severe damage to the natural environment" that is clearly excessive in regard to the military situation.[64] This provision was drafted so narrowly that it might not have applied to the use of Agent Orange by the United States in Vietnam and it has no applicability to ecocide in peacetime. Polly Higgins devoted her life to making ecocide a peacetime crime under the Rome Statute. She and others believed that an international crime was needed to deter, for example, widespread deforestation such as that which has occurred in the Amazon.[65]

Chapter 12 of this book covers ecocide.

D. Indigenous Legalities

Indigenous peoples have coexisted in harmony with the land for millennia. Their laws, customs, and way of life are based upon respect and care for nature. While Indigenous peoples comprise less than five percent of the world's population, they manage or have tenure over 25 percent of land, with such land accounting for 80 percent of global biodiversity.[66]

[63] Clyde Haberman, *Agent Orange's Long Legacy, for Vietnam and Veterans,* N.Y. Times (May 16, 2014), https://www.nytimes.com/2014/05/12/us/agent-oranges-long-legacy-for-vietnam-and-veterans.html; David Zierler, The Invention of Ecocide: Agent Orange, Vietnam, and the Scientist Who Changed the Way We Think About the Environment 95 (2011).

[64] Rome Statute of the International Criminal Court, 2187 U.N.T.S. 90 (emphasis added) (hereinafter "Rome Statute). As of Dec. 15, 2019, there were 123 parties. The United States signed the Rome Statute but is not a party. Rome Statute, U.N.T.C., Chap. XVIII, No. 10, https://treaties.un.org/Pages/ViewDetails.aspx?src=TREATY&mtdsg_no=XVIII-10&chapter=18&clang=_en#12 (last visited Dec. 15, 2019).

[65] As early as 1973 there were proposals for the peacetime crime of ecocide and at the national level. Vietnam became the first country to do so. *See* Chapter 12, "Ecocide."

[66] Gleg Raygorodetsky, *Indigenous Peoples Defend Earth's Biodiversity—But They're in Danger,* National Geographic (Nov. 16, 2018), https://www.nationalgeographic.com/environment/2018/11/can-Indigenous-land-stewardship-protect-biodiversity.

As the natural world suffers, so too have Indigenous peoples. Environmental degradation and climate disruption disproportionately impact the human rights of Indigenous peoples,[67] who often live in those ecosystems most impacted by environmental declines. There is also an onslaught of violence perpetrated against Indigenous defenders of the environment,[68] including the murder of Indigenous Goldman Environmental Prize winners Isidro Baldenegro López from Mexico (2005 winner for protecting ancient forests) and Berta Cáceres in Honduras (2015 winner for opposing a dam).[69] To protect Indigenous rights is to protect the environment and vice versa.

International law has begun to develop the foundations of Indigenous rights recognition and enforcement. There have been numerous international instruments recognizing Indigenous rights in recent decades — the Indigenous and Tribal Peoples Convention, 1989 ("ILO-convention 169") and the UN Declaration on the Rights of Indigenous Peoples (UNDRIP) amongst them. There have also been landmark court victories both in national and international venues by Indigenous peoples seeking to enforce their rights and correct injustices,[70] although their struggle for rights continues. Many believe that addressing Indigenous rights as they relate to the environment is necessary to help solve the global ecological crisis.

Indigenous people enter Earth law not only in respect to protecting their rights, but also for their insights into human-Earth relations. Since the ways that Indigenous peoples govern themselves are different than in conventional Western law, in this book we use the term "Indigenous legalities."

Several chapters in this book concern Earth law and Indigenous people: Chapter 18 (Colombia); Chapter 19 (Brazil/Mexico); Chapter 22 (New Zealand); Chapter 24 (Africa); and Chapter 25 ("Indigenous Legalities").

E. International Earth Law Developments

Since the 1970s, international law has attempted to introduce a series of stronger environmental protections, and there are dozens of international laws that aim to protect

[67] Division of Environmental Law and Conventions, *United Nations Environment Program*, Human Rights and the Environment, http://web.unep.org/divisions/delc/human-rights-and-environment (last visited Aug. 23, 2019).

[68] *See* Earth Law Center, *2016 Update: Fighting for Our Shared Future: Protecting Both Human Rights and Nature's Rights* (2016), https://static1.squarespace.com/static/55914fd1e4b01fb0b851a814/t /586d58835016e13b1e98820a/1483561101515/ELC+Co-Violations+Report+-+2016+Update.pdf.

[69] Nina Lakhani, *Second Winner of Environmental Prize Killed Months After Berta Cáceres Death*, The Guardian (Jan. 18, 2017), https://www.theguardian.com/world/2017/jan/18/isidro-baldenegro-lopez-killed-goldman -environmental-prize-mexico-berta-caceres.

[70] *See, e.g.*, United Nations Human Rights Office of the High Commissioners, *Land and Human Rights; Annotated Compilation of Case Law*, UN Doc HR/PUB/15/5 (2015), https://www.ohchr.org/Documents/ Publications/Land _HR-CaseLaw.pdf; *see also* Senwung Luk, *The Law of the Land: New Jurisprudence on Aboriginal Title*, The Supreme Court Law Review: Osgoode's Annual Constitutional Cases Conference 67 (2014).

the environment.[71] There are also numerous non-binding international legal instruments, from the 1972 Stockholm Declaration to the 2016 United Nations Sustainable Development Goals.

However, just as domestic environmental law is criticized for not successfully reducing environmental harm, so too are traditional international laws frequently condemned for lacking the capacity and force to rein in human consumption, production, pollution, and devastation of the living world.

Civil society declarations and agreements are leading the way in highlighting an Earth-centered approach to international law. In 2002, nearly a decade of work by thousands of people in civil society resulted in the Earth Charter, which recognizes that "all beings are interdependent and every form of life has value regardless of its worth to human beings."[72] In 2010, thousands of civil society leaders meeting in Cochabamba, Bolivia, wrote the Universal Declaration for the Rights of Mother Earth.[73] It is used as a guide by many rights of nature and Earth jurisprudence advocates around the world. This book surveys emerging international principles of ecocentric law, including the Global Pact for the Environment.

The United Nations Harmony with Nature initiative has recognized the importance of Earth jurisprudence and aims to weave its concepts and approaches into the work and consciousness of the United Nations. The 2019 United Nations Harmony with Nature report describes the growing support of Earth-centered laws and policies worldwide as follows:

> 20. Federal, state and local governments around the world are increasingly adopting laws that recognize the rights of Nature and the natural world to exist and flourish. In many cases, these new laws are the product of collaboration between non-governmental organizations, civil society associations, legislators and legislative bodies, working together to draft, adopt and implement laws recognizing Nature as a subject of rights and/or a legal "person", protected by law.
>
> 21. Likewise, non-governmental organizations and civil society associations have successfully expanded their efforts to obtain judicial recognition of Nature's rights and of rulings that protect the natural world. Additionally, countries with Nature's rights already incorporated into their laws are implementing those rights through judicial decisions protecting Nature.
>
> 22. Customary and Indigenous laws continue to serve as models for the expansion of Western positive law toward respecting Nature and Nature's rights. An increasing

[71] These include, among others, the Basel Convention on the Control of Transboundary Movements of Hazardous Waste and Their Disposal, the Convention on Biological Diversity, the Convention on International Trade in Endangered Species of Wild Fauna and Flora, the Ramsar Convention on Wetlands of International Importance especially as Waterfowl Habitat, the Stockholm Convention on Persistent Organic Pollutants, the United Nations Convention on the Law of the Sea, the United Nations Framework Convention on Climate Change, and the Vienna Convention for the Protection of the Ozone Layer.

[72] Earth Charter (2002), Principle I.1.a, https://earthcharter.org/discover/the-earth-charter.

[73] *See* Linda Sheehan, *Implementing the Rights of Nature Through Sustainability Bills of Rights*, 13 New Zealand J. of Pub. Intl. L. 99-100 (2015).

number of Indigenous groups have taken formal action to incorporate into their governing laws what they have long understood as the basic truth of life: humans are part of the natural world and must live in harmony with Nature.[74]

Chapter 15 of this book covers United Nations Sustainability Initiatives.

F. Other Approaches Global and Local

In addition to the foregoing approaches, chapters in this book cover a way of considering the ethical issues in wildlife through the eyes of a bear (Chapter 14), ecocentric environmental governance (Chapter 16), amendments to the Constitution of Ecuador recognizing the rights of nature (Chapter 17), and developments in Earth law in Colombia (Chapter 18), Brazil and Mexico (Chapter 19), India (Chapter 20), Israel (Chapter 21), and New Zealand (Chapter 22). These chapters present a number of other approaches, both global and local.

IV. CONCLUSION

This chapter describes how Earth law is both a departure from modern environmental law as well as a new context for its extension. It also explores how Western legal systems became separated from humans' role within nature, and how this separation is resulting in global environmental declines. Finally, the chapter surveys Earth law topics that are covered in this book to provide the reader with a taste of how current legal movements are working to create a more ecocentric legal system.

Chapter 3, "Conceptual Frameworks of Earth Law," describes in more detail the legal and philosophical theories upon which Earth law is based. It also explores the work of Thomas Berry, whose principles of Earth jurisprudence have inspired many of the authors of this book. As Thomas Berry famously said, "The universe is composed of subjects to be communed with, not primarily of objects to be used."

Consider whether society can once again realize this truth through the evolution of our legal system toward Earth law.

STUDY QUESTIONS

1) One critique of Western laws is that they treat nature as a machine that humans can tinker with and control. What analogy might you give for the treatment of nature under Earth law?

[74] United Nations General Assembly, "Harmony with Nature: Report of the Secretary-General," UN Doc. A/74/236 (Jul. 26, 2019).

2) Rights of nature laws are seen as Western-style positivist laws that may not be suitable in some jurisdictions. Can you think of any legal system where a rights-based approach might not be appropriate?

3) In his dissenting opinion in *Sierra Club v. Morton*, Justice Douglas expressed his opinion that the Mineral King Valley in Sequoia National Park should have legal rights. How would you respond to this poetic commentary published in the American Bar Association Journal in 1973 by John Naff?

> If Justice Douglas has his way—
> O come not that dreadful day—
> We'll be sued by lakes and hills
> Seeking a redress of ills
> Great mountain peaks of name prestigious
> Will suddenly become litigious
> Our brooks will babble in the courts,
> Seeking damages for torts
> How can I rest beneath a tree
> If it may soon be suing me?
> Or enjoy the playful porpoise
> While it's seeking habeas corpus?
> Every beast within his paws
> Will clutch an order to show cause
> The Courts besieged on every hand,
> Will Crowd with suits by chunks of land.
> Ah! But vengeance will be sweet
> Since this must be a two-way street.
> I'll promptly sue my neighbor's tree
> For shedding all its leaves on me.

4) Of the various Earth law approaches surveyed in this chapter, which do you think are most promising? Why?

5) As an ever-emerging body, Earth law is still in its relative infancy. Do you think any approaches to Earth law will be mainstream, if not universally adopted? If so, do you think this will take closer to 10 years or 100 years? If not, why do you think they will not become mainstream?

CHAPTER 3

Conceptual Frameworks of Earth Law[1]

I. INTRODUCTION

The subtitle of this book is "A Guide for Practitioners." The intent of the editors is to offer law students the best tools that have been developed for practicing Earth law with the goal of having students further develop the field through their various practices. There are opportunities to practice Earth law as litigators; judges; advisors of governments, businesses, nonprofit organizations, and individuals; lobbyists and members of bar committees; and scholars teaching and interpreting laws, analyzing legal systems, and working for reforms of both. Further, Earth law concerns legal ethics and how lawyers set up, conduct, and are remunerated for their practices. Given the difficulty of constraining and regulating conduct through positive law alone, Earth law also concerns customs and norms, the symbols and rituals of law, and what has been called *customary law,* unwritten laws governing behavior.

Earth law focuses on the role of law in the survival, health, and well-being of humans and the larger community of life and life systems in the context of the Anthropocene (discussed below). Its purpose is to provide the legal framework needed for humans to: (1) live within planetary boundaries, (2) prospectively care for ecosystems, (3) preserve biodiversity, (4) restore damaged ecosystems and loss of biodiversity, (5) protect human environmental rights, and (6) justly share the burdens of mitigating and adapting to climate change and other environmental stresses. A distinctive feature of Earth law is that nature is taken into consideration in its own right and the benefits, protections, and remedies afforded by law are extended to nature in its own right. In a sense, nature becomes a third party in every legal process. Earth law also gives new attention to human environmental rights and justice.

This chapter explores the distinctive characteristics of Earth law approaches and delves into questions and assumptions underlying them. It begins by examining the role of humans in nature as we enter the Anthropocene epoch, which is notable for its fundamental degradation of Earth's life systems. It then turns to foundational questions regarding the goals of our legal system to determine its alignment with the aim of restoring ecological balance. It also delves into the various definitions of optimal and

[1] Authored by Herman F. Greene, President of the Center for Ecozoic Societies, and Alessandro Pelizzon, Senior Lecturer at the Southern Cross University School of Law and Justice.

equitable outcomes of ecological legal approaches and then explores the role of law in society. Finally, it examines the role of ethics, the social contract, and myriad goals of justice and peace. The inquiry into Earth law involves the convergence of all these aspects, with the ultimate aim of restoring and protecting this planet's life.

There are ten sections in this chapter:

(1) Understanding the Anthropocene Epoch
(2) Earth Law, Philosophy, and Jurisprudence
(3) What Is Nature? The Nature-Culture Divide
(4) What Is Good Nature? Preservationist and Conservationist Views; Earth Systems Science and the Gaia Theory
(5) Anthropocentrism, Biocentrism, Ecocentrism, or Cosmocentrism?
(6) Rights, Responsibilities, and Reciprocity
(7) Property Rights, Individual Rights, Communal Rights, and the Commons
(8) Representing Nature: Dyadic Thinking, Systems Thinking, Customary Law, and Culture
(9) The Role of Law and Legal Ethics
(10) The New Social Contract: Culture, Democracy, Justice, Equity, and Peace

II. UNDERSTANDING THE ANTHROPOCENE EPOCH

Earth law is the resumption in a new historical context of what Eric Freyfogle called "our oldest task," that of "living on land without degrading it."[2] That new context is the Anthropocene epoch, which was beginning, but not clearly evident, when modern environmental law came into being in the 1960s and 70s. It has not been taken into account as environmental law has developed and been practiced since that time.

The term *Anthropocene epoch* was coined by Paul Crutzen and Eugene Stoermer in an article published in 2000,[3] where they proposed a name for a new geological epoch to succeed the Holocene epoch. The Holocene is the roughly 10,000-year period that began after the last ice age. All human civilization has developed during the Holocene Epoch. Crutzen and Stoermer identified large-scale changes humans have made on Earth and to the atmosphere and argued, considering these still-growing impacts, the role of humans should be recognized by naming the current epoch the Anthropocene.[4]

[2] Eric T. Freyfogle, Our Oldest Task: Making Sense of Our Place in Nature 1 (2017). He attributes the definition of our oldest task to Aldo Leopold, Engineering and Conservation, *in* The River of the Mother of God and Other Essays by Aldo Leopold (Susan Flader and J. Baird Callicott eds., 1991).
[3] Paul J. Crutzen & Eugene F. Stoermer, *The Anthropocene*, IGBP Newsletter 17 (May 2000).
[4] Anthropocene Working Group of the International Commission on Stratigraphy, *Results of Binding Vote*, http://quaternary.stratigraphy.org/working-groups/anthropocene (last visited Sept. 29, 2019) (hereafter, the "AWG Report"); Meera Subramanian, *Anthropocene Now: Influential Panel Votes to Recognize Earth's New Epoch*, Nature (May 21, 2019), https://www.nature.com/articles/d41586-019-01641-5. If the International Commission on Stratigraphy confirms the designation of the Anthropocene as a new epoch, it will be the first time that it has prospectively named a geological period, one in which the stratigraphic accumulation will occur largely in the future.

In May 2019, the Anthropocene Working Group (AWG) of the International Commission on Stratigraphy (ICS) voted to recognize the new epoch as beginning around 1950 and said it intended to submit a formal proposal for recognition of the epoch to the ICS in 2021. The AWG identified the Anthropocene epoch (often referred to simply as the Anthropocene) by phenomena related to it, as follows:

> An order-of-magnitude increase in erosion and sediment transport associated with urbanization and agriculture; marked and abrupt anthropogenic perturbations of the cycles of elements such as carbon, nitrogen, phosphorus, and various metals together with new chemical compounds; environmental changes generated by these perturbations, including global warming, sea-level rise, ocean acidification and spreading oceanic "dead zones"; rapid changes in the biosphere both on land and in the sea, as a result of habitat loss, predation, explosion of domestic animal populations and species invasions; and the proliferation and global dispersion of many new "minerals" and "rocks" including concrete, fly ash and plastics, and the myriad "technofossils" produced from these and other materials.[5]

To make the case for the designation of the Anthropocene as a geological epoch (in geology, an epoch is a period of thousands of years), the AWG stated: "Many of these changes will persist for millennia or longer, and are altering the trajectory of the Earth System, some with permanent effect. They are being reflected in a distinctive body of geological strata now accumulating, with potential to be preserved into the far future."[6]

Clive Hamilton, in *Defiant Earth,* made one of the strongest statements on the foreboding aspects of the Anthropocene when he wrote: "The idea of the Anthropocene was conceived by Earth System scientists to capture the very recent rupture in Earth history arising from the impact of human activity on the Earth System as a whole."[7] His analysis of the implications of the Anthropocene for humans serves as a background for discussing the special elements of Earth law.

Hamilton called for a new anthropocentrism.[8] The old anthropocentrism saw human mastery of Earth as a moral right, whereas the new anthropocentrism sees human mastery as a fact that puts humans in a place of responsibility and peril not heretofore imagined:

> We may have acquired it foolishly, but we now have a responsibility for the Earth as a whole and pretending otherwise is itself irresponsible. So the question is not whether human beings stand at the center of the world, but *what kind of human being stands at the center of the world* and *what is the nature of that world*. . . .
>
> Contrary to the comforting expectations that in the Anthropocene we can have "the kind of nature we wish to have," as we enter the new epoch, we will meet an Earth that

[5] Subramanian, *supra* note 4. As a general matter, the Anthropocene epoch may be understood as "the period of Earth's history during which humans have a decisive influence on the state, dynamics and future of the Earth system." For stratigraphic purposes, however, it will be defined by geological signals in Earth's strata. *Id.*

[6] *Id.*

[7] Clive Hamilton, Defiant Earth: The Fate of Humans in the Anthropocene 9 (2017).

[8] Here we are following Hamilton's analysis. Whether any kind of anthropocentrism is the right approach for Earth law is discussed later in this chapter.

> is further and further from the Earth we might want. And against the belief that "the world we will inhabit is the one we have made," the world we will have to live with is the Earth we have turned against us.[9]

Regarding nature, Hamilton wrote that the cosmology of the Anthropocene must be based on a concept of agency that extends beyond humans to the freedom woven into nature itself. In this view, nature is a "dynamic, self-organizing system, characterized by emergent properties." Emergent properties "cannot be found in any individual element [of the Earth system] and evade all cause-and-effect explanations. . . . The future always evades full predictability and inevitably holds surprises."[10] Earth is not simply a passive victim of human neglect and abuse; it has more than equal reactive power. Earth is not just a benign mother; it has a dangerous quality that we must respect.

The new anthropocentrism acknowledges that humans are agents more powerful than ever, yet it also confirms our ultimate inseparability from the forces of the natural world we inhabit. "The new anthropocentric self does not float free like the modern subject, but is always woven into nature, *a knot in the fabric of nature*."[11]

Though so enmeshed, we humans are, according to Hamilton, the exceptional agents in relation to nature, and we differ from the other agents in that we act with volition. In the Anthropocene, "Our inescapable responsibility for the Earth defines us as moral beings, [even more than] our own welfare, our virtues, and our duties to one another." Hamilton observes that a characteristic of humans is that we are world-making creatures. We imagine and then create buildings, companies, states, cities, and so on. "For humankind, how to create worlds while remaining within nature's limits is the supreme challenge."[12]

The promise that Hamilton offers to humans in the Anthropocene is that we, in a unique way, manifest the spontaneous creativity of nature. Our "creative powers embody the possibility that they be used to *enhance* the life-enriching potential of the Earth as well as to improve the human condition. Nature therefore contains within it the possibility of mutually harmonious human-Earth enhancement."[13]

III. EARTH LAW, PHILOSOPHY, AND JURISPRUDENCE

Jurisprudence concerns the philosophy of law.[14] Contemporary approaches to jurisprudence include: (1) natural law: law exists independently of positive law and is

[9] *Id.* at 43, 47-48 (footnote omitted, italics added).
[10] *Id.* at 137-138.
[11] *Id.* at 52.
[12] *Id.* at 52, 152.
[13] *Id.* at 144 (emphasis in original).
[14] Jurisprudence is "a search for wisdom through the study and evaluation of the structure, purpose, assumptions, and values of law." Judith Koons, *At a Tipping Point: Defining an Earth Jurisprudence for Social and Ecological Justice*, 58 Loyola L. Rev. 349, 363 (2012).

accessible to reason (since the eighteenth century this has largely been tied to the natural rights of humans); (2) analytic jurisprudence (or clarificatory jurisprudence) with two sub-categories: (a) legal positivism: law comes from basic social facts and there is no necessary connection to morality, and (b) legal realism: the real-world practice of law is what law is, and this practice can be studied using the methods of natural science; (3) critical legal studies: related to legal realism, but the focus is on power relations and oppression in the legal system; and (4) normative jurisprudence (or evaluative jurisprudence): What is the purpose of law? How can it be improved?

In terms of the above, Earth law is related to normative jurisprudence, critical legal studies, and natural law. The philosophical issues in Earth law, however, go beyond those covered in contemporary jurisprudence. Hamilton raises two such issues: "What kind of human being stands at the center of the world?" and "What is the nature of the world?" In philosophy, these are questions of philosophical anthropology and philosophical cosmology. The modern world (meaning the world since 1500) has given philosophical answers to these questions that are so embedded in our consciousness and institutions that we are barely aware of them. These answers are now called into question by the Anthropocene.

Because Earth law challenges some fundamental assumptions, it is instructive to reflect on the capacity of humans to shift dramatically their world views and their systems of organizing society. Judith Koons provides a brief historical account of how our current understandings of humans and nature developed. Following Koons's analysis, there are three key periods: (1) the Enlightenment period, (2) the Industrial Revolution, and (3) the twentieth-century rise of the modern corporation and of environmental law.[15] For the purposes of this chapter, we will add a fourth period, one that is coming into being, which is (4) the ecological period. While there is no consensus that the fourth period will be considered to be the ecological period, Anthropocene is the name advanced here because the changing and deteriorating conditions of nature as it affects human civilization is the paramount concern of this emerging period. *Ecological* has a normative connotation, but here it is used to indicate the centrality of human-Earth relations in this period whether the outcome is benign for humans and other beings or not. While many have argued that the alarm about the conditions of nature that gave rise to the designation of the Anthropocene is overblown, the conviction that this is not the case is a touchstone for Earth law. As noted above, Earth law concerns prospectively caring for ecosystems. This is not only because caring for ecosystems is a morally good thing to do, but also because the Anthropocene requires ameliorative action based on foresight—action must be taken to address ecological problems before they become too great to handle. Contemporary environmental law has a bias toward taking remedial action after problems arise rather than acting prospectively to avoid problems.

In the first period, as described by Koons, leaders of the Enlightenment privileged human reason and rejected traditional religious dogma and values. Humans were separated from nature. Nature was studied as a machine to be controlled and exploited for human use. In this period, Western discovery and colonialism arose. Certain people

[15] *Id.* at 357-362.

were objectified, conquered, killed, enslaved, and made, together with their lands, subservient to European interests (or in the case of settler colonialism,[16] the interests of the settlers). Concepts of liberty, progress, human rights, property, and social contract arose during this period.

In the second period, the period of the Industrial Revolution, the legal system shifted to support industrial development, and humans and nature were subordinated to industrial growth. Power shifted from agrarians to merchants and industrial barons. Economic utility became a paramount value, and a cost-benefit analysis was applied to weigh damage to person and property against the gains obtained.

In the third period, corporations and capital markets became the drivers of economic growth, economic activity was globalized, and corporations gained extensive political influence. The chief task of corporations was to maximize returns for the benefit of shareholders and management. The legal system continued to privilege economic growth, and the environmental laws that arose to make this growth safer were made explicitly or implicitly subject to cost-benefit analysis. While many corporate leaders objected to environmental regulation and liability, these environmental laws spurred innovation (supported, in some cases, by limited liability protections) and accompanied a period of economic growth unmatched in history—the period of the Great Acceleration in the second half of the twentieth century extending to the present.[17]

The fourth period, the ecological period, will be greatly affected by the Anthropocene. According to the Ecological Footprint Network, humankind currently has an ecological footprint that is 170 percent as large as the carrying capacity of Earth.[18] According to another measure, that of the nine planetary boundaries identified by Will Steffen and others,[19] humans have exceeded the boundaries for (1) flows of nitrogen and phosphorous, (2) land-system change, (3) genetic diversity, and (4) climate change, and are nearing the boundary on (5) ocean acidification. There are two other sectors in which the authors were unable to specify boundaries, those being (6) chemical pollution and the release of novel entities and (7) atmospheric aerosol loading. The two remaining categories, (8) ozone depletion and (9) freshwater use, were assessed as safe.

[16] "Settler colonialism is a distinct type of colonialism that functions through the replacement of Indigenous populations with an invasive settler society that, over time, develops a distinctive identity and sovereignty. Settler colonial states include Canada, the United States, Australia, and South Africa." Adam Barker & Emma Battell Lowman, *Settler Colonialism*, Global Social Theory, https://globalsocialtheory.org/concepts/settler-colonialism/ (last visited Oct. 6, 2019).

[17] Will Steffen and others documented rapid acceleration of economic growth and human impact on Earth generally. *See* graphs at IGBP, *Great Acceleration*, http://www.igbp.net/globalchange/greatacceleration.4.1b8ae20512db692f2a680001630.html (last visited Sept. 29, 2019).

[18] Global Footprint Network, *Ecological Footprint*, https://www.footprintnetwork.org/our-work/ecological-footprint (last visited Sept. 18, 2019).

[19] Will Steffen et al., *Planetary Boundaries: Guiding Human Development on a Changing Planet*, Science, Feb. 13, 2015, https://science.sciencemag.org/content/347/6223/1259855. *See also* Stockholm Resilience Center, *The Nine Planetary Boundaries*, https://www.stockholmresilience.org/research/planetary-boundaries/planetary-boundaries/about-the-research/the-nine-planetary-boundaries.html (last visited Sept. 18, 2019).

Many scientists write that humans are causing the sixth mass extinction in the history of this planet.[20] Further, among many other evidences of ecological degradation, the United Nations' Intergovernmental Panel on Climate Change has stated that Earth has warmed by 1.0°C from pre-industrial times (pre–1750),[21] and, according to the United Nations Environmental Program, we are on a path to 3.2°C of warming,[22] a climate very different from the one to which both human civilization and many other species have adapted. All these situations are the result of human impact on Earth over the last 250 years and especially the last 50. Because of the unsustainability of our present situation and the reactive power of Earth, nature will force itself upon human societies, and thus upon their legal systems, as the most fundamental concern. Nature will be perceived in three ways—as a destructive force to which humans must respond, as degraded life systems in need of restoration, and as a resilient source of physical and spiritual sustenance.

The most common response to the demands of the Anthropocene is that people must move from conventional economic development to sustainable development. *Sustainable development* means economic development with greater attention to environmental concerns and social issues. To date, for the most part, sustainable development has been based on a weak notion of sustainability, one that places economic growth first, people (or society) second, and the environment third. Based on a strong notion of sustainability, the order is reversed with the environment first, society second, and economics third.

Earth law takes the strong sustainability approach based on the premise that the health of Earth is a precondition to the health of society and economics. To improve health, the economy should be subservient to social well-being and cultural values rather than society and culture being subservient to the economy. It is a fundamental choice and it changes everything. In the second and third historical periods discussed above, the focus of law has been on defining human-economy relations. In the fourth period, the focus of law will be on defining human-Earth relations and this will have implications for all fields of law and all aspects of human societies.

Now let us look more closely at the questions Hamilton asked concerning philosophical anthropology ("What kind of human being stands at the center of the world?") and philosophical cosmology ("What is the nature of that world?"). According to the *New World Encyclopedia*, "[p]hilosophical anthropology is the philosophical discipline that inquires into the essence of human nature and the human condition. In making this inquiry, it [philosophical anthropology] seeks to unify or critique philosophically the diverse scientific methods and humanistic approaches to answering the question of human nature."[23] Concerning philosophical cosmology, Rémi Brague explained it this way: "As humans construct their understanding of the physical aspects of nature, they also construct their understanding of what it means to exist in this

[20] *See generally*, Center for Biological Diversity, *The Extinction Crisis*, https://www.biologicaldiversity.org/programs/biodiversity/elements_of_biodiversity/extinction_crisis/ (last visited Oct. 25, 2019).
[21] IPCC, *2018: Summary for Policymakers*, *in* Global Warming of 1.5°C 4 (2018).
[22] UNEP, 2018: Emissions Gap Report 10 (2018).
[23] *Philosophical Anthropology*, New World Encyclopedia, https://www.newworldencyclopedia.org/entry/ Philosophical_anthropology (last visited Sept. 22, 2019).

physical reality. Thus, from the standpoint of philosophical cosmology, the 'world' is more than a description of physical reality, it is a reflection on the nature of the world and what it means for humans to be in the world."[24]

Many philosophical assumptions undergird the present practice of law. As Earth law comes into being, those assumptions will be rethought. For example, in contemporary law, nature is converted into real property owned by humans and this property is fixed in space and time. Plate tectonics, wind, erosion, sea-level rise, floods, and more, however, have taught us that property is not fixed in space or time. In contemporary law, property is thought of primarily as land, and what happens on the owner's land is inconsequential to the planet so long as the owner's immediate neighbor is not harmed. We have learned, however, that Earth is an integral, living system. It is not just Earth's material structure that keeps the planet habitable but also the activities of living beings, which, for example, keep the level of oxygen in the atmosphere at about 20 percent. In contemporary law, humans, for the most part, are regarded as the only subjects that matter, and, otherwise, nature is composed of objects to be used. We have learned, however, that while humans have a unique kind of intelligence, other animals too have intelligence and, even where intelligence is not present in any meaningful sense, sentience goes far down the life scale. Every living being, human and nonhuman, has a unique role to play in the community of life.[25]

Technological and scientific developments present yet another set of issues that may greatly define the emerging fourth period. These issues concern potential modifications of humans and intelligent robots. Scientists have developed and are developing the ability to change our species through genetic modification, biomechatronics,[26] and brain-computer interfaces. Scientists are also developing artificial intelligence to extend human capacities and to replace humans in various decision-making and control functions. Some scientists are also working on robots that would have intelligence and physical capacities superior to humans. Robots may never be developed to be human, *i.e.* having the ability to experience—the way humans do—empathy, emotions, meaning, purpose, judgment, and wisdom. Nevertheless, robots have been and will continue to be developed to replace humans in many situations. All these changes will have ecological consequences as well as human consequences. Bill McKibben, in his 2019 book *Falter: Has the Human Game Begun to Play Itself Out?*, gives two imperatives for the future: (1) to keep the human game going, and (2) to keep it human.[27] Earth law is committed to both.

[24] Rémi Brague, The Wisdom of the World: The Human Experience of the Universe in Western Thought 5-6 (Teresa Lavender Fagan, trans., 2003).

[25] "Ownership" of land is also based on philosophical assumptions. These assumptions are critiqued, among other places in this book, in Chapter 4, "Property Law in the United States," Chapter 16, "Ecocentric Governance: The New Ecological Social Contract," and Chapter 25, "Indigenous Legalities."

[26] "Biomechatronics is the interdisciplinary study of biology, mechanics, electronics and control. It focuses on the research and design of assistive, therapeutic and diagnostic devices to compensate (partially) for the loss of human physiological functions or to enhance these functions." University of Twente, *What Is Biomechatronics?*, https://www.utwente.nl/en/education/master/programmes/systems-control/specialization/biomechatronics (last visited Oct. 2, 2019).

[27] Bill McKibben, Falter: Has the Human Game Begun to Play Itself Out? 17 (2019).

Thus, questions of "what kind of human being stands at the center of the world?" and "what is the nature of the world?" come very much to the fore in Earth law and answers given to these questions will shape Earth law. If the reasonable/economic/individual human is the standard for the responsible person in the third historical period above, who is the responsible person in the fourth period, the ecological period? In the ecological period, would all those interacting with nature—farmers, developers, governmental agencies, and laborers—be responsible not just for human safety but also for ecological safety? Would we continue to think of landowners as being responsible only for their individual plot of land because it is theirs and not for the surrounding ecosystems and bioregions? Would we continue to think of the world as a series of transactions between individual humans or human entities affecting only parties to the transactions rather than a world that is a dynamic, evolving, organic system of interrelations in which every transaction affects all? Would we replace history with geostory (the geobiological evolutionary story of Earth of which human history is only one aspect)? Would lawyers, legislators, administrators, and judges need to become ecologists?

IV. WHAT IS NATURE? THE NATURE-CULTURE DIVIDE

Earth law understands nature as one integrated, organic, evolutionary whole, which includes humans.[28] Yet, in many situations, Earth law distinguishes the human world from nature because the overall concern of Earth law is human-Earth or human-nature relations.

So, what is nature when it is distinguished from the human world? Nature may be thought of as all of the physical world, including all living beings other than humans, all minerals (all inorganic matter) other than human artifacts, and all forces and processes other than human-initiated forces and processes. Granted, this distinction is artificial because human activities affect nature's activities and vice versa.

While it is necessary in many cases to distinguish nature and humans in Earth law, it is also important to understand the arguments against nature-culture dualism (*culture* meaning the human world), also called the nature-culture divide. This issue receives considerable attention in philosophy, environmental ethics, environmentalism, and other fields. The dualism results in problematic uses of the term *nature* in Western society.

[28] Bruno Latour suggests a way of understanding such a world as one of highly complex relations between humans and nonhumans, both with the same amount of ontological agency, resulting in a non-hierarchical structure. Erhen Helmut Pflugfelder, *Is No One at the Wheel: Nonhuman Agency and Agentive Movement, in* Thinking with Bruno Latour in Rhetoric and Composition 120 (Paul Lynch & Nathaniel Rivers eds., 2015). Deep ecology rejects the inherent dualism of the idea of humans in the environment, rather imagining a relational total field whereby all things exist within a field of intrinsic relations in which the nature of any one thing cannot be described independently of its relation to others and, ultimately, to the field as a whole. Arne Naess, *The Shallow and the Deep, Long-Range Ecology Movement: A Summary*, 16 Inquiry: An Interdisciplinary J. of Phil. 95 (1973).

Nature may be:

- Objectified for study and use, or, in other words, understood through subject (human)-object (nature) relationships;
- Regarded as primitive or backward;
- Regarded as unfeeling and unknowing;
- Regarded as subordinate in status;
- Regarded as the source of base human impulses and temptations;
- Associated with Indigenous people (and such people may be regarded as inferior);
- Regarded as the world of the profane as contrasted with the divine;
- Regarded as the environment of humans;
- Regarded as dirty, threatening, obdurate, and/or stingy — a source of hardships and catastrophe — and thus something to be dominated, controlled, and overcome;
- Regarded as lacking worth, especially lacking economic worth absent human improvement and development;
- Associated with women or more generally the feminine and as being inferior to men or more generally the masculine, with both nature and women being subject to abuse; and
- Regarded as limiting or, conversely, as boundless.[29]

While Earth lawyers as a pragmatic matter will need to distinguish humans and nature in many situations, when they do so, they should endeavor to avoid misunderstandings based on culturally inscribed notions of nature-culture dualism.

V. WHAT IS GOOD NATURE? PRESERVATIONIST AND CONSERVATIONIST VIEWS; EARTH SYSTEMS SCIENCE AND THE GAIA THEORY

If Earth law is to preserve, protect, and restore nature, what nature is the object of its care? Is there *good* nature that needs to be protected and preserved and *bad* nature that needs to be restored? The answer is that Earth law does involve decisions about what is healthy nature or desirable nature, and nature of this type — good nature — is the object of its care. This section discusses aspects of making such determinations.

Two different notions of good nature have historically guided environmental law. One is the preservationist approach espoused by John Muir (1838–1914), founder of the Sierra Club. The other is the *wise use* or the conservationist approach espoused by Gifford Pinchot (1865–1946), first chief of the U.S. Forest Service in 1905. The early issues addressed by Muir and Pinchot largely concerned the use of public lands in

[29] René Descartes played an important role in dualistic thinking about nature and culture when he wrote that the human mind was not physical and had a special relationship with the divine, whereas everything else, including the human body, was physical, had extension, and was a mechanism. A corollary of this was that only humans and, more specifically, only their minds or souls had moral worth.

the United States. Muir wanted to preserve wilderness. Pinchot also wanted to avoid widespread exploitation, but for different reasons. Pinchot felt the land should be managed for optimal use based on the greatest good for the greatest number of people. To Pinchot, *optimal use* included wilderness value, but also grazing, mining, forestry, hunting, waterpower, and other uses.

The preservationist movement continues and seeks to preserve areas in their *natural* state, thereby protecting land, water, and natural forces and processes from human interference and pollution. For preservationists, good nature means nature in an undisturbed state or restored to a prior natural state. The wise-use movement continues also and favors private property rights, less environmental regulation, increased human access to public lands, and opposition to government intervention. Wise use is associated with maximum sustainable yield, which holds that renewable natural resources may be exploited so long as the exploitation does not result in long-term depletion. For conservationists, good nature means nature that provides the most human benefits.

Traditionally what constitutes good nature concerns nature *in situ*, or in other words, what is good nature in a particular locale? In the Anthropocene, the traditional question remains, but the question must also be asked and answered on larger scales. Questions arise concerning what kind of nature and how much nature is needed on a global and a bioregional basis, among other needs,

- To provide carbon sinks for anthropogenic greenhouse gas emissions?
- To preserve biodiversity?
- To protect coastal lands from flooding?
- To sustain fish stocks and other marine life?
- To regulate climate?
- For disease control?
- For waste treatment and filtration?
- For biochemical and genetic resources?
- For essential raw materials?
- For cultural services, including recreational, cognitive, aesthetic, and spiritual services?
- To sustain ocean currents and other flows?
- For human agriculture, living spaces, and other uses?

Good nature in the Anthropocene presumably would mean the type and amount of nonhuman nature needed to perform the above ecosystem services.[30] This

[30] The United Nations' *Millennium Ecosystem Assessment* provides these definitions:

> **Ecosystem.** An ecosystem is a dynamic complex of plant, animal, and microorganism communities and the nonliving environment interacting as a functional unit. Humans are an integral part of ecosystems. Ecosystems vary enormously in size; a temporary pond in a tree hollow and an ocean basin can both be ecosystems.
>
> **Ecosystem services.** Ecosystem services are the benefits people obtain from ecosystems. These include provisioning services such as food and water; regulating services such as regulation of floods, drought, land degradation, and disease; supporting services such as soil formation and

guideline, while a good one, is, however, difficult to apply when determining which local areas should serve these bioregional and global needs.

Until the twentieth century, nature was thought of in largely local terms; for example, weather was thought to be the result of local variations. Donella Meadows's modeling of Earth's resources, Lovelock's Gaia theory, the view of Earth from the moon, the results of Antarctic ice-core drilling, and many other scientific developments ultimately led to understanding Earth as a system. Hamilton wrote:

> The new Earth System thinking . . . is the integrative meta-science of the whole planet understood as a unified, complex, evolving system beyond the sum of its parts. It is a transdisciplinary and holistic approach assimilating earth sciences and life sciences, as well as the "industrial metabolism" of humankind, all within a systems way of thinking with special focus on the non-linear dynamics of a system. It represents a markedly novel way of thinking about the Earth that supersedes ecological thinking.[31]

This holistic understanding of Earth as a system does not, however, in itself offer a way of understanding what good nature is, especially at the level of particular localities. The science is descriptive, not prescriptive. Science with some degree of certainty can model Earth's processes and resources and how they will change given certain inputs, but alone it cannot decide what an optimal state for Earth is and how this could be maintained. For example, an advocate may soundly argue that based on science a local woodland is an *ecosystem* and should be protected with the implication that this term ecosystem is decisively normative. Another advocate could soundly argue that suburban lawns are also ecosystems as are vast fields of corn, pastures, feedlots, and even confined animal feeding operations and should be protected. Which of these are good nature and based on what criteria? Science is necessary for decision-making in the Anthropocene even though it may be contested or misused.

While the science of the Anthropocene emphasizes the importance of weighing the value of nature on global and bioregional levels, legal controversies are generally locally situated. One's perspective on good nature in resolving the controversy may be determined by where one lives and one's social position and culture. Property owners may agree that good nature, in terms of their bioregion, would include wildlife

> nutrient cycling; and cultural services such as recreational, spiritual, religious and other nonmaterial benefits.
>
> **Well-being**. Human well-being has multiple constituents, including basic material for a good life, freedom and choice, health, good social relations, and security. Well-being is at the opposite end of a continuum from poverty, which has been defined as a "pronounced deprivation in well-being." The constituents of well-being, as experienced and perceived by people, are situation-dependent, reflecting local geography, culture, and ecological circumstances.

MILLENNIUM ECOSYSTEM ASSESSMENT, ECOSYSTEMS AND HUMAN WELL-BEING: A FRAMEWORK FOR ASSESSMENT—SUMMARY 3 (2005), http://www.millenniumassessment.org/documents/document.48.aspx.pdf.

[31] Hamilton, *supra* note 7, at 11-12. "Ecology studies the local and regional; Earth System science studies the Earth as a total system." *Id.* "[T]he Earth System . . . involves the co-evolution of its spheres: the atmosphere, the hydrosphere (watery parts), the cryosphere (icy parts), the biosphere (life and its surrounds), and the lithosphere (the Earth's crust)." *Id.* at 14. Earth is not a collection of ecosystems, rather it is "a single, total functioning system." *Id.* at 34.

corridors yet dispute that a corridor should be on their property. A country may agree that CO_2 emissions are harmful yet claim the *right to develop* and that this right should not be carbon-constrained. A company may agree that deforestation is harmful yet claim the right to clear forests for palm oil plantations.

Further, in the Anthropocene, human rights to freedom of action may run counter to social constraints imposed to maintain good nature. Some people will see environmentalism as a threat to freedom . . . even as ecofascism.[32] These views, however unreasonable as they may seem, will challenge the Earth law movement. Surely Bruno Latour was right when he said that decisions regarding good nature would arise out of a political process, not as the result of some transcendent, commonly agreed-upon truth . . . not even science, which will be contested.[33] Earth law will arise out of this same political process—the work of practitioners of Earth law will be an important part of it.

There is one principle of Earth system science advanced by James Lovelock and Lynn Margulis in their *Gaia theory* which may serve as a very useful guideline for resolving the global-local/situated tensions in agreeing on what is good nature for purposes of Earth law. As Latour explains, the *Gaia theory*—the idea that Earth is self-regulating in a manner akin to an organism—has been misunderstood as meaning that there is some transcendent global organizing mechanism performing the self-regulation in the way that human bodies are self-regulating, when, in truth, the self-regulation of Earth occurs as a result of multiple intercommunicating actors engaging in reciprocal co-evolution.[34] What is needed now, Latour says, is "the relocalization of the Globe, [a] move from the Globe to the quasi-feedback loops that tirelessly design it in a way that is broader and denser each time."[35]

What Latour means is that while we have come to understand Earth as a global system, in reality, the system is composed of countless self-organizing subsystems interacting and co-evolving with each other. Nature over billions of years somehow arrived at this system of self-organizing subsystems that have been able to maintain a measure of stability in the face of internal and external challenges. In other words, these systems have been able to maintain a dynamic equilibrium or dynamic homeostasis . . . what is popularly known as the *balance of nature.*[36] Human civilization, as presently constituted,

[32] *See, e.g.,* Václav Klaus, *Global Warming Hysteria or Freedom and Prosperity?*, EUPORTÁL, Sept. 23, 2007, http://www.euportal.cz/Articles/1852-global-warming-hysteria-or-freedom-and-prosperity-.aspx. *See generally Ecofascism,* WIKIPEDIA, https://en.wikipedia.org/w/index.php?title=Ecofascism&oldid=921779464 (last visited Oct. 22, 2019), and JONAH GOLDBERG, LIBERAL FASCISM: THE SECRET HISTORY OF THE AMERICAN LEFT FROM MUSSOLINI TO THE POLITICS OF MEANING (2007). Some even see calls for global environmental controls, including climate controls, as the beginning of world government and the apocalypse. *See, e.g.,* Joseph Candel, *New World Order Update,* COUNTDOWN TO ARMAGEDDON, Dec. 31, 2015, https://countdown.org/en/entries/blogs/new-world-order-update, and StevieRay Hansen, *Green New Deal – Boldest Tactic Yet to Advance UN Agenda* 21, HNEWSWIRE, Oct. 10, 2019, https://hnewswire.com/green-new-deal-boldest-tactic-yet-to-advance-u-n-agenda-21.

[33] Bruno Latour, *Facing Gaia: Six Lectures on the Political Theology of Nature,* GIFFORD LECTURES ON NATURAL RELIGION, Feb. 18-28, 2013, at 114, https://macaulay.cuny.edu/eportfolios/wakefield15/files/2015/01/LATOUR-GIFFORD-SIX-LECTURES_1.pdf.

[34] The penchant for describing other transcendent organizing mechanisms extends to terms such as "society as a whole," the "social context," "culture," "globalization," "capitalism," "nature," and "Earth." "Each time, we are presupposing the existence of a superorganism." Latour, *supra* note 35, at 135.

[35] *Id.* at 136.

[36] *See* EDWARD GOLDSMITH, THE WAY: AN ECOLOGICAL WORLDVIEW 150 (Rev. ed., 1998).

however, has interrupted these homeostatic processes. A goal of Earth law as well as other like disciplines is to restore this balance by reshaping human culture and social structures such that they mimic nature's self-organizing local systems in ways that are coherent with those systems. People who fear that environmentalism imposes oppressive, top-down restraints should find some relief in Latour's proposition that the key to sustaining good nature is ecologically responsive localism, though it is necessary to remember that in nature the homeostatic processes take place simultaneously at both macro (more global) and micro (more local) scales within larger systems and subsystems that are co-evolving with each other. Thus, if humans are to mimic nature's processes, Earth law will need to enable responsive globalism and regionalism as well as responsive localism.

VI. ANTHROPOCENTRISM, BIOCENTRISM, ECOCENTRISM, OR COSMOCENTRISM?

Anthropocentrism puts humans at the center of the world and considers humans to be superior to and separate from nature.[37] Consequently, since humans are the measure of all things, as the Greek philosopher Protagoras stated,[38] the value of everything other than humans is measured by human values, desires, and utility. Many authors locate the roots of anthropocentrism within the Judeo-Christian tradition as reinforced by Cartesian dualism and other modern Western philosophy.[39] The secular successes of humans since the industrial revolution, the globalization of economics, the emergence of a Westernized universal global culture, and the resulting disruption of traditional cultures have spread or augmented anthropocentrism globally.

While extreme anthropocentrism entails a profoundly utilitarian, materialistic, and deterministic view of nature, another version of anthropocentrism exists that does not see itself in contradiction with an environmental approach. The former version supports an approach in which nature is seen as unlimited resources and unlimited sinks to be exploited at will in order to further unending economic growth; the latter acknowledges that the well-being of humans is both connected to and dependent on the well-being of the environment. In the latter, human needs are still central, but they are articulated around principles of human health, well-being, and sustainability.

A *biocentric* approach, in contrast, recognizes the inherent value of all living organisms, irrespective of their utility for humans.[40] Although not operating from an explicitly biocentric perspective himself, Christopher Stone's argument, in which *trees* were to be considered worthy of standing, introduced a biocentric perspective into legal

[37] Fundamental to the idea that humans are superior is the notion that *Homo sapiens*, because of their consciousness, morality, and ability to reason, are the culmination of evolution or at the top of the tree of life.
[38] Plato attributed the sentence "man is the measure of all things" to the sophist Protagoras in his dialogue *Theatetus*.
[39] *See, e.g.*, Lynn White, Jr., *The Historical Roots of Our Ecologic Crisis*, 155 Science 1203 (1967).
[40] Peter Singer's *Animal Liberation* arguably first introduced a biocentric perspective in environmental discourse, at least to a larger audience. Peter Singer, Animal Liberation (1975).

discourse.[41] An *ecocentric* approach, as understood by deep ecologists,[42] goes further, and values the natural world independently of (or potentially even contrary to) any value it may hold for human desires. The meaning of ecocentrism in the context of law and legal systems will develop as lawyers and policymakers continue to identify and confront the limitations of anthropocentrism.

The philosophical axis around which Earth law initiatives are articulated covers a spectrum, from an instrumentalist view of the environment as a store of goods that is necessary for human sustenance, sustainability, and even survival, to the idea of the environment as inherently worthy of recognition, respect, and protection irrespective of—and potentially in opposition to—human interests.

A proposed shift from an anthropocentric to a biocentric or ecocentric perspective raises several normative questions. Is it ever possible to transcend anthropocentrism in legal theory and/or in legal practice? At a deeper level, is it ever possible, as Aldo Leopold suggested, for humans to "think like a mountain?"[43] Some authors suggest that if the human mind is the term of reference for both observation and theory alike,[44] then it is impossible to transcend and move beyond an inevitably *anthropic* (i.e., human) perspective. To paraphrase Leopold's invitation, it may be possible to think *like* a mountain, but it will never be possible to think *as* a mountain. Thus, the attempt to transcend anthropocentrism does not permit an escape from inevitable anthropic perspectives but rather challenges the "centrism," the idea that human interests ought to take priority in ethical decisions concerning the environment.

Law is anthropocentric in another sense in that the object of law is the regulation of human activities, not nonhuman activities or processes; for example, a fictional act to regulate the operation of gravity would be comedic at best. It may be helpful, then, to distinguish clearly between anthropocentricism inasmuch as it concerns human attitudes, orientations, perspectives, and philosophies, which can be theoretically transcended and moved toward biocentrism and ecocentrism, and anthropocentrism inasmuch as it concerns developing norms for human conduct and regulation thereof, which is inherently human-centered. Thus, while it may never be possible to think as a mountain, Earth law requires humans to rethink the mountain itself and human relationships to it.

Like biocentrism and ecocentrism, *cosmocentrism* might be thought of as another extension of awareness beyond anthropocentrism for science now embeds Earth in the evolutionary journey and dynamics of the universe, and space law is an emerging field of study. Cosmocentrism is included here, however, primarily to represent a more

[41] Christopher Stone, *Should Tees Have Standing?–Towards Legal Rights for Natural Objects*, 45 S. CAL. L. REV. 450-501 (1972).

[42] Naess, *supra* note 30.

[43] Aldo Leopold, *Thinking Like a Mountain, in* A SAND COUNTY ALMANAC: AND SKETCHES HERE AND THERE 137-141 (1949). Leopold makes the point that humans tend to have a short-term view of things. We may see what is happening to wildlife on a mountain, such as the killing of wolves, but not be able to understand its consequences. "Only a mountain has lived long enough to listen objectively to the howl of a wolf." *Id.* at 137. He continues that the hunter may rejoice that the death of wolves will mean more deer, but the mountain will know the deeper meaning of what happens when deer lose their predators.

[44] *See, e.g.,* JOHN D. BARROW & FRANK J TIPLER, THE ANTHROPIC COSMOLOGICAL PRINCIPLE (1988); Margaret Davies's "theory dependence of observation" in MARGARET DAVIES, ASKING THE LAW QUESTION (3rd ed., 2008).

ancient way of understanding Earth as a cosmic phenomenon. Many Indigenous people have based their understanding of their place in the world on cosmogonic and cosmological myths. The theory of ontological politics recognizes that differences in *ontological understandings*—meaning understandings of the nature of reality and of relationality—among different peoples have political and, thus, legal consequences. The Spanish word *cosmovisión*—the manner of seeing the world—is often used with reference to how people in pre-Columbian societies of Mesoamerica viewed the world and, also, with reference to how their descendants carry those cosmovisions today. Contemporary law, on the other hand, assumes an analytical, scientifically oriented Western worldview. Symbols and rituals in legal institutions from courtrooms to legislative and administrative buildings and lawyers' offices are generally devoid of a cosmic vision.

Earth law is concerned with re-understanding and re-framing human roles and relations in the universe (cosmos), Earth (ecology), and the community of life (biology). With the qualification given above that human law cannot avoid being anthropic, Earth law strives to move from anthropocentrism to bio-, eco-, and cosmocentrism.

The subtitle of this book is "emerging ecocentric law," and in various chapters of this book, authors write of ecocentric in contrast to anthropocentric approaches to law. The way in which *ecocentric* is used does not correspond to any formal meaning given to the term by others. It is not used to mean the opposite of anthropocentrism. *Ecocentric* means that humans are a part of and dependent on a larger community of life called Earth, and law must operate to ensure the health and safety of the total community of life, even for the sake of the human part of it.[45] Earth law codifies the responsibility of legal subjects to behave in this manner.

VII. RIGHTS, RESPONSIBILITIES, AND RECIPROCITY

The concept of *nature's rights* or the *rights of nature* is prominent in the practice of Earth law.[46] Thomas Berry, an influential person in the development of Earth law, in his *Ten Principles for the Revision of Jurisprudence*, gave this description of the rights of nature:

1. Rights originate where existence originates. That which determines existence determines rights.
2. Since it has no further context of existence in the phenomenal order, the universe is self-referent in its being and self-normative in its activities. It is

[45] Thomas Berry wrote that we must move from a human-centered to an Earth-centered norm of reality and value. The human system is a subsystem of the Earth system; therefore, we must recognize that "the community of all living species, including the human, is the greater reality and the greater value [than that of the community of the human species alone]. The primary concern of the human community must be the preservation and enhancement of this comprehensive community, even for the sake of [the human community's] own survival." Thomas Berry, The Great Work: Our Way into the Future 58 (1999).

[46] For additional discussion of this idea, *see, inter alia*, Chapter 2, "The Origins of Earth Law," and Chapter 9, "The Rights of Nature Movement in the United States."

also the primary referent in the being and the activities of all derivative modes of being.

3. The universe is composed of subjects to be communed with, not primarily of objects to be used. As a subject, each component of the universe is capable of having rights.
4. The natural world on the planet Earth gets its rights from the same source that humans get their rights: from the universe that brought them into being.
5. Every component of the Earth community, both living and nonliving, has three rights: the right to be, the right to habitat or a place to be, and the right to fulfill its role in the ever-renewing processes of the Earth community.
6. All rights in nonliving form are role-specific; rights in living form are species-specific and limited. Rivers have river rights. Birds have bird rights. Insects have insect rights. Humans have human rights. Difference in rights is qualitative, not quantitative. The rights of an insect would be of no value to a tree or a fish.
7. Human rights do not cancel out the rights of other modes of being to exist in their natural state. Human property rights are not absolute. Property rights are simply a special relationship between a particular human "owner" and a particular piece of "property"; so that both might fulfill their roles in the great community of existence.
8. Since species exist only in the form of individuals, rights refer to individuals, not simply in a general way to species.
9. These rights as presented here are based on the intrinsic relations that the various components of Earth have to each other. The planet Earth is a single community bound together with interdependent relationships. No living being nourishes itself. Each component of the Earth community is immediately or mediately dependent on every other member of the community for the nourishment and assistance it needs for its own survival. This mutual nourishment, which includes the predator-prey relationship, is integral with the role that each component of the Earth has within the comprehensive community of existence.
10. In a special manner, humans have not only a need for but also a right of access to the natural world to provide for the physical needs of humans and the wonder needed by human intelligence, the beauty needed by human imagination, and the intimacy needed by human emotions for personal fulfillment.[47]

The above is a well-known statement of the rights of nature, but it is not definitive. There are other ways that the rights of nature have been expressed. Some governments have amended their constitutions to include the rights of nature. For example, in 2008, the Republic of Ecuador adopted a Constitution with far-reaching provisions regarding the rights of nature. In Title II, Chapter 7, the Ecuadorian Constitution states:

[47] Thomas Berry, *Ten Principles for the Revision of Jurisprudence*, Evening Thoughts 149-150 (2006).

Chapter 7th: Rights for Nature

> **Art. 71.** Nature or Pachamama, where life is reproduced and exists, has the right to exist, persist, maintain and regenerate its vital cycles, structure, functions and its processes in evolution.
>
> Every person, people, community or nationality, will be able to demand the recognitions of rights for nature before the public organisms. The application and interpretation of these rights will follow the related principles established in the Constitution.
>
> The State will motivate natural and juridical persons as well as collectives to protect nature; it will promote respect towards all the elements that form an ecosystem.
>
> **Art. 72.** Nature has the right to restoration. This integral restoration is independent of the obligation on natural and juridical persons or the State to indemnify the people and the collectives that depend on the natural systems.
>
> In the cases of severe or permanent environmental impact, including the ones caused by the exploitation of non-renewable natural resources, the State will establish the most efficient mechanisms for the restoration, and will adopt the adequate measures to eliminate or mitigate the harmful environmental consequences.
>
> **Art. 73.** The State will apply precaution and restriction measures in all the activities that can lead to the extinction of species, the destruction of the ecosystems or the permanent alteration of the natural cycles.
>
> The introduction of organisms and organic and inorganic material that can alter in a definitive way the national genetic patrimony is prohibited.
>
> **Art. 74.** The persons, people, communities and nationalities will have the right to benefit from the environment and from natural wealth that will allow well-being.
>
> The environmental services cannot be appropriated; its production, provision, use and exploitation, will be regulated by the State.[48]

Other rights of nature provisions have been proposed or adopted by nations and subdivisions of government within nations.[49] Further, the rights of nature have appeared in United Nations Documents and Conferences.[50] On April 22, 2010, approximately 40,000 people at the World People's Conference on Climate Change and the Rights of Mother Earth adopted the "Universal Declaration of the Rights of Mother Earth."[51]

The rights of nature approach, while popular, has had little success in practice. Obstacles include procedural issues concerning standing for nature in court cases[52] and who has the right to represent nature,[53] but there are also very basic issues in defining the rights of every aspect of nature. Berry says every species has its own rights

[48] Global Alliance for the Rights of Nature, *Rights of Nature Articles in Ecuador's Constitution*, https://therightsofnature.org/wp-content/uploads/pdfs/Rights-for-Nature-Articles-in-Ecuadors-Constitution.pdf (last visited Oct. 13, 2019).

[49] Some of these provisions are discussed, *inter alia*, in Chapter 9, "The Rights of Nature Movement in the United States."

[50] *See generally* United Nations, *Harmony with Nature*, http://www.harmonywithnatureun.org/rightsOfNaturePolicies/ (last visited Oct. 13, 2019).

[51] Global Alliance for the Rights of Nature, *Universal Declaration of the Rights of Mother Earth* (April 22, 2010), https://therightsofnature.org/wp-content/uploads/pdfs/FINAL-UNIVERSAL-DECLARATION-OF-THE-RIGHTS-OF-MOTHER-EARTH-APRIL-22-2010.pdf.

[52] *See* Chapter 5, "Standing."

[53] *See* Chapter 6, "Legal Guardianship Arrangements."

appropriate to its role in nature. Given that there are millions of species, the task of spelling out these rights is daunting. Berry also says that each species and each individual in each species has a right to be. Most human activity involves violating the right to be of some individuals of some species. A blank prohibition on the killing of humans, with limited exceptions, is enforceable, but obviously a blanket prohibition on the killing of any members of all species is not. Another problem is defining relative rights. Humans have rights, but these rights are always relative to the rights of other people. Defining the relative rights of each aspect of nature in relation to the rights of each other aspect is doubly daunting.[54]

Given the difficulties of the rights of nature approach, some Earth law practitioners prefer a human-responsibilities approach. Conventional environmental law is generally based on human responsibilities. Humans are responsible for acting in such a way that they do not harm other people by damaging their environments in ways prohibited by law. Major agreements among nations regarding climate change, biodiversity, and other matters are also based on responsibilities of the parties

Rights versus Responsibilities cannot, however, always be seen as opposing approaches because rights and responsibilities are often interrelated. Rights, once recognized, impose responsibilities on others with respect to those rights. And, in many situations, responsibilities imposed are grants of rights to others. If, for example, a parent has responsibility to provide support to their child, then the child has the right to be supported by their parent. Which of the two approaches is emphasized, however, makes a difference. If a person, under the obligations approach, had an obligation to protect native species on their land by removing invasive species, then, if there were a recognized list of invasive species and a neighbor were to spot an invasive species on that land, the neighbor could sue for enforcement of the obligation against the offending landowner. If, on the other hand, under the rights of nature approach, a native species had the right to live without undue incursion by invasive species, and a person were to spot an invasive species on their neighbor's land, then the person would have to bring suit on behalf of the native species. The court would have to hear the claim that the invasive species was harming the native species and, if upheld, fashion a remedy to protect the native species. Then, perhaps, a guardian would need to be appointed to ensure continued protection of the native species.

Lawyers are familiar with rights and responsibilities, but not so much with *reciprocity*, which is a third way of defining relations between humans and nature that is familiar to many Indigenous people. Reciprocity is a norm under which one responds to a positive action by carrying out another positive action. Many Indigenous people have seen Earth as bestowing many benefits that require a response in kind. The duty of the reciprocal act is grounded in gratitude, which is more appealing than responsibility grounded in duty, even though, looked at another way, the reciprocal act is a duty. Reciprocity has been interpreted in other ways too, such as tit-for-tat, an eye-for-an-

[54] The nature's rights approach has had some success where individual parts of nature have been recognized as legal persons, such as giving personhood to the River Ganges in India, which has afforded additional ways to protect the river from pollution. *Mohd Salim v. State of Uttarakhand & Others*, No. 126 of 2014, Uttaranchal High Court (Mar. 20, 2017), at ¶19. The ruling has been stayed by the Supreme Court, as discussed in Chapter 20, "India."

eye, and reciprocal concessions. In these interpretations, the element of gratitude is missing. Reciprocity grounded in gratitude may be a fruitful concept in the development of Earth law. It is not to date, however, a recognized concept in Western legal systems.

VIII. PROPERTY RIGHTS, INDIVIDUAL RIGHTS, COMMUNAL RIGHTS, AND THE COMMONS

The challenge to traditional conceptions of property law, as advanced by many Earth law advocates, is more profound than simply suggesting the introduction of a number of limits to existing rights of owners of property. Nicole Graham suggests that natural landscapes do not merely exist as a background upon which human activities are cast, but rather are shaped, even created, by the dominant legal paradigm, which, through the subtle operation of property regimes, imposes a set of parameters that define the spectrum of environments allowed to exist.[55]

Though legal property regimes clearly affect land, they also de-physicalize nature and create a paradigm of placelessness.[56] If nature is but an *object* of someone's property rights, and if property rights, such as the right to control the use of the land, are conceptually disconnected from the life community related to the land (the nature, above, on, in, and passing through the land), then most forms of ecological destruction become legally invisible within this network of de-physicalized property relations. The emergence of nature as a *subject* of legal rights separate from the rights of property owners has occurred, in large part, against these dominant, de-physicalized property regimes.

Similar observations might be made of the macro effects of taxation policies, corporation law, health law, or environmental law itself. Laws create lawscapes. The dominant means of resisting either the negative aggregate effects of legal regimes or tortious or other unlawful offenses is through asserting individual human or human-entity rights. A member of an Indigenous community in Colombia may make claims, for example, on their own behalf for personal injury where a mining operation contaminates drinking water or for trespass if a company clearing forest for a palm oil plantation has violated property laws or creates a nuisance on adjacent property, but the community as a whole may have no rights (known in this collective form as communal rights) to control its destiny by having the right to determine what takes place in the area affecting the community. The Community Environmental Legal Defense Fund (CELDF) in the United States has helped cities and towns draft home-rule statutes declaring the rights of the community to a healthy environment and renewable energy, among other things, are superior to corporate rights in the home-rule area.[57]

[55] *See generally* NICOLE GRAHAM, LAWSCAPE: PROPERTY, ENVIRONMENT, LAW (2011).

[56] *Id.* at 5.

[57] Note that many of the CELDF statutes have been successfully challenged by corporate interests. *See* Chapter 9, "The Rights of Nature Movement in the United States."

A related issue concerns the role of the commons in Earth law. Traditionally, the commons concerned the "control of access to and extraction of resources seen as limited but essential for the survival of local communities."[58] In environmental law, concerns arose about the misuse of resources in the public domain with open access.[59] A particular issue concerned externalities such as pollution discharged into the air or waterways. A more recent and increasingly important understanding of the commons acknowledges the interests of multiple stakeholders in environmental goods and services, which leads to a demand for regulation or control of the areas of common interests, which may be global or bioregional. The new conception of the commons concerns, among other things,

- Sinks for pollution (including carbon sequestration);
- Biodiversity (ecosystems, species, genes, and existence values);
- Watershed protection (flood control and freshwater supply);
- Disaster mitigation (landslides and avalanches);
- Soils (soil erosion, pollution, and water runoff);
- Climate (reduction of greenhouse gases);
- Clean air (reduction of pollution);
- Forests (sequestration of carbon and oxygen and cloud production);
- Oceans (avoidance of dead zones, acidification, fish stocks, and water currents);
- Ice (albedo effect, and water source); and
- Aesthetics and recreation (preservation of beauty, access, and protection of nature).

Protection of this new understanding of the commons will in most cases infringe on individual or entity property rights and, when considered on a global basis, will also infringe on national sovereign rights. For example, in the summer of 2019, countries in Europe appealed to the president of Brazil to reduce the burning of forests in the Amazon on the basis that those forests supplied 20 percent of the world's oxygen. President Macron of France, implying that the Amazon was part of the global commons, tweeted "Our house is burning. . . . It's an international crisis."[60] Further protection of the new conception of the commons raises concerns about who has the duty to protect the commons, how this duty will be exercised, and who will bear the costs of protection

[58] Erling Berge, *Environmental Protection in the Theory of the Commons* (2003), presented at "Trans-Nationalizing the Commons and the Politics of Civil Society" (Chiang Mai, Thailand, July 11-14, 2003), https://dlc.dlib.indiana.edu/dlc/bitstream/handle/10535/1101/Erling_Berge.pdf.

[59] Arguments related to these concerns often draw on a now-famous article, Garett Hardin, *The Tragedy of the Commons*, 162 SCIENCE 1242 (1968). The broad application, made by many, of Hardin's argument that when property is not controlled by ownership, it results in overuse or other abuses is controversial. Burns Weston and David Bollier, writing about "The Tragedy of the Market," offer a different perspective than Hardin's. BURNS WESTON & DAVID BOLLIER, GREEN GOVERNANCE: ECOLOGICAL SURVIVAL, HUMAN RIGHTS, AND THE LAW OF THE COMMONS 6-14 (2012).

[60] Rachel Koning Beals, *Brazil Says It's Lacking Resources to Fight Amazon Fire as Europe's Leaders Urge a G-7 Response*, MARKETWATCH, Aug. 23, 2019, https://www.marketwatch.com/story/brazil-says-its-lacking-resources-to-fight-amazon-fire-as-europes-leaders-urge-a-g-7-response-2019-08-23.

and the burden of infringement of pre-existing rights. If nature's rights are thrown into the mix, many additional issues arise.

IX. REPRESENTING NATURE: DYADIC THINKING, SYSTEMS THINKING, CUSTOMARY LAW, AND CULTURE

The last three sections of this chapter consider problems that the current legal system presents for Earth law. The rule of law is a great accomplishment of civilization that has deep roots. The reason so many terms in law are given in Latin, such as *habeas corpus*, is because the concepts first appeared in ancient Roman law. Many have come to think of our systems of laws, whether they are common-law systems or civil-law systems, as *the law*. Yet, if law is understood to include a more general notion of how societies regulate human behavior in accordance with normative standards, then there are other past and present means of doing so, including religion, culture, customary law, and non-Western legal systems. In our time, we would also need to add science in that scientific findings have important effects on public policy and the behavior of people whether or not those findings result in written laws.

In modern societies, the state has a monopoly on the legitimate use of physical force within a given territory. A key characteristic of law, conventionally understood, is that the law may be enforced by the coercive powers of the state. Related characteristics are that people who obey the law will not be subject to coercive state action, and they may rely on coercive state action to protect them against unlawful violations of their recognized legal rights, including their recognized environmental rights.

This way of thinking about the law places a premium on what the written law or a legally enforceable agreement says and forces either-or (dyadic) choices as to whether a law has been followed or not, or whether a party to an agreement has complied with an agreement or not.[61] This dyadic approach has merit and goes a long way in structuring human relationships. It has limitations, however, when applied to Earth law and may be one of the reasons why the rights of nature approach has had little success in practice. Dyadic thinking is based on subject-object relationships and contributes to the othering of nature. In addition, nature is a dynamic system of co-evolving systems and does not yield to either-or logic.

Arthur Tansley first used the term *ecosystem* in 1935. A system has many interacting parts and positive and negative feedback loops. Early system models emphasized structure, adaptation, and dynamic equilibrium or steady states — in other words, they emphasized how given structures became stabilized and could remain in a steady state indefinitely. This was important in the application of cybernetic models and specialized systems theory to the maintenance of complex machinery, but insufficient for biology. Even so, the complex-machinery understanding is prevalent in how people,

[61] Granted there are many other factors involved, beyond determining what the law or an agreement requires, in obtaining outcomes in conventional law including, without limitation, legal procedure, rules of evidence, selective enforcement, and ability to cover the costs of making a claim or defending against a claim.

including many scientists and lawyers, think about nature. Application of this type of systems model leads to a belief that nature, like a machine, can be broken down into parts, rules can be developed for the operations of the parts, and relative rights can be assigned to the parts.

Later systems models have moved beyond equilibrium or steady-state models to non-equilibrium or dynamic models that better reflect nature.[62] Nature is neither a static order, nor is it composed of closed systems. It is highly dynamic with dissipative systems that exchange matter and energy with neighboring systems and with larger systems of which they are subsystems and, in each case, co-evolve with them. Evolution takes place simultaneously at both macro and micro scales. The result of this openness is the emergence of novel properties, relations, and systems.[63] Human systems that enter into nature's dynamic system of systems, which are co-evolving with each other, especially in the Anthropocene, contribute greatly to the emergence of novel properties, relations, and systems in nature.

Rather than dealing with issues of what a person can or cannot do as described by static written laws and dyadic decision-making, the bases of Earth law include the principle of relationality and the human duties of care and reciprocity. Legal questions based on this philosophy can more effectively address what it means to be responsible within a given situation. Given the complexity and dynamism of nature, one's sense of what would be responsible in a given situation could not be determined solely by going through a checklist of either-or choices and would need to arise in part from an intuitive sense of what is right after considering the circumstances or context in which the situation occurs.

The problem of unsolved problems in artificial intelligence is context. Computers using if-then logic may be programmed to achieve certain objectives and may even *learn* in achieving those objectives, but they are not able, and may never be able, to understand context in exchanging information with humans and, by extension, with and about natural systems. When law is understood as a series of dyadic decisions, it runs into the same problems that AI based on binary computer logic encounters, which is to say law loses context. For Earth law to lose context would mean

[62] These models have included the Gaia theory of Lovelock and Margulis discussed in the text accompanying note 35 *supra*; Ilya Prigogine's theory of dissipative structures that operate far from equilibrium, which proposes a new ordering principle called order through fluctuation, *see generally* ILYA PRIGOGINE & ISABELLE STENGERS, ORDER OUT OF CHAOS: MAN'S NEW DIALOGUE WITH NATURE (1984); Humberto Maturana's and Francisco Varela's theory of autopoiesis, *see also* FRANCISCO VARELA & HUMBERTO MATURANA, AUTOPOIESIS AND COGNITION: THE REALIZATION OF THE LIVING (1980); and other ideas such as nonlinear dynamical systems, complex adaptive systems, phase transitions, emergence, and chaos theory.

[63] Erich Jantsch expressed this as follows: "The result of this openness is the self-transcendence of evolution in a 'meta evolution,' the evolution of evolutionary mechanisms and principles." ERICH JANTSCH, THE SELF-ORGANIZING UNIVERSE: SCIENTIFIC AND HUMAN IMPLICATIONS OF THE EMERGING PARADIGM OF EVOLUTION 8 (1980). Clive Hamilton puts it this way: The cosmology of the Anthropocene must be based on the concept of agency that extends beyond humans to the freedom that is woven into nature itself. In this view, nature is a "dynamic, self-organizing system, characterized by emergent properties. [Emergent properties] cannot be found in any individual element [of the Earth system] and evade all cause-and-effect explanations. . . . The future always evades full predictability and inevitably holds surprises." Hamilton, *supra* note 7, at 137-138.

concentrating on the particular, which is separate from the surrounding environment and culture.[64]

Indigenous ways of dealing with violations of communal norms avoided dyadic, either-or decision-making and there is much to be learned from them. Decisions were made by a council and began with invocation, symbol, ceremony, and context. Questions concerned what the group's obligations were to preserve the community, including the larger community of life. Decision-making was collaborative, not adversarial, and was attentive to the varying contexts and changing circumstances in which decisions needed to be made. A taboo was understood as breaking the norms needed to sustain the community. When someone violated these norms, the primary concern was not punishment of the offender but rather how to bring the offender back into the community of mutual obligations. To be an outcast—to be cast out of the community—was the ultimate penalty. To be expelled from the community is also a form of punishment described in the Old and New Testament. The community and each member of the community depended on and was supported by the mutual performance of obligations.

Today we live in a complex world filled with interactions and transactions. Most humans will not live in Indigenous or fundamentalist religious communities with a single culture in a limited geographical area. Still, Indigenous practices provide a compelling vision for Earth law. While it is not clear how a legal system based on relationality, care, duty, reciprocity, and context would operate in the emerging field of Earth law, these terms are evocative and will inform the discussions in the final two sections of this chapter.

X. THE ROLE OF LAW AND LEGAL ETHICS

Law is a system of rules that is enforced by a state or other society to maintain public order and promote public welfare by:

- Regulating behavior (enforcing obligations);
- Settling disputes;

[64] An IBM website explains how humans easily grasp context and emotion but why this is difficult for computers:

> Computers have not yet made the great strides [needed] in natural language understanding and dialogue. . . . Without this, most computer responses are painstakingly scripted by engineers using if-then rules. "It's really difficult to anticipate every way a conversation may go, and if you leave out some critical paths, then you end up with the system saying, 'I don't understand'." . . .
>
> The key is to better embed a sense of context in conversational systems. Context involves many interconnected layers of accumulated knowledge that humans acquire and apply in conversation with little effort but computers cannot yet amass—the purpose of a conversation, where the person you're speaking with has likely just been or where they are now, applicable learnings from previous interactions with people who had the same purpose, general information about the world as it relates to this purpose, what has been said previously in the course of the current and past conversations with this person and so much more.

IBM, *How Conversation (With Context) Will Usher in the AI Future,*" https://www.ibm.com/watson/advantage-reports/future-of-artificial-intelligence/ai-conversation.html (last visited Oct. 25, 2019).

- Redressing injury and grievance;
- Punishing illicit (forbidden) conduct;
- Protecting against harm, including violation of rights;
- Preserving assets; and
- Enabling social transactions and decision-making.

Earth law adds to this list, ensuring that Earth remains a viable habitat for humans, other species, and future generations, with the understanding that this involves prospectively caring for ecosystems, preserving biodiversity, restoring damaged ecosystems and loss of biodiversity, and justly sharing the burdens of mitigating and adapting to climate change and other environmental stresses.

Developments that have already taken place in Earth law, as discussed in this book, raise questions about whether Earth law can operate within the strictures of conventional Western law. For example, plaintiffs in atmospheric trust litigation cases argue for expansion of the doctrine of the public trust to include protection of the atmosphere from greenhouse gas (GHG) emissions. The most important of these cases in the United States is *Juliana v. United States*. In this case, the plaintiffs, a group of young people, alleged that agencies of the U.S. government had—with knowledge that the life, liberty, and happiness of the plaintiffs would be endangered—permitted, encouraged, and otherwise enabled fossil fuel production and the use and escalation of atmospheric CO_2 emissions to the detriment of the plaintiffs in violation of their constitutional rights to due process under the Fifth Amendment and to equal protection under the 14th Amendment, and, further, that the defendants had violated the public trust doctrine secured by the Ninth and Tenth Amendments to the Constitution.

The public trust doctrine goes back to the Code of Justinian in ancient Rome. It is a limitation on the power of the sovereign and an imposition of a duty on the sovereign. The fundamental idea is that the sovereign must protect—that is, hold in trust—the resource base on which present and future generations depend. It is a duty that cannot be abdicated, and petition may be made to courts to hold the sovereign accountable.

With respect to this doctrine, there are at least two areas where the *Juliana* case breaks new ground. First, one interpretation of the public trust doctrine in the United States is that it only applies to states, not to the federal government itself. There are existing legal theories and precedents for arguing that there is a federal public trust doctrine as well, so this area is not as novel as the next. Second, the public trust doctrine has never been invoked to require such a sweeping set of remedies as those proposed in *Juliana,* namely that the defendants be enjoined from further violation of the Constitution and the public trust, and that defendants "prepare and implement an enforceable national remedial plan to phase out fossil fuel emissions and draw down excess atmospheric CO_2 so as to stabilize the climate system and protect the vital resources on which plaintiffs now and in the future will depend."[65]

This case raises questions about whether the plaintiffs' claims are justiciable on the ground that they involve political issues that should be resolved by the legislative and

[65] First Amended Complaint for Declaratory and Injunctive Relief at 94, *Juliana v. United States*, No. 6:15-cv-01517-TC (D. Or., Eugene Div., Sept. 10, 2015).

executive branches of government rather than the judicial branch and, also, whether the plaintiffs lack standing on the basis of lack of redressability—*lack of redressability* means a court is not able to fashion a remedy for the injuries claimed. To overcome these defenses requires sufficient evidence to support the argument that the situation presented is extraordinary and the courts are the last resort for the plaintiffs. There must be persuasive evidence that the other political branches have proven to be incapable of dealing with climate destabilization. It is not enough to prove that the government facilitated the use of fossil fuels, which has led to the destabilization. Their prayer for relief through the issuance of an injunction, which must always be justified on the basis of the need for this extraordinary remedy, argues that the extraordinary injunction they seek is justified by the exceptionally extraordinary need to address climate change.[66]

Another example of where Earth law has broken with conventional Western law is in constitutional amendments and statutes in Bolivia, Ecuador, and other jurisdictions that grant rights to nature and, in some cases, give any citizen the ability to enforce the rights.

A final example, though many others could be given, concerns co-governance between states and indigenous people. Under the 1840 Treaty of Waitangi, signed by representatives of the British Crown and Māori chiefs, New Zealand became part of the British Empire. For over 700 years, Māori lived in harmony with and depended on the Whanganui River. It was their *awa tupua*, river of sacred power. Although the Treaty guaranteed the Māori the paramount authority they had exercised for time immemorial over their lands, habitations, and all that they treasured, it was dishonored from its inception. In 1975 the Treaty of Waitangi Act established the Waitangi Tribunal to hear claims of the Crown's violations to address those concerns. In 2017, Parliament passed legislation declaring that *Te Awa Tupua*—the river and all its physical and metaphysical elements—is an indivisible, living whole, and henceforth possesses "all the rights, powers, duties, and liabilities" of a legal person. The law appoints two guardians to serve as its voice in legal proceedings.

Earth law has come into being out of the conviction that humans are facing an existential crisis because they are living in a way that violates the *great law*—the laws of nature—and that human laws must conform to the great law with due recognition of the extraordinary measures that need to be taken at this time. It further recognizes the inability of conventional Western law to address the present and threatened harms, much of which will be irreversible. Within this context, a dimension of time is frighteningly relevant. Given the proximity and imminence of tipping points and feedback loops of nature, Earth Law practitioners must ask how the law can best be invoked—deficient as it may be—to prevent actions that would irrevocably unravel life-sustaining systems.

[66] The most recent ruling in this case was by a three-judge panel of the U.S. Ninth Circuit Court of Appeals, which by a 2-1 vote on January 17, 2020, ruled that a court could not consider the case based on lack of redressability and the plaintiffs would need to pursue relief in the legislative and executive branches of government. *Juliana v. United States*, No. 6:15-cv-01517-AA (9th Cir., Jan. 20, 2020) (No. 18-36082). On March 2, 2020, attorneys for the youth plaintiffs filed a petition for rehearing *en banc* with the Ninth Circuit Court of Appeals.

XI. THE NEW SOCIAL CONTRACT: CULTURE, DEMOCRACY, JUSTICE, EQUITY, AND PEACE

A body of law in response to the novel environmental conditions of the Anthropocene is not optional, but the form that this body of law will take is. Law can continue to take nature against the grain, seeking mastery and control of it, or law may be based on working with nature under a new social contract. The latter is Earth law.

Enlightenment thinking, the Industrial Revolution, technology, markets, capitalism, liberalism, and representative democracy have led to great historical achievements. Because they have brought about unprecedented economic growth and material wealth, they are now sustained by the narratives that endless growth is possible, and that technology can overcome any limits nature imposes. Bruce Jennings speaks for many when he observes that we now have a social contract—the old social contract—in which "ordinary citizens, the *demos*, have given elites political control in exchange for the promise and performance of economic growth and material affluence."[67] This contract is now fraying because a greater and greater concentration of wealth is occurring while many find their living and working conditions stagnating or declining. At the same time, the old social contract is being reinforced because people at both the bottom and the top of the scale express a desperation to keep the old social contract in place by entrusting leadership to those who will roll back environmental and health regulations in hopes of spurring further industrial growth and trickle-down benefits.

As discussed in Section III of this Chapter, many believe this is no longer tenable. We are crossing thresholds we dare not cross. The old social contract can no longer ensure the health, safety, and welfare of people because of natural limits that technology cannot transcend. As Lester Brown wrote, these limits are not susceptible to political negotiation.[68] Climate change is either real or it is not. The outcome will not change because a political party does not believe in climate change. The situation presents a novel political problem, however, because those who push for a new social contract cannot prove with certainty what will happen as a result of global warming in the future or that technology will be unable to solve or avoid the problems that might arise. The pattern in the past has been to wait for disaster to happen, then deal with it. Response to climate change, however, requires acting in uncertainty and incurring present sacrifice to avoid disasters that will happen later if action is not taken now.

Already, there are natural interventions that require immediate responses: fires, extreme heatwaves, droughts, water shortages, flooding of small islands and low-lying coastlines, and much more. These are more than warnings of what will happen; they are present disasters. Jennings observes that the narrative that we can continuously adapt nature to human will and activity is an illusion born of hubris: "Earlier natural limits were overcome not because they were truly superseded, but most often because

[67] Bruce Jennings, Ecological Governance 19 (2016).

[68] "We are crossing natural thresholds that we cannot see and violating deadlines that we do not recognize. These deadlines, determined by nature, are not politically negotiable." Lester Brown, Plan B 2.0: Rescuing a Planet under Stress and a Civilization in Trouble 5 (2006).

science and technology found ways to tap into natural pathways and potentialities so that the resilience of natural systems could handle the burden human extraction and excretion [i.e., waste disposal,] were placing on them."[69] He then asks the supreme question of our time: "Have we reached at last a kind of thermodynamic and ecosystemic bedrock? . . . Can we reengineer the global atmosphere, or is geophysical fluid dynamics at last saying to us: 'Enough is enough, change your way of living or reap the whirlwind!'?"[70]

There will be laws in response to changes in nature that come out of the old social contract and there will be laws in response that come out of a new *ecological* social contract. Earth law, as presented in this coursebook, comes out of the latter. This could be seen as a kind of capitulation, a settling for less. Clearly the authors of this book reject that characterization. We see it as an optimal choice, one that is a recognition of what we have learned about Earth from our science, an acceptance of reality, an embrace of Earth community, and a doorway to freedom, within the limits of nature, to cultural and social revitalization and to the flourishing of life on Earth.[71]

The shift from one social contract to the next will not take place all at once. The changes will be contested and will accelerate over an extended period of time. The changes do not just involve law, but law and lawyers are necessary to bring about the needed changes. Lawyers bring a particular set of skills to the transition. Ultimately the result will be decided, not in theory, but as the subtitle of this book suggests, in practice.

The Anthropocene will test the ability of democracies to make long-range plans to deal with future threats. Further, as discussed above, Earth law must ultimately be based on a new ecological social contract and a new political alignment. The impulses individually and at the level of international relations to domination, control, material consumption, the accumulation of wealth, and military power are real, but, if we are to have a habitable planet and a viable human future, they must give way to collaboration and shared responsibility for the care of our planet. The crisis to which Earth law is a response is one of peril and possibility—the ending of the old and the discontinuous transition to a new era of greater justice, equity, and peace. All disciplines will be affected. Law will be an essential part of the transition.

STUDY QUESTIONS

(1) The second paragraph of this chapter describes the purposes of Earth law. Earth law is "the legal framework needed so that humans

a. live within planetary boundaries,

[69] Jennings, *supra* note 69, at 24.
[70] *Id.*
[71] For more on the new ecological social contract, see Chapter 16, "Ecocentric Governance: The New Ecological Social Contract,"

b. prospectively care for ecosystems
c. preserve biodiversity,
d. restore damaged ecosystems and loss of biodiversity, and
e. justly share the burdens of mitigating and adapting to climate change and other environmental stresses."

How would you define Earth law? Would you distinguish it from environmental law, and, if so, how?

(2) Proponents of the designation *Anthropocene epoch* argue that we have moved into a new geo-biological period in Earth's history. While people commonly speak of an ecological crisis, this may be misleading because a crisis is usually thought of as a short-term situation but, if we have entered the Anthropocene epoch, we have entered a new ecological condition that will be of long duration. Would you distinguish the ecological conditions that brought into being environmental law in the 1960s from the conditions that are bringing Earth law into being in the 2020s? If so, how?

(3) In contemporary Western studies of jurisprudence, the focus has been on justice and procedural issues and not on the philosophical foundations of law. In what ways, if any, do you think the Anthropocene epoch and Earth law challenge the existing philosophical foundations of Western law?

(4) There are many components, living and nonliving, of nature (which includes humans). If nature has rights, how would a court decide among conflicting rights? For example, consider a situation in which an Indigenous community in Alaska has hunted whales for centuries. The community particularly prizes hunting a certain species of whales that has dwindled to the point where it is now endangered. If you were the judge in a lawsuit challenging the community's hunting of the whales, what considerations would guide you in determining whether the rights of the Indigenous people to hunt or the rights of the whales should prevail?

(5) Assuming that nature has rights, name some of those rights and describe how those rights might be protected in the legal system? Assuming that humans have obligations to or responsibilities for nature, name some of those responsibilities and how those responsibilities might be enforced in the legal system?

(6) Earth law is sometimes called *ecocentric law*. How would law change if it were ecocentric rather than anthropocentric? Western law emphasizes individual and human-entity rights and freedoms. Ecologists emphasize protection of nature against harms by humans. These harms are currently regarded as both economic and legal externalities and, as such, are not taken into account. Further, ecologists call attention to global, regional, and local effects in assessing these harms. If ecology were the basis of law, how would legal thinking be changed? Suppose a developer has applied for a permit to build 500 homes in an old-growth forest.

The development is opposed by a nonprofit environmental group. Give traditional arguments for the developer and the nonprofit group. If the tribunal were governed by Earth law, how would your arguments change?

(7) Many environmental disputes are decided not on the merits but on the basis of who has the money to engage in prolonged litigation. Great attention in these disputes is given to whether damaging behavior is prohibited by the letter of the law, whether proper procedure has been followed, whether a court has jurisdiction, and whether the law provides for a remedy. Given the complexity of nature, is it possible to protect nature based on the rule of (the letter of the) law? Should there be special ecological courts for deciding these disputes? How could the legal system be modified to have the latitude to deal with the complexity of nature and of human-nature relations so that more attention is given to the harm caused and restorative justice rather than to positive law and procedure while still protecting the rights of defendants?

(8) If you were to draw up a new ecological social contract, what elements would you include in that contract?

SECTION TWO

ADDRESSING THRESHOLD CHALLENGES

This section addresses two basic threshold issues that are fundamental to the development of Earth law: First, how do we stop treating nature as human property and take nature into account in its own right? Second, who speaks for nature?

With regard to the first question, Chapter 4, "Property Law in the United States," addresses the conflicts between a constitutionally recognized right to property and adopting a rights of nature paradigm, such as the right of an ecosystem, a tree, or a black bear (see Chapter 14) to thrive in their own habitat or rangeland. This concept is also explored in Chapter 9, "The Rights of Nature Movement in the United States," in the context of efforts to develop rights of nature laws in the United States. How can the law protect ecosystems if the U.S. Constitution, as with others worldwide, holds private property sacrosanct? As you read Chapter 4, consider if property owners have a *jus abutendi*, a right to destroy their property, regardless of the profusion of non-human life forms it might contain and support. Should one be able to sue to stop their neighbor from cutting down a tree on their property since it supports a rich diversity of insects and birds while providing benefits to humans as well?

To highlight these challenges, Chapter 4 examines a case by one private property owner against another (*Boomer*), a case by a private property owner against the government (*Lucas*), and a case by the government as a property owner of grazing lands in U.S. territory that became Arizona against an environmental organization litigating to acquire property rights over these lands and let them lie fallow (*Forest Guardians*).

These cases pit property rights against the rightless natural environment: and they demonstrate how owners' property rights are a barrier to establishing nature as a rights holder and even for protecting nature in general. As you review the chapter, keep in mind that the objective need not be the *elimination* of property rights; rather, the objective is to place reasonable limits on property rights for the benefit of non-human life and life systems.

The other two chapters in this section, "Standing" (Chapter 5) and "Guardianship Arrangements in Rights of Nature Legal Provisions" (Chapter 6), address the second issue of who speaks for nature. Both standing and human guardianship of nature are essential for ecosystems to have legal representation. Rights of nature laws in Ecuador, Bolivia, and a few local ordinances in the United States grant standing for judicial review to anyone interested in speaking for nature. In contrast, laws in New Zealand, India, Colombia, and other countries recognize the personhood of specific ecosystems and appoint legal guardians to represent their rights. Legal guardianship bodies have been composed of governmental bodies, community leaders who live within rights-bearing ecosystems, indigenous peoples, or a combination thereof.

Thus far, guardianship appears to provide stronger legal representation for nature in practice. Guardianship is not limited to protecting nature reactively by petitioning for judicial review in courts; rather it also involves proactive measures for the benefit of nature in policy-making forums. Moreover, standing becomes an issue only when people voluntarily step forward to represent nature, while guardianship is obligatory — the institution appointed as guardian of nature *must* act to protect the ecosystem. Thus, the guardians of the Whanganui River in New Zealand not only have standing to represent the river in courts when the need arises but also, as its legally appointed guardians, they are obligated to take other proactive measures to protect the river.

Where legal guardianship has been granted, standing in judicial forums is derived from the existence of guardianship. In other words, guardianship also grants standing. But as discussed in the chapter on standing, where guardianship has not been granted standing is a preliminary issue that the courts, in most jurisdictions, have to decide based upon defined criteria. In the United States, standing has proven to be a major barrier to plaintiffs in rights of nature and other Earth law cases.

CHAPTER 4

Property Law in the United States[1]

I. INTRODUCTION

Property law regulates the definition, use, and disposal of real estate and chattels (movable possessions). In the United States, the protection of private property has long been viewed as a central aspect of a free society, if not its very basis. The founders wrote this concern into Article V of the U.S. Constitution: "No person shall . . . be deprived of life, liberty, or property, without due process of law; nor shall private property be taken for public use, without just compensation" (this was later extended to states via the Fourteenth Amendment). Property rights are often viewed as the condition for individual liberty and economic gain. But what happens when conflicts arise between property rights and environmental well-being? How can the law protect ecosystems if private property is sacrosanct? And what is left out of the picture when we focus on the individual ownership of land, animals, and goods?

This chapter presents the jurisprudential basis of private property rights in the United States and focuses on two cases in which property rights ran up against environmental regulation. These cases are emblematic of the tension between property law and Earth law: As the scholarly analyses excerpted below discuss, prioritizing the health and rights of nature requires adjusting the human-environmental relationship embedded in our existing property regimes.

II. PHILOSOPHICAL BACKGROUND

U.S. law, in both its common law and constitutional forms, is derived largely from ideas developed during the European Enlightenment of the seventeenth and eighteenth centuries. A major influence on the founders and subsequent generations was John Locke, an English philosopher and political theorist who sought to defend individual rights against monarchical and religious establishments. As explained throughout this book, Earth law does not focus on individual rights; its focus is the rights of the Earth community, which includes nature and future generations. However, Earth law shares Locke's vision of social development based on the idea of the "social contract," an arrangement by which individuals agree to certain restrictions on their natural

[1] Authored by Ted Hamilton, Attorney and Co-Founder of Climate Defense Project, and Zachary Klein, Law Fellow at the National Sea Grant Law Center.

freedom in order to promote security and development in the broader social context. The development of Earth law depends on individuals recognizing the benefits of limiting, even relinquishing, individual rights in consideration for the security and development of healthy ecosystems.

In 1688, in his *Second Treatise of Government,* Locke famously wrote that "in the beginning all the World was *America*"[2]—in other words, that all people once lived in the ungoverned state that Locke imagined to be the condition of Native American Indigenous peoples. According to Locke's social contract theory, to protect what was considered an individual's natural right to private property, established by one's own labor (primarily via agriculture), systems enforced by governments were developed to secure the benefits earned.

John Locke, *Second Treatise of Government,* Chapter V: Of Property

26. God, who hath given the World to Men in common, hath also given them reason to make use of it to the best advantage of Life, and convenience. The Earth, and all that is therein, is given to Men for the Support and Comfort of their being. And though all the Fruits it naturally produces, and Beasts it feeds, belong to Mankind in common, as they are produced by the spontaneous hand of Nature; and no body has originally a private Dominion, exclusive of the rest of Mankind, in any of them, as they are thus in their natural state: yet being given for the use of Men, there must of necessity be a means *to appropriate* them some way or other before they can be of any use, or at all beneficial to any particular Man. The Fruit, or Venison, which nourishes the wild *Indian,* who knows no Inclosure, and is still a Tenant in common, must be his and so his, *i.e.,* a part of him, that another can no longer have any right to it, before it can do him any good for the support of his Life.

27. Though the Earth, and all inferior Creatures be common to all Men, yet every Man has a *Property* in his own *Person.* This no Body has any Right to but himself. The *Labour* of his Body, and the *Work* of his Hands, we may say, are properly his. Whatsoever then he removes out of the State that Nature hath provided, and left it in, he hath mixed his *Labour* with, and joyned to it something that is his own, and thereby makes it his *Property.* It being by him removed from the common state Nature placed it in, hath by this *labour* something annexed to it, that excludes the common right of other Men. For this *Labour* being the unquestionable Property of the Labourer, no man but he can have a right to what that is once joyned to, at least where there is enough, and as good left in common for others. . . .

32. But the *chief matter of Property* being now not the Fruits of the Earth, and the Beasts that subsist on it, but the *Earth it self;* as that which takes in and carries with it all the rest: I think it is plain, that *Property* in that too is acquired as the

[2] John Locke, *Second Treatise of Government, in Two Treatises of Government* vol. 2, §49 (1688).

former. *As much Land* as a Man Tills, Plants, Improves, Cultivates, and can use the Product of, so much is his *Property*. He by his Labour does, as it were, inclose it from the Common. Nor will it invalidate his right to say, Every body else has an equal Title to it; and therefore he cannot appropriate, he cannot inclose, without the Consent of all his Fellow-Commoners, all Mankind. God, when he gave the World in common to all Mankind, commanded Man also to labour, and the penury of his Condition required it of him. God and his Reason commanded him to subdue the Earth, *i.e.*, improve it for the benefit of Life, and therein lay out something upon it that was his own, his labour. He that in Obedience to this Command of God, subdued, tilled and sowed any part of it, thereby annexed to it something that was his *Property*, which another had no Title to, nor could without injury take from him.

The U.S. legal system inherited Locke's notion that individual title to property is prior to, and does not depend on, government action. In its simplified form, this idea means that the law can only protect and regulate property—it cannot create or destroy it. Is this an accurate picture of history? Many people think not. In the article excerpted below, property law theorist Joseph William Singer critiques Lockean property rights through the lens of American Indian law. Singer explains how European nations and the United States asserted dominion over North America based on the supposed inferiority of Indigenous uses of land: native peoples failed to develop the land according to Locke's vision, and so it was justifiable to turn the territory over to settlers who would make better economic use of it. For Singer, this reveals the irreducibly political basis of property rights, which are created and distributed by (rather than predating and giving rise to) government.

Joseph William Singer, *Sovereignty and Property*,
86 NW. U. L. REV. 1, 18-19, 50-51 (1991-1992)

Scholars ordinarily understand Locke as presenting an argument for property rights based on possession and labor in the state of nature; the state of nature, in this conception, represents a philosophical, rather than an historical concept. . . . In the beginning, Locke explained, "all the world was America." Locke's *Second Treatise of Government* provides a philosophical foundation for European conquest and possession of the New World. It did so by distinguishing between Indian relations with the land and European conceptions of property in land. American Indians, according to Locke, had not established property rights in land both because they had wasted it by not developing it and because they did not recognize the same kinds of possessory rights associated with fee ownership. . . .

> Focusing on American Indian property... gives us a rather different picture of the origin of property rights than that to which most of us are perhaps accustomed. The historical basis of original acquisition of property in the United States is not individual possession in the state of nature, with government stepping in only to protect property rights justly acquired. Rather, it is redistribution by the government from those who were thought not to need the property or to be misusing it to those who were thought to need it—a different picture, indeed.... The state therefore both defines property rights and defines limits on its ability to alter the definition and distribution of property rights. Property is derived from sovereignty, but also creates sovereignty.

STUDY QUESTIONS

(1) What assumptions does Locke make about the original state of human society (when "all the World was *America*")? What rights are inherent for each individual, and where do they come from? Who and what is left out of this picture?

(2) Locke's account relies upon the idea of labor as an essential element of property rights. How well does this idea match our current ideas about property?

(3) Consider Locke's assertion that "*As much Land* as a Man Tills, Plants, Improves, Cultivates, and can use the Product of, so much is his *Property*. He by his Labour does, as it were, inclose it from the Common.... God and his Reason commanded him to subdue the Earth...." Can Locke's social contract theory be reconciled with the fact that property, once "inclosed" and even when secured by law and the force of government, can be reclaimed by nature? In the context of Earth law, it is axiomatic that nature will reclaim property, both public and private, ignoring human constructs of property rights. How might a new social contract embed the fact that any right of real property ownership is conditioned on nature's right to reclaim the property?

III. RIGHTS IN CONFLICT WITH ENVIRONMENTAL REGULATION

The Anglo-American legal tradition has historically emphasized the sanctity of private property ownership, providing remedies for interference with private property by both public (government) and private entities. The two primary manners in which a private party interferes with another's private property are *trespass* and *nuisance*. Trespass refers to a private party entering onto the property of another without permission or causing someone or something else to do the same. Nuisance, on the other hand, does not require entry onto another's property, but rather interference with a private party's use and enjoyment of their property. When a plaintiff brings suit over ongoing interference with the use and enjoyment of their property by another and the court finds that this interference is a nuisance for legal purposes, the plaintiff is typically entitled to a permanent *injunction*, by which a court remedies the interference by ordering the defendant to totally cease engaging in the activity causing interference henceforth. The notion of *servitude in land* raised by the court in the case below refers to the legal mechanism that roots the benefits and obligations of land ownership in the land itself so that these benefits and obligations carry over to future owners and occupiers. Thus, an injunction to stop a nuisance may take the form of a servitude in land to prevent similar nuisance being inflicted in the future, regardless of who ends up owning the affected property or causing the nuisance.

The following case, *Boomer v. Atlantic Cement Co.*, arose from a dispute between a cement factory in upstate New York and nearby property owners who alleged that dirt, smoke, and vibrations from the plant were negatively affecting their properties. At first glance, this pitted the cement factory's right to use its property for legal and productive purposes against the adjacent landowners' right to use and enjoy their properties. However, the court in *Boomer* recognized that these property interests reflected a clash of major public priorities: on one hand, the importance of the cement factory to the region's economy; on the other, the prevention of the environmental and public health risks posed to the local community by the factory's pollution and similarly negative externalities. As you read *Boomer*, consider whether justice between the litigating parties reflects justice for the community at large and how the court attempts to reconcile the two.

Boomer v. Atlantic Cement Co.

26 N.Y.2d 219 (1970)

BERGAN, Judge.

Defendant operates a large cement plant near Albany. These are actions for injunction and damages by neighboring land owners alleging injury to property from dirt, smoke and vibration emanating from the plant. A nuisance has been found after trial, temporary damages have been allowed; but an injunction has been denied.

The public concern with air pollution arising from many sources in industry and in transportation is currently accorded ever wider recognition accompanied by a growing sense of responsibility in State and Federal Governments to control it. Cement plants are obvious sources of air pollution in the neighborhoods where they operate.

But there is now before the court private litigation in which individual property owners have sought specific relief from a single plant operation. The threshold question raised by the division of view on this appeal is whether the court should resolve the litigation between the parties now before it as equitably as seems possible; or whether, seeking promotion of the general public welfare, it should channel private litigation into broad public objectives....

Effective control of air pollution is a problem presently far from solution even with the full public and financial powers of government. In large measure adequate technical procedures are yet to be developed and some that appear possible may be economically impracticable. It seems apparent that the amelioration of air pollution will depend on technical research in great depth; on a carefully balanced consideration of the economic impact of close regulation; and of the actual effect on public health. It is likely to require massive public expenditure and to demand more than any local community can accomplish and to depend on regional and interstate controls.

A court should not try to do this on its own as a by-product of private litigation and it seems manifest that the judicial establishment is neither equipped in the limited nature of any judgment it can pronounce nor prepared to lay down and implement an effective policy for the elimination of air pollution. This is an area beyond the circumference of one private lawsuit. It is a direct responsibility for government and should not thus be undertaken as an incident to solving a dispute between property owners and a single cement plant—one of many—in the Hudson River valley.

The cement making operations of defendant have been found by the court of Special Term to have damaged the nearby properties of plaintiffs in these two actions. That court, as it has been noted, accordingly found defendant maintained a nuisance and this has been affirmed at the Appellate Division. The total damage to plaintiffs' properties is, however, relatively small in comparison with the value of defendant's operation and with the consequences of the injunction which plaintiffs seek.

The ground for the denial of injunction, notwithstanding the finding both that there is a nuisance and that plaintiffs have been damaged substantially, is the large disparity in economic consequences of the nuisance and of the injunction. This theory cannot, however, be sustained without overruling a doctrine which has been consistently reaffirmed in several leading cases in this court and which has never been disavowed here, namely that where a nuisance has been found and where there has been any substantial damage shown by the party complaining an injunction will be granted.

The rule in New York has been that such a nuisance will be enjoined although marked disparity be shown in economic consequence between the effect of the injunction and the effect of the nuisance....

One alternative is to grant the injunction but postpone its effect to a specified future date to give opportunity for technical advances to permit defendant to eliminate the nuisance; another is to grant the injunction conditioned on the payment of permanent damages to plaintiffs which would compensate them for the total economic loss to their property present and future caused by defendant's operations. For reasons which will be developed the court chooses the latter alternative.

If the injunction were to be granted unless within a short period—e.g., 18 months—the nuisance be abated by improved methods, there would be no assurance that any significant technical improvement would occur.

The parties could settle this private litigation at any time if defendant paid enough money and the imminent threat of closing the plant would build up the pressure on defendant. If there were no improved techniques found, there would inevitably be applications to the court at Special Term for extensions of time to perform on showing of good faith efforts to find such techniques.

Moreover, techniques to eliminate dust and other annoying by-products of cement making are unlikely to be developed by any research the defendant can undertake within any short period, but will depend on the total resources of the cement industry nationwide and throughout the world. The problem is universal wherever cement is made.

For obvious reasons the rate of the research is beyond control of defendant. If at the end of 18 months the whole industry has not found a technical solution a court would be hard put to close down this one cement plant if due regard be given to equitable principles.

On the other hand, to grant the injunction unless defendant pays plaintiffs such permanent damages as may be fixed by the court seems to do justice between the contending parties. All of the attributions of economic loss to the properties on which plaintiffs' complaints are based will have been redressed.

The nuisance complained of by these plaintiffs may have other public or private consequences, but these particular parties are the only ones who have sought remedies and the judgment proposed will fully redress them. The limitation of relief granted is a limitation only within the four corners of these actions and does not foreclose public health or other public agencies from seeking proper relief in a proper court.

It seems reasonable to think that the risk of being required to pay permanent damages to injured property owners by cement plant owners would itself be a reasonable effective spur to research for improved techniques to minimize nuisance....

Thus it seems fair to both sides to grant permanent damages to plaintiffs which will terminate this private litigation. The theory of damage is the 'servitude on land' of plaintiffs imposed by defendant's nuisance. (*See United States v. Causby*, 328 U.S. 256, 261, 262, 267, 66 S. Ct. 1062, 90 L. Ed. 1206, where the term "servitude" addressed to the land was used by Justice Douglas relating to the effect of airplane noise on property near an airport.)

The judgment, by allowance of permanent damages imposing a servitude on land, which is the basis of the actions, would preclude future recovery by plaintiffs or their grantees (*see Northern Indiana Public Serv. Co. v. W. J. & M. S. Vesey, Supra*, p. 351, 200 N.E. 620).

This should be placed beyond debate by a provision of the judgment that the payment by defendant and the acceptance by plaintiffs of permanent damages found by the court shall be in compensation for a servitude on the land.

Although the Trial Term has found permanent damages as a possible basis of settlement of the litigation, on remission the court should be entirely free to ex-examine this subject. It may again find the permanent damage already found; or make new findings.

The orders should be reversed, without costs, and the cases remitted to Supreme Court, Albany County to grant an injunction which shall be vacated upon payment by defendant of such amounts of permanent damage to the respective plaintiffs as shall for this purpose be determined by the court.

STUDY QUESTIONS

(1) The court in *Boomer v. Atlantic Cement Co.* characterizes the threshold question before it as a balancing of equity and the general public welfare. First, consider how the court intends for these labels to apply to the parties before it. Is this an accurate characterization of the property interests in conflict? How, if at all, might each label apply to the other party? How might the court's analysis have unfolded today given changes over the past 50 years in how one might measure the value of the "servitude on the land"? How could one argue today the "other public or private consequences" resulting from the nuisance complained of by these plaintiffs?

(2) The *Boomer* court ultimately required the cement factory to pay permanent damages to the plaintiffs rather than granting the permanent injunction that the plaintiffs had originally sought. The court reasoned that this would redress "all of the attributions of [the plaintiffs'] economic loss" while incentivizing the technological innovation that would be required to abate the nuisance emanating from the cement factory. (1) How might a plaintiff in *Boomer* use this compensation to alleviate the earlier and ongoing harm and inconvenience arising from the cement factory's activities? How, if at all, might financial compensation alone— even, for argument's sake, excessively generous financial compensation—prove to be an inadequate remedy to a plaintiff in *Boomer* who has just learned of the court's decision? Can you put a price on comfort and peace of mind in one's home? How could the plaintiffs mobilize the compensation they received to achieve such ends? (2) Although the *Boomer* court explicitly intended to incentivize the technological progress necessary to minimize ongoing harm to the plaintiffs, to what extent might this payment merely represent the cost of doing business for the Atlantic Cement Company moving forward?

(3) The dissent in *Boomer* noted that the majority had downplayed the severity of the plant's air pollution and argued that it was wrong to allow the company to continue perpetuating harms simply because it paid a fee.[3] Daniel A. Farber argues

[3] *Boomer v. Atlantic Cement Co.*, 26 N.Y.2d 219, 229-230 (1970) (Jasen, J. dissenting).

that the majority opinion in fact "firmly set aside the public's interest in environmental quality" in favor of a narrow economic calculus; after the company paid out several times the amount of damages estimated in the appellate opinion (thanks to complicated property value assessments decided by the trial court on remand), the plant continued to cause health problems even as its operations were subject to new regulations such as those under the Clean Air Act.[4] What do these additional facts and perspectives say about the majority's resolution of the case? Do common law solutions to environmental problems rely too heavily on assumptions of good faith and perfect information? What are the limits of a judicial approach that prioritizes assessment of economic value in its decision-making?

Rather than interference with private property by another private entity, as was the case in *Boomer*, the following case, *Lucas v. S.C. Coastal Council*, 505 U.S. 1003, 1005–32 (1992), considers interference with private property by the government, the state of South Carolina. Governments generally interfere with property rights in two ways: first, the seizure of private property through *eminent domain*, which requires the government to compensate the former property owner for title thereto; and second, *regulatory taking*, by which the government does not come into possession of the property, but rather negatively affects its economic value by restricting how that property can be used. Unlike eminent domain, to which the Fifth Amendment's Due Process Clause straightforwardly applies, regulatory taking has proved more confounding to U.S. courts. Regulatory takings were first recognized as compensable by the U.S. Supreme Court's seminal decision in *Pennsylvania Coal Co. v. Mahon*, 260 U.S. 393, (1922). As explained, deterring the change in the law was a concern that such compensation would disincentivize federal and state governments from introducing regulations that were necessary for public welfare—potentially impeding, if not outright infringing, the police powers reserved to the states by the Tenth Amendment to the Constitution.

In *Lucas*, the plaintiff brought suit against the South Carolina Coastal Council, which was responsible for granting permits for beachfront development. The state's Beachfront Management Act prevented the plaintiff from constructing residences on lots that he owned due to the effect that the construction would have on "critical areas" identified in South Carolina's Coastal Zone Management Act, including public beaches. As you read *Lucas*, consider the state's environmental interests when enacting the statutes in question and how, if at all, South Carolina could have exercised its police power to protect the state's environmental interests without the need for compensation. As in *Boomer*, does this merely represent the cost of doing business for state regulators? How do the cases deal differently with the cost of doing business when it comes to environmental protection?

[4] Daniel A. Farber, *The Story of Boomer: Pollution and the Common Law*, 32 Ecology L.Q. 113 at 121, 130-131 (2005).

Lucas v. S.C. Coastal Council

505 U.S. 1003, 1005-32 (1992)

Justice SCALIA delivered the opinion of the Court.

In 1986, petitioner David H. Lucas paid $975,000 for two residential lots on the Isle of Palms in Charleston County, South Carolina, on which he intended to build single-family homes. In 1988, however, the South Carolina Legislature enacted the Beachfront Management Act, S.C. Code Ann. §48-39-250 *et seq.* (Supp. 1990), which had the direct effect of barring petitioner from erecting any permanent habitable structures on his two parcels. *See* §48-39-290(A). A state trial court found that this prohibition rendered Lucas's parcels "valueless." App. to Pet. for Cert. 37. This case requires us to decide whether the Act's dramatic effect on the economic value of Lucas's lots accomplished a taking of private property under the Fifth and Fourteenth Amendments requiring the payment of "just compensation." U.S. Const., Amdt. 5. . . .

III

A

Prior to Justice Holmes's exposition in *Pennsylvania Coal Co. v. Mahon,* 260 U.S. 393, 43 S. Ct. 158, 67 L. Ed. 322 (1922), it was generally thought that the Takings Clause reached only a "direct appropriation" of property, *Legal Tender Cases,* 12 Wall. 457, 551, 20 L. Ed. 287 (1871), or the functional equivalent of a "practical ouster of [the owner's] possession," *Transportation Co. v. Chicago,* 99 U.S. 635, 642, 25 L. Ed. 336 (1879). *See also Gibson v. United States,* 166 U.S. 269, 275-276, 17 S. Ct. 578, 580, 41 L. Ed. 996 (1897). Justice Holmes recognized in *Mahon,* however, that if the protection against physical appropriations of private property was to be meaningfully enforced, the government's power to redefine the range of interests included in the ownership of property was necessarily constrained by constitutional limits. 260 U.S., at 414-415, 43 S. Ct., at 160. If, instead, the uses of private property were subject to unbridled, uncompensated qualification under the police power, "the natural tendency of human nature [would be] to extend the qualification more and more until at last private property disappear[ed]." *Id.,* at 415, 43 S. Ct., at 160. These considerations gave birth in that case to the oft-cited maxim that, "while property may be regulated to a certain extent, if regulation goes too far it will be recognized as a taking." *Ibid.*

Nevertheless, our decision in *Mahon* offered little insight into when, and under what circumstances, a given regulation would be seen as going "too far" for purposes of the Fifth Amendment. In 70-odd years of succeeding "regulatory takings" jurisprudence, we have generally eschewed any "'set formula' " for determining how far is too far, preferring to "engag [e] in... essentially ad hoc, factual inquiries." [Citations omitted.] We have, however, described at least two discrete categories of regulatory action as compensable without case-specific inquiry into the public interest advanced in support of the restraint. The first encompasses regulations that compel the property owner to suffer a physical "invasion" of his property. In general (at least with regard to permanent invasions), no matter how minute the intrusion, and no matter how weighty the public purpose behind it, we have required compensation. For example, in *Loretto v. Teleprompter Manhattan CATV Corp.,* 458 U.S. 419, 102 S. Ct. 3164, 73 L. Ed. 2d 868 (1982), we determined that New York's law requiring landlords to allow television cable companies to emplace cable facilities in their apartment buildings constituted a taking, *id.,* at 435-440, 102 S. Ct., at 3175-3178, even though the facilities occupied at most only 1½ cubic feet of the landlords' property, *see id.,* at 438, n. 16, 102 S. Ct., at 3177. *See also United States v. Causby,* 328 U.S. 256, 265, and n. 10, 66 S. Ct. 1062, 1067, and n. 10, 90 L. Ed. 1206 (1946) (physical invasions of airspace); cf. *Kaiser Aetna v. United States,* 444 U.S. 164, 100 S. Ct. 383, 62 L. Ed. 2d 332 (1979) (imposition of navigational servitude upon private marina).

The second situation in which we have found categorical treatment appropriate is where regulation denies all economically beneficial or productive use of land. [Citations omitted.] As we have said on numerous occasions, the Fifth Amendment is violated when land-use regulation "does not substantially advance legitimate state interests *or denies an owner economically viable use of his land.*" ...

We have never set forth the justification for this rule. Perhaps it is simply, as Justice Brennan suggested, that total deprivation of beneficial use is, from the landowner's point of view, the equivalent of a physical appropriation.... Surely, at least, in the extraordinary circumstance when *no* productive or economically beneficial use of land is permitted, it is less realistic to indulge our usual assumption that the legislature is simply "adjusting the benefits and burdens of economic life," *Penn Central Transportation Co.,* 438 U.S., at 124, 98 S. Ct., at 2659, in a manner that secures an "average reciprocity of advantage" to everyone concerned, *Pennsylvania Coal Co. v. Mahon,* 260 U.S., at 415, 43 S. Ct., at 160. And the *functional* basis for permitting the government, by regulation, to affect property values without compensation—that "Government hardly could go on if to some extent values incident to property could not be diminished without paying for every such change in the general law," *id.,* at 413, 43 S. Ct., at 159—does not apply to the relatively rare situations where the government has deprived a landowner of all economically beneficial uses.

On the other side of the balance, affirmatively supporting a compensation requirement, is the fact that regulations that leave the owner of land without economically beneficial or productive options for its use—typically, as here, by requiring land to be left substantially in its natural state—carry with them a heightened risk that private property is being pressed into some form of public service under the guise of mitigating serious public harm. [Citations omitted.] As Justice Brennan explained: "From the government's point of view, the benefits flowing to the public from preservation of open space through regulation may be equally great as from creating a wildlife refuge through formal condemnation or increasing electricity production through a dam project that floods private property." *San Diego Gas & Elec. Co., supra,* 450 U.S., at 652, 101 S. Ct., at 1304 (dissenting opinion). The many statutes on the books, both state and federal, that provide for the use of eminent domain to impose servitudes on private scenic lands preventing developmental uses, or to acquire such lands altogether, suggest the practical equivalence in this setting of negative regulation and appropriation....

We think, in short, that there are good reasons for our frequently expressed belief that when the owner of real property has been called upon to sacrifice *all* economically beneficial uses in the name of the common good, that is, to leave his property economically idle, he has suffered a taking.

The trial court found Lucas's two beachfront lots to have been rendered valueless by respondent's enforcement of the coastal-zone construction ban. Under Lucas's theory of the case, which rested upon our "no economically viable use" statements, that finding entitled him to compensation. Lucas believed it unnecessary to take issue with either the purposes behind the Beachfront Management Act, or the means chosen by the South Carolina Legislature to effectuate those purposes. The South Carolina Supreme Court, however, thought otherwise. In its view, the Beachfront Management Act was no ordinary enactment, but involved an exercise of South Carolina's "police powers" to mitigate the harm to the public interest that petitioner's use of his land might occasion....By neglecting to dispute the findings enumerated in the Act or otherwise to challenge the legislature's purposes, petitioner "concede[d] that the beach/dune area of South Carolina's shores is an extremely valuable public resource; that the erection of new construction, *inter alia,* contributes to the erosion and destruction of this public resource; and that discouraging new construction in close proximity to the beach/dune area is necessary to prevent a great public harm."...In the court's view, these concessions brought petitioner's challenge within a long line of this Court's cases sustaining against Due Process and Takings Clause challenges the State's use of its "police powers" to enjoin a property owner from activities akin to public nuisances....

It is correct that many of our prior opinions have suggested that "harmful or noxious uses" of property may be proscribed by government regulation without the requirement of compensation. For a number of reasons, however, we think the South Carolina Supreme Court was too quick to conclude that that principle decides the present case. The "harmful or noxious uses" principle was the Court's early attempt to describe in theoretical terms why government may, consistent with the Takings Clause, affect property values by regulation without incurring an obligation to compensate—a reality we nowadays acknowledge explicitly with respect to the full scope of the State's police power....We made this very point in *Penn Central Transportation Co.,* where, in the course of sustaining New York City's landmarks preservation program against a takings challenge, we rejected the petitioner's suggestion that *Mugler* and the cases following it were premised on, and thus limited by, some objective conception of "noxiousness":

> "[T]he uses in issue in *Hadacheck, Miller,* and *Goldblatt* were perfectly lawful in themselves. They involved no 'blameworthiness, . . . moral wrongdoing or conscious act of dangerous risk-taking which induce[d society] to shift the cost to a particular individual.' Sax, Takings and the Police Power, 74 Yale L.J. 36, 50 (1964). These cases are better understood as resting not on any supposed 'noxious' quality of the prohibited uses but rather on the ground that the restrictions were reasonably related to the implementation of a policy—not unlike historic preservation—expected to produce a widespread public benefit and applicable to all similarly situated property." 438 U.S., at 133-134, n. 30, 98 S. Ct., at 2664, n. 30.

"Harmful or noxious use" analysis was, in other words, simply the progenitor of our more contemporary statements that "land-use regulation does not effect a taking if it 'substantially advance[s] legitimate state interests'. . . ." [Citations omitted.]

The transition from our early focus on control of "noxious" uses to our contemporary understanding of the broad realm within which government may regulate without compensation was an easy one, since the distinction between "harm-preventing" and "benefit-conferring" regulation is often in the eye of the beholder. It is quite possible, for example, to describe in *either* fashion the ecological, economic, and esthetic concerns that inspired the South Carolina Legislature in the present case. One could say that imposing a servitude on Lucas's land is necessary in order to prevent his use of it from "harming" South Carolina's ecological resources; or, instead, in order to achieve the "benefits" of an ecological preserve. . . . Whether Lucas's construction of single-family residences on his parcels should be described as bringing "harm" to South Carolina's adjacent ecological resources thus depends principally upon whether the describer believes that the State's use interest in nurturing those resources is so important that *any* competing adjacent use must yield.

When it is understood that "prevention of harmful use" was merely our early formulation of the police power justification necessary to sustain (without compensation) *any* regulatory diminution in value; and that the distinction between regulation that "prevents harmful use" and that which "confers benefits" is difficult, if not impossible, to discern on an objective, value-free basis; it becomes self-evident that noxious-use logic cannot serve as a touchstone to distinguish regulatory "takings"—which require compensation—from regulatory deprivations that do not require compensation. *A fortiori* the legislature's recitation of a noxious-use justification cannot be the basis for departing from our categorical rule that total regulatory takings must be compensated. If it were, departure would virtually always be allowed. The South Carolina Supreme Court's approach would essentially nullify *Mahon's* affirmation of limits to the noncompensable exercise of the police power. Our cases provide no support for this: None of them that employed the logic of "harmful use" prevention to sustain a regulation involved an allegation that the regulation wholly eliminated the value of the claimant's land....

Where the State seeks to sustain regulation that deprives land of all economically beneficial use, we think it may resist compensation only if the logically antecedent inquiry into the nature of the owner's estate shows that the proscribed use interests were not part of his title to begin with. This accords, we think, with our "takings" jurisprudence, which has traditionally been guided by the understandings of our citizens regarding the content of, and the State's power over, the "bundle of rights" that they acquire when they obtain title to property. It seems to us that the property owner necessarily expects the uses of his property to be restricted, from time to time, by various measures newly enacted by the State in legitimate exercise of its police powers; "[a]s long recognized, some values are enjoyed under an implied limitation and must yield to the police power." *Pennsylvania Coal Co. v. Mahon,* 260 U.S., at 413, 43 S. Ct., at 159. And in the case of personal property, by reason of the State's traditionally high degree of control over commercial dealings, he ought to be aware of the possibility that new regulation might even render his property economically worthless (at least if the property's only economically productive use is sale or manufacture for sale). *See Andrus v. Allard,* 444 U.S. 51, 66-67, 100 S. Ct. 318, 327, 62 L. Ed. 2d 210 (1979) (prohibition on sale of eagle feathers). In the case of land, however, we think the notion pressed by the Council that title is somehow held subject to the "implied limitation" that the State may subsequently eliminate all economically valuable use is inconsistent with the historical compact recorded in the Takings Clause that has become part of our constitutional culture.

Where "permanent physical occupation" of land is concerned, we have refused to allow the government to decree it anew (without compensation), no matter how weighty the asserted "public interests" involved, *Loretto v. Teleprompter Manhattan CATV Corp.,* 458 U.S., at 426, 102 S. Ct., at 3171—though we assuredly *would* permit the government to assert a permanent easement that was a pre-existing limitation upon the land owner's title. [...] We believe similar treatment must be accorded confiscatory regulations, *i.e.,* regulations that prohibit all economically beneficial use of land: Any limitation so severe cannot be newly legislated or decreed (without compensation), but must inhere in the title itself, in the restrictions that background principles of the State's law of property and nuisance already place upon land ownership. A law or decree with such an effect must, in other words, do no more than duplicate the result that could have been achieved in the courts—by adjacent landowners (or other uniquely affected persons) under the State's law of private nuisance, or by the State under its complementary power to abate nuisances that affect the public generally, or otherwise.

On this analysis, the owner of a lake-bed, for example, would not be entitled to compensation when he is denied the requisite permit to engage in a landfilling operation that would have the effect of flooding others' land. Nor the corporate owner of a nuclear generating plant, when it is directed to remove all improvements from its land upon discovery that the plant sits astride an earthquake fault. Such regulatory action may well have the effect of eliminating the land's only economically productive use, but it does not proscribe a productive use that was previously permissible under relevant property and nuisance principles. The use of these properties for what are now expressly prohibited purposes was *always* unlawful, and (subject to other constitutional limitations) it was open to the State at any point to make the implication of those background principles of nuisance and property law explicit. . . . In light of our traditional resort to "existing rules or understandings that stem from an independent source such as state law" to define the range of interests that qualify for protection as "property" under the Fifth and Fourteenth Amendments, . . . this recognition that the Takings Clause does not require compensation when an owner is barred from putting land to a use that is proscribed by those "existing rules or understandings" is surely unexceptional. When, however, a regulation that declares "off-limits" all economically productive or beneficial uses of land goes beyond what the relevant background principles would dictate, compensation must be paid to sustain it.

The "total taking" inquiry we require today will ordinarily entail (as the application of state nuisance law ordinarily entails) analysis of, among other things, the degree of harm to public lands and resources, or adjacent private property, posed by the claimant's proposed activities, *see, e.g.*, Restatement (Second) of Torts §§ 826, 827, the social value of the claimant's activities and their suitability to the locality in question, *see, e.g., id.*, §§ 828(a) and (b), 831, and the relative ease with which the alleged harm can be avoided through measures taken by the claimant and the government (or adjacent private landowners) alike, *see, e.g., id.*, §§ 827(e), 828(c), 830. The fact that a particular use has long been engaged in by similarly situated owners ordinarily imports a lack of any common-law prohibition (though changed circumstances or new knowledge may make what was previously permissible no longer so, *see id.*, §827, Comment *g*. So also does the fact that other landowners, similarly situated, are permitted to continue the use denied to the claimant.

It seems unlikely that common-law principles would have prevented the erection of any habitable or productive improvements on petitioner's land; they rarely support prohibition of the "essential use" of land, *Curtin v. Benson*, 222 U.S. 78, 86, 32 S. Ct. 31, 33, 56 L. Ed. 102 (1911). The question, however, is one of state law to be dealt with on remand. We emphasize that to win its case South Carolina must do more than proffer the legislature's declaration that the uses Lucas desires are inconsistent with the public interest, or the conclusory assertion that they violate a common-law maxim such as *sic utere tuo ut alienum non laedas* [Use your own property in such a way that you do not injure another's.] As we have said, a "State, by *ipse dixit*, may not transform private property into public property without compensation. . . ." *Webb's Fabulous Pharmacies, Inc. v. Beckwith*, 449 U.S. 155, 164, 101 S. Ct. 446, 452, 66 L. Ed. 2d 358 (1980). Instead, as it would be required to do if it sought to restrain Lucas in a common-law action for public nuisance, South Carolina must identify background principles of nuisance and property law that prohibit the uses he now intends in the circumstances in which the property is presently found.

> Only on this showing can the State fairly claim that, in proscribing all such beneficial uses, the Beachfront Management Act is taking nothing.
>
> The judgment is reversed, and the case is remanded for proceedings not inconsistent with this opinion.
>
> *So ordered.*

As Justice Scalia acknowledges in his discussion of "noxious uses" and the "background principles" of property law, the relationship between property rights and public values is intimate and complicated. Property rights are a powerful tool to anyone who holds them, but these rights have always been—and continue to be—constrained by public values, that is, by the legal remedies available to persons who are negatively affected by particular property or the use thereof. As the New Jersey Supreme Court stated in *State v. Shack*, 58 N.J. 297, 303 (1971), "Property rights serve human values. They are recognized to that end, and are limited by it."

Indeed, as far as Justice Scalia and the other members of the Court's majority in *Lucas* are concerned, South Carolina's Beachfront Management Act would have been uncontroversial if the state had been able to demonstrate that the statute would achieve the same result as a *private nuisance* suit by adjacent landowners or a *public nuisance* suit brought by an eligible government entity. Other principles of property law that go unmentioned in Justice Scalia's opinion, such as the *public trust doctrine* and the dual common law doctrines of *public necessity* and *private necessity*, further capture the context and nuances of property rights serving the public interest, as well as the limits thereto.

In the following excerpt, environmental law scholar and Tulane Law professor Oliver Houck examines the Supreme Court's decision in *Lucas* against the backdrop of colonial conquest and modern resource scarcity in the United States and the Western Hemisphere more broadly. As you read, consider the source(s) of the legal inadequacies that Houck identifies and how modern lawmakers can address or overcome them.

Oliver A. Houck, *Why Do We Protect Endangered Species, And What Does That Say About Whether Restrictions On Private Property To Protect Them Constitute "Takings"?*, 80 Iowa Law Review 297 (1995)

In *Lucas*, the South Carolina Supreme Court found, and the United States Supreme Court accepted, that a coastal set-back ordinance had denied Lucas all economically feasible use of his land. At issue in the Supreme Court decision was the state court's holding that, since the ordinance was designed to prevent serious public harm and to alleviate the equivalent of a nuisance, the government was not required to pay compensation. Fearing that expansion of such a rationale could swallow all private property rights, the majority set out to limit it. In its way, however, stood precedents compelling the Court to acknowledge that certain activities could be legitimately prohibited without compensation.

The result was a compromise. The opinion limited government restrictions not requiring compensation to certain prescribed activities: those that a private owner would not have been allowed to undertake in the first place, variously described as those that were "not part of his title to begin with; those that were not "previously permissible under relevant property and nuisance law principles"; and those that could be abated by the state "under its complimentary power to abate nuisances that affect the public generally, or otherwise," under "background principles" of law. Lest courts expansively construe even this narrow leeway, the majority offered two examples of permissible prohibitions: a restriction on landfill that would flood others' land and the removal of a nuclear plant from an earthquake fault. In sum, to prevail in a takings case the government could not be preventing simply any public harm; it must be preventing something recognized as harmful for quite a long time and, by some measure, as major harm. . . .

Rereading American history, one is struck by the frequent spectacle of small bands of men (never women) standing in black robes or suits of mail at the mouths of unexplored rivers against a horizon of wilderness. Swords raised, small pennants flying, they are bravely shouting into the wind and nailing to a tree various proofs that all of the lands, waters, wildlife, indigenous peoples, and other resources within sight, and within the drainage of anything well beyond sight, belong now and forevermore to various kings, queens and other monarchs, rulers so distant they would not receive the news for several years and would not be able to identify the claims for several decades, if then, before new realities overtook them.

A few centuries of practice has reduced American real estate claims to more modest title documents filed with recorders of deeds. These documents do great service to regulate the affairs of men and to stimulate their quiet enjoyment and prosperity. But at bottom something remains in the process that is as arrogant and unrealistic as the claims of Hernando de Soto and his kind. The ownership of land is a fiction essential to the functioning of American society. Like all fictions, however, it can be taken too far. The idea that anyone, through the payment of money and the completion of other rituals, may dispose of the millions of living things that occupy his titled property, heedless of the role these things play in the life of everything around it, is an anachronism supportable only in a world ignorant of its dependence on all life, and in which its inhabitants could not imagine the major, even catastrophic impacts of human actions. The bell for this anachronism is tolling. Recognition of the needs of endangered species and their relationship to our own needs will only hasten the day.

The day that is coming does not feature the demise of property rights, as feared as that spectacle may be in quarters as high as the Supreme Court, or even their significant diminution. The day will herald limits to these rights, however, and among them will be the recognition that no one owns the right to extinguish a form of life on earth.

* * *

Supreme Court cases that came after *Lucas* have limited the effect of the Court's decision, with important implications for property rights and the protection of natural resources. Through *Palazzolo v. Rhode Island*, 533 U.S. 606 (2001), and *Tahoe-Sierra Preservation Council, Inc. v. Tahoe Regional Planning Agency*, 535 U.S. 302 (2002), for example, the Supreme Court clarified that the *Lucas* total takings analysis applies only when the affected property owner can demonstrate a complete elimination of all value or total loss of the use of the property in question. These developments have afforded government entities greater leeway to exercise their police powers without compensation than initially expected in the wake of *Lucas*, but the property rights pendulum has yet to swing back to pre-*Lucas* precedent, let alone to the environmentally-oriented lengths envisioned by Professor Houck in the excerpt above.

STUDY QUESTIONS

(1) *Lucas v. S.C. Coastal Council* draws attention to the conflation of eminent domain—by which the government seizes the title to private property—and regulatory taking—whereby the government does not actually take title to private property, but rather negatively impacts the value of private property through regulations, ordinances, etc. Compensation is always required when eminent domain occurs; however, compensation was traditionally not required when the government merely regulated the use of property without seizing title thereto. Why do you think U.S. courts eventually embraced compensation for regulatory takings? Is this the *cost of doing business* for the federal and state governments? Compare and contrast what the cost of doing business represents to government entities with the cost of doing business for industry, such as the Atlantic Cement Company.

(2) Consider the observation by the court that "if the protection against physical appropriations of private property was to be meaningfully enforced, the government's power to redefine the range of interests included in the ownership of property was necessarily constrained by constitutional limits. If, instead, the uses of private property were subject to unbridled, uncompensated qualification under the police power, the natural tendency of human nature [would be] to extend the qualification more and more until at last private property disappear[-ed]." Is this reasoning sound? How does the government redefine the range of interests included in the ownership? How might the government redefine the range of interests included in the ownership of property, consistent with constitutional limits, to recognize human rights to a healthy environment? Are there flaws in the proposition that if "the uses of private property were subject to unbridled, uncompensated qualification under the police power, the natural tendency of human nature [would be] to extend the qualification more and more until at last private property disappear[ed]"?

(3) The Court determined, as a purely technical matter, that "[b]y neglecting to dispute the findings enumerated in the Act or otherwise to challenge the legislature's purposes, petitioner 'concede[d] that the beach/dune area of South Carolina's shores is an extremely valuable public resource; that the erection of new construction, *inter alia,* contributes to the erosion and destruction of this public resource; and that discouraging new construction in close proximity to the beach/dune area is necessary to prevent a great public harm.' " How might the factual argument have unfolded if Lucas challenged the government's characterization of the public benefit of the regulation?

IV. STATE REGULATION OF LAND USE

Federal and state governments are actively involved in determining the extent of property rights and in promoting certain environmental interests and values. Especially in the western United States, large swathes of land are owned by these governments and leased to private parties to promote resource extraction, agriculture, and economic development. Can this scheme—in which property-owning governments determine how land should be used—be adapted to promote environmental protection?

In the case below, the state of Arizona owned *trust lands* that, under the state constitution, were to be leased out to private cattle grazers, with the profits benefiting public schools (the beneficiaries). A conservation group, Forest Guardians, entered a bid for grazing leases, hoping to preserve the land from use. The commissioner in charge of the bids denied their bid, finding their purposes to be contrary to the constitutional scheme. The state Supreme Court reversed that decision. As you read the opinion, pay close attention to the various property classifications, such as "commercial use," that the state makes, and consider how these relate to environmental values. What is the relationship between public policy, government ownership, and economic interest? How easily does environmental protection fit into the scheme laid out in the Arizona constitution?

Forest Guardians v. Wells

201 Ariz. 255 (2001)

FELDMAN, JUSTICE.

¶1 The State Land Commissioner (Commissioner) denied the applications of Forest Guardians and Jonathan Tate (collectively Plaintiffs), who were the highest bidders for grazing leases on three parcels of land that are part of the state's school land trust, which is administered by the State Land Department (Department). That denial was premised on the conclusion that the statutory scheme did not permit the issuance of grazing leases for the purpose of restoring the land. The trial court affirmed on review of the agency decision, as did the court of appeals. We granted review and now vacate the court of appeals' opinion and reverse the trial court's judgment.

¶2 In 1910, Congress passed the Arizona New Mexico Enabling Act (the Enabling Act), which authorized the citizens of the Arizona and New Mexico territories to form state governments. *See* Act of June 20, 1910, Pub. L. 219 (ch. 310), 36 Stat. 557. By that act, the United States granted the future state of Arizona approximately ten million acres of land to be held in trust and to be used only for the support of the common schools of the state (school trust lands). *See* Enabling Act §28. The Department, under the supervision of the Commissioner, an officer appointed by the governor and confirmed by the legislature, administers the school trust lands for the state. *See* A.R.S. §§ 37-102, 37-132. 1

¶3 In 1997, Forest Guardians applied for a ten-year lease on approximately 5,000 acres of school trust grazing land in Coconino County. The then-current lessee also applied to renew its lease to graze eighty-five head of cattle on the land for $2,150 per year. Forest Guardians' offer was approximately twice that amount. Forest Guardians also applied for a ten-year lease of approximately 162 acres of land in Santa Cruz County. That land had also been previously leased, and the lessee had applied for renewal at $50.16 per year. Forest Guardians offered to pay five times that amount. Jonathan Tate applied for a ten-year lease on approximately 16,000 acres of trust land in Pinal County, offering to pay twice the amount the then-current lessee offered for renewal of its lease.

¶4 Though the Commissioner had classified all the parcels of land at issue as grazing land, Plaintiffs did not intend to graze livestock on any of the parcels in question. Instead, they informed the Commissioner, Forest Guardians by cover letter and Tate in his application, that the land would be rested for the entire term of the ten-year leases. Thus, Forest Guardians requested that the Commissioner permit Forest Guardians to use the land "for purposes other than domestic livestock grazing, as is permitted by [Department regulations]." Forest Guardians' letter explained that non-use for the ten-year term would restore the properties, thus allowing grazing in the future and enhancing the corpus of the trust, while its higher bids would satisfy the Commissioner's other legal obligation to obtain the highest revenue for the school trust lands. Throughout a subsequent administrative proceeding, Plaintiffs argued that by "not stocking the land[, Plaintiffs] will increase [its] value . . . to conservationists, prospective livestock interests and trust beneficiaries." *See* Recommended Decision of Administrative Law Judge (ALJ Decision), Findings of Fact, at ¶18 (March 9, 1998) (No. 97F-032-LAN).

¶5 The Department notified Plaintiffs that their applications would be rejected because they did not propose to use the land for grazing—the purpose for which it had been classified. It informed Plaintiffs that they would have to file an application to have the lands reclassified for commercial rather than grazing use if they wished to lease trust land for preservation or restoration. Plaintiffs responded that they would neither withdraw their applications nor submit applications for reclassification and issuance of commercial leases.

They continued to request the Commissioner to accept their bids and issue leases for resting or non-use of the grazing lands. *Id.* at ¶¶19-21. The Commissioner eventually denied Plaintiffs' lease applications "on the basis" that Plaintiffs "did not intend to range livestock" and asserted that, under the Commission's rules, such non-use would be consistent only with commercial leasing. *Id.* at ¶22. Plaintiffs, however, were unwilling to apply for commercial leases, explaining that they were not willing to pay the higher fees that would be required for commercial leases and rentals. *Id.* at ¶30. According to the Department, Plaintiffs' failure to apply for reclassification for commercial uses would prevent the trust from receiving additional lease income based on the higher, commercial use standard and thus was "not in the best interests of the State Trust." Denial of Application, ¶¶3d (No. 146-97/98) and 3 (No. 147-97/98) (October 10, 1997). Accordingly, Plaintiffs' applications were denied.

¶6 On Plaintiffs' appeal from the denial, the administrative law judge (ALJ) concluded that the Commissioner did not violate his fiduciary duty by rejecting Plaintiffs' applications because Plaintiffs' intended restorative use of the land did not meet the Department's criteria for a grazing lease and because Plaintiffs declined to apply for issuance of commercial leases. ALJ Decision, Conclusions of Law, ¶8. By order, the Commissioner adopted the ALJ's recommended decision. *See* Decision and Order (April 1, 1998) (No. 447-97/98).

¶7 Plaintiffs then sought judicial review by special action filed in the superior court. *See* A.R.S. §§ 12-901 to 12-914. The trial judge affirmed the Commissioner's decision, and Plaintiffs appealed. The court of appeals' majority held that the land must be used for the purpose for which it was classified and that the use could not be changed unless it was reclassified....

¶14... [W]e turn to the ultimate question: Does article X of the Arizona Constitution permit the Commissioner to reject as inappropriate a high bid for a grazing lease, without considering possible benefit to the land in question or the trust lands in general, merely because the high bidder proposes to rest and restore land that the Commissioner has classified as usable only for grazing?

C. *Grazing use and conservation*

¶15 The statutes controlling administration of the trust require the Commissioner to classify and appraise all school trust lands for the purpose of sale or lease. *See* A.R.S. §37-132(A)(5). Among the available classifications are grazing and commercial uses. *See* A.R.S. §37-212(B)(2) and (4). Grazing land is defined as land that "can be used only for the ranging of animals." A.R.S. §37-101(7). Commercial land is land that "can be used principally for business, institutional, religious, charitable, governmental or recreational purposes, or any general purpose other than agricultural, grazing, mining, oil, homesite or rights-of-way." *Id.* The lands are appraised according to their classification, which is determined by considering their highest and best use. The lands at issue were appraised at full market value for grazing lands, the lowest category of use. A.R.S. §37-285(B)2 and (E). But as the Department argues, if commercial use "is an option," the lands would have to be appraised for that higher use, which would probably result in a higher minimum rental. *See* A.R.S. §37-281.02. This case shows, however, that higher rental may well discourage prospective bidders who seek to restore lands that have been overgrazed or otherwise damaged.

¶16 In this court, the Department nevertheless argues that the statutes do not permit the lease of grazing lands to an applicant "who states an intent from the outset never to graze for the full term of the lease." Department's Supplemental Brief at 6. Commercial use, however, includes "general purposes," which, the Department says, could encompass restoration and recreational uses. *See* A.R.S. §37-101(7). The Department maintains that because Plaintiffs refused to apply for reclassification, the Commissioner correctly rejected their applications.

¶17 Although the Department's position has surface appeal in terms of administration, it will not wash when examined in light of our constitution, the existing statutory scheme for leasing school trust lands, and the Commissioner's fiduciary duties as trustee of those lands. First, Plaintiffs do not seek to change the long-term use of the land from grazing to commercial use. Grazing leases are limited to ten years, while commercial leases may run for as long as ninety-nine years. *See* A.R.S. §§ 37-281, 37-281.02; *see also* Ariz. Const. art. X, §9. Plaintiffs seek only ten-year leases with no permanent change in use or classification of the property. Moreover, we find nothing in the definition of commercial land to suggest that it permits the type of non-use Plaintiffs propose.

¶18 Second, on this record, Plaintiffs' proposed use does not really conflict with a grazing use. According to Plaintiffs, they intend only to rest the property from overgrazing, thus making it more valuable for future grazing. Testimony at the hearing before the ALJ described at least one parcel as having been overgrazed and reduced to a "moonscape" in need of restoration. Reporter's Transcript (RT), 2/3/98, at 28. Photographs were introduced to support this description. Forest Guardians intended to undertake restoration work, such as fencing off the land to prevent livestock grazing, planting trees, and limiting human access that would interfere with restoration. *Id.* at 29-30. The Department, however, argued to the ALJ that Plaintiffs were simply trying to get the land at a grazing rate when the non-use "could command a higher rate" for commercial use. *Id.* at 91. "Moonscapes [were] irrelevant. Non-use was not grazing use." *Id.* But the Arizona Education Association's amicus brief cites the Department's 1999–2000 annual report to show that while ninety percent of the school trust land (or 7,433,000 acres out of the present total of approximately 7,900,000 acres) is classified as grazing land, A.R.S. §37-285(H) permits the Department to "authorize non-use for part or all of the grazing use upon request of the lessee at least sixty days prior to the beginning of the billing date." The evidence before the ALJ indicated that at any given time, the Department has granted non-use permission to grazing lessees covering a very significant number of acres of grazing land. The Department Range Selection Manager conceded that non-use permits could have covered up to one million acres. The Department has in fact adopted regulations permitting a grazing lessee to apply for a non-use permit. *See* A.A.C. R12-5-705(O).

¶19 Finally, the land was classified for grazing because it has no other practicable use. *See* A.R.S. §37-101(7). Yet the Department refuses to consider Plaintiffs' applications unless they apply for commercial reclassification, even though that classification does not expressly permit a non-use, as does §37-285(H), and a commercial classification might drive prospective bidders away because of the higher appraisal and higher rentals. *See* Department's Reply to Appellant's Response to Department's Motion for Summary Judgment at 6 (February 17, 1998) (No. 97F-031-LAN). Plaintiffs are unwilling to pay those higher rentals for land that has no real commercial value. It appears, in fact, that no one other than the present lessee and Plaintiffs would be interested in leasing the parcels for any purpose. *Id.* at 6-7.

D. Resolution

¶20 Neither the Enabling Act nor our constitution requires classification of property—only that any disposition be made to the highest and best bidder. Property classification, of course, may be an aid to proper administration of the trust, and our constitution permits the legislature to adopt statutory rules for administration that instruct the Commissioner to classify trust lands by present, potential, or appropriate use. But permissive administrative concern and practice must conform to the core fiduciary trust duties imposed by our law. Thus, the fiduciary duties imposed by article X of our constitution forbid the Department and the Commissioner from applying the statutes in such a way as to routinely issue non-use permits to grazing lessees who apply after signing the lease while automatically denying them to the highest, and arguably best, bidder simply because that bidder makes known its intent.

¶21 The Commissioner, rather, is required to consider and accept the "highest and best bidder." Ariz. Const. art. X, §8. What is highest is decided arithmetically; in the present case, Plaintiffs' bids were highest. What is best is a mixed question of fact and law on which the Commissioner has considerable discretionary decision-making power. *See Jeffries v. Hassell,* 197 Ariz. 151, 3 P.3d 1071 (App.1999). We do not diminish that discretion. But restoration and preservation are already and must continue to be considered legitimate uses for land that, according to the Commissioner's classification, has no higher and better use than grazing. Otherwise, grazing lessees could continue to graze stock until the land is damaged and its value destroyed. This fact, no doubt, is one of the reasons why the statutes and regulations presently permit issuance of non-use permits for grazing land....

¶23 Under the circumstances presented by this case, we believe the Commissioner's fiduciary duty required him to *consider* Plaintiffs' bids and ascertain whether they were best for the corpus of the trust and its beneficiaries. We are mindful that the high bid is not necessarily the best bid. *See Havasu Heights Ranch & Dev. Corp. v. Desert Valley Wood Prod., Inc.,* 167 Ariz. 383, 392, 807 P.2d 1119, 1128 (App.1990) ("The 'best interest' standard does not require blind adherence. . . ."). But the Commissioner could not reject the high bids without first examining the facts and exercising a fact-based discretion to determine whether those bids would advance the interests of the trust and its beneficiaries. *Brown v. City of Phoenix,* 77 Ariz. 368, 376, 272 P.2d 358, 363-64 (1954). The Department, in other words, cannot use the classification system in such a manner as to discourage or automatically reject those who seek to lease grazing lands for restorative purposes. Such a summary refusal to even consider whether Plaintiffs' offers were in the best interests of the trust was a clear violation of the fiduciary duties imposed by the state constitution. . . .

CONCLUSION

¶27 . . . The Commissioner may not reject such a proposal by the high bidder as inappropriate for land useful only for grazing when those who lease for grazing are routinely permitted to make such uses. Nor may the Department apply the classification statutes so as to discourage conservationists and others from bidding on grazing land by requiring them to have the land reclassified and pay the higher rentals resulting from commercial classification. If the parcels in question are usable for something more or better than grazing (including restoration and preservation), then the Department should, as it is permitted to do, institute reclassification procedures and open the land to commercial bidders. But the lands in question are far from having any use as sites for a Neiman Marcus, a Wal Mart, or a ski resort. . . .

¶28 The court of appeals' opinion is vacated and the superior court's judgment is reversed. The case is remanded to the trial court with instructions to enter judgment requiring the Commissioner to determine whether Plaintiffs' high bids were, in the long term, best for the school trust lands and their beneficiaries. If so, the Commissioner shall accept the bids and issue the leases.

STUDY QUESTIONS

(1) The effort by Forest Guardians to preserve grazing land from use was one of many conservationist efforts in the last several decades to intervene in public bidding processes in order to prevent economic activity such as oil and gas development, timber cutting, or mining. As the Forest Guardian opinion acknowledges, such efforts run contrary to the original intent of public land leasing schemes.

Is this an appropriate way to go about environmental protection? Was the state Supreme Court correct in allowing the conservationist effort to proceed? What about the impact on cattle ranchers should such projects grow more common?

(2) The Forest Guardians' success in this case was an anomaly; in most instances, conservationist bids have been tossed out, and many states have changed their laws and regulations to force winning bidders to use the land as intended.[5] What does this say about the role that governments play as property owners? What are the limits of using existing property law to advance environmental goals? Is this a problem that can be fixed by amending the laws that govern public lands leases, or is a more fundamental shift needed?

V. CONCLUSION

The cases discussed in this chapter reveal the increasing tension between the emergence of Earth law and the system of deeply embedded property rights based on the longstanding doctrine that one can use their own property in any way that does not injure another or another's property rights. As Earth law develops, within the constraints of current property law, practitioners may focus on the legal corollary of the rights of property ownership, both public and private: the duties, or at least the responsibilities—to preserve, sustain, and renew the characteristics of the property that are necessary to its fulfilling its role in the life-sustaining Earth community. In "The Land Ethic," a chapter of his seminal 1949 book *A Sand County Almanac*, American environmentalist and University of Wisconsin professor Aldo Leopold calls for a radical reorientation of humanity's interactions with the Earth. Leopold observes that "we abuse the land because we regard it as a commodity belonging to us" and laments the absence of an "ethic dealing with [humankind's] relationship to the land and to the non-human animals and plants which grow upon it." In response, Leopold proposes a so-called "Land Ethic" to influence human interaction with the Earth, with the Ethic consisting of self-imposed limitations on the freedom to exploit natural resources for the ultimate purpose of "chang[ing] the role of *Homo Sapiens* from conqueror of the land-community to plain member and citizen of it." Of particular import is the Land Ethic's explicit recognition of nature's "right to continued existence" and, more broadly, natural resources' right to "continued existence in a natural state." Leopold proposes the following formula: "A thing is right when it tends to preserve the integrity, stability, and beauty of the biotic community. It is wrong when it tends otherwise."[6] Although Leopold was neither a lawyer nor purporting to write in any legal capacity, his Land Ethic remains influential within the global environmental law and policy community and indelibly pervades contemporary advocacy for the development of Earth law.

[5] *See* Bryan Leonard & Shawn Regan, *Legal and Institutional Barriers to Establishing Non-Use Rights to Natural Resources,* 59 Nat. Resources J. 135 (2019).

[6] Aldo Leopold, A Sand County Almanac (1970), xviii, 238, 240, 262.

CHAPTER 5

Standing[1]

I. WHAT IS STANDING AND WHY IS IT IMPORTANT?

The law of standing determines whether a litigant has a sufficient personal interest in the outcome of a lawsuit to be heard by a court. In 1972, in *Sierra Club v. Morton,*[2] the Supreme Court considered whether the Sierra Club had standing to challenge the federal administrative action that approved a $35 million development project in the Sequoia National Forest. The Court found the Sierra Club lacked standing. It was groundbreaking litigation and carried an extraordinary financial and precedential cost. The Court found that the environmental injury to the Sequoia National Park, and, specifically, the Mineral King Valley where the development was proposed to take place, was not a relevant factor in assessing the Sierra Club's standing. Rather, the Court explained, standing "requires more than an injury to a cognizable interest. It requires that the party seeking review be himself among the injured." The precedent stands today, despite a thoughtful dissenting opinion that "the question of 'standing' would be simplified and also put neatly into focus if we fashioned a federal rule that allowed environmental issues to be litigated in the name of [the place] about to be despoiled, defaced or invaded. . . ."[3]

In the ensuing five decades, standing has been a persistent obstacle to the presentation of claims seeking to preserve and protect the environment, ecosystems, and their nonhuman constituents. The cases discussed in this chapter reflect the development and delineation of the legal criteria applied to determine whether a claimant has a right to be recognized by a court as a holder of justiciable legal rights.

Ultimately, one may characterize decisions based on standing as a reflection of the Court's interest in deciding the substantive issues presented. As Chief Justice Marshall stated in 1803: "It is emphatically the province and duty of the judicial department to say what the law is."[4] Dismissing a case based on the standing doctrine is a means for a court to avoid saying what the law is. As will be seen, the intricacy of the standing doctrine is a reflection of the evolution of the Supreme Court's interest in making an issue one the Court—as opposed to the other branches of the federal government—will decide. As the Ninth Circuit Court of Appeals observed in *Juliana v. United States,* the

[1] This chapter was authored by Tony Zelle, President of the Earth Law Center. The contributions to this chapter by Victoria Lichet and Addison Luck are gratefully acknowledged.
[2] *Sierra Club v. Morton,* 405 U.S. 727 (1972), discussed in detail *infra,* Section III.
[3] *Id.* at 741.
[4] *Marbury v. Madison,* 5 U.S. 137 (1803).

federal government's climate policies may pose a "clear and present danger" capable of destroying the nation, but it is up to the executive branch and Congress, not the U.S. courts, to do something about it.[5]

In *The Doctrine of Standing as an Essential Element of the Separation of Powers*, 17 Suffolk University Law Review 881, 882 (1983), Justice Antonin Scalia wrote:

> The Supreme Court has described standing as "a sufficient stake in an otherwise justiciable controversy to obtain judicial resolution of that controversy." In more pedestrian terms, it is an answer to the very first question that is sometimes rudely asked when one person complains of another's actions: "What's it to you?"

Standing provides the means to seek protection through the judicial system, at law or in equity, of one's claimed interest. Conferring standing on a party is a means by which the judicial system declares that the party is a holder of a legal right, at least a procedural right, to have its interests or value heard by a court. Without standing, no other procedural or substantive right that may be claimed can be adjudicated.

Federal standing requirements originate in Article III, Section II of the U.S. Constitution, which limits the jurisdiction of the federal judiciary to "cases" and "controversies":

> The judicial Power shall extend to all Cases, in Law and Equity, arising under this Constitution, the Laws of the United States, and Treaties made, or which shall be made, under their Authority;—to all Cases affecting Ambassadors, other public Ministers and Consuls;—to all Cases of admiralty and maritime Jurisdiction;—to Controversies to which the United States shall be a Party;—to Controversies between two or more States;—between a State and Citizens of another State;—between Citizens of different States;—between Citizens of the same State claiming Lands under Grants of different States, and between a State, or the Citizens thereof, and foreign States, Citizens or Subjects.

In *Baker v. Carr*, 369 U.S. 186 (1962), the Court described the basic test for standing as being whether a plaintiff has a "personal stake" in the outcome:

> Have the appellants alleged such a personal stake in the outcome of the controversy as to assure that concrete adverseness which sharpens the presentation of issues upon which the court so largely depends for illumination of difficult constitutional questions? This is the gist of the question of standing. It is, of course, a question of federal law.[6]

[5] *Juliana v. U.S.*, No. 18-36082 D.C. No. 6:15-cv-01517-AA (9th Cir., Jan. 17, 2020) ("Not every problem posing a threat—even a clear and present danger—to the American Experiment can be solved by federal judges.... The dissent correctly notes that the political branches of government have to date been largely deaf to the pleas of the plaintiffs and other similarly situated individuals. But, although inaction by the Executive and Congress may affect the form of judicial relief ordered when there is Article III standing, it cannot bring otherwise nonjusticiable claims within the province of federal courts.... Contrary to the dissent, we do not find this to be a political question, although that doctrine's factors often overlap with redressability concerns.")

[6] State courts in the United States may have different criteria for establishing standing. For example, the California Constitution—unlike the Federal Constitution—has no case or controversy requirement. However, federal standing requirements supersede state requirements in cases taken up by federal courts. The Supreme Court has promoted uniformity of standing among states and established the preemption of federal interpretations of federal law and the Constitution (*see, e.g., Martin v. Hunter's Lessee*, 14 U.S. 304 (1816)).

Thirty years later, in *Lujan v. Defenders of Wildlife,* 504 U.S. 555 (1992), the Supreme Court encapsulated the modern standing test:

> Over the years, our cases have established that the irreducible constitutional minimum of standing contains three elements: first, the plaintiff must have suffered an "injury in fact" — an invasion of a legally-protected interest which is (a) concrete and particularized, . . . and (b) "actual or imminent, not 'conjectural' or 'hypothetical,' " . . . Second, there must be a causal connection between the injury and the conduct complained of—the injury has to be "fairly . . . trace[able] to the challenged action of the defendant, and not . . . th[e] result [of] the independent action of some third party not before the court." Third, it must be "likely," as opposed to merely "speculative," that the injury will be "redressed by a favorable decision." (Citations omitted.)

The definition of "cases" and "controversies" as these terms are used in Article III have been refined by the terms *ripeness* (a dispute must be sufficiently developed in terms of its *prima facie* elements before the Court will address it),[7] *mootness* (a case must have controversy at all stages of review),[8] and *justiciability.*[9]

In *Baker,* the Supreme Court held that federal courts should not hear cases that deal directly with issues that the Constitution makes the sole responsibility of the executive branch or the legislative branch. This *political question doctrine* is frequently asserted to contest the standing of plaintiffs in cases brought to prevent environmental damage and to redress damage resulting from climate change. The doctrine is based on the parameters the Supreme Court sets for itself in the context of the Constitution's balance of powers. On the facts of each particular case, a court determines whether a judicial proceeding would interfere with the functions that the Constitution has reserved for the executive and/or the legislative branches.[10]

In addition to the standing requirements derived from Article III, the Supreme Court has developed additional "prudential" standing requirements. A court may rely upon these principles of prudence to refuse to adjudicate claims having broad social import.[11] The prudential standing requirements are "not meant to be especially

[7] *See Laird v Tatum,* 408 U.S. 1 (1972).

[8] *See United States v. Munsingwear,* 340 U.S. 36 (1950).

[9] A court will dismiss a case based on the justiciability doctrine when it determines that the conduct challenged is assigned by the Constitution to the executive or legislative departments of the government and presents what the Supreme Court describes as a "political question." In an early case applying the political question test for justiciability, *Oetjen v. Central Leather Co.,* 246 U.S. 297 (1918), the Supreme Court explained that the conduct of foreign relations is committed by the Constitution to the executive and legislative—the political—departments of the government, and the propriety of what may be done in the exercise of this political power is not subject to judicial inquiry or decision.

[10] *See, e.g., Am. Elec. Power Co. v. Connecticut,* 564 U.S. 410 (2011); *Kivalina v. ExxonMobil Corp.,* 696 F.3d 849 (9th Cir. 2012).

[11] *Gladstone Realtors v. Village of Bellwood,* 441 U.S. 91, 99-100 (1979) ("[A] plaintiff may still lack standing under the prudential principles by which the judiciary seeks to avoid deciding questions of broad social import where no individual rights would be vindicated and to limit access to the federal courts to those litigants best suited to assert a particular claim.").

demanding"[12] and are discretionary.[13] Moreover, Congress may legislate away prudential restraints and confer standing to the extent permitted by Article III.[14] The three prudential standing doctrines are:

1. The prohibition against litigating generalized grievances; a plaintiff may not air general injuries that are suffered by a large class of citizens;
2. The prohibition against litigating the rights of a third party; and
3. The plaintiff's interest must fall within the zone of interests that the statute was designed to protect.[15]

The Cornell Law School Legal Information Institute explains:

> The Court has identified three rules as prudential ones, only one of which has been a significant factor in the jurisprudence of standing. The first two rules are that the plaintiff's interest, to which she asserts an injury, must come within the "zone of interest" arguably protected by the constitutional provision or statute in question and that plaintiffs may not air "generalized grievances" shared by all or a large class of citizens. The important rule concerns the ability of a plaintiff to represent the constitutional rights of third parties not before the court.[16]

When combined, the Article III's standing requirements and the prudential standing requirements act as a gatekeeper for federal jurisdiction and have been described as the Doctrine of Standing.[17]

STUDY QUESTIONS

(1) How might one argue that the detailed technical criteria that have been developed to determine standing can or cannot be reconciled with Chief Justice Marshall's 1803 assertion that: "It is emphatically the province and duty of the judicial department to say what the law is."?

[12] *Match-E-Be-Nash-She-Wish Band of Pottawatomi Indians v. Patchak*, 567 U.S. ___, No. 11-246, slip op. at 15 (2012).

[13] *Cf. Warth v. Seldin*, 422 U.S. 490, 500-501 (1975); *Craig v. Boren*, 429 U.S. 190, 193-194 (1976).

[14] *Warth v. Seldin*, 422 U.S. 490, 501 (1975).

[15] *Allen v. Wright*, 468 U.S. 737, 751 (1984).

[16] Legal Information Institute, *Prudential Standing Rules*, Cornell University (last visited Jan. 31, 2020), https://www.law.cornell.edu/constitution-conan/article-3/section-2/clause-1/prudential-standing-rules.

[17] Micah J. Revell examines whether the prudential standing requirements are soundly based on principles of jurisdiction and identifies a conflict between the 9th Circuit Courts of Appeals and the D.C. Circuit. In *Indep. Living Ctr. of S. Cal., Inc. v. Shewry*, 543 F.3d 1050, 1065 n.17 (9th Cir. 2008), the court stated: "Unlike the Article III standing inquiry . . . prudential standing is not a jurisdictional limitation on our review." In contrast, in *Grocery Mfrs. Ass'n v. EPA*, 693 F.3d 169, 179-80 (D.C. Cir. 2012), *rehg. denied*, 704 F.3d 1005 (D.C. Cir. 2013), *cert. denied*, 133 S. Ct. 2880 (2013), *cert. denied*, 133 S. Ct. 2880 (2013), and *cert. denied*, 133 S. Ct. 2881 (2013), the court ruled: "[T]he theory plainly fails to demonstrate prudential standing. . . . We therefore dismiss all petitions for lack of jurisdiction." (internal quotation marks omitted). Micah J. Revell, *Prudential Standing, the Zone of Interests, and the New Jurisprudence of Jurisdiction*, 63 Emory L. J. 221 (2013).

(2) Consider the particular standing requirements of ripeness, concreteness, and the particularity of a plaintiff's injuries. Speaking as counsel for a river, a forest, a chimpanzee, or an ecosystem to which the privilege of standing has not been conferred, how would you answer Justice Scalia's colloquial construction of the key issue: "What's it to you?"

(3) The legal meaning of "case" as used in Article III, Section II of the U.S. Constitution is well-understood, if not as well-defined. What is a "controversy," as that term is used in this section? Is there any "controversy" in which a party has standing that is not a "case"?

II. HISTORY OF STANDING IN THE U.S. FEDERAL COURT SYSTEM

A. *United States v. 422 Casks of Wine*, 26 U.S. 547 (1828)

Four hundred and twenty-two casks of Malaga wine—falsely labeled as sherry to avoid import tax liability—were seized by the government when the ship on which it was carried, *The Sarah*, came to port in Louisiana.[18] The court exercised *in rem* jurisdiction over the government's claim that the ownership was forfeited as a result of the failure to pay the tax. Represented by an agent, the owners of the wine, Hazard and Williams, claimed they had standing in the case, and therefore could contest the seizure on the merits, as the wine was their property and they had legal title to it. The Court ruled:

> In such suits, the claimant is an actor, and is entitled to come before the Court in that character only, in virtue of his proprietary interest in the thing in controversy; this [claimed proprietary interest in the seized property] alone gives him *persona standi in judicio* [standing]. It is necessary that he should establish his right to that character, as a preliminary to his admission as a party, *ad litem* [in a guardian capacity], capable of sustaining the litigation.

This ruling set precedent for a claimant to have standing "in virtue of" (and based solely on) their claimed right of property ownership. It also set an early U.S. precedent for the appointment of a guardian to act on behalf of another. As a preliminary procedural matter, the Court required the claimant to state its proprietary interests and held that that the claimant may be represented by an agent if the agent can prove their authority is capable of contesting the merits.

STUDY QUESTION

What significance may lie in the fact that the determination of standing was based on a claimed right of property ownership?

[18] The case was first heard as *The Sarah*, the name of the ship on which the wine was seized.

B. *Trustees of Dartmouth College v. Woodward*, 17 U.S. 518 (1819)

In this case, the New Hampshire legislature passed a law converting Dartmouth College from a private corporation to a public institution, which would enable the governor of New Hampshire to appoint trustees. The Supreme Court held the law was unconstitutional:

> The charter granted by the British Crown to the trustees of Dartmouth College, in New Hampshire, in the year 1769, is a contract within the meaning of that clause of the Constitution of the United States, art. 1, s. 10, which declares that no state shall make any law impairing the obligation of contracts. The charter was not dissolved by the Revolution.
>
> An act of the State Legislature of New Hampshire altering the charter without the consent of the corporation in a material respect, is an act impairing the obligation of the charter, and is unconstitutional and void.
>
> Under its charter, Dartmouth College was a private, and not a public, corporation. That a corporation is established for purposes of general charity, or for education generally does not, *per se,* make it a public corporation, liable to the control of the legislature.

STUDY QUESTION

How did the Court's decision in *Trustees of Dartmouth College v. Woodward* set the stage for the development of corporate personhood and rights of corporations?

C. *Dred Scott v. Sandford*, 60 U.S. 393 (1856)

In a decision that was later nullified by the Thirteenth and Fourteenth Amendments, the Supreme Court held that former slaves did not have standing in federal courts because they lacked U.S. citizenship, even after they were freed.

The Court explained that the record must show that the case is one in which, by the Constitution and laws of the United States, the court had jurisdiction. Since the undisputed factual record established that Scott's ancestors were brought to this country and sold as slaves, the Court concluded that Scott was not a "citizen" within the meaning of the Constitution of the United States. The Court reasoned that when the Constitution was adopted, slaves were recognized by the law as property, were not regarded in any of the states as members of the community which constituted the state, and were not numbered among any state's "people or citizens." Consequently, the special rights and immunities guaranteed by the Constitution to citizens did not apply to them. And by not being "citizens" within the meaning of the Constitution, they were not entitled to sue in that character in a court of the United States.

Table 1: A Primer on Constitutional Construction

In *Dred Scott*, the Court stated: "The Constitution of the United States recognises slaves as property" and "The change in public opinion and feeling in relation to the African race which has taken place since the adoption of the Constitution cannot change its construction and meaning." This statement is an example of *originalism*, a method of judicial construction of the Constitution based on the assertion that statements in the Constitution must be interpreted based on the original understanding of the drafters at the time it was ratified. *Textualism* is another method of interpretation that focuses on the plain meaning of the text of a legal document. Textualists do not typically inquire into questions regarding the intent of the drafters when deriving meaning from the text. In "Modes of Constitutional Interpretation"[19] several other methods for discerning the meaning and reasoned construction of legal text are discussed. *Judicial precedent* is the most commonly cited source for discerning constitutional meaning and is based on the Supreme Court's prior decisions. A *pragmatic approach* to construction involves the Court weighing the probable practical consequences of one interpretation of the Constitution against other interpretations. Another approach to examining the meaning of the Constitution is based on *moral reasoning*. This approach is based on the belief that moral concepts underly the constitutional text at issue and that these concepts should inform the Court's interpretation. *Structuralism* is another mode of constitutional interpretation. It draws inferences from the design of the Constitution: the relationships among the three branches of the federal government (the separation of powers); the relationship between the federal and state governments (federalism); and the relationship between the government and the people.

STUDY QUESTIONS

(1) Would the Court have reached a different conclusion in *Dred Scott* if it had applied a textualist methodology?

(2) What are the benefits and drawbacks of these various approaches to interpreting the U.S. Constitution in the context of standing?

(3) What interpretive approaches do you think would be most effective in developing the rationale to support a decision that confers standing on a party that has not previously been recognized to be a holder of legal rights?

[19] Brandon J. Murrill, *Modes of Constitutional Interpretation* (2018), 7-5700, http://www.crs.gov R45129.

D. The Fourteenth Amendment

The Equal Protection Clause and the Due Process Clause of the Fourteenth Amendment propelled the evolution and expansion of standing in the federal courts. The Fourteenth Amendment, Section 1 states:

> All persons born or naturalized in the United States, and subject to the jurisdiction thereof, are citizens of the United States and of the state wherein they reside. No state shall make or enforce any law which shall abridge the privileges or immunities of citizens of the United States; nor shall any state deprive any person of life, liberty, or property, without due process of law; nor deny to any person within its jurisdiction the equal protection of the laws.

The Fourteenth Amendment explicitly granted citizenship to "all persons born or naturalized in the United States." By conferring protection from laws adopted by states that would "abridge the privileges and immunities" vested by U.S. citizenship, the Fourteenth Amendment conferred standing on African Americans born in the United States or who have been naturalized. The constitutional establishment of substantive legal rights—due process and equal protection— resulted in standing for "any person" deprived of life, liberty, or property by state action.

1. *Yick Wo v. Hopkins*, 118 U.S. 356 (1886)

In *Yick Wo v. Hopkins*, the Court reversed its holding in *Dred Scott* that standing depended on citizenship.[20] *Yick Wo* arose out of an 1880 San Francisco ordinance that made it illegal to operate a laundry in a wooden building without a permit from the San Francisco Board of Supervisors. The ordinance was conferred by the board with discretion to grant or withhold the permits. At the time, about 95 percent of the city's 320 laundries were operated in wooden buildings. Approximately two-thirds of those laundries were owned by Chinese people. While virtually all non-Chinese applicants were granted a permit, only one permit was granted of the 200 applications from Chinese owners. The Court held the ordinance was unconstitutional and explained:

> The Fourteenth Amendment to the Constitution is not confined to the protection of citizens. It says: "Nor shall any State deprive any person of life, liberty, or property without due process of law; nor deny to any person within its jurisdiction the equal protection of the laws."
>
> These provisions are universal in their application to all persons within the territorial jurisdiction, without regard to any differences of race, of color, or of nationality, and

[20] *Yick Wo v. Hopkins,* 118 U.S. 356 (1886) was also the first case in which the Supreme Court ruled that a law that is race-neutral on its face but is administered in a prejudicial manner is an infringement of the Equal Protection Clause in the Fourteenth Amendment to the U.S. Constitution.

the equal protection of the laws is a pledge of the protection of equal laws. It is accordingly enacted . . . that:

> all persons within the jurisdiction of the United States shall have the same right in every State and Territory to make and enforce contracts, to sue, be parties, give evidence, and to the full and equal benefit of all laws and proceedings for the security of persons and property as is enjoyed by white citizens and shall be subject to like punishment, pains, penalties, taxes, licenses, and exactions of every kind, and to no other.

The questions we have to consider and decide in these cases, therefore, are to be treated as invoking the rights of every citizen of the United States equally with those of the strangers and aliens who now invoke the jurisdiction of the court.

2. *Santa Clara County v. Southern Pacific Railroad,* 118 U.S. 394 (1886)

In *Santa Clara County v. Southern Pacific Railroad,* railroad corporations challenged the constitutionality of a California tax law that treated property owned by corporations differently than property owned by individuals. The Court held that the defendant corporations were persons within the intent of the clause in Section 1 of the Fourteenth Amendment to the Constitution of the United States, which forbids a state to deny to any person within its jurisdiction the equal protection of the laws. Before oral argument, Chief Justice White stated:

> The Court does not wish to hear argument on the question whether the provision in the Fourteenth Amendment to the Constitution which forbids a state to deny to any person within its jurisdiction the equal protection of the laws applies to these corporations. We are all of opinion that it does.

Nearly a century later, Justice William Rehnquist commented on the lack of a stated rationale for this unanimous opinion of the Court. In a dissenting opinion in *First National Bank of Boston v. Bellotti,* 435 U.S. 765, 822 (1978), he wrote:

> This Court decided at an early date, with neither argument nor discussion, that a business corporation is a 'person' entitled to the protection of the Equal Protection Clause of the Fourteenth Amendment. . . . Early in our history, Chief Justice Marshall described the status of a corporation in the eyes of federal law:
>
> > A corporation is an artificial being, invisible, intangible, and existing only in contemplation of law. Being the mere creature of law, it possesses only those properties which the charter of creation confers upon it, either expressly, or as incidental to its very existence. These are such as are supposed best calculated to effect the object for which it was created.
>
> *Dartmouth College v. Woodward,* 4 Wheat. 518, 636 (1819)

Professor Christopher Stone points out that the idea that a corporation could be a person was a surprising innovation: "[W]e forget how jarring the notion was to early jurists, 'that invisible, intangible and artificial being, that mere legal entity' [as] Chief Justice Marshall wrote of the corporation."[21] Nonetheless, Justice Rehnquist observed: "It soon became accepted that the property of a corporation was protected under the Due Process Clause of that same Amendment."[22]

STUDY QUESTION

How might the development of corporate standing and of procedural and substantive rights for corporations support the recognition of standing and the development of procedural and substantive rights for nature?

3. *In re Gault*, 387 U.S. 1 (1967)

In the United States, a person under 18 years of age does not have standing. The legal rights of a child, or in more precise legalese, a minor, must be asserted and defended by a guardian. However, lack of standing has not been a significant obstacle to the development of children's rights in the United States after the Supreme Court recognized a number of constitutional rights held by children under the Fourteenth Amendment in *In re Gault.*

Gault, a 15-year-old from Arizona, was determined to have violated ARS §13-377, which provides that a person who "in the presence of a woman or child... uses vulgar, abusive or obscene language is guilty of a misdemeanor...." He was found to be a juvenile delinquent and sent to a reform school. The Supreme Court held that in the process of adjudicating the charge against him, Gault was denied the right to an adequate notice of charges, was not advised of his safeguards against self-incrimination, and was deprived of the right to counsel and the right to confrontation and cross-examination of the witness providing evidence against him.

Despite Gault's lack of standing to assert any rights on his own behalf, the Court held Gault had constitutional rights to due process and equal protection. The Court reasoned:

> Appellants charge that the Juvenile Court proceedings were fatally defective because the court did not advise [Gault] or his parents of their right to counsel, and proceeded with the hearing, the adjudication of delinquency, and the order of commitment in the absence of counsel for the child and his parents or an express waiver of the right thereto. The Supreme Court of Arizona pointed out that "[t]here is disagreement [among the various jurisdictions] as to whether the court must advise the infant that he has a right to counsel." It noted its own decision in *Arizona State Dept. of Public Welfare*

[21] Christopher Stone, *Should Trees Have Standing? Toward Legal Rights for Natural Objects*, 45 S. CAL. L. REV. 450, 452 (1972).
[22] *See, e.g., Smyth v. Ames*, 169 U.S. 466, 522 (1898).

v. Barlow, 80 Ariz. 249, 296 P.2d 28 (1956), to the effect "that *the parents* of an infant in a juvenile proceeding cannot be denied representation by counsel of their choosing." (Emphasis added.) It referred to a provision of the Juvenile Code which it characterized as requiring "that the probation officer shall look after the interests of neglected, delinquent and dependent children," including representing their interests in court. The court argued that "the parent and the probation officer may be relied upon to protect the infant's interests." Accordingly, it rejected the proposition that "due process requires that an infant have a right to counsel." It said that juvenile courts have the discretion, but not the duty, to allow such representation; it referred specifically to the situation in which the Juvenile Court discerns conflict between the child and his parents as an instance in which this discretion might be exercised. We do not agree. Probation officers, in the Arizona scheme, are also arresting officers. They initiate proceedings and file petitions which they verify, as here, alleging the delinquency of the child, and they testify, as here, against the child. And here the probation officer was also superintendent of the Detention Home. The probation officer cannot act as counsel for the child. His role in the adjudicatory hearing, by statute and, in fact, is as arresting officer and witness against the child. Nor can the judge represent the child. There is no material difference in this respect between adult and juvenile proceedings of the sort here involved. In adult proceedings, this contention has been foreclosed by decisions of this Court.. A proceeding where the issue is whether the child will be found to be "delinquent" and subjected to the loss of his liberty for years is comparable in seriousness to a felony prosecution. The juvenile needs the assistance of counsel to cope with problems of law, to make skilled inquiry into the facts, to insist upon regularity of the proceedings, and to ascertain whether he has a defense and to prepare and submit it. The child "requires the guiding hand of counsel at every step in the proceedings against him." Just as in *Kent v. United States, supra,* at 561-562, we indicated our agreement with the United States Court of Appeals for the District of Columbia Circuit that the assistance of counsel is essential for purposes of waiver proceedings, so we hold now that it is equally essential for the determination of delinquency, carrying with it the awesome prospect of incarceration in a state institution until the juvenile reaches the age of 21.

STUDY QUESTIONS

(1) How might the assertion that nature, like the child, "requires the guiding hand of counsel at every step in the proceedings" help to develop legal rights for nature without conferring standing on nature? Can the development of rights for nature be as successful as it has been for children despite children's lack of standing? How and why might it be more difficult?

4. *Roe v. Wade,* 410 U.S. 113 (1973)

Roe v. Wade is a landmark case establishing women's rights to terminate their pregnancy by abortion. To reach this substantive issue, however, the Court had to determine that at least one of the parties challenging the Texas law, which only allowed abortions to save the life of the pregnant woman, had standing. The Court recognized that determining the legality of the abortion law would not provide a remedy to Roe because the issue was moot (Jane Roe was no longer pregnant when the Supreme Court heard the case). In addressing the issue of standing, Justice Blackmun wrote:

> We are next confronted with issues of justiciability, standing, and abstention. Have Roe and the Does established that "personal stake in the outcome of the controversy," that insures that the dispute sought to be adjudicated will be presented in an adversary context and in a form historically viewed as capable of judicial resolution?
>
> A. *Jane Roe*. . . .
>
> Viewing Roe's case as of the time of its filing and thereafter until as late as May, there can be little dispute that it then presented a case or controversy and that, wholly apart from the class aspects, she, as a pregnant single woman thwarted by the Texas criminal abortion laws, had standing to challenge those statutes. . . . The "logical nexus between the status asserted and the claim sought to be adjudicated," and the necessary degree of contentiousness, are both present.
>
> The appellee . . . suggests that Roe's case must now be moot because she and all other members of her class are no longer subject to any 1970 pregnancy.
>
> The usual rule in federal cases is that an actual controversy must exist at stages of appellate or certiorari review, and not simply at the date the action is initiated.
>
> But when, as here, pregnancy is a significant fact in the litigation, the normal 266-day human gestation period is so short that the pregnancy will come to term before the usual appellate process is complete. If that termination makes a case moot, pregnancy litigation seldom will survive much beyond the trial stage, and appellate review will be effectively denied. Our law should not be that rigid. Pregnancy often comes more than once to the same woman, and in the general population, if man is to survive, it will always be with us. Pregnancy provides a classic justification for a conclusion of nonmootness. It truly could be "capable of repetition, yet evading review."
>
> We, therefore, agree with the District Court that Jane Roe had standing to undertake this litigation, that she presented a justiciable controversy, and that the termination of her 1970 pregnancy has not rendered her case moot.
>
> . . . .
>
> C. *The Does*. In view of our ruling as to Roe's standing in her case, the issue of the Does' standing in their case has little significance. The claims they assert are essentially the same as those of Roe, and they attack the same statutes. Nevertheless, we briefly note the Does' posture.
>
> . . . [The Does are] a married couple who have, as their asserted immediate and present injury, only an alleged "detrimental effect upon [their] marital happiness" because they are forced to "the choice of refraining from normal sexual relations or of endangering Mary Doe's health through a possible pregnancy." Their claim is that, sometime in the future, Mrs. Doe might become pregnant because of possible failure of contraceptive

measures, and, at that time in the future, she might want an abortion that might then be illegal under the Texas statutes.

This very phrasing of the Does' position reveals its speculative character. Their alleged injury rests on possible future contraceptive failure, possible future pregnancy, possible future unpreparedness for parenthood, and possible future impairment of health. Any one or more of these several possibilities may not take place, and all may not combine. In the Does' estimation, these possibilities might have some real or imagined impact upon their marital happiness. But we are not prepared to say that the bare allegation of so indirect an injury is sufficient to present an actual case or controversy. The Does' claim falls far short of those resolved otherwise in the cases that the Does urge upon us. . . .

The Does therefore are not appropriate plaintiffs in this litigation. Their complaint was properly dismissed by the District Court, and we affirm that dismissal.

STUDY QUESTIONS

(1) In finding an exception to the mootness element of the case or controversy requirement, the Court began by noting: "Pregnancy is a significant fact in the litigation" and reasoned that "[i]n the general population, if man is to survive, it [the fact of pregnancy] will always be with us." What arguments can be made based on the analogy that if humankind is to survive, nature will "always be with us?" In cases seeking to establish rights for nature, when is the mootness element an obstacle to standing?

(2) Consider an air or water pollution case in which pollution discharges in conformance with a government permit are well below the permissible limit. The long-term effects of the pollutant's accumulation and dispersal are uncertain, though it is certain that there will be accumulation and dispersal. What arguments can be made to avoid a determination, as reached by the Court in *Roe*, concerning the Doe claimants, that potential future damage to nature is too speculative to meet the case or controversy requirement?

E. Administrative Procedure Act (1946)

Section 702 of the Administrative Procedure Act (APA, 5 U.S.C. §702) meaningfully expanded the scope of standing in cases arising out of decisions made by government agencies. In addition, the APA has provided the foundation for many cases seeking to prevent or curtail environmental damage based on the protection of the rights of persons to enjoy natural ecosystems and their constituents in their existing condition. It states in pertinent part:

A person suffering legal wrong because of agency action, or adversely affected or aggrieved by agency action within the meaning of a relevant statute, is entitled to judicial

> review thereof. . . . The United States [and its Departments and Agencies] may be named as a defendant in any such action. . . . Nothing herein (1) affects other limitations on judicial review or the power or duty of the court to dismiss any action or deny relief on any other appropriate legal or equitable ground; or (2) confers authority to grant relief if any other statute that grants consent to suit expressly or impliedly forbids the relief which is sought.

The APA defines "person" as "an individual, partnership, corporation, association, or public or private organization other than an agency."

1. *Citizens Committee for the Hudson Valley v. Volpe*, 425 F.2d 97 (2d Cir. 1970)

One of the early decisions construing the APA's expansion of standing for persons challenging governmental action is *Citizens Committee for the Hudson Valley v. Volpe.* In this case, the court held that persons "aggrieved" by agency action pursuant to a statute that does not expressly authorize a citizen suit are entitled to review on similar terms by the APA.

The Citizens Committee for the Hudson Valley and the Sierra Club challenged the U.S. Army Corps of Engineers' issuance of a permit authorizing a dredge-and-fill operation that was considered necessary in order to construct a 10-mile roadway along the Hudson River. The plaintiffs sought (1) a declaration that the permit as issued was beyond the scope of the Army's authority, and (2) injunctive relief to prohibit the issuance of any permit or the commencement of any construction in the absence of congressional consent and approval of the secretary of transportation. The court examined whether the Sierra Club and the Citizens Committee had standing and held that the public interest in environmental resources is a legally protected interest giving them—as responsible representatives of the public—standing to obtain judicial review of agency action.

The court's reasoning began with a discussion of prior Supreme Court decisions that considered the meaning of "adversely affected or aggrieved" in the context of the APA. Neither the Citizens Committee nor the Sierra Club claimed that the proposed expressway or the issuance of the dredge-and-fill permit threatened any direct personal or economic harm to them. "Instead they asserted the interest of the public in the natural resources, scenic beauty and historical value of the area immediately threatened with drastic alteration, claiming that they were 'aggrieved' when the Corps acted adversely to the public interest. They are, as the federal defendants observe, serving as 'private Attorney Generals to protect the public interest.'"[23]

The court recognized that conferring standing on private attorneys general in "public actions" challenging administrative activity is neither a new nor unusual concept. It also noted the significance of the fact that standing in such cases is based on judicial interpretation of the statutory term " 'aggrieved' as descriptive of persons entitled to review. It then described the discretion of the Supreme Court to apply the

[23] *Citizens Committee for the Hudson Valley v. Volpe*, 302 F. Supp. 1083 (S.D.N.Y. 1969).

"complicated specialty of federal jurisdiction" of which the standing issue is a part and "the solution of whose problems is in any event more or less determined by the specific circumstances of individual situations." It quoted Chief Justice Burger who, as a judge of the D.C. Circuit Court of Appeals in 1953, characterized the concept of standing as "a practical and functional one designed to insure that only those with a genuine and legitimate interest can participate in a proceeding."[24] It focused its inquiry on "the nature of the interest these plaintiffs are seeking to protect, and the appropriateness of their claim to represent the public in demanding that protection," based on the "connection between the official action challenged and some legally protected interest of the party challenging the action."

Applied to the case, the court described "the specific circumstances of individual situation" as "the prospect of massive alteration of the Hudson River shoreline and of the physical environment for some ten miles along the river's bank." After finding that the parties challenging the Army Corps of Engineers' action "have proved the genuineness of their concern by demonstrating that they are 'willing to shoulder the burdensome and costly processes of intervention' in an administrative proceeding" and "by their activities and conduct" have demonstrated a special interest in the preservation of the natural resources of the Hudson Valley, the court framed the legal issue: "It remains for us to examine whether there is legal justification for their intervention—whether there is a 'legally protected interest' at stake which they can assert because of their special concern."

In holding that the Citizen's Committee and other plaintiffs were "aggrieved" and met the injury-in-fact standard, the court stated:

> Section 702 of the Administrative Procedure Act provides that a person "aggrieved by agency action within the meaning of a relevant statute, is entitled to judicial review thereof." These plaintiffs, alleging that the Corps and the Secretary of the Army ignored their environmental concerns, are "aggrieved" within the meaning of at least three "relevant statute[s]." The Department of Transportation Act declares "the national policy that special effort should be made to preserve the natural beauty of the countryside . . . ," and requires consideration of recreational resources and historical values before the Secretary can approve projects under its jurisdiction. The Hudson River Basin Compact Act . . . embodies the conclusion of Congress that the Hudson River basin contains resources of "immense economic, natural, scenic, historic and recreational value to all the citizens of the United States," and instructs all agencies to consider those resources in planning or approving activities affecting the area.
>
> . . .
>
> Thus administrative as well as congressional concern for natural resources in the present exercise of federal authority is evident. We hold, therefore, that the public interest in environmental resources—an interest created by statutes affecting the issuance of this permit—is a legally protected interest affording these plaintiffs, as responsible representatives of the public, standing to obtain judicial review of agency action alleged to be in contravention of that public interest.

[24] *Office of Communication of United Church of Christ v. F.C.C.*, 359 F.2d 994, 1002 (D.C. Cir. 1966).

STUDY QUESTION

To establish standing for nature, future generations, or for other rightless beings, how effective might it be to rely on the statement that the concept of standing is "a practical and functional one designed to insure that only those with a genuine and legitimate interest can participate in a proceeding?" Is it consistent with the Court's observation that the law of standing is a 'complicated specialty of federal jurisdiction, the solution of whose problems is in any event more or less determined by the specific circumstances of individual situations' "?

III. NATURE'S STANDING

A. *Sierra Club v. Morton*, 405 U.S. 727 (1972)

The dissenting opinions by Justice Blackmun and Justice Douglas in *Sierra Club v. Morton*, 405 U.S. 727 (1972) sounded a rallying cry for the legal environmental movement in the early 1970s. They remain the Supreme Court's most progressive statement in the context of nature's standing. The majority's decision held the Sierra Club did not have standing under the APA to challenge the Forest Service's approval of a plan by the Disney Corporation to develop 80 acres of the Sequoia National Forest. Justice Blackmun wrote:

> The Court's opinion is a practical one espousing and adhering to traditional notions of standing as somewhat modernized by *Data Processing Service v. Camp*, 397 U.S. 150 (1970); *Barlow v. Collins*, 397 U.S. 159 (1970); and *Flast v. Cohen*, 392 U.S. 83 (1968). If this were an ordinary case, I would join the opinion and the Court's judgment and be quite content.
>
> But this is not ordinary, run-of-the-mill litigation. The case poses—if only we choose to acknowledge and reach them—significant aspects of a wide, growing, and disturbing problem, that is, the Nation's and the world's deteriorating environment with its resulting ecological disturbances. Must our law be so rigid and our procedural concepts so inflexible that we render ourselves helpless when the existing methods and the traditional concepts do not quite fit and do not prove to be entirely adequate for new issues?

The Sierra Club challenged the administrative decision based on §10 of the APA, 5 U.S.C. §702, which provides: "A person suffering legal wrong because of agency action, or adversely affected or aggrieved by agency action within the meaning of a relevant statute, is entitled to judicial review thereof." Framed by Justice Stewart, who delivered the opinion of the Court:

> The first question presented is whether the Sierra Club has alleged facts that entitle it to obtain judicial review of the challenged action. Whether a party has a sufficient stake in an otherwise justiciable controversy to obtain judicial resolution of that controversy is what has traditionally been referred to as the question of standing to sue.

The legal framework for review was established in *Data Processing Service* and *Barlow,* which held that a person has standing to obtain judicial review of federal agency action under the APA where they allege that the challenged action had caused them injury in fact, and where the alleged injury was to an interest "arguably within the zone of interests to be protected or regulated" by the statutes that the agencies were claimed to have violated.[25] Within this framework, the Court explained:

> The injury alleged by the Sierra Club will be incurred entirely by reason of the change in the uses to which Mineral King will be put, and the attendant change in the aesthetics and ecology of the area. Thus, in referring to the road to be built through Sequoia National Park, the complaint alleged that the development "would destroy or otherwise adversely affect the scenery, natural and historic objects and wildlife of the park and would impair the enjoyment of the park for future generations." We do not question that this type of harm may amount to an "injury in fact" sufficient to lay the basis for standing under §10 of the APA. Aesthetic and environmental well-being, like economic well-being, are important ingredients of the quality of life in our society, and the fact that particular environmental interests are shared by the many rather than the few does not make them less deserving of legal protection through the judicial process. But the "injury in fact" test requires more than an injury to a cognizable interest. It requires that the party seeking review be himself among the injured.

The Court held the Sierra Club lacked standing because it

> failed to allege that it or its members would be affected in any of their activities or pastimes by the Disney development. Nowhere in the pleadings or affidavits did the Club state that its members use Mineral King for any purpose, much less that they use it in any way that would be significantly affected by the proposed actions of the respondents.

The Court distinguished cases in which lower courts conferred standing upon organizations that demonstrated "an organizational interest in the problem" of environmental or consumer protection. It explained that an organization may represent its members' interests in a proceeding for judicial review, but only when a member is injured. It concluded: "But a mere 'interest in a problem,' no matter how longstanding the interest and no matter how qualified the organization is in evaluating the problem, is not sufficient by itself to render the organization 'adversely affected' or 'aggrieved' within the meaning of the APA."

Justice Douglas disagreed, writing a bold dissenting opinion that has greatly influenced the rights of nature movement in the decades since:

> The critical question of "standing" would be simplified and also put neatly in focus if we fashioned a federal rule that allowed environmental issues to be litigated before federal agencies or federal courts in the name of the inanimate object about to be despoiled, defaced, or invaded by roads and bulldozers and where injury is the subject of public outrage. Contemporary public concern for protecting nature's ecological equilibrium should lead to the conferral of standing upon environmental objects to sue for their

[25] *Sierra Club v. Morton,* 405 U.S. 727, 733 (1972) citing *Data Processing Service v. Camp,* 397 U. S. 150 (1970) and *Barlow v. Collins,* 397 U. S. 159 (1970).

> own preservation. *See* Stone, *Should Trees Have Standing? Toward Legal Rights for Natural Objects*, 45 S. Cal. L. Rev. 450 (1972). This suit would therefore be more properly labeled as *Mineral King v. Morton.*
>
> Inanimate objects are sometimes parties in litigation. A ship has a legal personality, a fiction found useful for maritime purposes. The corporation sole—a creature of ecclesiastical law—is an acceptable adversary and large fortunes ride on its cases. The ordinary corporation is a "person" for purposes of the adjudicatory processes, whether it represents proprietary, spiritual, aesthetic, or charitable causes.
>
> So it should be as respects valleys, alpine meadows, rivers, lakes, estuaries, beaches, ridges, groves of trees, swampland, or even air that feels the destructive pressures of modern technology and modern life. The river, for example, is the living symbol of all the life it sustains or nourishes—fish, aquatic insects, water ouzels, otter, fisher, deer, elk, bear, and all other animals, including man, who are dependent on it or who enjoy it for its sight, its sound, or its life. The river as plaintiff speaks for the ecological unit of life that is part of it. Those people who have a meaningful relation to that body of water—whether it be a fisherman, a canoeist, a zoologist, or a logger—must be able to speak for the values which the river represents and which are threatened with destruction. (Citations and footnotes omitted.)

In contrast to "[t]hose who have that intimate relation with the inanimate object about to be injured, polluted, or otherwise despoiled [who] are its legitimate spokesmen," Justice Douglas observed that "the pressures on agencies [responsible for environmental regulation] for favorable action one way or the other are enormous" and these agencies "are notoriously under the control of powerful interests who manipulate them through advisory committees, or friendly working relations, or who have that natural affinity with the agency which in time develops between the regulator and the regulated." He described the U.S. Forest Service as "notorious for its alignment with lumber companies, although its mandate from Congress directs it to consider the various aspects of multiple use in its supervision of the national forests."

Cognizant of the political question doctrine, which was not considered in the majority decision after it determined the injury-in-fact requirement was not met, Justice Douglas explained that conferring standing on nature "does not mean that the judiciary takes over the managerial functions from the federal agency." Rather, "[i]t merely means that before these priceless bits of Americana (such as a valley, an alpine meadow, a river, or a lake) are forever lost or are so transformed as to be reduced to the eventual rubble of our urban environment, the voice of the existing beneficiaries of these environmental wonders should be heard." In concluding, Justice Douglas described "the issue of 'standing' in the present case and controversy" by citing Aldo Leopold who wrote: "The land ethic simply enlarges the boundaries of the community to include soils, waters, plants, and animals, or collectively: the land."[26]

Though Justice Stewart wrote the plurality opinion rejecting the Sierra Club's appeal, he suggested in a footnote that the Sierra Club could amend its complaint to include allegations that members made regular trips to Mineral King Valley and

[26] Aldo Leopold, A Sand County Almanac 204 (1949).

therefore would be injured by the proposed development. The Sierra Club heeded the suggestion, amended its complaint, and the case proceeded. As it was proceeding, the U.S. Forest Service undertook a further environmental assessment that resulted in a limitation of the size of the development. Disney abandoned the project and the case was dismissed. Mineral King Valley was annexed to Sequoia National Park in 1978 and remains undeveloped today.

While there are other ways for the law to address the "[c]ontemporary public concern for protecting nature's ecological equilibrium," "the conferral of standing upon environmental objects to sue for their own preservation" remains a critical step yet to be taken. In the law review article cited by Justice Douglas, *Should Trees Have Standing? Towards Legal Rights for Natural Objects*, University of Southern California Law School Professor Christopher Stone explained why nature should have standing and how that could happen.

B. Should Trees Have Standing? Toward Legal Rights for Natural Objects

Reflecting on the historical development of standing and the development of legal rights, Stone observes that although infanticide was once a widespread socially accepted practice: "We have been making persons of children although they were not, in law, always so. And we have done the same, albeit imperfectly some would say, with prisoners, aliens, women (especially of the married variety), the insane, Blacks, fetuses, and Indians."[27] He continues:

> Nor is it only matter in human form that has *come* to be recognized as the possessor of rights. The world of the lawyer is peopled with inanimate right-holders: trusts, corporations, joint ventures, municipalities, Subchapter R partnerships, and nation-states, to mention just a few. . . . We have become so accustomed to the idea of a corporation having "its" own rights, and being a "person" and "citizen" for so many statutory and constitutional purposes, that we forget how jarring the notion was to early jurists. . . . Throughout legal history, each successive extension of rights to some new entity has been, theretofore, a bit unthinkable. We are inclined to suppose the rightlessness of rightless "things" to be a decree of Nature, not a legal convention acting in support of some status quo.[28]

To analogize the potential development of nature's rights with the historical development of women's rights, Stone cites a 1968 legal treatise entitled *Land Ownership and Use*, for the once generally accepted legal proposition that "after all, land, like woman, was meant to be possessed."[29] He explains that "each time there is a movement to confer rights onto some new 'entity,' the proposal is bound to sound odd or frightening or

[27] Stone, *supra* note 21, at 451.
[28] *Id.* at 452-453.
[29] Curtis Berger, Land Ownership and Use 139 (1968).

laughable."[30] He notes that the concept of subjectivity is irreconcilable with nature as long as it is legally, economically, and politically objectified.

Stone identifies four criteria that define what it means to be a holder of legal rights. The first is systemic: (1) "[A]n entity cannot be said to hold a legal right unless *some public authoritative body* is prepared to give *some amount of review* to actions that are colorably inconsistent with that 'right.' " Additionally, to "count jurally," (2) a thing (a corporation, a trust, a municipality, nature) must be able to institute a legal action; (3) injury to the thing itself must be the basis for the measurement of damages or other redress; and (4) the relief must run to the benefit of the thing.[31]

Stone describes a rightless polluted stream to illustrate the criteria. Lacking standing, it cannot seek redress from the polluter. It is detached from the economic interest assessment that determines whether there will be an award of money damages or equitable relief. "Whether under language of 'reasonable use,' 'reasonable methods of use,' 'balance of convenience' or 'the public interest doctrine,' what the courts are balancing, with varying degrees of directness, are the economic hardships on the upper riparian (or dependent community) of abating the pollution vis-à-vis the economic hardships of continued pollution on the lower riparians."[32] The polluted stream is not the beneficiary of a favorable judgment.

Stone discusses the guardianship approach to the representation of nature in its own right and addresses the two primary objections. He responds to the argument that a human guardian's expression of the "needs" of a river, forest, species, or ecosystem is speculative by noting that more speculative relationships are already recognized in legal practice: "I am sure I can judge with more certainty and meaningfulness whether and when my lawn wants (needs) water, than the Attorney General can judge whether and when the United States wants (needs) to take an appeal from an adverse judgment by a lower court."[33] And he responds to the argument that the Department of the Interior, conceived as a guardian of the public lands, is an adequate guardian noting: (1) its jurisdiction is limited to the federal public lands; and (2) environmental litigation involving federal statutes demonstrates the department is not fit for the purpose of serving as nature's guardian.[34] Describing the availability of attorneys general as protectors of the environment within the existing structure, Stone notes that their statutory powers are limited and their discretion is guided by politically directed interests in advancing and reconciling a broad variety of important social goals, which would not inhibit the decision-making and advocacy of a guardian charged solely with the protection of nature's interests.

[30] Stone, *supra* note 21, at 455.
[31] *Id.* at 458 (emphasis in original).
[32] *Id.* at 461.
[33] *Id.* at 471.
[34] *See Cowpasture River Preservation Assn. v. U.S. Forest Serv.*, No. 18-1144 (4th Cir. Dec. 13, 2018) ("We trust the United States Forest Service to 'speak for the trees, for the trees have no tongues.' Dr. Seuss, The Lorax (1971). A thorough review of the record leads to the necessary conclusion that the Forest Service abdicated its responsibility to preserve national forest resources. This conclusion is particularly informed by the Forest Service's serious environmental concerns that were suddenly, and mysteriously, assuaged in time to meet a private pipeline company's deadlines.")

Stone asks rhetorically, "Why should the environment be of importance only indirectly, as lost profits to someone else? Why not throw into the balance the cost *to the environment?*" He then explains:

> The argument for "personifying" the environment, from the point of damage calculations, can best be demonstrated from the welfare economics position. Every well-working legal-economic system should be so structured as to confront each of us with the full costs that our activities are imposing on society. Ideally, a paper-mill, in deciding what to produce—and where, and by what methods—ought to be forced to take into account not only the lumber, acid and labor that its production "takes" from other uses in the society, but also what costs alternative production plans will impose on society through pollution. . . . Unfortunately, so far as the pollution costs are concerned, the allocative ideal begins to break down, because the traditional legal institutions have a more difficult time catching and confronting us with the full social costs of our activities. . . . Indeed, one way—the homocentric way—to view what I am proposing so far, is to view the guardian of the natural object as the guardian of unborn generations, as well as of the otherwise unrepresented, but distantly injured, contemporary humans.[35]

This is a remarkable foreshadowing of current litigation to recognize the rights of future generations, exemplified by the *Juliana* case and discussed in detail in Chapter 8, "Rights of Future Generations." Further analyzing the question of recognizing injuries to nature *per se*, Stone explains:

> Wherever it carves out "property" rights, the legal system is engaged in the process of *creating* monetary worth. One's literary works would have minimal monetary value if anyone could copy them at will. Their economic value to the author is a product of the law of copyright; the person who copies a copyrighted book has to bear a cost to the copyright-holder because the law says he must. Similarly, it is through the law of torts that we have made a "right" of—and guaranteed an economically meaningful value to—privacy. (The value we place on gold—a yellow inanimate dirt—is not simply a function of supply and demand—wilderness areas are scarce and pretty too—but results from the actions of the legal systems of the world, which have institutionalized that value; they have even done a remarkable job of stabilizing the price). I am proposing we do the same with eagles and wilderness areas as we do with copyrighted works, patented inventions, and privacy: *make* the violation of rights in them to be a cost by declaring the "pirating" of them to be the invasion of a property interest. If we do so, the net social costs the polluter would be confronted with would include not only the extended homocentric costs of his pollution (explained above) but also costs to the environment *per se*.[36]

The proliferation of litigation in the past 20 years involving intellectual property, and the value judges and juries have assigned to that property, reinforces Stone's notion that once a right is legally recognized, the courts provide an effective system for placing a value on rights.[37]

[35] STONE, *supra* note 21, at 474-475.

[36] *Id.* at 476.

[37] *See, e.g.*, *Apple Inc. v. Samsung Electronics Co.* 580 U.S. ____, 137 S. Ct. 429; 196 L. Ed. 2d 363 (2016). In this case, the parties fought about the ownership of intellectual property rights related to Apple's smartphones. The parties spent hundreds of millions of dollars in the course of the seven-year litigation before the case settled in 2018.

Examining the idea of nature as a beneficiary in its own right, Stone concludes:

> The idea of assessing damages as best we can [based on the valuation of nature as measured by the invasion of a property interest] and placing them in a trust fund is far more realistic than a hope that a total 'freeze' can be put on the environmental status quo.[38]

Further, evaluating the legal concept of "irreparable damage," a criteria for injunction relief, Stone writes:

> [I]f we are going to revitalize the 'irreparable damages' doctrine, and expect it to be taken seriously, we have to recognize that what will be said to constitute 'irreparable damage' to the ionosphere, because of its importance to all life, or to the Grand Canyon, because of its uniqueness, is going to rest upon normative judgments that ought to be made explicit.[39]

After delineating the characteristics of being a holder of rights, and exploring the implications that would be entailed by making the environment a holder of rights,[40] Stone fleshes out "a significant body of [substantive] rights for [the environment] to invoke when it gets to court."

> In this regard, the lawyer is constantly aware that a right is not, as the layman may think, some strange substance that one either has or has not. One's life, one's right to vote, one's property, can all be taken away. But those who would infringe on them must go through certain procedures to do so; these procedures are a measure of what we value as a society. Some of the most important questions of "right" thus turn into questions of degree: how much review, and of which sort, will which agencies of state accord us when we claim our "right" is being infringed?
>
> We do not have an absolute right either to our lives or to our driver's licenses. But we have a greater right to our lives because, if even the state wants to deprive us of that "right," there are authoritative bodies that will demand that the state make a very strong showing before it does so, and it will have to justify its actions before a grand jury, petit jury (convincing them "beyond a reasonable doubt"), sentencing jury, and, most likely, levels of appellate courts.[41]

Reflecting on the National Environmental Policy Act as an example of this sort of rights-making through the elaboration of procedural safeguards, Stone observes that remanding a cause to an agency for further findings—following a successful challenge of an agency decision—may seem ineffectual or only a delay of the inevitable. However, he notes, "the lawyer and the systems analyst know that these demands for further findings can make a difference. It may encourage the institution whose actions threaten the environment to really *think about* what it is doing, and that is neither an

[38] Stone, *supra* note 21, at 480.

[39] *Id.* at 486.

[40] "Natural objects would have standing in their own right, through a guardian; damage to and through them would be ascertained and considered as an independent factor; and they would be the beneficiaries of legal awards." *Id.* at 481.

[41] *Id.* at 482.

ineffectual nor a small feat." He suggests that "the constitutional power would not be lacking to mandate that all private corporations whose actions may have significant adverse effect on the environment make findings of the sort now mandated for federal agencies."[42]

Considering the development of common law rights for nature, Stone suggests that "courts, in making rulings that may affect the environment, should be compelled to make findings with respect to environmental harm—showing how they calculated it and how heavily it was weighed—even in matters outside the present Environmental Protection Act." In shifting the focus of courtroom testimony and concern to the calculation of harm to the environment (as opposed to the harm of owner of property), "the appellate courts, through their review and reversals for 'insufficient findings,' would give content to, and build up a body of, environmental rights, much as content and body has been given, over the years, to terms like 'Due Process of Law.' " He concludes that "a society that grew concerned enough about the environment to make it a holder of rights would be able to find quite a number of 'rights' to have waiting for it when it got to court."[43]

Stone observes that to say nature has legal rights is of no more operational significance than saying humans have rights. Rather, "[t]o solve any concrete case, one is always forced to more precise and particularized statements. . . ."[44] Solving legal problems on a case-by-case basis is the way the common law works, and the incremental development of precedent is the system in place "to confront . . . the world-wide crises of a global organism." Stone concludes his prescient examination of conferring standing on nature with an expression of commitment to the system of common law:

> To shift from such a lofty fancy as the planetarization of consciousness to the operation of our municipal legal system is to come down to earth hard. Before the forces that are at work, our highest court is but a frail and feeble—a distinctly human—institution. Yet, the Court may be at its best not in its work of handing down decrees, but at the very task that is called for: of summoning up from the human spirit the kindest and most generous and worthy ideas that abound there, giving them shape and reality and legitimacy.[45]

STUDY QUESTIONS

(1) Stone discusses the need for both standing and substantive rights for nature while also addressing the challenges that might arise and potential solutions to those challenges. How accurate were Stone's predictions? Have the challenges been met in the way Stone expected? Have they been overcome? What additional obstacles have emerged? Can Earth law be effectively developed in the United

[42] *Id.* at 484. Emphasis in original.
[43] *Id.* at 485, 487.
[44] *Id.*, at 487.
[45] *Id.* at 500.

States if nature is not juridically embodied with rights? Consider how arguments asserting rights for nature have been and might be developed constitutionally, legislatively, and through the common law.

(2) In his provocative essay, *If Nature Had Rights*, Cormac Cullinan presents a general standard by which nature's rights might be balanced against other legal persons' recognized rights:

> We may find it more useful to condone or disapprove of human conduct by considering the extent to which an action increases or decreases the health of the whole community and the quality or intimacy of the relationships between its members. As Aldo Leopold's famous land ethic states, "a thing is right when it tends to preserve the integrity, stability, and beauty of the biotic community. It is wrong when it tends otherwise." From this perspective, individual and collective human rights must be contextualized within, and balanced against, the rights of the other members and communities of Earth.

Is this a workable standard? What evidence can be offered to establish whether "an action increases or decreases the health of the whole community and the quality or intimacy of the relationships between its members"? What challenges might be faced defining "the whole community"?

(3) Before oral argument in *Santa Clara County v. Southern Pacific Railroad*, 118 U.S. 394 (1886), Chief Justice White stated:

> The Court does not wish to hear argument on the question whether the provision in the Fourteenth Amendment to the Constitution which forbids a state to deny to any person within its jurisdiction the equal protection of the laws applies to these corporations. We are all of opinion that it does.

Nearly a century later, Justice William Rehnquist commented on the lack of a stated rationale for that unanimous opinion of the Court. In a dissenting opinion in *First National Bank of Boston v. Bellotti*, 435 U.S. 765, 822 (1978), he wrote:

> This Court decided at an early date, with neither argument nor discussion, that a business corporation is a "person" entitled to the protection of the Equal Protection Clause of the Fourteenth Amendment.

By the time the Court decided *Santa Clara County v. Southern Pacific Railroad*, the role of corporations in shaping the future of business and the relationships between corporations and then-currently recognized juridical "persons" was so important that it was seen as imperative to confer standing on corporations. What are the arguments for and against the assertion that in light of the role of nature in shaping the future (in the context of climate change, loss of biodiversity, viral pandemics, etc.) and the relationships between nature and currently recognized juridical beings, in particular corporations and sovereign beings, it is appropriate, if not imperative, to recognize standing for nature?

C. Citizen-Suit Provisions as a Proxy for Nature's Standing

Since 1972, the Supreme Court has not revisited the issue of standing for nature. However, the Court has construed "citizen-suit" provisions in environmental statutes broadly enough to confer standing on individuals and groups seeking to protect nature by enforcing government agencies' compliance with the prescriptions of environmental protection statutes.

1. *Lujan v. Defenders of Wildlife,* 504 U.S. 555 (1992)

In *Lujan v. Defenders of Wildlife,* the Court confronted numerous obstacles presented by the standing doctrine in the context of a claim that the geographical scope of the Endangered Species Act of 1973 (ESA) was not limited to the United States and the high seas. It decided the case based on respondents' failure to make the requisite demonstration of injury and redressability.

Section 7(a)(2) of the ESA divides responsibilities regarding the protection of endangered species between the Secretary of the Interior and the Secretary of Commerce, and requires each federal agency to consult with the relevant secretary to ensure that any action funded by the agency is not likely to jeopardize the continued existence or habitat of any endangered or threatened species. Both secretaries initially promulgated a joint regulation extending the coverage of Section 7(a)(2) to actions taken in foreign nations, but a subsequent joint rule limited the section's geographic scope to the United States and the high seas. Defenders of Wildlife and other environmental organizations filed an action seeking a declaratory judgment that the new regulation erred as to the ESA's geographic scope and an injunction requiring the Secretary of the Interior to promulgate a new rule restoring his initial interpretation.

Defenders of Wildlife asserted standing based on the interests of some of its members in endangered species purportedly threatened by agency-funded international projects. Their claim to injury was that the lack of consultation with respect to certain funded activities abroad, which they alleged "increas[es] the rate of extinction of endangered and threatened species." Writing for the Court, Justice Scalia cited *Sierra Club v. Morton* for the proposition that: "Of course, the desire to use or observe an animal species, even for purely aesthetic purposes, is undeniably a cognizable interest for purpose of standing."

The decision begins with reflection on the separations of powers, on which the Court comments: "[T]he Constitution's central mechanism of separation of powers depends largely upon common understanding of what activities are appropriate to legislatures, to executives, and to courts." The Court observed that whether the operation of particular legislation "will, or will not, extend beyond the legislative sphere . . . is not infrequently a question of real nicety in legislative bodies." Quoting James Madison, the Court added that "the executive power [is] restrained within a narrower compass [than the legislature] . . . , and the judiciary described by landmarks still less uncertain."[46]

The decision then recites the mantra of standing requirements: (1) that plaintiff suffered an "injury in fact"—an invasion of a legally protected interest which is (a) concrete and particularized, (b) "actual or imminent, not 'conjectural' or 'hypothetical,'" (2) that there is a causal connection between the injury and the conduct complained of, and (3) that it is "likely," as opposed to merely "speculative," that the injury will be "redressed by a favorable decision."

The Court began its reasoning after noting that "the party invoking federal jurisdiction bears the burden of establishing these elements." It explained:

> To survive the Secretary's [Lujan's] summary judgment motion, respondents had to submit affidavits or other evidence showing, through specific facts, not only that listed species were in fact being threatened by funded activities abroad, but also that one or more of respondents' members would thereby be "directly" affected apart from their "'special interest' in th[e] subject."

The Court then described the affidavits' failure to meet this burden, noting they "plainly contain no facts, however, showing how damage to the species will produce 'imminent' injury" to the individual members of Defenders of Wildlife. The Court observed:

> And the affiants' profession of an "inten[t]" to return to the places they had visited before—where they will presumably, this time, be deprived of the opportunity to observe animals of the endangered species—is simply not enough. Such "some day" intentions—without any description of concrete plans, or indeed even any specification of *when* the some day will be—do not support a finding of the "actual or imminent" injury that our cases require.

The Court also rejected three "novel standing theories" proposed by Defenders of Wildlife. The first, referred to as "ecosystem nexus," proposed that any person who uses any part of a "contiguous ecosystem" adversely affected by a funded activity has standing even if the activity is located a great distance away. The Court found this inconsistent with its holding in *National Wildlife Federation*," which held that a plaintiff claiming injury from environmental damage must use the area affected by the challenged activity, and not an area roughly 'in the vicinity' of it."[47] The Court also rejected the "animal nexus" approach, which argued that anyone who has an interest in studying or seeing the endangered animals anywhere on the globe has standing. Finally, the Court rejected the "vocational nexus" approach, under which anyone with a professional interest in such animals can sue. The Court found these standing theories to be "beyond all reason."

[46] James Madison, *These Departments Should Not Be So Far Separated as to Have No Constitutional Control over Each Other*, The Federalist No. 48 (Feb. 1, 1788), https://www.congress.gov/resources/display/content/The+Federalist+Papers#TheFederalistPapers-48.
[47] *Lujan v. Nat'l Wildlife Fed'n*, 497 U.S. 871 (1990).

> It is clear that the person who observes or works with a particular animal threatened by a federal decision is facing perceptible harm, since the very subject of his interest will no longer exist. It is even plausible—though it goes to the outermost limit of plausibility—to think that a person who observes or works with animals of a particular species in the very area of the world where that species is threatened by a federal decision is facing such harm, since some animals that might have been the subject of his interest will no longer exist. [Citation omitted.] It goes beyond the limit, however, and into pure speculation and fantasy, to say that anyone who observes or works with an endangered species, anywhere in the world, is appreciably harmed by a single project affecting some portion of that species with which he has no more specific connection.

In addition to failing to show injury, the Court found that Defenders of Wildlife failed to demonstrate redressability. "Instead of attacking the separate decisions to fund particular projects allegedly causing them harm, the respondents chose to challenge a more generalized level of government action (rules regarding consultation), the invalidation of which would affect all overseas projects. This programmatic approach has obvious practical advantages, but also obvious difficulties insofar as proof of causation or redressability is concerned." The Court explained:

> [S]uits challenging, not specifically identifiable Government violations of law, but the particular programs agencies establish to carry out their legal obligations . . . [are], even when premised on allegations of several instances of violations of law, . . . rarely if ever appropriate for federal court adjudication.

The Court concluded that:

> Since the agencies funding the projects were not parties to the case, the District Court could accord relief only against the Secretary: he could be ordered to revise his regulation to require consultation for foreign projects. But this would not remedy respondents' alleged injury unless the funding agencies were bound by the Secretary's regulation, which is very much an open question.

Because no individual agencies were parties to the suit, no individual agency would be obliged to honor an incidental legal determination the suit produced.

Finally, while deciding the case based on the lack of an injury in fact and the lack of redressability, the Supreme Court also refuted the court of appeals' finding that respondents had standing because they had suffered a "procedural injury" of the kind established by the ESA's citizen-suit provision. After explaining the flaws in the court of appeals' reasoning that "the injury-in-fact requirement had been satisfied by congressional conferral upon *all* persons of an abstract, self-contained, noninstrumental 'right' to have the Executive observe the procedures required by law," the Court stated:

> We have consistently held that a plaintiff raising only a generally available grievance, about government—claiming only harm to his and every citizen's interest in proper application of the Constitution and laws, and seeking relief that no more directly and tangibly benefits him than it does the public at large—does not state an Article III case or controversy.

2. *Bennett v. Spear*, 520 U.S. 154 (1997)

In *Bennett v. Spear*, the Supreme Court considered the citizen-suit provision of the ESA, which authorizes "any person" to commence a suit on their own behalf to enforce compliance with the act. The petitioners' claims challenged the U.S. Forest Service's Biological Opinion concerning minimum water levels required to protect an endangered species of sucker fish. The complaint asserts that petitioners' use of the Klamath Project's reservoirs and related waterways for "recreational, aesthetic and commercial purposes, as well as for their primary sources of irrigation water" will be "irreparably damaged" and that the restrictions on water delivery recommended by the U.S. Forest Service's Biological Opinion "adversely affect plaintiffs by substantially reducing the quantity of available water." In essence, petitioners claim a competing interest in the water, which the Biological Opinion declares necessary for the preservation of the endangered fish.

The Supreme Court focused on two questions: (1) whether the prudential standing rule known as the "zone-of-interests" test applies to claims brought under the citizen-suit provision of the ESA; and (2) if so, whether petitioners have standing under that test notwithstanding that the interests they seek to vindicate are economic rather than environmental.

The Court described the prudential limitations on standing as "judicially self-imposed limits on the exercise of federal jurisdiction," which are "founded in concern about the proper—and properly limited—role of the courts in a democratic society." It distinguished them from their constitutional counterparts, which cannot be modified or abrogated by Congress.

The *zone-of-interests test* determines whether plaintiff's grievance falls within the zone of interests protected or regulated by the statutory provision or constitutional guarantee invoked in the suit.[48] The Court noted that the breadth of the zone of interests varies according to the provisions of law at issue, so that what comes within the zone of interests of a statute for purposes of obtaining judicial review of administrative action under the "generous review provisions" of the APA may not do so for other purposes. For the ESA, the Court emphasized the broad scope of its citizen-suit provision, which says that "any person may commence a civil suit"—an authorization of remarkable breadth when compared with the language Congress ordinarily uses. It contrasted the ESA's citizen-suit provision with other environmental statutes that have more restrictive formulations, such as "[any person] having an interest which is or may be adversely affected," in the Clean Water Act (CWA), 33 U.S.C. §1365(g). The Court explained that the plain meaning of "any person"

> is greatly augmented by two interrelated considerations: that the overall subject matter of this legislation is the environment (a matter in which it is common to think all persons have an interest) and that the obvious purpose of the particular provision in question is to encourage enforcement by so-called "private attorneys general"—evidenced by its elimination of the usual amount-in-controversy and diversity-of-citizenship requirements, its provision for recovery of the costs of litigation (including even expert witness

[48] *See, e.g., Service Organizations, Inc. v. Camp,* 397 U.S. 150 (1970).

> fees), and its reservation to the Government of a right of first refusal to pursue the action initially and a right to intervene later.

The Court further explained that although the plaintiffs were seeking to prevent application of environmental restrictions rather than to implement them, there is no textual basis for saying that the expansion of standing requirements contained in the citizen-suit provision applies to environmentalists alone.

3. *Friends of the Earth, Inc. v. Laidlaw Environmental Services*, 528 U.S. 167 (2000)

In *Friends of the Earth, Inc. v. Laidlaw Environmental Services,* environmental groups brought an action against the holder of a National Pollutant Discharge Elimination System (NPDES) permit based on the discharge of mercury in excess of the permitted level. The Court granted certiorari to resolve the inconsistency between the Fourth Circuit's decision in this case, finding petitioners' claims moot, and the decisions of several other Courts of Appeals, which held that a defendant's compliance with its permit after the commencement of litigation does not moot claims for civil penalties under the CWA. The Supreme Court found that the citizen suit provision in the CWA conferred standing on the environmental groups and further held that the action was not rendered moot by the permit holder's cessation of discharge in excess of the permitted level. Justice Ginsburg, who wrote the opinion, described the case as presenting "an important question concerning the operation of the citizen-suit provisions of the Clean Water Act." The CWA's citizen-suit provision authorizes "a suit to enforce any limitation in an NPDES permit [to] be brought by any 'citizen,' defined as 'a person or persons having an interest which is or may be adversely affected.'"

The South Carolina Department of Health and Environmental Control, acting under the CWA, granted Laidlaw a NPDES permit. The permit authorized Laidlaw to discharge treated water into the North Tyger River, but limited, among other things, the discharge of pollutants into the waterway. Laidlaw began to discharge various pollutants into the waterway; these discharges, particularly of mercury, an extremely toxic pollutant, repeatedly exceeded the limits set by the permit. By the time Friends of the Earth (FOE) filed a lawsuit based on the CWA's citizen-suit provision, Laidlaw had reached a settlement with the South Carolina Department of Health and Environmental Control to pay a fine of $100,000 and to comply with the discharge limits. The district court declined to order injunctive relief because Laidlaw, after the lawsuit began, had achieved substantial compliance with the terms of its permit. However, it found that the amount of the settlement did not reflect the economic gain by Laidlaw through its violation of the permit and concluded that a civil penalty of $405,800 was appropriate.

The decision by the Court of Appeals assumed, *arguendo,* that FOE initially had standing, but reversed the district court's decision based on its determination that "the case had become moot once Laidlaw complied with the terms of its permit and the plaintiffs failed to appeal the denial of equitable relief." On further appeal, the Supreme Court considered both whether FOE met the statute's criteria of an adversely affected person and whether the case met an exception to the mootness requirement.

In addressing the first issue, the Court found the sworn affidavits submitted by FOE adequately established that its members had sustained or faced the threat of an injury in fact from Laidlaw's activities, noting: "We have held that environmental plaintiffs adequately allege injury in fact when they aver that they use the affected area and are persons 'for whom the aesthetic and recreational values of the area will be lessened' by the challenged activity." Evaluating the redressability requirement, the Court rejected Laidlaw's argument that the civil penalties that the South Carolina Department of Health and Environmental Control was authorized to assess offer no redress to private plaintiffs because they are paid to the government. It stated:

> It can scarcely be doubted that, for a plaintiff who is injured or faces the threat of future injury due to illegal conduct ongoing at the time of suit, a sanction that effectively abates that conduct and prevents its recurrence provides a form of redress. Civil penalties can fit that description. To the extent that they encourage defendants to discontinue current violations and deter them from committing future ones, they afford redress to citizen plaintiffs who are injured or threatened with injury as a consequence of ongoing unlawful conduct.

Turning to the question of mootness, the Court stated that the "well settled" principle that "a defendant's voluntary cessation of a challenged practice does not deprive a federal court of its power to determine the legality of the practice." The standard for determining "whether a case has been mooted by the defendant's voluntary conduct is stringent: 'A case might become moot if subsequent events made it absolutely clear that the allegedly wrongful behavior could not reasonably be expected to recur.' " The Court explained that the exception to mootness that arises when the defendant's allegedly unlawful activity is "capable of repetition, yet evading review" imposes on the party asserting mootness a " 'heavy burden of persua[ding]' the court that the challenged conduct cannot reasonably be expected to start up again." The Court distinguished the "circumstances in which the prospect that a defendant will engage in (or resume) harmful conduct may be too speculative to support standing, but not too speculative to overcome mootness." It concluded that both the closure of the facility during the course of the litigation and "Laidlaw's earlier achievement of substantial compliance with its permit requirements, might moot the case, but—we once more reiterate—only if one or the other of these events made it absolutely clear that Laidlaw's permit violations could not reasonably be expected to recur." Because the effect of both Laidlaw's compliance with the discharge permit and the facility closure on the prospect of future violations were disputed factual matters that were not aired in the lower courts, the Court held that they remained open for consideration on remand.

4. *Massachusetts v. Environmental Protection Agency*, 549 U.S. 497 (2007)

In *Massachusetts v. Environmental Protection Agency*, a group of states, cities, and environmental conservation organizations claimed that the EPA abdicated its responsibility under the Clean Air Act (CAA) to regulate the emissions of greenhouse gases, including carbon dioxide. The CAA's citizen-suit provision states: "[A]ny person may commence a civil action on his own behalf. . . against the Administrator where there is alleged a failure of the Administrator to perform any act or duty under this chapter which is not discretionary with the Administrator. . . ."[49] The petition for certiorari to the Supreme Court raised two questions: Whether the EPA had the statutory authority to regulate emissions from new motor vehicles; and if so, whether its stated reasons for refusing to do so were consistent with the statute. The Court was persuaded to grant the writ by "the unusual importance of the underlying issue." It held that Massachusetts, due to its "stake in protecting its quasi-sovereign interests," had standing to sue the EPA.

The CAA requires the EPA to prescribe standards for the emission of any air pollutant from new motor vehicles which, in the judgment of the agency, will cause or contribute to air pollution, "which may reasonably be anticipated to endanger public health or welfare."[50] In 1999, a group of private organizations filed a rulemaking petition asking the EPA to regulate "greenhouse gas emissions from new motor vehicles."[51] On Sept. 8, 2003, the EPA entered an order denying the rulemaking petition based on its determination that: (1) contrary to the opinions of the EPA's former general counsels, the CAA does not authorize the EPA to issue mandatory regulations to address global climate change; and (2) that even if the agency had the authority to set greenhouse gas emission standards, it would be unwise to do so at this time. The EPA reasoned that because climate change had its own "political history," and in light of the economic and political repercussions of imposing emission standards, it lacked the power to do anything. "In essence, EPA concluded that climate change was so important that unless Congress spoke with exacting specificity, it could not have meant the agency to address it."[52] The EPA argued that any regulation of motor vehicle emissions was a "piecemeal approach" to climate change, which "would conflict with the President's 'comprehensive approach' to the problem."[53]

The Supreme Court focused on two issues, the political question doctrine and the injury-in-fact requirement. Rejecting the EPA's political question argument, the Court stated:

> Article III of the Constitution limits federal-court jurisdiction to "Cases" and "Controversies." Those two words confine "the business of federal courts to questions presented in an adversary context and in a form historically viewed as capable of resolution through the judicial process." . . . It is therefore familiar learning that no justiciable "controversy" exists when parties seek adjudication of a political question . . . when they ask for an advisory opinion . . . or when the question sought to be adjudicated has been mooted by subsequent developments. . . . This case suffers from none of these defects.

[49] Clean Air Act, 42 U.S.C. §7604(a) (1988).
[50] *Id.* at §7408(a)(1)(A).
[51] *See* International Center for Technology Assessment's petition for rulemaking and collateral relief seeking the regulation of greenhouse gas emissions from new motor vehicles under §202 of the Clean Air Act, October 20, 1999, https://www.ciel.org/Publications/greenhouse_petition_EPA.pdf.
[52] *Massachusetts v. EPA*, 549 U.S. 497 (2007).
[53] *Id.*

> The parties' dispute turns on the proper construction of a congressional statute, a question eminently suitable to resolution in federal court. Congress has moreover authorized this type of challenge to EPA action. *See* 42 U.S.C. §7607(b)(1) [the CAA's citizen-suit provision]. That authorization is of critical importance to the standing inquiry: "Congress has the power to define injuries and articulate chains of causation that will give rise to a case or controversy where none existed before."

The Court further explained that "a litigant to whom Congress has 'accorded a procedural right to protect his concrete interests,' . . . —here, the right to challenge agency action unlawfully withheld, §7607(b)(1)—'can assert that right without meeting all the normal standards for redressability and immediacy.'" Construing the effect of the citizen-suit provision, the Court stated: "When a litigant is vested with a procedural right, that litigant has standing if there is some possibility that the requested relief will prompt the injury-causing party to reconsider the decision that allegedly harmed the litigant."

The Court noted: "It is of considerable relevance that the party seeking review here is a sovereign State and not, as it was in *Lujan*, a private individual." Citing a case decided 100 years earlier, in which Georgia sought to protect its citizens from air pollution originating outside its borders, the Court explained:

> This is a suit by a State for an injury to it in its capacity of *quasi*-sovereign. In that capacity the State has an interest independent of and behind the titles of its citizens, in all the earth and air within its domain. It has the last word as to whether its mountains shall be stripped of their forests and its inhabitants shall breathe pure air.[54]

The Court reasoned:

> Just as Georgia's "independent interest . . . in all the earth and air within its domain" supported federal jurisdiction a century ago, so too does Massachusetts' well-founded desire to preserve its sovereign territory today. . . . That Massachusetts does in fact own a great deal of the "territory alleged to be affected" only reinforces the conclusion that its stake in the outcome of this case is sufficiently concrete to warrant the exercise of federal judicial power.

Finally, the Court concluded:

> When a State enters the Union, it surrenders certain sovereign prerogatives. . . . These sovereign prerogatives are now lodged in the Federal Government, and Congress has ordered EPA to protect Massachusetts (among others) by prescribing standards applicable to the "emission of any air pollutant . . . which may reasonably be anticipated to endanger public health or welfare." 42 U.S.C. §7521(a)(1). Congress has moreover recognized a concomitant procedural right to challenge the rejection of its rulemaking petition as arbitrary and capricious. §7607(b)(1). Given that procedural right and Massachusetts' stake in protecting its quasi-sovereign interests, the Commonwealth is entitled to special solicitude in our standing analysis.

[54] *Georgia* v. *Tennessee Copper Co.*, 206 U.S. 230, 237 (1907).

> With that in mind, it is clear that petitioners' submissions as they pertain to Massachusetts have satisfied the most demanding standards of the adversarial process. EPA's steadfast refusal to regulate greenhouse gas emissions presents a risk of harm to Massachusetts that is both "actual" and "imminent." *Lujan*, 504 U.S., at 560 (internal quotation marks omitted). There is, moreover, a "substantial likelihood that the judicial relief requested" will prompt EPA to take steps to reduce that risk. *Duke Power Co. v. Carolina Environmental Study Group, Inc.*, 438 U.S. 59, 79 (1978).

Turning to the injury-in-fact requirement, the Court cited *Lujan* for the proposition that a litigant must demonstrate that it has suffered a concrete and particularized injury that is either actual or imminent, that the injury is fairly traceable to the defendant, and that it is likely that a favorable decision will redress that injury. The Court explained that the fact that climate change risks are widely shared "does not minimize Massachusetts' interest in the outcome of this litigation." It reasoned: "Because the Commonwealth 'owns a substantial portion of the state's coastal property,' . . . it has alleged a particularized injury in its capacity as a landowner."

The Court rejected the EPA's causation argument that its decision not to regulate greenhouse gas emissions from new motor vehicles contributes so insignificantly to petitioners' injuries that the agency cannot be hauled into federal court to answer for them. The Court explained:

> But EPA overstates its case. Its argument rests on the erroneous assumption that a small incremental step, because it is incremental, can never be attacked in a federal judicial forum. Yet accepting that premise would doom most challenges to regulatory action. Agencies, like legislatures, do not generally resolve massive problems in one fell regulatory swoop. . . . They instead whittle away at them over time, refining their preferred approach as circumstances change and as they develop a more-nuanced understanding of how best to proceed. . . . That a first step might be tentative does not by itself support the notion that federal courts lack jurisdiction to determine whether that step conforms to law.

Likewise, the Court refuted the EPA's argument that no emissions standards it might issue would remedy the claimed injury, noting that although "regulating motor-vehicle emissions will not by itself reverse global warming, it by no means follows that we lack jurisdiction to decide whether EPA has a duty to take steps to slow or reduce it." The uncontested affidavits established that rising sea levels associated with global warming had harmed and would continue to harm Massachusetts. Thus, the Court concluded: "The risk of catastrophic harm, though remote, is nevertheless real. That risk would be reduced to some extent if petitioners received the relief they seek. We therefore hold that petitioners have standing to challenge the EPA's denial of their rulemaking petition."

STUDY QUESTIONS

(1) Do citizen-suit provisions in environmental protection statutes meaningfully change the standing analysis in claims brought under the APA? What benefits

and drawbacks do citizen-suit provisions present in advocating for the recognition of standing for nature.

(2) In *United States ex rel. Chapman v. F.P.C.*, 345 U.S. 153, 156 (1953), the Court stated: "[T]he law of standing is a 'complicated specialty of federal jurisdiction, the solution of whose problems is in any event more or less determined by the specific circumstances of individual situations.'" In *Office of Communication of United Church of Christ v. F.C.C.*, 359 F.2d 994, 1002 (D.C. Cir. 1966), then D.C. Circuit Court Judge (and subsequently Chief Justice) Warren Burger wrote: "Since the concept of standing is a practical and functional one designed to insure that only those with a genuine and legitimate interest can participate in a proceeding, we can see no reason to exclude those with such an obvious and acute concern. . . ." How might these expressions of the concept of standing be reconciled? If they are irreconcilable, what do you find to be most persuasive about the divergent conceptualization of the legal issue of standing?

5. *Juliana v. U.S.*, No. 18-36082 D.C. No. 6:15-cv-01517-AA

In *Juliana,* the Ninth Circuit Court of Appeals considered the issue of standing in a claim brought by 21 young citizens, an environmental organization, and a "representative of future generations." The complaint asserts violations of (1) the plaintiffs' substantive rights under the Due Process Clause of the Fifth Amendment; (2) the plaintiffs' rights under the Fifth Amendment to equal protection of the law; (3) the plaintiffs' rights under the Ninth Amendment; and (4) the public trust doctrine. The plaintiffs sought declaratory relief and an injunction ordering the government to implement a plan to "phase out fossil fuel emissions and draw down excess atmospheric [carbon dioxide]." The court of appeals summarized the lower court's decision stating:

> The district court denied the government's motion to dismiss, concluding that the plaintiffs had standing to sue, raised justiciable questions, and stated a claim for infringement of a Fifth Amendment due process right to a "climate system capable of sustaining human life." The court defined that right as one to be free from catastrophic climate change that "will cause human deaths, shorten human lifespans, result in widespread damage to property, threaten human food sources, and dramatically alter the planet's ecosystem." The court also concluded that the plaintiffs had stated a viable "danger-creation due process claim" arising from the government's failure to regulate third-party emissions. Finally, the court held that the plaintiffs had stated a public trust claim grounded in the Fifth and the Ninth Amendments.

The three-judge panel considered the three requirements for whether plaintiffs had Article III standing to pursue their constitutional claims. First, the court held that the district court correctly found that plaintiffs claimed concrete and particularized injuries. Second, it held that the district court properly found the Article III causation requirement satisfied for purposes of summary judgment because there was at least a genuine factual dispute as to whether a host of federal policies were a "substantial factor" in causing the plaintiffs' injuries. Framing the redressability issue, the third requirement for Article III standing, the court began "by stressing what the plaintiffs do and do not assert":

> They do not claim that the government has violated a statute or a regulation. They do not assert the denial of a procedural right. Nor do they seek damages under the Federal Tort Claims Act, 28 U.S.C. §2671 et seq. Rather, their sole claim is that the government has deprived them of a substantive constitutional right to a "climate system capable of sustaining human life," and they seek remedial declaratory and injunctive relief.

The central issue framed by the court was "whether, even assuming such a broad constitutional right exists, an Article III court can provide the plaintiffs the redress they seek—an order requiring the government to develop a plan to 'phase out fossil fuel emissions and draw down excess atmospheric CO_2.'" In a 2-1 decision, Judge Andrew Hurwitz wrote: "Reluctantly, we conclude that such relief is beyond our constitutional power. Rather, the plaintiffs' impressive case for redress must be presented to the political branches of government." The court explained:

> The crux of the plaintiffs' requested remedy is an injunction requiring the government not only to cease permitting, authorizing, and subsidizing fossil fuel use, but also to prepare a plan subject to judicial approval to draw down harmful emissions. The plaintiffs thus seek not only to enjoin the Executive from exercising discretionary authority expressly granted by Congress, *see, e.g.*, 30 U.S.C. §201 (authorizing the Secretary of the Interior to lease land for coal mining), but also to enjoin Congress from exercising power expressly granted by the Constitution over public lands, *see* U.S. Const. art. IV, §3, cl. 2 ("The Congress shall have Power to dispose of and make all needful Rules and Regulations respecting the Territory or other Property belonging to the United States.").
>
> . . . .
>
> The plaintiffs concede that their requested relief will not alone solve global climate change, but they assert that their "injuries would be to some extent ameliorated." Relying on *Massachusetts v. EPA*, the district court apparently found the redressability requirement satisfied because the requested relief would likely slow or reduce emissions. *See* 549 U.S. at 525–26. That case, however, involved a procedural right that the State of Massachusetts was allowed to assert "without meeting all the normal standards for redressability;" in that context, the Court found redressability because "there [was] some possibility that the requested relief [would] prompt the injury-causing party to reconsider the decision that allegedly harmed the litigant." *Id.* at 517–18, 525–26 (quoting *Lujan*, 504 U.S. at 572 n.7). The plaintiffs here do not assert a procedural right, but rather a substantive due process claim. [Footnote omitted.]
>
> We are therefore skeptical that the first redressability prong is satisfied. But even assuming that it is, the plaintiffs do not surmount the remaining hurdle—establishing that the specific relief they seek is within the power of an Article III court. There is much to recommend the adoption of a comprehensive scheme to decrease fossil fuel emissions and combat climate change, both as a policy matter in general and a matter of national survival in particular. But it is beyond the power of an Article III court to order, design, supervise, or implement the plaintiffs' requested remedial plan.
>
> . . .

> Although the plaintiffs' invitation to get the ball rolling by simply ordering the promulgation of a plan is beguiling, it ignores that an Article III court will thereafter be required to determine whether the plan is sufficient to remediate the claimed constitutional violation of the plaintiffs' right to a "climate system capable of sustaining human life." We doubt that any such plan can be supervised or enforced by an Article III court. And, in the end, any plan is only as good as the court's power to enforce it.

The majority's opinion considers a dissenting opinion from Judge Josephine Staton in detail:

> Our dissenting colleague quite correctly notes the gravity of the plaintiffs' evidence; we differ only as to whether an Article III court can provide their requested redress. In suggesting that we can, the dissent reframes the plaintiffs' claimed constitutional right variously as an entitlement to "the country's perpetuity," Diss. at 35–37, 39, or as one to freedom from "the amount of fossil-fuel emissions that will irreparably devastate our Nation," *id.* at 57. But if such broad constitutional rights exist, we doubt that the plaintiffs would have Article III standing to enforce them. Their alleged individual injuries do not flow from a violation of these claimed rights. Indeed, any injury from the dissolution of the Republic would be felt by all citizens equally, and thus would not constitute the kind of discrete and particularized injury necessary for Article III standing. *See Friends of the Earth,* 528 U.S. at 180–81. A suit for a violation of these reframed rights, like one for a violation of the Guarantee Clause, would also plainly be nonjusticiable. [Citation omitted.]
>
> More importantly, the dissent offers no metrics for judicial determination of the level of climate change that would cause "the willful dissolution of the Republic," Diss. at 40, nor for measuring a constitutionally acceptable "perceptible reduction in the advance of climate change," *id.* at 47. Contrary to the dissent, we cannot find Article III redressability requirements satisfied simply because a court order might "postpone[] the day when remedial measures become insufficiently effective." *Id.* at 46; [citation omitted]. Indeed, as the dissent recognizes, a guarantee against government conduct that might threaten the Union—whether from political gerrymandering, nuclear proliferation, Executive misconduct, or climate change—has traditionally been viewed by Article III courts as "not separately enforceable." *Id.* at 39. Nor has the Supreme Court recognized "the perpetuity principle" as a basis for interjecting the judicial branch into the policy-making purview of the political branches. *See id.* at 42. Contrary to the dissent, we do not "throw up [our] hands" by concluding that the plaintiffs' claims are nonjusticiable. *Id.* at 33. Rather, we recognize that "Article III protects liberty not only through its role in implementing the separation of powers, but also by specifying the defining characteristics of Article III judges." *Stern v. Marshall,* 564 U.S. 462, 483 (2011). Not every problem posing a threat—even a clear and present danger—to the American Experiment can be solved by federal judges. As Judge Cardozo once aptly warned, a judicial commission does not confer the power of "a knight-errant, roaming at will in pursuit of his own ideal of beauty or of goodness;" rather, we are bound "to exercise a discretion informed by tradition, methodized by analogy, disciplined by system.'" Benjamin N. Cardozo, *The Nature of the Judicial Process* 141 (1921).

In her dissenting opinion, Judge Staton, a California district judge sitting by designation pursuant to 28 U.S.C. §291,[55] wrote:

> Plaintiffs bring suit to enforce the most basic structural principle embedded in our system of ordered liberty: that the Constitution does not condone the Nation's willful destruction. So viewed, plaintiffs' claims adhere to a judicially administrable standard. And considering plaintiffs seek no less than to forestall the Nation's demise, even a partial and temporary reprieve would constitute meaningful redress. Such relief, much like the desegregation orders and statewide prison injunctions the Supreme Court has sanctioned, would vindicate plaintiffs' constitutional rights without exceeding the Judiciary's province. For these reasons, I respectfully dissent.

The decision in *Juliana* clearly delineates the redressability challenge faced by claimants in the context of climate change litigation. However, as noted in the dissent, the federal judiciary has conferred standing on plaintiffs seeking relief that required extensive action by the executive branch in cases involving desegregation and statewide prison actions. This comparison recalls the words of Chief Justice Marshall, who stated in 1803: "It is emphatically the province and duty of the judicial department to say what the law is."[56] If the executive and legislative branches of the government continue to fail to address the threats of climate change to the United States and its citizens, the Supreme Court will likely have an opportunity to reassert its authority "to say what the law is."

STUDY QUESTIONS

(1) Consider Staton's dissent "Plaintiffs bring suit to enforce the most basic structural principle embedded in our system of ordered liberty: that the Constitution does not condone the Nation's willful destruction. So viewed, plaintiffs' claims adhere to a judicially administrable standard." How effective might it be to rely on this implicit duty embedded in the Constitution that would oblige courts to prevent the other branches from bringing the nation to its demise?

(2) Considering the historical course of the development of the standing doctrine, what similarities exist in those cases in which the Supreme Court decided to confer legal personhood on a new entity?

(3) What elements of the factual record in *Juliana* might have been presented differently to avoid the determination that "it is beyond the power of an Article III court to order, design, supervise, or implement the plaintiffs' requested remedial plan"?

[55] *See* 28 U.S.C. §291(b). The chief judge of a circuit or the circuit justice may, in the public interest, designate and assign temporarily any circuit judge within the circuit, including a judge designated and assigned to temporary duty therein, to hold a district court in any district within the circuit.
[56] *Marbury v. Madison*, 5 U.S. 137 (1803).

IV. CONCLUSION

In review, as a barrier to the development of the rights of nature in the United States, legal standing for nature has, so far, been insurmountable. Since *Sierra Club v. Morton* was decided, the federal courts have repeatedly deferred all responsibility to the legislative and executive branches to decide how much more destruction of the Earth will take place. However, by conferring standing on former slaves, non-citizens, women, and corporations, among others, the Supreme Court has demonstrated its recognition that the law can be radically and immediately changed when previously rightless beings acquire legal personhood. Moving forward in the effort to establish standing for nature, the linchpin may be found in answering the question Justice Scalia presented in framing the issue. He described the judicial determination of standing "[i]n more pedestrian terms, [as the] answer to the very first question that is sometimes rudely asked when one person complains of another's actions: 'What's it to you?' "[57] When the Supreme Court is prepared to accept that the answer is the preservation of Earth's systems that support all biological life, it will likely conclude that it is well within the Court's province and duty to confer standing on nature.

[57] Antonin Scalia, *The Doctrine of Standing as an Essential Element of the Separation of Powers*, 17 Suffolk U. L. R. 881, 882 (1983).

CHAPTER 6

Guardianship Arrangements in Rights of Nature Legal Provisions[1]

I. INTRODUCTION

Over the last decade, dozens of laws have been adopted around the world recognizing ecosystems (e.g., forests, watersheds, river systems, etc.) as legal subjects with rights as opposed to rightless objects, resources, or property. This recognition of ecosystems as legal subjects is akin to the status of corporations and other legally recognized nonhuman beings. Known generally as *rights of nature laws*—a key component of the emerging field of Earth law—these legal provisions confer standing as well as procedural and substantive rights on ecosystems that cannot speak for themselves in human forums. This raises the practical question of who should be able to speak for these ecosystems and represent their interests in legal, political, and social forums. Existing rights of nature legal provisions vary in how they structure arrangements for humans to represent these ecosystems, which this chapter refers to as *guardianship arrangements.* Specifically, such guardianship arrangements vary in who can legally represent ecosystems to protect their rights, whether anyone is obligated to do so, and whether guardians are embedded in governance institutions so that ecosystems' rights are not only protected reactively through the courts but also proactively through policymaking processes.[2]

Different guardianship arrangements stem in part from differences in how rights-bearing nature is defined. When rights are recognized for specific ecosystems, such as a river or a forest, it is easier to specify particular guardians and embed them in ecosystem management institutions. When rights-bearing nature is defined more

[1] This chapter was authored by Craig M. Kauffman, Ph.D. Associate Professor of Political Science at the University of Oregon, with the assistance of Linda Wendling.

[2] These and other differences are detailed in Craig M. Kauffman & Pamela L. Martin, *Constructing Rights of Nature Norms in the US, Ecuador, and New Zealand,* 18 Global Env't Pol. 43 (2018).

broadly, such as when rights are recognized for "all of nature" (conceptualized as *nested ecosystems*), choosing appropriate guardians becomes more complicated as a nested ecosystem encompasses a variety of dynamic characteristics, all of which are interrelated in complex, multiscale connections. This chapter examines these issues through a comparative analysis of guardianship arrangements established by a selection of existing rights of nature legal provisions.

Two distinct models have emerged for how to structure rights of nature legal provisions, including guardianship arrangements (*see* Table 1). The first illustrates rights of nature laws in Ecuador and the United States among others. In Model 1, rights-bearing nature is defined extremely broadly; all of nature within the legal jurisdiction is recognized as having rights. These laws identify the specific rights held by nature, such as the rights to exist, to maintain the functioning of ecosystem cycles, and to be restored when damaged. Under some of these laws, any person may stand to speak for nature. The law of Ecuador, unlike any U.S. laws, creates the role of *ombudsman* specifically to investigate and report on allegations of rights of nature violations brought by people and communities; however, representation of nature's interests is voluntary—no person is legally obligated to speak for nature. Consequently, the Model 1 tends to address rights of nature reactively, with people seeking to defend nature's rights in court when violations are imminent or after they have occurred.

The second model is illustrated by rights of nature legal provisions in New Zealand, Colombia, and India, among other places. In Model 2, particular ecosystems are recognized as legal persons, establishing them as rights-bearing subjects. In most cases, legal provisions do not delineate specific rights other than those held by all legal persons. To protect those rights, not only are specific guardians appointed to speak on behalf of the ecosystem, but those guardians are obliged to do so in both legal and policy arenas. Moreover, guardians are often embedded in newly created governance institutions charged with managing the ecosystem in a way that ensures the health and well-being of the ecosystem. These arrangements are intended to give the ecosystem a voice in decision-making processes regarding the management of the ecosystem, allowing rights of nature to be considered and protected proactively.

This chapter illustrates the different approaches to institutionalizing rights of nature generally, and guardianship specifically, by providing key excerpts of representative rights of nature legal provisions from different countries. Section I addresses guardianship agreements in Model 1 by examining key passages from rights of nature laws in Ecuador and the United States. The section notes differences stemming from the fact that rights of nature are recognized in Ecuador's constitution, while rights of nature are mainly recognized in the United States through local ordinances. Section II examines guardianship in Model 2 by looking at passages from legal provisions in New Zealand, Colombia, and India.

Table 1: Two Models for Structuring Guardianship Arrangements

	Model 1	Model 2
Illustrative Country	a) Ecuador b) United States	a) New Zealand b) Colombia c) India
Scope of Protection	All of nature (conceptualized as nested ecosystems within the legal jurisdiction) has rights	Rights of particular ecosystems are recognized
Legal Rights	Nature's rights are explicitly delineated	An ecosystem is granted legal personhood status
Legal Representation	Anyone can speak for nature, but no one is obliged to	Specific guardians are obliged to represent ecosystem
Redress	Rights of nature are protected when violations are reported	Guardians are embedded in integrated ecosystem management institutions

II. GUARDIANSHIP MODEL 1A: ECUADOR

Perhaps the most prominent example of the first model is Ecuador's 2008 Constitution. It provides a relatively vague and expansive definition of rights-bearing nature. Article 71 of the constitution defines nature as the Andean Indigenous deity "Pachamama [typically translated in English as Mother Earth], where life is reproduced and occurs." No other definition of rights-bearing nature is offered, implying that rights are inherent to all of the Earth's ecosystems.

Ecuador's constitution presents rights of nature as one component of a set of interrelated rights, along with individual rights and community rights, which together constitute tools for building "a new form of public coexistence, in diversity and in harmony with nature," rooted in the Andean Indigenous concept of *sumak kawsay*.[3] This is not merely a concept of living well (it is often translated into Spanish as *buen vivir*), but a way of life that celebrates and reveres Pachamama. It acknowledges humans' inseparable relationship with nature and the vital role that nature plays in human existence. For this reason, the specific rights of nature identified in the constitution reflect a holistic approach to conceptualizing nature's intrinsic value and an emphasis on maintaining balance within natural systems. Title II, Chapter 7, of the constitution recognizes that nature has rights to exist, to maintain the integrity of its

[3] It is beyond the scope of this chapter to fully explain the depth of *sumak kawsay*. For a fuller exposition of the concept, *see* Antonio Luis Hidalgo-Capitán, Alejandro Guillén García, & Nancy Deleg Guazha, *Sumak Kawsay Yuyay: Antología del Pensamiento Indigenista Ecuatoriano sobre Sumak Kawsay*, Huelva y Cuenca: FIUCUHU (2014).

ecosystems, and to regenerate "its life cycles, structure, functions and evolutionary processes." Nature also has the right to be restored if injured, independently of human claims for compensation.

A. Ecuador's Guardianship in Ecuador's 2008 Constitution

The principle of guardianship is established in Article 71 of Ecuador's constitution, which states: "All persons, communities, peoples and nations can call upon public authorities to enforce the rights of nature. To enforce and interpret these rights, the principles set forth in the Constitution shall be observed, as appropriate. The State shall give incentives to natural persons and legal entities and to communities to protect nature and to promote respect for all the elements comprising an ecosystem."

While the constitution allows anyone to speak on behalf of nature, it does not require them to do so. It does, however, establish two specific obligations of the state. In regards to nature's right to be restored when damaged, Article 72 states, "In those cases of severe or permanent environmental impact, including those caused by the exploitation of nonrenewable natural resources, the State shall establish the most effective mechanisms to achieve the restoration and shall adopt adequate measures to eliminate or mitigate harmful environmental consequences."

Secondly, Article 73 requires the state to act according to the precautionary principle, providing, "The State shall apply preventive and restrictive measures on activities that might lead to the extinction of species, the destruction of ecosystems and the permanent alteration of natural cycles." This article is important for establishing certain state responsibilities to act as guardian.

B. Ecuador's 2015 General Organic Code of Processes

In 2015, a secondary law was passed, which empowered the National Ombudsman's office (in Spanish, *the Defensoría del Pueblo*) to represent nature's interests.[4] The national ombudsman was given the authority to act on its own initiative, thereby expanding its standing. Nature itself cannot be sued in court or reprimanded. The ombudsman's office is responsible for handling all allegations brought by people and communities alleging a violation of the rights of nature. Claims for remedial and restorative measures, and the subsequent implementation, are submitted for the approval of the national environmental authority (Ministry of Environment). If claims for environmental, personal, or property damage are brought separately under the application of other laws, there will not be a "double recovery" under the rights of nature claims permitted unless the state or other public authority takes responsibility for remediation.[5]

[4] Republic of Ecuador, 2015 General Organic Code of Processes, Arts. 38-39.

[5] *Id.* at Art. 40.

C. Ecuadorian Guardianship in Action

Ecuador's guardianship arrangement has meant that many different types of actors have attempted to speak for nature. Lawsuits seeking remedy for violations against the rights of nature have been filed by individual lawyers and citizens, community groups, social activists, and government agencies like the Ministry of Environment. Judges have *sua sponte* recognized the rights of nature in their rulings in cases where rights of nature violations were not claimed either by claimants or defendants. While the national ombudsman has written reports documenting rights of nature violations, it has no power to enforce its recommendations or findings without bringing a formal lawsuit.

In one sense, Ecuador's guardianship model can be considered strong in that it empowers anyone to speak for nature. But, in another sense, it is weak since no one is obligated to represent nature or fight for its rights. The system relies on volunteerism. It also sets up a reactive system in which people are expected to appeal to public authorities, typically through the legal system, to stop an ongoing or impending violation of the rights of nature. Those acting for nature require funding and other resources, which are not provided for in the constitution. Consequently, the system sets up a collective-action problem in which the benefits of protecting nature's rights are broadly diffused, but some individual or group of individuals must incur the costs of doing so.

III. GUARDIANSHIP MODEL 1B: U.S. MUNICIPALITIES

Municipalities around the United States, from Pittsburgh, Pennsylvania, to the Santa Monica, California, have passed local laws creating rights for ecosystems. Most of these follow the same model as that seen in Ecuador, recognizing specific rights held by all ecosystems within the political jurisdiction and granting all citizens the authority to speak for nature. For example:

Home Rule Charter of the City of Pittsburgh, Pennsylvania

§618.03 Statements of Law—Rights of Pittsburgh Residents and the Natural Environment. (b) Rights of Natural Communities. Natural communities and ecosystems, including, but not limited to, wetlands, streams, rivers, aquifers, and other water systems, possess inalienable and fundamental rights to exist and flourish within the City of Pittsburgh. Residents of the City shall possess legal standing to enforce those rights on behalf of those natural communities and ecosystems.

Santa Monica's approach addresses environmental protections in terms of sustainability and city planning:

An Ordinance of the City Council of the City of Santa Monica Establishing Sustainability Rights

WHEREAS, in the last fifty years, national and state governments have attempted to address the [environmental] crisis by adopting specific environmental protection laws,

> such as the Clean Water Act, Clean Air Act, National Environmental Policy Act and California Environmental Quality Act, that limit pollution and resource consumption; but those laws also have proven inadequate to provide long-term protection of our rights to clean air, water, and soil, and sustainable food systems, and the rights of natural ecosystems; and
>
> WHEREAS, the inadequacy of these laws results, in part, from the underlying legal assumption that the natural world is "property," which may be used by its owners—be they individuals, corporations, or other entities—for their own, private, short-term economic benefit, generally with minimal regard for the health of the environment;...

It should be noted that these laws cannot bar development but can only address zoning-type issues by presenting a cost-benefit analysis. This has played out in two Pennsylvania ordinances that have been rejected by the courts after challenges to their constitutionality. The Home Rule Charter of Grant Township Pennsylvania is representative of most U.S. rights of nature laws in that it gives all residents the right to enforce the protective provisions of the charter "in the name of the ecosystem or natural community as the real party in interest," and damages are intended to be restorative.

This Home Rule Charter was adopted after an earlier ordinance was found to be invalid and preempted by various other state laws and township codes. It is unlikely that assertions of right under the charter will be any more successful as the federal magistrate judge in the original Ordinance case noted: "Even after the Ordinance was adjudged pre-empted by state law, Grant Township sought to make an end run around that judicial determination by amending its form of government and adopting the pre-empted and constitutionally deficient provisions in the form of a Home Rule Charter."[6]

Substantively, the ordinance attempted to establish "their sovereign right of local community self-government"[7] to secure their "right to the scenic, historic, and aesthetic values of the Township, including unspoiled vistas and a rural quality of life."[8] Article III enumerates the various prohibited activities which would interfere with the residents' environmental rights.

> **Article III—Prohibitions and Enforcement**
>
> **Section 301. Depositing of Waste from Oil and Gas Extraction.** It shall be unlawful within Grant Township for any corporation or government to engage in the depositing of waste from oil and gas extraction.
>
> **Section 302. State and Federal Authority.** No permit, license, privilege, charter, or other authorization issued to a corporation, by any State or federal entity, that would violate the prohibitions of this Charter or any rights secured by this Charter, shall be deemed valid within Grant Township.

[6] *Pa. Gen. Energy Co, LLC v. Grant Twp.*, C.A. No. 1:14-cv-209. (W.D. Pa. 2019), Order for Attorney's Fees.
[7] Home Rule Charter of the Township of Grant, Indiana County, Pennsylvania, Art. 1; Sec. 103.
[8] *Id.* at Sec. 105.

Section 303. Summary Offenses. Any corporation or government that violates any provision of this Charter shall be guilty of an offense and, upon conviction thereof, shall be sentenced to pay the maximum fine allowable under State law for that violation. Each day or portion thereof, and each violation of a section of this Charter, shall count as a separate violation.

Section 304. Standing for Township and Residents. Grant Township, or any resident of Grant Township, may enforce the rights and prohibitions of the Charter through an action brought in any court possessing jurisdiction over activities occurring within Grant Township. In such an action, Grant Township or the resident shall be entitled to recover all costs of litigation, including, without limitation, expert and attorney's fees.

Section 305. Enforcement of Natural Community and Ecosystem Rights. Ecosystems and natural communities within Grant Township may enforce their rights, and this Charter's prohibitions, through an action brought by Grant Township or residents of Grant Township in the name of the ecosystem or natural community as the real party in interest. Actions may be brought in any court possessing jurisdiction over activities occurring within Grant Township. Damages shall be measured by the cost of restoring the ecosystem or natural community to its state before the injury, and shall be paid to Grant Township to be used exclusively for the full and complete restoration of the ecosystem or natural community.

The district court in *Pennsylvania General Energy Company, LLC v. Grant Township,*[9] found that the Home Rule Charter was preempted by several provisions of the Second Class Township Code, rules under the Oil and Gas Act, the Limited Liability Company Law, and the Pennsylvania Constitution, and therefore was declared invalid.

As discussed in Chapter 9, *infra,* the rules of preemption have been a stumbling block for American municipalities attempting to assert their historic "home rule" rights to control and protect local natural resources and ecosystems.

IV. GUARDIANSHIP MODEL 2A: NEW ZEALAND'S TE AWA TUPUA ACT

New Zealand pioneered a very different approach to institutionalizing rights of nature compared to Ecuador and the United States. This second model is illustrated by New Zealand's 2017 Te Awa Tupua Act, which recognizes the Whanganui River as a living, spiritual being with legal personhood status. The Whanganui River is known by the Indigenous Māori as Te Awa Tupua and is understood to be an integrated whole from the mountains to the sea. As a tourist attraction and filmmaking site (*The Lord of the*

[9] *Pa. Gen. Energy Co, LLC v. Grant Twp,* C.A. No. 14-209ERIE (W.D. Pa. 2015).

Rings's Mount Doom is New Zealand's Mount Ngauruhoe, the origin of the Whanganui River), it has suffered degradation through diversion for a hydroelectric power scheme and dynamiting to make it easier for tourist boats. The Act does not specify particular rights held by Te Awa Tupua, but simply states that the river possesses "all the rights, powers, duties, and liabilities of a legal person."

The Te Awa Tupua Act emerged from treaty settlement negotiations resolving claims by the Whanganui Iwi (tribe) in relation to the Whanganui River under the Treaty of Waitangi. The settlement agreement, Tūtohu Whakatupua, was signed on August 30, 2012. The terms of the treaty settlement were given the force of national law through the 2017 Te Awa Tupua Act. After defining Te Awa Tupua ("River"), both in terms of its physical geography and the intrinsic values that represent its essence, the Act specifies the procedures for appointing guardians called Te Pou Tupua ("guardians"), as well as their obligations to the River.

In order to effectuate the act, an *Office of the Guardian* was established with all the powers necessary to protect and preserve the river. There is an extensive set of conditions for nomination to this office, which is composed of two people, one selected by the Crown government and one selected by Māori iwi with ties to the river. Not only are these guardians charged with protecting the intrinsic value of the river, but they are able to assert landowner rights for those lands vested in the river. Fund administration and treaty/contract powers are also granted to the Office of the Guardian.

The guardians are responsible for engaging with, and reporting to, the iwi and hapū [Māori clan] on matters relating to the river "as a means of recognizing the inalienable connection of those iwi and hapū with Te Awa Tupua." Promotion and the protection of the status of the river with the public, agencies, or other bodies may be appropriate by developing or reviewing relevant guidelines or policies. The river also has the right to participate in any statutory process affecting it.

The Te Awa Tupua Act also provides for support to be given to the guardians by an advisory group called Te Karewao (hereinafter "the advisors") and a 17-member strategy group called Te Karewao (hereinafter the "strategists") who must also act in the interests of the river. The strategist group is composed of "representatives of persons and organizations with interests in the Whanganui River, including iwi, relevant local authorities, departments of State, commercial and recreational users, and environmental groups." The primary function of strategists is to approve a collaboratively developed and integrated watershed management plan (Te Heke Ngahuru).

These guardians, advisors, and strategists act as an integrated support system that is embedded in a collaborative governance body tasked with managing the protected ecosystem, and that "management" is characterized as protecting the river's "health and well-being" as a natural being. In New Zealand's model, decision-making takes the ecosystem's rights and interests into consideration and requires collaborative planning among the stakeholders.

V. GUARDIANSHIP MODEL 2B: COLOMBIA'S ATRATO RIVER

The Atrato River lies in Colombia's Chocó region. One of the most biodiverse regions on the planet, the Chocó region, particularly the Atrato River, has been severely degraded from the mining of heavy metals and other industrial activities. In November 2016, Colombia's constitutional court declared the Atrato River basin to be a legal person possessing the rights to "protection, conservation, maintenance, and restoration." While Colombia's constitution does not explicitly recognize rights of nature, Judge Jorge Ivan Palacio ruled that the rights of nature are part of a set of "biocultural rights" that may be inferred from guarantees in the Colombian constitution for biodiversity, cultural, and humanitarian protections. This rights of nature interpretation was asserted in the opinion rendered in a protection action filed by the Center of Studies for Social Justice (Tierra Digna) on behalf of the Greater Community Council of the Popular Farmer Organization of the Alto Atrato (Cocomopoca), the Greater Community Council of the Integral Farmer Association del Atrato (Cocomacia), the Association of Community Councils of Bajo Atrato (Asocoba), the Inter-Ethnic Forum of Solidarity Chocó (FISCH), and others against the Presidency of the Republic and others.[10]

The court's decision underscores the concept of biocultural rights:

> [T]he rights that ethnic communities have to administer and exercise autonomous guardianship over their territories—according to their own laws and customs—and the natural resources that make up their habitat, where their culture, their traditions and their way of life are developed based on the special relationship they have with the environment and biodiversity.[11]

It also notes that the constitution recognizes special protection for Indigenous and Afrodescendant ethnic groups, which are distinct from the "dominant culture."[12] The ruling gave the Chocó region's ethnic and Indigenous organizations the authority to represent the collective will of the peoples of the Chocó region.

Judge Palacio then outlined the constitution's "social state of rights" that encompass human dignity, social justice, well-being, protections for vulnerable peoples, cultural and ethnic diversity, and protection of the environment and natural resources.[13] He argued that these constitutional principles form an ecological constitution that justifies the protection not only of a pluralist society with diverse cultures but also of the environment in which those peoples live.[14] Alluding to rights of rivers movements circulating globally, Judge Palacio noted the spiritual importance of natural resources and the environment for many cultures. He argued that the cultural,

[10] *Tierra Digna v. Presidency of Colombia,* Judgment T-622/16 (The Atrato River Case), Constitutional Court of Colombia (2016) (translated by and available at Dignity Rights Project).
[11] *Id.* at 43.
[12] *Id.* at 17.
[13] *Id.* at 21. Other court sentences cited as providing a foundation for this ruling include T-426 1992; T-505 1992; SU-747 1998; C-1064 2001.
[14] *Id.* at 26, 28.

economic, social, and environmental rights recognized in the constitution combined to form a set of biocultural rights.

Judge Palacio based his decision to give the Atrato River legal personhood status on the concept of *biocultural rights*. This concept emphasizes that the rights of peoples and nature are inextricably linked.[15] Consequently, Judge Palacio argued that such rights should prevent (or proactively control) environmental destruction and should support conservation, restoration, and sustainable development.[16]

Citing the precedent established by New Zealand's rights of nature laws, the court issued orders to implement provisions that, not coincidentally, mirror almost exactly the key provisions in New Zealand's Te Awa Tupua Act. Below are key excerpts from the court ruling that pertain to the mandated guardianship arrangement. Throughout the text, the court repeated the theme of interconnectivity and necessity of preserving biodiversity "beyond the human scenario," and therefore, that "justice for nature" must be protected in terms of its status as a protected being with rights.[17]

Until these guardians were in place, the national and local governments charged with protecting the environment had not approached their actions holistically, and the river's degradation had revealed these gaps in protection. Therefore, the court directed more attention to the "profound relationship between biological and cultural diversity."[18] Public policy that is focused on the preservation of the entire ecosystem and cultivation of biodiversity could create a stable and healthy environment. The river's entire ecosystem is "a living entity composed of other multiple forms of life and cultural representations."[19] The state and society must "enter into relationships with them [(the components of the ecosystem)] in fair and equitable terms, leaving aside any concept that is limited to the simply utilitarian, economic, or efficient."[20]

> **9.32.** To that extent, considering the scope of protection of international treaties signed by Colombia in the field of environmental protection, the Ecological Constitution and biocultural rights (sections 5.11 to 5.18), which preach the joint and interdependent protection be human with nature and its resources, is that the Court will declare that the Atrato River is subject to rights that imply its protection, conservation, maintenance and, in the specific case, restoration. *For the effective fulfillment of this declaration, the Court will arrange for the Colombian State to exercise legal guardianship and representation of the rights of the river in conjunction with the ethnic communities that inhabit the Atrato River Basin in Chocó; in this way, the Atrato River and its basin—henceforth—will be represented by a member of the plaintiff communities and a delegate of the Colombian State.* Additionally, and with the purpose of ensuring the protection, recovery and due conservation of the river, both parties must design and set up a commission of Atrato River guardians whose integration and members will be developed in the section of orders to proffer in this ruling.[21]

[15] *Id.* at 35-36.
[16] *Id.* at 36.
[17] *Id.* at 99.
[18] *Id.* at 100.
[19] *Id.* at 98.
[20] *Id.*
[21] *Id.* at 100 (emphasis added, page numbers deleted).

Recognizing that the ecosystem is not siloed from human existence, the court emphasized the special relationships between the natural environment and the Indigenous, tribal, and Afrodescendant peoples are co-dependent. Therefore, these peoples do not assert dominion over the environment. This unifying character should be respected when addressing the preservation of not only its physical existence but also the culture associated with the ecosystem.

After such lengthy discussion of the individual, living character of the river's ecosystem, the court found that the mining companies and the state entity defendants had "violated the fundamental rights to the territory and culture of the ethnic communities [which encompasses] the rights to life, health, water, food security, a healthy environment."[22] To enable a holistic, long-term vision for sustainability, the court opined that it is "imperative to strengthen a constitutional pedagogy that favors the values of biological diversity and cultural heterogeneity, with the aim of mobilizing towards a new human rationality based on the protection and respect of nature as an expression of evolution and civilization."[23] To this end, the court ordered:

> **10.2.**
>
> **1.** The Atrato River, its basin and tributaries will be recognized as an *entity subject to rights of protection, conservation, maintenance and restoration* by the State and ethnic communities, as indicated in the motivating part of this provision in the Sections 9.27 to 9.32. [emphasis added]
>
> Consequently, *the Court will order the national government to exercise legal guardianship and representation of the rights of the river* (through the institution designated by the President of the Republic, which could be the Ministry of the Environment) together with the ethnic communities that inhabit the basin of the Atrato River in Chocó; *in this way, the Atrato River and its basin—henceforth—will be represented by a member of the (plaintiffs) and a delegate of the Colombian Government, who will be the guardians of the river.* For this purpose, the Government, headed by the President of the Republic, must make the appointment of its representative within the month following the notification of this ruling. In that same period of time, the active communities must choose their representative.
>
> Additionally, and with the purpose of ensuring the protection, recovery and due conservation of the river, the legal representatives of the same shall design and conform, within three (3) months following the notification of this order, a *commission of guardians of the Atrato River,* integrated by the two appointed guardians and an advisory team integrated by invitation of the Humboldt Institute and WWF Colombia, who have developed the Bita River protection project in Vichada [337] *who therefore, have the necessary experience to guide the actions to take.* This advisory team can be formed and receive support from all public and private entities, universities (regional and national), research centers on natural resources and environmental organizations (national and international), community and civil society wishing to join the protection project of the Atrato River and its basin.

22 *Id.* at 103-104.
23 *Id.* at 106.

> Notwithstanding the foregoing, the *panel of experts* that will be responsible for verifying compliance with the orders of this Judgement (number 8) may also supervise, accompany and advise the work of the Atrato river guardians.[24]

The remainder of the orders relates to the functioning of the oversight (including the monitoring of precise indicators) and restoration of the River's ecosystem. The plans contemplated participation of the ethnic communities to honor their relationship, knowledge of, and reliance on the environment for their way of life. Recognizing the time-sensitiveness of restoration, the court ordered:

> . . . the Office of the Attorney General to convene within three (3) months after the notification of this ruling a *panel of experts* to advise on the follow-up and execution process—according to its experience in the specific topics—, always with the participation of the plaintiff communities, in order to establish timelines, goals and indicators of compliance necessary for the effective implementation of the orders here stated.[25]

In July 2017, Colombia's president appointed the Ministry of Environment as the government's designee to the Guardian Council for the Atrato River, and the council was formed in May 2018. The Guardian Council also contains 14 community members from the Chocó region, including 7 permanent members and 7 replacements. These guardians were chosen based on their leadership in the organizations involved in the court ruling in the Chocó region. Five committees representing appropriate government institutions were created to coordinate and implement policies relating to the river, including decontamination under the Ministry of Environment; eradication of illicit mining under the Ministry of Defense; food security under the Ministry of Housing; and toxicology and epidemiology studies under the Ministry of Health. Colonel Juan Francisco Pelaez of Colombia's Anti-Illicit Mining Unit said that the constitutional decision to give rights to the Atrato River has improved his coordination with the military and the treasury. He also noted that the structural changes provide institutional solutions to these complex problems.[26] Interviews with the communities and guardians have indicated that the court's decision was well-received, although delays in implementation and the lack of funding resources have slowed action.[27]

VI. GUARDIANSHIP MODEL 2C: INDIA'S GANGA AND YAMUNA RIVERS

On March 20, 2017, the Uttarakhand High Court in the Indian State of Uttarakhand issued a ruling declaring that "the Rivers Ganga and Yamuna, all their tributaries, streams, every natural water flowing with flow continuously or intermittently of these rivers, are declared as juristic/legal persons/living entities having the status of a legal

[24] *Id.* at 110 (emphasis added).

[25] *Id.* at 112 (emphasis added).

[26] *El Coronel que Protégé al Rio Atrato*, La Semana, Dec. 15, 2017.

[27] Roncucci, Regine, Rights of Nature and the Pursuit of Environmental Justice in the Atrato Case 72 (Wageningen University & Research, July 2019).

person with all corresponding rights, duties and liabilities of a living person in order to preserve and conserve [the] river[s] Ganga and Yamuna."[28] Based on these rights, the court ordered government agencies to take specific actions to "promote the health and wellbeing of these rivers."

The 2017 Uttarakhand High Court ruling came after decades of failed government programs designed to clean up the Ganga River. The Ganga is one of the most sacred rivers for Hindus, believed by many to contain divine properties. It is also strategically important, as many cities are built on its banks and millions of people depend on it for their survival. The Ganga and the Yamuna, the Ganga's longest tributary, are also highly polluted. The government's first attempt to clean up the Ganga was the 1985 National Ganga Action Plan. The second was the National Ganga Basin Authority's 2009 Mission Clean Ganga. Both were unqualified failures. The latest attempt to restore the Ganga is Namami Gange ("Obeisance to Ganga" in Sanskrit), an initiative launched in 2014 by the Hindu nationalist government led by the Bharatiya Janata Party.

The Uttarakhand High Court ruling is interesting in many ways. From a procedural perspective, the original lawsuit never asked to declare the rivers as legal persons; the judges took this step unilaterally. The process leading to the Court's historic ruling began when Mohammed Salim, a man living in the village of Kuhlal (in Uttarakhand), complained to Uttarakhand state authorities about encroachments on the banks of a canal emerging out of the Ganga in the state capital. Frustrated by the lack of action, in 2014, Salim filed a public interest lawsuit with the Uttarakhand High Court to stop the construction and mining, to have the encroachments removed, and to address the high levels of pollution in the Ganga and its tributaries.[29] The process dragged on for several years and, despite numerous court orders directing Uttarakhand state authorities to remove the encroachments, no action was taken by the state, leading the court to recognize the rivers as legal persons with rights. In justifying this extraordinary step, the court noted: "The extraordinary situation has arisen since [the] Rivers Ganga and Yamuna are losing their very existence. This situation requires extraordinary measures to be taken to preserve and conserve [the] Rivers Ganga and Yamuna."

The court cited as precedent the New Zealand government's awarding of legal personhood status to the Whanganui River. Consequently, the institutionalization of rights of nature is similar to that in New Zealand. However, there are some important differences in regard to guardianship stemming from the legal doctrine invoked to justify appointing guardians.

After establishing the rivers as legal persons whose well-being is threatened due to neglect, the court invoked the legal doctrine of *in loco parentis* (Latin for "in the place of a parent") to make a set of government bodies and officers responsible for acting on behalf of the rivers for their protection and conservation. Courts commonly use this

[28] *Mohd Salim v. State of Uttarakhand*, Writ Petition (PIL) No.126 of 2014, (High Court of Uttarakhand at Nainital, March 2017), 11.

[29] *State of Uttarakhand & Ors v. Mohd Salim & Ors.*, Special leave petition submitted to the Supreme Court of India Civil Appellate Jurisdiction against the judgement and final order dated March 20, 2017 in Writ Petition No. 126 of 2014, passed by the Honorable High Court of Uttarakhand at Naintal, 2017.

legal principle to appoint guardians for children or incapacitated people who cannot defend themselves. Adopting the same logic, the court appointed Chief Secretary of Uttarakhand, the Advocate General of Uttarakhand, and the Director of Namami Gange, the central government initiative, to clean up the river, as guardians. Excerpts of the ruling regarding guardianship are provided below.

Salim v. State of Uttarakhand

Writ Petition (PIL) No. 126 of 2014
High Court of Uttarakhand at Nainital (India)
March 20, 2017

[. . .]

18. The constitution of Ganga Management Board is necessary for the purpose of irrigation, rural and urban water supply, hydro power generation, navigation, industries. There is utmost expediency to give legal status as a living person/legal entity to Rivers Ganga and Yamuna r/w Articles 48-A and 51A(g) of the Constitution of India.

19. Accordingly, while exercising the *parens patriae* jurisdiction, the Rivers Ganga and Yamuna, all their tributaries, streams, every natural water flowing with flow continuously or intermittently of these rivers, are declared as juristic/legal persons/living entities having the status of a legal person with all corresponding rights, duties and liabilities of a living person in order to preserve and conserve the rivers Ganga and Yamuna. The Director of Namami Gange,[30] the Chief Secretary of the State of Uttarakhand and the Advocate General of the State of Uttarakhand are hereby declared *persons in loco parentis* as the human face to protect, conserve and preserve Rivers Ganga and Yamuna and their tributaries. These Officers are bound to uphold the status of Rivers Ganges and Yamuna and also to promote the health and well-being of these rivers.

20. The Advocate General shall represent at all legal proceedings to protect the interest of Rivers Ganges and Yamuna.

21. The presence of the Secretary, Ministry of Water Resources, River Development & Ganga Rejuvination is dispensed with.

[. . .]

[30] The Namami Gange Programme is an Integrated Conservation Mission, approved as a "Flagship Programme" by the Union Government in June 2014, established to accomplish the effective abatement of pollution and the rejuvenation and the conservation of the Ganga River. It is administered by the Ministry of Jal Shakti by the Department of Water Resources, River Development & Ganga Rejuvenation. *See Namami Gange Programme,* https://nmcg.nic.in/NamamiGanga.aspx/ (last visited July, 15, 2020).

Despite its reliance on New Zealand's 2017 Te Awa Tupua Act, the Uttarakhand High Court ruling lacks several important features of the guardianship model established by that act. First, rather than having local stakeholder groups in the watersheds nominate guardians to protect the rivers, the court, following the usual procedure when *in loco parentis* is invoked, appointed state officials to serve as guardians. Also, the ruling did not embed the guardianship body within a multi-stakeholder, collaborative, integrated watershed management body. These differences have undermined efforts to protect the rights of rivers in India when compared to New Zealand and Colombia.

In May 2017, the State of Uttarakhand, along with India's central government and others, filed a petition with India's Supreme Court to overturn the Uttarakhand High Court ruling. In this action, the entities appointed by the court to be the guardians of the Ganga and Yamuna rivers sought to have the Supreme Court overturn the ruling naming them as the rivers' legal guardians. The objection to the ruling given in the petition provides insight into the source of concern among Uttarakhand authorities, with important considerations for structuring guardianship arrangements. These objections are presented in the excerpts below.

State of Uttarakhand & Ors v. Mohd Salim & Ors.

Special Leave Petition
Supreme Court of India
2017

It is respectfully submitted that the Hon'ble High Court has erred in passing the impugned order in a writ petition which was disposed of on 05.12.2016. That the High Court, while hearing the matter for compliance of its earlier order dated 05.12.2016 with respect to the constitution of the Ganga Management Board and removal of illegal encroachment done by the respondent no. 2 and 3, has passed the impugned order and, declaring the Rivers Ganga and Yumna as living entities, further went on to appoint Director Namami Gange, the Chief Secretary of the State of Uttarakhand and Advocate General of the State of Uttarakhand persons *in loco parentis* as the human face to protect, conserve and preserve the Rivers Ganga and Yamuna and their tributaries. These officers are bound to uphold the status of Rivers Ganges and Yamuna and also to promote the health and well-being of these rivers. Further, the High Court has directed that the Advocate General shall represent at all legal proceedings to protect the interest of the Rivers Ganga and Yamuna.

That it is respectfully submitted that in view of the para. 19 of the impugned order passed by the Hon'ble High Court, the River Ganga, Yamuna and their assistant tributaries which are flowing naturally are all declared as legal persons/ and living entities. Hence, in that view all rights, duties and responsibilities of a legal person are now made available to the Ganga and Yamuna so that proper preservation and efficacious protection be made available to these rivers. Hence, if the provisions of the para 19 of the impugned order dated 20.03.2017 is to be implemented in its true spirits in the state of Uttarakhand, then the following will be the resultant effect/legal repercussions;

1. Ganga and Yamuna are interstate rivers and these rivers flow in different states. As per the provisions under item no. 56 of the union list of the 7th Schedule (Article 246) of the Constitution, it is the sole constituent right of the Union Government to frame out the rule for efficacious management of all the interstate rivers. Hence, having resultant effect to others states as to whether the state of Uttarakhand High Court can declare the river Ganga and Yamuna as a legal person/living entity or not?

    (i) It is in respect of these two interstate rivers, the Director, Namami Gange, Government of India, Chief Secretary State of Uttarakhand and the Advocate General of the State are all declared as persons *in loco parentis.* Hence, in view of the aforesaid light, if there arises any dispute in respect to any kind of different illegalities being committed in other states, then as to whether the Chief Secretary may pass any instruction against any other States or Union of India or not?

    (ii) It is because; Ganga and Yamuna rivers are now declared as legal persons/living entities. Hence, in case of the coming of a flood vis-a-vis someone dying in these rivers due to such flood, then as to whether the effective party can file suit for damages against the Chief Secretary of the State and as to whether the State Government is liable to bear such financial burden?

    (iii) The two rivers and all tributaries mixing in these rivers belong to one State is now declared as a legal unit. Hence, for seeking declaration of all other different rivers and their tributaries lying on all other different states as legal persons/living entities, whether it is possible to file separate court case/litigation?

    (iv) Whether in view of the previous direction of the National Green Tribunal, it is for removal of the illegal encroachment/construction within 200 meters from the bank of the aforesaid two rivers, it is the duty of the Chief Secretary to submit the case before the court of law?

    (v) Whether in case of floods and resultant effect of human casualties vis-a-vis in case of encroachment of the river bank area; court cases can only be filed in the name of Chief Secretary, State of Uttarakhand?

That it is respectfully submitted that the State Government feeling aggrieved by the order dated 05.12.2016 passed by the High Court has preferred Special Leave Petition No. CC 8202-8203/2017, which was listed on 05.05.2017 when this Hon'ble Court has been pleased to issue notice and stayed the order dated 05.12.2016. Hence the present Special Leave Petition.

* * *

In July 2017, India's Supreme Court agreed to hear the petition and temporarily stayed the Uttarakhand High Court ruling until the Supreme Court issues its decision. No decision had been issued at the time of writing (June 2020.)

VII. GUARDIANSHIP MODEL 2D: INDIA'S RIGHTS OF THE ANIMAL KINGDOM

The following matter is being presented as a contrast to the above rights of nature given to a resource rather than, as here, to a class of sentient beings. The same underlying guardianship theory was applied. Readers are encouraged to examine the differences both between the covered entities and the guardianship enforcement provisions in the two cases.

On April 7, 2018, the Uttarakhand High Court issued another ruling recognizing the rights of nature in regard to a separate writ petition, this one protesting the abuse of horses used to transport cargo from Nepal to India. In this ruling, the court recognized rights for the entire animal kingdom. Like its ruling for the Ganga and Yamuna rivers, the court recognized all members of the animal kingdom as legal entities with all the rights, duties, and liabilities of a legal person. However, this judgment mandated a different guardianship arrangement than that proposed in its disputed ruling for the Ganga and Yamuna rivers. The excerpt on guardianship follows.

Narayan Dutt Bhatt v. Union of India & Others

Uttarakhand High Court
Writ Petition No. 43 of 2014.

[. . .]

99. Accordingly, the writ petition is disposed of by issuing the following mandatory directions:

   A. The entire animal kingdom, including avian and aquatic, are declared as legal entities having a distinct persona with corresponding rights, duties and liabilities of a living person. All the citizens

> throughout the State of Uttarakhand are hereby declared persons *in loco parentis* as the human face for the welfare/protection of animals . . .
>
> * * *

It is worth noting that the Uttarakhand High Court again invoked the doctrine of *in loco parentis* to order court-appointed guardians for the entire animal kingdom instead of having guardians be voluntarily nominated by different stakeholder groups. However, rather than appointing state officials, the court appointed all citizens as guardians in a somewhat similar move to one used in the Ecuador model. This choice makes sense given the previous experience with state officials rejecting their status as guardians and the collective-action problem inherent in naming all citizens as guardians (described above in regard to Ecuador's guardianship arrangement). It may be that the court saw this collective-action problem as an advantage in this case, since it would reduce the likelihood that the appointed guardians would appeal the ruling. Since everyone is a guardian, the obligation to speak for nature is broadly diffused, reducing individual accountability and, thus, the incentive of individual citizens to appeal the ruling.

VIII. CONCLUSION

The above case studies show how guardianship arrangements in existing rights of nature legal provisions can be categorized into two models. In the first, anyone can speak for nature, but no one is specifically obligated to do so. In the second, specific guardians are appointed and obligated to represent and advocate for nature's rights, often within legal and policy arenas. The first guardianship model tends to be used when rights-bearing nature is defined broadly (e.g., all of nature or the entire animal kingdom). The second model is typically used when rights are recognized for particular ecosystems. Both models are useful contributions to Earth law as nonhuman voices become stronger both within law and society.

Which model provides stronger protections for the rights of nature is debatable. Theoretically, when authority to represent nature is distributed broadly, the barriers to defending nature's rights are lower. However, empowering people to protect nature by invoking the rights of nature is not the same thing as requiring them to do so. When rights are not accompanied by the assignment of responsibilities, rights of nature legal provisions may be weakened. New Zealand's rights of nature laws, for example, emphasize the concept of responsibility much more than that of rights. These laws create statutory guardians charged with promoting and protecting the interests, well-being, and rights of the river Te Awa Tupua and the forest Te Urewera. While this legal design limits who can represent nature, advocates argue that this guardianship model is stronger because it appoints representatives who are legally mandated to advocate for nature's interests and protect its rights, not only in courts but also in policy and social forums.

STUDY QUESTIONS

(1) "Who speaks for the trees?" is the famous question on environmental representation posed in *The Lorax.* The legal community has long grappled with answering questions to determine who best represents nature in the courts and otherwise. Which of the guardianship models above do you think provides a better representation for nature? What are their relative strengths and shortcomings? Do you think that a governmental body can represent nature as a neutral party? What about an environmental organization with its own subjective interests and biases?

(2) Do you think there should be objective qualifications to serve as a legal guardian of nature, or is it a better model to let anyone serve as a legal guardian? Objective qualifications could be professional (e.g., level of education and years of experience) or based upon an affiliation with a particular community or people (e.g., Indigenous peoples that live within the boundaries of a particular ecosystem). Or, alternatively, should legal guardians be appointed on a case-by-case basis with rough guidelines?

(3) In the Atrato River case, the court acknowledged the rights of the Atrato River based on biocultural rights, which recognize the importance of community stewardship over nature in accordance with customary laws. In turn, the court reasoned that biocultural rights arise from recognized cultural, economic, social, and environmental rights. How strong is the court's reasoning? Is there any flaw in the reasoning? How could similar biocultural rights be established in the United States? How might biocultural rights provide a foundation for the rights of nature to be recognized in the United States?

(4) Should legal guardians be appointed to represent particular ecosystems? How does this change if all ecosystems are recognized as having rights? What are the pros and cons of a system of guardianship based upon political boundaries, such as a city, county, or state?

(5) As a purely theoretical exercise: Do you think legal guardians of nature should also have legal duties to their charges and should be brought into court when such legal duties are violated in the same way that parents as guardians of their children can face charges of neglect? What duties would natural entities, such as rivers, even have? Could they be similar to those duties that humans have toward each other as in torts for example? Under this rights of nature approach, could you sue a river for a flood that destroyed your house? Why or why not?

SECTION THREE

LITIGATION STRATEGIES

Now having explored barriers to Earth law, Section III moves on to litigation strategies. Let's say that you have read Judge Aiken's decision in the *Juliana* case that "Plaintiffs likely could not obtain the relief they seek through citizen suits brought under the Clean Air Act, the Clean Water Act, or other environmental laws,"[1] which has fortified your decision to lay aside codified environmental laws in favor of an approach rooted in Earth law to protect your clients. What strategies will you choose to convince the court that the foundation of your lawsuit, while not based on anthropocentric Western law, is robust enough to lead to a judgment in your favor? The chapters in this section explore a number of litigation strategies that could strengthen your case for Earth law.

Chapter 7, "Public Trust Doctrine," tackles the ancient doctrine, which arose from the legal system of the Roman empire. It requires a sovereign, or state, to hold in trust designated elements of nature for the benefit of people. Traditionally, it was applied as a guard against the privatization of navigable water and wildlife. But, in recent years, the public trust doctrine has taken a much broader application, with lawyers filing lawsuits to require governments to limit or reverse the degradation of river systems, air, wetlands, groundwater, and more. The doctrine has also been used as the legal framework for atmospheric trust litigation, which argues the atmosphere is the subject of a public trust that imposes a duty upon the government to protect it for the public.[2] As you read the chapter, also note the public trust doctrine's limitations. As Chapter 13 on the necessity defense points out, "While this long-term strategy [the public trust doctrine] is undoubtedly important, in the short term, it likely will be insufficient by itself to protect the myriad resources that are rapidly being depleted and degraded."

Inherently linked to the public trust doctrine is the subject of Chapter 8, "Rights of Future Generations." The chapter defines "future generations" and reviews numerous legal instruments that recognize governments' obligations to protect the environment for the benefit of future generations. The chapter also lays bare the unique problems of standing for future generations: Who speaks for those who do not yet exist? Drawing from the *Juliana* case and the earlier chapter on standing, this chapter argues that future generations of humans meet all the requirements of standing. Once standing is established, the public trust doctrine is one underlying litigation strategy to argue

[1] *Juliana v. United States*, 217 F. Supp. 3d 1224, 1261 (D. Or. 2016).
[2] *Id.*

that the government's obligation to protect ecosystems and planetary systems extends to future generations.

Chapter 9, "The Rights of Nature Movement in the United States," explores how Earth law in the United States is emerging through practitioners seeking systemic change by giving legal rights to nature. Some U.S. rights of nature precedent takes the form of ordinances passed by communities exposed to fracking, toxic dumping, and other threats to humans and nature. Where standard legal strategies to overcome environmental injury based on federal and state environmental laws have proven unsuccessful, "movement lawyering" has coalesced communities and provided opportunities to fight in the courts for the rights of ecosystems. While some successes have been achieved, the efforts have identified additional hurdles that may bar the way forward. Other precedent takes the form of local ordinances and resolutions that embody rights of nature into the DNA of a community. Beyond local ordinances, another source of Earth law in the United States is the legislation of Indigenous Americans. For example, the Yurok tribe in California adopted a "Resolution Establishing the Rights of the Klamath River," which is in line with the United Nations Declaration of the Rights of Indigenous Peoples.

Chapter 10, "Human Rights and Rights of Nature: A Symbiotic Relationship," addresses the overlay between human rights violations and ecological devastation. It points out that the same acts destroying ecosystems and disrupting planetary systems also violate human rights. The chapter emphasizes the rights of Indigenous peoples, who are disproportionately the victims of ecosystem loss. The chapter is based on the 2015 and 2016 co-violations reports by Earth Law Center entitled *Fighting for Our Shared Future — Protecting Human Rights and Nature's Rights*, which documented over 200 case studies from around the world that implicate both human rights and nature's rights. A key litigation strategy is to prosecute violations of both human rights and rights of nature would be to pursue them in international human rights forums, based on the argument that acts of environmental harm also violate human rights. As an alternative, Indigenous peoples, together with social and environmental organizations, have created the International Rights of Nature Tribunal based on actual case studies — the hitch being that any decision is solely declaratory.

Chapter 11, "Nonhuman Rights," addresses the work of the Nonhuman Rights Project (NhRP) to gain the release of chimpanzees, elephants, and certain other nonhuman animals held in captivity. Linking to previous discussions on nature as property, this chapter chronicles how the NhRP uses the common law to transform nonhuman animals from *things*, lacking the capacity for rights, to *persons* and *rights holders*, by petitioning the courts for habeas corpus relief on behalf of captive chimpanzees. As explained in Chapter 11, historically, legal systems have "divided the world . . . into persons" and "things." The treatment of things under the law can be horrific, such as in the case of chattel slavery, which underscores how entire classes of humans were recently seen as incapable of possessing rights. Perhaps animals will undergo a similar transformation under the law to secure enforceable rights. Toward that goal, the NhRP aims "to persuade the American courts to accept the first nonhuman animal as a legal person. . . ." The chapter argues that promoting rights for nonhuman animals would lead to rights for the natural systems upon which they depend.

Chapter 12 explores the concept of ecocide, using the 2019 destruction of the Brazilian Amazon rainforest as a case study. The movement to recognize ecocide as an international crime was the initiative of the Polly Higgins, a U.K. barrister, who died in 2019 after building a movement but before realizing her ultimate goal. The crime of ecocide has already been adopted by 12 countries as part of their criminal codes. Meanwhile, the debate continues on the international criminalization of acts of mass destruction of nature. Proponents of the idea are currently working to turn ecocide into an international crime under the jurisdiction of the International Criminal Court, a step that would impose liability on governments. As you read the chapter, consider how the barriers to gaining formal international recognition of ecocide stem from the anthropocentric approach that still views nature as a commodity.

Turning from strategies that proactively seek to protect nature in the courts, this section's last chapter, Chapter 13, "Climate Change Civil Disobedience and the Necessity Defense," analyzes the necessity defense as a strategy for defending climate change activists who are arrested for actions of civil disobedience. The chapter reviews how environmental activists have mobilized the necessity defense to justify their acts of civil disobedience, particularly for climate change. Necessity defendants need to prove that their allegedly criminal actions were necessary to prevent imminent public harm caused by climate change, and their acts of civil disobedience were less harmful than climate change itself. Moreover, and returning to the strategies discussed in preceding chapters, the defendant must also prove that no reasonable legal alternative existed. As U.S. climate change cases such as *Juliana* lose in the courts and the U.S. government balks on meaningful climate action, CO2 levels continue to rise, strengthening the argument that some defendants have no choice but to engage in acts of civil disobedience in defense of a stable climate.

CHAPTER 7

Public Trust Doctrine[1]

I. INTRODUCTION

The public trust doctrine is an actively developing foundation for Earth law within the existing Anglo-American legal system. As detailed in Chapter 4, the common law treats almost all things—land, animals, trees, language, and ideas—as property to be owned by persons and governments. But since the time of Justinian and the Roman Empire, the public trust doctrine has protected water, air, wildlife, and the shores of the sea from privatization as property. The historic protection from privatization has evolved into environmental protection from pollution and degradation. Ultimately, the public trust doctrine puts the duty on sovereign governments to steward water for the benefit of life that depends on it and empowers courts to hold governments accountable.

II. THE HISTORIC PUBLIC TRUST DOCTRINE AND LIMITATIONS OF PRIVATE PROPERTY

Anglo-American law treats water, the land beneath navigable waters, and wildlife and fisheries as *publici juris*—meaning private persons cannot own or possess them as property. English and American courts have long established that private persons cannot own or possess water and "natural resources" such as fish and wildlife as property:

> Flowing water, as well as light and air, are in one sense "*publici juris*." They are a boon from providence to all, and differ only in their mode of enjoyment. Light and air are diffused in all directions, flowing water in some. When property was established, each one had the right to enjoy the light and air diffused over, and the flowing water through, the portion of soil belonging to him. The property in the water itself was not in the proprietor of the land through which it passes, but only the use of it, as it passes along, for the enjoyment of his property, and as incidental to it. . . .
>
> [Thus riparian landowners] had no property in the water itself, but a simple usufruct as it passes along. . . .
>
> The right to have the stream to flow in its natural state without diminution or alteration is an incident to the property in the land through which it passes; but flowing water is *publici juris*,—not in the sense that it is a *bonum vacans* [property without an owner], to

[1] Authored by Noah Hall, Wayne State University Law School.

> which the first occupant may acquire an exclusive right, but that it is public and common in this sense only; that all may reasonably use it who have a right of access to it, that none can have any property in the water itself except in the particular portion which he may choose to abstract from the stream and take into his possession, and that during the time of his possession only.[2]

Lord Hailsham of St. Marylebone, in *Halsbury's Laws of England*, stated it succinctly:

> Although certain rights as regards flowing water are incident to the ownership of riparian property, the water itself, whether flowing in a known and defined channel or percolating through the soil, is not, at common law, the subject of property or capable of being granted to anybody.[3]

That water and other crucial resources cannot be owned as private property is long established in the common law, from England to the United States, and often without reference to the public trust doctrine. Private property rights in these resources are *usufructuary*—a right of use only (but a property right nonetheless). So what are the limitations on government privatizing water or giving, by lease or permit, this public resource to private interests? The Supreme Court addressed these questions by invoking the public trust doctrine in *Illinois Central Railroad Co. v. Illinois*, 146 U.S. 387 (1892). The factual background of this case was the practice by the State of Illinois in the 1860s to give the Illinois Central Railroad Company authority to develop the Chicago Harbor in Lake Michigan, including development of the submerged lands. In 1869, the Illinois legislature granted Illinois Central Railroad Company ownership of the harbor with an absolute and perpetual title to large tracks of the harbor's submerged lands. In 1873, the Illinois legislature repealed the grant, setting the stage for this legal dispute.

Illinois Central Railroad Co. v. Illinois

146 U.S. 387 (1892)

MR. JUSTICE FIELD delivered the opinion of the court. The CHIEF JUSTICE, having been of counsel in the court below, and MR. JUSTICE BLATCHFORD, being a stockholder in the Illinois Central Railroad Company, did not take any part in the consideration or decision of these cases. MR. JUSTICE SHIRAS dissented, in which dissent MR. JUSTICE GRAY and MR. JUSTICE BROWN concurred.

The state of Illinois was admitted into the Union in 1818 on an equal footing with the original states, in all respects.... The boundaries of the state were prescribed by congress and accepted by the state in its original constitution.... It is sufficient for our purpose to observe that they include within their eastern

[2] *Wood v. Waugh*, 3 Ex. 748, 775 (1848)

[3] *Halsbury's Laws of England - LexisNexis*. Retrieved 18 September 2017, Lexisnexis.co.uk.

line all that portion of Lake Michigan lying east of the mainland of the state and the middle of the lake, south of latitude 42 degrees and 30 minutes.

It is the settled law of this country that the ownership of and dominion and sovereignty over lands covered by tide waters, within the limits of the several states, belong to the respective states within which they are found, with the consequent right to use or dispose of any portion thereof, when that can be done without substantial impairment of the interest of the public in the waters, and subject always to the paramount right of congress to control their navigation so far as may be necessary for the regulation of commerce with foreign nations and among the states. This doctrine has been often announced by this court, and is not questioned by counsel of any of the parties.

The same doctrine is in this country held to be applicable to lands covered by fresh water in the Great Lakes, over which is conducted an extended commerce with different states and foreign nations. These lakes possess all the general characteristics of open seas, except in the freshness of their waters, and in the absence of the ebb and flow of the tide. In other respects they are inland seas, and there is no reason or principle for the assertion of dominion and sovereignty over and ownership by the state of lands covered by tide waters that is not equally applicable to its ownership of and dominion and sovereignty over lands covered by the fresh waters of these lakes. . . .

The state prays a decree establishing and confirming its title to the bed of Lake Michigan, and exclusive right to develop and improve the harbor of Chicago by the construction of docks, wharves, piers, and other improvements, against the claim of the railroad company that it has an absolute title to such submerged lands by the act of 1869, and the right, subject only to the paramount authority of the United States in the regulation of commerce, to fill all the bed of the lake within the limits above stated, for the purpose of its business, and the right, by the construction and maintenance of wharves, docks and piers, to improve the shore of the lake for the promotion generally of commerce and navigation. . . .

The question, therefore, to be considered, is whether the legislature was competent to thus deprive the state of its ownership of the submerged lands in the harbor of Chicago, and of the consequent control of its waters; or, in other words, whether the railroad corporation can hold the lands and control the waters by the grant, against any future exercise of power over them by the state.

That the state holds the title to the lands under the navigable waters of Lake Michigan, within its limits, in the same manner that the state holds title to soils under tide water, by the common law, we have already shown; and that title necessarily carries with it control over the waters above them, whenever the lands are subjected to use. But it is a title different in character from that which the state holds in lands intended for sale. It is different from the title which the United States hold in the public lands which are open to preemption and sale. It is a title held in trust for the people of the state, that they may enjoy the navigation of the waters, carry on commerce over them, and have liberty of fishing therein, freed from the obstruction or interference of private parties. The interest of the people in the navigation of the waters and in commerce over them may be improved in many instances by the erection of wharves, docks, and piers therein, for which purpose the state may grant parcels of the submerged lands; and, so long as their disposition is made for such purpose, no valid objections can be made to the grants.... But that is a very different doctrine from the one which would sanction the abdication of the general control of the state over lands under the navigable waters of an entire harbor or bay, or of a sea or lake. Such abdication is not consistent with the exercise of that trust which requires the government of the state to preserve such waters for the use of the public. The trust devolving upon the state for the public, and which can only be discharged by the management and control of property in which the public has an interest, cannot be relinquished by a transfer of the property. The control of the state for the purposes of the trust can never be lost, except as to such parcels as are used in promoting the interests of the public therein, or can be disposed of without any substantial impairment of the public interest in the lands and waters remaining.... The state can no more abdicate its trust over property in which the whole people are interested, like navigable waters and soils under them, so as to leave them entirely under the use and control of private parties, except in the instance of parcels mentioned for the improvement of the navigation and use of the waters, or when parcels can be disposed of without impairment of the public interest in what remains, than it can abdicate its police powers in the administration of government and the preservation of the peace....

The harbor of Chicago is of immense value to the people of the state of Illinois, in the facilities it affords to its vast and constantly increasing commerce; and the idea that its legislature can deprive the state of control over its bed and waters, and place the same in the hands of a private corporation, created for a different purpose, one limited to transportation of passengers and freight between distant points and the city, is a proposition that cannot be defended.

The area of the submerged lands proposed to be ceded by the act in question to the railroad company embraces something more than 1,000 acres, being, as stated by counsel, more than three times the area of the outer harbor, and not only including all of that harbor, but embracing adjoining submerged lands, which will, in all probability, be hereafter included in the harbor. It is as large as that embraced by all the merchandise docks along the Thames at London; is much larger than that included in the famous docks and basins at Liverpool; is twice that of the port of Marseilles, and nearly, if not quite, equal to the pier area along the water front of the city of New York. And the arrivals and clearings of vessels at the port exceed in number those of New York, and are equal to those of New York and Boston combined. Chicago has nearly 25 percent of the lake carrying trade, as compared with the arrivals and clearings of all the leading ports of our great inland seas.... Surely an act of the legislature transferring the title to its submerged lands and the power claimed by the railroad company to a foreign state or nation would be repudiated, without hesitation, as a gross perversion of the trust over the property under which it is held....

Any grant of the kind is necessarily revocable, and the exercise of the trust by which the property was held by the state can be resumed at any time.... [T]he power to resume the trust whenever the state judges best is, we think, incontrovertible....

We cannot, it is true, cite any authority where a grant of this kind has been held invalid, for we believe that no instance exists where the harbor of a great city and its commerce have been allowed to pass into the control of any private corporation. But the decisions are numerous which declare that such property is held by the state, by virtue of its sovereignty, in trust for the public. The ownership of the navigable waters of the harbor, and of the lands under them, is a subject of public concern to the whole people of the state. The trust with which they are held, therefore, is governmental, and cannot be alienated, except in those instances mentioned, of parcels used in the improvement of the interest thus held, or when parcels can be disposed of without detriment to the public interest in the lands and waters remaining.

STUDY QUESTIONS

(1) The result of *Illinois Central* is that the grant of the Chicago Harbor's submerged lands to the railroad company was struck down, with the court developing the public trust doctrine for its authority. Thus, the American public trust doctrine was, first and foremost, a guard against the privatization of public resources—meaning navigable water and wildlife. How might this historic function be invoked to advance Earth law principles in all waters and other contexts?

(2) *Illinois Central* identifies three basic public uses of navigable waterways protected by the public trust doctrine: navigation, commerce, and fishing. Consider the historic period of the case. Are these public uses still important today? Are there other public uses that should be included? How could public values such as stewardship shape new public uses protected by the public trust doctrine?

(3) As explored in detail in the next chapter, the public trust doctrine has been applied as a legal tool to protect the environment for future generations by focusing on their right to use and enjoy, as well as the government's duty to conserve and preserve, the trust resources. Advocates contend that a balanced and healthy ecology is essential to the public trust, and they seek to continue to expand its scope from navigable waters to a planetary trust or nature's trust. What elements of the established public trust doctrine support its application in this broader context? What elements limit its application to the historic public uses and navigable waters?

(4) *Illinois Central* did not prohibit all private uses of the water and submerged lands. For example, it explicitly acknowledged the common law riparian right to wharf out for navigation, as long as the developer does not interfere with public navigation. What other private uses could be properly balanced with public uses under the public trust doctrine? Can private uses be reviewed for sustainability and harmony with ecology as part of the balancing?

(5) *Illinois Central* suggests that the public trust doctrine has a foundation in federal law, vaguely citing the United States Constitution. But in a more recent opinion, *PPL Montana, LLC v. Montana*, 565 U.S. 576, 603-04 (2012), the Supreme Court indicated that the public trust doctrine is a matter of state law. The case involved a dispute between the state of Montana and an electric power company over ownership of riverbeds, and the Montana Supreme Court had invoked the public trust doctrine. The Supreme Court of the United States rebuked:

> As a final contention, the State of Montana suggests that denying the State title to the riverbeds here in dispute will undermine the public trust doctrine, which concerns public access to the waters above those beds for purposes of navigation, fishing, and other recreational uses. This suggestion underscores the State's misapprehension of the equal footing and public trust doctrines.
>
> The public trust doctrine is of ancient origin. Its roots trace to Roman civil law and its principles can be found in the English common law on public navigation and fishing rights over tidal lands and in the state laws of this country. Unlike the equal-footing doctrine, however, which is the constitutional foundation for the navigability rule of riverbed title, the public trust doctrine remains a matter of state law, subject as well to the federal power to regulate vessels and navigation under the Commerce Clause and admiralty power. While equal-footing cases have noted that the State takes title to the navigable waters and their beds in trust for the public, the contours of that public trust do not depend upon the Constitution. Under accepted principles of federalism, the States retain residual power to determine the scope of the public trust over waters within their borders, while federal law determines riverbed title under the equal-footing doctrine.

The source of law for the public trust doctrine is a legal question with tremendous practical importance. *Illinois Central* has been referred to as "the lodestar in American public trust law." It reaffirmed that each state in its sovereign capacity holds permanent title, which cannot be conveyed to any private party, to all submerged lands within its borders and that it holds these lands in public trust. It has been cited by the courts of at least 35 states in their articulation of the public trust doctrine. However, is this really just a state law doctrine? What is the source of state sovereignty? What discretion do states have, if any, to define the subject of the trust? Can a state completely abdicate its duties as trustee? While some states have purported to do so, other states have expanded the public trust doctrine beyond navigable waters and the traditional public purposes. The California case involving Mono Lake, excerpted below, is a leading example, and Chapter 8.4 has additional examples.

III. THE PUBLIC TRUST DOCTRINE AND THE PROTECTION OF WATER AND NATURE

With the rise of modern environmentalism that led to the adoption of the National Environmental Policy Act in 1970, the amendment of the Clean Air Act (originally passed in 1963), and the enactment of the Clean Water Act in 1972, the public trust doctrine began to evolve and expand beyond a mere limitation on private property into an obligation for government stewardship. Courts have invoked the public trust doctrine to impose affirmative duties on the government to protect water and other crucial natural resources. The following case is the leading state precedent.

National Audubon Society et al. v. The Superior Court of Alpine County

658 P.2d 709 (Cal. 1983) ***(en banc)***

BROUSSARD, JUSTICE.

Mono Lake, the second largest lake in California, sits at the base of the Sierra Nevada escarpment near the eastern entrance to Yosemite National Park. The lake is saline; it contains no fish but supports a large population of brine shrimp which feed vast numbers of nesting and migratory birds. Islands in the lake protect a large breeding colony of California gulls, and the lake itself serves as a haven on the migration route for thousands of Northern Phalarope, Wilson's Phalarope, and Eared Grebe. Towers and spires of tufa on the north and south shores are matters of geological interest and a tourist attraction.

Although Mono Lake receives some water from rain and snow on the lake surface, historically most of its supply came from snowmelt in the Sierra Nevada. Five freshwater streams—Mill, Lee Vining, Walker, Parker and Rush Creeks—arise near the crest of the range and carry the annual runoff to the west shore of the lake. In 1940, however, the Division of Water Resources, the predecessor to the present California Water Resources Board, granted the Department of Water and Power of the City of Los Angeles (hereafter DWP) a permit to appropriate virtually the entire flow of four of the five streams flowing into the lake. DWP promptly constructed facilities to divert about half the flow of these streams into DWP's Owens Valley aqueduct. In 1970 DWP completed a second diversion tunnel, and since that time has taken virtually the entire flow of these streams.

As a result of these diversions, the level of the lake has dropped; the surface area has diminished by one-third; one of the two principal islands in the lake has become a peninsula, exposing the gull rookery there to coyotes and other predators and causing the gulls to abandon the former island. The ultimate effect of continued diversions is a matter of intense dispute, but there seems little doubt that both the scenic beauty and the ecological values of Mono Lake are imperiled.

Plaintiffs filed suit in superior court to enjoin the DWP diversions on the theory that the shores, bed and waters of Mono Lake are protected by a public trust. . . .

This case brings together for the first time two systems of legal thought: the appropriative water rights system which since the days of the gold rush has dominated California water law, and the public trust doctrine which, after evolving as a shield for the protection of tidelands, now extends its protective scope to navigable lakes. Ever since we first recognized that the public trust protects environmental and recreational values, the two systems of legal thought have been on a collision course. . . .

In our opinion, the core of the public trust doctrine is the state's authority as sovereign to exercise a continuous supervision and control over the navigable waters of the state and the lands underlying those waters. This authority applies to the waters tributary to Mono Lake and bars DWP or any other party from claiming a vested right to divert waters once it becomes clear that such diversions harm the interests protected by the public trust. . . .

1. BACKGROUND AND HISTORY OF THE MONO LAKE LITIGATION.

DWP supplies water to the City of Los Angeles. Early in this century, it became clear that the city's anticipated needs would exceed the water available from local sources, and so in 1913 the city constructed an aqueduct to carry water from the Owens River 233 miles over the Antelope–Mojave plateau into the coastal plain and thirsty city. . . .

After purchasing the riparian rights incident to Lee Vining, Walker, Parker and Rush Creeks, as well as the riparian rights pertaining to Mono Lake, the city applied to the Water Board in 1940 for permits to appropriate the waters of the four tributaries. At hearings before the board, various interested individuals protested that the city's proposed appropriations would lower the surface level of Mono Lake and thereby impair its commercial, recreational and scenic uses.

The board's primary authority to reject that application lay in a 1921 amendment to the Water Commission Act of 1913, which authorized the board to reject an application "when in its judgment the proposed appropriation would not best conserve the public interest." (Stats. 1921, ch. 329, §1, p. 443, now codified as Wat. Code, §1255.) The 1921 enactment, however, also "declared to be the established policy of this state that the use of water for domestic purposes is the highest use of water" (*id.*, now codified as Wat. Code, §1254), and directed the Water Board to be guided by this declaration of policy. Since DWP sought water for domestic use, the board concluded that it had to grant the application notwithstanding the harm to public trust uses of Mono Lake. . . .

DWP expects that its future diversions of about 100,000 acre-feet per year will lower the lake's surface level another 43 feet and reduce its surface area by about 22 square miles over the next 80 to 100 years, at which point the lake will gradually approach environmental equilibrium (the point at which inflow from precipitation, groundwater and nondiverted tributaries equals outflow by evaporation and other means). At this point, according to DWP, the lake will stabilize at a level 6,330 feet above the sea's, with a surface area of approximately 38 square miles. Thus, by DWP's own estimates, unabated diversions will ultimately produce a lake that is about 56 percent smaller on the surface and 42 percent shallower than its natural size.

Plaintiffs consider these projections unrealistically optimistic. They allege that, 50 years hence, the lake will be at least 50 feet shallower than it now is, and hold less than 20 percent of its natural volume. Further, plaintiffs fear that "the lake will not stabilize at this level," but "may continue to reduce in size until it is dried up." Moreover, unlike DWP, plaintiffs believe that the lake's gradual recession indirectly causes a host of adverse environmental impacts. Many of these alleged impacts are related to an increase in the lake's salinity, caused by the decrease in its water volume. . . .

Plaintiffs predict that the lake's steadily increasing salinity, if unchecked, will wreak havoc throughout the local food chain. They contend that the lake's algae, and the brine shrimp and brine flies that feed on it, cannot survive the projected salinity increase. To support this assertion, plaintiffs point to a 50 percent reduction in the shrimp hatch for the spring of 1980 and a startling 95 percent reduction for the spring of 1981. . . .

DWP's diversions also present several threats to the millions of local and migratory birds using the lake. First, since many species of birds feed on the lake's brine shrimp, any reduction in shrimp population allegedly caused by rising salinity endangers a major avian food source. . . . Second, the increasing salinity makes it more difficult for the birds to maintain osmotic equilibrium with their environment.

The California gull is especially endangered, both by the increase in salinity and by loss of nesting sites. Ninety-five percent of this state's gull population and 25 percent of the total species population nests at the lake. Most of the gulls nest on islands in the lake. As the lake recedes, land between the shore and some of the islands has been exposed, offering such predators as the coyote easy access to the gull nests and chicks. In 1979, coyotes reached Negrit Island, once the most popular nesting site, and the number of gull nests at the lake declined sharply. . . .

Plaintiffs allege that DWP's diversions adversely affect the human species and its activities as well. First, as the lake recedes, it has exposed more than 18,000 acres of lake bed composed of very fine silt which, once dry, easily becomes airborne in winds. This silt contains a high concentration of alkali and other minerals that irritate the mucous membranes and respiratory systems of humans and other animals. . . .

Furthermore, the lake's recession obviously diminishes its value as an economic, recreational, and scenic resource. Of course, there will be less lake to use and enjoy. The declining shrimp hatch depresses a local shrimping industry. The rings of dry lake bed are difficult to traverse on foot, and thus impair human access to the lake, and reduce the lake's substantial scenic value. Mono Lake has long been treasured as a unique scenic, recreational and scientific resource, but continued diversions threaten to turn it into a desert wasteland like the dry bed of Owens Lake. . . .

2. THE PUBLIC TRUST DOCTRINE IN CALIFORNIA.

"By the law of nature these things are common to mankind—the air, running water, the sea and consequently the shores of the sea." (Institutes of Justinian 2.1.1.) From this origin in Roman law, the English common law evolved the concept of the public trust, under which the sovereign owns "all of its navigable waterways and the lands lying beneath them 'as trustee of a public trust for the benefit of the people.' " The State of California acquired title as trustee to such lands and waterways upon its admission to the union; from the earliest days its judicial decisions have recognized and enforced the trust obligation.

Three aspects of the public trust doctrine require consideration in this opinion: the purpose of the trust; the scope of the trust, particularly as it applies to the nonnavigable tributaries of a navigable lake; and the powers and duties of the state as trustee of the public trust. We discuss these questions in the order listed.

(a) The purpose of the public trust.

The objective of the public trust has evolved in tandem with the changing public perception of the values and uses of waterways. As we observed in *Marks v. Whitney, supra,* 6 Cal. 3d 251 [*Marks v. Whitney,* 6 Cal. 3d 251, 259, 491 P.2d 374, 380 (1971)], "[p]ublic trust easements [were] traditionally defined in terms of navigation, commerce and fisheries. They have been held to include the right to fish, hunt, bathe, swim, to use for boating and general recreation purposes the navigable waters of the state, and to use the bottom of the navigable waters for anchoring, standing, or other purposes." We went on, however, to hold that the traditional triad of uses—navigation, commerce and fishing—did not limit the public interest in the trust res. In language of special importance to the present setting, we stated that "[t]he public uses to which tidelands are subject are sufficiently flexible to encompass changing public needs. In administering the trust the state is not burdened with an outmoded classification favoring one mode of utilization over another. There is a growing public recognition that one of the most important public uses of the tidelands—a use encompassed within the tidelands trust—is the preservation of those lands in their natural state, so that they may serve as ecological units for scientific study, as open space, and as environments which provide food and habitat for birds and marine life, and which favorably affect the scenery and climate of the area."

Mono Lake is a navigable waterway. It supports a small local industry which harvests brine shrimp for sale as fish food, which endeavor probably qualifies the lake as a "fishery" under the traditional public trust cases. The principal values plaintiffs seek to protect, however, are recreational and ecological—the scenic views of the lake and its shore, the purity of the air, and the use of the lake for nesting and feeding by birds. Under *Marks v. Whitney, supra,* it is clear that protection of these values is among the purposes of the public trust.

(b) The scope of the public trust.

Early English decisions generally assumed the public trust was limited to tidal waters and the lands exposed and covered by the daily tides; many American decisions, including the leading California cases, also concern tidelands. It is, however, well settled in the United States generally and in California that the public trust is not limited by the reach of the tides, but encompasses all navigable lakes and streams.

Mono Lake is, as we have said, a navigable waterway. The beds, shores and waters of the lake are without question protected by the public trust. The streams diverted by DWP, however, are not themselves navigable. Accordingly, we must address in this case a question not discussed in any recent public trust case—whether the public trust limits conduct affecting nonnavigable tributaries to navigable waterways. . . .

We conclude that the public trust doctrine, as recognized and developed in California decisions, protects navigable waters from harm caused by diversion of nonnavigable tributaries.

(c) Duties and powers of the state as trustee.

In the following review of the authority and obligations of the state as administrator of the public trust, the dominant theme is the state's sovereign power and duty to exercise continued supervision over the trust. One consequence, of importance to this and many other cases, is that parties acquiring rights in trust property generally hold those rights subject to the trust, and can assert no vested right to use those rights in a manner harmful to the trust. . . .

[Prior California] cases amply demonstrate the continuing power of the state as administrator of the public trust, a power which extends to the revocation of previously granted rights or to the enforcement of the trust against lands long thought free of the trust. Except for those rare instances in which a grantee may acquire a right to use former trust property free of trust restrictions, the grantee holds subject to the trust, and while he may assert a vested right to the servient estate (the right of use subject to the trust) and to any improvements he erects, he can claim no vested right to bar recognition of the trust or state action to carry out its purposes....

Thus, the public trust is more than an affirmation of state power to use public property for public purposes. It is an affirmation of the duty of the state to protect the people's common heritage of streams, lakes, marshlands and tidelands, surrendering that right of protection only in rare cases when the abandonment of that right is consistent with the purposes of the trust.

3. THE CALIFORNIA WATER RIGHTS SYSTEM.

... [T]he function of the Water Board has steadily evolved from the narrow role of deciding priorities between competing appropriators to the charge of comprehensive planning and allocation of waters. This change necessarily affects the board's responsibility with respect to the public trust. The board of limited powers of 1913 had neither the power nor duty to consider interests protected by the public trust; the present board, in undertaking planning and allocation of water resources, is required by statute to take those interests into account.

4. THE RELATIONSHIP BETWEEN THE PUBLIC TRUST DOCTRINE AND THE CALIFORNIA WATER RIGHTS SYSTEM.

As we have seen, the public trust doctrine and the appropriative water rights system administered by the Water Board developed independently of each other. Each developed comprehensive rules and principles which, if applied to the full extent of their scope, would occupy the field of allocation of stream waters to the exclusion of any competing system of legal thought....

In our opinion, both the public trust doctrine and the water rights system embody important precepts which make the law more responsive to the diverse needs and interests involved in the planning and allocation of water resources. To embrace one system of thought and reject the other would lead to an unbalanced structure, one which would either decry as a breach of trust appropriations essential to the economic development of this state, or deny any duty to protect or even consider the values promoted by the public trust. Therefore, seeking an accommodation which will make use of the pertinent principles of both the public trust doctrine and the appropriative water rights system, and drawing upon the history of the public trust and the water rights system, the body of judicial precedent, and the views of expert commentators, we reach the following conclusions:

a. The state as sovereign retains continuing supervisory control over its navigable waters and the lands beneath those waters. This principle, fundamental to the concept of the public trust, applies to rights in flowing waters as well as to rights in tidelands and lakeshores; it prevents any party from acquiring a vested right to appropriate water in a manner harmful to the interests protected by the public trust.

b. As a matter of current and historical necessity, the Legislature, acting directly or through an authorized agency such as the Water Board, has the power to grant usufructuary licenses that will permit an appropriator to take water from flowing streams and use that water in a distant part of the state, even though this taking does not promote, and may unavoidably harm, the trust uses at the source stream. The population and economy of this state depend upon the appropriation of vast quantities of water for uses unrelated to in-stream trust values. California's Constitution, its statutes, decisions, and commentators all emphasize the need to make efficient use of California's limited water resources: all recognize, at least implicitly, that efficient use requires diverting water from in-stream uses. Now that the economy and population centers of this state have developed in reliance upon appropriated water, it would be disingenuous to hold that such appropriations are and have always been improper to the extent that they harm public trust uses, and can be justified only upon theories of reliance or estoppel.

c. The state has an affirmative duty to take the public trust into account in the planning and allocation of water resources, and to protect public trust uses whenever feasible. Just as the history of this state shows that appropriation may be necessary for efficient use of water despite unavoidable harm to public trust values, it demonstrates that an appropriative water rights system administered without consideration of the public trust may cause unnecessary and unjustified harm to trust interests. As a matter of practical necessity the state may have to approve appropriations despite foreseeable harm to public trust uses. In so doing, however, the state must bear in mind its duty as trustee to consider the effect of the taking on the public trust, and to preserve, so far as consistent with the public interest, the uses protected by the trust.

Once the state has approved an appropriation, the public trust imposes a duty of continuing supervision over the taking and use of the appropriated water. In exercising its sovereign power to allocate water resources in the public interest, the state is not confined by past allocation decisions which may be incorrect in light of current knowledge or inconsistent with current needs.

The state accordingly has the power to reconsider allocation decisions even though those decisions were made after due consideration of their effect on the public trust. The case for reconsidering a particular decision, however, is even stronger when that decision failed to weigh and consider public trust uses. In the case before us, the salient fact is that no responsible body has ever determined the impact of diverting the entire flow of the Mono Lake tributaries into the Los Angeles Aqueduct. This is not a case in which the Legislature, the Water Board, or any judicial body has determined that the needs of Los Angeles outweigh the needs of the Mono Basin, that the benefit gained is worth the price. Neither has any responsible body determined whether some lesser taking would better balance the diverse interests. Instead, DWP acquired rights to the entire flow in 1940 from a water board which believed it lacked both the power and the duty to protect the Mono Lake environment, and continues to exercise those rights in apparent disregard for the resulting damage to the scenery, ecology, and human uses of Mono Lake.

It is clear that some responsible body ought to reconsider the allocation of the waters of the Mono Basin. No vested rights bar such reconsideration. We recognize the substantial concerns voiced by Los Angeles—the city's need for water, its reliance upon the 1940 board decision, the cost both in terms of money and environmental impact of obtaining water elsewhere. Such concerns must enter into any allocation decision. We hold only that they do not preclude a reconsideration and reallocation which also takes into account the impact of water diversion on the Mono Lake environment....

This opinion is but one step in the eventual resolution of the Mono Lake controversy. We do not dictate any particular allocation of water. Our objective is to resolve a legal conundrum in which two competing systems of thought—the public trust doctrine and the appropriative water rights system—existed independently of each other, espousing principles which seemingly suggested opposite results. We hope by integrating these two doctrines to clear away the legal barriers which have so far prevented either the Water Board or the courts from taking a new and objective look at the water resources of the Mono Basin. The human and environmental uses of Mono Lake—uses protected by the public trust doctrine—deserve to be taken into account. Such uses should not be destroyed because the state mistakenly thought itself powerless to protect them.

STUDY QUESTIONS

(1) The *Mono Lake* case expanded both the physical and legal scope of the public trust doctrine. First, the court recognized the realities of hydrological and ecological connections in the watershed and went beyond the historic "navigable waters" to address harms stemming from the use of small tributaries. Second, the court acknowledged modern values of environmental protection and incorporated an environmental ethic into the state's public trust obligations. Is this judicial activism or sound development of common law? Should the public trust doctrine remain static, or should it evolve with new disputes and values?

(2) The *Mono Lake* decision expanded the public trust doctrine and established affirmative duties for environmental protection. But did Mono Lake ultimately prevail? Does the court pick a winner or just rebalance the relative rights? Consider the condition of Mono Lake today. After over thirty years, Mono Lake is still well below its natural level, although likely in far better shape than it would have been without some public trust protection. See the current condition of Mono Lake at http://www.monolake.org/today/water.

(3) The Hawai'i' constitution, Art. XI, §1, states that:

> For the benefit of present and future generations, the State and its political subdivisions shall conserve and protect Hawaii's natural beauty and all natural resources, including land, water, air, minerals and energy sources, and shall promote the development and utilization of these resources in a manner consistent with their conservation and in furtherance of the self-sufficiency of the State. All public natural resources are held in trust by the State for the benefit of the people.

The Hawai'i Supreme Court has reinforced that "the public trust doctrine applies to all water resources without exception or distinction" and has indicated that these more general constitutional public trust concepts extend to environmental and biodiversity protection.[4] How might this development of the public trust doctrine complement the advancement of guardianship models (explored in Chapter 6) that are being developed at the local and state level in the United States? How might progressive applications of the public trust doctrine benefit from the growing importance of traditional Indigenous views of nature? These views are discussed briefly in Chapter 3 and, in more detail, in later chapters that cover the legal developments in Colombia, Ecuador, and Brazil. For more on this topic, see Chapter 18 and Lawrence H. Miike, *Water and the Law in Hawaii* (2004).[5]

[4] *Kauai Springs, Inc. v. Planning Commission of the County of Kauai*, SCWC-29440 (Haw. 2014).

[5] Miike, Lawrence H. *Water and the Law in Hawaii.* Honolulu: University of Hawai'i Press, 2004. Accessed June 2, 2020, www.jstor.org/stable/j.ctvvmxkg.

CHAPTER 8

Rights of Future Generations[1]

I. INTRODUCTION

Do future generations of humans have a legally cognizable right to an Earth that can sustain life? Who—if anyone—owes a duty to protect the Earth for future generations? And to what extent? And what defines a "generation," let alone a "future generation"?

Some legal theorists have argued that future generations "cannot have rights because they do not yet exist and therefore cannot have anything, including rights."[2] Future human beings are indeterminate and contingent, and, as such, lack identity; we cannot know their names or collective size, nor their needs, desires, or tastes. Indeed, we cannot even be sure that "they" ever will exist.[3] The corollary argument drawn from these assertions is that current generations cannot have obligations to account for or protect those rights. More darkly, opponents of rights of future generations ask whether "the future will be too grim to allow future [humans to even] come into existence?"[4]

This chapter addresses these questions by first defining "generation" and offering a legal framework to identify "future generations." Second, it reviews examples of explicit cultural and legal norms that recognize a duty to protect Earth for future generations, as articulated by Indigenous societies, the U.S. environmental movement, international institutions, and governments around the world. Third, it discusses the public trust doctrine as a means to enforce governments' obligations to protect nature for the benefit of current and future generations. Fourth, it explores the question of whether future generations possess constitutional rights to a habitable Earth. Finally, the last section considers the possibility of future generations gaining standing to assert their rights and enforce the duties owed to them in the courts.

[1] This chapter was authored by Stacy Jane Schaefer, Associate Director of Land Conservation at the Maryland Department of Natural Resources. Gratitude to Ruihan (Yvette) Wang, Indiana University Maurer School of Law '19, for her research and valuable contributions to this chapter.

[2] *See* Burns H. Weston & Tracy Bach, *Recalibrating the Law of Humans with the Laws of Nature: Climate Change, Human Rights, and Intergenerational Justice*, 17 (2009) [hereinafter CLI Paper on Intergeneration Justice] (pointing out arguments against the right of future generations).

[3] *Id.*

[4] Neil H. Buchanan, *What Kind of Environment Do We Owe Future Generations?*, 15 Lewis & Clark L. Rev. 339, 344, 346 (2011).

II. DEFINITION OF "GENERATION" AND IDENTIFICATION OF THE "FUTURE GENERATIONS" CLAIMANT

To delve into the question of whether future generations hold legally cognizable rights and whether any enforceable duties are owed to them, a sensible start is the legal framework in which the meaning of "future generation" has been considered. The Merriam-Webster dictionary defines a generation as "a body of living beings constituting a single step in the line of descent from an ancestor; a group of individuals born and living contemporaneously."[5] An identified *current* generation is necessarily tied to identifiable past generations as well as future generations. That is, it encompasses the time continuum from the birth of one generation to the birth of that generation's offspring and so on.

Defining future generations in the context of constitutional protections will likely warrant consideration beyond dictionary sources[6] and there is legal authority in tax and estate law. For example, the generation-skipping transfer tax was enacted by Congress in 1976 to prevent families from avoiding the estate tax for one or more future generations by making bequests directly to recipients two or more generations younger than the donor.[7] The IRS Code defines "two or more generations" as at least 37.5 years and recognizes a new generation every 25 years.[8] Social science research also constructs a timeline in which each successive generation has an identified position, as shown below.[9]

	The Silent Generation	Baby Boomers	Gen X	Millennials Gen Y	Gen Z	Gen AA	Gen BB
Born	1928–1945	1946–1964	1965–1980	1981–1996	1997–2015	2015–2039	2039–2059

Identifying future generations by estimating the average number of years on a time continuum has legal precedence as well as precedence in other disciplines. While

[5] "Generation," Merriam-Webster Dictionary, https://www.merriam-webster.com/dictionary/generation (last visited Mar. 1, 2020).

[6] *But see Rapanos v. U.S.*, 547 U.S. 715, 728 (2006), in which Justice Scalia writing for a plurality determined the meaning of "waters" as used in the Clean Water Act §1362(7) by relying on Webster's New International Dictionary 2882 (2d ed. 1954): "...'the waters' refers more narrowly to water '[a]s found in streams and bodies forming geographical features such as oceans, rivers, [and] lakes,' or 'the flowing or moving masses, as of waves or floods, making up such streams or bodies.'"

[7] *See* Tax on Generation-Skipping Transfers, 26 U.S.C. §§ ?2601-2664.

[8] IRS, Instructions for Form 709 (2019), Determining the Generation of a Donee, https://www.irs.gov/pub/irs-pdf/i709.pdf.

[9] Information found in the table with generation names and dates is from Michael Dimock, *Defining Generations: Where Millennials End and Generation Z Begins*, Pew Research Center (Jan. 17, 2019), https://www.pewresearch.org/fact-tank/2019/01/17/where-millennials-end-and-generation-z-begins/ and Kasasa, *Boomers, Gen X, Gen Y, and Gen Z Explained* (Apr. 22, 2019), https://www.kasasa.com/articles/generations/gen-x-gen-y-gen-z.

there may be other approaches, this demonstrates that there are practical methods of defining what constitutes "future generations."

STUDY QUESTIONS

(1) What types of impacts have past generations made on the current generation with respect to the environment and nature? Do you think they have violated your rights? What duty(ies) did they have when they violated the right(s)? When did the violation(s) occur, and when were you injured? When was your generation injured? If rights of future generations are established as a matter of law and impose duties on governments to protect the rights of future generations, what duties may governments impose on people and corporations whose conduct violates those rights?

(2) The question of whether one or more future generations has legal rights is separate and distinct from the question of whether an unborn child has legal rights. The answer to the latter question is based on the constitutional construction that establishes individual rights (a woman's privacy and reproductive rights),[10] while the latter may be based on constitutional rights of public trust doctrine duties. How else might one contrast or compare the rights of future generations with the rights of an unborn child and reproductive rights?

III. THE CONCEPT OF A DUTY TO PROTECT THE EARTH FOR FUTURE GENERATIONS

The term "future generations" and the concept that there is an obligation of some sort to protect them appears in many different legal subjects and political and social pronouncements. And the more specific concept of a duty to protect the Earth for the benefit of future generations is neither new nor restricted to any one culture or nation. This section provides a brief survey of customary, international, and domestic government edicts that speak to protecting the Earth for future generations. What follows is a selective series of examples from around the world.

A. Indigenous Customary Law

As discussed in Chapter 3, "Indigenous decision-making was often phrased in terms of what the group's obligations were to preserve its human community and its larger community of life." This worldview necessitates consideration of future generations, as is done by many Indigenous peoples.

[10] *Roe v. Wade*, 410 U.S. 113, 158, (1973) ("the word 'person,' as used in the Fourteenth Amendment, does not include the unborn").

A current expression of protecting the Earth for future generations appears as the "Seventh Generation Principle"—that current decision-making should result in a sustainable world seven generations later—set out in the Bemidji Statement, which combines the wisdom of the Native American Haudenosaunee tribe with the precautionary principle:

> The first mandate . . . is to ensure that our decision-making is guided by consideration of the welfare and well-being of the seventh generation to come. . . . Indigenous Peoples have learned over thousands of years to live in harmony with the land and the waters. It is our intent to survive and thrive on this planet for this and many generations to come.[11]

Other Indigenous leaders speak of future generations from an ecocentric perspective. The Indigenous rights magazine *Cultural Survival* wrote about this perspective in 2009: "When women like Pauline Whitesinger, an elder at Big Mountain, and Carrie Dann, a Western Shoshone land rights activist, speak of preserving the land for future generations, they are not just talking about future generations of humans. They are talking about future generations of plants, animals, water, and all living things."[12]

Another example of a legal obligation owed to future generations is found in the customary legal system of the Indigenous Māori in New Zealand. The Māori's *tikanga* recognizes both a physical and spiritual connection of the people to the Whanganui River ecosystem in which they have lived for centuries. The belief that "Ko au te awa. Ko te awa ko au" (I am the river. The river is me.) is reflected in the 1840 Te Awa Tupua Treaty.[13] As the Waitangi Tribunal explained in its report on the Whanganui River treaty claim, the Māori consider the Whanganui River "the central bloodline of their one heart."[14] The Māori tikanga asserts that humans are connected to the world and that interconnectedness carries the responsibilities and rights as one would attribute to fellow family members.

B. The U.S. Environmental Movement of the 1960s and 1970s

In 1969, a U.S. Senate Report on the National Environmental Policy Act stated that "[t]he Nation has in many areas overdrawn its bank account in life-sustaining natural elements."[15] From this recognition, Congress enacted numerous federal statutes such as the Clean Air Act, Clean Water Act, and Endangered Species Act to realign the American government's commitment to protecting the environment. In 1970, the Environmental Protection Agency was created.

[11] *The Bemidji Statement on Seventh Generation Guardianship*, 14th Protecting Mother Earth Conference, Jul. 6-9, 2006, http://www.precaution.org/lib/06/prn_bemidji.060627.htm.
[12] Wilma Mankiller, *Being Indigenous in the 21st Century*, Cultural Survival (Mar. 2009).
[13] The Te Awa Tupua Act emerged from treaty settlement negotiations resolving historical Treaty of Waitangi claims of the Whanganui Iwi (tribe) in relation to the Whanganui River. The settlement agreement, Tūtohu Whakatupua, was signed August 30, 2012. Whanganui Iwi & The Crown, Tūtohu Whakatupua (2012).
[14] Waitangi Tribunal, The Whanganui River Report, 379 (1999).
[15] S. Rep. No. 91-296 at 16 (1969).

The 1970 National Environmental Policy Act (NEPA) is the closest U.S. environmental law has come to explicitly representing the interests of future generations. NEPA, called America's "basic national charter for the protection of the environment,"[16] was enacted with broad bipartisan support in the both executive and legislative branches.[17] The text of NEPA begins by "recognizing the profound impact of man's activity on the interrelations of all components of the natural environment."[18] It "declares that it is the continuing policy of the Federal Government... to create and maintain conditions under which man and nature can exist in productive harmony, and fulfill the social, economic, and other requirements of present *and future generations* of Americans."[19] The Senate author of NEPA stated for the Congressional Record that "[t]he basic principle of this policy [NEPA] is that we must strive in all that we do, to achieve a standard of excellence in man's relationship to his physical surroundings" and "[a] statement of environmental policy is more than a statement of what we believe as a people and as a nation.... it serves a constitutional foundation... for guidance in making decisions which find environmental values in conflict with other values."[20] President Richard Nixon hailed NEPA as providing the "direction" for the country to "regain a productive harmony between man and nature"[21] and declared "I think that 1970 will be known as the year of the beginning, in which we really began to move on the problems of clean air and clean water and open spaces *for the future generations of America.*"[22]

The initial strength of this movement and the potential it had to create "a productive harmony between man and nature" for the benefit of current and future generations has proved to be short-lived. To date, no federal court has found a statutory right of future generations to an inhabitable Earth. In *Strycker's Bay Neighborhood Council v. Karlen*, 444 U.S. 223, 227 (1980), the Supreme Court established that while NEPA sets out "significant substantive goals for the Nation," it only "imposes upon agencies duties that are essentially procedural."[23] According to the Supreme Court, "once an agency has made a decision subject to NEPA's procedural requirements, the only role for a court is to ensure that the agency has considered the environmental consequences; it cannot 'interject itself within the area of discretion of the executive as to the choice of the action to be taken.' "[24] Based on this understanding, U.S. courts have foreclosed substantive review of agency actions, even if such actions are significantly detrimental to nature and to present and future generations of Americans.

[16] 42 U.S.C.A. §4331(a) (1969).
[17] 40 C.F.R. §1500.1(a).
[18] 42 U.S.C.A. §4331(a).
[19] *Id.* (emphasis added).
[20] Senator Henry Jackson, 115 Cong. Rec. S. 17451, Dec. 20, 1969.
[21] Richard M. Nixon, Statement About the National Environmental Policy Act of 1969, 1 Pub. Papers 2 (Jan. 1, 1970).
[22] EPA, 40th Anniversary of the Clean Air Act, https://www.epa.gov/clean-air-act-overview/40th-anniversary-clean-air-act (emphasis added).
[23] *Strycker's Bay Neighborhood Council, Inc. v. Karlen*, 444 U.S. 223, 227 (1980) (internal citation omitted).
[24] *Id.* at 227-228 (internal citation omitted) (emphasis added).

C. *Juliana v. United States*

In 2016, after decades of being ignored under NEPA and other environmental laws, future generations came knocking on the courtroom doors. In the case *Juliana v. United States*, 217 F. Supp. 3d 1224, 1260-61 (D. Or. 2016), "Future Generations" of humans were among the petitioners, along with 21 young persons and the nonprofit organization Earth Guardians, suing the U.S. government for allowing CO2 levels to rise to dangerous levels.[25] The plaintiffs alleged that these actions violate their right to a stable climate system, which is retained by the people under the Ninth Amendment and essential to the Fifth Amendment's guarantee that the government shall not deprive any person of life, liberty, or property without due process of law.[26] The plaintiffs also alleged that these actions violate the public trust doctrine.[27] James Hansen, the former NASA scientist who has warned about climate change since the 1980s, served as the appointed legal guardian (or "representative") of Future Generations.

In January 2020, the U.S. Ninth Circuit Court of Appeals voted 2-1 to dismiss the lawsuit, ruling that the plaintiffs lacked Article III standing to sue because the plaintiff's injuries were not redressable by the exercise of judicial power. Rather, the court concluded, "the plaintiffs' impressive case for redress must be presented to the political branches of government."[28] By confining the grounds for the decision to the issue of redressability, the court did not decide whether the Future Generations were rights-bearing legal entities who, through a legal guardian, may yet be afforded constitutional protections.

In the dissent, Judge Staton highlighted what might persuade another court and perhaps a future-generation Supreme Court that the Constitution requires the exercise of judicial power to redress the injury of climate change:

> What sets this harm apart from all others is not just its magnitude, but its irreversibility. The devastation might look and feel somewhat different if future generations could simply pick up the pieces and restore the Nation. But plaintiffs' experts speak of a certain level of global warming as "locking in" this catastrophic damage. Put more starkly by plaintiffs' expert, Dr. Harold R. Wanless, "[a]tmospheric warming will continue for some 30 years after we stop putting more greenhouse gasses into the atmosphere. But that warmed atmosphere will continue warming the ocean for centuries, and the accumulating heat in the oceans will persist for millennia" (emphasis added). Indeed, another of plaintiffs' experts echoes, "[t]he fact that GHGs dissipate very slowly from the atmosphere . . . and that the costs of taking CO2 out of the atmosphere through non-biological carbon capture and storage are very high means that the consequences of GHG emissions should be viewed as effectively irreversible" (emphasis added). In other words, "[g]iven the self-reinforcing nature of climate change," the tipping point may well have arrived, and we may be rapidly approaching the point of no return.[29]

[25] *See* First Amended Complaint for Declaratory and Injunctive Relief, *Juliana. v. United States of America*, Case No.: 6:15-cv-01517-TC (D. Or. 2015).
[26] *Id.*
[27] *Id.*
[28] Opinion, *Juliana. v. United States of America* Case No.: 6:15-cv-01517-AA (D. Or. 2020).
[29] *Id.* at 34-35.

Finally, expressing a belief that the U.S. government has some duty to consider the needs of future generations, Judge Staton also discusses the roots of the U.S. Constitution. As Judge Staton recalled,

> When the Articles of the Confederation proved ill-fitting to the task of safeguarding the Union, the framers formed the Constitutional Convention with "the great object" of "preserv[ing] and perpetuat[ing]" the Union, for they believed that "the prosperity of America depended on its Union." The Federalist No. 2, at 19 (John Jay) (E. H. Scott ed., 1898); *see also* Letter from James Madison to Thomas Jefferson (Oct. 24, 1787). [Citation omitted.] . . . In light of this animating principle, it is fitting that the Preamble declares that the Constitution is intended to secure "the Blessings of Liberty" not just for one generation, but for all future generations—our "Posterity."[30]

STUDY QUESTIONS

(1) During the 1960s–1970s American Environmental Movement, the two political branches of government—the executive and legislative—enthusiastically and very publicly sought to protect nature for current and future generations. Recall that the Supreme Court then interpreted NEPA as securing only procedural rights as opposed to substantive environmental protection rights for current and future generations. In the context of the Environmental Protection Agency's alleged failure to fulfill its mandate, the court also established a doctrine of judicial deference to agency discretion. How important was this decision in affecting the efforts of the environmental movement and, more generally, the attitudes of the American public and those seeking work in government agencies to advance the purpose stated in the statutes? What political developments may have contributed to the dissolution of the bipartisan commitment to the environment reflected in the stated purpose of NEPA?

(2) Fifty years after NEPA was enacted, in *Juliana v. U.S.*, the Ninth Circuit Court of Appeals observed that "the political branches of government have to date been largely deaf to the pleas of the plaintiffs" to, in the words of NEPA, "maintain conditions under which man and nature can exist in productive harmony, and fulfill the social, economic, and other requirements of present and future generations of Americans." Nonetheless, the court held the case could not proceed based on constitutional limitations of federal judicial powers:

> Not every problem posing a threat—even a clear and present danger—to the American Experiment can be solved by federal judges. As Judge Cardozo once aptly warned, a judicial commission does not confer the power of "a knight-errant, roaming at will in pursuit of his own ideal of beauty or of goodness;" rather, we are bound "to exercise a discretion informed by tradition, methodized by

[30] *Id.* at 38-39.

analogy, disciplined by system." Benjamin N. Cardozo, The Nature of the Judicial Process 141 (1921)."

What factors might lead another federal court to find that judicial action to remedy the failure of the political branches of government to adhere to the stated purposes of NEPA is constitutionally permissible?

D. International Soft Law

In the contemporary international legal system, there are declarations, conventions, and resolutions that speak to the protection of the environment for future generations. Some of these legal instruments are summarized in the following chart.

Legal Instrument	Rights of Future Generations Text
1972 Stockholm Declaration on the Human Environment	"[Humanity] bears a solemn responsibility to protect and improve the environment for present and future generations."[31]
Article 4 of the UNESCO Declaration of the Responsibilities of the Present Generations Towards Future Generations	"Preservation of life on Earth. The present generations have the responsibility to bequeath to future generations an Earth which will not one day be irreversibly damaged by human activity. Each generation inheriting the Earth temporarily should take care to use natural resources reasonably and ensure that life is not prejudiced by harmful modifications of the ecosystems and that scientific and technological progress in all fields does not harm life on Earth."[32]
Rio Declaration on Environment and Development	"The right to development must be fulfilled so as to equitably meet developmental and environmental needs of present and future generations."[33]
The 1992 Convention on the Protection and Use of Transboundary Watercourses and International Lakes	"Water resources shall be managed so that the needs of the present generation are met without compromising the ability of future generations to meet their own needs."[34]

[31] Declaration of the United Nations Conference on the Human Environment, princ. 1, U.N. Doc. A/CONF. 48/14, *reprinted in* 11 I.L.M. 1416 (1972).

[32] United Nations Educational, Scientific and Cultural Organization (UNESCO), *Declaration on the Responsibilities of the Present Generations Towards Future Generations*, arts. 4-5, Records of the General Conference, Paris, Oct. 21-Nov. 12, 1997.

[33] U.N. Conference on Environment and Development, princ. 3, U.N. Doc. A/CONF. 151/5/Rev. 1, *reprinted in* 31 I.L.M. 874 (1992).

[34] The Convention on the Protection and Use of Transboundary Watercourses and International Lakes, Art. 2(5)(c), Mar. 17, 1992, 1936 U.N.T.S. 269, 31 I.L.M. 1312.

Legal Instrument	Rights of Future Generations Text
North American Agreement on Environmental Cooperation Preamble, Sept. 13, 1993, 32 I.L.M. 1480	"CONVINCED of the importance of the conservation, protection and enhancement of the environment in their territories and the essential role of cooperation in these areas in achieving sustainable development for the wellbeing of present and future generations."
Stockholm Convention on Persistent Organic Pollutants Preamble, paragraph 2, May 22, 2001, 40 I.L.M. 532	"Aware of the health concerns, especially in developing countries, resulting from local exposure to persistent organic pollutants, in particular impacts upon women and, through them, upon future generations."
Article 3 of the Framework Convention on Climate Change from the United Nations Conference on Environment and Development	"The Parties should protect the climate system for the benefit of present and future generations of humankind."[35]

The international laws, declarations, and statements referenced above are functionally "soft laws" because they allow an organization to declare its intentions without being directly enforceable in a court of law. Despite its nonbinding nature, soft law helps to generate shared norms and leads to binding hard law in the future, as it has with human rights. Soft law can communicate "future intentions to enact hard law, allowing people to adjust their behavior in advance of binding statutes and in some cases avoiding constitutional requirements that apply to hard law . . . if people adjust their behavior in anticipation of hard law, hard law enactment might not be necessary."[36]

Future generations are strongly considered in global sustainability efforts.[37] The *Report of the World Commission on Environment and Development: Our Common Future*, released in 1987, defines the principle of sustainable development as "development that meets the needs of the present without compromising the ability of future generations to meet their own needs."[38] This has become the mantra of the international community's sustainability work. In some limited contexts, the principle of sustainable

[35] United Nations Conference on Environment and Development: Framework Convention on Climate Change, May 9, 1992, INC/FCCC, 5th Sess., 2d Part, at Annex I, U.N. Doc. A/AC.237/18 (Part II) Add. 1, *reprinted* in 31 I.L.M. 851.

[36] Jacob E. Gersen & Eric A. Posner, *Soft Law: Lessons from Congressional Practice*, 61 Stan. L. Rev. 573, 586 (2008).

[37] *See generally* Environment & Society Portal, *UN World Commission on Environment and Development*, www.environmentandsociety.org/mml/un-world-commission-environment-and-development-ed-report-world-commission-environment-and (last visited Mar. 1, 2020).

[38] Report of the World Commission on Environment and Development: Our Common Future, ch. 2 para. 1 (World Comm'n on Env't & Dev. ed., 1987), available at *https://sustainabledevelopment.un.org/content/documents/5987our-common-future.pdf.*

development may have reached the level of customary international law.[39] While it lacks the element of "rights," it does establish that current generations have a "responsibility" to future generations.

In sum, the use of soft law in the international arena is an important element of the legal framework for protecting the rights of future generations. As commentators have noted, "Despite their lack of formal legal status, international soft laws can ultimately have real effect—by working their way into customary international law or by providing the framework for informal interstate cooperation."[40] Certainly international law instruments will continue to play a major role in the development of rights of future generations.

STUDY QUESTIONS

(1) Some of the international declarations and conventions cited above emphasize how humans should endeavor to avoid depletion of natural resources to ensure their availability for future generations. How might this imply a responsibility to the Earth as well as to future generations of humans? Why is the beneficiary of the duty important? How does it make a difference to the potential beneficiaries when nature is described as "natural resources" as opposed to the "environment"?

(2) If the U.S. Supreme Court adopted Article 4 of the *UNESCO Declaration of the Responsibilities of the Present Generations Towards Future Generations* that "each generation inheriting the Earth temporarily should take care to use natural resources reasonably," as an enforceable hard law standard, *who* would determine what is reasonable in the context of protection for future generations? What factors might be considered? How might those standards change as the condition of Earth changes? How will the rapidity and accelerating changes in the condition of the Earth affect the development of standards for what is reasonable in the use of natural resources? How does one balance the interests of present generations with the interests of future generations? How might the standard of reasonable care be defined?

(3) How could an attorney in the United States representing the rights of future generations make use of international soft laws?

(4) What arguments might support the assertion that the rights of future generations should be considered customary international law?

[39] *See, e.g.*, Varamon Ramangkura, *Thai Shrimp, Sea Turtles, Mangrove Forests and the WTO: Innovative Environmental Protection under the International Trade Regime*, 15 Geo. Int'l Envtl. L. Rev. 677, 682 (2003).
[40] Gersen & Posner, *supra* note 36, at 575.

(5) How strong is the argument that a court need not *create* future generations' fundamental rights because the government is *already obligated as a sovereign* to protect and promote the pre-existing right of its citizens to inherit a land capable of sustaining life?

IV. THE PUBLIC TRUST DOCTRINE: FROM CONCEPT TO A LEGALLY ENFORCEABLE DUTY TO PROTECT THE ENVIRONMENT FOR FUTURE GENERATIONS

As discussed in the preceding chapter, the public trust doctrine is built on the principle that the power of governing is a trust committed by the people to the government, no part of which can be granted away. Not even statutes can supersede a government's public trust obligations to protect the environment.[41] With respect to future generations, a sovereign's public trust obligations prevent it from "depriving a future legislature of the natural resources necessary to provide for the well-being and survival of its citizens."[42]

The public trust doctrine has a prominent role in the development of Earth law within our legal system because it requires sovereign governments to protect the land, water, wildlife, and other parts of nature for the benefit of the public. In this context, this section looks more closely at what an attorney asserting the right of future generations to a habitable Earth could argue under the public trust doctrine. Specifically, such an attorney could assert that (1) the government is a trustee, (2) future generations are beneficiaries, (3) the environment or nature as broadly defined is the subject (or the "res"), and (4) the government has a fiduciary duty to sustain certain ecological processes.

A. Trustees: All Levels of Government

The United States is a democracy that can be described as a dual sovereignty. That is, the Constitution gives the state governments all powers that are not assigned exclusively to the federal government.[43] Since the doctrine of public trust is built on the principle that the power of governing is a trust committed by the people to the government, it is logical that in the United States, both the state and federal governments serve the role as trustee consistent with each government's respective authority. To put it simply, they are co-trustees of the environment. With that introduction, let us look at the rights of future generations at the state and then the federal level.

[41] *Juliana*, 217 F. Supp. 3d at 1260.
[42] *Id.* at 1253 (internal citations omitted).
[43] U.S. Const. amend. X ("the powers not delegated to the United States by the Constitution, nor prohibited by it to the States, are reserved to the States respectively, or to the people.").

1. Domestic state governments as trustee of the environment for future generations

As explored in Chapter 7, the public trust doctrine is most familiar in the context of states. The next chapter, "The Rights of Nature Movement in the U.S.," examines state constitutions in the context of developing law to explicitly recognize fundamental rights of nature. By way of example, the Pennsylvania Constitution provides as follows:

> The people have a right to clean air, pure water, and to the preservation of the natural, scenic, historic and esthetic values of the environment. Pennsylvania's public natural resources are the common property of all the people, *including generations yet to come.* As trustee of these resources, the Commonwealth shall conserve and maintain them for the benefit of all the people."[44]

The Hawai'i' Constitution likewise provides:

> For the benefit of present *and future generations,* the State and its political subdivisions shall conserve and protect Hawaii's natural beauty and all natural resources, including land, water, air, minerals and energy sources, and shall promote the development and utilization of these resources in a manner consistent with their conservation and in furtherance of the self-sufficiency of the State. All public natural resources are held in trust by the State for the benefit of the people.[45]

While these written sources of law establish strong precedent for the development of rights of future generations, it is important to remember that a state's obligations under the public trust doctrine are inherent and thus not reliant on codification by the legislature.[46]

2. The Federal government as trustee of the environment for future generations

As discussed above, there is ample support for public trust claims as they pertain to state governments. However, the public trust doctrine has not been widely applied at the federal level.[47] While the state government's public trust obligations are more explicitly stated, the federal government's public trust obligations, including to future generations, are increasingly important due to the global scope of ecological threats.

[44] Pa. Const. art. I, §27 (emphasis added).

[45] Haw. Const., art. XI, §1.

[46] In *Parks v. Cooper,* the South Dakota Supreme Court made precisely this point, holding that "history and precedent have established the public trust doctrine as an inherent attribute of sovereign authority." *Parks v. Cooper,* 676 N.W.2d 823 (S.D. 2004).

[47] Zachary L. Berliner, *What About Uncle Sam? Carving a New Place for the Public Trust Doctrine in Federal Climate Change Litigation,* Penn Law: Legal Scholarship Repository 340 (2017). Some argue that the public trust doctrine does not apply to the federal government at all. Mary Wood rebuts this assumption in Mary Christina Wood, Nature's Trust: Environmental Law for a New Ecological Age 133 (2014). *See also United States v. 1.58 Acres of Land Situated in City of Bos., Suffolk Cty., Com. of Mass.,* 523 F. Supp. 120, 124 (D. Mass. 1981) ("The state's administration of the public trust is subject to the paramount rights of the federal government to administer its trust with respect to matters within the federal power").

For example, the *Juliana* case seeks public trust accountability for future generations to be borne by the federal government since climate change is best addressed through sweeping federal action. NEPA is another example where the federal government was envisioned as serving a trustee role on behalf of future generations.

3. Indigenous tribes as trustees of the environment for future generations

Tribal sovereignty in the United States is the concept of the inherent authority of Indigenous tribes to govern themselves within the borders of the United States. Professor Wood explains that "[a]s the original governments across the land, tribes possess inherent sovereignty pre-existing the federal government or any state."[48] In the development of Earth law, tribes may take their rightful place as co-trustees with federal or state governments of shared ecological assets.

The role of trustee for the Earth and future generations is inherent in Indigenous customary law. Recall the Bemidji Statement:[49]

> The health and well-being of our grandchildren are worth more than all the wealth that can be taken from these lands. By returning to the collective empowerment and decision making that is part of our history, we are able to envision a future that will restore and protect the inheritance of this, and future generations.
>
> Therefore, we will designate Guardians for the Seventh Generation.

Chapter 25, "Indigenous Legalities," and Chapter 6, "Guardianship Arrangements in Rights of Nature Provisions," discuss this concept in greater detail.

B. Beneficiaries: Current and Future Generations

Looking to the future through a connected time continuum is at the center of the public trust doctrine. As the Supreme Court explained in *Newton v. Mahoning Cnty. Comm'rs,* 100 U.S. 548, 559 (1879) "[e]very succeeding legislature possesses the same jurisdiction and power with respect to [the public trust] as its predecessors." A government's public trust obligations prevent it from "depriving a future legislature of the natural resources necessary to provide for the well-being and survival of its citizens."[50]

In establishing the United States Constitution, the Founding Fathers were explicit about forming a government structure that secured "the Blessings of Liberty to ourselves and our Posterity."[51] The word *posterity* means descendants and future generations. Recall Professor Wood's point that including posterity in the Preamble to the Constitution "underscores an inalienable duty ingrained in government itself as part of its constituted purpose: to govern for the *endurance* of the nation, and thus for the benefit of future generations as well as present ones."

[48] Wood, *supra* note 47, at 136.
[49] *The Bemidji Statement, supra* note 11.
[50] *Juliana v. United States,* 217 F. Supp. 3d 1224 1253 (D. Or. 2016).
[51] U.S. Const. pmbl.

Judge Staton's dissent in the 2020 Ninth Circuit *Juliana* case observes that the harm from climate change is unique in "not just its magnitude, but its irreversibility" and that the "devastation might look and feel somewhat different if future generations could simply pick up the pieces and restore the Nation." Judge Staton also observed that the "perpetuity of the Republic" is a fundamental underpinning of the U.S. Constitution's structure that serves as the "guardian of all other rights." Simply stated, without the organized society known as the United States, "all the liberties protected by the [United States] Constitution" are "meaningless." In emphasizing this point, the dissent recalled President George Washington's 1783 Circular Letter of Farewell to the Army in which Washington recognized, "the destiny of unborn millions" rested on the fate of the nation itself.[52]

Other nations' courts have recognized the principle. In *Reliance Natural Res., Ltd. v. Reliance Indus., Ltd.*, the Supreme Court of India explained:

> [t]he concept of people as a nation does not include just the living; it includes those who are unborn and waiting to be instantiated. Conservation of resources, especially scarce ones, is both a matter of efficient use to alleviate the suffering of the living and also of ensuring that such use does not lead to diminishment of the prospects of their use by future generations."[53]

Similarly, as discussed below, the Philippines Supreme Court has made clear that "The right to a balanced and healthful ecology . . . concerns nothing less than self-preservation and self-perpetuation."[54]

C. The Subject of the Trust — the "Res" or "Corpus"

Public trust doctrine case law has expanded "the trust" far beyond navigable waters. Beginning with the proposition that "the essential feature of the public trust [is] the right of the people to have the waters protected for their use," the Supreme Court of Hawaii, in *In re Water Use Permit Applications,* 9 P.3d 409, 458 (Haw. 2000), went a step further and held "the state water resources trust . . . demands adequate provision for traditional and customary Hawaiian rights, wildlife, maintenance of ecological balance and scenic beauty, and the preservation and enhancement of the waters for various uses in the public interest." The "body" of the trust (*corpus* is Latin for "body") has traditionally been described as the property protected by the trust. Also known as the *trust res,* through the judicial development of the public trust doctrine, the corpus has been recognized to include legal rights.

Some cases have cast the subject of the trust in terms of the current and future condition of the environment as an ecological whole. In *Robinson Twp., Washington Cty. v. Commonwealth,* 83 A.3d 901, 955 (Pa. 2013), the court found that "the concept

[52] George Washington's Circular Letter of Farewell to the Army (June 8, 1783).

[53] *Reliance Natural Res., Ltd. v. Reliance Indus., Ltd.*, (2010) I.N.S.C. 374, pt. IV, para. 94 (India), http://www.indiankanoon.org/doc/1070490.

[54] *Minors Oposa,* 33 I.L.M. at 187-188.

of public natural resources includes not only state-owned lands, waterways, and mineral reserves, but also the resources that implicate the public interest, such as ambient air, surface and groundwater, wild flora, and fauna (including fish) that are outside the scope of purely private property." Similarly, in *Just v. Marionette County,* 56 Wis. 2d 7, 16-17 (1972), the court explained the development of the breadth of the public trust doctrine in relation to advancements in scientific understandings of complex and interrelated ecosystems:

> The state of Wisconsin under the trust doctrine has a duty to eradicate the present pollution and to prevent further pollution in its navigable waters . . . What makes this case different from most condemnation or police power zoning cases is the interrelationship of the wetlands, the swamps and the natural environment of shorelands to the purity of the water and to such natural resources as navigation, fishing, and scenic beauty. Swamps and wetlands were once considered wasteland, undesirable, and not picturesque. But as the people became more sophisticated, an appreciation was acquired that swamps and wetlands serve a vital role in nature, are part of the balance of nature and are essential to the purity of the water in our lakes and streams. Swamps and wetlands are a necessary part of the ecological creation and now, even to the uninitiated, possess their own beauty in nature."[55]

Professor Wood's *Nature's Trust* paradigm supports a similarly broad application of the public trust doctrine. She argues for a holistic conception of the *res,* or subject of the trust, that "[encompasses] all natural assets and ecology."[56] This approach, she argues, "brings the public trust doctrine in alignment with Nature's own laws and resurrects the original doctrine with the range necessary to carry out its purpose not only for this generation, but also for those to come."[57]

D. The Fiduciary Duty: To Sustain the Welfare of Current and Future Generations

Once the government is established as a trustee, present and future people as the beneficiaries, and balanced and healthy systems as the subject of the trust, the last component to determine is the *fiduciary duty.* Courts have considered what fiduciary duty entails in many contexts: attorney-client disputes, financial advisor-customer disputes, insurer-policyholder disputes, and disputes in trusts and estates law.[58] While the description of the duties vary, in all contexts the duties owed to the beneficiaries are both procedural and substantive. Over thirty years ago, advocating for the concept of

[55] 56 Wis. 2d. at 16-17.

[56] Wood, *supra* note 47, at 144.

[57] *Id.*

[58] *See, e.g.,* Terry Jennings, *Fiduciary Litigation in Texas,* 69 Tex B.J. 844, 850 (2006) (discussing the rise in fiduciary break claims against attorneys); *see also* Arthur B. Laby, *Fiduciary Obligations of Broker-Dealers and Investment Advisers,* 55 Vill. L. Rev. 701 (2010) (discussing the fiduciary duties of broker-dealers and investment advisers); *see also Certain Interested Underwriters at Lloyd's v. Bear, LLC,* 259 F. Supp. 3d 1050, 1054 (S.D. Cal. 2017) (discussing a breach of fiduciary duty for insurance brokers).

a planetary trust, Professor Edith Brown Weiss put forth her vision of the government's duty that was based in part on the 1980 *World Conservation Strategy*:[59]

> The basic purpose of the [the Planetary Trust] is to sustain the welfare of future generations. This purpose can be broken down into three sub-purposes: to sustain the life-support systems of the planet; to sustain the ecological processes and environmental conditions necessary for the survival of the human species; and to sustain a healthy and decent environment.[60]

In *Nature's Trust*, written 20 years later with the environment substantially more degraded, Professor Mary Wood posits a more demanding duty than identified by Weiss. She delineates six substantive fiduciary duties of a public trust trustee:

1) to protect the environment;
2) to conserve the "natural inheritance of future generations";
3) to maximize the "societal value of natural resources";
4) to restore the environment where it is degraded;
5) to "recover natural resource damages from third parties that injured the environment"; and
6) to refrain from privatizing the trust except in limited circumstances.[61]

Wood concludes with an inspiring vision of a nature's trust concept:

> If citizen beneficiaries and courts hold public officials accountable to these obligations, environmental management will aim toward replenishment, rather than depletion, of the natural commonwealth—and the people's interests, rather than corporate interests, will rank supreme in ecological decision making. Viewed in aggregate, these obligations present a necessary paradigm shift in environmental law.[62]

Establishing a fiduciary duty to protect the Earth we live on today for sustainable life by future generations is an extraordinarily difficult legal objective, despite its conceptual existence since the time of the Roman Empire and in Indigenous customary law before then. As the law responds to the increasingly dire need for a legal solution that may protect the future of nations and their posterity, the development of the public trust doctrine into a nature's trust or planetary trust can play a meaningful role.

[59] 1980 *World Conservation Strategy* states that "resource conservation has three specific objectives: (1) to maintain essential ecological processes and life-support systems; (2) to preserve genetic diversity; and (3) to ensure the sustainable utilization of species and ecosystems." World Conservation Strategy: Living Resource Conservation for Sustainable Development, pt. 1, para 7 (Int'l Union for Consv. of Nature and Natural Resources, ed., 1980).

[60] Edith B. Weiss, *The Planetary Trust: Conservation and Intergenerational Equity*, 11 Ecology L.Q. 495, 508-509 (1984).

[61] Wood, *supra* note 47, at 167.

[62] *Id.*

STUDY QUESTIONS

(1) In their articulation of the public trust, are the state supreme court decisions *In re Water Use Permit Applications; Robinson Twp., Washington Cty. v. Commonwealth; Marks v. Whitney; and Just v. Marionette County* cited above consistent with the International Union for Conservation of Nature Species Survival Commission's statement? What is at the core of these judicial opinions and the IUCN plea? How do they relate to protecting the rights of future generations?

(2) How do the statements made in these cases tie into Professor Brown's *Planetary Trust* and Professor Wood's *Nature's Trust* reviewed above? And how might this all tie into the fiduciary duty owed to future generations?

(3) How might a planetary trust be different in application if instead of the six substantive fiduciary duties delineated by Wood, there was only one: to conserve the natural inheritance of future generations? How might the "inheritance" be defined in practice?

V. CONSTITUTIONAL RIGHTS FOR FUTURE GENERATIONS

At the national level, Bolivia, Norway, and South Africa constitutionally recognize the rights of future generations to a healthy environment. The Constitution of Bolivia states: "Every person has the following fundamental rights . . . to enjoy a healthy environment, ecologically balanced and adequate for his wellbeing, safeguarding the rights of future generations." The Constitution of the Kingdom of Norway states: "Every person has a right to an environment that is conducive to health and to a natural environment whose productivity and diversity are maintained. Natural resources should be managed on the basis of comprehensive long-term considerations whereby this right will be safeguarded for future generations as well." The Republic of South Africa's Bill of Rights, found in Chapter 2 of its Constitution, provides that "Everyone has the right—to have the environment protected, for the benefit of present and future generations. . . ."

While the development of Earth law based on national constitutional recognition of rights of future generations may be more well-grounded than other approaches, it seems unlikely that the U.S. Congress will soon pass such an amendment. Nevertheless, there is ample opportunity to develop the rights of future generations in the state context.

A. U.S. State-Level Constitutional Rights for Future Generations

As discussed above, some state constitutions provide for protection of the environment for the current and future generations. Pennsylvania's Supreme Court interpreted its

Commonwealth's constitutional guarantee in *Pennsylvania Environmental Defense Foundation v. Commonwealth of Pennsylvania*, 161 A.3d 911 (Penn. 2017). The Court found that the state has a constitutional obligation to manage state parks and forests, including the oil and gas they contain, as a trustee, with present and future generations as the named beneficiaries of the trust. As part of the reasoning for its decision, the Court described the history and purpose of Section 27 as follows:

> That Pennsylvania deliberately chose a course different from virtually all of its sister states speaks to the Commonwealth's experience of having the benefit of vast natural resources whose virtually unrestrained exploitation, while initially a boon to investors, industry, and citizens, led to destructive and lasting consequences not only for the environment but also for the citizens' quality of life. Later generations paid and continue to pay a tribute to early uncontrolled and unsustainable development financially, in health and quality of life consequences, and with the relegation to history books of valuable natural and esthetic aspects of our environmental inheritance. The drafters and the citizens of the Commonwealth who ratified the Environmental Rights Amendment, aware of this history, articulated the people's rights and the government's duties to the people in broad and flexible terms that would permit not only reactive but also anticipatory protection of the environment for the benefit of current and future generations.[63]

During the case, a question arose as to whether Section 27 is self-executing, meaning whether the judiciary can enforce the provision without the aid of a legislative enactment. An amicus curiae in the case, the Republican caucus, argued that the rights enumerated in Section 27 are *not* self-executing and therefore needed implementing legislation to become effective for the benefit of current and future generations. However, the Court disagreed:

> There can be no question that the Amendment itself declares and creates a public trust of public natural resources for the benefit of all the people (including future generations as yet unborn) and that the Commonwealth is made the trustee of said resources, commanded to conserve and maintain them. No implementing legislation is needed to enunciate these broad purposes and establish these relationships; the [A]mendment does so by its own ipse dixit.[64]

This case set a precedent for applying the public trust doctrine to protect the rights of future generations at the state level in the United States. Federally, recognizing the rights of future generations has been more of a challenge.

B. U.S. Federal-Level Constitutional Rights for Future Generations

Unlike some other countries, the U.S. Constitution does not articulate a fundamental right for future generations to a habitable Earth. Nor has the Supreme Court yet found

[63] *Penn. Environmental Defense Fdn. v. Commonwealth of Penn.*, 161 A.3d 911, 918 (Pa. 2017).
[64] *Id.* at 937.

such a right arising from the Constitution. However, scholars[65] and litigators[66] alike have argued that the Fifth Amendment's Due Process Clause and Fourteenth Amendment's Equal Protection Clause require the federal government to uphold the right to a healthy environment, including a stable climate system, for both present and future generations.

"Future generations," as represented by guardian James Hansen, asserted their constitutional right to a stable climate in *Juliana v. United States.* However, the U.S. district court dismissed the case for lack of standing before ruling on whether future generations were capable of holding this right.[67] As long as lawyers continue litigating on behalf of future generations, opportunities to develop Earth law expand.

C. *Minors Oposa:* A Landmark Decision in the Philippines

As the constitutional embodiment of rights of future generations continues to progress, more courts will also examine the concept. The most deeply developed common law recognizing the rights of future generations is the Philippines Supreme Court's decision in *Minors Oposa v. Sec. of the Dept of Env. & Natural Resource.* This opinion provides an expansive and comprehensive interpretation of the rights of future generations to a healthy environment in the absence of any constitutional authority. In this case, the Philippine Supreme Court was presented with the question of whether the Philippine Constitution confers a right to a "balanced and healthful ecology" for not just the current generation of its people, but also future generations. The 2018 *Companion to Global Judicial Handbook on Environmental Constitutionalism: Selected Cases and Materials, Selected Edited Judicial Opinions from Around the Globe* provides a comprehensive edited version of *Minors Oposa,* which is excerpted below.

Juan Antonio, Anna Rosario and Jose Alfonso Oposa & Others v. The Honorable Fulgencio S. Factoran, Jr.

(Supreme Court of the Philippines, 1993)

The court recognized the principle of intergenerational justice and granted standing to petitioners, who represented their generation and generations of unborn Filipinos in a petition opposing timber license agreements.

[65] *See, e.g.,* Ylam Nguyen, *Constitutional Protection for Future Generations from Climate Change,* 23(1) Hastings West Northwest J. of Envtl. L. & Pol'y 183 (2017).

[66] *See* First Amended Complaint for Declaratory and Injunctive Relief, *Juliana v. United States of America,* Case No.: 6:15-cv-01517-TC (D. Or. 2015).

[67] *Juliana,* 9th Cir. at 21 (comparing *Clean Air Council v. United States,* 362 F. Supp. 3d 237, 250-253 (E.D. Pa. 2019) (finding no constitutional right), with *Juliana,* 217 F. Supp. 3d at 1248-1250; see also *In re United States,* 139 S. Ct. at 453 (reiterating "that the 'striking' breadth of plaintiffs' below claims 'presents substantial grounds for difference of opinion' ").

This petition bears upon the right of Filipinos to a balanced and healthful ecology which the petitioners dramatically associate with the twin concepts of "inter-generational responsibility" and "inter-generational justice." Specifically, it touches on the issue of whether the said petitioners have a cause of action to "prevent the misappropriation or impairment" of Philippine rainforests and "arrest the unabated hemorrhage of the country's vital life support systems and continued rape of Mother Earth."

The principal petitioners [include] all minors duly represented and joined by their respective parents, [and the minors] further asseverate that they "represent their generation as well as generations yet unborn." Consequently, it is prayed for that judgment be rendered:

... ordering defendant, his agents, representatives and other persons acting in his behalf to—

(1) Cancel all existing timber license agreements in the country;

(2) Cease and desist from receiving, accepting, processing, renewing or approving new timber license agreements. and granting the plaintiffs "... such other reliefs just and equitable under the premises."

The complaint starts off with the general averments that the Philippine archipelago of 7,100 islands has a land area of thirty million (30,000,000) hectares and is endowed with rich, lush and verdant rainforests in which varied, rare and unique species of flora and fauna may be found; these rainforests contain a genetic, biological and chemical pool which is irreplaceable; they are also the habitat of Indigenous Philippine cultures which have existed, endured and flourished since time immemorial; scientific evidence reveals that in order to maintain a balanced and healthful ecology, the country's land area should be utilized on the basis of a ratio of fifty-four per cent (54%) for forest cover and forty-six per cent (46%) for agricultural, residential, industrial, commercial and other uses; the distortion and disturbance of this balance as a consequence of deforestation have resulted in a host of environmental tragedies, such as (a) 15 water shortages resulting from drying up of the water table, otherwise known as the "aquifer," as well as of rivers, brooks and streams, (b) salinization of the water table as a result of the intrusion therein of salt water, incontrovertible examples of which may be found in the island of Cebu and the Municipality of Bacoor, Cavite, (c) massive erosion and the consequential loss of soil fertility and agricultural productivity, with the volume of soil eroded estimated at one billion (1,000,000,000) cubic meters per annum—approximately the size of the entire island of Catanduanes, (d) the endangering and extinction of the country's unique, rare and varied flora and fauna, (e) the disturbance and dislocation of cultural communities, including the disappearance of the Filipino's Indigenous cultures, (f) the siltation of rivers and seabeds and consequential destruction of corals and other aquatic life leading to a critical reduction in marine resource productivity, (g) recurrent spells of drought as is presently experienced by the entire country, (h) increasing velocity of typhoon winds which result from the absence of windbreakers, (i) the floodings of lowlands and agricultural plains arising from the absence of the absorbent mechanism of forests, (j) the siltation and shortening of the lifespan of multi-billion peso dams constructed and operated for the purpose of supplying water for domestic uses, irrigation and the generation of electric power, and (k) the reduction of the earth's capacity to process carbon dioxide gases which has led to perplexing and catastrophic climatic changes such as the phenomenon of global warming, otherwise known as the "greenhouse effect."

As their cause of action, they specifically allege that:

CAUSE OF ACTION

7. Plaintiffs replead by reference the foregoing allegations.

8. Twenty-five (25) years ago, the Philippines had some sixteen (16) million hectares of rainforests constituting roughly 53% of the country's land mass.

9. Satellite images taken in 1987 reveal that there remained no more than 1.2 million hectares of said rainforests or four per cent (4.0%) of the country's land area.

10. More recent surveys reveal that a mere 850,000 hectares of virgin old growth rainforests are left, barely 2.8% of the entire land mass of the Philippine archipelago and about 3.0 million hectares of immature and uneconomical secondary growth forests.

11. Public records reveal that the defendants' predecessors have granted timber license agreements ("TLA's") to various corporations to cut the aggregate area of 3.89 million hectares for commercial logging purposes. . . .

12. At the present rate of deforestation, i.e. about 200,000 hectares per annum or 25 hectares per hour—nighttime, Saturdays, Sundays and holidays included—the Philippines will be bereft of forest resources after the end of this ensuing decade, if not earlier.

13. The adverse effects, disastrous consequences, serious injury and irreparable damage of this continued trend of deforestation to the plaintiff minors' generation and to generations yet unborn are evident and incontrovertible. As a matter of fact, the environmental damages enumerated in paragraph 6 hereof are already being felt, experienced and suffered by the generation of plaintiff adults.

14. The continued allowance by defendant of TLA holders to cut and deforest the remaining forest stands will work great damage and irreparable injury to plaintiffs—especially plaintiff minors and their successors—who may never see, use, benefit from and enjoy this rare and unique natural resource treasure. This act of defendant constitutes a misappropriation and/ or impairment of the natural resource property he holds in trust for the benefit of plaintiff minors and succeeding generations.

15. Plaintiffs have a clear and constitutional right to a balanced and healthful ecology and are entitled to protection by the State in its capacity as parens patriae.

16. Plaintiff[s] have exhausted all administrative remedies with the defendant's office. On March 2, 1990, plaintiffs served upon defendant a final demand to cancel all logging permits in the country. . . .

17. Defendant, however, fails and refuses to cancel the existing TLA's to the continuing serious damage and extreme prejudice of plaintiffs.

18. The continued failure and refusal by defendant to cancel the TLA's is an act violative of the rights of plaintiffs, especially plaintiff minors who may be left with a country that is desertified (sic), bare, barren and devoid of the wonderful flora, fauna and Indigenous cultures which the Philippines had been abundantly blessed with.

20. Furthermore, defendant's continued refusal to cancel the aforementioned TLA's is contradictory to the Constitutional policy of the State to—a. effect "a more equitable distribution of opportunities, income and wealth" and "make full and efficient use of natural resources (sic)." (Section 1, Article XII of the Constitution); b. "protect the nation's marine wealth." (Section 2, ibid); c. "conserve and promote the nation's cultural heritage and resources (sic)" (Section 14, Article XIV, id.); d. "protect and advance the right of the people to a balanced and healthful ecology in accord with the rhythm and harmony of nature." (Section 16, Article II, id.)

21. Finally, defendant's act is contrary to the highest law of humankind—the natural law—and violative of plaintiffs' right to self-preservation and perpetuation.

22. There is no other plain, speedy and adequate remedy in law other than the instant action to arrest the unabated hemorrhage of the country's vital life support systems and continued rape of Mother Earth.

On 22 June 1990, the original defendant, Secretary Factoran, Jr., filed a Motion to Dismiss the complaint based on two (2) grounds, namely: (1) the plaintiffs have no cause of action against him and (2) the issue raised by the plaintiffs is a political question which properly pertains to the legislative or executive branches of Government.

Petitioners contend that the complaint clearly and unmistakably states a cause of action as it contains sufficient allegations concerning their right to a sound environment based on Articles 19, 20 and 21 of the Civil Code (Human Relations), Section 4 of Executive Order (E.O.) No. 192 creating the DENR, Section 3 of Presidential Decree (P.D.) No. 1151 (Philippine Environmental Policy), Section 16, Article II of the 1987 Constitution recognizing the right of the people to a balanced and healthful ecology, the concept of generational genocide in Criminal Law and the concept of man's inalienable right to self-preservation and self-perpetuation embodied in natural law. Petitioners likewise rely on the respondent's correlative obligation per Section 4 of E.O. No. 192, to safeguard the people's right to a healthful environment.

This case, however, has a special and novel element. Petitioners minors assert that they represent their generation as well as generations yet unborn. We find no difficulty in ruling that they can, for themselves, for others of their generation and for the succeeding generations, file a class suit. Their personality to sue in behalf of the succeeding generations can only be based on the concept of intergenerational responsibility insofar as the right to a balanced and healthful ecology is concerned. Such a right, as hereinafter expounded, considers the "rhythm and harmony of nature." Nature means the created world in its entirety.

Such rhythm and harmony indispensably include, inter alia, the judicious disposition, utilization, management, renewal and conservation of the country's forest, mineral, land, waters, fisheries, wildlife, off-shore areas and other natural resources to the end that their exploration, development and utilization be equitably accessible to the present as well as future generations. Needless to say, every generation has a responsibility to the next to preserve that rhythm and harmony for the full enjoyment of a balanced and healthful ecology. Put a little differently, the minors' assertion of their right to a sound environment constitutes, at the same time, the performance of their obligation to ensure the protection of that right for the generations to come.

The locus standi of the petitioners having thus been addressed, We shall now proceed to the merits of the petition.

After a careful perusal of the complaint in question and a meticulous consideration and evaluation of the issues raised and arguments adduced by the parties, we do not hesitate to find for the petitioners and rule against the respondent Judge's challenged order for having been issued with grave abuse of discretion amounting to lack of jurisdiction. . . .

We do not agree with the trial court's conclusions that the plaintiffs failed to allege with sufficient definiteness a specific legal right involved or a specific legal wrong committed, and that the complaint is replete with vague assumptions and conclusions based on unverified data. A reading of the complaint itself belies these conclusions. The complaint focuses on one specific fundamental legal right—the right to a balanced and healthful ecology which, for the first time in our nation's constitutional history, is solemnly incorporated in the fundamental law. Section 16, Article II of the 1987 Constitution explicitly provides:

Sec. 16. The State shall protect and advance the right of the people to a balanced and healthful ecology in accord with the rhythm and harmony of nature.

This right unites with the right to health which is provided for in the preceding section of the same article:

Sec. 15. The State shall protect and promote the right to health of the people and instill health consciousness among them.

While the right to a balanced and healthful ecology is to be found under the Declaration of Principles and State Policies and not under the Bill of Rights, it does not follow that it is less important than any of the civil and political rights enumerated in the latter. Such a right belongs to a different category of rights altogether for it concerns nothing less than self-preservation and self-perpetuation—aptly and fittingly stressed by the petitioners—the advancement of which may even be said to predate all governments and constitutions. As a matter of fact, these basic rights need not even be written in the Constitution for they are assumed to exist from the inception of humankind. If they

> are now explicitly mentioned in the fundamental charter, it is because of the well-founded fear of its framers that unless the rights to a balanced and healthful ecology and to health are mandated as state policies by the Constitution itself, thereby highlighting their continuing importance and imposing upon the state a solemn obligation to preserve the first and protect and advance the second, the day would not be too far when all else would be lost not only for the present generation, but also for those to come—generations which stand to inherit nothing but parched earth incapable of sustaining life.
>
> The right to a balanced and healthful ecology carries with it the correlative duty to refrain from impairing the environment. . . . The said right implies, among many other things, the judicious management and conservation of the country's forests. Without such forests, the ecological or environmental balance would be irreversibly disrupted.

STUDY QUESTION

What might be the most promising ways to test U.S. state-level constitutional rights for future generations? To gain recognition of federal-level constitutional rights for future generations? To develop rights of future generations through common law in the United States?

VI. STANDING FOR FUTURE GENERATIONS CLAIMS IN THE UNITED STATES

As explained in Chapter 5, standing is a constitutional doctrine that determines whether an aggrieved person is allowed to bring a claim (i.e., "stand") before the court. Article III, Section 2, Clause 1 delineates only the substantive limits of "[t]he Judicial Power" of the federal court system as the adjudication of "Cases" and "Controversies" concerning "the Laws of the United States, and Treaties." From this basic limitation, the Supreme Court has developed the requisite elements of standing over time through its case law. By way of review, standing has three elements:

1. **Injury**: The plaintiffs' alleged injury in fact must consist of an invasion of a legally protected interest, which is (a) concrete and particularized, and (b) "actual or imminent, not 'conjectural' or 'hypothetical.'" According to the Supreme Court, the element of "injury in fact" is a "hard floor of Article III jurisdiction that cannot be removed by statute."[68]
2. **Causation**: The plaintiff must allege a causal connection between the injury and the conduct complained of—the injury has to be fairly traceable to the

[68] *Summers v. Earth Island Inst.*, 555 U.S. 488, 497 (2009).

challenged action of the defendant, and not the result of the independent action of some third party not before the court.[69]

3. **Redressability**: It must be "likely," as opposed to merely "speculative," that the injury will be "redressed by a favorable decision."[70]

The requirement of standing "tends to assure that the legal questions presented to the court will be resolved, not in the rarified atmosphere of a debating society, but in a concrete factual context conducive to a realistic appreciation of the consequences of judicial action."[71] This section explores the challenges and potential that an Earth law practitioner representing future generations faces with respect to each of these elements.

A. Injury in Fact

The injury to a future generation plaintiff is the damage and destruction of the Earth's life-sustaining biosphere. As we explored earlier, that injury might rest on claims that the government body(ies) breached their fiduciary duties to protect natural resources under the public trust doctrine. The injury might likewise be asserted as a violation of constitutional rights. Either way, it is imperative for an attorney to plead a cognizable injury in fact to future generations for purposes of Article III standing. Challenges to meeting this first element of the standing test include establishing the environmental harm or imminent threat to an ecosystem as an "injury in fact" and proving the injury within the plaintiff's lifetime.

Attorneys for future generation plaintiffs can learn from the difficulties that members of the present generation have had establishing an injury in fact in the context of Article III standing. For example, establishing that an injury is sufficiently "imminent" to constitute an injury in the Article III context requires a plaintiff to establish that it will occur within their lifetime. In *Lujan v. Defenders of Wildlife*, 504 U.S. 555 (1992), the Court ruled that the plaintiffs had not shown how extinction of endangered animals would produce any imminent injury to the plaintiff since they did not have any definite, concrete plans to return to the countries and native habitats of the animals.[72] In 2004, the Eighth Circuit in *Shain v. Veneman*, 376 F.3d 815, 818 (8th Cir. 2004) found that the plaintiff lacked standing to challenge the building of a sewage-treatment plant on a 100-year flood plain because the possibility of a 100-year flood was not an "imminent harm." In so holding, the court stated: "If the possibility of a 100-year flood is remote in the abstract, the possibility the flood will occur while [the plaintiffs] own or occupy the land becomes a matter of sheer speculation. Indeed, one wonders whether any of the parties (or the court) in this case will be alive the next time a 100-year flood occurs upon the land."

[69] *Lujan v. Defs. of Wildlife*, 504 U.S. 555, 560-561 (1992).

[70] *Id.*

[71] *Valley Forge Christian Coll. v. Americans United for Separation of Church & State, Inc.*, 454 U.S. 464, 472, (1982).

[72] *Lujan*, 504 U.S. at 564.

The Supreme Court has consistently recognized that threatened rather than actual injury can satisfy Article III standing requirements.[73] In *Friends of the Earth v. Laidlaw*, the Supreme Court held that the *threat* of injury in fact is sufficient to confer standing and that citizen affidavits attesting to reduced use of a waterway out of reasonable fear and concern of pollution.[74] Relying on Laidlaw, in *Ecological Rights Foundation v. Pac. Lumber*, 230 F.3d 1141, 1148 (9th Cir. 2000), the court of appeals wrote that that "the 'injury in fact' requirement in environmental cases is not... reducible to inflexible, judicially mandated time or distance guidelines, as *Laidlaw* makes clear."[75] Finally, in *Friends of the Earth, Inc. v. Gaston Copper Recycling Corp.*, 204 F.3d 149, 160 (4th Cir. 2000), the court found that a threatened injury arising from water pollution was enough to establish injury in fact. "[A plaintiff] need not wait until his lake becomes barren and sterile or assumes an unpleasant color and smell before he can invoke the protections of the Clean Water Act."[76]

However, while severe damage to ecosystems—from neighborhood wetlands to vast national forests—will occur within the lifetimes of future generations, will the courts be able to say a harm is "actual and imminent" when the lifetime of the plaintiff has not even begun? Turning back to *Juliana*, although Court of Appeals for the Ninth Circuit did not address this issue directly, it did agree with the plaintiffs that "... the federal government has long promoted fossil fuel use despite knowing that it can cause catastrophic climate change ...". It also found that the injury requirement was met for "at least some plaintiffs," such as one who was forced to leave her home due to water scarcity. However, the court did not specifically address the injury to future generations.

In practice, tying the harms of future generations to those harms faced by current generations seems to be a viable solution. In *Mass. v. EPA*, the Supreme Court considered affidavits alleging future harm to the state of Massachusetts through the year 2100 from climate change, which of course would implicate future generations. "The severity of that injury will only increase over the course of the next century: If sea levels continue to rise as predicted, one Massachusetts official believes that a significant fraction of coastal property will be 'either permanently lost through inundation or temporarily lost through periodic storm surge and flooding events.' "[77] The Court then tied this future harm to current harm, finding that "at least according to petitioners' uncontested affidavits—the rise in sea levels associated with global warming has already harmed and will continue to harm Massachusetts. The risk of catastrophic harm, though remote, is nevertheless real."[78] In this case, arguing that environmental harms impact both present and future generations seemed to work in practice.

[73] *See, e.g., Valley Forge*, 454 U.S. at 472; *Gladstone Realtors v. Vill. of Bellwood*, 441 U.S. 91, 99 (1979).
[74] *Id.* (emphasis supplied).
[75] *Id.* at 1151.
[76] *Id.*
[77] *Massachusetts v. EPA*, 549 U.S. 497, 522-523 (2007).
[78] *Id.* at 526.

STUDY QUESTIONS

(1) The Eighth Circuit's *Shain v. Veneman* decision demonstrates what might be described as "gatekeeping" of scientific evidence by the judiciary. In *Shain v. Veneman,* how could that court know, particularly in light of climate change, when the area would or would not flood?

(2) In *Lujan,* on what basis does the Court conclude that species extinction and damage to ecosystems (in itself) has no perceptible effect on human plaintiffs? Does the opinion reflect an understanding or appreciation of ecology? Why or why not? How might a court have considered these cases applying the precautionary principle?

(3) In the United States, an individual state possesses quasi-sovereign interests and, as such, can bring suits by acting as *parens patriae* (Latin for "parent of the nation in law") on behalf of its citizens. This legal doctrine may permit a state's attorney general to present a cognizable claim to protect future generations. Do you think a state government can adequately represent the interests of future generations? If not, who should have that responsibility?

B. Causation: Injury Fairly Traceable to Challenged Conduct

The second element of the standing test examines the connection between the alleged misconduct and the injury. The chain of causation for a future generation plaintiff rests on the core allegation that the government, by failing to protect the Earth's biosphere, has breached its fiduciary duty to protect the subject of the trust pursuant to the public trust doctrine. In so doing, the government has also violated the fundamental rights of current and future generations to a habitable Earth (at least and perhaps only within its national borders). In addition to presenting evidence of harmful conduct that ties injury to current and future generations together, meeting the causation element of the standing test may require closely tracing the present conditions complained of into the future.

Establishing that the injury to future generations is "fairly traceable to the challenged conduct," is the intergenerational connection discussed under the "injury in fact" element applied in the causation context. Antonio Oposa, the attorney who brought suit on behalf of himself, his children (Minors Oposa), and others, including "unnamed children of the future," provided the Philippines Supreme Court with Brown Weiss's *Intergenerational Equity* article as "proof" that the legal concept of intergenerational equity was real.[79] Whether as a direct result of reading the article or not, the court's holding expresses the concept:

[79] Oliver A. Houck, *Light From The Trees: The Stories of Minors Oposa and The Russian Forest Cases,* 19 Geo. Int'l Envtl. L. Rev. 321, 335 n.111 (2007).

> the right to a balanced and healthful ecology belongs to a different category of rights altogether for it concerns nothing less than self-preservation and self-perpetuation . . . Without "a balanced and healthful ecology," future generations "stand to inherit nothing but parched earth incapable of sustaining life;" moreover, "the right to a balanced and healthful ecology carries with it the correlative duty to refrain from impairing the environment.[80]

In the context of tracing the challenged conduct to future generations' injuries, the degree of difficulty will increase the farther into the future the future generations' claims extend. One way to establish how future harm may be connected to present-day wrongs is to rely on what science can reasonably estimate. In *Daubert v. Merrell Dow Pharmaceuticals, Inc.*,[81] the Supreme Court established what is now known as the "Daubert standard" for courts to use in assessing the reliability of scientific evidence. The key factors include: 1) Whether the expert's technique or theory can be or has been tested—that is, whether the expert's theory can be challenged in some objective sense, or whether it is instead simply a subjective, conclusory approach that cannot reasonably be assessed for reliability; 2) whether the technique or theory has been subject to peer review and publication; the known or potential rate of error of the technique or theory when applied; 3) the existence and maintenance of standards and controls; and 4) whether the technique or theory has been generally accepted in the scientific community.[82]

In the context of recognizing the causal connections between present actions and the effects on future generations, current science on the impacts of present actions on the future might allow courts to consider the interests of the future generations claimant within the next hundred years. The United Nations Intergovernmental Panel on Climate Change (IPCC), which draws on expert opinions from around the world, has made detailed estimates and projections concerning climate change through the year 2100.[83] In finding "the risk of catastrophic harm, though remote, is nevertheless real," the Supreme Court in *Mass. v. EPA* relied on the work of the IPCC in recognizing the harm, demonstrated through climate modeling, facing the petitioner over the next 100 years.[84]

C. Redressability — Will Judicial Relief Requested Relieve the Harm

The third element of the standing test is redressability. Under this element, an attorney representing future generations must establish the connection between the alleged injury and the requested judicial relief. To establish Article III redressability, the plaintiffs must show that the relief they seek is both (1) substantially likely to redress their

[80] *Id.* at 188.
[81] *Daubert v. Merrell Dow Pharmaceuticals, Inc.*, 509 U.S. 579 (1993).
[82] *Id.* at 592-595.
[83] Climate Model: Temperature Change (Hadley b1): 1870-2100, NOAA, https://sos.noaa.gov/datasets/climate-model-temperature-change-hadley-b1-1870-2100/ (last visited on Nov. 26, 2019) (data from three of the IPCC models tracks the temperature change from 1870 to 2100).
[84] *Mass. v. EPA*, 549 U.S. 497 (2007).

injuries; and (2) within the court's power to award. Redress need not be guaranteed, but it must be more than "merely speculative."[85]

In addition, the redressability element can be met by showing that the requested remedy would slow or reduce the alleged injury. As explained in *Mass. v. EPA*, "while it may be true that regulating motor-vehicle emissions will not by itself reverse global warming, it by no means follows that we lack jurisdiction to decide whether EPA has a duty to take steps to slow or reduce it."[86]

The recent Ninth Circuit decision in *Juliana* held that the plaintiffs did not meet this second prong of "establishing that the specific relief they seek is within the power of an Article III court." The court reasoned:

> There is much to recommend the adoption of a comprehensive scheme to decrease fossil fuel emissions and combat climate change, both as a policy matter in general and a matter of national survival in particular. But it is beyond the power of an Article III court to order, design, supervise, or implement the plaintiffs' requested remedial plan. As the opinions of their experts make plain, any effective plan would necessarily require a host of complex policy decisions entrusted, for better or worse, to the wisdom and discretion of the executive and legislative branches."

As explained in this section, Article III standing requirements and the jurisprudential considerations that have been developed through the arc of application of this constitutional law present challenges to Earth law practitioners who represent future generations claimants. They may be difficult to overcome; however, encouragement directly from the Supreme Court lies in Chief Justice Marshall's statement in *Marbury v. Madison,* 5 U.S. 137 (1803): "It is emphatically the province and duty of the judicial department to say what the law is." Dismissing a case based on the standing doctrine is a means for a court to avoid saying what the law is. If the time comes that the Supreme Court determines that it is up to the judiciary to exercise its constitutional power to protect the nation, and its people, present and future, from further destruction of Earth's sustaining power, it will discern that the rights of future generations lies in the Founding Fathers' original intent, or will through other means of judicial construction recognize the existence of these rights.

STUDY QUESTIONS

(1) Consider the additional issue that would have been presented if the youth and future generation plaintiffs in *Juliana* were joined by a state. Recall the majority opinion's distinguishing *Juliana* from the *Mass v. EPA* decision:

> That case, however, involved a procedural right that the State of Massachusetts was allowed to assert "without meeting all the normal standards for redressability;" in that context, the Court found redressability because "there [was] some possibility

[85] *Lujan,* 504 U.S. at 561.
[86] 549 U.S. at 525.

that the requested relief [would] prompt the injury-causing party to reconsider the decision that allegedly harmed the litigant." [Citation omitted.] The plaintiffs here do not assert a procedural right, but rather a substantive due process claim."[87]

(2) Decisions based on the technical legal criteria for standing can be viewed as form over substance. In the context of claims by future generations, what judicial objectives are served by adherence to formality? What arguments might persuade a court that the benefit of considering a future generations claim on the merits requires an exception to the adherence to legal formalities?

VII. CONCLUSION

Future generations face an existential threat—the damage and destruction of the Earth's life-sustaining systems. As explored in this chapter, a legally cognizable injury can rest on claims that governments have breached their fiduciary duties to the governed as is established by the public trust doctrine; the injury might concurrently be asserted as a violation of fundamental rights to life, liberty, or the pursuit of happiness under the due process clauses.

Many judges will agree with the proposition that both sovereigns and private actors should act to preserve our planet for the health and well-being of future generations. Yet, it will difficult to find judges who will impose duties on sovereigns and private actors based on the rights of, or a duty of care owed to, future generations. Federal courts in the United States continue to defer to the political branches of government and continue to interpret the Article III standing elements as a barrier to plaintiffs seeking to protect the environment for present and future generations. Compounding this problem is the federal judiciary's hesitancy to interpret its constitutional embedded power to balance that of the legislative and executive branches.

Advancing the application of the public trust doctrine to protect future generations will require lawyers to convince judges to embrace the wisdom reflected in Indigenous customary law and culture and what modern science has established through ecology and other disciplines—all life on Earth is interconnected with the Earth systems that created life. As observed in the CLI Paper on Intergeneration Justice: "The planet earth does not suffer and submit beyond a point. Thereafter, it rejects species that do not comply with its rules, which supervene all legal systems. The earth is the ultimate court of appeals."[88]

[87] *Juliana*, 9th Cir. at 572.

[88] Burns H. Weston & Tracy Bach, *Recalibrating the Law of Humans with the Laws of Nature: Climate Change, Human Rights, and Intergenerational Justice*, xi (2009).

CHAPTER 9

The Rights of Nature Movement in the United States[1]

I. INTRODUCTION

Traditional legal practice models do not prepare lawyers to practice law in a way that changes the law. One way that Earth law is being developed is by practitioners who work within social movements seeking systemic change, namely, changing ecosystems and other parts of the natural world from property to beings with rights.

The development of rights for nature in the United States is starting at the grassroots: in townships, cities large and small, and counties. It is now building toward state-level lawmaking, even while opposed by powerful corporate special interests. This chapter examines strategy, tactics, and skills that have been utilized to develop rights of nature law in the United States through movement lawyering. It considers how rights of nature in the United States may follow the course of the development of the rights of corporations, which once were as rightless as nature is today, and how corporations exercise the rights they now have to thwart efforts to grant rights to nature. It will also examine rights of nature expressed in the laws of Native American nations.

II. HOW DID WE GET HERE?

Like its European antecedents, U.S. law reflects the concept of human exceptionalism and dominion over nature. The U.S. legal system is based on federal supremacy and the protection of individual property. The capitalistic economy developed based on the belief that there will always be enough "natural resources" to support "economic growth."[2] These foundational principles reflect the rootstock of the United States' legal system, which values nature as a tradeable commodity based on its economic

[1] Authored by Elizabeth M. Dunne and Lindsey Schromen-Wawrin, attorneys in private practice who have litigated several cases on behalf of ecosystems.

[2] The term "natural resources" is ingrained in our legal culture and has long been a matter of common usage. Viewing nature as resources, and only in that way, is anathema to Earth law. Similarly, Earth law does not abide measuring wealth and economic achievement solely by calculation of gross domestic product.

worth.[3] In stark contrast, Earth law does not treat nature merely as property, rather it recognizes value in nature itself.

A. The Colonial Legacy

How did we get here? Beginning in the late-fifteenth century, European explorers claimed sovereignty and ownership over the "New World"—already inhabited by millions of Indigenous Americans—based on the assumption that the Earth was human property to be acquired through conquest or bargained for and exploited for economic gain and national pride. Under the Doctrine of Discovery,[4] the land was theirs for the taking. They killed and displaced Indigenous people. Needing labor, they kidnapped, enslaved, and killed Africans. The legal system that Europeans brought to the "New World" protected their right to claim its land as their own and validated genocide, slavery, and plunder of the environment.

The U.S. Constitution enshrined strong protections for commerce and property rights. The Contract and Commerce Clauses protect private agreements and the flow of commerce. The Bill of Rights, which was fashioned to protect individual freedom against governmental tyranny, particularly safeguards private property. These bedrock legal principles all foster economic growth through private endeavor. With these protections in place, a vast expanse of resource-rich lands to the West, and a history built on conquest and colonialism as a legal right (and, through the eyes of the church, a moral right), the United States grew with little protection for nature. Environmental laws enacted in the last 50 years have made environmental protection a national policy but left many gaps in coverage and enforcement (*see* Foreword and Chapter 1 – "History of Environmental Law").[5]

B. The Indigenous and Ecological Heritage

What one might consider the origins of Earth law depends on where one looks. Indigenous communities have practiced Earth law in the United States for centuries. Indigenous governance is at odds with the Western laws that settlers brought which uphold human rights to property without adequate concern for the rights of other members of the Earth community and our responsibilities to them.[6] The ancient wisdom of Indigenous people is an important part of Earth law.

[3] *See generally* BEN G. PRICE, HOW WEALTH RULES THE WORLD: SAVING OUR COMMUNITIES AND FREEDOMS FROM THE DICTATORSHIP OF PROPERTY (2019); JANE ANNE MORRIS, GAVELING DOWN THE RABBLE: HOW "FREE TRADE" IS STEALING OUR DEMOCRACY (2008); TERRY BOUTON, TAMING DEMOCRACY: "THE PEOPLE," THE FOUNDERS, AND THE TROUBLED ENDING OF THE AMERICAN REVOLUTION (2009).

[4] In *Johnson v. M'Intosh*, 21 U.S. 543 (1823), Chief Justice John Marshall explained the way colonial powers laid claim to lands belonging to foreign sovereign nations in the preceding centuries. Legal scholars are suspicious of Marshall's factual accuracy. *See, e.g.,* presentations by Stuart Banner & Lindsay Robertson, *Fact or Fiction?: The United States Courts' Use of History to Shape Native Law Jurisprudence*, NATIONAL MUSEUM OF THE AMERICAN INDIAN (Oct. 7, 2011), video available from http://americanindian.si.edu/connect/symposia/archive.

[5] *See generally* MARY CHRISTINA WOOD, NATURE'S TRUST: ENVIRONMENTAL LAW FOR A NEW ECOLOGICAL AGE (2013).

[6] *See generally* GUSTAVO ESTEVA & MADHU SURI PRAKASH, GRASSROOTS POST-MODERNISM: REMAKING THE SOIL OF CULTURES (1998).

For this reason, the development of Earth law in the United States does not have a simple linear history but rather continues to evolve through the melding of ancient wisdom with reawakened and newly found consciousness. The organization Honor the Earth describes how rights of nature brings these together:

> Since Indigenous communities constantly negotiate from a place of reduced efficacy, it is essential to identify methods of engagement that do not compromise Indigenous thought patterns while also providing better land protection. A movement that may allow this engagement is the advancement of the Rights of Nature.[7]

Ecologist Aldo Leopold in the 1940s was among the first non-natives to call for the rights of nature. His statement on this also shows how ancient insights and newly found consciousness come together:

> There is as yet no ethic dealing with man's relation to land and to the animals and plants which grow upon it. Land, like Odysseus' slave-girls, is still property. The land-relation is still strictly economic, entailing privileges but not obligations. . . .
>
> All ethics so far evolved rest upon a single premise: that the individual is a member of a community of interdependent parts. . . .
>
> The land ethic simply enlarges the boundaries of the community to include soils, waters, plants, and animals, or collectively: the land.[8]

There are many twentieth century authors, philosophers, and cultural historians who have led the way in re-thinking the human relationship with the natural world as reflected in our current legal system. Today, a growing body of lawyers and others—including many contributors to this book—carry forward their thinking by calling for systems change that would harmonize the legal system with the needs of nature.

This being said, because the United States adopted the framework of an English (settler) legal system, we have to address legal developments within that paradigm, as it is this paradigm that currently prevails.

III. MOVEMENT LAWYERING

A. Background on Movement Lawyering

Movement lawyering is a theory of legal practice in which lawyers work within (rather than for) social movements fighting for systemic change.

A traditional legal education teaches us to reify and enforce statutes, rules, and above all, case law. While these are important skills for practicing lawyers, ultimately, these laws are only some of the rules that govern human behavior. Cultural and social

[7] Honor the Earth, *The Rights of Nature*, www.honorEarth.org/Indigenous_rights [perma.cc/RER3-4APN].
[8] Aldo Leopold, *The Land Ethic* 1-3, 7, 10-12, *in* A Sand County Almanac (1949).

rules, "norms," govern human behavior as well. An underexplored but critical area of legal education is the origin of our legal structures and how those structures change based on these norms. Certainly, the law influences culture and society. But more often, the law is dragging behind social progress, with judicial opinions ultimately legitimizing a new norm that society has already accepted. Felicity Jones, playing Ruth Bader Ginsberg in the film *On the Basis of Sex* (2019), which tells the story of Ginsberg's early cases against gender discrimination, embodied this reality when she says to the court, "We're not asking you to change the country; that's already happened without any court's permission."

Purvi Shah, a leading theorist and practitioner of movement lawyering, and Chuck Elsesser, co-founder of the Community Justice Project, have critiqued the different legal models typically used to drive social justice. They describe the *civil legal-aid model,* which considers the lack of lawyers as the major problem with the legal system; the *test-case* or *impact litigation model,* which pursues systemic social change through carefully targeted class action litigation; and the *social-rescue model,* which believes that poverty is the result of the failure of social and other support services, including legal services.[9] Shah and Elsesser write the following criticism:

> The first two of these models believe in the underlying justness of the legal system—if you can simply have a lawyer to enforce the law, or have the right case argued to the right judge justice will result. The third model assumes that poor people . . . are simply "broken people" who need comprehensive services to be "fixed." Not one of these models takes into account the long-standing systems of class and racial discrimination and oppression, which have resulted in systemic powerlessness of whole communities. Many of the classic conflicts between organizers and traditional legal services lawyers can be attributed to this disconnect between their differing theories of social change. Traditionally, lawyers and organizers have vastly different analyses on why our world is the way it is.[10]

Shah and Elsesser then introduce their own model of community lawyering:

> We use legal advocacy to build the power of communities to challenge and eradicate these systems of inequality. In this model, rather than saviors or gatekeepers, lawyers are tacticians in the struggle for change. We call it community lawyering. . . .
>
> By using legal advocacy to support organizing, community education, and leadership development, community lawyering allows lawyers to have a much larger impact than any one lawsuit. . . .
>
> [W]e also believe that community lawyers must be engaged in a regular practice of self-scrutiny and self-reflection. If lawyers want to practice law in a respectful, responsible and accountable manner, we believe you have to be constantly evaluating your work to determine if it perpetuates racism, sexism, homophobia, classism and elitism. To that

[9] Joseph Phelan, *Purvi & Chuck: Community Lawyering,* ORGANIZING UPGRADE (June 1, 2010), http://archive.organizingupgrade.com/index.php/modules-menu/community-organizing/item/71-purvi-amp-chuck-community-lawyering [perma.cc/4UK4-57WU].
[10] *Id.*

> end, we believe that community lawyers should be engaged in a process of political study and growth collectively with organizers. Poor communities of color face multiple and intersecting injustices and good lawyering requires a deep understanding of race, class, and power. [11]

While Shah and Elsesser focus on economic and social justice, these frameworks also apply to environmental and ecological justice and the rights of nature.

B. Rights of Nature Movement Lawyering

Today, many organizations and networks participate in the movement in the United States to develop Earth law. Some of these organizations use strategies that can be described as movement lawyering. Not unexpectedly—in a legal system rooted in corporate rights, state and federal preemption, and, ultimately, human dominion over nature—this approach has faced strong pushback. But along the way, a blossoming grassroots movement has emerged, equipped with many lessons of how rights of nature can take hold in the United States.

Some of the organizations involved in the legal development of rights of nature in the United States include Earth Law Center, the Community Environmental Legal Defense Fund, Indigenous Environmental Network, Honor the Earth, Movement Rights, the Global Alliance for the Rights of Nature, Center for Earth Jurisprudence, Center for Environmental Ethics and Law, the Ecological Law and Governance Association, Boulder Rights of Nature, International Rivers, and the National Lawyers Guild's Environmental Justice Committee and National Lawyers Guild's International Committee's Environmental Human Rights Committee. These organizations are pursuing diverse strategies to catalyze the shift toward a legal system that incorporates Earth law. Many different approaches are being taken, each with strengths, weaknesses, and opportunities.

C. Federal Rule of Civil Procedure 11

Practitioners of movement lawyering in the U.S. rights of nature field may find themselves representing ecosystems in courts based upon relatively untested or unprecedented legal theories. Because representing ecosystems in court requires arguing for a good faith change in the law, Federal Rule of Civil Procedure 11 ("FRCP 11") and the Rules of Professional Conduct must be understood. Typically, lawyers make arguments in court based on the law at the time. However, the FRCP and state corollaries allow litigants to make "claims, defenses, and other legal contentions [that] are warranted... by a nonfrivolous argument for extending, modifying, or reversing existing law or for establishing new law." Fed. R. Civ. P. 11(b)(2). The 1993 Notes of Advisory Committee on Rules state:

[11] *Id.*

> Arguments for extensions, modifications, or reversals of existing law or for creation of new law do not violate subdivision (b)(2) provided they are "nonfrivolous." This establishes an objective standard, intended to eliminate any "empty-head pure-heart" justification for patently frivolous arguments. However, the extent to which a litigant has researched the issues and found some support for its theories even in minority opinions, in law review articles, or through consultation with other attorneys should certainly be taken into account in determining whether paragraph (2) has been violated. Although arguments for a change of law are not required to be specifically so identified, a contention that is so identified should be viewed with greater tolerance under the rule.

American Bar Association Model Rule of Professional Conduct 3.1 "Meritorious Claims & Contentions" similarly recognizes the value of good faith arguments for changes in the law. It reads, in part: "[a] lawyer shall not bring or defend a proceeding, or assert or controvert an issue therein, unless there is a basis in law and fact for doing so that is not frivolous, which includes a good faith argument for an extension, modification or reversal of existing law."

Because lawyers advocating for rights of nature are seeking to extend, modify, or reverse existing law, adversaries may rely on the threat of Rule 11 sanctions both to gain leverage and, if they are successful on the merits, to punish proponents of rights of nature. As explored below in Section VI, Federal Lawsuit for the Rights of the Colorado River Ecosystem, lawyers arguing for rights of nature face this risk.

IV. CASE STUDIES IN LOCAL LAWMAKING

Thus far, movement lawyering for the rights of nature in the United States has taken form largely through ordinances and resolutions at the local level—in townships, counties, and cities large and small. Advocates have also attempted to integrate rights of nature into state law.

Because of the federalized structure of the U.S. legal system, proponents of Earth law has the strongest legal authority if recognized through national constitutional-amendments and enforceable international agreements. However, in the face of inadequate federal action to protect the Earth, and based on the beliefs that the residents of local communities have a right to a healthy local environment and that nature has inherent rights, local governments have used legal theories that draw from local authority to develop Earth law in the United States. This local lawmaking follows a tradition of local grassroots movements based on a strong democratic ideal: the idea that a community should get to decide to make stronger laws to protect its land, water, and air, and its inhabitants' rights to live in a healthy ecosystem.

In addition, tribal nations have written and begun to enforce laws recognizing the rights of nature.

This section examines strategy, tactics, and skills that have been used in movement lawyering for the rights of nature in the United States.

A. Introduction to Local Rights-Based Lawmaking

Beginning in the early twenty-first century, the rights of nature movement took root at the local level, spearheaded largely by community groups, local governments, and supportive legal organizations like the Community Environmental Legal Defense Fund (CELDF).[12] Their approach has focused on passing laws recognizing human rights and ecosystem rights as superior to corporate interests. These laws address the injustice of corporations (a form of organized property) possessing enforceable rights while basic rights for ecosystems do not even exist.[13]

This strategy was based on the premise that conventional environmental law does not recognize a community's authority to say no to a federal or state permitted project. This meant that while administrative successes might stall a project (such as by denying a permit because of failure to follow NEPA or state corollaries), a business entity intent on a development project would eventually return with a completed permit application.

This approach reframed the problem from being one of pollution to one of corporate control over the community's ability to decide whether it can protect its own air, water, and soil. In other words, it's a democracy problem, not a pollution problem. In effect, this strategy attempts to move environmental law from a regulatory law framework of permits and administrative procedures, to a constitutional law framework of decision-making authority and rights. Thus, the problem was not merely corporate power, but the structure of law (legal principles such as the dormant commerce clause, Dillon's Rule, ceiling preemption, and corporate constitutional rights) that enables and authorizes that corporate power and prevents the people from having any say in their own communities' ability to expand their human rights and ecological rights.[14]

As a result, some of these local laws expressly limited corporate constitutional rights and asserted that the local law is not preempted by less protective state or federal laws. This strategy has sometimes resulted in aggressive pushback by corporate opponents. In some cases, opponents convinced courts to invalidate the local laws to maintain the paradigm in which corporate rights take precedence over the rights of communities and ecosystems. These cases provide the opportunity to consider whether the benefits of challenging the root problems outweighs the burdens of targeting corporate rights. The key argument for taking the more aggressive approach is that while there may be setbacks in the short run, it lays the foundation for future success. Historically successful rights movements have faced setbacks in the beginning when they challenged root problems.

[12] Both authors of this chapter have worked with the Community Environmental Legal Defense Fund to represent local communities enforcing rights of nature provisions in local laws.

[13] For discussion, see Erin Fitz-Henry, *Challenging Corporate "Personhood": Energy Companies and the "Rights" of Non-Humans*, 41 Political & Legal Anthropology Rev. 85 (Sept. 2018).

[14] *See generally* Community Environmental Legal Defense Fund, Community Rights Do-It-Yourself Guide to Lawmaking, https://perma.cc/HGQ8-XALF.

B. Grant Township, Pennsylvania

This section begins with a case study of a local Community Bill of Rights Ordinance passed by Grant Township in 2014, which included recognition of the rights of nature—including the rights of Little Mahoning Creek. As you read this section, consider some of the practical questions faced by lawyers representing an ecosystem, including: Who should be named as the party? How is that party represented, or, put another way, who speaks for the ecosystem? If the ecosystem has been damaged, how are the damages proved? What risks are presented making novel arguments and pressing those arguments if they have been rejected? The community of Grant Township adopted a community rights ordinance that included a recognition of rights of nature. Pennsylvania General Energy Company contested the validity of the ordinance and these practical questions were explored in the ensuing litigation.

1. Representing the Little Mahoning Watershed as an ecosystem

In 2014 and again in 2017, the Pennsylvania Department of Environmental Protection approved an application by Pennsylvania General Energy Company (PGE) and issued a permit for PGE to inject runoff from its fracking operations in a 7,000 foot-deep, abandoned well in Grant Township (the Yanity Well). The well is near Little Mahoning Creek. Residents of the tiny township, with a population of about 700, were concerned with the risks the project posed to their drinking water, their health, the creek, and its watershed. Grant Township adopted a community rights ordinance that included recognition of the rights of nature.

As to nature, the law provides: "Natural communities and ecosystems within Grant Township, including but not limited to, rivers, streams, and aquifers, possess the right to exist, flourish, and naturally evolve." After listing these rights, the ordinance also attempts to diminish federal, state, and corporate power when it conflicts with the protections for ecosystems and residents in Grant Township: "any state or federal authorization, through permit or otherwise, which would allow violation of the ordinance is invalid within Grant Township" and that "corporations violating or seeking to violate the ordinance, shall not be deemed legal 'persons.' "[15]

PGE filed a federal lawsuit to overturn the Grant Township Ordinance.[16] PGE claimed relief under 42 U.S.C. Section 1983 (the federal Civil Rights Law) because the ordinance deprived it of its constitutionally protected rights. It also claimed the Grant Township Ordinance was preempted by state law. Grant Township filed a counterclaim, alleging that PGE's lawsuit violated the township's people's rights to local community self-government as secured by the American Declaration of Independence, the Pennsylvania Constitution, the federal constitutional framework, and the Community Bill of Rights Ordinance itself.[17]

[15] Home Rule Charter of the Township of Grant, Indiana County, Pa. § 106, § 401 (2015), https://perma.cc/SY5N-9F9Q.

[16] *Pennsylvania General Energy Company, L.L.C. v. Grant Township*, No. 1:14-cv-209 (W.D. Pa. 2017) (hereafter, "General Energy case").

[17] Grant Township's Answer and Counterclaim in General Energy case, *supra* note 16, at Docket 10 (Oct. 13, 2014).

A nonprofit organization of township residents, the East Run Hellbenders Society (named after the hellbender salamander, which is native to the area), and the ecosystem in the township, the Little Mahoning Watershed, moved to intervene as real parties in interest.[18] PGE vehemently opposed the motion and argued:

> Watershed (the "Watershed"), allegedly, and the East Run Hellbenders Society, Inc. (the "Hellbenders") (collectively, the "Intervenors") seek to intervene in the above-captioned matter.... Incredibly, the Motion to Intervene seeks, apparently for the first time in American jurisprudence, for a condition of nature, in this case the Watershed, to intervene in a lawsuit.
>
> The Watershed does not meet the definition of a "person" under the Federal Rules of Civil Procedure, and lacks the most fundamental capacities necessary to be a participant in the judicial process. The Watershed is neither an appropriate candidate for party status in a court of law, nor feasibly represented. The Watershed obviously cannot consent to this intervention, cannot be a party to a lawsuit and cannot be provided the ethical protections represented parties are afforded by the Pennsylvania Rules of Professional Conduct....
>
> A watershed lacks consciousness, intelligence, cognition, communicability, or agency. A watershed can neither recall nor forget; neither articulate nor remain silent; neither agree nor dispute. The Watershed cannot decide to intervene, cannot accept representation or engage with counsel as a client, and cannot appear in court or testify. It cannot knowingly participate in the adversarial system of justice.[19]

The Little Mahoning Watershed replied to this specific argument:

> Adequate client representation is no joking matter, yet the irony here must be pointed out. PGE's lawyers represent a legal fiction, which is itself incapable of doing the things PGE's lawyers require an ecosystem to be able to do:
>
> A [business entity] lacks consciousness, intelligence, cognition, communicability, or agency. A [business entity] can neither recall nor forget; neither articulate nor remain silent; neither agree nor dispute. The [business entity] cannot decide to intervene, cannot accept representation or engage with counsel as a client, and cannot appear in court or testify. It cannot knowingly participate in the adversarial system of justice.
>
> Pennsylvania General Energy Company, L.L.C., a limited liability company, cannot do any of those things (its members, managers, and lawyers do them). Yet, we pretend that it is PGE acting. PGE's lawyers' argument is that our system of justice allows lawyers to accommodate legal fictions, but not accommodate the living ecosystems upon which we

[18] Federal Rule of Civil Procedure 24(a)(2) sets forth the standard for intervention as of right. It provides that:

> [o]n timely motion, the court must permit anyone to intervene who ... claims an interest relating to the property or transaction that is the subject of the action, and is so situated that disposing of the action may as a practical matter impair or impede the movant's ability to protect its interest, unless existing parties adequately represent that interest.

[19] Pennsylvania General Energy Company's Response to Motion to Intervene by East Run Hellbenders Society, Inc. and Little Mahoning Watershed at 1, 2, 4, in General Energy case, *supra* note 16, at Docket 45 (Dec. 8, 2014).

> all depend and within which we are a part, even when those ecosystems are recognized by law to have rights. If that is indeed true, then it is the greatest legal fiction of all.[20]

The District Court did not rule on whether the Little Mahoning Watershed was a proper party, and instead denied the intervention motion by holding that the Watershed's interests would be adequately represented by an existing party, the township. On appeal, the Third Circuit affirmed on the same grounds, and only addressed the ecosystem as a party separately in a footnote expressing doubt as to its capacity to sue or be sued as prescribed in FRCP 17(b).

> We do not see, however, how a watershed could be considered a proper party under Rule 17. Under that Rule, in order to be a party to a lawsuit, the purported litigant must have the capacity to sue or be sued. On this point, the rule speaks only in terms of individuals, corporations and others permitted by state law to sue or be sued. *See* Fed. R. Civ. P. 17(b). The plain language of Rule 17 does not permit an ecosystem such as the Little Mahoning Watershed to sue anyone or be sued by anyone, and for that reason alone we have misgivings with the Watershed being listed as a party in this litigation.[21]

Little Mahoning Watershed filed a motion for rehearing, arguing that FRCP 17(b) defers the question of who has capacity to the "law of the state" which requires finding that the Little Mahoning Watershed has capacity under the applicable law, namely, the Grant Township ordinance. In this motion, the proposed intervenors argued:

> The panel Opinion misreads Rule 17(b) to reach this conclusion. Rule 17(b) provides that "capacity to sue or be sued . . . for all other parties [not individuals or corporations, is determined] by the law of the state where the court is located." Courts apply local law, in addition to state law, when considering capacity under "the law of the state where the court is located." [Citation omitted.]
>
> Here, there is a law on point that provides ecosystems, such as the Little Mahoning Watershed, with the capacity to sue. The Ordinance provides "[a]ny action brought by either a resident of Grant Township or by the Township to enforce or defend the rights of ecosystems or natural communities secured by this Ordinance shall bring that action in the name of the ecosystem or natural community . . . ." App. at 38 (Ordinance § 4(c)). This is the relevant law for determining whether the Little Mahoning Watershed has capacity under Rule 17(b), and it clearly confers capacity on an ecosystem to defend its rights by appearing in court with the help of "either a resident of Grant Township or . . . the Township."
>
> The Federal Rules of Civil Procedure do not bar the ecosystem's participation in this suit.[22]

[20] Reply to Response to Motion to Intervene by East Run Hellbenders Society, Inc. and Little Mahoning Watershed at 10-11, (footnotes omitted), in General Energy case, *supra* note 16, at Docket 54 (Dec. 18, 2014).

[21] *Pa. Gen. Energy Co. v. Grant Twp.*, No. 15-3770, at note 2 (3rd Cir., July 27, 2016).

[22] Motion for Rehearing in *Penn. Gen. Energy Co. LLC v. Grant Twp.*, filed Aug. 10, 2016, in 3d Cir. No. 15-3770.

The Third Circuit denied the motion for rehearing.

The underlying litigation over Grant Township's Ordinance lasted over three years. While the Ordinance's rights of nature provision was not at issue, the court invalidated other portions of the Ordinance, namely the prohibition against the disposal of fracking waste, and ultimately agreed with PGE that the Ordinance violated some of its constitutional rights. The court's decision illustrates the challenges communities face when confronting corporate rights head on and in asking the courts to uphold laws that give more power to communities and ecosystems than corporations.

But, Grant Township's story does not end there. Shortly after the court invalidated portions of the Ordinance, the people of Grant Township enacted a Home Rule Charter by popular vote. The Charter contains the same provisions as the Ordinance. This time, the Pennsylvania Department of Environmental Protection sued the township alleging that state law preempted the Charter's prohibition against the disposal of fracking waste. The Commonwealth Court of Pennsylvania rejected the township's argument that the Charter was a valid exercise of the people's right to local self-government, but recognized that the township may be able to show at trial that the state laws at issue—the Oil and Gas Act and Solid Waste Management Act—and DEP's enforcement of these statutes, violate the Environmental Rights Amendment in Article 1, section 27 of Pennsylvania's Constitution and that they are therefore powerless to preempt the Township's Charter. A few weeks after the court's ruling, the DEP rescinded PGE's permit for the injection of fracking waste. In doing so, DEP recognized that the injection of oil and gas waste fluid into the well would violate the Home Rule Charter. It remains to be seen whether PGE will file its own lawsuit to challenge the Charter. In the meantime, the township has remained fracking waste free.

Communities and their lawyers should consider the risks versus rewards of laws that directly confront corporate rights, preemption, or both and the resources required to sustain what may become protracted litigation.

STUDY QUESTIONS

(1) Courts have considered the characteristics of being a legal person to include: (1) the ability to contract, (2) the ability to own property, (3) the ability to sue, and (4) the ability to be sued. What arguments might be made for and against holding nature legally accountable? How might a monetary judgment against an ecosystem be enforced? Where legal persons, humans, corporations, governmental bodies are members of an ecosystem, could they be held liable under rules of joint and several liability? Should ecosystems, if recognized as legal persons, be able to contract? To own property? How do they participate in a lawsuit if they cannot contract (e.g., agree to a settlement)? Should "legal person" be the concept that we try to fit ecosystems into, or do we need a new concept in the law to accommodate ecosystems?

(2) How does an ecosystem speak in court? For the Little Mahoning Watershed, the human residents of the ecosystem—members of the East Run Hellbenders Society—volunteered to speak for the ecosystem's interests. What other options are there for getting ecosystems heard in court?

For instance, in *Seneca Resources Corporation v. Highland Township* (W.D. Pa., No. 1:16-CV-289) and *Capri v. Jenkins* (Lincoln Cty., No. 17CV23360, filed June 6, 2017), human members of the ecosystem, independent of the intervening community groups, represented the best interests of the Crystal Springs Ecosystem and Siletz River Ecosystem, respectively. In such a case, the Ecosystem's rights and interests are advanced by persons focused solely on the Ecosystem's unique interests.

(3) If you were representing the Little Mahoning Watershed, would you have appealed the denial of its motion to intervene? Why or why not? Does your answer consider the interests of the Little Mahoning Watershed, as well as the movement as a whole? If those are in conflict, what legal advice would you provide? How can the client make the decision?

(4) In 2010, Pittsburgh, Pennsylvania, became the first large city to adopt a local ordinance recognizing the rights of nature by adopting Pittsburgh's Community Protection from Natural Gas Extraction Ordinance. Section 618.01 of the ordinance "bans commercial extraction of Marcellus Shale natural gas within the City of Pittsburgh. . . ." Section 618.023 explicitly recognizes rights of nature. Pittsburgh's law also purports to deprive corporate violators of existing legal rights conferred by federal or state law. Today, there are no gas wells within the Pittsburgh city limits. However, there are about 10,000 gas wells within the state, and large clusters of the wells lie in the city's suburbs, some within 4 miles of the city boundary. Why do you think this law has not been challenged? Do you think it will ever be enforced? If you could amend the law, how would you do so?

C. Lake Erie Bill of Rights, Toledo, Ohio

While many local governments passed laws recognizing rights for ecosystems in the years between 2006 and 2019, this grassroots movement gained global attention when the people of Toledo, Ohio, voted to adopt a Lake Erie Bill of Rights (LEBOR) into their city charter.[23]

[23] *See generally, e.g.*, Community Environmental Legal Defense Fund, *Rights of Nature, Episode 2*, video at youtu.be/-G8tHAkd1DM; Sigal Samuel, *Lake Erie now has legal rights, just like you: Ohio voters passed groundbreaking legislation that allows citizens to sue on behalf of the lake when it's being polluted*, Vox (Feb. 26, 2019), article and video at www.vox.com/future-perfect/2019/2/26/18241904/lake-erie-legal-rights-personhood-nature-environment-toledo-ohio [perma.cc/U384-UJHD]; or for a comedic take, Michael Kosta, *The Fight to turn Lake Erie into a Person*, The Daily Show with Trevor Noah (July 16, 2019), www.cc.com/video-clips/dh6i82/the-daily-show-with-trevor-noah-the-fight-to-turn-lake-erie-into-a-person.

LEBOR recognizes the rights of the Lake Erie Ecosystem in proclaiming that, "Lake Erie, and the Lake Erie watershed, possess the right to exist, flourish and naturally evolve."[24] It also recognizes that the people of Toledo have the right to a clean and healthy environment, including a clean and healthy Lake Erie. LEBOR prohibits any corporation or government from violating these rights. LEBOR states that the city or any city resident has standing to sue in state court to enforce these rights and prohibition. LEBOR also provides that Lake Erie itself may enforce its rights, as a named plaintiff and real party in interest, through a suit brought by the city or any resident of the city. A corporation or government that violates LEBOR's rights or prohibition provisions is subject to criminal fines and strict liability for all harms resulting from its violations, including damages for the cost of restoring Lake Erie.

The impetus for LEBOR, in 2014, was a harmful algae bloom caused by fertilizer pollution carried by runoff into Lake Erie. Toledo residents went three days without drinking water because the city's water intake in the lake was polluted.

The day after LEBOR passed, Drewes Farms Partnership, supported by industrial agricultural interest groups, sued the City of Toledo to attempt to overturn the law.[25] The complaint sought a declaratory judgment and injunction, arguing violations of the First, Fifth, and Fourteenth Amendments as well as preemption. The complaint included a plea for a civil rights attorneys' fee award—as a corporation seeking to defend its constitutional rights in a claimed Section 1983 action.[26]

Lake Erie Ecosystem (with rights recognized under the new charter amendment) and Toledoans for Safe Water (the community group that petitioned for the ballot measure) attempted to intervene under FRCP 24. The district court denied intervention on the grounds that Lake Erie Ecosystem did not have capacity to sue or be sued under FRCP 17, and that Toledoans for Safe Water did not have a substantial legal interest in defending the charter amendment, one of the FRCP 24(a) elements, because Toledoans interest was shared by the people of Toledo as a whole.[27] Meanwhile, the State of Ohio intervened in the trial court action against the City of Toledo.

Meanwhile, corporate interests took action against LEBOR in the state legislature. After the charter amendment passed, the Ohio Chamber of Commerce submitted a late addition to a budget bill to the state legislature, which promptly adopted it.[28] This legislation, now codified at O.R.C. § 2305.011, provided:

[24] The full text of the Lake Erie Bill of Rights charter amendment is available as document 1-1 in *Drewes Farms Partnership v. City of Toledo*, N.D. Ohio Case No. 3:19-cv-00434-JZ (filed Feb. 27, 2019), docket at www.courtlistener.com/docket/14573310/drewes-farms-partnership-v-city-of-toledo-ohio.

[25] *Drewes Farms Partnership v. City of Toledo*, Ohio, N.D. Ohio, 2019, No. 19-cv-00434, docket *supra*.

[26] *See* 42 U.S.C. § 1988.

[27] Order on Motion to Intervene, Doc. 23.

[28] H. Claire Brown, *How Ohio's Chamber of Commerce Killed an Anti-Pollution Bill of Rights*, The Intercept (Aug. 29, 2019), http://theintercept.com/2019/08/29/lake-erie-bill-of-rights-ohio [perma.cc/NZ5Y-LRWY].

Sec. 2305.011. (A) As used in this section:

1. "Nature" means the phenomena of the physical world collectively, including plants, animals, the landscape, other features and products of the Earth, the natural environment or wilderness, and generally areas that are not human or human creations, have not been substantially altered by humans, or that persist despite human intervention.
2. "Ecosystem" means a complex community of living organisms in conjunction with their physical environments, all interacting and linked together as a system through nutrient cycles and energy flows in a particular unit of space.

   b. Nature or any ecosystem does not have standing to participate in or bring an action in any court of common pleas.
   c. i. No person, on behalf of or representing nature or an ecosystem, shall bring an action in any court of common pleas.
      ii. No person shall bring an action in any court of common pleas against a person who is acting on behalf of or representing nature or an ecosystem.
      iii. No person, on behalf of or representing nature or an ecosystem, shall intervene in any manner, such as by filing a counterclaim, cross-claim, or third-party complaint, in any action brought in any court of common pleas.
   d. Nothing in this section shall be construed to prevent the state or any of its agencies from enforcing the laws pertaining to environmental pollution, conservation, wild animals, or other natural communities or ecosystems.

As the Ohio Chamber of Commerce lobbyist implied, this new state law was in direct response to concerns that policymaking like the Lake Erie Bill of Rights would spread, and that state preemption would be an effective tool to stop it.

Undeterred, three Toledo residents filed suit against the State of Ohio for violations of the Lake Erie Bill of Rights.[29] The trial court dismissed their action on the State's motion to dismiss. As they prepared an appeal, the federal district court decided *Drewes Farms Partnership v. City of Toledo*, on February 27, 2020, a year after the people had voted to enact LEBOR.

The federal district court ruled that "LEBOR is unconstitutionally vague and exceeds the power of municipal government in Ohio." The court explained:

> LEBOR's environmental rights are even less clear than the provisions struck down in [*Coates v. City of Cincinnati*, 402 U.S. 611 (1971), *Belle Maer Harbor v. Charter Twp. of Harrison*, 170 F.3d 553 (6th Cir. 1999), and *Springfield Armory, Inc. v. City of Columbus*, 29 F.3d 250 (6th Cir. 1994)]. What conduct infringes the right of Lake Erie and its watershed to "exist, flourish, and naturally evolve"? How would a prosecutor, judge, or jury decide? LEBOR offers no guidance. Similar uncertainty shrouds the right of Toledoans to a "clean and healthy environment." The line between clean and unclean, and between healthy and unhealthy, depends on who you ask. Because of this vagueness, Drewes Farms reasonably fears that spreading even small amounts of fertilizer violates

[29] *Ferner v. Ohio*, Lucas County Court of Common Pleas No. G-4801-CI-0201902904-000.

> LEBOR. Countless other activities might run afoul of LEBOR's amorphous environmental rights: catching fish, dredging a riverbed, removing invasive species, driving a gas-fueled vehicle, pulling up weeds, planting corn, irrigating a field—and the list goes on. LEBOR's authors failed to make hard choices regarding the appropriate balance between environmental protection and economic activity. Instead, they employed language that sounds powerful but has no practical meaning. Under even the most forgiving standard, the environmental rights identified in LEBOR are void for vagueness.[30]

In the state court lawsuit, the three Toledo residents filed their appeal anyway.[31] The Lake Erie Bill of Rights in Toledo, Ohio, put the concept of ecosystem rights into the mainstream. Once one can conceptualize a thing having rights, it is very difficult to go back.

D. Santa Monica, California

In 2013, Earth Law Center, Global Exchange, and other organizations and partners worked together to advocate for the first-ever West Coast rights of nature ordinance—the Sustainability Rights Ordinance in Santa Monica, California. This section explores its roots and discusses how its approach to rights of nature differs from the prior case studies.

In 2011, the City of Santa Monica Task Force on the Environment recommended that the city support and join the world-wide effort to address the mounting environmental crisis by recognizing the rights of people, natural communities and ecosystems to exist, regenerate and flourish in a sustainable environment.

The city council responded to the task force recommendation by unanimously adopting a resolution "Declaring the City's Commitment to Sustainable Rights."[32] Legislative findings supporting the resolution document the inadequacy of current environmental laws and the need for a paradigm shift to recognizing nature's rights. Further, the findings recognize the rights of the Santa Monicans to a clean and sustainable environment and expressly support "local recognition of the fundamental rights of natural communities and ecosystems to exist, thrive and evolve"[33] by "modifying local law and policy as needed to better protect and sustain, for current and future generations, the natural environment upon which we all depend."[34] In addition to adopting the resolution, the council directed city staff to prepare a Sustainability Rights Ordinance.

[30] *Drewes Farms Partnership v. City of Toledo, supra* note 23, at 5-6.
[31] Docket at https://bit.ly/39DzAwM.
[32] Santa Monica, CA, City Council of Santa Monica Declaring the City's commitment to Sustainable Rights (Jan. 24, 2012), https://www.smgov.net/departments/council/agendas/2012/20120124/s2012012408-B-1.htm.
[33] *Id.* § 2.
[34] *Id.* § 3.

The staff report concluded by proposing to highlight the city's commitment to sustainability rights for both humans and the natural world by creating a new article of the municipal code to collect and/or reference all of the city's existing environmental laws, which were scattered throughout the voluminous code, as well as environmental laws adopted in the future—the goal being to create a cohesive body of municipal environmental governance, readily accessible and available as a model for other cities.

The ordinance was adopted unanimously by the city council. Its legislative findings declare:

> Santa Monica's welfare is inextricably bound to the welfare of the natural environment; the expanding environmental crisis demonstrates the necessity of examining societal and legal assumptions about humans' relationship to the environment; and the rights of humans and natural communities and ecosystems must both be legally recognized.[35]

The substantive provisions of the ordinance recognize the "fundamental and inalienable rights of natural communities and ecosystems to exist and flourish"[36] and the rights of Santa Monica residents to clean marine waters, clean indoor and outdoor air, a sustainable food system, a sustainable climate, a flourishing biodiverse environment, waste systems that do not degrade the environment, and a sustainable energy future based on renewable energy. The ordinance requires a biennial report to the community and a public hearing on the state of the local environment, the realization of the rights secured by the ordinance, and the effectuation of provisions of the Sustainable City Plan. In March 2020, the city released its 2019 Sustainability Rights Report which includes its progress on various sustainability metrics that give effect to rights of nature.[37]

Santa Monica's resolution and ordinance do not purport to diminish corporate rights secured by state or federal law or to protect city laws against federal or state preemption claims. Instead, the ordinance provides that its several purposes include "to the full extent legally possible, subordinating the short term, private, financial interests of corporations and others to the common, long-term interest of achieving environmental and economic sustainability." Additionally, the ordinance provides that "corporate entities, and their directors and managers, do not enjoy special privileges or

[35] Santa Monica, CA, An Ordinance of The City Council of the City of Santa Monica Establishing Sustainability Rights (Apr. 9, 2013), https://www.smgov.net/departments/council/agendas/2013/20130409/s20130409_07A1.htm (hereafter, "Sant Monica Sustainability Rights Ordinance").

[36] Id, § 4.75.040(b).

[37] City of Santa Monica, Sustainability Rights Report: A Biennial Report of Ecosystem Health Metrics, https://www.smgov.net/uploadedFiles/Departments/OSE/Categories/Sustainability/SustainabilityProgressReport10.pdf. The report documented Santa Monica's long-standing commitment to environmental leadership, as evidenced by its creation and funding of a wide range of successful environmental programs, its successful utilization of environmental protection laws to hold polluters accountable for environmental damage, the City's adoption of numerous local environmental laws, and its adoption of the Sustainable City Plan in 1994. The report also highlighted the growing recognition, by the local environmental community and national environmental leaders, of the need to embrace the new approach of the nature's rights movement, "an approach that would recognize the rights of both humans and the natural environment to exist and flourish."

powers under the law that subordinate the community's rights to their private interests."[38]

Following its passage, the Sustainability Rights Ordinance was incorporated into the city's Sustainable City Plan as a guiding principle for administration of the plan. Additionally, the City Council created a new municipal code article devoted to environmental sustainability, with the Sustainability Rights Ordinance as its foundational introduction. Consistent with its decision to use the concept of nature's rights as a foundational principle for future environmental work, the next environmental ordinance adopted by the city (prohibiting private water wells), referenced the Sustainability Rights Ordinance as a policy basis for the new enactment. Santa Monica's ordinance recognizing nature's rights has enhanced the city and its inhabitants through its incorporation in existing environmental laws, policies and programs, as a guiding legal, philosophical and ethical principle that reinforces ecocentric awareness.

Consider how the different local rights of nature models differ. For example, compare the Santa Monica Sustainability Rights Ordinance to the Lake Erie Bill of Rights. One major difference is that Santa Monica's model does not limit corporate rights or fight permitted projects that cause pollution. For this reason, some rights of nature advocates felt the ordinance did not go far enough. But other advocates support this model because it can strengthen environmental protections and works to transform community consciousness without risking lawsuits for preemption or corporate rights violations. Another distinction is that the Sustainability Rights Ordinance applies to the jurisdiction of Santa Monica, whereas LEBOR sought to protect an entire watershed. It is important for Earth lawyers to understand the distinctions, and to think about new approaches, too.

STUDY QUESTIONS

(1) In promoting recognition of nature's rights, what are the advantages and disadvantages of local laws and resolutions, that proclaim aspirations, rather than establish prohibitions? How can such laws be effectuated? What factors might propel or impede the way resolutions and policy statements may lead to changed conditions on the ground?

(2) Governments often pass resolutions on topics of public concern: making a statement without creating law. A resolution is a useful tool for building awareness about the issue. The downside is that it does not create any enforceable law. A resolution might also expressly state that it will be followed by an ordinance. However, that provision itself is also unenforceable, and unless it is followed by strategic community organizing, resolutions often merely provide elected officials

[38] Sant Monica Sustainability Rights Ordinance, § 4.75.030.

with an opportunity to placate public pressure with words rather than deeds. What might lawyers do to promote the development of enforceable laws based on resolutions?

(3) In 2019, the town of Crestone, Colorado adopted a resolution recognizing that "the Town of Crestone does officially recognize that nature, natural ecosystems, communities, and all species possess intrinsic and inalienable rights which must be effectuated to protect life on Earth." While nonbinding, in what ways might you promote rights of nature in Crestone to ensure it is part of the community consciousness?

(4) The federal district court in *Drewes Farms Partnership* invalidated LEBOR for vagueness grounds. If those same provisions were part of the Ohio Constitution, how might that have impacted the consideration by the court? The people of Toledo adopted LEBOR as part of their City Charter; what are the arguments for and against interpreting the city charter provisions like constitutional text?

(5) What lessons can movement lawyers take from the *Drewes Farms Partnership* decision for: (a) legal strategy and (b) organizing strategy?

(6) How and why might the Earth law advocacy in Toledo, Ohio, and in Santa Monica, California, help or hurt the Earth law movement? In what other ways might movement lawyering contribute to the body of Earth law and the reformation of the legal system?

(7) What would your strategic and tactical advice be on how to advance the development of rights of nature if your client were: (a) the City of Santa Monica, (b) a community group in Santa Monica, (c) the City of Toledo, (d) a community group in Toledo? What legal advice would you give to an opponent of rights of nature in these communities?

V. DEVELOPING ECOCENTRIC LAW IN STATE CONSTITUTIONS

About fifty years ago, people in many states enacted Environmental Rights Amendments into their state constitutions. These amendments guaranteed humans' rights to a healthy environment. By way of example, the Constitution of Pennsylvania, Art. I, § 27, states:

> The people have a right to clean air, pure water, and to the preservation of the natural, scenic, historic and esthetic values of the environment. Pennsylvania's public natural resources are the common property of all the people, including generations yet to come. As trustee of these resources, the Commonwealth shall conserve and maintain them for the benefit of all the people.

While these provisions are important advances in human environmental rights, they do not extend the community of rights-bearing entities beyond people. In contrast, the recognition of nature's rights seeks, in the words of Aldo Leopold, to "enlarge[] the boundaries of the community to include soils, waters, plants, and animals, or collectively: the land." Human environmental rights and nature's rights are compatible advances in environmental and ecological justice. The mechanisms for their interaction and mutual reinforcement is an important consideration for the continuing development of Earth law. The proliferation of local lawmaking may stimulate additional state-level lawmaking to advance Earth law. Below are brief case studies of several of those campaigns.

A. Vermont

In 2012, Vermont was the first U.S. state where a group, the Vermont Rights of Nature Campaign, sought to establish an amendment to the Vermont constitution that would grant legal rights to Nature. A constitutional amendment has yet to take hold, but, so far, two Vermont municipalities have adopted resolutions urging the state legislature to amend the Vermont constitution to include rights of nature. The resolutions call for an amendment that would "recognize in the law the natural, inherent and inalienable rights of forests, natural areas, waterways, and fish and wildlife populations of Vermont to exist, thrive and evolve."

B. Colorado

Since 2014, Colorado organizers have pushed for a Colorado Community Rights Amendment to the Colorado constitution. The proposed amendment adds "Section 32. Right of Local Community Self-Government" to the Colorado constitution.[39] The proposed amendment includes in that right "the power of the people, and the power of their governments, to enact local laws that protect health, safety, and welfare by recognizing or establishing rights of natural persons, their local communities, and nature; and by securing those rights using prohibitions and other means deemed necessary by the community, including measures to establish, define, alter, or eliminate competing rights, powers, privileges, immunities, or duties of corporations and other business entities operating, or seeking to operate, in the community." The intent of the amendment to expand, and not restrict, rights is expressed in part 3(b) which says: "Such local laws do not weaken protections for natural persons, their local communities, or nature provided by state, federal, or international law."

[39] *See* proposed amendment text at Colorado Community Rights Network, *Colorado Community Rights Amendment*, https://cocrn.org/colorado-community-rights-amendment [perma.cc/5Y2R-G64J].

C. New Hampshire

In 2018, community organizers persuaded legislators to bring forward a resolution for a state constitutional amendment to recognize the right of local community self-government to establish, *inter alia*, rights of nature. A resolution was introduced, which if passed would put the proposed amendment on the general ballot.[40] The proposed amendment incorporates language from Article 10 of the New Hampshire Bill of Rights, enacted in 1784, which states:

> [Art.] 10. [Right of Revolution.] Government being instituted for the common benefit, protection, and security, of the whole community, and not for the private interest or emolument of any one man, family, or class of men; therefore, whenever the ends of government are perverted, and public liberty manifestly endangered, and all other means of redress are ineffectual, the people may, and of right ought to reform the old, or establish a new government. The doctrine of nonresistance against arbitrary power, and oppression, is absurd, slavish, and destructive of the good and happiness of mankind.[41]

The proposed resolution provided that: "the people of New Hampshire have an inherent and inalienable right of local, community self-government in each county, municipality, city, and town to enact local laws that protect health, safety, and welfare by recognizing or establishing rights of natural persons, their local communities, and nature." The proposed resolution also would have conferred on local communities the right to "establish, define, alter, or eliminate competing rights, powers, privileges, immunities, or duties of corporations and other business entities operating, or seeking to operate, in the community." The House of Representatives voted and deemed the proposed resolution "Inexpedient to Legislate."[42]

D. Oregon

Organizers in Oregon have advanced a similar state constitutional amendment by initiative.[43] Like with local lawmaking, the procedural mechanisms for lawmaking vary by jurisdiction. For example, both Colorado and Oregon have direct constitutional amendment by the people, while New Hampshire requires that proposed amendments originate in the state legislature.

[40] See specific bill text at www.gencourt.state.nh.us/bill_status/billText.aspx?sy=2018&id=1554&txtFormat=html[perma.cc/9AVK-SETS]; and see community advocacy at New Hampshire Community Rights Network, www.nhcommunityrights.org/state-constitutional-change.html [perma.cc/3VDU-UNWF].

[41] https://www.nh.gov/glance/bill-of-rights.htm.

[42] https://legiscan.com/NH/bill/CACR19/2018.

[43] The initiative text is available at: 2015 filing at http://egov.sos.state.or.us/elec/web_irr_search.record_detail?p_reference=20160030.LSCYYYSELF-GOVERNMENT [perma.cc/935B-W9EU], http://oregonvotes.org/irr/2016/030text.pdf [https://perma.cc/G4FH-28Q4]; the 2016 filing at http://egov.sos.state.or.us/elec/web_irr_search.record_detail?p_reference=20160055.LSCYYYSELF-GOVERNMENT, http://oregonvotes.org/irr/2016/055text.pdf [https://perma.cc/9KJS-DRXH]. *See also* Community Advocacy *at* Oregon Community Rights Network, http://orcrn.org.

STUDY QUESTIONS

(1) Many of these state constitutional amendments advance ecocentric law in connection with expanded local lawmaking power. What are the advantages and disadvantages to making that connection?

(2) How would you draft a state constitutional amendment to recognize earth rights? What would your amendment's strengths and weaknesses be?

VI. FEDERAL LAWSUIT FOR THE RIGHTS OF THE COLORADO RIVER ECOSYSTEM

In 2017, the nonprofit organization Deep Green Resistance filed a complaint in federal district court in Colorado, naming the Colorado River Ecosystem as plaintiff and the state and governor as defendants.[44] The relief sought includes a declaratory judgment that, among other things, the Colorado River Ecosystem possesses rights to: exist, flourish, regenerate, be restored and naturally evolve; protections of the Due Process and Equal Protection Clauses; and First Amendment protections, including the right to petition the government.

Unlike the Little Mahoning Watershed's attempt to intervene under the authority of an ordinance, the Colorado River Ecosystem filed suit based on the ecosystem's fundamental and inherent rights. It was the first lawsuit in the United States filed by an ecosystem without another plaintiff.[45]

The amended complaint asserted:

> [I]t is within the Court's authority to recognize that Plaintiff Colorado River Ecosystem enjoys rights, including those belonging to 'persons.' . . .
>
> Recognizing the Colorado River Ecosystem as a "person" is indeed no stretch at all. It is dictated by the logic that ecosystems are living, and that human life is inextricably intertwined with, and dependent upon, ecosystems. Honoring this symbiotic relationship is much more profound than the idea that corporations are made up of people and that they, therefore, enjoy many of the same rights.[46]

[44] *Colorado River Ecosystem v. State of Colorado*, No. 17-cv-2316 (D. Co.), at http://www.courtlistener.com/docket/6158241/colorado-river-ecosystem-the-v-state-of-colorado.

[45] Julie Turkewitz, "Corporations Have Rights. Why Shouldn't Rivers?" N.Y. TIMES, Sept. 26, 2017, https://www.nytimes.com/2017/09/26/us/does-the-colorado-river-have-rights-a-lawsuit-seeks-to-declare-it-a-person.html. *Cetacean Community v. Bush*, 386 F.3d 1169 (9th Cir. 2004), denied whales, dolphins, and porpoises statutory standing under several federal statutes (ESA, MMPA, NEPA, APA), but held that Article III constitutional standing did not bar the cetaceans from having standing (had they also had statutory standing). This case does not concern ecosystems as parties but is a useful analogy and precedent for getting past Article III.

[46] Amended Complaint, pages 19-20, ECF No. 19, filed Nov. 16, 2017, filed in *Colorado River Ecosystem v. State of Colorado*, No. 17-cv-2316 (D. Co.), available at http://www.courtlistener.com/docket/6158241/colorado-river-ecosystem-the-v-state-of-colorado.

The relief requested focused on obtaining a declaratory judgment from the court that:

> a. The Colorado River Ecosystem is a "person" capable of possessing rights;
>
> b. The Colorado River Ecosystem possesses the rights to exist, flourish, regenerate, be restored, and naturally evolve;
>
> c. That [Deep Green Resistance] members, Owen Lammers, Living Rivers Executive Director, and John Weisheit, the Colorado Riverkeeper, may serve as guardians, or "next friends," for the Colorado River Ecosystem;
>
> d. That Plaintiff Colorado River Ecosystem is protected by the Due Process and Equal Protection Clauses of the Fourteenth Amendment and the Petition Clause of the First Amendment of the U.S. Constitution; and
>
> e. That certain activities permitted by, or carried out by Defendant, may violate the rights of the natural communities creating the Colorado River, and that the Plaintiff may proceed to file for injunctive relief to enjoin Defendant from taking action related to those activities, or to force Defendant to take certain actions, as violations of the rights of Plaintiff Colorado River Ecosystem.
>
> 114. Plaintiff Colorado River Ecosystem further seeks to enjoin Defendant from continuing to violate its inherent rights to exist, flourish, regenerate, be restored, and to naturally evolve and its rights under the First and Fourteenth Amendments by failing to recognize its legal status as a "person."[47]

The State of Colorado, represented by the Office of the Attorney General, filed motions to dismiss, challenging the complaint on various constitutional and other grounds including, but not limited to, federal immunity, lack of standing, and lack of jurisdiction under a federal statute. Colorado also asserted that the complaint and amended complaint failed to present a justiciable legal issue and instead made a policy argument, which was more appropriate for legislative determination.

The attorney general then wrote a letter to plaintiffs' counsel, notifying him that she would seek sanctions based on the pursuit of frivolous claims unless the suit was withdrawn. Plaintiff's counsel agreed to dismissal and filed an "Unopposed Motion to Dismiss Amended Complaint with Prejudice,"[48] which stated:

> The Complaint represented a good faith attempt to introduce the Rights of Nature doctrine to our jurisprudence. The rights of nature—specifically, the legal standing of natural entities—was first recognized by the Honorable William O. Douglas in his dissent in *Sierra Club v. Morton* and is being increasingly utilized as a legal doctrine by countries around the world.

[47] *Id.* at 32-33.

[48] *Colorado River Ecosystem v. State of Colorado*, No. 1:17-cv-02316 (D. Colo. plaintiffs' motion Dec. 3, 2017; order dismissing case Dec. 4, 2017), http://www.courtlistener.com/docket/6158241/colorado-river-ecosystem-the-v-state-of-colorado.

The undersigned continues to believe that the doctrine provides American courts with a pragmatic and workable tool for addressing environmental degradation and the current issues facing the Colorado River.

That said the expansion of rights is a difficult and legally complex matter. When engaged in an effort of first impression, the undersigned has a heightened ethical duty to continuously ensure that conditions are appropriate for our judicial institution to best consider the merits of a new canon.

STUDY QUESTIONS

(1) Would you have brought this case on behalf of the Colorado River Ecosystem? If not, why not? If so, how would you have responded to the state attorney general's Rule 11 notice letter?

(2) Aggressive legal tactics, such as seeking sanctions against lawyers using new or emerging legal theories in defense of ecosystems and communities, should be anticipated. To some extent, violence may also be anticipated, especially in developing countries, as examined in Chapters 10: Human Rights and Rights of Nature: A Symbiotic Relationship, Chapter 18: Colombia, Chapter 19: Brazil and Mexico, and Chapter 25: Africa. Global Witness, founded in 1993, a pioneering NGO in seeing the link between natural resources, conflict and corruption, found that an environmental defender is murdered almost every other day on average.[49] What impact does the strong pushback against environmental defenders, including lawyers, have on the overall movement to protect the environment? What risks would you take in order to develop Earth law?

(3) What are the advantages and disadvantages to ecosystems appearing in court when recognized by a statute or ordinance, versus based on an inherent rights theory?

(4) The premise of the Colorado River Ecosystem case illustrates how the U.S. governance system revolves around "persons." How might this claim fit with an ecocentric governance framework (explored in Chapter 16: Ecocentric Environmental Governance)? Is it better to seek to expand the definition of "person" or to develop new concepts that move away from the current options of "natural person" (humans) and "artificial person" (entities)?

(5) Given that the law of standing currently allows humans with a special connection to nature to speak on nature's behalf in court, and given that nature must speak through a human, why is it important for nature, itself, to have standing and "personhood"?

[49] Jonathan Watts, *Environmental Activist Murders Double in 15 Years*, The Guardian (Aug. 5, 2019).

(6) In some countries, courts have recognized the rights of nature even without legislation explicitly establishing such rights, such as in Colombia, where the rights of the Atrato River, the Colombian Amazon, and other ecosystems were recognized as part of sweeping rights-based rulings. What strategies might work best in the local jurisdictions you are familiar with?

VII. TRIBAL GOVERNMENTS AND NATIVE HAWAIIANS—THE SPIRITUAL DIMENSION OF SACRED PLACES

A. Native American Nations' Recognition of Nature's Rights

In 2003, the Navajo Nation tribal council amended its code to emphasize the rights of all creation. Title 1 of the code states "all creation, from Mother Earth and Father Sky to the animals, those who live in the water, those who fly, and plant life have their own laws, and rights and freedom to exist."

In 2017, the Ponca Nation in Oklahoma recognized the rights of Nature in the context of a law prohibiting fracking. Tribal representative, Casey Camp-Horinek, said, "We are proud to be moving into the future by honoring our original instructions to respect all life on our Mother Earth."

In 2018, the White Earth Band of Ojibwe, whose homelands are in Minnesota, adopted a law recognizing the rights of wild rice, which the Ojibwe call *Manoomin.*[50] *Manoomin* is central to Ojibwe culture. According to the resolutions adopting the law, these rights were recognized because " 'it has become necessary to provide a legal basis to protect wild rice and fresh water resources as part of our primary treaty foods for future generations.' "[51] The law begins: "Manoomin, or wild rice, within all the Chippewa ceded territories, possesses inherent rights to exist, flourish, regenerate, and evolve, as well as inherent rights to restoration, recovery, and preservation." The law was based in part on the decision by the Supreme Court in *Minnesota v. Mille Lacs Band of Chippewa Indians,* 526 U.S. 172 (1999). The Court considered whether the descendants of several bands of Chippewa that entered a treaty with the United States in 1837 retained the usufructuary rights recognized by the treaty. The State of Minnesota claimed that the Indigenous people lost these rights through an executive order

[50] Wild rice is an annual plant that grows from seed each year. While it can be cultivated, it is native to Minnesota, Wisconsin, Michigan and Idaho in the United States. and the aquatic areas of the Boreal Forest regions of Northern Ontario, Alberta, Saskatchewan and Manitoba in Canada. It begins to grow in lakes and streams after ice out in the spring. Cross pollination occurs naturally usually in late July. Rice kernels begin to fill with a milky substance in late July to early August. These kernels harden to become the seed (or grain) of the plant. Ripe wild rice seed will eventually fall into the water if not harvested. Seeds sink and settle into the sediment at the bottom of the lake or river. With favorable conditions, seeds will grow into wild rice plants beginning the next spring, though wild rice seed also has the ability to remain dormant until favorable conditions are encountered. This dormancy can last for years if the seed remains in the water.

[51] White Earth Band of Ojibwe, Press Release: *Chippewa Establish Rights of Manoomin on White Earth Reservation and Throughout 1855 Ceded Territory* (Jan. 11, 2019), https://healingmnstories.files.wordpress.com/2019/01/right-of-manoomin-media-statement.pdf (quoting resolutions of the White Earth Band of Ojibwe).

in 1850, an 1855 treaty, and the admission of Minnesota into the Union in 1858. The Court held: "After an examination of the historical record, we conclude that the Chippewa retain the usufructuary rights guaranteed to them under the 1837 Treaty."[52]

In 2019, the Yurok Tribe of the Pacific Northwest adopted a "Resolution Establishing the Rights of the Klamath River," making it the first river in the United States to have its rights recognized by governmental action. The resolution describes the relationship between Weroy (the Klamath River) and the Yurok people: "since time immemorial Yurok culture, ceremonies, religion, fisheries, subsistence, economics, residence, and all other lifeways are intertwined with the health of the River, its ecosystem and the multiple species reliant on a thriving Klamath River ecosystem."[53] It also declares that the Yurok people have sovereign rights to conserve and protect their territory, including the river, its ecosystem and species, and to sustainably harvest plants, salmon and other fish, animals, and other life-giving foods and medicines. The declaration notes that its provisions comport with international legal norms set forth in the United Nations Declaration of the Rights of Indigenous Peoples.

Noting their sacred responsibilities to the river and its ecosystem and the present threats to the environment, the enactment recognizes "the Rights of the Klamath River to exist, flourish, and naturally evolve; to have a clean and healthy environment free from pollutants; to have a stable climate free from human-caused climate change impacts; and to be free from contamination by genetically engineered organisms." Finally, the council declared that the resolution serves as notice to all entities threatening the river that the threats have necessitated the provision of a legal basis to protect the river and that the council will adopt an ordinance to achieve that purpose.

B. Native Hawaiians Petition on behalf of Moʻoinanea

An Earth law approach also reflects a responsibility to care for sacred places. In 2019, Native Hawaiians, and those standing with them in solidarity, gathered at the base of Mauna Kea on the Big Island of Hawaiʻi to not only protest the installation of a gigantic telescope atop their sacred mountain, but also to speak against the desecration of sacred places, the displacement of Indigenous peoples, and the present imbalance between humans and the rest of nature.

Eight years prior, in litigation over the permit to build the telescope, Native Hawaiians brought the sacred into the hearing room by filing a petition on behalf of Moʻoinanea. That petition identified Moʻoinanea as a "nature spirit and guardian of Lake Waiau [who] presently resides on the summit of Mauna a Wakea" and requested that she be allowed to participate in the legal proceedings pertaining to the permit decision.

[52] *Id.* at 1.
[53] Yurok Tribal Council. Resolution Establishing the Rights of the Klamath River, Res. No. 19-40 (May 9, 2019), http://files.harmonywithnatureun.org/uploads/upload833.pdf.

The final decision by the State of Hawai'i's Board of Land and Natural Resources ("BLNR") describes the request:

> On February 23, 2011, Mr. Flores also filed a petition for contested case on behalf of "Mo'oinanea et al." That petition identified Mo'oinanea as a "nature spirit and guardian of Lake Waiau [who] presently resides on the summit of Mauna a Wakea." The petition stated that Mo'oinanea "has never been previously consulted regarding this and other projects on this sacred mountain," and "wishes her expressed concerns to be disclosed." It stated that Mo'oinanea's "insight" is needed "to avoid obstructing the piko/portal on the summit of Mauna a Wakea that connects with Ke Akua (The Creator) and 'Aumakua (Ancestors)," which "is a major portal for the life forces that flow into this island." The petition recites that Mo'oinanea "has a substantial interest in this matter, resides on the summit of Mauna a Wakea, and can demonstrate that she and others will be directly and immediately affected by the requested action"; it further asserts that "her interest in the proceeding is clearly distinguishable from that of the general public." Exhibit A-318.[54]

The BLNR denied the request, refusing to allow Mo'oinanea to participate because she was not a "person" as defined in the law and therefore lacked standing.[55]

The BLNR provided a very literal analysis in support of its decision to preclude Mo'oinanea's participation:

> A plain English reading can be applied to the definition of "person" under the Hawai'i Administrative Procedures Act. *See County of Hawai'i v. Civil Serv. Comm'n*, 77 Haw. 396, 400, 885 P.2d 1137, 1141 (1994).
>
> Webster's Dictionary defines a "person" as a "human being, individual." Webster's Dictionary 877 (9th ed. 1983).
>
> Black's Law Dictionary defines a person as follows: "In general usage, a human being (i.e., natural person) . . .". Black's Law Dictionary 1028 (5th ed. 1979).
>
> A plain English reading shows that Mo'oinanea, identified in the petition submitted on its behalf as a "nature spirit and guardian of Lake Waiau who resides on the summit of Mauna a Wakea," does not qualify as a "person" under the Hawai'i Administrative Rules.

[54] BNLR, Findings of Fact, Conclusions of Law and Decision and Order at 5. The full decision is available at www.malamamaunakea.org/uploads/management/plans/TMT_FinalDecision_HA-11-05.pdf [perma.cc/UUJ5-86WP].

[55] Haw. Admin. R. § 13-1-10 (limiting who can appear in a representative capacity in proceedings before the BLNR as "persons"). Applicable Hawai'i law defines "person" similarly to most federal and state laws. *See* Haw. Admin. R. § 13-1-2 (" 'Petitioner' means the person or agency on whose behalf a petition or application is made," and " 'Person' means as appropriate individuals, partnerships, corporations, associations, or public or private organizations of any character other than agencies."); and Haw. Rev. Stat. § 91-1 (" 'Persons' includes individuals, partnerships, corporations, associations, or public or private organizations of any character other than agencies.").

Under Haw. Admin. R. § 13-1-10, Petitioners Flores and Case do not have authority to appear on behalf of Mo'oinanea. Under Section 13-1-10, a person can only appear on his or her own behalf, or represented by counsel.

For these reasons, Mo'oinanea lacked standing to be a party to the contested case proceeding in this matter.[56]

STUDY QUESTIONS

(1) Allowing Mo'oinanea to formally participate in the BLNR proceedings would have honored Native Hawaiian cultural practices. The result shows the disconnect between our current prevailing legal construct and this reality. Would it help to amend the definition of "person" to include nature spirits, along with natural communities and ecosystems? What needs to be done to align statutory text with societal values? Do you think there would be opposition to efforts to amend the definition of "person"? Do you think it is better to amend the definition of "person" or to create entirely new categories of entities recognized as having a voice (standing) in court or administrative proceedings?

(2) Assuming the rights of nature continue to develop in the United States, there are likely to become more robust guardianship bodies in order to better represent the rights and interests of ecosystems. Why would strong representation from Native Americans and Native Hawaiians be important within these guardianship bodies?

(3) As you read in Chapter 23, the Māori tribe of Whanganui and the Crown recognized the rights of the Whanganui River in a treaty agreement. Māori leaders have said that this was not a "rights of nature" model per se. Rather, it was a manifestation of the longstanding relationship between the Whanganui iwi ("tribe") and the Whanganui River that is unique to their culture and beliefs. What problems do you see with classifying Indigenous movements that include personhood or rights for ecosystems as "part of the rights of nature movement?" How might that apply to tribal governments and Native Hawaiians? How can Earth lawyers be respectful of Indigenous cultures?

(4) After reading about the petition that named Mo'oinanea in Hawai'i , do you think that Western law is simply incompatible with Earth law principles? Or can the two approaches be harmonized?

[56] *Supra* note 54.

VIII. NATURE'S RIGHTS AND POPULATION ECOLOGY

Ecological sciences look at systems at different scales. *Population ecology* focuses on an individual species, the number of organisms in that species, and how that population is changing over time and why. For example, a population ecologist may study American Crow (*Corvus brachyrhynchos*) behavior and how that behavior affects the population of crows in an area. *Community ecology* looks at a group of species in an area. For example, a community ecologist may study how crows interact with other birds and their habitats. *Systems ecology* focuses on all the biotic and abiotic parts of the natural world: the whole ecosystem. For example, a systems ecologist may study how crows change their habitat through altering the behavior of other birds and thus their seed distribution patterns.

Most of the laws examined above have focused on Earth rights at an ecosystem scale, protecting Lake Erie, for example. The White Earth Band of Ojibwe's recognition of wild rice, or *Manoomin*, *supra* at 254-255, explores recognizing the rights of specific nonhuman entities. Historian Roderick Frazier Nash, in *The Rights of Nature: A History of Environmental Ethics* (1989), examines the development of environmental ethics beginning with early animal welfare laws that focused more on treatment of individual organisms, and moving toward the land ethic, or ecosystem recognition, of Aldo Leopold, *supra* at 233. In extant U.S. law, the Endangered Species Act is a form of population scale protection, but it is limited in that it only comes into effect after a species is listed as threatened or endangered, as if we recognize a species' value only when we are about to lose it. But even with the Endangered Species Act, many species continue to go extinct.[57] Something is not working.

In Washington state, a group called Legal Rights of the Salish Sea has embarked on a campaign to recognize the rights of the Southern Resident Orcas.[58] The Southern Resident Orcas, an apex predator in the Salish Sea, are on the brink of extinction. The group is circulating a Declaration of the Rights of the Southern Residents that recognizes not only the rights of the Southern Residents, but also the rights of the ecosystems, including the Salish Sea, Fraser River Watershed, Columbia River Basin, and Snake River Watershed, upon which salmon, the Southern Residents' food, depend for their survival. In this way, the Southern Resident Orcas show the connection between multiple ecosystems. The campaign's goal is to educate and build support for a rights-based approach, leading to legal changes at the local, state, national, and international level.[59]

[57] *See generally* ELIZABETH KOLBERT, THE SIXTH EXTINCTION: AN UNNATURAL HISTORY (2014).

[58] *See* Legal Rights for the Salish Sea, http://legalrightsforthesalishsea.org/ [http://perma.cc/D88G-CUTB].

[59] Nimiipuu Protecting the Environment, Earth Law Center, and partners have launched a separate but related campaign to recognize the rights of the Snake River. This campaign also takes a whole ecosystem perspective by supporting concurrent rights' recognition for Southern Residents. *See* Earth Law Center, *Rights for a Free Snake River* (Feb. 24, 2020), https://www.earthlawcenter.org/blog-entries/2020/2/rights-for-a-free-snake-river.

STUDY QUESTIONS

(1) Consider how plant and animal species-specific laws advance the Earth law movement as a whole. In EVENING THOUGHTS: REFLECTING ON EARTH AS SACRED COMMUNITY, Appendix 2 ("Ten Principles for Jurisprudence Revision"), Thomas Berry said that we can talk about species' specific rights while recognizing that specific species are part of, and have a role in, the entire Earth community. Berry described one of the three rights by virtue of belonging to the Earth community as the right to fulfill a particular role in the ever-renewing processes of the Earth community. What are the advantages and disadvantages to focusing on a particular species rather than an entire ecosystem?

(2) Chapter 11 covers "Nonhuman Rights" with a focus on the quest of the Nonhuman Rights Project to seek habeas corpus relief for captive animals in the State of New York based on principles of state common law. How does this legal strategy compare to the one taken for rights of *Manoomin* and Southern Resident Orcas?

IX. CONCLUSION

Looking to the future of the rights of nature movement in the United States, consider the following excerpt from Christopher Stone's *Should Trees Have Standing*:

> The fact is, that each time there is a movement to confer rights onto some new "entity," the proposal is bound to sound odd or frightening or laughable. . . . [T]here will be resistance to giving the thing "rights" until it can be seen and valued for itself; yet, it is hard to see it and value it for itself until we can bring ourselves to give it "rights"—which is almost inevitably going to sound inconceivable to a large group of people.
>
> The reason for this little discourse on the unthinkable, the reader must know by now, if only from the title of the paper. I am quite seriously proposing that we give legal rights to forests, oceans, rivers and other so-called "natural objects" in the environment—indeed, to the natural environment as a whole.[60]

Movement lawyers advocating rights of nature laws have thought the unthinkable and will not go back. Representing ecosystems and advancing rights of nature in the United States requires taking a long view. Seeking fundamental systemic change requires transforming the legal system's relationship with the earth. Nature is not property. Legal history demonstrates that when only certain parties have standing to litigate about ecosystem's rights, those parties become susceptible to succumbing to regulatory capture and to compromising those rights with economic impacts or to bartering one ecosystem for another. Developing rights of nature within local, state

[60] Christopher D. Stone, *Should Trees Have Standing? — Toward Legal Rights for Natural Objects*, 45 S. CAL. L. REV. 450, 455-56 (1972).

and federal legislative processes is no less susceptible to compromise. Rights of nature advocates will face difficult decisions in preserving and strengthening the paradigm shifting elements of this work.

As lawyers work to advance the rights of nature in the United States, the issues below may frame the context:

- Will ecosystems become another kind of legal "person"? If so, how might they fit within the present division between "natural persons" and "artificial persons"? Is it necessary to create a new category of legal being for rivers, forests, species, and whole ecosystems?
- How will ecosystems and the human communities that are part of them interact legally?
- Could recognizing ecosystem rights invoke constitutional takings? Will it require amendment of the U.S. Constitution to prevent this, as was done with the Fourteenth Amendment? (Section 4 states: "But neither the United States nor any state shall assume or pay any . . . claim for the loss or emancipation of any slave; but all such debts, obligations and claims shall be held illegal and void.")
- How might rights of nature, Indigenous rights, human rights, including the right to a healthy environment, and other rights-based frameworks support and conflict with one another?

Considering these questions, and more, will facilitate the work of lawyers and others to create a legal system that honors and respects the earth on which we all depend.

STUDY QUESTIONS

(1) Giving rights to a particular ecosystem makes sense from an ecological perspective. But political boundaries (e.g., a state border) often do not closely follow nature's own boundaries (e.g., a watershed). How might this be tackled in developing rights of nature laws?

(2) Boulder Rights of Nature is a grassroots organization based in Boulder County, Colorado, that works to advance rights of nature. One of its current projects is establishing legal rights for the Boulder Creek Watershed. What strategies and tactics could be developed to achieve this, considering the previous study question and other challenges faced by rights of nature advocates? What stakeholders should be involved? If there were a legal guardianship body developed on behalf of the watershed, who would be invited to be a part of the body? What new ideas might become part of the rights of nature movement in the United States?

(3) Recalling the guardianship models examined in Chapter 6: Legal Guardianship and Representation, consider the potential conflicts. For example, the interests

of a river that is part of the ecosystem may be in maintaining a higher flow rate than farmers, also part of the ecosystem, who want to use the water for irrigation. The interests of some aquatic life may thrive under a reduced flow, others only if the flow is higher. How might the guardian work to represent the rights and interests of ecosystems? Is that the right approach as guardianship implies that the ecosystem is incapacitated?

(4) How do you see rights of nature playing out in the United States in the next 10 years? 50 years? 100 years?

CHAPTER 10

Human Rights and Rights of Nature: A Symbiotic Relationship[1]

I. LAND AND ENVIRONMENTAL DEFENDERS

In 2016, Berta Cáceres, the internationally recognized Honduran community and environmental activist and recipient of the 2015 Goldman Environmental Prize,[2] was murdered in her home in La Esperanza, Honduras. World-renowned for her Indigenous rights and environmental activism, Cáceres was murdered for her leadership role in the grassroots campaign to stop the Agua Zarca hydroelectric dam, planned for construction on the biodiversity-rich Gualcarque River, which is sacred to the local Indigenous Lenca people.[3] The dam would devastate the Gualcarque's sensitive aquatic ecosystem that sustains the Lenca people. Cáceres's outspoken advocacy and public exposure made her a target for the Honduran government and the corporations involved. In the years since the 2009 military coup, Honduras has become notorious for its violence against environmental and social activists, including protestors fighting massive hydroelectric dams constructed to power mines owned and controlled by multinational corporations.[4] Often slated for ecologically valuable Indigenous territories, these government-backed projects damage aquatic and riparian ecosystems and flood Indigenous lands, impairing or destroying both natural and human communities.

Cáceres was one of thousands of land and environmental defenders active across the globe protesting the ravage of natural areas and local communities by mega industrial projects at the risk of being killed or seriously injured. The organization Global Witness tracks the killings of these activists, to whom it gives the name "land and environmental defenders" as defined below:[5]

[1] This chapter was authored by Rachelle Adam, Faculty of Law, Hebrew University.

[2] According to its website, "The Goldman Environmental Prize honors the achievements and leadership of grassroots environmental activists from around the world, inspiring all of us to take action to protect our planet." Goldman Environmental Prize, *About the Prize*, https://www.goldmanprize.org/about (last visited Jan. 15, 2020).

[3] *See* Earth Law Center, *2016 Update: Fighting for Our Shared Future: Protecting Human Rights and Nature's Rights*, 22 (2016), https://www.earthlawcenter.org/co-violations-of-rights.

[4] *Id.* at 20.

[5] Global Witness, *At What Cost? Irresponsible Business and the Murder of Land and Environmental Defenders in 2017*, 12 (2018).

> WHO ARE LAND AND ENVIRONMENTAL DEFENDERS? When communities have their land taken from them, forests cut down or rivers polluted without their permission or even knowledge, they are given little choice but to take a stand. As soon as they speak up, they are no longer only affected communities: they become land or environmental defenders. A land or environmental defender is anybody who takes peaceful action, either voluntarily or professionally, to protect environmental or land rights. They are often ordinary people who may well not define themselves as "defenders." Some are Indigenous or peasant leaders living in remote mountains or isolated forests, protecting their ancestral lands and traditional livelihoods from mining projects, large-scale agribusiness, hydro-dams and luxury hotels. Others are park rangers, tackling poaching and illegal logging. They could also be lawyers, journalists or NGO staff working to expose environmental abuse and land-grabbing. Land and environmental defenders often clash with political, business and criminal interests, who collude to steal their natural resources. These powerful forces often seek to marginalise defenders, branding their actions "anti-development." Many defenders face years of death threats, criminalisation, intimidation and harassment, but receive little or no protection from authorities. These activists defend internationally recognised human rights, such as the right to a healthy environment, the right to participate in public life, the right to protest and the right to life. As such, they are a subset of human rights defenders who governments are obliged to protect, as set out in the UN Declaration on Human Rights Defenders. Business must respect their rights too, as per the UN Guiding Principles on Business and Human Rights.

While many land and environmental defenders come from Indigenous communities directly threatened by catastrophic projects sited in their ancestral lands, all humans are dependent on nature to survive. "Nature" encompasses healthy and thriving ecosystems and biodiversity that supply us with our most basic and critical needs, including clean air, clean water, food, and medicine. The dependence of every one of us on nature for survival is globally recognized by the emergence of environmental rights and the expansion of human rights to include a healthy environment, water, food, health, sanitation, and shelter. These emerging environmental rights are understood as part of the universal goal of achieving well-being for all humanity, as already recognized by many international human rights declarations and conventions.[6]

Yet while we recognize our absolute need for nature, our view of nature remains stubbornly anthropocentric, and we continue to treat it as a commodity under our control and ownership. Nature is still viewed as the entrenched property of humans and the supplier of resources required for the relentless economic growth that remains the overriding goal of international society. The outcome is that we are destroying the very infrastructure that keeps us alive and flourishing. Hence, by laying waste to nature, we are endangering ourselves, especially those human populations who are directly supported by nature without the buffer of technology to protect them.

As Christopher Stone argues in his iconic essay *Should Trees Have Standing? Toward Legal Rights for Natural Objects*, the good news is that society has evolved to abhor the evil and brutality of the human-created institutions of slavery and discrimination based on race, gender, or age, progressively extending human rights by crafting laws to protect

[6] *Id.*

us from these travesties.[7] Yet, in sharp contrast to the extension of rights to all humans, nature remains rightless. Despite the many years that have passed since Stone's classic work in 1972, we are not yet at a place where we recognize and respect other species, ecosystems, or biodiversity generally as co-habitants of planet Earth and co-travelers in time. Triggered by the Industrial Revolution 250 years ago and sharply escalating after World War II, these explosive expansions—of population, economic growth, and consumption—are now spiraling out of control, and, as discussed in this section, the initial victims are local communities and, of course, nature itself.

Indeed, under human legal systems, rightless nature can neither protest its rightless status nor seek to gain its own right to protect itself (although the havoc that climate change is currently wreaking demonstrates that nature has its own ways of fighting back). Standing up for beleaguered nature, land and environmental defenders are risking their lives to stop government and corporate activities in agribusiness, energy, extractive mining, dams, and other industries that devastate both natural systems and local communities.

As discussed above, many environmental defenders are members of Indigenous tribes that are directly dependent on nature and thus are the people hardest hit by its loss. Demonstrating a biocentric, or ecocentric, perspective, they have lived in harmony with their natural surroundings for thousands of years. Indigenous culture, religion, and livelihoods are uniquely interconnected with nature because of the communities' dependence on the goods and services that it supplies them. Indigenous peoples have been at the forefront of the rights of nature movement, which builds upon the worldview of connectedness that these Indigenous cultures embrace. Environmental defenders intertwine their human rights with rights for nature, understanding that to protect human rights, nature's rights must be ensured. Yet, pitted against the formidable power of governments and corporations that treat nature as property that can be taken by force, hundreds—if not thousands—of environmental defenders have been murdered or seriously injured in pursuing this goal.

II. CO-VIOLATIONS OF RIGHTS

In response to this worsening situation, in 2015 and again in 2016, Earth Law Center published co-violation reports, entitled *Fighting for Our Shared Future: Protecting Human Rights and Nature's Rights.* The project is based on an analysis of over 200 case studies of environmental defenders from around the world.[8] The premise of the reports is that human rights violations are strongly correlated with violations of the rights of nature were such rights to be widely recognized. The following excerpts from the 2016 report demonstrate the interconnection between human rights and rights of nature. As you

[7] Christopher Stone, *Should Trees Have Standing? Toward Legal Rights for Natural Objects,* 45 S. CA. L. REV. 450-501 (1972).

[8] *See* Earth Law Center, *Fighting for Our Shared Future: Protecting Human Rights and Nature's Rights* (2016), https://static1.squarespace.com/static/55914fd1e4b01fb0b851a814/t/586d58835016e13b1e98820a/1483561101515/ELC+Co-Violations+Report+-+2016+Update.pdf.

read these excerpts,[9] consider the report's criticism of current environmental laws in treating "nature as property." Also consider the global "legalization" of greenhouse gas emissions by regulating them rather than banning them entirely.

> Destructive activities that impact both humans and nature are increasing alarmingly. Many of the associated injuries amount to simultaneous violations, or "co-violations," of both nature's rights and human rights, including in particular Indigenous rights. We define a "co-violation" of rights as a situation in which governments, industries, or others violate both the rights of nature and human rights, including Indigenous rights, with the same action. . . .
>
> Climate change once again provides an important set of co-violation examples. Climate change threatens the following human rights, among others: to life; to adequate food, water, and sanitation; to adequate housing; and to self-determination. The rights of particularly vulnerable populations are of special concern, including: women, children, persons with disabilities, those living in extreme poverty, Indigenous peoples, and displaced persons. Global Humanitarian Forum estimates that 26 million people worldwide have been forced to move from their homes due to climate change.[10] Because women constitute up to 80% of global refugee and displaced populations, this results in up to 20 million women worldwide displaced due to global warming. . . .
>
> Despite these and other escalating climate-related harms, national and international climate change laws and conventions continue to legalize massive amounts of greenhouse gas emissions while only calling for modest, and usually voluntary, reductions. While the international community fails to address climate change and other drivers of co-violations, humans and nature continue to suffer the consequences. . . .
>
> Our overarching legal and economic systems accelerate co-violations by treating nature and workers as "resources" to fuel short-term profit maximization for the few. Nature is particularly mistreated in light of its characterization as merely "property" to be bought, sold, and ultimately degraded for profit. Reinforcing this misperception is the fact that our modern environmental laws themselves implicitly accept this claim of "nature as property." They legalize nature's destruction by dictating *how much* of the environment we can degrade, thus validating the continuing onslaught. Instead, we need laws grounded in the inherent rights of the natural world to exist, thrive, and evolve. The evolution of human rights provides precedent for recognizing the fundamental rights of nature. Human progress can be measured by the ever-widening circle of those whom we understand to possess dignity and rights, work that is ongoing today. As described in the Universal Declaration of Human Rights (UDHR), such understanding is "the foundation of freedom, justice and peace in the world." . . .
>
> By extending the sphere of rights outward to encompass all of Earth's beings, with which we co-evolved, we are logically and morally continuing the work we began by recognizing the inherent rights of all humans.

[9] *See id.* at 4, 5, 7-8, 9-10.

[10] This estimate was made in 2009. IISD, *Global Humanitarian Forum Addresses Human Impact of Climate Change*, http://sdg.iisd.org/news/global-humanitarian-forum-addresses-human-impact-of-climate-change (last visited Feb. 19, 2020).

The concept of nature's rights in law is not new. Christopher Stone famously wrote about it in his groundbreaking essay of the early 1970s, listing four elements as necessary to effectively recognize the rights of nature in law:

- Rights must be subject to redress by a public body;
- The entity must have standing to institute legal actions on its own behalf (a guardian can stand in for the entity as needed);
- Redress must be calculated for the entity's own damages; and
- Relief must run to the benefit of the injured entity. . . .

[H]ow we treat the natural world often mirrors how we treat each other. For example, governments and industries around the world are increasingly harassing, threatening, attacking, imprisoning, and even killing defenders of environmental and human rights. The United Nations found that human rights defenders working on "land and environmental issues in connection with extractive industries and construction and development projects in the Americas" face the highest risk of death of all human rights advocates worldwide. Organizations such as Global Witness and EJOLT, and the Yes to Life No to Mining Campaign, are providing invaluable reports of rights violations against people and the environment in the name of profit. These continued violations of fundamental rights have to stop. We must hold governments and industry accountable for actions that impact human and environmental wellbeing. Among other steps, we must:

- Reformulate our laws to recognize and implement environmental rights;
- Bolster identification and enforcement of human rights, Indigenous rights, and environmental rights violations; and
- Shift to ecological economics models, which respect people and planet. . . .

As the case studies in this report demonstrate, unless our governance systems recognize the inherent rights of *all* beings in law, we will fail to recognize them in practice. . . . [citation omitted]. Our key findings with regard to trends in the co-violation of human rights, Indigenous rights, and nature's rights include the following:

- Co-violations are frequently connected to the extractive and energy industries;
- Violations of the rights of Indigenous peoples and environmental destruction are often strongly associated;
- Co-violations occur globally, but they have been arising more often in the Global South; and
- Governments often side with private industry over people and natural systems whose rights may be violated . . . .

Based on this process, we recommend the following actions by the United Nations and international community:

- Recognize in law and implement the fundamental rights of nature, including through UN General Assembly adoption of the Universal Declaration of the Rights of Mother Earth;
- Support swift enforcement of International Rights of Nature Tribunal judgments;[11]

[11] *See infra* Section III, pp. 273-275 for a description of the International Rights of Nature Tribunals.—Eds.

- Create "International Rights of Nature" courts to hear cases involving nature's rights violations; and
- Incorporate rights of nature principles into existing human rights instruments and bodies. . . .

Such co-violations result when the law prioritizes corporate interests over human and nature's rights. Legal systems throughout the world were developed to protect corporations. The underlying legal rationale is that without broad protections, corporations cannot continue to perform their function of growing the economy. The fundamental predicate of this reasoning is that growing the economy will continue to improve the welfare of the human species. The violation of human and nature's rights in the Lago Agrio Canton on Ecuador's norther border with Colombia exemplifies the flaws of this paradigm.

As a result of the human and ecological devastation caused by Texaco Corporation's[12] drilling for oil between 1964 to 1992, Lago Agrio is often described as the "Chernobyl in the Amazon." The dumping of hundreds of thousands of barrels of crude oil and billions of gallons of oil-contaminated wastewater ravaged a vast rainforest ecosystem that included more than 100,000 members of numerous Indigenous communities. The land and water has been destroyed and the lives of Indigenous peoples and rural communities have been plagued by "an epidemic of birth defects, miscarriages, and an estimated 1,400 cancer deaths."[13]

Legal action seeking remediation for the environmental damage and recompense for the 30,000 human victims began in 1993 in the United States District Court for the Southern District of New York. After 9 years of litigation, Chevron succeeding in moving the case to Ecuador based on *forum non conveniens* grounds. The court's decision relied on Chevron's agreement to comply with any final judgment issued in Ecuador. Ecuador's Supreme Court issued a final judgment in 2013 awarding the victims $9.5 billion. Chevron refused to honor the judgment and engaged in a staggering number of legal measures to void the judgment and punish the plaintiffs, including litigation attacking the legitimacy of the legal process in Ecuador and accusing the lawyer representing the victims of fraud.[14] The Chevron case opens the window into the extraordinary challenges in pursuing justice for co-violation cases and holding corporations responsible for human and ecological devastation.

Human rights bodies are beginning to create new mechanisms to combat violations against humans and nature perpetrated by corporations that regularly escape responsibility. For example, in 2014, the UN Human Rights Council decided "to establish an open-ended intergovernmental working group on transnational corporations and other business enterprises with respect to human rights, whose mandate shall be

[12] Texaco was acquired by Chevron in 2001. CNN Money, *FTC Oks Chevron Deal* (Sept 7, 2001), https://money.cnn.com/2001/09/07/deals/chevron_texaco.

[13] Texaco Toxico.net, Open Letter to Chevron Shareholders About Voting at Annual General Meeting 2018, http://texacotoxico.net/en/open-letter-to-chevron-shareholders-about-voting-at-annual-general-meeting-2018-on-item-8-and-item-10; Aldo Orellana López, *Chevron vs Ecuador: International Arbitration and Corporate Impunity* (March 27, 2019), http://isds.bilaterals.org/?chevron-vs-ecuador-international.

[14] *Chevron Corp. v. Donziger*, No. 14-0826 (2d Cir. 2016).

to elaborate an international legally binding instrument to regulate, in international human rights law, the activities of transnational corporations and other business enterprises."[15] The resulting intergovernmental working group on transnational corporations and other business enterprises with respect to human rights has had five negotiating sessions as of 2020.[16]

Civil society groups have also played an increasing role in highlighting the atrocities by corporations, governments, and other actors against land defenders, with the goal of building awareness of the global problem and solutions. Global Witness's 2017 report, *At What Cost? Irresponsible Business and the Murder of Land and Environmental Defenders in 2017,* documents the murder of 207 defenders.[17]

> The food on our plates, the rings on our fingers and the wooden furniture in our homes: all too often there is a violent reality behind household items we use every day. As agribusiness booms, tropical forests are logged and mining continues to deliver huge revenue to major global corporations, there are increasingly brutal attacks on land and environmental defenders.
>
> In Colombia, Hernán Bedoya was shot by a paramilitary group 14 times. He was killed after protesting against palm oil and banana plantations on land stolen from his community. In the Philippines, near the town of Lake Sebu, the military descended on a small community, leaving eight dead, wounding five and causing 200 to flee.
>
> And in one of the largest-scale attacks of 2017, Gamela Indigenous people were assaulted in Brazil. Machetes and rifles were used in an attempt to forcibly seize control of their land, leaving 22 severely injured, some with their hands cut off. Months later, nobody had faced justice for this appalling incident, reflecting a wider culture of impunity and inaction to support defenders by the Brazilian government.
>
> Rather than taking steps to crack down on these attacks, President Michel Temer and the Brazilian legislature are actively weakening the laws and institutions designed to protect land rights and Indigenous peoples. At the same time, they have set about making it easier for big business—apparently unperturbed by the devastating human and environmental cost of their activities—to accelerate their exploitation of fragile ecosystems. . . .
>
> But it's not just in Brazil where governments and business are turning their backs on those fighting to protect their land and way of life. As our sixth Annual Report shows, around the world too many of those who perpetrate and are complicit in attacks on defenders are literally getting away with murder.
>
> Governments and business have failed to act responsibly, ethically and even legally, making them a major driving force behind a litany of crimes against activists last year.

[15] UN Human Rights Council, Res. 26/9 (2014), para. 1.

[16] UN Human Rights Council, Fifth Session of the Open-Ended Intergovernmental Working Group on Transnational Corporations and Other Business Enterprises with Respect to Human Rights, https://www.ohchr.org/EN/HRBodies/HRC/WGTransCorp/Session5/Pages/Session5.aspx.

[17] Global Witness, *At What Cost? Irresponsible Business and the Murder of Land and Environmental Defenders in 2017,* 6-7, 9, 10 (2018), https://www.globalwitness.org/en/campaigns/environmental-activists/at-what-cost.

They are part of the reason 207 defenders were killed in 2017, making it the worst year on record. And why many, many more were attacked, threatened or criminalised for showing the courage to speak out for their communities, their way of life and our environment.

Their inaction helped fuel the surge in killings of people protesting against large-scale agriculture, as the global rush for land gathered pace.

And their willingness to turn a blind eye has permitted the systemic impunity that lets perpetrators know they will almost certainly never be brought to justice. In fact, governments are often complicit in the attacks. One of the most shocking facts outlined in this report is the number of killings committed by government security forces at the behest of their political bosses and in league with industry.

The data painstakingly gathered and presented in this report—and the case studies included—are almost certainly a sizeable underestimate, given the many challenges in identifying and reporting killings. Yet even as it stands, it shows that governments and business have a very serious case to answer.

But we can all do more.

Ultimately, attacks against land and environmental defenders stem from our voracious appetite for agricultural goods like palm oil and coffee, and for fossil fuels, minerals and timber. Extracting these resources requires an increasing amount of land, turning it into a highly prized commodity. Communities who have lived and worked on the land for generations are often the losers in this quest for natural resources.

Companies have a responsibility to their customers, who should have confidence that the products they buy are not fueling human rights abuses, cultural destruction or environmental devastation. And we, the consumers, have a responsibility to demand that these companies live up to their responsibilities.

When rich tropical forest is levelled for monoculture crops, delicate ecosystems that could capture carbon emissions are lost forever. When land is exploited for mining, soil and fresh water are poisoned, jeopardising the health and the future of nearby communities. These abuses are tolerated, facilitated and sometimes even perpetrated by irresponsible business and investors, together with corrupt or negligent governments, who are hell-bent on meeting consumer demand and maximising profit. . . .

We're calling on governments and business to take responsibility, prioritise defenders, and:

- Tackle the root causes of violence against defenders, especially the lack of free, prior and informed consent from communities for the use of their land and natural resources.
- Support and protect defenders at risk so they can carry out their advocacy in safety.
- Ensure accountability so that those responsible for attacks on defenders are brought to justice; and so that there are consequences for those who fail to protect activists and for companies who don't do proper due diligence of their supply chains.

Consumers can play their part too, demanding guarantees that the products they buy are not associated with land-grabbing, forcible evictions or attacks on defenders.

Despite the odds they face, the global community of environmental and land defenders is not going away—it's only getting stronger. We will campaign alongside them, taking their struggle to the corridors of power and the boardrooms of corporations. We will not tire in our fight to ensure that their voices are heard. . . .

In 2017, Global Witness documented 207 killings of land and environmental defenders—ordinary people murdered for defending their forests, rivers and homes against destructive industries. This is six more murders than in 2016, making it the worst year on record.

As the killing has increased, some governments, businesses and intergovernmental organisations have begun to acknowledge the gravity of the situation. But their promises and rhetoric have yet to translate into convincing policies and concrete change, leaving defenders in fear of their lives. . . .

This is, in part, driven by one deadly trend: the number of people killed while protesting against large-scale agriculture more than doubled compared to 2016. For the first time, agribusiness surpassed mining as the most dangerous sector to oppose, as 46 defenders who protested against palm oil, coffee, tropical fruit and sugar cane plantations, as well as cattle ranching, were murdered in 2017.

Opposition to mining and oil operations (40 killings), poaching (23 murders) and logging (23 cases) were the other main reasons defenders were killed last year. . . .

Linked to the spike in agribusiness-related deaths, Global Witness observed a rise in multiple killings (7 incidents in total) of land and environmental defenders, many of whom were disputing large-scale agriculture projects. Brazil was the scene of three horrific massacres, during which 25 defenders died. Eight Indigenous activists were massacred in the Philippines, while Mexico, Peru and the Democratic Republic of Congo also saw incidents where more than four defenders died at the same time.

These massacres sent the message that not only community leaders will be targeted: nobody is safe. This has a huge impact, given that whole communities—or large parts of them—are often involved in struggles to protect their land from being grabbed. . . .

The term "agribusiness" features heavily in this report as the industry most linked to killings of land and environmental defenders. Any business that earns most or all of its revenues from agriculture is known as an "agribusiness." They tend to be large-scale business operations involved in farming, processing and manufacturing, as well as potentially packaging and distributing products.

Some key agribusiness products include cattle (beef and dairy), cotton, palm oil, soy and sugar cane. Palm oil is in about half of all packaged products sold in the supermarket, including chocolate, margarine, ice cream, shampoo and lipstick. Sugar extracted from sugar cane is prevalent in many of the foods we eat, and increasingly a source of biofuels and bioplastics. Most commercially produced beef, fish, chicken and dairy products were fed on soy, with 80% of the world's soybean crop fed to livestock. . . .

A widespread culture of impunity has made it difficult to identify those responsible for the killings, and sends a signal to would-be perpetrators that they will not be made to pay for their crimes. Worse still, Global Witness data shows that it is often government security forces committing the crimes. They were linked to around a quarter of the murders last year—30 linked to the army and 23 to the police. Criminal gangs, security guards, landowners, poachers and other non-state actors were suspected of carrying out at least 90 killings. . . .

Once again, Latin America saw the highest number of murders, accounting for almost 60% of the total. According to Global Witness data, Brazil recorded the most killings of any country ever with 57 people killed, 80% of them while protecting the natural riches of the Amazon. In Colombia 24 defenders were murdered in 2017, as conflicts over land raged on. Mexico and Peru saw a jump in killings from three to 15 and two to eight respectively. There were fewer murders in Honduras—five compared to 14 in 2016—but the growing repression of civil society has restricted what defenders can say and do. Nicaragua registered the most murders per capita, with four defenders killed.

In Asia, the most alarming developments took place in the Philippines, which saw 48 killings—almost a 71% rise on 2016 and the most murders ever recorded in Asia in a single year. President Duterte's aggressively anti-human-rights stance and a renewed military presence in resource-rich regions are fuelling the violence. Almost half of the killings in the Philippines were linked to struggles against agribusiness.

Of the 19 land and environmental defenders reported killed across Africa, 17 lost their lives while defending protected areas against poachers and illegal miners—12 in the Democratic Republic of Congo alone.

Of course, many other countries and regions could be suffering elevated numbers of killings which have not been documented or which we have been unable to verify. . . .

Fewer Indigenous people were killed in 2017—falling to 25% of the total, from 40% in 2016. However, with Indigenous groups making up just 5% of the world's population, they remain massively overrepresented among defenders killed. And it is not only killings: in one of the most brutal attacks, Gamela Indigenous people were assaulted with machetes and rifles by Brazilian farmers, leaving 22 of them severely injured, some with their hands cut off. In Mexico, 13 out of 15 defenders killed were Indigenous—murdered defending their ancestral territories.

Although nine out of every 10 murdered activists last year were male, women defenders faced gender-specific threats including sexual violence. They were often subjected to smear-campaigns, threats against their children, and attempts to undermine their credibility; sometimes from within their own communities, where macho cultures might prevent women from taking up positions of leadership. . . .

Our data on killings is likely to be an underestimate, given that many murders go unreported, particularly in rural areas. Our methodology requires cases to be verified according to a strict set of criteria . . . which can't always be met by a review of public information like newspaper reports or legal documents, nor through local contacts. Having a strict methodology means our figures don't represent the scale of the problem, and we are working to improve this.

III. INTERNATIONAL RIGHTS OF NATURE TRIBUNALS

In light of government indifference and even involvement in these brutalities, what chances are there to prosecute the perpetrators and end the human and environmental devastation? As an alternative to government judicial forums mandated to issue decisions under current anthropocentric laws exclusively, the Global Alliance for the Rights of Nature, together with Indigenous groups and other social and environmental organizations, spearheaded a brave and creative initiative of "International Rights of Nature Tribunals" to hear and decide cases of violations of human rights and rights of nature. The Tribunal is a non-governmental "people's tribunal," in which leading academics, environmental activists, Indigenous leaders, and others hear cases and write judgments in enforcement of the rights of nature and other ecocentric legal doctrines based on specific case studies. These include destructive mining projects in the heart of the Amazon, mega-dams in Latin America, fracking across the United States, the oil pollution of the Niger Delta in Nigeria, and many others. It is modeled on other people's tribunals, such as the Russell Tribunal, also known as the International War Crimes Tribunal, that was organized by Nobel Prize winner and British philosopher Bertrand Russell to investigate and evaluate American military intervention in Vietnam, ultimately finding they had committed war crimes.[18] As with the International Rights of Nature Tribunal, the Russell Tribunal did not have recognized legal authority but was necessary to raise awareness and push for accountability and reform in the absence of sufficient governmental action.

Five such tribunals have been held so far, in Quito, Ecuador, in January 2014, in Lima, Peru, in December 2014, in Paris, France, in November 2016, in Bonn, Germany, in November 2017, and in Santiago, Chile, in 2019. The 2016 and 2017 tribunals were held concurrently with Conferences of the Parties of the United Nations Framework Convention on Climate Change. Among Earth Law Center's recommendations in its co-violations reports is to "support swift enforcement of International Rights of Nature Tribunal Judgments." The following excerpt from Earth Law Center's *Fighting for Our Shared Future* report describes the work of these forums in greater depth:[19]

> Organized by civil society around the world, International Rights of Nature Tribunals re-frame and adjudicate prominent environmental and social justice cases within a rights of nature context. While the Tribunals do not yet have formal legal authority, the adjudication process:

[18] Cody J. Foster, *Did America Commit War Crimes in Vietnam?*, THE N.Y. TIMES (Dec. 1, 2017), https://www.nytimes.com/2017/12/01/opinion/did-america-commit-war-crimes-in-vietnam.html.
[19] Earth Law Center, *supra* note 8, at 41-42.

- Generates sophisticated legal analysis of diverse cases from a nature's rights perspective, applying the UDRME [Universal Declaration of Rights of Mother Earth] tenets and nature's rights laws as legal guidelines;
- Educates governments, advocacy groups, and the interested public on the tenets of the rights of nature and how they can be applied;
- Recommends actions such as enforcement and mitigation based on rights of nature violations; and
- Enables others to ultimately develop formal legal structures that recognize the inherent rights of nature.

The Tribunals are particularly guided by the Universal Declaration of Rights of Mother Earth (UDRME) Article 2(1)(j), which states that: "Mother Earth and all beings of which she is composed have the following inherent rights: . . . the right to full and prompt restoration for the violation of the rights recognized in this Declaration caused by human activities." As discussed by 2015 Tribunal Chair Cormac Cullinan of South Africa:

> [i]magine if there were an international tribunal that concerned itself with the fundamental rights of all beings, including humans, and decided matters on the basis of what was best for the Earth community as a whole, regardless of politics; an Earth Tribunal of respected individuals that drew on the wisdom of humanity as whole, respected the laws of Nature and was not beholden to governments or corporations.
>
> The establishment of the International Tribunal for the Rights of Nature is intended to give effect to this dream. This bold venture by the members of the Global Alliance for the Rights of Nature is a creative response to the current impasse at the international level which has led to a widening chasm between what global civil society wants done and what governments are willing to agree to and implement. . . .

Tribunals such as the International Rights of Nature Tribunals have a long tradition of addressing fundamental issues of justice beyond the reach of traditional courts, including military interventions and human rights abuses. By recognizing these groundbreaking tribunals for rights of nature and calling for the enforcement of their judgments, the United Nations and other international bodies would help ensure that the international community addresses some of the world's most insidious co-violations of both nature's rights and human rights.

Yet meanwhile the UN, as an organization composed of sovereign states, has refrained from recognizing these forums. Moreover, it is improbable that such a decision would even make it to the agenda of the UN General Assembly as it would, of course, create a major conflict with current international and national laws and judicial forums governed by established laws based on the independent interests of nations. As such, decisions of rights of nature tribunals are not being implemented and enforced since police power remains in the hands of governments that do not recognize their validity. For the very same reason, tribunals have also not been used as platforms for governments to initiate investigations and judicial proceedings at the national level of the violations at issue.

In searching for other ways to prosecute violations of both human rights and rights of nature, co-violations could be theoretically pursued in international human rights forums by arguing that acts of environmental devastation are violating human rights and, in particular, the right to a healthy environment. While nature would not be a petitioner to argue for its own rights, the outcome could be the same. The main criteria in searching for an appropriate human rights forum would be its capacity to review petitions from individuals and non-governmental organizations, rather than solely from states. While the International Court of Justice is limited to hearings between sovereign states, both the UN Human Rights Council and the European Court of Human Rights, as well as regional commissions of human rights, accept complaints from individuals, victims of human rights violations, and concerned non-governmental organizations. The subsequent section explores several such cases from the Inter-American Commission of Human Rights (IACHR or "commission") and the Inter-American Court of Human Rights ("the court"), which together make up the human rights protection system of the Organization of American States (OAS). Following the report of an alleged human rights violation, a complaint is lodged with the commission, who rules on the admissibility of the case. The commission then prepares a list of recommendations and, if the state fails to amend the violation, or if the commission determines the case is of particular importance or legal interest, refers the case to the court. The court ultimately rules on whether a state has violated human rights.

IV. HUMAN RIGHTS PROTECTION SYSTEM OF THE ORGANIZATION OF AMERICAN STATES

A. Yanomami Community—Brazil

The commission has reviewed many cases of human rights violations as a result of environmental injury resulting from government expropriation of lands and activities such as mining, dams, logging, and agriculture. In 1979, the Indian Law Resource Center petitioned the commission on behalf of the Yanomami Indigenous community regarding human rights violations by Brazil.[20] The International Network for Economic, Social and Cultural Rights (ESCR-Net), which connects over 280 non-governmental organizations and initiatives from more than 75 countries, summarized the case as follows:

> The case was based on the construction of a road and mining licenses granted in Indigenous land, which had led to a massive presence of foreigners in the said territory and had had serious effects on the community's well-being, including the alteration of their traditional organization, emergence of female prostitution, epidemics and

[20] Indian Law Resource Center, https://indianlaw.org/content/about-center.

> diseases, forced displacement to lands unsuitable to their ways of life, and death of hundreds of Yanomamis.[21]

The IACHR issued its decision in 1985. The ESCR-Net stated in a summary:

> The IACHR found the State was responsible for failing to take timely and effective measures to protect the Yanomamis' human rights. The IACHR concluded such failure had led to alterations in the community's well-being and violations to the right to life, liberty, security, residence and movement, and to the preservation of health and well-being. . . . The IACHR recommended the State, in line with domestic legislation, to proceed to demarcate the Yanomami Park, to continue adopting preventive and remedial sanitary measures aimed at protecting the life and health of the Yanomami. . . .[22]

ESCR-Net noted the following updates as to the enforcement of the case:

> In 1992, the land of the Yanomamis was finally demarcated as "Yanomami Park." In a 1995 visit to Brazil, the IACHR was able to prove on site the presence of federal agency surveillance and healthcare stations in the Yanomami area. However, the Yanomamis' personal and collective integrity, as well as their environment, continue to be subject to aggression by intruding miners. State protection is weak and inconsistent.[23]

B. Mayagna Awas (Sumo) Tingni Community—Nicaragua

In 1995, the Indigenous Mayagna Awas (Sumo) Tingni community from the Atlantic coastal area of Nicaragua submitted a petition to the commission. The petition charged Nicaragua for failing to demarcate Awas Tingni's communal land and to take the necessary measures to protect the community's property rights over its ancestral lands and natural resources, including 62,000 hectares of tropical forest planned for commercial development. The petition alleged that Nicaraguan law has been "absolutely ineffective to prevent the State from allowing the foreign firm SOLCARSA to destroy and exploit the lands which for years have belonged to the Awas Tingni community," and that "the Community suffered the continuation of a logging concession which negatively affected their traditional land tenure and their natural resources."[24]

In 1998, the commission submitted the case to the court. Only state parties and the commission may refer cases to the court, which is authorized to adjudicate cases brought against state members of the OAS that have accepted the court's jurisdiction, subject to the commission's initial overview of the case. Hence, the American human rights system, by limiting submission of cases to the court by state parties or the commission, differs from the European human rights system: as mentioned above, the European Court on Human Rights provides for submission of petitions by individuals and non-governmental organizations.

[21] ESCR-Net https://www.escr-net.org/caselaw/2006/comunidad-yanomami-caso-no-7615-resolucion-no-1285-eng (last viewed June 9, 2020). *Yanomami v. Brazil,* Case No. 7615, Resolution No. 12/85, Inter-Am. Comm. H.R. (Mar. 5, 1985).
[22] *Id.*
[23] *Id.*
[24] *Mayagna (Sumo) Awas Tingni Cmty. v. Nicaragua,* Case No. 79, Inter-Am. Ct. H.R., Ser. C (2001).

In 2001, the court issued its ruling on *Mayagna (Sumo) Awas Tingni Cmty. v. Nicaragua*:

> Nicaragua had violated the right to judicial protection and to property. The Court noted that the right to property acknowledged by the American Convention of Human Rights originated in Indigenous tradition and, therefore, the State had no right to grant concessions to third parties in their land. Consequently, the Court decided that the State had to adopt the necessary measures to create an effective mechanism for demarcation and titling of the Indigenous communities' territory, in accordance with their customary law, values, customs and mores. The Court also decided that, until such mechanism was created, the State had to refrain from any acts that might affect the existence, value, use or enjoyment of the property located in the geographic area where the members of the Indigenous community live and carry out their activities.[25]

Nicaragua ignored the court's decision, and, in 2003, the Indigenous community petitioned the court for a decision ordering the government to comply with the ruling. The case was finally resolved in 2008 when the Nicaraguan government titled the land under dispute in the name of the Awas Tingni. This was the first community to obtain a land title under the Nicaraguan law that mandated the government to demarcate Indigenous land on Nicaragua's Atlantic coast.[26]

In addition, "[t]his was the first case in which an international tribunal with legally binding authority found a Government in violation of the collective land rights of an Indigenous group, setting an important precedent in international law."[27]

C. Saramaka People—Suriname

In Suriname, in 2000, the non-Indigenous community of Saramaka people, liberated slaves who had lived on the land since the early eighteenth century, submitted a complaint to the commission regarding violations of their human rights by logging and mining concessions operating under government approval in Saramaka territory without consultation or consent.[28] The complaint specifically referred to "Chinese and other multinational logging and mining companies which were extracting resources with the explicit permission of the State."[29] In 2006, the commission submitted the case to the court and, in 2007, the court issued a ruling that while not Indigenous, the Saramaka people held rights similar to those of Indigenous peoples, including the right to their land through possession, and title was not required. It ruled that Suriname had to

[25] *Id.*

[26] UN News, *Nicaragua's Titling of Native Lands Marks Crucial Step for Indigenous Rights — UN Expert* (Dec. 17, 2008), https://news.un.org/en/story/2008/12/285592.

[27] *Id.*

[28] Application Filed by the Inter-American Commission on Human Rights with the Inter-American Court of Human Rights in Case 12.338, 12 Saramaka Clans Against the Republic of Suriname, Inter-Am. Ct. H.R. (June 23, 2006).

[29] Richard Price, *Saramaka People v Suriname: A Human Rights Victory and its Messy Aftermath*, CULTURAL SURVIVAL (July 29, 2012), https://www.culturalsurvival.org/news/saramaka-people-v-suriname-human-rights-victory-and-its-messy-aftermath.

grant the Saramaka people a collective title to their land, to refrain from any activities in the territory until title was granted, to review current concessions, to adopt legislation and undertake other measures to protect the Saramaka's human rights and avoid further violations, and to pay them compensation for the injury that these violations caused them, including environmental damage. The court also ruled that major development projects require prior and informed consent. While the court's 2007 decision was considered a landmark decision, it has only been partially enforced.[30]

D. Lhaka Honhat Communities—Argentina

In 1998, after years of demanding that Argentina refrain from subdividing their land, the Indigenous Lhaka Honhat people in Argentina submitted a complaint to the IACHR. They alleged that Argentina had violated their right to property because the state failed to give their communities effective title to their ancestral territory, along with "having carried out works, demarcations, measurements, and other activities that affected the integrity of the territory... [and] consented to and tolerated the illegitimate actions of private parties, such as the tending of wire fences, logging, bovine cattle grazing and the like."[31] For several years Argentina held negotiations with the Lhaka Honhat but then withdrew. This led the IACHR to warn Argentina that if dialogue failed, the commission would submit the case to the court.

In 2012, the IACHR found Argentina in violation of the community's rights and issued an order for reparations, which Argentina ignored. Finally, the IACHR submitted the case to the court.[32] In 2019, the court made an on-site visit to the Indigenous communities and the lands at conflict and found that roaming livestock and the placement of fences by European-descended settlers within the communities' territory directly affected more than 10,000 people's way of life and customs. In addition, the members of the court participated in an assembly of the chiefs of the Lhaka Honhat communities, with representatives traveling from different corners of the territory in question, to explain the impact and transformation of their way of life provoked by the settlers' activities.[33]

In February 2020, the court issued its decision in the case, *Lhaka Honhat Association vs. Argentina*.[34] It found that Argentina had violated Indigenous communities' right to a healthy environment, to their property, cultural identity, food, and water, and obligated the state to undertake detailed measures to rectify the situation. The plaintiffs had argued that the state had violated its obligation to ensure their right to communal

[30] *Id.*

[31] Report No. 2/121m Case 12.094, Indigenous Communities of the Lhaka Honhat (Our Land) Association Merits Argentina, Inter-Am. Ct. H.R. (Jan. 26, 2012).

[32] Asociación de Comunidades Aborígenes Lhaka Honhat, Caso No. 12.094, Inter-Am. Comm. H.R. (Aug. 29, 2012).

[33] CELS, *Lhaka Honhat: The Inter-American Court Visited the Indigenous Communities* (May 20, 2019), https://www.cels.org.ar/web/en/2019/05/lhaka-honhat-the-inter-american-court-visited-the-Indigenous-communities.

[34] *See* Maria Antonia Tigre, *Lhaka Honhat Association vs. Argentina: the human right to environment in the Inter-American Court* https://gnhre.org/2020/04/10/lhaka-honhat-association-vs-argentina-the-human-right-to-environment-in-the-inter-american-court/ (as of June 6, 2020, the judgment had not yet been translated into English).

property, due to the construction of infrastructure projects and fossil fuels exploration on their lands without free, prior and informed consultation. They further argued that the state had violated their human rights by allowing illegal logging, land enclosures, and cattle raising, activities that severely hampered their traditional way of life based on hunting, gathering, farming and fishing.

In 2017 the court had issued an advisory opinion on the right to a healthy environment (Advisory Opinion 23/17 of 2018[35]) but this was the first contentious case on the issue. The Court, relying on its advisory opinion, determined that rights incorporated in the American Convention on Human Rights had been violated, including the rights to cultural identity, a healthy environment, and adequate food and water. Referring to its advisory opinion in interpreting the right to a healthy environment, the court reiterated that this right protects forests, rivers, seas and other natural elements as entities with their own inherent worth. Adopting an ecocentric perspective and again based on its 2017 advisory opinion, the court restated its willingness to recognize the rights of nature beyond its practical value to humans.[36]

On the one hand, the long period of time from the initial 1998 submission to the court's final decision in 2020 displays the IACHR and the court as slow-moving institutions. But on the other, the intermediacy of these institutions and their role as watchdogs have succeeded in keeping these issues both under negotiation with the state and on the public agenda. Moreover, the final judgment is a decision for both the right to a healthy environment and rights of nature.

E. Kaliña and Lokono Peoples—Suriname

In 2007, again in Suriname, the Kaliña and Lokono Indigenous people alleged human rights violations as a result of the state's failure to recognize their property rights over their ancestral territories, following the establishment of nature reserves, the issuance of land titles, and the granting of mining concessions.[37] They petitioned the IACHR, which issued a decision in 2013 requesting Suriname to remedy the situation. Following Suriname's non-compliance with the decision, in 2014 the IACHR submitted a complaint to the court which in 2016 issued a decision in favor of the Kaliña and Lokono, The court's "treatment of the rights of Indigenous peoples in relation to environmental protected areas, and associated international environmental law, is especially noteworthy."[38] As further explained:

> The Court . . . extensively cites international environmental law, reading provisions of the Convention on Biological Diversity (CBD) into its interpretation of the ACHR . . .

[35] Advisory Opinion OC-23/18, Inter-Am. Ct. H.R., (ser. A) No. 23 (Nov. 15, 2017) [hereinafter OC-23/17].
[36] *Supra* note 34.
[37] *Case of the Kaliña and Lokono Peoples v. Suriname,* Report No. 79/13, Case 12.639, Inter-Am Ct. H.R. (July 18, 2013).
[38] Fergus MacKay, *The Case of the Kaliña and Lokono Peoples v. Suriname and the UN Declaration on the Rights of Indigenous Peoples: Convergence, Divergence and Mutual Reinforcement,* 11(1) ERASMUS LAW REVIEW 31-42 (2018), https://papers.ssrn.com/sol3/papers.cfm?abstract_id=3174650.

and stresses, as a general proposition, that "the rights of the Indigenous peoples and international environmental laws should be understood as complementary, rather than exclusionary, rights." It is important to note that, although the CBD purports to guarantee some Indigenous rights, there is no corresponding enforcement mechanism. The Court's ruling provides an opportunity to enforce some CBD provisions through the lens of the ACHR.[39]

F. Advisory Opinion on Human Rights and the Environment—Colombian Petition Concerning the Application of the American Convention on Human Rights

In 2018, the IACHR published its "Advisory Opinion OC-23/17" on the obligations of states to prevent environmental harm to ensure the right to a healthy environment, as well as the rights to life and to personal integrity, to peoples living both within and beyond their borders.[40] The court had been requested by Colombia to determine

> how the Pact of San José [the American Convention on Human Rights] should be interpreted when there is a danger that the construction and operation of major new infrastructure projects may have severe effects on the marine environment in the Wider Caribbean Region and, consequently, on the human habitat that is essential for the full enjoyment and exercise of the rights of the inhabitants of the coasts and/or islands of a State Party to the Pact, in light of the environmental standards recognized in international customary law and the treaties applicable among the respective States.[41]

The government of Colombia explained that:

> The protection of the human rights of the inhabitants of the islands of the Wider Caribbean Region and, consequently, the prevention and mitigation of environmental damage in this area, is an issue of particular interest to Colombia, because part of its population lives on the islands that form part of the Archipelago of San Andrés, Providencia and Santa Catalina and they therefore depend on the marine environment for their survival, and economic, social and cultural development. . . .
>
> Owing to the ecological and oceanographic interconnectedness of the Wider Caribbean Region—a well-documented situation—it is vitally important that the problems of the marine environment be dealt with taking into consideration the effects on relevant areas and the ecosystem as a whole, with the cooperation of the other States that could be affected. . . .[42]

The Court based its decision on Article 11 of the Additional Protocol to the American Convention on Human Rights in the Area of Economic, Social and Cultural Rights (Protocol of San Salvador), and Article 26 of the Convention. Article 11 guarantees that "Everyone shall have the right to live in a healthy environment and to have

[39] *Id.* at 41-42.
[40] OC-23/17.
[41] *Id.* ¶ 1.
[42] *Id.* ¶ 2.

access to basic public services" and "The States Parties shall promote the protection, preservation, and improvement of the environment."[43]

In 2017, as a human rights forum, the court tackled the impact of a transboundary environmental injury on the rights of people living outside of the state that was source of the harm. Based on the human rights to a healthy environment, to life, and to personal integrity, the court expanded the definition of "subject to jurisdiction" and determined that states are obligated to prevent environmental injury and protect the human rights not only of its own peoples, but also of those living beyond its borders.

As you read these excerpts from the advisory opinion, and in the context of co-violations of human rights and rights of nature discussed in this chapter, note the court's emphasis on the "interdependence and indivisibility of human rights and environmental protection," its references to international environmental instruments and their connection to human rights, and the obligation of states to prevent environmental harm in order to protect human rights. Note, in particular, the court's emphasis on the "special vulnerability" of Indigenous and tribal peoples as victims of environmental harm.

Inter-American Court of Human Rights Advisory Opinion OC-23/17 of November 15, 2017 Requested by the Republic of Colombia[44]

...

VI

ENVIRONMENTAL PROTECTION AND THE HUMAN RIGHTS RECOGNIZED IN THE AMERICAN CONVENTION

46. This Opinion constitutes one of the first opportunities that the Court has had to refer extensively to the State obligations arising from the need to protect the environment under the American Convention (supra para. 23). Even though the object of the request made by Colombia, as previously defined (supra paras. 32 to 38), refers specifically to the State obligations derived from the rights to life and to personal integrity, the Court finds it pertinent to include some initial and introductory considerations on: (A) the interrelationship between human rights and the environment, and (B) the human rights affected by environmental degradation, including the right to a healthy environment. The purpose of the considerations in this chapter is to provide a

[43] Article 11 to the Additional Protocol to the American Convention on Human Rights in the Area of Economic, Social and Cultural Rights (Protocol of San Salvador), Organization of American States (OAS), 16 November 1999.
[44] All footnotes preserved from original.—Eds.

context and a general background to the answers to the specific questions posed by Colombia that follow.

A. The interrelationship between human rights and the environment

47. This Court has recognized the existence of an undeniable relationship between the protection of the environment and the realization of other human rights, in that environmental degradation and the adverse effects of climate change affect the real enjoyment of human rights. . . .[45]

48. Specifically, in cases concerning the territorial rights of Indigenous and tribal peoples, the Court has referred to the relationship between a healthy environment and the protection of human rights, considering that these peoples' right to collective ownership is linked to the protection of, and access to, the resources to be found in their territories, because those natural resources are necessary for the very survival, development and continuity of their way of life.[46] The Court has also recognized the close links that exist between the right to a dignified life and the protection of ancestral territory and natural resources. In this regard, the Court has determined that, because Indigenous and tribal peoples are in a situation of special vulnerability, States must take positive measures to ensure that the members of these peoples have access to a dignified life—which includes the protection of their close relationship with the land—and to their life project, in both its individual and collective dimension.[47] The Court has also emphasized that the lack of access to the corresponding territories and natural resources may expose Indigenous communities to precarious and subhuman living conditions and increased vulnerability to disease and epidemics, and subject them to situations of extreme neglect that may result in various violations of their human rights in addition to causing them suffering and undermining the preservation of their way of life, customs and language . . . [citation omitted].

52. In addition, there is extensive recognition of the interdependent relationship between protection of the environment, sustainable development, and human rights in international law. This interrelationship has been asserted since the Stockholm Declaration on the Human Environment (hereinafter "Stockholm Declaration") which established that "[e]conomic and social development is essential for ensuring a favourable living and working environment for man and for creating conditions on earth that are necessary for the

[45] *Cf. Case of Kawas Fernández v. Honduras. Merits, reparations and costs.* Judgment of April 3, 2009. Series C No. 196, ¶ 148.

[46] *See, inter alia, Case of the Yakye Axa Indigenous Community v. Paraguay. Merits, reparations and costs.* Judgment of June 17, 2005. Series C No. 125, ¶ 137; *Case of the Sawhoyamaxa Indigenous Community v. Paraguay. Merits, reparations and costs.* Judgment of March 29, 2006. Series C No. 146, ¶ 118; *Case of the Saramaka People v. Suriname. Preliminary objections, merits, reparations and costs.* Judgment of November 28, 2007. Series C No. 172, ¶¶ 121 and 122; and *Case of the Kaliña and Lokono Peoples v. Suriname, supra,* ¶ 173.

[47] *Cf. Case of the Yakye Axa Indigenous Community v. Paraguay, supra,* ¶ 163; and *Case of the Kaliña and Lokono Peoples v. Suriname, supra,* ¶ 181.

improvement of the quality of life," and asserting the need to balance development with protection of the human environment [citations omitted]. Subsequently, in the Rio Declaration on Environment and Development (hereinafter "the Rio Declaration"), the States recognized that "[h]uman beings are at the centre of concerns for sustainable development, "and also underlined that "[i]n order to achieve sustainable development, environmental protection shall constitute an integral part of the development process" [citation omitted]. Following this, the Johannesburg Declaration on Sustainable Development established three pillars of sustainable development: economic development, social development and environmental protection [citation omitted]. Also, in the corresponding Plan of Implementation of the World Summit on Sustainable Development, the States "acknowledge[d] the consideration being given to the possible relationship between environment and human rights, including the right to development."[48]

54. Numerous points of interconnection arise from this relationship of interdependence and indivisibility between human rights, the environment, and sustainable development owing to which, as indicated by the Independent Expert, "all human rights are vulnerable to environmental degradation, in that the full enjoyment of all human rights depends on a supportive environment."[49] In this regard, the Human Rights Council has identified environmental threats that may affect, directly or indirectly, the effective enjoyment of specific human rights, affirming that: (i) illicit traffic in, and improper management and disposal of, hazardous substances and wastes constitute a serious threat to a range of rights, including the rights to life and health;[50] (ii) climate change has a wide range of implications for the effective enjoyment of human rights, including the rights to life, health, food, water, housing and self-determination,[51] and (iii) "environmental degradation, desertification and global climate change are exacerbating destitution and desperation, causing a negative impact on the realization of the right to food, in particular in developing countries."[52]

[48] *Cf.* Plan of Implementation of the World Summit on Sustainable Development, adopted at the World Summit on Sustainable Development, Johannesburg, September 4, 2002, UN Doc. A/CONF.199/20, ¶ 5.
[49] Human Rights Council, Preliminary Report of the Independent Expert on the Issue of Human Rights Obligations Relating to the Enjoyment of a Safe, Clean, Healthy and Sustainable Environment, John H. Knox, December 24, 2012, UN Doc. A/HRC/22/43, ¶ 19. [Remainder of citation omitted.]
[50] *Cf.* Commission on Human Rights, Resolution 2005/15, . . . UN Doc. E/CN.4/RES/2005/15; Human Rights Council, Resolution 9/1, . . . September 24, 2008, UN Doc. A/HRC/RES/9/1; Human Rights Council, Resolution 18/11 . . . adopted on September 27, 2011, A/HRC/18/L.6. [Remainder of citation omitted.]
[51] *Cf.* Human Rights Council, Resolution 35, entitled "Human Rights and Climate Change," adopted on June 19, 2017, UN Doc. A/HRC/35/L.32 . . . [remainder of citation omitted].
[52] *Cf.* Human Rights Council, Resolution 7/14, "The Right to Food," adopted on March 27, 2008, A/HRC/7/L.6; Human Rights Council, Resolution 10/12, entitled "The Right to Food," adopted on March 26, 2009, A/HRC/RES/10/12; and Human Rights Council, Resolution 13/4, entitled "The Right to Food," adopted on March 24, 2010, A/HRC/RES/13/4. [Remainder of citation omitted.]

55. Owing to the close connection between environmental protection, sustainable development and human rights (*supra* paras. 47 to 55), currently (i) numerous human rights protection systems recognize the right to a healthy environment as a right in itself, particularly the Inter-American human rights system, while it is evident that (ii) numerous other human rights are vulnerable to environmental degradation, all of which results in a series of environmental obligations for States to comply with their duty to respect and to ensure those rights. Specifically, another consequence of the interdependence and indivisibility of human rights and environmental protection is that, when determining these State obligations, the Court may avail itself of the principles, rights and obligations of international environmental law, which, as part of the international *corpus iuris* make a decisive contribution to establishing the scope of the obligations under the American Convention in this regard (*supra* paras. 43 to 45)....

B. Human rights affected by environmental degradation, including the right to a healthy environment

...

58. The Court underscores that the right to a healthy environment is recognized explicitly in the domestic laws of several States of the region [citation omitted], as well as in some provisions of the international *corpus iuris,* in addition to the aforementioned Protocol of San Salvador (*supra* para. 56), such as the American Declaration on the Rights of Indigenous Peoples; the African Charter on Human and Peoples' Rights; the ASEAN Human Rights Declaration, and the Arab Charter on Human Rights [citations omitted].

59. The human right to a healthy environment has been understood as a right that has both individual and also collective connotations. In its collective dimension, the right to a healthy environment constitutes a universal value that is owed to both present and future generations. That said, the right to a healthy environment also has an individual dimension insofar as its violation may have a direct and an indirect impact on the individual owing to its connectivity to other rights, such as the rights to health, personal integrity, and life. Environmental degradation may cause irreparable harm to human beings; thus, a healthy environment is a fundamental right for the existence of humankind.

60. The Working Group on the Protocol of San Salvador[53] indicated that the right to a healthy environment, as established in this instrument, involved

[53] The Working Group to examine the periodic reports of the States Parties established in the Protocol of San Salvador (hereinafter "the Working Group" or "the "GTPSS") was installed in May 2010 to examine the reports presented by the States Parties and to forward its recommendations and comments on the situation in the States as regards compliance with the provisions of the Protocol of San Salvador. [Remainder of citation omitted.]

the following five State obligations: (a) guaranteeing everyone, without any discrimination, a healthy environment in which to live; (b) guaranteeing everyone, without any discrimination, basic public services; (c) promoting environmental protection; (d) promoting environmental conservation, and (e) promoting improvement of the environment.[54] It also established that the exercise of the right to a healthy environment must be governed by the criteria of availability, accessibility, sustainability, acceptability and adaptability [citation omitted], as in the case of other economic, social and cultural rights.[55] In order to examine the State reports under the Protocol of San Salvador, in 2014, the OAS General Assembly adopted specific progress indicators to evaluate the status of the environment based on: (a) atmospheric conditions; (b) quality and sufficiency of water sources; (c) air quality; (d) soil quality; (e) biodiversity; (f) production of pollutant waste and its management; (g) energy resources, and (h) status of forestry resources... [citation omitted].

* * *

62. The Court considers it important to stress that, as an autonomous right, the right to a healthy environment, unlike other rights, protects the components of the environment, such as forests, rivers and seas, as legal interests in themselves, even in the absence of the certainty or evidence of a risk to individuals. This means that it protects nature and the environment, not only because of the benefits they provide to humanity or the effects that their degradation may have on other human rights, such as health, life or personal integrity, but because of their importance to the other living organisms with which we share the planet that also merit protection in their own right. In this regard, the Court notes a tendency, not only in court judgments, but also in Constitutions, to recognize legal personality and, consequently, rights to nature.

63. Thus, the right to a healthy environment as an autonomous right differs from the environmental content that arises from the protection of other rights, such as the right to life or the right to personal integrity....

66. The Court considers that the rights that are particularly vulnerable to environmental impact include the rights to life, personal integrity, private life, health, water, food, housing, participation in cultural life, property, and the right to not be forcibly displaced [citations omitted]. Without prejudice to

[54] *Cf.* GTPSS, "Progress Indicators: Second Group of Rights," November 5, 2013, OEA/Ser.L/XXV.2.1, GT/PSS/doc.9/13, ¶ 26.

[55] *Cf.* GTPSS, "Progress Indicators: Second Group of Rights," November 5, 2013, OEA/Ser.L/XXV.2.1, GT/PSS/doc.9/13, ¶ 29. See, similarly, but in relation to other rights, *Case of Gonzales Lluy et al. v. Ecuador. Preliminary objections, merits, reparations and costs.* Judgment of September 1, 2015. Series C No. 298, ¶ 235; and *Case of I.V. v. Bolivia. Preliminary objections, merits, reparations and costs.* Judgment of November 30, 2016. Series C No. 329, ¶ 164.

the foregoing, according to Article 29 of the Convention,[56] other rights are also vulnerable and their violation may affect the rights to life, liberty and security of the individual,[57] and infringe on the obligation of all persons to conduct themselves fraternally,[58] such as the right to peace, because displacements caused by environmental deterioration frequently unleash violent conflicts between the displaced population and the population settled on the territory to which it is displaced. Some of these conflicts are massive and thus extremely grave.

67. The Court also bears in mind that the effects on these rights may be felt with greater intensity by certain groups in vulnerable situations. It has been recognized that environmental damage "will be experienced with greater force in the sectors of the population that are already in a vulnerable situation"; hence, based on "international human rights law, States are legally obliged to confront these vulnerabilities based on the principle of equality and non-discrimination." Various human rights bodies have recognized that Indigenous peoples, children, people living in extreme poverty, minorities, and people with disabilities, among others, are groups that are especially vulnerable to environmental damage, and have also recognized the differentiated impact that it has on women [citations omitted]. In addition, the groups that are especially vulnerable to environmental degradation include communities that, essentially, depend economically or for their survival on environmental resources from the marine environment, forested areas and river basins,[59] or run a special risk of being affected owing to their geographical location, such as coastal and small island communities.[60] In many cases, the special vulnerability of these groups has led to their relocation or internal displacement [citation omitted].

. . . .

[56] *See* Article 29(b), (c), and (d) of the American Convention, which establish that: "No provision of this Convention shall be interpreted as: [...] (b) restricting the enjoyment or exercise of any right or freedom recognized by virtue of the laws of any State Party or by virtue of another convention to which one of the said states is a party; (c) precluding other rights or guarantees that are inherent in the human personality or derived from representative democracy as a form of government, or (d) excluding or limiting the effect that the American Declaration of the Rights and Duties of Man and other international acts of the same nature may have."

[57] In this regard, Article I of the American Declaration of the Rights and Duties of Man stipulates that: "Every human being has the right to life, liberty and the security of his person."

[58] In this regard, see the Preamble to the American Declaration of the Rights and Duties of Man, which indicates that: "All men are born free and equal, in dignity and in rights, and, being endowed by nature with reason and conscience, they should conduct themselves as brothers one to another."

[59] *See, inter alia,* United Nations General Assembly, Resolution 66/288, "The Future We Want," July 27, 2012, UN Doc. A/RES/66/288, ¶ 30; United Nations General Assembly, Resolution 64/255, Report of the Special Rapporteur on Adequate Housing as a Component of the Right to an Adequate Standard of Living, and on the Right to Non-Discrimination in this Context, August 6, 2009, UN Doc. A/64/255, ¶¶ 26, 27, and 30 to 34, and Convention on Biological Diversity, entered into force on December 29, 1993, preamble.

[60] In particular, the effects of climate change may result in saltwater flooding, desertification, hurricanes, erosion and landslides, leading to scarcity of water supplies and affecting food production from agriculture and fishing, as well as destroying land and housing. [Rest of citation omitted.]

A. The rights to life and to personal integrity in relation to environmental protection

A.1 Meaning and scope of the rights to life and to personal integrity in the face of potential environmental damage

108. The Court has affirmed repeatedly that the right to life in the American Convention is essential because the realization of the other rights depends on its protection.[61] Accordingly, States are obliged to ensure the creation of the necessary conditions for the full enjoyment and exercise of this right.[62]

109.... Among the conditions required for a decent life, the Court has referred to access to, and the quality of, water, food and health, and the content has been defined in the Court's case law, indicating that these conditions have a significant impact on the right to a decent existence and the basic conditions for the exercise of other human rights [citations omitted]. The Court has also included environmental protection as a condition for a decent life... [citation omitted].

112. Regarding the right to personal integrity, the Court reiterates that the violation of an individual's right to physical and mental integrity has various connotations of degree and ranges from torture to other types of ill-treatment or cruel, inhuman or degrading treatment, the physical and mental effects of which vary in intensity according to endogenous and exogenous factors (such as duration of the treatment, age, sex, health, context and vulnerability) that must be examined in each specific situation.[63]

113. Furthermore, in the specific case of Indigenous and tribal communities, the Court has ruled on the obligation to protect their ancestral territories owing to the relationship that such lands have with their cultural identity, a fundamental human right of a collective nature that must be respected in a multicultural, pluralist and democratic society.[64]

114. The Court notes that although each right contained in the Convention has its own sphere, meaning and scope,[65] there is a close relationship between

[61] *Cf. Case of the "Street Children" (Villagrán Morales et al.) v. Guatemala. Merits, supra,* ¶ 144*; and Case of Ortiz Hernández et al. v. Venezuela. Merits, reparations and costs.* Judgment of August 22, 2017. Series C No. 338, ¶ 100.

[62] *Cf. Case of the "Street Children" (Villagrán Morales et al.) v. Guatemala. Merits, supra,* ¶ 144; and *Case of Chinchilla Sandoval et al. v. Guatemala, supra,* ¶ 166.

[63] *Cf. Case of Loayza Tamayo v. Peru. Merits.* Judgment of September 17, 1997. Series C No. 33, ¶¶ 57 and 58; and *Case of Ortiz Hernández et al. v. Venezuela, supra,* ¶ 102.

[64] *Mutatis mutandi, Case of the Kichwa Indigenous People of Sarayaku v. Ecuador, supra,* ¶ 217; and *Case of the Río Negro Massacres v. Guatemala. Preliminary objection, merits, reparations and costs.* Judgment of September 4, 2012. Series C No. 250, ¶ 160.

[65] *Cf. Case of Manuel Cepeda Vargas v. Colombia. Preliminary objections, merits, reparations and costs.* Judgment of May 26, 2010. Series C No. 213, ¶ 171; and *Case of Mohamed v. Argentina. Preliminary objection, merits, reparations and costs.* Judgment of November 23, 2012. Series C No. 255, ¶ 119.

> the right to life and the right to personal integrity. Thus, there are times when the lack of access to conditions that ensure a dignified life may also constitute a violation of the right to personal integrity;[66] for example, in cases involving human health.[67] Moreover, the Court has recognized that certain projects and interventions in the environment in which people live can constitute a risk to their life and personal integrity.[68] Therefore, the Court considers it pertinent to examine jointly the State obligations in relation to the rights to life and to personal integrity that may be affected by environmental damage. Consequently, the Court will now establish and reaffirm the meaning and scope of the general obligations to respect and to ensure the rights to life and to personal integrity (*infra* paras. 115 to 121) and will then establish the specific environmental obligations derived from this general obligation (*infra* paras. 123 to 242), as solicited by Colombia in its request for an advisory opinion.

* * *

In summary, the Court determined that:

> **4.** For the purposes of Article 1(1) of the American Convention, it is understood that individuals whose rights under the Convention have been violated owing to transboundary harm are subject to the jurisdiction of the State of origin of the harm, because that State exercises effective control over the activities carried out in its territory or under its jurisdiction, in accordance with paragraphs 95 to 103 of this Opinion.
>
> **5.** To respect and to ensure the rights to life and to personal integrity of the persons subject to their jurisdiction, States have the obligation to prevent significant environmental damage within or outside their territory and, to this end, must regulate, supervise and monitor activities within their jurisdiction that could produce significant environmental damage; conduct environmental impact assessments when there is a risk of significant environmental damage; prepare a contingency plan to establish safety measures and procedures to minimize the possibility of major environmental accidents, and mitigate any significant environmental damage that may have occurred, in accordance with paragraphs 127 and 174 of this Opinion. . . .

* * *

[66] *Mutatis mutandi, Case of the "Juvenile Re-education Institute" v. Paraguay, supra,* ¶ 170; and *Case of Chinchilla Sandoval v. Guatemala, supra,* ¶¶ 168 and 169.

[67] *Cf. Case of Albán Cornejo et al. v. Ecuador. Merits, reparations and costs.* Judgment of November 22, 2007. Series C No. 171, ¶ 117; and *Case of Chinchilla Sandoval v. Guatemala, supra,* ¶ 170.

[68] *Cf. Case of the Kichwa Indigenous People of Sarayaku v. Ecuador, supra,* ¶ 249; and *Case of the Kaliña and Lokono Peoples v. Suriname, supra,* ¶ 222.

VI. CONCLUSION

The Inter-American human rights system has addressed a substantial number of human rights violations caused by environmental harm, while the Inter-American Court of Human Rights' landmark 2017 advisory opinion and 2020 decision in the case between Argentina and Indigenous communities, also display its willingness to recognize nature's own right to a healthy environment. The European and African human rights systems also contend with cases involving human rights violations as a result of environmental injury. Yet, governments, for the most part, ignore these decisions of human rights forums where, in many instances, they themselves are the perpetrators. New approaches are necessary to hold governments accountable for upholding human rights and, where recognized, the rights of nature.

In a search for alternative approaches, following Berta Cáceres's murder in 2016, the Civic Council of Popular and Indigenous Organizations of Honduras (COPINH), the grassroots organization that she co-founded, took legal action against the Dutch development bank FMO over its involvement in the construction of the Agua Zarca dam in Honduras. The lawsuit claims that the bank had a duty of care towards Cáceres, her children, and other members of the community that no harm would accrue to them as a result of the dam project. The bank and its officials had failed in their responsibilities toward the Indigenous community who were seriously harmed by the project and ignored the violations of human rights by the company building the dam and, specifically, the warnings raised by Cáceres herself. Moreover, they had not performed the due diligence required to ensure that their financial support of the project would not abet violations of the community's human rights. The objective of the lawsuit was to create a precedent for other European banks considering the financing of similar projects.[69]

As a result of her murder, the Dutch bank stopped loans to the project pending a review, and, in 2017, it withdrew from the project, along with the Finnish Fund for Industrial Cooperation and the Central American Bank of Economic Integration.[70]

Campaigns against investment and development banks financing companies that violate human rights are proving to be one successful method of stopping these projects, as are divestment initiatives such as that initiated by Greenpeace, Earth First!, and BankTrack against investors in the Dakota Access Pipeline campaign. BankTrack investigates and reports on bank financing of projects causing egregious harm to communities and to the environment and maintains a list of these banks on its website. It also leads campaigns to prevail upon banks to end the financing of such projects and to meet their international commitments regarding human rights and the environment.[71]

[69] *Bank Faces Lawsuit Over Honduras Dam Project as Spirit of Berta Cáceres Lives On*, (May 18, 2018), THE GUARDIAN, https://www.theguardian.com/global-development/2018/may/18/bank-faces-lawsuit-over-honduras-dam-project-spirit-of-berta-caceres-fmo-agua-zarca; https://www.bothends.org/en/Our-work/Dossiers/Agua-Zarca-Indigenous-fight-against-dam-costs-lives/.

[70] *Id.*

[71] BankTrack, *Campaigns*, https://www.banktrack.org/campaigns (last visited Feb. 20, 2020).

These campaigns protesting human rights violations as a result of ecological harm are instrumental in achieving recognition for rights of nature. While all humans need thriving ecosystems and biodiversity for survival, our view of nature remains anthropocentric, and we continue to view it as property and a source of resources for unlimited economic growth. Under the current legal system, nature cannot protest violations of its rights to flourish and thrive. Instead, environmental defenders face life-threatening risks to stop ecological catastrophes from destroying both natural systems and local communities. These defenders intertwine their own human rights with rights for nature, understanding that to protect human rights, nature's rights must be ensured. As detailed in this chapter, they use a creative diversity of legal forums and lawsuits in pursuing justice for violations of both. Their work will be bolstered by Earth law and the transformation of current laws to support an ecocentric worldview that recognizes rights of nature and gaining formal legal status for nature.

STUDY QUESTIONS

(1) Christopher Stone, in his essay *Should Trees Have Standing? Toward Legal Rights for Natural Objects,* writes that "[a] society in which it is stated . . . that 'rivers have legal rights' would evolve a different legal system than one which did not employ that expression." What do you think he meant by this—that law's role is primarily in creating new norms? How would this work for rights for nature? Earth Law Center's 2015 Co-violation Report, which emphasizes the importance of adopting the Universal Declaration on the Rights of Mother Earth, brings as an analogy the 1948 Universal Declaration of Human Rights, which triggered an entirely new branch of international law—human rights law. How might the adoption of the Universal Declaration of Rights of Mother Earth follow the success of the UDHR by inspiring a new branch of international rights of nature laws? What factors might stand in the way?

(2) In many co-violation incidents, governments and industries blame environmental defenders for violating the human "right to development," be it creating more energy sources, extracting more minerals and other resources from Earth, creating more farmland, etc. What would you argue in reply to this argument? Do you see this is as a possible clash and source of conflict between human rights and rights for nature?

(3) The extensive burning of the Amazon in 2019 to create more pastureland for animals and more farmland, supported by government policy, has triggered a global response threatening Brazil if it doesn't take steps to stop the devastation. So far the threats have related to trade between Brazil and the rest of the world. What could happen if Brazil ignores the threats and keeps on burning? If you were a world leader participating in a summit addressing this issue, and the scientists advising the summit are telling you that the world is facing a catastrophe if the Amazon burning doesn't stop, would you go so far as to support an

international force invading Brazil to stop the destruction? How would you support this? Would you define the burning as ecocide? To help answer this question, read the following excerpt from the Earth Law Center's 2015 Co-violations Report:

> Nature's rights can also be considered through existing court structures. For example, an area that is the focus of escalating global advocacy is the effort to recognize and act on the crime of "ecocide" in international criminal law, as the fifth crime prosecutable before the International Criminal Court (ICC) in the same manner as crimes against humanity (such as genocide and war crimes). "Ecocide" cases represent the most severe cases of environmental destruction and health-related damages. They are those which threaten the safety of the planet, and so must be recognized as a crime.[72] (*See also* Chapter 12, "Ecocide.")

(4) Do you agree with the argument raised in the Earth Law Center's 2015 Co-violations Report that "Our modern environmental laws themselves implicitly accept this claim of nature as property. They legalize nature's destruction by dictating *how much* of the environment we can degrade, thus validating the continuing onslaught. Instead, we need laws grounded in the inherent rights of natural world to exist, thrive, and evolve"?[73] How might the following statement from the report help you to determine your position?

> Despite these and other escalating climate-related harms, national and international climate change laws and conventions continue to legalize massive amounts of greenhouse gas emissions while only calling for modest, and usually voluntary, reductions. While the international community fails to address climate change and other drivers of co-violations, humans and nature continue to suffer the consequences.[74]

(5) Our current legal system, including its environmental laws, is geared to support governments in their drive for increasing economic growth. Therefore, this system also supports corporations as catalysts for economic growth. As such, environmental defenders are targets of attack by police and army forces, whose mandate it is to enforce government laws. The problem is particularly acute in countries where democracy is weak, governments are riddled by corruption, and human rights are violated with impunity. In light of legal systems supporting the global economic model of unlimited growth, is the key factor in bringing about change to adjust the current economic model? How might that take place? Considering the obstacles in creating economic change, how might the adoption and enforcement of laws granting rights to nature promote that change? How might it curtail the fundamental change of the current economic model?

(6) By reminding ourselves that the economic model of unlimited growth feeds on high consumption rates, we expose our own role in violations of human rights and rights of nature. Global Witness tells us that while governments and

[72] Earth Law Center, *supra* note 8, at 43.
[73] *Id.* at 8.
[74] *Id.* at 7.

corporations are certainly guilty of atrocities against environmental defenders, "we can all do more. Ultimately, attacks against land and environmental defenders stem from our voracious appetite for agricultural goods like palm oil and coffee, and for fossil fuels, minerals and timber."[75] What does this say about us as consumers? Should we be admonishing the manufacturers of our favorite products and threaten that we will not buy them if they are "fueling human rights abuses, cultural destruction or environmental devastation?"[76] What laws might be developed to promote cutting down on our rates of consumption? How can global grassroots efforts coalesce to eventually change the current economic model and, at the same time, protect human rights and rights of nature?

(7) In 2015, Berta Cáceres accused then U.S. Secretary of State Hillary Clinton of supporting the 2009 coup in Honduras and the subsequent election of the current president, Juan Orlando Hernández Alvarado. While the international community was demanding the return of President Emanuel Zelaya and restitution of democracy, the United States legitimized the fraudulent elections that would install the coup regime. What arguments might be made based on the U.S. support for the 2009 Honduran coup and subsequent elections that the United States bears legal responsibility for the murder of environmental and social activists and the environmental degradation by foreign corporations that has ensued? To the extent U.S. international policy is part of, or even the core of, the problem, how might the solution lie in coordinating campaigns for international and national laws for rights of nature with political campaigns to change U.S. policy?

(8) In the Lago Agrio case, over the course of nearly 30 years, Chevron spent tens if not hundreds of millions of dollars to avoid liability for the impact of its business activities on nature and human life. While Chevron's ultimate objective was to avoid financial responsibility for the damage caused by Texaco's oil drilling activities, its ulterior motive was discouraging other lawsuits. Thus Chevron filed a Strategic Lawsuit Against Public Participation (a "SLAPP" suit) against Steven Donziger, the lawyer representing the victim, for the purpose of chilling the interests by terrifying other potential litigants. How might you deal with the threat of being personally targeted by a large corporate defendant? How chilling might the effect of sanctions be on lawyers practicing Earth law?

[75] *Supra* note 17 at 6.
[76] *Id.* at 7.

CHAPTER 11

Nonhuman Rights[1]

I. INTRODUCTION

He never asked for it, but Tommy has been something of a celebrity for much of his life. In 1987, he appeared alongside the Hollywood actor Matthew Broderick in the film *Project X* about the U.S. space program. Then, he became a well-known circus performer in upstate New York. After that career came to an end sometime in the 2000s, Tommy was moved to a trailer lot in Gloversville, New York, where he was made to live inside a metal cage with green bars. Eventually, his companions all died, leaving him with only a television for company. All of this is perfectly legal in the United States under current municipal, state, and federal law.

Tommy's confinement and commercial exploitation are legal because he is not a human being (with the right not to be unjustly imprisoned) but a chimpanzee (with no legal rights whatsoever). Like every nonhuman animal in the United States, Tommy is currently treated as a "thing" under the law. Being a thing in this context means he lacks the capacity for rights.[2] Tommy is protected to some extent by existing anti-cruelty, welfare, and conservation statutes, but none of these avenues provide relief from his solitary confinement.

There is an effort underway to change the legal status of Tommy and other nonhuman animals so that they can possess fundamental legal rights, including to their bodily liberty. In December 2013, Tommy was once again thrust into the spotlight as the first-ever nonhuman animal in the world to seek a common law writ of habeas corpus.[3] The litigation to free Tommy to a sanctuary[4] is the work of the Nonhuman Rights Project (NhRP), a U.S.-based civil rights organization whose stated mission is to change the common law legal status of at least some nonhuman animals from things, which lack

[1] This chapter was authored by Kevin R. Schneider, Esq., Executive Director of the Nonhuman Rights Project (NhRP), a U.S.-based nonprofit civil rights organization founded by Steven M. Wise, Esq., in 1996.

[2] *See* Dave Fagundes, *What We Talk About When We Talk About Persons: The Language of a Legal Fiction*, 114 Harv. L. Rev. 1745, 1746 (2001).

[3] Tommy, and the legal fight to see him freed, is featured in the 2016 HBO/Pennebaker Hegedus documentary film "Unlocking the Cage." For a full timeline of Tommy's case, including links to all filings, affidavits, and decisions, see https://www.nonhumanrights.org/client-Tommy.

[4] Unfortunately, captive chimpanzees generally cannot be sent back to nature because they lack the complex set of skills necessary for survival. The same is true with many captive wildlife species, especially those who naturally live in complex social units among their kin. While sanctuary can never replace the natural life that was taken from them, it can provide animals with a meaningful degree of autonomy, free choice, and companionship.

the capacity for any rights, to "persons" who possess the capacity for at least a single right.

This chapter takes the habeas corpus litigation to free Tommy and other chimpanzees in New York as a jumping-off point for broader discussions about how the law is responding to demands for the recognition of the rights of nonhuman animals and the natural world. The issue of whether a chimpanzee is entitled to habeas corpus goes to questions at the heart of rights of nature jurisprudence by illuminating foundational legal questions:

- Are legal rights coextensive with the human species?
- Who or what counts under the law, and whose rights will the law affirmatively act upon to protect?
- What is the role of the common law in expanding legal protections?
- How should science impact judicial decision-making and policymaking?
- What principles should guide the assignment of rights?
- Where should society draw the line when it comes to recognizing other species and the natural world as rights-bearers?

This chapter focuses on five New York state trial and appellate court opinions issued between 2014 and 2018. Tommy is involved in three of the five opinions and the others involve chimpanzees Kiko (Niagara Falls) and Hercules and Leo (Stony Brook). These cases represent the beginning of the world's first concerted effort to achieve common law legal personhood for any nonhuman animal. The theory of the NhRP is that a narrow but deep case presenting a profound claim for the rights of even one animal is the best means by which to call the fundamental legal situation into question. This chapter mirrors that ethic by focusing on Tommy's case (as well as those of Kiko, Hercules, and Leo).

Every case in this chapter began with the filing of a petition for a common law writ of habeas corpus. *Habeas corpus* is Latin for "produce the body" (sometimes translated differently, though to the same effect). Habeas corpus is one of the oldest writs (cause of action, form of petitioning for redress) in the English common law tradition. Often referred to as the "Great Writ," habeas corpus came into being around the time of the Magna Carta as a means to protect individuals from arbitrary detention. Habeas corpus, to the extent it has not been abrogated by statute, is composed of common law as opposed to statutory law and, as such, remains a unique area in which judges have flexibility to expand the scope of the law without need for legislative approval.[5] The writ can also be sought by "order to show cause," where it does not call for the physical production of the detained, as is (obviously) the case in the NhRP's litigation on behalf of chimpanzees and other nonhuman animals.

Common law, originating in England beginning around the mid-twelfth century with roots in Roman law and other traditions, forms the foundation of American law and many other English-speaking jurisdictions. Under this system, judicial decisions

[5] It is important to note that legislatures can generally override the decisions of common law courts within their jurisdictions by statute, and, so, other measure need to be taken in order to protect court victories.

accrete over time as precedent and inform the decisions of judges in future disputes, and that "living body of law" is collectively known as the *common law*. In contrast with constitutional law, statutory law, and regulatory law, in which judges are interpreting statutes or provisions written by legislators or administrators, the common law is the law that judges make.

Judges are bound to a greater or lesser extent by common law rules rendered by judges before them, but they may also choose to decline to follow such rules as changed circumstances require. While the common law is an older and, in some ways, less relevant body of law in some areas, such as federal law and international law, which are dominated by statutes, regulations, treaties, and detailed civil law codes, it still remains vitally important across a wide range of legal disputes, and the time-tested principles it has described are often relied on outside the traditional confines of the common law. The common law will be familiar to students of torts and property, in particular, since these branches are predominately composed of common law rules that at one time did not exist but which were created over the generations in response to changes in human experience, economics, morality, and scientific understanding (e.g., property, contracts, common law marriage, negligence principles, etc.).[6]

The common law, by its nature, builds upon itself over time. While there is no concrete mechanism within the common law responsible for this evolutionary process, it is nonetheless an integral part of it.[7] Common law judges are empowered to "legislate" from the bench in certain circumstances to shape the future path of the law and can choose to depart from prior precedent. Crucial for the present conversation, common law judges are empowered to transform legal things into legal persons under some circumstances, including through the common law writ of habeas corpus. The NhRP's litigation work is based in large part on the monumental 1772 anti-slavery precedent of *Somerset v. Stewart*,[8] in which, for the first time, a common law judge recognized the legal personhood and rights of an African slave, thereby setting him free and putting into motion the beginning of the end of the transatlantic slave trade. The common law writ of habeas corpus, which includes the *Somerset* precedent, was imported into the American colonies and "lies in all cases of imprisonment by commitment, detention, confinement or restraint, for whatever cause, or under whatever pretence."[9] In a similar spirit, the United States Supreme Court has emphasized that the writ's "scope and flexibility" and "its capacity to reach all manner of illegal detention," as well as "its ability to cut through barriers of form and procedural mazes . . . have always been emphasized and jealously guarded by courts and lawmakers."[10] In short, habeas corpus appears a uniquely powerful vehicle for presenting a claim that an entity lacking rights

[6] Civil law and other non-common law systems will need to be addressed separately, but there are some early indications that the "thing/person" paradigm generally prevails in these systems as well (*see, e.g., In re Cecilia* Third Court of Guarantees, Mendoza, Argentina, File No. P-72.254/15).

[7] *But see* Oliver Wendell Holmes, *The Path of the Law*, 10 HARV. L. REV. 457 (1897) (describing a still-influential view of the law as a positivist structure that gives supremacy to statutes and constitutions over common law).

[8] *Somerset v. Stewart*, 98 ER 499 (1772) as described in Steven M. Wise, *Though the Heavens May Fall: The Landmark Trial That Led to the End of Human Slavery* (2005).

[9] *People v. McLeod*, 3 Hill 635, 647 note j (N.Y. 1842).

[10] *Harris v. Nelson*, 394 U.S. 286, 291 (1969).

should be entitled to at least one right, namely, the right to liberty protected by the common law writ of habeas corpus.

Habeas corpus was created to protect autonomy. Tommy is autonomous. The crux of the argument for Tommy is that autonomy is a sufficient, but not necessary, basis for personhood and the right to bodily liberty under the common law of habeas corpus. Tommy's case is built on the foundation of scientific research into the emotional and cognitive complexity of chimpanzees that first came into focus through the work of Dr. Jane Goodall, whose observations of the chimpanzees of the Gombe Stream National Park in Tanzania Gombe forest in Uganda changed forever humanity's perceptions of the other species with whom we share the planet.[11] We now know chimpanzees to be "autonomous beings."[12] What autonomy means in real-life terms for chimpanzees, in part, is that they are self-aware[13] and act in an intentional manner;[14] possess an autobiographical self,[15] episodic memory,[16] long-term spatial memory and awareness,[17] and self-consciousness (chimpanzees can recognize their younger selves in photographs);[18] are capable of numerosity,[19] sequential learning,[20] mental state modeling,[21] and understanding the experiences of others[22] (for example, a chimpanzee named Santino, who is an "inmate" of a zoo in Furuvik, Sweden, stockpiles hidden stashes of rocks to use as missiles against gawking zoo visitors out of apparent and understandable spite and regularly thwarts the efforts of zoo staff to stop him from amassing these stockpiles);[23] possess the ability to understand and carry out duties and responsibilities while knowingly assuming obligations and then honoring them;[24] engage in referential and intentional communication (what some call "language," including the ability to learn human sign language and spontaneously teach it to other

[11] Jane Goodall, The Chimpanzees of Gombe: Patterns of Behavior (1986).

[12] T.L. Beauchamp & V. Wobber, *Autonomy in Chimpanzees*, 35 Theoretical Med & Bioethics 117 (2014).

[13] Takaaki Kaneko & Masaki Tomonaga, *The Perception of Self-Agency in Chimpanzees (Pan Troglodytes)*, 278 Proceedings of the Royal Society B. 3694-3702 (2011).

[14] Josep Call & Michael Tomasello, *Distinguishing Intentional from Accidental Actions in [Orangutans, Chimpanzees] and Human Children (Homo Sapiens)*, 112(2) J. of Comparative Psych. 192-206 (1998).

[15] Michael J. Beran et al., *Sequential Responding and Planning in Chimpanzees (Pan Troglodytes) and Rhesus Macaques (Macaca Mulatta)*, 30(3) J. of Experimental Psych.: Animal Behavior Processes 203-212 (2004).

[16] *See, e.g.*, Gema Martin-Ordas et al., *Keeping Track of Time: Evidence for Episodic-Like Memory in Great Apes*, 13 Animal Cognition 331-340 (2010).

[17] Karline Janmaat, Simone Ban, & Christophe Boesch, *Chimpanzees Use Long-Term Spatial Memory to Monitor Large Fruit Trees and Remember Feeding Experiences Across Seasons*, 86 Animal Behaviour 1183-1205 (2013).

[18] Daniel J. Povinelli, Alyssa B. Rulf, & Donna T. Bierschwale, *Self-Recognition in Chimpanzees (Pan Troglodytes): Distribution, Ontogeny, and Patterns of Emergence*, 107 J. of Comparative Psych 347-372 (1993).

[19] S.T. Boysen & G. Berntson, *Numerical Competence in a Chimpanzee* [], 103(1) J. of Comp. Psych 23-31 (1989).

[20] Michael J. Beran et al., *Sequential Responding and Planning in Chimpanzees (Pan Troglodytes) and Rhesus Macaques (Macaca Mulatta)*, 30(3) J. of Experimental Psych.: Animal Behavior Proc, 203-212 (2004).

[21] Brian Hare et al., *Chimpanzees Know What Conspecifics Do and Do Not See*, 59 Animal Behaviour 771-785 (2000).

[22] Josep Call et al., *'Unwilling' Versus 'Unable': Chimpanzees' Understanding of Human Intentional Action*, 7(4) Developmental Sci. 488-498 (2004).

[23] *See, e.g., Mathias Osvath, Spontaneous Planning for Future Stone Throwing by a Male Chimpanzee*, 19 Current Biology R190-R191 (2009).

[24] *See* Jane Goodall Affidavit, Supreme Court of the State of New York, County of New York, at https://www.nonhumanrights.org/content/uploads/2015/12/36.-Affidavit-Of-Jane-Goodall-Ph.d-Dbe.pdf (last visited June 30, 2020).

chimpanzees without human invention);[25] have a symbolic culture and engage in tool-use and tool-making[26] and pass these on for generations (sometimes hundreds of generations);[27] possess imagination, empathy,[28] and an understanding of cause and effect;[29] behave in ways that seem both lawful and rule-governed;[30] have moral inclinations and a level of moral agency;[31] ostracize individuals who violate social norms and respond negatively to inequitable situations;[32] have a social life that is cooperative and represents a purposeful and well-coordinated social system;[33] routinely enter into contractual agreements, keep promises and secrets, and prefer fair exchanges;[34] have an awareness of death and perform death-related duties;[35] and show concern for others' welfare (for example, even adult male chimpanzees, assumed to be gruff, have been observed adopting and caring for unrelated orphaned baby chimpanzees).[36] In short, chimpanzees recognize themselves as unique individuals, reflect on the past, appreciate the present, and plan for the future.[37] Yet, to the law, these remarkable beings remain things.

Autonomy is a supreme value in the common law. Apart from habeas corpus, which has long acted as the guarantor of liberty and protector of the autonomy of persons, there are many cases in the common law tradition enshrining the importance of autonomy. Some of the most prominent examples of this principle come from "right to die" cases, in which the courts have reliably sided with the wishes of a person of sound mind to refuse life-saving treatment, thereby placing autonomy and individual choice above even the protection of human life in the panoply of fundamental interests.[38]

Tommy is but one chimpanzee representing a broader movement. The fundamental questions raised in Tommy's case are reverberating around the world, as courts begin to wrestle with claims for the legal personhood and rights of animals and nature.

[25] *See, e.g.*, David A. Leavens, William D. Hopkins, & R.K. Thomas, *Referential Communication by Chimpanzees (Pan Troglodytes)*, 118 J. of Comparative Psych. 48-57 (2004).

[26] *See, e.g.*, Christophe Boesch, Josephine S. Head, & Martha M. Robbins, *Complex Tool Sets for Honey Extraction Among Chimpanzees in Loango National Park, Gabon*, 56 J. of Human Evolution 560-569 (2009).

[27] *See, e.g.*, Julio Mercader et al., *4,300-Year-Old Chimpanzee Sites and the Origins of Percussive Stone Technology*, 104 Proceedings of the Nat'l Acad. of Sci. 3043-3048 (2007).

[28] *See, e.g.*, Christophe Boesch, *Dead or Alive? Towards a Notion of Death and Empathy*, *in* Wild Cultures: A Comparison Between Chimpanzee and Human Cultures 155-175 (2012).

[29] Victoria Horner & Andrew Whiten, *Causal Knowledge and Imitation/Emulation Switching in Chimpanzees (Pan Troglodytes) and Children (Homo Sapiens)*, 8 Animal Cognition 164-181 (2005).

[30] Frans de Waal, Peacemaking Among Primates (1990).

[31] *See, e.g.*, Brosnan, S.F. *Justice and Fairness Related Behaviors in Nonhuman Primates*, 110(2) Proceedings of the Nat'l Acad. of Sci 10416-10423 (2013).

[32] *Id.*

[33] Victoria Horner et al., *Spontaneous Prosocial Choice by Chimpanzees*, 108(33) Proceedings of the Nat'l Acad. of Sci. 13847-13851 (2011).

[34] Darby Proctor et al., *Chimpanzees Play the Ultimatum Game*, 110(6) Proceedings of the Nat'l Acad. of Sci. 2070-2075 (2013).

[35] *See, e.g.*, Boesch, *supra* note 28, at pp. 155-175.

[36] Christophe Boesch et al., *Altruism in Forest Chimpanzees: The Case of Adoption, 5(1)* PLoS ONE e8901 (2010).

[37] Mathias Osvath & H. Osvath, *Chimpanzee (Pan Troglodytes) and Orangutan (Pongo Abelii) Forethought: Self-Control and Pre-Experience in the Face of Future Tool-Use*, 11 Animal Cognition 661-674 (2008).

[38] *See, e.g.*, *Superintendent of Belchertown State Sch. v. Saikewicz*, 373 Mass. 728, 370 N.E.2d 417 (1977); *Erickson v. Dilgard*, 44 Misc. 2d 27, 252 N.Y.S.2d 705 (Sup. Ct. 1962) (New York common law values autonomy over life itself, permitting competent adults to decline life-saving treatment).

Outside the United States. courts have already recognized that some nonhuman animals have legal rights. In 2014, the Indian Supreme Court held that animals in general possess constitutional and statutory rights.[39] In 2016, in a case almost identical to Tommy's, an Argentine trial court granted a writ of habeas corpus to a chimpanzee named Cecilia, designated her a "nonhuman legal person" with "nonhuman rights," and ordered her release from the Mendoza zoo and subsequent transfer to a sanctuary.[40] Rejecting the claim that Cecilia could not avail herself of habeas corpus because she was not a human, the court recognized that "societies evolve in their moral conducts, thoughts, and values" and concluded that classifying autonomous "animals as things is not a correct standard."[41]

Courts and legislatures are also beginning to recognize parts of the natural environment as persons. In 2018, the Colombia Supreme Court designated the Colombian part of the Amazon rainforest "as an entity subject of rights," in other words, a person.[42] In 2017, the New Zealand Parliament designated New Zealand's Whanganui River Iwi as a person that owns its riverbed.[43] In 2014, New Zealand's Te Urewera park was designated a "legal entity, having all the rights, powers, duties, and liabilities of a person."[44] Municipalities around the United States are starting to vote in favor of rights for lakes[45] and may soon do so for at least some nonhuman animals.[46] All of this is occurring rapidly and against a social backdrop of unprecedented calls for action on climate change, species loss, deforestation, threats to Indigenous tribes and cultural knowledge, and other issues, all of which are increasingly seen as inextricably linked.

There are important critiques of the habeas corpus approach that should be considered. Does premising a case for the rights of a nonhuman animal on their "human-like" intelligence risk creating an unreasonably high bar for other species, thus dooming them to remain rightless?[47] Does basing a case like this on historical common law re-entrench harmful property-driven, colonialist ideas of personhood and individualistic liberty?[48] How will the change in status of a handful of "autonomous" animals change the reality for the vast majority suffering on industrial farms or driven toward extinction as a result of human activity? Is it wrong to premise

[39] *Animal Welfare Board of India v. A. Nagaraja & Ors.*, (2014) 6 SCR 468 ¶ 77 at 4, 7, 9 (India).

[40] Third Court of Guarantees, Mendoza, Argentina, File No. P-72.254/15 at 22-2, 24 (as translated from original Spanish by attorney Ana Maria Hernandez).

[41] *Id.* at 5, 19-20, 23-24.

[42] *See* Claudia Fonseca, *Supreme Court Orders Immediate Protection of the Colombia Amazon*, República de Colombia: Corte Suprema de Justicia (Apr. 5, 2018).

[43] *Innovative Bill Protects Whanganui River with Legal Personhood*, New Zealand Parliament (March 28, 2017), https://www.parliament.nz/en/get-involved/features/innovative-bill-protects-whanganui-river-with-legal-personhood/ (accessed January 20, 2019).

[44] Te Urewara Act 2014, Subs 3, s 11(1) (N.Z.).

[45] The citizens of Toledo voted in a municipal election to grant Lake Erie rights to "exist, flourish, and continue to evolve," but it was later overturned by a federal district court judge as "unconstitutionally vague" and beyond "the power of municipal government in Ohio." *Drewes Farms Partnership v. Toledo* (Feb. 27, 2020).

[46] *See* Steven M. Wise et al., *The Power of Municipalities to Enact Legislation Granting Legal Rights to Nonhuman Animals Pursuant to Home Rule*, 67 Syracuse L. Rev. 31, 69 (2017).

[47] *See, e.g.*, Martha C. Nussbaum, *Working with and for Animals: Getting the Theoretical Framework Right*, 94 Denv. L. Rev. 609, 615 (2017).

[48] Will Kymlicka, *Social Membership: Animal Law Beyond the Property/Personhood Impasse*, Dalhousie L. J. 40, 123-155 (2017).

the expansion of rights to animals on court precedents challenging slavery and other historical wrongs done to humans?[49] Must animals be persons in order to be protected, or would such recognition do damage to notions of human rights and exceptionalism?[50] These are important strategic and ethical questions to be sure. However, if we cannot achieve recognition of even a single fundamental right for a "human-like" beings such as Tommy (who are not domesticated, are few in number, and whose economic significance is nil), what hope does any other species really have?[51] Moreover, habeas corpus is but one means to pursue the rights of nonhuman animals. While a viable habeas claim requires that the petitioner be autonomous (i.e., have an interest in bodily liberty), this will not be the case for future endeavors, especially those achieved by legislative means, where the legislature can choose any arbitrary basis it pleases on which to premise legal personhood and rights. If it can be done for corporations, it can be done for chimpanzees. And rivers. And more.

II. RIGHTS VERSUS WELFARE

Tommy is, as discussed, a legal thing, but not all things are created alike in our legal system. As a living breathing animal, Tommy might be thought of in legal terms as a "special" kind of thing, subject to various welfare, conservation, and other laws that are meant to prevent outright abuse and neglect.[52] So, while Tommy and his television are both things in the eyes of the law and property of their human owner, in practice, they are treated very differently (there is no "television welfare" law, obviously). However, welfare laws are silent to this because Tommy lacks the capacity for rights; the legal options for helping him under existing law appear limited.[53]

Under the prevailing animal welfare paradigm, as long as Tommy's human owners treat him according to minimum welfare standards—for example, minimum cage size, adequate food and water, and avoidance of outright physical abuse or neglect—and comply with the minimal registration and inspection requirements, they can confine him alone without any others of his own kind. In other words, a human can legally

[49] Lori Gruen, Entangled Empathy: An Alternative Ethic for Our Relationships with Animals (2014).

[50] *See, e.g.*, Richard L. Cupp Jr., *A Dubious Grail: Seeking Tort Law Expansion and Limited Personhood as Stepping Stones Toward Abolishing Animals' Property Status*, 60 SMU L. Rev. 3 (2007).

[51] *See* Sue Donaldson & Will Kymlicka, Zoopolis: A Political Theory of Animal Rights (2011).

[52] *See, e.g.*, New York's Agriculture and Markets Law §353 (prohibits the "torture" or "unjustifiable killing" of certain animals); Federal Endangered Species Act, 16 U.S.C. §§ 1531-1543 (2012) (prohibits certain behavior involving listed animals, including captive chimpanzees); Federal Animal Welfare Act, 7 U.S.C. §§ 2131-2159 (2012) (regulating the use of certain laboratory and food animals).

[53] Courts are routinely constrained by the status of nonhuman animals in cases presented before them and occasionally voice their frustration at being legally handcuffed from considering the best interests of the animal(s). *See, e.g.*, *Finn v. Anderson*, N.Y.S.3d *2-3, 2019 N.Y. Slip Op. 29131 (City Court of Jamestown, Chautauqua County 2019) ("Under New York Law, irrespective of how strongly people feel about their pets, cats and dogs have been viewed as 'personal property—sometimes referred to as "chattel"—just like a car or a table'.... While it appears the Appellate Division, Fourth Department, has not addressed the issue, this Court concludes that it is time to declare that a pet should no longer be considered 'personal property' like a table or car." (Citations omitted.)).

subject Tommy to a life we would consider inherently wrong (and illegal) were Tommy a human being. Under the welfare view, humans should treat animals with some consideration, but animals remain things that may be exploited and even killed if that suffering is deemed "justified" or "necessary," a concept explored in Chapter 14, "Bears Among Us: Earth Law and Animal-Human Coexistence."

In any sphere, not all life is law, and it should be noted here that the legal thinghood of animals only represents part of our complex relationships with nonhuman animals as a broad class (there are a million or so species of animals on the planet and roughly half of them are beetles).[54] Anybody who grew up with a dog or other beloved family pet knows from experience that animals are far from just things in our hearts and imaginations. Our cultural relationship with nonhuman animals is vast and the product of a long and intertwined history—to the level of impacting each other's genetic evolution.[55] Indeed, human civilization never would have been possible if not for the countless contributions of animals as food, fiber, labor, companions, and otherwise.[56]

Nor does the thinghood of animals mean that every animal lives a life of suffering—indeed far from it. The welfare and protection laws that do exist, not to mention the billions of dollars spent on pets every year, are compelling evidence of human concern for at least some nonhuman animals, and this is also reflected in public opinion polls, which show a marked increase in support for "animal rights."[57] Organizations to promote the well-being of animals, beginning with the Royal Society for the Prevention of Cruelty to Animals in England in 1824, demonstrate a long-running social concern and commitment to preventing harm to animals.[58]

Society clearly cares about the lives and suffering of (at least some) animals. Yet, despite widespread social concern and the passage of hundreds of animal protection laws, even caring humans frequently operate with a double standard, an attitude reinforced and enabled by the structure of the law. For many thousands of species and trillions of individuals, their categorical thinghood under the law has devastating real-world ramifications. In many instances, being a thing means that your life may be taken at any instant. Or, like Tommy, even if you are a protected endangered species, you may be kept in a small cage alone for decades until you die. Worse, an alarming number of animal and plant species go extinct every year or get closer to extinction. Looked at this way, it appears there are severe limits to the welfare approach, and social concern and empathy alone are evidently not enough to protect nonhuman animals any more than they would humans.

From the rights perspective, the fundamental problem with the welfare paradigm is that it relies upon and perpetuates the assumption that human beings are the only

[54] Steven M. Wise, Drawing the Line: Science and the Case for Animal Rights (2003).
[55] Carl Safina, Beyond Words: What Animals Think and Feel (2016).
[56] David Grimm, Citizen Canine: Our Evolving Relationship with Cats and Dogs (2015).
[57] *See, e.g.*, the view on animal rights poll in Garrett Broad, *There Is Broad Public Support for Animal Rights*, Patch, https://patch.com/us/across-america/there-broad-public-support-animal-rights (last visited June 30, 2020).
[58] *See* Cass R. Sunstein, *A Tribute to Kenneth L. Karst: Standing for Animals (with Notes on Animal Rights)*, 47 UCLA L. Rev. 1333 (2000).

proper rights holders in our legal system. This can be seen in the context of environmental law as well, where legal protections fall short of their stated goals for a variety of reasons, ranging from industry capture and lobby influence to the drift of regulatory authority away from Congress and toward the executive branch, which may not be inclined to maintain long-term environmental commitments passed by its predecessors.[59] Looked at this way, the current system could be called "environmental welfare," insofar as it protects the environment to some extent but never calls into question the right of humans to own, control, and manage the environment. While aspects of the environment are protected by various state, federal, and local laws, at the end of the day, in the United States nature itself does not, and cannot, have rights at present.

Do animals (or nature) really need to be persons to be adequately protected? Or do only humans really require that status, with a corresponding duty to see that animals are responsibly treated (broadly, the "welfare" approach)? It is true that animals and the environment are protected to a greater or lesser extent by existing animal welfare and conservation laws, among other protections; and organizations continue to carry on laudable efforts to improve these laws and their enforcement. But the fact remains that currently these efforts cannot create rights or recognition of personhood (that is, the capacity for rights). For that reason, this chapter explores the common law habeas corpus approach of the NhRP as a profoundly different entry point to begin the process of assigning rights beyond the human species. The legal, philosophical, and procedural arguments raised will be informative to rights of nature practitioners now and in the future. In the words of one state high court judge featured in this chapter, the very process of demanding habeas corpus relief for a single chimpanzee calls into question "our relationship with all the life around us."[60]

III. THE LEGAL CONCEPT OF A PERSON

There is not now nor has there ever been a universally accepted definition of what makes a legal person; in fact, there is great discord. Under the common law there is no single definition of person and no checklist of attributes an entity must possess in order to be a person. The process of assigning rights in a liberal democratic society is far more complex than that, as evidenced, for example, by fights over human slavery and abortion. What is clear is that legal personhood, while influenced by natural law understandings of the person as an individual human (or more likely, as the historical record demonstrates, white upstanding male), has never been about biology. As evidence of this fact, for the vast majority of the 2,000-plus-year history of the person/thing dichotomy, most human beings were not persons under the law. In New York, for example, human slaves were not persons until the last slave in the state was freed

[59] *See, e.g.*, White House, *Trump Dumps Paris Climate Accord* (June 1, 2017), https://www.whitehouse.gov/briefings-statements/statement-president-trump-paris-climate-accord/.

[60] *In the Matter of Nonhuman Rights Project, Inc., on Behalf of Tommy v. Patrick C. Lavery, et al.*, and *In the Matter of Nonhuman Rights Project, Inc., on Behalf of Kiko, Appellant, v. Carmen Presti et al.*, Motion No. 2018-26 (N.Y. Ct. App. May 18, 2018), https://www.nycourts.gov/ctapps/Decisions/2018/May18/M2018-268opn18-Decision.pdf.

in 1827[61] and were not persons throughout the United States until 1865.[62] Women were not persons for many purposes of the common law until well into the twentieth century.[63] Jews were once not persons,[64] and the first time a Native American sought a writ of habeas corpus, the U.S. government claimed he was not a person either.[65] Against this backdrop of legalized human oppression, various nonhuman entities have been treated as legal persons for hundreds of years in the form of associations, corporations, limited liability companies, churches, holy relics, and ships. The companies that owned slaves were persons, while the slaves they owned were not.

Legal personhood is nothing more or less than the capacity for rights. While this does not comport with the everyday understanding of what a person is, nor can it hope to ever capture the complex nuance and emotional content of our social, religious, philosophical, and other traditions, it makes perfect sense in the logic of the law because personhood is a legal fiction, not a biological concept.[66] For Dean Roscoe Pound, the "significant feature of legal personality is the capacity for rights."[67] "Legal persons" possess inherent value; "legal things," possessing merely instrumental value, exist for the sake of "legal persons."[68] A "person," the noted legal scholar John Salmond observed, "is any being whom the law regards as capable of rights or duties."[69] And while some "persons" can legally be bought, sold, or even destroyed (corporations and ships), the fundamental premise holds: only persons may have rights.

The history of personhood is inextricably tied to the struggle for the rights of all human beings. Much of the history of the social justice movements of the past 200 years is both reflected in and amplified by the evolution of the law and specifically by the outward expansion of legal personhood.[70] Every human being in the world is now recognized as a "person," but for the majority of modern human history, this was not the case. As the American constitutional law scholar Laurence Tribe has written, "To the degree that competing conceptions of personhood are nonetheless deemed at least pertinent even if not decisive, it is important to remember that legal definitions of what and who constitutes a 'person' do much 'more than just regulate behavior' when it

[61] *See, e.g., Trongett v. Byers*, 5 Cow. 480 (N.Y. Sup. Ct. 1826); *Smith v. Hoff*, 1 Cow. 127, 130 (N.Y. 1823); *In re* Mickel, 14 Johns. 324 (N.Y. Sup. Ct. 1817); *Sable v. Hitchcock*, 2 Johns. Cas. 79, 83 (N.Y. Sup. Ct. 1800).

[62] *See, e.g., Jarman v. Patterson*, 23 Ky. (7 T.B. Mon.) 644, 645-46 (1828) (noting how "[s]laves, although they are human beings . . . [are] not treated as a person, but (*negotium*), a thing").

[63] *See* Robert J. Sharpe & Patricia I. McMahon, The Persons Case — The Origins and Legacy of the Fight for Legal Personhood 71 (2007) (detailing how "[m]arried women had no legal rights" in the ownership of their family home); William Blackstone, Commentaries on the Law of England 430 (1765-1769) (noting "the very being or legal existence of the woman is suspended during the marriage").

[64] R.A. Routledge, *The Legal Status of the Jews in England* 1190-1790, 3 J. of Legal Hist. 91, 94 (1982) (explaining how thirteenth-century Jews were chattels of the king).

[65] *United States ex rel. Standing Bear v. Crook*, 25 F. Cas. 695, 697 (D. Neb. 1879).

[66] *See, e.g., Byrn v. N.Y.C Health & Hosp. Corp.*, 31 N.E. 2d 194, 201 (N.Y. 1972) (denying legal personhood to previable fetuses and noting that legal personhood does not "necessarily correspond to the natural order").

[67] Roscoe Pound, Jurisprudence 197 (1959).

[68] William Blackstone, Commentaries on the Laws of England 16 (1765-1769).

[69] P. J. Fitzgerald, Salmond on Jurisprudence 62 (1966); *see Wartelle v. Women's & Children's Hosp.*, 704 So. 2d 778, 780 (La. 1997) (stating a " 'Person' is a term of art [used] . . . to signify a subject of rights or duties").

[70] *See, e.g., Somerset v. Stewart* 98 ER 499 (1772); The Emancipation Proclamation; The Thirteenth and Fourteenth Amendments to the U.S. Constitution; the UN Declaration of Human Rights.

comes to 'America's most divisive social issues': they express 'conceptions of [the] relative worth of the objects included and excluded by personhood,' and these expressions of 'law's values' in turn shape social norms and values."[71]

While in everyday parlance the word "person" evokes the image of a singular human being, legal personhood has never been about biology. By way of analogy, a person is like a cup, a "container" for rights. Once the cup is secured (i.e., the entity is recognized under law as a person), the courts (and society at large) can begin the process of "filling" that cup, even one right at a time. Of course, not every person, human or otherwise, will have exactly the same set of rights. This is obvious when one considers that legal personhood embraces the whole range of human capacities. Every born human being is by definition a legal person, and every human, including a child or developmentally disabled adult, has fundamental rights to liberty and due process, regardless of their level of conscious awareness of the world and their actions, even those with absolutely no demonstrable conscious awareness of the world. But, of course, that child or disabled adult may not have the right to vote or drive or marry. The flexibility of personhood likewise allows corporations and other associations to be treated as paradigmatic legal persons that can enjoy rights and take on duties, despite the fact that they are fictitious non-biological entities that may themselves be owned, bought, and sold.

It should be emphasized, as may be obvious from considering the example of the corporation or a ship as a legal person, that being a "person" alone does not necessarily entitle an entity to the full panoply of what are considered basic "human rights," including rights to free speech, association, and so on.[72] Also note that there is a distinct and fundamental difference between *common law corporate personhood*, which is on balance a socially beneficial construct, and *corporate personhood* under the Fourteenth Amendment Due Process Clause, as first set forth through a headnote in *Santa Clara* (without discussion).[73] (That decision and subsequent Supreme Court decisions expanding corporate rights to free speech and religious freedom under the U.S. Constitution are the rightful cause of contemporary concern over the undue political influence of large corporations. The underlying concept of common law legal personhood, however, is not the true culprit).

In contrast to landmark corporate personhood decisions (e.g., *Citizens United*), which are fought in the federal courts and which rely on expansive interpretations of the U.S. Constitution, the work of the NhRP is focused exclusively on state courts using arguments based on state common law. The federal Constitution is arguably irrelevant to the question of whether a given entity is considered a legal person for purposes of

[71] Laurence Tribe as amicus curiae, *Nonhuman Rights Project, Inc. v. Lavery* 152 A.D.3d 73, 54 N.Y.S.3d 392 (N.Y. App. Div. 2017) citing Fagundes, *supra* note 2, at 1759-1760. *See also* Laurence H. Tribe, *Ten Lessons Our Constitutional Experience Can Teach Us About the Puzzle of Animal Rights: The Work of Steven M. Wise*, 7 Animal L. 1 (2001).

[72] *Citizens United v. Federal Election Comm'n*, 558 U.S. 310 (2010); *Burwell v. Hobby Lobby Stores, Inc.*, 573 U.S. 682 (2014); *Santa Clara County v. Southern Pacific R.R. Co.*, 118 U.S. 394 (1886).

[73] *Santa Clara County v. Southern Pacific R. Co.*, 118 U.S. 394 (1886).

state common law habeas corpus.[74] Moreover, the common law is all but nonexistent in the federal courts, which are, by definition, courts of limited jurisdiction under Article III of the Constitution. There are benefits and drawbacks to this approach, such as, mainly, the trade-off between common law flexibility and limited jurisdictional reach on the state court side against a seemingly more rigid and limited federal court system that could in theory produce a decision with binding and preemptive effect nationwide.

With the above in mind, one might ask, what are the advantages of using the avenue of legal personhood for some nonhuman animals to develop ecocentric law more broadly? One answer is that human rights provide the best template available for imagining the rights of nonhuman animals. With respect to the development of human rights over the past few centuries, history and legal logic show that personhood matters immensely. Personhood is now universally regarded as a fundamental basis for human rights. For example, Article 6 of the Universal Declaration of Human Rights and Article 16 of the International Convention on Social and Political Rights guarantee that every human shall be a "person." If even one nonhuman animal is conferred with legal personhood, it will provide a precedent to expand rights of nature.

Personhood is a remarkably flexible concept. The legal imagination that created it can quite easily encompass a variety of nonhuman entities as legal persons: A century ago, Professor John Chipman Gray observed that "[t]here is no difficulty in giving legal rights to a supernatural being and thus making him or her a legal person."[75] To the point, Gray noted there may be "systems of law in which animals have legal rights... animals may conceivably be legal persons."[76]

Of course, not all of life is captured, reflected, or ultimately governed by the law. And changing the status of a given entity or class of beings from thing to person will not instantly and magically transform that being nor necessarily lead to improved fortunes or enhanced quality of life. Indeed, hundreds of thousands of slaves were freed by the Emancipation Proclamation and subsequently by the Thirteenth and Fourteenth Amendments to the Constitution following the Civil War, but in the South they were exposed to the horrific vicissitudes of Jim Crow and other means of segregation and subjugation. But still, it appears undeniable that, in the struggle for universal human rights, the legal recognition of rights and personhood codifies, enforces, and protects the most fundamental rights of human beings, namely, the right not to be held in bondage.

[74] *But see Nonhuman Rights Project, Inc. v. R.W. Commerford & Sons, Inc.*, 192 Conn. App. 36, 46, 216 A.3d 839, 845 (2019) (upholding denial of habeas corpus petition brought on behalf of three captive elephants on grounds of, *inter alia*, the "social compact" created by the Connecticut constitution).
[75] John Chipman Gray, The Nature and Sources of the Law 39 (1921).
[76] *Id.* at 42-43.

IV. THE VALUE OF HABEAS CORPUS

Human autonomy is protected under the common law by the writ of habeas corpus. As one of the oldest writs in the common law, it has always been meant to safeguard the liberty and free movement of persons. Its origins go back at least as far as the Magna Carta of 1215. As part of this impressive pedigree, habeas corpus also has a unique history of being used by courts to transform legal things into legal persons, thereby taking a human being with no right to be free and recognizing him as a person with the right to be free.[77]

The position advanced by the NhRP is, essentially, that if a being is demonstrably autonomous then they should have rights protecting that autonomy, regardless of their species. While it is now near-universally recognized that many, if not most, nonhuman animals are conscious and aware beings with intentions,[78] autonomy is far more complex (and apparently much less common), and sentience does not have the same place in the common law as autonomy. The legal problem then becomes, how can a nonhuman animal cross the common law threshold from thing to person?

The common law, while flexible and open to radical change at times, has always regarded nonhuman animals as things, with roots going back at least 2,000 years to Roman law. While there are many gradations within that paradigm (*ferae naturae*[79]), the law has nonetheless always treated nonhuman animals as things that are incapable of rights.[80] While the law around animals has remained more or less static, science has demonstrated beyond reasonable doubt—especially over the past 50 years—that chimpanzees and other nonhuman animals share many cognitive abilities that were once thought to be uniquely human. The science summarized above paints a picture of the rich interior and social lives that chimpanzees enjoy when left to their own devices or allowed to live in sufficiently large, secluded, and social captive situations like sanctuaries; it also shows how much can be taken from them in captive environments. An imprisoned individual like Tommy is not only thwarted from exercising most or all of the above capacities, but he is also *aware* of the fact that his will is being thwarted and likely suffers immensely as a result—just as a conscious human would if left in solitary confinement.

It may seem odd to seek to address a modern problem with ancient law. But as the arc of opinions in this chapter shows, the process of rigorously and studiously engaging the common law wheels of justice creates a powerful vehicle for the transformation of individual entities or groups. It also drives powerful conversations about the deep meaning of the law, and, in the context of nature's rights and nonhuman rights

[77] *See Somerset* and progeny, *supra* note 69.

[78] *See, e.g.*, The Cambridge Declaration on Consciousness, http://fcmconference.org/img/CambridgeDeclarationOnConsciousness.pdf (last visited Feb. 15, 2019) (declaring nonhumans have the capacity for consciousness and intentional behaviors).

[79] Latin for "of a wild nature," meaning there can be no absolute ownership. *See* Karen Bradshaw, *Animal Property Rights*, 89 U. Colo. L. Rev. 809 (2018).

[80] *See* Justin F. Marceau, *Killing for Your Dog*, 83 Geo. Wash. L. Rev. 943, 947 (2015) (noting that common law doctrines and statutes were developed at a time when the relationships between humans and animals were different).

specifically, a more reflective and informed look at the duties we owe to other species and the natural world. The rich tradition of the common law, while pockmarked with many unjust decisions, provides fertile ground on which to demand legal recognition for a wider set of beings and, in the process, discard the designation of "species" as the basis of one more outmoded and invidious form of discrimination. Habeas corpus is, to date, the primary vehicle common law judges have used to transform things to persons (and civil law judges as well; *see Cecilia, supra*, Section I).

V. NONHUMAN RIGHTS PROJECT LITIGATION

With the above legal, moral, public policy, and scientific arguments, and based on decades of legal scholarship,[81] the NhRP filed the world's first common law habeas corpus petitions on behalf of nonhuman animals in December 2013—specifically, on behalf of every known chimpanzee in the state of New York.[82] As part of these petitions, the NhRP included affidavits from some of the world's leading primatologists and scientific experts on chimpanzee behavior and cognition, summarized *supra* in Section I.

Below, in chronological order, are five decisions in the NhRP's litigation campaign in New York, beginning with the first-ever appellate decision to consider the question of whether a nonhuman animal may be a person entitled to habeas corpus, which came about after the denial of Tommy's petition in December 2013. The second appellate decision followed close after, in the case of the chimpanzee Kiko, who lives in a small storefront property in upstate New York described by its owners as a "sanctuary." The third is a trial court opinion that followed the world's first common law habeas corpus hearing in the name of a nonhuman animal (in fact, two animals, research chimpanzees Hercules and Leo). The fourth opinion, another appellate decision, rejected the combined second appeals of Tommy and Kiko. That opinion was appealed and led to the fifth and final opinion in this chapter, a concurring opinion from a member of the New York Court of Appeals, which marked the first time an American high court judge opined on the question of legal personhood for nonhuman animals.

[81] *See, e.g.*, Steven M. Wise, *Animal Law — The Casebook*, 6 ANIMAL L. 251 (2000); Steven M. Wise, *Rattling the Cage Defended*, 43 B.C. L. REV. 623, 624 (2002); Steven M. Wise, *Animal Rights, One Step at a Time, IN* ANIMAL RIGHTS: CURRENT DEBATES AND NEW DIRECTIONS (Cass R. Sunstein & Martha C. Nussbaum eds., 2004); Steven M. Wise, *The Entitlement of Chimpanzees to the Common Law Writs of Habeas Corpus and De Homine Replegiando*, 37 GOLDEN GATE U. L. REV. 219, 220 (2007); Steven M. Wise, *Legal Personhood and the Nonhuman Rights Project*, 17 ANIMAL L. 1 (2010); Steven M. Wise, *The Capacity of Non-Human Animals for Legal Personhood and Legal Rights, IN* THE POLITICS OF SPECIES: RESHAPING OUR RELATIONSHIPS WITH OTHER ANIMALS (Raymond Corbey & Annette Lanjouw eds., 2013).

[82] Habeas corpus is a special proceeding that does not follow the form of a normal civil lawsuit. It follows a "two-step" process: first, the petitioner or someone acting on their behalf petitions a court for the writ of habeas corpus; second, if the court agrees that a *person* is being detained without just cause, it will order the detainer to court to justify that detention, and if there is no justification, order the person's release (or transfer). As such, in order for the court to ever take that step of ordering a hearing, they must first be convinced that they are dealing with a detained *person* or at least an entity which *could be a person.*

The Nonhuman Rights Project, Inc., on Behalf of Tommy v. Lavery et al.,

Supreme Court, Appellate Division, Third Department, New York 2014
124 A.D.3d 148, 998 N.Y.S.2d 248

OPINION OF THE COURT

PETERS, P.J.

The subject of this litigation is a chimpanzee, known as Tommy, that is presently being kept by respondents on their property in the City of Gloversville, Fulton County. On behalf of Tommy, petitioner sought an order to show cause to commence a habeas corpus proceeding pursuant to CPLR article 70 on the ground that Tommy was being unlawfully detained by respondents. In support, petitioner submitted the affidavits of several experts in an effort to establish that, in general, chimpanzees have attributes sufficient to consider them "persons" for the purposes of their interest in personal autonomy and freedom from unlawful detention. Collectively, these submissions maintain that chimpanzees exhibit highly complex cognitive functions—such as autonomy, self-awareness and self-determination, among others—similar to those possessed by human beings. Following an ex parte hearing, Supreme Court found that the term "person" under CPLR article 70 did not include chimpanzees and issued a judgment refusing to sign an order to show cause. Petitioner appeals.[83,84]

This appeal presents the novel question of whether a chimpanzee is a "person" entitled to the rights and protections afforded by the writ of habeas corpus. Notably, we have not been asked to evaluate the quality of Tommy's current living conditions in an effort to improve his welfare. In fact, petitioner's counsel stated at oral argument that it does not allege that respondents are in violation of any state or federal statutes respecting the domestic possession of wild animals (*see, e.g.,* ECL 11-0512). According to petitioner, while respondents are in compliance with state and federal statutes, the statutes themselves are inappropriate. Yet, rather than challenging any such statutes, petitioner requests that this Court enlarge the common-law definition of "person" in order to afford legal rights to an animal. We decline to do so, and conclude that a chimpanzee is not a "person" entitled to the rights and protections afforded by the writ of habeas corpus.

[83] As Supreme Court's judgment finally determined the matter by refusing to issue an order to show cause to commence a habeas corpus proceeding, it is appealable as of right. *See* CPLR 7011; *see generally People ex rel. Seals v. New York State Dept. of Correctional Servs.*, 32 AD3d 1262, 1263 [2006]; *People ex rel. Tatra v McNeill*, 19 AD2d 845, 846 [1963]). [Originally formatted as footnote "1." — EDS.]

[84] During the pendency of this appeal, this Court granted petitioner's motion for a preliminary injunction enjoining respondents from removing Tommy to Florida (2014 NY Slip Op. 77524[U] [2014]). [Originally formatted as footnote "2." — EDS.]

The common law writ of habeas corpus, as codified by CPLR article 70, provides a summary procedure by which a "person" who has been illegally imprisoned or otherwise restrained in his or her liberty can challenge the legality of the detention (CPLR 7002 [a]). The statute does not purport to define the term "person," and for good reason. The "Legislature did not intend to change the instances in which the writ was available," which has been determined by "the slow process of decisional accretion" (*People ex rel. Keitt v. McMann*, 18 N.Y.2d 257, 263 [1966]) [citation omitted]). Thus, we must look to the common law surrounding the historic writ of habeas corpus to ascertain the breadth of the writ's reach.

Not surprisingly, animals have never been considered persons for the purposes of habeas corpus relief, nor have they been explicitly considered as persons or entities capable of asserting rights for the purpose of state or federal law (*see, e.g., Lewis v. Burger King,* 344 Fed. Appx. 470, 472 [10th Cir. 2009], *cert. denied,* 558 U.S. 1125 [2010]; *Cetacean Community v. Bush,* 386 F.3d 1169, 1178 [9th Cir. 2004]; *Tilikum ex rel. People for the Ethical Treatment of Animals, Inc. v. Sea World Parks & Entertainment, Inc.*, 842 F. Supp. 2d 1259, 1263 [S.D. Cal 2012]; *Citizens to End Animal Suffering & Exploitation, Inc. v. New England Aquarium,* 836 F. Supp. 45, 49-50 [D. Mass. 1993]). Petitioner does not cite any precedent—and there appears to be none—in state law, or under English common law, that an animal could be considered a "person" for the purposes of common-law habeas corpus relief. In fact, habeas corpus relief has never been provided to any nonhuman entity (*see, e.g., United States v. Mett,* 65 F.3d 1531, 1534 [9th Cir. 1995], *cert. denied,* 519 U.S. 870 [1996]; *Waste Mgt. of Wisconsin, Inc. v. Fokakis,* 614 F.2d 138, 139-140 [7th Cir. 1980], *cert. denied,* 449 U.S. 1060 [1980]; *Sisquoc Ranch Co. v. Roth,* 153 F.2d 437, 441 [9th Cir. 1946]; *Graham v. State of New York,* 25 A.D.2d 693, 693 [1966]).

The lack of precedent for treating animals as persons for habeas corpus purposes does not, however, end the inquiry, as the writ has over time gained increasing use given its "great flexibility and vague scope" (*People ex rel. Keitt v. McMann,* 18 N.Y.2d at 263 [internal quotation marks and citation omitted]). While petitioner proffers various justifications for affording chimpanzees, such as Tommy, the liberty rights protected by such writ, the ascription of rights has historically been connected with the imposition of societal obligations and duties. Reciprocity between rights and responsibilities stems from principles of social contract, which inspired the ideals of freedom and democracy at the core of our system of government (*see* Richard L. Cupp, Jr., *Children, Chimps, and Rights: Arguments from "Marginal" Cases,* 45 Ariz. St. L.J. 1, 12-14 [2013]; Richard L. Cupp, Jr., *Moving Beyond Animal Rights: A Legal/Contractualist Critique,* 46 San Diego L Rev 27, 69-70 [2009]; *see also In re Gault,* 387 U.S. 1, 20-21 [1967]; *United States v. Barona,* 56 F.3d 1087, 1093-1094 [9th Cir. 1995], *cert. denied,* 516 U.S. 1092 [1996]). Under this view, society extends rights in exchange for an express or implied agreement from its members to submit to social responsibilities. In other words, "rights [are] connected to moral agency and the ability to accept societal responsibility in exchange for [those] rights" (Richard L. Cupp, Jr., *Children, Chimps, and Rights: Arguments from "Marginal" Cases,* 45 Ariz. St. L.J. 1, 13 [2013]; *see* Richard L. Cupp, Jr., *Moving Beyond Animal Rights: A Legal/Contractualist Critique,* 46 San Diego L Rev 27, 69 [2009]).

Further, although the dispositive inquiry is whether chimpanzees are entitled to the right to be free from bodily restraint such that they may be deemed "persons" subject to the benefits of habeas corpus, legal personhood has consistently been defined in terms of both rights *and duties.* Black's Law Dictionary defines the term "person" as "[a] human being" or, as relevant here, "[a]n entity (such as a corporation) that is recognized by law as having the *rights and duties* [of] a human being" (Black's Law Dictionary 1162 [7th ed 1999] [emphasis added]). It then goes on to provide:

"So far as legal theory is concerned, a person is any being whom the law regards as capable of rights and duties. . . . Persons are the substances of which rights and duties are the attributes. It is only in this respect that persons possess juridical significance, and this is the exclusive point of view from which personality receives legal recognition" (Black's Law Dictionary 1162 [7th ed 1999], citing John Salmond, Jurisprudence 318 [10th ed 1947]; *see* John Chipman Gray, The Nature and Sources of the Law, ch II at 27 [2d ed 1963] [stating that the legal meaning of a "person" is "a subject of legal rights and duties"]).

Case law has always recognized the correlative rights and duties that attach to legal personhood (*see, e.g., Smith v. ConAgra Foods, Inc.,* 431 S.W.3d 200, 203-204 [Ark. 2013], *citing Calaway v. Practice Mgt. Servs., Inc.,* 2010 Ark. 432 [2010] [defining a "person" as "a human being or an entity that is recognized by a law as having the rights and duties of a human being"]; *Wartelle v. Women's & Children's Hosp., Inc.,* 704 So. 2d 778, 780 [La. 1997] [finding that the classification of a being or entity as a "person" is made "solely for the purpose of facilitating determinations about the attachment of legal rights and duties"]; *Amadio v. Levin,* 509 Pa. 199, 225, 501 A.2d 1085, 1098 [1985, Zappala, J., concurring] [noting that " '(p)ersonhood' as a legal concept arises not from the humanity of the subject but from the ascription of rights and duties to the subject"]).[85] Associations of human beings, such as corporations and municipal entities, may be considered legal persons, because they too bear legal duties in exchange for their legal rights (*see, e.g., Pembina Consol. Silver Mining & Milling Co. v. Pennsylvania,* 125 U.S. 181, 189 [1888]; *Western Sur. Co. v. ADCO Credit, Inc.,* 251 P.3d 714, 716 [Nev. 2011]; *State of Washington v. A.M.R.,* 147 Wash. 2d 91, 94, 51 P.3d 790, 791 [2002]; *State of West Virginia v. Zain,* 207 W. Va. 54, 61-65, 528 S.E.2d 748, 755-759 [1999], *cert. denied,* 529 U.S. 1042 [2000]).

Needless to say, unlike human beings, chimpanzees cannot bear any legal duties, submit to societal responsibilities or be held legally accountable for their actions. In our view, it is this incapability to bear any legal responsibilities

[85] To be sure, some humans are less able to bear legal duties or responsibilities than others. These differences do not alter our analysis, as it is undeniable that, collectively, human beings possess the unique ability to bear legal responsibility. Accordingly, nothing in this decision should be read as limiting the rights of human beings in the context of habeas corpus proceedings or otherwise.

and societal duties that renders it inappropriate to confer upon chimpanzees the legal rights—such as the fundamental right to liberty protected by the writ of habeas corpus—that have been afforded to human beings.

Our rejection of a rights paradigm for animals does not, however, leave them defenseless. The Legislature has extended significant protections to animals, subject to criminal penalties, such as prohibiting the torture or unjustifiable killing of animals (*see* Agriculture and Markets Law §353), the abandonment of animals in a public place (*see* Agriculture and Markets Law §355), the transportation of animals in cruel or inhuman manners (*see* Agriculture and Markets Law §359 [1]) or by railroad without periodically allowing them out for rest and sustenance (*see* Agriculture and Markets Law §359 [2]), and the impounding of animals and then failing to provide them sustenance (*see* Agriculture and Markets Law §356). Notably, and although subject to certain express exceptions, New Yorkers may not possess primates as pets (*see* ECL 11-0103 [6] [e] [1]; 11-0512). Thus, while petitioner has failed to establish that common-law relief in the nature of habeas corpus is appropriate here, it is fully able to importune the Legislature to extend further legal protections to chimpanzees.

Lahtinen, Garry, Rose and Lynch, JJ., concur.

Ordered that the judgment is affirmed, without costs.

STUDY QUESTIONS

(1) While acknowledging the evidence of chimpanzees as "self-aware" and "autonomous" beings, the *Lavery* court denied habeas corpus relief to Tommy on the basis that the common law and social contract theory dictate that only those who can take on legal duties and responsibilities may be "persons," with all nonhuman animals presumably relegated to the status of "things" that are incapable of possessing the right to common law habeas corpus or any other right. While reference is made to Black's Law Dictionary and other sources, this was the first time that an English-speaking court, or perhaps any court, has made such a statement and put this condition on legal personhood. Is social contract theory a sound basis for deciding whether an entity is deserving of legal personhood?

(2) In rejecting legal personhood and habeas corpus relief for chimpanzees, the *Lavery* court cites numerous New York statutes designed to protect animals in various ways. Are the existing statutory protections for animals sufficient? For example, what is "necessary" killing, as generally allowed for under all "animal welfare" laws including those cited by the court? Do these laws adequately protect a chimpanzee like Tommy, given what we now know about the cognitive capacities of chimpanzees and their ability to suffer in captivity, especially solitary captivity?

(3) The *Lavery* court acknowledges that the ascription of legal personhood is a policy matter made without respect for the species or biological nature of a given entity

but rather by its ability to bear duties and responsibilities correlating to its rights. Then, in footnote 3, the court acknowledges that "some humans are less able to bear legal duties or responsibilities than others," but that, generally speaking, humans have the "unique ability" to appreciate legal duties and responsibilities. What about those millions of humans who have *no* ability to bear legal duties and responsibilities, such as children or comatose adults, or those humans who suffer a mental impairment and will *never* have the ability to shoulder duties?

(4) While the thinghood of nonhuman animals is not the cause of their plight, per se, it is a powerful reflection of it and normalizes and makes efficient their use and destruction. As discussed *supra*, legal fights over (human) personhood have frequently been proxy battlegrounds for deeper social tensions and conflicts (and continue to be so in the context of abortion, and may soon reach areas like artificial intelligence as well). To what extent might this be happening here, and how much might these kinds of tensions be at play in other courts' rulings?

(5) Assuming that legal personhood is a necessary prerequisite for rights of nature, how would these claims fare under the *Lavery* standard?

* * *

Two days prior to the issuance of the *Lavery* decision, the neighboring Fourth Department intermediate appellate court heard arguments in the case of Kiko, a chimpanzee held captive in Niagara Falls, New York. The NhRP had initially sought the writ on December 4, 2013, the day after filing for Tommy, and it was denied by the trial court as in Tommy's case. The NhRP appealed Kiko's decision, and, following argument, the Fourth Department issued the following decision on January 2, 2015.

Nonhuman Rights Project, Inc., on Behalf of Kiko v. Presti et al.,

Supreme Court, Appellate Division, Fourth Department, New York 2015
124 A.D.3d 1334, 999 N.Y.S.2d 652

Appeal from a judgment (denominated order) of the Supreme Court, Niagara County (Ralph A. Boniello, III, J.), entered December 11, 2013 in a proceeding pursuant to CPLR article 70. The judgment dismissed the petition.

It is hereby ordered that the judgment so appealed from is unanimously affirmed without costs.

Memorandum: Petitioner, an organization seeking better treatment and housing of, inter alia, nonhuman primates, commenced this proceeding seeking a writ of habeas corpus on behalf of Kiko, a chimpanzee. Rather than seeking Kiko's immediate release, however, the petition alleges that Kiko is illegally confined because he is kept in unsuitable conditions, and it seeks to have Kiko's confinement transferred to a different facility selected by the

North American Primate Sanctuary Alliance. On appeal from a judgment dismissing the petition, petitioner contends that Kiko is entitled to the relief sought. Contrary to petitioner's contention, we conclude that Supreme Court properly dismissed the petition.

Regardless of whether we agree with petitioner's claim that Kiko is a person within the statutory and common-law definition of the writ, " 'habeas corpus relief nonetheless is unavailable as [that] claim [ ], even if meritorious, would not entitle [Kiko] to immediate release' " (*People ex rel. Gonzalez v. Wayne County Sheriff*, 96 A.D.3d 1698, 1699 [2012], *lv denied* 21 N.Y.3d 852 [2013]; *see People ex rel. Shannon v. Khahaifa*, 74 A.D.3d 1867, 1867 [2010], *lv dismissed* 15 N.Y.3d 868 [2010]; *People ex rel. Hall v. Rock*, 71 A.D.3d 1303, 1304 [2010], *appeal dismissed* 14 N.Y.3d 882 [2010], *lv denied* 15 N.Y.3d 703 [2010]). It is well settled that a habeas corpus proceeding must be dismissed where the subject of the petition is not entitled to immediate release from custody (*see People ex rel. Kaplan v. Commissioner of Correction of City of N.Y.*, 60 N.Y.2d 648, 649 [1983]; *People ex rel. Douglas v. Vincent*, 50 N.Y.2d 901, 903 [1980]). Here, petitioner does not seek Kiko's immediate release, nor does petitioner allege that Kiko's continued detention is unlawful. Rather, petitioner seeks to have Kiko placed in a different facility that petitioner deems more appropriate. Consequently, even assuming, arguendo, that we agreed with petitioner that Kiko should be deemed a person for the purpose of this application, and further assuming, arguendo, that petitioner has standing to commence this proceeding on behalf of Kiko, this matter is governed by the line of cases standing for the proposition that habeas corpus does not lie where a petitioner seeks only to change the conditions of confinement rather than the confinement itself (*see generally People ex rel. Dawson v. Smith*, 69 N.Y.2d 689, 690-691 [1986]; *Matter of Berrian v. Duncan*, 289 A.D.2d 655, 655 [2001]; *People ex rel. McCallister v. McGinnis*, 251 A.D.2d 835, 835 [1998]). We therefore conclude that habeas corpus does not lie herein.

Present—Smith, J.P., Peradotto, Lindley, Valentino and Whalen, JJ.

STUDY QUESTIONS

(1) In its short opinion, the *Presti* court was clear not to rule on the issue of nonhuman personhood, instead finding that habeas relief is not available when trying to move a person from one condition of confinement to another. Is this a more positive outcome (from the perspective of nonhuman animal rights) than *Lavery* insofar as it does not appear to create an absolute bar to nonhuman animals being persons in the way *Lavery* does?

(2) Because they come from complex societies in their natural environment, under most circumstances, captive chimpanzees like Kiko cannot simply "go back to the wild," and, of course, release into New York would be dangerous for the chimpanzee and the public. Given this, is sanctuary (several acres, with other

chimpanzees, and not open to visitors) a suitable option? How does this compare with a prison inmate (or his attorney) who files a habeas petition to be sent instead to a mental hospital or similar facility, arguing incapacity or otherwise? Or, historically, a freed child slave or apprentice being sent to an orphanage (even, at times, over the protest of the child)?

(3) The Third Department Appellate Division cited *Presti* in a case that did not involve nonhuman animals and stated: "[I]t is common knowledge that personhood can and sometimes does attach to nonhuman entities like ... animals[.]" *People v. Graves*, 163 A.D.3d 16, 21 (4th Dept. June 15, 2018). How can this be reconciled with *Presti*? Was the *Presti* court implicitly acknowledging that Kiko was or could be a person? Why might an appellate court in the same state as *Lavery* reach such a radically different conclusion when presented with a near-identical case?

* * *

On December 5, 2013, immediately after filing petitions for Tommy and Kiko, the NhRP brought a petition in Suffolk County on behalf of Hercules and Leo, two research chimpanzees detained at the State University of New York at Stony Brook on Long Island who were being used in locomotion experiments. That petition was likewise denied by the trial court and the NhRP appealed to the Second Department intermediate appellate court.[86] Instead of pursuing an appeal to the state's highest court via the Second Department, the NhRP instead sought a new habeas corpus petition in New York County in March 2015, which falls under the intermediate appellate jurisdiction of the First Department. In April 2015, Supreme Court Justice Barbara Jaffe issued the world's first-ever writ of habeas corpus for a nonhuman animal when she ordered a hearing for Hercules and Leo, though later striking the word "habeas corpus" to make clear that the chimpanzees were not required to be produced in court. Justice Jaffe's order required the detainers of Hercules and Leo, Stony Brook University, to appear in court and defend their detention. Because it is a state institution, the university was represented throughout the proceedings by the New York attorney general's office. This was the first time a court anywhere in the world issued a common law habeas corpus petition on behalf of a nonhuman animal. The hearing was held in May 2015, after which the following opinion issued.

The Nonhuman Rights Project, Inc., on behalf of Hercules and Leo v. Samuel L. Stanley Jr., M.D.

Supreme Court, New York County 2015
49 Misc. 3d 746, 16 N.Y.S.3d 898, 322 Ed. Law Rep. 440

JAFFE, J.

Petitioner brings this proceeding pursuant to CPLR article 70 and under the common law for a writ of habeas corpus on behalf of Hercules and Leo, two

[86] *Matter of Nonhuman Rights Project, Inc. v. Stanley*, 2014 N.Y. Slip Op. 68434(U) (2nd Dept. 2014).

chimpanzees now in the custody of respondent State University of New York at Stony Brook (University). It seeks an order directing respondents to demonstrate the basis for detaining Hercules and Leo, and an order directing their release and transfer to a sanctuary in Florida.

. . .

III. DISCUSSION

"The great writ of habeas corpus lies at the heart of our liberty" (*Figueroa v. Walsh,* 2008 WL 1945350 [E.D.N.Y. 2008]), and is deeply rooted in our cherished ideas of individual autonomy and free choice (*Rivers v. Katz,* 67 N.Y.2d 485, 493, 504 N.Y.S.2d 74, 495 N.E.2d 337 [1986]; *People ex rel. DeLia v. Munsey,* 117 AD3d 84, 90 [2d Dept. 2014]). As "[t]he remedy against illegal imprisonment," the writ is described as "the greatest of all writs" and "the great bulwark of liberty." (*People ex rel. Tweed v. Liscomb,* 60 N.Y. 559, 566 [1875].) The writ of habeas corpus "has been cherished by generations of free men who had learned by experience that it furnished the only reliable protection of their freedom." (*Hoff v. State of New York,* 279 N.Y. 490, 492 [1939].) It must, therefore, be liberally construed "in harmony with its grand purpose." (*Tweed,* 60 N.Y. at 568-569.)

According to some scholars, the writ is rooted in Roman law and "[t]he authority for it in the Anglo–American legal system is found in the 39th clause of Magna Carta." (*People ex rel. Lobenthal v. Koehler,* 129 A.D.2d 28, 30, 516 N.Y.S.2d 928 [1st Dept. 1987] [citation omitted]; *see Tweed,* 60 N.Y. at 565). Authority for it is traced to 1166, with the Assize of Clarendon (*Rosa v. Senkowski,* 1997 WL 436484, *5 [S.D.N.Y. 1997]), well before Magna Carta (*Tweed,* 60 N.Y. at 565).

The writ "is a part of the common law of this State'" (*Munsey,* 117 A.D.3d at 90, 983 N.Y.S.2d 35, *citing People ex rel. Lobenthal v. Koehler,* 129 A.D.2d at 30, 516 N.Y.S.2d 928), and courts have, "by the slow process of decisional accretion, made increasing use of 'one of the hallmarks of the writ . . . its great flexibility and vague scope'" (*People ex rel. Keitt v. McMann,* 18 N.Y.2d 257, 263, 273 N.Y.S.2d 897, 220 N.E.2d 653 [1966] [citations omitted]). Safeguarded by the United States and New York Constitutions (N.Y. Const., Art. 1, §4; U.S. Const., Art. 1, §9, cl. 2), the writ "cannot be abrogated, or its efficiency curtailed, by legislative action" (*Tweed,* 60 N.Y. at 566).

. . . *B. Standing*

In asserting standing to seek a writ of habeas corpus on behalf of Hercules and Leo, petitioner relies on CPLR 7002 (a) which provides that a petition for a writ of habeas corpus may be made not only by "[a] person illegally imprisoned or otherwise restrained in his [or her] liberty," but also by "one acting on his [or her] behalf." (Petitioner's mem of law.) Respondents deny that petitioner has standing to bring this proceeding absent a substantial relationship between it and the chimpanzees. (Respondents' mem of law.)

(1) As the statute places no restriction on who may bring a petition for habeas corpus on behalf of the person restrained, and absent any authority for the proposition that the statutory phrase "one acting on his behalf" is modified by a requirement for obtaining standing by a third party, petitioner has met its burden of demonstrating that it has standing. (*See Matter of Larner,* 68 App. Div. 320, 322 [2d Dept. 1902] [only requirement under habeas statute is that application for release "shall be signed 'either by the person for whose relief it is intended, or by some person in his behalf' "]; *cf. State of N.Y. ex rel. Harkavy v. Consilvio,* 7 N.Y.3d 607 [2006] [assuming without deciding that Mental Hygiene Legal Service had standing to initiate habeas proceeding on behalf of involuntarily committed persons]; *People ex rel. DeLia,* 117 A.D.3d 84 [same].) In any event, petitioner demonstrates an interest in vindicating what it perceives to be the rights of these chimpanzees.

. . .

F. Legal personhood

The substance of the petition requires a finding as to whether a chimpanzee is a legal person entitled to bring a writ of habeas corpus.

"Person" is not defined in CPLR article 70, or by the common law of habeas corpus. Petitioner agrees that there exists no legal precedent for defining "person" under article 70 or the common law to include chimpanzees or any other nonhuman animals, or that a writ of habeas corpus has ever been granted to any being other than a human being. Nonetheless, as the Third Department noted in *People ex rel. Nonhuman Rights Project, Inc. v. Lavery,* the lack of precedent does not end the inquiry into whether habeas corpus relief may be extended to chimpanzees. (124 A.D.3d 148, 150-151 [3d Dept. 2014].)

"Legal personhood" is not necessarily synonymous with being human. (*Byrn v. New York City Health & Hosp. Corp.,* [citation omitted]). Nor have autonomy and self-determination been considered bases for granting rights. In any event, petitioner denies that it seeks human rights for chimpanzees. Rather, it contends that the law can and should employ the legal fiction that chimpanzees are legal persons solely for the purpose of endowing them with the right of habeas corpus, as the law accepts in other contexts the "legal fiction" that nonhuman entities, such as corporations, may be deemed legal persons, with the rights incident thereto. The determination of legal personhood, it maintains, is a matter of policy and not a question of biology, and in this case, policy requires that Hercules and Leo be recognized as legal persons with rights. (Petition ¶ 3; petitioner's mem of law at 30.)

While not clearly articulating the policy underlying a supposed mandatory recognition of chimpanzees as persons beyond the guarantee of fundamental rights to liberty for all persons, petitioner argues that because chimpanzees possess fundamental attributes of personhood in that they are demonstrably autonomous, self-aware, and self-determining, and otherwise are very much like humans, "justice demands" that they be granted the fundamental rights of liberty and equality afforded to humans. (*Id.* at 32-33.)

Amicus curiae correctly observes that while corporations and partnerships have been deemed persons for certain purposes, those entities are composed of humans, hence the legal fiction of personhood accorded them. It also cites certain Penal Law provisions that refer exclusively to persons as human beings, "and where appropriate, a public or private corporation, an unincorporated association, a partnership, a government or a governmental instrumentality." (Penal Law §10.00 [7].) Amicus thus argues that the expanded definition of person in a restricted context connotes a legislative intent that the definition not be further expanded, and that the extension of the right to be named as a beneficiary that is accorded to animals pursuant to EPTL 7-8.1 does not require a different result, as nowhere in that statute are animals defined as persons. (Amicus curiae brief by Center for the Study of The Great Ideas in opp to petition for writ of habeas corpus, dated May 4, 2015.)

And yet, the concept of legal personhood, that is, who or what may be deemed a person under the law, and for what purposes, has evolved significantly since the inception of the United States. Not very long ago, only caucasian male, property-owning citizens were entitled to the full panoply of legal rights under the United States Constitution. Tragically, until passage of the Thirteenth Amendment of the Constitution, African American slaves were bought, sold, and otherwise treated as property, with few, if any, rights. Married women were once considered the property of their husbands, and before marriage were often considered family property, denied the full array of rights accorded to their fathers, brothers, uncles, and male cousins. (*See generally,* Saru M. Matambanadzo, *Embodying Vulnerability: A Feminist Theory of the Person,* 20 Duke J. Gender L. & Policy 45, 48-51 [2012]). "If rights were defined by who exercised them in the past, then received practices could serve as their own continued justification and new groups could not invoke rights once denied." (*Obergefell v. Hodges,* ____ U.S. ____, 135 S. Ct. 2584, 2602, 192 L. E. 2d 609 [2015].)

The past mistreatment of humans, whether slaves, women, Indigenous people or others, as property, does not, however, serve as a legal predicate or appropriate analogy for extending to nonhumans the status of legal personhood. Rather, the parameters of legal personhood have long been and will continue to be discussed and debated by legal theorists, commentators, and courts, and will not be focused on semantics or biology, or even philosophy, but on the proper allocation of rights under the law, asking, in effect, who counts under our law. (*Byrn,* 31 N.Y.2d at 201, 335 N.Y.S.2d 390, 286 N.E.2d 887.)

For purposes of establishing rights, the law presently categorizes entities in a simple, binary, "all-or-nothing" fashion. "Persons have rights, duties, and obligations; things do not." (*See generally* Jessica Berg, *Of Elephants and Embryos: A Proposed Framework for Legal Personhood,* 59 Hastings L J 369, 372, 403 [2007]; Note, *What We Talk About When We Talk About Persons: The Language of a Legal Fiction,* 114 Harv L Rev 1745 [2001]; *see also* Atiba R. Ellis, *Citizens United and*

Tiered Personhood, 44 J Marshall L Rev 717, 727-731 [2011].) Animals, including chimpanzees and other highly intelligent mammals, are considered as property under the law. They are accorded no legal rights beyond being guaranteed the right to be free from physical abuse and other mistreatment (*see, e.g.*, Agriculture and Markets Law Article 26, §§ 353, 353–a, 362), and the right to humane living conditions (*id.* §§ 353–b, 353–d, 356), although they may be included in orders of protection. (*See* Fam. Ct. Act §842[i].) In one instance, Oregon's highest court found that a horse was a "person" under a statute permitting warrantless searches of property where there was a reasonable belief that a person was suffering serious injury or harm. In that case, the court upheld the conduct of a police officer who had entered property and seized an obviously emaciated horse, although it "exercise[d] judicial restraint and [left] for another day questions unnecessary to the resolution of this case, such as whether the emergency aid exception [to the warrant requirement] extends to animals." (*State of Oregon v. Fessenden*, 355 Or .759, 774-775, 333 P.3d 278, 287 [2014].)

Moreover, some animals, such as pets and companion animals, are gradually being treated as more than property, if not quite as persons, in part because legislatures and courts recognize the close relationships that exist between people and their pets, who are often viewed and treated by their owners as family members. (*See generally Feger v. Warwick Animal Shelter*, 59 A.D.3d 68, 71-72 [2d Dept. 2008] ["Companion animals are a special category of property" and courts recognize their "cherished status"]; *see also People v. Garcia*, 29 A.D.3d 255 [1st Dept .2006] [goldfish are companion animals protected by animal cruelty law]; *Raymond v Lachmann*, 264 A.D.2d 340, 341 [1st Dept .1999] [recognizing cherished status of pets and considering cat's interests by awarding possession of her to defendant as "best for all concerned," notwithstanding plaintiff's actual ownership interest]; *Travis v. Murray*, 42 Misc. 3d 447 [Sup. Ct., NY County 2013] [recognizing, in dispute over custody of dog in divorce proceeding, that dogs are seen as family members, and declining to apply strict property analysis, applying something akin to "best interests of the child" standard].) At least one New York court, recognizing that "a pet is not just a thing but occupies a special place somewhere in between a person and a piece of personal property," found that a dog's owner may be entitled to emotional distress damages for the wrongful destruction and loss of her dog, thereby departing from contrary precedent. (*Corso v. Crawford Dog & Cat Hosp.*, 97 Misc. 2d 530, 531 [Civ. Ct., Queens County 1979]; *cf. Mongelli v. Cabral*, 166 Misc. 2d 240, 244-245 [Yonkers City Ct. 1995] [absent equitable jurisdiction in small claims part, and as substantial justice not served if claim dismissed and pursued in higher court, claimant awarded damages unless defendants return Peaches, a cockatoo, "in good health, along with her cage, her bowls and her toys"].)

Consonant with these recent trends, New York enacted section 7-8.1 ("Trusts for pets") of the Estates, Powers and Trusts Law (EPTL), providing that a domestic or pet animal may be named as a beneficiary of a trust. (Petitioner's mem of law at 54-56; *see* Jesse McKinley, *Dog-Related Bills Flood Albany as*

Major Legislation Stalls, NY Times, June 11, 2015, http://www.nytimes.com/2015/06/12/nyregion/dog-related-bills-flood-albany-as-major-legislation-stalls.html [noting that dogs' interests "are exceptionally well represented in Albany this year"].)

Some commentators have described the current legal status of animals as "quasi-persons, being recognized as holding some rights and protections but not others." (*E.g.*, Matambanadzo, *Embodying Vulnerability: A Feminist Theory of the Person,* 20 Duke J. Gender L. & Policy at 61.) Petitioner claims, however, that its effort to elevate the legal status of chimpanzees, and some other animals, above the level of things or mere property, is not addressed by animal welfare legislation.

The determination of whether an entity or being counts as a legal person is largely context-specific, and not necessarily consistently made.

"In the United States' common law tradition there is no discrete body of law containing all of the applicable provisions of legal personhood. Legal persons constitute a diverse community that includes various individuals, entities and collectives in different ways for different jurisdictions. To add to this diversity, the common law of legal personhood is disparate and diffuse, found in cases, statutes and treatises." (Saru M. Matambanadzo, *Embodying Vulnerability: A Feminist Theory of the Person,* 20 Duke J Gender L & Poly at 64-65; *see also* Note, *What We Talk About When We Talk About Persons: The Language of a Legal Fiction,* 114 Harv L Rev 1745, 1746 [2001].)

"Often . . . arguments for animal rights proceed by way of analogy. First, biological human beings are entitled to rights. Second, animals share many of the characteristics of human beings, at least to some lesser degree. Therefore, animals are entitled to at least some of the same rights as human beings. Obviously, this argument only works if the shared characteristics are relevant to the ascription of rights—otherwise the analogy loses its force. . . . Extending the concept of the person to animals therefore merely indicates that they share relevant characteristics with human beings and deserve rights on that basis." (Jens David Ohlin, Note, *Is the Concept of the Person Necessary for Human Rights?*, 105 Colum L Rev 209, 222 [2005].)

This seems to be the argument advanced by petitioner, namely, that chimpanzees should be accorded rights consonant with their abilities, and that their autonomy and self-determination merit the right to be free from illegal detention, and to that extent, the status of legal personhood.

Relying on the so-called "social contract" and the common law in determining that chimpanzees are disqualified from receiving the status of legal personhood, the Third Department in *People ex rel. Nonhuman Rights Project, Inc. v. Lavery* determined, in effect, that according chimpanzees the status of legal personhood is inappropriate as they are incapable of bearing any legal responsibilities and societal duties. (124 A.D.3d 148, 151-152, 998 N.Y.S.2d 248). The Court also noted, among other sources of support, that the definition of "person" in Black's Law Dictionary (1257-1258 [9th ed 2009]) includes "human being," or "natural person," and "[a]n entity (such as a corporation) that is recognized by law as having most of the rights and duties of a human being," also described as an "artificial person." It thus found that petitioner had failed to establish that Tommy was entitled to be granted common-law relief in the nature of habeas corpus, adding that petitioner "is fully able to importune the Legislature to extend further legal protections to chimpanzees." (124 A.D.3d at 153.)

The parties differ as to whether I am bound by that determination.

G. Stare decisis

Petitioner denies that *Lavery* binds me, maintaining that the Third Department applied the wrong legal standard for determining legal personhood when it applied the rights and duties paradigm, and that absent "settled law" on the issue, a lower court has no legal obligation to follow the decisions of the appellate courts. It does not, however, argue that there is a conflict between the decisions of the Third and Fourth Departments; each reached the same result on different grounds. Rather, it maintains that both decisions are wrong on the law, that the law relied on by those courts is not settled, and that the Third Department in particular is wrong because habeas corpus relief has and continues to be granted to persons who are not part of the "social contract," such as slaves and noncitizens (*see Rasul v. Bush,* 542 U.S. 466, 484-485, 124 S. Ct. 2686, 159 L. Ed. 2d 548 [2004] [Guantanamo detainees entitled to habeas]; petitioner's mem of law at 61-62).

Petitioner observes that "sister common law countries" have recognized that a legal person need not have duties or responsibilities, citing instances where a river, a sacred text, a mosque, and a religious idol were designated as persons. (Petitioner's mem of law at 63.) According to petitioner, "a 'person' need not even be alive." (*Id.*) Thus, petitioner argues, the Third Department confused its "demand for the 'immunity-right' of bodily liberty, to which the ability to bear duties and responsibilities is irrelevant, with a 'claim-right.'" (*Id.* at 64.)

Respondents argue that absent a decision to the contrary by the Court of Appeals or the First Department, I am bound by the Third Department's determination in *Lavery* that, given a chimpanzee's inability to take on duties or responsibilities, chimpanzees are not entitled to legal personhood. (Resps. Memo. of Law).

. . .

State trial courts must follow a higher court's existing precedent "even though they may disagree." (*People v. Rivera,* 5 N.Y.3d 61, 72 n. 2, 800 N.Y.S.2d 51, 833 N.E.2d 194 [2005] [Kaye, Ch. J., dissenting] [internal citations omitted], *cert. den.* 546 U.S. 984, 126 S. Ct. 564, 163 L. Ed. 2d 473 [2005]). . . .

. . .

Relying on *Byrn v. New York City Health & Hosps. Corp.* (31 N.Y.2d 194 [1972]), petitioner asserts that the Third Department in Lavery failed to recognize that the determination of whether a chimpanzee is a legal person is a policy question, not a biological one. (Petitioner's mem of law at 64.)

In *Byrn*, the Court held that question of "[w]hether the law should accord legal personality... in most instances devolves on the Legislature." (*Id.* at 201.) It also observed that "[t]he Constitution does not confer or require legal personality... ; the Legislature may, or it may do something less,... and provide some protection far short of conferring legal personality." (*Id.* at 203.) Similarly, the Court in *Lavery* held that petitioner failed to establish that common-law relief in the nature of habeas corpus was appropriate, and referenced the legislature as the appropriate forum for obtaining additional protections. (*Lavery*, 124 A.D.3d at 153.) As *Lavery* does not appear to be inconsistent with *Byrn* in that regard or any other, I am bound by *Lavery*.

Even were I not bound by the Third Department in *Lavery*, the issue of a chimpanzee's right to invoke the writ of habeas corpus is best decided, if not by the legislature, then by the Court of Appeals, given its role in setting state policy. (*See Matter of Hynes v. Tomei*, 237 A.D.2d 52, 60-61 [2d Dept. 1997], *revd on other grounds* 92 N.Y.2d 613 [1998], *citing People v. Keta*, 165 A.D.2d 172, 178 [2d Dept. 1991], *revd on other grounds sub nom. People v. Scott*, 79 N.Y.2d 474 [1992] [Court of Appeals is "the State's policy-making tribunal"]; *see also Matter of Eckart*, 39 N.Y.2d 493, 499 [1976] [if recent holding interpreting a statute is contrary to line of well-reasoned opinions, court need not wait for legislature to repair damage]; *see also People ex rel. Tweed v. Liscomb*, 60 N.Y. 559, 566 [1875] [writ of habeas corpus safeguarded by the United States and New York Constitutions and "cannot be abrogated, or its efficiency curtailed, by legislative action"].)[87]

IV. CONCLUSION

The similarities between chimpanzees and humans inspire the empathy felt for a beloved pet. Efforts to extend legal rights to chimpanzees are thus

[87] Respondents also argue that according personhood to Hercules and Leo "could set a precedent for the release of other animals held in captivity, whether housed at a zoo, in an educational institution, on a farm, or owned as a domesticated pet, and enmesh New York courts in continuing litigation over the applicability of habeas corpus to other animals." (Respondents' mem of law.)

The floodgates argument is not a cogent reason for denying relief. (*See Enright v. Eli Lilly & Co.*, 77 N.Y.2d 377, 393 [1991] ["floodgates of litigation" alarm unpersuasive in view of Court's "repeated admonitions that it is not 'a ground for denying a cause of action that there will be a proliferation of claims' and 'if a cognizable wrong has been committed that there must be a remedy, whatever the burden of the courts.' "], quoting *Tobin v. Grossman*, 24 N.Y.2d 609, 615 [1969].)

Respondents also maintain that as petitioner does not seek the release of the chimpanzees from the University, but their transfer to a chimpanzee sanctuary, it has no legal recourse to habeas corpus. (Respondents' mem of law.) There is, however, authority to the contrary in the First Department. (*See McGraw v. Wack*, 220 A.D.2d 291, 292-293 [1st Dept. 1995] [observing that Court of Appeals approved, *sub silentio*, use of writ of habeas corpus to secure transfer of mentally ill individual to another institution], *citing Matter of Mental Hygiene Legal Servs. v. Wack*, 75 N.Y.2d 751 [1989].) Consequently, I am not bound by the decision of the Fourth Department in *Matter of Nonhuman Rights Project, Inc. v. Presti* (124 A.D.3d 1334, 1335 [4th Dept. 2015], *lv denied* 126 A.D.3d 1430 [4th Dept. 2015]).

understandable; some day they may even succeed. Courts, however, are slow to embrace change, and occasionally seem reluctant to engage in broader, more inclusive interpretations of the law, if only to the modest extent of affording them greater consideration. As Justice Kennedy aptly observed in *Lawrence v. Texas,* albeit in a different context, "times can blind us to certain truths and later generations can see that laws once thought necessary and proper in fact serve only to oppress." (539 U.S. 558, 579 [2003].) The pace may now be accelerating. (*See Obergefell v. Hodges,* 576 U.S. —, —, 135 S. Ct. 2584, 2595 [2015] [granting right to marry to same-sex couples and acknowledging that institution of marriage has evolved over time notwithstanding its ancient origins].)

For now, however, given the precedent to which I am bound, it is hereby ordered that the petition for a writ of habeas corpus is denied and the proceeding is dismissed; it is further ordered that respondents' cross motion to change venue is denied; and it is further ordered that petitioner's motion to strike the affidavit of Styliani-Anna Tsirka and respondents' motion to strike the additional evidence offered by petitioner are denied as moot.

STUDY QUESTIONS

(1) The *Stanley* court makes reference to the "right" of animals in New York "to be free from physical abuse and other mistreatment" and "the right to humane living conditions." This is after making clear that all nonhuman animals are "things." By definition, it would appear that a "thing" cannot have a right, and what the court is referring to are actually statutory protections that fall short of "rights." Can a thing have rights? Or is the court simply uncomfortable admitting that animals have no rights and are, in fact, incapable of having them?

(2) What does it mean to be "more than property," as the *Stanley* court refers to pets like dogs and cats? If an entity can only be a thing or a person, what might the court mean here? In theory, courts and legislatures are free to create a third (or more) category of entity, a "nonhuman legal person," for example. *See Cecilia, supra.* Is this a more viable option than personhood for protecting the rights of nature and nonhuman animals? Is there other value in seeking to force the legal system to adapt preexisting categories to these new classes of rights holders?

(3) The *Stanley* court found itself bound by the decision of the Third Department in *Lavery* that the social contract theory dictates only humans can be persons and have rights. Was this appropriate? But for *Lavery,* how do you think the court would have ruled on the question of personhood? If it had not found binding precedent, what other grounds may the court have relied upon to push the issue to the legislature or court of appeals, as it noted toward the end?

(4) The *Stanley* court observed: "The past mistreatment of humans, whether slaves, women, Indigenous people or others, as property, does not, however, serve as a legal predicate or appropriate analogy for extending to nonhumans the status of legal personhood." Is this too narrow a way of looking at human/civil rights precedent? How well-founded is it to use human rights as an analogy for nonhuman rights? What are the advantages and drawbacks of relying on analogies to human rights in the broader effort to develop rights of nature? How might one draw an analogy to the development of human rights in the context of seeking rights for a river or an entire ecosystem?

(5) The *Stanley* judge noted that the NhRP was not seeking "human rights" for the chimpanzees but rather rights to coordinate with their nature as autonomous beings by arguing that "autonomy" is a sufficient, but not necessary, condition for rights. The judge then went on to state that there is no support for autonomy as a basis for personhood or rights. Is autonomy a reasonable ground on which to premise personhood and rights? How might one argue it is implicit in constitutional grants of rights and protections of personal liberties? Considering that every human being is a person, regardless of their individual level of conscious awareness or autonomy, should at least autonomous nonhuman animals be recognized as persons? Should there be other grounds for rights aside from autonomy, and what might those be?

Following Justice Jaffe's opinion, Hercules and Leo were moved back to their owners in December of 2015, the New Iberia Research Center in Lafayette, Louisiana, where they were born into the research trade. (They were later transferred to a chimpanzee sanctuary in Northern Georgia where they will be able to live out the remaining four to five decades of their lives in conditions that approximated their natural homes as best as is possible in North America.) Around the time Hercules and Leo were being shipped back to Louisiana, the NhrP brought new petitions on behalf of Tommy and Kiko—this time taking advantage of liberal venue rules in New York to file in Manhattan despite both chimpanzees remaining upstate, as in the previous filings (*Lavery* and *Presti*, respectively). Because these were the first new filings since the *Lavery* opinion, the NhRP included new affidavits and supplemental affidavits from several of its other scientific experts setting forth evidence of chimpanzees taking on "duties and responsibilities," both in relations with each other and with humans. These affidavits were intended to specifically address the alleged requirement in *Lavery* that an entity (or, more precisely, a representative member of that entity's species) must be capable of shouldering duties and responsibilities in order to be a person, as relied upon by Justice Jaffe in *Stanley*. Because both cases were filed in the same court that heard the Hercules and Leo petition, both cases were assigned once again to Justice Jaffe, pursuant to rules of judicial economy. However, she denied both petitions and refused to order another hearing on the grounds they were "successive petitions" and did not present new facts or circumstances to warrant another hearing despite the addition of 60 pages of new expert affidavits on the issue of duties and responsibilities. The NhRP appealed both decisions, and the First Department joined the cases together for appeal, after which the following opinion issued.

Nonhuman Rights Project, Inc. ex rel. Tommy v. Lavery (Lavery II),

Supreme Court, Appellate Division, First Department, New York 2017
152 A.D.3d 73, 54 N.Y.S.3d 392

OPINION OF THE COURT

WEBBER, J.

Petitioner seeks reversal of the motion court's judgment declining to extend habeas corpus relief to two adult male chimpanzees, Tommy and Kiko.

Petitioner is a Massachusetts nonprofit corporation whose stated mission is "to change the common-law status of at least some nonhuman animals from mere 'things,' which lack the capacity to possess any legal rights, to 'persons,' who possess such fundamental rights as bodily integrity and bodily liberty, and those other legal rights to which evolving standards of morality, scientific discovery, and human experience entitle them" to—certain fundamental rights which include entitlement to habeas relief.[88]

The petition as to Tommy was brought in December 2015. It is alleged that Tommy, who is owned by respondents Circle L Trailer Sales, Inc. and its officers, is in a cage in a warehouse in Gloversville, New York. The petition as to Kiko was brought in January 2016. Kiko, who is owned by respondents the Primate Sanctuary, Inc. and its officers and directors, is allegedly in a cage in a cement storefront in a crowded residential area in Niagara Falls, New York.

These are not the first petitions for habeas relief filed by petitioner on behalf of Tommy and Kiko. In December 2013, petitioner filed a petition on behalf of Kiko, in Supreme Court, Niagara County. There, the trial court declined to sign an order to show cause seeking habeas relief and the Fourth Department affirmed (citation omitted) [See above, *Presti*]. Also in December 2013, petitioner brought a habeas proceeding on behalf of Tommy, in Supreme Court, Fulton County. There, the trial court declined to sign an order to show cause and the Third Department affirmed the decision (*People ex rel. Nonhuman Rights Project, Inc. v. Lavery*, 124 A.D.3d 148 [3d Dept. 2014], *lv denied* 26 N.Y.3d 902 [2015]).

Petitioner has also brought a habeas petition seeking the release of two chimpanzees not at issue here, Hercules and Leo, who, according to petitioner are confined for research purposes, at the State University of New York at Stony Brook. In that proceeding, Supreme Court, Suffolk County, declined to sign an order to show cause and in 2014, the Second Department dismissed petitioner's appeal (*Matter of Nonhuman Rights Project, Inc. v. Stanley*, 2014 N.Y. Slip Op. 68434[U] [2d Dept. 2014]).

Without even addressing the merits of petitioner's arguments, we find that the motion court properly declined to sign the orders to show cause since

[88] Assuming habeas relief may be sought on behalf of a chimpanzee, petitioner undisputedly has standing pursuant to CPLR 7002 (a), which authorizes anyone to seek habeas relief on behalf of a detainee. [Originally formatted as footnote "1." — EDS.]

these were successive habeas proceedings which were not warranted or supported by any changed circumstances (*see People ex rel. Glendening v. Glendening*, 259 App. Div. 384, 387 [1st Dept. 1940], *affd* *76284 N.Y. 598 [1940]; *People ex rel. Woodard v. Berry*, 163 A.D.2d 759 [3d Dept. 1990], *lv denied* 76 N.Y.2d 712, 715 [1990]; *see also People ex rel. Lawrence v. Brady*, 56 N.Y. 182, 192 [1874]).

CPLR 7003 (b) permits a court to decline to issue a writ of habeas corpus if "the legality of the detention has been determined by a court of the state on a prior proceeding for a writ of habeas corpus and the petition presents no ground not theretofore presented and determined and the court is satisfied that the ends of justice will not be served by granting it."

Petitioner has filed four identical petitions in four separate state courts in four different counties in New York. Each petition was accompanied by virtually the same affidavits, all attesting to the fact that chimpanzees are intelligent, and have the ability to be trained by humans to be obedient to rules, and to fulfill certain duties and responsibilities. Petitioner has failed to present any new information or new ground not previously considered. The "new" expert testimony presented by petitioner continues to support its basic position that chimpanzees exhibit many of the same social, cognitive and linguistic capabilities as humans and therefore should be afforded some of the same fundamental rights as humans.

Any new expert testimony/affidavits cannot be said to be in response to or counter to the reasoning underlying the decision of the Court in *People ex rel. Nonhuman Rights Project, Inc. v. Lavery* (124 A.D.3d at 148). In declining to extend habeas relief to chimpanzees, the Court in *Lavery* did not dispute the cognitive or social capabilities of chimpanzees. Nor, did it, as argued by petitioner, take judicial notice that chimpanzees cannot bear duties and responsibilities. Rather, it concluded:

"[U]nlike human beings, chimpanzees cannot bear any legal duties, submit to societal responsibilities or be held legally accountable for their actions. In our view, it is this incapability to bear any legal responsibilities and societal duties that renders it inappropriate to confer upon chimpanzees the legal rights—such as the fundamental right to liberty protected by the writ of habeas corpus—that have been afforded to human beings" (*id.* at 152).

The gravamen of petitioner's argument that chimpanzees are entitled to habeas relief is that the human-like characteristics of chimpanzees render them "persons" for purposes of CPLR article 70. This position is without legal support or legal precedent.

In support of its argument, petitioner submits several expert affidavits, including one by Dr. Jane Goodall, the well-known primatologist, purportedly showing, based on academic research and hands-on experience, that chimpanzees have many human-like capabilities. These include recognizing themselves in reflections; setting and acting toward goals such as obtaining food; undergoing cognitive development with brains having similar structures to those of humans; communicating about events in the past and their intentions for the future, such as by pointing or using sign language; exhibiting an awareness of others' different visual perspectives, such as by taking food only when it is out of their competitors' line of sight; protecting others in risky situations, such as when relatively strong chimpanzees will examine a road before guarding more vulnerable chimpanzees as they cross the road; deceiving others (implying that they are able to anticipate others' thoughts); making and using complex tools for hygiene, socializing, communicating, hunting, gathering, and fighting; counting and ordering items using numbers; engaging in moral behavior, such as choosing to make fair offers and ostracizing chimpanzees who violate social norms; engaging in collective behavior such as hunting in groups of chimpanzees adopting different roles; showing concern for the welfare of others, particularly their offspring, siblings, and even orphans they adopt; protecting territory and group security; resolving conflicts; and apologizing.

"The common law writ of habeas corpus, as codified by CPLR article 70, provides a summary procedure by which a 'person' who has been illegally imprisoned or otherwise restrained in his or her liberty can challenge the legality of the detention" (*id.* at 150, quoting CPLR 7002 [a]). While the word "person" is not defined in the statute, there is no support for the conclusion that the definition includes nonhumans, i.e., chimpanzees. While petitioner's cited studies attest to the intelligence and social capabilities of chimpanzees, petitioner does not cite any sources indicating that the United States or New York Constitutions were intended to protect nonhuman animals' rights to liberty, or that the legislature intended the term "person" in CPLR article 70 to expand the availability of habeas protection beyond humans. No precedent exists, under New York law, or English common law, for a finding that a chimpanzee could be considered a "person" and entitled to habeas relief. In fact, habeas relief has never been found applicable to any animal (*see, e.g., United States v. Mett,* 65 F.3d 1531 [9th Cir. 1995], *cert. denied,* 519 U.S. 870 [1996]; *Waste Mgt. of Wisconsin, Inc. v. Fokakis,* 614 F.2d 138 [7th Cir. 1980], *cert. denied,* 449 U.S. 1060 [1980]; *Sisquoc Ranch Co. v. Roth,* 153 F.2d 437, 441 [9th Cir. 1946]).

The asserted cognitive and linguistic capabilities of chimpanzees do not translate to a chimpanzee's capacity or ability, like humans, to bear legal duties, or to be held legally accountable for their actions. Petitioner does not suggest that any chimpanzee charged with a crime in New York could be deemed fit to proceed, i.e., to have the "capacity to understand the proceedings against him or to assist in his own defense" (CPL 730.10 [1]).

. . . .

Petitioner argues that the ability to acknowledge a legal duty or legal responsibility should not be determinative of entitlement to habeas relief, since, for example, infants cannot comprehend that they owe duties or responsibilities and a comatose person lacks sentience, yet both have legal rights. This argument ignores the fact that these are still human beings, members of the human community.

Similarly, petitioner's argument that the word "person" is simply a legal term of art is without merit. As evidence, petitioner points to the doctrine of corporate personhood. In support of this argument, petitioner cites *Santa Clara County v. Southern Pacific R. Co.* (118 U.S. 394 [1886]), where the United States Supreme Court reaffirmed that a corporation is a person for purposes of the Fourteenth Amendment and, thus, its property cannot be taxed differently from the property of individuals. The underlying reasoning was that the corporation's property was really just the property of the individual shareholders who owned the corporation, and therefore should be protected in the same manner. Again, an acknowledgment that such laws are referenced to humans or individuals in a human community.

Petitioner's additional argument that "person" need not mean "human," as evidenced by a river in New Zealand designated as a legal person owning its own riverbed pursuant to a public agreement with Indigenous peoples of New Zealand and pre-independence Indian court decisions recognizing various sacred entities as legal persons, is not relevant to the definition of "person" here in the United States and certainly is of no guidance to the entitlement of habeas relief by nonhumans in New York.

Even assuming, however, that habeas relief is potentially available to chimpanzees, the common-law writ of habeas corpus does not lie on behalf of the two chimpanzees at issue in these proceedings. Petitioner does not seek the immediate production of Kiko and Tommy to the court or their placement in a temporary home, since petitioner contends that "there are no adequate facilities to house [them] in proximity to the [c]ourt." Instead, petitioner requests that respondents be ordered to show "why [the chimpanzees] should not be discharged, and thereafter, [the court] make a determination that [their] detention is unlawful and order [their] immediate release to an appropriate primate sanctuary." Petitioner submits an affidavit from the executive director of Save the Chimps stating that this organization agrees to provide a permanent sanctuary to any and all chimpanzees released by court order. Save the Chimps maintains that the warm, humid climate in southern Florida is "ideal for chimpanzees," as it is similar to the species' native Africa.

Since petitioner does not challenge the legality of the chimpanzees' detention, but merely seeks their transfer to a different facility, habeas relief was properly denied by the motion court (*see Matter of Nonhuman Rights Project, Inc. v. Presti*, 124 A.D.3d at 1334; *compare People ex rel. Dawson v. Smith*, 69 N.Y.2d 689 [1986], with *People ex rel. Brown v. Johnston*, 9 N.Y.2d 482 [1961]).

. . . .

While petitioner's avowed mission is certainly laudable, the according of any fundamental legal rights to animals, including entitlement to habeas relief, is an issue better suited to the legislative process (*see Lewis v. Burger King*, 344 Fed. Appx. 470, 472 [10th Cir. 2009], *cert. denied*, 558 U.S. 1125 [2010]).

Accordingly, the judgment (denominated an order) of the Supreme Court, New York County (Barbara Jaffe, J.), entered January 29, 2016, declining to sign an order to show cause seeking the transfer of Kiko to a primate sanctuary, and the judgment (denominated an order) of the same court and Justice, entered July 8, 2016, effective nunc pro tunc as of December 23, 2015, declining to sign an order to show cause seeking such relief on behalf of Tommy, should be affirmed, without costs.

Renwick, J.P., Mazzarelli, Manzanet-Daniels and Feinman, JJ., concur.

STUDY QUESTIONS

(1) In dispensing with the "argument from marginal cases," the *Lavery II* court referenced the "human moral community" as a basis for personhood. Given the sordid history of personhood that left most of humanity as things for hundreds of years, as set out in detail by Justice Jaffe in *Stanley*, above, what do you make of this line of argument?

(2) The ruling of the *Lavery II* court was that the petitions were properly dismissed by the trial court as "identical" and "successive petitions," despite the addition of new evidence that chimpanzees can, in fact, bear duties and responsibilities, both among themselves and in relation to humans in various contexts. The rest of the opinion appears to be dicta. What do you think of the court's ruling and why it felt compelled to embellish beyond the decisive procedural issue?

(3) The *Lavery II* court cites the *Santa Clara* case, which extended Fourteenth Amendment personhood and protections to corporations, and states that the "underlying reasoning was that the corporation's property was really just the property of the individual shareholders who owned the corporation, and therefore should be protected in the same manner." Is it accurate to describe an entity such as a corporation as "just the property of the individual shareholders"? *See* Meir Dan-Cohen, *Rights, Persons, and Organizations: A Legal Theory for Bureaucratic Society* (2nd ed. 2016) (invalidating the notion that a corporation or other large entity is merely an amalgamation of the rights and duties of its constituent human owners/members); *See, e.g.*, Shawn J. Bayern, *Of Bitcoins, Independently Wealthy Software, and the Zero-Member LLC*, 108 Nw. U.L. Rev. 1485 (2014) (describing rapid growth of nontraditional corporate forms including zero-owner LLCs and autonomous cryptocurrency-enabled trading algorithms). Under U.S. law, corporations are both things that can be created and dissolved, divided into transferrable pieces (shares), and bought and sold. How might this support an analogy on which court might recognize the rights of Stanley, Tommy, Kiko, Hercules, or Leo? How might this analogy be employed to argue for rights of nature generally?

(4) The *Lavery II* court recites a litany of scientific evidence about the cognition of chimpanzees and then refers to the ability of chimpanzees to be trained to be "obedient to demands." Given the weight of the scientific evidence of

chimpanzee cognition and behavior in both captivity and the wild, including a demonstrated sense of fairness among themselves and in interactions with humans, is this a fair reading by the court?

(5) The *Lavery II* court rejected the value of foreign precedent. In an increasingly interconnected world faced by threats like global warming and deforestation that do not respect national boundaries, how might one argue that the persuasive authority of the courts of other countries should not be so summarily discounted? Some countries, like South Africa, constitutionally require courts to consider foreign case law. What benefits and detriments does this present in the context of developing Earth law?

The above decision was appealed in early 2018 to the highest court in New York, the court of appeals. That court denied leave to hear the appeal, but one judge of the court, Judge Eugene Fahey, wrote the following concurring opinion, in which for the first time an American high court judge opined on the issue of nonhuman personhood, even though he did not vote to hear the case or otherwise rule on the merits.

Nonhuman Rights Project, Inc., on Behalf of Tommy v. Lavery et al. (Lavery II),

New York Court of Appeals 2018
31 N.Y.3d 1054,100 N.E.3d 846

Memorandum.
Motion for leave to appeal denied.

Concur: Chief Judge DiFiore and Judges Rivera, Fahey, Garcia and Wilson, Judge Fahey in an opinion. Judges Stein and Feinman taking no part.

FAHEY, J. (concurring). The inadequacy of the law as a vehicle to address some of our most difficult ethical dilemmas is on display in this matter.

In these habeas corpus proceedings brought by petitioner Nonhuman Rights Project on behalf of Tommy and Kiko, two captive chimpanzees, petitioner seeks leave to appeal from an order of the Appellate Division, First Department affirming two judgments of Supreme Court declining to sign orders to show cause to grant the chimpanzees habeas relief. The adult chimpanzees, according to the habeas petition, have been confined by their owners to small cages in a warehouse and a cement storefront in a crowded residential area, respectively.

If this Court were to grant petitioner leave to appeal, I would be most likely to vote to affirm pursuant to CPLR 7003 (b) (Successive petitions for writ). Accordingly, I concur in the Court's decision to deny leave.

However, I write to underscore that denial of leave to appeal is not a decision on the merits of petitioner's claims. The question will have to be addressed eventually. Can a nonhuman animal be entitled to release from confinement through the writ of habeas corpus? Should such a being be treated as a person or as property, in essence a thing?

"A person illegally imprisoned or otherwise restrained in his liberty within the state, or one acting on his [or her] behalf... may petition without notice for a writ of habeas corpus to inquire into the cause of such detention and for deliverance" (CPLR 7002 [a]). The lower courts in this appeal and related cases, in deciding that habeas corpus is unavailable to challenge the legality of the chimpanzees' confinement, rely in the first instance on dictionary definitions. The habeas corpus statute does not define "person," but dictionaries instruct us that the meaning of the word extends to any "entity... that is recognized by law as having most of the rights and duties of a human being" (Black's Law Dictionary [10th ed 2014], person [3]; *see also e.g.* Oxford English Dictionary Online [Oxford University Press 2018], person [7] [http://www.oed.com (last accessed May 4, 2018)] ["An individual... or corporate body... recognized by the law as having certain rights and duties"]).

The Appellate Division then reasoned that chimpanzees are not persons because they lack the "capacity or ability... to bear legal duties, or to be held legally accountable for their actions" (citation omitted) [stating that chimpanzees "cannot bear any legal duties, submit to societal responsibilities or be held legally accountable for their actions"]). Petitioner and amici law professors Laurence H. Tribe, Justin Marceau, and Samuel Wiseman question this assumption. Even if it is correct, however, that nonhuman animals cannot bear duties, the same is true of human infants or comatose human adults, yet no one would suppose that it is improper to seek a writ of habeas corpus on behalf of one's infant child (*see People ex rel. Wehle v. Weissenbach,* 60 N.Y. 385 [1875]) or a parent suffering from dementia (*see, e.g., Matter of Brevorka ex rel. Wittle v. Schuse,* 227 A.D.2d 969 [4th Dept. 1996]). In short, being a "moral agent" who can freely choose to act as morality requires is not a necessary condition of being a "moral patient" who can be wronged and may have the right to redress wrongs (*see generally* Tom Regan, *The Case for Animal Rights* 151-156 [2d ed 2004]).

The Appellate Division's conclusion that a chimpanzee cannot be considered a "person" and is not entitled to habeas relief is in fact based on nothing more than the premise that a chimpanzee is not a member of the human species (*see Nonhuman Rights Project, Inc.,* 152 A.D.3d at 78 [stating that petitioner's argument "that the ability to acknowledge a legal duty or legal responsibility should not be determinative of entitlement to habeas relief, since, for example, infants cannot comprehend that they owe duties or responsibilities and a comatose person lacks sentience, yet both have legal rights... ignores the fact that these are still human beings, members of the human community"]). I agree with the principle that all human beings possess intrinsic dignity and value, and have, in the United States (and territory completely controlled thereby), the constitutional privilege of habeas corpus, regardless of whether they are United States citizens (*see Boumediene v. Bush,* 553 U.S. 723 [2008]), but, in elevating our species, we should not lower the status of other highly intelligent species.

The better approach in my view is to ask not whether a chimpanzee fits the definition of a person or whether a chimpanzee has the same rights and duties as a human being, but instead whether he or she has the right to liberty protected by habeas corpus. That question, one of precise moral and legal status, is the one that matters here. Moreover, the answer to that question will depend on our assessment of the intrinsic nature of chimpanzees as a species. The record before us in the motion for leave to appeal contains unrebutted evidence, in the form of affidavits from eminent primatologists, that chimpanzees have advanced cognitive abilities, including being able to remember the past and plan for the future, the capacities of self-awareness and self-control, and the ability to communicate through sign language. Chimpanzees make tools to catch insects; they recognize themselves in mirrors, photographs, and television images; they imitate others; they exhibit compassion and depression when a community member dies; they even display a sense of humor. Moreover, the amici philosophers with expertise in animal ethics and related areas draw our attention to recent evidence that chimpanzees demonstrate autonomy by self-initiating intentional, adequately informed actions, free of controlling influences (*see* Tom L. Beauchamp, Victoria Wobber, *Autonomy in Chimpanzees,* 35 Theoretical Med & Bioethics 117 [2014]; *see generally* Jane Goodall, *The Chimpanzees of Gombe: Patterns of Behavior* 15-42 [1986]).

Does an intelligent nonhuman animal who thinks and plans and appreciates life as human beings do have the right to the protection of the law against arbitrary cruelties and enforced detentions visited on him or her? This is not merely a definitional question, but a deep dilemma of ethics and policy that demands our attention. To treat a chimpanzee as if he or she had no right to liberty protected by habeas corpus is to regard the chimpanzee as entirely lacking independent worth, as a mere resource for human use, a thing the value of which consists exclusively in its usefulness to others. Instead, we should consider whether a chimpanzee is an individual with inherent value who has the right to be treated with respect (*see generally* Regan, *The Case for Animal Rights* 248-250).

The Appellate Division's approach to these proceedings is mistaken in another respect. Petitioner seeks the transfers of the chimpanzees to a primate sanctuary, rather than the wild. The Appellate Division held that habeas relief was properly denied, because petitioner "does not challenge the legality of the chimpanzees' detention, but merely seeks their transfer to a different facility" (*Nonhuman Rights Project, Inc.,* 152 A.D.3d at 79; *see also Matter of Nonhuman Rights Project, Inc. v. Presti,* 124 A.D.3d 1334, 1335 [4th Dept. 2015], *lv denied* 26 N.Y.3d 901 [2015]). Notably, the Appellate Division erred in this matter, by misreading the case it relied on, which instead stands for the proposition that habeas corpus *can* be used to seek a transfer to "an institution separate and different in nature from the . . . facility to which petitioner had been committed," as opposed to a transfer "within the facility" (*People ex rel. Dawson v. Smith,* 69 N.Y.2d 689, 691 [1986]). The chimpanzees' predicament is analogous to the former situation, not the latter.

The reliance on a paradigm that determines entitlement to a court decision based on whether the party is considered a "person" or relegated to the category of a "thing" amounts to a refusal to confront a manifest injustice. Whether a being has the right to seek freedom from confinement through the writ of habeas corpus should not be treated as a simple either/or proposition. The evolving nature of life makes clear that chimpanzees and humans exist on a continuum of living beings. Chimpanzees share at least 96% of their DNA with humans. They are autonomous, intelligent creatures. To solve this dilemma, we have to recognize its complexity and confront it.

In the interval since we first denied leave to the Nonhuman Rights Project (*see* 26 N.Y.3d 901 [2015]; 26 N.Y.3d 902 [2015]), I have struggled with whether this was the right decision. Although I concur in the Court's decision to deny leave to appeal now, I continue to question whether the Court was right to deny leave in the first instance. The issue whether a nonhuman animal has a fundamental right to liberty protected by the writ of habeas corpus is profound and far-reaching. It speaks to our relationship with all the life around us. Ultimately, we will not be able to ignore it. While it may be arguable that a chimpanzee is not a "person," there is no doubt that it is not merely a thing.

STUDY QUESTIONS

(1) Judge Fahey's concurring opinion states that "while it may be arguable that a chimpanzee is not a person, there is no doubt that it is not merely a thing." How does this comport with the court's observation in *Stanley* and the discussion *supra* that the common law only provides two categories: thing and person? Do you think we need to create a third category of rights holders for nonhuman animals? Or can we expand the definition of person to include at least some nonhuman animals? *See People v. Gordon*, 61 Misc. 3d 966, 971-72, 85 N.Y.S. 3d 725, 729-30 (N.Y. Crim. Ct. 2018) (upholding a charge of neglect for failing to care for a dog and discussing Judge Fahey's concurring opinion, "This view comports with an emerging awareness of the injustice of treating animals as 'things,' and present efforts to change the status of non-human animals from 'things' to legally recognized "persons," for the purpose of habeas corpus protection.").

(2) Judge Fahey cites the amicus curiae briefs filed in support of the NhRP's arguments by Laurence Tribe, Justin Marceau, and Samuel Wiseman, and that of a group of philosophers. Judge Fahey also cites the animal rights philosopher Tom Regan twice, believed to be the first time any court has cited his work in a written opinion. How important to you think these outside authorities were to the judge in deciding to issue his concurring opinion?

(3) Recall the discussion of *Black's Law Dictionary*'s definition of person, particularly in the Third Department's opinion in *Lavery*. Here, on the contrary, Judge Fahey rejected reliance on "dictionary definitions" when discussing whether a species of nonhuman animal should be entitled to the right to bodily liberty protected by common law habeas corpus, referring in particular to the *Lavery* court's reliance on the *Black's Law Dictionary* definition of "person" for the premise that a person is the subject of "rights *and* duties," as opposed to "rights *or* duties," as argued by the NhRP and amici. Following the *Lavery* decision and prior to the First Department's opinion in *Lavery II*, the NhRP wrote a letter to Bryan Garner, the editor-in-chief of *Black's Law Dictionary*, to inform him that its definition was based on a misprint in *Salmond On Jurisprudence* and to request that it amend the quoted text to make clear that Salmond said a person may be the subject of rights *or* duties (that is, an entity need not be able to bear both right and duties in order to be a person). Mr. Garner wrote back immediately and reported that the definition is "marked for correction" in the next edition of the dictionary, and it was corrected in the 11th edition released in 2019, with the "and" replaced by an "or." Should dictionary definitions matter? If they do, is *Black's Law Dictionary* now in conflict with the Third Department and other courts that hold that duties and responsibilities are necessary for rights and personhood?

(4) Fahey was just giving a concurring opinion, but is this still significant?

VI. CONCLUSION

The nonhuman rights movement is part of the struggle for rights that is occurring all over the world—through the courts, legislative and administrative bodies, and social movements. It fits into the larger context of Earth law as one approach in which we may extend the sphere of rights beyond humans to include other living species. By seeking legal personhood and habeas corpus relief for chimpanzees and other animals through the common law, the movement for nonhuman rights seeks to chip away at the anthropocentric bias of the U.S. legal system.

CHAPTER 12

Ecocide[1]

We find ourselves as ethically destitute just when, for the first time, we are faced with ultimacy, the irreversible closing down of the Earth's functioning in its major life systems. Our ethical traditions know how to deal with suicide, homicide, and even genocide; but these traditions collapse entirely when confronted with biocide, the extinction of the vulnerable life systems of the Earth, and geocide, the devastation of the Earth itself.

—Thomas Berry[2]

I. INTRODUCTION

Ecocide refers to the destruction of ecosystems and the species they support on a massive scale. The definitions of the term vary, but in all cases, they concern the widespread killing or degradation of nature such as that which occurred when the United States sprayed the jungles of Vietnam with Agent Orange.[3] The term "ecocide" is derived from the Greek words *oikos,* meaning household, and the French suffix *-cide,* which is derived from the Latin *caedere,* meaning to chop, hew, cut down, or slaughter. The impetus to develop enforceable law to criminalize ecocide comes from the sense that (1) incremental measures, such as identifying specific toxic chemicals and regulating their use, fail to address the magnitude of environmental degradation that is occurring; and (2) ecocide, like genocide, is of international concern and should be subject to transborder enforcement. As will be discussed in this chapter, many jurisdictions have passed laws against ecocide.

This chapter begins with a discussion of deforestation of the rainforest in the Amazon as a case study of ecocide, moves to a history of the crime, and ends with a discussion of who is the victim, what is the harm, who is the responsible party, and what is the penalty.

[1] This chapter was authored by Bedirhan Erdem, Ph.D. cand. and Uğur Orhan, Ph.D. cand. and Research Assistant of Criminal Law and Criminal Procedure Law at the Bilkent University.
[2] Thomas Berry, The Great Work: Our Way into the Future 104 (1999).
[3] "Agent Orange" was a powerful herbicide and defoliant chemical used for the purpose of depriving the Viet Cong of forest cover. The relation of its use to ecocide is discussed *infra* in the text accompanying notes 14-17 of this chapter.

II. A CASE STUDY: 2019 DEFORESTATION OF THE BRAZILIAN AMAZON RAINFOREST

The Amazon rainforest covers over a billion acres in Brazil, Venezuela, Colombia, Ecuador, and Peru. It has been called the "lungs of the world" as it produces more than 20 percent of the world's oxygen. Half of the world's species and a fifth of the world's fresh water is in the Amazon Basin. Eighty percent of the developed world's diet originated in the rainforest. There are 3,000 varieties of fruit in the rainforest; only 200 are now in use in the developed world, whereas Indigenous people use over 2,000. Numerous drugs have been derived from Amazonian plants, and the healing potentials of many others have not been evaluated. Approximately 200,000 Indigenous people live in the rainforest.[4] The Amazon is also a "cloud factory" in that it produces organic aerosol particles that serve as the nuclei for water vapor that drives the hydrological cycle in the Amazon and beyond.[5] Further, the clouds cool the Amazon. The Amazon absorbs 2 billion tons of CO2 per year, about 5 percent of annual emissions.[6] Because of these services, the entire world has an interest in keeping the rainforest intact.

On the other hand, some Brazilians have an interest in developing the rainforest for agricultural purposes, including conversion of the rainforest into croplands, pastures, and palm oil or other tree plantations. Distributors, users, and consumers of products resulting from such conversion, as well as those who provide financial and other services related to production and distribution, have a short-term economic interest in such conversion. In conventional economic terms, the existence value of the Amazon is small, while its potential to produce monetary returns through conversion for agricultural uses and other forms of development is large.

Twelve percent of what was Amazonian rainforest, about 93 million acres (an area bigger than Texas), has been converted to farmland. An area of forest the size of a soccer field is being cleared every minute.[7] Each year there are many naturally occurring fires in the Amazon, but there are even more human-caused fires as land is cleared for agriculture. The burning releases huge amounts of greenhouse gases and reduces the ability of the Amazon to perform its ecological functions. Some of those services, such as the production of cloud cover and rain, are essential for the rainforest to exist. Carlos Nobre, a climate scientist at the University of Sao Paolo, estimates that if another 25 percent of the forest is destroyed, the entire area will become a savannah.[8]

Deforestation in the first eight months of 2019 rose 76 percent over the previous year's rate, reaching the highest pace since 2010.[9] Many have blamed the acceleration

[4] Raintree, *Rainforest Facts*, http://www.rain-tree.com/facts.htm (last visited Dec.4, 2019).

[5] Max-Planck-Gesellschaft, *The Amazon Rainforest—A Cloud Factory* (Sept. 20, 2010), https://www.mpg.de/622290/pressRelease20100920.

[6] Anna Jean Kaiser, *AP Explains: Role of the Amazon in Global Climate Change*, AP News (Aug. 27, 2019), https://apnews.com/384fdb5ee7654667b53ddb49efce8023.

[7] David Shukman, *"Football Pitch" of Amazon Forest Lost Every Minute*, BBC (July 2, 2019), https://www.bbc.com/news/science-environment-48827490.

[8] Kaiser, *supra* note 6.

[9] BBC, *The Amazon in Brazil Is on Fire—How Bad Is it?*, BBC, (Aug. 30, 2019), https://www.bbc.com/news/world-latin-america-49433767.

on actions taken by Brazil's President, Jair Bolsonaro, who took office on January 1, 2019. In his campaign for office, Bolsonaro promised to open up Brazil's protected lands for commercial development, and, since taking office, he has continued to encourage development while pulling back on enforcement measures like fines and seizure or destruction of illegal equipment.[10] Brazil lost 3,769 square miles of rainforest in the 12 months leading up to July 2019.[11]

Deforestation of the Amazon rainforest is deadly to many species and ecosystems and has an impact beyond the Amazon on Earth and its life systems. People within and outside of Brazil are extremely concerned about what is happening. The situation made its way to the agenda of the Group of Seven (G7) summit held in France in August 2019, where the parties pledged $20 million to fight the fires. Germany and Norway froze aid to the Amazon, and President Emmanuel Macron of France threatened to block a trade deal with Brazil. Two hundred investment funds called on companies to reduce their reliance on deforestation, and several companies announced boycotts of Brazilian beef and leather. In response, Bolsonaro declared the deforestation was cultural and would never stop, concerns about the Amazon were overblown, and international interference was an assault on Brazil's sovereignty.[12]

The deforestation of the Amazon in Brazil raises many of the issues related to the crime of ecocide:

- Is it ecocide if a forest is converted to agricultural land or savannah since each one is a life system? Or, more generally, how does one determine that ecocide has occurred?
- How does ecocide relate to the "right to development"?[13]
- Assuming ecocide has occurred, when multiple parties are involved in the illicit activity—in the above case, Bolsonaro, land clearers, farmers, sources of financial investment, multinational corporations who buy products, and consumers—with which party or parties does criminal liability lie?

[10] Leticia Casado & Erneso Londono, *Under Brazil's Far-Right Leader, Amazon Protections Slashed and Forests Fall*, N.Y. TIMES (July 28, 2019), https://www.nytimes.com/2019/07/28/world/americas/brazil-deforestation-amazon-bolsonaro.html.

[11] Marina Lopez, *Brazil's Bolsonaro Calls Amazon Deforestation "Cultural," Says It "Will Never End,"* THE WASH. POST (Nov. 20, 2019), https://www.washingtonpost.com/world/the_americas/brazils-bolsonaro-calls-amazon-deforestation-cultural-says-it-will-never-end/2019/11/20/ba536498-0ba3-11ea-8054-289aef6e38a3_story.html.

[12] *Id.*

[13] Under the United Nations' Declaration of the Right to Development:

> 1. The right to development is an inalienable human right by virtue of which every human person and all peoples are entitled to participate in, contribute to, and enjoy economic, social, cultural and political development, in which all human rights and fundamental freedoms can be fully realized.
> 2. The human right to development also implies the full realization of the right of peoples to self-determination, which includes, subject to the relevant provisions of both International Covenants on Human Rights, the exercise of their inalienable right to full sovereignty over all their natural wealth and resources.

G.A. Res, 41/128, Declaration of the Right to Development (Dec. 4, 1986).

- Does the crime of ecocide require criminal intent, or is it a strict liability offense?
- Who can prosecute ecocide?
- What international tribunal or tribunals can adjudicate an ecocide case?
- What is the punishment for an ecocide violation?
- What remedies are available for restoring a damaged ecosystem?

These issues are discussed in the remainder of this chapter.

III. HISTORY OF ECOCIDE

A. First Use of the Term Ecocide

During the war in Vietnam, the U.S. Army, with major help from U.S. chemical companies, implicitly declared an immense herbicidal warfare program in order to defoliate the forest of Vietnam so that guerilla fighters could not live or hide there. During the operation, known as "Operation Ranch Hand," 20 million gallons of Agent Orange and other chemicals were sprayed over an area the size of the state of Massachusetts.[14] Although the declaration of herbicidal war was implicit, the chemical warfare itself was explicit and a clear example of "war against nature."[15] But war against nature is not the same as war against humans, because unwarranted slaughtering of humans violates *jus cogens* norms, or core human rights. Killing nature is not considered to be a crime of this kind.

The anger toward the U.S. strategy triggered a response from scientists (mostly biologists and botanists). They used the term "ecocide" as part of their anti-war agenda to denounce the environmental disaster caused by the Pentagon's Operation Ranch Hand.[16] A plant biologist, Arthur W. Galston, was the originator of the term "ecocide." He defined it as "willful and permanent destruction of environment in which a people can live in a manner of their own choosing."[17] Since the introduction of the term, there has been an ongoing debate about the criminalization of acts involving the extensive destruction of nature.

B. The Rome Statute and Wartime Ecocide

At the international level, there is no crime explicitly called "ecocide." However, the Rome Statute of the International Criminal Court regulates ecocide as a crime in wartime without using that name. The Rome Statute, which came into force in 2002 and is the main legal instrument in international criminal law, states:

[14] Clyde Haberman, *Agent Orange's Long Legacy, for Vietnam and Veterans*, N.Y. Times (May. 16, 2014), https://www.nytimes.com/2014/05/12/us/agent-oranges-long-legacy-for-vietnam-and-veterans.html.

[15] David Zierler, The Invention of Ecocide: Agent Orange, Vietnam, and the Scientist Who Changed the Way We Think About the Environment 95 (2011).

[16] *Id.* at 15.

[17] *Id.* at 19.

Article 8 War Crimes

[. . .]

2. For the purpose of this Statute, "war crimes" means:

[. . .]

(b) Other serious violations of the laws and customs applicable in international armed conflict, within the established framework of international law, namely, any of the following acts:

[. . .]

[iv] Intentionally launching an attack in the knowledge that such attack will cause incidental loss of life or injury to civilians or damage to civilian objects *or widespread, long-term and severe damage to the natural environment* which would be clearly excessive in relation to the concrete and direct overall military advantage anticipated . . . .[18]

In addition, the earlier Convention on the Prohibition of Military or Any Other Hostile Use of Environmental Modification Techniques (ENMOD), which entered into force on 5 October 1978,[19]also regulates ecocide in wartime without specific reference to that term in Article I:

Each State Party to this Convention undertakes not to engage in military or any other hostile use of environmental modification techniques having widespread, long-lasting or severe effects as the means of destruction, damage or injury to any other State Party.[20]

The "Understandings" relating to the treaty define the terms "widespread," "long-term," and "severe damage":

Understanding relating to Article I

It is the understanding of the Committee that, for the purposes of this Convention, the terms "widespread", "long-lasting" and "severe" shall be interpreted as follows:

(a) "widespread": encompassing an area on the scale of several hundred square kilometers;

[18] Rome Statute of the International Criminal Court., 2187 U.N.T.S. 90 (emphasis added) [hereinafter "Rome Statute]. As of December 15, 2019, there were 123 parties. The United States signed the Rome Statute but is not a party. Rome Statute, U.N.T.C., Chap. XVIII, No. 10, https://treaties.un.org/Pages/ViewDetails.aspx?src=TREATY&mtdsg_no=XVIII-10&chapter=18&clang=_en#12 (last visited Dec. 15, 2019).

[19] As of December 15, 2019, there were 78 parties to ENMOD, including the United States. Convention on the Prohibition of Military or Any Other Hostile Use of Environmental Modification Techniques, *opened for signature* May. 18, 1977, U.N.T.C., Chap. XXIV, No. 1, https://treaties.un.org/Pages/ViewDetails.aspx?src=TREATY&mtdsg_no=XXVI-1&chapter=26&clang=_en (last visited Dec. 15, 2019).

[20] Convention on the Prohibition of Military or Any Other Hostile Use of Environmental Modification Techniques, art. I, 1108 U.N.T.S. 153.

(b) "long-lasting": lasting for a period of months, or approximately a season;
(c) "severe": involving serious or significant disruption or harm to human life, natural and economic resources or other assets.[21]

Article II defines environmental modification techniques as "any technique for changing—through the deliberate manipulation of natural processes—the dynamics, composition or structure of the earth, including its biota, lithosphere, hydrosphere and atmosphere, or of outer space."[22] In sum, international law already recognizes wartime ecocide without reference to that term.

C. Ongoing Effort to Define Peacetime Ecocide

While the Rome Statute and ENMOD in effect regulate ecocide in wartime, there is no international agreement on peacetime ecocide. Many scholars have, however, proposed that the crime of ecocide should not be limited to military acts. Table 1, below, lists some of the proposed definitions of ecocide that would apply, at least in part, to non-military activities of humans:

Table 1

Author	Definition
Richard Falk	"To disrupt or destroy, in whole or in part, a human ecosystem." [23]
Benjamin Whitaker	"Adverse alterations, often irreparable, to the environment—for example through nuclear explosions, chemical weapons, serious pollution and acid rain, or destruction of the rain forest—which threaten the existence of entire populations, whether deliberately or with criminal negligence." [24]
Polly Higgins	"The extensive damage to, destruction of or loss of ecosystem(s) of a given territory, whether by human agency or by other causes, to such an extent that peaceful enjoyment by the inhabitants of that territory has been or will be severely diminished." [25]

[21] International Committee of the Red Cross, text of Convention on the Prohibition of Military or Any Other Hostile Use of Environmental Modification Techniques, Understandings, https://ihl-databases.icrc.org/applic/ihl/ihl.nsf/Treaty.xsp?action=openDocument&documentId=2AC88FF62DB2CDD6C12563CD002D6EC1 (last visited Jan. 20, 2020).

[22] Convention on the Prohibition of Military or Any Other Hostile Use of Environmental Modification Techniques, art II. 1108 U.N.T.S. 153.

[23] Richard Falk offers a "Proposed International Convention on the Crime of Ecocide," which would define ecocide as any of a list of acts done "with intent to disrupt or destroy, in whole or in part, a human ecosystem." Richard A. Falk, *Environmental Warfare and Ecocide — Facts, Appraisal and Proposals*, 4 Bulletin of Peace Proposals 80 app. at 95-96 (1973).

[24] Benjamin Whitaker, Special Rapporteur on the Economic and Social Council, *Revised and Updated Rep. on the Question of The Prevention and Punishment of The Crime of Genocide*, ECOSOC, P33, UN Doc. E/CN.4/Sub.2/1985/6.

[25] Polly Higgins, Eradicating Ecocide 63 (2d. ed. 2015).

Author	Definition
Lynn Berat	"Intentional destruction, in whole or in part, of any portion of the global ecosystem, via killing members of a species; causing serious bodily or mental harm to members of the species; inflicting on the species conditions of life that bring about its physical destruction in whole or in part: and imposing measures that prevent births within the group or lead to birth defects." [26]
Mark Gray	"Serious, extensive, or long-lasting ecological damage, that has an international dimension and is wasteful."[27]
Laurent Neyret	"Any... intentional acts when they threaten the security of the planet and are committed as part of a widespread or systematic action." [28]
Franz Broswimmer	"Acts that intend to disrupt or destroy species development and an entire ecosystem." [29]

An important difference among these proposals is that some require criminal intent (*mens rea)* and others are based on strict liability. Polly Higgins argued that ecocide should be a strict liability crime because (1) it is the consequence that is in question, not the conduct; (2) the gravity of the destruction and damage justifies conviction without proof of criminal intent; (3) without strict liability, enforcement would be largely ineffective; and (4) strict liability rightly places the focus on prevention of the crime and not the blame of the accused.[30]

D. Ecologically Induced Genocide

Ecocide may also be considered as cultural genocide because Indigenous peoples, who have a strong connection to natural habitats, are especially vulnerable to the expansion of transnational production and consumption patterns.[31]

Martin Crook and Damien Short have written about "ecologically induced genocide."[32] This may occur when " 'ecologically destructive interventions'—for example, killing or destroying animals, fish, or crops... [–] 'undermine the life, existence and

[26] Lynn Berat, *Defending the Right to a Healthy Environment: Toward a Crime of Geocide In International Law*, B.U. Int'l. L. J. (1993).

[27] Bronwyn Lay, Laurent Neyret, Damien Short, Michael Urs Baumgartner & Antonia A. Oposa, Jr., *Timely and Necessary: Ecocide Law as Urgent and Emerging*, 28 J. Juris 431, 434 (2015).

[28] *Id.*

[29] Franz Broswimmer, Ecocide: A Short History of the Mass Extinction of Species 75, 109 (2002).

[30] Higgins, *supra* note 25, at 68.

[31] Damien Short, Redefining Genocide: Settler Colonialism, Social Death and Ecocide 35,36 (2016); Deniz Tekayak, *Protecting Earth Rights and the Rights of Indigenous Peoples: Towards an International Crime of Ecocide*, 14 Fourth World J. 2, 9 (2016).

[32] Martin Crook & Damien Short, *Marx, Lemkin and the Genocide-Ecocide Nexus*, 18 Int'l J. of Hum. Rts. 298, 299 (2014).

resistance of Indigenous populations' and can be identified as an example of 'textbook counterinsurgency "starvation" tactics' that may form 'part of a larger extermination strategy.' "[33]

Genocide always has a cultural element and is distinguishable from mass killing. For example, in World War II, there was mass killing as a result of the atomic bombs dropped on Nagasaki and Hiroshima, but this was not considered genocide as it did not involve the extermination of a population with a shared culture. In contrast, the attempt of Nazi Germany to exterminate Jews was genocide. The U.S. Holocaust Memorial Museum defines genocide as follows: "Genocide is an internationally recognized crime where acts are committed with the intent to destroy, in whole or in part, a national, ethnic, racial, or religious group."[34]

There is growing attention to the genocide-ecocide nexus. For example, in 2016, the Office of the Prosecutor of the International Criminal Court, whose remit includes genocide, stated that it would concern itself with crimes involving land grabbing and environmental harm. In a policy paper on case selection and prioritization, the office stated: "The Office will give particular consideration to prosecuting Rome Statute Crimes that are committed by means of, or that result in, *inter alia*, the destruction of the environment, the illegal exploitation of natural resources or the illegal dispossession of land."[35]

It is not clear how a crime or crimes related to ecologically induced genocide would be written. The ultimate crime is genocide, and ecocide is the means, or a means, of achieving it. It is possible that a separate crime might be specified of ecocide with the intent to bring about genocide, or the death of a society or an Indigenous community. As indicated above, the International Criminal Court already recognizes that ecocide may be taken into account in prosecuting genocide.

E. Proposed Ecocide Amendment to the Rome Statute

Under the Rome Statute, the jurisdiction of the International Criminal Court is limited to "the most serious crimes of concern to the international community as whole,"[36] specifically

1. The Crime of Genocide
2. Crimes Against Humanity
3. War Crimes
4. The Crime of Aggression.[37]

[33] Martin Crook, Damien Short, & Nigel South, *Ecocide, Genocide, Capitalism and Colonialism: Consequences for Indigenous Peoples and Global Ecosystems Environments*, 22 Theoretical Criminology 298, 299 (2018) (quoting A. Dunlap, *The "Solution" Is Now the "Problem": Wind Energy, Colonization and the "Geocide Ecocide Nexus" in the Isthmus of Tehuantepec, Oaxaca*, 22 Int'l J. of Hum. Rts. 550, 557 (2018)).
[34] U.S Holocaust Memorial Museum, *What Is Genocide?*, https://www.ushmm.org/genocide-prevention/learn-about-genocide-and-other-mass-atrocities/what-is-genocide (last visited Dec. 16, 2019).
[35] Office of the Prosecutor, International Criminal Court, Policy Paper on Case Selection and Prioritization, ¶ 41 (Sept. 15, 2016).
[36] Rome Statute, *supra* note 18, at art. V, 2187 U.N.T.S. 90.
[37] *Id.*

Polly Higgins devoted her life to eradicating ecocide and led an effort to establish ecocide as the fifth crime under the jurisdiction of the International Criminal Court. In 2010, she submitted a draft model ecocide law to the United Nations. This draft law defined ecocide as follows: "Ecocide is the extensive damage to, destruction of or loss of ecosystem(s) of a given territory, whether by human agency or other causes to such an extent that peaceful enjoyment by the inhabitants of that territory has been or will be severely diminished."[38]

The website on ecocide law operated by the U.K. nonprofit Ecological Defence Integrity (EDI), co-founded by Polly Higgins in 2017, gives the following justification for this fifth crime:

> The inclusion of Ecocide law as international law prohibits mass damage and destruction of the Earth and, as defined above, creates a legal duty of care for all inhabitants that have been or are at risk of being significantly harmed due to Ecocide. The duty of care applies to prevent, prohibit and pre-empt both human-caused Ecocide and natural catastrophes. Where Ecocide occurs as a crime, remedy can be sought through national courts and the International Criminal Court (ICC) or a similar body.
>
> Currently there is no overriding mandatory duty of care (sometimes called a fiduciary duty) to prohibit, prevent significant hazards or harm, or to pre-empt by assisting those who are facing Ecocide. Governments, business and finance are not legally bound to be accountable for some of the biggest Ecocides, despite the risk to both humans and nature. By creating a crime of Ecocide, the enforcement of a global primary duty (to stop activities that cause significant harm) ensures that all subsequent decisions are made whereby people and planet are put first. By criminalising Ecocide at an international level, a global duty of care is created.[39]

The International Criminal Court began operation in 2002. Proceedings against 22 people have been completed and about as many are ongoing. As of December 2019, with respect to the 22 completed proceedings, "two [of the accused] are serving sentences, four have finished their sentences, two have been acquitted, six have had the charges against them dismissed, two have had the charges against them withdrawn, one has had his case declared inadmissible, and four have died before trial."[40]

Thus, in terms of trials and convictions, the International Criminal Court has had limited impact. In addition, China, the United States, Russia, South Africa, Israel, the Philippines, and other significant nations either never were parties or have withdrawn from the Rome Statute, and thus are not subject to the jurisdiction of the International Criminal Court. Nevertheless, the statute and the court are important and have an impact on international norms of conduct.

[38] Ecocide Law, *Proposed Amendment to the Rome Statute*, https://ecocidelaw.com/the-law/what-is-ecocide (last visited Dec. 17, 2019).

[39] *Id.*

[40] *International Criminal Court*, Wikipedia, https://en.wikipedia.org/w/index.php?title=International_Criminal_Court&oldid=930467742 (last visited Dec. 17, 2019).

F. National Codes Criminalizing Ecocide

Eleven countries have criminalized ecocide. Table 2, below, lists the countries and, with respect to each country, the date of adoption of the statute, the title of the statute, and the description of the crime:

Table 2

Country and Date of Adoption	Title of Statute	Description of Crime
Armenia (2003)	Crimes Against Peace and Human Security	"Mass destruction of flora or fauna, poisoning the environment, the soils or water resources, as well as implementation of other actions causing an ecological catastrophe." (Art. 394)
Belarus (1999)	Crimes Against Peace and Security of Mankind and War Crimes	"Mass destruction of flora and fauna, or air or water poisoning or any other intentional acts that may cause and ecological catastrophe." (Art. 131)
Georgia (1999)	Offense Against Humankind	"Ecocide i.e. contamination of the atmosphere, soil, water resources, mass destruction of fauna or flora, or any other act that could have led to an ecological disaster." (Art. 1999)
Kazakhstan (1997)	Crimes Against Peace and Human Security	"Mass destruction of vegetable or animal world, poisoning of the atmosphere, land and water resources, as well as commission of other actions, caused or could cause ecological disaster or environmental emergency." (Art. 169)
Kyrgyzstan (1997)	Crimes Against the Peace and Security of Mankind	"Massive destruction of the animal or plant kingdoms, contamination of the atmosphere or water resources, and also commission of other actions capable of causing an ecological catastrophe." (Art. 374)
Republic of Moldova (2002)	Crimes Against the Peace and Security of Humanity, War Crimes	"Deliberate mass destruction of flora and fauna, poisoning the atmosphere or water resources, and the commission of other acts that may cause or caused an ecological disaster." (Art. 136)
Russian Federation (1996)	Crimes Against the Peace and Security Mankind	"Massive destruction of the animal or plant kingdoms, contamination of the atmosphere or water resources, and also

Country and Date of Adoption	Title of Statute	Description of Crime
		commission of other actions capable of causing an ecological catastrophe." (Art. 358)
Tajikistan (1998)	Crime Against the Peace and Safety of Mankind	"Mass destruction of flora and fauna, poisoning the atmosphere or water resources, as well as commitment of other actions which may cause ecological disasters." (Art. 400)
Ukraine (2001)	Criminal Offenses Against Peace, Security of Mankind and International Legal Order	"Mass destruction of flora and fauna, poisoning of air or water resources, and also any other actions that may cause an environmental disaster." (Art. 441)
Uzbekistan (1994)	Crimes Related to Environment Protection and Conservancy	"Pollution or damage of land, water, or atmospheric air, resulted in mass disease incidence of people, death of animals, birds, or fish, or other grave consequences." (Art. 196)
Vietnam (1990)	Crimes of Undermining Peace, Against Humanity and War Crimes	"Those who, in peace time or war time, commit acts of... as well as other acts of genocide or acts of ecocide or destroying the natural environment." (Art. 342)

IV. KEY ISSUES IN ECOCIDE

In this third and final section, we will consider three key issues in prosecuting ecocide, as follows: Who is the victim and what is the harm or violation? Who is the responsible party? And what is the penalty?

A. Who Is the Victim of Ecocide?

1. Existing law

It is necessary to define the victim(s) and the harm or loss suffered in order to prosecute criminal acts and assess penalties, including the performance of restorative acts to the harmed ecosystem.

There are two methods of identifying the victim: one is harm and the other is violation.[41] In the harm method, the question is, "Who was harmed directly?" In the violation method, the question is, "Who was the holder or bearer of the legally protected right or interest (including the right to or interest in existence) that was violated?" In regard to the latter question, as discussed elsewhere in this coursebook, nature is not traditionally considered to be a holder of legally protected rights or interests.

The 1985 UN General Assembly Declaration of Basic Principles of Justice for Victims of Crime and Abuse of Power defines a victim as follows:

> "**Victims**" means persons who, individually or collectively, have suffered harm, including [(harm method)] physical or mental injury, emotional suffering, economic loss or [(violation method)] substantial impairment of their fundamental rights, through acts or omissions that are in violation of criminal laws operative within Member States, including those laws proscribing criminal abuse of power.[42]

The above definition is limited to humans, so the harm or violation suffered would pertain only to humans. In the Rome Statute and in ENMOD, the offending act may involve "widespread, long-lasting or severe" harm to *nature*, as well as harm to humans.

In regard to the national statutes described in Table 2, *supra*, ten of the countries consider ecocide as a crime against the peace and security of humankind and thus take the same human-centered perspective as the UN General Assembly did in the above definition of victims of crime. Uzbekistan, in contrast, takes an ecocentric perspective in making ecocide a crime related to environment protection and conservancy.

2. Nature as victim under the proposed ecocide amendment to the Rome Statute in the United Kingdom 2011 mock trial

As noted above, Higgins proposed an ecocide amendment to the Rome Statute in 2010. She also proposed a model act with application to the United Kingdom.[43] Under the Model U.K. Ecocide Act, ecocide involves damage to ecosystems that affect peaceful enjoyment by the inhabitants, with inhabitants being defined as "any living species dwelling in a particular place." The Ecocide Act also specifies the ways in which the crime of ecocide breaches the rights to life of humanity and nature, endangers the lives of future generations, and harms the cultural life of Indigenous communities.

[41] Tuğrul Katoğlu, *Ceza Hukukunda Suçun Mağduru Kavramının Sınırları*, 61 AÜHFD 657, 693 (2012).

[42] G.A Res, 40/34, Declaration of Basic Principles of Justice for Victims of Crime and Abuse of Power (Nov. 29, 1985).

[43] Ecocide Act, https://ecocidelaw.com/wp-content/uploads/2012/06/Earth-is-Our-Business-Appendix-II.pdf (last visited December 15, 2019) [hereinafter the "Model U.K. Ecocide Act"].

In 2011, Higgins organized a mock trial in the Supreme Court in London to test the viability of the model statute. While this was a mock trial, it has value as a study of how an inclusive ecocide law might be applied. The mock criminal trial concerned alleged offenses under the Act by the CEOs of two fictional companies, Global Petroleum Company and Glamis Group, related to the operation of an offshore drilling unit by Global Petroleum in the Gulf of Mexico and operations in the Canadian tar sands by both companies. The indictment of the CEO of Global Petroleum Company read, in part, as follows:

> [I]n his role as Chief Executive Officer, **Mr. Bannerman of Global Petroleum Company (GPC)** had authority over and responsibility for a semi-submersible Mobile Offshore Drilling Unit when an explosion on the platform caused an oil spill in excess of 250 million gallons of crude oil into the sea resulting in extensive destruction, damage to or loss of ecosystem(s) covering an area in excess of 200 square kilometers of ocean, to such an extent that the peaceful enjoyment by the inhabitants of that territory has been severely diminished thereby:
>
> 1. putting birds at risk of injury;
> 2. causing injury to 2,086 birds; and
> 3. causing the death of 2,303 birds
>
> contrary to sections 1(1) and 1(2) of the Ecocide Act of 2010.[44]

The paragraph clearly shows the application of the Ecocide Act to nonhuman victims. Mr. Bannerman was cleared of charges related to offshore drilling, but both Mr. Bannerman and the CEO of Glamis Group were found guilty of ecocide for the killing of birds in the tar sands operations of the two companies.[45]

B. Who Is the Responsible Party?

When acts of ecocide have occurred and the victims have been identified, the responsible party must be connected with the crime. In some cases, there is one dominant actor, such as BP in the 2010 Deepwater Horizon oil spill in the Gulf of Mexico. In others, such as in the case study at the beginning of this chapter concerning the 2019 burning of the Brazilian Amazon, there are multiple actors. In the Amazon burning, some would blame the government of Brazil or President Bolsonaro for not enforcing environmental laws or taking other preventive measures. Others would blame large corporations who are buying products produced on converted Amazon land or establishing farms and processing facilities in the Amazon. Others would blame the

[44] Ecocide Law, *Bannerman & Tench Indictment* (Sept. 30, 2011), https://ecocidelaw.com/resources/documents/.

[45] A description of the mock trial and the trial documents are available at https://ecocidelaw.com/the-law/mock-trial/ (last visited Dec. 17, 2019).

individuals actually doing the burning. Even in the BP oil spill, although BP was the dominant actor, there were many other companies and individuals involved. Who should be charged with the crime?

1. Individuals as responsible parties

In many ecocide cases, the damage is done by people acting through corporations or other legal entities, including states. The legal entities are more capable of paying fines or carrying out recovery and restoration efforts than individuals within those entities. Yet, for cases brought before the International Criminal Court under the Rome Statute, only natural persons may be tried. This is a carryover from one of the Nuremberg Principles that governed war crimes trials after World War II. The principle adopted by the Nuremberg Tribunal was as follows: "Crimes against international law are committed by men, not by abstract entities, and only by punishing individuals who commit such crimes can the provisions of international law be enforced."[46]

In keeping with this principle, the Rome Statute states:

Article 25

Individual criminal responsibility

1. The Court shall have jurisdiction over natural persons pursuant to this Statute.[47]

* * *

2. Corporations as responsible parties

The drafters of the Rome Statute did, however, consider including a provision addressing the criminal responsibility of corporations.[48] The proposed article read as follows:

> Without prejudice to any individual criminal responsibility of natural persons under this Statute, the Court may also have jurisdiction over a juridical person for a crime under this Statute. Charges may be filed by the Prosecutor against a juridical person, and the Court may render a judgement over a juridical person for the crime charged, if:

[46] United Nations, *Overview of the Rome Statute of the International Criminal Court*, https://legal.un.org/icc/general/overview.htm (last visited Dec. 18, 2019).

[47] Rome Statute, *supra* note 18, at art. 25, 2187 U.N.T.S. 90. Some states also follow the principle that entities cannot be criminally liable. For example, "according to German law criminal liability always requires fault on the part of the offender (known as '*Schuldprinzip*') whereby fault cannot exist on the part of the corporate itself (*societas delinquere non potest*)." Jamie Nowak, *Corporate Criminal Liability in Germany*, Norton Rose Fulbright Corporate and Commercial Disputes Review 3 (April 2016), https://www.nortonrosefulbright.com/en/knowledge/publications/800922a0/corporate-criminal-liability-in-germany.

[48] Andrew Clapham, Human Rights Obligations of Non-State Actors 245 (2013).

(a) The charges filed by the Prosecutor against the natural person and the juridical person allege the matters referred to in subparagraphs (b) and (c); and
(b) The natural person charged was in a position of control within the juridical person under the national law of the State where the juridical person was registered at the time the crime was committed; and
(c) The crime was committed by the natural person acting on behalf of and with the explicit consent of that juridical person and in the course of its activities; and
(d) The natural person has been convicted of the crime charged.

For the purpose of this Statute, "juridical person" means a corporation whose concrete, real, or dominant objective is seeking private profit or benefit, and not a State or other public body in the exercise of State authority, a public international body, or an organization registered and acting under the national law of a State as a non-profit organization.

The proceedings with respect to a juridical person under this article shall be in accordance with this Statute and the relevant Rules of Procedure and Evidence. The Prosecutor may file charges against the natural and juridical persons jointly or separately. The natural person and the juridical person may be jointly tried. If convicted, the juridical person may incur the penalties referred to in article 76. These penalties shall be enforced in accordance with the provisions of article 99.[49]

* * *

Under regional agreements, corporations have been regarded as legal persons in order to hold them criminally responsible for their actions.[50] An example is provided in Article 9 of the Council of Europe's 1998 Convention on the Protection of the Environment through Criminal Law:[51]

Article 9 – Corporate liability

Each Party shall adopt such appropriate measures as may be necessary to enable it to impose criminal or administrative sanctions or measures on legal persons on whose behalf an offence referred to in Articles 2 or 3 has been committed by their organs or by members thereof or by another representative.

Under Article 14, however, in order for the convention to enter into force, it had to be ratified by three states who are members of the Council of Europe. Only 13 of the 47 members of the Council signed the convention and only Estonia ratified it.[52] Thus, it is not in force. The failure to ratify the Convention is an example of the

[49] Working Paper on Article 23, Paragraphs 5 and 6. Draft Statute of An International Criminal Court, A/Conf-183/C-1/WGGP/L-5/Rev-2; William A. Schabas, The International Criminal Court: A Commentary on the Rome Statute 564 (2016).

[50] Rosalyn Higgins, Problems And Process: International Law And How We Use It 54 (1993). *See also* M. Cherif Bassiouni, The Introduction to International Criminal Law 100 (2nd ed. 2013). *See also* Vanessa Schwegler, *The Disposable Nature: The Case of Ecocide and Corporate Accountability*, 9 Amsterdam L.F. 71, 93 (2017).

[51] Council of Europe, Convention on the Protection of Environment through Criminal Law, C.E.T.S. No. 172.

[52] Chart of Signatures and Ratifications of Treaty 172, https://www.coe.int/en/web/conventions/full-list/-/conventions/treaty/172/signatures?p_auth=XCxa6gU0 (last visited Dec. 19, 2019).

international resistance to imposing criminal liability on corporations for environmental and human rights violations.[53]

In the Model U.K. Ecocide Act, individuals, corporations, and other legal entities, but not states, may be prosecuted for ecocide.[54] Under that act, a person "in a passion of superior responsibility" for a legal entity, including a state, is responsible for offenses committed by people under their authority.[55] Further, if a superior person of a legal entity is convicted of an offense by reason of their role in a legal entity, the legal entity is jointly responsible for the offense.[56] The Act has a very broad reach.

3. Methods for holding legal entities responsible for committed crimes

There are several methods for attributing culpability to corporations, with most common law and civil law jurisdictions using one of three approaches: (1) identification; (2) aggregation; or (3) culture.[57]

The identification method equates the acts of specific natural persons to the acts of a corporation.[58] The natural persons are generally determined to be those who are members of a decision-making body or individuals with sufficient authority who possess the criminal intent (*mens rea)* for the offense.[59] In a civil law system, the will of legal entities is expressed through the entities' "organs" (directors and managers of a corporation). A crime occurs in relation to an offense committed for the benefit of a legal entity through the participation of the organs of that legal entity.

The aggregation method, rather than putting authorized corporate personnel or organs at the center of culpability, searches the collective knowledge to satisfy the test of *mens rea.*[60] If the total guilt aggregated from the officials involved in a particular offense reaches the required level of culpability, the corporation may be held criminally responsible even though each individual's *mens rea* separately is not enough to justify imposing a punishment.[61]

Under the culture method, for example in the Australian model of corporate responsibility,[62] corporations may be held liable in regard to their organizational structure and the operating mechanism that led to noncompliance with the law.[63] According to the Australian Criminal Code, the corporate culture is "an attitude, policy, rule, course of conduct or practice existing within the body corporate generally or in

[53] Clapham, *supra* note 48, at 76-77.
[54] Model U.K. Ecocide Act, *supra* note 43, at art. 17.
[55] *Id.* at art. 13.
[56] *Id.* at art. 17.
[57] Nina H.B Jørgensen, The Responsibility of States for International Crimes 75 (2006).
[58] A.P Simester et al., Simester and Sullivan's Criminal Law Theory and Doctrine 279 (2016).
[59] *Id.* at 280.
[60] Jørgensen, *supra* note 57, at 76.
[61] Simester & Spencer, *supra* note 58, at 285.
[62] Joanna Kyriakakis, *Prosecuting Corporations for International Crimes: The Role for Domestic Criminal Law, in* Int'l Criminal Law and Philosophy 115 (Larry May & Zachary Hoskins eds., 2010).
[63] *Id.*

the part of the body corporate in which the relevant activities take place."[64] In this code, corporate culture is a basis for corporate responsibility in addition to the identification method.

4. Liability of entities under existing environmental laws

Existing environmental laws give states the ability to address some forms of ecocide at both the entity and individual level, although they fall short of offering a comprehensive ecocide framework. The BP oil spill, for example, involved the Deepwater Horizon drilling rig that was operating in the Gulf of Mexico and drilling an exploratory well 18,360 feet below sea level about 41 miles south of Louisiana. BP was the operator and principal developer of the project. On April 20, 2010, high-pressure methane gas expanded into the marine riser and rose into the drilling rig, where it ignited and exploded. Eleven workers were killed and 17 were wounded. The rig sank two days later, and oil leaked from the well for 87 days. The flow rate was as high as 62,000 barrels per day and the total oil spilled was estimated at 4.9 million barrels.[65] The oil was dispersed over an area of 68,000 square miles that included coastal wetlands, beaches, and the Gulf of Mexico. In addition, chemicals with relatively unknown ecological impacts were sprayed to increase dispersion and absorption of the oil. The disaster affected the coasts of Texas, Louisiana, Mississippi, Alabama, and Florida, and toxic waste remains in these coastal lands to this day. The oil spill affected the livelihoods of fishermen, people in the tourist industry, and many others, and it had a devastating effect on marine life and coastal life.[66]

BP was investigated by the U.S. government under the Oil Pollution Act of 1990.[67] This act contains provisions intended to avoid future oil spills, as well as provisions requiring removal of spilled oil and assigning liability for damages caused and the cost of cleanup. Categories of damage covered include natural resource damages, damages to real or personal property, loss of subsistence use, loss of government revenues, loss of profits or impaired earning capacity, damaged public services, and damage assessment costs.[68] The Oil Pollution Act provides for strict liability of the responsible party for settlement of claims.[69] To settle claims from this oil spill, BP set up a $20 billion "Gulf Coast Claims Facility," and billions of dollars have been paid to claimants from this facility. Claims have included private claims for damages to property, loss of income, and environmental cleanup and restoration costs incurred by governmental agencies.[70]

[64] Australia Crim. Code Act 1995, Div. 12, Sec. 12. 3, Art. 6.

[65] U.S COAST GUARD, ON SCENE COORDINATOR REPORT: DEEPWATER HORIZON OIL SPILL 33 (2011).

[66] *Deepwater Horizon Oil Spill*, https://en.wikipedia.org/wiki/Deepwater_Horizon_oil_spill (last visited Dec. 19, 2019).

[67] Oil Pollution Act, 33 U.S.C. § 2701 et seq. (1990).

[68] *Id.* at § 2702.

[69] *Id.* at § 2702, but subject to the defenses given in § 2703.

[70] *See generally* Colin McDonell, *The Gulf Coast Claims Facility and the Deepwater Horizon Litigation: Judicial Regulation of Private Compensation Schemes*, 64 STANFORD L. REV. 765 (2012).

In addition to action against BP under the Oil Pollution Act, the U.S. federal government brought claims under the Clean Water Act resulting in a settlement under which BP was obligated to pay a $4.5 billion fine. Further, more than a hundred private lawsuits were filed against BP and other corporations that had a nexus with the oil spill. The settlement of these claims was in the neighborhood of $10 billion. As of 2015, BP's costs related to the oil spill had reached $54 billion.[71] Further criminal charges were brought against companies and individuals involved in the loss.

The litigation related to the BP oil spill was extensive and involved a tremendous amount of time and resources by many companies, governmental agencies, and individual claimants. In this case, claimants received substantial payments for damages, extensive environmental cleanup, restoration, and recovery projects that were undertaken, and large criminal fines against the corporations were collected. No one, however, served prison time.[72]

5. States as responsible parties

States may be perpetrators of ecocide, may fail to take actions to prevent the ecocide, or may fail to penalize perpetrators of ecocide. However, there are no statutes or treaties under which states may be prosecuted for ecocide. At present, the restraint of states from committing ecocide would come from pressures or sanctions by other states, companies, or individuals who had determined this was necessary. For example, as stated previously in the 2019 Amazon fires case, Germany and Norway, objecting to the encouragement of the burning by the Brazilian government and the lack of enforcement by the Brazilian government of laws that would restrict the land conversion and forest burning, froze aid to the Amazon, and President Macron of France threatened to block a trade deal with Brazil. In addition, 200 investment funds called on companies to reduce their reliance on deforestation and several companies announced boycotts of Brazilian beef and leather.

C. What Is the Penalty?

After the conviction of a defendant of ecocide, the question is, what penalty or obligation should be imposed? There are five theories of criminal punishment: (1) Under the *incapacitation theory*, the perpetrator should be removed from society so that the perpetrator cannot do further harm; (2) Under the *retributive theory*, the perpetrator of a crime should suffer for the perpetrator's act in proportion to the harm caused; (3) Under the *rehabilitation theory*, the perpetrator should be placed in a situation where they may change their ways and re-enter society; (4) Under the *deterrence theory*, the perpetrator should be punished in such a way that the punishment deters others from committing the same crime; and (4) Under the *restorative theory*, the perpetrator should

[71] *Deepwater Horizon Oil Spill*, *supra* note 66 (citing Ed Crooks & Christopher Adams, *BP: Into Uncharted Waters*, Financial Times (Jul. 9, 2015), https://www.ft.com/content/0a71ce8c-24b9-11e5-9c4e-a775d2b173ca).
[72] *Id.*

be obligated to reconcile with the victim and the community at large, such as by repairing the harm caused.[73] Governments in their legislative roles and courts in their judicial roles often combine two or more of these theories in determining penalties.

1. Treatment under the Rome Statute

The Rome Statute contains the following penalties for convicted individual criminals: (1) imprisonment for a number of years or a life sentence in egregious cases; (2) a fine; and (3) forfeiture of property proceeds and assets derived directly or indirectly from the crime.[74] The Rome Statute also authorizes the establishment of a trust fund funded by the fines and forfeited property for the benefit of the victims.[75]

2. National codes

Under the national ecocide codes identified in Table 2, most statutes impose imprisonment as the penalty. Judicial fines or restorative or reparative measures are not common sanctions. Vietnam provides for capital punishment for acts of ecocide. The killing of a human being as punishment, however, is difficult to support with respect to ecocide when the underlying reason for making it an offense is to protect the life of nature with all its inhabitants.

Table 3, below, lists different national penal provisions.

Table 3

COUNTRY	PUNISHMENT
Armenia	. . . is punished with imprisonment for the term of ten to fifteen years.
Belarus	. . . shall be punished by imprisonment for a term of ten to fifteen years.
Georgia	. . . shall be punished by imprisonment for a term of twelve to twenty years.
Kazakhstan	. . . shall be punished by imprisonment for the term of ten to fifteen years.
Kyrgyzstan	. . . shall be punishable by deprivation of liberty for a term of twelve to twenty years.
Republic of Moldova	. . . shall be punished by imprisonment from ten to fifteen years.

[73] Haluk Toroslu, Ceza Müeyyidesi 36-39 (2010).
[74] Rome Statute, *supra* note 18, at art. 77.
[75] *Id.* at art. 79.

COUNTRY	PUNISHMENT
Russian Federation	. . . shall be punishable by deprivation of liberty for a term of twelve to twenty years.
Tajikistan	. . . is punishable by imprisonment for a period of fifteen to twenty years.
Ukraine	. . . shall be punishable by imprisonment for a term of eight to fifteen years.
Uzbekistan	. . . shall be punished with a fine from one hundred to two hundred minimum monthly wages or deprivation of certain rights up to five years, or correctional labor up to three years. The same acts resulted in death of a person shall be punished with arrest from three to six months, or imprisonment up to three years and deprivation of certain rights.
Vietnam	. . . shall be sentenced to between twelve years and twenty years of imprisonment, life imprisonment or capital punishment.

3. Penalization of corporations

The punishments under the Rome Statute and the above national codes cover penalties for responsible individuals in corporations but not penalties for corporations themselves. Such penalties could include fines and forfeiture of property proceeds and assets derived directly or indirectly from the crime. As with the Rome Statute, the codes could authorize the establishment of trust funds funded by the fines and forfeited property for the benefit of the victims and for environmental cleanup and restoration.[76] While not covered under any present statutes, penalties could also include replacement of management, removal of the corporate charter, a forced merger, or a forced sale of assets, including a partial sale of a line of business and its assets.

V. ECOCIDE'S IMPORTANCE FOR EARTH LAW

As discussed above, ecocide, by reason of its inclusion in the Rome Statute (albeit never explicitly named by that term), is an established part of international law as a war crime, but not yet as a peacetime offense. Under the laws of various nations, ecocide is an offense regardless of whether it occurs in connection with armed conflict or in peacetime. Under these laws, the offense of ecocide only occurs when there is "extreme" or "severe" damage to nature. The Rome Statute requires finding a military

[76] In the BP oil spill, BP set up a trust fund for the benefit of the victims of the spill as well as for environmental cleanup and restoration. Deepwater Horizon Litigation, WIKIPEDIA, https://en.wikipedia.org/wiki/Deepwater_Horizon_litigation (last visited July 21, 2020).

attack was launched that resulted in "*widespread, long-term* and *severe* damage to the natural environment." The Model U.K. Ecocide Act would require finding "*extensive* damage to, destruction of or loss of ecosystem(s) of a given territory, whether by human agency or other causes to such an extent that peaceful enjoyment by the inhabitants of that territory has been or will be *severely* diminished."

The impetus for adding a new crime comes from a widely held sense that something wrong is happening or has happened and there should be a law against it, and people who violate the law should be criminally punished. Arguably, there is a widespread sense that devastation of large portions or aspects of nature, causing extensive harm to human or nonhuman inhabitants of the area, should be punishable as a crime. Yet, defining and applying the crime of ecocide has been limited. This may be because the devastation of nature is often connected with something that is considered a social good: the defeat of an enemy in war or economic "development" in peacetime. Thus, the pollution of water and land incident to extracting oil from tar sands in Canada may be viewed by some as ecocide while, for others, it may be seen as a negative side effect of producing a needed commodity—a side effect that may be held in check by pollution control regulations under conventional environmental law. Another prominent issue limiting the adoption and prosecution of ecocide relates to criminal intent. As noted above, the Model U.K. Ecocide Act makes ecocide a strict liability crime, presumably because of the difficulty of proving that perpetrators act with the intent of seriously degrading nature. Another issue has been that where ecocide has been adopted, only individuals, not legal entities, are subject to prosecution.

Five justifications for criminal punishment were discussed above, namely (1) incapacitation; (2) retribution; (3) rehabilitation; (4) deterrence; and (5) restoration. Punishment for ecocide may deter people from perpetrating the crime, and imposing obligations of restoration may be a way of addressing the harm caused by the crime. The benefits of incapacitation, retribution, and rehabilitation offer less support for punishment for ecocide. This is because, as with genocide, the primary reasons for punishing ecocide are completely preventing recurrence of the crime and bringing as much healing as possible when the crime has occurred.

Ecocide fits awkwardly in anthropocentric law, which regards nature as something for the use of humans. When the use of nature yields benefits to humans, the harm to nature tends to be considered an externality not to be taken into account except regarding the extent that humans are harmed as a result. On the other hand, ecocide fits very well in Earth law, or ecocentric law, where the integrity of the Earth community in its diverse and interrelated manifestations is the primary concern. Earth law offers a new framework for what is reasonable and permissible, and what is not. It assumes an ecological consciousness. In the case of ecocide, it assumes that you should know when your actions will cause widespread and severe damage to nature, and it is not reasonable for you to act without regard for the integrity of the natural systems. Such awareness may not come easily to the modern human, yet it would be wrong to say that it does not exist.

Let us end this chapter by returning to where we began, with the 2019 deforestation of the Brazilian rainforest. May the actors involved in the burning of the rainforests and those who finance them or profit from their activities claim that they were ignorant of the potential harm they were causing? Ecocide, as with genocide, is not an everyday crime. Ecocide is an egregious crime, one that unfortunately fits the scale of the destruction that is taking place in the functioning of Earth, such as the accumulation of enormous amounts of plastics in oceans resulting from the disposal of fishing nets and plastic bags, the destruction of boreal forests, the pollution of soil and water with toxic mine tailings resulting from extracting oil from tar sands, and the accumulation of greenhouse gases in the atmosphere and acid in the ocean resulting from fossil fuel production and consumption.

Defining ecocide may be difficult, but law often deals with problems of where to draw the line and determining who should be accountable. It seems likely that the scale of environmental degradation will increase for some time. The importance of the crime of ecocide increases in proportion to the scale of this devastation. People should not feel they are innocent and above the law when they destroy the planet. Ecocide will call them to their duty of care.

STUDY QUESTIONS

(1) How would you define ecocide? When should ecocide be a crime?

(2) Since economic development often involves the large-scale conversion of land or, through aquaculture, large-scale conversion of oceans and other bodies of water, how should ecocide be distinguished from economic development? Or should they not be distinguished because economic development is not a defense to ecocide?

(3) Two general arguments are made for creating the crime of ecocide:

   a. One is that current environmental laws do not address the magnitude of harm being caused to the Earth system and ecocide laws are more capable of doing so than conventional environmental laws. In consideration of four objectives of Earth law—ensuring that humans live within planetary boundaries, prospectively caring for ecosystems, restoring damaged ecosystems, and justly sharing the burdens of mitigating and adapting to climate change and other environmental stresses—how could ecocide laws help?

   b. The other is that ecocide, like genocide, is of international concern and should be subject to transborder enforcement. Do you agree that ecocide, like genocide, should be an international crime?

(4) Why do you think the Rome Statute limits ecocide to acts of war?

(5) Is ecocide too vague to be considered a peacetime offense? In peacetime, could strengthening environmental laws provide adequate protection for offenses related to environmental protection, conservation, species protection, and the

health of all species, or is a peacetime crime of ecocide needed? What arguments would you make for the necessity of a peacetime offense of ecocide?

(6) Polly Higgins gave four reasons why ecocide should be a strict liability offense: (1) it is the consequence that is in question, not the conduct; (2) the gravity of the destruction and damage justifies conviction without proof of criminal intent; (3) without strict liability, enforcement would be largely ineffective; and (4) strict liability rightly places the focus on prevention of the crime and not the blame of the accused. Should ecocide be a strict liability offense, or should criminal intent (*mens rea*) be an element of the crime?

(7) Should legal entities be subject to prosecution for ecocide? Consider the discussion in this chapter and the provisions of the Model U.K. Ecocide Act. On what basis should legal entities be considered responsible parties?

(8) What should the penalties for ecocide be?

(9) Does ecocide involve political questions that should best be resolved by the legislative and executive branches?

(10) In terms of restorative justice, are courts capable of fashioning remedies for the harm caused by ecocide?

CHAPTER 13

Climate Change Civil Disobedience and the Necessity Defense[1]

I. INTRODUCTION

Activists are increasingly recognizing that long-term approaches are not enough to address the urgency of threats to the environment and that attorneys must respond accordingly. Much of the legal thinking on the environment is aimed at institutional change. For example, public trust litigation (*see* Chapter 7) aims to require governments, such as the United States, to take positive action to protect common resources—most crucially, the climate system. As another example, the rights of nature movement (*see, e.g.,* Chapter 9) seeks systems change by recognizing non-human living beings and natural entities, such as entire watersheds or forests, as living entities with rights. While these long-term strategies to build a body of Earth law are important, shorter term strategies are needed to address urgent environmental threats. This is especially true with regard to the threat of climate change: As the defendant in a case discussed below asserts, scientists and activists are starting to recognize that "the window for action on climate change has narrowed to the point that immediate, emergency action is necessary."[2]

While the Paris Climate Agreement purportedly seeks to limit warming to below 1.5°C, recent studies suggest that the emissions reduction targets laid out in the accord will not be enough to reach this goal and even those targets are not being met.[3] Failure to do so will have catastrophic consequences for human civilization and nature alike, including ecosystems collapsing, poorer nations and regions becoming uninhabitable, and water availability decreasing sharply in vast areas and increasing sharply in others.[4]

[1] This chapter was authored by Lance N. Long, Professor of Law at Stetson University College of Law, Ted Hamilton, Co-Founder and Staff Attorney with Climate Defense Project, Ph.D. candidate, Comparative Literature, Yale University, and Zachary Klein, Law Fellow at the National Sea Grant Law Center.

[2] *Washington v. Ward*, 438 P.3d 588, 595 (Wash. Ct. App. 2019).

[3] UNEP, Emissions Gap Report 2019, https://newclimate.org/wp-content/uploads/2019/11/EGR2019.pdf.

[4] David Spratt & Ian Dunlop, *Existential Climate-Related Security Risk: A Scenario Approach*, Breakthrough – National Centre for Climate Restoration Policy Paper (May 2019), https://docs.wixstatic.com/ugd/148cb0_a1406e0143ac4c469196d3003bc1e687.pdf.

Moreover, the United States has renounced its commitment and formally begun to withdraw from the Paris Climate Agreement.[5] As federal agencies roll back environmental regulations and as energy companies continue to promote ever-increasing and unsustainable production of fossil fuels, activists have been using civil disobedience and nonviolent direct action to slow, and hopefully stop, this dangerous trend. In doing so they are putting their lives and liberty on the line. Acts of civil disobedience may help hold the line while a slower-moving body of Earth law that addresses the root causes of climate change moves forward.

Working alongside these activists are their attorneys, who are attempting to legally and socially legitimize the actions the activists are taking. One of the primary legal strategies used in the United States to defend acts of civil disobedience is known as the *necessity defense.* This common law and, in some jurisdictions, statutory defense will be explored in this chapter. Specifically, this chapter will show how environmental activists have marshaled the necessity defense to justify their acts of nonviolent civil disobedience.

The necessity defense, which has roots in English common law and appears in many legal traditions is an argument used by criminal defendants to justify or excuse charged conduct. Necessity defendants argue that their allegedly criminal actions were necessary to prevent an injury to themselves or others and that it is in society's best interest to acquit them of any wrongdoing. Like self-defense or the insanity defense, the necessity defense is usually considered an affirmative defense, in which the defendant accepts the prosecution's facts but offers additional facts that warrant a not-guilty finding.

Although the defense differs from state to state and between federal circuits, it usually requires the following elements:

- The defendant faced an imminent harm to themselves or others;
- The defendant's actions were less harmful than the harm to be avoided (defendant chose the lesser of two evils);
- The defendant reasonably thought that their actions would be effective in avoiding or mitigating the imminent harm; and
- The defendant had no reasonable legal alternatives to violating the law.

In the twentieth and twenty-first centuries, this defense has been commonly asserted in cases involving marijuana use, driving under the influence, and prison escape. In recent decades, the necessity has often, and controversially, been used by political protesters seeking to justify acts of civil disobedience. In particular, criminal defendants charged for opposing war, nuclear power and arms, and illegal government action, and for supporting civil rights, began using the defense. They soon discovered that juries accepted their arguments about the social good accomplished by their illegal actions and would often acquit defendants based on a political necessity defense.

[5] Rebecca Hersher, *U.S. Formally Begins to Leave the Paris Climate Agreement,* NPR (Nov. 4, 2019), https://www.npr.org/2019/11/04/773474657/u-s-formally-begins-to-leave-the-paris-climate-agreement.

One of the most notable uses of the defense occurred in 1987, when Abbie Hoffman, Amy Carter, and 13 other people occupied an administration building at the University of Massachusetts and sat in road-blocking buses carrying arrested protestors from the building. The defendants were protesting illegal conduct by the CIA in Central America and were acquitted of trespass and disorderly conduct charges stemming from their occupation.

Beginning in the mid-2000s, climate activists began using the *climate necessity defense* to justify their acts of civil disobedience. The typical climate necessity argument is straightforward. Framed in light of the typical common law defense, climate necessity defendants argue that:

- Climate change is not only imminent, but it is occurring now and is causing severe harms to the planet and its people;
- Their acts of civil disobedience are much less harmful than the harms caused by climate change;
- Civil disobedience is demonstrably effective in mitigating or avoiding specific climate change harms, in building public support for climate change policy, and in influencing political decision-makers; and
- Traditional alternatives such as voting, lobbying, and organizing have failed to prevent climate change harms, making civil disobedience necessary.

As discussed in the three cases that follow, climate necessity defendants face many obstacles, such as courts' reluctance to recognize the efficacy of civil disobedience or the non-existence of legal alternatives; pre-trial evidentiary tests; and judicial and prosecutorial resistance to climate change science and evidence of political failure to address climate change. Nonetheless, climate necessity defenses are increasingly common, and, in the past two years, some state appellate courts have recognized the validity of the defense.

II. NEW YORK CITY

Because climate necessity defenses are usually offered in lower-level criminal courts and do not result in written opinions, full judicial consideration of the defense's elements is rare. An instance of such full consideration in a case involving air pollution can be found in *People v. Gray*. In this New York City criminal court case, defendants were protesting the dangers of air pollution to bikers and pedestrians on the Queensboro Bridge in New York City and were charged with disorderly conduct for blocking the entrance of a bridge roadway. The prosecution agreed to allow the defendants to present a necessity defense in exchange for the defendants agreeing to not contest the elements of the crime. The judge acquitted the defendants in a nonjury trial, finding that they had proven all elements of the necessity defense.

People v. Gray

571 N.Y.S.2d 851, 866 (Crim. Ct. 1991)

The necessity defense is fundamentally a balancing test to determine whether a criminal act was committed to prevent a greater harm. The common elements of the defense found in virtually all common-law and statutory definitions include the following: (1) the actor has acted to avoid a grave harm, not of his own making; (2) there are not adequate legal means to avoid the harm; and (3) the harm sought to be avoided is greater than that committed. A number of jurisdictions, New York among them, have included two additional requirements—first, the harm must be imminent, and second, the action taken must be reasonably expected to avert the impending danger.

Extensive research revealed that while Judges in New York (with one partial exception, discussed *infra)* have so far declined to rule that a necessity defense has been sufficiently established to allow the trier of fact to consider it in their deliberations in cases involving defendants who have engaged in citizen intervention/civil disobedience, numerous State Trial Judges in other jurisdictions, as well as some Federal District Court Judges, have so charged juries or acquitted defendants after bench trials in similar cases.

Moreover, when the necessity defense is actually submitted to the trier of fact in such cases, defendants have usually been acquitted [Citations omitted]. There are also a number of cases in which charges were dropped after the Judge's rulings that a necessity defense would be permitted. . . .

I. THE CHOICE OF EVILS REQUIREMENT

. . . In this case, the defendants are all members of an organization called Transportation Alternatives, an organization devoted to the promotion of nonvehicular, ecologically sound means of transportation. Through their testimony and that of their expert witnesses, it was clear that these defendants' actions were motivated by the desire to prevent what they called the "asphyxiation of New York" by automobile-related pollution. Specifically, the harm they seek to combat is the release of ever higher levels of pollution from vehicular traffic, and the unnecessary death and serious illness of many New Yorkers as a result.

Defendants also articulated a motivation to put an end to an extremely hazardous situation that had resulted on the Queensboro Bridge south outer roadway, subsequent to the implementation of the regulation opening that roadway to vehicular traffic during the evening rush hour. Since many pedestrians and bicyclists continued to use that roadway, the defendants testified that they also acted to prevent serious injuries to those individuals who continued to use alternative forms of transportation on the bridge. . . .

In this case, as well as in most necessity cases, it is clear that defendants chose the correct societal value. It is beyond question that both the death and illness of New Yorkers as a result of additional air pollution, and the danger to cyclists and pedestrians posed by vehicles on the south outer roadway, are far greater harms than that created by the violation of disorderly conduct. . . .

II. THE IMMINENCE OF GRAVE HARM REQUIREMENT

In evaluating whether defendants' perceptions of the harm they sought to avoid in this case were reasonable, the court must decide whether they had a well-founded belief in imminent grave injury. [Citations omitted.]

Such determination is almost always a question for the trier of fact. [Citations omitted.]

Defendants in the instant case presented several witnesses, as well as submitting studies, to establish the existence of a grave and imminent harm. Defendants themselves testified that the [Department of Transportation] regulation, if obeyed, would prove to be a devastating disincentive to New Yorkers who use alternative or nonvehicular means of transportation between the Boroughs of Manhattan and Queens. The only road open to bicyclists and pedestrians is practically inaccessible to them during the hours most critical to their return home. In contrast to this disincentive to nonpolluting forms of transportation, another lane is open to vehicular traffic.

Defendants clearly articulated their belief that encouraging automobiles at a rush hour traffic "choke-point" while discouraging walkers and cyclists produces a specific, grave harm that is not only imminent, but is occurring daily. This belief was supported by the testimony of expert witnesses and studies submitted into evidence. . . .

Unlike many of the cases in this area, where the harm sought to be prevented was perceived as too far in the future to be found "imminent," the grave harm in this case is occurring every day. The additional pollution breathed by all New Yorkers (in a city that is already out of compliance with the minimal standards set by the EPA [Environmental Protection Agency]), as a result of the fact that more road space will be devoted to vehicles and its corollary that those hundreds of individuals who would otherwise bicycle or walk are discouraged from using nonpolluting forms of transportation is a concrete harm being suffered by the population at this moment. . . .

III. THE NO LEGAL ALTERNATIVE REQUIREMENT

A key requirement of the necessity defense is that no reasonable legal option exists for averting the harm. Once again, the proper inquiry here is whether the defendant reasonably believed that there was no legal alternative to his actions. The defense does not legalize lawlessness; rather it permits courts to distinguish between necessary and unnecessary illegal acts in order to provide an essential safety valve to law enforcement in a democratic society.

It has been asserted that because a democracy creates legal avenues of protest, alternatives must always exist. In the opinion of this court, however, to dispense with the necessity defense by assuming that people always have access to effective legal means of protest circumvents the purpose of the defense.

When courts rule as a matter of law that defendants always have a reasonable belief in other adequate alternatives, they are asserting that regardless of how diligent a party is in pursuing alternatives, no matter how much time has been spent in legitimate efforts to prevent the harm, no matter how ineffective previous measures have been to handle the emergency, the courts in hindsight can always find just one more alternative that a citizen could have tried before acting out of necessity....

In this case, the defendants were individuals who were thoroughly familiar with the process by which decisions concerning transportation in New York are made, and who, despite their long history of an advocacy and consultative role in such matters, were completely excluded from the decision-making process concerning the closing of a very important roadway for nonpolluting forms of transportation. Where, at the first opportunity, every traditional method of petitioning, letter writing, phone calling, leafletting and lobbying was vigorously pursued by these defendants to no avail, it cannot be said as a matter of law that they did not reasonably believe their legal alternatives to be exhausted....

IV. THE CASUAL RELATIONSHIP REQUIREMENT

New York is among the jurisdictions that require a defendant's actions to be reasonably designed to actually prevent the threatened greater harm....

As with the other elements of this defense, the test consistent with the purposes of this defense is one of reasonable belief. Defendants' initial burden is to offer sufficient evidence of a reasonable belief in a causal link between their behavior and ending the perceived harm.

The New York statute and most common-law formulations use the term "necessary" rather than "sufficient." In the opinion of this court, a defendant's reasonable belief must be in the necessity of his action to avoid the injury. The law does not require certainty of success....

While this court agrees that there are numerous examples in United States history which support the reasonable belief of a causal connection between citizen intervention and the prevention of harm, the defendants in this case need not go beyond their own experiences....

Pursuant to the foregoing opinion, this court finds that the People have not disproved the elements of the necessity defense in this case beyond a reasonable doubt. Defendants are therefore acquitted.

STUDY QUESTIONS

(1) In *People v. Gray*, the court summarily concluded that "it is clear that defendants chose the correct societal value." To what degree does this conclusion depend on this particular judge's personal perspective on societal values? In an effort to counsel a client, how might one assess trial judges to determine the viability of a climate necessity defense? What evidence might be marshaled to persuade a judge as to the "correctness" of the societal value of preventing climate change?

(2) One of the most difficult hurdles for civil disobedience to clear when raising the necessity defense is showing the absence of any reasonable legal alternatives. In finding that the defendants met their burden for this element, the court states: "It has always been asserted that because a democracy creates legal avenues of protests, alternatives must always exist. In the opinion of this court, however, to dispense with the necessity defense by assuming [this] circumvents the purpose of the defense." What other legal obstacles exist that prevent individuals from effecting meaningful change through the democratic process generally? With respect to climate change specifically?

* * *

III. UTAH

One of the first American climate necessity defenses was offered by Tim DeChristopher in 2009. Posing as a bidder, DeChristopher disrupted a Bureau of Land Management (BLM) auction for oil and gas drilling rights to several parcels of pristine red-rock country in southeastern Utah, resulting in charges of false statement and violation of the Federal Onshore Oil and Gas Leasing Act. The Utah federal district court granted the prosecution's motion in limine to bar the necessity defense—a common pre-trial tactic in which litigants ask the court to preemptively bar evidence or testimony in the interest of efficiency or preventing bias or confusion — because DeChristopher's actions did not meet the requirements. DeChristopher then appealed to the Tenth Circuit, which in the following 2012 opinion upheld the district court's decision.

United States v. DeChristopher

No. 2:08-CR-183, 2009 WL 3837208 (D. Utah Nov. 16, 2009), ***upheld in United States v. DeChristopher*****, 695 F.3d 1082, 1087-88 (10th Cir. 2012)**

District court opinion.

This matter is before the court on the government's motion in limine to bar defendant Tim DeChristopher ("DeChristopher") from presenting a necessity defense at trial, including any evidence in support of such a defense....

On December 19, 2008, DeChristopher went to the Utah BLM office in Salt Lake City, Utah. Outside the BLM office, environmental activists organized a protest. Inside the office, DeChristopher registered to bid on oil and gas leases. In order to register as a bidder, DeChristopher was required to fill out and sign a "Bidder Registration Form." The Bidder Registration Form required DeChristopher to certify that: (1) he was a good-faith bidder, (2) he had the intention to acquire an oil and gas lease on the offered lands, (3) a winning bid constituted a legally binding commitment to accept the lease, and (4) in the event of winning a bid, he was obligated to pay the BLM by the end of the day a percentage of the lease's purchase price, whether or not the lease was subsequently issued. The Bidder Registration Form also informed DeChristopher of the criminal consequences of tampering with the bidding process.

At the lease sale, DeChristopher placed bids on dozens of oil and gas leases. Initially, DeChristopher would drive up the bid price and then pull out before he had won the bid. But then he began to bid on the oil and gas leases until he won the bid. In total, DeChristopher won fourteen leases totaling $1.7 million. DeChristopher claims he acted to combat the "government's violation of its own laws and regulations and the consequential exacerbation of global warming and climate change, and destruction of irreplaceable natural and cultural resources." . . .

On April 1, 2009, a grand jury returned a two-count indictment against DeChristopher, charging him with (1) violating the Federal Onshore Oil and Gas Leasing Reform Act, and (2) providing false statements. Both before and after the return of the indictment against him, DeChristopher and his actions at the BLM lease sale received considerable attention by the print and broadcast media. He gave numerous interviews, at times with his lawyer standing at his side, in which he declared that he was justified in his actions because of his concerns about the environment. In these statements DeChristopher indicated that he would defend his behavior as necessary or legally justified. . . .

I. LEGAL STANDARD

A criminal defendant has the right to have a jury resolve disputed factual issues.[6] However, where the evidence, even if believed, does not establish all of the elements of a legal defense, the court need not submit the defense to a jury.[7] Accordingly, a motion in limine can determine the admissibility of the necessity defense.[8] The sole issue before this court is whether the evidence, as described in DeChristopher's written proffer, is insufficient as a

[6] *Sandstrom v. Montana,* 442 U.S. 510, 523 (1979).

[7] *United States v. Bailey,* 444 U.S. 394, 416-17 (1980).

[8] *United States v. Patton,* 451 F.3d 615, 638 (10th Cir. 2006); *United States v. Aguirre-Torres,* 3 Fed. Appx. 852, 854 (10th Cir. 2001); *see also United States v. Seward,* 687 F.2d 1270, 1277-78 (10th Cir. 1982), *cert. denied,* 459 U.S. 1147 (1983).

matter of law to support the necessity defense.[9] If it is, then the court should exclude the defense and the evidence offered in support.[10]

II. THE NECESSITY DEFENSE

Successful use of the necessity defense requires the defendant to prove that: (1) he was faced with a choice of evils and chose the lesser evil; (2) he acted to prevent imminent harm; (3) he reasonably anticipated a direct casual [sic] relationship between his conduct and the harm to be averted; and (4) he had no legal alternatives to violating the law.[11] If a defendant's offer of proof is deficient with regard to any of the four elements, the defense of necessity fails.[12] This case does not qualify for the necessity defense.

A. Choice of Evils

The necessity defense requires that a defendant prove that he was faced with a choice of evils and chose the lesser evil.[13] DeChristopher's written proffer asserts that his actions were a lesser evil compared to the greater evil of the government's violation of the law surrounding the BLM lease sale and the "consequential exacerbation of global warming and climate change, and destruction of irreplaceable natural and cultural resources." [14] The court finds that DeChristopher fails to satisfy the "choice of evils" requirement for at least two reasons.

First, a harm or evil that may or may not occur is insufficient for purposes of the necessity defense.[15] Indicating that harms that are insufficiently concrete are not cognizable as harms for purposes of the necessity defense.[16] "[Defendant] must be able to show some direct harm... not a theoretical future harm to all of us that may or may not occur."[17]

Second, the court agrees with the United States Court of Appeals for the Ninth Circuit in that the court does "not sit to render judgments upon the legality of the conduct of the government at the request of any person who asks us to because he happens to think that what the government doing is wrong.... To [do so] would... put [the court] in the position of usurping the functions that the Constitution has given to the Congress and to the President."[18] "The necessity defense was never intended to excuse criminal activity by those who

[9] *Patton,* 451 F.3d at 638; *see also Seward,* 687 F.2d at 1276.

[10] *Patton,* 451 F.3d at 638; *see also Seward,* 687 F.2d at 1276.

[11] *United States v. Turner,* 44 F.3d 900, 902 (10th Cir. 1995); *see also United States v. Schoon,* 971 F.2d 193, 195 (9th Cir. 1991).

[12] *Id.* at 902.

[13] *Id.* at 902.

[14] Def.'s Written *Proffer* 5-7.

[15] *Schoon,* 971 F.2d at 198.

[16] *United States v. May,* 622 F.2d 1000, 1009 (9th Cir.).

[17] *Cert. denied,* 449 U.S. 984 (1980).

[18] *May,* 622 F.2d at 1009; *see also United States v. Kabat,* 797 F.2d 580, 591 (8th Cir. 1986).

disagree with the decisions and policies on the lawmaking branches of government; in such cases the 'greater harm' sought to be prevented would be the course of action chosen by elected representatives, and a court in allowing the defense would be making a negative political or policy judgment about that course of action." Accordingly, DeChristopher's necessity defense fails because he did not face a definite and/or cognizable choice of two evils.

B. Imminent Harm

The necessity defense requires the defendant to show that the harm to be avoided was so imminent that, absent the defendant's criminal acts, the harm was certain to occur.[19] In DeChristopher's written proffer, he asks the court to relax the "imminent harm" requirement. The court declines to do so. The term "imminent harm" connotes a real emergency or crisis.[20] Even assuming arguendo that the BLM's lease sale was "evil," the evidence does not support a finding of imminent harm because issuance of the oil and gas leases offered at the BLM lease sale was not certain to occur. There were approximately 1,600 protests filed including at least one for every parcel offered for lease. The BLM does not issue an officially protested lease until after the protest has been investigated and affirmatively resolved. This can be a lengthy process with an uncertain outcome. Furthermore, unlike the destructive forces of fire referred to by DeChristopher in his written proffer, the suggested consequences of the BLM lease sale were not certain to occur or immediately dangerous. Thus, the court finds that DeChristopher's necessity defense fails because the evidence does not establish "imminent harm."

C. Sufficient Causal Relationship

A defendant must demonstrate that he reasonably anticipated a direct causal relationship between his actions and the harm to be averted.[21] DeChristopher attests that he reasonably anticipated his actions would "thwart" the BLM's unlawful lease sale, and also avert its consequential exacerbation of global warming and climate change, and its destruction of irreplaceable natural and cultural resources. However, DeChristopher fails as a matter of law to establish that driving the bid price up on some parcels and winning only fourteen of over a hundred parcels sold could be reasonably anticipated to directly stop the BLM's "unlawful" lease sale and avoid its purported consequences. Unlike a person demolishing a home to create a firebreak, DeChristopher's actions were more akin to placing a small pile of dirt in the fire's path. The court finds that DeChristopher's necessity defense fails because he cannot establish that his actions would directly bring about the ends he claims to have sought.

[19] *Kabat*, 797 F.2d at 591 (*citing Bailey*, 444 U.S. at 410).
[20] *Seward*, 687 F.2d at 1276.
[21] *Turner*, 44 F.3d at 902.

D. The Availability of Other, Legal Alternatives to Violating the Law

As long as defendant's perceived "crisis" permitted a selection from among several solutions, some of which did not involve criminal acts, the necessity defense must fail.[22] Here, DeChristopher could have filed protests during the 30-day protest period. DeChristopher could have also demonstrated with the environmental activists outside the BLM office. Moreover, DeChristopher could have involved himself with the coalition of environmental groups that filed a federal lawsuit in the District of Columbia that eventually precluded the issuance of certain leases included in the BLM lease sale. Consequently, the court finds that DeChristopher's necessity defense fails because there were reasonable, legal alternatives open to DeChristopher other than his alleged criminal acts.

E. Conclusion

For the foregoing reasons, the court finds that the evidence is insufficient as a matter of law to support the necessity defense. Accordingly, the government's motion in limine to bar DeChristopher from presenting a necessity defense at trial, including any evidence in support of such a defense is GRANTED.

STUDY QUESTIONS

(1) The *DeChristopher* court ultimately concluded that three of the four elements of necessity were not met: (1) legally cognizable harm, (2) no legal alternatives, and (3) sufficient causal relationship. What are the strengths and flaws of the court's reasoning, particularly of the "sufficient causal relationship" factor, in light of the information presented in the note?

(2) DeChristopher's climate necessity defense was denied prior to trial on a motion in limine by the prosecution; the jury never had the opportunity to hear the defendant's theory of the case. Is a motion in limine an appropriate means of deciding such central questions in a case? What are the benefits and drawbacks of litigating the climate necessity defense in pre-trial motions? In a trial setting, in both state and federal courts, it is a deeply embedded tenet that judges are responsible for making decisions about the law, while juries are responsible for deciding issues of fact. Where is the line between the law and the facts in DeChristopher's case? Should the jury be able to decide for itself whether evidence is relevant?

[22] *Seward*, 687 F.2d at 1276.

(3) Ultimately, while DeChristopher was convicted and served 21 months of a two-year sentence, his defense received significant media attention and even led to an investigation into the lack of environmental assessments performed before the auction. As a result of this investigation, all the drilling leases in the area were eventually cancelled. How does this post-conviction development reflect upon the court's holding regarding the element of "sufficient causal relationship?" How might this tangible effect of DeChristopher's protest impact future necessity defense arguments?

(4) Notice that the *Gray* court and the *DeChristopher* court articulate the elements of the necessity defense almost identically. Do both courts fairly analyze the necessity defense in reaching opposing conclusions? To what extent were the different outcomes due to the differing facts in each case? To what extent were the courts analyzing the necessity defense to reach a pre-determined outcome? Which court present the more sound legal analysis of the necessity defense?

* * *

IV. WASHINGTON

In a significant set of ongoing cases, five activists responding to a call to action from the Standing Rock anti-pipeline protest camp in North Dakota simultaneously turned off valves controlling the flow of tar sands oil from Canada through pipelines in Minnesota, North Dakota, Montana, and Washington. All five activists prepared climate necessity defenses to the array of felony and misdemeanor charges they faced.

The first trial for the so-called "Shut It Down" actions involved felony charges of burglary and criminal sabotage against Ken Ward, a long-time environmental protestor. After receiving notice of the defense's intent to argue necessity, the prosecution filed a motion in limine to preclude necessity defense-related evidence, to which the defense responded with a brief and a list of expert witnesses prepared to testify regarding climate science, energy economics, tar sands, and the effectiveness of civil disobedience. At the pre-trial hearing, the judge denied the necessity defense, finding that Ward had legal alternatives to his act of protest and expressing concerns that the trial would turn into a referendum on the science of climate change; in his oral ruling, the judge called the question of the effects of global warming a matter of "tremendous controversy."

Ward proceeded to trial, testifying about his beliefs and motivations and winning judicial notice of several charts depicting the causes and risks of climate change. The trial ended in a hung jury. The prosecution then decided to retry Ward, and the judge enforced his earlier denial of necessity defense despite a motion for reconsideration. A new jury hung once again on the sabotage charge but convicted on burglary. In the following opinion, the Washington Court of Appeals takes up Ward's appeal and explains its reasoning for reversing the trial court's denial of Ward's right to present a necessity defense.

Washington v. Ward

438 P.3d 588 (Wash. Ct. App. 2019)

Appellate opinion

Washington recognizes a common law necessity defense. The defense may be raised when a defendant demonstrates that they reasonably believed the commission of the crime was necessary to avoid or minimize a harm, the harm sought to be avoided was greater than the harm resulting from a violation of the law, the threatened harm was not brought about by the defendant, and no reasonable legal alternative existed.

Kenneth Ward appeals his conviction for burglary in the second degree after he broke into a Kinder Morgan pipeline facility and turned off a valve, which stopped the flow of Canadian tar sands oil to refineries in Skagit and Whatcom Counties. Ward intended to protest the continued use of tar sands oil, which he contends significantly contributes to climate change, and the inaction by governments to meaningfully address the crisis of climate change. Ward argues that he was deprived of his Sixth Amendment right to present his only defense—necessity—after the trial court granted the State's motion in limine excluding all testimony and evidence of necessity. We agree and reverse.

I

Kinder Morgan transports tar sands oil from Canada into the United States by pipeline. On October 11, 2016, Kinder Morgan was notified by telephone that persons "would be closing a valve, one of our main line valves in the Mount Vernon area within the next 15 minutes." Following the call, Ward cut off a padlock and entered the Kinder Morgan pipeline facility off of Peterson Road in Burlington. Ward then closed a valve on the Trans-Mountain pipeline and placed sunflowers on the valve. At the same time, other protesters closed similar valves in North Dakota, Montana, and Minnesota. Collectively, the protests temporarily stopped the flow of Canadian tar sands oil from entering into the United States.

Ward was arrested at the pipeline facility and charged with burglary in the second degree, criminal sabotage, and criminal trespass in the second degree. Ward admitted his conduct but argued that his actions were protected under a necessity defense. The trial court granted the State's pretrial motion in limine to preclude all witnesses and evidence offered in support of Ward's necessity defense.

Ward's first trial ended with a hung jury. The State then recharged Ward with burglary in the second degree and criminal sabotage. Ward moved for reconsideration of the trial court's order granting the State's motion in limine. In support of his motion, Ward offered argument, the curriculum vitae for eight proposed expert witnesses, and voluminous scientific evidence documenting the impacts of climate change, that climate change is primarily caused by greenhouse gas emissions resulting from human activity, and the contribution of burning tar sands oil. The trial court denied Ward's motion for reconsideration and excluded all testimony and evidence in support of Ward's necessity defense. A second jury found Ward guilty of burglary but were unable to return a verdict on criminal sabotage. Ward appeals.

II

Ward argues that the trial court denied his constitutional right to present a defense by granting the State's motion in limine striking all testimony and evidence of necessity. We agree....

The Sixth Amendment to the United States Constitution and article 1, sections 21 and 22 of the Washington Constitution guarantee a defendant the right to trial by jury and to defend against criminal allegations.[23] "The right of an accused in a criminal trial to due process is, in essence, the right to a fair opportunity to defend against the State's accusations."[24] "A defendant's right to an opportunity to be heard in his defense, including the rights to examine witnesses against him and to offer testimony, is basic in our system of jurisprudence."[25]

Below, the trial court prohibited Ward from presenting evidence or witnesses on the necessity defense. If Ward submitted a sufficient quantum of evidence to show that he would likely be able to meet each element of the necessity defense, then the trial court's exclusion of evidence in support of his sole defense violated Ward's constitutional rights.

III

"[A]n act is justified if it by necessity is taken in a reasonable belief that the harm or evil to be prevented by the act is greater than the harm caused by violating the criminal statute."[26] Necessity is available when "the pressure of circumstances cause the accused to take unlawful action to avoid a harm which social policy deems greater than the harm resulting from a violation of the law... [but not where] a legal alternative is available to the accused."[27]

To successfully raise the necessity defense the defendant must prove, by a preponderance of the evidence, that: (1) they reasonably believed the commission of the crime was necessary to avoid or minimize a harm, (2) the harm sought to be avoided was greater than the harm resulting from a violation of

[23] *State v. Darden*, 145 Wn. 2d 612, 620, 41 P.3d 1189 (2002).

[24] *Chambers v. Mississippi*, 410 U.S. 284, 294, 93 S. Ct. 1038 35 L. Ed. 2d 297 (1973).

[25] *Jones*, 168 Wn.2d at 720.

[26] *State v. Aver*, 109 Wn.2d 303, 311, 745 P.2d 470 (1987).

[27] *State v. Gallegos*, 73 Wn. App. 644, 651, 871 P.2d 621 (1994) (citing *State v. Diana*, 24 Wn. App. 908, 913-14, 604 P.2d 1312 (1979)).

the law, (3) the threatened harm was not brought about by the defendant, and (4) no reasonable legal alternative existed.[28]

The State argues that Ward's offer of proof failed to establish the elements of the necessity defense. A challenge to the sufficiency of evidence "admits the truth thereof and all inferences that can reasonably be drawn therefrom."[29] "It requires the trial court and appellate courts to interpret the evidence most favorably for the defendant."[30] In this light, we review Ward's offer of proof as to each element of the necessity defense.

A

Ward presented sufficient evidence that he reasonably believed the crimes he committed were necessary to minimize the harms that he perceived. Ward's offer of proof included evidence of how past acts of civil disobedience have been successful, evidence of previous climate activism campaigns, and evidence of his own personal successes in effectuating change through civil disobedience. Specifically, Ward offered evidence that he has been working with environmental issues for more than 40 years but that the majority of his efforts failed to achieve effective results. Ward asserted that because of these failures he "came to understand that the issue of climate change would require other than incremental change" and that "direct action was necessary to accomplish these goals." Ward offered three experts—Eric de Place, Bill McKibben, and Martin Gilens—who were prepared to testify as to the efficacy of civil disobedience and how such actions have become necessary in the climate movement. Ward argued that to decide whether his actions were "reasonably calculated to be effective in averting the imminent harm of climate change requires [the] expert testimony and evidence" that he was prepared to present to the jury, and that whether his beliefs were reasonable was a question for the jury, not the trial court, to decide.

The State argues that it was unreasonable for Ward to believe that the commission of this crime was necessary to avoid or minimize harm. The State asserts, first, that all Ward did was temporarily inconvenience Kinder Morgan's employees so it was unreasonable to think that his actions would actually avoid or minimize the broader harms associated with climate change. And second, that because Ward had legal alternatives available it was unreasonable for him to believe that his actions were necessary to avoid or minimize harm.

Whether Ward's beliefs were reasonable was a question for the jury.[31] ("It is the province of the jury to determine such issues" as whether the defendant acted with reasonable grounds.) And further, Ward did not have to prove that the harm he sought to avoid or minimize was actually avoided or minimized but instead that the reason he broke the law was in an attempt to avoid or

[28] *Gallegos*, 73 Wn. App. at 650; *see also* 11 Washington Practice: Washington Pattern Jury Instructions: Criminal 18.02, at 292 (4th ed. 2016), (WPIC).
[29] *State v. Cole*, 74 Wn. App. 571, 578, 874 P.2d 878 (1994).
[30] *Cole*, 74 Wn. App. at 578-79.
[31] *State v. Negrin*, 37 Wn. App. 516, 524, 681 P.2d 516 (1984).

minimize harm.[32] Describing the second prong as "the harm sought to be avoided [, not the harm actually avoided,] was greater than the harm resulting from a violation of the law." Ward's past successes in effectuating change through civil disobedience in conjunction with the proposed expert witnesses and testimony about Ward's beliefs were sufficient evidence to persuade a fair minded, rational juror that Ward's beliefs were reasonable.

B

Ward also offered sufficient evidence to show that the harms of global climate change were greater than the harm of breaking into Kinder Morgan's property. Ward asserted that the extent of the harm resulting from his actions were the loss of a few locks and the temporary inconvenience to Kinder Morgan's employees. Compared to this, Ward introduced "voluminous scientific evidence of the harms of climate change." This evidence included information establishing climate change is real and detrimentally effecting Washington, and that tar sands oil poses a specifically acute threat to our environment. Further, Ward offered to present testimony from climate scientists, Drs. James Hansen, Richard Gammon, and Celia Bitz, supporting his defense.

C

Whether the harms of global climate change was brought about by Ward was not an issue in this case. Nevertheless, Ward proffered evidence and expert testimony establishing the harms associated with global climate change and the root causes of global climate change.

D

Ward also offered sufficient evidence to create a question of fact on whether there were reasonable legal alternatives. Ward argued that the window for action on climate change has narrowed to the point that immediate, emergency action is necessary. Ward offered evidence of his more than 40 years being involved in various environmental movements, the numerous attempts he has made to address climate change, and how most of those efforts have failed. Ward additionally offered proposed testimony by pipeline industry expert Eric de Place, professor and climate campaigner Bill McKibben, and professor of political science Martin Gilens, to the effect that the fossil fuel industry's influence over political institutions renders traditional legal avenues unreasonable as a means of addressing the climate emergency.

State v. Parker discussed the "no reasonable alternative" element.[33] Parker was charged with felon in possession of a gun. Parker claimed that he carried the gun because he had been shot the previous July and his assailants were still

[32] *Gallegos,* 73 Wn. App. at 650.
[33] *State v. Parker,* 127 Wn. App. 352, 353, 111 P.3d 1152 (2005).

at large. Division Two of this court held that in order to show he had no reasonable alternative, Parker has to demonstrate "that he had actually tried the alternative or had no time to try it, or that a history of futile attempts revealed the illusionary benefits of the alternative."[34] Here, in contrast with Parker, Ward offered evidence that he had tried the alternatives and they were unsuccessful. Whether Ward's evidence was sufficient to establish that his history of failed attempts to address climate change revealed the futility of supposed reasonable alternatives was a question for the jury. Viewed in the light most favorable to Ward, and admitting the truth of his evidence and all reasonable inferences therefrom, Ward's offer of proof created a question for the jury.[35] Because Ward met his initial burden of showing that he would likely be able to submit a sufficient quantum of evidence on each element of necessity to make it a jury question whether he established that element beyond a reasonable doubt, the trial court violated his constitutional right by granting the State's motion in limine. . . .

We reverse and remand.

* * *

STUDY QUESTIONS

(1) With regard to reasonable belief, the trial court stated that "Ward's past successes in effectuating change through civil disobedience in conjunction with the proposed expert witnesses [testifying to the efficacy of civil disobedience] and testimony about Ward's belief were sufficient evidence to persuade a . . . juror that Ward's beliefs were reasonable." How might increased judicial recognition of the climate necessity defense affect others' decision to engage in climate disobedience in the future? Could this increased participation in turn have an impact on how often the defense is recognized? Why or why not?

(2) The court found Ward's prior unsuccessful attempts to effect change through political avenues were critical to establishing the "no reasonable legal alternatives" element. Imagine you are an attorney advising a client who wants to engage in civil disobedience to protest a liquid natural gas (LNG) export facility being built in your community. What actions should your client take prior to engaging in such an action to increase the probability of a court finding this element has been satisfied? Is voting sufficient? Calling one's political representatives? How long should your client persist in these activities before resorting to civil disobedience?

[34] *Parker*, 127 Wn. App. at 355.
[35] *Cole*, 74 Wn. App. at 578-579.

(3) In analyzing whether Ward "reasonably believed the commission of the crime was necessary to avoid or minimize a harm," the court stated that "[w]hether Ward's beliefs were reasonable was a question for the jury." Is that standard appropriate for every element of the necessity defense? In other words, does every element of the necessity defense present a question for the jury, or are some particularly appropriate for a decision by the court?

(4) In what contexts might the presentation of the necessity defense in future climate civil disobedience cases advance the interests of other conceptual and technical elements of Earth law?

V. CONCLUSION

As the foregoing cases indicate, the climate necessity defense is gaining some traction. Even where the necessity defense is not successful, it is being more fully considered in courts addressing the issue. The trend is encouraging for plaintiffs who seek to use civil disobedience to more immediately address catastrophic climate change. In keeping with the spirit of Earth law, these efforts compel the legal system to reckon with the scope and scale of environmental degradation and to take seriously the obligation to care for the planet—in this instance, through sustained social movement pressure and legal advocacy that links environmental well-being to political change. It also provides a tool that might compel some climate activists to take action against certain climate change drivers while systematic legal solutions, such as those embodied in long-term Earth law strategies, are put into place.

SECTION FOUR

TRANSFORMING THE LAW

Each of the following three chapters discusses the transformation of current legal systems into systems adapted to promoting and implementing emerging Earth law. In Chapter 14, "Bears Among Us: Earth Law and Animal-Human Coexistence," Professor Reed Loder hones in on the inadequacy of current legal, social and ethical structures for dealing with human relations with wild animals. She explains how human "superiority over, and separation from, the nonhuman world [which] is part of our longstanding cultural legacy . . . merges with contempt for beings, like bears." Examining how humans both understand and empathize with the traumatic experiences of a mother bear's forced geographic relocation and separation from her still-weaning cubs, she discusses how the biocentrism of Earth law can better protect bears that share our habitats and rangelands. Notably, this concept of wildlife protection does not depend on a species being listed as "threatened" or "endangered" under the Endangered Species Act. The fundamental Earth law concept of the dignity of all beings and species, as depicted in this chapter, challenges the legally embedded concept of human domination over nature and nonhuman animals. This development of Earth law will reinforce the growing ecocentric ethic as a social mechanism that imposes responsibility on humans to treat ecosystems, species, and individual animals with kindness, dignity, and respect.

Chapter 15, "United Nations Sustainable Development Initiatives," chronologically reviews sustainable development initiatives of the United Nations. The term *sustainable development* came into wide usage with the 1987 "Bruntland Report." It is intended to balance protecting the environment and improving quality of life for humans. The United Nations promoted sustainable development in three Earth summits held since 1992. In 2015 the UN General Assembly adopted its 2015–2030 development agenda consisting of 17 Sustainable Development Goals (SDGs). The sustainable development approach is primarily anthropocentric in orientation. Even though it has gained widespread support from governments, businesses, and civil society, large-scale ecological degradation like biodiversity loss and climate change has accelerated. In response to the demands of many countries and civil society groups to instill ecocentric principles, including rights of nature, into the implementation of the SDGs, the United Nations launched the "Harmony with Nature" initiative. This promotes an ecocentric approach through resolutions of the UN General Assembly and Harmony with Nature conferences and educational programs. Shifting the sustainable development approach to an ecocentric orientation is proving to be a difficult process. Global ecocentric governance will require more than high-level discussions at the United Nations.

It will also require a commitment of the individual and collective will of the people, which is discussed in Chapter 16.

Chapter 16 examines ecological governance with a focus on social contract theory. The theories of Thomas Hobbes, John Locke, and Jean-Jacques Rousseau lay the groundwork of the current "consumptive social contract." This contract is fraying as inequality increases and globalization falters, but the real challenges to it are natural limits. The chapter considers the work of Bruno Latour and Bruce Jennings who present ideas for a new *ecological* social contract, which includes nature and abides by nature's limits. This is not a one-time agreement for people to be governed by a common sovereign under the rule of law. It is societal agreement to be engaged in an ongoing process of seeking the common good not only for humans but also for the entire Earth community—present and future. The potential for institutional reform is discussed, as is the crucial role of lawyers in bringing into being this new social contract.

This second part of Chapter 16 involves a case study of Bolivia's rich structure of rights of nature laws. Drawn from the heritage of its Indigenous people, these laws offer a sharp contrast to the U.S. legal system, which has been committed from its inception to privatizing and protecting property rights. The Bolivian experience illustrates the complex relations among law, economics, politics, culture, and the challenges involved in bringing into being an ecological social contract. In the conclusion to the chapter, there is a brief study of nature's rapid derailment of the human economy through a coronavirus, COVID-19, which exploded during the final stages of writing this book. While it is too early to draw any conclusions as to the long-term significance, the COVID-19 pandemic has provided a timely opportunity to consider the efficacy of the current social contract.

As you read these chapters, think of the significance of a governance system that extends protection to nonhuman species and ecosystems, in which the economy is a subsystem of nature and economic growth is limited to planetary boundaries. How would it impact your lives directly? How would your current law studies need to adapt to a legal system supporting ecological governance? Consider, in particular, your courses on constitutional law, property law, and criminal law. How would key doctrines and principles need to change, or disappear, to accommodate the new system? In what ways would practicing law under this new system differ from the current practice of law?

CHAPTER 14

Bears Among Us: Earth Law and Animal-Human Co-existence[1]

Editors' Note: This chapter tells the story of a black bear in New Hampshire who lives in the wild but is losing her habitat because of the expansion of human settlement into her territory. Consequently, she has been subjected to displacement and relocation to separate her from humans. The chapter opens by discussing why the general state of human relations with wild animals is inadequate from an Earth law perspective. Superiority over and separation from the nonhuman world is part of our longstanding cultural legacy; Earth law challenges this framework.

In contrast to the approach of conservationists, whose primary concern is to protect species and prevent extinctions, this chapter concerns the suffering of an individual bear. It examines why humans respond differently to the suffering of an individual animal than to the threat of extinction to a species. It notes the tension between animal rights advocates and conservation biologists whose field is biased toward wholes like populations, species, and ecosystems, and asks, "Does the fate of one bear matter in an Earth law regime?" This chapter concerns reframing attitudes toward wild beings and co-existence with them. Earth law involves ethical recognition of the rights of animals to kindness and dignity and laws that support these rights.

As you read about the bear, note the discussion of a paradigm shift from the anthropocentric perspective that has fostered human exploitation of animals to a biocentric approach based on ethics and moral consideration. How would such an approach influence the current treatment of wildlife, for example, as food, for entertainment, and as a trade commodity? Would it awaken a meaningful reconsideration of human's perceived superiority over the rest of the animal kingdom? Compare the call for an ethic of compassion and morality in our relationship with wild animals to the current model of wildlife law and policy based on sustainability and conservation. Are these two approaches contradictory? Complementary? From the perspective of this chapter the approaches are generally complementary, although not always recognized as such.

Despite its focus on preserving species, current wildlife policy has failed to effectively reduce the accelerating rate of extinctions. The objectificaion of nonhuman

[1] This chapter was authored by Reed Loder, Professor of Law at Vermont Law School.

animals is deeply ingrained in law and society. This chapter considers how a more compassionate approach to wildlife could help to change the culturally reinforced insensitivity of humans to nonhuman animals.

I. A PARTICULAR BEAR: WHY AN EARTH LAW CASE STUDY?

This chapter tells a story of a mother bear and her multiple generations of cubs. It is neither a fairy tale nor a story of purely local significance. This is a probe into remaking wild animal and human relations from an Earth law perspective. The focus is not on laws but on reframing attitudes toward wild beings and co-existence with them. These are primarily ethical issues. Laws reflect assumptions about what things have value, which, in turn, affects the treatment of others under the laws. Thus, the core of laws is ethics. Laws provide minimum standards of conduct required by society under those values.

Earth law emphasizes that among all members of the Earth community are interconnected (*see* Chapter 3, "Conceptual Frameworks of Earth Law") and all voices in the Earth community must be heard in law and policy decisions. For centuries, humans have dominated and exploited animals and viewed themselves as superior. They have eliminated wild beings at will and developed attitudes of fear and disdain toward them. As a result, we are facing the sixth great extinction in Earth's history and an unprecedented loss of biodiversity.[2]

This chapter discusses why the general state of human relations with wild animals is inadequate from an Earth law perspective. Next, it summarizes the story of "Mink," an American Black Bear. Based on this summary, the chapter delves into the importance of considering conflicts between bears and humans from the bear's perspective, instead of taking an exclusively monolithic human viewpoint. To understand the animal standpoint, the chapter provides information about the life cycle of bears from biology and about animal experiences from cognitive ethology, which is the study of the mental lives of animals. It is ethically necessary to take that information into account in policy and law to avoid inflicting harm on animals and their species. Other arguments for improving animal and human relations include those contributions animals make to the ecosystems of which they are part and the values animals lend to the places we are responsible for tending—both of which are Earth law concerns.

Several terminological points precede this exploration. First, nonhuman animals are referred to as "animals" as a shorthand device, which in no way fails to recognize humans as members of the kingdom *Animalia*. Second, the terms "morality" and "ethics" are used interchangeably in this chapter, although some people may affix different meanings to the terms. Finally, this chapter capitalizes the names of certain animal species and gives personal pronouns to animals to reflect their status in Earth law as subjects, not objects.

[2] Damian Carrington, *Earth's Sixth Mass Extinction Event under Way, Scientists Warn*, The Guardian (July 10, 2017), https://www.theguardian.com/environment/2017/jul/10/earths-sixth-mass-extinction-event-already-underway-scientists-warn.

II. HUMANS AND WILD BEARS GENERALLY

When wild animals and humans mix, humans almost invariably have the upper hand. Humans have eradicated or severely degraded wild animal habitats through voracious development and have often eliminated animals when they venture too close. Human motivations are ambivalent when it comes to carnivores, especially large ones like bears (while technically omnivores, bears are classified as carnivores). As Earth law emphasizes, superiority over and separation from the nonhuman world is part of our longstanding cultural legacy,[3] and it merges with contempt for beings, such as bears, who are powerful enough to injure or kill us or damage our property.[4]

At the same time, humans are fascinated with these creatures at an observable distance. So, no matter how many times they are cautioned not to do so, they are willing to risk encounters by leaving food, garbage, and bird feeders accessible past the time bears emerge from hibernation.[5] The bears and other animals that are attracted to these easy sources of high calorie food often become labeled as "nuisances" and are then subject to extermination. Think about this for a moment—extermination for being a nuisance. We are not discussing animals with diseases or those who have attacked people or other animals—although there are bears with such histories. We cannot imagine treating pesky humans in this draconian manner, yet it is a ready solution for some wild creatures among us. This attitude reveals that we devalue these animals and make them subject to our whims.

This balance of power would change under an Earth law approach. Laws would better protect bears sharing our habitat, even if they were not listed as "threatened" or "endangered" under the Endangered Species Act.[6] Also, the term human habitat would be expanded to take account of the nonhuman inhabitants and systems within a community.

III. THE STORY OF ONE BEAR AND HER PROGENY

My first bear encounter was in the late New Hampshire winter of 2016. I heard thumping outside and opened the curtain to reveal a large black bear tearing a bird feeder from the porch eaves. Standing not four feet from the bear, I tapped the window to discourage the animal. The bear whirled around on its hind legs and placed a paw on the glass. Thrilled and frozen, I was close enough to see long curved claws on the windowpane and white hairs mixed with black on the bear's cheeks. The bear grabbed the

[3] *See, e.g.*, Thomas Berry, The Great Work: Our Way into the Future 4, 24, 41, 43, 45-46, 72, 91, 102, 104 (1999); Cormac Cullinan, Wild Law: A Manifesto for Earth Justice 44, 49, 51, 62-64, 170 (2nd ed. 2011); David R. Boyd, The Rights of Nature: A Legal Revolution That Could Save the World xxiii (2017).

[4] Berry, *supra* note 3, at 122.

[5] Benjamin Kilham & Ed Gray, Among the Bears: Raising Orphan Cubs in the Wild 226-229 (2002) [hereinafter *Among the Bears*].

[6] 16 U.S.C. Sec. 1531(b).

feeder and ran off on all fours. So, I thought, ended my once-in-a-lifetime, close-up bear experience.

During the following late winter, a commotion on the porch revealed a sea of black fur with a mass of intertwined bodies. Thus began the story of the sow and her three yearlings that would captivate my region. That bear crew frequented the Upper Valley of New Hampshire, including the towns of Hanover and Lebanon. Although neighbors in Lebanon, where I live, posted daily website backyard sightings of the sow and yearlings, the animals became "The Hanover Bears" in news reports.[7] Hanover residents began reporting bears raiding dumpsters and garbage, sitting in private yards, and even trying locks on doors. Town Manager Julia Griffin launched a campaign to convince people to secure their homes, use "bear-proof" garbage receptacles, take down bird feeders, and remove all traces of food.[8] According to Griffin, the problem in this college town was off-campus students, who were transient and impossible to educate about bears despite their attendance at Dartmouth. Griffin and local officials declined to pass an ordinance requiring simple bear deterrence measures as being too time-consuming and expensive for the town.[9]

The idea of Hanover "owning" the bears evolved into a notion of exclusive responsibility for their fate. The straw broke when two yearlings entered the open kitchen of a house near Mink Brook, their main habitat. They were foiled in their search for food and fled upon hearing noise in the house.[10] This was the final straw for Griffin, and the newspapers announced with no preparation—the bears would be "euthanized" to protect the public.[11] According to the Director of the New Hampshire Fish and Game Department, Andrew Timmins: "When their behavior reaches a certain point, it is tough to be wild bears again."[12] "A fed bear is a dead bear" is an old slogan warning that human curiosity and carelessness spawn "nuisance" bear status and ultimately animal execution.[13]

A New Hampshire resident, pleading for relocation of the bears, started a petition on an online website. Almost 10,000 people from all over America signed the petition. Suddenly headlines changed and the issue went national: "Online Petition Helps Save Family of New Hampshire Bears," proclaimed CBS-Boston.[14]

[7] *See, e.g.,* Cam Tranchemontagne, *Watch: Hanover Bears to Be Trapped, Relocated,* WMUR (May 26, 2017), https://www.wmur.com/article/watch-hanover-bears-to-be-trapped-relocated-1495853575/9940418; John P. Gregg, *Mink, the Hanover Bear Spotted in Woodstock Village,* VALLEY NEWS (April 11, 2019), https://www.vnews.com/Bear-removed-from-Hanover-now-in-Woodstock-area-24781656.

[8] Nik DeCosta-Klipa, *How New Hampshire's Governor Saved 4 Bears from Near-Certain Death,* B NEWS (May 30, 2017), https://www.boston.com/news/animals/2017/05/30/how-new-hampshires-governor-saved-4-bears-from-near-certain-death.

[9] *Id.* Rob Wolfe, *N.H. Wildlife Officials' Plans to Euthanize Family of Bears Near Dartmouth College Faces Backlash,* VALLEY NEWS (May 24, 2017), https://www.vnews.com/Backlash-over-plans-to-euthanize-Hanover-NH-bears-near-Dartmouth-College-10292552.

[10] DeCosta-Klipa, *supra* note 8.

[11] Wolfe, *supra* note 9.

[12] *Facets: How State, Local and Private Worked Together to Keep a Bear Family Safe,* DAILY UV (last visited July 2, 2018), https://dailyuv.com/profile/1931/954782.

[13] Timmins, *Bear and Human Conflicts – A Need for Change,* NEW HAMPSHIRE FISH AND GAME DEPARTMENT (May 13, 2014), https://www.wildlife.state.nh.us/wildlife/documents/bear-human-conflicts.pdf.

[14] *Id.*

Democratic governors ran New Hampshire for 18 of 20 years until Chris Sununu's term began in 2017. Governor Sununu won only about 26 percent of the Hanover vote.[15] Regardless of animal protection, this was a propitious political opportunity for Sununu. "Don't worry, we aren't going to kill the bears," the governor soothed the public in a surprise announcement, blithely overriding the decision of Town Manager Julia Griffin and Andrew Timmins of the Fish and Game Department, without advance notice to either party.[16] Sununu ordered that the bears be trapped and released in the northern portion of the state.[17] A Quebec hunter legally shot one of the yearlings just 18 days after the three were relocated without the sow, who managed to evade capture.[18]

Many marveled when the sow emerged from her den in late winter of 2018 with four new adorable cubs. In response to a blog question, "Where did this notion that bears are cuddly come from, since they're savage, strong, and brutal animals?" Shelley Stein answered, "First of all, they have the cutest babies in the world. Look at them. Look at how fuzzy and warm they look. They have round little bodies, short little limbs, and sweet little faces. Seriously, anyone who doesn't think baby bears are adorable is an asshole."[19]

Bears have some features that lend themselves to neoteny, with adult features resembling the young. These include high foreheads, round cheeks, and stubby and short legs. People find these human, baby-like traits endearing and often favor animals with such appearance.[20]

Cubs in this new litter of "Hanover cubs" each weighed about five to seven pounds and they were three months old when they emerged. Bear specialists fixed the sow with a large red-orange tracking collar. Their plan was to relocate mom and young to another site in New Hampshire when the snow dissipated and food became more available.[21]

As early spring turned to summer officials seemed to relent on relocation. Andrew Timmins voiced concerns that dominant bears at the new site would thwart the relocated bears' access to quality foods and that the sow would likely try to return home, which would by then already be occupied by other bears already known to be present in the area.[22] Deputy Fire Chief of the Hanover Fire Department Michael Hinsley

[15] *See* William M. Gardner, *Governor – 2016 General Election* (last visited Feb. 14, 2020), http://sos.nh.gov/2016GovGen.aspx?id=8589964201 (excel file).

[16] DeCosta-Klipa, *supra* note 8.

[17] Allie Morris, *Hanover Bears Still Mired in Politics,* Concord Monitor (June 5, 2017), reprinted in Valley News, July 2, 2018, http://www.vnews.com/Nuisance-Hanover-bears-still-mired-in-politics-10501764.

[18] Jordan Cuddemi, *Relocated Bear Was Shot, Killed in Quebec,* Valley News (Nov. 1, 2017), https://www.vnews.com/One-of-Three-Bear-Cubs-Has-Died-Lebanon-NH-13477066.

[19] Shelley Stein, *Where Did This Notion That Bears Are Cuddly Come From, Since They're Savage, Strong, And Brutal Animals?,* Quora (last visited Feb. 14, 2020), https://www.quora.com/Where-did-this-notion-that-bears-are-cuddly-come-from-since-theyre-savage-strong-and-brutal-animals.

[20] *See* Steve Baker, Picturing the Beast: Animals, Identity, and Representation 181 (2001).

[21] Jordan Cuddemi, *Hanover Asks Residents to Secure Potential Food Sources as Mama Bear Returns with New Cubs,* Valley News (April 13, 2018), https://www.vnews.com/Experts-Put-GPS-Tracker-on-Mother-Bear-from-Hanover-16798720 [hereinafter *Hanover Asks*].

[22] Britta Greene, *Fate of Hanover's Rogue Mama Up In the Air (Again),* New Hampshire Public Radio (June 4, 2018), https://www.nhpr.org/post/fate-hanovers-rogue-mama-bear-air-again#stream/0 [hereinafter *Fate*].

stated that the bear was not a threat to residents. Tolerance did not extend to places considered resident turf, however. "She crossed the line," Hinsley said when the bear appeared on the Hanover High School Football Field.[23]

Despite apprehensions in Hanover about "Mink," now so named for the sow's home in Mink Brook Reserve, the decision to relocate a bear family that had not recently raided human food was questionable. Bears are natural opportunists, however. Someone soon photographed Mink in an open dumpster with two cubs foraging for food.[24] Although Timmins acknowledged that only 1 percent of people in town had failed to secure food sources, he set an impossibly high standard of compliance that would require: "100 percent of Hanover to clean up (its) acts."[25] Julia Griffin, who had favored euthanasia, concluded that they were "fighting a losing battle."[26]

Mink had run out her chances, it seemed, when she had eluded relocation the year before. The plan was ready for the sow to be relocated near the Canadian border, notwithstanding the known risk that she might attempt to return. Fortunately, the cubs would go to regional bear expert Ben Kilham to be "rehabilitated" from their wayward habits and eventually be released into the wild. Acknowledging that the sow would be "frantic" without her cubs, Timmins warned that Mink's failure to "integrate into the wild," and her return to Hanover would eventually result in her being euthanized.[27] He lamented not euthanizing her the year before.[28] Once relocated, Mink, seeking her cubs and home, traveled rapidly, but she was off course. Timmins admitted, "There are several other bears working the edges of Hanover,"[29] so he could not say how killing or relocating Mink would have ended human and bear conflicts in Hanover.

Winter passed uneventfully. In April of 2019, the local newspaper reported that Mink had hibernated "across the river" in Vermont.[30] Several weeks later Mink swam the Connecticut River to New Hampshire.[31] Her perseverance and strength demonstrated her attachment to place as nothing else could. People sighted and photographed her with the distinctive red radio collar, looking sleek and robust.

Is it really just conjecture that people would think of Mink as having a story with elements of pain, sorrow, and injustice? Why would they assume Mink underwent an

[23] Katherine Underwood, *Mama Bear May Not Be Relocated from Area Near Dartmouth College*, NECN (June 5, 2018), https://www.necn.com/news/new-england/Mama-Bear-May-Not-Be-Relocated-From-Area-Near-Dartmouth-College-Hanover-NH-484615241.html.

[24] John P. Gregg, *Mink, the Hanover Bear, Spotted in Woodstock Village*, Valley News (Apr. 11, 2019), https://www.vnews.com/Bear-removed-from-Hanover-now-in-Woodstock-area-24781656 [hereinafter *Mink*]; *Family of Bears Captured, Transported Out of Hanover*, Valley News (June 29, 2018), https://www.vnews.com/Hanover-Bears-Captured-Transported-Out-of-Town-18527420 [hereinafter *Family*].

[25] Jordan Cuddemi, *Relocated Bear Trying to Find Home*, Valley News (July 7, 2018), https://www.vnews.com/Hanover-Sow-Very-Active-18666804 [hereinafter *Relocated Bear*].

[26] *Family*, *supra* note 24.

[27] *Id.*

[28] *Relocated Bear*, *supra* note 25.

[29] *Id.*

[30] Britta Greene, *Mink, the Famous Hanover Bear, Has Returned to the Upper Valley*, New Hampshire Public Radio (Apr.12, 2019), https://www.nhpr.org/post/mink-famous-hanover-bear-has-returned-upper-valley#stream/0.

[31] Siobhan Lopez, *"Mink," Hanover's Most Famous Bear Is Back in Town*, WMUR (May 18, 2019), https://www.wmur.com/article/mink-hanovers-most-famous-bear-is-back-in-town/27516785.

ordeal and experienced trauma over the sudden loss of her cubs and home place of 15 years? Why is it even important to imagine Mink's perspective? If important, how is it possible for humans to grasp anything accurate about a bear's point of view? That we can think of Mink as a subject in this manner is important ethically to the way we imagine the lives of other animals we do not encounter. They are members of the wider community of subjects that Earth law encompasses.

IV. THE IMPORTANCE OF THE ANIMAL'S PERSPECTIVE

As Earth law emphasizes, humans, believing themselves to have unique capacities, have long separated themselves from animals.[32] Species differentiations are based on actual distinctions, but these have been used by humans to bolster feelings of superiority, enabling them to use animals for human benefit without considering their suffering.[33] *Cognitive ethology*, or the comparative and evolutionary study of animal minds, and evolutionary biology have shown that many animals have complex cognitive abilities, including tool use, culture, reasoning, and flexible problem-solving; recognition of other individuals; and sophisticated forms of communication that only humans were once thought to possess.[34] Yet, people still fail to recognize unique species attributes, such as the speed of the cheetah or eyesight of the eagle that human beings lack, and continue to measure animal capacities in human terms. An animal will never measure up to a human-centered assessment of nonhuman capacities because different species have evolved to cope with varied developmental and environmental conditions.[35] In taking the animal's perspective, this section looks first to biology to understand how bears exist within suitable habitats, and then it considers what the science of ethology teaches about the mental lives of animals.

A. American Black Bear Biology and Life Cycle

One important way to understand an animal's perspective is through life cycle and biological makeup. This shows how the animal lives within physical and environmental constraints. The specific subjects of this story are American black bears (*Ursus americanus*),[36] the bears in North America with the widest range and the only bears inhabiting the eastern United States from Maine to Florida.[37] All bear species face strain, but

[32] Cullinan, *supra* note 3, at 44, 49, 51.

[33] *See* Bernard E. Rollin, Animal Pain in The Animal Ethics Reader, 114-115 (Susan J. Armstrong & Richard G. Botzler eds., 3rd ed. 2017).

[34] *See* Marc Bekoff & Paul W. Sherman, Reflections on Animal Selves in Animal Passions and Beastly Virtues: Reflections on Redecorating Nature 2, 3 (Marc Bekoff ed., 2006) [hereinafter *Passions*] at 3.

[35] Paul Taylor, Biocentric Egalitarianism, *in* Environmental Ethics: Readings in Theory and Application 187, 188 (Louis P. Pojman, Paul Pojman & Katie McShane eds., 7th ed., 2017) at 187-188.

[36] Gary Brown, The Bear Almanac: A Comprehensive Guide to the Bears of the World 14-15 (2009).

[37] *Where Do Bears Live in North America?*, Geology.com, https://geology.com/stories/13/bear-areas (last visited Nov. 1, 2019).

the black bear is faring best in North America[38] because of its impressive flexibility and adaptability.[39] Thus we are not considering an endangered or threatened animal, and people hunt black bears in many states.[40] Instead of vanishing, this is one of many animals that persists in North America while losing habitat to human development and finding it more challenging to carry out the typical life processes of its kind.[41]

American black bears are omnivores and food opportunists who seek many varieties of nourishment from diverse sources depending on availability within their range.[42] A range differs from a territory in that a range does not have fixed boundaries. Often, black bears have overlapping ranges when a particular food source, such as berries, is plentiful.[43] Thus, unfamiliar bears feed together without undue aggression, probably because the scarcity of a particular food makes tolerance worthwhile.[44] If humans expose garbage or other sources of potential food, bears will investigate and tap those sources.[45]

During the warmer months, black bear activities largely revolve around foraging. Although bears are omnivorous, about 85 percent of their diet is vegetation, consisting of roots, berries, herbs, and nuts. The bear's diet varies significantly by season, depending on availability of food sources, which bears move around to find. In fact, seeking food is the principal bear occupation during at least half of the year.[46]

For this, black bears have a keen sense of smell that "allows location of mates, avoidance of humans and other bears, identification of cubs, and the locations of food sources." Recent research shows that bears have "reasonably good" vision, possibly equivalent to that of humans; bears show good depth perception and peripheral vision, can see well at night, and see color.[47] American black bears have small round ears back on the head and have good hearing.[48]

People notoriously overestimate the size of bears they observe,[49] perhaps because of the creature's girth in relation to its legs, and perhaps simply because an encounter with a bear is astonishing. The average size of American black bears varies by region, individual condition, and sex, with male bears about one-third larger than females.[50] The average size of an adult male is 200 to 300 pounds.[51] Like humans, bears walk

[38] *See* BROWN, *supra* note 36, at 50, 281, 308.
[39] *Id.* at 97-98, 281.
[40] *Id.* at 142-143, 146-147 (describing hunting in Idaho).
[41] *See* ROSIE WOODROFFE, STRATEGIES FOR CARNIVORE CONSERVATION: LESSONS FROM CONTEMPORARY EXTINCTIONS IN CARNIVORE CONSERVATION 61, 65-66, 69 (John L. Gittleman, Stephan M. Funk *et al.* eds., 2001).
[42] John Beecham & Jeff Rohlman, *Shadow in the Forest: Idaho's Black* Bear 104-108 (1994).
[43] BROWN, *supra* note 36, at 164, 166.
[44] *See Among the Bears, supra* note 5, at 270-271.
[45] *Id.* at 270-271, 227-228.
[46] BROWN, *supra* note 36, at 166, 169.
[47] *Id.* at 82, 84, 166.
[48] *Id.* at 86, 166.
[49] *Among the Bears, supra* note 5, at 101.
[50] BROWN, *supra* note 36, at 57-59.
[51] GEORGE LAYCOCK, THE WILD BEARS 191 (1986) (describing the long practice of Park visitors feeding grizzlies and black bears).

plantigrade (flat-footed) with heel and foot on the ground. They are slightly pigeon-toed and walk with a shuffling gait, which makes them appear clumsy. Their front feet have five toes with curved non-retractable claws that are used for varied activities like digging, fighting, lifting, and movement. Black bears are extremely strong, agile, and swift runners despite their clumsy appearance. Black bears are remarkable climbers and sows teach their cubs to climb trees to avoid danger even before the cubs are proficient at walking. Bears are also strong and enthusiastic swimmers.[52]

The average lifespan of a wild American black bear is 14 to 20 years. Typically, a sow has her first litter at age five, and the usual number of cubs is two. Black bears mate from late May into June and July.[53] A mature female ordinarily has cubs every other year.[54] Older, sexually mature males have the privilege of mating because younger males are unable to compete.[55] Once mating is complete, male black bears show no interest in their offspring.[56]

The sow, on the other hand, is focused on her young. "There is a deep family bond. The mother is affectionate, devoted, protective (aggressive toward threats), sensitive, strict, and attentive to the training of her cubs."[57] Although mating happens in summer, birth occurs in January or February while the mother is hibernating in her den. Although the egg is fertilized at copulation, it is not implanted in the uterine wall until hibernation. Delayed implantation prevents the sow from having cubs during the pre-hibernation period when she must feed extensively to build enough fat to sustain her through the winter. During torpor (not the deepest form of hibernation), the sow will not eat, drink, or expel waste, and she will lose about one-third of her body weight. The newborn cubs, weighing only half a pound, will nurse during hibernation, absorbing warmth from the mother's body in the den, which is constructed to retain heat. Sow and cubs emerge in April, and, during the summer, the sow teaches the young all they need to know about hunting food and the life of a bear. The cubs usually hibernate with the sow a second winter and stay with her until she is ready again to mate.[58]

An interesting trait of black bears is their ability to navigate. Bears who have relocated very long distances can somehow return to their home place even without any prior knowledge of the route that would facilitate mapping.[59] Mink illustrated this. Did she return out of some kind of instinct or imprint? Or, was she determined in a more emotional and cognitive way to find her cubs and home? Experts do not know much about this skill of navigation.

[52] Brown, *supra* note 36, at 47, 48, 74, 77, 127, 128-129, 146.
[53] *Id.* at 96, 135.
[54] *Among the Bears*, *supra* note 5, at 30.
[55] Brown, *supra* note 36, at 135.
[56] *Id.* at 99.
[57] *Id.*
[58] *Id.* at 99, 135, 138, 204, 206.
[59] *Id.* at 125-126.

B. Bear Social and Emotional Lives: Ethology

Contemporary ethology suggests that bears have complex cognitive and emotional lives.[60] Although they are often deemed solitary animals, female bears in particular form loose social groups by admitting select individuals into their ranges, often their former female young.[61] They help other individuals but also, at other times, retaliate for slights. For example, Benjamin Kilham, the orphan bear rehabilitator in New Hampshire, has observed two adult females arranging a lasting adoption of a young bear. Kilham also reports instances of retaliation against him, once for neglecting to bring food when visiting a wild bear he had reared as an orphan. He returned to his truck to find both rearview mirrors missing![62]

Bears generally are highly intelligent and secretive. Enos A. Mills, a famous Rocky Mountain bear tracker in the late nineteenth and early twentieth century, learned that a grizzly bear he was pursuing was actually silently tracking him. He also observed bears quietly contemplating a sunset or rainbow and witnessed their sense of humor and play many times in the form of antics such as sliding down snowy hills and deliberately ascending to repeat the slide. After years of close proximity to grizzlies, Mills concluded that they were the most intelligent nonhuman mammals.[63]

Some would call such attributions *anthropomorphizing* or imposing human traits on nonhuman beings. This used to be a cardinal sin in ethology, as Jane Goodall discovered as a student when she named the chimps she studied and described their behavior as purposive.[64] Ethology today does not shun descriptions of animal behavior in human terms,[65] provided the observer recognizes that similar manifestations of mental life are most likely experienced differently from nonhuman to human. Brain imaging has demonstrated activity in similar regions of the brain when animals display behavior resembling a human, and brain chemistry reveals similar neurochemicals in the brains of nonhumans when they appear to be experiencing pain, joy, fear, anger, and other emotional states.[66] Laboratory experiments show that many animals are aware of the future in returning to caches of food,[67] recognizing individuals of their species over time,[68] and deceiving other individuals about the location of desirable objects.[69]

Some people persist in attributing such behavior to instinct or imprinting, but the learned quality of much of the conduct belies this explanation. Indeed, diversity in the ways members of the same species in different locations perform certain tasks, such as

[60] *See Among the Bears, supra* note 5, at 166, 241-244, 252-254, 258, 260-261, 272.

[61] Benjamin Kilham, In the Company of Bears: What Black Bears Have Taught Me About Intelligence and Intuition, 19, 28, 95 (2013).

[62] *Id.* at 28, 45, 46, 47, 88, 102.

[63] Enos A. Mills, The Grizzly 72, 79, 99-100 (1976).

[64] *See* Marc Bekoff, Minding Animals: Awareness, Emotions, and Heart, x, 41, 48-49 (2002) [hereinafter *Minding*].

[65] Frans De Waal, Mama's Last Hug: Animal Emotions and What They Tell Us About Ourselves 50-51 (2019).

[66] *See Passions, supra* note 34, at 16-17, 29.

[67] Donald R. Griffin & Gayle B. Speck, New Evidence of Animal Consciousness, *in* the Animal Ethics Reader, 143-144 (Susan J. Armstrong & Richard G. Botzler eds., 3rd ed. 2017)

[68] *See* De Waal, *supra* note 65, at 142-143 (long-term animal friendships). *See Minding, supra* note 64, at 4.

[69] *Minding, supra* note 64, at 91.

chimpanzees using different tools to gather ants for food,[70] suggests that groups develop cultural variations in their life activities that are transmitted through their distinct social groups. According to primate expert Franz De Waal, it is understandable and "parsimonious" to describe carefully observed animal behavior in emotive or cognitive terms because contemporary ethology shows continuity between humans and animals.

The behavior itself is most telling. When we observe an animal grimacing or whimpering in response to an event that would cause pain in a human, we infer from similar human responses that the animal is experiencing pain. Although some scientists still insist that the pain response and the conscious experience of pain (or fear, joy, jealousy, etc.) are different and we are not entitled to assume that the scientific evidence of pain responses means that the animal has the conscious experience, the prevailing scientific view is that it is more accurate to conclude, based on multiple forms of evidence, that the animal has the experience as well as the bodily response.[71]

Of course, no one can demonstrate with certainty that an animal is experiencing any particular thought or emotion, just as no one is certain what another human is thinking or feeling.[72] With many humans, however, we have the benefit of language to communicate mental states. If you tell me you are happy and you are smiling and showing enthusiasm, I have compelling reasons to believe that you are experiencing happiness. Further, I can compare how I act when I feel happy and conclude that what you call "happiness" is very similar to the state I label "happy" in myself. This is not true with all humans (e.g., infants or those who have lost the ability to communicate in words). Yet, we do not conclude that an infant or wordless person who is smiling and laughing is not actually experiencing the mirth that behavior suggests. Even highly verbal humans communicate much information through facial expressions, body language, and non-language vocalizations. Many animals have sophisticated modes of complex communication that do not replicate human methods but can be deciphered upon repeated observation of the animal in various contexts.[73]

Black bears use an array of movements, such as nuzzling, standing on hind legs, charging, sitting, rubbing, stretching, stiff-walking, and varied vocalizations from snorting, grunting, huffing, woofing, jaw clicking, and more.[74] These actions have varied meanings when used in combination, and the context is crucially important in interpreting the meaning.[75] For example, a sow handling cubs might use some movements and noises that in other situations would indicate aggression but in this context is discipline for training purposes.[76] Analogously, *canids* at play use some of the movements they employed in fighting, but they signal to the play partner through ritualized

[70] A. Whiten, J. Goodall et al., Cultures in Chimpanzees, in the Animal Ethics Reader, 183 (Susan J. Armstrong & Richard G. Botzler eds., 3rd ed. 2017).
[71] De Waal, *supra* note 65, at 51, 48-51, 111, 113, 114.
[72] *See* Rollin, *supra* note 33, at 112.
[73] Griffin & Speck, *supra* note 67, at 141, 143-45.
[74] *See Among the Bears*, *supra* note 5, at 21, 62-63, 111-112, 122,128, 138-139, 142-143, 248-249.
[75] *Id.* at 243.
[76] *See* Brown, *supra* note 36, at 147.

"bowing" and other cues that their intent is not to inflict harm but to have fun.[77] Play signals are also important to bears.

To appreciate the complexity and variety of animal minds, it is necessary to see the world as much as possible from the animal's perspective. It is also important to consider the evolutionary origins of particular behaviors—to ask why some patterns of activity have added value to the species' survival.[78] These steps will not produce certain knowledge immune to revision. Over time, however, careful study can teach us much about animal lives that is too easy to disregard from a human-centered perspective.

C. Ethical Implications of Animals' Perspectives

Immersion into animals' perspectives is ethically vital to the treatment they receive from humans. Within Earth law, perspectival information is important to recognizing the diverse rights of all members of the Earth community because rights are closely linked to conditions that enable flourishing. Attention to an individual animal reveals that each one is unique and, even within a species, there are great variations. This orientation means that each animal matters, and fair treatment is an ethical responsibility for humans because of the power we wield over the creature world and our capacity for conscious self-reflection.

Empathy is an important cognitive and moral skill for understanding nonhumans better. Through empathy a person is able to *understand* the point of view of others including their emotions. Empathy for another's perspective does not entail sympathetically *sharing* that perspective, however. A psychopath can use skills of empathy to torture animals or human victims because they understand the subjects' exact vulnerabilities. If the person who understands another's stressful emotions also shares those feelings and is motivated out of concern to assist the one in distress, that person has both sympathy and empathy.[79]

Empathy as a tool of moral understanding does not necessarily yield accurate knowledge of the other. This is because the person placing herself in the other's position is herself differently situated. Being differently situated biases one's perception of another.[80] The risk is always present of projecting one's own beliefs, feelings, and judgments onto the other, thereby distorting the other's perspective.[81] This is sometimes called "false empathy."[82] Lawyers are susceptible to this tendency. They are required to act in their client's best interests and give primacy to the client's values and goals. For example, in a case concerning the right to refuse drug treatment, a client who

[77] *Passions*, *supra* note 34, at 125-127.
[78] *Id.* at 1, 7, 28 (emotions have evolutionary value for survival).
[79] De Waal, *supra* note 65, at 103, 106.
[80] *See, e.g.*, Richard Delgado, *Rodrigo's Eleventh Chronicle: Empathy and False Empathy*, 84 Calif. L. Rev. 61, 78 (1996).
[81] *Id.* at 74.
[82] *Id.* at 70-71.

has bipolar disorder might reject the medication that has controlled manic states because of side effects from the drug, such as a flattened mood. The patient's doctors insist that the patient has done well on medication and should continue the regimen, and they will recommend this in a legal hearing on the right to refuse treatment. The lawyer, who is supposed to promote the client's autonomy and follow the client's considered judgment,[83] might be hesitant to follow the client's expressed wishes because of apprehension that the client might act rashly or even become suicidal without medication. The lawyer might decide that the client is behaving irrationally against their best interest, and thus apply personal norms to someone whose experience the lawyer cannot fully comprehend.

This problem is compounded with an animal because humans lack full understanding of the animal's complex communications and the problems the animal encounters in daily living. This is why understanding the biology and life cycle of an animal is relevant to ethics and policy. This is also why it is important to research animal behavior and mental capacities, both through intensive observations of animals in their natural settings and through neurological comparisons to other animals. On the other hand, most people are confident in attributing emotions and mental states to their companion animals, which suggests that barriers to animal-human communication may not as great as some scientists claim.[84]

Reading Mink's emotional experience in being relocated and separated from her young is not very susceptible to error because bear experts know a great deal about a sow's relationships to her cubs. Besides being fiercely protective, sows display great affection and care toward cubs by teaching them about food sources, disciplining them for their protection, and playing, hibernating, and remaining with them for a lengthy period.[85] A sow nursing, like Mink, would be wholly devoted to her five-month-old cubs at the time of her relocation. This is not an emotionally ambiguous context of interpretation. Recall that bear expert Andrew Timmins predicted that Mink would be "frantic" without her cubs.[86]

Attending to the animal's perspective also helps researchers avoid over-generalizations. Openness to the inevitable need to revise information is crucial because animals often behave in surprising ways that require further investigation.[87] Individual animal differences can reveal a range of capacities within a species.[88] Careful observation of different populations can also demonstrate cultural diversity, such as the way that a particular group of animals learns to gather food.[89]

[83] MODEL RULES OF PROF'L CONDUCT r. 1.2 (AM. BAR ASS'N. 1983).
[84] *See Passions, supra* note 34, at 26, 29, 30.
[85] BROWN, *supra* note 36, at 147.
[86] *Family, supra* note 24.
[87] *See Passions, supra* note 34, at 18 (Jane Goodall's observations of chimpanzee tool use leading to further research).
[88] *Id.* at 18, 272 (importance of animals as individuals with diverse personalities).
[89] *See* DE WAAL, *supra* note 65, at 159 (cultural learning about foods and access).

D. Cultural Influences on Understanding Animals' Perspectives

Openness and humility are moral virtues for anyone trying to understand fellow creatures and how to behave toward them. For the sake of repairing our planetary condition and survival, Earth law emphasizes that humans must undo entrenched tendencies to dominate nonhuman nature. Since pre-history, evidence shows that people have made normative judgments about animals in their worlds. For example, people often judge large predators negatively.[90]

On the other hand, some humans have associated bears with virility and power and admired those traits. In ancient Germanic culture, bears were regarded as strong and nearly invincible animals, and male warriors proved their prowess through hand-to-hand combat with male bears. Further, some experts think ancient European caves contain evidence of a religion of the bear, or at least of the bear as "a creature apart" with unique powers.[91]

As Christianity rose to the foreground of European culture, people sought ways to denigrate bears. Historian, Michel Pastoureau, who studied the bear's shifting cultural position in European history, found that the lion displaced the bear as the king of strength in the High Middle Ages. Christianity persistently eviscerated pagan ideas, especially those about a continuum between animals and humans. Legends across cultures depict sexual attraction between male bears and women and describe sexual relations resulting in hybrid human-bear offspring. The bear-male son often returns to the human domain and becomes known as a warrior and hero.[92]

Europeans massacred bears, eradicated their forest habitats, and drove the animals to the distant mountains. Later, some captured bears and brought them to cities, where they forced bears to perform unnatural antics, like walking upright, doing "handstands," and performing skits, which made them appear foolish and stupid. Indeed, there is a long tradition of stories and fables about inept bears. Bears also became entertainers at circuses and carnivals and spectacles in zoos. Bears became pathetic objects of mockery, docility, and servility. These intelligent animals were so out of place in these roles.[93]

European settlers in America killed black bears with abandon, sometimes for food and fat, but often because they could not accept the right of these powerful creatures to occupy the same places as humans. Sometimes killing was simply for the challenge.[94]

[90] *See, e.g.*, Kent H. Redford, Large Carnivores and Conservation of Biodiversity 5 (Justina C. Ray, Kent H. Redford, Robert S. Steneck & Joel Berger eds., 2005) (carnivores' power over humans part of attitude) [hereinafter *Large Carnivores*].

[91] Michel Pastoureau, The Bear: History of a Fallen King 1-2, 25, 35-39 (George Holoch, trans., 2011).

[92] *Id.* at 72, 80-81, 89-92, 135-138.

[93] *Id.* at 89-91, 118, 161-168, 171-176, 248, 250.

[94] Laycock, *supra* note 51, at 212.

Although bears are omnivorous and prefer vegetation, roots, and insects to meat, the practice of some bears of consuming the flesh of the dead of their own species provokes human repugnance: "[T]he bear shows, a gruesome and cannibal fondness for the flesh of his own kind," said President Theodore Roosevelt. It is important to interpret such behavior of bears non-judgmentally and as the way animals make their way in the world because of species-related traits. Black bears consume any available food, including carrion, upon emerging from hibernation while spring vegetation is scarce.[95]

Although instances of black bears attacking and killing humans are "virtually nonexistent,"[96] every incident captures media attention.[97] Although a bear avoids physical altercations, when cornered or surprised, it may attack.[98] Unfortunately, some people generalize from the very rare instances of bears harming people to draw the conclusion that bears do not belong in a shared environment.

There is also danger in flipping attitudes toward animals. Some now view once-maligned wolves as environmental heroes or symbols. Lovers and haters exist side by side—sometimes even in the same conflicted people. Bears, too, have lovers and haters. Voyeurism has led to the demise of bears attracted and then habituated to human food and residences.

Empathy for animals should not lead to freighting them with human characteristics that endear or repel them to people. Appreciating bears is largely about seeing them as different biological beings with lives and agency of their own. Operating against bear conservation is the glib human tendency to endow wild animals with human-like traits that moralize attitudes toward them. Repairing our relations with the Earth is aided by an awareness of cultural history as it makes us less likely to fall prey to entrenched prejudices.

V. ETHICAL DECISION-MAKING ABOUT CO-EXISTENCE WITH BEARS

It is time for ideas to coalesce on improving human and nonhuman co-existence ethically and legally. These ideas should be useful to address future situations similar to the Mink case study, which can be anticipated now that humans have encroached so pervasively on animal habitats. The ideas also have comparative relevance for different cases of exploring the relationship between humans and nonhumans.

[95] *See* Brown, *supra* note 36, at 169.
[96] *Among the Bears, supra* note 5, at 242; *See also* Brown, *supra* note 36, at 271.
[97] *See* Brown, *supra* note 36, at 271 (headlines treating bears as "serial killers").
[98] *Id.* at 116, 276.

A. Relevant Ethical-Legal Factors in Mink's Case: Illustrative Questions

In assessing Mink's situation within an Earth law framework, the questions that follow are relevant. Does the fate of one bear matter in an Earth law regime, or should the focus be on species, populations, and ecosystems? What are the relative interests at stake for those affected here, primarily those of the human residents, an adult female bear, and her young? Are there alternatives to extreme measures like euthanasia or relocation that compromise fewer values for bears? How should information from ethology and biology affect decision-making about bears? How will decisions affect the dignity of animals? What are possible concerns of justice involving historical and current treatment of the animal? How will decisions alter the holistic and wild characteristics of affected places? Do humans owe any affirmative duties to the animals besides preventing future harms? The discussion that follows considers only some of these questions.

B. Individuals or Wholes: A Contextual Approach

Approaches that emphasize population, species, and ecosystem levels will have little perceived significance in the daily lives of people who encounter individual bears who are raiding their bird feeders and garbage. It is important to note Earth law's tendency to take the holistic approach[99] because this raises concerns regarding the interests of individual beings to animals as only being important when they affect larger processes and systems. These are not unlike concerns that animal rights advocates have about conservation biologists whose field is biased toward wholes like populations, species, and ecosystems.[100] Even though Earth law has tended to focus on rights of nature for systems such as rivers, in some contexts, the rights of individuals are paramount because fundamental interests in being, having habitat, and fulfilling their roles in the Earth community—three primary rights Thomas Berry attributed to *all* members of the larger universe community—are at stake.[101] In bestowing rights on individuals to exist and flourish, however, it is always important to consider holistic limits such as ecological burdens of animal over-population on system-carrying capacities. As Earth law develops, it will allow for contextual shifts in attention between individuals and wholes without a fixed priority on a holistic perspective. Shifting contextual attention is partly what makes an Earth law approach so challenging to define, but it is inherent in recognizing the rights of all components of the Earth community.

Given that the Mink case study involves co-existence between people and particular bears occupying overlapping habitats, the primary focus should be on the rights of the animals in *relationship* with people, with preservation of the ecosystem and wild processes always in the background as limiting and enhancing factors. In this case, as in many others, protecting individual animals simultaneously improves the ecology of the landscape.

[99] CULLINAN, *supra* note 3, at 100.
[100] *See Passions, supra* note 34, at 226-227, 229.
[101] *Id.* at 101.

C. Relative Interests, Harms, and Benefits

1. Trivial human interests in convenience and aesthetics

For humans, limitations on their interests are relatively trivial in preventing harm to Mink and her progeny. It is a matter of small inconvenience to secure doors, birdseed, and garbage. Aesthetic interests in observing birds and bears in the backyard are important but not vital. Happily, avoiding serious physical threats to humans from these large animals is consistent with measures to protect them.

2. Vital bear interests in life, reproduction, and mental well-being

From the bear's perspective, the interests in the case study are vital—literally life and death. The slogan, "A fed bear is a dead bear," reflects this. Humans are largely responsible for creating "nuisance" bears, a condition with unethical origins not acknowledged. Bears forage large areas in search of food, especially during pre-hibernation when they must increase their weight to sustain themselves and possibly newborn cubs during winter,[102] and they forage even larger stretches in times of drought or berry and nut shortages.[103] Bears will avail themselves of accessible food close to humans if convenient, and proximity to humans is frequently a death sentence. Thus humans can be ethically responsible for bear mortality out of wanton carelessness or even amusement in watching bears.

Sows and their young also have vital interests in the reproductive cycle. Pregnant bears euthanized as "problems" do not reproduce. Yearling bears are most at risk as they leave their mother's protection and seek new ranges. Nursing cubs depend completely on their mother for food and to learn foraging and other survival skills. When we deem a nursing sow a "nuisance" and sentence her to death or relocation, we are also dooming her dependent cubs. Fortunately, wildlife officials knew of Mink's cubs, and an orphan-bear rehabilitator accepted the laborious care of the cubs.

The separation of Mink from her cubs was emotionally traumatic, which wildlife expert Timmins acknowledged,[104] and this mental harm is another strong animal interest and ethical factor. Wildlife observers have noted the fast bond and affectionate behavior between a sow and her cubs.[105] It is ethically appropriate to respect bears' complex emotional and cognitive capacities, given current knowledge from ethology. From an Earth ethics perspective, such respect is not based only on similarities to humans (e.g., in the recognizable mother-young bond). Wild animals have unique characteristics and functioning and deserve respect in their own right.[106] For example, bears should not be judged for sending off yearlings, sometimes forcefully, even though yearlings face grave risks. This animal reproduces few of its own kind, usually

[102] BROWN, *supra* note 36, at 164-166, 154.
[103] *Among the Bears, supra* note 5, at 156-157, 263.
[104] *Family, supra* note 24.
[105] *See, e.g.*, BROWN, *supra* note 36, at 147.
[106] *See* Reed Elizabeth Loder, *Animal Dignity*, 23 ANIMAL L. 1, 35-36 (2016).

just every other year, and the sow's undivided attention to her cubs is how some bears survive and continue the cycle of species life.

D. Assessing Alternatives: Less Harmful Effective Options

In encounter cases, human fears and prejudices take over, and people expect public officials to take decisive action, which often means killing or relocating the "problem" bear. People might demand this despite their carelessness in leaving food accessible and doors ajar—they demand a lethal solution to a problem they could have prevented.

Local law is one mechanism to alter the balance of interests and repair the relationship between wild bears and humans. Towns could pass laws that impose reasonable fines on people who deliberately feed bears, leave bird feeders outside after the first of March, fail to secure trash receptacles, and make homes or garages accessible. Such a "bear ordinance" would remind people to develop new, relatively simple, habits. An ordinance could also require commercial trash companies to provide bear-proof receptacles either by new stock or retrofitting existing containers. Education should accompany lawmaking. Residents should be instructed in preventing human-bear confrontations that could result in physical injuries to human or animal. Hanover officials took measures that directly harmed vital animal interests when there was a legal option available that would have protected those interests with minimal inconvenience to humans.

Local government is responsible for fostering the collective well-being of human and wild animal co-existence. Simple and lightly burdensome legal requirements could save many bears and a few humans from destructive confrontations.[107] When Mink's yearlings entered an open kitchen, the Hanover town administrator precipitously ordered the animals euthanized. Yet, that administrator had contributed to the problem by rejecting an ordinance.[108] Ordering euthanasia without first using the legal authority of local government was unjustified. Although residents might be annoyed if fined, over time most would adjust and likely see benefits in their new behaviors. If local governments are unwilling to adopt such ordinances, legislation at the state level could accomplish the same result.

Deliberative democracy will be important to the development of Earth law because the ideas are bold, comprehensive, and need discussion to take hold. The process leading to the Hanover euthanasia decision was ethically bereft. Indeed, there was no process—just an announcement. Town officials apparently had no thoughts about including people in adjacent towns (where the bears also frequented) or the public's opinions of the situation. Encouraging discussion often leads to creative and jointly acceptable ideas, not only about the issue at hand but also for future planning. Without facilitating public participation, Hanover officials left few options open for communication, and the response was an indignant petition demanding relocation of Mink over

[107] *See* Timmins, *supra* note 13 (recommending such law-making).
[108] Wolfe, *supra* note 9.

euthanasia. This tied the officials' hands for future decisions about wild animals because the public will not soon forget Mink, who unwittingly became a star. The method used to make an animal vanish placed her in the limelight and exposed a flawed democratic process.

The media also has an ethical obligation to provide accurate information about newsworthy animals by dispelling, not reinforcing, harmful stereotypes and irrational fears. Media should avoid politicizing animals and treating them as the property of the places they happen to visit, such as by calling Mink and her cubs "The Hanover Bears."

The individual humans living in the area also fell short of fulfilling their duties. Deliberative democracy requires that people be committed to improving the community. Humans are adept in changing habits. They alter diet and exercise to promote health, take courses to improve employment prospects, seek psychic self-improvement to feel better, and consult relationship professionals to become better partners. Why should habits toward wild animals be exempt from self-improvement regimes with so much at stake for the animals? When people realize the stakes, they respond, albeit often weakly. The thousands of people who signed the "Save Mink" petition probably encouraged the governor's intervention. The idea of killing innocent bears provoked ripple effects of moral outrage—a righteous kind of anger geared toward positive social change. Yet, the death order would never have been issued if people had collectively done the small, easy things that would have prevented a bear from becoming a "nuisance" in the first place. People should work on remaking their relations with wildlife to *prevent* foreseeable crises.

Humans owe bears the least harmful negative responses if it becomes necessary to interfere with their lives. This rules out relocation and execution in almost all cases. Ben Kilham describes deterrence methods, such as electric fencing, loud noises, and trapping that are somewhat useful[109] and should at least be tried before more extreme measures. People also need to educate themselves about realistic threats from bears as they use the outdoors and take protective measures to avoid or deter bears while hiking, such as carrying noisemakers or sprays to ward off bears, and not traveling alone on bear trails.

E. Bear Dignity: The Right to Be

This case study shows that sometimes the focus of concern should be on individual beings like Mink. The idea of animal dignity stretches our moral imagination toward understanding nonhuman perspectives and builds respect for nature that is unlike us. The concept of dignity also matters because wrongs to nonhuman nature are often not reducible to utilitarian harms, although they do include these.

Animals like bears have much to teach us. Exposing Mink's life reveals a being with a complex emotional and physical life that is partly species related and partly a matter of Mink's own determination—her personality. Animal dignity is a complex idea that is highly contextual and multi-faceted. Explanations of dignity are elusive even in the

[109] *Among the Bears*, *supra* note 5, at 239.

human context; animal dignity resembles but does not duplicate human dignity. Suffice it to say here that dignity relates to the capacity to exercise autonomy and agency, the importance of presenting oneself in a certain manner to the outside world, the opportunity to fulfill the traits that make one the kind of being one is, and the distinctive ability to express one's individual identity.

What do we know about the agency of black bears? We can marvel at their resourcefulness, their extraordinary care of their young, and their ability to adapt to ever-changing circumstances. They are definitely curious about us as fellow beings, but they demonstrate that they prefer tending to their own kind and survival when possible and unraveling the considerable challenges of their forested environment: "Black Bears are shy, secretive animals who live in the dense woods. . . ."[110] Bears' dignity is largely related to their species' being.

Bears share in the aspect of dignity that makes outward presentation important. Bears are famous for posturing and displaying formidable powers, but this show usually leads to retreat, which reinforces the bear's preference to avoid humans. This kind of display reveals animals adapted to defensive presentations rather than inherently aggressive reactions. Tamed bears, coerced to entertain humans, show discomfort. They often appear dejected and humiliated—the self-presentation of a being diminished. Some circus bears reveal this countenance, as when Professor Susan Cataldi observed Russian circus bears clothed in female domestic garments and walking upright on their hind feet, pushing baby carriages. Cataldi rightly identified the lost dignity of these bears as she glimpsed sadness in them and their situation.[111]

It is often easier to understand dignity through recognizing such violations and then identifying what caused the affront. In Mink's case, so many things went wrong. She and her yearlings escaped extermination by the political happenstance of a governor responding to a surprisingly vehement petition. Later, officials wrenched her from her cubs and deposited her in a strange land while still nursing. She managed to forage as hibernation drew nigh and then spent an unusual but not forgetful winter without cubs. Upon emergence, she found her way back to Mink Brook and survived. The story may have a happy interlude with Mink hibernating and emerging once more with newborn cubs.[112] Yet, the events inflicted on Mink and her young were indignities besides being conventional harms. They disrupted her agency, autonomy, her all-important sow relationships with her young, her avoidant nature, and her fierce attachment to place, all of which comprised her bear and Mink identity. Mink has earned freedom after years in the spotlight and ongoing hardships. She has taught us much about bonds between sow and young, indomitable persistence in the face of extreme

[110] KILHAM, *supra* note 61, at xviii.

[111] Susan Laba Cataldi, *Animals and the Concept of Dignity: Critical Reflections on a Circus Performance*, 7 ETHICS & ENVT. 1, 106, 113-114 (2002).

[112] Since writing this chapter, I am delighted to report that Mink has returned! In the late spring of 2020 she reappeared in her old turf with three male cubs. Since then, folks in my neighborhood have enjoyed seeing and photographing her while her cubs were "treed," but everyone has kept a respectful distance. By mid-June 2020, no one has reported any incidents with garbage or unlocked houses, which perhaps shows how much people have learned about coexisting with this creature among us. The local conversation has changed from fear and trepidation to admiration and awe.

hardship and loss, the enduring attachment to place that people and animals share, and strength as an agent exerting powers. For this, we owe Mink deep gratitude, awe, and respect.

Mink has displayed remarkable dignity that her large red GPS collar belies. Everyone recognizes Mink by her jewelry; she has not shown interest in celebrity or in increased interactions with humans. Town and wildlife officials track her every move, although they generally keep her whereabouts classified until someone announces a sighting.

Privacy is part of human dignity, and constant surveillance of people in prison or captivity is a punitive experience. Do bears have a right to privacy? They are thought to be solitary animals, although current research suggests more sociability than previously thought.[113] Solitary and sociable are terms that apply relative to other bears, however, and no one disputes that bears largely prefer concealed lives in the depths to presence among humans. Perhaps such behavior shows that bears value privacy, although not as a conscious idea.

We now live with bears like Mink in a shared domain. Mink belongs near the Mink Brook she chose 15 years ago as her home. She belongs there as much as humans do. People should tolerate, but discourage, contact with Mink. They should let Mink resume whatever wildness she can savor without jeopardizing her safety or unnecessarily subjecting her to the human gaze. We should know enough now about Mink and bears to understand that this is part of bear dignity, an idea that is encompassed in Thomas Berry's rights to be and to fulfill one's nature.

F. Ethics and Character of Place

The unfortunate responses to Mink show how far we have humanized our places. The places bears inhabit will be impoverished if humans continue to exert their pattern of dominance. People are privileged to live among wild fauna and flora. Nearly imperceptibly, the abundance of wildness is shrinking everywhere. We are finally beginning to internalize that we are losing life and its communities at an alarming rate, including insects, birds, and meadows where bobolinks and other grassland birds used to fill the air with effervescent songs.

Some people have turned inward to electronic devices to the point of addiction and have distanced themselves from the nature that used to be children's default play arena.[114] What all of this does to the human psyche is hard to measure, but those who recall a different world know and lament the difference. Many people's ethic toward the environment is expressed in descriptions of early-life experiences of the wild that inspired their respect and desire to protect what remains. That "wild" can range from a city park, to a populated campsite or beach, to a remote mountain or forest. The common experience is of something greater than the human that shapes one's values and commitments and becomes part of one's personal identity. Is it ever too late for

[113] *Among the Bears, supra* note 5, at 353.

[114] Richard Louv, Last Child in The Woods: Saving Our Children from Nature-Deficit Disorder 31, 65-66, 137 (2008).

anyone to experience the wonder and mysteries of nature? Prison gardening, farming, and animal-raising programs show that people deprived of such experiences value them greatly. The capacity for wonder probably evolved with our humanness, as beings inherently connected with and dependent upon the natural environment. Something will be lost in the soul of our landscapes if we squeeze out the beings that retain otherness and wildness.

Black bears lack significant economic importance except in hunting revenues, limited fur trapping, and illegal trade in body parts or products such as bile, so most people do not think of the animals as having significant utility. Thus, it is hard to persuade people to preserve bears for their instrumental or use value in the way many people measure the value of nature as a resource. American black bears are faring best among all bear species,[115] so it is easy to place low priority on their protection relative to many animals on the brink. The role of large carnivores in ecological systems is thus important in promoting bear conservation. Ecological consequences follow from eradicating large animals like bears. Large carnivores are sometimes protected, or introduced into an area, because maintaining or restoring the complex and large habitat these beings require also supports the life of other animals and plants.[116] Conservation biologists sometimes consider large predators as a "tool" for preserving the biodiversity of natural systems. They are often the first species humans eradicate from a region, and their absence can indicate other risks to biodiversity.[117] This ecosystem approach is consistent with Earth jurisprudence.

At an accelerating rate, humans have encroached on wildlands with increasing populations and development, greatly curtailing the spaces left for wild beings to flourish. Some animals like bears have also entered the "human" domain to survive and have disproportionately suffered the consequences of human and nonhuman interactions. In their book, *Zoopolis: A Political Theory of Animal Rights*, Sue Donaldson and Will Kymlicka discuss the rapidly growing "liminal" places that animals such as coyotes, large cats, Canada Geese, foxes, and others now occupy.[118] "Liminal" animals are "denizens" because they normally do not seek out sociability, but rather live among us out of necessity, opportunistically, or because they have found a particular niche.[119] Wild animals in these spaces change human obligations, according to Donaldson and Kymlicka.[120] Our duties toward denizens are mostly geared to preventing harm by avoiding exploitation, allowing animals to self-regulate in habitat and reproduce within reasonable limits, limiting unwanted human contact, and respecting their security of

[115] Brown, *supra* note 36, at 281 (International Union for Conservation of Nature and Natural Resources, IUCN, classifies the American black bear as "survival ensured"; Red List, Appendix B).
[116] *Id.* at 38.
[117] Justina C. Ray, *Large Carnivorous Animals as Tools for Conserving Biodiversity: Assumptions and Uncertainties, in Large Carnivores and the Conservation of Biodiversity* 34-35, 44-45 (Justina C. Ray, Kent H. Redford, Robert S. Steneck & Joel Berger eds., 2005). at 44-45.
[118] Sue Donaldson & Will Kymlicka, Zoopolis: A Political Theory of Animal Rights 210, 219 (2011) (describing "liminal" animals as living among people neither as wild nor domesticated).
[119] *Id.* at 217-221.
[120] *Id.* at 212, 216, 220.

space.[121] Some of these duties clearly apply to bears, like Mink, entering human residential spaces. For example, Donaldson and Kymlicka discourage relocations of animals, rehabilitation of animal orphans, and feeding, or making food accessible to animals who then become "less wary of humans and are labeled 'nuisances.' "[122]

Philosopher Clare Palmer also views animal ethics as relational in her book *Animal Ethics in Context.* Palmer views human responsibility toward animals on a continuum, with the greatest duties owed to animals who are almost completely dependent on humans for their breeding, care, and daily functioning. Pets would be first candidates for such stringent responsibilities, with domesticated, captive animals a close second. Even a normally "wild" animal can be the subject of strong human obligations if removed from autonomous circumstances and made captive and dependent on humans.[123] Zoo animals would be examples. On the other hand, a feral animal, typically a pet, such as a cat or dog, functioning independently of human oversight might be farther along the continuum toward "wild."

Bears do not fall on the fully wild end of the ethical continuum, nor do they seek to be liminal. A long-term perspective shows that humans have reduced bear habitat, making increased interactions with humans inevitable. Collective human responsibilities toward bears rise with diminishing wildness. This duty must be discharged at the federal, state, and local governmental levels, with the pressure of groups and individuals committed to conserving large carnivorous species.

VI. LONG RANGE DUTIES OF AFFIRMATIVE ASSISTANCE TO BEARS

Some would object that assisting even partly wild animals is wrong, and the proper stance is to leave wild beings alone to fend for themselves. This "hands-off" attitude is entrenched to the point that it can serve as a facile excuse for inaction. Clare Palmer opens her book with a true story of tens of thousands of migrating wildebeests crossing Kenya's Mara River in a location with very steep embankments. Thousands of wildebeests perished while reporters, camera crews, and safari tourists watched and documented the debacle instead of attempting to divert the herd a short distance.[124] This event exposes the largely unquestioned attitude that wild animals should not receive human assistance and that a "let it be" principle better serves nature. Although a non-interventionist approach to the wild is a reasonable default position, there are incidences when the ease of assistance might prevent severe harm to animals, and in the case of the wildebeests, might have saved as many as 10,000 members of the species.

[121] *Id.* at 217, 227, 229, 233, 239-241 (human efforts to respect animal space, avoiding deportation and exploitation, and fairly accommodating human and animal interests).
[122] *Id.* at 243-244.
[123] Clare Palmer, Animal Ethics in Context 43, 63, 64,78, 92-95 (2010).
[124] *Id.* at 1, 2-3, 84, 89.

A compelling case for limited active assistance applies to the many American black bears in situations like Mink and her progeny. Although Mink did engage in opportunistic feeding behavior and can be seen beyond the Mink Brook Nature Reserve wandering two towns, she mostly fends for herself without relying on humans. She is not fully wild because her home range overlaps with human residences and activities, but not by her design. Generally, New England black bears are further from the wild pole than Kenyan wildebeests because humans have saturated and appropriated much of their habitat. Through negative although partially inadvertent causal influences on their ways of being, humans have acquired special duties to bears. Under Earth law principles, our duty is to repair our relations by restoring some of the damage we have wrought.

A. Duties of Habitat: Restoring Corridors

Humans owe a significant affirmative obligation to bears based on past collective actions of taking more than we needed to live comfortably, to the point of impairing the rights of these animals to be, have habitat, and fulfill their nature, three basic Earth law rights.[125] Collectively, we owe bears basic mechanisms to prevent lethal and harmful conditions. Corrective (backward-looking) justice must include recreating contiguous spaces large enough to accommodate bear migration for reproduction, seasonal foraging, and hibernation. Bounded parks will not do. Because corridors have disappeared or become fragmented through human development, urban and rural local planning projects and regional state compacts should make corridor restoration a priority.

Road mortality is a vulnerability of bears, and roads also affect habitat connectivity. Discussions about fixing this problem should be win-win for humans and animals because both perish in large-animal collisions. Heartening work is underway in some states (and Europe) to establish infrastructure to reduce this harm. Road overpasses and underpasses allow animals to cross highways and facilitate their movement for feeding and reproduction.[126] While infrastructure is expensive, the relative costs of highway injury and mortality must be considered. Human convenience has generated the elaborate system of roads that have jeopardized both animals and humans themselves. Simultaneously, human roads have cut off animal migration. The causal human impact on the nonhuman environment is a source of ethical obligation in both corrective and forward-looking justice.

B. Duties of Habitat: Land Use Planning

Overall spatial duties are more complicated. Expecting humans to set aside large enough areas to reduce bear and human contacts on a large scale is presently unrealistic because of expense and other environmental priorities, still networks of smaller

[125] Berry, *supra* note 3, at 80 (right to be, right to habitat, and right to fulfill role in natural system).
[126] *See* Starre Vartan, *How Wildlife Bridges Over Highways Make Animals – and People – Safer*, National Geographic (Apr. 16, 2019), https://www.nationalgeographic.com/animals/2019/04/wildlife-overpasses-underpasses-make-animals-people-safer/.

but connected preserves are feasible.[127] Because habitat fragmentation is a central problem for many species and ecosystems, cooperation by private landowners and use of federal and state public lands, as well as general public support, will be necessary to restore habitat.[128] Finding compromise solutions may be pragmatically important for meaningful results, and democratic processes of collaboration might facilitate environmental progress in other matters.

Particular land-use infrastructure decisions should prospectively take into account the need for sufficient relatively undisturbed habitat so that bears can meet their wide-ranging seasonal nourishment needs. For example, humans can select a location for ridgeline wind turbines that does not run through beech tree groves so bears will have a more secure source of fall nuts to build protein and fat for hibernation. Such a factor could be significant enough to alter the preferred siting of a wind energy facility.[129] Because of the historic human injustice of shrinking and fragmenting bear habitat, it is fair to compensate with extra attention to animal needs. This might mean that humans should forego the most desirable wind facility site in favor of a workable site that does less harm to wildlife. At least they should consider ways to mitigate harm in planning and designing the site they select. Preserving open spaces for bears supports many components of ecosystems, including other fauna, vegetation, and pure water sources. Such preservation serves multiple human and nonhuman purposes and supports core Earth law principles.

These land-use decisions go beyond justice and permeate all that we do as humans. The motivation goes deeper than correcting past wrongs. Albert Schweitzer, physician and theologian, urged that all individuals, to the extent of their ability, owe some affirmative assistance to other living beings simply because all life participates in the necessity of taking life for survival. The appropriate ethical response to this universal necessity is not justice, according to Schweitzer, but rather "reverence" for the unity of life. When possible, each person should improve the lives of others, even doing something as simple as rescuing an insect from a water puddle.[130]

VII. CONCLUSION

Learning to make room for nonhuman beings, including large animals saddled with stereotypes about ferocity, is a step toward reverence and a rebalanced human relationship to the nonhuman community that has gone so far astray in viewing the world from ownership and property perspectives. Humans are not separate and superior; we are privileged to inhabit diverse landscapes alongside different creatures with whom we should share basic rights. Feeling humble and grateful amidst such creatures, instead

[127] Woodroffe, *supra* note 41, at 91-92.
[128] *See, e.g.*, Beecham & Rohlman, *supra* note 42, at 90-92, 212.
[129] *See* Reed Elizabeth Loder, *Breath of Life: Ethical Wind Power and Wildlife*, 10 VT. J. ENV'L, L. 507, 510, 515, 519, 531 (2009).
[130] ALBERT SCHWEITZER, REVERENCE FOR LIFE, *IN* ENVIRONMENTAL ETHICS: READINGS IN THEORY AND APPLICATION 170-172 (Louis P. Pojman, Paul Pojman & Katie McShane eds., 7th ed., 2017).

of dominant and free to use them at will as a resource, is a vital step for planetary survival as we seek to avert irreparable damage to Earth's land, atmosphere, and waters.

Earth jurisprudence is progressing in heartening ways by shaking some legal frameworks at their cores. It is helpful to apply the visions and concepts of this perspective to more particular contexts to illustrate how the theory might work practically. The case of Mink reveals some complex overlapping factors for understanding obligations under an Earth law perspective, which is helpful in imagining cases that might come before legislators and judges. Illustrations can also impart courage to lawyers to advance bold, transformative ideas.

The development of Earth law will benefit from contextual attention to individual animals, including their dignity, a value derived from recognition of one's right to be and to realize one's nature. Individual beings should sometimes be the focus of discussions within an overall systems perspective. Making individuals prominent does not have to compromise ecosystems and processes. Improving landscapes for black bears will generate collateral improvements for forest ecology. Respecting the Earth community encompasses all components of that community. These embellishments to Earth law may inspire an even more compelling and adoptable vision.

STUDY QUESTIONS

(1) The chapter argues that our ethical obligations to animals arise in part from empathy, which allows us to recognize that animals have characteristics similar to those that create duties toward humans. Is empathy—an emotion—an appropriate foundation for legal thinking?

(2) Bears are relatively easy for humans to empathize with. Can the same argument create legal status for other natural beings? Could squirrels, insects, trees, rocks, for example, also gain legal recognition in this way?

(3) How should information from ethology and biology affect legal decision-making about bears?

(4) What affirmative duties should apply to humans in relation to wild animals such as Mink? To liminal animals such as raccoons?

(5) The chapter proposes that a planned wind turbine farm be relocated if it interferes with bears' needs to gather nuts. What would happen if there were no other suitable locations for a planned infrastructure project? Do humans have priority over bears? What constraints would the view of Earth law described in this chapter place on humans when converting a part of nature to their own use?

(6) This chapter describes a duty to restore damaged natural habitat in order to remedy past abuses. How would this work in practice in a legal context?

CHAPTER 15

United Nations Sustainable Development Initiatives[1]

I. INTRODUCTION

Sustainable development is currently the predominant global model for protecting the environment while ensuring quality of life for humans. Efforts to promote sustainable development are taking place primarily within the United Nations (UN), a truly international governance body comprising 193 states. While non-governmental bodies continue to proliferate, in a global system based on the ultimate authority of sovereign states, the authority and power remains with the UN. Historically, the UN has taken a lead role in protecting the environment, starting from its sponsorship of the 1972 Stockholm Conference and then in subsequent global environmental conferences. It has drafted and negotiated the vast majority of post-1972 international environmental conventions, as well as a substantial number of soft law instruments comprising today's global environmental toolbox.

Yet, as discussed in this chapter, sustainable development is dominated by anthropocentrism. Sustainable development is for the betterment of people. Nature's value is rated by the services it supplies to humans, rather than for its own inherent worth. UN efforts to move beyond sustainable development to an Earth law paradigm have been minimal, and UN policy, determined by its member states, continues to promote economic growth and development. UN initiatives currently underway for promoting Earth law and rights of nature are taking place within the "Harmony with Nature" initiative, promoting a biocentric approach to implementing the UN Sustainable Development Goals, through resolutions of the UN General Assembly (UNGA), and hosting Harmony with Nature dialogues on the relationship between humans and nature.[2]

This chapter is divided into two main parts. The first explores the benefits and shortcomings of UN sustainable development initiatives as well as emerging principles in the field, including harmony with nature. The second part explores the Global Pact

[1] Authored by Earth Law Center; Yann Aguila, a partner at Bredin Prat (Paris) and chair of the Environmental Law Commission of the *Club des Juristes*; and Shehana Gomez, associate lecturer at the Open University and co-convener of the UK Environmental Law Association's wild law special interest group.

[2] United Nations, *Chronology*, Harmony with Nature, http://www.harmonywithnatureun.org/chronology/ (last visited Mar. 6, 2020).

for the Environment, a proposed international treaty that would strengthen state duties to protect nature.

II. OVERVIEW OF THE UNITED NATIONS

The UN was founded in 1945 in the aftermath of World War II. Beyond its globally-recognized leadership in issues of peace, security, and human rights, its reach includes activities through specialized agencies as diverse as the World Health Organization and the World Bank. The United Nations Environmental Programme (UNEP) promotes and coordinates the United Nations' environmental initiatives.

The UN Charter establishes six principal organs: the General Assembly, the Security Council, the Economic and Social Council, the Trusteeship Council, the International Court of Justice, and the Secretariat.[3] Of those, the Economic and Social Council bears primary responsibility for implementing sustainable development.[4] The General Assembly comprises all 193 member nations and is the main deliberative and policymaking organ of the United Nations.[5]

Notable UN-related bodies active in areas related to Earth law are UNEP, the United Nations Development Program (UNDP), the Intergovernmental Panel on Climate Change (IPCC), the High-level Political Forum on Sustainable Development (High-level Political Forum or HLPF), the UN Forum on Forests, and the United Nations Program on Harmony with Nature, among others.

Earth law may be developed by forging a new social contract that involves both humans and nature. The United Nations is playing an important role in the development of this contract, and that role is the subject of this chapter.

III. UNITED NATIONS SUSTAINABILITY EFFORTS

Sustainable development is the defining paradigm of UN environmental work. The famous definition given by the 1987 Brundtland Report is that "sustainable development meets the needs of current generations without compromising the ability of future generations to meet their needs as well."[6] This section reviews the origins of that goal and UN progress to achieve it in chronological order, beginning with the 1972 Stockholm Conference for the Human Environment ending with the 2019 session of the High-level Political Forum.

[3] UN Charter, Art. 8.

[4] United Nations, *About Us,* United Nations Economic and Social Council, https://www.un.org/ecosoc/en/about-us (last visited Mar. 6, 2020).

[5] United Nations, *Role of the General Assembly,* United Nations Peacekeeping, https://peacekeeping.un.org/en/role-of-general-assembly (last visited Mar. 6, 2020).

[6] World Commission on Environment and Development, *Our Common Future* 37 (WCED 1987) ["the Brundtland Report"].

A. United Nations Conference on the Human Environment, Stockholm 1972

The 1972 UN Conference on the Human Environment (UNCHE), or the Stockholm Conference, was the UN's first environmental megaconference. It sought to address global environmental and conservation issues, focusing on escalating industrial pollution and its impact on the environment.[7]

Because the conference was the initiative of the developed world, the UNCHE generated deep suspicion among developing countries. Many viewed the Stockholm Conference as a plot of developed countries to solve the environmental problems that they had created by their high standard of living (dependent on ravenous consumption of natural resources) by denying developing countries a right to develop and achieve the same standard of living.[8] The suspicion with which developing countries responded to the UNCHE was also rooted in the fierce guard that they had adopted against perceived threats to their national sovereignty.[9]

Prior to the conference, as an outlet for the increasing tension, UNCHE Secretary-General Maurice Strong convened a meeting on environment and development held in Founex, Switzerland. This sparked the earliest major discussions on sustainable development. The meeting's outcome document, the Founex Report on Development and Environment, found that the environmental devastation of developing countries derives from poverty, in sharp contrast to developed countries, whose pollution derives from the excesses of development and who can "afford" conservation.[10] Addressing environmental problems of developing countries meant economic development, which developed countries should help them achieve.[11]

Addressing global needs while recognizing the unique challenges of developing countries became a key theme of the Stockholm Conference. The key output was the Stockholm Declaration, which contains 26 principles "to inspire and guide the peoples of the world in the preservation and enhancement of the human environment."[12] Principle 11 epitomized the viewpoint of many developing countries: "The environmental policies of all States should enhance and not adversely affect the present or future development potential of developing countries, nor should they hamper the attainment of better living conditions for all. . . ."

[7] The Problems of the Human Environment, G.A. Res. 2398 (XXIII) (Dec. 3, 1968).

[8] Martin Holdgate, The Green Web 111 (1999).

[9] Susan Bragdon, *National Sovereignty and Global Environmental Responsibility: Can the Tension Be Reconciled for the Convention on Biological Diversity?,* 33 Harvard Int'l L.J. 381, 383 (1992).

[10] *See* United Nations, Development and Environment ("Founex Report"), Report of a Panel of Experts convened by the Secretary-General of the UN Conference on the Environment, June 4-12, 1971.

[11] *See* Report Submitted by a Panel of Experts Convened by the Secretary-General of the UNCHE, *Maurice Strong Papers,* 40/395 (June 4-12, 1971).

[12] United Nations Conference on the Human Environment, *Declaration of the United Nations Conference on the Human Environment,* UN Doc. A/CONF.48/14/Rev.1 (June 5-16, 1972).

The Stockholm Declaration is at times unabashedly anthropocentric. Consider the following excerpt from the preamble, which is rooted in human superiority over nature:

> The natural growth of population continuously presents problems for the preservation of the environment, and adequate policies and measures should be adopted, as appropriate, to face these problems. *Of all things in the world, people are the most precious.* It is the people that propel social progress, create social wealth, develop science and technology and, through their hard work, continuously transform the human environment. Along with social progress and the advance of production, science and technology, *the capability of man to improve the environment increases with each passing day.*[13]

While Stockholm Declaration principles call for environmental protections, they are often tempered with human-centered perspectives and a right to pollute. Some of these include Principle 2 (calling for safeguarding to flora and fauna but only "for the benefit of present and future generations"), Principle 6 (calling for a halt to toxic and other discharges but only where they exceed the assimilative capacity of the environment), and Principle 21 ("States have, in accordance with the Charter of the United Nations and the principles of international law, the sovereign right to exploit their own resources pursuant to their own environmental policies . . .").

The Stockholm conference also afforded an opportunity for the UN to promote international environmental law. Three international biodiversity agreements reached the final UNCHE agenda: the 1971 Ramsar Convention on Wetlands of International Importance, and the draft texts of the future 1972 World Heritage Convention and the 1973 Convention on International Trade in Endangered Species of Wild Fauna and Flora (CITES). The 1972 Convention for the Prevention of Marine Pollution by Dumping of Wastes and Other Matter (London Convention) was also on the UNCHE's agenda.

The UNCHE's emphasis on international conventions was repeated at a later UN environmental megaconference: The 1992 UNCED Rio Summit, which opened for signing both the Convention on Biological Diversity (CBD) and the UN Framework Convention on Climate Change (UNFCCC). The CBD promotes biological conservation and sustainable use along with fair and equitable sharing of genetic resources. The UNFCCC is the framework agreement for combating climate change under which the 2015 Paris Agreement was negotiated and adopted.

B. World Charter for Nature, 1982

In 1982, the UN General Assembly adopted the World Charter for Nature, the work of the International Union for Conservation of Nature (IUCN), the world's largest environmental network. In stark contrast to the Stockholm Declaration, the World Charter for Nature adopts an ecocentric or "deep sustainability" view and remains the UN's

[13] *Id.* at preamble.

strongest statement on the integrity of nature.[14] The charter dates from the IUCN's 1975 Twelfth General Assembly in Kinshasa, Zaire, where President Mobutu of Zaire raised the idea while pointedly blaming developed countries for environmental problems that arise from colonialism and capitalism:

> Industrialized countries put the blame on those who have not yet reached that stage, for not controlling the growth of their populations. . . . At the same time, however, they forget that their populations, although representing one-third of mankind, consume ninety percent of the planet's resources. . . . We, who have been colonized, were taught that civilization of our former masters was the best one. . . . the crisis is one of civilization. . . . Thanks to zairianisation, we have become the owners of our lands. . . . If I had any advice for you, I would suggest the establishment of a Charter of Nature . . . insofar as Zaire is concerned, we are ready to help you succeed. . . . The jungle of liberal capitalism is finished. Every citizen in this world must defend his heritage, the area in which he lives, against those modern savages, the killers of Nature who do not hesitate to slaughter her to swell their wallets."[15]

Following Mobutu's proposal, the same IUCN General Assembly adopted a resolution recommending that governments promote a World Charter for Nature. UN General Assembly deliberations began shortly thereafter.[16] While many African countries were supportive of the initiative in light of Zaire's leading role,[17] Latin American countries believed the charter favored conservation over social and economic needs. As it had done in debates surrounding the Stockholm Conference, Brazil framed the debate as the Global North's exploitation of the Global South's natural resources. However, in the end, the charter's vision of a more harmonious relationship with nature prevailed, and the UN General Assembly adopted the charter by a vote of 111-1 with 18 abstentions. The United States was the only "no" vote.

The Charter calls upon a moral code of conduct to guide human action in a way that treats other organisms with respect. It was perhaps the first official UN document to use the concept of "harmony with nature" in its preamble. The following are key excerpts from the Charter.

World Charter for Nature

UN GA RES 37/7

The General Assembly,

Reaffirming the fundamental purposes of the United Nations

[14] 1982 World Charter for Nature, G.A. Res. 37/7 (Oct. 28, 1982).

[15] IUCN G.A., 12th Sess., Conf. 3 at 217-222, Supplementary Paper No 44-E (Sept. 8-18, 1975).

[16] Peru cautioned that "the use and exploitation of all natural resources of each country constitute a right inherent in the sovereignty of each state, emphasizing socio-economic development." *Id.* at 25. Also, Argentina warned that "the principle of sovereignty of States . . . is at stake." *Id.* at 19, 29, 34.

[17] The charter had received significant support from African nations; in submitting the draft charter Zaire represented 31 African countries. *Id.*

Aware that:

(a) Mankind is a part of nature and life depends on the uninterrupted functioning of natural systems which ensure the supply of energy and nutrients,

(b) Civilization is rooted in nature, which has shaped human culture and influenced all artistic and scientific achievements, and living in harmony with nature gives man the best opportunities for the development of his creativity, and for rest and recreation,

Convinced that:

(a) Every form of life is unique, warranting respect regardless of its worth to man, and, to accord other organisms such recognition, man must be guided by a moral code of action. . . .

Persuaded that:

(a) Lasting benefits from nature depend upon the maintenance of essential ecological processes and life support systems, and upon the diversity of life forms, which are jeopardized through excessive exploitation and habitat destruction by man,

(b) The degradation of natural systems owing to excessive consumption and misuse of natural resources, as well as to failure to establish an appropriate economic order among peoples and among States, leads to the breakdown of the economic, social and political framework of civilization.

. . .

Adopts, to these ends, the present World Charter for Nature, which proclaims the following principles of conservation by which all human conduct affecting nature is to be guided and judged.

I. General Principles

1. Nature shall be respected and its essential processes shall not be impaired.

2. The genetic viability on the earth shall not be compromised; the population levels of all life forms, wild and domesticated, must be at least sufficient for their survival, and to this end necessary habitat shall be safeguarded.

3. All areas of the earth, both land and sea, shall be subject to these principles of conservation; special protection shall be given to unique areas, to representative samples of all the different types of ecosystems and to the habitat of rare or endangered species.

4. Ecosystems and organisms, as well as the land, marine and atmospheric resources that are utilized by man, shall be managed to achieve and maintain optimum sustainable productivity, but not in such a way as to endanger the integrity of those other ecosystems or species with which they coexist.

. . .

II. Functions

6. In the decision-making process it shall be recognized that man's needs can be met only by ensuring the proper functioning of natural systems and by respecting the principles set forth in the present Charter.

. . .

III. Implementation

14. The principles set forth in the present Charter shall be reflected in the law and practice of each State, as well as at the international level. . . .

. . .

21. States and, to the extent they are able, other public authorities, international organizations, individuals, groups and corporations shall: . . .

(d) Ensure that activities within their jurisdictions or control do not cause damage to the natural systems located within other States or in the areas beyond the limits of national jurisdiction;

(e) Safeguard and conserve nature in areas beyond national jurisdiction.

. . .

22. Taking fully into account the sovereignty of States over their natural resources, each State shall give effect to the provisions of the present Charter through its competent organs and in co-operation with other States.

* * *

While the 1982 World Charter for Nature declared that "Nature shall be respected and its essential processes shall not be impaired," the 1987 Brundtland Report, which launched the current global model of sustainable development, largely contradicts these principles by emphasizing development over protection of the environment. We read about this next.

C. Brundtland Report, 1987

The 1987 Report of the World Commission on Environment and Development: Our Common Future, also called the Brundtland Report, was an attempt to reconcile the objectives of economic development and protection of the environment. The report argued that sustainable development could be achieved through the "three pillars": economic growth, social equality, and environmental sustainability. It also focused on the need to eradicate poverty as a fundamental requirement of sustainable development. While this was not the first time the term "sustainable development" had been used, the term entered the global lexicon as a result of this report.

The chairperson of the commission, Prime Minister Gro Harlem Brundtland of Norway, candidly acknowledged the tension of sustainable development. These were, among others, tensions between rich nations and poor nations, between global governance and national sovereignty, between economic development and environment, and between economic growth and equity. Ms. Brundtland described the approach taken by the commission in resolving this conflict as follows:

> When the terms of reference of our Commission were originally being discussed in 1982, there were those who wanted its considerations to be limited to "environmental issues" only. This would have been a grave mistake. The environment does not exist as a sphere separate from human actions, ambitions, and needs, and attempts to defend it in isolation from human concerns have given the very word "environment" a connotation of naivety in some political circles. The word "development" has also been narrowed by some into a very limited focus, along the lines of "what poor nations should do to become richer"...
>
> But the "environment" is where we all live; and "development" is what we all do in attempting to improve our lot within that abode. The two are inseparable.... Further, development issues must be seen as crucial by the political leaders who feel that their countries have reached a plateau towards which other nations must strive. Many of the development paths of the industrialized nations are clearly unsustainable. And the development decisions of these countries, because of their great economic and political power, will have a profound effect upon the ability of all peoples to sustain human progress for generations to come....[18]

Thus, from the beginning, sustainable development has been a compromise between those who want to privilege the environment and those who want to privilege economic development. Economic development would be primary, and social and environmental concerns would condition development. As with many of the environmental laws critiqued in Chapter 1, "Modern Environmental Law," sustainable development was born from an undeniably anthropocentric and economy-focused paradigm. This model largely persists today.

D. United Nations Conference on Environment and Development, Rio de Janeiro, 1992

The 1992 Earth Summit (also known as the Rio Conference) was a watershed moment in international environmental law. In attendance were 172 governments, including 108 heads of state, as well as huge numbers of civil society groups.[19] Building on the Brundtland Report, the Earth Summit set forth a comprehensive agenda—over 300 pages

[18] The Brundtland Report, *supra* note 6.

[19] United Nations, *Outcomes on Sustainable Development*, https://www.un.org/en/development/devagenda/sustainable.shtml (last visited Mar. 11, 2020).

long—for sustainable development called Agenda 21: Programme of Action for Sustainable Development (Agenda 21).[20] The conference's short outcome document was called the Rio Declaration.

While the Rio Declaration emphasizes the need to protect nature, Principle 1 makes clear that human interests are paramount: "Human beings are at the centre of concerns for sustainable development. They are entitled to a healthy and productive life in harmony with nature." The declaration goes on to highlight common environmental concepts such as the precautionary principle (Principle 15), the polluter pays principle (Principle 16), and the need for environmental impact statements (Principle 17), among others. One other principle that has gained significant traction in recent years is Principle 10 on environmental access rights: access to information, access to public participation, and access to justice, as key pillars of sound environmental governance. This principle is the basis of two subsequent treaties: the 1998 Aarhus Convention in Europe[21] and the 2018 Escazú Agreement in Latin America.[22]

Beyond Agenda 21 and the Rio Declaration, the Earth Summit produced the Forest Principles, a nonbinding document on the conservation and sustainable use of forests.[23] Further, the UNFCCC and the CBD were both opened for signature. Finally, based on a recommendation contained in Agenda 21, the UN Commission on Sustainable Development was established shortly after the conference. It led the UN's sustainable development efforts until it was replaced by the High-level Political Forum in 2013.

E. Millennium Summit and the Millennium Development Goals 2000

The September 2000 UN Millennium Summit was held in New York over a three-day period at the UN headquarters in New York. Attended by 149 heads of state and high-ranking officials, its primary purpose was a show of strength for the United Nations at the start of the 21st century. The key output of the Summit was the Millennium Declaration, adopted by the UN General Assembly three days later.[24] While this declaration mostly relates to economic and human development, it also addresses environmental concerns. Section I, "Values and principles" opens as follows:

> 1. We, heads of State and Government, have gathered at United Nations Headquarters in New York from 6 to 8 September 2000, at the dawn of a new millennium, to reaffirm

[20] United Nations Conference on Environment and Development, *Agenda 21: Earth Summit—The United Nations Programme of Action from Rio,* 9, UN Doc A/CONF.151/26/Rev.1 (Vol. I) (June 3-14, 1992).

[21] Aarhus Convention of June 25, 1998, 2161 U.N.T.S. 447. Formally the "UNECE Convention on Access to Information, Public Participation in Decision-making and Access to Justice in Environmental Matters."

[22] Escazú Agreement C.N.195.2018.TREATIES-XXVII.18 of 9 April 2018. Formally the "Regional Agreement on Access to Information, Public Participation and Justice in Environmental Matters in Latin America and the Caribbean."

[23] United Nations Conference on Environment and Development. *Non-Legally Binding Authoritative Statement of Principles for a Global Consensus on the Management, Conservation and Sustainable Development of All Types of Forests,* A/CONF.151/26 (Vol. III) 480 (June 3-14, 1992).

[24] United Nations Millennium Declaration, G.A. Res. 55/2 (Sept. 8, 2000).

our faith in the Organization and its Charter as indispensable foundations of a more peaceful, prosperous and just world.

...

IV. Protecting our common environment.

21. We must spare no effort to free all of humanity, and above all our children and grandchildren, from the threat of living on a planet irredeemably spoilt by human activities, and whose resources would no longer be sufficient for their needs.

22. We reaffirm our support for the principles of sustainable development, including those set out in Agenda 21, agreed upon at the United Nations Conference on Environment and Development.

23. We resolve therefore to adopt in all our environmental actions a new ethic of conservation and stewardship and, as first steps, we resolve:...

- To intensify our collective efforts for the management, conservation and sustainable development of all types of forests.
- To press for the full implementation of the Convention on Biological Diversity and the Convention to Combat Desertification in those Countries Experiencing Serious Drought and/or Desertification, particularly in Africa.
- To stop the unsustainable exploitation of water resources by developing water management strategies at the regional, national and local levels, which promote both equitable access and adequate supplies....

* * *

Drawing on the Millennium Declaration, the world leaders who participated in the Summit adopted the Millennium Development Goals (MDGs). Eight goals were to be reached by the year 2015:

(1) eradicate extreme poverty and hunger;
(2) achieve universal primary education;
(3) promote gender equality and empower women;
(4) reduce child mortality;
(5) improve maternal health;
(6) combat HIV/AIDS, malaria and other diseases;
(7) ensure environmental sustainability; and
(8) develop a global partnership for development.

In 2002, the Secretary-General of the UN and the administrator of the UN Development program launched the Millennium Project to support the MDGs in meeting their target date of 2015. Beginning in 2012, the UN began a process to develop the Post-2015 Agenda. This effort led to the SDGs, or, sustainable development goals, adopted in 2015, which supplanted the MDGs and placed a greater emphasis on the environment (*see* subsection I).

F. The Earth Charter (2000)

In 2000, the United Nations Educational, Scientific and Cultural Organization (UNESCO) adopted the Earth Charter[25] at its headquarters in Paris. The Earth Charter is "... an ethical framework for building a just, sustainable, and peaceful global society in the 21st century...."[26] The Earth Charter rejects anthropocentrism in its goal "to inspire in all people a new sense of global interdependence and shared responsibility for the well-being of the whole human family, the greater community of life, and future generations."[27] While not an official UN document, it is regarded as an important statement of environmental values by UNESCO and has since been endorsed by thousands of organizations representing millions of people.[28] As you read the following Earth Charter principles, consider how they differ from the sustainable development mandate of Agenda 21, the MDGs, and so forth:

The Earth Charter

PRINCIPLES

I. RESPECT AND CARE FOR THE COMMUNITY OF LIFE

1. Respect Earth and life in all its diversity.

   a. Recognize that all beings are interdependent and every form of life has value regardless of its worth to human beings.

   b. Affirm faith in the inherent dignity of all human beings and in the intellectual, artistic, ethical, and spiritual potential of humanity.

...

4. Secure Earth's bounty and beauty for present and future generations.

   a. Recognize that the freedom of action of each generation is qualified by the needs of future generations.

   b. Transmit to future generations values, traditions, and institutions that support the long-term flourishing of Earth's human and ecological communities....

...

[25] Earth Charter Commission, *The Earth Charter* (2000), https://earthcharter.org/discover/the-earth-charter/ (last visited Mar. 6, 2020).
[26] *Id.*
[27] Earth Charter, *The Earth Charter Global Movement*, https://earthcharter.org/act (last visited Mar. 11, 2020).
[28] Earth Charter, *History of the Earth Charter*, https://earthcharter.org/discover/history-of-the-earth-charter (last visited Mar. 14, 2020).

7. Adopt patterns of production, consumption, and reproduction that safeguard Earth's regenerative capacities, human rights, and community well-being.

a. Reduce, reuse, and recycle the materials used in production and consumption systems, and ensure that residual waste can be assimilated by ecological systems.

b. Act with restraint and efficiency when using energy, and rely increasingly on renewable energy sources such as solar and wind.

c. Promote the development, adoption, and equitable transfer of environmentally sound technologies.

d. Internalize the full environmental and social costs of goods and services in the selling price, and enable consumers to identify products that meet the highest social and environmental standards.

e. Ensure universal access to health care that fosters reproductive health and responsible reproduction.

f. Adopt lifestyles that emphasize the quality of life and material sufficiency in a finite world.

. . .

III. SOCIAL AND ECONOMIC JUSTICE

9. Eradicate poverty as an ethical, social, and environmental imperative.

a. Guarantee the right to potable water, clean air, food security, uncontaminated soil, shelter, and safe sanitation, allocating the national and international resources required.

b. Empower every human being with the education and resources to secure a sustainable livelihood, and provide social security and safety nets for those who are unable to support themselves.

c. Recognize the ignored, protect the vulnerable, serve those who suffer, and enable them to develop their capacities and to pursue their aspirations.

. . .

IV. DEMOCRACY, NONVIOLENCE, AND PEACE

14. Integrate into formal education and life-long learning the knowledge, values, and skills needed for a sustainable way of life.

a. Provide all, especially children and youth, with educational opportunities that empower them to contribute actively to sustainable development.

b. Promote the contribution of the arts and humanities as well as the sciences in sustainability education.

c. Enhance the role of the mass media in raising awareness of ecological and social challenges.

d. Recognize the importance of moral and spiritual education for sustainable living.

15. Treat all living beings with respect and consideration.

a. Prevent cruelty to animals kept in human societies and protect them from suffering.

b. Protect wild animals from methods of hunting, trapping, and fishing that cause extreme, prolonged, or avoidable suffering.

c. Avoid or eliminate to the full extent possible the taking or destruction of non-targeted species.

. . .

G. World Summit on Sustainable Development, Johannesburg, 2002

The 2002 World Summit on Sustainable Development (WSSD) in Johannesburg was the third UN megaconference on the environment. In the ten years following the Rio Summit, the global environmental crisis had worsened, and the implementation of the Rio Declaration and Agenda 21 were deemed to be inadequate. The summit's planners decided to reinvigorate their sustainable development commitment with a focus on five priorities: water and sanitation, energy, health, agriculture, and biodiversity. The summit adopted the Johannesburg Declaration on Human Development, a general statement of political commitment to sustainable development, and the Johannesburg Plan of Implementation, which included a specific timetable to achieve their goals.[29] Unlike the previous two megaconferences, no initiatives were taken for negotiating new environmental conventions.[30]

Despite these agreements, the summit was considered by many to be a setback on environmental issues. For example, the implementation plan adopted at the summit was criticized by the Heinrich Böll Foundation "for not having real new commitments, targets and funding for implementation provided." Critics also argued that the summit continued to promote unfettered economic growth as the main strategy to alleviate poverty instead of advancing new economic models that better support sustainability.[31]

[29] World Summit on Sustainable Development, *Johannesburg Declaration on Sustainable Development*, A/CONF.199/20, (September 4, 2002), http://www.un-documents.net/jburgdec.htm.

[30] David Hunter, James E. Saltzman, & Durwood Zaelke, International Environmental Law & Policy 181 (2015).

[31] *See, e.g.*, "What Are the Outcomes of the World Summit?" (2002), http://www.worldsummit2002.org/ (accessed June 10, 2012).

Against this backdrop, some countries began to call for new international frameworks that would better protect the environment, including the UN Harmony with Nature Initiative, as discussed next.

H. The UN Harmony with Nature Initiative

Alongside its agenda for sustainable development, the UN has also taken steps to build awareness of Earth law concepts. In 2009, the UNGA approved a resolution proclaiming April 22 as International Mother Earth Day. The following excerpts are from the statement of then President of Bolivia Evo Morales to the General Assembly on living in harmony with nature:

UN General Assembly
80th plenary meeting, Wednesday, 22 April 2009

Statement of President Evo Morales, Bolivia

> We recall that, in past centuries, there was a continuous struggle for human rights.... [W]ith today's declaration of International Mother Earth Day, planet Earth, Mother Earth, has also won her rights. And this new century, the twenty-first, should be the century of Mother Earth's rights. [...] If we are to live in harmony with nature, we need to recognize that not only we human beings have rights, but that the planet does as well. Animals, plants and all living beings have rights that we must respect. What is happening to us now with climate change is the direct result of not respecting the rights of Mother Earth.
>
> The United Nations must ensure that the rights of Mother Earth and of all living beings are respected.... Many people, in particular certain lawyers—forgive me for saying so—will say that only human beings have rights. In our view, it is difficult to accept that. [...] Another important thing that I would like to point out is the importance of coexisting with nature, because human life is not possible without Mother Earth. [...] In Bolivia, in particular among the local Indigenous peoples that I am familiar with, Mother Earth is sacred to life. That is why we undertake sacred rituals of tribute to our rivers, forests, lakes and animals and have many tunes to express our respect for Mother Earth. [...]
>
> I would like to propose four rights of great importance to humankind.
>
> - First is the right to life. [...] We human beings must recognize that Mother Earth and all living beings have a right to exist and that our rights end when we set off the extinction or elimination of nature.
> - Second is the right of regeneration for the planet's biocapacity. [...] Human activity on the planet and its resources cannot be unlimited. Development cannot be infinite. [...]
> - Third is the right to a clean life. That means the right of Mother Earth to live without pollution....
> - Fourth is the right to harmony and balance with and among all and everything....
>
> Until now, human beings have been prisoners of development capitalism, which states that man is the sole owner of the planet. Now it is time to recognize that the Earth

does not belong to us. It is the other way around: we belong to the Earth, and it is our mission in the world to watch over the rights, not only of human beings, but of Mother Earth and of all living beings.

* * *

Later that year, in December 2009, the UN General Assembly adopted its first resolution on Harmony with Nature:

Resolution adopted by the General Assembly on 21 December 2009
64/196. Harmony with Nature

The General Assembly, Expressing its concern over the documented environmental degradation and the negative impact on nature resulting from human activity, Recalling the 1982 World Charter for Nature, Reaffirming the Rio Declaration on Environment and Development, Reaffirming also Agenda 21 . . . the Johannesburg Declaration on Sustainable Development and the Plan of Implementation of the World Summit on Sustainable Development . . .

Convinced that humanity can and should live in harmony with nature,

1. Invites Member States, the relevant organizations of the United Nations system, and international, regional and subregional organizations to consider, as appropriate, the issue of promoting life in harmony with nature and to transmit to the Secretary-General their views, experiences and proposals on this issue;

. . .

3. Decides to include in the provisional agenda of its sixty-fifth session a sub-item entitled "Harmony with Nature", under the item entitled "Sustainable development". . . .[32]

* * *

Universal Declaration of the Rights of Mother Earth

Just one year after President Morales made his impassioned speech for protecting Mother Earth to the UN General Assembly, in April 2010, Bolivia held the first World People's Conference on Climate Change and the Rights of Mother Earth in Cochabamba. This gathering included over 35,000 people representing 140 countries—civil society leaders, 56 governmental delegations, Indigenous peoples, climate activists, and others—all of whom sought bold collective action after the failures

[32] *See* full resolution at https://undocs.org/A/RES/64/196.

of the 2009 Climate Change Conference in Copenhagen (COP 15). Among the initiatives presented at the World People's Conference was a Universal Declaration for the Rights of Mother Earth (UDRME), which called for the UN and all countries to recognize the rights of nature.

The UDRME asserts that the rights of nature arise from its very existence on the planet. Its preamble recognizes the "critical importance and urgency of taking decisive, collective action to prevent humans causing climate change and other impacts on Mother Earth that threaten the wellbeing and survival of humans and other beings." It then goes onto describe the specific rights held by Mother Earth. Some of the recognized rights include the right to life and to exist (Art. 2(1)(a), the right to be respected (Art. 2(1)(b)), the right to integral health (Art. 2(1)(g), and the right to full and prompt restoration for violation of the rights recognized (Art. 2(1)(j)).

A petition for the UN to adopt the Universal Declaration of the Rights of Mother Earth has gained almost 300,000 signatures. It also continues to guide rights of nature developments worldwide.

Building from International Mother Earth Day, the UN began hosting "interactive dialogues" that brought together global experts on harmony with nature, including many Earth law practitioners. The first dialogue, in December 2010, convened to support the UN Conference on Sustainable Development in Brazil (2012) by providing guidance on best practices to promote a holistic approach to sustainable development in harmony with nature, as well as criteria and indicators to measure progress.[33]

Since then, an interactive dialogue has occurred annually on Mother Earth Day. Each dialogue is preceded by a report of the Secretary-General on Harmony with Nature and then followed by a Resolution on Harmony with Nature that is adopted by the UN General Assembly. All of this work is informed by a body of experts, called Knowledge Network Experts, who keep the UN apprised of global developments on living in harmony with nature. These interactive dialogues, reports, and resolutions, along with the Knowledge Network Experts, serve as the foundation of the Harmony with Nature Initiative at the United Nations.

Unlike most UN programs, the Harmony with Nature Initiative acknowledges ecocentric legal movements worldwide and builds knowledge and capacity around their growth. Consider how the 2011 resolution on Harmony with Nature ties in UN sustainability work to Earth law principles you have read about in this book:

[33] UN Doc A/RES/65/164 (Dec. 2010).

Resolution adopted by the General Assembly on 22 December 2011
66/204. Harmony with Nature

The General Assembly,

Expressing concern about documented environmental degradation and the negative impact on nature resulting from human activity, and recognizing the need to strengthen scientific knowledge on the effects of human activities on ecosystems,

Recognizing that gross domestic product was not designed as an indicator for measuring environmental degradation resulting from human activity and the need to overcome this limitation with regard to sustainable development and the work carried out in this regard,

. . .

Reaffirming that fundamental changes in the way societies produce and consume are indispensable for achieving global sustainable development and that all countries should promote sustainable consumption and production patterns, with the developed countries taking the lead and with all countries benefiting from the process, taking into account the Rio principles, including the principle of common but differentiated responsibilities, as set out in principle 7 of the Rio Declaration on Environment and Development,

Recognizing that many ancient civilizations and Indigenous cultures have a rich history of understanding the symbiotic connection between human beings and nature that fosters a mutually beneficial relationship,

. . . .

6. Encourages all countries and the relevant bodies of the United Nations system to develop and strengthen the quality and quantity of basic statistical data on the three pillars of sustainable development, and invites the international community and the pertinent bodies of the United Nations system to assist the efforts of developing countries by providing capacity-building and technical support;

7. Invites the relevant entities of the United Nations system to work with other relevant actors, including non-governmental organizations, experts and the academic community, as appropriate, both to identify new ways and means to overcome the limitations of gross domestic product with regard to sustainable development and to better measure the environmental degradation resulting from human activity;[34] . . .

* * *

[34] G.A. Res. 66/204, at 1-3 (Dec. 22, 2011).

The 2012 Resolution on Harmony with Nature goes even further by acknowledging, although not explicitly endorsing, the global movement for the rights of nature:

Resolution adopted by the General Assembly on 21 December 2012
67/214. Harmony with Nature

The General Assembly,

. . .

4. Welcomes the launching of the Harmony with Nature website on the occasion of the United Nations Conference on Sustainable Development...

5. Recognizes that planet Earth and its ecosystems are our home and that "Mother Earth" is a common expression in a number of countries and regions, and that some countries recognize the rights of nature in the context of the promotion of sustainable development, and is convinced that, in order to achieve a just balance among the economic, social and environmental needs of present and future generations, it is necessary to promote harmony with nature;

6. Calls for holistic and integrated approaches to sustainable development that will guide humanity to live in harmony with nature and lead to efforts to restore the health and integrity of the Earth's ecosystems;

12. Recognizes the need for broader measures of progress to complement gross domestic product in order to better inform policy decisions, and in this regard notes the ongoing work of the Statistical Commission on a work programme to develop broader measures of progress and to conduct a technical review of existing efforts in this area;[35]...

* * *

In sum, the UN Harmony with Nature Initiative attempts to direct global sustainability efforts towards new paradigms of law and culture that would allow humans to live in harmony with nature. This program serves as an imperative link between UN sustainability work and Earth law.

Continuing in chronological order, we now turn back to the UN's more conventional sustainable development work, picking up at the next UN megaconference on sustainable development: Rio+20.

I. United Nations Conference on Sustainable Development (Rio+20)—Rio de Janeiro, 2012

The United Nations Conference on Sustainable Development (UNCSD), or Rio+20, was the third megaconference on sustainable development. As with the previous conferences, its goal was to balance global economic and environmental goals. The

[35] G.A. Res. 67/214, at 3 (Dec. 21, 2012).

outcome document of Rio+20, entitled The Future We Want, sets out new measures to implement sustainable development. Importantly, it called for Sustainable Development Goals (SDGs) that would build from the existing MDGs to implement a post-2015 development agenda. Consider the following excerpt from The Future We Want that largely reaffirms the sustainable development mandate that has prevailed since the Stockholm Conference in 1972:

> 1. We, the Heads of State and Government and high-level representatives, having met at Rio de Janeiro, Brazil, from 20 to 22 June 2012, with the full participation of civil society, renew our commitment to sustainable development and to ensuring the promotion of an economically, socially and environmentally sustainable future for our planet and for present and future generations.
>
> 2. Eradicating poverty is the greatest global challenge facing the world today and an indispensable requirement for sustainable development. In this regard we are committed to freeing humanity from poverty and hunger as a matter of urgency.
>
> 3. We therefore acknowledge the need to further mainstream sustainable development at all levels, integrating economic, social and environmental aspects and recognizing their interlinkages, so as to achieve sustainable development in all its dimensions.

Despite its emphasis on existing commitments rather than forging new ones, the Future We Want did pay homage to harmony with nature:

> 39. We recognize that planet Earth and its ecosystems are our home and that "Mother Earth" is a common expression in a number of countries and regions, and we note that some countries recognize the rights of nature in the context of the promotion of sustainable development. We are convinced that in order to achieve a just balance among the economic, social and environmental needs of present and future generations, it is necessary to promote harmony with nature. We call for holistic and integrated approaches to sustainable development that will guide humanity to live in harmony with nature and lead to efforts to restore the health and integrity of the Earth's ecosystem.

1. Peoples' sustainability treaties

Rio+20 was considered a highly inclusive megaconference, with 44,000 badges issued for official meetings, most of those going to members of civil society. However, many civil society groups were concerned that state actors in Rio were advancing a weak international agenda on sustainable development. To provide a stronger vision of sustainability, a consultative process with hundreds of civil society organizations resulted in fourteen "Peoples' Sustainability Treaties" that set a bold agenda for achieving a sustainable world.[36] One of these was a Peoples' Sustainability Treaty on Rights of Mother Earth.[37] Note the response of this Declaration to Decisions of the Conference itself supported "green economies."

[36] *See* Peoples' Sustainability Treaties, https://sustainabilitytreaties.org.

[37] Peoples' Sustainability Treaty on Rights of Mother Earth, https://sustainabilitytreaties.org/draft-treaties/rights-of-mother-earth.

Peoples' Sustainability Treaty on Rights of Mother Earth

1. Preface

The undersigned recognize and acknowledge the following:

We are all part of Mother Earth, an indivisible, living community of interrelated and interdependent beings with a common destiny. Mother Earth is the source of life, nourishment, and learning and provides these as well as spirituality and all else we need to live well.

Existing governance systems that assume that humans are separate from the environment have wrought great destruction, degradation, and disruption of Mother Earth, putting life as we know it today at significant risk through habitat destruction, species elimination, climate change, and other threats. Existing economic systems treat the natural world as property that can be exploited and degraded, rather than as an integral ecological partner with its own rights to exist and thrive, leading to dangerously unbalanced relationships among humans and Mother Earth and her other inhabitants.

The United Nations-commissioned 2011 report, *Towards a Green Economy,* defines a "green economy" as one that "seeks to minimise the impact of economic activity on the environment," and thereby fails to ensure either the necessary reversal of ongoing environmental degradation or the eventual health of Mother Earth. The "green economy" mistakenly presumes that we can "protect" Mother Earth by further forcing environmental policies to fit within an economic system that is causing the destruction in the first place, such as through privatization of the natural world.

Mother Earth-based governance, rather than economy- or development-based governance, is necessary to recognize the rights of ecosystems and species – including humans – to exist, thrive and evolve. In an interdependent living community, it is not possible to recognize the rights of only human beings without causing an imbalance within Mother Earth. To guarantee human rights, it is necessary to recognize and defend the rights of Mother Earth and all beings in her, and that there are existing cultures, practices, and laws that do so.

There exists now an urgency to take decisive, collective action to transform structures and systems that cause habitat destruction, species elimination and abuse, climate change, and other ongoing, imminent and immediately dangerous threats and damage to Mother Earth.

. . .

2. Principles

Principle #1: Inherent Rights of Mother Earth

Mother Earth and all ecosystems and species of which she is composed [have certain fundamental rights].

. . .

Principle #2: Responsibilities of human beings to Mother Earth and the overall well-being of human and environmental communities

Every human being is responsible for respecting and living in harmony with Mother Earth.

The economy must serve and advance the overall well-being of human and environmental communities, rather than the maximization of private wealth; communities must not suffer a loss of overall well-being to serve the incessant driver of economic growth that is fueling the destruction of the Earth's ecosystems and species.

Human community well-being includes not only a functioning economy but also thriving ecosystems and species as well as diverse cultures, strong societal/familial relations, healthy food, clean drinking water, adequate sanitation, safe housing, necessary medical care, democratic governance, full education, meaningful and appropriately rewarded labor, support for spirituality, respectful treatment of animals, and other elements.

Environmental community well-being includes thriving relationships with human partners, as well as strong ecosystem and species biodiversity and well-being, clean water, healthy nutrients, and sound and connected habitats.

Principle #3: Focus on "sustainable communities" and a balanced respect for all life

"Sustainable development" and the "green economy" should be re-focused instead as "sustainable communities," a term which includes both human communities and the wider communities of the natural world, to ensure that all elements of sustainable communities are promoted, rather than subsumed to the overarching driver of the economy.

A balanced respect for all life, and the recognition that all life has the right to exist, persist, and evolve as an interrelated and interdependent system, is essential to ensure both sustainable communities and a healthy, thriving planet overall.

* * *

A positive outcome of Rio+20 for many civil society attendees was a resolve to build the political will for transformative change—including by shaping the post-2015 UN development agenda toward harmony with nature. However, few left Rio+20 with a feeling that what was needed had been accomplished.

J. UN SDG Summit of 2015

In 2015, the General Assembly adopted the post-2015 development agenda, called the 2030 Agenda for Sustainable Development, which describes the 17 SDGs. A crucial difference between the MDGs and the SDGs is that the former set goals only for developing countries. The SDGs, in contrast, apply to all countries.

The SDGs are as follows:

Goal 1: No Poverty
Goal 2: Zero Hunger
Goal 3: Good Health and Well-being
Goal 4: Quality Education
Goal 5: Gender Equality
Goal 6: Clean Water and Sanitation
Goal 7: Affordable and Clean Energy
Goal 8: Decent Work and Economic Growth
Goal 9: Industry, Innovation and Infrastructure
Goal 10: Reduced Inequality
Goal 11: Sustainable Cities and Communities
Goal 12: Responsible Consumption and Production
Goal 13: Climate Action
Goal 14: Life Below Water
Goal 15: Life on Land
Goal 16: Peace and Justice Strong Institutions
Goal 17: Partnerships to achieve the Goal

* * *

In August 2016, the UN Secretary-General released a Harmony with Nature note addressing the SDGs. As you will read, the SDGs can be contextualized in the goal of achieving harmony with nature.

Harmony with Nature, Note by the Secretary-General

UN Doc A/71/266 (1 August 2016)

. . .

1. On 22 December 2015, the General Assembly adopted resolution 70/208, its seventh resolution on "Harmony with Nature", in which it requested the Secretary General to initiate, in 2016, a virtual dialogue on Harmony with Nature among, inter alia, experts on Earth jurisprudence worldwide, including those who have been active in the interactive dialogues of the General Assembly, in order to inspire citizens and societies to reconsider how they interact with the natural world in order to implement the Sustainable Development Goals in harmony with nature, noting that some countries recognize the rights of nature in the context of the promotion of sustainable development, and requested that the experts submit a summary to the General Assembly at its seventy-first session and that the virtual dialogue be hosted on the website on Harmony with Nature.

2. A first step in recognizing the rights of nature took place in June 2012 at the United Nations Conference on Sustainable Development, held in Rio de Janeiro, Brazil, where Heads of State and Government adopted the outcome document, entitled "The future we want", recognizing that the Earth and its ecosystems are our home and that some

countries recognize the rights of nature in the context of the promotion of sustainable development. They also agreed that, in order to achieve a just balance among the needs of present and future generations, it is necessary to promote harmony with nature.[38]

3. Subsequently, in its resolution 70/1, adopted on 25 September 2015, the General Assembly adopted the post-2015 development agenda, the 2030 Agenda for Sustainable Development, which contains 17 Sustainable Development Goals, including Goal 12, target 12.8, which seeks to "ensure that people everywhere have the relevant information and awareness for sustainable development and lifestyles in harmony with nature". In the context of the 2030 Agenda, the 2016 virtual interactive dialogue advances the implementation of target 12.8 by providing information and recommendations from experts in Earth-centred governance, also known as Earth jurisprudence.

K. High-level Political Forum 2019

The first post-2015 UN Summit on the SDGs, the High-level Political Forum, was held four years later in New York, on September 24 to 25, 2019. A report released ahead of the summit found that the current trajectory of progress would be insufficient to fulfill the SDGs.[39] The following excerpt is from the foreword by the Secretary-General, Antonio Guterres:

> Since its inception in 2015, the 2030 Agenda has provided a blueprint for shared prosperity in a sustainable world—a world where all people can live productive, vibrant and peaceful lives on a healthy planet. The year 2030 is just over a decade away, and we must ask ourselves if our actions today are laying the right foundation to achieve the Sustainable Development Goals (SDGs). The Sustainable Development Goals Report 2019 provides evidence-based insights to answer this question.
>
> The report demonstrates that progress is being made in some critical areas, and that some favorable trends are evident. . . .
>
> Notwithstanding that progress, this report identifies many areas that need urgent collective attention. The natural environment is deteriorating at an alarming rate: sea levels are rising; ocean acidification is accelerating; the past four years have been the warmest on record; one million plant and animal species are at risk of extinction; and land degradation continues unchecked. We are also moving too slowly in our efforts to end human suffering and create opportunity for all: our goal to end extreme poverty by 2030 is being jeopardized as we struggle to respond to entrenched deprivation, violent conflicts and vulnerabilities to natural disasters. Global hunger is on the rise, and at least half of the world's population lacks essential health services. More than half of the world's children do not meet standards in reading and mathematics; only 28 per cent of persons with severe disabilities received cash benefits; and women in all parts of the world continue to face structural disadvantages and discrimination.

[38] G.A. Res. 70/208 at 3, (Dec. 22, 2015).

[39] United Nations, *Sustainable Development Goals Report 2019,* United Nations, https://unstats.un.org/sdgs/report/2019/ (last visited Mar. 6, 2020).

It is abundantly clear that a much deeper, faster and more ambitious response is needed to unleash the social and economic transformation needed to achieve our 2030 goals. From our advances, we know what works. This report therefore highlights areas that can drive progress across all 17 SDGs: financing; resilience; sustainable and inclusive economies; more effective institutions; local action; better use of data; and harnessing science, technology and innovation with a greater focus on digital transformation. In everything we do, we must diligently ensure that policy choices leave no one behind, and that national efforts are supported by effective international cooperation, grounded in a commitment to diplomacy and crisis prevention. . . .

* * *

IV. DEEP SUSTAINABILITY—AN ALTERNATIVE APPROACH

The mainstream UN sustainable development paradigm is only one interpretation of sustainability—one that is unabashedly anthropocentric and focused on development. Other approaches to sustainability take a more holistic approach to humanity's place on the planet, more in line with the teachings of Earth law. Consider the following excerpt from John Ikerd, a professor emeritus at the University of Missouri, which describes deep sustainability as being "co-centric" rather than either anthropocentric or ecocentric.

Deep Sustainability: Rediscovering Our Connectedness

John Ikerd

All and all, today's environmental movement has not been succeeding. We have been winning battles, some critical ones, but losing the war."[40] These are the words of Gustave Speth, founder of the World Resources Institute, co-founder of the Natural Resource Defense Council, and advisor to Presidents Carter and Clinton. He pointed to a variety of ecological indicators in his 2008 book, *The Bridge at the Edge of the World,* to drive this point home: air and water pollution, fossil energy and fossil water depletion, greenhouse gas emissions, and loss of biodiversity. Speth concluded that environmental organizations have failed because they have spent their time, energy, and money battling the symptoms of ecological degradation rather than attacking its root causes. Today's environmental crisis is ultimately rooted in our dysfunctional relationships with the other living and non-living things of the earth. To avert the impending global ecological disaster, we must delve *deeper* into the nature of our interconnectedness.

The concept of "deep sustainability" goes deeper than environmentalism. It even goes beyond current approaches to sustainability, which focus on resource protection and conservation and substitution of renewable for nonrenewable sources of energy. Deep sustainability explores the ethical, philosophical, and spiritual roots of ecological, social,

[40] JAMES GUSTAVE SPETH, THE BRIDGE AT THE EDGE OF THE WORLD vii (2008).

and economic sustainability.[41] It is rooted in new ways of thinking, knowing, learning, and being in the world: ways not only essential for avoiding a global ecological catastrophe but also for progress toward a new and better world of the future.

Deep sustainability represents an intellectual conceptualization of the wisdom of Indigenous peoples throughout the world in that it reemphasizes the importance of our interconnectedness with nature and with each other. It calls on us to reestablish *intimate, caring* relationships with the earth and with other people. It recognizes that we need to connect with others not solely to meet our physical or material needs but also because we need to care and be cared for, to love and be loved. It trusts that a new set of ethical and cultural values can and will evolve from these loving and caring *personal* relationships.

. . .

Sustainability may well be the defining question of the twenty-first century: "How can we meet the needs of all in the present without diminishing opportunities for those of the future." Sustainability is about meeting the basic needs of all, with equity and justice, both within and across future generations. Sustainability requires economic, social, and ecological integrity, all three; but sustainability ultimately is rooted in nature. Everything that is of use to humans, including everything of economic value, ultimately comes from nature. Furthermore, beyond self-sufficiency, we must rely on relationships with other people, meaning society, to help us benefit from nature's bounty. To meet needs that cannot be met through *personal* relationships, we must rely on *impersonal* economies. To sustain our economies, societies, and ultimately humanity, we must maintain the health and productive capacity of both society and nature.

In failing to respect the *intrinsic* value of our connectedness with and within nature, we have allowed questions of ecological and social sustainability to degenerate to their lowest common dominator: money or economic value. Certainly, our relationships with nature have economic value; nature is the ultimate source of all economic value. However, nature also has intrinsic values that far exceed its economic value to humans. Economic value, as we know it today, is inherently individual, instrumental, and impersonal. It accrues to individuals or collections of individuals, rather than to communities or societies as wholes. It is instrumental, in that an economic transaction is always a means to an end, rather than something done because of its inherent worth. Economic value is also *impersonal,* because if something cannot be bought, sold, or traded among people, it has no economic value.

. . .

At the very least, governments should be willing to identify and "internalize" the economic costs of ecological degradation: they should make "polluters pay" the economic costs they impose on society. They should also "cap" greenhouse gas emissions, and if the cap is sufficiently low to reverse global climate change, even allow trading of CO2 emission rights. They should also assign economic values to activities that *enhance* the

[41] John Ikerd, Lonnie Gamble, & Travis Cox, *Deep Sustainability; The Essentials,* Deep Sustainability, https://sites.google.com/site/sustainabilitydeep/ (last visited Mar. 6, 2020).

economic productivity of nature. However, while government policies that force markets to reflect full economic values are *necessary*, internalizing externalities is not *sufficient* to ensure sustainability. We should do the necessary, but should not allow "the necessary" to become an obstacle to "the sufficient."

Unfortunately, we have allowed our preoccupation with economic value to become an obstacle to sustainability, mainly because economic relationships *depersonalize* our relationships with other people as well as with nature. We buy, sell, and trade, rather than maintain personal relationships. We must ultimately account for the *social* and *ethical* costs of our failures to care for society and nature, not just the economic costs. We can begin by reminding ourselves that our ecological failures have *personal* consequences, and personal costs cannot be measured in terms of economic value. Our dependence on fossil energy provides a convenient illustration of the personal consequences of our dysfunctional economic relationship with nature.

. . .

The worldview of *deep sustainability* goes beyond social justice and extends the concept of ecological justice to all things of the earth. All things of nature have rights; the rights of all species, including human rights, reflect their unique purposes within the whole of nature. In today's world of scientific materialism, the other things of nature have no subjectivity or being and thus have no inherent "right" to exist or purpose apart from their potential usefulness to humanity. Ironically, this worldview guides even today's environmental movement. In spite of claims to the contrary, the environmental movement is anthropocentric. Most environmentalists implicitly accept that the world exists primarily, if not solely, for the purpose of sustaining the well-being of humanity. "Deep ecologists," on the other hand, claim an eco-centric worldview, showing no more concern for humans than for any other species or non-living thing on earth. Deep ecologists would depopulate the earth of humans, if necessary, to sustain the rest of nature.

Deep sustainability is "co-centric" rather than anthropocentric or eco-centric. It is not eco-centric because it is concerned specifically with humans – the present and future well-being of humanity. However, it is not anthropocentric or human centered, in spite of its specific concern for the human species. The deep sustainability worldview recognizes that human well-being and the sustainability of humanity is inseparably and critically interrelated with the well-being of the other non-living and living beings of the earth. Deep sustainability is rooted in a deep reverence and respect for all things of nature – living and non-living – specifically but not solely humans. Nature does not exist for the sole benefit of humans any more than humans exist for the sole benefit of the other things of nature. Humanity is not sustainable unless human societies contribute to, or at least do not detract from, the overall health and well-being of the whole of nature of which humans are a part. . . . [42]

[42] John Ikerd, *Deep Sustainability; Rediscovering Our Connectedness*, About Place Journal, https://aboutplacejournal.org/issues/voices/section-1/john-ikerd/ (last visited Mar. 6, 2020).

V. EMERGING PARADIGMS: A GLOBAL PACT FOR THE ENVIRONMENT

A. Introduction: What Is the Global Pact initiative?

We have now reviewed about 35 years of UN sustainability initiatives along with several alternatives. Looking to the future, what will be the next major development of the UN's work to protect the environment?

One possibility is a Global Pact for the Environment ("Global Pact"), introduced in 2017. The Global Pact proposes the adoption of a legally binding international treaty that would give force to the environmental law principles enshrined in the Rio Declaration that emerged from the 1992 UNCED. The Global Pact would guide global and national environmental action for all states and citizens, as well as the private sector.

Why is a new legal instrument necessary? The Global Pact's proponents argue that, at present, international environmental law lacks an overarching, legally binding umbrella text to clarify and define principles, obligations, and rights with respect to environmental law and the global environment. As a result, international environmental law suffers from "gaps"[43] and ineffective and uneven implementation across global and national governance structures.

In 2017, an international group of legal experts proposed a draft text for a Global Pact based on the mutually interdependent source principles of the right to a healthy environment and the duty to take care of the environment. These source principles give rise to other environmental principles recognized in the Rio Declaration, including (1) the states' duty of prevention and remediation of environmental harms, (2) the polluter pays principle, and (3) the citizens' right to environmental information and public participation in environmental decision-making. Further, the draft Global Pact includes corollary principles such as non-regression[44] and official recognition of civil society's role in environmental protection.

This section discusses the history, purpose, and principles of the proposed Global Pact.

B. Why Is a Global Pact for the Environment Necessary?

Human-impacted global ecocide is so undeniably severe and increasingly alarming that many scholars consider our impact as having brought about a new geologic era: the Anthropocene.[45] It is clear that existing international environmental laws have not

[43] G.A. Res. 72/277, 2 *Towards a Global Pact for the Environment* (May 10, 2018).

[44] The principle of non-regression is an international law principle requiring that norms which have previously been adopted by States not be revised, if this implies going backwards on the subject of standards of protection of collective and individual rights.

[45] Maria-Antonia Tigre, Gaps in International Environmental Law: Toward a Global Pact for the Environment xx, 2019.

been enough to mitigate humanity's destructive impact on our planet. With only 10 years to implement the UN's 2030 Agenda for Sustainable Development, which requires unprecedented global cooperation to protect, conserve, and restore planetary systems,[46] the advocates for a Global Pact consider it crucial to ensure we can meet this global commitment and reclaim hope for a healthy sustainable future. At present, they argue that international environmental law lacks a foundational and legally binding document that ensures environmental law principles can be evenly integrated and effectively implemented in global and national legal systems.

1. Global environmental constitutionalism

Arguably, as a constitutional text for environmental law, a global pact would transform principles into compulsory environmental actions and serve as an inviolable source of law for international and domestic legal systems. Over time, a global pact would guide environmental constitutionalism and contribute to the incorporation of environmental norms into the constitutional tier of national legal systems, leading to stronger domestic environmental laws and steering effective implementation that would radiate out to the regional and international governance systems.[47] The movement for environmental constitutionalism has already seen many countries incorporate environmental principles into their constitutions, such as Brazil, China, France, Mexico, and many others.[48] A global pact would serve as the binding, overarching text necessary to guide all countries to elevating environmental protection and sustainable development as pillars of domestic, regional, and international governance.

2. Turning soft law into hard law

A global pact would give binding force to the Rio Declaration principles to ensure these principles have universal recognition, harmonized understanding, and effective application across comparative legal systems.

As a soft-law instrument, the Rio Declaration is not binding, and thus the jurisprudential and practical effects of some of these essential principles have failed to be applied and enforced effectively.[49] For example, the precautionary principle (Rio Principle 15) is instructive as to how conflicting interpretations of soft law can prevent

[46] G.A. Res. 70/1 Transforming Our World: The 2030 Agenda for Sustainable Development; Intergovernmental Panel on Climate Change, *2019 Refinement to the 2006 IPCC Guidelines for National Greenhouse Gas Inventories* (June 19, 2019); United Nations 2030 Agenda for Sustainable Development, *The Sustainable Goals Report 2019* (2019).

[47] *See* James R. May & Erin Daly, Global Environmental Constitutionalism (2015); David Boyd, The Environmental Rights Revolution (2012).

[48] *See, e.g.*, Mexico: *Case XXVII.309 CS.*, SJFG, 10th Period, Book 37, December 2016, 1840 (relying on Principle 15 of the Rio Declaration to interpret the right to a healthy environment enshrined in Article 4 of the Mexican Constitution); Brazil: Constitution of Brazil, Art. 225; China: Chinese Constitution, Art. 26; France: French Charter for the Environment (included in its "block of constitutionality"), Arts. 2, 3, 5; Ecuador 2008 Constitution, Arts. 71-74, 395-399, 400-415.

[49] Yann Aguila & Jorge E. Viñuales, A Global Pact for the Environment: Legal Foundations (2019).

environmental law principles from realizing their full potential. On the legal question of whether the precautionary principle is a recognized norm of customary international law, the International Law of the Sea Tribunal stated that the precautionary principle is an "emerging norm,"[50] while the International Court of Justice suggested that this principle "may be relevant" for interpretation purposes.[51]

A global pact would settle the question of which environmental principles are recognized as norms and therefore create binding obligations on states. This would ensure that these foundational principles are universally accepted and would allow for an accelerated application and implementation of these principles across all legal systems.

C. History of the Initiative for a Global Pact for the Environment

The idea of creating a global framework for environmental protection like the Global Pact has evolved since the 1970s. The Stockholm Conference of 1972 was seen as the constitutional moment of international environmental law and inspired widespread promulgation of domestic environmental laws;[52] however, the resulting Stockholm Declaration was a soft-law instrument without legal force.

The 1992 Rio Declaration on Environment and Development[53] was the major leap forward for the idea of a global pact because this declaration set forth constitutional principles for global environmental governance.[54] Significantly, the Rio Declaration stated the now-essential customary international law principles of prevention (Rio Principle 2), conducting an environmental impact assessment (Rio Principle 17), and the duty to cooperate (Rio Principles 18 and 19). Other key environmental principles stated, many of which were environmental principles of first impression,[55] are (1) common but differentiated responsibilities (Rio Principle 7), (2) the precautionary principle (Rio Principle 15), (3) polluter pays, (4) notification of emergencies, (5) notification and consultation in case of risk, and (6) peaceful settlement of disputes. Many of these environmental principles have catalyzed the development of customary norms and have been transposed into a wide range of global treaties and instruments.

Inspired by the Rio Declaration, the International Union for the Conservation of Nature (IUCN) released the first of its consistently updated drafts of an International Covenant on Environment and Development in 1995.[56]

[50] *Responsibilities and Obligations of States Sponsoring Persons and Entities with Respect to Activities in the Area, Advisory Opinion,* ITLOS Rep. 10 ¶ 135 (Feb. 11, 2011).

[51] *Pulp Mills on the River Uruguay (Argentina v. Uruguay),* Judgment, I.C.J. ¶ 164 (April 20, 2010).

[52] *See* Robert Lutz, *The Laws of Environmental Management: A Comparative Study,* 24 Am. J. of Comp. L. 3, 447 (1976).

[53] United Nations Conference on Environment and Development. *Rio Declaration on Environment and Development,* UN Doc. A/CONF.151/26 (vol. 1) (June 3-14, 1992).

[54] Pierre-Marie Dupuy & Jorge Viñuales, International Environmental Law 60 (2018).

[55] *See* Alexandre Kiss, *The Rio Declaration on Environment and Development, in* The Environment After Rio: International Law and Economics (Luigi Campiglio et al. eds., 1994).

[56] The IUCN, in collaboration with the International Council of Environmental Law, has pursued work on a Draft Covenant, which now has several editions. *See* IUCN, *Draft International Covenant on Environment and Development* (2017).

In November 2015, the legal think tank *Club des Juristes* released a report recommending the adoption of a universal pact to merge international environmental law in a binding instrument that would (1) impose environmental obligations on states and non-state actors, (2) confer environmental rights to citizens, and (3) create an inviolable legal instrument in national courts.[57] The adoption of the Paris Agreement inspired high-level international support for the pact from Laurent Fabius[58] (President of the 21st Conference of the Parties to the UN Framework Convention on Climate Change) and led to the 2017 convening of an international network of over 100 environmental law experts from more than 40 countries who finalized a final draft text for the Global Pact in June 2017. Laurent Fabius, who chaired the expert meeting that finished the draft text, presented it to French President Emmanuel Macron at a high-profile symposium featuring former UN Secretary-General Ban Ki-Moon, French Minister of the Environment Nicolas Hulot, and many other political figures, diplomats, experts, and students.[59] In September 2017, the draft text network of experts, now known as the International Group of Experts for the Pact (IGEP) published a white paper, *Toward a Global Pact for the Enviroment*[60] (GPE), to further advance governmental and civil society support for the Global Pact.

In September 2017, over 40 heads of state expressed their support at the Summit on a Global Pact for the Environment.[61] In May 2018, the United Nations General Assembly adopted the Enabling Resolution[62] Towards a Global Pact for the Environment,[63] which was resoundingly accepted by the global community, with 143 states voting to adopt the resolution, and only five votes against, the United States, the Russian Federation, Syria, the Philippines, and Turkey. The Enabling Resolution called on the United Nations Secretary-General to prepare a report[64] and to set up a working group to make recommendations to the UN General Assembly on the matter, including the possibility of convening an intergovernmental conference to adopt an international instrument.[65]

The Secretary-General's November 2018 report found that international environmental law could indeed be strengthened "through a comprehensive and unifying

[57] *See* Yann Aguila, *La Adopción de un Pacto Internacional para la Protección del Medio Ambiente* 13 Misión Juridica: Revista de Derecho y Ciencias Sociales 431 (2017).

[58] Laurent Fabius was the President of the 21st Conference of the Parties to the UN Framework Convention on Climate Change, the Minister of Foreign Affairs of France in 2015, and is now the President of the Constitutional Court of France.

[59] *See* Y. Aguila, *"Vers un Pacte Mondial pour l'Environnement : Acte Fondateur à Paris le 24 juin 2017,"* 25 La Semaine Juridique 718 (2017).

[60] Y. Aguila et al., *White Paper: Toward a Global Pact for the Environment*, Le Club des Juristes (2017).

[61] *See* Emmanuel Macron, *Speech by M. Emmanuel Macron, President of the Republic: Summit on the Global Pact for the Environment*, France Diplomatie (Sept. 19, 2017).

[62] UNGA 'Towards a Global Pact for the Environment' UN Doc A/RES/72/277 (10 May 2018).

[63] *See* United Nations, *General Assembly Decides to Establish Working Group Aimed at Identifying Gaps in International Environmental Law* (May 10, 2018), https://www.un.org/press/en/2018/ga12015.doc.htm.

[64] The resolution asked the Secretary-General to submit "a technical and evidence-based report that identifies and assesses possible gaps in international environmental law and environment-related instruments with a view to strengthening their implementation." Enabling Resolution, *supra* note 62, ¶ 1.

[65] Enabling Resolution, *supra* note 62, ¶ 2.

international instrument that gathers all the principles of environmental law."[66] The Global Pact's working group met at the UN Environment Programme's Nairobi headquarters for three substantive meetings during 2019, resulting in a recommendation to states to make a "political declaration" on the matter in 2022, the 50th anniversary of the Stockholm Conference.[67] While this delays the Global Pact's adoption, supporters remain hopeful that continued mobilization might see the formal adoption of the Global Pact in 2022.[68]

D. Principles Recognized in the Draft Global Pact for the Environment

The draft Global Pact for the Environment must be seen as a preliminary work base. The authors have deliberately used general and concise wording, as it is a document intended to be reshaped and negotiated by the various states before being adopted.

1. The Right to a Healthy Environment

Every person has the right to live in an ecologically sound environment adequate for their health, well-being, dignity, culture and fulfillment.

2. The Duty to Take Care of the Environment

Every State or international institution, every person, natural or legal, public or private, has the duty to take care of the environment. To this end, everyone contributes at their own levels to the conservation, protection, and restoration of the integrity of the Earth's ecosystem.

3. Integration and Sustainable Development

Parties shall integrate the requirements of environmental protection into the planning and implementation of their policies and national and international activities, especially in order to promote the fight against climate change, the protection of oceans and the maintenance of biodiversity. They shall pursue sustainable development. To this end, they shall ensure the promotion of public support policies, patterns of production and consumption both sustainable and respectful of the environment.

4. Intergenerational Equity

International equity shall guide decisions that may have an impact on the environment. Present generations shall ensure that their decisions and action do not compromise the ability of future generations to meet their own needs.

[66] United Nations Secretary-General, *Gaps in International Environmental Law and Environment-Related Instruments: Towards a Global Pact for the Environment,* UN Doc. A/73/419 2 (Nov. 30, 2018).
[67] Ana Maria Lebada, *Global Environment Pact Recommendations Forwarded to the UNGA* (2019).
[68] *Follow-Up to the Report of the Ad Hoc Open-Ended Working Group Established Pursuant to General Assembly Resolution 72/277,* UN GAOR, UN Doc A/RES/73/333 (Aug. 30, 2019).

5. Prevention

The necessary measures shall be taken to prevent environmental harm. The Parties have the duty to ensure that activities under their jurisdiction or control do not cause damage to the environments of other Parties or in areas beyond the limits of their national jurisdiction. They shall take the necessary measures to ensure that an environmental impact assessment is conducted prior to any decision made to authorise or engage in a project, an activity, a plan, or a program that is likely to have a significant adverse impact on the environment

6. Precaution

When there is a risk of serious or irreversible damage, lack of scientific certainty shall not be used as a reason for postponing the adoption of effective and proportionate measures to prevent environmental degradation.

7. Environmental Damages

The necessary measures shall be taken to ensure an adequate remediation of environmental damages. Parties shall immediately notify other States of any natural disasters or other emergencies that are likely to produce sudden harmful effects on the environment of those States. Parties shall promptly cooperate to help concerned States

8. Polluter Pays

Parties shall ensure that prevention, mitigation and remediation costs for pollution, and other environmental disruptions and degradation are, to the greatest possible extent, borne by their originator.

9. Access to Information

Every person, without being required to state an interest, has a right of access to environmental information held by public authorities. Public authorities shall, within the framework of their national legislations, collect and make available to the public relevant environmental information.

10. Public Participation

Every person has the right to participate, at an appropriate stage and while options are still open, in the preparation of decisions, measures, plans, programmes, activities, policies and normative instruments of public authorities that may have a significant effect on the environment.

11. Access to Environmental Justice

Parties shall ensure the right of effective and affordable access to administrative and judicial procedures, including redress and remedies, to challenge acts or omissions of public authorities or private persons which contravene environmental law, taking into consideration the provisions of the present Pact.

12. Education and Training

The Parties shall ensure that environmental education, to the greatest possible extent, is taught to members of the younger generation as well as to adults, in order to inspire in everyone a responsible conduct in protecting and improving the environment. The Parties shall ensure the protection of freedom of expression and information in environmental matters. They support the dissemination by mass media of information of an educational nature on ecosystems and on the need to protect and preserve the environment.

13. Research and Innovation

The Parties shall promote, to the best of their ability, the improvement of scientific knowledge of ecosystems and the impact of human activities. They shall cooperate through exchanges of scientific and technological knowledge and by enhancing the development, adaptation, dissemination and transfer of technologies respectful of the environment, including innovative technologies.

14. Role of Non-State Actors and Subnational Entities

The Parties shall take the necessary measures to encourage the implementation of this Pact by non-State actors and subnational entities, including civil society, economic actors, cities and regions taking into account their vital role in the protection of the environment.

15. Effectiveness of Environmental Norms

The Parties have the duty to adopt effective environmental laws, and to ensure their effective and fair implementation and enforcement.

16. Ecological Resilience

The Parties shall take necessary measures to maintain and restore the diversity and capacity of ecosystems and human communities to withstand environmental disruptions and degradation and to recover and adapt.

17. Non-Regression

The Parties and their sub-national entities refrain from allowing activities or adopting norms that have the effect of reducing the global level of environmental protection guaranteed by current law.

18. Cooperation

In order to conserve, protect and restore the integrity of the Earth's ecosystem and community of life, Parties shall cooperate in good faith and in a spirit of global partnership for the implementation of the provisions of the present Pact.

* * *

VI. CONCLUSION

Sustainable development is a comprehensive term covering environmental conservation and economic, social, and cultural development. While the term is vague, it brings everyone to the table. Sustainable development is in the global lexicon, and whatever the differences in usages, it uniformly stands for an alternative mode of development that is sustainable, within the limits of nature, and addresses poverty and inequity. Without dramatic changes in the development path within the next forty years, there will be environmental and social catastrophe.

Yet sustainable development alone cannot reverse the current ecological crisis. The UN needs to undertake a shift to a paradigm of global environmental governance that transcends its anthropocentric model of sustainable development by promoting, ecocentrism; harmony with nature; and binding environmental instruments, such as through the Global Pact for the Environment. As an international organization rather than a supranational organization, this shift in the work of the UN is dependent on the organization's member states' collective decision to incorporate principles of Earth law within the sustainable development model, and, most important, to implement these principles on a national basis.

* * *

STUDY QUESTIONS

(1) Recalling the origins of sustainable development in the preparations for the 1972 Stockholm Convention, would you see it as an idea crafted specifically to supplicate the developing countries into supporting the Stockholm Conference, or rather a concept whose time had come and would have been launched onto the international agenda in any case? To understand the conflict between the developing and developed countries as the background against which sustainable development became the paradigm for today's global governance, trace the positions of the developing countries throughout the events and policy papers discussed in this chapter.

(2) Article 20.4 of the CBD states: "The extent to which developing country Parties will effectively implement their commitments under this Convention will depend on the effective implementation by developed country Parties of their commitments under this Convention related to financial resources and transfer of technology and will take fully into account the fact that economic and social development and eradication of poverty are the first and overriding priorities of the developing country Parties." Article 4.2(6) of the UNFCCC contains similar text. Do you feel that the successful negotiation of this text by developing countries was simply a means for them to escape implementing these two major conventions, or is it a justifiable mechanism considering the vast economic

growth of the developed countries that is the key underlying factor for the global environmental crisis? What do these articles disclose as to how developing countries define sustainable development?

(3) How would you rate the three global environmental megaconferences of 1992, 2002, and 2012? Given that the environmental crisis shows no sign of letting up, nevertheless, how would you define their contribution to global governance? If their goal too was to balance global economic and environmental goals, think of reasons why the global economy is growing without limits while global environmental devastation is worsening and proving so hard to reverse.

(4) Agenda 21 set out the blueprint for sustainable development, but it hasn't been implemented as planned. Is the failure of the developed countries to undertake financial commitments to the developing countries an impassable obstacle? What other circumstances contribute to its disappointing track record? Can sustainable development work in a competitive global economy based on unlimited growth and consumption?

(5) The UN Harmony with Nature Initiative seeks to root sustainable development in a number of Earth law principles. Do you think that Earth law and sustainable development through the UN can be reconciled? What other measures would you suggest for incorporating rights for nature into international legal instruments? Would you recommend a binding convention on rights for nature? Do you think rights of nature can be upheld in a way that respects the goal of developing countries to alleviate poverty? How might you articulate the advantages and disadvantages?

(6) How would you address the non-governmental organizations' criticism of "green economies" at the 2012 UNCSD? Do you think "green economies" is the most viable solution, or should economic development not be the goal at all? For example, a different goal would be a "green society" or a "thriving society." Think of a few more examples.

(7) John Ikerd's description of deep sustainability describes it as being "co-centric" rather than anthropocentric or ecocentric. Similarly, many of the legal movements that comprise Earth law can be described as being on a spectrum between ecocentric and anthropocentric law, often incorporating elements of both while trying to find a balance that upholds the well-being of all life on the planet. Do you think it is possible for sustainability to be "co-centric," representing both anthropocentrism and ecocentrism at once, or must it be one or the other?

(8) Generally, international environmental conventions have failed in reversing the environmental crisis. Do you think that a Global Pact for the Environment as described in this chapter would be an appropriate response to the current state of the environment? In your opinion, what are the flaws and the strengths of a Global Pact for the Environment?

(9) As the chapter explains, the proposed Global Pact includes relatively few new principles. Most of the ideas have already been stated in various treaties, conventions, and declarations. Does that mean the Global Pact is likely to see little resistance to adoption? Or, does it mean that the Global Pact is unnecessary since most of the principles that it is promoting already enjoy binding legal status through international conventions?

(10) What other creative ways can you think of to integrate Earth law principles into international fora? For example, what if "nature" was recognized as having rights and then had its own delegation to negotiate environmental treaties, such as the UNFCCC? Or what if "nature" (as represented by legal guardians) held a seat in the UN General Assembly—or multiple seats for the oceans, forests, watersheds, and so forth? Would this create a more equitable "eco-democracy" that gave a voice to nature? Would nations object to this structure, and if so, how could that be overcome?

CHAPTER 16

Ecocentric Governance: The New Ecological Social Contract[1]

I. INTRODUCTION

Earth law encompasses all legal structures and mechanisms that protect, stabilize, and restore the functional interdependency of Earth's life and life-support systems. Ecocentric or ecological governance (the two terms are used interchangeably) is an essential part of Earth law and is the subject of this chapter. Topics covered include the new ecological social contract, the role of lawyers in ecological governance, and the rights of nature laws in Bolivia as a case study in implementing ecocentric governance.

In a very general sense, the social contract is the mutual agreement of people in a society to be governed at this time, in a certain way, and by certain rules. A social contract theory gives an explanation of what this mutual agreement is, and, also, what people should expect from the government and its laws. In a time of stability, the social contract is in place—like the air people breathe, it is there but they do not give attention to it. In a time of great historical change from one period to another, however, the existing contract receives attention, as it must be reaffirmed or be recreated.

The early twenty-first century is such a period of great historical change—perhaps the greatest since agricultural civilization began 11,000 years ago. Like then, both human history and Earth's geobiological history are changing—then from the Pleistocene (the last ice age) to the Holocene epoch, and now from the Holocene to the still warmer Anthropocene epoch (see Chapter 3, Section II, "Understanding the Anthropocene Epoch"). The Holocene was a period of relatively stable climate and humans were generally able to take nature for granted. In the Anthropocene, climate is changing rapidly along with Earth's life and life-support systems. The existing human-only social contract is being called into question. There is now a need for a social contract that includes nature, an ecological social contract.

[1] This chapter was authored by Herman Greene, President of the Center for Ecozoic Studies and an editor of this coursebook.

II. THE ECOLOGICAL SOCIAL CONTRACT

A. Bruno Latour: The Social Contract with Nature

Bruno Latour in his 2013 Gifford Lectures on *Facing Gaia* sets the stage for considering a new ecological social contract.[2]

Latour states we should not be alarmed if the current disruption of planetary life leads to social upheaval ending the human-only social contract because it was not designed to hold together in the present encounter with Gaia.[3] We might be upset, frustrated, and dismayed, but not any more alarmed than we would be if slowly rising sea levels caused the collapse of a failing sea wall. We have known about the disruption of planetary life and the strains it is placing on societies for a long time.

Latour continues by saying that because humans are now facing planetary limits, they have entered a new Hobbesian condition of a "war of all against all." The protagonists now include plants, animals, fires, storms, and carbon emissions, as well as the various human factions—all are seeking their places in Earth's limited space. This new "state of nature" is not the condition described by Hobbes that existed prior to the formation of the human social contract long ago; rather, it is a present condition that has arisen because the human social contract is incomplete.[4] A new social contract that includes nature is needed and it has to be assembled bit by bit. The laws of the new polity have to be invented and be self-imposed because "[w]ithout decision, there is no body politics, no liberty, [no] autonomy."[5]

In his 2018 book, *Down to Earth: Politics in the New Climatic Regime,* Latour expands on the nature of politics in the Anthropocene. In addition to right and left, he posits there are now two new political poles—"Out-of-This-World" and "Terrestrial." People inclined to Out-of-This-World seek to escape the existing planetary situation through climate denial, alternative facts, populism, fascism, offshore tax havens, gated communities, and even settling other planets. Due to the pull of the Out-of-This-World perspective, humanity is losing a common world of reality in relation to what is happening to Earth. Restoring this common world depends on those who are inclined to the Terrestrial.

Being Terrestrial, as explained by Latour, does not have an obvious meaning such as becoming green, natural, ecological, or environmental. These movements have not been able to mobilize politically on a sufficient enough scale to effectuate change in

[2] Bruno Latour, *Facing Gaia: Six Lectures on the Political Theology of Nature* (2013), https://eportfolios.macaulay.cuny.edu/wakefield15/files/2015/01/LATOUR-GIFFORD-SIX-LECTURES_1.pdf.

[3] In Greek mythology, Gaia was the goddess of the Earth. Latour's use of the term comes from James Lovelock's and Lynn Margulis's Gaia theory. Gaia is the self-regulating planetary system. She is nurturing to humans but may also kill them—she is both mother and other.

[4] Latour, *supra* note 2, at 103.

[5] Latour, *supra* note 2, at 104. Latour calls people to recognize and take constructive responsibility for political decisions regarding Earth's ecology. People who believe ecology is apolitical or just a scientific matter are making a mistake. If the right political decisions are not made, there won't be any polity, freedom, or autonomy left for humans because Earth will become uninhabitable.

the social contract; rather, they have resulted in decades of frozen political positions. Those who choose the Terrestrial have no established political party or institutional form (though they are necessarily active in political parties and institutions). They are neither left nor right, conservative nor liberal, reactionary nor progressive, global nor local. Their pull to the Earth sharpens these conflicts, deploys them differently, and seeks allies on all sides by calling attention to issues that are more basic than those dominating current political discourses. Rather than asking how to grow (or degrow) the economy, expand the pie, or redistribute wealth, Terrestrials ask, "How is humanity in the twenty-first century going to be able to subsist on Earth?" Their goal is not to save the Earth, to protect it, or to live in harmony with it; it is to learn how to *become dependent* on it. They do not defend nature; they are nature defending themselves. The Terrestrials are not engaged in modernity's pursuit of some infinite horizon where everyone will have all they want and do as they wish; instead, they are engaged in a journey to Earth—to becoming bound by Earth's limits (Earthbound).

Terrestrials will construct the new social contract with nature.

B. Bruce Jennings on Ecological Governance

Bruce Jennings, like Bruno Latour, writes about a new social contract. The major theme of Jennings's 2016 book, *Ecological Governance: Toward a New Social Contract with the Earth,* is that humans need to move from the current consumptive social contract to a new ecological social contract.

1. Governance is more than government, and the meaning of the social contract

Jennings distinguishes governance from government: "Governance is the overall process of coordinating, shaping, and directing individual and collective agency. [It] is inherently normative and value-laden.... [It] embodies the character of the collectivity, representing the kind of society an association of people aspires to be or become.... [I]ts work is the construction of institutionalized normative practice and symbolic orders of meaning."[6] Governance involves more than the government; it involves economic, religious, cultural, and many other civil society institutions.

The social contract is at the base of governance. "[It] refers to the fundamental norms of common consent that provide social cohesion. It is the mutual agreement that provides grounds for our moral ideals and our sense of worth and happiness."[7] The social contract limits freedom in that people agree to common rules because they need each other for survival and flourishing, and, by doing so, freedom arises that would not otherwise be possible.

[6] Bruce Jennings, Ecological Governance: Toward a New Social Contract with the Earth 173-174 (2016).
[7] *Id.* at 16.

2. Social contract theories: Hobbes, Locke, and Rousseau

The three great writers on the social contract are Thomas Hobbes (1588–1679), John Locke (1632–1704), and Jean-Jacques Rousseau (1712–1778). For Hobbes, humans are driven by the passions—especially fears about survival—not reason. They have no innate virtue and originally lived, as depicted in Hobbes' masterpiece *Leviathan,* in a state of nature that was nasty and brutish—a war of all against all. People lacked a deterrent against attack and common rules for cooperation, so they voluntarily entered into a social contract to obtain a common sovereign for defense and enforcement of the rules. In Hobbes's view, once established, the power of the sovereign is absolute and without moral limit—only an absolute sovereign can avoid the anarchy of the state of nature. The sovereign, which may be one person or an assembly of people, defines the laws and morality. Science and commerce are encouraged but not religion or metaphysical beliefs. Peace, tranquility, order, and, in Hobbes's words, "commodious living" are the purpose of civil society.[8]

Locke's social contract theory also begins with a state of nature. In it, people are equal and pursue life, health, liberty, and possessions (property). They are not amoral as imagined by Hobbes, rather they are subject to the laws of God and nature, yet they may be selfish and violent. Humans are free, but they are threatened by others. The alternative to life in this condition is a representative government subject to the will of the majority that protects the basic human rights to life, liberty, and property under the rule of law administered by an impartial judge. People are governed by their consent. They grant to the state a monopoly on the use of force (reserving the right to self-defense). If the state, however, endeavors to breach their rights to life, liberty, and property, they have a right of revolution. Government is limited; its main obligations are to protect the rights of its citizens, especially their property rights, and provide for the common defense.

Rousseau, like Hobbes and Locke, saw the formation of the social contract as an act of reciprocal agreement to live in a society governed by laws, rules, and political authority (the "State"), but unlike in Hobbes, people never completely transfer power to the State. They continually reaffirm and reenact the social contract to hold the State in check. Rousseau did not see the source of conflict that leads to the contract in the nature of humans but rather in the frictions of social existence as people culturally and psychologically develop. Thus, conflict "is a contingent cultural and historical condition, not a natural one."[9]

Unlike Hobbes and Locke, Rousseau did not imagine a pure state of nature preceding the social contract. Rather he saw humans moving into societies as a natural process. The social contract is a means to orderly living, moral development, and human flourishing. The State responds to a need of living in society—in other words,

[8] Jennings interprets Hobbes's version of the social contract as the birth of the social contract of consumption in which free and equal people transfer authority to a sovereign for economic growth and material well-being. *Id.* at 41.

[9] *Id.* at 42.

of living in mutual dependence and fellowship of others—but the State may also be a source of oppression. Rousseau sought to construct a theory of the social contract by which people would have the benefit of society yet remain as free as before the contract. His conception of freedom is not the ability to do what one wants without restraint—this is enslavement to the passions. Freedom is the ability to act in accord with higher laws, rules of universal application that make community, care, and association possible. The State may, in like manner, act in accord with such universal laws. When it treats its members equally in accord with the common good, it augments, rather than diminishes, individual freedom.

Yet, it is up to the people to ensure that the State does this. Sovereignty resides not in the State, but in the general will (*la volunté général*) of the people. As G. D. H. Cole puts it, "[T]he State is based not on any original convention, [nor] on any determinate power, but on the living and sustaining rational will of its members."[10] This is not the sum total of the individual wills of the people—Rousseau calls this the "will of all." The general will is the imperishable sense of the common good in accord with a moral ideal that calls the association into being and is operative within it. It is not an abstract ideal; it exists by reason of the active willing of it. "[T]he General Will is realized not when that is done which is best for the community, but when, in addition, the community as a whole has willed the doing of it. Then General Will demands not only good government, but also self-government—not only rational conduct, but good-will."[11] This sovereignty is inalienable because the people, not the government, are the absolute and they ultimately control their own destiny.

Jennings describes the general will as follows:

> [The general will] is not a person or an office; it is a moral culture and a spirit of community and solidarity. It is a capacity for a radically demanding impartiality of moral intention and the scrupulously public use of political power. . . . It is socially and politically embodied in a participatory republic, that is, in a set of interlocking governance institutions that rest on the periodic re-creation of the general will by a popular assembly of all citizens. And the general will is culturally embedded in a special form of moral imagination and civic virtue, one informed by the independent judgment of each citizen and by a strong widespread sense of common need, vulnerability, and equal concern and respect.[12]

The social contract, sovereignty, and the general will are all in continuous processes of becoming. Association is needed for moral development and fulfillment. For the promise of this association to be realized, people must commit themselves to it and actively engage in it for the common good. The actual will of the people is corrigible but through enlightened public participation may move toward the ideal general will. "The will must be 'general' in two senses: in the sense in which Rousseau

[10] G.D.H. Cole, *Introduction, in* Jean-Jacques Rousseau, The Social Contract & Discourses xxiv (G.D.H. Cole, trans., 1920).
[11] *Id.* at xxxix.
[12] Jennings, *supra* note 6, at 43.

used the word, it must be general in its object, i.e. universal; but it must also be generally held, i.e. common to all or to the majority."[13]

The general will is always present as a motivating force, even when it is not realized. The reason it is not achieved is because of factionalism and *amour-propre*—"vanity, self-regard, the tendency to get one's sense of self from being seen and approved of by others, insincerity and inauthenticity."[14] What is needed is *pitié*, which corresponds to empathy or compassion, the ability to go beyond oneself, and the consideration of the needs of others. Thus, after describing the general will, Jennings states: "[It] is a precarious achievement in human history... the highest expression of our communal humanity, and it arises from *the development of humanity out of nature through culture*."[15] Therefore, there is a need for a cultural order to cultivate the good that is in human nature and provide education for enlightened political engagement so that the common good or ideal general will might be realized.

3. Jennings's new ecological social contract

Building on Rousseau's work, Jennings extends the social contract from one among humans to one among humans and nature. He states: "The sphere of right, or justice, as I understand it, includes (1) the moral community of both human and nonhuman life and (2) the ecological commons—the symbiotic, interdependent systems, both natural and social, upon which human being and becoming depend."[16] Thus, the general will is not just that of humans but of humans and nature, and, further, the cultural order that cultivates and educates humans includes nature's order and activity.[17] His work responds to Latour's call for a social contract with nature. Even though there is an already existing human social contract, planetary limits have put humans and other living beings in a new "state of nature" that is no longer viable.

[13] COLE, *supra* note 10, at xl. That the general will must be generally held requires commitment to a democratic process and respect for the wisdom of the people as a whole even if it does not agree with one's personal position or interest. This should, however, not be understood as meaning that all decisions arrived at through a democratic process express the general will.

[14] JENNINGS, *supra* note 6, at 45. *Amour-propre* literally means "self-love," but for Rousseau the term carries this negative meaning and not the will to survive and respectfully care for oneself, which he instead calls *amour-soi.* Jennings later further describes *amour-propre* as "an insecure and duplicitous identity, and strategically self-regarding and manipulative behavior." *Id.* at 54.

[15] *Id.* at 44 (emphasis in the original).

[16] *Id.* at 9.

[17] In general, in modernity nature is considered amoral and the good must come solely from human morality. Rémi Brague observes: "The image of the world that emerged from physics after Copernicus, Galileo, and Newton is of a confluence of blind forces, where there is no place for consideration of the Good." RÉMI BRAGUE, THE WISDOM OF THE WORLD: THE HUMAN EXPERIENCE OF THE UNIVERSE IN WESTERN THOUGHT 185 (Teresa Lavender Fagan, trans., 2003). Further, as the good was no longer understood to be in nature, it had to be introduced by humans "by force, by taking nature against the grain ...." *Id.* at 209. Numerous people, including Jenkins, have challenged this amoral assessment of nature and its activity on the basis of the goodness of the order and development of the evolutionary universe as revealed in the purposive, teleological, symbiotic, cooperative, sentient, interior, or subjective aspects of nature. Jenkins holds up Robert Nadeau in support of his assessment. Jennings, *supra* note 6, at 62. Others include Thomas Berry, Teilhard de Chardin, and Lynn Margulis.

Thus, a new ecological social contract is needed for orderly living, moral development, and the flourishing of all species.

According to Jennings, the existing social contract of consumption is the product of the history of modernity. This begins in the sixteenth century with emancipation from the constraints of feudalism. The Enlightenment of the seventeenth and eighteenth centuries gave rise to empiricism, materialism, science, technology, reason, utilitarianism, diversity, tolerance, secular liberalism, separation of church and state, lack of transcendent value in public culture, and loss of the commons. The Industrial Revolution of the nineteenth and twentieth centuries meant the market economy and commodification of nature and labor. This led to a development model based on carbon-intensive energy use, technology, and consumerism. In the Great Acceleration, the period following World War II,[18] the political economy shifted from egalitarian liberalism to market liberalism (neoliberalism) predicated on the assumption that the optimal results for human civilization would be obtained by continuous economic growth. The fundamental values of modernity are freedom, equality, human rights, pursuit of happiness, and possessive individualism. In the consumptive social contract, ordinary citizens give political and business elites control in exchange for the promise of economic growth and improved material conditions.

At the heart of this social contract is a political economy.[19] "A political economy is a structure of power and a form of large-scale social coordination."[20] It is the way that society organizes itself to meet human needs and material aspirations. It is socially constructed based on values and assumptions and the availability of materials and technologies. It is a rule-based system for the use and conservation of resources and the production and distribution of goods and services. The political economy of the social contract of consumption assumes unlimited resources, unlimited sinks,[21] and continuous economic growth through industrial development. The opponent of this political economy is natural limits.

> [T]he accelerating global extractive assault on planetary resources and ecosystems, as well as the unprecedented extensions of our technological reach, do not truly represent progress and the triumph of human freedom or the human destiny. Why not? [Because] they are not sustainable or viable as a road to the future. . . . While seeming to extend human freedom, economic behavior and technology are laying the groundwork for its repression; while seemingly representing the advanced expression of human capability, they are actually undermining what is most precious in humanness.[22]

[18] *Planetary Dashboard Shows "Great Acceleration" in Human Activity Since 1950*, IGPD, http://www.igbp.net/news/pressreleases/pressreleases/planetarydashboardshowsgreataccelerationinhumanactivitysince1950.5.950c2fa1495db7081eb42.html (last visited April 21, 2020).

[19] A political economy is more than a description of natural resources and the means by which goods and services are produced and distributed within a given society. A political economy includes the public policies and social values that give rise to and sustain a particular economy.

[20] Jennings, *supra* note 6, at 22.

[21] A "sink" is a place where human waste may be recycled without harm to the environment.

[22] Jennings, *supra* note 6, at 27-28.

The dilemma for leaders today is that, on the one hand, "[s]ocial order and stability in virtually every nation rests on economic activity based on the intensive procurement and use of energy-rich fossil fuels. . . . [This] has made possible most of modern technology and industrial civilization;"[23] and on the other hand, the procurement and use of these fuels and the industrial systems they support poses an imminent threat to civilization. Modernity's storyline is that natural limits can be always be overcome by technological innovation or substitution of materials or sources. Jennings points out, however, that earlier natural limits were not overcome; rather, humans found natural pathways that would handle the burden of human extraction and production of waste and pollution at those times.[24] Are humans now facing absolute natural limits, sometimes called "planetary boundaries," that make the continuation of the consumptive social contract not only unwise in the near term but also impossible in the medium and long term? For Jennings, the answer is presumptively yes.

In consideration of this presumption, Jennings, as a social contract theorist,[25] puts forward an ecological social contract as being normatively the best for our times. In rejecting the idea that only technological changes are needed, he aligns with and quotes Pope Francis in *Laudato Si'*:

> Ecological culture cannot be reduced to a series of urgent and partial responses to the immediate problems of pollution, environmental decay and the depletion of natural resources. There needs to be a distinctive way of looking at things, a way of thinking, policies, an educational programme, a lifestyle and a spirituality which together generate resistance to the assault of the technocratic paradigm. . . . To seek only a technical remedy to each environmental problem which comes up is to separate what is in reality interconnected and to mask the true and deepest problems of the global system.[26]

This quote offers a segue into a discussion of the importance of value systems in a social contract. People enter a social contract for survival and defense (negative reasons) and also, as social beings, to be whom they aspire to be for happiness, fulfillment, and meaning, and for how they can extend the capabilities for flourishing to others (positive reasons).[27] Thus, also at the heart of a social contract are "ethical principles, rules, and norms, which, when they are accepted and practiced widely enough, become an orienting and directing force in society."[28] These standards grow out of tradition and are maintained by habit, but are also created by reflection. When a

[23] *Id.* at 158.
[24] *Id.* at 24.
[25] For Jennings, social contract theory has a normative task, which is to lay out "what it takes to be an appropr iate general form of cultural being [in order to] provide a regulative ideal, against which any particular existing cultural arrangements can be judged." *Id.* at 51. Culture is the socially transmitted systems of meanings and beliefs through which we interpret our experience and assign value to it. In social contract theory it also includes political culture, which is the way power is organized through systems, institutions, and symbols, and the mode of orderly cooperation of large groups of people who share a sense of common interest and membership. Humans in their original condition lack a political culture. Social contract theory tells "how a place is to be created (civil society) in which the potential creatures we are can become actual and fully human, however that is to be characterized—rational, cooperative, productive, moral." *Id.* at 49.
[26] Pope Francis, *Laudato Si': Care for Our Common Home* § 111 (2015) (quoted by Jennings, *supra* note 6, at 151).
[27] Jennings, *supra* note 6, at 89.
[28] *Id.*

historical shift occurs, such as is occurring in the early twenty-first century, the changes can be quite radical.

Jennings's appeal to morality is an important factor in the move to a new ecological social contract as there must be a moral justification for people to forego the benefits of the consumptive social contract.[29] Without widespread consent, there is no new ecological social contract, there is only a partisan group within society that holds ecological values. The new contract involves reasoned conviction, a measure of contentment, and an appeal to ideals of a higher order. The social contract is not a bargained agreement for personal benefit; it is a moral community.

With this as background, Jennings offers what he takes to be the key terms of the ecological social contract:

> These terms are: (1) creating a system of wealth that moves beyond affluence and scarcity to plentitude and frugality; (2) creating a system of property that moves beyond commodities to commons; (3) creating a system of freedom or liberty that moves beyond noninterference and independent self-sufficiency to relationality and interdependence; and (4) creating a system of citizenship that moves beyond self-interested advantage to trusteeship for right relationship and right recognition.[30]

The transition from the consumptive social contract to the ecological social contract will be difficult: "A new social contract for ecological governance will need to navigate conflicting social and economic interests and blocking coalitions on many fronts. It must be continually recreated and renewed."[31] "[It]must provide the transitional generation of citizens with a way to respond positively to the foreclosing of an unsustainable growth future they have been taught to expect."[32] It must show that it can achieve justice in terms of equity for present generations and for future generations. And it must offer the promise of sustainability and care for nature.

Jennings is concerned about the future of democratic societies. He foresees three possible types of governance orientations in an ecological political economy. The first is *ecological authoritarianism*. "[E]cological authoritarians maintain that the successful governance in an ecological era will require centralized, elitist, and technocratic management at least in the areas of economic and environmental policy."[33]

The second is *ecological discursive democracy*. "[It] involves institutionalization and empowerment of participatory and discursive governance within a diverse and pluralistic society and culture.... [It] grows directly out of concerted action with others, shaped by debate and deliberation." It differs from the current interest group democracy, which involves the aggregation of interests of different groups in a diverse population with conflicting interests. These groups compete for the attention of elected officials. The role of the citizen centers around voting, with only a few playing a larger role through financial contributions or involvement in political action groups. In

[29] *Id.* at 128.
[30] *Id.* at 9.
[31] *Id.* at 175.
[32] *Id.*
[33] *Id.* at 182.

contrast to discursive democracy, "the citizen role is actively and extensively participatory at multiple levels." In Jennings's view, interest group democracy "is prone to incrementalism and preservation of the status quo." "[It] is not succeeding and is structurally incapable of presiding over the transition from a consumptive growth-oriented political economy to an ecological political economy."[34]

The third is *ecological constitutionalism.* Ecological constitutionalism "would involve the creation of several elite governing entities that can check and balance the more representative institutions such as the presidency or legislature."[35] There are already examples of such entities, with the most familiar being the judiciary. The Federal Reserve is another example with authority over monetary policy. Yet another example is independent administrative agencies that are protected from political influence. The kinds of entities that would be needed for an ecological political economy might be special environmental courts modeled on the business courts that already exist in various states, administrative agencies with different powers than existing environmental protection agencies, or civil society groups that exercise only soft power.[36]

Jennings believes that the best overall outcome is probably a combination of discursive democracy and ecological constitutionalism.

A final theme of note in Jennings's work is recovery of the political, which is a concern of Latour's as well. The present consumptive social contract gives individual freedom[37] but not relational freedom.[38] It works against relational freedom, which is the ability to act in solidarity with others for the common good. Relational freedom is what is needed to meet the demands of the future. In the ecological social contract, "the problem of politics is not to seek power, but to resist it; and not to deny vulnerability and dependency but to embrace them creatively. The problem of [this] politics is to resist the kind of power and domination that actually render its agents impotent and enthralled. The problem of [this] politics is to accept restraints on behalf of communal agency and relational freedom."[39] "It needs the vocabulary of solidarity, mutuality, reciprocity, community and the common good."[40]

[34] *Id.* at 140, 180-184.

[35] *Id.* at 185.

[36] Jennings holds up the Earth Charter Initiative as an example of such a civil society group. *See* Earth Charter Initiative, https://earthcharter.org/ (last visited March 30, 2020). The Earth Charter was created by a highly participatory process and is well regarded as a vision for society. At present, it lacks the soft power to act as a check on governments and economies. Whether a soft-power ethics group could check the power of corporations and governments is an open question.

[37] According to Jennings, the consumptive social contract is based on negative freedom. Negative freedom is "*self-directed individual agency free from interference by others in the pursuit of the subjective satisfaction of needs that are ontologically and psychologically limitless and insatiable.*" *Id.* at 128 (emphasis in the original).

[38] "[R]elational liberty is freedom in and through relationships of interdependency. More specifically [it is] *freedom through transactions and relationships of interdependency with others that exemplify justice (parity of membership, voice, and participation) and solidarity (mutuality of civic concern and respect).*" *Id.*, at 130-131 (emphasis in the original).

[39] *Id.* at 194.

[40] *Id.* at 134.

STUDY QUESTIONS

(1) Bruno Latour says Earth (Gaia) is both mother (nurturing) and other (has a dangerous quality). How does this distinction help Earth law to recognize that nature is both nurturing and threatening?

(2) Latour says that by bringing issues down to Earth and asking basic questions about a viable future for humans and their dependence on Earth, Terrestrials sharpen the distinctions between left and right, conservative and liberal, reactionary and progressive, and global and local, and cast them in a new light. How might this be so?

(3) How does Jennings distinguish between government and governance?

(4) Describe the consumptive social contract and its most critical elements.

(5) Describe the ecological social contract and its most critical elements.

(6) Both Latour and Jennings say the social contract among humans alone is incomplete and needs to include nature. Do you think this means that the human social contract needs to take nature more fully into account, or that there needs to be a contract among humans and nonhuman nature? If the latter, how would it be possible for humans to have a contract with nonhuman nature? What would nature's role be in the general will?

* * *

III. THE ROLE OF LAWYERS IN ECOLOGICAL GOVERNANCE

The remainder of this chapter concerns the role of lawyers in ecological governance, and how they might play a part in developing a new social contract. It covers the place of lawyers in society; accepting Earth as a client; Earth lawyers and the ecological social contract; Earth lawyers and the reform of law; and a case study of the rights of nature laws in Bolivia.

A. The Place of Lawyers in Society

For most lawyers, governmental bodies and their laws form the backdrop of their practices. They devote little of their attention to governance itself (with notable exceptions, such as lobbyists). Many students come to law school expecting to learn social theory and political advocacy and find instead they learn "THE LAW." Their task is to learn the law and understand how law applies to factual situations. After law school, they apply this skill in their practices by acting as advocates for their clients, which means helping clients achieve their goals within the bounds of the law.

As lawyers carry on their practices, they may, over time, become less clear as to how much THE LAW is determinative. In court, opposing lawyers argue the facts and the law, yet claim different results. In appeals courts, legal arguments are made and then some judges rule one way and others another. Further, practicing lawyers may find situations where law is not determinative in terms of achieving justice. It may become clear that the legal system is a means of power and exclusion and that it is closely tied to the goal of progress through continuous and unlimited economic growth. It may also become clear how law structures relationships by creating *lawscapes* of land and societies. For many lawyers, practicing Earth law and making a living will seem in conflict. What is good for the Earth may not be what clients want and what clients want may not be good for the Earth. Practicing lawyers will find that the rules of professional ethics do not cover many of the ethical issues related to Earth law.

An attorney is an agent, yet in respect of Earth law (though less so in respect of environmental law), attorneys may feel at a loss for agency, or, in other words, in their ability to act on behalf of Earth. This is because their practices may seem unrelated to Earth law or even counter to it. Further, if they consciously undertake an Earth law practice, they will face obstacles in the way the legal system is structured. For example, doctrines of property law and issues of standing, as discussed in Chapters 4 and 5 of this book, impose impediments.

Yet, who is better positioned than lawyers to bring into being ecological governance?

Lawyers have special skills in analysis, organization, and expression of thought, in organization of entities, in negotiation of transactions, and in settlement of disputes. Many have skills in overcoming factionalism and roadblocks to move things forward and in forming and maintaining alliances. They are granted enviable status in society—any lawyer knows the power of saying, "I'm a lawyer." On the whole, lawyers are affluent members of society. Historically, they have played prominent roles in elective and appointed positions of government. They also play prominent roles in social organizations from churches to foundations to think tanks to administrations of universities. Bar associations and legal societies have influence on the appointment of judges, and they are consulted on legislation and public policy.

And, most important of all, lawyers are trained in the law and are embedded in the legal system.

B. Taking on Earth as a Client: A Reality Check

A quality that is important to the practice of law is being realistic. Practicing lawyers receive little to no reward for what they think ought to be the case. They are measured for the most part by the results they achieve. Law is an intense intellectual exercise in that lawyers are called on to understand complex factual situations and weigh legal, social, and economic factors in advising and representing their clients to provide the best outcomes. Lawyers may agree or disagree with their clients' goals, values, and decisions, yet, so long as they maintain the relationship, they seek to further their clients' goals within the law. In doing so, the task of the lawyer is to assess and act on what is *realistically* possible.

What if a lawyer's client were Earth and the client's goal was to survive and thrive? Your client wants your representation in promoting change from anthropocentric to ecocentric governance. This representation involves a level of complexity not heretofore imagined. Still, the lawyer might draw on the skills they have acquired—listen, learn, assess what and who you can rely on and what are the obstacles, *be realistic* . . . .

You will find that as an Earth lawyer, you will receive highly conflicting accounts of the state of the planet, the needs of the planet, and how Earth law should be practiced. This will not only be the case with the planet but also with the particular environmental situations of humans and other species. Believing one knows how to save Earth or even the right way to practice Earth law is a liability not an asset. Earth lawyers are seekers, information hounds, critical thinkers, and dreamers. They are participants in a process of healing that will outlive them. In deciding what to do, they should ask, "Will this engender life?"

They should be realistic while still reaching for and planning to accomplish what has not been done before.

C. Earth Lawyers and the Ecological Social Contract

The overarching task of every Earth lawyer is to bring into being the new ecological social contract. Without this, no matter how many Earth law victories are won, the objective of Earth law will not be achieved. To be an Earth lawyer, one does not need to be an environmental lawyer. Any lawyer may be an Earth lawyer. An Earth lawyer is a lawyer who is willing to take as starting points that nature has limits, that the consumptive social contract is unsustainable, and that a new ecological social contract is needed. Earth lawyers commit to bringing a new ecological social contract into being by thought, word, and deed.

They cannot do this acting alone; they can do this only in concert with other like-minded people in law and in other walks of life. Ultimately for the contract to come into being, it will require the consent of the whole society. In a globally connected world, it will require the consent of all people. This would not mean that each person in the world would have to give conscious consent to an express written social contract any more than this was required to bring into being the present consumptive social contract. It would mean people consciously or unconsciously would become part of a new moral culture and a new political economy. In a spirit of community and solidarity, they would accept new ways of doing things as well as the institutions that embody them and make them possible. It would mean people would have a level of satisfaction that in this new arrangement they could be what they aspire to be and they could extend the capabilities for flourishing to others.

As noted above, lawyers bring special skills, abilities, social status, and roles to this task. If they are corporate lawyers, they could guide their clients in understanding that the failures of the old are the opportunities of the new. They could help their clients see that profits are a means to providing needed goods and services and employment, not an end in themselves, that the granting of a public charter is the grant of a public trust, and that the fiduciary responsibilities of officers and directors extend to the entire community of life. Corporate lawyers and other lawyers involved in business law, such as employment, banking, securities, tax, real estate, and business litigation lawyers, are involved at a high level in all the activities of the consumptive political economy. They could model humility and the values of the ecological political economy in their own personal lives, in their practices, and in their law firms. The choices they could make in how they live, the conferences they attend, and the roles they take on in the community would make a difference. The table conversations they could have with their clients would as well. While it might seem difficult to bring up Earth law, people are interested in the Earth and how they can make a difference. By being Earth lawyers, they would attract clients who are moving on the path to an ecological political economy. They could draw the line when what their clients are doing is wrong—even if it is legal. They could practice the spirit of the law as well as the letter of the law. If needed, they could discontinue the representation of clients. Business lawyers could engage in the reform of laws and the establishment of the new institutions for the ecological social contract. They could become engaged in civic, political, and religious associations with other members of society.

Earth lawyers who are not business lawyers could find similar ways of bringing into being a new ecological social contract. For example, intellectual property lawyers could seek to reform patent law so that it benefits the ecosystems from which many "human inventions" are derived.[41] Estate planning lawyers could work with their clients to bequeath some or all of their estate for the permanent benefit of nature, as well as for the benefit of Indigenous peoples and others whose land has been taken. Criminal lawyers could call for the recognition of ecocide as a crime, both in the International Criminal Court and in national legal systems. Civil rights lawyers could lend their expertise to emerging rights-based movements for nature. Voting rights lawyers could help conceptualize and implement effective voting schemes on behalf of nonhuman ecosystems and animals. Environmental lawyers could continue enforcing environmental laws while calling for passage of a new generation of ecocentric laws. Every lawyer could have a role.

Lawyers, however, cannot help by intention alone. They must engage in the task in thought, word, and deed.[42]

[41] The Interspecies Technology Transfer Consortium seeks to do just this. *See* Earth Law Center, *Interspecies Technology Transfer Consortium*, https://www.earthlawcenter.org/international-1?rq=interspecies%20technology (last visited Apr. 19, 2020).

[42] Using different terminology, Thomas Berry calls this task the "Great Work" of our time. It may be helpful for Earth Lawyers to think of this overarching task of bringing into being a new ecological social contract as the Great Work. *See generally* THOMAS BERRY, THE GREAT WORK: OUR WAY INTO THE FUTURE (1999).

D. Earth Lawyers and the Reform of Law: Normative Jurisprudence

Much of this book is devoted to litigation strategies in Earth law. Attorneys today are arguing for the rights of nature, the public trust, the rights of future generations, and environmental human rights. Litigation is essential for the advancement of Earth law.

This section of this chapter, however, covers a different aspect of Earth law—the role of Earth lawyers in the reform of positive law and in the means of enforcing such law. *Positive law* for purposes of this chapter means written laws, such as statutes, regulations, constitutions, and civil and criminal procedure. Enforcement of positive law means making such law operational and effective.

Law schools focus on what the law is, not what it should be. While practicing lawyers and legal scholars do advocate for changes in law, these reforms tend to be within a narrow frame of reference consistent with the consumptive social contract, such as reforms to advance the economic interests of clients. (Notable exceptions include lawyers advancing justice and welfare reforms for humans and nature.) Normative jurisprudence "both criticizes [existing] positive law and suggests reforms on the basis of stated moral values and legalistic ideals."[43] It concerns "[t]he nature of the legal good—what makes law good and virtues a good law ought to have."[44] Interpreting Thomas Aquinas's famous statement in *Summa Theologica*, "An unjust law is no law at all," one would say a law must have a moral justification for it to be binding. Normative jurisprudence seeks to understand the moral justification for particular laws or the lack of the same and proposes good law on the basis of moral claims.

What is a moral claim? At its simplest, a *moral claim* is a statement made of a kind that when a person hears the statement, she responds, "Yes, this is my duty. It is something I ought to do." Laws need to be largely self-enforcing. For example, people are asked to file tax returns that state their true income and then they are taxed on this income. Only rarely will they be audited if they do not accurately represent their income. Fear of potential enforcement activity motivates compliance, but even more, it is the sense that obeying the law is what one ought to do to provide for the public welfare. If people do not feel this moral obligation and they feel enforcement is unlikely, compliance will be low.

Jennings, following on Rousseau, however, offers a broader conception of moral obligation. Laws are not just what is written on paper; they are willed into being and are maintained by an active will. When they no longer serve a public purpose, they may remain on the books but have no effect. Some laws come into being by "particular wills" and are maintained by them. Some laws come into being by the general will, but when their time is past, they are maintained by particular wills and perhaps will later be reformed by the general will.

The way that the concept of the general will changes moral justification is that its morality is more than one's personal sense of what I ought or ought not do. It is a morality derived from a public discourse about the common good. It is always more

[43] Robin West, Normative Jurisprudence: An Introduction i (2011).
[44] *Id.* at 7.

than one's personal knowledge or determination—this is why citizens read op-eds, talk with friends about their concerns, go to school, listen to the news, enter into conversations in religious and social groups, read magazines, and pray and meditate in concert with others. Some of the considerations that emerge will be quite narrow; these are the particular wills, or those that only take into account the needs of one group or interest. Other considerations are broader as they are seeking not only the good of a particular group or interest but the greater good. The general will does not adhere to some abstract higher value or position, such as a doctrine, an ideology, a particular religious teaching or belief, the views of a talk show host, or a political party or faction. It comes out of enlightened public discourse—the willing of the people for the common good. "[T]he most general will is always the most just also, and [it is found in] the voice of the people."[45]

There is no final arbiter and no deity who announces this general will. It is an ongoing process of discernment, it is always at work, and it is always right in the sense of Martin Luther King, Jr.'s statement that "the arc of the moral universe is long, but it bends toward justice"—that bend, however, occurs only through the active participation of people in discerning and willing the common good.[46] This discerning does not, however, result in a final, clear consensus agreement. The discerning is an ongoing process and what the general will is will be expressed in diverse ways; nonetheless, this discerning will be a unifying force for good. It will only be understood in retrospect, and, even then, interpretations will vary.

Thus, in this understanding, Aquinas's statement that "an unjust law is no law at all" would mean the unjust law is not supported by the general will and will not stand. Normative jurisprudence in this understanding would mean that moral claims in support of reformed law and enforcement thereof should be based on the general will and not some particular interest or moral frame.

What Jennings adds to Rousseau is that the public discourse extends to nature and, therefore, necessarily beyond human language. The cosmos takes on a moral character and nature becomes a source of wisdom.[47] For Rousseau, human freedom is found in the common good for humans; for Jennings, human freedom is found in the common good for the Earth community, including humans, where rivers, birds, and winds also speak and listen, and we humans listen and speak to them, as well. It is worth recalling that for Jennings and Rousseau, freedom is not primarily license (negative freedom), it is relational freedom. One gives up the freedom of the state of nature in order to have the greater freedom that comes from being in relation with others. The distinction is easily understood by reference to the dynamics of the nuclear family. If all family members insist on doing just what they want, there is no family, only discord. When family members take into account the needs of others, there is the freedom to live in supportive and responsive relationships.

[45] Jean-Jacques Rousseau, *Discourse on Political Economy*, *in* The Social Contract & Discourses 254 (G.D.H. Cole trans., 1920). Rousseau's actual statement of the second clause is "and that the voice of the people is in fact the voice of God." *Id.*

[46] *See* Mychal Denzel Smith, *The Truth About "The Arc of the Moral Universe,"* Huffington Post (Jan. 18, 2018), https://www.huffpost.com/entry/opinion-smith-obama-king_n_5a5903e0e4b04f3c55a252a4.

[47] This is a breach with modernity's understanding of nature and the cosmos as amoral; *see supra* note 17.

It will be a challenge for Earth lawyers to listen to Earth's nonhuman languages in considering the general will; yet, if Jennings is right, their success will depend on it. This will involve outside-the-box thinking. Consider this extension of the franchise to nonhuman beings proposed by experimental philosopher Jonathon Keats at San José State University:

> If the general will includes the will of animals and plants, even bacteria, shouldn't they also be enfranchised in democratic decision-making? Although this question may at first seem to be purely philosophical, there are ways to do this in practice. For instance, science has the tools to measure stress hormones in many species. Changes in aggregate stress might potentially be polled, revealing how those species are reacting to the current body of law. An increase in stress hormone levels in enough organisms might count as a call for change in the legal *status quo*. Data could inform the choices made by human voters or legislators who are voluntarily acting as proxies on a non-binding basis. At a greater extreme, taking the general will to mean the will of Gaia, and according Gaia with the right to self-determination, it could be argued that the votes of animals and plants themselves ought to be counted officially in the choice of representatives or in legislative decisions.[48]

No nation has yet granted nature the right to vote in this way. The Bolivian case study below, however, shows how Indigenous people in Bolivia sought to give nature a voice in government—a voice they had long included in their polity.

E. The Rights of Nature in Bolivia

1. The historical experience

Bolivia is a land-locked country located in western-central South America. It has had a tumultuous history, including a brutal period of Spanish colonial rule followed, during independence, by many changes of government and wars with neighboring countries. Bolivia is one of the poorest countries in the Western Hemisphere as measured by standard economics. Mining has been a key feature of the Bolivian economy for centuries and remains so today.

A majority of Bolivians identify as Indigenous. In 2005, Bolivia elected its first Indigenous president, Evo Morales. His victory was seen as an outcome of decades of struggle against neoliberal politics. Morales brought with him Indigenous values of living well (*suma qamaña/vivir bien*) and respect for Mother Earth (*Pachamama*[49]). In 2006, with the backing of a coalition of Indigenous organizations called the "Unity Pact," Morales convened a Constitutional Assembly with the goal of forming a plurinational state—

[48] This idea has recently been explored by the independent experimental philosopher Jonathon Keats, who has prototyped a system for "phytodemocracy" in collaboration with researchers at San José State University.

[49] For Quechua-speaking people, Pachamama is not equivalent to "nature" or even "Mother Earth" as conventionally understood. It has a cosmological scope encompassing the Earth/time, the Sun and the Moon, the Goddess of Fertility, and the prime origin of all-life as well. DICCIONARIO QUECHUA ESPAÑOL, QUECHUA EDICIÓN DE LA MUNICIPALIDAD DEL CUSCO (Perú) (1995).

one made up of many different "national" groups within Bolivia, including those of Indigenous people.

In 2009, Bolivia adopted a new constitution. Its preamble recognized the principles of *vivir bien,* protection of Mother Earth, equity, and redistribution of social wealth, and declared Bolivia was being founded anew:

> We have left the colonial, republican and neo-liberal State in the past. We take on the historic challenge of collectively constructing a Unified Social State of Pluri-National Communitarian law, which includes and articulates the goal of advancing toward a democratic, productive, peace-loving and peaceful Bolivia, committed to the full development and free determination of the peoples. . . .
>
> We found Bolivia anew, fulfilling the mandate of our people, with the strength of our Pachamama and with gratefulness to God.[50]

The Constitution did not formally grant rights to Mother Earth, but it did grant environmental rights to the people:

> Everyone has the right to a healthy, protected, and balanced environment. The exercise of this right must be granted to individuals and collectives of present and future generations, as well as to other living things, so they may develop in a normal and permanent way.
>
> Any person, in his own right or on behalf of a collective, is authorized to take legal action in defense of environmental rights, without prejudice to the obligation of public institutions to act on their own in the face of attacks on the environment.[51]

When Morales began his second term in 2009, he was already well-known in international circles. In that year he attended the United Nations Climate Change Conference in Copenhagen, where he blamed climate change on capitalism, called for strong commitments to climate mitigation, and demanded that the Global North pay its climate debt to the Global South. Unsatisfied with the results of the conference, Morales invited people to come to Cochabamba in April 2010 for the World People's Conference on Climate Change and the Rights of Mother Earth (the "World People's Conference"). In an often-festive atmosphere, 33,000 people assembled and worked on issues such as climate change, equity and justice, alternative development paths, the rights of nature, Indigenous rights, patriarchy, and food sovereignty. At the end of the conference, a draft Universal Declaration of the Rights of Mother Earth was adopted with a goal of having the declaration adopted by the United Nations.

In December 2010, Bolivia passed the Law of the Rights of Mother Earth ("the Mother Earth Rights Law"). In Chapter II, Article 3, Mother Earth (*Pachamama*) was defined as follows:

> Mother Earth is a dynamic living system comprising an indivisible community of all living systems and living organisms, interrelated, interdependent and complementary,

[50] Const. of the Plurinational State of Bolivia, Preamble (2009).
[51] *Id.* at arts. 33 & 34.

which share a common destiny. Mother Earth is considered sacred, from the worldviews of nations and peasant indigenous peoples.

In Chapter III, Article 7, Mother Earth was given the following rights:

1. **To life**: The right to maintain the integrity of living systems and natural processes that sustain them, and capacities and conditions for regeneration.
2. **To the diversity of life**: It is the right to preservation of differentiation and variety of beings that make up Mother Earth, without being genetically altered or structurally modified in an artificial way, so that their existence, functioning or future potential would be threatened.
3. **To water**: The right to preserve the functionality of the water cycle, its existence in the quantity and quality needed to sustain living systems, and its protection from pollution for the reproduction of the life of Mother Earth and all its components.
4. **To clean air**: The right to preserve the quality and composition of air for sustaining living systems and its protection from pollution, for the reproduction of the life of Mother Earth and all its components.
5. **To equilibrium**: The right to maintenance or restoration of the interrelationship, interdependence, complementarity and functionality of the components of Mother Earth in a balanced way for the continuation of their cycles and reproduction of their vital processes.
6. **To restoration**: The right to timely and effective restoration of living systems affected by human activities directly or indirectly.
7. **To pollution-free living**: The right to the preservation of any of Mother Earth's components from contamination, as well as toxic and radioactive waste generated by human activities.

In Article 8, the plurinational state was given the following duties, among others:

- Develop public policies and actions of prevention, early warning, protection, and precaution;
- Develop balanced forms of production and patterns of consumption, while safeguarding the regenerative capacity and integrity of the cycles, processes and vital balance of Mother Earth;
- Develop policies to protect Mother Earth from the multinational and international scope of exploitation of its components, from the commodification of living systems or the processes that support them, and from the structural causes and effects of global climate change; and
- Develop policies to ensure the long-term energy sovereignty and gradual incorporation of clean and renewable alternative sources into the energy matrix.

In Article 9, these duties, among others, were imposed on natural persons and public or private legal entities:

- Uphold and respect the rights of Mother Earth;
- Promote harmony with Mother Earth in all areas of her relationship with other human communities and the rest of nature in living systems;

- Participate actively, individually or collectively in generating proposals designed to respect and defend the rights of Mother Earth;
- Assume production practices and consumer behaviour in harmony with the rights of Mother Earth;
- Ensure the sustainable use of Mother Earth's components; and
- Report any act that violates the rights of Mother Earth, living systems, and/or their components.

Article 10 called for the establishment of the Office of Mother Earth "to ensure the validity, promotion, distribution and compliance of the rights of Mother Earth established in this Act." There were no other enforcement mechanisms in the act.

Bolivia enacted a much more extensive law for the protection of Mother Earth in October 2012, the Framework Law of Mother Earth and Integral Development for Living Well (the "Framework Law," and together with the Constitution and the Mother Earth Rights Law, the "Mother Earth laws"). Article 2 of the Framework Law stated that it had come into being within the powers assigned in the Constitution and the Mother Earth Rights Law and provided that "[i]t constitutes a Framework Law and of preferential application for the development of specific laws, policies, norms, strategies, plans, programs and projects."

Both the Mother Earth Rights Law and the Framework Law were negotiated between the government and the Unity Pact. In 2010, following the World People's Conference, the Unity Pact prepared a draft law on the rights of Mother Earth based on the proceedings of that conference. Only a portion of the draft was approved and included in the 2010 Mother Earth Rights Law. Members of the Unity Pact felt that the abbreviated law may have been passed to bolster Bolivia's image at the Climate Change Conference held in Cancun, Mexico, in 2010. The government insisted, however, that the Mother Earth Rights Law paved the way for a comprehensive framework law to give effect to the intentions of the 2010 law. The Framework Law passed by the legislature in 2012 contained a watered-down version of the Unity Pact draft and had extensive pro-development provisions. The legislature took the lead in drafting the Framework Law and excluded certain Indigenous organizations. Others dropped out of the legislative process and only a few remained involved in the end.[52]

The Framework Law, in Article 1, contained this statement of purpose:

> The purpose of this Law is to establish the vision and foundations of *integral development* in harmony and balance with Mother Earth to Live Well, guaranteeing the continuity of the regeneration capacity of the components and systems of life of Mother Earth, recovering and strengthening local knowledge and ancestral knowledge, within the framework of the complementarity of rights, obligations and duties; as well as the objectives of *integral development* as a means to achieve Living Well, the bases for planning, public management and investments and the strategic institutional framework for its implementation. (Emphases added.)

[52] *See* Paola Villavicencio Calzadilla & Louis J. Kotzé, *Living in Harmony with Nature? A Critical Appraisal of the Rights of Mother Earth in Bolivia,* 7 Transnational Evntl. L. 397, 412 (2018).

Thus, the Framework Law introduces the concept of "integral development" in an effort to reconcile ecocentric respect and care for Mother Earth and anthropocentric development. The difficulty is illustrated by the term "extractivism," which means "those activities which remove large quantities of natural resources that are not processed (or processed only to a limited degree), especially for export."[53] Extractivism as part of integral development was recast as "neo-extractivism" by the Morales government. The intent was to put mining and oil and gas production in Bolivia in a subordinate position to the other values of building the plurinational state and also set them within a chronology where neo-extractivism would be a bridge to *vivir bien*. Critics, however, argued that neo-extractivism simply "maintain[ed] and reproduce[d] key elements of the extractivism that date[d] back to colonial times."[54]

The Framework Law did contain many provisions in line with the Mother Earth Rights Law, but it also placed an obligation on the government to pursue mining, hydrocarbon extraction, and industrialization, always cautioning that these should be undertaken with respect and care for Mother Earth. Note that Bolivia has a high population growth rate, two-thirds of its population lives in cities, and, in conventional economic terms, many of its people are poor. It is especially vulnerable to climate change. Water supply for cities and agriculture derives in part from tropical glaciers in the Andes Mountains, which are melting. The Morales government, in line with the pro-development provisions of the Framework Law, did succeed in increasing economic growth and redistributing some wealth.

In 2019, Morales ran for a fourth time as president under questionable authority as the constitution provided for only two terms. (His first term predated the constitution.) The vote was held on October 20. Morales won the vote, but election fraud was suspected. Supporters of Carlos Mesa, Morales's opponent, protested and convened nationwide strikes. Supporters of Morales engaged in counterstrikes. The Organization of American States was brought in to audit the election, found serious irregularities, and called for a new election. Morales agreed, but the military suggested he resign. Police units mutinied along with presidential guards. Morales fled the capital. Mexico, declaring Morales the legitimate president, sent a jet to pick him up and take him to Mexico, where he lives at the time of this writing. After three supporters of Morales in line for presidential succession resigned, Jeanine Áñez, who had been endorsed by the military, proclaimed herself president. She made clear that she intended to purge Morales's legacy. During his presidency Morales had been opposed by conservative forces in Bolivia and by the United States for his left-wing policies and for issues relating to Bolivian narcotics trafficking. Now the conservatives are back in power.

This report on Bolivia and its rights of nature laws illustrates the complexity of the relationships of law, economics, politics, and culture, and the challenges involved in changing the social contract. It is instructive for Earth lawyers, among other ways, as set out below.

[53] Alberto Acosta, *Extractivism and Neoextractivism: Two Sides of the Same Curse*, *in* BEYOND DEVELOPMENT: ALTERNATIVE VISIONS FROM LATIN AMERICA 61, 62 (M. Lang & D. Mokrani eds., 2013), https://www.tni.org/files/download/beyonddevelopment_extractivism.pdf (last visited April 3, 2020).
[54] *Id.* at 73.

2. A model to be developed

The Bolivian rights of nature laws on their face (as positive law) are a remarkable achievement. They

- Offer a vision of a better way of life, *vivir bien*;
- Recognize a diversity of cultures and the rights of Indigenous people;
- Call for a plurinational polity;
- Recognize that all human development must take place within planetary limits;
- Call for respect for Mother Earth, for the rights of Earth's life systems to perform their functions, and for other species to flourish; and
- Integrate meeting human needs through development with respect and care for Earth.

Paola Villavicencio and Louis Kotzé wrote this about the laws:

> Bolivia's effort to legally protect the rights of Mother Earth is a significant milestone. The country's Constitution, its Law of the Rights of Mother Earth, and the Framework Law are concrete examples in which the law attempts to turn away (if not always successfully) from anthropocentric hierarchies while embracing care for Mother Earth as an ethical obligation of ecological stewardship. On paper at least, the legal protection of the rights of non-human entities provides an opportunity for society to redirect its behaviour away from growth-without-limits paradigms towards an altogether more careful ecological approach.[55]

The Framework Law might be criticized for being a set of principles rather than a precise legal document, yet this is what framework laws are. They set general principles without necessarily including specific goals or targets or enforcement mechanisms. They are written with the understanding that they will be followed by additional laws, protocols, resolutions, and decisions.[56] The Framework Law is a document along the lines of the United Nations' World Charter for Nature[57] and the Earth Charter.[58] The Framework Law goes beyond those, however, in that it grounds principles that are generally in accord with these international documents in Bolivia's own history, cultures, and traditions and applies them to the governance of Bolivia. Bolivia's Mother Earth laws taken together are documents of governance in the broad sense of the term used by Jennings. They are an articulation of a new ecological social contract and a rejection of the social contract of consumption.

[55] Villavicencio & Kotzé, *supra* note 52, at 423.

[56] *See* Daniel Bodansky, The Framework Convention/Protocol Approach 9 (1999), https://www.researchgate.net/publication/289507490_Framework_ConventionProtocol_Approach (last visited April 4, 2020).

[57] G.A. Res. 37/7, World Charter for Nature (Oct. 28, 1982).

[58] The Earth Charter (Earth Charter Commission, 2000), Earth Charter International, https://earthcharter.org/wp-content/uploads/2020/03/echarter_english.pdf (last visited Apr. 7, 2020).

3. A critical appraisal

After praising Bolivia's Mother Earth laws on their face, Villavicencio and Kotzé conclude their article as follows:

> [T]here are important general insights that present themselves from the Bolivian experience. . . . [O]ne such insight is that law has limitations, and one must remain realistic about its potential to counter deeply vested political, social and economic interests. Law will always remain merely one ingredient (albeit a powerful one) in the social institutional regulatory toolbox. However, where it does provide for radical formulations (such as rights of nature), it prompts us to start having conversations about ways in which to accommodate such novel juridical constructs in our social, economic, religious, legal and political structures, including ways to implement them and ways of resolving the many normative and practical contradictions that are likely to arise when the interests that the rights of nature seek to protect collide with those championed by the neoliberal developmental agenda[, which is the] ultimate test for law in relation to protecting the rights of Mother Earth.[59]

Bolivia's rights of nature laws were hailed as a breakthrough on environmental and Earth law websites, in progressive publications, and on websites that highlight promising developments. Here are the headlines from one newspaper:

Bolivia enshrines natural world's rights
with equal status for Mother Earth
Law of Mother Earth expected to prompt radical new
conservation and social measures in South American nation[60]

Earth law websites continue to hold up Bolivia's laws as an example of where the rights of nature are taking hold. The history of Bolivia discussed above, however, presents a far more complex picture. Even when Morales was in power, Villavicencio and Kotzé questioned whether the laws were merely window dressing intended to elevate Bolivia's status on the world stage while it continued to pursue development and extractivism.[61] They observed that as of August 2018 (when Morales was still in office), "the Bolivian government has neither approved new environmental legislation consistent with the Law of the Rights of Mother Earth and the Framework Law, nor repealed major laws that are inconsistent with those laws; nor has it established the Office for the Protection of Mother Earth."[62]

In her doctoral dissertation, Carla Sbert Carlsson examined emerging ecological law in various nations with particular attention to how this law dealt with mining. She examined Bolivia's Mother Earth laws based only on their texts through a three-fold ecological lens of ecocentrism, ecological primacy, and ecological justice and found

[59] Villavicencio & Kotzé, *supra* note 52, at 423.
[60] John Vidal, *Bolivia Enshrines Natural World's Rights with Equal Status for Mother Earth*, The Guardian (Apr. 10, 2011), https://www.theguardian.com/environment/2011/apr/10/bolivia-enshrines-natural-worlds-rights.
[61] Villavicencio & Kotzé, *supra* note 52, at 416.
[62] *Id.* (footnote omitted).

on the whole that the laws were ecocentric.[63] Then she looked at how the laws worked in practice based on an analysis of the Salar de Uyuni lithium industrialization project. This project was announced by Morales in 2008 and involved several stages—from developing a mine to eventually producing lithium batteries. Salar de Uyuni is the world's largest salt flat. It is the legacy of a prehistoric lake that went dry leaving a desert-like 1,000-kilometer landscape. It contains one of the world's largest deposits of lithium and also holds sodium, potassium, magnesium, and borax. Bolivia's Mother Earth laws do not establish licensing requirements, nor are there any regulations under the laws that apply to the mining project. Instead, regulation of the mine is governed by the 1992 Law of the Environment. The mine, which is currently active, is managed by a state agency known as Yacimientos de Litio Bolivianos (YLB). YLB refers on its website to authorizations concerning the project but does not mention Bolivia's Mother Earth laws.

Sbert Carlsson attempts to apply the principles of the Mother Earth laws to the project. For example, the mining activity involves using large amounts of water and the disposal of large amounts of brine as a waste product. The water is "fossil water" drawn from wells and is nonrenewable. She questions whether drawing so much water contravenes the requirement in the Mother Earth laws that economic activities are limited by the capacity of Mother Earth to regenerate herself. She also considers whether mining, since it is a nonrenewable activity that negatively affects wildlife, is consistent with justice for future generations and other species. She notes that lithium is considered essential to a global transition to renewable energy, but she does not weigh this as a balancing factor.[64]

After examining conflicting rights among beings, she states: "This complexity and the general difficulty of establishing proof in environmental cases, begs the question whether the Rights of Mother Earth Law could be implemented effectively even with the most dedicated effort; and if not, whether legal recognition of the rights of nature (in this detailed way at least) is a viable path for ecological law."[65]

Her overall conclusion regarding the application of the Mother Earth laws to the mining project was as follows: "In sum, it is hard to conclude from this case study that the potentially transformative recognition of the rights of Mother Earth and direction towards living well in Bolivian laws have had any bearing on the actual implementation of a project as nationally important as that of lithium industrialization."[66]

4. Lessons for Earth lawyers from Bolivia

For a non-Bolivian, one's initial reaction to what has happened in Bolivia may be that it is a unique situation or that it has application only to circumstances in Bolivia, in South

[63] *See* Carla Sbert Carlsson, Mining from the Lens of Ecological Law: Obstacles and Opportunities for Re-Formation 224-245 (2019) (unpublished Ph.D. in law thesis, University of Ottawa), https://www.academia.edu/39149609/Mining_from_the_Lens_of_Ecological_Law_Obstacles_and_Opportunities_for_Re-formation.
[64] *Id.* at 245-264.
[65] *Id.* at 253.
[66] *Id.* at 258.

America, or in the Global South generally. There are some aspects that can be characterized this way, yet there are also lessons applicable to all places. Some of these lessons are as follows.

Bolivia's laws of Mother Earth offer a model for how to draft constitutions and legislation for an ecological age. The values in the legislation are that of the new ecological social contract. It was a signal accomplishment to have passed these laws. This would not currently be possible in, for example, the "advanced" United States. In 1982, the United Nations' World Charter for Nature was approved by 111 nations, 18 abstained, and only the United States voted against it. The United States either did not sign or did not ratify the Convention on the Law of the Sea (1990), Convention on Biological Diversity (1992), the Kyoto Protocol (climate mitigation) (1997), the Rome Statute of the International Criminal Court (1998), or the Paris Agreement (climate mitigation) (which became effective in November 2016—the convention was signed by the Obama administration, in April 2016, but it was not ratified by the U.S. Senate and, in August 2017, the United States withdrew from the agreement).[67] The Trump administration, as of December 2019 (after three years in office), had rolled back 95 previously enacted environmental laws.[68]

Earth lawyers in the United States must consider whether or in what way its environmental laws are a step toward ecological governance. What are the values in those laws and how well do they map the values Jennings calls for in ecological governance? In drafting its Mother Earth laws, Bolivia drew on the wisdom of its Indigenous peoples; what might drafters of Earth laws in the United States draw on from its history and culture? What in U.S. culture, if anything, corresponds to *vivir bien*? In a country committed to economic growth measured by GDP, of which 70 percent is accounted for by consumer spending, what would a non-consumptive political economy look like?

Another area for reflection is whether the Bolivian experience is a judgment on rights of nature laws. Have Earth lawyers promoted the passage of these laws without critically reflecting on the complexity of applying them? If one takes the position that an ecocentric perspective requires that rights of nature laws make no distinctions among the various beings in nature—as Sbert Carlsson did in applying the ecocentric part of her ecological lens to the Mother Earth laws—can they provide legal guidance at all?[69] Given the impossibility of developing statues detailing the rights and duties respecting each being and component of nature, can a framework law such as that in Bolivia play a guiding role in policy?

The Bolivian experience also calls for reflection on the role of the written ecocentric laws in relation to governance as a whole. For written laws to be effective, they must

[67] *List of Treaties Unsigned or Unratified by the United States*, WIKIPEDIA, https://en.wikipedia.org/w/index.php?title=List_of_treaties_unsigned_or_unratified_by_the_United_States&oldid=946035018 (last visited Apr. 5, 2020).

[68] Nadja Popovich, Livia Albeck-Ripka, & Kendra Pierre-Louis, *95 Environmental Rules Being Rolled Back under Trump*, N.Y. TIMES (Dec. 21, 2019), https://www.nytimes.com/interactive/2019/climate/trump-environment-rollbacks.html.

[69] Her ecocentric lens was: "Ecocentrism, recognize and respect the value of all beings and the interconnectedness among them, equally promoting the interests of human and nonhuman members of the Earth community." Sbert Carlsson, *supra* note 63, at 224 (emphasis added).

be supported by law enforcement, the judicial system, and the administrative branch. Laws must be largely self-enforcing by voluntary compliance. For laws to be self-enforcing, the public generally must find them and the political system just and fair. Economic considerations, both domestic and international, come into play. People must feel they have a means of support and that they can prosper. "Prosper" can be framed as less consumptive living (*vivir bien*), but this has to be an established expectation.

It could be said that environmental law treats the symptoms, not the disease, and the Bolivian Mother Earth laws are intended to treat the disease. The latter is what is needed. Earth lawyers must ask how they can *realistically* build on the Bolivian experience. Neither law schools nor law practices prepare lawyers for the challenges of Earth law. Conventional law practices reward lawyers who learn "either-or" law and then use it to solve problems for their clients.[70] What is needed now is relational-evolutionary jurisprudence. Winning and losing have a different meaning in this jurisprudence. Winning means creative adjustment to ever-changing circumstances; losing means failing to adapt. A client's success can never be separated from the success of the system as a whole. "Resilience" is a term that has gained some currency as a description of success in an ecological age. "Vitality" is another such term. It is the task of Earth lawyers to create and practice resilient, vital law.

IV. CONCLUSION: DEPENDING ON THE INTERCONNECTED WEB OF LIFE

In late 2019, an infectious virus, SARS-CoV-2 (commonly referred to as COVID-19), caused by a particular coronavirus was first identified in Wuhan, a city of 11 million in central China. Because COVID-19 has a nearly identical genome sequence as a bat coronavirus, a theory for the origin of the disease is that it was transmitted from a bat to a human.[71] Further, there is a theory that the virus started in a particular wet market in Wuhan.[72] After infection of a single human being there, the disease spread rapidly to people in nearly every nation in the world. As of this writing, there is no vaccine for the disease and no cure. Social isolation and quarantine have been determined to be the best ways to reduce its spread. As a result, on a global basis, economic activity has fallen precipitously, millions have lost their jobs, health systems have become overburdened, and large numbers of people have died and continue to die.

[70] This has been called "mechanical jurisprudence." See Fritjof Capra & Ugo Mattei, The Ecology of Law: Toward a Legal System in Tune with Nature and Community 101-103, 173 (2015).

[71] Peng Zhou et al., *A Pneumonia Outbreak Associated with a New Coronavirus of Probable Bat Origin*, 579 Nature 270 (2020), https://doi.org/10.1038/s41586-020-2012-7.

[72] Aylin Woodward, *China Just Banned the Trade and Consumption of Wild Animals. Experts Think the Coronavirus Jumped from Live Animals to People at a Market*, Business Insider (Feb. 25, 2020), https://www.businessinsider.com/china-bans-wildlife-trade-consumption-coronavirus-2020-2.

At first this may not be thought of as an environmental issue, but many are seeing a connection. According to Kate Jones, Chair of Ecology and Biodiversity at University College London,

> [V]iruses are on the rise . . . because there are so many of us and we are so connected. The chance of more [spillovers into humans] happening is higher because we are degrading these landscapes. Destroying habitats is the cause, so restoring habitats is a solution. . . . It's not OK to transform a forest into agriculture without understanding the impact that has on climate, carbon storage, disease emergence and flood risk. . . . You can't do those things in isolation without thinking about what that does to humans.[73]

In 1970, the first Earth day occurred and modern environmental law began. Then the global population was 3.2 billion; now, 50 years later, there are nearly 8 billion people. In 1970, there were around 200 million cars and trucks; today, there are more than 1.5 billion. By almost every measure human impact on Earth has skyrocketed. Before 1970, fires that consumed 100,000 acres were rare in the United States, but since then, there have been dozens. In the summer of 2019, fires in Siberia consumed 17 million acres and, in Australia, in 2019 and 2020, fires burned more than 10 million acres. At present, deforestation is accelerating, coral reefs are dying, oceans are acidifying, sunny day flooding is occurring, storms are becoming more frequent and fiercer, and ice is melting. According to the WWF's 2018 *Living Planet Report*, population sizes of vertebrate species have declined on average by 60 percent since 1970 (but there has not been as large of a percentage drop in absolute numbers across species).[74] In Germany, a study found that the biomass of insects in certain protected areas has dropped by 76 percent in three decades.[75]

Crops depend on pollinators that are in decline. Drones have been tested to carry pollen, which raises the question of whether humans are still dependent on the interconnected web of life? Will humans always be able to find substitutes for what is lost in nature? For Earth lawyers the answer to the latter question is clear: It is a foolish wager to rely on.

Much has already been set in motion. Earth lawyers will not be surprised to be living in an age of cascading crises. They will not dismiss them. Instead, they will look for patterns and they will seek to understand the lessons in them. In a twist on Soren Kierkegaard's statement that "life is not a problem to be solved but a reality to be experienced," they will understand that our planet is not a problem to be solved but a reality to be lived.

Different theories of the social contract are being played out. Some following Hobbes see the state as sovereign "defin[ing] the laws and morality. Peace, tranquility,

[73] Nick Paton Walsh & Vasco Cotovio, *Bats Are Not to Blame for Coronavirus. Humans Are*, CNN (Mar. 20, 2020), https://www.cnn.com/2020/03/19/health/coronavirus-human-actions-intl/index.html.
[74] WWF, Living Planet Report 7 (2018).
[75] *See* Elizabeth Kolbert, *The Case for Catastrophe*, National Geographic 14-21 (Apr. 2020).

order, and, in Hobbes's words 'commodious living' are the purpose of civil society."[76] Others following Locke hold that the "State's main obligations are to protect the rights of its citizens, especially their property rights, and provide for the common defense."[77] The consent of citizens is conditional and they are ever vigilant lest the state should trample on their rights. Those following Rousseau hold that "[t]he State responds to a need of living in society—in other words of living in mutual dependence and fellowship of others."[78] People are fully committed to the social contract yet remain sovereign. Governance is a moral community guided by the general will of the people.

Jennings extends Rousseau: The State responds to the needs of living in mutual dependence and fellowship *with all members of the Earth community*. The formation of this new ecological social contract is only beginning. As Latour wrote: "[It] has to be assembled bit by bit. The laws of the new polity have to be invented and self-imposed because "[w]ithout decision, there is no body politics, no liberty, [no] autonomy."[79] Rousseau sought to construct a theory of the social contract where humans would be as free as in their natural state. People are now coming to see that they cannot be free without an ecological social contract.

Earth lawyers will play a crucial role in shaping this new contract, and they will place their wager on the interconnected community of life.

STUDY QUESTIONS

(1) What is an Earth lawyer?

(2) What special skills, abilities, social status, and roles do lawyers bring to the task of creating a new ecological social contract?

(3) What can lawyers do to bring into being a new ecological social contract?

(4) What is normative jurisprudence? An "objective" legal system allows transactions and resolution of conflicts without direct reference to morals. What is the role of morals in law practice? Will "ecological morals" cause conflict?

[76] *See supra* text accompanying note 8. This is the role played by the Communist party in China. In part in response to the threat of COVID-19, in March 2020, the Hungarian parliament voted to allow Hungarian Prime Minister Viktor Orban to rule by decree. In the United States, in the impeachment hearings of President Trump in 2019-2020, the president refused to cooperate with the legislative branch. This was an extension of the theory of the unitary executive, which "argues that the president's constitutionally allocated executive responsibilities may not be restricted by Congressional or Judicial action." *The Unitary Executive,* SCHMOOP.COM, https://www.shmoop.com/study-guides/civics/executive-branch/unitary-executive (last visited Apr. 17, 2020).

[77] *See supra* text following note 8.

[78] *See supra* text following note 9.

[79] *See supra* text accompanying note 5. As to the character the politics of the new social contract according to Jennings, *see supra* text accompanying notes 42 and 43.

(5) How may lawyers and society engage the nonhuman language discourse of nature?

(6) How may Earth lawyers be guided by the general will of the Earth community?

(7) What lessons do you take from the Bolivian experience?

(8) Human history is filled with catastrophes, such as the current COVID-19 crisis. Do you anticipate cascading catastrophes, and, if so, what is the meaning of this for you? How will this affect Earth law?

SECTION FIVE

A GLOBAL SURVEY OF EARTH LAW

Section V addresses Earth law's actual implementation through lawmaking and litigation at the national level. The case studies reviewed in this section are marked by diverse legal strategies used to stop and reverse injury to forests, rivers, streams, springs, and other ecosystems. Moreover, each chapter reveals a distinctive legal system within which the strategies unfold. We discussed implementation of Earth law in the United States in Section III, Chapter 9, and using that as a basis for comparison, we now turn to a discussion of litigating and applying Earth law in other countries to better understand how implementation at the ground level actually works.

As you review the case studies, note their similarities as well as the distinctions. The chapters on Ecuador (Chapter 17), Colombia (Chapter 18), and Brazil (Chapter 19) reveal an encouraging number of cases recognizing rights of nature. Yet, the legal framework within which these cases play out varies for each country. Earth law litigation in Ecuador springs from the country's Constitution, which grants nature broad rights. While Colombia and Brazil do not embody rights of nature in their Constitutions or statutes laws, their courts, particularly in Colombia, are creating a rich body of case law through ecocentric interpretation of existing legislation to recognize the rights of nature. In groundbreaking decisions, the Colombian courts have recognized the Atrato River Basin and the Colombian Amazon as legal subjects of rights in order to stop destructive mining and deforestation, respectively. The case study on Brazil addresses the failure of its environmental laws and the efforts underway to remedy the situation by promoting rights of nature laws. Yet, without waiting for new laws, courts in Brazil are moving ahead with Earth law, recently recognizing a nonhuman animal (a parrot) as a subject of rights. The emergence of Earth law in Mexico is unfolding in part through the expansion of legal frameworks for human rights. Similar to Brazil's constitution, which recognizes the human right to an "ecologically balanced environment" and supports Indigenous practices for living in harmony with nature, Mexico's constitution also grants humans environmental rights, including a specific Indigenous right for maintaining and improving their environment. While both Brazil's and Mexico's constitutions are anthropocentric and, unlike Ecuador's, do not recognize rights of nature, their codification of the human right to a healthy environment is fostering the development of Earth law. In Mexico, three state governments have included rights of nature within their constitutions and other are not far behind.

Although this section does not include a chapter on Bolivia, in 2009 Bolivia's president was a key figure in the U.N. Harmony with Nature initiative, as reviewed in Chapter 15, "United Nations Sustainable Development Initiatives." Bolivia adopted the Law of the Rights of Mother Earth (2010) and the Framework Law of Mother Earth and Integral Development for Living Well (2010). One reason for omitting a Bolivia chapter is the abject failure experienced in enforcing the laws that grant nature a diversity of rights.

Indigenous rights-based movements are explored in Chapter 24, "Africa." Similar to Latin American countries, efforts in Africa to promote Earth law spring from the continent's local traditions and customs of living in harmony with Mother Earth and the focus on restoring Indigenous knowledge and practices at the community and local levels. Africa's Earth law movement has evolved under the leadership of a civil society intent on reviving customary laws and Indigenous practices as the basis for a new Earth jurisprudence.

Continuing the focus on Indigenous laws and customs, Chapter 25, "Indigenous Legalities," addresses American indigenous knowledge and practices and their potential for transforming Western legal systems in the face of the current ecological crisis. Unlike many Indigenous people's belief systems, Western law is based on an "ontology of separation" between nature and culture that is incompatible with ecocentric law. The chapter also reviews how Western colonialism has impacted Indigenous laws and how colonialism endures.

Earth law in India (Chapter 20) and New Zealand (Chapter 22) are based on the model of legal personhood for nature. In New Zealand, the 2014 Te Urewera Act recognizes the former Te Urewera National Park as its own legal entity, and a 2017 treaty agreement between the government and the Māori tribe of Whanganui also recognizes the Whanganui River as its own legal entity. Guardians were appointed in both cases to represent the rivers, in India by the court and in New Zealand through legislation. Specifically citing the personhood for nature in New Zealand, an Indian court recognized the legal personhood of the Ganges River (a decision that was later overturned by the country's Supreme Court) as well as rights for the entire animal kingdom in 2017.

While these countries have already left their mark as practitioners of Earth law, note the situation in Israel (Chapter 21), where both Earth law legislation and litigation is almost non-existent. Similar to Colombia and Brazil, the Israel country study demonstrates how Earth law can evolve without specific laws when courts have the will to interpret existing legislation to counter harm to nature. Moreover, the Israeli case also shows that courts might hand down precedential judgements that in reality create rights for nature without mentioning these rights or other Earth law doctrines and concepts.

In the Netherlands (Chapter 23), implementation of Earth law received an enormous boost by the 2020 decision of the country's Supreme Court in the *Urgenda* case, in which current and future generations successfully established the Dutch government's duty to prevent dangerous climate change. The Supreme Court cited human rights conventions and the Intergovernmental Panel on Climate Change in ordering the Dutch government to meet its obligations under international law (the Paris Agreement) in order to avoid severe environmental harm.

Drawing all these cases together is the strong consensus on the need to transform nature—currently objectified as human property—into an independent entity with its own legal personhood or rights. Changing nature from an object of law into its subject underlies the assumption that existing laws cannot reverse the unfolding ecological tragedy. Hence, the case studies share the objective of replacing the current legal system with an ecocentric one that will recognize nature's inherent value, rather than its current worth to humans as a resource to feed the global economy.

As you read the chapters in this section, consider how litigation can generate transformative change at the ground level and the specific impact of each case on ecosystems at risk. Also try to interlink the cases discussed in Chapter 9 on U.S. Earth law, for example, with the litigation models presented in the Colombian and Dutch case studies. Do these models offer a more effective strategy to litigate Earth law in the United States, or are foreign (non-U.S.) legal systems simply more likely to make ecocentric legal interpretations? Effectively promoting Earth law requires an in-depth understanding of the different litigation and policy models being used to secure rights for ecosystems and their applicability to other incidents of ecological harm.

CHAPTER 17

Ecuador[1]

I. INTRODUCTION

In 2008, Ecuador made history by becoming the world's first country to recognize the rights of nature in its Constitution. The Constitution was drafted beginning in 2007 by the Ecuadorian Constituent Assembly, comprising 130 delegates representing all of Ecuador's regions.[2] The majority of elected delegates were members of President Rafael Correa's center-left social democratic movement, *Patria Altiva i Soberana* (Proud and Sovereign Homeland or PAIS). In July 2018, the Assembly approved a draft constitution with 494 articles. In September 2008, a constitutional referendum was approved by 63.93 percent of Ecuador voters.

In Ecuador, rights of nature reflects the belief system of its population, especially its Indigenous peoples, who have lived in harmony with nature since time immemorial. Other supporters of rights of nature include lawyers and non-governmental organizations (NGOs) seeking stronger environmental protection to combat an influx of extractive industries. Many view rights of nature as an emerging success story of eco-centric law in practice. But others find its impact to be more symbolic than practical. These contradictory visions may explain the uneven way in which rights of nature has developed in Ecuador over the last 12 years.

This chapter explores rights of nature developments in Ecuador. It begins by discussing why rights of nature received constitutional recognition and what it means to Ecuadorians. It then reviews rights of nature decisions handed down by the Ecuadorian courts. Finally, the chapter looks ahead to how rights of nature might progress in Ecuador in the near future.

[1] This chapter was authored by Julio Prieto Méndez, lawyer for the Union of the people affected by Texaco (UDAPT), and Hugo Echeverria, Professor of Law at the University of San Francisco (Quito) and a rights of nature attorney in Ecuador. A special thank you to Sarah Stoughton for her research, writing, and translation assistance and to Jordan Michelson for his writing contributions.

[2] *See* THE CARTER CENTER, FINAL REPORT ON ECUADOR'S APPROBATORY CONSTITUTIONAL REFERENDUM OF SEPT. 28, 2008 4 (2008).

II. A CLASH BETWEEN INDIGENOUS BELIEF SYSTEMS AND WESTERN NORMS

Rights of Nature was a current flowing through Ecuadorian veins long before the country's 2008 Constitution. Indigenous peoples in Ecuador, comprised of 14 separate nationalities, have traditionally recognized underlying rights of nature principles through their practices, customs, and laws.[3] For example, they regard forests as living entities and thus reject development or intervention that threatens forest ecosystems.[4] One group, the Sarayaku people, believe that forests are already "developed" because they contain natural paths, well-defined hunting seasons and areas, and rotating *chakras* (the Indigenous Quechua word for small farms) that have existed for generations.[5] The Sarayaku have developed their communities and shaped the forest in harmony with nature's rhythms.

Western benchmarks of development—roads, electricity, and jobs from extractive industries—are considered unnecessary by the Sarayaku. This Sarayaku philosophy is consistent with the concept of the rights and responsibilities of rights of nature law as it has begun to be developed in Ecuador.

However, Ecuador is home to many different cultures, and rights of nature is not ingrained into the ethos of most of the population. Even though many Ecuadorians are of mixed Indigenous and European heritage,[6] Ecuador's society is heavily influenced by Western culture, including its emphasis on continuous development and economic growth. Ecuador is thus a story of two competing visions: embracing age-old belief systems of living in harmony with nature and pursuing economic progress at the expense of nature.

Some Ecuadorians are critical of rights of nature. For them, it is easy to understand the legal interest in protecting *something* because of its value to human life, but rights of nature proposes to respect *someone*, because *she* deserves respect. These concepts can be radical and threatening to some humans. Consider the following argument from Farith Simon Campaña:

[3] "In Bolivia and Ecuador, these and other references serve occasionally as academic corroboration of long-standing Indigenous demands that build on a deeply ingrained, animated relationship between humans and nature, expressed as mutual caring and learning beyond rational accounts" (internal citations omitted). JOHANNES M. WALDMUELLER & LAURA RODRÍGUEZ, HANDBOOK OF DEVELOPMENT ETHICS INVITED ENTRY CHAPTER: *BUEN VIVIR* AND RIGHTS OF NATURE 12 (Jay Drydyk & Lori Keleher eds., 2008).

[4] As ample scholarship has demonstrated, the Amazon, for instance, is neither an untouched nor unspoiled ecosystem but in fact has been profoundly shaped by human impact during thousands of years. *Id.* at 19 (internal citations omitted).

[5] The Sarayaku cosmovision is called *Kawsay Sacha o Selva Viviente,* [meaning] "Living Rainforest," and is based on a life in harmonious coexistence with nature. As Franco Viteri, the Sarayaku leader, says: "The forest is already 'developed', the forest is life.'" Leah Temper*, Sarayaku Wins Case in the Inter-American Court of Human Rights but the Struggle for Prior Consent Continues,* ENVIRONMENTAL JUSTICE ORGANISATIONS, LIABILITIES, AND TRADE (Aug. 21, 2012), http://www.ejolt.org/2012/08/sarayaku-wins-case-in-the-inter-american-court-of-human-rights-but- the-struggle-for-prior-consent-continues.

[6] SILVERIANO CHISAGUANO, LA POBLACIÓN INDÍGENA DEL ECUADOR [INDIGENOUS POPULATION IN ECUADOR] 26 (2006).

> Avoiding the destruction of the Earth by humans is important, but [we should not] accept any regulatory reform as valid just because it sounds "revolutionary" without examining its possible consequences, especially when the possibility exists to weaken human rights protections.
>
> . . . What should judges give more weight to when in conflict: the rights of nature or the rights of individuals and communities? Do human beings and nature have the same ontological value? [discussing what sort of things exist in the social world and assumptions about the form and nature of that social reality]. . . .
>
> [E]verything suggests that we will soon be studying, defending, and explaining the importance of the most basic human rights, remembering the need to consider the human being as the center of everything.[7]

By contrast, other Ecuadorians embrace the idea that humans are *part* of nature, not the center or owner of it. As explained by Ramiro Ávila Santamaría, "You cannot separate the concept of being human from nature; both are one, hence hurting nature is hurting oneself. . . . [R]espect for nature has a direct impact on respect for human beings and, on the other hand, disrespect of any human being inevitably means disrespect of nature."[8]

In sum, even within Ecuador where rights for nature have been constitutionally recognized, viewpoints vary significantly. The ultimate success of the rights of nature legal paradigm will depend in large part on the extent to which and how Ecuadorean judges, politicians, lawyers, and citizens embrace nature's rights in practice.

III. ECUADOR'S 2008 CONSTITUTION

This section explores the text of Ecuador's 2008 Constitution. It begins with a discussion of *Sumak Kawsay*, meaning "good living," which is a fundamental pillar of Ecuador's Constitution. It then discusses constitutional rights of nature protections and concludes by discussing Ecuador's recognition of human environmental rights.

A. *Sumak Kawsay*

Indigenous peoples were central to shaping Ecuador's Constitution.[9] For example, the National Indigenous Confederation of Ecuador (CONAIE) successfully fought to

[7] Farith Simon Campaña, Derechos de la Naturaleza: ¿Innovación Trascendental, Retórica Jurídica O Proyecto Político? [The Rights of Nature: The Transcendent Innovation Legal Rhetoric or Political Project?] 37 (2013) (translated from Spanish).

[8] Ramiro Ávila Santamaria, el Derecho de la Naturaleza: Fundamentos, 16-17 (2010).

[9] Julio Prieto, Derechos de la Naturaleza: Fundamento, Contenido Y Exigibilidad Jurisdiccional [Rights of Nature: Rationale and Jurisdictional Enforcement] (2013).

ensure that the Constitution reflected the multi-ethnic character of Ecuador and its various belief systems.[10] One of those belief systems is the concept of *Sumak Kawsay*, usually translated as *good way of living* (*buen vivir* in Spanish). The Preamble of the Constitution states that the sovereign people of Ecuador "hereby decide to build a new form of public coexistence, in diversity and in harmony with nature, to achieve the good way of living, the *sumak kawsay*." *Sumak Kawsay*, however, is a deeper concept than the literal translation of the words conveys. As described by Raúl Llasag Fernández,

> In order to make visible other forms of knowledge and wisdom, without intending to essentialize, but to make possible the intercultural dialogue, [it is necessary to] look at the conception of Pachamama for Indigenous peoples of Ecuador, aware that there is diversity of Indigenous peoples and diversity of realities, therefore, diversity of conceptions of Pacha- mama and *Sumak Kawsay*, but they are articulated by fundamental principles that make them common." *Sumak Kawsay* is an Indigenous idea that represents living in harmony with pachamama, or nature.[11]

Luis Macas explains the meaning of the words *Sumak* and *Kawsay* as follows:

> *Sumak* is the fullness, the sublime, excellent, magnificent, beautiful, and superior. *Kawsay* is life, is being. However, it is dynamic, changing, it is not passive []. Therefore, *Sumak Kawsay* would be life in fullness. Life in material and spiritual excellence. The magnificent and the sublime are expressed in harmony, in the internal and external balance of a community.[12]

To a linear-thinking legal mind, the definition of *Sumak Kawsay* may seem impossibly imprecise. That is because the true meaning of *Sumak Kawsay* escapes a simple translation, and it is too difficult to capture in Western thought. Truly understanding *Sumak Kawsay* requires "look[ing] at the conception of Pachamama for Indigenous peoples of Ecuador, aware that there is a diversity of Indigenous peoples and diversity of realities, [and] therefore, a diversity of conceptions of Pachamama and *Sumak Kawsay*."[13]

Nonetheless, the various conceptions of *Sumak Kawsay* do share common fundamental principles. Andean philosopher Javier Lajo has identified five such principles:

1. There is no life without wisdom (*Tucu Yachay*);
2. We all come from Mother Earth (*Pachamama*);
3. Life is healthy (*Hambi Kawsay*);
4. Life is collective (*Sumak Kamaña*); and
5. We all have an ideal or dream (*Hatun Muskuy*).[14]

[10] *Id.* at 28; *see also* Katherine Bowen Scofield, Indigenous Rights and Constitutional Change in Ecuador 1-3 (2017) (Indiana University Dissertation).

[11] Daniela Bressa Florentin, *Buen Vivir in Ecuador*, in The Politics of Wellbeing: Theory, Policy and Practice 132 (Ian Bache & Karen Scott eds., 2018).

[12] Luis Macas, *Sumak Kawsay: La Vida en Plenitud*, J. of Am. Lat. Mov 14-16 (2010).

[13] Ibáñez-Elam, at 284.

[14] Javier Lajo, *Recuperemos el Sumak Kawsay -el Vivir Bien-, por un 'Orden Andino'*, America Latina en Movimiento (July 15, 2008), https://www.alainet.org/es/active/25273.

Ultimately, the Ecuadorian Constituent Assembly embraced *Sumak Kawsay* as one of the pillars of its new Constitution. In large part, rights of nature emerged directly from this mindset. Aside from supporting *Sumak Kawsay*, constitutional drafters identified many other benefits of rights of nature: it supported plurinationalism (the existence of several different nations in a political state), helped address the ecological crisis, and might curb dominant capitalistic influences, amongst others.[15] Thus rights of nature was included in the 2008 Constitution, as discussed in the next subsection.

B. Rights of Nature and Related Environmental Protections

Based in part upon the concept of *Sumak Kawsay*, Ecuador's Constitution established rights of nature protections in Title II, Chapter 7—Articles 71-74, entitled "Rights of Nature." The substantive rights constitutionally recognized as belonging to nature are specifically those in Articles 71 and 72:

> **Art 71**. Nature, or Pacha Mama, where life is reproduced and occurs, has the right to integral respect for her existence and for the maintenance and regeneration of her life cycles, structure, functions and evolutionary processes.
>
> All persons, communities, peoples and nations can call upon public authorities to enforce the rights of nature. To enforce and interpret these rights, the principles set forth in the Constitution shall be observed, as appropriate.
>
> The State shall give incentives to natural persons and legal entities and to communities to protect nature and to promote respect for all the elements comprising an ecosystem.
>
> **Art 72**. Nature has the right to be restored. This restoration shall be apart from the obligation of the State and natural persons or legal entities to compensate individuals and communities that depend on affected natural systems.
>
> In those cases of severe or permanent environmental impact, including those caused by the exploitation of nonrenewable natural resources, the State shall establish the most effective mechanisms to achieve the restoration and shall adopt adequate measures to eliminate or mitigate harmful environmental consequences.

These are the bedrock guarantees of nature's rights in Ecuador, although their exact meaning is still subject to interpretation. For example, when is a project deemed to have interfered with the "maintenance" of Pachamama's "life cycles, structure, functions and evolutionary processes"? Is it a strictly science-based determination? Does a court just "know it when it sees it?" Further, nature has a right to be restored in Article 72—but to be restored to what state? The courts are already grappling with many of these questions.

Continuing, Article 73 establishes certain affirmative duties on the Ecuadorian government—which includes executive, legislative, and judicial branches—to protect nature, with an emphasis on preventing *permanent* harm to nature:

[15] For a more detailed description of the debate leading to the adoption of the 2008 Constitution, *see* Constituent Ecuadorian Assembly. Act N.º 58, June 6, 2008. *See also* Prieto, *supra* note 19, at 40-46.

> **Art. 73**. The State shall apply preventive and restrictive measures on activities that might lead to the extinction of species, the destruction of ecosystems and the permanent alteration of natural cycles.
>
> The introduction of organisms and organic and inorganic material that might definitively alter the nation's genetic assets is forbidden.

Finally, Article 74 establishes that humans still have a right to benefit from the environment, with *Sumak Kawsay* (translated here as "good way of living") as the end in view:

> **Art 74**. Persons, communities, peoples, and nations shall have the right to benefit from the environment and the natural wealth enabling them to enjoy *the good way of living.*

Environmental services shall not be subject to appropriation; their production, delivery, use and development shall be regulated by the State. The rights of nature provisions in Articles 71-74 are strengthened by subsequent articles addressing the legal relationship between humans and nature. Here, the Constitution addresses both the human duties and responsibilities that are necessary to uphold the rights of nature (Art. 83), and once again calls for a harmonious coexistence with nature through the lens of *Sumak Kawsay* (Art. 275):

> **Art. 83.** Ecuadorians have the following duties and obligations, without detriment to others provided for by the Constitution or by law:....
>
> 6. To respect the rights of nature, preserve a healthy environment and use natural resources rationally, sustainably and durably.

> **Art. 275.** The development structure is the organized, sustainable and dynamic group of economic, political, socio-cultural and environmental systems which underpin the achievement of the good way of living (*Sumak Kawsay*)....The good way of living shall require persons, communities, peoples and nationalities to effectively exercise their rights and fulfill their responsibilities within the framework of interculturalism, respect for their diversity, and harmonious coexistence with nature.

To some, it may sound as though rights of nature would prohibit any activity that impacts the environment, but this is not the case. Not every environmental impact has the potential to threaten or harm the integrity of nature's existence and the maintenance and regeneration of her life cycles, structure, functions and evolutionary processes—those fundamental protections established by the Constitution. Rights of nature represents a rebalancing, not an elimination, of human activities that impact the environment, with the goal of protecting and restoring basic ecological processes. Therefore, lifestyles such as those suggested by the Sarayaku people are not the only acceptable lifestyle under this environmental approach, although they do provide helpful guidance. On the other hand, activities that fail to respect these norms—regardless of whether a valid permit or license has been issued—would be in violation of nature's constitutional rights.

C. Ecuadorian Environmental Constitutionalism

In addition to *Sumak Kawsay*, two other "pillars of support" for rights of nature may be recognized in Ecuador's Constitution: (1) constitutional environmental principles that developed in Ecuador since the 1990s, such as the human right to a healthy environment, and (2) international environmental law, such as sustainable development agreements, the Convention on Biological Diversity, and the 1982 World Charter for Nature.[16] As an example of the latter, Principle 1 of the World Charter proclaims that "***Nature shall be respected*** and its essential processes shall not be impaired." This language is echoed in Article 71 of Ecuador's 2008 Constitution, which upholds nature's rights and requires the State to promote respect towards nature. It may be helpful to consider Ecuadorian environmental constitutionalism in the context of three pillars: Indigenous law (including *Sumak Kawsay*), constitutional law, and international environmental law.

Aside from Articles 71-74 assertion of rights of nature principles, Ecuador's Constitution applies other principles of environmental law that support rights of nature. For example, Article 395 is frequently cited in rights of nature decisions that also involve basic human rights. Pay special attention to Article 395.3, which commands the State to allow affected populations to participate in planning and monitoring activities impacting the environment:

> **Art. 395.** The Constitution recognizes the following environmental principles:
>
> 1. The State shall guarantee a sustainable model of development, one that is environmentally balanced and respectful of cultural diversity, conserves biodiversity and the natural regeneration capacity of ecosystems, and ensures meeting the needs of present and future generations.
> 2. Environmental management policies shall be applied cutting across all sectors and dimensions and shall be mandatorily enforced by the State at all of its levels and by all natural persons or legal entities in the country's territory.
> 3. The State shall guarantee the active and permanent participation of affected persons, communities, peoples and nations in the planning, implementation and monitoring of all activities exerting environmental impacts. . . .

Furthermore, Articles 395.4 and 396 establish the *in dubio pro natura* (when in doubt, favor nature) principle and the precautionary principle, respectively. The first states a general constitutional rule that nature should be protected above other interests when there is doubt about how legal provisions should be applied. It is primarily enforced by the judicial branch when interpreting environmental rules, but it is also mandatory for decisions of the legislative and executive branches. Meanwhile, Article 396 establishes that the state has a duty to protect the environment whenever there is uncertainty about environmental impacts.

[16] *See* Hugo Echeverría, The Rights of Nature, Fundación Pachamama, Recognizing Rights for Nature in the Ecuadorian Constitution 2 (n.d.) (discussing the 1998 Constitution's protection of the right to a healthy environment) and Rights of Nature: the Ecuadorian Case, 78-79 (2017).

> **Art. 395.4.** In the event of doubt about the scope of legal provisions for environmental issues, it is the most favorable interpretation of their effective force for the protection of nature that shall prevail.
>
> **Art. 396.** The State shall adopt timely policies and measures to avoid adverse environmental impacts where there is certainty about the damage. In the case of doubt about the environmental impact stemming from a deed or omission, although there is no scientific evidence of the damage, the State shall adopt effective and timely measures of protection.

The Constitution also establishes the *human* right to live in a healthy environment that is distinct from, but related to, the rights of nature provisions:

> **Art. 14.** The right of the population to live in a healthy and ecologically balanced environment that guarantees sustainability and the good way of living (*Sumak Kawsay*) is recognized. Environmental conservation, the protection of ecosystems, biodiversity and the integrity of the country's genetic assets, the prevention of environmental damage, and the recovery of degraded natural spaces are declared matters of public interest.
>
> **Art. 66.** The following rights of persons are recognized and guaranteed:...
> **27.** The right to live in a healthy environment that is ecologically balanced, pollution-free and in harmony with nature.

Observe that nature's rights and human environmental rights are completely separate under Ecuador's Constitution. They are different rights belonging to different rights-holders. However, they are complementary in practice because human environmental rights cannot be upheld without respect for nature. Still, consider whether a rights of nature paradigm should establish a single set of rights for the entire Earth community—including both humans and the rest of nature. If the goal is for humans and nature to live together in harmony, should we move away from the *us* (humans) and *them* (nature) mentality? Or if human environmental rights and rights of nature are separated, should different components of nature also have their own tailored rights—forest rights, animal rights, ocean rights, and so forth?

IV. RIGHTS OF NATURE COURT CASES

Through March 2020, more than 32 legal decisions in Ecuador have involved the rights of nature.[17] Of those, at least seven cases have reached Ecuador's Constitutional Court. Article 429 of the Constitution states that the Constitutional Court is Ecuador's highest authority on constitutional interpretation, so its decisions set precedents that greatly contribute to the development of rights of nature. This section explores the rights of nature cases decided by this Court.

[17] *Casos en Ecuador*, Observatorio Juridico de Derechos de la Naturaleza (last visited Mar. 27, 2020), https://www.derechosdelanaturaleza.org.ec/casos-en-ecuador.

A. *Biodigesters* Case, Ruling No. 0567-08-RA (2009)[18]

The *Biodigesters* case, submitted in 2007, was the first to be resolved from a rights of nature perspective by the Constitutional Court. The case was brought as an *amparo* action, which seeks to protect an individual's rights while also upholding the Constitution for its own sake.[19] The case concerned an agro-industrial pig farm that planned to install six biodigesters, which turn hog waste into methane gas. The plaintiffs, neighbors of the farm, complained about a suite of environmental harms arising from the pig farm, including air pollution, water pollution from wastewater discharges, and otherwise poor environmental management. However, the only remedy sought by the lawsuit was to suspend installation of the biodigesters, which can produce toxic odors.

The Court denied the *amparo*, arguing that the installation of biodigesters does not, in itself, violate the human right to live in a healthy environment. The Court further argued that biodigesters fall under the Clean Development Mechanism of the Kyoto Protocol, since they replace the use of fossil fuels with biogas recycled from animal manure.

While the plaintiffs lost on the biogas issue, the Court took a broader look at the agro-industrial farm's environmental impacts, namely its wastewater discharges, which for years had been reported to authorities without an effective response. The Court, for the first time ever, applied the 2008 Constitution's rights of nature protections, which by the time of the ruling had just gone into effect. The Court stated that it would "consider all the elements of the case, and [all] the parties involved, ***amongst which is Nature***" because the existence of life—not only human life, but *all* living species—depends upon water.[20] The Court continued by reaffirming the rights of nature and recognizing the State's affirmative duty to enforce these rights:

> The integral and effective respect of her existence must be fulfilled by safeguarding each and every one of her systems, processes, and natural elements, considering it above all as being part of an imperative precaution for the maintenance and regeneration of vital cycles, structure, functions, and evolutionary processes....
>
> For this reason, we cannot set aside...articles 71 and 72 of the Supreme Law of the State, which states that Nature has the right to have her existence fully respected...as well as the right to be restored when natural systems are affected. Even more so when, according to the same foundational Charter, as set out in articles 3 and 277, it is the State's duty to protect natural assets and guarantee the rights of individuals, communities, and Nature....

In support of rights of nature, the Court also applied the concept of *in dubio pro natura*, meaning "in case of doubt, favor nature:"

> We must bear in mind that this guarantee of protection of nature enjoys the principle of autonomy, that is, it must be considered holistically as an end and not as a means to

[18] Corte Constitutional [C.C.] [Constitutional Court], La Primera Sala julio 16, 2009 J.P: R. Pinoargote, No. 0567- 08-RA, Registro Oficial Suplemento 23 (Ecuador).

[19] A writ of *amparo* is similar to the *acción de tutela* (tutelage action) discussed in Chapter 18, "Colombia."

[20] Case No. 0567-08-RA, *supra* note 18.

> which her own behavior is inevitably respected; [to understand] otherwise would be to omit the validity of [nature's] rights and legal protection[s]. For that purpose, we also invoke the principle *in dubio pro natura*, which entails [principles of] prevention as much as precaution and integral restoration with respect to the effects caused by human activity. It is an obligation of this Court, as a guardian of compliance with the constitutional mandates, to realize the will of the constituent in that our Fundamental Charter grants rights to nature as part of a bio-centrist and non-anthropocentric judicial philosophy; thus, in case of doubt, environmental principles and legal provisions should be applied to the protection of nature in the most favorable way....

Finally, the Court ordered the creation of a commission, to be comprised of the plaintiffs, supervisory bodies, and the defendant, which would monitor the operations of the biodigesters and ensure compliance with environmental laws.

Having ruled in favor of rights of nature for the first time in the *Biodigesters* case, the Constitutional Court later addressed the potential tension between nature's rights and human interests as demonstrated in the *Galápagos Islands* case that follows.

B. *Galápagos Islands* Case, Ruling No. 017-12-SIN-CC (2012)[21]

The Galápagos Islands are a biodiversity hotspot that is home to an extraordinary amount of endemic species (those found nowhere else on Earth), including the giant Galápagos tortoise, marine iguana, flightless cormorant, and many others. In 1998, the Galápagos Islands were established as a *special regime* under the framework of the Special Law for Galápagos (LOREG or Ley de Régimen Especial para la Conservación y Desarrollo Sustentable de la Provincia de Galápagos). This special regime allows restrictions on the rights of free residence, property, and commerce, in order to protect this global biodiversity hotspot. It also established a Galápagos Marine Reserve extending 40 miles off the coastline in which industrial fishing was prohibited.

The constitutionality of LOREG's restrictions were challenged in 2001 by the Association of Industrial Tuna Fishermen. The plaintiffs argued that the prohibition of industrial fisheries in the Galápagos Marine Reserve violated the labor rights of fishermen. The Constitutional Court disagreed, finding that LOREG was in accordance with the special regime of governance established by Ecuador's 1998 Constitution and reaffirmed by its 2008 Constitution.

In 2012, the Constitutional Court again reviewed the law, this time regarding the constitutionality of restrictions on the rights of residence and mobility of people in

[21] Corte Constitutional [C.C.] [Constitutional Court], julio 11, 2015 J.P: F. Franco, No. 017-12-SIN-CC, (Ecuador).

the Galápagos Islands. The Court, affirming the decision of the former Constitutional Tribunal, this time ruled from a rights of nature perspective:

> [The Court's position in favor of the LOREG is even] more relevant if we consider that the Constitution of the Republic of 2008 establishes a chapter on the 'rights of nature' that the State is obliged to promote and guarantee.

Highlighting the constitutional recognition of rights of nature, the Court wrote:

> Even though the challenged Law predates the Constitution of 2008, it's not only in accordance with the former Constitution—as the Constitutional Tribunal ruled—but also with the current Constitution, whose article 258 ratifies the special regime of governance for the province of Galápagos, whose main objective is to preserve the natural, scientific and educational values of the Islands. [The Law is defensible] *a fortiori* [i.e., with even stronger evidence than before] if the Constitution sets the highest standards of environmental protection (rights of nature) . . . —standards that the State is obliged to protect and guarantee.

The Court therefore denied the petition for review and confirmed the constitutionality of the law governing the Galápagos Islands.

C. *Mangroves* Case, Ruling No. 166-15-SEP-CC (2015)[22]

This case arises from a shrimp farm operating within a protected mangroves area. In Ecuador, there are 161,835 hectares of mangroves in five estuarine areas. One of these is the highly biodiverse Cayapas–Mataje, located in northwest Ecuador and home to the world's tallest mangroves. Cayapas–Mataje is a protected ecological reserve under Ecuadorian law and is a designated Ramsar site under the Convention on Wetlands of International Importance (Ramsar Convention). Under the Ramsar Convention, member states designate significant important wetlands—i.e., Ramsar sites—and then must take special measures to protect them.[23]

The plaintiff, Ecuador's Ministry of Environment, invoked rights of nature to justify its efforts to remove shrimp farmers from the ecological reserve. The shrimp farmers, a powerful economic interest group in Ecuador, sued the government in provincial court for violating their property rights. The provincial court sided with the shrimp farmers. However, its reasoning failed to address several environmental law issues. For example, the provincial court did not consider the special constitutional protections afforded to mangroves as a "fragile ecosystem," which was the result of a 30-year effort that was explicitly to protect mangroves from shrimp farming. The provincial court also failed to discuss rights of nature.

[22] Corte Constitutional [C.C.] [Constitutional Court], La Primera Sala agosto 28, 2015 J.: A. Loor, Sentencia. 166-15-SEP-CC, Official Record No. 575 (Ecuador).

[23] Hugo Echeverría, *When Courts Meet Nature: A Real Case on Rights of Nature*, VT J. of Evntl. L—Ecoperspectives Blog (2018), http://vjel.vermontlaw.edu/courts-meet-nature-real-case-rights-nature.

The plaintiff asked the Constitutional Court to review the provincial court's decision by means of an "extraordinary protection action" (*acción extraordinaria de protección*), which allows for the review of constitutional rights that are violated by a court order.

The Constitutional Court of Ecuador reviewed the case and concluded that the lower court's decision was invalid because it only addressed property rights instead of also considering rights of nature, which was a particularly large omission in a protected and fragile ecosystem. The Court elaborated that all constitutional rights are of equal legal significance in Ecuador, including the rights of nature. As stated by the Court:

> This Constitutional Court has been emphatic in highlighting the importance of rights to nature, which result in the obligation of the State and its officials to encourage and promote respect for all the elements that are part of an ecosystem, as well as for Nature's right to be respected in her entirety. These aspects have obviously not been observed . . . in a case whose central issue is the installation of a shrimp farm within the Cayapas-Mataje ecological reserve, a place possessing a system of mangroves with a wide variety of species of fauna and flora.

The Court also emphasized the ecocentric nature of Ecuador's rights of nature provisions. In the following excerpt, consider whether you agree with the Court's assessment that nature can be treated both as a subject (i.e., a holder of rights) and an object (i.e., property) under the Constitution, or whether nature can only be treated as a legal subject in all contexts:

> [R]ights of nature constitutes one of the most interesting and relevant innovations from the current Constitution, as it departs from the traditional "nature-object" conception, which considers nature as property and focuses its protection exclusively through the human right to enjoy a healthy natural environment, [and instead supports] a rationale that recognizes rights in favor of nature herself. The innovation refers to a change of paradigm on the basis of which, as a living being, nature is considered a rights holder. In this sense, it is important to highlight that the Constitution creates [two treatments of] nature and the environment in general . . . [not only] as a legal object, but also as a legal subject, independent and holding its own and specific rights. . . . The foregoing reflects, within the legal relationship between humans and nature, a biocentric vision in which nature is prioritized, as opposed to the classic anthropocentric conception in which the human being is the center and measure of all things [and] where nature was considered a mere provider of resources.

Next, the Court highlighted the duty of all citizens to uphold nature's rights and called upon the State to support this role:

> As can be seen from the constitutional norm, it is important that citizens play a fundamental role in protecting the rights of nature, since every person can require the administrative and judicial authorities to observe and fulfill these rights[.] [Therefore,] the State is called to promote citizens' participation to utilize those mechanisms focused on [nature's] protection. In this sense, all citizens enjoy legal standing to represent nature when her rights are being violated.

Ultimately, the Court concluded that the failure to consider nature's rights in the previous ruling breached the constitutional standards of reasonableness and judicial logic needed in a judgment. Therefore, the Court annulled the provincial court's ruling and ordered it to re-try the case.

Rights of nature prevailed in each of the case studies discussed above. The next section explores a major case where an Ecuadorian Court favored economic development over the rights of nature.

V. SHORTCOMINGS OF RIGHTS OF NATURE IN THE COURTS: THE *MIRADOR MINE* CASE[24]

Aside from the Constitutional Court cases analyzed above, rights of nature has had mixed results in Ecuador. This section highlights a few of the challenges faced construing constitutionally-granted rights of nature. It then discusses the *Mirador Mine* case as an example.

Craig Kauffman and Pamela Martin identify four "pathways" through which rights of nature has been applied in Ecuador:

1. Civil society pressure (civil society actions such as lawsuits),
2. Instrumental government action (government actions such as lawsuits),
3. Bureaucratic institutionalization (bureaucratic activities such as routine administrative actions), and
4. Professional interpretations by judges.[25]

Kauffman and Martin tracked the efficacy of each pathway in the early years of rights of nature in Ecuador, with unexpected results: "Surprisingly, civil society pressure was the least successful pathway, as activists lost high-profile lawsuits," prevailing only in local, less politically charged cases.[26] These norm-driven rights of nature advocates were undercut by politicization, contentious relationships with the government, and an absence of judicial knowledge about how to interpret rights of nature:

> The idea that individual and corporate property rights must be curtailed in some cases to uphold Nature's rights was not only foreign to most judges, but ran counter to their legal training. As a result, judges in civil society lawsuits have generally ruled that economic development activities are protected by individual rights (e.g., property rights, right to work) that supersede Nature's rights.[27]

[24] *See* Judgment No. 1711120130317, Case No. 3160, Provincial Court of Pichincha, Republic of Ecuador (20 June 2013) [Mirador Mine Case].
[25] Craig M. Kauffman and Pamela L. Martin, *Can Rights of Nature Make Development More Sustainable? Why Some Ecuadorian lawsuits Succeed and Others Fail,* 92 World Development 130-142, 134 (2017).
[26] *Id.* at 131-132.
[27] *Id.* at 134.

The *Mirador Mine* case exemplifies many of the hurdles faced by rights of nature in the courts. The case was pursued by Indigenous and environmental activists eager to test the rights of nature provisions in the Ecuadorian Constitution. They settled on the Condor-Mirador Mine, an open-pit mining project authorized by the Ecuadorian government in the Zamora-Chinchipe province of the Ecuadorian Amazon. The Mirador Mine is a massive Chinese-backed $1.4 billion open-pit copper and gold mine on Indigenous Shuar and Cañari-Kichwa land. At the time of the lawsuit, it was still in the development stages. The mine threatened to destroy large areas of primary rainforest and pollute and dewater local rivers, including the Wawayme and Quimi Rivers. The rights of nature violations were blatant:

> The mining company's own environmental impact study acknowledged that the open-pit mine would cause impacts listed as rights of nature violations in the Constitution. These include the total removal of ecosystems, including the habitats on which endangered endemic species rely, likely causing the extinction of one or more species. Also, contaminating surface and groundwater with heavy metals and toxic products would be catastrophic for surrounding watershed ecosystems.[28]

Additionally, the plan would require the forcible removal of local Indigenous communities who had been on the land for generations. Some activists resisting the mine were even met with violence. Shuar leader José Isidro Tendetza Antún was found murdered just days before he was to present on rights of nature at a civil society-led tribunal, which many believe was the result of his protests of the mine.[29]

In 2013, activists and local communities filed a protective action in the 25th Civil Court in Pichincha province against Ecuacorriente, the mining company. The action sought to suspend the mining project and order a new environmental impact study. The petitioners invoked the precautionary principle as well as Article 73 of Ecuador's Constitution, which requires the State to "apply preventive and restrictive measures on activities that might lead to the extinction of species, the destruction of ecosystems and permanent alteration of natural cycles."

Despite what these advocates considered a strong and unequivocal case for rights of nature, the judge ruled that the Mirador Mine did not violate rights of nature. The ruling was based on two premises. First, that the affected area was not a protected area and therefore did not have any rights (despite being contrary to express constitutional language that *all* of nature has rights regardless of its protected status). Second, that in this case protecting nature was a *private* goal, whereas the mining company was acting in the public interest by advancing development. The public interest outweighed the private one, ruled the judge. An appeal was unsuccessful.

After the lawsuit, the project moved forward and is now operational. The Mirador Mine concessions sprawl for some 10,000 hectares, where all vegetation and superficial levels of soil will eventually be removed. Already, 1,200 hectares of primary rainforest

[28] *Id.* at 134-135 (internal citations omitted).

[29] Dan Collyns, *Was this Indigenous Leader Killed Because He Fought to Save Ecuador's Land?*, The Guardian (June 2, 2015).

have been cut down. Many Indigenous peoples were forcibly evicted and continue to protest.[30]

Why did rights of nature fail in this case? Some believe that political influence and lack of judicial independence were the culprits. Others argue that many judges simply do not understand the concept of rights of nature, and therefore cannot successfully balance nature's rights against other constitutional rights. Another possibility is that courts are willing to disregard rights of nature (as well as Indigenous rights) when large amounts of money are at stake. The Ecuadorian government has already received $85 million in royalties from EcuaCorriente for the Mirador Mine.[31]

VI. THE FUTURE OF RIGHTS OF NATURE IN ECUADOR

This section explores emerging developments of rights of nature in Ecuador, including new Constitutional Court cases and legislative reform.

A. Rights of Nature in the Constitutional Court Agenda

In February 2019, a new Constitutional Court took the bench in Ecuador.[32] In May 2019, the new Court selected an important case that addresses the extent of the constitutional protections for the rights of nature. The case pertains to the Dulcepamba River.

The Constitutional Court can select cases that are novel or relevant to constitutional rights protections. The Court's rulings on such selected cases have an *erga omnes* effect—meaning it is enforceable against all, not just the parties to the case.[33] The Court's reasoning provides substantive content for those constitutional rights addressed in the case. In this specific case, the Court has already announced that it will address standards and limits regarding the exploitation of nature and its impact on rights of nature. The Court's decision on rights of nature, still pending at the time of this writing, is expected to have a meaningful long-term impact.

The selected case concerns the San Jose del Tambo Hydroelectric Project, which was built on the Dulcepamba River. Developing the hydroelectric project required significant physical changes to the Dulcepamba River, including diverting the riverbed close to the community of San Pablo de Amalí. This ultimately caused a major flood in 2015 that shattered houses, destroyed farmland, and killed two women and a child.

[30] Matthew C. DuPée, *Ecuador Has Big Plans for Its Mining Industry. But at What Environmental Cost?*, World Politics Rev. (Aug. 12, 2019), https://www.worldpoliticsreview.com/articles/28110/ecuador-has-big-plans-for-its-mining-industry-but-at-what-environmental-cost.

[31] Jose Llangari, *Ecuador Begins Large-Scale Mining at Mirador Copper Project*, Reuters (July 18, 2019).

[32] U.S. Department of State, Ecuador 2019 Human Rights Report 6 (2019) https://www.state.gov/wp-content/uploads/2020/02/ECUADOR-2019-HUMAN-RIGHTS-REPORT.pdf.

[33] Allan R. Brewer-Carías, Constitutional Protection of Human Rights in Latin America: A Comparative Study of Amparo Proceedings 151 (2009).

As for the river itself, the hydroelectric project has devastated native species in this biologically rich region of the Andes Mountains.

In 2019, the case was admitted for review by the Constitutional Court. As explained, the Court will not only provide an *inter partes* judgment (i.e., a judgment between the parties), but also will issue *erga omnes* dictum on the standards, limits, and conflicts between rights of nature and the exploitation of nature, such as through hydroelectric dam projects.

Numerous civil society organizations have submitted *amicus curiae* briefs in support of a strong rights of nature ruling by the Constitutional Court.[34] One *amicus* brief submitted by a coalition of environmental organizations requested the relief described below. As you read it, consider whether you think this relief would fulfill the vision of rights of nature in Ecuador's Constitution.

> [T]he Environmental Organizations respectfully request the [following relief from the] Constitutional Court of Ecuador:
>
> a. That, in the present case, the Dulcepamba River be recognized as a subject of rights and that the Court firmly apply the Constitutional mandate contained in articles 71, 72, 73 and 74, which sets forth the rights of nature to exist, to the maintenance and regeneration of its life cycles, structure, functions, and evolutionary processes, as well as the right to be restored. This brings with it an obligation to the Ecuadorian State not only to respect but to protect and guarantee these rights to nature.
>
> b. That the human right to water of the communities of San Pablo de Amalí be recognized. And also, that water be recognized as a vital element of nature, essential for the life of the communities of Dulcepamba River watershed, in the Province of Bolívar, and throughout the country as established in Articles 12 and 318 of the Ecuadorian Constitution. The alterations to the Dulcepamba River put at risk both the human right to water and the rights of nature.
>
> c. That the Court recognizes the specific rights of the rivers, and especially of the Dulcepamba River. The fundamental rights of the rivers are: (1) the right of flow (grounded in the ecological flow recognized in the Ecuadorian legislation); (2) the right to exercise their essential functions within their ecosystems; (3) the right to be free from all contamination; (4) the right to feed and be fed by their tributaries; (5) the right to native biodiversity; (6) the right to restoration; and (7) the right to independent appointment of one or more

[34] *See, e.g.*, Amicus Curiae: Earth Law Center, Great Lakes Environmental Law Center, International Rivers, & CEDENMA, submitted to the Constitutional Court of Ecuador, Case No. 502-19-JP (2019).

legal guardians, who act solely in the name of river rights, with at least one legal guardian as representative.[35]

d. That the Court appoint one or more legal guardians on behalf of the Dulcepamba River. The legal guardians must be independent, qualified, appropriate, with human and financial capacity, and act solely in the name of the rights and interests of nature. Although Article 71 of the Constitution establishes that: "any person, community, people, or nation may demand from the public authority the fulfillment of the rights of nature," the Environmental Organizations recommend giving nature a voice, a human face and the ability to appear before the Court. . . .

e. That it guarantees the right to the ecological restoration of the Dulcepamba River as provided for in Article 72 of the Constitution of Ecuador, by issuing (a) an order to enjoin and dismantle the Hidrotambo SA project as it is incompatible with the Rights of Nature, the human right to water, and the Human and Economic, Social and Cultural Rights of the communities of San Pablo de Amalí; and, (b) a restoration order that must be applied in accordance with Article 396 of the Ecuadorian Constitution. . . .

f. That it orders the Ecuadorian government to fulfill its obligation to guarantee the rights of nature established in article 277 of the Constitution of Ecuador and eliminate possibilities for dilution of the rights of nature. To do this, the government must ensure that state agencies coordinate to protect and promote the validity of the rights of nature. . . .

g. That it instructs the National Assembly that the Organic Environmental Code must include positive, concrete, and effective mechanisms for each state institution to protect the rights of nature in its administrative acts. . . .

h. That it orders the creation of an independent subcommittee composed of environmental scientists and engineers, responsible for evaluating current and future hydroelectric projects for the prevention of negative impacts, the possible need for dismantling, and the restoration of nature. The establishment of a subcommittee dedicated to the above would ensure that the environmental effects of the dams are considered and that new dams are only constructed in exceptional circumstances when necessary to obtain a vital social, ecological or energy objective that cannot be achieved by other reasonable means.[36]

* * *

[35] Note that these rights are based on a civil society initiative to create and implement a Universal Declaration of the Rights of Rivers. *See* Earth Law Center, *Universal Declaration of the Rights of Rivers*, https://www.earthlawcenter.org/river-rights.

[36] Hugo Echeverria, interview by author, Mar. 20, 2019.

B. Legislative Reform

In December 2019, a proposal to reform the Environmental Code of Ecuador, including changes to the rights of nature, was submitted to the Ecuadorian legislature. The proposal asserts that rights of nature are constitutional rights and therefore must be given substantive content via legislation. To this end, it puts forward reforms to the current law, which does not provide for such content. The initiative is open to public comment as well as legislative debate.

To date, despite numerous victories, many regard rights of nature as mainly being symbolic.[37] However, through legislative reform, as well as through landmark court decisions, rights of nature can fully take shape, gaining greater clarity on how it can be applied in a way commensurate with other human constitutional rights. If this occurs, 12 years after its recognition in Ecuador, rights of nature may become the ecocentric legal regime envisioned by its constitutional drafters.

VII. CONCLUSION

As stated, the recognition of rights of nature constitutes an important legal development for many reasons, including the acceptance of a new paradigm of a human-nature relationship. This is a difficult goal, one that requires more than the 12 years that have passed since rights of nature achieved constitutional recognition. Many human rights-based movements still struggle for recognition. In Ecuador, one promising development is simply that nature's rights are being fought for in courts—and, sometimes, nature is the prevailing party. This is more than can be said in almost every other country in the world. Additionally, the Constitutional Court is on the verge of a major rights of nature decision, which could further clarify these issues—and, with it, a greater application of rights of nature.

STUDY QUESTIONS

(1) *Sumak Kawsay* (roughly translated to *buen vivir* in Spanish and *good living* in English) is a worldview held by the Quechua peoples of the Andes. What worldview exists in your own country or region that might serve as the backbone of a constitutional amendment that includes rights of nature protections?

(2) Article 74 of Ecuador's Constitution establishes that nature has a right to be restored. You have been appointed as a rights of nature ombudsman and your first task is to create a plan for enforcing Article 74. How would you go about putting this into practice? Would you try to restore ecosystems that have been

[37] Ricardo Crespo, *La Naturaleza Como Sujeto de Derechos: ¿Símbolo o Realidad Jurídica?*, 12 Iuris Dictio 31-37 (2009).

harmed perpetually for decades? Or would you focus on more recent impacts, such as from ongoing mining projects? What limitations would you establish to nature's right to restoration, if any?

(3) The *Mangroves* case emphasized the Ecuadorian government's duty to enforce the rights of nature. Do you think national governments can properly uphold the rights of nature when they have so many competing interests — especially short-term economic considerations — that might run afoul of basic rights of nature principles? Do you think entire new forms of governance are necessary in order to put rights of nature into practice? Would a new branch of government be necessary, or perhaps greater ecosystem representation within existing branches of government?

(4) The *Mirador Mine* case indicates that not all Ecuadorean courts are ready to place the rights of nature above economic interests, even if the rights of nature should prevail by the letter of the law. How did the *Mirador* court justify its ruling? Do you think it was correct? What does this say for the potential of rights of nature to be the driving force behind systems change in the economic system?

(5) There have been several cases in Ecuador addressing animal rights issues, such as a 2017 case resulting in a criminal conviction for illegal shark finning based in part on rights of nature.[38] Consider how rights of nature differs from the rights of a specific animal. All species play important roles, but certain species are particularly critical to ecosystem balance — pollinator species, keystone predators, and so forth. Should rights of nature protections favor these animals and disfavor others, such as overpopulated animals? Domestic animals, such as sheep or chickens, do not play an important role in maintaining ecosystem balance at all. Are they still rightless under a rights of nature paradigm?

(6) You have been invited to speak about rights of nature by a governmental task force in your country charged with amending its constitution. They want to know how the lessons learned in Ecuador could inform their own consideration of adopting the rights of nature. What would you tell them? Would you put any limitations on rights of nature? How would you address the challenge of practical enforcement?

[38] Earth Law Center, *Rights of Nature to Save the Endangered Sharks of the Galápagos* (July 9, 2018), https://www.earthlawcenter.org/blog-entries/2018/7/rights-of-nature-to-save-the-endangered-sharks-of-the-galapagos.

CHAPTER 18

Nature's Rights in Colombia: An Emerging Jurisprudence[1]

I. AN INTRODUCTION TO COLOMBIA

In response to the significant threats its ecosystems face, the Colombian legal system has developed new ways of protecting nature. This chapter explores how Colombia's development of Earth law has granted specific ecosystems a special form of protection by making them subjects of rights. Two such ecosystems are the Atrato River Basin and the Colombian Amazon, which have both been given the status of a legal person. These judicial decisions reflect the Colombian courts' willingness to apply new, bold environmental and human rights legal paradigms.

A. Colombia's Environment

Colombia sits on the northwestern border of South America, surrounded by Panama to the northwest; Venezuela to the east; and Ecuador, Peru, and Brazil to the south. Colombia ranks as the second most biodiverse country in the world, and first in bird and orchid species.[2] A significant number of Colombia's megadiverse ecosystems transcend national borders.[3] For example, the megadiverse Chocó-Darién ecoregion runs from eastern Panama to northwest Ecuador. This ecoregion contains a variety of important ecosystems that serve as habitat for thousands of plant and animal species, many of them endemic (or unique) to that region.[4] The best-known example is the

[1] This chapter was authored by Camila Bustos, a J.D. candidate at Yale Law School, and Whitney Richardson, a social science researcher who focuses on human rights and environmental politics.

[2] Chris Bell, *Here's Why Colombia Is One of the Most Biodiverse Countries on Earth*, Culture Trip (Mar. 7, 2018), https://theculturetrip.com/south-america/colombia/articles/heres-why-colombia-is-one-of-the-most-biodiverse-countries-on-earth/ (most diversity in bird and orchid species); Varun Kuman, *17 Megadiverse Countries in the World*, Red Rank (Dec. 22, 2018), https://www.rankred.com/top-10-megadiverse-countries-in-the-world/ (ranked second-most biodiverse country).

[3] *See Other Ecoregions of South America*, Yale School of Forestry & Environmental Studies, https://globalforestatlas.yale.edu/amazon/ecoregions/other-ecoregions (last visited Jan. 23, 2020) (this is significant in its implications for international jurisdiction, and challenges associated with demarcating the legal personhood of ecosystems).

[4] Luis Fernando Gómez N. et al., Landscape Management in Chocó-Darién Priority Watersheds 5 (Luis Fernando Gómez N. et al. eds., 2014), http://www.wwf.org.co/?221730/Documento-Landscape-Management-in-Choco-Darien-Priority-Watersheds.

Amazon—the world's largest tropical rainforest—which spans nine countries. In terms of animal life, the Amazon is home to at least 25 percent of the world's known land species.[5]

B. The Colombian Legal System

The judiciary of Colombia does not have a single supreme entity to oversee the lower courts, but rather has four courts (the "High Courts"), which are the supreme tribunals of decision in their respective fields. The four high courts are the Constitutional Court (head of the constitutional jurisdiction), the Supreme Court (head of the ordinary jurisdiction), the Council of State (head of the administrative jurisdiction), and the Superior Council of Judicature (head of the disciplinary jurisdiction). Unlike the United States, Colombia is a civil law system based on codes and laws, which are passed and updated by a bicameral legislature. Although Colombia does not recognize precedent the same way common law countries do, judicial decisions by its Constitutional Court and its Supreme Court of Justice have gained increasing recognition by regional courts in recent years. Nevertheless, decisions by the national courts are often cited as authority, informing judges' interpretation of the law. The judiciary does not have the legislative power to create new laws; it only restates existing national obligations. In addition to consulting codes and statutes, Colombian judges look at the National Constitution of 1991 when ruling on legal questions.

Article 1 of the National Constitution states that "Colombia is a social state of law under the rule of law, organized in the form of a unitary republic, decentralized, with autonomy of its territorial entities, democratic, participatory, and pluralistic."[6] While Article 1 describes Colombia as being a decentralized republic, Colombia still has a centralized government responsible for making laws.

Colombia is divided into 32 departments. Unlike "states" in the United States and elsewhere, "departments" in Colombia do not have legislative or judicial authority. They do, however, enjoy autonomy in the administration of sectional issues and in the planning and promotion of economic and social development within their respective territories.[7]

C. The 1991 Constitution

The 1991 National Constitution emerged from a widespread sense that Colombia needed modern and robust democratic institutions, stronger human rights guarantees, a new framework to tackle violence and inequality, and an end to corruption.[8] It was

[5] Secretariat of the Convention on Biodiversity, Forest Biodiversity—Earth's Living Treasure 8 (2010).

[6] Constitución Política de Colombia 1991, art. 1.

[7] *Id.* at art. 298.

[8] *See* Julieta Lemaitre Ripoll, El Derecho Como Conjuro: Fetichismo Legal, Violencia y Movimientos Sociale 96 (2009) (The student movements published a manifesto calling for a national referendum titled "We Can Still Save Colombia," which rapidly became the way the movement identified itself).

drafted and approved by a Constitutional Assembly comprised of 70 delegates from diverse backgrounds, including politicians, former guerrilla members, Indigenous leaders, academics, and people representing the interests of business and labor.[9]

The Colombian Constitution has strong protections of citizens' rights. It includes not only fundamental rights but also economic and social rights. It also recognizes the ethnic and cultural diversity of Colombia, including the languages and dialects of ethnic groups.[10] Indigenous peoples are explicitly permitted to form special jurisdictions outside the national jurisdiction.[11]

Some of the constitutional protections of fundamental rights include the right to life; protection from torture, cruel, inhumane, or degrading treatment or punishment; equal protection and treatment; freedom of conscience; freedom of religion; and others.[12] Article 13, in particular, makes explicit the notion that the state will give special protection to individuals who, on account of their economic, physical, or mental condition, are in vulnerable circumstances.

The second chapter of the Constitution identifies social, economic, and cultural rights. These rights include the right to a family, equal rights and opportunities for men and women, the rights of children, collective bargaining, public health, education, food, and others.[13] Of special interest is Article 63, which states that property in public use, natural parks, communal lands of ethnic groups, and other types of property are "inalienable, imprescriptible, and not subject to seizure."

The third chapter describes collective rights and the environment. This chapter has been referred to as an "Ecological Constitution," where protection of the environment and biodiversity is characterized as a "higher interest."[14] It contains 30 provisions in total that enshrine a series of principles, mandates, and obligations focused on: "(1) protecting the environment in an integral manner, and (2) guaranteeing a model of sustainable development."[15] Reference to the "Ecological Constitution"

[9] David Rampf and Diana Chavarro, The 1991 Colombia National Constituent Assembly: Turning Exclusion Into Inclusion, or a Vain Endeavour? 8 (2014).

[10] Constitución Política de Colombia 1991, arts. 7, 10.

[11] *Id.* at art. 246 ("the authorities of Indigenous peoples may exercise their jurisdictional functions within their territorial jurisdiction in accordance with their own laws and procedures" as long as they are not contrary to national laws and the Constitution).

[12] *Id.* at arts. 11-16, 18-19, 29, 37.

[13] *Id.* at arts. 5, 42-44, 49, 55, 67.

[14] Corte Constitucional [C.C.] [Constitutional Court], Sala Sexta de Revisión noviembre 10, 2016, M.P: J Palacio, Sentencia T-622, (p. 31) (Colom.).

[15] *Id.* For additional information on the Constitución Ecológica, *see* Corte Constitucional [C.C.] [Constitutional Court], Sala Plena de la Corte Constitucional mayo 23, 2018, M.S: C. Schlesinger, Sentencia C-048, Gaceta de la Corte Constitucional [G.C.C.] (Colom.); Corte Constitucional [C.C.] [Constitutional Court], Sala Plena de la Corte Constitucional mayo 18, 2016, M.S: L. Pérez, Sentencia C-259, Gaceta de la Corte Constitucional [G.C.C.] (Colom.); Corte Constitucional [C.C.] [Constitutional Court], Sala Tercera de Revisión abril 3, 2008, M.P: J. Triviño, Sentencia T-299 (Colom.); Corte Constitucional [C.C.] [Constitutional Court], abril 12, 2000, M.P: V. Mesa, Sentencia 431 (Colom.); Consejo de Estado [C.E.] [State Council], Cámara Regional de la Construcción de Cundinamarca noviembre 5, 2013, C.P: M. Lasso, Fallo 66203, Gaceta del Consejo de Estado [G.C.E.] (Colom.); Juzgado 34 Administrativo de Bogotá [J. Admtivos] [34th Administrative Court of Bogota], agosto 6, 2019, J: O. Marín, Fallo 00222 (Colom.); Juzgado 39 Administrativo de Bogotá [J. Admtivos] [39th Administrative Court of Bogota], marzo 1, 2019, J: L. Guevara, Fallo 02488 (Colom.).

is made within court judgments recognizing nature's rights, and these articles serve as a critical component in the decision-making process.[16]

Human environmental rights are recognized in Article 79, which establishes that "every individual has the right to enjoy a healthy environment. The law will guarantee the community's participation in the decisions that may affect it."[17] In this way, the Constitution conceives the right to a healthy environment as both a collective right and an individual one.

The Constitution also provides several mechanisms for Colombians to vindicate their rights. For example, *tutelas*, translated as guardianship arrangements, function as a mechanism to protect fundamental rights at the individual level.[18] Since they are designed to address the threat and violation of fundamental rights, *tutela* actions are expected to be filed within a reasonable time after a threat and/or violation takes place and to be resolved promptly. They may be filed whenever an individual has exhausted other avenues or has no other means of judicial redress. *Tutelas* are handled by the Constitutional Court.

Beyond individual rights, the Constitution creates a right to collective actions to protect collective rights and interests related to the environment and public health. These include *acciones populares* (or popular actions) and *acciones de grupo* (or group actions).[19] After the ratification of the Constitution, Law 472 of 1998 defined the procedures for both actions. Popular actions are preventative in nature, and they serve to address activities that may result in harm to a large number of individuals. Group actions are reactive in nature, and they seek redress for harms that have already been caused to a large number of individuals. Both types of collective action are handled by the State Council.

D. The Role of Socioeconomic Rights Jurisprudence

In recent years, Colombian jurisprudence on constitutional issues and socioeconomic rights has gained international prominence for its progressive outcomes. The Constitutional Court, in particular, has made progressive rulings on the rights of internally displaced persons,[20] the right to health,[21] and prison conditions,[22] amongst others. While

[16] Corte Constitucional [C.C.] [Constitutional Court], Sala Sexta de Revisión noviembre 10, 2016, M.P: J Palacio, Sentencia T-622, (p. 31-35) (Colom.); Corte Suprema de Justicia [C.S.J.] [Supreme Court of Colombia], Sala Civil Especializada en Restitución de Tierras del Tribunal Superior del Distrito Judicial de Bogotá abril 5 2018, M.P: L. Villabona, Sentencia 4360 (p. 18) (Colom.).

[17] Constitución Política de Colombia 1991, art. 79.

[18] *Id.* at art. 86.

[19] *Id.* at art. 88. (Articles 86 and 88, together read to say that a community may bring an *acción popular*, but an individual in the community may still file a *tutela* to protect his or her fundamental rights).

[20] Corte Constitucional [C.C.] [Constitutional Court], Sala Tercera de Revisión enero 22, 2004, M.P: M. Espinosa, Sentencia T-025 (Colom.).

[21] Corte Constitucional [C.C.] [Constitutional Court], Sala Segunda de Revisión julio 31, 2008, M.P: M. Espinosa, Sentencia T-760, Gaceta de la Corte Constitucional [G.C.C.] (Colom.).

[22] Corte Constitucional [C.C.] [Constitutional Court], Sala Tercera de Revisión abril 28, 1998, M.P: E. Muñoz, Sentencia T-153, Gaceta de la Corte Constitucional [G.C.C.] (Colom.).

implementation has been far from perfect, these decisions have had positive effects on public policy, public participation, and institutional coordination.[23] These judicial decisions are the backdrop against which the cases described in this chapter have developed.

II. AN OVERVIEW OF RECENT JURISPRUDENCE

The Colombian courts have issued recent landmark decisions advancing the concept of nature's rights.[24] In 2015, the Constitutional Court issued a groundbreaking decision protecting the Tayrona Park in Colombia, home to four distinct Indigenous groups and a unique ecosystem made of jungles, beaches, and mangrove swamps. The Court recognized that rivers, mountains, forests, and the atmosphere must be protected not because of their utility but because of their own independent rights to exist.[25] The Court said it was imperative to transform humanity's relationship with the rest of the natural world and applied an ecocentric perspective, expressly criticizing a purely anthropocentric approach.[26] A year later, the Court issued a groundbreaking decision recognizing the Atrato River Basin as a subject of rights.[27] Since then, a growing number of Colombian courts have followed suit, recognizing the rights of ecosystems in response to violations of human environmental rights. As mentioned earlier in this chapter, it should be noted that under the civil law system in Colombia, judicial decisions do not translate into formal laws or binding precedents. As Paola Villaviencio explains:

> although no legislation on rights of nature had been adopted at that time in Colombia, the courts ruled in favor of such natural entities and through two landmark decisions changed their traditional status and recogni[z]ed them as rights-bearing subjects, thereby demonstrating that rights of nature/ecosystems can be recognized by both legislative and judicial channels.[28]

[23] César Rodriguez-Garavito, *Beyond the Courtroom: The Impact of Judicial Activism on Social and Economic Rights in Latin America*, 89 Texas L. Rev. 1670, 1676 (2011). *See* César Rodríguez-Garavito and Diana Rodríguez Franco, Cortes y Cambio Social: Cómo la Corte Constitucional Transformó el Desplazamiento Forzado en Colombia (Marta Rojas ed., 1st ed. 2010).

[24] Prior to judicial recognition of nature's rights in Colombia, the land was recognized as a victim of the long-running armed conflict between the government and paramilitary groups in the Victims & Land Restitution Law (Law 1448 of 2011) and granted the right to restitution. Also, the Special Jurisdiction for Peace (JEP) has publicly recognized the environment as a victim of the armed conflict. This recognition applies a customarily anthropocentric term to an environmental entity and implies an understanding of the environment as a living subject with the capacity to be harmed.

[25] Corte Constitucional [C.C.] [Constitutional Court], Sala Sexta de Revisión septiembre 21, 2015, M.P: J. Palacio, Sentencia T-606 (Colom.); David R. Boyd, The Rights of Nature: A Legal Revolution That Could Save the World 225 (2019).

[26] *Id.* at 225-226.

[27] Corte Constitucional [C.C.] [Constitutional Court], Sala Sext de Revsión noviembre 10, 2016, M.P. J. Palacio, Sentencia T-622 (Colom.).

[28] Paola Villavicencio Calzadilla, *Case Note: A Paradigm Shift in Courts' View on Nature: The Atrato River and Amazon Basin Cases in Colombia*, 15 L., Envtl. and Dev. J. 1, 3 (2019).

Colombian courts are not drawing on existing Colombian interpretations of any nature's rights laws when reviewing legal challenges on environmental rights. Instead, they are prescribing a new interpretation to these laws based on constitutional principles and evolving social understandings. The international legal wave recognizing nature as a legal subject of rights is one of the influences that has led Colombian courts to apply an ecocentric lens when reviewing environmental rights cases. Colombia joins an emerging jurisprudence "built on ecocentric rights-based approaches to environmental protection" that challenges traditional legal paradigms.[29]

Within Colombian jurisprudence, judicial decisions by the Colombian High Courts have established a legal analytical framework for recognizing nature's rights, with regional courts now also starting to apply an ecocentric perspective when adjudicating cases. Through 2019, judicial decisions that have recognized nature's rights include:

- The Atrato River Basin (2016, Constitutional Court);
- The Colombian Amazon (2018, Supreme Court);
- Páramo de Pisba (2018, Administrative Court of Boyacá);
- The Plata River (2019, Colombian Municipal Civil Court of La Plata);
- Three rivers in Tolima including the Coello, Combeima, and Cocora (2019, Administrative Tribunal Court of Tolima);
- The Cauca River Basin (2019, Superior Court of Medellín); and
- The Pance River Basin (2019, Third Court of Enforcement of Sentences and Security Measures of Cali).

This recognition of nature's rights by the courts has also built momentum in the departments of Nariño and Boyacá, culminating in the incorporation of rights of nature into their governance frameworks in 2019.[30] Within the rights of nature framework, judicial decisions have recognized bees and an individual iconic Andean bear named El Chucho as subjects of rights, although these rulings are still subject to further review.[31]

The cases concerning the Atrato River Basin, the Colombian Amazon, the Cauca River, and the three rivers in Tolima will be examined closely. The *Atrato River Basin* case and the *Colombian Amazon* case have been picked because of their significance in sparking similar rulings by regional courts, as well their illustration of themes in environmental legislation. The *Cauca River Basin* case and the case of the three rivers in Tolima, both handled by regional courts, demonstrate how Earth jurisprudence has

[29] *Id.*

[30] Nuevo Siglo, *Boyacá y Nariño Firman Acuerdo para Prohibir Asbesto y Plásticos de un Solo Uso*, DINERO (Aug. 10, 2019, 12:01 AM), https://www.dinero.com/pais/articulo/gobernadores-de-boyaca-y-narino-firman-pacto-por-la-naturaleza-como-sujeto/275442.

[31] For instance, in November 2018, the Tribunal Superior of Cartagena revoked an earlier ruling which declared bees as subject of rights. *Abejas en Colombia, sin Protección Jurídica*, SEMANA SOSTENIBLE (May 20, 2019), https://sostenibilidad.semana.com/medio-ambiente/articulo/abejas-en-colombia-sin-proteccion-juridica/44262. Further, in August 2019, the Constitutional Court of Colombia held a public hearing on a motion issued by the Supreme Court in 2016 granting habeas corpus to the bear Chuco. Corte Constitucional, YOUTUBE (Aug. 8, 2019), https://www.youtube.com/watch?v=_X0BHUJWPwo (footage from the public hearing).

been applied by regional courts to address long-term, ongoing environmental conflicts across Colombia.

III. THE ATRATO RIVER BASIN

In 2016, Colombia's Constitutional Court recognized the Atrato River Basin (located within the megadiverse[32] northwest Chocó department) as a subject of rights. Although jurisprudence of the Constitutional Court had previously referred to nature as a "subject of legal rights," the Atrato decision was the first time a designated ecosystem was recognized as a legal subject of rights in Colombia.[33] These rights include the right to be protected, conserved, maintained, and restored.[34]

The ruling came in response to a *tutela* against the Colombian state filed by the Colombia-based Center for Social Justice Studies (Tierra Digna) on behalf of an alliance of Chocó resident organizations, including people of African descent and Indigenous and *mestizo campesino* communities.[35] The action was intended to hold the state accountable for violating local peoples' constitutional rights against well-documented, ongoing illegal mining activity.[36] These constitutional rights include the fundamental right to life[37] as well as to "health, water, food security, healthy environment, and the culture and the territory of active ethnic communities."[38] Illegal mining activity in the region utilizes toxic chemicals, such as mercury, which severely contaminates the surrounding ecosystem. The basin's unfettered contamination has been linked to the deaths of at least 37 minors; the poisoning of 64 people by ingesting

[32] The term megadiverse refers to regions hosting a high concentration of the world's biodiversity. UN Environment World Conservation Monitoring Centre, *Megadiverse Countries*, Biodiversity A-Z (Nov. 20, 2014), https://www.biodiversitya-z.org/content/megadiverse-countries. The Chocó region is known as a biogeographic region. Ninety percent of Chocó is considered a special conservation area, and the Atrato River Basin contains one of the world's highest water yields. Corte Constitucional [C.C.] [Constitutional Court], Sala Sexta de Revisión noviembre 10, 2016, M.P: J Palacio, Sentencia T-622, (p. 6) (Colom.).

[33] Villavicencio, *supra* note 28, at 3 n. 2, mentions several examples of rulings, including "No C-595 of 27 July 2010 on a constitutional challenge filed by Juan Gabriel Rojas López, Expediente D-7977; C-632 of 24 August 2011 on a constitutional challenge filed by Luis Eduardo Montealegre Lynett, Expediente D-8379; and, Protection Ruling (Sentencia de Tutela) T-080 of 20 February 2015 on an action of tutela (Acción de Tutela) filed by Fundepúblico y otros v. Sala Civil y de Familia del Tribunal Superior del Distrito Judicial de Cartagena, Expediente T-4.353.004."

[34] Corte Constitucional [C.C.] [Constitutional Court], Sala Sexta de Revisión noviembre 10, 2016, M.P: J Palacio, Sentencia T-622, (p. 158) (Colom.).

[35] Eighty-seven percent of the people of Chocó are of African descent, 10 percent Indigenous, and 3 percent mestizo farmers. Tierra Digna filed on behalf of the following organizations: the Higher Community Council of the High Atrato Peasant People's Organization (Cocomopoca), the Community Council Major of the Peasant Association Atrato (Cocomacia), the Association of Low Atrato Community Councils (Asocoba), the Interethnic Forum Solidarity Choco (FISCH) and others. Corte Constitucional [C.C.] [Constitutional Court], Sala Sexta de Revisión noviembre 10, 2016, M.P: J Palacio, Sentencia T-622, (p. 1) (Colom.).

[36] Corte Constitucional [C.C.] [Constitutional Court], Sala Sexta de Revisión noviembre 10, 2016, M.P: J Palacio, Sentencia T-622, (p. 7) (Colom.).

[37] Constitución Política de Colombia 1991, art. 11.

[38] Corte Constitucional [C.C.] [Constitutional Court], Sala Sexta de Revisión noviembre 10, 2016, M.P: J Palacio, Sentencia T-622, (p. 1) (Colom.).

contaminated water; and the loss of critical food and water resources, leading to dehydration, malnutrition, and other ailments.[39]

The *tutela* was first filed on January 27, 2015, before the Administrative Tribunal of Cundinamarca. In response, several defendants requested that the Court deny the *tutela* due to lack of standing and on procedural grounds, arguing that a *tutela* is an inappropriate mechanism to bring the case. Various defendants argued that the responsibility to take action lies with other authorities.[40]

Due to its constitutional functions and its obligation to defend human rights in Colombia, the Ombudsman's Office[41] intervened to expand on the plaintiff's legal claims. The ombudsman affirmed that the severe socio-ecological impacts of mining in the region violated the fundamental rights of the plaintiffs' populations.[42] The ombudsman further emphasized that ethnic communities have special constitutional protections, including the right to be protected through a *tutela* action. Finally, the ombudsman declared that a popular action was not a sufficient means to handle the case because a popular action deals only with collective rights, while a *tutela* deals with fundamental rights.[43]

On Feb. 11, 2015, the first instance court ruled against the plaintiffs by denying the *tutela* action on procedural grounds. The Administrative Tribunal of Cundinamarca (*Tribunal Administrativo de Cundinamarca*) held that, at its core, the suit sought protection of collective rights. Consequently, the Court recommended that the plaintiffs file a popular action suit. The plaintiffs appealed the decision.[44] On April 21, 2015, the second instance court once again ruled against the plaintiffs by denying the *tutela* action on procedural grounds. The State Council (*Consejo del Estado*) held that the suit sought to protect collective rights and that the plaintiffs "failed to demonstrate irreparable harm or ineffectiveness of the class actions for protection of the rights that they considered violated."[45] On Nov. 13, 2015, the Sixth Chamber of Review of the Constitutional Court (*Sala Sexta de Revisión de la Corte Constitucional*) ordered input from several universities, NGOs, and international organizations on several matters related to the case. The Court also ordered and carried out a judicial inspection in Quibdó and some sectors of the Atrato River Basin in early 2016.[46]

[39] *Id.* at 9.

[40] *Id.* at 10-12.

[41] The Ombudsman's Office of Colombia, established by the Constitution, (Spanish: Defensoría del Pueblo) is the national government agency charged with overseeing the protection of civil and human rights. The ombudsman is appointed by the President, and elected by the Chamber of Representatives of Colombia, to head this agency.

[42] Defensoría del Pueblo (Ombudsman), Resolución No. 64: Crisis Humanitaria en el Departamento del Chocó 2014 (2014).

[43] Corte Constitucional [C.C.] [Constitutional Court], Sala Sexta de Revisión noviembre 10, 2016, M.P: J Palacio, Sentencia T-622, (p. 13) (Colom.).

[44] The appeal was made on the following grounds: "(i) ignorance [by the first instance court] of the violation and threat to the fundamental rights of the communities in the class action; (ii) irregularities in the judicial process of the acción de tutela; and (iii) the execution of other judicial actions that have not been effective." *Id.* at 14.

[45] *Id.*

[46] *Id.* at 15.

In its decision recognizing the rights of a designated ecosystem, the Court found that the serious effects of illegal mining exploitation violated multiple fundamental rights in the Atrato River Basin. It also declared that human populations, which are interdependent with respect to the natural world, must "assume the consequences of their actions and omissions with nature."[47] This decision marks the first instance of a Colombian court designating an ecosystem as a legal subject, with (in essence) the right to life.[48] The Court pointed out that key principles considered during the decision-making process included the role of international Earth jurisprudence, the principle of interdependence, biocultural rights of specially protected ethnic groups, and the principle of *inter communis* (between the commons which, in contrast to *inter partes*, means the ruling applies to everyone in similar circumstances). As you read the opinion, notice how each principle guides the Court's reasoning.

Center for Social Justice Studies et al. v. Presidency of the Republic et al.

Constitutional Court of Colombia (2016)[49]
Judgment T-622
Bogotá, D.C., Nov. 2nd, 2015

OPINION OF THE COURT

Palacio Palacio, I. J.

9. ANALYSIS OF THE CONCRETE CASE.

Introduction.

In the case submitted to the Court, the plaintiffs filed a writ of *acción de tutela* to stop the intensive and large-scale use of various methods of illegal mining and logging, including heavy machinery—dredges and backhoes—and highly toxic substances — like mercury — in the Atrato River (Chocó), its basins, swamps, wetlands and tributaries. Which, in this court's opinion, have been intensifying for several years and which are having harmful and irreversible consequences on the environment, affecting with it the fundamental rights of ethnic communities and the natural balance of the territories they inhabit.

[47] *Id.* at 99.
[48] It should be noted that legal recognition came in the form of a court order defined in the sentence.
[49] This opinion was translated by the Dignity Rights Project at Delaware Law School in the United States, available at: http://files.harmonywithnatureun.org/uploads/upload838.pdf. Citations and cross-references to other sections not reproduced here have been removed from the original.

To this, they add that the mechanized mining exploitation—which has been developing on a large scale illegally since the end of the nineties by different actors—mainly affects the upper and middle basin of the Atrato River and even its mouth in the gulf of Urabá, as well as its main tributaries... concretely, through the use of heavy machinery such as suction dredgers... hydraulic elevators and backhoes, which in turn destroy the riverbed and perform indiscriminate dumping of mercury and other substances and supplies required (such as cyanide, gasoline and fats, etc.) for the development of these activities in the Atrato and its tributaries, in addition to the dispersion of vapors that mercury treatment throws in the mining entanglements.

In this sense, the plaintiffs consider that state-run entities (both at the local level and at the national level) are responsible for the violation of their fundamental rights to life, human dignity, health, water, [food security], a healthy environment, the culture and the territory due to its omission to not take effective actions to stop the development of such illegal mining activities, which have generated the configuration of a serious humanitarian and environmental crisis in the region....

Resolution of the legal problem raised.

9.3. In a preliminary manner, the Court considers that in order to resolve the legal problem, it must: (i) outline some reference reports that describe the grave situation of illegal mining in the Department of Chocó; (ii) present the effects observed in the judicial inspection carried out in Chocó in January 2016; (iii) raise a series of conclusions on the legal matters submitted for its consideration, and finally, (iv) make some considerations about public policy regarding illegal mining.

9.4. By way of illustration, the Chamber must begin by pointing out that the serious humanitarian, socio-cultural and environmental situation in which the Department of Chocó is immersed, is historic. The origins of the humanitarian crisis in the region are old, deep and structural. Some of the factors that have been identified in the literature that has studied the subject in detail suggest that poverty in Chocó is the result of: (i) a colonial legacy of weak or non-existent political-administrative institutions; (ii) difficult geographic and climatic conditions that increase the costs of production and "isolate" the district from the rest of the country and, at the same time, favor the settlement of illegal armed groups; (iii) an extractive economic structure focused exclusively on the exploitation of natural resources, in particular, the mining of gold, silver and platinum; and (iv) the isolation of the district from national economic activity.

9.5. To this historical situation of poverty, marginalization, institutional isolation and the accumulation of a large number of unsatisfied basic needs—in a region of the country that has been historically affected by violence, displacement and internal armed conflict—has been added in the last decades the incursion of new illegal armed groups and the exponential increase of illegal mining, which, in the words of the Ombudsman's Office, "has generated an unprecedented humanitarian crisis in Chocó that demands the joint action of the entire State, its institutionalism and territorial entities at all levels to give attention and final solution to the serious crisis that this Department is experiencing."...

9.11. The worsening of the problems described, due to the overflow of illegal mining in recent years, has meant that the vigilance and control bodies, without exception, have repeatedly called the national government's attention to the critical situation that affects the Department of Chocó, especially with respect to mining that takes place illegally.

State entities have had the possibility of knowing the dimension of the effects on fundamental rights that occurs in this region of the country where the plaintiffs live, by virtue of the phenomenon of illegal mining....

9.14. In terms of health effects, the Plaintiffs stated that as a consequence of the use of mercury in illegal mining activities, "the most serious damage to communities—in terms of health and environmental degradation of rivers and forests—occur in the areas surrounding the Atrato River and its tributaries, in the territories of Río Quito, Soledad, Villa Conto, San Isidro and Paimadó, among others; damages that they estimate occurred in about 84% of the collective territory of the communities. They explain that, according to studies from the Pacific Environmental Research Institute—IIAP—, there have been reports of spontaneous abortions, vaginal, skin and fungal diseases caused by the presence of mercury, methylmercury and cyanide in the river waters."

In the same way, they indicated that "as a consequence of the presence of mercury and other toxic chemical substances in the waters of the Atrato River there is a proliferation of new vaginal and cutaneous diseases. For these communities, the river is the center of their social and cultural life: it is there where they identify themselves as a people, where they wash their clothes, bath, play, swim, fish and share cultural and recreational activities."

They indicated that "the level of mercury found by the IIAP in the populations is alarming and refers to a study that was carried out on 160 people in the basin of the Atrato River and its tributaries (Quito River). According to which, the level of mercury found in the blood is 60 [parts] per million, when the minimum world average, what is considered acceptable, is 0.5 [parts] per million, and in Colombia it is 1.0 per person."...

9.15. In terms of effects on the environment (rivers, swamps and forests), representatives of the plaintiff ethnic communities argued that the harmful effects of mercury used in illegal mining activities, which is specified as follows: "(i) by direct contact with the skin; (ii) by contamination of the atmosphere when the substance is burned (by generating steam and then acid rain precipitation); (iii) contamination of water sources when mercury is poured into rivers accumulates in water, plants and fish, which are the basis of the way of life and food practices of ethnic communities. It is added that the ethnic communities that inhabit the banks of the Atrato River (high, medium and low zones) suffer directly from the effects of mercury and cyanide pollution, as all their hygienic, nutritional, social and cultural activities are carried out in the river, in the absence of basic infrastructure of aqueduct and basic sanitation."

In this regard, it is added that "the contamination by chemical substances also affects the forests and added to this the forestry exploitation that has been carried out for years in the zone — in particular in the region of the Bajo Atrato- without effective state control."

To this it is also added that, "this environmental degradation not only responds to a problem of collective rights but also to a systematic violation of fundamental rights such as a dignified life, health, freedom of movement, territory, and autonomy. It warns of a profound transformation of the traditional ways of life of the communities (agriculture, fishing, hunting) due to mining."...

9.17. About the damages to the rights, to the culture, and the territory, one of the community leaders of Paimadó (Chocó) affirmed, during the visit to that region that, "it is very sad to walk today along the Quito river — which is drying up — from Atrato to Paimadó or Manacruz because illegal mining has not only changed the course of the river but has also ended up with traditional forms of subsistence based on agriculture and the crops of yam, yucca and plantain. The ancestral trees such as borojó, chontaduro, the 'bread tree', the 'pato' and the banana tree are no longer available and cannot be transported due to the way in which mining has destroyed the river."

In a complementary sense, the Ombudsman's Office indicated that the illegal mining activity in the Atrato River Basin and its tributaries has caused the decrease of agricultural work, as a traditional form of subsistence, "to the point that all the food consumed is taken from populated centers like Quibdó and Beté." The Office added that this situation has also affected the social and ecological function of the collective territory, "because its use for the traditional practice of agriculture was suspended." This is how the foods that were ancestrally cultivated for consumption such as chontaduro, borojó, cacao, banana, among others, their basic foods, are no longer cultivated in the areas most impacted by illegal mining, also because these activities generate infertility on earth....

9.22. Likewise, the destruction of the environment and the threat to biodiversity in the region subject to the facts of this action was corroborated not only by the Chamber but also by all the accompanying entities, as referred to in sections 9.14 to 9.17. For the Court, there is no doubt that illegal mining is seriously affecting the fundamental rights to life, health and a healthy environment of the ethnic communities that inhabit the Atrato River Basin and its tributaries. And that this violation has impacts direct and indirect on the Chocoano ethnic communities....

> 9.23. . . . the Chamber should reiterate that . . . the protection of rivers, forests, food sources and biodiversity (healthy environment) has a direct and interdependent relationship with the guarantee of the rights to life and health (as well as culture and territory), within what has been called biocultural rights. Precisely, the central elements of this approach establish an intrinsic link between nature and culture, and the diversity of the human species as part of nature and manifestation of multiple forms of life. From this perspective, the conservation of biodiversity necessarily leads to the preservation and protection of the ways of life and cultures that interact with it.
>
> Consequently, public policies on the conservation of biodiversity must adapt and focus on the preservation of life, its various manifestations, but mainly in the preservation of the conditions for that biodiversity to continue deploying its evolutionary potential in a stable and indefinite manner, as the Court has indicated in abundant jurisprudence. Similarly, the obligations of the State to protect and conserve the lifestyles of Indigenous peoples, black and farmer, mean guaranteeing their conditions of being, perceiving and apprehending the world. . . .
>
> 9.25. In consideration of the aforementioned, for the Court it is necessary to conclude that the illegal mining activity, having the potential to cause harm to health and to the environment, as has been seen in the case of the ethnic communities that inhabit the basin of the Atrato River, it is subject to the application of the precautionary principle. This applies when — although there is a principle of technical certainty — there is scientific uncertainty regarding the harmful effects of a measure or activity. In that case, the solution that avoids the damage must be preferred and not the one that can allow it. This principle is not only designed to protect the right to the environment but also the right to health when there is a threat of violation. . . .
>
> [T]he precautionary principle implies in very simple terms, that in case of scientific doubt, it does not abstain and, on the contrary, protects the right to a healthy environment and health in connection with life.
>
> Specifically, the application of the precautionary principle in the present case will have as objectives, (i) to prohibit the use of toxic substances such as mercury[50] in mining activities, whether legal or illegal; and (ii) declare that the Atrato River is subject to rights that imply its protection, conservation, maintenance and, in the specific case, restoration. . . .
>
> 9.26. By way of conclusion and with respect to this particular point, the Court finds that the Defendant entities have violated the rights to life, health and a healthy environment of the Plaintiff communities by allowing the

[50] In 2018, the Colombian government banned the use of mercury from all gold mining activities. A full ban of the use of mercury is to take effect by 2023. Adriaan Alsema, *Colombia Bans Mercury in Gold Mining*, Colombia Reports (July 16, 2018), https://colombiareports.com/colombia-imposes-ban-on-mercury-in-gold-mining/. Colombia has some of the highest rates of mercury contamination in the world; however, this issue is not considered to be monitored adequately. *See* OECD, Environmental Performance Reviews - Colombia, Highlights 2014 (2014).

indiscriminate dumping of mercury and other toxic chemical substances necessary for the realization of illegal mining activities in the Atrato River, its tributaries and surrounding territories by not taking concrete and articulated measures to avoid it, having full knowledge of the situation, that is, by omission in the fulfillment of its legal and constitutional duties. As a result, the responsible entities will be ordered to adopt a series of emergency measures to deal with this serious violation of the fundamental rights to life, health and a healthy environment, which will be indicated in the relative section to the orders.

b. About the pollution of the Atrato River, its tributaries, forests and food sources produced by the development of illegal mining activities in the region.

9.27. Violation of the right to water as a water source. At this point, it is clear to the Court that, as proven by the evidence in the case file and in the judicial inspection—which were outlined in sections 9.14 to 9.17—the illegal mining that takes place in the Atrato River Basin and its tributaries challenges any idea of rational use of water and forest resources, and constitutes an open violation of the fundamental right to water (as a consequence of its serious contamination) that threatens not only ethnic communities, the Department of Chocó or the environment, but also one of the most important water and biodiversity sources in the world, and thus, present and future generations. . . .

Additionally, it cannot be overlooked that the right to water is a sine qua non requirement for the exercise of other rights, while "water is necessary to produce food (right to food); to ensure environmental hygiene (right to health); to procure life (right to work) and to enjoy certain cultural practices (right to participate in cultural life)."Therefore, pollution—especially with mercury and cyanide—and carrying out illegal mining activities in the Atrato River Basin and its tributaries not only violates the right to water and other components of the right to a healthy environment (as has already been stated), but also violates the essential standards of availability, accessibility and water quality established in General Comment No. 15, because this type of mining is harmful, the production of food (trees, crops and fish), the health conditions, the traditional ways of life and the cultural practices of the Plaintiff ethnic communities.

Precisely, the biggest challenge of contemporary constitutionalism on environmental matters, is to achieve the safeguard and effective protection of nature, associated cultures, ways of life, and biodiversity, not just for the simple material, genetic or productive utility that these can represent to humans, but because being a living entity composed of other multiple forms of life and cultural representations, are subjects of individual rights, which makes them a new imperative of integral protection and respect on the part of States and societies. In short, only from an attitude of deep respect and humility with nature, its members and its culture, is it possible to enter into relationships with them in fair and equitable terms, leaving aside any concept that is limited to the simply utilitarian, economic, or efficient.

In effect, nature and the environment are a transversal element of the Colombian constitutional order. Its importance lies, of course, in attention to the human beings that inhabit it and the need to have a healthy environment to live a dignified life and in well being conditions, but also in relation to the other living organisms with whom the planet is shared, understood as stocks worthy of protection in themselves. It is about being aware of the interdependence that connects us to all living beings on earth; that is, recognizing ourselves as integral parts of the global ecosystem - biosphere, rather than from normative categories of domination, simple exploitation or utility. A position that takes on special relevance in Colombian constitutionalism, taking into account the principle of cultural and ethnic pluralism that supports it, as well as the knowledge, uses, and ancestral customs bequeathed by Indigenous and tribal peoples.

Precisely, in relation to the natural and cultural wealth of the nation, Article 8 of the Political Charter establishes as a fundamental obligation of the State and of society to watch over the care of our natural and cultural riches. Additionally, in the chapter on collective rights (Articles 79 and 80) and specific obligations (Article 95-8), the general parameters that guide the relationship between the human being and his living environment are established: natural, environmental and biodiverse. In this sense, as a consequence of the attributions consecrated at the head of the State, society and individuals in the above-mentioned articles, the obligation to protect the environment is established in order to prevent and control the environmental deterioration factors, procuring its conservation, restoration and sustainable development. . . .

9.28. In this context, it is necessary for the Chamber to advance in the interpretation of the applicable law and in the forms of protection of fundamental rights and their subjects, due to the great degree of degradation and threat in which it found the Atrato River Basin. Fortunately, at the international level a new legal approach called biocultural rights is being developed, whose central premise is the relationship of profound unity and interdependence between nature and human species, and that has as a consequence a new socio-legal understanding in which nature should be taken seriously and with full rights. That is, as a subject of rights.

9.29. In this order of ideas, the issue that is considered in this order by the Court—on the serious effects produced by the intensive development of activities of illegal mining exploitation with damage to multiple fundamental rights in the Atrato River Basin (Chocó)—, has clearly evidenced that human populations are those that are interdependent of the natural world—and not the other way around—and that they must assume the consequences of their actions and omissions with nature. It is about understanding this new sociopolitical reality with the aim of achieving a respectful transformation with the natural world, as it has happened before with civil and political rights (first generation); the economic, social and cultural (second generation), and environmental rights (third generation). Now is the time to begin taking the first steps to effectively protect the planet and its resources before it is too late, or the damage is irreversible, not only for future generations but for the human species.

9.30. In this way, respect for nature must start from the reflection on the meaning of existence, the evolutionary process, the universe and the cosmos. That is, a system of thought based on a conception of the human being as an integral part, and not as a simple dominator, would allow a process of self-regulation of the human species and their impact on the environment, recognizing their role within the circle of life and evolution from an ecocentric perspective. It is from this consideration, for example, that respect for animal rights has been cemented. In this way, it is a matter of establishing a legal instrument that offers greater justice to nature and its relations with human beings, based on the collective recognition of our species, as suggested by biocultural rights.

In this same sense, biocultural diversity as an approach, based, as has been seen, in an ecocentric perspective, implies that policies, norms and interpretations about biodiversity conservation recognize the link and interrelation that exists between culture and nature. It extends the participation of ethnic communities in the definition of public policies and regulatory frameworks, and guarantees the conditions conducive to the generation, conservation and renewal of their knowledge systems, within the framework of a SRL [Colombian Social Rule of Law].

The importance of the biological and cultural diversity of the nation for the next generations and the survival of our natural and cultural wealth poses to the Colombian State the need to adopt comprehensive public policies on conservation, preservation and compensation that consider the interdependence between biological and cultural diversity. In this way, biocultural diversity represents the most integral and comprehensive approach to ethnic and cultural diversity in the face of effective protection.

9.31. In other words, justice for nature must be applied beyond the human scenario and must allow nature to be subject to rights. Under this understanding, the Chamber considers it necessary to take a step forward in the jurisprudence towards the constitutional protection of one of our most important sources of biodiversity: the Atrato River. This interpretation finds full justification in the best interests of the environment that has been widely developed by constitutional jurisprudence and that is made up of numerous constitutional clauses that constitute what has been called the "Ecological Constitution" or "Green Constitution". This set of provisions makes it possible to affirm the transcendence of the healthy environment and the interdependent link with human beings and the State.

From the above, a series of obligations of protection and guarantee of the environment are derived from the State, who is first in responsibility for its protection, maintenance and conservation, which must materialize through responsible environmental public policies (sustainable governance), issuance of CONPES documents, legislation and National Development Plans, among others; without prejudice to the duty of protection and care that also assists civil society and the communities themselves to take care of natural resources and biodiversity. In this sense, the Chamber considers it pertinent to call attention to the ethnic communities that inhabit the Atrato River Basin so that they protect, within the exercise of their customs, uses and traditions, the environment of which they are its first guardians and responsible for it. . . .

9.32. To that extent, considering the scope of protection of international treaties signed by Colombia in the field of environmental protection, the *Ecological Constitution* and biocultural rights, which preach the joint and interdependent protection be human with nature and its resources, is that the Court will declare that the Atrato River is subject to rights that imply its protection, conservation, maintenance and, in the specific case, restoration. For the effective fulfillment of this declaration, the Court will arrange for the Colombian State to exercise legal guardianship and representation of the rights of the river in conjunction with the ethnic communities that inhabit the Atrato River Basin in Chocó; in this way, the Atrato River and its basin — henceforth — will be represented by a member of the plaintiff communities and a delegate of the Colombian State. Additionally, and with the purpose of ensuring the protection, recovery and due conservation of the river, both parties must design and set up a commission of Atrato River guards whose integration and members will be developed in the section of orders to proffer in this ruling.

As a complement to the above, it is necessary to remember that the central premise on which the conception of bioculturality and biocultural rights is based, is the relation of profound unity between nature and human species. This relationship is expressed in other complementary elements such as: (i) the multiple ways of life expressed as cultural diversity are inextricably linked to the diversity of ecosystems and territories; (ii) the richness expressed in the diversity of cultures, practices, beliefs and languages is the product of the co-evolutionary interrelation of human communities with their environments and constitutes an adaptive response to environmental changes; (iii) the relationships of different ancestral cultures with plants, animals, microorganisms and the environment actively contribute to biodiversity; (iv) the spiritual and cultural meanings of Indigenous peoples and local communities about nature are an integral part of biocultural diversity; and (v) the preservation of cultural diversity leads to the conservation of biological diversity, so that the design of policy, legislation and jurisprudence should be focused on the conservation of bioculturality [316]. These elements, from now on, should be considered as parameters for the protection of the rights of the environment and nature, from a biocultural perspective. . . .

10.2. Next, the orders to proffer in the present sentence are outlined:

1. The Atrato River, its basin and tributaries will be recognized as an entity subject to rights of protection, conservation, maintenance and restoration by the State and ethnic communities, as indicated in the motivating part of this provision in the Sections 9.27 to 9.32. . . .

2. The Ministry of the Environment, the Ministry of Finance, the Ministry of Defense, Codechoco and Corpourabá, the Governments of Chocó and Antioquia, and the defendant municipalities will be ordered . . . and in conjunction with the Plaintiffs, within a year after the notification of the sentence is designed and put in place a plan to decontaminate the water sources of Chocó, beginning with the basin of the Atrato River and its tributaries. . . .

3. Likewise, the Ministry of Defense, the National Police - Unit against Illegal Mining, the National Army of Colombia, the General Prosecutor's Office of the Nation, the governors of Chocó and Antioquia and the defendant municipalities will be ordered, in conjunction with the Plaintiff ethnic communities and with the support of the Ministry of Foreign Affairs, to design and implement, within six (6) months after notification of this ruling, a joint action plan to neutralize and eradicate definitely illegal mining activities that are carried out not only in the Atrato River and its tributaries, but also in the Department of Chocó. In this regard, the Court reiterates that it is the obligation of the Colombian State to prosecute and eradicate definitively any illegal mining activity that takes place in the country.

The aforementioned actions must include the seizure and neutralization of dredges, and in general of the machinery used in these tasks, the restriction and prohibition of the transit of inputs such as fuel and associated chemical substances (mercury, cyanide) and the judicialization of responsible persons and organizations. Also, this process will be accompanied by the Ministry of Foreign Affairs in what has to do with the situation of foreigners who engage in illegal mining activities. . . .

4. In addition to the foregoing, the Ministry of Agriculture, the Ministry of the Interior, the Ministry of Finance, the Department of National Planning, the Department for Social Prosperity, the Governors of Chocó and Antioquia and the municipalities will be ordered [340] that in a concerted manner with the plaintiff ethnic communities, design and implement within the six (6) months following the notification of this ruling an integral plan of action [341] that allows the recovery of traditional forms of subsistence and food. This plan of action will be in the framework of the concept of ethno-development that ensures minimum food safety in the area, which has ceased to be realized by the contamination of the waters of the Atrato River and by the intensive development of illegal mining activity.

This plan should also be *aimed at restoring the rights of the ethnic communities that inhabit the Atrato River Basin*, especially in relation to the recovery of their

> culture, participation, territory, identity, way of life and productive activities, including fishing, hunting, agriculture, fruit harvesting and artisanal mining. In this sense, the measures taken must be focused on guaranteeing: (i) the food sovereignty of the communities and (ii) preventing their involuntary displacement from the area due to illegal mining activities and environmental damage.
>
> These measures should include clear and precise indicators that allow an effective evaluation and monitoring of the measures adopted. . . .
>
> *It is so ordered.*

* * *

The breadth and depth of legal analysis in the *Atrato River Basin* case was unprecedented when it was decided in 2016. Since then, in Colombia and elsewhere, ecocentric considerations are becoming more common. The case also cast a critical new light on human rights to sustainable ecosystems and the cultural rights of Indigenous communities.

Although biocultural rights are not explicitly defined within Colombian legislation, the Court found that there are cultural rights belonging to special protected ethnic groups. In its interpretation of the case, the Court recognized the interdependence between the fundamental right to life and a healthy environment in the local context of the Chocó community of plaintiffs (primarily consisting of specially protected groups).[51] The Court noted the culture's distinct relationship with the Atrato River Basin, which provides them with nearly all of their vital needs, including drinking water, food, a bathing site, recreation, and so on. The Chocó communities' reliance upon the well-being of the Atrato led the Court to make an additional link—namely, the interdependence between this specially protected ethnic group and the local ecosystem. The Court recognized that the Atrato functions as an extension of the local community and, therefore, saw the two as intrinsically linked. This understanding reflects a biocentric interpretation of existing cultural rights in the Constitution. This is a first signal by the Constitutional Court of a potential ecocentric shift in understanding the rights of special protected groups.

IV. THE AMAZON

In 2018, the Supreme Court of Colombia applied the ecocentric reasoning that had been adopted by the Constitutional Court in the *Atrato River Basin* case. Ruling on a constitutional challenge against deforestation in the Amazon rainforest, the Court issued a landmark decision that recognized the Colombian Amazon as a subject of rights.[52]

[51] Corte Constitucional [C.C.] [Constitutional Court], Sala Sexta de Revisión noviembre 10, 2016, M.P: J Palacio, Sentencia T-622, (p. 14) (Colom.) (from notes preceding translated sentence).

[52] Corte Suprema de Justicia [C.S.J.] [Supreme Court of Colombia], Sala Civil Especializada en Restitución de Tierras del Tribunal Superior del Distrito Judicial de Bogotá abril 5 2018, M.P: L. Villabona, Sentencia 4360 (p. 18) (Colom.). "Colombian Amazon," la Amazonia colombiana, refers to the Amazon region as a whole.

The case was filed with the support of the Center for the Study of Law, Justice, and Society (Dejusticia) on behalf of 25 plaintiffs, including children and young people from the regions in the country most vulnerable to climate change. Through a *tutela* action, the plaintiffs claimed that deforestation in the Amazon violated their constitutional right to a healthy environment and thus threatened their fundamental rights to life, health, food, and water, as well as the rights of future generations.[53] The defendants included the President of Colombia, the Ministry of Environment, the Ministry of Agriculture, the National Parks, the regional autonomous corporations (the entities in charge of environmental governance by region), and local mayors and governments.

At the time of filing, deforestation in the Amazon had increased by 44 percent between 2016 and 2017, despite Colombia's national and international commitments to tackle deforestation.[54] The Colombian government had committed to a 20 percent reduction in its emissions by 2030 under the United Nations Framework on Climate Change, which meant significantly curbing deforestation.[55] Furthermore, the government had issued a joint statement with Norway, the United Kingdom, and Germany in 2010 committing to reduce deforestation to net zero by 2020.

The arguments of the plaintiffs were two-fold. First, deforestation in the Amazon results in severe consequences to local and national ecosystems. For instance, a significant source of drinking water in Colombia's central region comes from a special ecosystem known as *páramos*, which ultimately depends on the Amazon to regulate its water cycle. Second, deforestation in Colombia amounts to approximately two-thirds of all greenhouse gas emissions in Colombia, with most deforestation concentrated in the Amazon forest. Thus, deforestation has significant implications for climate change and the resulting impacts.

On February 12, 2018, the first instance court ruled against the plaintiffs by denying the *tutela* action on procedural grounds. The High Court of the Judicial District of Bogotá (*Tribunal Superior del Distrito Judicial de Bogotá — Sala Civil*) held that the appropriate vehicle for the plaintiffs' claims was not a *tutela* action, but rather a popular action. The plaintiffs appealed the decision, arguing that even if there were collective impacts stemming from deforestation in the Amazon, their fundamental rights were threatened and thus a *tutela* action was the appropriate mechanism for their claims. On April 5, 2019, the Supreme Court reversed the decision by the Court of first instance and issued a ruling in favor of the plaintiffs.

The Court applied the ecocentric approach the Constitutional Court had applied to the Atrato Case.[56] In its reasoning, the court moved away from an anthropocentric and utilitarian perspective by describing nature as its own autonomous being. The Court pointed out the key principles that it considers when issuing a decision, including the precautionary principle, intergenerational equity, and solidarity. As you read,

[53] The plaintiffs defined future generations as those who would become adults during the period of 2041 to 2070, when it is estimated that Colombia will experience a 1.6 °C increase in average temperatures.
[54] The main drivers of deforestation in the Amazon region include illegal mining, land grabbing, illicit crop cultivations, logging, and infrastructure such as roads for agro-industries.
[55] Colombia committed to a reduction of 30 percent contingent on international aid.
[56] Villavicencio, *supra* note 28, at 7.

pay attention to how the Court applies each principle to the case, guiding its reasoning.

Future Generations v. Ministry of Environment et al.

Supreme Court of Justice
STC4360-2018
Bogotá, D.C., April 5th, 2018

OPINION OF THE COURT

Tolosa Villabona, P. J.

1. BACKGROUND

1. The plaintiffs plead for the protection of "supralegal" rights, highlighting those of "enjoying a healthy environment," life, and health, allegedly violated by the accused. . . .

2.1. As a first step, they identify themselves as ". . . a group of 25 children, adolescents and young adults . . . between 7 and 25 years old, who live [in] [2] cities that are part of the list of cities at greatest risk by climate change . . . [with] a life expectancy of 78 years on average (75 years for men and 80 years for women), which is why they expect to develop [their] adult lives between the years 2041-2070 and [their] old age from the year 2071 onwards. In these periods of time, according to the climate change scenarios presented by the IDEAM,[57] the average temperature in Colombia is expected to increase by 1.6º C and 2.14º C, respectively . . .".

2.2. They explain that in the Paris Agreement and Law 1753 of 2015, the government acquired national and international commitments to achieve ". . . reduction of deforestation and the emission of greenhouse gases in a context of climate change . . . ," among which, they emphasize the duty to reduce "the net rate of deforestation to zero in the Colombian Amazon for the year 2020." . . .

Additionally, the "Comprehensive Strategy for Control of Deforestation and Forest Management in Colombia," reported that ". . . the country lost 178,597 hectares in 2016, that is, deforestation increased by 44% compared to the figure reported for 2015 . . . ," and of that number, 70,074 hectares were in the Amazon.

[57] *See* Instituto de Hidrología, Meteorología y Estudios Ambientales, http://www.ideam.gov.co/ (Institute of Hydrology, Meteorology and Environmental Studies) (footnote added).

They denounce as causes of this phenomenon "...land grabbing (60-65%), illicit crops (20-22%), illegal extraction of mineral deposits (7-8%), infrastructure, agro-industrial crops, and illegal extraction of wood...."

2.4. They affirm that "...deforestation in the Amazon has consequences not only in that region but also in the ecosystems of the rest..." of the national territory, among which they list: "...1) The negative alteration of the water cycle; 2) the alteration of the grounds that capture and absorb water when it rains (and the resulting floods that this generates); 3) the changes in the water supplies that arrive at the *páramos*[58] and provide water to the cities where the plaintiffs live; [and] 4) global warming due to the carbon dioxide emissions, which are stored in the forests in conditions of no deforestation...."

2.5. According to what is argued, the above is possible because those summoned have not adopted the appropriate measures to deal with this eventuality and, in addition, this has dire consequences for the places of their residence, altering their living conditions and depriving them of the chance to "enjoy a healthy environment".

They claim to be part of "...the future generation that will face the effects of climate change in the periods 2041-2070 and 2071-2100...."

2.6. In their opinion, the present petition is "suitable for the protection" of the guarantees invoked, for which they present numerous jurisprudential precedents from the Constitutional Court, specifically, they ensure compliance "with the criteria established for this in judgment SU-1116 of 2001".

Additionally, they state that "... *acción popular* as an alternative means of defense is not adequate and effective enough...," as "both fundamental and collective rights are affected."...

1.3. The appeal.

The plaintiffs formed it insisting on their disagreements, particularly, they believe that the *acción popular* is not the "ideal remedy" to settle the controversy raised and, furthermore, claiming to have proved the "irremediable damage"....

2. DISCUSSION

[The opinion summarizes the procedural differences between *tutela* and *acción popular*, recognizing that constitutional jurisprudence has established a right to the *tutela* action when the impairment of group interests infringes,

[58] Páramo is a special alpine tundra ecosystem in Colombia. *See, e.g., Páramo*, ENCYCLOPEDIA BRITANNICA, https://www.britannica.com/science/paramo (footnote added).

consequently, upon individual rights. The action must meet several requirements including (i) a connection between the violation of collective rights and the violation of one or more of the primary, fundamental, and individual rights, (ii) the person filing must be the person directly affected, (iii) the threat of the rights must not be hypothetical, and (iv) the judicial order must seek to restore individual rights and not the collectives ones, even if these are implicit in the decision.]

...By virtue of what has been said, it can be preached that the fundamental rights of life, health, minimum subsistence, freedom, and human dignity are substantially linked and determined by the environment and the ecosystem. Without a healthy environment, subjects of law, and sentient beings in general, will not be able to survive, much less protect those rights, for our children or for future generations. Neither can the existence of the family, society, or the State itself be guaranteed.

The increasing deterioration of the environment is a serious assault to current and future life and all other fundamental rights; it gradually depletes life and all rights related to it. The inability to exercise the fundamental rights to water, to breathe pure air, and to enjoy a healthy environment negatively affects the current populace; it increases the lack of fresh water and decreases the ability to enjoy a dignified life....

Humanity is mainly responsible for this scenario, its global hegemonic position led to the adoption of an anthropocentric and selfish model, whose characteristic features are harmful to environmental stability, namely: i) the excessive demographic growth; ii) the adoption of a rapid system of development guided by consumerism and the current political-economic systems; and iii) the excessive exploitation of natural resources.

5. However, gradually an awareness of the duty to change our behaviors has begun creating itself. There is a surge of movements favorable to a new ideology of an "ecocentric anthropic" society, which overcomes the excessive "homo mensura" "autistic" anthropocentrism; which takes into consideration the environment, the idea of progress, and the notion of sustainable development to achieve "...a balance between economic growth, social welfare, and environmental protection, under the understanding that present actions must ensure the possibility of making use of resources in the future...."

5.1. "...[G]iven the existence of [the] risks and problems of a global nature...," the judiciary must advocate in the Constitutional State; for the effective recognition of the rights that in principal may seem "...oriented to the protection of collective interests and the satisfaction of generalized needs...," substantially points to the defense of the essential rights of the individual....

The foregoing means that all individuals of the human species must stop exclusively thinking of self-interest. We are obligated to consider how our works and daily behavior also affect society and nature....

5.2. As noted, the scope of protection of the fundamental principles is each person, but also the "other." The "neighbor" is alterity; its essence: the other people that inhabit the planet, covering also animal and plant species.

But, in addition, it includes the subjects not yet born, who deserve to enjoy the same environmental conditions lived by us....

5.3. The environmental rights of future generations are based on (i) the ethical duty of solidarity of the species and on (ii) the intrinsic value of nature.

The first is explained by the fact that natural goods are shared by all inhabitants of Planet Earth, and by their descendants or future generations who do not yet have them physically, but who are tributaries, recipients, and owners of them, even if they, in a contradictory way, are increasingly insufficient and limited. Thus, without the current existence of an equitable and prudent approach to consumption, the human species may find itself compromised in the future due to the scarcity of essential life resources. In this way, solidarity and environmentalism "are related until they become the same."

Thus, the establishment of the duty of human solidarity with nature constitutes the essential meaning of "the true values that routinely facilitate life" both in its present and future dimensions. This idea establishes a dynamic and tangible ethic of environmental values, adjusted and compatible with "...the conservation needs of nature in the most favorable sense needed to maintain the lives of human beings [forever]...."

The second transcends from the anthropocentric perspective, and focuses on "anthropic-ecocentric" criterion, which places the human being on par with the environmental ecosystem, whose purpose is to avoid arrogant, dismissive, and irresponsible treatment of environmental resources, in its entirety, to satisfy materialistic ends, without any protectionist or conservationist respect.

The establishment of the duty of direct solidarity with nature is built on a value, on itself; this, by affinity with the knowing subject or external "object" by which it is defined, because the human being "forms part of nature 'being', likewise, nature."

This is the main idea on which the concept of the intrinsic value of the environment is based: respect for oneself implies, in itself, "respect for the part of oneself that is composed by nature, and which, in time, future generations will form a part of."

What has been stated then, develops a binding legal relationship regarding the environmental rights of future generations, such as an "omission," whose impact translates into a limitation to the freedom of action of present generations, while simultaneously implicitly demanding new burdens of environmental commitments, to the extent that they assume the care and custody of natural resources and the future world."

6. In view of the foregoing, numerous regulations have emerged in the international arena, *hard and soft law,* which constitute a global ecological public order and serve as guiding criteria for national legislation, as well as for resolving citizens' complaints about the destruction of our habitat, in favor

of the protection of the subjective rights of people, of both present and future generations.[59] . . .

7. In Colombia, the 1991 Constitution updated our stance on environmental issues, from which a national ecological public order was constructed, in which several precepts were established on the matter, such as: the prevalence of the "general interest" (Article 1); the duty to protect the "natural assets of the nation" (Article 8); public health (Article 49); the "ecological dimension" of private property (Article 58); the qualification of "natural parks" as property that is "inalienable, imprescriptible and not subject to seizure" (Article 63); one function of education was defined as ". . . train the Colombian when it comes to . . . the protection of the environment . . ." (Article 67); the fundamental right to ". . . enjoy a healthy environment" and duty of the state ". . . to protect the diversity and integrity of the environment . . ." (Article 79); the imposition upon the State duty to ". . . plan the handling and use of natural resources, to guarantee their sustainable development . . .".

The Constitutional Court played an important role with its pronouncements, and designed a jurisprudential line welcoming the concepts and advances that have emerged on the subject in the international and academic scene.

In this sense, it has analyzed the Constitution's postulates from a "green" perspective, cataloging the Political Charter as an "Ecological Constitution" and elevating the environment into the category of fundamental rights. . . .

10. The conservation of the Amazon is a national and global obligation, it is the main environmental axis of the planet, and has been called the "lung of the world . . . ."

The international community has generated various commitments to achieve its conservation; the Amazon Cooperation Treaty (TCA) should be highlighted, as its main objective is the ". . . promotion of the harmonious development of the Amazon, and the incorporation of its territories to the respective national economies, which is essential for maintaining the balance between economic growth and environmental preservation . . ."

Likewise, in the aforementioned Framework Convention on Climate Change in Paris in 2015, where Colombia, among other responsibilities, agreed to reduce "deforestation in the Colombian Amazon," with this purpose, it promoted the "Sustainable Colombia Initiative" and the "Vision Amazon". . . .

11. Under the above assumptions, the Court will study the appropriateness of the protection, establishing, for that purpose, whether the violation

[59] The opinion summarizes legal instruments such as the International Covenant on Economic, Social, and Cultural Rights of 1966, Convention on the Prohibition of Military or Any Other Hostile Use of Environmental Modification Techniques of 1976, additional Protocol I to the Geneva Conventions, The Stockholm Declaration of 1972, the Rio Declaration, the Framework Convention on Climate Change. (Footnote added.)

of the collective right to enjoy a healthy environment implicates a violation of fundamental rights, alleged as violated by the plaintiffs. . . .

In this regard, the Chamber must determine, at the venue of the dispute, whether there is a causal link between climate change generated by the progressive reduction of forest cover, caused by the expansion of the agricultural frontier, narco-crops, mining, and illicit logging; and the supposed negative effects on the health of people residing in the Colombian territory; and, next, it will have to establish if the rampant degradation of the jungle forests directly undermines the rights to dignified life, the water, and the health of the tutelantes. . . .

This previous reality, in contrast with the environmental legal principles of (i) precaution; (ii) intergenerational equity; and (iii) solidarity, leads the Court to the following conclusions:

11.1. Regarding the first of the aforementioned principles, there is no doubt that there is a risk of harm, since, according to the IDEAM, the increase in GHG [greenhouse gas] emissions caused by the deforestation of the Amazon rainforest would generate an increase in Colombia's temperature, between "0.7 and 1.1 degrees Celsius between 2011 and 2040," while for the period "between 2041 and 2070," an increase of "1.4 and 1.7" degrees centigrade is calculated, and to reach up to 2.7 degrees Celsius "in the period between 2071 and 2100."

Likewise, the mass reduction of the Amazon forest would break the ecosystem's connection with the Andes, causing the probable extinction or threat of subsistence of the species inhabiting that corridor, generating "damage to its ecological integrity."

Additionally, according to the IDEAM, the GHG emissions due to deforestation would cause, with respect to rainfall, two types of consequences. The first, an increase in several regions of the country, a situation that would trigger an increase in water levels, and therefore, runoff, generating the spread of water-borne pollutants. The second, a deficit in other national departments, causing a decrease in the water supply, as well as prolonged droughts.

Regarding the irreversibility of the damage and the scientific certainty, both additional components of the precautionary principle, they are evident since the GHG emitted as a result of deforestation, constitutes 36% of the forestry sector, becoming an uncontrolled component of CO2 emissions; information supported, in detail, by the studies carried out by the IDEAM, the Ministry of Foreign Affairs, the Ministry of Environment and Sustainable Development, and the UNDP [United Nations Development Programme], among many others.

11.2. In terms of intergenerational equity, the transgression is obvious, as the forecast of temperature increase is 1.6 degrees in 2041 and 2.14 in 2071; future generations, including children who brought this action, will be directly affected, unless we presently reduce the deforestation rate to zero.

11.3. The principle of solidarity, for the specific case, is determined by the duty and co-responsibility of the Colombian state to stop the causes of GHG emissions caused by the abrupt forest reduction of the Amazon; thus, it is imperative to adopt immediate mitigation measures, and to protect the right to environmental welfare, both of the plaintiffs, and of the other people who inhabit and share the Amazonian territory, not only nationals, but also foreigners, together with all the inhabitants of the globe, including the ecosystems and living beings.

11.3 [sic]. The discussed reality, in addition to transgressing the regulations pertaining to the Environmental Charter of the country, and the international instruments that make up the global ecological public order, constitutes a serious ignorance of the obligations acquired by the State in the Framework Convention on Climate Change of Paris 2015, where Colombia, among other commitments, undertook an agreement to reduce "deforestation in the Colombian Amazon," with the objective to reduce deforestation to zero in that region by 2020. . . .

It is up to the authorities to respond effectively to the specific questions of the problem, among which, it is important to highlight the urgent need to adopt mitigation and corrective measures: i) for the excessive expansion of illicit crops and illegal mining that unreasonably destroy the Amazonian forest; ii) to fill the void left by the FARC and paramilitaries to make an active state presence in favor of the conservation of Amazonian territories that in the context of armed conflict were conquered by insurgent groups, merciless predators, irrational colonizers, and generally, people and organizations outside the law; iii) to prevent and mitigate the growing fires, deforestation, and unreasonable expansion of the agricultural frontier; iv) for the lack of prevention of the consequences inherent to constructing roads, granting titles to property and mining concessions; v) for the expansion of large-scale agro-industrial and livestock farming; vi) for the preservation of this ecosystem due to its importance in regulating the global climate; vii) for the lack of scientific calculations of the release of tons of carbon through burning and the loss of biomass, which constitutes the vegetation cover; and viii) to confront climate change due to the destruction of the Amazon rainforest in the national territory.

12. Therefore, the excessive intensification of this problem is evident, showing: the ineffectiveness of the governmental measures adopted to confront it, and, from that perspective, granting the protection for the breach of fundamental guarantees such as water, air, dignified life, and health, among others, in connection with the environment.

In this regard, this Chamber follows the thesis held by the Constitutional Court in the T-622 of 2016, related to the recognition of nature as a real subject of rights, a position consistent with the relevance of the environment and its conservation, from the eco-centric perspective defined in previous sections. . . .

13. It is clear that despite several international commitments, legislation, and jurisprudence on the subject, the Colombian State has not efficiently tackled the problem of deforestation in the Amazon.

13.1. Currently, the three autonomous regional corporations with jurisdiction in the Amazonian territory, have not made efforts to reduce the concentrated area of deforestation, which registers 47.23% of the AT-D, distributed between the Corporation for the Sustainable Development of the South of the Amazon (Corpoamazonia) at 24.47%; the Corporation for the Sustainable Development of the North and the East of the Amazon (CDA) at 11.10%; and the Corporation for the Sustainable Development of the Area of Special Management La Macarena (Cormacarena) at 11.67%.

In this way, the aforementioned environmental authorities are not fulfilling their duty to evaluate, control, and monitor natural resources, nor to impose and execute sanctions in the event of a violation of environmental protection norms in their jurisdiction; despite being able to, in case they lack sufficient resources, request support from other agencies at the national and local level, in order to protect natural resources.

13.2. Deforestation in the Colombian Amazon also occurs in places under the protection of National Natural Parks of Colombia (PNN), specifically in the Sierra de la Macarena, Nukak, Tinigua and La Paya parks, "which occupy the places 3, 5, 6 and 9, respectively, of the Parks with a higher concentration of AT-D in 2017."

The deforestation in natural national parks is proof of the negligence in fulfilling the legal functions which were assigned to the Natural National Parks of Colombia (PNN), noting that the reduction of forest mass in protected areas is a situation that by regulation, must be controlled and sanctioned by said authority, it being empowered, in case of not being able to fulfill this task, to demand collaboration with other authorities of the national, departmental, and municipal rank.

13.3. The departments with jurisdiction in the Amazonian territory, such as Amazonas, Caquetá, Guaviare, and Putumayo are also failing to fulfill the functions that the law imposes on them regarding the environmental protection of the Colombian Amazon. It is well known, they have the duty to assist the Regional Autonomous Corporations [(CAR)] with authority in their territories; the percentage of deforestation is their responsibility to mitigate in concert with the CAR.

13.4. Regarding the municipalities that have Amazonian land according to the AT-D newsletter, in particular, La Macarena, Valle del Guamuez, Puerto Asís, San Vicente del Caguán, Vistahermosa, San José del Guaviare, Puerto Guzmán, Orito, Puerto Rico, Mapiripán Cartagena del Chairá, Calamar, Uribe, Solano, Puerto Leguízamo, El Retorno, Miraflores, and Florencia, contained high levels of deforestation in 2017, without them, as observed in the reports related to this action, counteracting the situation.

The foregoing transgresses the fulfillment of legal and regulatory assignments, established by Article 3 of Law 1551 of 2012, which assigns municipalities "to ensure the proper handling of natural resources and the environment, in accordance with the Constitution and the law."...

14. Therefore, in order to protect this ecosystem vital for our global future, just as the Constitutional Court declared the Atrato River, the Colombian Amazon is recognized as a "subject of rights," entitled to protection, conservation, maintenance and restoration led by the State and the territorial agencies.

Consequently, we grant the relief, and order the Presidency of the Republic, the Ministry of Environment and Sustainable Development, and the Ministry of Agriculture and Rural Development, in coordination with the actors of the National Environmental System and the participation of the plaintiffs, the affected communities, and the interested population in general, within the four (4) months following today's notice, to formulate a short, medium, and long term action plan to counteract the rate of deforestation in the Amazon, tackling climate change impacts.

The purpose of this plan will be to mitigate the early deforestation warnings issued by the IDEAM.

Likewise, it will be ordered of the Presidency of the Republic, the Ministry of Environment and Sustainable Development, and the Ministry of Agriculture and Rural Development, within a period of five (5) months following today's notice, with the active participation of the plaintiffs, the affected communities, scientific organizations or environmental research groups, and the interested population in general, to formulate the construction of an "*intergenerational pact for the life of the Colombian Amazon (PIVAC)*" to adopt measures aimed at reducing deforestation to zero and greenhouse gas emissions, and has national, regional, and local implementation strategies of a preventative, mandatory, corrective, and pedagogical nature, directed towards climate change adaptation.

It will also be ordered of all the municipalities of the Colombian Amazon, within a period of five (5) months following today's notice, to update and implement the Land Management Plans, and when relevant, include an action plan to reduce deforestation to zero in its territory, which should encompass preventative, mandatory, corrective, and pedagogical measurable strategies, oriented towards climate change adaptation.

The Corporation for the Sustainable Development of the South of the Amazon (Corpoamazonia), the Corporation for the Sustainable Development of the North and the East of the Amazon (CDA), and the Corporation for the Sustainable Development of the Special Management Area La Macarena (Cormacarena), will be ordered, within a period of five (5) months from today's notice, with respect to its jurisdiction, to create an action plan to counteract

> the deforestation problems reported by the IDEAM through police, judicial, or administrative measures.
>
> Additionally, within their duties, the defendants will have to, in the forty-eight (48) hours following the completion of this ruling, increase actions tending to mitigate deforestation while carrying out the modifications contained in the aforementioned mandate. Within the responsibilities assigned, they must urgently present the complaints before the corresponding administrative and judicial entities.
>
> *It is so ordered.*

V. THE CAUCA RIVER

The plaintiffs filed a *tutela* against Empresas Publicas de Medellin[60] (EPM), Antioquia (department in Colombia), the Ituango Hydroelectric S.A., the Ministry of Environment, the National Agency of Environmental Licenses (ANLA), and others to protect the fundamental rights of communities living near the Ituango Hydroelectric project. The project is located in Antioquia, along the Cauca River.[61] Hidroituango (the name of the project) has been under public scrutiny due to the social and environmental impacts of the dam. Despite EPM's attempts to keep an open dialogue with neighboring communities, there was little progress addressing the problems affecting the nearby villages and municipalities. In February 2019, a structural flaw led the company to take emergency measures, which resulted in a reduction in the water flow, causing a large part of the river to run dry.[62] This had significant impacts on fishing activities, transportation, and tourism in the area. In response, the plaintiffs filed a legal action seeking protection of their fundamental rights to health, water, and a healthy environment, and the neighboring communities' right to a dignified life.[63]

The court of first instance of the Fourth Civil Court of the Oral Circuit of Medellin (*Juzgado Cuarto Civil del Circuito de Oralidad de Medellín*) declined to grant the *tutela* after concluding that there was a clear and real intention on behalf of EPM to deal with the ongoing issues around Hidroiutango. The court found that there had been no omission by the defendants, which is a requirement for a *tutela* action to move forward. The plaintiffs appealed the case, alleging that the first instance judge failed to study the precedent of sentence T-622 of 2016 (the *Atrato River Basin* case). On appeal, the Superior Court of Medellin reversed the judgment.

[60] Empresas Publicas de Medellin operates as a utility company providing infrastructure and operational services for water and sewerage, telecommunications, electricity and gas, and garbage collection services.

[61] The Cauca River covers 1,350 km, reaching more than 150 municipalities in Colombia, with a total population of approximately 10 million people.

[62] *See* Taran Volckhausen, *Colombia's Disaster-Ridden Hydropower Project Runs Second Largest River Dry*, MONGABAY (Feb. 7, 2019), https://news.mongabay.com/2019/02/colombias-disaster-ridden-hydropower-project-runs-second-largest-river-dry/ ("[T]he Cauca[] was reduced to less than 10 percent of normal flow.").

[63] Neither plaintiff was part of the affected communities as was the case in the Atrato River Basin litigation. Nonetheless, the Court found that they met the requirements to bring a tutela action.

Castro Córdoba and David Ochoa v. Ministry of Environment et al.

Superior Court of Medellín
Judgment #38
Medellín, 2015.

OPINION OF THE COURT[64]

Sosa Londoño, J., J.

[The judgment discusses the facts and procedural posture. It then cites national[65] and international law on sustainable development and future generations.]

It is noteworthy that the regulations implicitly recognize the dignity of future generations and this principle constitutes, in essence, one of the distinguishing elements of the subjects of rights in modern legislation, which imposes an analysis around the concept and the determination that not only are future generations the subjects of rights, but of the possibility that the obligations that current generations have towards future generations can be protected through *tutela* actions. . . .

[The opinion cites the United Nations Charter, the United Nations Conference on the Human Environment (The Stockholm Declaration), the World Charter for Nature, the Rio Declaration on Environment and Development, the Vienna Declaration and Program of Action, and UNESCO's Declaration on the Responsibilities of the Present Generations Towards Future Generations.]

5.2 Sentence C-256 of 1994 said that the constitutional basis of the legal requirement for a declaration of impact or environmental defect is found in the constitutional right that all people have, those of present and future generations, to enjoy a healthy environment. . . .

5.3 When Sentence C-649 of 1997 stated the rights possessed by all persons, current and future generations alike, it reiterated that the right to enjoy a healthy environment emerges from articles . . . of the Constitution, which is the basis for the obligation that environmental law has imposed on people to present an environmental . . . impact statement . . . on the consequences that the development or execution of a specific project or activity may have on the environment or on natural resources. The consequences explain "the need to protect for current and future generations the basic elements . . . to guarantee a healthy environment through the preservation and restoration of the ecosystem . . ."

[64] Translation by authors.
[65] L. 99/93, diciembre 22, 1993, DIARIO OFICIAL [D.O.] (Colom.); L. 388/97, julio 18, 1997, DIARIO OFICIAL [D.O.] (Colom.).

5.4 Sentence C-126 of 1998 reminds us that the Constitution produced an "ecologization" of private property, which has noteworthy consequences not only for the social function of property but also because the powers of individual property owners are limited by the rights of those who have yet to be born, that is, by future generations, requiring and empowering the legal order to adopt greater restrictions on appropriations of natural resources and the powers of property owners themselves. . . .

6. Based on the previous doctrinal and jurisprudential precedent, and granting the preamble of the United Nations Charter and the instruments mentioned . . . future generations, [have] a fundamental right to a healthy environment [and] are true subjects of rights.

But nothing would be done by simply recognizing the rights of future generations under the category of subjects . . . if there were not at the same time a way for those rights to be exercised, in other words, [the courts] must grant from now on actions for the defense of their interests, and although it could be thought that in this case the appropriate mechanism is the *acción popular,* given the nature of the requests made in the writ of amparo, mainly the third, regarding the declaration of the Cauca River as a subject of rights, judgment T-622 of 2016 as a precedent imposes a different interpretation. . . .

8. As stated in the complaint, there is no doubt about the existence of an unprecedented crisis that affected the . . . fauna and flora that depend directly on the good state of the river, a natural ecosystem that, as the 1972 United Nations Conference in Stockholm declared, must be preserved for the benefit of future generations. . . . [Arising from this precedent,] another no less important subject of rights emerges: the same river to which EPM owes a series of commitments to remedy the damages that the contingency produced on its ecosystem.

This is not about elaborating on the argument for the protection of natural wealth, the concept of the ecological or green constitution, since the Constitutional Court already did so through its judgment T-622 of 2016, . . . but about the special protection that the Cauca River deserves as a source of food, environment, and diversity, but especially of the right to water as a hydrological source, of conserving its future value. . . .

The river has suffered from the behavior, the intervention of human beings, foreseeable or not, taking its flow to a historical minimum. . . . [The crisis] demands, claims, a recovery process, (if one is highly optimistic in the medium term, but in reality, in the long term), and therefore merits not only current compensation, but . . . the materialization of future generations as a subject of rights. . . .

[T]here was mention of the intergenerational equity that can be expressed in that future generations have the right to an adequate inheritance that allows them a level of life not less than that of the current generation, which is a principle that is directly related to the ethical base of the environmental order and the *solidarity* concept, this latter enshrined in Article 1 of the 1991 Political Charter.... In summary, this court essentially declares:

(i) That future generations are the subject of rights requiring very special protection, (ii) that they have fundamental rights to dignity, water, food security, and a healthy environment, and (iii) that the river Cauca is the subject of rights, which implies, as was done with the Atrato River, its protection, conservation, maintenance, and restoration under the authority of the Public Municipal Entity and the State.

10. The orders to be issued will be similar to those ordered by the Court in judgment T-622 of 2016. Without a doubt, EPM is responsible for the violation of the fundamental rights of future generations to their life, water, food security, healthy environment, but as the abundant documentary evidence that has been collected shows that effective actions [by the company] have begun to stop the damage suffered by the river downstream, no order will be issued to initiate such actions.

Consequently, the National Government will be ordered to exercise the protection and legal representation of the rights of the river (through the institution designated by the President, which could well be the Ministry of Environment), together with the communities and people who were present at the preventive monitoring hearing of the Ituango Hydroelectric project held on February 27, 2019.... In this way, the Cauca River and its watershed will be represented from now on by a member of these participants and a delegate of the Colombian Government, who will be the guardians of the river....

[The guardians will receive support from public or private entities, universities, research centers, environmental organizations (national or international), grassroots groups, etc.]

It is ordered that the General Prosecutor of the Nation, the Ombudsman, and the Office of the Controller General of the Republic ... in accordance with their legal and constitutional powers, carry out a process of accompaniment and monitoring compliance and execution of orders already indicated ... [these offices] will submit semester reports of their activities and compliance indicators.

11. Finally, since the judgment will only be effective once it is extended to all persons or communities that reside in the Cauca river basin, its tributaries, and neighboring territories, the Court grans *inter communis* effects to the decision.

It is so ordered.

VI. THE COELLO, COMBEIMA, AND COCORA RIVERS

Isaac Vargas Morales, acting as Municipal Official of Ibague, filed a popular action against the Ministry of Environment, the Colombian Geological Survey, AngloGold Ashanti Colombia, Continental Gold, and others, seeking to stop mining activity in the river basins of the Coello Greater River, the Combeima River, and the Cocora River. Gold mining around the rivers' basins affects the quality and quantity of water used for human consumption. It also affects the agricultural, industrial, and livestock sectors, which are crucial for the economy and food security of the population of Ibague and other municipalities. In essence, the complaint alleged that the environmental licenses granted to mining companies threaten the Coello, Cocora, and Combeima Rivers and, in turn, the collective rights to enjoyment of the public space, free of pollution; the enjoyment of a healthy and ecologically balanced environment; the prevention of technically foreseeable disasters; and public safety and health.

Vargas Morales v. Ministry of Environment et al.

File number: 73001-23-00-000-2011-00611-000
Administrative Court of the Department of Tolima
Ibague, Tolima May 30th, 2019

OPINION OF THE COURT

ROJAS VILLA, J., J.

[The opinion discusses in depth the national and international sources of law on sustainable development and the right to water, including international human rights law and comparative law. It then describes the precautionary principle. According to a 2011 technical report, the risks associated with gold mining exploration and exploitation include increased soil erosion, loss of regular water flows, impacts on food production, and an increase in the kind and number of landslides, among others.] . . .

At this stage of the judicial process, it seems plausible to affirm that if these risks are materialized, the damage would be of such magnitude that they would pose a serious detriment to the environment and natural resources. A critical result if one considers that, in addition, strategic ecosystems are being affected which . . . play a crucial role for the subsistence of ecosystems, crops, and communities of the region. . . .

[T]his Chamber finds that the acute environmental, social, and economic problem resulting from the granting of mining titles in the basin of the rivers Coello, Cocora and Combeima makes evident a fundamental threat of serious damage to the ecological balance and the preservation of natural resources that cannot be [ignored by] the Constitutional Judge of Popular Action. . . .

> [Following the principle of proportionality, the Court denied the suspensions of the mining titles requested by plaintiffs.]
>
> The Chamber declares the violation of the collective [rights] to enjoy the public space free of pollution, a healthy and ecologically balanced environment, prevention of technically foreseeable disasters, and public safety and health of the communities living in the basin of the Coello river. . . .
>
> The Chamber will adopt the necessary measures to protect the hydric resource that is indispensable for the residents of the Municipality of Ibague and a great part of the Department of Tolima. . . .
>
> [Opinion cites the 2016 Atrato river decision.]
>
> The Chamber will adopt the arguments developed by the Honorable Constitutional Court to recognize that the Coello, Combeima and Cocora rivers, their basis and tributaries as individual entities, subject of rights to the protection, conservation, maintenance, and restoration in charge of the State and communities.
>
> Consequently, it will order the national Government to exercise guardianship and legal representation of the rights of the rivers (through the institution that the President of the Republic designates, which could well be the Ministry of Environment and Sustainable Development) together with the communities that live in the basis of the Coello, Combeima, and Cocora rivers; in this way, the three rivers and their basins, from now on, will be each represented by a member of their communities and a delegate from the Colombian Government, whom will be the guardians of the river. . . .[66]
>
> Additionally, this plan will include a series of clear indicators that allow to measure their efficacy and must be designed and executed in a consensual manner with the residents of the area, while guaranteeing the participation of communities . . . under the 169 Convention of the ILO.
>
> [Opinion orders the creation of action plans as well as toxicologic and epidemiological studies of the Coello, Combeima, and Cocora rivers, its tributaries, and communities.]
>
> It will be ordered that the General Prosecutor of the Nation, the Ombudsman, and the Office of the Controller General of the Republic, in accordance with their legal and constitutional powers, carry out a process of accompaniment and of monitoring compliance and execution of orders already indicated . . . in the short, medium, and long term. . . .

VII. PÁRAMO DE PISBA

In 2018, a Colombian court (*Tribunal Administrativo de Boyacá*) declared that the Páramo de Pisba was a subject of rights, making it the third recognized rights-bearing

[66] The opinion also orders the creation of an advisory team composed of the Alexander von Humboldt Institute of Biological Resources Research, WWF Colombia, and other research organizations, civil society groups, etc. (footnote added).

ecosystem in the country. The recognition of this páramo (a unique alpine tundra ecosystem) raised questions, such as, if this ecosystem has rights, shouldn't all of them? In the case of the Páramo de Pisba, it is important to note the context of the ecosystem. Seven percent of Colombians rely on water supplies regulated by páramos. Only five countries in the world have páramo ecosystems, and Colombia has the most.

The evolution of their legal protection began in 2011, when the basis for the law of the páramos (*Ley 1450, Artículo 202*[67]) first appeared within the context of the National Development Plan. The initial law set to demarcate the boundaries of páramos and prohibited new contracts for the cultivation of the land, farming, mining and exploration for minerals and carbon, and construction of oil and gas refineries. In 2018, Law 1930 (*Ley 1930*)[68] was signed by Congress. Article 1 states, "The object of the present law is to establish páramos as strategic ecosystems and to set guidelines that favor their integrality, preservation, restoration, sustainable use, and generation of knowledge." The Law contains 6 chapters and 33 articles, pertaining to the maintenance and protection of páramos, in relation to retaining their integrity.

A few months later, the Boyacá Tribunal's decision (*Expediente 15238 3333 002 2018 00016 01I)* recognized Páramo de Pisba as a subject of rights, with the right to maintenance, protection, conservation, and restoration.[69] The decision came in response to a *tutela* filed by residents demanding their fundamental rights to participation in the process of zoning and determining the boundaries of the páramo.

In its decision, the court declared the Ministry of the Environment and Sustainable Development as the legal representative of Páramo de Pisba.[70] The court then gave the ministry one year to determine the boundaries of the páramo, inviting all actors to participate in the process, according to minimum standards.[71] The judge cautioned that the outcome of the process cannot infringe on the rights of the Páramo de Pisba.[72] With notice to the mining companies operating across the department, the court ordered that all people affected by the rezoning should be compensated, particularly those groups who have historically been subject to discrimination.[73]

VIII. CONCLUSION

The cases discussed in this chapter, along with others in Colombia that advance the development of Earth law have fostered a broader discussion in Colombia of the relationship between nature and humans. Supporters of nature's rights point to the evolving understandings of rights and legal personhood throughout history. At one time,

[67] L. 1450/11, junio 16, 2011, Diario Oficial [D.O.] (Colom.).

[68] Congreso de la República Colombia. Ley 1930, "Por media de la cual se dictan disposiciones para la gestión integral de los páramos en Colombia" (2018).

[69] Expediente 15238 3333 002 2018 00016 01I makes reference to the Atrato Case (see p. 25).

[70] *Id.* at 68

[71] *Id.* at 68-69.

[72] *Id.* at 35.

[73] *Id.* at 70.

children, women, and many other groups were not considered legal persons in the way they are now. Today, in an increasing number of jurisdictions, ecosystems, river basins, and individual animals are the subjects of rights.

These achievements raise important questions. For example, what is the impact of granting rights to nature when guardians or representatives are required to sue on their behalf? Might the creation of new legal obligations in regard to natural systems be redundant and needlessly complicate decision-making if human rights to a healthy environment could provide the same remedies? Would focusing on human rights yield more effective results than working towards the creation of such new obligations. Consider the argument that nature's rights are not an appropriate framework to further environmental protection because ecosystems and their nonhuman components cannot exercise rights or be subject to duties in the ways that humans and legal entities such as corporations can.

Villavicencio and others, writing in support of these new obligations, have found that recent judgments shed light on the inefficiency of the Colombian government, institutional gaps at the local and national levels, and the insufficient protection of nature and ecosystems.[74] They signal a new approach in which judges recognize the rights of ecosystems so that local communities and other stakeholders may enforce their protection, conservation, maintenance, and restoration, even in the absence of action by the legislative branch.[75] Furthermore, they provide an opportunity for civil society actors to engage in monitoring and create follow-up mechanisms to aid the implementation of a judgment. While the plaintiffs in many of these cases did not expressly request that the courts designate ecosystems as the subjects of rights, the courts have affirmatively recognized their legal personhood and made progress to reinforce a rights of nature paradigm.[76]

Rights evolve in a matrix of legal systems and frameworks and need to be considered in tandem with these factors. Despite the judgments' tendency to give emphasis to the enforcement of nature's rights, the challenges of effectuating these rights is complicated in the context of inequality, ongoing violence, and a social transition in Colombian society that was engulfed in armed conflict before the Constitution was adopted in 1991.

There may also be tensions between the rights of nature and the fundamental rights of vulnerable populations. Challenges between the rights of nature and of vulnerable populations have begun to emerge in the implementation of some of the recent case decisions in Colombia. For example, in the case of the Atrato River, various residents thought to be associated with the protection of the river have been targeted for assassination and threatened with violence.[77] While the threats and violence against

[74] Villavicencio, *supra* note 28, at 9.
[75] *Id.*
[76] *Id.* at 10.
[77] Threats of violence against environmental defenders and rights activists are endemic in Colombia. In recent years, Colombia has ranked among the five most dangerous countries worldwide for environmental defenders and rights activists. *Colombia: 'Terrible Trend' of Rights Defenders Killed, Harassed; UN Calls for 'Significant Effort' to Tackle Impunity*, UN News (May 10, 2019), https://news.un.org/en/story/2019/05/1038281.

environmental defenders are not a new phenomenon, the judicial order may be increasing this risk. At this time, there does not appear to be any governmentally recognized system to protect residents from these ongoing threats of violence.[78] An analysis of these tensions does not imply a flaw in the judgments per se. It simply indicates that the individuals and entities responsible for the implementation process are encountering foreseeable challenges in carrying out the courts' decisions.

Tensions are also present in the implementation of the judicial orders on deforestation in the Amazon region. There is a complex web of groups with a presence in these territories, including regional autonomous corporations (CARs), Indigenous groups, foreign landowners, *campesinos* (peasant farmers), and illegal armed actors. While certain groups have special rights to operate in the territory, such as the CARs, or special constitutional protections, as is the case with Indigenous people, others, such as illegal armed groups and foreign landowners or investors, have power in the territory. In this simplified matrix, it is important to note that Colombian *campesinos* do not have constitutional protections, despite long-standing movements advocating for their rights. In the case of the Amazon, attention should be paid to who is prosecuted for deforestation and how certain groups may be disproportionately penalized. Similarly, plans to tackle deforestation cannot develop without providing comprehensive programs to help build alternative livelihoods that do not rely on deforestation. In 2019, the Colombian government made deforestation a national security issue; the impacts will further shed light on how this tension between rights evolves and is reconciled in practice.[79]

In sum, while there are challenges to implementing judgments recognizing nature's rights, the Colombian cases represent an extraordinary advancement in the field of Earth law and chart a promising future for both litigation and legislation. Recently, Representative Juan Carlos Lozada Vargas introduced a bill to amend the Constitution to make nature a subject of rights in accordance with the recent judicial decisions.[80] In addition, these decisions are spurring meaningful legal debate, pushing institutions to respond, and inspiring activists to imagine new ways to leverage the law for social and environmental change. These developments will continue to shape the field of Earth law.

[78] Redacción Colombia 2020, *¿Nos Van a Matar a Todos por Defender el Río Atrato?": Líder Social del Chocó*, El Espectador (Feb. 26, 2019 2:22 PM), https://www.elespectador.com/colombia2020/pais/nos-van-matar-todos-por-defender-el-rio-atrato-lider-social-del-choco-articulo-857687.

[79] *En Este Gobierno, la Falta de Agua, la Pérdida de la Biodiversidad y la Contaminación Ambiental, se Convirtieron en una Preocupación de Seguridad Nacional*, Ministerio de Ambiente y Desarrollo Sostenible 2020 (2019), http://www.minambiente.gov.co/index.php/noticias/4279-en-este-gobierno-la-falta-de-agua-la-perdida-de-la-biodiversidad-y-la-contaminacion-ambiental-se-convirtieron-en-una-preocupacion-de-seguridad-nacional-gracias-a-la-nueva-politica-de-defensa-y-seguridad-para-la-equidad.

[80] *See "Por el cual se modifica el artículo 79 de la Constitución Política de Colombia. [Naturaleza como sujeto de derechos]"*, Universidad de los Andes (2019) https://congresovisible.uniandes.edu.co/proyectos-de-ley/por-el-cual-se-modifica/10116/ (Proyecto de Acto Legislativo "por el cual se modifica el artículo 79 de la Constitución Política de Colombia).

STUDY QUESTIONS

(1) *Interpretation of international principles.* Colombia's legal system integrates several principles of international environmental law and environmental justice into its legislation and jurisprudence, such as the precautionary principle, the prevention principle, distributive justice, participatory justice, environmental equity, and intergenerational equity, among others. How does the judiciary enlarge these principles beyond their traditional interpretations in the *Atrato* judgment? For instance, the judiciary expanded the precautionary principle, which is often applied in the environmental context, to human health. How can this expanded view of the precautionary principle be used to develop legislation suited to protect human and non-human nature?

(2) *Establishing a new regime.* The *Atrato* judgment set the legal framework for ecosystem rights-based jurisprudence in Colombia, namely the right to be maintained, protected, conserved, and eventually restored. While most rights frameworks applicable to individual rights typically include duties, nature cannot itself execute assigned duties or be held liable for harms done. Recognizing both nature's intrinsic and instrumental values as a holistic package, is it appropriate to posit that — in the absence of assigning nature traditional legal duties — the intrinsic values and ecological goods and services provided by nature may supersede the need for prescribed legal duties? In the *Atrato* case, the Court has assigned humans with the responsibility to act on behalf of nature, with the understanding that a protected and respected natural environment preserves and enhances human quality of life. How can the reasoning presented by this case contribute to our understanding of a nature's rights regime?

(3) *Challenges in implementation.* It is important to note that a significant portion of the state defendants in this case do not have a regional presence in Chocó, despite their prescribed obligations to coordinate or collaborate on activities in the region. How might this complicate the implementation of the court's orders? Do you think authorities without a preexisting regional presence can realistically meet the demands of the court order? Further, the case deals in large part with illegal activity and alludes to illegal armed actors in the region. Due to armed conflict and state absence in the region, Chocó residents continue to live alongside illegally armed actors. How might this further complicate full implementation of the judgment?

(4) *Nature's rights.* In its decision, the Court repeatedly underscored interdependence between the fundamental human right to life and other constitutional rights, including the right to a clean, healthy environment. This emphasis can be seen as a signal to the broader judicial branch to recognize this interdependence. Additionally, the case presents an ecocentric understanding of human dependence on nature, linking this interdependence to emerging Earth jurisprudence and setting a legal precedent for nature's rights around the

globe. Yet, nature's rights were not a part of the requested relief. What rational arguments did the Court use to make a case for nature's rights? Are any existential arguments included to justify the order to protect nature's rights? How do you understand the Court's interpretation of the petitioner's claims?

(5) *Soft law v. hard law.* While Colombia's legal system integrates international agreements through what is known as *bloque de constitucionalidad,* some of the sources that the plaintiffs in the *Amazon* case included in their complaint to assert the government's legal obligation were not international conventions or other legally binding treaties. For instance, the joint statement that had set zero net deforestation as a goal for the year 2020 was simply a statement reiterating the support that Germany, the United Kingdom, and Norway offered to Colombia in the fight against deforestation. Similarly, the plaintiffs referred to several principles of international environmental law such as the precautionary principle, the solidarity principle, and intergenerational equity among others, of which only some are included in the Constitution. What was the importance of these principles in the Court's reasoning? Does it make a difference that some of these principles were enshrined in national law while others were not? How did the national commitments under the Paris Agreement informed the opinion's reasoning?

(6) *Challenges in litigating climate change.* As in other climate change lawsuits around the world, the plaintiffs in the *Amazon* case risked the Court finding that it did not have jurisdiction over the case because the question of deforestation and climate change policy was a "political question" reserved for the executive and legislative branches to handle. Alternatively, the Court could have found that the violations alleged by the plaintiffs were nonjusticiable, although the jurisprudence on socioeconomic rights in Colombia made this scenario much less likely than in countries like the United States. What do you make of the Court's non-treatment of the separation of powers principle? What other obstacles do you think the plaintiffs faced? In addition, climate change litigation faces the challenge of establishing causality between greenhouse gas emissions and the impacts attributed to the defendants' (in)action. Climate change is a global problem cause by global GHG emissions, which can rarely be traced to particular emitters. How did the Court overcome the obstacle of causality?

(7) *Intragenerational equity.* While the *Amazon* plaintiffs brought their claims on behalf of present and future generations, the Court did not rule on their standing nor did it adopt a definition of future generations. The claimants used the very specific definition of future generations; namely, "those individuals who would become adults between the years 2041 and 2070," which is the period in which the country expects to see an increase in average temperatures of more than 1.6°C according to official data. Why do you think they defined "future generations" this way? If future generations were defined to include unborn children would this have caused standing issues? Could this have potential implications in other areas of law?

(8) *Science and the law.* Both the *Amazon* complaint and the Supreme Court's opinion drew heavily on climate science and the government's official submissions to the United Nations Framework on Climate Change. The government of Colombia relies on the Institute of Hydrology, Meteorology and Environmental Studies (IDEAM), the agency tasked with producing environmental data in the country. This made it very difficult for the defendants to question any of the science that was presented. Instead, the defendants argued on procedural grounds, pointing out that the *tutela* was not the ideal mechanism to bring the plaintiffs' claim. What do you think is the role of science in climate litigation cases, or in litigation dealing with the rights of nature more broadly?

(9) *Separation of powers.* Other climate change litigation cases around the world have demanded more ambition with respect to national plans to mitigate emissions.[81] This inherently raises questions about the separation of powers principle. In the *Amazon* case, the Court issued a series of orders mandating the executive branch to develop and implement action plans. However, the order fails to mention the Ministry of Finance, arguably the most important ministry. What other actors should the opinion have involved? Do you think these orders violate the separation of powers principle? Are they effective?

(10) *Challenges of structural judgments.* Similar to the *Atrato River Basin* case, the *Amazon* judgment attempts to tackle complex and structural dynamics in Colombia: ongoing conflict, an absent state, weak institutions, the presence of illegal actors, land grabbing, and rampant inequality, among others. Do you think a judicial order is an appropriate way to deal with these problems? What should be the role of the judiciary branch in tackling systemic issues like deforestation in the Amazon or chronic environmental injustice in ethnic territories? How should other branches of government engage with the problem? Furthermore, the case raises questions about monitoring and compliance, which are ongoing challenges at the time of writing. What issues may emerge during the implementation of structural judgments like the one in the *Amazon* case?

(11) *The role of precedent.* In both of the cases dealing with rivers, the regional courts adopted an ecocentric framework. How do previous decisions shape the reasoning of the courts here? Do you think that their application of previous judgments is compelling?

(12) *Legal fetishism.* Julieta Lemaitre Ripoll has coined the theory of legal fetishism to describe a situation of "desiring and enjoying the law not as a means to an end,

[81] Cases have been filed in Canada, Germany, Norway, France, Switzerland, Ireland and the Netherlands among others. For more information, *see Climate Change Litigation Databases*, The Sabin Center for Climate Change Law, http://climatecasechart.com/.

but rather as an end in itself."[82] While in general environmental practitioners praise recent jurisprudence applying an ecocentric approach, several concerns have been raised. Some critics posit that the Colombian legal system already has sufficient tools to protect nature and thus advocates should pay more attention to the implementation of legislation or judicial sentences. Similarly, some critics find that there are strong constitutional protections but significant gaps in both institutional coordination and fulfillment of fundamental rights on a daily basis.[83] What do you make of these critiques? Are there any arguments for the symbolic effect or impact of the sentences discussed in this chapter?

(13) *Legislating nature's rights.* As of the time of publication, a member of Congress had introduced a constitutional amendment to modify Article 79 and guarantee the recognition of nature as a subject of rights. What do you think about constitutional reform as opposed to further jurisprudence on this issue? What is the value of introducing and potentially passing a constitutional amendment on this issue? Are there drawbacks?

[82] Julieta Lemaitre Ripoll, *Legal Fetishism: Law, Violence, and Social Movements in Colombia,* 77 Rev. Jur. U.P.R. 331 (2008).
[83] *See* United Nations Environment Programme, Environmental Rule of Law: First Global Report viii (2019).

CHAPTER 19

Earth Law in Latin America: A Glimpse of Brazil and Mexico[1]

I. INTRODUCTION

Latin America is a world leader in the rights of nature movement. Already, you have learned about developments in Ecuador and Colombia—two trailblazers in the development of Earth law. Other countries in Latin America also recognize the rights of nature in some capacity, and many more have proposed to do the same.[2]

In addition to Ecuador and Colombia, an important embodiment of rights of nature in Latin America comes from Bolivia. In 2010, Bolivia's Plurinational Legislative Assembly passed the Law of the Rights of Mother Earth, which recognized nature's rights to life, to the diversity of life, to water, to clean air, to equilibrium, to restoration, and to pollution-free living.[3] This law was followed up by the 2012 Framework Law of Mother Earth and Integral Development for Living Well,[4] which required the creation of a Mother Earth Ombudsman Office (Defensoria de la Madre Tierra) to bolster Bolivia's existing rights of nature protections. Unfortunately, in practice, Bolivia has largely failed to uphold its bold rights of nature agenda. As lamented by Pablo Solon, former UN ambassador from Bolivia: "We might expect neoliberal extractivist politicians to do this. But it's particularly painful when it is done by former comrades who wave a banner of Mother Earth in the air while crushing those very rights under foot."[5]

Two other Latin American countries that recognize nature's rights in some capacity are Brazil and Mexico. Both Brazil and Mexico have a unique perspective on emerging Earth law movements in Latin American nations. They were combined into a single

[1] The chapter's section on Mexico was authored by Raúl Gutiérrez Patiño (Transdisciplinary University Center for Environmental Sustainability of the Iberoamerican University (CENTRUS)) with modifications and additions by Earth Law Center (particularly on the Rights of Nature) and research by Camelia Stanciu (founder of Balance Earth). The section on Brazil was authored by Nikoletta Pikramenou, Ph.D.
[2] Rights of nature have been proposed nationally in Argentina, (UN Harmony with Nature, Rights of Nature Law, Policy and Education, http://www.harmonywithnatureun.org/rightsofnature), and a coalition of lawyers in Peru recently proposed a law recognizing the rights of rivers.
[3] *Ley de Derechos de la Madre Tierra*, Law 071 of the Plurinational State (2010).
[4] *La Ley Marco de la Madre Tierra y Desarrollo Integral para Vivir Bien*, Law 300 of the Plurinational State (2012).
[5] Shannon Biggs & Nick Buston, *Bolivia Must Practice What it Preaches*, The Ecologist (May 24, 2019), https://theecologist.org/2019/may/24/bolivia-must-practice-what-it-preaches.

chapter to encourage a comparison of their respective approaches. There are many similarities and some important distinctions, as well.

Despite their different biomes — tropical Brazil is famous for its rainforest and savannah while Mexico straddles the tropic of Cancer and has significant areas of arid and desert habitat — Brazil and Mexico share significant similarities from an environmental perspective. Both are classified as mega-diverse countries with an incredible array of plant and animal species. And while both have national constitutions that emphasize a human-centered attitude to the environment, in both nations, there are budding grassroots movements to strengthen Indigenous philosophies, ecocentrism, and the rights of nature.

This chapter discusses Brazil first and then Mexico. For each, it starts by examining the law's treatment of the environment and how Earth law can be derived from the existing legal systems. Both sections also discuss the development of Earth law at the local or statewide level. Finally, both sections look at the current and possible future roles of Indigenous peoples in the development of the countries' legal systems.

There are differences between Brazil and Mexico, as well. Notably, the two countries discuss unique theories for expanding current laws to achieve greater ecocentrism: the Brazil section discusses incorporating Indigenous traditions into the existing Western framework, whereas the Mexico section discusses extending human rights frameworks to include nature. Additionally, the Brazil section includes a unique case about legal rights for a parrot.

As you read these case studies, consider how new rights-based movements are born. It may be through the passage of an innovative local law that inspires other governments to follow suit. Or perhaps the judiciary, in a display of bravery and creativity, issues a decision based on a new legal theory. In both cases, grassroots movements are often the engine—activists, lawyers, civil society groups, and others fighting against the injustices of the legal system. Finally, as the rights of nature movements in Brazil and Mexico grow, consider how an Earth lawyer might guide them over the coming years to ensure their success.

PART I: BRAZIL

II. THE ENVIRONMENT IN BRAZIL'S CONSTITUTION

Brazil is the largest country in South America. It shares its borders with the majority of countries on the continent and boasts an extensive Atlantic coastline. Given its variety of terrain and abundance of diverse species and habitat, it is among the world's 17 mega-diverse countries.[6] As of the 2010 census, there were approximately 900,000 Indigenous people in Brazil distributed among 305 ethnic groups. Of its total

[6] Amber Pariona, *Habitats and Ecosystems of Brazil*, WorldAtlas (Apr. 25, 2017), https://www.worldatlas.com/articles/habitats-and-ecosystems-of-brazil.html.

area, 13.8 percent of the lands have been reserved for Indigenous peoples, the majority of which are concentrated in the Amazon.[7]

The current Federal Constitution of the Federative Republic of Brazil was promulgated in 1988, becoming a symbol of the process of national democratization as the country exited 21 years of military dictatorship. It describes Brazil as a legal democratic state founded on sovereignty, citizenship, dignity of the individual, social values of work and of free enterprise, and political pluralism.

A. Ecologically Balanced Environment

Brazil's Constitution explicitly recognizes the importance of an ecologically balanced environment. However, the value of nature is justified solely in anthropocentric terms for its benefit to humans. The Constitution also gives special safeguards to the country's Indigenous peoples, which allows space for the development of an ecocentric approach to law by supporting traditional Indigenous practices that are in harmony with natural systems. With this introduction, we now look at some of the specific provisions.

Title VIII of the Brazilian Constitution addresses "The Social Order" and includes Chapter VI on the environment and Chapter VIII on "Indians," as the chapter calls Indigenous peoples. Brazil's Constitution reflects many progressive values. However, unlike the Constitution of Ecuador, the Brazilian Constitution does not recognize nature as a subject of rights with legal standing of its own. Instead, care for the environment is justified in terms of the benefits to humans. Consider Article 225, which establishes a strong ecological foundation but simultaneously treats the environment as an "asset of common use":

> All have the right to an ecologically balanced environment, which is an asset of common use and essential to a healthy quality of life, and both the Government and the community shall have the duty to defend and preserve it for present and future generations.[8]

STUDY QUESTION

Although seemingly anthropocentric, how might one argue that first word of Article 225, "all," applies to the entire Earth community, not only humans? Or that protections for "future generations" might include nonhumans? What opposing arguments might be made?

***

[7] María de Lourdes Beldi de Alcántara, Brazil, in The Indigenous World 135.

[8] CF 88 at art. 225.

Article 225, para. 1 establishes specific government duties intended to ensure the effectiveness of the right to an ecologically balanced environment, including the following:

- To "preserve and restore the essential ecological processes and provide for the ecological treatment of species and ecosystems";
- To "promote environmental education in all school levels and public awareness of the need to preserve the environment"; and
- To "protect the fauna and the flora, with prohibition, in the manner prescribed by law, of all practices which represent a risk to their ecological function, cause the extinction of species, or subject animals to cruelty."[9]

Article 225, para. 2 requires those who exploit mineral resources to restore environmental degradation, and para. 3 requires those who conduct procedures and activities considered harmful to the environment to repair the damages caused.[10]

Article 225, para. 4 adds additional protections for specifically named ecosystems, although critics have called these protections "merely symbolic."[11] The wording does not prohibit extractivism and has even been construed to encourage it:

> The Brazilian Amazonian Forest, the Atlantic Forest, the Serra do Mar, the Pantanal Matogrossense and the coastal zone are part of the national patrimony[12], and they shall be used, as provided by law, under conditions which ensure the preservation of the environment, therein including the use of mineral resources.[13]

B. Indigenous Rights

Indigenous peoples are prominent in Brazil, particularly in the Brazilian Amazon, where they constitute 23 percent of the population.[14] Brazil's Constitution affords certain rights to Indigenous peoples in Chapter VIII, Articles 231-232 on "Indians." As explored in detail in Chapter 25, "Indigenous Legalities," and throughout this book, empowering Indigenous cultures' care for ecological balance is important for Earth law development.

Article 231 establishes that "Indians shall have their social organization, customs, languages, creeds, and traditions recognized, as well as the original rights to the lands

[9] *Id.* at ¶ 1.
[10] *Id.* at ¶¶ 2-3, Sect. I, VI, VIII.
[11] Andrea Steuer Zago & Lionel Pimentel Nobre, *The Brazilian Citizen Constitution, the Environment and Taxation,* 20 Loyola of Los Angeles Intl. & Comp. L. Rev. 507, 519 (1998).
[12] The preservation of cultural and historical "patrimony" is typically referred to "heritage" in English. Collins, John F. "Historical and Cultural Patrimony in Brazil: Recent Work in Portuguese." *Latin American Research Review* 44, no. 1 (2009): 291-301. www.jstor.org/stable/20488182.
[13] CF 88, Art. 225, ¶ 4.
[14] Shannon Simms, *The Land Battle Behind the Fires in the Amazon,* The Atlantic (Aug. 27, 2019).

they traditionally occupy."[15] It also recognizes the inexorable link between Indigenous peoples and the land: "Lands traditionally occupied by Indians are . . . those indispensable to the preservation of environmental resources necessary for their well-being and for their physical and cultural reproduction, according to their uses, customs and traditions."[16] Moreover, it voids acts that attempt to exercise dominion and rights over the Indigenous lands or to exploit them.

However, Article 231, para. 6 also creates loopholes that could deprive Indigenous peoples of their land where there is a "relevant public interest":

> Acts with a view to occupation, domain and possession of the lands referred to in this article or to the exploitation of the natural riches of the soil, rivers and lakes existing therein, are null and void, producing no legal effects, ***except in case of relevant public interest of the Union***, as provided by a supplementary law and such nullity and voidness shall not create a right to indemnity or to sue the Union, except in what concerns improvements derived from occupation in good faith, in the manner prescribed by law.[17]

The next section explores how the Indigenous rights and the environment have fared under the strongly pro-development administration of President Jair Bolsonaro.

III. DEVELOPMENTS IN BRAZIL UNDER BOLSONARO

While Brazil's Constitution opens up the possibility of an ecocentric approach to law, there has been only limited success in practice. Instead of implementing constitutional protections for the environment, some national legislation has done the opposite—such as a 2012 law that weakened forest conservation under Brazil's 1965 Forest Code.[18] Many other environmental initiatives continue to prioritize economic development over human and environmental well-being. For example, Brazil's 2007 energy infrastructure plan, established with scant public input, prioritizes dam construction in the Amazon without fully considering environmental and social impacts, amongst other shortcomings.[19]

The attack on the environment and Indigenous rights has intensified since President Jair Bolsonaro came to power in 2019. For example, in his first year of office, he issued a decree to transfer authority to protect Indigenous territory to the Ministry of Agriculture, "which is well known to defend the interests of businesses that want access to previously restricted and protected Indigenous lands."[20] Bolsonaro also supports the transformation of the Amazon rainforest into land for cattle and crops. With the industry empowered by Bolsonaro's rhetoric to destroy rainforests for quick profit, "the

[15] *Id.* at Art. 231.
[16] *Id.* at Art. 231, ¶ 1.
[17] *Id.* at Art. 231, ¶ 6 (emphasis added).
[18] Editorial, *Don't Bypass Brazil's Environmental Protection*, 539 NATURE 139 (2016).
[19] Editorial, *supra* note 13.
[20] *Indigenous Peoples in Brazil*, International Work Group for Indigenous Affairs (IWGIA), https://www.iwgia.org/en/brazil (last visited Feb. 15, 2020).

Amazon is completely lawless," said Carlos Nobre, a climate scientist at the University of São Paulo.[21]

In another effort to circumvent constitutional protections, on March 4, 2019, Admiral Bento Albuquerque, the new minister of Mines and Energy, announced plans to permit mining on Indigenous land, even without the approval of impacted communities. He said the restricted Indigenous areas "have become centers of conflict and illegal activities, that in no way contribute to sustainable development or to sovereignty and national security."[22]

People and ecosystems both suffer as a result of Brazil's backsliding on Indigenous rights. Chief Antonia Mello of the Munduruku people described how "the actions of the Brazilian government [are] allowing the assassination of [our] community's way of life, a way of life that had lived in harmony with Mother Earth for hundreds of years."[23]

Many Indigenous groups are fighting back. Even before Bolsonaro assumed office, the Association of Indigenous Peoples of Brazil (APIB)[24] released a letter stating, "We do not accept being treated as inferior beings. . . . We are only different, and it is the Federal Government's obligation, according to the Constitution, to respect our 'social organization, customs, languages, beliefs and traditions.'"[25] In early 2020, the APIB sued Bolsonaro for making racist comments. Bolsonaro had said, "The Indian has changed, he is evolving and becoming more and more, a human being like us."[26] Previously, Bolsonaro had characterized Indigenous peoples as "animals in zoos" who need to be assimilated into Brazilian society. Some Indigenous leaders even believe he is planning ethnocide by eliminating their cultures and existence.[27]

Bolsonaro has also weakened public participation in governance. Through national councils and conferences, civil society has long helped formulate public policy. On April 12, 2019, Bolsonaro signed a decree extinguishing national councils, committees, and commissions created by decrees of previous presidents and limited the creation of new ones.[28] Among the national councils targeted were those aiming to uphold racial equality, sustainable rural development, and biodiversity. On June 12, 2019, Brazil's Supreme Court issued an injunction blocking parts of the decree, finding that Bolsonaro cannot abolish bodies supported by law and created through the deliberations of the National Congress.[29]

[21] Matt Sandy, '*The Amazon is Completely Lawless': The Rainforest After Bolsonaro's First Year*, The N.Y. Times (Dec. 5, 2019).

[22] Sue Branford & Maurício Torres, *Brazil's Bolsonaro Government Wants to Circumvent the Constitution to Allow Mining on Indigenous Lands*, Pacific Standard (March 15, 2019).

[23] Global Alliance for the Rights of Nature, *Third International Rights of Nature Tribunal-Paris*, https://therightsofnature.org/rights-of-nature-tribunal-paris (last visited Jan. 31, 2020).

[24] "Articulação dos Povos Indígenas do Brasil" in Spanish.

[25] *Povos Indígenas a Bolsonaro: "Não Admitimos ser Tratados como Seres Inferiores,"* Brasil de Fato (Dec. 6, 2018).

[26] Anthony Boadle, *Brazil's Indigenous to Sue Bolsonaro for Saying They're Evolving*, Reuters (Jan. 24, 2020).

[27] *Id.*

[28] *Decree 9.759 Ending National Councils & Social Participation Policy in Brazil*, Participedia (2019), https://participedia.net/case/5832.

[29] Ricardo Della Coletta & Flávia Faria, *Bolsonaro Suffers First Supreme Court Defeat*, Folha de S. Paulo (June 13, 2019).

Together, these actions by Bolsonaro signify a disregard for environmental and Indigenous rights in Brazil. As with the United States under the Trump Administration, the authority of Bolsonaro to significantly weaken environmental protections underscores the need for an enforceable system of *inalienable* rights for Earth and its inhabitants. Such rights could develop in the courts, as the next section explores.

IV. ECOCENTRISM IN BRAZILIAN COURTS

This section explores a recent case that extended rights to a nonhuman animal. As you consider the Brazilian court's approach, recall the reasoning in the decisions by the New York courts discussed in Chapter 11, "Nonhuman Rights."

In the 2019 case *In re IBAMA*, the Superior Court of Justice (STJ)[30] recognized the rights of a nonhuman animal based on the principle of individual dignity found in the Brazilian Constitution. The case involved the capture, confinement, and mistreatment of a native parrot.[31] The Court found that the parrot's living conditions were not acceptable, but instead of merely confiscating the parrot to be housed elsewhere, the Court deliberated on the rights of the parrot and what would be in its own best interest.

Although the Court could have decided to release the parrot into its natural habitat or to a qualified zoo, it ultimately found that the bird, having lived domestically with the Ibama family for over two decades, would best remain in their custody and care. To separate the parrot from its caregiver would break a certain "affective bond" in violation of "the ecological dimension of human dignity, since the multiple changes in the environment perpetuate the stress of the animal, putting in doubt the feasibility of a readaptation to a new environment."[32]

To arrive at this decision, the Court looked to Article 225, Section VII of the Constitution, which obligates the government to "protect the fauna and the flora, prohibiting . . . all practices that jeopardize their ecological functions, cause extinction of species, or subject animals to cruelty."[33] The meaningful contribution to the body of Earth law recognizes the inherent dignity and needs of the parrot as an individual—much the same as they would consider the unique needs of a child in a custody case. The Court also recognized the empathic interspecies bond between the parrot and the family. As explored in detail in Chapter 11, legal recognition of the dignity of even a single member of a nonhuman animal species opens the opportunity to extend that

[30] "Superior Tribunal de Justiça" in Spanish.

[31] *In re IBAMA* R Ext. 1.797.175-SP, 2. STJ, em 21.03.2019, http://files.harmonywithnatureun.org/uploads/upload820.pdf.

[32] *Id.* at 8. The Court made clear that this decision to permit the original infraction of keeping a wild bird did not establish any precedent to incentivize or allow the capture and retention of wild animals as a practice.

[33] CF 88, Art. 225, ¶ 4.

sound rationale to protect the entire natural world. *In re IBAMA* provides a foothold to justify universal recognition of the rights of nature in Brazil.[34]

In re IBAMA (2019)

Superior Court of Justice REsp 1.797.175/SP

DECISION

IV

From the ecological perspective of the principle of human dignity and the recognition of non-human animals as subjects of law. . . .

In this context, one should reflect on the Kantian, anthropocentric and individualistic concept of human dignity, that is, to focus also on non-human animals as well as all forms of life in general, in the light of the biocentric jurisphilosophical [the philosophy of law] matrix (or ecocentric), capable of recognizing the web of life that permeates the relationship between human beings and nature. . . .

In other words, one can also speak of limitations on the fundamental rights of human beings based on the recognition of non-human interests. . . .

Thus, any prohibition against the practice of "objectification" should not, in principle, be limited only to human life, but must have its broad spectrum to also contemplate other life forms. . . .

The very idea of non-cruel treatment of animals must no longer be grounded in human dignity or human compassion, but rather in the very dignity inherent in the existence of nonhuman animals. It is a question of moral duty. . . .

This view of nature as an expression of life in its entirety enables constitutional law and other areas of law to recognize the environment and non-human animals as beings of their own value and therefore to deserve the respect and care that the legal system may attribute to them as having ownership of rights and dignity.

In fact, what we must rethink and discuss is that these nonhuman living beings are no longer just means that guarantee to human species their own dignity and survival. . . .

In the reasoning defended by Oliveira (2016),[35] nature is not something apart from the human species, and the rest of the beings of the planetary

[34] Germana de Oliveira Moraes, *Direitos dos Animais e da Natureza Levados a Sério: Comentários Sobre o Julgamento do Superior Tribunal de Justiça do Brasil (Recurso Especial 1.797.175-SP)*, 39 Revista do Programa de Pós-Graduação em Direito da UFC 173 (2018).

[35] Vanessa Hasson de Oliveira, Rights of Nature 115 (2016) (footnote added).

> community, as well as human beings, are nature itself in its universality and diversity.
>
> It is necessary to rethink a new rationality, distinct from the logic hegemonically traced and reproduced within ordinary instances, that appreciates demands, including this one which is the subject of discussion in this Superior Court, so that the State and Society can think in a radically different way from the already established legal standards.
>
> Moreover, with this reflection as a starting point, it is not difficult to conclude that the relationship to be established between the human being and nature is much more an interrelation marked by interdependence than a relationship of domination of the human being over the rest of the beings of the planetary community.
>
> Therefore, it is necessary to reflect on the internal field of infra-constitutional laws, in an attempt to point out ways to ripen the discussion about the recognition of dignity of nonhuman animals and, consequently, of the recognition of rights and to make the shift so that people can relate to each other and to the rest of living things.[36]

As you just read, *In re IBAMA* had a much broader application than a single parrot. The Court argued for the need to change the anthropocentric paradigm to a biocentric one—regardless of the anthropocentric nature of Brazil's Constitution. Citing this case in courts in the United States and other nations will inform judges of new approaches to ecocentric law, a critical responsibility of Earth law practitioners. Whether it is considered a persuasive authority will depend on the judge.

V. LOCAL RIGHTS OF NATURE INITIATIVES IN BRAZIL

There has been a growing movement since 2015 to recognize nature as a subject of rights at the local level in Brazil. As in the United States, one of the primary motivations is the belief that Brazil's national framework is inadequate to protect nature.

Considering that current environmental laws have been failing to adequately protect Brazilian ecosystems, there have been several grassroots movements to recognize nature as a subject of rights. The story begins with the city council of São Paulo's consideration of a draft bill[37] to amend its Organic Law (equivalent to a local constitution) to read as follows:

> The Municipality will promote the development of environmental policies, considering that members of nature possess intrinsic rights to life and maintenance of their ecosystems in interdependence with the dignified life of citizens, in order to achieve sustainability in the city.

[36] *In re IBAMA* at 4-5 (citation omitted).

[37] *Projeto de Emenda à Lei Orgânica 04-00005/2015 of councilor Eduardo Tuma (PSDB)*, Câmara Municipal de São Paulo.

The explanatory report for the draft bill stated that "the issue of the recognition of the rights of nature is intrinsically dependent on a new approach to the concept of sustainable development" and highlights the "need for a real paradigm shift."[38] It also stated that "Brazil has approached this understanding with discussions about Environmental Services which go far beyond defending nature's economic values and end up exposing its priceless, intangible value, even in relation to human beings." Humanity, the draft bill concluded, has a duty "to preserve life worthy of and on the planet."

The 2015 draft bill did not pass. But advocates tried once again, and in 2017 the city council of São Paulo successfully amended Article 180-A of the Organic Law of the Municipality to recognize nature as having "full, intrinsic and perpetual rights, inherent in its existence on the planet."[39] The bill also calls upon the government to promote policies, management tools, and partnerships to preserve and restore Brazil's environment and foster harmony with nature, including by addressing climate change. Finally, the bill establishes that any actions taken that would affect nature "should be supported by Science; observe the Precautionary Principle; and seek to involve the Legislative and Judiciary, the State and the Union, the other municipalities of the Metropolitan Region and civil society entities in general."

On May 16, 2018, another legal proposal for the rights of nature was presented in São Paulo, this time to the São Paulo Commission of Legality.[40] The draft bill, which has not yet been approved at the time of this book's publication, "received a positive evaluation from the main commission and is expected to gain further support for future implementation within the legal system."[41]

Other municipalities besides São Paulo have also embraced the rights of nature. The municipality of Bonito in the state of Pernambuco passed an amendment to its Organic Law in 2017 that adopts the rights of nature in Article 236:

> The Municipality recognizes the right of nature to exist, thrive and evolve, and should act in order to assure all members of the natural community, human and non-human, of the Municipality of Bonito, the right to an ecologically healthy and balanced environment and to the maintenance of ecosystemic processes necessary to good quality of life, being the Public Power, as well as the collectivity, in charge of defending and preserving it for the present and future generations of the members of the earth community. . . . In order to ensure this right, the Municipality shall promote the amplification of its public policies in environmental, health, educational and economic areas so as to provide conditions for the establishment of a life in harmony with Nature, and it shall articulate with other states, regional and federal competent bodies, as well as with other municipalities, if it is the case, in order to solve common problems related to the protection of Nature.[42]

One year later, the municipality of Paudalho in the state of Pernambuco also amended its Organic Law to recognize rights of nature, using wording almost identical

[38] *Justificativa-PLO 0005/2015*, Câmara Municipal de São Paulo.
[39] *Projeto de Emenda à Lei Orgânica 04-00005/2017 of councilor Natalini (PV)*, Câmara Municipal de São Paulo.
[40] *PLO-Projeto de Emenda Lei Organica 7/2018 de 16/05/2018*, Câmara Municipal de São Paulo.
[41] UN Harmony with Nature Initiative, *Rights of Nature Law, Policy and Education*, http://www.harmonywithnatureun.org/rightsOfNaturePolicies (last visited Jan. 31, 2020).
[42] *Emenda à Lei Orgânica No 01/2017*, Câmara Municipio de Bonito.

to Bonito. The change aimed to ensure that public policies align with the "establishment of a life in harmony with Nature."[43] As a result of the amendment to the Organic Law, the San Severino Ramos Natural Water Spring was granted rights to exist, thrive, and evolve in accordance with the law's rights of nature provisions—the first specific ecosystem to be granted rights in Brazil.

Finally, on March 28, 2018, the municipality of Fortaleza proposed a draft bill to amend its Organic Law in order to grant recognition to the rights of nature. It states: "All beings of Nature have the right to an ecologically balanced environment, [which is] a good for common use for the people and essential to a healthy quality of life and to natural ecosystemic processes."[44] This law is still pending as of the time of publication.

These developments are all recent. It remains to be seen how these laws will impact local environmental protections in practice and whether they will spark systemic change throughout Brazil. However, the existence of the movement in Brazil is itself meaningful and is likely to lead to the development of more ecocentric law in the near future.

VI. BRAZIL'S INDIGENOUS PEOPLE JOIN TO SHOW A PATH FORWARD

In 2017, two major environmental gatherings in Brazil set a strong foundation for the future of Earth law. Indigenous peoples played a major role in each. The first event was a large environmental forum that produced a "Letter to Nature" defining their rights of nature vision. The second was the Great Assembly of the Alliance of Mother Nature's Guardians.

First, in July 2017, participants of the Brazil Environmental Management Forum—including the Ministry of the Environment, Indigenous leaders, civil society representatives, and others[45]—adopted a "Letter for Nature," entitled *The Rights of Nature and Public Policies in Cities.* The letter-writing process was led by Vanessa Hasson, a Brazilian lawyer, civil society leader, and rights of nature advocate.[46] The letter was also heavily influenced by Indigenous leaders from the University of Ancient Wisdom, the Acunhanhe Institute, and the Shawãdawa community.

The Letter for Nature invited forum participants to recognize the inherent rights of nature and reflect upon their responsibility to strengthen public policies that harmonize with nature. The Letter for Nature also warns that current policies and

[43] *Emenda à Lei Orgânica No 03, de 5 Janeiro de 2018,* Câmara Municipal de Paudalho.

[44] *Emenda Modificativa No. 0011/2018 ao Projeto de Emenda à Lei Orgânica Municipal No 09/2017,* Câmara Municipal de Fortaleza, Article 244.

[45] *Brazil's Public Administrators Sign for the Rights of Nature,* World Conscious Pact (Sept. 18, 2017), https://worldconsciouspact.org/rights-of-nature/brazils-public-administrators-sign-for-the-rights-of-nature/.

[46] Vanessa Hasson is the founder of Methods of Supporting Environmental and Social Practices (MAPAS).

legislation are insufficient to address the global climate emergency, which may result in "catastrophic ruptures, risking functions essential to the maintenance and reproduction of life, including human life." As a solution, the Letter for Nature highlights the rights of nature and also encourages society to return to traditional, Indigenous, natural knowledge that emphasizes the connections between nature and humans.

In accordance with the Brazil Constitution's mandate to promote environmental education, the Letter for Nature also encourages the expansion of rights of nature:

> 14. Formal education at every level should be oriented according to the basic principles of the Rights of Nature and of a way of life in harmony with Nature; multi/interdisciplinary theoretical and methodological approaches should be included in teaching curriculum and research methodology disciplines in both primary and secondary education and at undergraduate and postgraduate levels.[47]

Finally, to put these precepts into action, forum participants promised to "undertake their best efforts for the inauguration or expansion of public preservation policies of the environment." Such efforts should follow the principle of harmony with nature, "considering the intrinsic value of each of the members that constitute the Earth." As participants in the forum recognized, harmony with nature does not mean a complete reversion to pre-industrial conditions, but it does support the value of ancient human knowledge.

Building upon this effort, in October 2017, the first-ever Great Assembly of the Alliance of Mother Nature's Guardians was held in Brasília and attended by nearly 200 Indigenous representatives from around the world. Together, the delegates discussed rights of nature paradigms and other global issues impacting human rights and the environment.[48]

Prior to this event, the Constituent Assembly of the Alliance of Mother Nature's Guardians was held in Paris and resulted in the adoption of the Declaration of the Alliance of Guardians and Children of Mother Earth. The declaration stated: "We must evolve towards a paradigm based on Indigenous thought and philosophy, which grants equal rights to Nature and which honors the interrelationships between all life forms and the preservation of Mother Earth."[49]

In conclusion, Brazil is advancing numerous promising ecocentric legal paradigms—through the courts, local lawmaking, and multi-stakeholder gatherings. But simultaneously, the current government is attempting to circumvent laws and overturn policies in order to prioritize incessant extraction and development of ecosystems, injurious to Indigenous peoples and others.[50] Now, we will compare this dynamic with rights-based movements in Mexico.

[47] *Id.*

[48] Global Alliance for the Rights of Nature, *First Great International Assembly of the Alliance of Mother Nature's Guardians* (Sept. 29, 2017).

[49] Alliance of Guardians of Mother Nature, *The Declaration of the Alliance of Guardians and Children of Mother Earth.*

[50] Herton Escobar, *Brazil's Deforestation Is Exploding–and 2020 Will Be Worse*, Science (Nov. 22, 2019), https://www.sciencemag.org/news/2019/11/brazil-s-deforestation-exploding-and-2020-will-be-worse.

PART II: MEXICO

VII. INTRODUCTION TO MEXICO

Mexico is the fourth largest country in the Americas, after Canada, the United States, and Brazil. It is also counted among the world's 17 mega-diverse countries, having the second-largest number of ecosystems amongst them.[51] At 27.5 million people, Mexico's Indigenous population is the largest in the Americas and makes up 21.5 percent of the country's total.[52]

This section explores Mexico's constitutional protections of the environment, Indigenous rights, and the rights of nature. Overall, while Mexico's environmental enforcement is lacking, it has a legal and societal foundation for the development of Earth law.

VIII. ENVIRONMENTAL PROTECTIONS IN MEXICO

Mexico's Constitution explicitly recognizes the importance of the environment. However, as with Brazil, nature's value is viewed from a human perspective. Nonetheless, with the *In Re IBAMA* case, it is possible that Mexico's constitutional environmental rights could be extended to include rights of nature in the future.

Here are some of the most important environmental provisions in Mexico's Constitution:

- **Article 2(A):** Granting Indigenous peoples the right to maintain and improve their environment, and the preferential use of natural resources within sites they inhabit;
- **Article 4, para. V:** Establishing the right of "any person" to a healthy environment;
- **Article 25**: Requiring national development to be sustainable, and the use of resources to be for the general good while preserving the environment;
- **Article 27**: Allowing the government to impose restrictions, including on the use of natural resources and private property, that preserve and restore "environmental balance;"
- **Article 73**: Establishing the power of Congress to legislate in order to coordinate the actions of the three levels of government in environmental matters and to direct the General Board of Health on combating environmental pollution;

[51] Amber Pariona, *The World's 17 Mega-Diverse Countries,* WorldAtlas (July 25, 2018), https://www.worldatlas.com/articles/ecologically-megadiverse-countries-of-the-world.html.
[52] José de Val, Juan Mario Pérez Martínez & Carolina Sánchez Garcia, *Mexico,* The Indigenous World 2019 102 (David Nathaniel Berger ed., 2019).

- **Article 115, para. III**: Organizing states with municipal powers in environmental matters, including creating nature reserves; and
- **Article 122:** Giving special competence to Mexico City in environmental matters.[53]

(As with Brazil, consider how these constitutional protections can be relied upon to develop Earth law. For example, could an ecosystem be defined as a "person" and thus have a right to a healthy environment? Or could the Indigenous right to maintain and improve their environment necessitate their application of ecocentric laws?)

In addition to its constitutional protections, Mexico has passed several major environmental framework laws. (Note in the below examples how both laws not only protect but *restore* nature when it is harmed.) First, the General Law of Ecological Equilibrium and Environmental Protection (1988) defines the framework for all environmental laws in Mexico. Its overarching purpose is the "preservation ***and restoration*** of the ecological balance, as well as the protection of the environment. . . ."[54] Second, the Federal Law of Environmental Responsibility (2013) builds upon the General Law by creating a strong application of the "polluter pays principle." Its stated purpose is "to regulate the environmental responsibility that arises from the damages caused to the environment, as well as ***the repair and compensation of such damages.***"[55] This law also envisions the creation of environmental courts that are separate from other civil, administrative, and criminal courts.

Taking a broader view, some of the main principles of Mexico's environmental laws are sustainable development, conservation, preservation, and environmental restoration. Mexican law also supports the prevention principle. However, the precautionary principle, asserting that activities should be prohibited in case of doubt, is practically absent from Mexican environmental legislation.[56]

Finally, Mexico has numerous agencies that work to defend the environment. The Ministry of Environment and National Resources (SEMARNAT)[57] is mandated to ensure the protection, conservation, and use of nature with an emphasis on sustainable development. Additionally, the Federal Office of Environmental Protection (PROFEPA)[58] is the institution responsible for increasing compliance with environmental regulations and minimizing environmental deterioration. Neither agency represents the interests of nature directly.

[53] Comparative Constitutions Project, *Mexico's Constitution of 1917 with Amendments Through 2015* (Fernanda Gomez Aban trans.), https://www.constituteproject.org/constitution/Mexico_2015.p*df?lang=en.*

[54] General Law of Ecological Equilibrium and Environmental Protection (*Ley General del Equilibrio Ecológico y la Protección al Ambiente*), Art. 1 (1988).

[55] Federal Law of Environmental Responsibility (*Ley Federal de Responsabilidad Ambiental*).

[56] Tania García López, *La Constitución Mexicana y los Principios Rectores del Derecho Ambiental, in* La Constitución y el Medio Ambiente 36 (Emilio Rabasa ed., 2007).

[57] Secretaría de Medio Ambiente y Recursos Naturales (SEMARNAT).

[58] Procuraduría Federal de Protección al Ambiente (PROFEPA).

IX. DERIVING RIGHTS OF NATURE FROM HUMAN ENVIRONMENTAL RIGHTS?

As discussed later in this chapter, in Mexico, there are a handful of recent state constitutional amendments establishing rights of nature. Another way to develop Earth law in Mexico is through human environmental rights frameworks.

Many people in Mexico do not view rights of nature as being totally separate from human rights. Instead, rights of nature is seen as upholding human rights that rely upon healthy and functioning natural systems. According to José Gilberto Garza Grimaldo,"[t]he premises of human rights consist in balancing what is good for human beings and what is good for other species and for the planet itself, and to fully understand the meaning of the interdependence between all ecosystems and all that we share for our own survival."[59]

Article 1 of Mexico's Constitution establishes the foundation of human rights protection:

> [A]ll individuals shall be entitled to the Human Rights granted by this Constitution and the international treaties signed by the Mexican State, as well as to the guarantees for the protection of these rights. Such human rights shall not be restricted or suspended, except for the cases and under the conditions established by this Constitution itself.[60]

The anthropocentric nature of Mexico's Constitution can support the development of Earth law if the rights of nature can be presented as an interdependent manifestation of human rights. The Constitution, as well as "international treaties signed by the Mexican State," guarantee the security of human beings. This includes their environment, food, and health security. Earth laws that protect, stabilize, and restore the functional interdependency of ecosystems may be developed based on the human rights embodied in Mexico's Constitution.

Once again, consider how other nations have expanded their constitutional protections to include nature—such as in Colombia, where courts have inferred rights of nature from human environmental rights, cultural rights, and related principles (see Chapter 18). Or in Brazil, where the Superior Court of Justice applied anthropocentric constitutional protections to a single nonhuman animal—a parrot.

X. INDIGENOUS RIGHTS AND THE ENVIRONMENT

A starting point for ecocentrism in Mexico is the traditions of Indigenous communities. Pre-Hispanic Mexican law, which still resonates throughout the current legal system, includes the recognition of a different attitude to nature, and many of these

[59] José Gilberto Garza Grimaldo, *Los Derechos de la Naturaleza y sus Medios de Defensa* 137 (2015).
[60] Comparative Constitutions Project, *supra* note 53.

Indigenous principles can now be employed in extending the law to encompass the rights of nature.

According to Garza Grimaldo: "In Mexico, the original cultures addressed the relationship with nature through religious laws, where worship and offerings to natural forces and manifestations were part of their daily obligations, there being deities for each of the elements, for the sun, for Mother Earth, water, wind, volcanoes, plants and even animals and the cycles of time and life."[61]

Like Brazil, Mexico's Constitution carves out a special status for Indigenous peoples and upholds their land rights. Article 2 (notable in that it appears nearly at the beginning of the Constitution) recognizes that Mexico "is multicultural, based originally on its Indigenous peoples, described as descendants of those inhabiting the country before colonization and that preserve their own social, economic, cultural and political institutions, or some of them."[62] In turn, Article 2(A)(V) upholds Indigenous peoples' right to self-determination and autonomy, including their right to "maintain and improve their environment and lands."[63]

State-level constitutions establish even stronger language to uphold the traditional cultural practices of Indigenous peoples and recognize their contributions to environmental well-being. The constitution of the state of Campeche is one example. It guarantees the right of Indigenous peoples to self-determination and obligates the state government to put these rights into practice. As you read the state's specific duties, consider how these principles support Earth law:

> [The State of Campeche shall:]
>
> - [R]espect, preserve and maintain the knowledge, innovations, and practices of Indigenous communities that involve traditional lifestyles relevant to the conservation and sustainable use of biological diversity. . . .
> - [P]romote the wider application, with approval, and participation of those who possess such knowledge, innovations, and practices, and will encourage the benefits derived from the use of that knowledge, innovations, and practices to be shared equally. . . . [and]
> - Protect and encourage customary use of biological resources in accordance with traditional cultural practices that are compatible with the requirements of conservation or sustainable use; likewise, natural resources, sacred places and the material and intangible cultural heritage of peoples and communities are protected, with the active participation of communities. . . .

One final example of Indigenous rights in Mexico is the National Institute of Indigenous Peoples (in Spanish, Instituto Nacional de los Pueblos Indígenas, or INPI), a centralized agency established in 2018 that serves as the federal authority of matters related to Indigenous and Afro-Mexican peoples. Its duties are to create, define, execute, and coordinate policies and programs to guarantee Indigenous and Afro-Mexican rights. The INPI is also committed to "recognize and respect the formalities

[61] Grimaldo, *supra* note 59, at 143.
[62] Mexico's Constitution of 1917 with Amendments through 2015, Art. 2.
[63] *Id.* at Art. 2(A)(V).

established by the Indigenous normative systems, having the corresponding legal effects."[64] Irma Pineda Santiago, whom the INPI appointed to represent Mexico's Indigenous peoples at the United Nations, stated the importance of learning from Indigenous communities to protect the environment:

> When we look at Indigenous communities or where they have more control over the land, they conserve the environment better. . . . If the land is being better cared for, it must mean that Indigenous communities know how to do this. We need to learn from these Indigenous communities.[65]

Indigenous communities help advance Mexico's collective well-being through customs and worldviews that consider the comprehensive protection of ecosystems and the deep bond shared by all life. For example, María Gabriela González Cruz writes about the Indigenous-inspired concept of the "socio-ecosystem" as a means of looking holistically at the interrelationship between humans and the rest of nature:

> At the end of the 20th century some researchers, several of them Mexicans, showed that the fields of ecology and biodiversity conservation can develop not only in protected areas, but also in ecosystems inhabited by human societies. Ecologists and conservation biologists started communicating with anthropologists and sociologists and developed research that considered ecosystems and groups of humans together. As a result of this new vision, they formulated a concept which is still controversial: the socio-ecosystem.
>
> In the socio-ecosystem, the human beings and Nature are interconnected. Our actions as individuals and as a society have repercussions on nature. Similarly, natural systems define us culturally, and the changes that occur in nature have repercussions on our lifestyle.
>
> The concept of a socio-ecosystem can be very helpful for establishing protected areas and managing nature. In some regions of our country, such as the Yucatán Peninsula, the concept of a socio-ecosystem has already been applied in projects to develop Indigenous villages and to conserve biodiversity.
>
> This concept has helped us realize that our well-being and that of nature go hand in hand, and that it is possible to generate strategies that allow the integral development of human groups while we also seek the permanence of nature.[66]

Indigenous communities in Mexico also support the notion of *buen vivir*, or good living, which is discussed in depth in Chapter 17 on Ecuador. According to Carlos Cruz, the original peoples of Latin America "[b]elieve in good living (*buen vivir*), not in living better. Living better means having the best cell phone and the best car. To live good is to live holistically and nothing else."[67]

[64] Ley del Instituto Nacional de los Pueblos Indígenas (2019).

[65] Leigh Thelmadatter, *Voicing the Concerns of Mexico's Indigenous People, In their Own Language*, Mexico Daily News (Mar. 4, 2020).

[66] María Gabriela González Cruz, *El Socioecosistéma*, 163 Cómoves 34 (2012).

[67] Adela Salinas, *Constructores de Paz en México: Perspectivas, Procesos y Acciones que Desarticulan la Violencia* 97 (2019) (interview with Carlos Cruz).

Based on Indigenous rights protections discussed in this section, the Mexican government must respect the notion of *buen vivir* and other Indigenous ways of life that support nature's well-being. Mexico's recognition of Indigenous self-determination and legal pluralism also supports the advancement of ecocentric governance structures, including the rights of nature. For this reason, many advocates believe that strengthening Indigenous rights is paramount to restoring the planet to health.

XI. ENVIRONMENTAL NORMS IN STATE CONSTITUTIONS

All Mexican states establish constitutional environmental protections but with widely different approaches. Most, but not all, state constitutions take an anthropocentric perspective. Some state constitutions frame the environment as a resource demanding human extraction. Other state constitutions concepts of sustainable development in accordance with international environmental instruments, such as the 1992 Rio Declaration.[68] Finally, several state constitutions now recognize the rights of nature. This subsection explores a few of these different models.

A. Introduction to State Constitutional Provisions on the Environment

In most Mexican state constitutions, nature is addressed through the human right to a healthy environment. An example of this approach is seen in Article 7 of the constitution of the state of Aguascalientes, which establishes that "[e]veryone has the right to a healthy environment for their development and well-being, as well as the duty to protect and preserve it."[69] Article 8 of the constitution of the state of Veracruz has similar language.

In some cases, the environment is unequivocally linked to state socioeconomic development, and nature is treated as merely an exploitable human resource. For example, Article 9, section XXXI of the constitution of the state of Baja California Sur, establishes a government obligation to "[p]romote the integral development of all natural resources, among others: mining, fishing; and in addition, agricultural activities and tourism."[70]

Other states recognize a constitutional duty to achieve sustainable development. For example, Article 18, section VIII of the constitution of the state of Tamaulipas says that all people have an obligation "[to] respect and care for the natural heritage of the State and to make use of the natural resources susceptible to appropriation *without affecting the sustainable development of the State* in the terms provided by the laws."[71]

[68] The 1992 Rio Declaration recognized that human beings are "entitled to a healthy and productive life in harmony with nature" (Principle 1).

[69] Constitution of the State of Aguascalientes (*Constitución Política Del Estado De Aguascalientes*), art. 7o (2018).

[70] Political Constitution of The Free and Sovereign State from Baja California Sur (*Constitución Política del Estado Libre y Soberano de Baja California Sur*), Art. 9, Sect. XXXI (2008).

[71] Constitución Política del Estado de Tamaulipas, Art. 18, Sect. 8 (2019) (emphasis added).

While many of these state constitutions have been effective at establishing at least baseline protections for the environment, the anthropocentric perspective inhibits the development of Earth law. However, as discussed in the next section, several states have taken the additional step of explicitly recognizing the rights of nature.

B. Rights of Nature in Colima, Guerrero, and Mexico City

This section analyzes several rights of nature laws in Mexico. Currently, the constitutional systems of Guerrero, Mexico City, and Colima all recognize nature as a collective entity that is subject to rights with its own legal personality. All of these locations have also recognized a deep interdependency between rights of nature and human rights. As noted by María Valeria Berros, "In [the state of Guerrero and Mexico City], legal recognition of the human right to a healthy environment coexists with this explicit enlargement of nature rights."[72]

While recognizing rights of nature in law is a valuable foundation, institutions and governments must uphold them in practice.

1. Guerrero

On April 1, 2014, the state congress of Guerrero approved comprehensive constitutional reform that recognized, *inter alia*, the rights of nature. The proposal was presented and defended by the deputies Arturo Álvarez Angli and Alejandro Carabias Icaza. Its passage followed a seminar on the future of the rights of nature and humans in Mexico, held at the Autonomous University of Guerrero, in which over 20 keynote speakers discussed the need for fundamental reform to address a growing ecological and moral crisis.

Article 2 of Guerrero's constitution contemplates the rights of nature by stating the following:

> In the State of Guerrero, dignity is the basis of the human, individual and collective rights of the person. The higher values of the legal, political and social order are freedom, equality, social justice, solidarity, democratic and ideological pluralism, secularism, respect for diversity and respect for life in all its manifestations. . . . the State undertakes to protect the rights of nature in accordance with the respective law.[73]

Notice that the wording of Article 2 recognizes both principles of human rights and the rights of nature. This is important because there is no perceived conflict between these rights—to the contrary, they complement each other. If nature's rights are seen as supporting human rights, they are more likely to be recognized federally.

[72] María Valeria Berros, *Rights of Nature in the Anthropocene: Towards the Democratization of Environmental Law?* Charting Environmental Law Futures in the Anthropocene 26 (Michelle Lim ed., 2019).
[73] Constitución Política del Estado Libre y Soberano de Guerrero (2016), http://files.harmonywithnatureun.org/uploads/upload665.pdf.

2. Mexico City

On January 11, 2017, Mexico City (which is now a recognized state[74]) adopted rights of nature into its new constitution.[75] The constitutional amendment followed the First International Forum for the Rights of Mother Earth held in Mexico City on June 1–5, 2016. The forum was "centered around the importance of legislating the Rights of Mother Earth" and worked toward supporting and implementing rights of nature in Mexico City.

Article 13 of the new constitution establishes that nature, with all of its ecosystems and species, is a collective body that is the subject of rights. Those rights include "the right to the preservation and protection," which are to be guaranteed by the authorities of Mexico City. Article 13 also requires that a secondary law shall be passed "to recognize and regulate the protection of the rights of nature, as formed by all its ecosystems and species as a collective entity with collective rights." This secondary law has not yet been developed. Finally, the constitution asserts that citizens of Mexico City will be able to enforce nature's rights.

3. Colima

In June 2019, the congress of the state of Colima approved a state constitutional amendment recognizing the rights of nature. The initiative was presented by Congresswoman Blanca Livier Rodríguez Osorio, who is also president of the Commission for Environmental Protection.

The constitutional amendment establishes that nature, including all ecosystems and species, is a collective entity with fundamental rights. Nature's rights include the rights to exist, to restoration, to regeneration of its natural cycles, and to conservation of its ecological structure and functions. The constitutional amendment also establishes that the protection, preservation, and recovery of biodiversity, natural ecosystems, genetic heritage, and native species are a joint responsibility of the public, private, and social sectors.

The state of Colima received support from numerous organizations, including El Deber es Nuestro, Empoderamiento Climático, and Earth Law Center.

4. State of Mexico

The State of Mexico — Mexico's most populous state — has also taken an important step for rights of nature without yet giving official recognition to the concept itself. Article 18 of the constitution of the state of Mexico does not recognize the rights of

[74] In 2016, Mexico City officially became a state and now has its own congress, constitution, local governments, and fiscal rules. Viridiana Rios, *Mexico City Will Become A State*, Wilson Center (June 2, 2016), https://www.wilsoncenter.org/article/mexico-city-will-become-state.

[75] Constitución Política de la Cuidad de México (2017), http://www.infodf.org.mx/documentospdf/constitucion_cdmx/Constitucion_%20Politica_CDMX.pdf.

nature in so many words but asserts that "[t]he legislation and regulations that are issued for this purpose will emphasize the promotion of a culture of protection of nature, the improvement of the environment, the rational use of natural resources and the propagation of existing flora and fauna. . . ." Thus, this provision can be construed to advance Earth law; however, its effectiveness will depend on whether the judiciary will meaningfully consider non-anthropocentric viewpoints. A favorable indication: in August 2019, the Congress of the state of Mexico hosted a presentation on the rights of nature that included leading experts in Mexico and worldwide.[76]

XII. CIVIL SOCIETY FORGES A PATH FORWARD IN MEXICO

Much of the development of Earth law in Mexico is being driven by social movements. For example, many of the provisions for Mexico City's new constitution were crowdsourced from the internet, with civil society groups such as Derechos de la Madre Tierra Mexico (Rights of Mother Earth Mexico) and their allies making a strong plea for recognition of the rights of nature. As you learned, they were successful.

The following excerpt from an interview with "Coyote" Alberto Ruz, a leading figure in the Mexican environmental movements, describes how the rights of nature movement in Mexico and Latin America came about:

> **[Esperanza Project ("EP")]:** Can you explain to me why now is a ripe moment in time for the rights of nature and a shift toward biocentric jurisprudence?
>
> **Alberto:** When the environment and ecology became an important issue 30–40 years ago, the movement was "humans saving nature" for human benefit and enjoyment. It wasn't until 2008 when people from Bolivia and Ecuador, Raphael Correa and Evo Morales, started shifting the discussion to the Rights of Nature and preserving the environment for environment's sake. Raphael Correa and Evo Morales started incorporating Indigenous culture to understand our relationship with the Earth. I realized that we couldn't keep thinking of the Earth as a non-living being, from the occidental viewpoint, that the Earth exists solely as a resource for us. *La tierra no es de nosotros* [The earth is not ours]. Our life depends on Her but the last hundred years has been a steady deterioration of Mother Earth. *Silent Spring* [the 1962 book by Rachel Carson] is no longer a prophecy, we are living in it. Nature is telling us we are reaching the limits of human growth. Now, instead of degradation happening in remote areas of the globe, it's happening everywhere, in front of everyone's eyes. For centuries we have had collective amnesia about the negative impacts humanity has had on the environment. . . .
>
> **EP:** How can people support this movement in their own lives? Where can I look for answers to know if my choices align with the biocentric ethic?

[76] Redacción Así Sucede, *Urgen Acciones Para Revertir el Deterioro Ambiental: Especialistas*, Asi Sucede (Aug. 19, 2019).

Alberto: I first awoke to this idea when I was very young, 15 or 16 years old, and went on a camping trip where we set up tents and [made] fires and I realized that this all affected the environment. Even the rocks we moved. We need to become conscious of what we do every day. Look around you. What is your footprint? Don't wait for a university lecture to make changes in your lifestyle and habits. Learn to compost, learn where your water comes from. Start to educate yourself in small things and put them into practice and then other people will see what you are doing and make changes in their own lives. It's all about the ripple effect.

EP: How would you describe the progress you have seen over the years?

Alberto: Years ago when I started talking about the Rights of Nature in Mexico City everywhere I went people looked at me like: "What?!" It's a radical idea. And for me that radical idea came when I went to my first bioregional congress in Northwest Canada in 1988. That's when it first struck me that everything we were saying or writing or deciding or thinking was affecting the lives of the coyote, the life of the river, the life of the tree. In twenty years, from 1988 to 2008, we saw the first government (Ecuador) adopt the Rights of Nature into their constitution. It was a very small step in 1988 but if a country is doing it, it is a bigger step, and we continue to make progress. Evo Morales brought the concept to the United Nations in 2009 and that was the basis for the UN adopting a resolution on Harmony with Nature. And we are going back to the UN again this year because this is the way you change legislation and you change mentality, you change everything. It's a gradual change. Last year, we organized the first forum for the Rights of Earth in Mexico. Here we're doing another step, we're bringing people from all the different movements, articulations, organizations, networks, and alliances together. In talking to others you realize it's not only me who is thinking, "How I can protect the trees and the birds around my house?"

EP: How do we convince people to place the interest of other species equal to or above their own interests?

Alberto: The first thing is [to] take a step back and look at what we're doing and understand why it's so important other species exist because without the bees, butterflies and tiny insects, the whole chain upon which we depend is going to break and we are all going to go if it breaks. We are eight billion human beings right now and every day there is one less bear and one less lion and one less elephant and this is only the most visible of the species. The life of Us is destroying the life of all the Others. We are the predators now that are destroying life around us everywhere, every second. In the [United Mexican] States right now, I see it as a crossroads, we could be at the beginning of the world's first global dark age (and it's a perspective we cannot forget, we cannot dismiss and think it is just a political prophesy, because if this ripple effect happens in that direction it's going to happen everywhere). On the other side, we are seeing another global reaction. A sentence came to me from the book of one of my friends, *Despertar de la Mujer* which means "the awakening of the sleeping woman," which comes from a legend in our country

> Mexico that the moment when the sleeping woman (which is the volcano Iztaccíhuatl) wakes up, all of humanity is going to wake up. . . . I haven't heard such radical speech since the sixties but it is different from the radical of the sixties because this is a radical full of love, full of consciousness, of nurturing, of finding, and that is maybe what we needed in the planet right now to happen so that we could choose to say now is the time we cannot continue waiting for something to happen, we have to make it happen. So it might be a step in our evolution that will bring us to a planetary consciousness and at the same time a Mother Earth consciousness, which is the ultimate step. We have to make changes in our daily life and habits and that will lead to a change in culture and laws in order to avoid waking to our own extinction. The women need to lead the way.[77]

XIII. CHALLENGES IN MEXICO

Despite some strong foundational legal elements, there are major challenges for Mexico to further develop Earth law. The existing level of poverty in Mexico clouds the aims of conservation because it can mistakenly be viewed as adverse to human interests. Attitudes of this kind make it difficult to adopt general laws (which implement the constitutional provisions) specifically designed to defend and guarantee the rights of nature beyond anthropocentric considerations.

Conversely, the effects of climate change, disparities in quality of life, and overwhelming inequality all put additional pressure on nature. Oftentimes, society defaults to only safeguarding humans without adequate consideration of the environment. Unfortunately, this mindset is used to justify environmental degradation, drawing upon the so-called basic needs of the population as a crutch to justify misguided environmental exploitation. These challenges are bolstered by voracious and rampant capitalism, which continues to treat nature as a mere resource to feed the economic system.

In the face of this reality, we must also acknowledge the lack of responsibility shown by governments. Governments and their policies center on consumption as a means to guarantee quality of life. The result is a vicious circle of environmental degradation, the consequences of which are felt by the most vulnerable sectors of society.

Genuine strengthening of the rights of nature is a legitimate and valuable goal that is widely expressed in Mexico. Respect for the rights of nature is a test, not only for the rule of law but also for basic human and societal values. It falls to states and society as a whole to accept responsibility for changing the current course. The numerous state government enactments and the growing grassroots movement supporting rights of nature provide encouraging opportunities to develop Earth law.

[77] Keala Carter & "Coyote" Alberto Ruz Buenfil, *Towards a New Jurisprudence of the Earth*, ESPERANZA PROJECT (Feb. 23, 2017), www.esperanzaproject.com/2017/sustainability/ecovillages/coyote-alberto-on-the-rights-of-nature.

STUDY QUESTIONS

(1) In both Brazil and Mexico, Indigenous traditions have become a factor in developing law and policy for rights of nature. Given that these Indigenous traditions are based on an entirely different outlook than Western society, what could persuade judges and lawmakers to draw on this source?

(2) This chapter describes three approaches for developing Earth law: (1) passing rights of nature laws; (2) drawing on Indigenous traditions; and (3) extending the present protections of human rights to encompass nature. What are the advantages and disadvantages of each of these approaches in Brazil and Mexico?

(3) Discuss current issues with the regulatory frameworks in Brazil and Mexico. How do they impair the efforts to develop Earth law? How might Brazil and Mexico transform the regulatory system to better promote the development of Earth law?

(4) How might Brazilian and Mexican constitutional law be relied upon to develop Earth law? Are there provisions that may hinder the development of Earth law?

(5) The constitutional protections for nature in Brazil are found in Title 8. Title 8 also establishes the Social Security system, the Public Health system, and the Public Pension system. How might this placement help or hinder the promotion of rights of nature?

(6) What role does poverty play in the development of Earth law in Brazil and Mexico?

(7) How might the environmental courts that are separate from other civil, administrative, and criminal courts, envisioned by Mexico's Federal Law of Environmental Responsibility, promote the development of ecocentric law? How might that development be deterred by a separate court system?

CHAPTER 20

India[1]

I. INTRODUCTION

Rights of nature are increasingly seen as the backbone of a new generation of environmental laws. However, successful implementation and practical enforcement remain a challenge. In India, there have been at least two attempts by courts to recognize the rights of nature, but the results have been mixed. In one decision, the first of its kind in India, the Uttarakhand High Court recognized the legal rights of personhood for the Ganges (or "Ganga") and Yamuna (or "Jumna") rivers and related natural systems. The ruling has been stayed by the Indian Supreme Court, which has not indicated when it will resume proceedings. (Chapter 6, "Guardianship Arrangements in Rights of Nature Legal Provisions," also discusses this case.) The second decision, also by the Uttarakhand High Court, declared that the members of the animal kingdom, including avian and aquatic creatures, are legal entities and therefore have the same rights, duties, and liabilities as other juristic persons. This chapter will examine these cases to show the possibilities and difficulties posed by the "first generation" of rights of nature laws in India.

II. THE LEGAL LANDSCAPE IN INDIA

India is a federal union with 28 states and 8 union territories. The Indian legal system is a hybrid of civil, common, and customary law, coupled with Islamic ethical and religious law, all molded into a framework that is heavily influenced by the country's colonial past. India has a parliamentary system of government with three branches: the executive, the legislative and the judiciary. The operations of these three branches are dictated by the Constitution of India, which was adopted by the Constitutional Assembly on November 26, 1949, and came into effect on January 26, 1950.

The judiciary in India follows a common law, hierarchical structure, similar to that of the United States. The Supreme Court sits at the apex and is charged with the responsibility of interpreting the Indian Constitution. It is the final appellate court for all matters. At the next level are the high courts, which oversee judicial administration in India's states and union territories. Various other bodies have a right to appeal

[1] This chapter was authored by Earth Law Center staff and volunteers. A special thank you to Odaria Finemore, Jyoti Chaudhari, and Nikita Tanwar for their assistance.

to the high courts, including lower courts in the states and territories, the district courts, and *Lok Adalats* (agencies that resolve disputes through conciliation) at the village and *panchayat* (village council) level.[2] Part III of the Indian Constitution provides that both the Supreme Court and high courts have the special constitutional responsibility of enforcing the "fundamental rights" of citizens.

III. LANDMARK DECISION FOR THE RIGHTS OF RIVERS: THE *MOHAMMED SALIM* CASE

The rights of nature movement in India took a significant step in 2016 when the High Court of Uttarakhand ("High Court") gave legal status to the Ganga and Yamuna Rivers along with their tributaries, glaciers, and catchments. The case commenced as a citizen suit when local resident Mohammed Salim sued the State of Uttarakhand to remove illegal construction and encroachments along the banks of the Yamuna River. The Yamuna River, which originates in the Himalayan foothills, is the second-largest tributary of the Ganges River. Salim also alleged that the state governments of Uttarakhand and neighboring Uttar Pradesh were failing to cooperate with the government of India (hereinafter "the central government") to create a Ganga Management Board, which was mandated under the Uttar Pradesh Reorganization Act, 2000.[3]

In December 2016, the High Court ruled that the illegal encroachments and construction on government land be removed, that the governments of Uttarakhand and Uttar Pradesh join the Ganga Management Board and Upper Yamuna River Board within three months, and that all mining in the riverbed of the Ganga and its floodplains cease immediately.[4] Much of the decision focused on issues of federalism, such as the respective roles of state and federal government in water management.

However, the central government, as well the governments of Uttarakhand and Uttar Pradesh, failed to comply with the direction of the High Court, and in a further order issued in March 2017, the High Court judges expressed the court's "serious displeasure" at the two state governments.[5] While the earlier order had focused on issues of federalism, the court's second order decided that protecting the Ganga and Yamuna Rivers required the ambitious and unprecedented step of recognizing their "legal personhood" in part based on their spiritual significance to the Hindu people. The following are excerpts from the court's order, written by Justice Rajiv Sharma.

[2] National Informatics Centre, *Indian Judiciary*, Indian Courts, http://indiancourts.nic.in/index.html (last visited Mar. 13, 2020).
[3] *Mohd. Salim v. State of Uttarakhand and Others*, W.P.(C.) 126 of 2014, H.C. Uttarakhand, reserved judgment, ¶ 19 (Dec. 5, 2016).
[4] *Id.* at ¶ 25.
[5] *Id.* at ¶ 9.

Mohd. Salim v. State of Uttarakhand and Others

Writ Petition (PIL) No. 126 of 2014 (Mar 20. 2017)

10. The extraordinary situation has arisen since Rivers Ganga and Yamuna are loosing [sic] their very existence. This situation requires extraordinary measures to be taken to preserve and conserve Rivers Ganga and Yamuna.

11. Rivers Ganges and Yamuna are worshipped by Hindus. These rivers are very sacred and revered. The Hindus have a deep spiritual connection with Rivers Ganges & Yamuna. . . .

12. In 1969 (1) SCC 555 their Lordships of Hon. Supreme Court in *Yogendra Nath Naskar v. Commission of Income-Tax, Calcutta* have held that a Hindu idol is a juristic entity capable of holding property and of being taxed through its Shebaits [ministers and custodians of the idol] who are entrusted with the possession and management of its property. In paragraph no.6, their Lordships have held as under:

> 6. That the consecrated idol in a Hindu temple is a juridical person has been expressly laid down in Manohar Ganesh's case, I.L.R. 12 Bom. 247 . . . Such ascription of legal personality to an idol must however be incomplete unless it be linked [to human guardians]. . . . The Judicial Committee observed thus: 'It is only in an ideal sense that property can be said to belong to an idol and the possession and management must in the nature of things be entrusted with some person as shebait or manager. It would seem to follow that the person so entrusted must, of necessity, be empowered to do whatever may be required for the service of the idol and for the benefit and preservation of its property at least to as great a degree as the manager of an infant heir'—words which seem to be almost an echo of what was said in relation to a church in a judgment of the days of Edward I: 'A church is always under age and is to be treated as an infant and it is not according to law that infants should be disinherited by the negligence of their guardians or be barred of an action in case they would complain of things wrongfully done by their guardians while they are under age (Pollock and Maitland's 'History of English Law', Volume I, 483).[6]

* * *

The High Court's ruling continued by examining precedents recognizing other nonhumans, such as Hindu idols and deities, as "juristic persons" in Indian religious law. This provided legal support for the notion that the Ganges and Yamuna Rivers, both sacred rivers, could also be juristic persons under the law. . . .

> 14. In AIR 2000 SC 1421, their Lordships of Hon. Supreme Court in the case of *Shiromani Gurudwara Prabandhak Committee, Amritsar v. Shri Som Nath Dass &*

[6] *Id.* at ¶¶ 10-12.

others have held that the concept "Juristic Person" arose out of necessities in the human development. Recognition of an entity as juristic person is for subserving the needs and faith of society. In paragraph nos. 11, 13 and 14, their Lordships held as under:

> 11. The very words "Juristic Person" connote recognition of an entity to be in law a person which otherwise it is not. In other words, it is not an individual natural person but an artificially created person which is to be recognised to be in law as such. When a person is ordinarily understood to be a natural person, it only means a human person. Essentially, every human person is a person. If we trace the history of a "Person" in the various countries we find surprisingly it has projected differently at different times. In some countries even human beings were not treated as persons in law. Under the Roman Law a "Slave" was not a person. He had no right to a family. He was treated like an animal or chattel. In French Colonies also, before slavery was abolished, the slaves were not treated to be legal persons. They were later given recognition as legal persons only through a statute. Similarly, in the U.S. the African-Americans had no legal rights though they were not treated as chattel.
>
> 13. With the development of society, where an individual's interaction fell short, to upsurge social development, co-operation of a larger circle of individuals was necessitated. Thus, institutions like corporations and companies were created, to help the society in achieving the desired result. The very Constitution of State, municipal corporation, company etc. are all creations of the law and these "Juristic Persons" arose out of necessities in the human development. In other words, they were dressed in a cloak to be recognised in law to be a legal unit.
>
> Corpus Juris Secundum, Vol. LXV, page 40 says:
>
>> Natural person. A natural person is a human being; a man, woman, or child, as opposed to a corporation, which has a certain personality impressed on it by law and is called an artificial person. In the C.J.S. definition 'Person' it is stated that the word "person," in its primary sense, means natural person, but that the generally accepted meaning of the word as used in law includes natural persons and artificial, conventional, or juristic persons.
>
> Corpus Juris Secundum, Vol. VI, page 778 says:
>
>> Artificial persons. Such as are created and devised by human laws for the purposes of society and government, which are called corporations or bodies politic.

Salmond on Jurisprudence, 12th Edn., 305 says:

> A legal person is any subject-matter other than a human being to which the law attributes personality. This extension, for good and sufficient reasons, of the conception of personality beyond the class of human being is one of the most noteworthy feats of the legal imagination. . . . Legal persons, being the arbitrary creations of the law, may be of as many kinds as the law pleases. Those which are actually recognised by our own system, however, are of comparatively few types. Corporations are undoubtedly legal persons, and the better view is that registered trade unions and friendly societies are also legal persons though not verbally regarded as corporations. . . . If, however, we take account of other systems than our own, we find that the conception of legal personality is not so limited in its application, and that there are several distinct varieties. (Ellipses in original.) . . .

We may, therefore, define a person for the purpose of jurisprudence as any entity (not necessarily a human being) to which rights or duties may be attributed.

14. Thus, it is well settled and confirmed by the authorities on jurisprudence and Courts of various countries that for a bigger thrust of socio-political-scientific development evolution of a fictional personality to be a juristic person became inevitable. This may be any entity, living inanimate, objects or things. . . . This recognition is for subserving the needs and faith of the society. . . .

15. In AIR 1972 Allahabad 287, learned Single Judge of Allahabad High Court in case of *Moorti Shree Behari ji v. Prem Dass 7 others*[7] has held that a deity can sue as a pauper. In paragraph no. 6, it was held as under:

> 6. The question then that arises is why a deity who is [a] juristic person and can sue or be sued through its Pujari, Shebait or any other person interested, cannot sue as a pauper? To my mind when an incorporated limited company has been held by this Court capable of suing as a pauper, a fortiori it follows that a deity can also sue as a pauper. The learned Judge of the court below was in error in explaining away the Full Bench decision of this Court in the case of AIR 1959 All 540 (FB) (*supra*) on the observation that It related to a joint stock company, hence not applicable. The court below thus was in error in rejecting the application of the deity for that reason.

16. With the development of the society where the interaction of individuals fell short to upsurge the social development, the concept of juristic person

[7] The original document contains a typographical error. The case is *Moorti Shree Behari ji v. Prem Dass & Others.*

> was devised and created by human laws for the purposes of the society. A juristic person, like any other natural person is in law also conferred with rights and obligations and is dealt with in accordance with law. In other words, the entity acts like a natural person but only through a designated person, as their Lordships have held in the judgments cited hereinabove, that for a bigger thrust of socio-political-scientific development, evolution of a fictional personality to be a juristic person becomes inevitable. This may be any entity, living inanimate, objects or things. It may be a religious institution or any such useful unit which may impel the Courts to recognise it. This recognition is for subserving the needs and faith of the society. . . . Thus, to protect the recognition and the faith of society, Rivers Ganga and Yamuna are required to be declared as the legal persons/living persons.
>
> 17. All the Hindus have deep Astha [care, interest, faith] in rivers Ganga and Yamuna and they collectively connect with these rivers. Rivers Ganga and Yamuna are central to the existence of half of [the] Indian population and their health and well being. The rivers have provided both physical and spiritual sustenance to all of us from time immemorial. Rivers Ganga and Yamuna have spiritual and physical sustenance. They support and assist both the life and natural resources and health and well-being of the entire community. Rivers Ganga and Yamuna are breathing, living and sustaining the communities from mountains to sea.
>
> 18. The constitution of Ganga Management Board is necessary for the purpose of irrigation, rural and urban water supply, hydro power generation, navigation, industries. There is utmost expediency to give legal status as a living person/legal entity to Rivers Ganga and Yamuna r/w Articles 48-A and 51A(g) of the Constitution of India.
>
> 19. Accordingly, while exercising the *parens patrie* [sic] jurisdiction, the Rivers Ganga and Yamuna, all their tributaries, streams, every natural water flowing with flow continuously or intermittently of these rivers, are declared as juristic/legal persons/living entities having the status of a legal person with all corresponding rights, duties and liabilities of a living person in order to preserve and conserve river Ganga and Yamuna. The Director NAMAMI Gange, the Chief Secretary of the State of Uttarakhand and the Advocate General of the State of Uttarakhand are hereby declared *persons in loco parentis* as the human face to protect, conserve and preserve Rivers Ganga and Yamuna and their tributaries. These Officers are bound to uphold the status of Rivers Ganges and Yamuna and also to promote the health and well being of these rivers.

* * *

The High Court made important connections between Articles 48A and 51A(g) of the Indian Constitution and the rights of nature. These two articles provide as follows:

- **Article 48A:** "The State shall endeavor to protect and improve the environment and to safeguard the forests and wild life of the country."

- **Article 51A(g):** "It shall be the duty of every citizen of India to protect and improve the natural environment including forest, lakes, rivers and wildlife, and to have compassion for living creatures."

As applied to rights of nature, the High Court reasoned that achieving the environmental mandate of Articles 48A and 51A(g) for the Ganges and Yamuna Rivers required recognizing the two rivers as juristic persons. In other words, the current approach to environmental governance was not sufficient. "Today, the State and the citizens are under a fundamental obligation to protect and improve the environment, including forests, lakes, rivers, wildlife and to have compassion for living creatures," the High Court concluded.[8]

At the time of this writing, the Uttarakhand High Court's ruling in *Mohd. Salim* is pending in the Supreme Court of India, pursuant to a plea filed by the government of the state of Uttarakhand challenging the judgment on several legal and administrative grounds.[9] Among other contentions, the government of Uttarakhand argued that the ruling was "unsustainable in law." For example, they voiced concern over complicated legal questions that might arise once a river is recognized as having rights. If the river floods and destroys human property or someone drowns in its water, could the river itself be sued? And would the government of Uttarakhand be liable to pay damages on behalf of the river? Or, if not them, then who? Finally, the government of Uttarakhand raised jurisdictional issues. For example, because the rivers run through different states, policies pertaining to their protection should be formulated by the central government.

In response, on July 7, 2017, the Supreme Court of India ordered the proceedings and the High Court order to be stayed.

STUDY QUESTIONS

(1) One noteworthy aspect of the Uttarakhand High Court's judgment was its invocation of the principle of *parens patriae. Black's Law Dictionary* defines *parens patriae* as:

a. The State regarded as a sovereign; the state in its capacity as provider of protection to those unable to care for themselves.
b. A Doctrine by which a government has standing to prosecute a lawsuit on behalf of a citizen, especially on behalf of someone who is under a legal disability to prosecute the suit. The State ordinarily has no standing to sue on behalf of its citizens, unless a separate, sovereign interest will be served by the suit.[10]

[8] *K.M. Chinnappa, T.N. Godavarman Thirumalpad v. Union of India & Ors.*, (2002) (10) S.C.C. 606.
[9] *India's Ganges and Yamuna Rivers are 'Not Living Entities'*, BBC (Jul. 7, 2017).
[10] Shama Sinha, *Doctrine of Parens Patriae*, High Court and Supreme Court Judgments (Aug. 6, 2016), http://latestsupremecourtjudgments.blogspot.com/2016/08/doctrine-of-parens-patriae.html.

To this end, the High Court eventually appointed six government officials *in loco parentis* with a duty to protect, conserve, and preserve the two rivers and their tributaries in cooperation with seven local representatives. Having read the guardianship chapter and now learning about the case of *Mohd. Salim v. State of Uttarakhand and Others*, what challenges might impair the effectiveness of a guardianship body comprised of government officials in implementing the rights of nature? Based on the Court's reliance on the juristic status of Hindu idols, what role might be served by a religious or spiritual element in a guardianship body that represents the Ganges and Yamuna Rivers? What benefits might result from the religion-rooted perspective? What drawbacks might be encountered?

(2) In what other countries might rivers be recognized as having personhood or rights based upon religious and spiritual beliefs? Would more or fewer rivers be recognized as having rights if the highest law of the nations in the Americas was the law of the Indigenous Americans? If all sovereign nations in the Americas recognized rights of rivers, what conflicts might ensue when rivers flow through more than one country?

(3) The government of Uttarakhand argued that recognizing the personhood of a river could lead to immense legal complications, posing the example of whether humans should be able to sue a river if it floods. Can an entity have rights without duties? What might the duties be? What benefits to society, if any, might be achieved if rivers had legal duties?

(4) Do you agree with the Uttarakhand High Court's approach that legal personality is a useful alternative for river management? How would the legal personality approach change river management in the United States? How would the rights of rivers as legal personalities be balanced with human rights and interests? What is the proper balance? If you do balance, how do you avoid "balancing away" all of the important river protections, and at what point do rights of nature become no different than the current approach to protecting rivers?

IV. EXTENDING THE RIGHTS OF NATURAL ENTITIES: THE *MIGLANI* CASE

Following the Uttarakhand High Court's declaration that the Ganga and Yamuna Rivers are "juristic/legal persons/living entities having the status of a legal person," that same court in *Miglani v. State of Uttarakhand and Others* extended the ambit of juristic persons to a wide range of natural entities that feed into these rivers, such as other rivers, glaciers, waterfalls, streams, lakes, rivulets, jungles, meadows, forest wetlands, grasslands, dales, air, and forest wetlands.[11] Two natural entities were picked out for

[11] *Lalit Miglani v. State of Uttarakhand and Others*, W.P.(C.), No. 140 of 2015, H.C. Uttarakhand (Mar. 30, 2017).

special attention: glaciers and forests. Emphasizing the existential threat faced by the Gangotri and Yamnotri Glaciers, the High Court wrote as follows:

Miglani v. State of Uttarakhand and Others

W.P.(C.), No. 140 of 2015, H.C. Uttarakhand, March 30, 2017

Gangotri Glacier is situated in District Uttarakashi of the State of Uttarakhand. It is 330.2 kilometres long and between 0.5 to 2.0 kilometres wide. It is one of the largest glaciers in the Himalayas. However, it is receding since 1780. The receding is quick after 1971. According to the images of NASA, over the last 25 years, Gangotri glacier [sic] has retreated more than 850 meters, with a recession of 76 meters from 1996 to 1999 alone. River Ganga originates from Gangotri Glacier.

River Yamuna originates from Yamunotri Glacier. It is also situated in District Uttarkashi. Yamunotri Glacier is also receding at an alarming rate. These Glaciers are receding due to pollution as well as climate change. The urgent remedial steps are required to be taken to ensure that the receding of these Glaciers is stopped.

Both Ganga and Yamuna Rivers are revered as deities by Hindus. Glacial Ice is the largest reservoir of fresh water on Earth.[12]

In granting these various natural entities some of the same legal rights as a living person, the High Court in *Miglani* also proclaimed it is "the fundamental duty of all the citizens to preserve and conserve the nature in its pristine glory."[13] This duty went beyond the law: "Besides our constitutional and legal duties, it is our moral duty to protect the environment and ecology," wrote the court.[14]

The High Court again invoked the principle of *parens patriae*, which designates the government, or some other authority, as the legal representatives of citizens unable to protect themselves. The High Court of Uttarakhand cited various cases from the United States which applied or discussed the principle of *parens patriae*, including *Mormon Church v. United States, Kansas v. Colorado, Oklahoma ex. rel. Johnson v. Cook, Snapp & Son, Inc. v. Puerto Rico ex rel. Barez.*[15] Yet, despite the value of legal precedent and case law, the court concluded

[12] *Id.* at 5.
[13] *Id.* at 42.
[14] *Id.* at 59.
[15] *Mormon Church v. United States,* 136 U.S. 1 (1890); *Kansas v. Colorado,* 185 U.S. 125 (1902); *Oklahoma ex. rel. Johnson v. Cook,* 304 U.S. 387 (938); *Snapp & Son, Inc. v. Puerto Rico ex rel. Barez,* 458 U.S. 592 (1982).

that the best justification for the use of *parens patriae* in the *Miglani* case was the gravity of the threats and harms to the natural entities that would benefit from legal representation. Accordingly, the High Court named a number of officials as legal guardians. Recognizing the rights of communities living nearby, the High Court also permitted the chief secretary of Uttarakhand to appoint seven public representatives from the state to represent these communities.

The High Court concluded by emphasizing the importance of giving personhood to nature to address environmental degradation caused by humans: Rivers and Lakes have intrinsic right[s] not to be polluted. Polluting and damaging the rivers, forests, lakes, water bodies, air and glaciers will be legally equivalent to harming, hurting and causing injury to persons.

Rivers, Forests, Lakes, Water Bodies, Air, Glaciers and Springs have a right to exist, persist, maintain, sustain and regenerate their own vital ecology system. The rivers are not just water bodies. These are scientifically and biologically living.

The rivers, forests, lakes, water bodies, air, glaciers, [and] human life are unified and are [an] indivisible whole. The integrity of the rivers is required to be maintained from Glaciers to Ocean.

However, we would hasten to observe that the local inhabitants living on the banks of rivers, lakes and whose lives are linked with rivers and lakes must have their voice too.

The rivers sustained the aquatic life. The flora and fauna are also dependent on the rivers.

Rivers are gasping for breath. We must recognize and bestow the Constitutional legal rights to the 'Mother Earth'.

The very existence of the rivers, forests, lakes, water bodies, air and glaciers is at stake due to global warming, climate change and pollution.

Trees are the buffer zone necessary to protect the glaciers from direct and indirect heat. One tree sustains life of thousand[s] of insects. Birds chirp and make their nests on the trees. Trees are mini-reservoirs and have a capacity to store the water. The water stored by the trees is released slowly. The Oak tree preserves about 75,000 gallon[s] of pure water. Plucking of one leaf [or] grass blade also damages the environment universally.

The leading civilizations have vanished due to severe droughts. Water is the elixir of life and we must conserve and preserve every drop of water. The value of water should not be undermined only for the reason that it is still available in plenty.

The past generations have handed over the "Mother Earth" to us in its pristine glory and we are morally bound to hand over the same Mother Earth to the next generation.

All the persons have a constitutional and moral responsibility to endeavour to avoid damage or injury to nature (*in damno vitando*). Any person causing any injury and harm, intentionally or unintentionally to the Himalyas, [sic] Glaciers, rivers, streams, rivulets, lakes, air, meadows, dales, jungles and

> forests is liable to be proceeded against under the common law, penal laws, environmental laws and other statutory enactments governing the field. . . .
>
> Thus, the Himalayan Mountain Ranges, Glaciers, rivers, streams, rivulets, lakes, jungles, air, forests, meadows, dales, wetlands, grasslands and springs are required to be declared as the legal entity/legal person/juristic person/judicial person/moral person/artificial person for their survival, safety, sustenance and resurgence.[16]

STUDY QUESTIONS

(1) The High Court in *Miglani* cited numerous U.S. court decisions to help justify its use of the principle of *parens patriae.* Courts in Brazil and Colombia have relied on the decision of the High Court of Uttarakhand in *Salim v. State of Uttarakhand.* Do U.S. courts rely on decisions from other countries? Do you think this is appropriate? How might courts in the U.S. be persuaded to rely more often on decisions from other countries that embody Earth law principles? In state and federal courts in the United States, lawyers have relied on decisions made under other states' laws. Many are found to be persuasive and trends begin. Consider the development of product liability law. What additional hurdles are presented when the law is of another country? How might the law of foreign countries be relied on by U.S. courts to craft new legal solutions that fit today's most difficult challenges?

(2) Should community representatives serve as legal guardians of nature when they may represent the interests of the human community over the interests of nature? How can it be ensured that they act on behalf of the rights and interests of nature? There are innumerable conflicts of interests within ecosystems, perhaps the most obvious being predator-prey relationships. Are the rights of human communities that draw benefits from nature comparable to the rights of non-human predators with respect to their prey. How might these conflicts be resolved? Identify other conflicts and potential resolutions.

(3) One of the natural entities that received recognition of their rights was waterfalls. What rights might they have? Should their rights be considered in isolation, or only as part of a larger ecosystem?

(4) In *Miglani,* the High Court stated: "Besides our constitutional and legal duties, it is our moral duty to protect the environment and ecology," and "[a]ll the persons have a constitutional and moral responsibility to endeavour to avoid damage or injury to nature. . . ." What role does moral duty have in decisions made by trial and appellate judges in the United States? What role should moral duty play?

[16] *Id.*

V. THE RIGHTS OF THE ANIMAL KINGDOM: THE *NARAYAN DUTT BHATT* CASE

On July 4, 2018, the High Court of Uttarakhand held in *Narayan Dutt Bhatt v. Union of India and Others* that all members of the animal kingdom are legal persons.[17] The decision came in response to a petition filed for the protection and welfare of animals. The petitioner had sought to restrict the movement of horse carts known as "tongas" between Nepal and India through Banbasa in the Champawat district of India, due to the suffering experienced by the horses. As a remedy, the petitioner sought vaccinations and medical checkups for the horses for suspected infections prior to entry into India from Nepal. By consent of the parties, the petition's scope was enlarged to promote the protection and welfare of *all* animals. The High Court wrote as follows:

Narayan Dutt Bhatt v. Union of India and Others

W.P.(C.), No. 43 of 2014, H.C. Uttarakhand (July 4, 2018)

12. Learned counsel for the petitioner has vehemently argued that the Indian authorities have failed to regulate the entry of horse carts/tonga entering from Nepal to India. The horses are not medically examined. The fare and freight are not regulated. He has referred to the treaty [between India and Nepal] signed in the year 1991, revised in 2009. According to the treaty, the contracting party may impose restrictions for protecting public morals, protecting human, animal and plant life, safeguarding national treasures. He has also argued that there is overloading in the horse carts/tonga going from India to Nepal and vice-versa. The animals are treated with cruelty. The horses are abandoned in the Indian Territory. He then argued that the provisions of Prevention of Cruelty to Animals Act, 1960 and the rules framed thereunder and the provisions of Prevention and Control of Infectious and Contagious Diseases in Animals Act, 2009 have not been enforced. He also argued that the animals are transported in violation of Transport of Animals Rules, 1978. The animals are transported on foot to long distances causing immense pain and suffering to them. He also prayed that the entire animal kingdom may be conferred status of [a] legal entity/legal person.[18]

* * *

The High Court reviewed the relevant legislation, notably the Prevention of Cruelty to Animals Act, 1960, which states that a person commits cruelty to an animal if that person, amongst other actions,

[17] *Narayan Dutt Bhatt v. Union of India and Others*, W.P.(C.), No. 43 of 2014, H.C. Uttarakhand (July 4, 2018).
[18] *Id.*

> beats, kicks, over-rides, over-drives, over-loads, tortures or otherwise treats any animal so as to subject it to unnecessary pain or suffering or causes, or being the owner permits any animal to be so treated; or (employs in any work or labour or for any purpose any animal which, by reason of its age or any disease) infirmity; wound, sore or other cause, is unfit to be so employed or, being the owner, permits any such unfit animal to be employed.[19]

Additional legislation specifically applies to animals used in transportation, setting maximum loads and numbers of passengers, limiting working hours in hot weather, and imposing other restrictions.[20]

After examining animal cruelty legislation, the High Court then considered the question of animal suffering. Reviewing previous court decisions, it stated as follows:

> 75. Their Lordships of the Hon'ble Supreme Court . . . have held that an animal has also honour and dignity which cannot be arbitrarily deprived of and its rights and privacy have to be respected and protected from unlawful attacks. The principle of equality of all species found in Isha Upanishads [Sanskrit texts containing Hindu teachings] is the culture and tradition of the country, particularly the States of Tamil Nadu and Maharashtra. The PCA Act [Prevention of Cruelty to Animals Act, 1960] has been enacted with an object to safeguard the welfare of the animals and evidently to cure some mischief and age old practices, so as to bring into effect some type of reform, based on eco-centric principles, recognizing the intrinsic value and worth of animals. So far as animals are concerned, "life" means something more than mere survival or existence or instrumental value for human beings, but to lead a life with some intrinsic worth, honour and dignity.[21]

Next, the High Court considered works by a number of authors on the emotions, intelligence, language, self-awareness, and other capabilities of animals. These included David R. Boyd's book *The Rights of Nature*,[22] which the High Court quoted as follows:

> On the frontiers of legal change, there is a growing global movement to recognize non-human animals as legal persons, a radical change that would endow them with the variety of legal rights. Animal rights advocates are not saying primates, cetaceans, or elephants are people. A 'legal person' is not necessarily a human being, but rather an entity to which the law grants specific rights. A corporation is considered a legal person, as are ships, churches and municipalities. The rights and responsibilities of a legal person vary according to the nature of the entity. Corporations and human beings have different sets of legal rights and duties. For example, corporations may assert freedom of expression, but are not protected by the right to life."[23]

The High Court continued by tying its concept of a juristic person to the animal kingdom in terms similar to those employed in *Mohd. Salim v. State of Uttarakhand and*

[19] *Id.*, quoting Prevention of Cruelty to Animals Act, No. 59 of 1960, § 11. (Section numbers removed from quotation.)
[20] *Id.*, quoting Prevention of Cruelty to Draught and Pack Animals Rules, 1965.
[21] *Id.*
[22] David R. Boyd, The Rights of Nature (2017). (Footnote added.)
[23] *Narayan Dutt Bhatt*, *supra* note 26.

Others. It also cited religious perspectives on animals, including from Jainism and Buddhism, to support the notion of giving legal rights to animals.

> 83. We have to show compassion towards all living creatures. Animals may be mute but we as a society have to speak on their behalf. No pain or agony should be caused to the animals. Cruelty to animals also causes psychological pain to them. In Hindu Mythology, every animal is associated with a god. Animals breathe like us and have emotions. The animals require food, water, shelter, normal behavior, medical care, self-determination.
>
> 84. Due to damage caused to environment and ecology, the avian and aquatic life is also threatened. Major rivers have been reduced to the status of a sewer. Aquatic life cannot survive without water. The rivers have inherent right to flow in length as well as in width. The oceans are chocked with plastic. Many species are becoming extinct. The loss of one species causes immense damage to the entire ecosystem. Global warming has arrived and its impact can be seen in day-to-day existence. There are gaps in laws. New inventions are required to be made in law to protect the environment and ecology. The animals including avian and aquatic have a right to life and bodily integrity, honour and dignity. Animals cannot be treated merely as property. . . .
>
> 87. It would be pertinent at this stage to make reference of the book, "*Sacred Animals of India*", written by Nanditha Krishna. She has introduced every animal with the myths and legends that establish its religious status, followed by a short note on the ecological or social role of the animal, which made it important in people's lives. The learned author has also discussed the Ahimsa and Non-violence preached by Lord Mahavira, Lord Gautama Buddha as under:
>
> **Ahimsa or Non-Violence**
>
> The concept of ahimsa—or non-violence—is India's unique contribution to world culture. The Vedas and Upanishads were the first to speak of *ahimsa.* Although the Aryans were not vegetarians, the concept of non-killing appears in the earliest literature. The Rig Veda (10.87.16), condemns all forms of killing, even for food, preferring vegans to drinkers of milk:
>
>> The yatudhana who fills himself with the flesh of man,
>>
>> He who fills himself with the flesh of horses or of other animals,
>>
>> And he who steals the milk of the cow:
>>
>> Lord, cut off their heads with your flame.
>
> The Yajur Veda says that service to animals leads to heaven: 'No person should kill animals helpful to all and persons serving them should obtain heaven.' According to the Atharva Veda, the earth was created for the enjoyment of not only human beings but also for bipeds and quadrupeds, birds, animals and all other creatures. The emergence of all life forms from the Supreme Being is expressed in the Mundakopanishad from Him, too, gods are produced manifold, The celestials, men, cattle, birds.

These ideas led to the concept of ahimsa or non-violence. Much later, the Manusmriti says, 'He who injuries innocent beings with a desire to give himself pleasure never finds happiness, neither in life nor in death.' The Shrimad Bhagavatam says that a cruel person who kills others for his existence deserves to be killed, and cannot be happy, either in life or in death. The consequences, according to the Yajunavalkya Smriti are that 'the wicked person who kills animals which are protected has to live in hellfire for the days equal to the number of hairs on the body of that animal.' . . .

Although Sanatana Dharma did not require its adherents to be vegetarians, vegetarianism was recognized as a higher forms of living, a belief that continues in contemporary Hinduism where vegetarianism is considered essential for spiritualism. Around the sixth century BCE, two great religious preachers were born, who took the Upanishadic philosophy of good conduct and non-killing to the people in the common language: Mahavira the Jina (Victor), and Gautama the Budha [sic] (wise). The name traditionally used for Hinduism. Both emphasized that ahimsa or non-violence was essential for a good life. . . .

Mahavira was not the founder of Jainism: he was the twenty-fourth and last Tirthankara who revised the Jaina doctrines and established the central tenets of Jainism. . . . Mahavira [taught] the importance of right faith, right knowledge and right conduct, which includes non-violence (ahimsa)—not to cause harm to any living being. . . .

According to Jainism, ahimsa is not the mere causing of violence, but rather the "severance of any of the vitality in a mobile or immobile being." Ahimsa, as viewed by Jainism, is very comprehensive and takes into consideration the welfare of all beings on earth. Keeping anything in confinement, without consideration for its freedom to exist or live, is bandhana (captivity). Rearing animals without adequate shelter, air, light, space and food is atichara (bad conduct). Keeping animals, including dairy animals, tied with ropes or chains throughout the day is violence. The simple prayer of the Jainas is "let the law of the Jaina give all happiness to all the living beings of the world. All beings desire to live. They like pleasure, hate pain, shun destruction, like to live long. To all, life is dear." (Ramanujam 2006). . . .

The eightfold path taught by the Buddha [(Gautama)] emphasized abstinence from activities that bring harm to other living beings and non-killing. The Boddhisattva is one who is full of maitri (friendship) towards all animals and which aspires to achieve Buddha-hood. Said the Buddha, "As a mother would be very good towards her only child, her well-beloved son' so too you should be very good towards all creatures everywhere and to everyone." (Dwivedi, 1989) The Buddha himself sought refuge from his bickering disciples by living among the animals. The Jataka tales hold up the noble qualities of various animals as examples to emulate.

* * *

The High Court concluded:

96. It is the fundamental duty of all the citizens under Article 51-A of the Constitution of India to have compassion for living creatures. It should be the endeavour of the State under Article 48 of the Constitution to organize agriculture and animal husbandry on modern and scientific lines and take steps for preserving and improving the breeds. The State Government is required to protect and improve the environment and to

safeguard the forests and wild life of the counter as per Article 48-A of the Constitution of India.

97. The maximum weight prescribed under Rules 3 and 4 of the Prevention of Cruelty to Draught & Pack Animals Rules, 1965 is prima facie excessive. In India, by and large, the weather remains dry. It causes immense stress to the animals to drive vehicles by carrying maximum load, as prescribed under the Rules, 1965 in dry conditions. The need of the hour is to have the expert's opinion whether the maximum load prescribed under Rules 3 and 4 of Rules, 1965 is reasonable or not.

98. Their Lordships of the Hon'ble Supreme Court in "A. Nagaraja's" case have held that Article 21 of the Constitution, while safeguarding the rights of humans, protects life and the word "life" has been given an expanded definition and any disturbance from the basic environment which includes all forms of life, including animal life, which are necessary for human life, fall within the meaning of Article 21 of the Constitution. "Life" means something more than mere survival or existence or instrumental value for human beings, but to lead a life with some intrinsic worth, honour or dignity. All the animals have honour and dignity. Every species has an inherent right to live and are required to be protected by law. The rights and privacy of animals are to be respected and protected from unlawful attacks. Their Lordships have evolved the term "species' best interest." The Corporations, Hindu idols, holy scriptures, rivers have been declared legal entities and thus, in order to protect and promote greater welfare of animals including avian and aquatic, animals are required to be conferred with the status of legal entity/ legal person. The animals should be healthy, comfortable, well-nourished, safe, able to express innate behavior without pain, fear and distress. They are entitled to justice.

99. Accordingly, the writ petition is disposed of by issuing the following mandatory directions:

> A. The entire animal kingdom including avian and aquatic are declared as legal entities having a distinct persona with corresponding rights, duties and liabilities of a living person. All the citizens throughout the State of Uttarakhand are hereby declared persons *in loco parentis* as the human face for the welfare/protection of animals.

STUDY QUESTIONS

(1) In *Narayan Dutt Bhatt v. Union of India and Others*, the High Court examines in detail the concepts of *ahimsa* or nonviolence and explains that in "Jainism, ahimsa is not the mere causing of violence, but rather the 'severance of any of the vitality in a mobile or immobile being.'" Is there anything in the foundations of U.S. law that reflects these concepts? Compare and contrast this conceptual framework used by the High Court of Uttarakhand with the approach in U.S. law? "Personhood" as applied to nature attempts to apply personhood rights given to humans to nature. What is the benefit of this approach. What alternative

Earth law strategies exist to granting aspects of nature legal rights without granting them status as "legal persons"? Discuss and explain the pros and cons of these different approaches.

(2) Each of these cases discussed in this chapter come from the High Court of Uttarakhand. How does the case law created in one jurisdiction inspire or persuade courts in other jurisdictions?

CHAPTER 21

Israel[1]

I. INTRODUCTION

The emergence of Earth law in Israel plays out against the backdrop of the country's fragile geophysical conditions, a fast-growing economy, rapid population growth, and its high technological capacity, such as desalination and wastewater reuse. Early forays into Earth law, particularly the rights of nature, attempt to break out of the current legal paradigm crafted to support a governance system geared for unfettered growth. Earth law development in Israel focuses on demonstrating the costs of the current governance system for nature by reframing ecosystem devastation and biodiversity loss through the lens of the rights of natural entities to survive and flourish.

Israel's ecological crisis has spawned environmental activism, which has been highly litigious in its approach. Yet this activism, propelled by hundreds of organizations at both the local and national level, is still largely anthropocentric, focusing on protecting nature because of its services to humans rather than its own inherent value. No doubt, this approach is more pragmatic than ideological, since environmental campaigns are more likely to succeed if they appeal to the self-interest of the public by viewing nature as a supplier of critical goods and services.

Nevertheless, glimmerings of a rights of nature doctrine are emerging in Israel, and the country has made its own contribution, albeit small, in advancing global Earth law, illustrated by the two case studies discussed below. The first case study examines the 2004 amendment to the Water Law granting nature a right to water; the second examines the mountain gazelle's petition to Israel's High Court of Justice to protect its habitat from development.

II. NATURE'S RIGHT TO WATER UNDER ISRAELI LAW

In an arid country characterized by chronic water scarcity, 70 years of intense human activity has polluted the country's water sources with sewage and other waste, while capturing their use for industrial, agricultural, and residential purposes. By 1980,

[1] This chapter was authored by Rachelle Adam, Faculty of Law, Hebrew University.

Israel's water use had reached the total capacity of available freshwater.[2] Massive exploitation has ravaged Israel's streams, springs, winter ponds, and wetlands, resulting in their desiccation and the loss of aquatic habitats. Today only 3 percent remains of the wetlands that existed a century ago, most of it in national parks and nature reserves.

Israel has historically solved its water shortage by creating more water. The country makes extensive use of treated wastewater effluents for irrigation in agriculture. Today, roughly 90 percent of the wastewater generated is reused,[3] making Israel the world's leading country in water reuse. In addition, since the beginning of this century, Israel has ranked high in the production and use of desalinated water, which now comprises approximately 70 percent of its drinking water supply.[4] The question of the sustainability of such extensive reuse of effluents as well as massive desalination looms large over Israel's formidable success in overcoming its chronic water scarcity. Nevertheless, an admirable goal of government policy in its sweeping use of desalinated water is to cut back on pumping groundwater to allow the restoration of natural inflow to devastated streams and springs.

Overdrawing of groundwater has reduced aquifer levels and, subsequently, spring flow, transforming most of the perennial streams in central and northern Israel into intermittent streams whose only source of water is rain. Moreover, the conversion of coastal streams into sewage canals has damaged their rich biodiversity, including unique plant and animal species. Public anger over this ecological catastrophe, and the country's water crisis generally, finally erupted in the 1990s. In response, the government initiated an extensive stream restoration program as a national priority, supported by a decision from the year 2000 allocating 50 million cubic meters of water annually for stream inflow.[5]

Harnessing the momentum, a coalition of government officials and nature conservation organizations introduced the concept of "nature's rights to water," which captured the public's imagination and swiftly became a key talking point in the mainstream environmental dialogue. In 2002, a government masterplan for water management implementing allocations for stream restoration defined nature itself as a legitimate consumer of water. The concept of granting rights to water to Israel's much-abused streams and other wetlands began to drive government policy. In 2003, the government's Environment Ministry and Nature Reserves Authority issued a landmark policy paper called "Nature's Right to Water" officially recognizing streams' entitlement to their own natural inflow rather than to water from the national grid. Finally, in 2004, the concept was incorporated into Israel's Water Law.

The Water Law is a broad framework governing the country's water in its entirety—from production, allocation, and distribution to pollution, conservation,

[2] Arthur Wiener, *Levels of Control in Water Quality under Conditions of Scarcity, in Water Quality Management Under Conditions of Scarcity: Israel as a Case Study* 18 (Hillel I. Shuval ed., 1980).
[3] Zafrir Rinat, *Israeli Wastewater Policy Continues to Pay Off*, Haaretz (Mar. 23, 2015).
[4] Melanie Lidman, *Desalination Isn't the Magic Bullet: Water Authority Warns Israelis*, Times of Israel (Jun. 5, 2018).
[5] Government Decision No.46, Economics of the Ministerial Committee on Economic Issues from July 18, 2000; Government Decision 2117 from Aug. 3, 2000 (*see* paragraph on "water allocations for nature").

and restoration. At the law's adoption in 1959,[6] water was perceived as a commodity for development, and hence the law was initially crafted as a tool for intense urban, industrial, and agricultural development. Yet it evolved alongside the growing awareness of the environmental crisis, and in 1972 a chapter on pollution prevention was added.[7] In 1991, stronger enforcement provisions were added to the Water Law to strengthen pollution control.[8] And, in 2004, the law finally evolved to guarantee nature the right to water for "conservation and restoration of nature and landscapes, including springs, streams and wetlands."[9] The text of section 6 of the Water Law reads as follows:

> Any right for water is linked to one of the water purposes that are listed below: the right to water ceases upon the cessation of the purpose; and these are the water purposes:
>
> 1. Domestic needs;
> 2. Agriculture;
> 3. Industry;
> 4. Labor, trade and services;
> 5. Public services; and
> 6. Protection and restoration of nature and landscape values, including springs, rivers and wetlands (in this law—"nature and landscape values").

To ensure accountability and transparency, the director of Israel's Water Authority is required to "submit to the Economic Committee of the Knesset [the country's legislative body] by the first of April each year, a notification regarding the amount of water that was decided to allocate during the same year for the purpose of nature and landscape values according to Section 6 (6). . . ." Finally, the explanatory note to the bill clarified that the purpose of the amendment was to allow for both the conservation and restoration of nature and freshwater systems:

> Current efforts to restore nature and landscape values are not anchored in legislation since they are not listed in section 6 to the Water Law, 1959 . . . The said section determines, that any right to water must be linked to . . . domestic needs, agriculture, industry, labor, trade and services, and public services. It is proposed to add to the list . . . conservation and restoration of nature and landscape assets, including springs, streams and wetlands, so that in the framework of water allocations this purpose will also be taken into consideration.

Looking back today on the 2004 amendment to Israel's Water Law allows a broad perspective on the law's implementation and the challenges that arose. Adding nature's right to water to the law mandated the government to allocate water to nature itself. Furthermore, government policy has determined that the source of the allocations must be from the stream's own natural flow rather than water from the national grid. However, overdrawing from aquifers continues because of high human demand, while

[6] The Water Law, S.H.288 (1959). For the complete text of the Water Law translated to English, *see* https://www.sviva.gov.il/English/Legislation/Documents/Water%20Laws%20and%20Regulations/WaterLaw1959-Excerpts.pdf.
[7] Amendment to the Water Law, S.H.640 (1971).
[8] Amendment to the Water Law, S.H. 1361 (1991).
[9] Amendment to the Water Law, S.H. 1948 (2004).

drought has led to decreased recharging of aquifers, and hence the over-diversion of fresh water from springs and streams for human use continues. The resulting trend is a scarcity of instream flow and a severe decrease in spring resurgence in northern Israel, which lacks a desalination plant to replace freshwater appropriated for humans.[10]

While Israel's laws and official policy recognize nature's right to water, government policies aimed at expanding the economy and increasing gross domestic product together with a rapidly growing population have undermined its implementation. These challenges are likely to increase as Israel's population is projected to rise to 20 million by 2065, a rise from 8.7 million in 2019.[11] At present, the priority of human needs in the allocation of ecosystem goods and services is unquestioned and may intensify in this arid, ecologically fragile, and geographically small country.

The case study of Israel's Water Law demonstrates how laws recognizing the rights of nature can be rendered powerless when faced with formidable political forces demanding development for housing and jobs. Section 6 (6) of the Water Law has not succeeded in warding off the threats of stream desiccation. While it has ensured that the government allocates water to nature, humans still have priority over nature. Full enforcement of Section 6(6) of the Water Law would require, at least, meeting the basic water needs of ecosystems.

A recent development project underscores the flawed application of nature's right to water in Israel. In response to objections to a plan for a new neighborhood in Jerusalem that will dry up adjacent natural springs called *Ein Lavan* (White Spring), the government planning committee decided that "the public need for this plan justifies its approval, despite its impact on the springs."[12] Yet the committee could not ignore the government's own mandate to ensure water for the springs, and hence devised a plan to bring water from the national grid into the spring's pools. Thus, a shortcoming of the right-to-water amendment as written is that it does not commit the government to allocate the springs' own natural inflow as the source of water. In any petition for judicial review, Israeli courts would in all likelihood defer to the government experts who devised the plan and refrain from interfering.

On the other hand, the government recognized the ecological need to return natural inflow to streams. In June 2018, it approved the "Strategic Emergency Plan Addressing the Water Sector Under Drought Conditions." The plan calls for the construction of two additional desalination plants with the goal of almost doubling the current production amount to 1.1 billion cubic meters annually by 2030. One of the new desalination plants will be located in northern Israel, to allow for a decrease in pumping from aquifers and the return of natural inflow to streams and springs.

[10] *See* Assaf Soknik & Urit Skotlasky, *Nature's Right to Water? Dilemmas in Restoring Israel's Streams in Light of Changes in the Water Sector*, 4 ECOLOGY AND ENVT. 68-75 (Dec. 2017) http://www.magazine.isees.org.il/ArticlePage.aspx?ArticleId=715 (Hebrew); Government Decision No. 3866: Strategic Plan for Drought in the Water Sector, 2018-2030, https://www.gov.il/he/departments/policies/dec3866_2018 (Hebrew).

[11] *See* Lidar Grave Lazi, *Israel's Population to Reach 20 Million by 2065*, THE JERUSALEM POST (May 21, 2017), https://www.jpost.com/printarticle.aspx?id=492429#.

[12] Decisions from the Meetings of the Sub-Committee for Objections, July 18, 2019 & July 28, 2019, at p. 68, ¶ 2 (Hebrew)

Meanwhile streams and springs in Israel continue to fight for their survival. They remain silent stakeholders despite the improvement of their legal status entitling them to water allocations. To fill this gap, Israel's steams and springs require their own uniquely defined rights—such as rights to flow, to be free from pollution, to feed and be fed by sustainable aquifers, to restoration, and others.[13] And, of course, they require a right of standing so that they can have representation and protect themselves in a court of law when these rights are not enforced.

III. THE GAZELLE PETITION

A further case model of the rights of nature in Israel is the "Gazelle Petition." In this case, the endangered Israeli mountain gazelle, together with five humans, petitioned Israel's High Court of Justice to prevent the development of its habitat—and won. In contrast to nature's right to water now established in Israeli law, the human petitioners, residents of the neighborhood bordering the mountain gazelle habitat, could not point to a specific law granting the gazelle a right to its habitat. Instead, the petition was based on nature and wildlife protection laws that grant the gazelle a protected status, albeit one that falls short of statutory legal identity.

The following excerpts are from the article *Finding Safe Passage through a Wave of Extinctions: Israel's Endangered Mountain Gazelle* that narrates and analyzes the case.[14] As you read the excerpts, remember that the objective behind this precedential case was not only to protect the gazelles, but also to prevent development of forestland that happened to be the gazelles' habitat. Attaching the iconic gazelle as a petitioner transformed it into the poster child of the campaign, underscoring that protecting the gazelle means protecting the forest as well.

Finding Safe Passage through a Wave of Extinctions: Israel's Endangered Mountain Gazelle

In 2008, the Supreme Court of Israel overturned a decision by the country's highest planning authority to approve the development of 2,000 housing units on Mitspeh Neftoah, one of Jerusalem's few remaining natural areas (*See* HCQ 11745/04 466/05, *Reiss, Roth, Shachaf, Adam, Shefer, Gazella Gazella v. Nat'l Planning & Building Comm.* (2008) (Isr.)) The six petitioners were from a neighboring suburb: five of them were *Homo sapiens* and the sixth was the *Gazella gazella (G. gazella),*

[13] *See* Earth Law Center, *Universal Declaration of River Rights*, https://www.earthlawcenter.org/river-rights/.

[14] Rachelle Adam, *Finding Safe Passage through a Wave of Extinctions: Israel's Endangered Mountain Gazelle*, 19 J. of Intl. Wildlife L. & Poly. 136-158, 136, 137, 147, 148, 149, 150-151, 157 (2016).

Israel's mountain gazelle and one of the country's most iconic species. Although the range of the gazelle was once extensive, Israel is now the only country where the species is extant, and even there its future appears grim. [A small population of approximately 200 exists in Turkey.[15]] Gazelle numbers overall in Israel have spiraled sharply downwards from approximately 10,000 in 1985 to about 2,500 today.

The following analysis focuses on a stage in the conflict when local residents, together with the mountain gazelle, sued the government for breaking its own laws—and won. The court did not, however, mention the gazelle in its decision, nor did it raise the question of its standing to sue, making it a sort of elephant in the room. But neither did the court demand removal of the gazelle as a party to the case; the gazelle, thus, retains its legal status as petitioner.

The . . . petition explained that:

> Petitioner 6 is the Israeli gazelle. . . . At least 30 individuals of the species live in the area of Mitspeh Neftoah, and they will be directly injured by the plan's approval and development of the area, comprising a taking of its habitat. The Israeli gazelle is a protected nature asset in accordance with the National Parks and Nature Reserves Declaration (Protected Natural Assets),[16] 1979, as well as protected wildlife in accordance with the Wildlife Protection Act, 1955. . . .

The law, petitioners argued, "protects [the gazelle] and other protected species by granting them status as protected legal assets and protected wildlife . . . in theory they have standing to initiate legal action against those who would harm them. Yet a key distinction between the gazelles and ourselves is that they are voiceless and so cannot argue for themselves before the court. So we, as speech enabled human beings, stepped in as their guardians. . . . We argue that since the government has ignored the potential effects of the development plan on the gazelle population,. . . . the gazelles should become petitioners themselves. . . . Petitioner 6 argues and Petitioners 1–5 concur that the National Parks and Nature Reserves Law grants the Israeli gazelle a property right to its natural habitat and range areas, which it has occupied for thousands of years in Mitspeh Neftoah. Petitioner 6 will further argue that the law grants him statutory protection of his rights, as well as the right to address this honorable court sitting as a High Court of Justice, to avoid injury. The respondents' decision to approve the plan . . . will cause severe injury to Petitioner 6 and deprive him of his property rights of thousands of years to his habitat in Mitspeh Neftoah. . . .

[15] Lia Hadas et al., *Wild Gazelles of the Southern Levant: Genetic Profiling Defines New Conservation Priorities*, PLOS One at 2 (Mar. 11, 2015), https://doi.org/10.1371/journal.pone.0116401.

[16] "Natural Assets" is defined as "anything or class of things in nature, animal, vegetable or abiotic that originate in an area of the State or outside it.

Although the government took the view that the highest and best use of Mitspeh Neftoah was as a housing project, the petitioners wanted the court to accept that the land at issue had more essential uses as a provider of ecosystem goods and services, values of the utmost importance. The petition was, thus, an ambitious legal attempt to overcome the limitations of an anthropocentric legal system—a system that recognizes only those land uses that are *perceived* as most important for human beings and that prioritize land uses without proper regard for the natural systems that underpin life on the planet:

> Decision makers in Israel's planning institutions act solely out of anthropocentric considerations . . . totally ignoring other forms of life. . . . Furthermore, even if the only consideration that guides the planning committees is human welfare, we ourselves need other species. . . .

The court's decision cautiously avoided mention of the gazelles and of their legal status and standing before the court. It decided in favor of the petitioners, the court said, on two grounds. First, the respondents had exceeded their authority by approving an amendment to the district rezoning plan that violated National Outline Plan 22 for forests and forestation, in breach of the amount of forestland that the Plan permitted for development. Second, the government had discriminated against petitioners by violating their right to a fair hearing by allowing the Jerusalem district planner to participate in the National Planning Council's internal meeting on the examiner's findings, whilst at the same time refusing the petitioners' request to participate in the same meeting. Despite the government attorney's attempts to persuade the court that the flawed government actions and decisions were reparable through further deliberation and discussion, the court took the view that the process was so egregious that only a total and immediate revocation of the decisions already made could provide petitioners with relief.

This decision was remarkable because Israeli courts are loath to second-guess government experts and typically defer to them. In this instance, however, the court judged that the severity of the errors in the decision-making process overrode customary deference. In addition, and on a more substantive note, the court emphasized the high value of Israel's few remaining forestlands. Their scarcity, it said, obligates the government to conduct in-depth analysis and deliberations on the impact of their loss on the surrounding environment prior to decisions on rezoning forestlands for urban development. Not only was such an analysis not undertaken in this case, the court noted, but the information on which the government did rely was both erroneous and inaccurate.

By sidestepping the issue of the gazelle's right to standing in court, and by basing its decision on a violation of National Outline Plan 22, the court adroitly succeeded in protecting the gazelles while at the same time avoiding what could have been significant political controversy. The court's avoidance of the gazelle's legal standing is understandable as a matter of institutional self-preservation. It leaves in limbo, however, the question of just how effective Israel's existing wildlife protection laws can be in preventing extinctions. The day was won for the gazelle not by wildlife law but by planning law that has, for the most part, succeeded in balancing multiple demands for land use and keeping at bay the more egregious interests of private entities. . . .

Although the Supreme Court carefully avoided addressing the unusual petitioner and the provocative arguments raised in favor of its standing to be a petitioner, the precedent-making nature of the case did not go entirely unnoticed by the court. When petitioners submitted a request for an interim order restraining the government from moving ahead with the actual development until a final decision in the case, presiding Justice Elyakim Rubinstein took the opportunity to address the standing of Petitioner 6, *G. g. gazella.* The justice first hastily disposed of the petitioners' request for a restraining order, relying on the government attorney's reassurance that the detailed plan's approval was not pending and actual construction was far from tangible. He then eagerly turned his attention to the beguiling nonhuman petitioner:

> I would like to add that Petitioner 6 is the Israeli Gazelle. . . . I have considered if an animal itself—to differentiate it from organizations for animal welfare—can be a petitioner . . . In actual fact, the gazelle does have a protected legal status as a "protected nature asset and as protected wildlife . . . But is it possible to grant it standing as a petitioner? I think that the answer is no . . . [R]egarding this question we have to differentiate between the very deserving and important concept of animal protection as provided in various forms by Israeli legislation and case law, and the question of an animal as a direct party to a . . . judicial proceeding, since it cannot—amongst other issues—give power of attorney or think or analyze as humans do, or . . . pay court fees . . . if the petition is rejected, and of course I am not expressing any opinion in this matter.

Justice Rubinstein concluded by ordering the petitioners to "notify the court within 7 days if they are willing to remove 'Petitioner 6' while keeping their right to raise arguments concerning the plight of the gazelles." This obiter dicta received a great deal of media attention that misconstrued it as a final decision tossing the gazelles out of the courthouse. The human petitioners declined, however, to abandon the gazelles, and keeping them on board incurred no retaliatory decision or court fees, as had been gently threatened by Justice Rubinstein. In the end, the gazelle remained an official petitioner in the case.

The attempt to gain judicial recognition of the gazelle's right to standing in court was intended to gain for the species a legitimacy in courts of law that animals never enjoy. It reflects an underlying view that it is difficult, if not downright impossible, to save from extinction nonhuman species that we do not respect or simply just do not care about as much as making more room for more people. Preventing their extinction requires granting them moral consideration. Reasonably enough, the court would not go this far. It was vigilant in protecting its own integrity and in avoiding what might have led to public ridicule. The fact remains, however, that the gazelle has a legacy on record [as] a formal petitioner in Israel's High Court of Justice. Perhaps this signals the earliest glimmerings of Israeli society's recognition that it does have a duty to prevent the extinction of its own endangered wildlife.

IV. CONCLUSION

As shown by the above discussion of nature's right to water and the gazelle petition, Israel's experience with rights of nature has so far been limited. Yet if the human species is to live within ecological limits and save the environment from complete collapse, legally enforceable rights of nature may be a critical tool.

The role of rights of nature is to counter the entrenched assumption of humans as conquerors of nature, to challenge the belief that the Earth's resources are unlimited, that nature is indestructible and will recover from whatever we throw at it, and that we can populate, mine, dam, farm, fish, manufacture, and consume without limits. While flawed, a foundation for the development of Earth law in Israel has been laid by the legislative recognition of the rights of water and the judicial acceptance, at least nominally, of a gazelle in the courtroom. How Israel builds from this foundation may determine the fate of freshwater habitat, native species, and ecosystems.

STUDY QUESTIONS

(1) While streams, springs, and other wetlands in Israel are today legally entitled to water, as discussed above, the law has certainly not stopped the government from moving ahead with development that threatens the existence of springs in Jerusalem.[17] Relying on a statutory right to water, do you think that the threatened spring is entitled to petition the courts for judicial review? Take into consideration that while the law recognizes the right of the spring to water, it does not go further and declare the stream a legal person; the provision to declare streams, springs, and other wetlands legal entities that appeared in the original version of the bill did not make it to the final version of the amendment.

(2) After reading the case study on Israel's right to water, explain Israel's water technologies as both a solution to the country's widespread wetland desiccation and pollution, as well as a drawback in promoting the rights of nature to water. Will

[17] *See* Rachelle Adam, *Securing Rights for the Ein Lavan Natural Spring*, EARTH LAW CENTER (Nov. 15, 2018), https://www.earthlawcenter.org/blog-entries/2018/11/securing-rights-for-the-ein-lavan-natural-spring.

desalination and wastewater reuse contribute to normalizing the rights of ecosystems to water in Israel or is it more likely to have the reverse effect?

(3) Could the public trust doctrine support the spring's standing in court? Under Sec. 2 of the Water Law, "Israel's water sources belong to Israel's public, subject to the control of the state." Hence government officials are public trustees for protecting the country's ecosystems, streams, springs, plants, wildlife, and biodiversity, but with the public as the beneficiary and not for the actual ecosystem, stream, or spring. An alternative would be to turn the public into trustees with nature as the beneficiary, but this would entail new legislation, which can be politically difficult. How would you propose drafting a petition invoking the public trust doctrine under current legislation?

(4) In considering the New Zealand model of legal identity for rivers (*see* Chapters 6 and 22), would you suggest this model for Israel, as well, in addition to nature's right to water? Would this model help Israel's streams recover their instream flow from humans? Or would humans still have priority? Is the New Zealand model perhaps unworkable in Israel because of geographical, political, and cultural differences? Taking this further, do you foresee the development of a diversity of Earth law, in adaptation to the unique conditions of each country? If so, what expressions of Earth law do you see evolving?

(5) Israel's right of nature to water law demonstrates the fragility of law when pitted against human interests. The restoration of nature's own instream water to streams and springs in Israel is still contingent on humans drawing enough water for their own needs first. Thus, the law is not necessarily the ultimate protector of nature. Above all, human cultural values need to change, from an anthropocentric approach to an ecocentric one. How would you suggest changing our society's values, and would law have any role to play in this? Can law be a crafter of cultural values, rather than their reflection? In this context, do you agree with the petitioners that the gazelle had standing as a consequence of its status as protected wildlife and as a protected natural asset under Israel's nature and wildlife protection laws? Or do you think that standing can only be bestowed by a specific law clearly granting that right? Does the argument that the development plan threatens the gazelle's property rights strengthen the argument for standing, or do you think that arguing property rights for a nonhuman entity would be counterproductive because it reinforces the concept of ownership of nature?

(6) The petitioners argued that they were acting as guardians of the voiceless gazelles by arguing the gazelles' case in court, and that their decision to bring the gazelle as a formal petitioner was a result of the government ignoring the impact of the planned development on this specific gazelle population. Do you think that there is a contradiction in this argument, that if the petitioners considered themselves the gazelles' guardians and saw their role as speaking for them, the gazelle need not be a formal petitioner? How would you have written the judgment on this

specific point, drawing perhaps on guardian issues for minors and the incapacitated?

(7) The judgment in the Gazelle Petitioner case was written by Israel's then Chief Justice Dorit Benisch, probably the most environmentally-minded judge that has ever sat on Israel's Supreme Court. How much do you think this had to do with the petition's outcome? Would a less environmentally friendly judge have been more likely to demand that the human petitioners remove the gazelle as petitioner, as Justice Rubinstein suggested in the *obiter dictum* judgment in the interim order hearing? What does this say about the objectivity of the courts when hearing cases challenging existing values, such as rights of nature issues? And, if the human petitioners had not included the gazelle as a petitioner, do you think that the court would still have revoked the government's approval of the development plan? Taking into consideration that the gazelle was not mentioned in the judgment, how do you feel that it contributed to this highly successful case?

(8) Linking the two case studies discussed in this section, could a stream under threat by development plans also petition the court to protect its integrity as a stream? Lacking a statutory right for standing, would you also use Israel's nature protection laws to claim standing for the stream? Why would it be critical to verify if the stream is located in a statutory national park or nature reserve? Adding human petitioners is a sure way to hedge your bets if the nonhuman entity is removed from the petition by a court decision and the petition consequently collapses. What qualifications should the human petitioners ideally have in order to increase your chances of a favorable judgment together with the stream as petitioner?

CHAPTER 22

New Zealand[1]

"Nature wills that there is no end to life."[2]

I. INTRODUCTION

Aotearoa New Zealand (inclusive of both the Māori and the English names), is a relatively young and sparsely populated state. The 1840 Treaty of Waitangi between the English Queen and the Indigenous Māori provided the terms of English settlement and subsequent government. In 2020, as a result of mostly European settlement over the last 200 years, Māori make up approximately 15 percent of the population of about 5 million.[3] Those five million people are spread over a land area of approximately the size of Colorado.

In relation to its environmental laws and legal system, Aotearoa New Zealand is a common law, democratic country without a written constitution. Even though there is no single written New Zealand constitution, there are constitutional documents, including a New Zealand Bill of Rights Act 1990, and the foundational Treaty of Waitangi, signed by representatives of the British Crown and over 500 Māori chiefs in 1840. However, Aotearoa New Zealand also has a system of parliamentary sovereignty, similar to those in the United Kingdom and in Israel. Therefore, court decisions are important, as in any common law system, but courts do not have power to invalidate procedurally valid laws passed by Parliament, whereas Parliament can pass a law to override a court decision. While the separation of powers is taken extremely seriously, and New Zealand is repeatedly ranked as one of the least corrupt nations in the world,[4] the make-up of Parliament—and thus the system for appointing parliamentarians—determines the content of most of New Zealand's laws.

New Zealand is a party to most international environmental agreements and prides itself on being a strong protector of the environment. That pride may not

[1] This chapter was authored by Catherine J. Iorns Magallanes, BA, LLB (Hons) *Well*, LLM *Yale*, Professor of Law, Victoria University of Wellington, New Zealand.

[2] The first sentence of Te Kawa o Te Urewera, the management plan for Te Urewera, https://www.ngaituhoe.iwi.nz/te-kawa-o-te-urewera; discussed in Sect. 23.4B, *infra*.

[3] *See, e.g.*, Statistics New Zealand on population numbers and ethnicity: http://www.stats.govt.nz.

[4] *See, e.g.*, Transparency International, *Corruption Perceptions Index 2019*, https://www.transparency.org.nz/corruption-perceptions-index (last visited Mar. 16, 2020) (ranking New Zealand first equal with Denmark).

reflect its domestic results in practice.[5] It has a range of domestic environmental laws dealing with different subjects; the largest and most comprehensive statute creating an integrated management regime for most uses of land, air, and water is the Resource Management Act 1991. Separate legislation governs national parks, protected species, animal welfare, and most resource extraction. Separate legislation also governs some of the innovative environmental co-management and co-governance arrangements between government and the Māori.

New Zealand is also a party to most international human rights agreements and similarly prides itself on being a strong defender of human rights. Key domestic human rights laws include the Bill of Rights Act and the Human Rights Act; both are ordinary statutes and the Bill of Rights contains solely civil and political rights; none contain environmental rights. It is through New Zealand's human rights framework that many of the more ecocentric legal mechanisms have been made part of the law. Most significantly, this has taken place as a result of the systems New Zealand has adopted for resolving Indigenous grievances to breaches of the 1840 Treaty of Waitangi.

This chapter outlines three aspects of New Zealand legislation that contribute to the body of Earth law: references to the intrinsic value of nature, recognition that animals are sentient beings, and adoption of legal personality for nature.

II. LEGISLATIVE RECOGNITION OF THE INTRINSIC VALUE OF NATURE

Several significant pieces of New Zealand's environmental legislation contain recognition of the "intrinsic worth" or "intrinsic value" of nature. The key examples are the Reserves Act 1977, the National Parks Act 1980, the Conservation Act 1987, the Resource Management Act 1991, the Hazardous Substances and New Organisms Act 1996, and the Marine and Coastal Area (Takutai Moana) Act 2011. In addition, several other statutes specific to particular natural areas refer to intrinsic values of nature.[6]

References to the intrinsic worth or intrinsic value of nature occur most often as part of the general purpose of the statute or the principles by which decisions under the statute should be made. Interestingly, some statutes define these terms but others do not; those without definitions thus leave the terms to their ordinary meaning and definition by decision-makers and courts.

[5] For example, New Zealand has been ranked 18th/179 in the world for its proportional environmental impact (where 1 is the greatest environmental impact proportional to total resource availability—i.e., New Zealand is one of the worst 20 countries of the world). CJA Bradshaw, X Giam, & NS Sodhi, *Evaluating the Relative Environmental Impact of Countries*, 5(5) PLoS ONE e10440 (2010), https://doi.org/10.1371/journal.pone.0010440.

[6] *See, e.g.*, Water Conservation Orders in respect of the Kawerau and Rangitata Rivers, the two statutes conferring legal personality on Te Awa Tupua and Te Urewera referred to later in this chapter, some forest and heritage area legislation, and the Antarctica (Environmental Protection) Act 1994.

The Reserves Act 1977 provides for a range of types of reserves, including recreation, historic, scenic, nature, and scientific. Only the provision defining scenic reserves refers to their intrinsic worth:

19 Scenic Reserves

(1) It is hereby declared that the appropriate provisions of this Act shall have effect, in relation to reserves classified as scenic reserves—

(a) for the purpose of protecting and preserving in perpetuity for their intrinsic worth and for the benefit, enjoyment, and use of the public, suitable areas possessing such qualities of scenic interest, beauty, or natural features or landscape that their protection and preservation are desirable in the public interest.

The term *intrinsic worth* is not further defined in the statute, so it is left to take its ordinary (anthropocentric) meaning.[7] Nature's intrinsic worth, although ecocentric in abstraction, is still rooted in human enjoyment of nature. For example, the courts have determined that the view from a scenic reserve is part of its intrinsic worth;[8] this justified the Minister of Conservation granting a lease to enable construction of a gazebo on a scenic reserve to take advantage of the view. In determining when and where "protection and preservation are desirable," the decision-making is based on what is "desirable in the [human] public interest." Thus, the measure of intrinsic worth is established anthropocentrically.

The National Parks Act 1980 has a very similar purpose and reference to intrinsic worth, but for national parks:

Principles to be applied in national parks

4. Parks to be Maintained in Natural State, and Public to Have Right of Entry

(1) It is hereby declared that the provisions of this Act shall have effect for the purpose of preserving in perpetuity as national parks, for their intrinsic worth and for the benefit, use, and enjoyment of the public, areas of New Zealand that contain scenery of such distinctive quality, ecological systems, or natural features so beautiful, unique, or scientifically important that their preservation is in the national interest.

(2) It is hereby further declared that, having regard to the general purposes specified in subsection (1), national parks shall be so administered and maintained under the provisions of this Act that:

(a) they shall be preserved as far as possible in their natural state:

(b) except where the Authority otherwise determines, the native plants and animals of the parks shall as far as possible be preserved and the introduced plants and animals shall as far as possible be exterminated:

[7] The ordinary meaning of the text is interpreted in light of the purpose of the legislation: Interpretation Act 1999, § 5(1).

[8] *Summit Road Society (Inc.) v. Minister of Conservation*, 14 NZTPA 216 (1990) (N.Z.).

(c) sites and objects of archaeological and historical interest shall as far as possible be preserved:
(d) their value as soil, water, and forest conservation areas shall be maintained:
(e) subject to the provisions of this Act and to the imposition of such conditions and restrictions as may be necessary for the preservation of the native plants and animals or for the welfare in general of the parks, the public shall have freedom of entry and access to the parks, so that they may receive in full measure the inspiration, enjoyment, recreation, and other benefits that may be derived from mountains, forests, sounds, seacoasts, lakes, rivers, and other natural features.

As with the Reserves Act, the term *intrinsic worth* is not further defined in the statute, so it is similarly left to take its ordinary meaning. To date, it has not been considered by courts in any manner that has refined the meaning of the "intrinsic worth" of the parks.

The Conservation Act 1987 refers to *intrinsic values* three times when defining "conservation," "nature conservation," and "preservation":

> ***conservation*** means the preservation and protection of natural and historic resources for the purpose of maintaining their intrinsic values, providing for their appreciation and recreational enjoyment by the public, and safeguarding the options of future generations
>
> ***nature conservation*** means the preservation and protection of the natural resources of New Zealand, having regard to their intrinsic values and having special regard to indigenous flora and fauna, natural ecosystems, and landscape
>
> ***preservation***, in relation to a resource, means the maintenance, so far as is practicable, of its intrinsic values

Conservation is the goal and purpose of the Act, and the drafting makes it clear that intrinsic worth is a key factor in decisions about what to conserve, preserve, and protect. For example, the purpose of the Act is stated in its Long Title: "An Act to promote the conservation of New Zealand's natural and historic resources, and for that purpose to establish a Department of Conservation." The New Zealand Supreme Court has held that the definition of "conservation" and its inclusion in the purpose of the Act means that the existence of "intrinsic conservation values" are key to the existence and protection of conservation land; only where such values no longer exist can the protected status of conservation land be revoked.[9] Thus, intrinsic values, as vaguely defined and as anthropocentrically discerned as they may be, have enabled the strong protection sought by the Act.

[9] *Hawke's Bay Regional Investment Co Ltd v. Royal Forest and Bird Protection Society of New Zealand Inc* [2017] 1 NZLR 1041 (N.Z.). In this judicial review, the conservation status of land was unable to be revoked for a dam, as it still had inherent conservation value. The Minister's (highly politically charged) decision to revoke that conservation status was quashed.

The Marine and Coastal Area (Takutai Moana) Act 2011, also in the purpose of the Act:

> recognises, through the protection of public rights of access, navigation, and fishing, the importance of the common Marine and coastal area—
>
> (i) for its intrinsic worth; and
> (ii) for the benefit, use, and enjoyment of the public of New Zealand.

The meaning of "intrinsic worth" again is not provided in the legislation, nor is it addressed in commentaries on the legislation. It has not been considered by courts in the context of the Takutai Moana Act.

The Resource Management Act 1991 refers to "intrinsic values of ecosystems" in one of the sections containing the overriding principles governing decision-making section 7(d). These provisions are cited in their entirety below, as their hierarchy and comparison within the overall scheme is important to their interpretation. Helpfully, the term is defined in the statute:

> ***intrinsic values***, in relation to ecosystems, means those aspects of ecosystems and their constituent parts which have value in their own right, including—
>
> (a) their biological and genetic diversity; and
> (b) the essential characteristics that determine an ecosystem's integrity, form, functioning, and resilience." . . .
>
> **5. Purpose**
>
> (1) The purpose of this Act is to promote the *sustainable management* of natural and physical resources.
> (2) In this Act, sustainable management means managing the use, development, and protection of natural and physical resources in a way, or at a rate, which enables people and communities to provide for their social, economic, and cultural well-being and for their health and safety while—
>
> > (a) sustaining the potential of natural and physical resources (excluding minerals) to meet the reasonably foreseeable needs of future generations; and
> > (b) safeguarding the life-supporting capacity of air, water, soil, and ecosystems; and
> > (c) avoiding, remedying, or mitigating any adverse effects of activities on the environment.
>
> **6. Matters of National Importance**
>
> In achieving the purpose of this Act, all persons exercising functions and powers under it, in relation to managing the use, development, and protection of natural and physical resources, *shall recognise and provide* for the following matters of national importance:

(a) the preservation of the natural character of the coastal environment (including the coastal marine area), wetlands, and lakes and rivers and their margins, and the protection of them from inappropriate subdivision, use, and development:
(b) the protection of outstanding natural features and landscapes from inappropriate subdivision, use, and development:
(c) the protection of areas of significant indigenous vegetation and significant habitats of indigenous fauna:
(d) the maintenance and enhancement of public access to and along the coastal marine area, lakes, and rivers:
(e) the relationship of Māori and their culture and traditions with their ancestral lands, water, sites, waahi tapu, and other taonga:[10]
(f) the protection of historic heritage from inappropriate subdivision, use, and development:
(g) the protection of protected customary rights:
(h) the management of significant risks from natural hazards.

7. Other Matters

In achieving the purpose of this Act, all persons exercising functions and powers under it, in relation to managing the use, development, and protection of natural and physical resources, *shall have particular regard to*—

(a) kaitiakitanga:[11]

(aa) the ethic of stewardship:

(b) the efficient use and development of natural and physical resources:

(ba) the efficiency of the end use of energy:

(c) the maintenance and enhancement of amenity values:
(d) intrinsic values of ecosystems:
(e) [Repealed]
(f) maintenance and enhancement of the quality of the environment:
(g) any finite characteristics of natural and physical resources:
(h) the protection of the habitat of trout and salmon:
(i) the effects of climate change:
(j) the benefits to be derived from the use and development of renewable energy.

[10] The term *waahi tapu* is not defined in the RMA. The Heritage New Zealand Pouhere Taonga Act 2014 Act defines wāhi tapu to mean a place sacred to Māori in the traditional, spiritual, religious, ritual, or mythological sense. A *taonga* in Māori culture is a treasured thing, whether tangible or intangible.
[11] This is a Māori term meaning guardianship or stewardship and responsibility for land and resources. For discussion of the use of Māori terms in New Zealand legislation, *see, e.g.*, Catherine Iorns Magallanes, *The Use of "Tangata Whenua" and "Mana Whenua" in New Zealand Legislation: Attempts at Cultural Recognition*, 42(2) VICTORIA U. OF WELLINGTON L.R. 259-76 (2011).

8. Treaty of Waitangi

> In achieving the purpose of this Act, all persons exercising functions and powers under it, in relation to managing the use, development, and protection of natural and physical resources, shall take into account the principles of the Treaty of Waitangi (Te Tiriti o Waitangi).

The application of section 7(d), the "intrinsic values of ecosystems," has been considered by the courts in a few cases. This provision, significantly, does not have as much weight as those in section 6, which decision-makers "shall recognise and provide for"; they need only "have particular regard to" the intrinsic values of ecosystems.[12] Thus, intrinsic values are not as fundamental to the definition of what is to be protected or to decision-making under the Resource Management Act as they are in the context of the Conservation Act.

An illustration of section 7(d) being outweighed by other factors is provided by an Environment Court decision on an application for an open cast coal mine on a plateau containing rare plant species and a unique and endangered ecosystem within New Zealand. The Environment Court considered the application of section 7(d), with a focus on the ecosystem integrity:

> Section 7(d) requires particular regard for the intrinsic value of ecosystems. We have no doubt that if the mine is consented on the conditions proposed there will be a reduction in the value of ecosystems on the mine site. Connectivity and the current assemblages will be disrupted or lost by changes such as the loss of some plant species are likely to be permanently lost to the site, and some of those have considerable rarity value. The range and volume of invertebrates will be reduced for a considerable period, along with the various eco-system services they provide. We accept that elsewhere on the plateau weed-control and predator control will assist in protecting and enhancing the ecosystems present, but the very considerable likelihood of the complete loss of rare plant species from the mine site and the Barren Valley gives us particular concern in these terms, and we urged BCL [Buller Coal Limited] during the hearing to consider whether adverse effects on that area could be avoided if the proposal were otherwise consented.[13]

In addition, the Environment Court found that "there is clearly an adverse effect on the proposal on significant habitats of indigenous fauna," with it being "a century or more before similar habitats to those presently existing would be available on the mine site."[14] However, despite these factors, the court granted the mining consent, agreeing to the applicant's suggested biodiversity offsets in order to mitigate the clear biodiversity losses that would occur from the mining.

[12] For an overview of § 7 and how it operates within the RMA, *see Environmental Defence Society Inc v. New Zealand King Salmon Company Ltd* (2014) NZSC 41 at 26 (N.Z.). The matters in § 7 are important considerations to be born in mind at every stage of the planning process. *See McGuire v Hastings District Council*, NZRMA 557 at 21 (2001) (N.Z.).

[13] *West Coast Environmental Network Inc. v. West Coast Regional Council and Buller District Council* (2013) NZEnvC 47 at 319 (N.Z.).

[14] *Id.* at 324.

In the other RMA decisions to consider section 7(d), the courts did not discuss the meaning of "intrinsic value" in any detail but merely asserted that it would be upheld by the promotion of conservation measures. For example, in relation to the use of a particular poison to control introduced and invasive pests within a wildlife sanctuary, the parties disagreed about the effects of this poison on intrinsic values of ecosystems.[15] The High Court considered that pest eradication in the name of conservation "satisfies the RMA promotion of protection of natural resources and ecosystems with intrinsic value" because of the ultimate aim of protecting and conserving such ecosystems, but did not discuss any more detail.

As another example, in an appeal relating to a consent given for a solid waste landfill, intrinsic ecological values were identified as a reason in favor of imposing conditions in relation to the protection of indigenous vegetation.[16] Four hundred hectares of land surrounding the landfill would be revegetated and turned into a conservation area. The Environment Court was persuaded that the proposed conservation area would produce significant ecosystem benefits and "that the intrinsic values of the ecosystems would at least be maintained and, in all probability, significantly enhanced as a result of the restoration project and conservation management area."[17] There was no discussion of the intrinsic value, more just the assertion that it would be upheld.

In another case, the Environment Court stated that "[a] huge part of this case is about the intrinsic values of ecosystems."[18] However, there was similarly no separate discussion of what intrinsic value meant, just discussion — albeit extensive — of the preservation of indigenous flora and fauna. The case concerned hydroelectric power generation on a river, where a key concern was the effect of changed water flows on water quality in the river, on freshwater species within that river, and on the lower braided areas of the river and the wetlands downstream that were significant habitats for native flora and fauna. Local Māori guardians offered evidence that the *mauri*— the spiritual value — of the river would be significantly adversely affected. The Court agreed "that there will be a general adverse effect on the mauri" of the river. While that would be partly offset by conditions enhancing aquatics diversity, wetlands, and braided river birds, all of which contribute to that *mauri*, "there remains a net loss to the mauri of the river."[19] Despite this, the court considered that the proposal would be of net benefit to the community, in light of the renewable energy generation. The court was accordingly prepared to grant consents for the water diversions as long as conditions were amended to better protect wetlands and the braided river birds.[20]

The Hazardous Substances and New Organisms Act 1996 has a provision similar to that in the Resource Management Act, whereby "the intrinsic value of ecosystems" is

[15] *Brook Valley Community Group Inc v. The Trustees of the Brook Waimarama Sanctuary Trust* (2018) NZRMA 51, at 20 (N.Z.).

[16] *Transwaste Canterbury Ltd v. Canterbury Regional Council*, NZEnvC, Decision C29/2004 (22 March 2004) at 284 (N.Z.).

[17] *Id.* at 266.

[18] *Lower Waitaki River Management Society Inc v. Canterbury Regional Council & Meridian Energy Ltd*, NZEnvC, Decision C80/2009 (24 September 2009) at 231 (N.Z.).

[19] *Id.* at 457, 519.

[20] *Id.* at 558. It is noted that this judgment runs to 241 pages, with an additional 40 pages of Annexures. There are 560 paragraphs and more than 800 footnotes. The environmental issues are discussed in detail.

one of a list of six matters that decision-makers must "take into account" when exercising functions under the Act.[21] This Act also contains the definition of "intrinsic values" adopted in the RMA:

> **intrinsic values**, in relation to ecosystems, means those aspects of ecosystems and their constituent parts which have value in their own right, including—
>
> (a) their biological and genetic diversity; and
> (b) the essential characteristics that determine an ecosystem's integrity, form, functioning, and resilience.

Professional legal practice guides to this legislation suggest that interpretations of the equivalent "RMA provisions are likely to provide some guidance in interpreting these provisions of the HSNO Act."[22] In other words, the academic legal community expects the meaning of nature's intrinsic value will become to be understood as transcending specific laws.

III. LEGISLATIVE RECOGNITION THAT ANIMALS ARE SENTIENT BEINGS

In 2015, the New Zealand Parliament passed amendments to the 1999 animal welfare legislation, as a result of the first review of that legislation since 1999. On May 10, 2015, section 4 of the Animal Welfare Amendment Act (No. 2) explicitly included a recognition that animals are sentient. This followed campaigning from animal rights and welfare advocates, such that the government department responsible for the review recommended that it be recognized in the title to the Act and/or a preamble.

> **Title of the Animal Welfare Act 1999:**
>
> An Act—
>
> (a) to reform the law relating to the welfare of animals and the prevention of their ill-treatment; and, in particular,—
>
> (i) to recognise that animals are sentient:
>
> (ia) to require owners of animals, and persons in charge of animals, to attend properly to the welfare of those animals:
>
> (ii) to specify conduct that is or is not permissible in relation to any animal or class of animals:
> (iii) to provide a process for approving the use of animals in research, testing, and teaching:

[21] Hazardous Substances and New Organisms Act 1996, § 6(b).
[22] D Randal, "Hazardous Substances and New Organisms Act 1996", *Environmental and Resource Management Law Online*, LexisNexis, at 11.5 (Nov 2019).

(iv) to establish a National Animal Welfare Advisory Committee and a National Animal Ethics Advisory Committee:

(v) to provide for the development and issue of codes of welfare and the approval of codes of ethical conduct: . . .

The term sentient is not defined in the Act. The only other section where sentience is referred to is in relation to approvals for animals in research, testing, and teaching. A purpose of the provisions on the use of animals in research, testing, and teaching is "to replace animals as subjects for research, and testing by substituting, where appropriate, non-sentient or non-living alternatives."[23] Two of the criteria for assessing applications for animal use are accordingly: "the extent to which there has been— (i) assessment of the suitability of using non-sentient or non-living alternatives in the project; and (ii) replacement of animals as subjects with suitable non-sentient or non-living alternatives.[24] Consequently, the prime practical effect of the use of the word (and concept) "sentient" will be via statutory interpretation, as courts are required to interpret the text of all legislation "in light of its purpose."[25]

Neither the Explanatory Note to the Amendment Bill nor the parliamentary debates on it discussed the inclusion of "sentient," indicating that it was not officially seen as being of much significance. The government ministry responsible for the Act categorized it as merely a "minor and technical amendment"[26] and a symbolic gesture that "would not affect the detail of the rights, duties or obligations set out within the body of the Act."[27] Some critics have called it "political puffery to maintain New Zealand's reputation for the sake of appearances to overseas markets, and window dressing to appease New Zealand's animal welfare groups."[28]

In contrast, the New Zealand Veterinary Association says that the legal recognition of animal sentience for the first time in New Zealand law is one of the "key changes" to the legislation. Its inclusion "strongly reinforces that people are obliged to meet their animals' physical health and behavioural needs, and places New Zealand at the 'forefront of progressive animal welfare legislation.' "[29]

[23] Animal Welfare Act 1999, § 80.

[24] Animal Welfare Act 1999, § 100(1)(fa); inserted, on 9 November 2015, by § 41(3) of the Animal Welfare Amendment Act (No 2) 2015 (2015 No 49).

[25] Interpretation Act 1999, § 5(1).

[26] Ministry of Primary Industries, "Overview of the Animal Welfare Amendment Bill: Updated following the Select Committee Process," https://www.mpi.govt.nz/dmsdocument/6766.

[27] Ministry for Primary Industries *Animal Welfare Amendment Bill: Report for the Ministry of Primary Industries* (Feb. 2014) at 69.

[28] Ian Robertson & Daniel Goldsworthy, "To Feel or Not to Feel; That is the Legal Question" 2017 NZLJ 10, at 10.

[29] New Zealand Veterinary Association, Press release, "Landmark Animal Welfare Legislation Welcomed by Vets, Scoop (May 5, 2015), https://www.scoop.co.nz/stories/PO1505/S00047/landmark-animal-welfare-legislation-welcomed-by-vets.htm.

In between these positions, the chair of the National Animal Ethics Advisory Committee said it was "another step along the animal welfare journey" and "provided a stronger underpinning" for the other provisions in the legislation.[30]

A submission by the Society for the Prevention of Cruelty to Animals (SPCA) argued that the declaration of sentience was needed "because most New Zealand law treats animals as 'things' and 'objects' rather than as living creatures." A regional SPCA manager accordingly "hoped that recognising animals as sentient beings would add 'more weight' to abuse and neglect cases in court."[31] This may indeed have happened already, as the recognition "that animals are sentient" was acknowledged by the New Zealand Court of Appeal as one of the particular purposes of the act relevant to sentencing for a conviction of extreme animal cruelty.[32] However, it is hard to say that the same result could not have been achieved without that clause, as it was only one of quite a few things listed, and the animal's suffering was already a key aspect of the prosecution and sentencing.

Another concrete suggestion for a positive effect of the recognition of sentience is that it could expand the responsibilities of animal caregivers. At present, the expectations for compliance with animal welfare standards focuses on avoiding pain and suffering. Sentience incorporates the fact that animals can experience pleasure as well as pain, so some writers argue that it must extend the duties on caregivers to adequately provide for positive experiences for animals, not just avoid negative ones.[33]

Finally, some legal advocates suggest that this paves the way for the introduction of class actions on behalf of animals.[34] Perhaps the next "step along the animal welfare journey" that sentience paves, after recognition of animals as beings with feelings, is the recognition of animals as legal persons, with all the legal implications that that may have.[35] Through the unique relationship between the Māori and the New Zealand government, and thoughtful creative problem-solving, law has been developed to more effectively protect sentient beings. As courts consider and construe the meaning of "sentience," they will determine how broadly it may be construed.

[30] As quoted in Jonathan Carson, "New Zealand Legally Recognises Animals as 'Sentient' Beings," STUFF (May 9, 2015), https://www.stuff.co.nz/nelson-mail/68363264/new-zealand-legally-recognises-animals-as-sentient-beings.
[31] *Id.*
[32] *Auckland Royal New Zealand Society for the Prevention of Cruelty to Animals v. MacPherson* [2019] NZDC 4102 (N.Z.). In this case the defendant used sustained and extreme violence, breaking a dog's leg into pieces, with the extent of the injuries and lack of treatment causing the dog severe pain, distress, and suffering. The defendant was imprisoned and ordered to pay reparations for the veterinary and other costs.
[33] Robertson & Goldsworthy, *supra* note 28, at 12-13. This is in line with the expansion of the older Five Freedoms model to the Five Domains and a focus on quality of life overall.
[34] *Id.* at 10.
[35] See Chapter 11, "Nonhuman Rights," in this book.

IV. LEGAL PERSONALITY FOR NATURE

As with other settled countries around the world with surviving Indigenous peoples, Māori have made legal and political claims to lands and resources that they have lost through settlement. New Zealand is widely regarded as being at the forefront of initiatives to recognize Indigenous rights and resolve such claims, including the co-management and co-governance of New Zealand's land and resources with Māori.

New Zealand does not recognize any human right to a healthy environment, nor have existing human rights been extended to enable any remedies for violations through degraded environments. However, the recognition of Indigenous rights and the resolution of claims based on the land taken by the British from the Māori has led to the recognition of Indigenous environmental rights and responsibilities. Through the protection of Indigenous worldviews and Indigenous environmental management, this particular combination has entailed the adoption of measures for environmental protection that go beyond simple claims to rights to also implement complex notions of responsibility and guardianship on the part of individuals, communities, and the state. It is through this recognition and system for resolving the Indigenous people's grievances that the legislature has adopted the innovative use of legal personhood for natural features.

A. Māori Environmental Philosophies

Māori cultural beliefs view natural and geographical features as ancestors.[36] It is the responsibility of Māori today to act as guardians and care for their environmental ancestors, which will in turn protect and look after the people. The environment is believed to be inhabited by spirits, such that each environmental feature has its own spirit and life force; human actions must maintain this life force. Part of being ancestrally connected to nature means that humans are not considered separate from or above it, and they cannot own it. What is important for the interplay between human rights and the environment is that they are intertwined: human well-being exists in tandem with that of the nonhuman natural world, and each cares for the other. It is no coincidence that these beliefs are held by Indigenous peoples worldwide.

Over the last 40 years, the ability of Māori as Indigenous peoples to manage natural resources[37] in a way that is consistent with a Māori worldview has gradually been incorporated in New Zealand law through Treaty of Waitangi grievance settlements, judicial decisions, and domestic legislation, as well as through local, regional, and national policy.[38] It is noteworthy that this covers publicly owned lands and resources, not just ones currently owned by Māori, and that this has occurred within a Western

[36] For more detail, *see* Catherine Iorns Magallanes, *Māori Cultural Rights in Aotearoa New Zealand: Protecting the Cosmology that Protects the Environment*, 21(2) Widener L. Rev. 273-327 (2015).
[37] As with other chapters, "natural resources" is used here to describe the elements of nature commonly utilized by humankind, although the editors of this book acknowledge the need to begin describing nature beyond its economic utility to humans as a resource.
[38] Alan Ward, An Unsettled History: Treaty Claims in New Zealand Today 34 (1999).

legal system. In particular, Māori cosmology, including the spiritual relationship with the environment, has become a required consideration in most environmental decision-making and has even been given "primacy" as a matter of national importance when balancing competing factors.[39] Decision-makers under the Resource Management Act are also required to pay particular regard to traditional Māori *kaitiakitanga* (guardianship) or stewardship of natural resources.[40] This started with court decisions upholding the importance of the Treaty and is now enshrined in the Resource Management Act.[41]

Māori relationships with the natural world have also been recognized and protected through grievance settlement agreements between the New Zealand government and Māori, and these are enshrined in legislation. Over the last 30 years, the government and claimants have devised a wide range of options to recognize and restore Māori tribal spiritual, cultural, and traditional associations with the natural environment, as well as to recognize and restore Māori cultural authority.[42] They have included joint management of lands and resources between the government and Māori and tribal ownership of natural sites of great cultural significance to the tribes, including the beds of rivers and lakes.[43] The most significant of these measures has been the recent creation of separate legal personality for natural beings, such as rivers, with joint tribal/government representation and guardianship of that being's interests.[44]

Accordingly, legal personhood or personality to natural beings—such as rivers, mountains, and even broad areas of territory comprising ecosystems—is being increasingly argued and used as a tool to accord rights to nature and/or better implement human responsibility for it.[45] New Zealand has legislatively accorded personhood to a river and to what was a national park and, at the time of this writing, has agreed to do so for a mountain. The legislation does not explicitly recognize rights of nature in the sense rights are generally recognized in legal systems. It was not designed primarily to prevent or remedy environmental degradation. Rather, the legislation was designed to implement a Māori Indigenous vision of human responsibility for and relationship with our natural environment and was done to better uphold Indigenous people's rights. While the legislation recognizes the intrinsic value of the environment—i.e., in its own right—it also recognizes that people are part of the environment and it is intended to promote co-existence between people and all natural environments.

[39] *Environmental Defence Society, Inc. v. Mangonui County Council* (1989) 3 NZLR 257 (CA) (N.Z.).

[40] Resource Management Act 1991, § 7.

[41] Resource Management Act 1991, §§ 6-8.

[42] *See, e.g.,* Dean Cowie, *The Treaty Settlement Process, in* Treaty of Waitangi Settlements 48, 61 (J. Hayward & N. Wheen eds., 2012).

[43] *See, e.g.,* the Ngai Tahu Claims Settlement Act 1998; Office of Treaty Settlements (2015), (n 66) at 90-94.

[44] Te Awa Tupua (Whanganui River Claims Settlement) Act 2017 and Te Urewera Act 2014. *See also* Iorns Magallanes, *supra* note 36.

[45] *See, e.g,* S. Ravi Rajan, Catherine Iorns Magallanes & Kirsten Davies, *Identifying Human Rights and the Environment,* Encyclopedia of Human Rights and the Environment, 183, at notes 12-19 (James R May & Erin Daly eds., 2019).

B. Te Urewera[46]

Te Urewera National Park was created in the 1950s out of ancestral land confiscated from the Māori Tūhoe people.[47] This was the subject of a grievance against the government, the settlement of which culminated in the Te Urewera Act 2014.[48] Key to this settlement was Tūhoe regaining control of the Te Urewera National Park and the ability to exercise its *kaitiakitanga* (guardianship) over Te Urewera, along with explicit acknowledgment of the metaphysical relationship of Tūhoe with their ancestral land.[49] The method of achieving this was through the creation of legal personhood for the park, whereby Te Urewera would obtain its own separate identity, with the establishment of a legal guardian for Te Urewera. What was a national park can now be governed independently, with significant Tūhoe input and in accordance with Tūhoe protocol and custom.

Under this agreement, Te Urewera is no longer a national park. It is its own legal entity, with "all the rights, powers, duties, and liabilities of a legal person."[50] This legal status permits Te Urewera to hold title to land (i.e., title to itself), which is managed by its guardian, the Te Urewera Board, that acts "on behalf of, and in the name of, Te Urewera." A detailed discussion of this guardianship arrangement is presented in Chapter 6, "Legal Guardianship and Representation."

Board membership is a mix of Tūhoe trustees and government appointees. The Act grants the Board extensive powers and obligations, including the power to make by-laws and to grant activity permits within Te Urewera. Tūhoe spirituality is directly provided for in Board decision-making. The principles governing the implementation of the Act focus primarily on aspects of environmental protection but are also protective of Indigenous relationships with the park and of public access for the benefit of all New Zealanders.

The Board released their management plan for Te Urewera, *Te Kawa o Te Urewera,* in 2017 ("Te Kawa").[51] This plan shows a new vision of the rights and responsibilities between humans and the environment. The overriding purpose of Te Kawa is to delineate dignity and command respect for nature and to reaffirm the subordinate place of humans within it.[52] It emphasizes duty and "responsibility ... not power or rights" throughout the document. It expressly states: "[T]he Board through Te Kawa is disrupting the notion of our false superiority over the natural world ... we are returning to our place in nature, as her child."[53]

[46] This description of Te Urewera is adapted from Catherine Iorns Magallanes, "Human rights, responsibility and legal personality for the Environment in Aotearoa New Zealand", ENCYCLOPEDIA OF HUMAN RIGHTS AND THE ENVIRONMENT, 550, at 554-555 (James R May & Erin Daly, eds., 2019).

[47] Department of Conservation, *Te Urewera National Park Management Plan* 1 (2003). *See also* Ngai Tuhoe, *Te Urewera* (2015), http://www.ngaituhoe.iwi.nz/te-urewera.

[48] Tangata Whenua (2012) "Historic Treaty Settlement for Tuhoe," 11 September, 2012. Retrieved 30 June 2017 from http://news.tangatawhenua.com/2012/09/historic-treaty-settlement-for-tuhoe/.

[49] Te Urewera Act 2014, § 9(36).

[50] *Id.* at § 11(1).

[51] *Te Kawa o Te Urewera: The Te Urewera Management Plan* (2017), http://www.ngaituhoe.iwi.nz/Te-Kawa-o-Te-Urewera.

[52] *Id.* at p. 15.

[53] *Id.*

Excerpts from Te Urewera Act 2014

PART 1: TE UREWERA

Subpart 1—Background, Purpose, and Principles

3. Background to this Act

Te Urewera

(1) Te Urewera is ancient and enduring, a fortress of nature, alive with history; its scenery is abundant with mystery, adventure, and remote beauty.
(2) Te Urewera is a place of spiritual value, with its own mana and mauri.
(3) Te Urewera has an identity in and of itself, inspiring people to commit to its care.

Te Urewera and Tūhoe

(4) For Tūhoe, Te Urewera is Te Manawa o te Ika a Māui; it is the heart of the great fish of Māui, its name being derived from Murakareke, the son of the ancestor Tūhoe.
(5) For Tūhoe, Te Urewera is their ewe whenua, their place of origin and return, their homeland.
(6) Te Urewera expresses and gives meaning to Tūhoe culture, language, customs, and identity. There Tūhoe hold mana by ahikāroa; they are tangata whenua and kaitiaki of Te Urewera.

Te Urewera and all New Zealanders

(7) Te Urewera is prized by other iwi and hapū who have acknowledged special associations with, and customary interests in, parts of Te Urewera.
(8) Te Urewera is also prized by all New Zealanders as a place of outstanding national value and intrinsic worth; it is treasured by all for the distinctive natural values of its vast and rugged primeval forest, and for the integrity of those values; for its indigenous ecological systems and biodiversity, its historical and cultural heritage, its scientific importance, and as a place for outdoor recreation and spiritual reflection.

Tūhoe and the Crown: shared views and intentions

(9) Tūhoe and the Crown share the view that Te Urewera should have legal recognition in its own right, with the responsibilities for its care and conservation set out in the law of New Zealand. To this end, Tūhoe and the Crown have together taken a unique approach, as set out in this Act, to protecting Te Urewera in a way that reflects New Zealand's culture and values.
(10) The Crown and Tūhoe intend this Act to contribute to resolving the grief of Tūhoe and to strengthening and maintaining the connection between Tūhoe and Te Urewera.

4. Purpose of this Act

The purpose of Parts 5 to 7 is to establish and preserve in perpetuity a legal identity and protected status for Te Urewera for its intrinsic worth, its distinctive natural and cultural values, the integrity of those values, and for its national importance, and in particular to—

(a) strengthen and maintain the connection between Tūhoe and Te Urewera; and
(b) preserve as far as possible the natural features and beauty of Te Urewera, the integrity of its indigenous ecological systems and biodiversity, and its historical and cultural heritage; and
(c) provide for Te Urewera as a place for public use and enjoyment, for recreation, learning, and spiritual reflection, and as an inspiration for all.

5. Principles for implementing this Act

(1) In achieving the purpose of this Act, all persons performing functions and exercising powers under this Act must act so that, as far as possible,—

(a) Te Urewera is preserved in its natural state:
(b) the indigenous ecological systems and biodiversity of Te Urewera are preserved, and introduced plants and animals are exterminated:
(c) Tūhoetanga, which gives expression to Te Urewera, is valued and respected:
(d) the relationship of other iwi and hapū with parts of Te Urewera is recognised, valued, and respected:
(e) the historical and cultural heritage of Te Urewera is preserved:
(f) the value of Te Urewera for soil, water, and forest conservation is maintained:
(g) the contribution that Te Urewera can make to conservation nationally is recognised.

(2) In achieving the purpose of this Act, all persons performing functions and exercising powers under this Act must act so that the public has freedom of entry and access to Te Urewera, subject to any conditions and restrictions that may be necessary to achieve the purpose of this Act or for public safety. . . .

Subpart 3: Legal Identity of Te Urewera and Vesting of Te Urewera Land

Legal entity

11. Te Urewera Declared to be Legal Entity

(1) Te Urewera is a legal entity, and has all the rights, powers, duties, and liabilities of a legal person.
(2) However,—

(a) the rights, powers, and duties of Te Urewera must be exercised and performed on behalf of, and in the name of, Te Urewera—

(i) by Te Urewera Board; and
(ii) in the manner provided for in this Act; and

(b) the liabilities are the responsibility of Te Urewera Board, except as provided for in section 96. . . .

13. Te Urewera Land Inalienable

Te Urewera land must not be alienated, mortgaged, charged, or otherwise disposed of, except—

(a) in accordance with section 111; or
(b) if a lease or an easement is granted under section 62(1). . . .

PART 2: GOVERNANCE AND MANAGEMENT OF TE UREWERA

Subpart 1—Te Urewera Board

Purposes, functions, and powers of Board

17. Purposes of Board

The purposes of the Board are—

(a) to act on behalf of, and in the name of, Te Urewera; and
(b) to provide governance for Te Urewera in accordance with this Act.

18. Functions of Board

(1) The functions of the Board are—

(a) to prepare and approve Te Urewera management plan; and
(b) to advise the persons managing Te Urewera on the implementation of the management plan, including by means such as—

(i) issuing an annual statement of priorities for implementing the management plan:
(ii) undertaking any specified functions in relation to the annual operational plan for Te Urewera:
(iii) monitoring the implementation of the annual operational plan; and

(c) to initiate proposals and make recommendations for—

(i) adding land to, or removing land from, Te Urewera; and
(ii) acquiring interests in land; and
(iii) establishing specially protected areas, wilderness areas, and amenity areas within Te Urewera; and

(d) to make bylaws for Te Urewera; and
(e) to authorise activities that must not otherwise be undertaken in Te Urewera without an authorisation under Part 2; and
(f) to prepare or commission reports, advice, or recommendations on matters relevant to the purposes of the Board; and
(g) to promote or advocate for the interests of Te Urewera in any statutory process or at any public forum; and
(h) to liaise with, advise, or seek advice from any agency, local authority, or other entity on matters relevant to the purposes of the Board; and
(i) to perform any other function of the Board specified in this Act or in any other enactment; and
(j) to take any other action that the Board considers to be relevant and appropriate in achieving its purposes.

(2) In performing its functions, the Board may consider and give expression to—

(a) Tūhoetanga: [cultural characteristics specific to the Tūhoe]
(b) Tūhoe concepts of management such as—

(i) rāhui:
(ii) tapu me noa:
(iii) mana me mauri:
(iv) tohu.

(3) In this section, in accordance with the understanding of Tūhoe,—

mana me mauri conveys a sense of the sensitive perception of a living and spiritual force in a place

rāhui conveys the sense of the prohibition or limitation of a use for an appropriate reason

tapu means a state or condition that requires certain respectful human conduct, including raising awareness or knowledge of the spiritual qualities requiring respect

tapu me noa conveys, in tapu, the concept of sanctity, a state that requires respectful human behaviour in a place; and in noa, the sense that when the tapu is lifted from the place, the place returns to a normal state

tohu connotes the metaphysical or symbolic depiction of things. . . .

20. Decision Making Affecting Relationship of Iwi and Hapū with Te Urewera

(1) The Board must consider and provide appropriately for the relationship of iwi and hapū and their culture and traditions with Te Urewera when making decisions, including—

(a) the approval of Te Urewera management plan; and
(b) the adoption of the Board's annual statement of priorities; and
(c) the acceptance of the annual operational plan; and

(d) the making of a recommendation to add land to Te Urewera or remove land from Te Urewera; and
(e) the making of a recommendation to establish a specially protected area, a wilderness area, or an amenity area; and
(f) the grant of an activity permit or a concession in Te Urewera; and
(g) the imposition of controls on access to parts of Te Urewera; and
(h) the making of bylaws.

(2) The purpose of subsection (1) is to recognise and reflect—

(a) Tūhoetanga; and
(b) the Crown's responsibility under the Treaty of Waitangi (Te Tiriti o Waitangi)....

Subpart 2—Te Urewera Management Plan

Preparation, approval, purpose, and scope of plan

44. Obligation on Board to Prepare and Approve Management Plan for Te Urewera

(1) The Board must prepare and approve Te Urewera management plan in accordance with this subpart.
(2) Public notice, as required by clause 19(1)(c) of Schedule 2, must be given not later than 1 year after the settlement date that a draft management plan is to be prepared....

45. Purpose of Te Urewera Management Plan

The purpose of Te Urewera management plan is—

(a) to identify how the purpose of this Act is to be achieved through the management of Te Urewera; and
(b) to set objectives and policies for Te Urewera.

46. Contents of Te Urewera Management Plan

(1) The management plan must—

(a) state the objectives and policies for the integrated management of Te Urewera; and
(b) identify relevant values at places within Te Urewera, including values relating to—

(i) indigenous species, habitats, and ecosystems; and
(ii) cultural and historical heritage; and
(iii) recreational values; and
(iv) scenic, geological, soil, and landform features; and
(v) freshwater fisheries and freshwater fish habitats; and

(c) identify the outcomes planned for specified places within Te Urewera—

(i) that are consistent with the values under paragraph (b); and
(ii) that take into account relevant national species recovery and management objectives; and

(d) explain how any conflicts between planned outcomes will be resolved; and
(e) identify any effects of activities undertaken within Te Urewera and explain how adverse effects are to be minimised; and
(f) identify any places in Te Urewera that have been given international recognition in agreements ratified or given legal standing in New Zealand and provide for the management of those places accordingly, where this is consistent with the purpose of this Act; and
(g) identify whether there is a need to create specially protected areas, wilderness areas, or amenity areas; and
(h) identify the criteria for decision making in respect of Te Urewera, including decisions on applications for activity permits and concessions; and
(i) identify what regular monitoring and evaluation of Te Urewera ought to be undertaken; and
(j) identify the matters proposed to be regulated by bylaws. . . .

Subpart 4—Authorisation of Certain Activities in Te Urewera

Activity permits

58. Activities Requiring Activity Permit

The following activities must not be undertaken in Te Urewera unless they are authorised by an activity permit issued by the Board:

(a) taking, cutting, or destroying any plant, whether indigenous or exotic:
(b) disturbing, trapping, taking, hunting, or killing any animal, whether indigenous or exotic (other than sports fish):
(c) possessing dead protected wildlife for any cultural or other purpose:
(d) entering specially protected areas:
(e) making a road or altering an existing road:
(f) establishing accommodation:
(g) farming:
(h) recreational hunting:
(i) any activity that would otherwise be an offence under this Act.

In relation to liabilities, section 96 of the Act provides that Te Urewera is not liable for local government land taxes, nor for levies to fund any rural fire district authorities, nor for contamination of any Te Urewera land if the contamination occurred before it became a legal person.

C. The Management Plan: Te Kawa o Te Urewera[54]

The first words that greet you in (the English version of) Te Kawa o Te Urewera (Te Kawa) are "**Nature wills that there is no end to life,**" in bold 72-point font. As such a beginning indicates, Te Kawa is like no other management plan. It was deliberately written to establish the principles to guide the decisions of the board and the setting of operational management plans under the legislation. As board Chairman Tamati Kruger said at the time:

> Te Kawa does not work the same way as other management plans, which focus on setting rules and stock-taking. . . . That traditional approach can frame nature as a set of discrete resources to be managed and used. Te Kawa is different. It asks us to stop and reflect on Te Urewera and what that means as a living system. A living system we depend on for survival, culture, recreation, and inspiration. Te Urewera has its own identity that is legal, but also physical, environmental, cultural and spiritual. . . .
>
> Te Kawa sets out a vision for bringing all New Zealanders, including Tūhoe, into a closer relationship with Te Urewera, rather than setting out to manage the land itself . . . Te Kawa o Te Urewera is not about short term thinking. Te Urewera does not work to annual plans, but over seasons and centuries."[55]

We now turn to the text of the management plan itself. As you read, consider how it differs from the types of management plans that you might typically expect from your own local, regional, or national jurisdictions.

Extracts from Te Kawa o Te Urewera:

[Introduction:]

Te Kawa is about the management of people for the benefit of the land—it is not about land management.

It raises hope for a renewed collective responsibility for our people impact on the land and foresees our disciplined response to those impacts.

Together, we invite an inter-generational outlook to introduce new practice for principled based responsibility and management to meet our admiration and respect for Te Urewera. . . .

Te Kawa is not intended to operate in the same way as a usual management plan which focuses on rules. Rather, Te Kawa records principles as law, and traditions and beliefs as the sense of a better future. As in life, virtues shape our

[54] Te Kawa o Te Urewera (English version), https://www.ngaituhoe.iwi.nz/te-kawa-o-te-urewera>.

[55] Te Kawa o Te Urewera Draft Released, Scoop, https://www.scoop.co.nz/stories/AK1705/S00487/te-kawa-o-te-urewera-draft-released.htm.

responsibilities and choices guiding Te Urewera Board decisions on appropriate and responsible activities in Te Urewera. The application of these will also develop over time in the form of operational plans, activities and use terms, and other wide-ranging areas. . . .

1.1 THE PURPOSE OF TE KAWA

People need nature, land and waters for life, purpose and humanity. Nature enjoys people for their aspiration, endeavour and friendship. Te Kawa then describes the interrelationship between people and Te Urewera for a just life. An interplay that acknowledges our place and describes our renewed respect and intuition for the health and vitality of Te Urewera.

We know and we understand that nature is timeless, regenerative and operates by mauri and mana. Life's purpose is realised when we understand that life flow, for it brings us order, shows us how to dispense justice and know fairness, letting us see how to serve as worthy people deserving of benefit and entitlement. Without nature's principles alive in our relationships we too often suffer discord from irrelevant habits and cannot apply justice to achieve a natural balance. But, if we can share in these Te Urewera traditions and beliefs guiding our way to a responsible life, our ability as people to live with nature can be restored. And so that what we see in the world is that which we want to see in ourselves.

As tanata whenua [people of the land—ie Tūhoe guardians] and manuhiri [visitors], we know that Te Urewera-Papatūānuku[56] predates us and that we are of her creation living with and amongst all of her kin. As her children we are born with responsibility, we are not born with power and rights. The most difficult of virtues yet most important to accomplish is our sense of belonging, to know our place and contribution to creation.

In reaffirming this natural order the Board through Te Kawa is disrupting the notion of our false superiority over the natural world. In all decisiveness, we are returning to our place in nature, as her child.

TE UREWERA PRINCIPLES

• PAPATŪĀNUKU: LANDSCAPE

Balance: Nothing in the natural world is equal; nature itself operates on the basis of diversity. A human view of devastation can be for Te Urewera a process of recycling and regeneration. Nothing in nature is wasted; everything happens for a reason. Te Urewera has a scale beyond our perception in which to balance and order life.

[56] *Papatūānuku* refers to "Mother Earth."

• **MAURI: LIFE**

Mauri: A life force requiring generosity each to the other. This generosity opens the soul to want connection and collective benefit. To see the relationship between past and future, species and race, birth and death, individual and community, dreaming and science and through managing self-interest, see the common threads of all creations to realise true purpose through which to bring prosperity to life.

• **TAPU: WAI**

Resilience: Wai [water] is comprehensively hard and soft, serene and insurgent[;] she nourishes all that have needs for life. Fairness brings the discipline necessary for collective progress, sharing life, easing the pressure on those that might otherwise struggle, foreseeing and adapting for future life needs and standards as easily as creating new water courses.

• **AHUA: CHARACTER**

Nakau iti: Futures grow from selflessness and sacrifice today. Nature thus humanizes interest and inspirit each other not through biological makeup but through values, personality and vibe. Our care for each other inspires us to live together for purpose. All things are bound together, everything is connected, so the need for strict discipline and high regard for reciprocity.

• **TATAI: HERITAGE**

Time: Our sense of time creates our past and future. Our memory for unity, hope and generosity urges our will to live together. This memory spurs us into the future, unlearning, relearning, learning anew so that we are always current adapting to be necessary and relevant to each time span we are granted.

• **WHĀNAU: MANUHIRI AND TANATA WHENUA**

Discipline: No creature should believe they belong only to themselves. Our values and virtues help guard against inherent human impulses to dominate one another; to balance ego and self-interest. When strong, our habits defend against these pressures and the wellbeing of the collective outweighs the good of individual.

When our laws and rules depart from Te Urewera principles and from our practice of that alive in our traditions and beliefs, they lose moral integrity and authority. They make no sense; they cannot be said to be fair or just.

2.1 THE LEGAL PERSONALITY APPLIED

The role of Te Urewera Board is to act on behalf of, and in the name of, Te Urewera. In doing so the Board must engage with and embrace the Te Urewera identity.

Te Urewera Act recognises that Te Urewera has its own identity, in and of itself, inspiring people to commit to its care. Through this identity, the Act makes evident the presence and distinct personality that is Te Urewera as well her creations of the natural world. The Act does not establish the Te Urewera identity rather it liberates it from human speculation in order that nature and the natural world return to its primal role, revered and served by those of her children to whom she has given life.

The use of property rights by the western legal system has hidden from view the concept of nature; rendered her parts as natural resources now capable of rival priorities competing with other household choices. These human granted rights have displaced our devotion for Papatūānuku with ownership now serving individual advantage. These motives suppress the vision of Te Urewera as distinct life. Yet, property rights do not give life nor do they encourage the connectedness of all living things for life. In this altered relationship people struggle to unify to perceive the whole which is nature collectively. Needlessly our fracturing of nature has sponsored our own fragmentation. The use of property rights to regulate human disputes arising from human society is no longer permissible in and of Te Urewera. Te Urewera may never again be owned by people.

The National Parks Act was sympathetic to the voice of Te Urewera but also created a further dislocation between Te Urewera, its identity, and Tūhoe. By ignoring the presence and personality of Te Urewera, treating her as lands for the enjoyment of others, these mechanisms served to disorder the Te Urewera connection distorting the relationship between people, nature and identity.

The recognition of Te Urewera as a legal entity in Te Urewera Act redresses the Te Urewera identity. Te Urewera has primacy under the law, with the role of institutions, laws and people being to embrace, respect, and act in the interests of Te Urewera.

Now, Te Kawa seeks to start the journey of understanding and articulating the Te Urewera identity. That requires an understanding of traditions and beliefs, the role and place of people in Te Urewera, the concepts of tanata whenua and manuhiri, and the relationship between Tūhoe and Te Urewera. . . .

3.3 MANAGING HUMAN EXPECTATION

We recognise that Te Urewera, which includes the well-being and the experiences of the people that make her their home or a place to visit, is also influenced by activities that happen outside of her borders. Global warming, pest infestation, water and air quality, attitudes and aspirations of people all have the potential to adversely impact Te Urewera's living system. These problems are our problems; we have a stake in resolving them. Leaving such neglect and abuse for the next generation will not reflect honourably on any of us. Our investment in these issues today will count; they are relevant factors for our impact accounting.

If we believe that the permanency of the land is a precondition for our life, then as we invite the return of nature into our homes and relationships we will relearn her needs and through that our limits. Reciprocity and mutual respect are key elements of Te Kawa—the more selfless the interaction with Te Urewera, be they transient or generational, the richer the engagement and our security for enduring life.

3.4 OUR ASPIRATIONS

The aspiration is that in 20 years' time Te Urewera, Tūhoe and her Manuhiri who choose a relationship connection with Te Urewera will be supporting a local, national and global effort of living with the land, admiring the living system of nature and making us whole. . . .

4.2 ESTABLISHING TE UREWERA PRIORITIES

Te Urewera's living system has a balance and a rhythm that is mysterious and imperceptible to human senses. She is timeless and pulses to beat of her own. Understanding then what is a priority or urgency by Te Urewera opinion is somewhat illusory. Here a priority speaks to the common worry for excessive use by human activity and perhaps also our inactivity to better our habits for living with Te Urewera. Priority affects more than a present day state, its true focus the behavioural standards which we need and want to instill in ourselves. It is future oriented. These standards are the true guards against living excessively, that when strong naturally repel habits that lead to placing too great a burden on Te Urewera.

These priorities then are our urgent need to regrow Responsibility, to bring resilience into community, to raise humanity, lifting our sight to living by Te Urewera principle, her eternal standards that reveal themselves in a range of ways throughout Te Urewera. It counts on the actions of Tūhoe their commitment to her for all time, this is whakapapa-kinship in action; and on her manuhiri connections for similar. Her form and figure expect this adoration forever, where her Living System parts and their relationships with each other are felt, understood, respected and lived.

Yet Te Urewera has much to consider, where reversing trends of poor health is complex. History has seen the disruption of the Tūhoe contribution. She will delight to feel the return of regular and thoughtful footfall through river and across mauna [mountains], instilling a new generation understanding, revitalised values, bringing relevance to the myriad of pressures now faced. Experiencing the essence of her Living System—reconnecting passion and memory for the next kaitiaki. . . .

6.1.2 NEW ACTIVITY AND RESPONSIBLE INNOVATION WELCOMED

The potential of responsible innovation to improve the efficacy of operations and experiences within Te Urewera is embraced. New ideas are encouraged, approaches and technologies consistent with Te Urewera values welcomed, forever mindful of the potential risks and unintended consequences associated with unchecked innovations. . . .

Connection to and opportunity within this considers ideas such as:

- The potential for innovations and technologies around all aspects of delivering on Te Urewera priorities e.g. pest control, smart/sensing living systems.
- Manuhiri relationship and experience systems to inform planning decisions more efficiently to bring targeted development and manage and deliver better experiences for people.
- Openness to exploring new and better ways of doing things. Te Urewera has potential to benchmark the safe, responsible and robust testing of new ideas, technologies and other innovations consistent with Te Kawa principles.

6.2 BUSINESS OPPORTUNITIES—FRIENDSHIP AGREEMENTS

For appropriate commercial-type activities and large scale activities, more formal relationship will be required. The Board may grant a concession now referred to as a Friendship Agreement in the form of a lease, license, permit or easement, but only where the activity is not inconsistent with Te Kawa.

Friendship Agreements replace the previous concessions regime applied by the Department of Conservation. Associated processes for approving, monitoring and adapting these will have similarities to the previous concessions regime, but will be designed to achieve new and broader standards of integrity for our impact uses on the living system of Te Urewera.

A Te Urewera Friendship Agreement admits that opportunities are afforded only where we can demonstrate loyal affection to Te Urewera values and her need to continue her complex balancing act amongst her living system. The collaboration needed by holders of Friendship Agreements will enact and instill robust examples of the principles required of all interactions with Te Urewera.

Their design will ensure the mauri of Te Urewera is not diminished through external pressures, considerations or expectations.

Introducing a Friendship Agreement brings opportunity for those seeking a livelihood within Te Urewera, or to undertake an activity of scale or with a non-trivial impact. The Board in applying the terms of [section] 62 and schedule 3 of Te Urewera Act will only do so in a way that is consistent with Te Kawa;

(a) Explicitly considers how such an activity contributes to achieving the (i) purpose of Te Urewera Act; (ii) Te Urewera principles which are Te Kawa principles; (iii) Te Urewera Responsibilities and Prioritised Actions
(b) Clearly explains how the activity effects the living system of Te Urewera;
(c) Clearly provides adequate or reasonable methods of remedying, avoiding or mitigating the adverse effects on the living system of Te Urewera;
(d) Shares the benefits/risk on a sustainable basis between the parties, reflecting their respective contributions.
(e) Is enabling of Tūhoe participation, where they are or have the potential in the future to be best placed to own/manage an activity.
(f) Has positive obligations on parties granted an agreement to "use it, or lose it."

6.3 INTEGRITY AND COMPLIANCE

The Board will apply a monitoring oversight at the whole of living system level, at an individual activity operator level and at the manuhiri or partner satisfaction level. Key elements of the monitoring will include establishing a "dashboard" to highlight how the living system of Te Urewera is adapting, what real impact particular activities or factors are having, and where the priorities are for future action.

- The resilience of the living system of Te Urewera;
- Productivity and use in Te Urewera;
- Economic opportunities and innovation within Te Urewera;
- Tūhoe leadership and infrastructure.

6.4 EVOLVING OUR TE UREWERA EXPERIENCE

Providing for all who wish to have a deeper relationship with Te Urewera the opportunity to do so, through the facilitation of dialog and opportunity which will consider:

- Information provision—on Te Urewera and Tūhoe practices, cultures, expectations etc. so that willing manuhiri [visitors] can educate themselves;

- Opportunities for manuhiri [visitors] to announce themselves—either prior or at the time of their arrival—to Tūhoe who can listen to their goals and help them plan and get the most out of their visit. This is expected to be an important channel for identifying parties who wish to have a positive exchange with Tūhoe and Te Urewera and services as a first step in building the networks and dialogs for this to happen;
- Specific initiatives—Invitations for Tūhoe and manuhiri to participate in workshops and development programmes, e.g., a contribution to trapping pests, planting trees, restoring tracks;
- Information capture—manuhiri provided with a range of mechanisms to provide a contribution to the caretaking of Te Urewera;
- Partnerships (and sponsorships) which through introducing and mobilising new and complementary capabilities that can in combination create new potential and opportunities. . . .

7.3 COMPLIANCE

Our need for new standard[s] and responsibility needs new guidance. Natural tensions exist from old and new practices, between the individual and the collective, between use and preservation, science and culture and science and people, these things are in desperate need of sound reconciliation effort. The use of new whanau [extended family], hapū [sub-tribe], tribal, stakeholder and community leadership supported by new instinct and technology needs time to be developed. Raising our compliance standards will also need disciplined innovation which the Board accepts as an important current priority.

* * *

Te Kawa finishes with some lines from the T.S. Eliot poem "Little Gidding": "We shall not cease from exploration, and the end of all our exploring will be to arrive where we started and know the place for the first time." The poem also explains: "What we called the beginning is of the end, and to make an end is to make a beginning. The end is where we start from."

In summary, the Te Urewera legislation elevates the legal status of a national park to a legal entity with all of the rights, powers, duties, and liabilities of a legal person. It envisages a new relationship between humans and the environment based on a framework of rights and responsibilities. However, it is Te Kawa o Te Urewera—the management plan made under it—that redefines that relationship and creates a truly new beginning, where that relationship is in harmony with Earth law principles.

V. FROM THE WHANGANUI RIVER TO TE AWA TUPUA[57]

The Whanganui River has also been accorded legal personality by legislation, and has been provided with legal guardians to represent and uphold its interests. The Whanganui River is the ancestral river of a number of Whanganui Iwi (tribal groups). From the 1800s, the government assumed ownership of the river and undertook riverbed works, gravel extraction, and water diversions for a hydroelectric power scheme, despite persistent opposition from Whanganui Iwi. Grievances over the river were the subject of petitions to Parliament, Royal Commission reports, Waitangi Tribunal claims, and numerous court cases between 1938 until 2010. An agreement in resolution of these grievances was enacted in the Te Awa Tupua (Whanganui River Claims Settlement) Act 2017. . . .

This Act recognizes the indivisible connection between the Whanganui Iwi and the Whanganui River, as well as the river's metaphysical status as a living being:

> Te Awa Tupua is an indivisible and living whole, comprising the Whanganui River from the mountains to the sea, incorporating all its physical and metaphysical elements.

In an effort to implement the Māori understanding of the river as a living whole, connected to the Whanganui Iwi but incapable of being "owned" in an absolute sense, the Act grants the Whanganui River independent legal personhood as Te Awa Tupua: "Te Awa Tupua is a legal person and has all the rights, powers, duties, and liabilities of a legal person."

Title to the riverbeds of what was the Whanganui River and its tributaries, within a large catchment area, is vested in the name of Te Awa Tupua itself. The riverbed is defined:

> **bed**, in relation to the Whanganui River,—
>
> (a) means the space of land that the waters of the Whanganui River cover at its fullest flow without overtopping its banks; and
> (b) includes the subsoil, the plants attached to the bed, the space occupied by the water, and the airspace above the water.[58]

Importantly, the Act provides that guardians shall be appointed on behalf of the Whanganui River: two persons "of high standing," one appointed by the Crown and one appointed collectively by all tribes with interests in the river, are to be the river's guardians and must act in the name of Te Awa Tupua. This office of guardianship, called Te Pou Tupua, must "promote and protect the health and wellbeing of Te Awa Tupua," "act and speak on behalf of Te Awa Tupua," and act "in its interests and consistently with Tupua te Kawa [intrinsic values of the river]." The office of Te Pou Tupua embodies a co-governance arrangement, with both Māori and non-Māori

[57] This section is adapted from C. Iorns Magallanes, *supra* note 46, at 555-556.
[58] *Id.* at § 2.

members, and its powers enable stronger legal respect for the environment in line with Māori cosmology.

The Act anticipates the development of *Te Heke Ngahuru,* a "Whole of River Strategy," that addresses and advances the health and well-being of the Whanganui River. It also establishes *Te Korotete o Te Awa Tupua,* a "River Fund" of NZD $30 million that is designed to support the health and well-being of the river. Unlike Te Urewera, the Whanganui River was not a national park prior to being granted legal status. The environmental protection afforded to it under the Te Awa Tupua Act is thus greater than had previously been the case. Yet what is most important for the Whanganui Iwi is their understanding and belief that their health and well-being is dependent on the health and well-being of the river. It is expressed in their proverb, "*Ko au te awa, ko te awa ko au*" (I am the river and the river is me).[59] As the health of the river improves, so will the health of the people; the environment and human rights are intertwined and protected together.

Extracts from Te Awa Tupua Act 2017 detailing the guardianship bodies and their functions are provided in Chapter 6, "Guardianship Arrangements in Rights of Nature Legal Provisions." The legislation does not detail the means by which these bodies will interact with the bodies established under other legislation. This is currently being worked out as the Te Awa Tupua guardians undertake their roles.

Interestingly, the legal person is treated differently depending on which legislation it might be covered by or interact with:

17. Application of Other Acts to Te Awa Tupua

Te Awa Tupua is to be treated as—

(a) an institution for the purpose of applying for registration as a charitable entity under the Charities Act 2005:
(b) a public body for the purposes of clauses 30 and 30A of Schedule 7 of the Local Government Act 2002:
(c) a public authority for the purpose of section 33X of the Maritime Transport Act 1994:
(d) a registered collector of taonga tūturu[60] for the purposes of section 14 of the Protected Objects Act 1975:
(e) a public authority for the purposes of the Resource Management Act 1991:
(f) a body corporate for the purpose of applying to be a heritage protection authority under section 188 of the Resource Management Act 1991:
(g) a public body for the purposes of sections 4 and 35 of the Walking Access Act 2008.

An omission worth noting is that the waters of the river catchment have been excluded from this legislation's coverage. The river's water is thus not part of the legal person nor its property. This is due to a government position that no one owns

[59] *Id.* at § 69(3).

[60] *Taonga tūturu* means an object that (a) relates to Māori culture, history, or society; and (b) was, or appears to have been; (i) manufactured or modified in New Zealand by Māori; or (ii) brought into New Zealand by Māori; or (iii) used by Māori; and (c) is more than 50 years old.

freshwater in New Zealand, and that the government merely manages it for the good of all. The government therefore refused to recognise ownership of the water in the legislation, even by the natural entity itself. Despite this omission, the arrangements enacted in respect of Te Awa Tupua have created a new beginning. They have created a new relationship between local and national government, the area's residents, the river, and its guardians, if not also with the whole country that has celebrated its passage. It, too, is a relationship based on a new set of rights and responsibilities that are in line with Earth law principles.

VI. CONCLUSION

New Zealand is a modern, Western democracy with its values and the majority of its culture being familiar to other English-speaking Western democracies. In that sense, the adoption of statements of intrinsic value for nature and declarations of animal sentience were subject to the political and policy considerations that might arise in other such countries. It is thus instructive to consider the choices made in their legislative incorporation, as well as in their ongoing application by courts, and to consider opportunities to rely on the New Zealand lawmaking to develop Earth law in other countries.

New Zealand's recognition of Indigenous environmental rights and responsibilities has been more extensive and effective than in other countries that share the English language and Western culture. Consider, for example, the efforts in the United States promoted by CELDF, as discussed in Chapter 9, "The Rights of Nature Movement in the United States." The protection of Indigenous worldviews and Indigenous environmental management through statute—notably the adoption of responsibility, guardianship and legal personhood—is innovative. Globally, they are perceived as a threat by embedded economic interests and have not garnered the social and political backing needed to pass legislation. Nevertheless, the New Zealand experience in drafting legislation will provide both perspective and persuasive authority for practitioners of Earth law in other countries.

As with all legislation, the value of the New Zealand laws will depend on the statutory wording and the legislative history, which provide the parameters for what judicial and administrative decision-makers can do. Courts will determine the breadth of such parameters as they consider and construe their meanings. In considering the study questions below, focus on these parameters as you identify and argue their interpretation and application. The experience under statutes such as the Resource Management Act show that interpretations of the provisions implementing Māori culture and values are argued as thoroughly in courts as any other statutory provisions that are challenged on the basis of the meaning and application of the words. The specific wording must be paid careful attention.

Te Kawa is not itself legislation. It was adopted pursuant to the powers and guidelines within the statutory framework. It illustrates a new vision of the rights and responsibilities between humans and the environment, in line with Earth laws. The overriding dignity and respect for nature, along with the place of humans within it, and its emphasis on duty and responsibility rather than power or rights, provides an innovative opportunity for land management. Te Kawa illustrates what can be done to challenge "the notion of our false superiority over the natural world" and return us "to our place in nature, as her child."[61]

The study of Earth law in its many emergent forms enables us to explicitly identify and draft ecocentric legislation, to recognize whether it is being used as intended and effectively, and to take action to uphold and extend its application. These examples from Aotearoa New Zealand expand the ideas of what is possible.

STUDY QUESTIONS

Intrinsic worth and intrinsic values:

(1) Does the inclusion of reference to intrinsic worth or intrinsic value represent the inclusion of a deep ecology approach, which treats human life as just one of many interrelated components, all essential in their own separate and collective ways, of a larger global ecosystem? Can it have any effect if it operates within and must be balanced against other more mainstream values? How would you explain intrinsic value to a court? How would it be different in a general sense than in the case of a particular client, for example a river? How does the Resource Management Act 1991 delineate the range of matters that must be balanced by a decision-maker?

(2) How might the persuasive value of an argument based on intrinsic worth or intrinsic value be enhanced or diminished by the fact that they are mentioned as an overriding purpose and not elsewhere in the statute? How might a court instruct a jury on the weight to be given to intrinsic worth or intrinsic value? How might it be distinguished from extrinsic value?

(3) Should intrinsic worth and intrinsic values in relation to nature be interpreted consistently across the different statutes, or should each term take the meaning most appropriate for that statute? Note that a purposive approach to statutory interpretation suggests that each statute is considered on its own and that other statutes are irrelevant; the particular context and purpose of that single statute is key, unless it forms part of a statutory scheme and should be treated as interrelated.

(4) Are there any differences in the meanings of intrinsic worth or intrinsic value that would make any difference in practice? Think about the interpretation of scenic value from the place in the question; would an interpretation of "intrinsic value" in the National Parks Act ever be likely to be similar to that for the scenic reserves in the Reserves Act? Do you think constructing a gazebo to take advantage of the view would be likely to be approved for a national park?

[61] Te Kawa, *supra* note 51, at p. 15.

Sentence of animals:

(5) What real effect can a general statement of principle about sentience have when applying clear standards that are already specified in the legislation, or when developing the content of animal welfare codes or other rules under the Act? How might a court, in practice, change the manner in which it conducts its decision-making business to include a consideration of sentience? How might a legislative enactment, or a judicial enactment of procedural rules be developed? How much power do trial court judges have in your jurisdiction to use a purposive approach in interpreting legislation?

(6) If you were making a submission on the inclusion of a reference to animals being sentient in animal welfare legislation, how could it be worded, where would you place it, and what effect would you want it to have? Is there other legislation that might benefit from its inclusion? If so, how?

(7) If animal welfare codes needed to be revised in accordance with an expanded concept of animal quality of life, and requiring positive experiences, what effect would that have on the animal food industries, such as in relation to animal housing and transport?

(8) How should we balance sentience and animal welfare with controlling invasive, introduced pest species?

Indigenous rights and legal personality:

(9) Consider how the two different legal persons have been defined for Te Urewera National Park and Whanganui River. Should they be defined by geographical lines on a map or by ecosystem function? How significant might it be that freshwater is not owned by the legal persons nor under the control of their guardians?

(10) Does using Indigenous language terms import their different understanding of humans' relationships with nature—more in line with Earth law—or are they only as good as the judges interpreting the terms? The use of "*kaitiakitanga*" in the Resource Management Act will be considered and interpreted by decision-makers who are not Indigenous and may have little understanding of Indigenous cosmology. How might this be met? How would you avert a non-Indigenous interpretation based on the statutory wording that it is only needed to be paid regard to, rather than recognized and provided for by a decision-maker?

(11) Discuss the other uses of language in the legislation according to legal personality to nature. For example, note the use of "her" to refer to Te Urewera; what does this signify and incorporate? Note the use of the word "appointee" to the Te Urewera Board. Board members are appointed by the New Zealand government and by the Māori Tuhoe tribe; yet their job is to represent Te Urewera; might their source of appointment affect their views of the interests of Te Urewera? How would you assert your authority to speak as a guardian of a national park? How would you balance your authority with the guardian of a river that flowed through the park?

(12) Instead of a list of activities allowed in the area, Te Kawa refers to "experience" and "connection"; instead of "concessions," Te Kawa refers to "friendship agreements." Do you think the use of this wording will make any difference in the way these activities are conducted? How might they make a difference?

(13) In the context of legal personality discussed in section 2.1 of the Te Kawa extracts, how do property rights encourage fragmentation and discourage connectedness of nature and living things in it? What might dispute resolution within human society look like if it did not use property rights to resolve disputes?

(14) When you read that natural beings like parks and rivers are legal entities and have "all the rights, powers, duties, and liabilities of a legal person," what are the strengths and weaknesses of arguments based separately on: (1) rights, (2) powers, (3) duties and (4) liabilities? Why do you think the New Zealand legislation identifies all four?

(15) Do you think of New Zealand's laws discussed in this chapter are appropriately termed rights of nature laws? Why or why not? How do you distinguish rights of nature from other types of Earth laws?

(16) What benefit can the New Zealand legislation that accords personality to nature provide by way of a precedent for Earth laws in other countries? Consider this commentary on the laws examined in this chapter:

> These examples provide an excellent illustration of the interconnection between environment and human rights. Upholding Māori Indigenous rights to land, resources and culture has resulted in a new way to not only protect the environment but to reconceive our relationship with the environment, upholding human rights better in the process, as a virtuous circle. In respect of the legal personhood model in particular, the granting of legal personhood to a geographical feature represents a momentous shift from an external ownership model, which prioritises the uses that humans derive from a resource, to an Indigenous self-ownership model, which requires no human justification for environmental protection. While intimately connected with human rights, this is a very different vision of legal subjects and objects, and of rights and duties, from that which human rights law traditionally upholds. The notion of responsibility in these examples is used in contrast to the notion of rights, and these examples adopt a communal focus, rejecting individualistic notions of rights.[62]

(17) How might the New Zealand example of upholding human rights—Indigenous rights—provide persuasive authority for the development of Earth law in a jurisdiction you are familiar with? What are the elements of the development of the New Zealand laws that might have comparable elements in your jurisdiction? How might a focus on human responsibility over rights be achieved in a jurisdiction in which you may practice?

[62] *Supra* note 46, at 556-557.

CHAPTER 23

The Netherlands and the Future of Atmospheric Trust Litigation[1]

I. INTRODUCTION

This chapter examines the Dutch Supreme Court's 2019 decision in *The State of the Netherlands v. Urgenda Foundation* (*Urgenda*), the world's first case in which citizens successfully established their government's legal duty to address climate change. The Court ordered the Dutch government to slash greenhouse gas (GHG) emissions to 25 percent below 1990 levels by the end of 2020 in enforcement of the European Convention on Human Rights and other legal standards. This case provides a model for other courts to make similar landmark climate change decisions worldwide.

Section II examines the European Union's (EU) environmental regulatory framework, which sets GHG emission commitments; the fundamental rights set out in the ECHR; and EU law impediments to developing Earth law, which the Dutch Court's decision circumvented.

Section III explains the elements of the Constitution of the Netherlands and the Dutch legal system that are critical to the Supreme Court's reasoning in the *Urgenda* case.

Section IV compares and contrasts *Urgenda* with a U.S. climate change case: *Juliana v. United States*. *Urgenda* serves as a counterweight to the *Juliana* case, which the Ninth Circuit Court dismissed for lack of standing (*see* Chapter 7, "Public Trust Doctrine"). This section also highlights "atmospheric trust litigation" more broadly.

II. THE EUROPEAN CONVENTION ON HUMAN RIGHTS

EU environmental and human rights obligations are based on a series of legally binding treaties. Examples are the Treaty on the European Union, the Treaty on the Functioning of the European Union, and the Charter of Fundamental Rights of the European Union. In addition to the foundational treaties of the EU, which set out the constitutional rights and duties of its member states, there are other treaties that

[1] This chapter was authored by Valentijn Punt, Environmental Law Associate at Earth Law Center.

focus on specific areas, such as human rights, labor markets, the economy, and environmental protection.

The European Convention on Human Rights (ECHR or Convention) is one such treaty. It legally binds the 47 members of the Council of Europe, an international organization with the mission to uphold human rights and the rule of law. Of the Council's 47 members, 27 are members of the EU. The idea for the ECHR was shaped in 1948 during the "Congress of Europe," a gathering in the Hague where politicians, civil society, and representatives of trade unions, universities, and other institutions worked together to propose a list of basic human rights.[2] A number of articles were directly based on the United Nations' Universal Declaration of Human Rights.

The European Court of Human Rights (European Court) oversees enforcement of the provisions of the ECHR.[3] The European Court was set up in 1959 in Strasbourg and issues judgments that are legally binding on member states.[4]

Domestic courts of ECHR member states also have an obligation to apply the convention. This is because the ECHR is incorporated into the legislation of all member states and is therefore directly applicable at a national level. This becomes important in the *Urgenda* case.

There are two types of applications that can be brought to the European Court: (1) individual applications lodged by any person, group of persons, or nongovernmental organization (NGO); and (2) inter-state applications where one state brings a claim against another. The cases can only be brought against a state that has ratified the ECHR, and thus agreed to honor judgments made by the court. The execution of judgments is monitored by the Committee of Ministers of the Council of Europe.

The admissibility criteria for complaints before the European Court are defined in Articles 34 and 35 of the ECHR. Under Article 34, the applicant must be a person, NGO, or group of individuals claiming to be a "victim" of a violation of rights established in the ECHR. (The meaning of "victim" becomes relevant in the district court opinion of *Urgenda.*) Under Article 35, all domestic remedies must have been exhausted, the contested domestic court decision must have been made within the previous six months, and the applicant must have suffered a "significant disadvantage," amongst other requirements.[5]

In practice, enforcement of European Court decisions has been problematic. If the European Court finds that a right has been breached, it simply declares that a violation has occurred and oftentimes allows the country to determine its own plan for compliance. Sometimes the European Court does prescribe a remedy, such as ending

[2] *The Establishment of the European Movement,* CVCE.EU (July 4, 2020), https://www.cvce.eu/en/recherche/unit-content/-/unit/04bfa990-86bc-402f-a633-11f39c9247c4/272166ae-84b2-466b-9cfa-4df511389208.

[3] Council of Europe, European Convention on Human Rights, as amended by Protocols Nos. 11 and 14, Supplemented by Protocols Nos. 1, 4, 6, 7, 12, and 13 ETS 5 (1950), http://www.echr.coe.int/Documents/Convention_ENG.pdf [hereinafter ECHR].

[4] *Id.*

[5] Council of Europe, European Court of Human Rights, Practical Guide on Admissibility Criteria (updated on Aug. 31, 2019), https://www.echr.coe.int/Documents/Admissibility_guide_ENG.pdf.

the violation in question, making payment, or amending laws.[6] But overall, enforcement has been lacking. For example, a 2017 review found that 9,944 judgments by the European Court had not been implemented by the respective states.[7] Part of the problem is that European Court decisions do not force states to enact new or amend existing legislation. This is different from the Court of Justice of the European Union, for example, the judgments of which effectively override national law. There is no such relationship between the European Court and the EU: the Council of Europe is a separate organization of European nations unrelated to the EU. The general rule is for national courts to follow the European Court's decisions, but there are no practical means to force recalcitrant states to implement them.[8]

An aspect of the European Court that sets it apart from other human rights courts is that there is a follow-up system in the form of the Committee of Ministers. The challenge with the committee itself, however, is the fact that it is made up of high-level officials representing member states, and relationships between countries influence how committee members follow up on the enforcement of judgments.

There are 18 human rights set out in the ECHR, commonly known as the "Convention Rights." The articles most relevant to the *Urgenda* case are Articles 2 and 8. Article 2 concerns the right to life and states the following:

> 1. Everyone's right to life shall be protected by law. No one shall be deprived of his life intentionally save in the execution of a sentence of a court following his conviction of a crime for which this penalty is provided by law.
> 2. Deprivation of life shall not be regarded as inflicted in contravention of this Article when it results from the use of force which is no more than absolutely necessary:
>
>   (a) in defence of any person from unlawful violence;
>   (b) in order to effect a lawful arrest or to prevent the escape of a person lawfully detained;
>   (c) in action lawfully taken for the purpose of quelling a riot or insurrection.[9]

Article 8 establishes the right to privacy and family life and reads as follows:

> 1. Everyone has the right to respect for his private and family life, his home and his correspondence.
> 2. There shall be no interference by a public authority with the exercise of this right except such as is in accordance with the law and is necessary in a democratic society in the interests of national security, public safety or the economic well-being of the country, for the prevention of disorder or crime, for the protection of health or morals, or for the protection of the rights and freedoms of others.[10]

[6] Maria Issaeva, Irina Sergeeva & Maria Suchkova, *Enforcement of the Judgments of the European Court of Human Rights in Russia,* 15 Intl. J. on Human Rights (Dec. 2011).
[7] Ginger Hervey, *Europe's Human Rights Court Struggles to Lay Down the Law,* Politico.EU (Sept, 17, 2017, 4:05 AM, CET).
[8] Council of Europe, The Execution of Judgments of European Court of Human Rights, Human Rights Files, No. 19 (2d ed. 2008).
[9] ECHR, *supra* note 3.
[10] *Id.*

Articles 2 and 8 have been interpreted to protect against environmental harms that affect rights to life, home, and private life where such harms are caused by a state action or the state's failure to properly regulate private-sector activities. These articles also impose a positive obligation upon states to take the necessary precautionary measures to prevent future rights violations, especially when there is a known and imminent threat.[11] As reflected in the examination of the *Urgenda* case, the Dutch Supreme Court ruled that these articles require member states to take reasonable and sufficient steps to protect residents from the life-threatening consequences of climate change.

III. THE *URGENDA* CASE

This section begins by taking a closer look at the Dutch legal system. It then explores the merits of the *Urgenda* case at the Hague District Court, the Hague Court of Appeal, and the Dutch Supreme Court.

A. Background on Dutch Legal System

The Netherlands is a constitutional monarchy with a civil law legal system. The foundation of its national law is the Dutch Civil Code (DCC), which addresses most subjects of Dutch law. All other legislation is based on the principles set out in the DCC. Dutch judges have a high degree of discretion in interpreting these provisions, even when the text of a provision seems clear. An underlying principle of this discretion is the notion in the Dutch legal system of "reasonableness and fairness," which refers to a generally accepted standard of what is reasonable and fair in a given situation. In other words, if a party knew or should have known a certain fact, this principle requires them to act accordingly, with consideration of the societal and personal interests. This also means that regulations and binding legal instruments in general may not have a legal effect if, as written or as applied, they are deemed not to be objectively fair.[12]

The Dutch legal system has three types of courts. First, there are the district courts (*Rechtbank*), of which there are 19 and which are divided into five areas based on different sectors; these include the civil, administrative, and criminal sectors. Second, five courts of appeal (*Gerechtshof*) hear both civil and criminal cases where an appeal has been lodged against a judgment by a district court. Finally, the Supreme Court (*Hoge*

[11] *See* European Court of Human Rights, Environment and the European Convention on Human Rights, (Mar. 2020), https://www.echr.coe.int/Documents/FS_Environment_ENG.pdf.

[12] *See* Popke Sjoerd Bakker, Redelijkheid en billijkheid als gedragsnorm 147-153 (2012) (unpublished Ph.D. dissertation, Vrije Universiteit), https://research.vu.nl/ws/portalfiles/portal/42108308/complete+dissertation.pdf.

Raad) is the highest court in the Netherlands and hears cases in civil, criminal, and tax matters in cassation, which means that the Supreme Court is required by law to base its holdings on the facts as established by the lower courts.[13] In *Urgenda,* the case moved from the Hague District Court to the Hague Court of Appeal to the Supreme Court, with the Dutch government appealing each time. As described in the next section, ultimately these appeals were unsuccessful.

Also, the Dutch judicial branch has an independent advisor who is part of the judicial branch, called the procurator general. Along with the advocates general, the role of procurator general is to provide the Supreme Court with independent advice through advisory opinions. In civil cases such as *Urgenda,* provision of this advisory opinion is mandatory but the Dutch Supreme Court is not required to follow it. Such advisory opinions review the relevant facts, legal questions, scholarly opinions, case law, as well as the decision of the lower court that is being appealed.

B. Urgenda: Procedural History and Ruling

The *Urgenda* case was brought as a collective action. Dutch collective actions to protect a public interest can be initiated pursuant to Article 3:305a of the Dutch Civil Code. This provision allows a representative entity to initiate a collective action in a civil court based on the interests of natural persons, so long as those interests are the same as the entity's. The entity must be an association or foundation, and its articles of association and by-laws need to state that the aim of the entity is to represent a specified group of persons.

In the *Urgenda* case, the specified group of persons was extremely broad, with the Urgenda Foundation representing over 800 individuals. *Urgenda* also asserted its representation of future generations, both within and outside the Netherlands, of people impacted by climate change. Urgenda's articles of association met the threshold requirement to represent future generations in a collective action by explicitly recognizing that the Foundation's purpose is to "preserve the planet as a sustainable place for future generations to live." Additionally, a 2001 decision by the District Court of the Hague held that Article 3:305a of the DCC can serve as legal basis for actions brought on behalf of future generations.[14] However, the courts never addressed this issue in *Urgenda* and found the standing of Urgenda and its living Dutch co-plaintiffs to be sufficient.[15]

[13] *Cassation: The Main Task of the Supreme Court,* Hoge Raad der Nederlanden, https://www.rechtspraak.nl/Organisatie-en-contact/Organisatie/Hoge-Raad-der-Nederlanden/Supreme-court-of-the-Netherlands/Paginas/Cassation-the-main-task-of-the-Supreme-Court.aspx (last visited July 4, 2020).

[14] ECLI:NL:RBSGR:2001:AB1369, District Court The Hague (May 2, 2001) [3.5].

[15] Urgenda Foundation v. Kingdom of the Netherlands, Translation of Summons, 15, ¶ 28 (June 25, 2015), http://www.urgenda.nl/documents/FINAL-DRAFT-Translation-Summons-incase-Urgenda-v-Dutch-State-v.25.06.10.pdf.

C. Background and Overview of the Holding

The *Urgenda* case emerged from a dispute about Dutch obligations to reduce GHGs. Although the Dutch government and Urgenda agreed about the need to reduce GHG emissions, they differed about the exact reduction target. Urgenda believed it must be a 25 percent reduction compared to 1990 levels, whereas the Dutch government had targeted a 20 percent reduction. While the difference may seem small, the importance of the case is that the lawsuit sought to enforce science-based climate-change targets established by international consensus, regardless of how close the government was to meeting these targets.

Prior to the historic Supreme Court decision, the District Court of the Hague and the Hague Court of Appeal both ruled in favor of Urgenda. The two courts used different legal reasoning. These cases are discussed below in sequence.

1. District Court of the Hague (2015)

The first ruling, from the District Court of the Hague in 2015, found that the Dutch government breached its duty of care to its citizens under tort law by failing to adopt a 25 percent reduction criterion.[16] Dutch tort law establishes a duty of care that is similar to the "reasonable person" standard in U.S. tort law. The district court constructed the standard of care on the basis of international, European, and constitutional duties to which the Dutch government was committed—including Articles 2 and 8 of the ECHR, which uphold the right to life, and to respect privacy and family life, respectively; the United Nations Framework Convention on Climate Change; and Article 21 of the Dutch Constitution, which establishes the fundamental right to a clean environment. The district court further substantiated the breach of this duty of care based upon a review of Dutch climate change policy, which it deemed to be inadequate. The district court concluded that the Dutch government acted unlawfully by establishing a GHG reduction target that was less than 25 percent by 2020 compared to the year 1990.

One necessary element to establish a breach of the duty of care under tort law is a causal link between the challenged act or omission, and the damage suffered by the plaintiff. When it comes to climate change, this can be difficult to prove because one country's reduction in emissions is unlikely to prevent climate change by itself. Consider how the district court addressed this issue:

> From the above considerations, particularly in 4.79, it follows that a sufficient causal link can be assumed to exist between the Dutch greenhouse gas emissions, global climate change and the effects (now and in the future) on the Dutch living climate. The fact that the current Dutch greenhouse gas emissions are limited on a global scale does not alter the fact that these emission [sic] contribute to climate change. The court has taken into consideration in this respect as well that the Dutch greenhouse emissions have

[16] Urgenda Foundation v. The State of the Netherlands, Case No. C/09/456689/HA_ZA 13-1396 (Netherlands), Rechtbank Den Haag [District Court of The Hague, Chamber for Commercial Affairs] (June 24, 2015).

> contributed to climate change and by their nature will also continue to contribute to climate change.[17]

Despite ruling in Urgenda's favor, the district court found that Urgenda could not base its claims on Articles 2 and 8 of the ECHR directly—only indirectly through tort law—since a nonhuman organization cannot be a "victim" per the meaning of Article 34 of the ECHR: "After all, unlike with a natural person, a legal person's physical integrity cannot be violated nor can a legal person's privacy be interfered with."[18] While non-governmental organizations are explicitly recognized as possible "victims" under Article 34, the district court rejected the notion that they can be victims of specifically *physical* harms. The district court also declined to explicitly rule that the Dutch government had breached international treaty obligations (such as under the United Nations Framework Convention on Climate Change) or the Dutch Constitution. Instead, it relied upon these sources of law to interpret the duty of care under tort law. The Netherlands appealed.

2. Hague Court of Appeal (2018)

The second ruling, from the Hague Court of Appeal in 2018, upheld the district court ruling.[19] However, unlike the Hague District Court, the Hague Court of Appeal found that Urgenda, along with the many humans it represents, *could* directly enforce the ECHR without having to rely upon tort law. The court reasoned that the limitations of a "victim" under Article 34 of the ECHR only applies to admissibility to the European Court, not to Dutch courts. By contrast, Dutch law—specifically, Article 3:305a of the DCC—provides for class actions of interest groups such as this one. The court explained that individuals who fall under Dutch jurisdiction may invoke Articles 2 and 8 of the ECHR directly. The court then laid out the basic obligations of the Dutch government:

> In short, the State has a positive obligation to protect the lives of citizens within its jurisdiction under Article 2 ECHR, while Article 8 ECHR creates the obligation to protect the right to home and private life. This obligation applies to all activities, public and non-public, which could endanger the rights protected in these articles, and certainly in the face of industrial activities which by their very nature are dangerous. If the government knows that there is a real and imminent threat, the State must take precautionary measures to prevent infringement as far as possible. In light of this, the Court shall assess the asserted (imminent) climate dangers.[20]

[17] *Id.*
[18] *Id.*
[19] The State of the Netherlands v. Urgenda Foundation, The Hague Court of Appeal (Oct. 9, 2019), case 200.178.245/01, English translation at https://www.law.uh.edu/faculty/thester/courses/Climate-Change-2018/Urgenda%20Appeal%20Decision%20100918.pdf.
[20] *Id.* at ¶ 43.

The court then explored the science-based threats of climate change, the international obligations of the Netherlands, and the impact on human rights as derived from Articles 2 and 8 of the ECHR. Ultimately, the court concluded as follows:

> [T]he State has done too little to prevent a dangerous climate change and is doing too little to catch up, or at least in the short term (up to end-2020). Targets for 2030 and beyond do not take away from the fact that a dangerous situation is imminent, which requires interventions being taken now....
>
> [T]he Court is of the opinion that the State fails to fulfil its duty of care pursuant to Articles 2 and 8 ECHR by not wanting to reduce emissions by at least 25 percent by end-2020....
>
> All of the above leads to the conclusion that the State is acting unlawfully (because in contravention of the duty of care under Articles 2 and 8 ECHR) by failing to pursue a more ambitious reduction as of end-2020, and that the State should reduce emissions by at least 25 percent by end-2020. The State's grounds of appeal pertaining to the district court's opinion about the hazardous negligence doctrine [i.e., the tort claim] need no discussion under these state of affairs. The judgment is hereby upheld.[21]

The Netherlands again appealed.

3. Procurator General advisory opinion (2019)

Next, on September 13, 2019, the Procurator General of the Supreme Court (joined by the advocate general) released a formal advisory opinion supporting the ruling of the court of appeal.[22] It agreed that human rights law can be used to interpret the government's duty of care with respect to climate change. The advisory opinion also rejected the defenses of the Netherlands, including that climate change policy is a political issue that should be left to the legislative branch so as to not interfere with the separation of powers between branches of government. The Procurator General concluded as follows:

> The jurisdiction of the civil courts, under Dutch law, is independent from the question of whether the claim raises a political issue.... If the claimant bases its claim on a violation or impending violation of a right to which it is entitled or on an unlawful act committed against it, the civil courts do, in principle, have jurisdiction to take cognizance of that claim and render a substantive opinion on it. This also applies when the claim is directed against the State.

As discussed above, the Procurator General's advisory opinion is not binding but is considered by the Supreme Court.

[21] *Id.* at ¶¶ 71, 73, 76.

[22] In the Matter Between the State of the Netherlands and Stichting Urgenda, Procurator General of the Supreme Court of the Netherlands, No. 19/00135 (Sept. 13, 2019).

4. Dutch Supreme Court (2019)

Finally, in December 2019, the Supreme Court upheld the ruling of the Court of Appeal. As with the Court of Appeal, its reasoning derived from Dutch human rights obligations.[23] The Supreme Court agreed that "there is the threat of dangerous climate change and it is clear that measures are urgently needed."[24] Under Articles 2 and 8 of the ECHR, the Netherlands has a duty to protect the right to life and the right to private and family life of its residents. In its ruling, the Court also referred to the 2007 IPCC report, which found that a reduction in emissions of 25 to 40 percent by 2020 would be necessary to limit global warming to a 2ºC increase, and held that the Dutch government had provided insufficient reasons for adhering to a lesser 20 percent reduction.[25] The Supreme Court concluded as follows:

> This case involves an exceptional situation. After all, there is the threat of dangerous climate change and it is clear that measures are urgently needed, as the District Court and Court of Appeal have established and the State acknowledges as well. The State is obliged to do 'its part' in this context. Towards the residents of the Netherlands, whose interests Urgenda is defending in this case, that duty follows from Articles 2 and 8 ECHR, on the basis of which the State is obliged to protect the right to life and the right to private and family life of its residents. The fact that Annex I countries, including the Netherlands, will need to reduce their emissions by at least 25 percent by 2020 follows from the view generally held in climate science and in the international community, which view has been established by the District Court and the Court of Appeal. The policy that the State pursues since 2011 and intends to pursue in the future, whereby measures are postponed for a prolonged period of time, is clearly not in accordance with this, as the Court of Appeal has established.[26]

In making its historic ruling, the Dutch Supreme Court—agreeing with the Procurator General—rejected the Dutch government's defense that a sweeping climate change ruling would interfere with the separation of powers by reshaping the legislative process, thereby blurring the lines between the judicial and political spheres.[27] In *Urgenda*, the core of the government's argument was that ruling in favor of the claimants would violate the separation of powers by undermining the government's authority in the context of international politics and negotiation leverage.[28] However, the Supreme Court found the government's argument flawed because it did not distinguish the separation of powers doctrine from the system of political checks and balances.[29]

[23] Urgenda Foundation v. Kingdom of the Netherlands, Translation of Judgment, Dec. 20, 2019, ¶ 5.2.1, https://uitspraken.rechtspraak.nl/inziendocument?id=ECLI:NL:HR:2019:2007.
[24] *Id.* at ¶ 8.3.4.
[25] *Id.* at¶ 2.1.
[26] *Id.* at ¶ 8.3.4 (internal cross-references omitted).
[27] *Id.* at ¶ 2.2.3.
[28] Roger Cox, *A Climate Change Litigation Precedent: Urgenda Foundation v. The State of the Netherlands,* 34 J. of Energy & Natural Resources L. 143, 148 (2016).
[29] K J de Graaf & J H Jans, *The Urgenda Decision: Netherlands Liable for Role in Causing Dangerous Global Climate Change,* 27(3) J. of Envtl. L. 517, 523 (2015).

The Supreme Court stated:

> In the Dutch system of government, the decision-making on greenhouse gas emissions belongs to the government and parliament. They have a large degree of discretion to make the political considerations that are necessary in this regard. It is up to the courts to decide whether, in taking their decisions, the government and parliament have remained within the limits of the law by which they are bound. Those limits ensue from the ECHR, among other things. The Dutch Constitution requires the Dutch courts to apply the provision of this convention, and they must do so in accordance with the ECHR's interpretation of these provisions. This mandate to the courts to offer legal protection, even against the government, is an essential component of a democratic state under the rule of law.[30]

In sum, the Supreme Court ruled that requiring the Dutch government to protect its citizens from climate change does not infringe upon the separation of powers since it is only prescribing the outcome, not the means by which the government must achieve this outcome. While the Court determined that the law required the cuts in GHG emissions, the Dutch government could decide how to achieve them.

IV. COMPARING *URGENDA* TO *JULIANA*

This section considers the different results reached by the Dutch Supreme Court and the Ninth Circuit Court of Appeals in the United States in cases seeking the same relief: compelling the government to protect the fundamental rights of its citizens from the adverse consequences of climate change. It focuses on the argument made in both cases that climate change policy must be left to the political branches of government.

As discussed in Chapter 5, "Standing" and Chapter 8, "Rights of Future Generations," the Ninth Circuit dismissed *Juliana*— the "climate kids" lawsuit—for lack of standing. Similar to *Urgenda*, the plaintiffs sued the government for failing to address climate change, which they argued violated their federal constitutional rights and the public trust doctrine. However, the Ninth Circuit, in a 2-1 vote, found that the redress sought by the plaintiffs—a court order requiring the government to create a plan to phase out fossil fuels and draw down GHG emissions—would "require a host of complex policy decisions entrusted, for better or worse, to the wisdom and discretion of the executive and legislative branches."[31] Without redressability, a plaintiff in the United States does not have Article III standing. The Court concluded that "the plaintiffs' case must be made to the political branches or to the electorate at large."[32]

In stark contrast, the Dutch Supreme Court found that the judiciary could order the Dutch government to address climate change so long as the legislative branch

[30] Urgenda Foundation v. Kingdom of the Netherlands, Translation of Judgment, Dec. 20, 2019, Summary of Decision, https://uitspraken.rechtspraak.nl/inziendocument?id=ECLI:NL:HR:2019:2007.
[31] Juliana et al. v. United States, D.C. No. 6:15-cv-01517- AA, at 5 (2019). Note that petitioners filed a petition for rehearing of the Juliana case on March 2, 2020. See docket at http://climatecasechart.com/case/juliana-v-united-states/.
[32] *Id.* at 32.

decided upon the means. The Court considered it an inherently legal decision as to whether the plaintiff's rights had been violated even though the decision would have political consequences.[33]

The contrast between these two rulings underscores how a court's understanding of its own power within the scope of its government's separation of powers may determine the outcome. Additionally, the contrast highlights the breadth of a court's permissible interpretation of the political question doctrine. Courts in the United States and elsewhere will continue to be presented with claims seeking redress for the adverse consequences of climate change. Whether climate change policy, a political question, can be distinguished from the legal question of protecting constitutional rights, as framed in *Juliana*, or the legal question of protecting human rights, as delineated in *Urgenda*, may be a central issue for climate change litigation in other countries. In the final consideration, the problem with a court that recognizes a violation of constitutional or human rights but finds the violation is not redressable is simply a lack of judicial will. As this coursebook has previously expressed, in the words of United States Supreme Court Chief Justice Marshall: "It is emphatically the province and duty of the judicial department to say what the law is."[34] And this includes the laws regarding separation of powers and the role of the courts, whether expressed as an issue of standing, redressability, justiciability, political question, or otherwise.

V. IMPACT OF THE *URGENDA* HOLDING FOR CLIMATE LITIGATION

The *Urgenda* case was the first time a court imposed a duty on a national government to lower its GHG emissions. David Boyd, the United Nations Special Rapporteur on human rights and the environment, said the *Urgenda* case was "the most important climate change court decision in the world so far, confirming that human rights are jeopardized by the climate emergency and that wealthy nations are legally obligated to achieve rapid and substantial emission reductions."[35] What might this ruling mean for both the national government of the Netherlands and the rest of the world?

The Dutch government, notwithstanding the fact that it disagreed with the Supreme Court ruling, has actively pursued measures to reduce its GHG emissions. One of the first steps the Dutch government took in response to the Court's order was the shutdown of most coal-fired power plants in the Netherlands. The resulting energy loss will be replaced by natural gas-powered plants that emit half the amount of carbon dioxide, a reduction of about 9 million tons. In early 2020, it also passed an ambitious legislative act laying out a carbon plan for 2030. Some of the measures: (1) the introduction of a CO2 tax for large companies; (2) natural gas tax increase;

[33] *Id.* at ¶ 68.
[34] Marbury v. Madison, 5 U.S. 137 (1803).
[35] Isabella Kaminski, *Dutch Supreme Court Upholds Landmark Ruling Demanding Climate Action,* The Guardian (Dec. 20, 2019), https://www.theguardian.com/world/2019/dec/20/dutch-supreme-court-upholds-landmark-ruling-demanding-climate-action.

(3) stimulation of wind and solar energy projects; (4) zero-emission driving by 2050; (5) sustainable and CO2-free buildings, and natural gas phased out in new construction; (6) transition from gas to sustainable heat; and (7) investing €330 million with the aim of further reducing CO2 emissions in the agriculture sector through sustainable farming practices.[36]

Beyond the Netherlands, the *Urgenda* holding has promising international implications. Courts in France, Canada, Norway, Pakistan, Ireland, Belgium, Switzerland, New Zealand, and Colombia have all taken on similar cases that were inspired by *Urgenda*.[37] As importantly, the holding provides encouragement for Earth law practitioners in all countries challenged by inadequate action on climate change by the legislative or executive branches of government. Meaningful change can take place when the judicial branch responds to fundamental unfairness. The *Urgenda* decision also created an important precedent for national judiciaries to compel adherence to international climate change duties even if they are not perceived to be directly binding upon a state. This was emphasized by the United Nations High Commissioner for Human Rights, who published a release stating the following:

> The decision confirms that the Government of the Netherlands and, by implication, other governments have binding legal obligations, based on international human rights law. To undertake strong reductions in emissions of greenhouse gases. . . . The recognition by the highest Dutch Court that the Netherlands' human rights obligations provide a legal basis to compel stronger and more rapid action by the Government is vitally important. This landmark ruling provides a clear path forward for concerned individuals in Europe—and around the world—to undertake climate litigation in order to protect human rights . . . .[38]

VI. ATMOSPHERIC TRUST LITIGATION

Atmospheric trust litigation is a relatively recent development in climate justice exemplified by *Juliana*—a case where young plaintiffs sought to compel the government to take action with respect to climate change by means of the public trust doctrine. The basic idea is that the atmosphere is held in trust by the government for the benefit of the public, and therefore the government has a duty to protect the atmosphere. *Urgenda*, while it did not rely explicitly upon the public trust doctrine, had many characteristics that are common to atmospheric trust litigation cases.

The public trust doctrine itself originates from English common law and is an example of an environmental rights-based approach where the government is

[36] Baker McKenzie, *The Netherlands: Highlights of the Dutch Climate Agreement,* Global Compliance News (July 4, 2019), https://globalcompliancenews.com/highlights-dutch-climate-agreement-20190704/.

[37] *Global Climate Litigation,* Urgenda, https://www.urgenda.nl/en/themas/climate-case/global-climate-litigation/(last visited July 4, 2020). The nations referenced are those in which claims had been filed as of March 13, 2020.

[38] *Bachelet Welcomes Top Court's Landmark Decision to Protect Human Rights from Climate Change,* United Nations Human Rights Office of the High Commissioner (Dec. 20, 2019), https://www.ohchr.org/EN/NewsEvents/Pages/DisplayNews.aspx?NewsID=25450&LangID=E.

considered to be a steward of not only essential natural resources, but also of the public's right to protection of these resources.[39] While the public trust doctrine originally applied only to navigation, commerce, and fishing, its scope was later extended to include the protection of groundwater, wetlands, recreation, and wildlife, and, most recently, the protection of the atmosphere.[40]

As demonstrated in both *Juliana* and *Urgenda*, the main goals of atmospheric trust litigation include: (1) imposing a positive obligation on national governments to protect the atmosphere; (2) promoting the rights of both current and future generations; and (3) pursuing a more progressive role by the judicial branch to address climate change. In both cases, plaintiffs argued that the government has a duty to protect the public from the disastrous consequences of climate change for both current and future generations. Unfortunately, only *Urgenda* was successful.

There are, however, some challenges that come with atmospheric trust litigation. First, some courts may be reluctant to rule that the atmosphere should be categorized as a public trust resource since the public trust doctrine has not historically been applied in that context. The second challenge is that some courts, as illustrated by *Juliana*, may consider it too much of an interference in the political decision-making process to issue an injunction mandating certain GHG emission reductions.[41]

There are, however, indications that courts in many states are willing to consider atmospheric trust cases and to establish rights to a stable climate system for present and future generations. In the coming decades, court-mandated GHG emissions will likely become increasingly crucial to the fight against climate change.

VII. CONCLUSION

The *Urgenda* case demonstrates that there are creative ways for courts to consolidate domestic and international laws. In the end, courts have the responsibility to make sure that laws are executed faithfully, including those laws concerning the future of a country and the planet as a whole. The Dutch Court in *Urgenda* has led the way by exercising its authority to change the environmental standards in the Netherlands in accordance with an international treaty with which the government had failed to fully comply.

The *Urgenda* case shows that courts can help address climate change, in accordance with domestic and international legal obligations, while still avoiding political barriers. It did this by framing the holding as a legal decision with political consequences, rather than a political decision made by the judicial branch. This is an approach other courts can take where legislative and executive branches of government fail to take the urgent actions needed to respond to climate change to the detriment of the fundamental rights of their present and future citizens and in disregard of international conventions.

[39] Barton H. Thompson Jr., T*he Public Trust Doctrine: A Conservative Reconstruction & Defense,* 15 Se. ENVTL. L. J. 47, 67 (2006).
[40] Randall S Abate, *Atmospheric Trust Litigation: Foundation for a Constitutional Right to a Stable Climate System,* GEORGE WASHINGTON J. OF ENERGY AND ENVTL. L. (2019).
[41] *Id.*

In countries where the use of a duty of care test is inapplicable or less likely to succeed, as it did in *Urgenda*, each legal system will provide its own opportunities for creative legal arguments for the right to a stable climate, a healthy environment, and other ecocentrically focused rights for humans and nature. The existential threat of climate change, in its global scale, severity, and complexity, warrants something different from the precedent-based, backward-looking systems of common law and civil codes developed in the nineteenth and twentieth centuries. Remarkably, in 1803, Chief Justice John Marshall wrote in *Marbury v. Madison*:

> It is emphatically the duty of the Judicial Department to say what the law is. Those who apply the rule to particular cases must, of necessity, expound and interpret the rule. . . . It is scarcely necessary for the Court to disclaim all pretensions to such a jurisdiction. An extravagance so absurd and excessive could not have been entertained for a moment. . . . So, if a law be in opposition to the Constitution, if both the law and the Constitution apply to a particular case, so that the Court must either decide that case conformably to the law, disregarding the Constitution, or conformably to the Constitution, disregarding the law, the Court must determine which of these conflicting rules governs the case. This is of the very essence of judicial duty.[42]

STUDY QUESTIONS

(1) What factors will influence the extent to which the reasoning by the *Urgenda* Court is relied upon by other courts to address the adverse consequences of climate change? What might influence courts in the United States to take such a bold approach? What will inhibit it?

(2) What are the advantages and disadvantages of "judicial activism"—the notion that courts have a role to play in shaping issues of critical importance to society? How could the *Urgenda* decision be criticized as inappropriate judicial activism? How could it be characterized positively as an example of a court interpreting both national and international laws to establish a new precedent? How did the role of "reasonableness and fairness" in the Dutch legal system affect the decision in *Urgenta*? How would you respond to the argument that any case that makes new law is judicial activism?

(3) Do you think the Dutch Supreme Court was right to interpret national law by reference to the ECHR provisions? Respond to the argument that a national court should not rely on obligations a government owes to other nations to find obligations owed by that government to its citizens?

(4) Consider further the differences in the constitutional structure of the legal systems in the United States and the Netherlands. How did these differences shape the contrasting holdings in *Juliana* and *Urgenda*? Were the different results more a product of differences in the legal systems or in differing interpretations of applicable law?

[42] Marbury v. Madison, 5 U.S. 137 (1803).

CHAPTER 24

Africa[1]

I. INTRODUCTION

Africa is widely recognized as the continent within which humans first originated and evolved. It is home to a rich cultural heritage and tremendous biodiversity. It has also been subjected to colonialism and waves of invasions seeking to plunder its natural resources. Savannah grasslands and primeval jungles teeming with wildlife co-exist with the reality of pervasive habitat destruction, burgeoning cities, and reckless, destructive development.

Since colonial times, there has been widespread oppression and violation of Africa's Indigenous and traditional peoples,[2] their customary laws, and their ancestral lands. Contemporary Africa is beset with environmental degradation caused by deforestation, rampant mining, and other forms of extraction for minerals, metals, and fossil fuels, with resultant air, water, and soil pollution. Mega-infrastructure projects, unfettered development, and urban overcrowding have driven economic inequity, social oppression, and squalid living conditions for many. Governments compete for investors in their quest for growth, prosperity, and economic emancipation.[3] Like elsewhere in the world, they have failed to regulate, let alone stop, the destruction of nature, and attempts to preserve the cultural and traditional values that root African peoples are an ongoing challenge.

Africa is a plurilegal continent: its law is multi-layered and far more diverse than the various state laws alone. Its legal traditions, which have been practiced over millennia on the continent, are rooted in the customary governance systems of its Indigenous and traditional communities. These governance systems are underpinned by a different source of law from that of the dominant systems of state law. They are derived from the laws that govern life—the Earth's laws—based on generations of acute observation of and relationship with the ecosystems to which humans belong.

[1] This chapter was authored by Roger Chennells, a lawyer in South Africa, and The Gaia Foundation.

[2] In this chapter, we define "Indigenous and traditional communities" broadly as peoples of ethnic origin in Africa whose identities originate and are derived from their ancestral lands or territories regulated by their own customary governance systems. In African states, these Indigenous peoples/communities might be described variously as Indigenous or traditional and be organized as clans, communities, tribes, or kingdoms.

[3] *See, e.g.*, Africa Union, *Agenda 2063: The Africa We Want*, https://au.int/en/agenda2063/overview (last visited Feb. 18, 2020), which offers a "blueprint and master plan for transforming Africa into the global powerhouse of the future."

In response to the destructive effects of modern development, a growing movement of African Earth jurisprudence practitioners is promoting the revival and enhancement of Africa's rich cultural heritage of ecologically rooted traditions and Earth-centered customary governance systems. From Benin to Zimbabwe, they are guided by a philosophy of law or worldview, recognized by Thomas Berry at the turn of the century, which finds powerful cultural expression within traditional and Indigenous governance systems.[4]

This chapter provides a panorama of Africa through the lens of Earth law by focusing on the growing Earth jurisprudence movement in Sub-Saharan Africa and offering examples of Earth law re-emerging on the continent at local, national, and regional levels.

Section II discusses traditional African governance systems that predated the colonial invasions—the original Indigenous or *a priori*[5] legal systems by which humans regulated themselves and their relationship with nature over millennia. These early legal systems recognized the inherent rights of nature. Humans co-existed with nature within a respectful and interdependent relationship, as opposed to the current anthropocentric approach, which commodifies ecosystems and all their parts. This section also addresses the enduring importance of sacred natural sites embedded within the ancestral territories of Indigenous and traditional communities.

Section III gives a brief account of the colonial "Scramble for Africa,"[6] in which all but two African states—Liberia and Ethiopia (Abyssinia)—became European colonies and were robbed of their cultures and customary laws. The alliance of state and church denigrated Indigenous African culture and once-vibrant cosmologies, and ancient community governance systems were severely undermined by modern institutions and beliefs imported from Europe. In the 1960s, the "winds of change"[7] heralded the decolonization of African states and the drive for political and economic emancipation.

Section IV describes regional governance on the African continent by introducing the African Union (formerly the Organization for African Unity) as the continent-wide

[4] Thomas Berry drew inspiration for his book *The Great Work* from Indigenous cosmologies and customary laws which place Earth as the primary source of law or, in Berry's words, the "primary text." As noted throughout this book, Berry calls for a move from anthropocentric to ecocentric law. For example, he wrote that ecology must become the queen of the sciences, and not only of the sciences but also of the humanities, economics, and the studies of the professions. It should not be thought of as a separate course of study, but as "the foundation of all courses [and] programs. [Thus, for example,] ecology is not a part of medicine; [rather] medicine is an extension of ecology [because medicine is an extension of the healing powers of Earth]." The same can be said for law. THOMAS BERRY, THE GREAT WORK: OUR WAY INTO THE FUTURE 84 (1999).

[5] The Legal Information Institute gives this meaning to *a priori:* "A Latin term meaning 'from what comes before.'" With reference to African customary law, *a priori* law means norms of conduct inherent in Indigenous cultures that predated modern states.

[6] *See generally* THOMAS PAKENHAM, SCRAMBLE FOR AFRICA (1990).

[7] In a speech to the South African parliament on February 3, 1960, and after a visit to all the British colonies in Africa, U.K. prime minister Harold Macmillan said, "The wind of change is blowing through this continent. Whether we like it or not, this growth of national consciousness is a political fact." Harold Macmillan, *The Wind of Change* (Feb. 3, 1960), http://www.africanrhetoric.org/pdf/J%20%20%20Macmillan%20-%20%20the%20wind%20of%20change.pdf.

governing body and the African Commission on Human and Peoples' Rights (African Commission or ACHPR), together with its visionary "African Charter."[8] It also reviews the emergence of the Earth Jurisprudence movement in Africa, initiated in part by Africans visiting the Colombian Amazon to learn about revitalizing Indigenous culture and customary governance. This experience galvanized community and civil society leaders to "go back to roots" and commence similar processes to revive the connection between humans and nature in Africa.

Section V explores the development of Earth jurisprudence in Africa at regional, national, and local levels. It covers the pathway toward the African Commission's resolution on the recognition and protection of sacred natural sites and territories and the rights of custodian communities to protect those sites,[9] which encourages legal pluralism as called for by the African Charter. Legal and policy developments support the view that the original or *a priori* legal systems that predated colonialism have a vital place in African society and identity and should be recognized in local and national law as part of the decolonization process. Examples of case law and national legislation emphasize the importance of Indigenous legal systems and Earth-centered law as providing essential guidance to humans as to how to live as part of and in harmony with nature, our source of life.

Section VI ventures a conclusion, offering optimism for practitioners of Earth law while also acknowledging the challenges faced in Africa and across the planet in the current decisive decade, the 2020s.

II. AFRICA'S PRE-COLONIAL HERITAGE: CULTURAL DIVERSITY, CUSTOMARY GOVERNANCE, AND SACRED NATURAL SITES

Africa is recognized as the birthplace of the human species, *homo sapiens*, and the continent where we have spent the largest part of our collective history. Evolving with the land, the people of Africa are considered the most genetically[10] and culturally diverse[11] in the world. Different landscapes have fostered distinct ways of life and diverse cultural expressions—spiritual, musical, and other traditions, as well as stories of origin, ceremonies, and at least 2,000 languages. Embedded in these cultural expressions are deep understandings of the ecosystems that nurtured them. These gave rise to

[8] Organization of African Unity, The African Charter on Human and Peoples' Rights (hereafter the "African Charter") OAU Doc. CAB/LEG/67/3 rev. 5, 21 I.L.M. 58 (1982) (adopted June 27, 1981; entered into force October 21, 1986).

[9] ACHPR, Resolution on the Protection of Sacred Natural Sites and Territories, Res. 372 (LX) 2017, https://www.achpr.org/sessions/resolutions?id=414.

[10] Joel Achenbach, *Study Finds Africans More Genetically Diverse Than Other Populations*, The Wash. Post (May 1, 2009).

[11] Max Fisher, *A Revealing Map of the World's Most and Least Ethnically Diverse Countries*, The Wash. Post (May 16, 2013).

sophisticated knowledge and ecological governance systems, which enabled humans in Africa to maintain resilient landscapes over millennia.

The cosmology shared by Indigenous peoples in Africa and worldwide considers humankind as part of a "communion of subjects"[12] within Mother Earth,[13] through an intricate web of ceremony, respect, and lore[14] present since ancient times. The ethos of Indigenous governance systems is for humans to comply with the laws that govern life in order to maintain the integrity of our source of life, Mother Earth. Reverence for her bounty is emphasized through sharing intergenerational knowledge, practices, and ceremony. The understanding is that if we disturb her complex living systems, we will inevitably suffer consequences, as we are now witnessing across our planet. This recognition that the Earth system is lawful and ordered remains an integral part of Indigenous education, health, and governance.

Indigenous peoples, defined broadly from the French word *indigène* as "belonging to the Earth," developed complex systems of law over countless generations through their deep relationship with the wider web of life. Stories of origin, which are held by custodians of the community and shared at key events, commonly describe the tribe or culture's ancient and mythic origin and recognize the essential nurturing quality of the mother of all human and nonhuman beings. These stories orient Indigenous people in their ancestral lands[15] and play foundational roles in African customary law. These customary laws and customary governance systems contain common principles even though the details vary widely within Africa, as they do worldwide.

Sacred natural sites and territories (SNST) and their custodian communities[16] are the legacy of Africa's pre-colonial heritage. As places of ecological, cultural, and spiritual importance, they are at the heart of the traditional customs, laws, values, norms, and principles from which customary governance systems are derived. SNST include natural features, such as mountains, springs, lakes, forests, waterfalls, and caves. They include the horizontal domains of plants, animals, and ancestral spirits, as well as vertical domains reaching deep into the Earth, beyond the subsoil, rocks, and minerals, and up into the celestial constellations in the sky. They include places where spirits and ancestors are present, as inherent parts of the living Earth—focal points of the community's connection with the spiritual world, where rituals are practiced to express respect and gratitude. There is a profound relationship between custodian communities and their SNST. These communities read the law in the land and carry out rituals when justice or balance needs to be restored. The right of SNST not to be degraded or

[12] Thomas Berry, Evening Thoughts: Reflecting on Earth as Sacred Community 17 (2006).

[13] From an Indigenous perspective, the Earth is conceived of as "Mother Earth" rather than "nature."

[14] Ancient and complex governance systems provided both lore and law which governed human relationships as well as those between humans and the rest of nature, the more-than-human world.

[15] The terms "ancestral lands" and "territories" are used interchangeably, making the link between language used in the African Charter (ancestral lands) and language used in other international fora (sacred natural sites and territories).

[16] Indigenous communities and clans whose custodians are specifically responsible for one or more sacred natural site and territory.

developed has profound significance for the health of local ecosystems as well as the lives and cultures that depend on them.

It is a tragedy that many of these ancient community governance systems and cosmologies, which provided context, meaning, and identity for communities across Africa, did not survive the colonial onslaught.

III. THE SCRAMBLE FOR AFRICA AND BEYOND

Thomas Pakenham's 1990 book, *The Scramble for Africa,*[17] describes the colonization of Africa by European powers between 1876 and 1912, where nations vied with each other to annex territories, such as King Leopold II of Belgium, who annexed the Congo. Virtually the entire continent was colonized by Europe, with the exception of Liberia and Ethiopia. Other continents too had suffered this fate over centuries supported by the doctrine of *terra nullius,* which in effect held that Indigenous or customary governance systems did not constitute any form of recognizable governance. This doctrine conveniently enabled the annexation of vast tracts of land that were deemed to be ungoverned, and therefore ripe for the taking.

The reversal of colonialism gathered pace in the 1960s, heralded in Africa by the famous "winds of change" speech of Harold Macmillan announcing the end of the colonial era. Yet it was only in the 1990s that the *terra nullius* doctrine that enabled the entire colonial effort was finally discredited in the seminal Australian case of *Mabo and Others v. Queensland.*[18] This case focused on the importance of active customary law, and the judgment emphasized the fact that Indigenous or traditional governance systems do in fact represent authentic, legal governance, a conclusion that has gathered momentum in the twenty-first century. As the *Mabo* judgment held, the source of title to the traditional lands of the Aboriginal and Torres Straits Islanders was the Indigenous connection to the land through their unbroken customary law.

The "winds of change" and the *Mabo* case have been followed by a growing body of law in Africa that enables Indigenous and traditional communities to assert their rights and responsibilities to their customary laws and governance systems, which are rooted in Earth law. The revival of these African governance systems has developed against a backdrop of devastation for Indigenous communities and their ancestral lands, the consequence of modern African states that collaborate with foreign interests eager to extract "natural resources" from within their jurisdictions, part of the dominant rhetoric on incessant economic growth.

[17] Thomas Packenham, The Scramble for Africa: White Man's Conquest of the Dark Continent from 1876 to 1912 (1990).
[18] *Mabo and Others v. Queensland* (no2), HCA 23, (1992) 175 CLR 1, 1992.

IV. AFRICAN GOVERNANCE, PLURILEGAL SYSTEMS, AND AN EARTH JURISPRUDENCE MOVEMENT

The Organization for African Unity (OAU) was first formed as a continental legislative body in 1963 and was replaced by the African Union in 2002. The 55 member states together form a legislative body guided by a central vision, which includes promoting the characteristics of African communities and embracing Africa's culture and common heritage as it was prior to the colonial era.

The African Charter, adopted by the OAU in 1981,[19] reflects Africa's desire and struggle to shake off the yoke and chains of Western domination. It commits African member states to respect and maintain plurilegal systems as a means of decolonizing Africa's jurisprudence.

The African Charter, founded on both individual and communal rights and a commitment to decolonizing the continent rather than entrenching Western legal norms, is among the most visionary of rights-based charters. The preamble, reaffirming the pledge made by the OAU "to eradicate all forms of colonialism from Africa,"[20] promotes the vision of a continent free from the vestiges of colonialism. A further aspiration contained in the preamble is to restore "the virtues of their historical tradition and the values of African civilization."

The African Commission is a pan-African body founded in 1987 pursuant to the African Charter in service of the African Union. A role of the African Commission is to ensure that both individuals (humans) and communities (peoples) have their inherent rights, as enshrined in the African Charter, acknowledged and protected across Africa. Since its foundation, commissioners have met at least twice a year to report on progress and violations of these rights. The African Commission has a mandate to address and pressure African states directly on rights issues by passing resolutions and producing reports that highlight rights violations and by hearing cases of violations internally or referring them to the African Court or African Union. Two such cases, of the Endorois and the Ogiek in Kenya, are detailed below.

The African Commission's Working Group on Indigenous Populations/Communities (WGIP) has acknowledged that customary laws are, in today's world, treated as subordinate to written laws and commented:

> This is unfortunate given the wide cross-section of people who still rely on African customary law as a source of law, particularly Indigenous communities. Indeed, the fact that most Indigenous communities rely on their traditions and customs to seek recognition and protection of their human and peoples' rights and its relegation to the lowest echelons in the hierarchy of applicable law, means that most of these communities have to labour for recognition of their fundamental human rights.[21]

[19] African Charter, *supra* note 8.

[20] *Id.* art. 2, Sept. 13, 1963, https://www.refworld.org/docid/3ae6b36024.html (last visited Feb. 19, 2020).

[21] ACHPR, *Report of the African Commission's Working Group on Indigenous Populations/Communities: Research and Information Visit to Kenya,* 56 (Mar. 1-19, 2010).

Within this context and the vision of the African Charter, a civil society-led African Earth jurisprudence movement has been taking root. It is committed to enabling the revival of customary laws, Indigenous knowledge, and customs for the rights of humans, peoples, and nature. This movement had its origins in the year 2000, when The Gaia Foundation[22] began to consolidate a network of African civil society leaders who were committed to tackling the root cause of the many social and ecological crises we face and developing another way forward. In partnership with Gaia Amazonas,[23] in Colombia, these African leaders took part in learning journeys to experience the thinking and the work of Indigenous people in the Amazon rainforest. They also participated in other experiential learning processes at the Ngwenyama school for traditional healers in Botswana to reconnect African leaders to their rich bio-cultural heritage of ecological and spiritual knowledge, which they had largely rejected as a result of the colonial process.[24]

More than 150 African change-makers and community leaders have participated in these transformative and experiential learning experiences. Many now work with custodian communities to revive their bio-cultural knowledge and practices; to restore SNST and associated rituals, seed diversity, and food sovereignty; and to strengthen ecological governance systems derived from the laws of Earth. The Gaia Foundation later developed a three-year course to enable small groups of African civil society and community leaders to explore Earth jurisprudence in more depth. The course included wilderness experience and practices to learn the laws of Earth, and explorations of Western and African philosophical and legal traditions, as well as analysis of the impacts of the industrial growth economy and practices for reviving Indigenous knowledge systems. The graduates, African Earth jurisprudence practitioners, are now playing an important role in practice-based advocacy, working alongside traditional communities for the recognition of customary Earth-centered laws and policies from local to pan-African levels (as discussed further below).[25]

The movement is founded on the conviction that Earth-centered approaches to governance that align with the laws of nature are the only way forward for Africa and for the world. African Earth jurisprudence practitioners are accompanying elders, custodians, and their traditional communities on a journey of restoring Indigenous knowledge and practices, SNST, and custodial governance systems. Strategies are continually being sought for reclaiming Indigenous ways of being in partnership with, rather than in dominion over, nature. As the elders and communities gain confidence, they recognize the relevance and importance of their customary laws amidst the current crises, being reminded that their ancient ways and beliefs are neither backward nor primitive nor any of the other pejorative terms that have contributed to the widespread denigration

[22] The Gaia Foundation is an NGO with a global reach that is based in London, UK, and works to revive bio-cultural diversity, regenerate healthy ecosystems, and strengthen community self-governance for climate change resilience. society. *See* https://www.gaiafoundation.org.

[23] *See* https://www.gaiaamazonas.org.

[24] *See* the short film by the African Biodiversity Network and The Gaia Foundation, *A Story Worth Remembering? Unearthing Africa's Identity*, https://vimeo.com/30482538 (last visited Feb. 20, 2020).

[25] Gaia Foundation, *Trainings for Transformation: Africa's First Earth Jurisprudence Graduates*, www.gaiafoundation.org/what-we-do/earth-jurisprudence/trainings-for-transformation (last visited Feb. 20, 2020).

and demise of Indigenous cultures around the world. In Kenya, Benin, South Africa, Ethiopia, Zimbabwe, Cameroon, and Uganda, elders and their communities are now at the forefront of the revival of confidence in the original, *a priori* laws. They are opening pathways for others to follow and establishing precedents for legal recognition.

V. BUILDING A BODY OF AFRICAN JURISPRUDENCE ON EARTH LAW: A MULTIFACETED LEGAL STRATEGY FROM GRASSROOTS TO THE AFRICAN COMMISSION

The Earth jurisprudence movement in Africa is founded upon Indigenous and traditional communities for whom Earth jurisprudence is a living reality inherent in their cosmologies and customary laws. This bottom-up development informs law and policy at regional, national, and local levels, effecting legislative and societal change from the grassroots upwards. The Earth jurisprudence movement derives its resilience from its roots in the work of communities to restore their knowledge and practices, which are underpinned by an understanding of the laws of nature through direct relationship. By using a multifaceted legal strategy, it aims proactively at opening spaces at all levels of governance for recognition of a different source of law.

A. Regional Developments

Domestic laws in each state are generally in the thrall of the modern industrial growth and development paradigm, and this has a huge impact on communities and the ecosystems upon which they depend. Yet the fundamental vision of the African Charter, which is reflected in popular discourse, is to decolonize Africa and to enable Africa to revert to the original values of African civilization. Moreover, many constitutions within Africa promote cultural heritage and customary values as well as devolution, self-governance, and freedom of religion. In accord with the African Charter, across the continent, the following developments reflect the growing influence and application of Earth law.

1. Statement and call to action by African custodian communities, 2015

In 2012 and then again in 2015, custodian communities from Benin, Ethiopia, Kenya, South Africa, and Uganda met to discuss strategies to protect the continent's SNST, to share stories of how they were doing so, and to compile their common customary laws. Together with their allies, they decided to take their voices to the African Commission and seek recognition from Africa's most respected human rights institution.

Representatives of custodian communities from Tharaka, Meru, Kamba, Kikuyu, and Maasai in Kenya; Buganda and Bunyoro in Uganda; Bale and Sheka in Ethiopia; Venda in South Africa; and Adjarra, Avrankou, and Adjohoun in Benin, agreed on a

"Statement and Call to Action," on March 24, 2015, at Lake Langano, Ethiopia.[26] Their statement explained:

> The whole Earth is sacred. Within the body of our Earth there are places which are especially sensitive, because of the special role they play in our ancestral lands. We call these places sacred natural sites. Each sacred natural site plays a different but important role, like the organs in our body. All of life is infused with spirit. . . .
>
> Sacred natural sites and territories are sources of law. They are centres of knowledge and inter-generational learning. Our customary governance systems are established through our relationship with and responsibility for sacred natural sites and territories. Our customary laws are derived from the laws of the Earth, as interpreted from and applied at our sacred natural sites and territories. As custodians, we have a responsibility to ensure that our governance systems comply with the laws of the Earth, the laws that govern life. Our common customary laws that apply to all our sacred natural sites and territories are stated as follows:
>
>> Sacred natural sites are the source of life. Sacred natural sites are where we come from, the heart of life. They are our roots and our inspiration. We cannot live without our sacred natural sites and we are responsible for protecting them.[27]

2. Resolution on the Protection of Sacred Natural Sites and Territories

In response to the Statement and Call to Action, in 2017, the African Commission passed the "Resolution on the Protection of Sacred Natural Sites and Territories"[28] (ACHPR/Res.372). It was drafted in collaboration with the African Commission Working Group on Indigenous Populations/Communities. This landmark policy statement called on state parties to

> recognize sacred natural sites and territories, and their customary governance systems, as contributing to the protection of human and peoples' rights[;] uphold their obligations and commitments under regional and international law on sacred natural sites and territories and their customary governance systems, and the rights of custodian communities[; and] recognize and respect the intrinsic value of sacred natural sites and territories.

Building on a series of policy resolutions and recommendations achieved at IUCN World Conservation Congresses and other international fora, ACHPR/Res.372 heralded a new chapter in Africa's acknowledgment of the critical role that SNST and their associated customary governance systems play in the protection of African ecosystems and in the realization of African people's rights. Passage of the resolution was cause for celebration among custodians, civil society groups, and commissioners alike,

[26] https://www.gaiafoundation.org/wp-content/uploads/2015/09/CalltoAfricanCommission-1.pdf.

[27] Roger Chennels, Co-Authored by Carine Nadal/The Gaia Foundation, *Submission To The African Commission*: A Call for Legal Recognition of Sacred Natural Sites and Territories, and Their Customary Governance Systems 9-10 (2015).

[28] ACHPR/Res.372(LX)2017.

as, by strengthening recognition of the original laws that make up Africa's plurilegal systems, it represented an important step towards the decolonization of African legal systems and conservation practices.

The resolution has no enforceable provisions. However, the African Commission can pressure African states directly to ensure they are aware of and implement the resolution at national levels. Further, as a quasi-judicial body, the African Commission can hear cases about the violation of SNST. The African Commission can also refer cases to the African Court to hold violators to account. The resolution provides a basis for developing national policy frameworks and legislation for recognizing SNST and their customary governance systems. So far, only Benin has adopted a written law for the protection of SNST, a law on Sacred Forests, which is discussed below.[29]

3. Guiding principles and a draft African Model Law, 2018

Following ACHPR/Res.372, a "Draft African Model Law for the Recognition and Protection of Sacred Natural Sites and Territories" was developed by The Gaia Foundation, the African Biodiversity Network, and African Earth jurisprudence practitioners.[30] This document provides guiding principles for the domestication of ACHPR/Res.372 into national laws to protect and conserve SNST together with their related customary governance systems in Africa.

This proposed African Model Law offers an important vision of improving Africa's plurilegal systems through recognition of traditional institutions.[31] It highlights the need for guidelines for drafting laws protecting SNST that are adaptable in the varying ecological, cultural, social, and political realities of each African nation. It also explains how the recognition and protection of Africa's SNST and custodial governance systems supports the implementation of Agenda 2063,[32] the 2030 Agenda for Sustainable Development,[33] and the 2050 vision on biodiversity[34] of living in harmony with nature, along with contributing to an integrated, prosperous, and peaceful Africa.

[29] Republic of Benin Ministry of the Environment, Housing and Town Planning Ministry of Decentralisation, Local Governance, Administration and Country Planning Cabinets, Interministerial Order, N°0121/MEHU/MDGLAAT/DC/SGM/DGFRN/SA, Setting the Conditions for the Sustainable Management of Sacred Forests in the Republic of Benin (2014), https://sacrednaturalsites.org/wp-content/uploads/2014/09/Benin-Sacred-Forest-law-final-English-version-2014.pdf.

[30] The Gaia Foundation, African Biodiversity Network, and African Earth Jurisprudence Practitioners, *African Model Law For The Recognition And Protection Of Sacred Natural Sites And Territories: Introduction, Guiding Principles And The Model Law Text* (Working Draft—Oct. 2018), https://www.gaiafoundation.org/wp-content/uploads/2018/10/AfricanModelLawandGuidingPrinciples_WorkingDraft_bw_October2018.pdf.

[31] IPBES, *Regional Assessment Report on Biodiversity and Ecosystem Services for Africa* (2018), https://www.ipbes.net/assessment-reports/africa.

[32] Africa Union, *Agenda 2063: The Africa We Want*, https://au.int/en/agenda2063/overview.

[33] G.A. Res. 70/1, Transforming Our World: The 2030 Agenda for Sustainable Development (Sep. 25, 2015).

[34] IUCN, *A New Vision for Biodiversity Conservation Strategic Plan for the Convention On Biological Diversity* (CBD) 2011-2020 (2010), https://www.iucn.org/sites/dev/files/import/downloads/cbd_cop10__position_paper__strategic_plan_2011_2020_1.pdf; and Convention on Biological Diversity, Long-Term Strategic Directions to the 2050 Vision for Biodiversity, Approaches to Living in Harmony with Nature and Preparation for the post-2020 Global Biodiversity Framework (COP-14, Nov. 17-29, 2018), https://www.cbd.int/doc/c/0b54/1750/607267ea9109b52b750314a0/cop-14-09-en.pdf.

Article 5 of the draft African Model Law recognizes the following "inherent rights" of SNST:

- The right to life, and to exist.
- The right to be respected and maintain their physical, cultural, spiritual, and ecological integrity and resilience.
- The right to persist, maintain and regenerate their vital cycles, structure, functions, and evolutionary processes free from human alteration or interferences.
- The right to maintain their identity and integrity as distinct, interconnected networks within the territory, as self-regulating bodies consisting of different but interdependent and interrelated beings.
- The right to be sacred, to be recognised and to remain as such.
- The right to be free from contamination, pollution and toxic or radioactive waste as well as any activity which might undermine their integrity.
- The right to full and prompt restoration of any violation of the rights recognized in this law caused by human activities.

4. Jurisprudence of the African Commission on Human and Peoples' Rights and the African Court on Human and Peoples' Rights

The jurisprudence of the African Commission and the African Court on Human and Peoples' Rights ("African Court" or "ACtHPR")[35] are replete with references to legal pluralism, and the need to respect the ancestral or customary laws that predate modern law and find great resonance with Earth law.

The *Endorois* case[36] stands as a touchstone case in the interpretation of the African Charter regarding sacred ancestral lands and customary governance systems.

[35] The following excerpt is a helpful introduction to the African Court from its website:

> The African Court on Human and Peoples' Rights (the Court) is a continental court established by African countries to ensure the protection of human and peoples' rights in Africa. It complements and reinforces the functions of the African Commission on Human and Peoples' Rights.
>
> The Court was established by virtue of Article 1 of the Protocol to the African Charter on Human and Peoples' Rights on the Establishment of an African Court on Human and Peoples' Rights, (the Protocol) which was adopted by Member States of the then Organization of African Unity (OAU) in Ouagadougou, Burkina Faso, in June 1998. The Protocol came into force on 25 January 2004.
>
> As of now, only nine (9) of the thirty (30) States Parties to the Protocol [have] made the declaration recognising the competence of the Court to receive cases from NGOs and individuals. The nine (9) States are: Benin, Burkina Faso, Côte d'Ivoire, The Gambia, Ghana, Mali, Malawi, Tanzania and Republic of Tunisia.

ACtHPR, *Welcome to the African Court*, https://en.african-court.org/ (last visited Feb. 20, 2020).

[36] *Centre for Minority Rights Development (Kenya) and Minority Rights Group International on Behalf of Endorois Welfare Council v. Kenya*, ACHPR, 276/2003, https://www.hrw.org/sites/default/files/related_material/2010_africa_commission_ruling_0.pdf.

In 2003, a complaint was filed with the African Commission against the Kenyan Government for forcibly removing the Endorois, a Kenyan hunter-gatherer and pastoralist community, from their ancestral lands, and in particular for restricting their access to a sacred lake. In 2009, the African Commission became the first international tribunal to recognize Indigenous peoples in Africa and their rights as custodians to their ancestral lands. The African Commission interpreted Article 8 of the African Charter (freedom of conscience and religion) as follows: "religion is often linked to land, cultural beliefs and practices, and [the] freedom to worship and engage in such ceremonial acts is at the center of the freedom of religion."[37] The African Commission also interpreted the meaning of culture as "including the spiritual and physical association with ancestral land, knowledge, belief, morals, values, law, customs and any other practices."[38] The African Commission found that the Kenyan Government had violated the rights of the Endorois under the African Charter including Articles 8, 14, 17, 21, and 22—respectively, the right to religious practice, property, culture, free disposition of natural resources, and development—and recommended that Kenya:

(a) Recognize rights of ownership to the Endorois and restitute Endorois ancestral land.
(b) Ensure that the Endorois community has unrestricted access to Lake Bogoria and surrounding sites for religious and cultural rites and for grazing their cattle.
(c) Pay adequate compensation to the community for all the loss suffered.
(d) Pay royalties to the Endorois from existing economic activities and ensure that they benefit from employment possibilities within the Reserve.
(e) Grant registration to the Endorois Welfare Committee.
(f) Engage in dialogue with the complainants for the effective implementation of these recommendations.
(g) Report on the implementation of these recommendations within three months from the date of notification.[39]

In a subsequent case in 2017, the African Court ruled in favor of the Ogiek Indigenous community of Kenya, and in doing so, further strengthened the authority of customary governance within African plurilegal systems.[40] The eviction of the Ogiek people from their ancestral land in the Mau Forest in 2009 was found to violate multiple provisions of the African Charter, including freedom of religion (Article 8) and the right to culture (Article 17(2) and (3)). The court recognized that the Ogiek had a communal right to their ancestral land and affirmed the interconnection between the Forest and the Ogiek's cultural practices. Interestingly, the African Court rejected Kenya's argument that the eviction of the Ogiek was needed for the conservation of the Mau Forest and thereby effectively recognized the role played by Indigenous

[37] *Id.* at ¶ 166.
[38] *Id. at* ¶ 241.
[39] *Id.* at ¶ 80.
[40] *ACHPR v. Republic of Kenya*, ACtHPR, Application No. 006/2012 (2017).

peoples in the conservation of land. This was the first case in which the African Court ruled on an Indigenous peoples' rights case.[41]

Despite the holdings in the above two cases, the Kenyan government has not fully remedied the rights violations outlined in the judgments.

B. National Case Law—Examples from South Africa

At the state and national levels, a body of case law is developing based on the recognition of Indigenous peoples' customary rights. This trend has been a basis for rolling back several harmful development projects. It also empowers Indigenous peoples to serve as custodians of their ancestral land and all life therein. The three cases below exemplify such developments within South Africa.

1. *Richtersveld* Case (Rights to Land—South Africa)[42]

In this case, the Richtersveld Community, Nama-speaking Indigenous peoples, known collectively as Khoi-Khoi, sued Alexkor Ltd, a diamond-mining company owned by the government of the Republic of South Africa. The community asked for their ancestral land to be restored based on the Restitution of Land Rights Act 22 of 1994, which required them to prove loss of rights to land as a result of past racially discriminatory laws or practices. The Supreme Court of Appeal confirmed that the Richtersveld community was in exclusive possession of the land in question prior to annexation by the British Crown in 1847, deemed the practice of annexing the community's land to be racially discriminatory, and found that community was entitled to restitution. The decision was confirmed by the Constitutional Court, which recognized and emphasized the value of the Indigenous customs to support the return of the land to the community. The decision affirmed the application of customary law to protect the land interests of Indigenous peoples.

2. *Gongqose* Case (Fishing Rights—South Africa)[43]

This case started with the conviction for illegal fishing of members of the Hobeni Xhosa community in the Eastern Cape region of South Africa. The conviction was appealed to the Supreme Court of Appeal on the basis that customary rights were protected under Section 211(3) of the Constitution, which states: "The courts must apply customary law when that law is applicable, subject to the Constitution and any

[41] ESCR-Net, *African Court Upholds Land Rights for Kenya's Ogiek*, https://www.escr-net.org/caselaw/2017/african-commission-human-and-peoples-rights-v-republic-kenya-acthpr-application-no (last visited February 20, 2020).

[42] Richtersveld Community and Others v. Alexkor LTD and the Government of the Republic of South Africa, Supreme Court of Appeal Case No. 488/2001 (Mar. 24, 2003).

[43] Gongqose and Others v. Minister of Agriculture, Forestry & Fisheries and Others; Gongqose & Others v. State & Others (1340/16 & 287/17) [2018] ZASCA 87 (June 1, 2018).

legislation that specifically deals with customary law."[44] The court decided that the Marine Living Resources Act (the current law prohibiting extraction of mussels without a permit) did not extinguish the appellants' prior customary right of access to and respectful use of marine life. In other words, the court held that *a priori* customary laws, being maintained by the community, predated the modern law and provided a valid defense to charges in terms of subsequent statutory laws. The convictions of the appellants were set aside.

3. *Xolobeni* Case (Mining—South Africa)

In this case, an Australian mining company, Transworld Energy and Mineral Resources (TEM), was challenged over mining rights by the Xolobeni community in the Eastern Cape province of South Africa. The community first launched a legal claim against the Department of Mineral Resources and TEM over mining rights in 2007. After many years of litigation, during which mining laws and regulations were changed by the government, the High Court of South Africa (Gauteng Division, Pretoria) in 2018 awarded judgment in the community's favor. The court ordered that the government was required to obtain prior informed consent—not simply consulting the community—before granting mining rights, which in effect held that the community has the right to decide what happens with its land. The court's conclusion was based upon the combination of two domestic laws: the Interim Protection of Informal Land Rights Act (IPILRA), which states that no one can be deprived of land without their consent, and the Mineral and Petroleum Resources Development Act (MPRDA), which is intended to give equal access to mineral resources to all South Africans.[45]

C. National Legislation

Earth law is also finding expression within national legislation in Africa. Most laws relating to nature continue to place humans as central, such as South Africa's National Water Act (1998), which states in the preamble that "water is a natural resource that belongs to all people."[46] This anthropocentric perspective fails to reflect the countless other nonhuman beings whose lives depend on the health and integrity of water bodies in and around which they live. The following three examples are signs of a growing trend of ecocentric awareness, namely Benin's Sacred Forest Act, section 4 of the National Environment Act 2019 in Uganda, and two Rights of River Bills under review in Nigeria.

[44] Constitution of the Republic of South Africa, 1996—Chapter 12, Section 211(3).

[45] For additional information on this case, see Alex Mitchley, High Court Rules in Favour of Xolobeni Community in Historic Mining Rights Case, Mail & Guardian, Nov. 22, 2018, https://mg.co.za/article/2018-11-22-high-court-rules-in-favour-of-xolobeni-community-in-historic-mining-rights-case/; and Zelda Venter, Xolobeni Community Scores Huge Victory against Mining, IOL, Nov. 22, 2018, 11:51 AM, https://www.iol.co.za/news/south-africa/gauteng/watch-xolobeni-community-scores-huge-victory-against-mining-18223575.

[46] National Water Act No. 36 of 1998, Preamble.

1. Sacred Forests Act, Benin

In 2012, civil society and communities successfully advocated for the Benin Government to pass a national law for the sustainable "management" and legal recognition of sacred forests as protected areas. Benin is the first country in Africa to pass a national law that expressly recognizes sacred forests and their custodian communities. Indeed, the Interministerial Order is among the few laws in the world to recognize SNST and the community custodians. The Act offers an example to other African nations, heeding the call of ACHPR/Res.372 and responding to the growing number of international laws, policies, resolutions, and guidelines that urge for the protection of SNST and their custodian governance.

In a radical departure from the forest governance regimes promoted in other jurisdictions, "Interministerial Order No. 0121 setting the conditions for the sustainable management of the sacred forest in the Republic of Benin" (2012) recognizes sacred forests, burial forests, and sites where gods, spirits, and ancestors reside and provides for communities to protect, govern, and implement management plans for sacred forests. In addition, the order prohibits industrial farming, tree felling, bush clearing, and hunting, amongst other activities, within sacred forests. The Interministerial Order No. 0121 builds on Benin's Constitution, which recognizes the right to culture, freedom of religion, and customary laws and affirms the State's duty to safeguard spiritual and cultural traditions.

2. National Environment Act 2019, Uganda

In 2019, Uganda became the first African country to recognize the rights of nature within national state law. Section 4 of the National Environmental Act (NEA 2019) provides as follows:

(1) Nature has the right to exist, persist, maintain and regenerate its vital cycles, structure, functions and its processes in evolution.
(2) A person has a right to bring an action before a competent court for any infringement of rights of nature under this Act.
(3) Government shall apply precaution and restriction measures in all activities that can lead to the extinction of species, the destruction of the ecosystems or the permanent alteration of the natural cycles.
(4) The Minister shall, by regulations, prescribe the conservation areas for which the rights in subsection (1) apply.

This huge achievement reflects the beginning of a paradigm shift in ecological governance by recognizing that Ugandans' right to a healthy environment cannot be realized unless the health of nature herself is protected. It is the result of three years of sustained advocacy by Ugandan environmental and legal advocacy group ANARDE (Advocate for Natural Resources and Development) with the support of The Gaia Foundation, NAPE (National Association of Professional Environmentalists), AFRICE

(African Institute for Culture and Ecology), and the Open Society Initiative for East Africa.

The regulations referenced in subsection 4(4) of NEA 2019 are yet to be issued. By restricting the areas in which the rights of nature will apply this provision potentially severely limits the reach of the act. The forthcoming regulations to implement the rights of nature in Uganda mark a crucial next step in the establishment of Earth law in Africa and offer an opportunity to reverse the potentially restrictive effect of subsection 4(4). A broad and inclusive definition of "conservation areas" is crucial so that the rights of nature apply as extensively as possible.

3. River Ethiope Rights Bill and Nigeria Rights of Rivers Bill, Nigeria

In an effort to establish the River Ethiope as the first river in Africa to be recognized as a living entity with legal rights, the River Ethiope Trust Foundation (RETFON), Earth Law Center, and other partners drafted the River Ethiope Rights Bill, which is now undergoing a review process. The River Ethiope is situated in the Delta State of Nigeria and is a sacred river for followers of the traditional Olokun and Igbe religions. In parallel, the Nigeria Rights of Rivers Act has been presented to the upper chamber of the National Assembly of the Federal Republic of Nigeria, and it is being scheduled for review. In addition, comments on the Nigeria National Water Resources Act 2016 calling for rights of rivers integration into the law have been presented to the Nigerian Parliament and are currently under consideration.

D. Local Developments

The regional and national developments described above demonstrate that there is a growing body of African Earth law. Local and district level developments are key to furthering the legal strategy. The following two examples showcase grassroots initiatives for the revival and recognition of their customary governance systems and SNST.

In Uganda, the Buliisa District Council has passed a resolution recognizing Bagungu customary laws and governance systems—the first example of practical, local implementation of ACHPR/Res.372. The District Council and the Association of Custodian Clans of SNST in Bagungu are developing an ordinance that will demonstrate how plurilegal systems can be implemented at the district level.[47] In the preamble of their customary laws, the Bagungu state:

> Our source of law is Maweetu (Mother Earth, the Universe—all of Creation which is not human-made) which is read from our Mpuluma (sacred natural sites) and our Bugungu land, which has sustained us for generations. Our customary laws come from the

[47] Open Society Initiative for Eastern Africa (OSIEA) supports a project with Bagungu custodians to develop human, peoples' and nature's rights, accompanied by Ugandan organizations ANARDE (Advocates for Natural Resources and Development), AFRICE (African Institute for Culture and Ecology), NAPE (National Association of Professional Environmentalists), and The Gaia Foundation (U.K.).

> Bugungu Indigenous Laws of Origin, from our ancestors, from our detailed observation of the laws of our territory and from our relationship with our Butaka (territory), over generations. We understand how the patterns and cycles of life are part of a complex system which includes the solar, lunar and celestial cycles.[48]

In Kenya, local communities in Tharaka District are reviving their cultural identity, traditional farming, and indigenous seed diversity, and building the case for their SNST and customary governance to be recognized in-line with ACHPR/Res.372. Tharakan clan members developed a ten-point resolution, and the Tharaka-Nithi county government, recognizing that Indigenous knowledge is key for the restoration of local rivers and the drought-ravaged ecosystem, has indicated its support for this Earth-centered approach.

VI. CONCLUSION

Earth law is developing as a means to restore the cultural and natural heritage of Africa where customary laws derived from the laws of the Earth — the "primary text" — are now being recognized by courts and legislatures as part of Africa's plurilegal systems.

This chapter documents the origin and journey of African Earth jurisprudence practitioners and custodian communities, together with their allies, in a growing movement from grassroots to the international policy level to correct the wrongs of the past century and, in particular, wrongs that ravage Mother Earth and her communities. These Earth jurisprudence practitioners and Indigenous communities recognize a different conception and origin of law, identifying the Earth as the primary source of our human laws. The developments outlined above provide grounds for optimism for Earth law practitioners that Africa is increasingly moving to give effect to the vision of the African Charter, namely that it can find its soul in restoring its ancient cultural and natural heritage. The inspiration for this movement, as encapsulated by Earth jurisprudence, is provided by a new understanding and respect for the importance of customary governance systems, sacred natural sites, and ancestral lands across the continent.

STUDY QUESTIONS

(1) Mining is big business in Africa. Many mining companies exploiting minerals on the continent are foreign-owned, provide little benefit to local communities, and devastate surrounding ecosystems and the sustainable livelihoods they support. Is Earth law incompatible with this "extractive" economic paradigm? If so, why, what has to change, and who should get to decide what changes are needed?

[48] The Customary Laws of Bagungu Custodian Clan (2019).

(2) Uganda has already recognized the rights of nature through a national environmental law, although full implementation is pending. Meanwhile, the River Ethiope Rights Bill is an emerging possibility in Nigeria that would establish a sacred waterway as a rights-bearing entity. These are two different approaches, one through a national law applying to all of nature and the other a grassroots effort to protect a specific watershed. What are the challenges and opportunities of both approaches as examples for other locations?

(3) Indigenous peoples and Earth jurisprudence practitioners recognize Mother Earth as the primary source of law from which all human laws should derive. Thus in order to practice Earth law, we need to learn the laws of the Earth—what Thomas Berry called the "primary text." Earth jurisprudence practitioners therefore develop personal practices to cultivate close observation of and relationship with the natural world to which they belong. What personal practices might you cultivate to support your understanding of the laws of the Earth?

CHAPTER 25

Indigenous Legalities[1]

I. INTRODUCTION

Over the last few decades, Indigenous communities in Latin America have faced the interrelated crises of climate change, natural resource extraction, and violence.[2] Indigenous struggles, ranging from mobilizations on the ground to various forms of legal activism at local, national, and international levels, are part of an ongoing grassroots movement to resist the worst consequences of development and Western modernity.

Western modernity is, broadly speaking, characterized by the separation between humans and the larger community of life. It endorses a paradigm of expert knowledge[3] at the expense of "non-modern" legal systems that are based on oral tradition and the intimate relationship between humans and nature. In addition, Western modernity often produces and reinforces power asymmetries between social groups and growth-oriented economic systems.

Western environmental law is often framed as an independent set of norms and procedures to regulate the human use of an external entity: nature. This model, however, remains grounded in what scholar John Law has called a "one-world world"

[1] This chapter was authored by Iván Darío Vargas Roncancio, M.Sc., and Ph.D. candidate in Natural Resource Science—Renewable Resources and Fellow of the Leadership for the Ecozoic Program at McGill University, and *Taita* Hernando Chindoy Chindoy an Indigenous traditional authority of the Inga people of Colombia, and a university expert on Indigenous issues, *Universidad Carlos III,* Madrid, 2013. Research assistance by Daan de Bruijn, law student at Amsterdam University College. The authors give special acknowledgement to the Inga Indigenous people of Colombia, the Wasikamas of Aponte-Nariño, and the editors of this volume. Also, to the Leadership for the Ecozoic program at McGill University—especially Dina Spigelski and Peter Brown, and Colciencias in Colombia for their support, and law and environment student Daan de Bruijn at the Amsterdam University College for her outstanding research assistance for this chapter. Last but not least, thanks to James Magnus for proofreading several translations for this chapter.

[2] Arturo Escobar, *Sentipensar con la Tierra: Las Luchas Territoriales y la Dimensión Ontológica de las Epistemologías del Sur,* 11(1) Revista de Antropologia Iberoamericana 11, 14 (2016).

[3] Since the invention of the discourse of economic development after World War II and the problematizing of "poverty" (in other words the ways of life of most of the world's people at that time), expertise in "economic development" has been particularly pertinent. Part and parcel of that expertise was how to bring Western legal conventions of property and contract, among others, to bear to promote the market economy. *See* Arturo Escobar, *The Problematization of Poverty: The Tale of Three Worlds and Development, in* ENCOUNTERING DEVELOPMENT: THE MAKING AND UNMAKING OF THE THIRD WORLD 21-54 (1995).

ontology,[4] which suggests that regardless of cultural variations and belief systems, humans and nature occupy one single real world made up of *discrete* and *separate* entities. This vision—which we call an "ontology of separation" between nature and culture—poses significant challenges for ecocentric legal practice.[5]

This chapter will offer a point of view of what Anishinaabe[6] legal scholar Aaron Mills calls "Indigenous legalities" as a way to respond to these features of Western legalities.[7] By Indigenous legalities, we do not mean only Indigenous legal *traditions*—a set of customs, norms, and procedures to regulate social behavior but also the local "lifeworlds," which are "distinct ways of knowing and being in the world,"[8] including forms of laws for humans and nature.

Drawing from these principles, the chapter surveys some of the main tenets, methodologies, and sources of Indigenous legalities in the Americas as a contribution to the emergent field of Earth law. Indigenous legal theory and practice must draw from the living and knowledge systems where the legal order is already embedded. Part of this task consists in taking seriously the systems of norms, procedures, and practices informed by the multiplicity of lifeworlds referred to as Indigenous legalities. In many countries, such as Colombia and Ecuador, law at the state level already incorporates Indigenous legalities. Such countries are said to have *plurilegal systems.*

Following Indigenous legal practice in the Andean-Amazonian region, the life-enhancing vision endorsed by the authors of this chapter embraces a relational, rather than separationist, view of the world. This view underscores the radical interdependency between human and nonhuman beings, pays attention to the benefits of plurilegal systems, and recognizes the intelligence and communicative capacities of the nonhuman world.

Earth law challenges the narratives and premises of Western law and, in particular, environmental law. Indigenous legalities contribute to the emergent field of Earth law by emphasizing a paradigm shift away from anthropocentricism to ecocentrism. The purpose of this chapter is to enable students to understand the contribution of Indigenous legalities to Earth law and prepare practitioners to be advocates for Indigenous peoples and Indigenous legalities. Section II concerns the differences between Western law and Indigenous legalities; Section III concerns the sources and methods of Indigenous legalities; Section IV presents Colombian and Inter-American case law regarding Indigenous legalities; and Section V offers a vision of Indigenous legalities

[4] For the purposes of this chapter, ontology means a set of claims about the nature of reality. John Law, Paper presented at the Center for the Humanities, Wesleyan University, Middletown, CT (Sept. 19, 2011), http://www.heterogeneities.net/publications/Law2011WhatsWrongWithAOneWorldWorld.pdf.

[5] *See* Ivan Vargas Roncancio et al., *From the Anthropocene to Mutual Thriving: An Agenda for Higher Education in the Ecozoic,* 11 Sustainability 3312 (2019).

[6] *Anishinaabe* is an ethnic term generally referring to the shared culture of the native tribes of the Great Lakes area in both America and Canada.

[7] Aaron Mills, *Miinigowiziwin: All That Has Been Given for Living Well Together: One Vision of Anishinaabe Constitutionalism,* University of Victoria Dissertation, iii (2019), https://dspace.library.uvic.ca/bitstream/handle/1828/10985/Mills_Aaron_PhD_2019.pdf?sequence=1&isAllowed=y.

[8] *Id.* at 24.

in the Andean-Amazonian context today: the *Wuasikamas* law, or the "law for the guardianship of Earth" of the Inga people of Colombia.

II. COLONIALITY AND THE LAW

This chapter builds upon the body of work that reverses the predominant colonial relation between Western modernity and Amerindian (i.e., Indigenous American) worlds. It primarily concerns how Amerindian ways of knowing and being can transform Western legal systems, rather than how Western law impacts Indigenous life and legal systems. Indigenous legalities offer a useful lens to transform Western law in the face of the ecological crises. To illuminate the ways that Indigenous legalities can transform Western legal systems, one must first understand how Western colonial systems have impacted Indigenous lifeworlds and legalities and how this colonization persists.

Following the famous Valladolid debate in Spain in 1550–1551 about the treatment of Indigenous peoples in the newly colonized lands of the Americas, the *derecho indiano* (Spanish colonial law) formalized the treatment of Indigenous others as "things," depriving them of their humanity. The Valladolid debate was the first moral and legal dispute in European history to discuss the appropriate course of treatment of Indigenous peoples under the Spanish Crown. One of the outcomes was eliminating local epistemologies—that is, ways of representing reality through rituals, social practices, and legal systems.

The book *Comparative Legal Traditions* illustrates how Western law tends to undermine Indigenous legalities.[9] The narrative begins with an account of how Roman law was the beginning of "civilized" legal systems and remains today a primary source for understanding and interpreting legal developments. The progress of Western law continued with the tradition of canon law—a set of norms derived from the regulation of Christian conduct—and the formation of national laws in the mid-sixteenth century.

Contextualizing the "modern" legal tradition, *Comparative Legal Traditions* goes on to describe the legal structures, principles, and legal actors of a civil law republic, the tenets of common law and parliamentary government, the separation of powers, and the enforcement of judicial review, amongst other topics.[10] While the book gives a thorough description of legal tradition in the Western context, one should ask: What is missing from this picture? The answer is that this standard legal narrative ignores Indigenous peoples' systems of law. It also does not cover how Indigenous peoples influenced and shaped legal institutions in the Western context. Suffice it to say what was omitted is highly relevant to understanding the multiplicity of Indigenous legalities in colonial contexts and their importance in facing today's ecological crisis.

Other relevant omissions in the account given in *Comparative Legal Traditions* include the complete disregard for the violent histories of imperial and colonial domination, as well as the pervasive transplantation of Western culture and

[9] MARY ANN GLENDON, PAOLO CAROZZA, & COLIN PICKER, COMPARATIVE LEGAL TRADITIONS (2006).
[10] *Id.*

re-appropriation of Indigenous cultures that are fundamental parts of Western legal history. This text, as well as the standard Western narrative of the legal system, also omit the role that pre-Roman law and culture, including Middle Eastern law and culture, played in the formation of Roman law, and the colonial character of legal structures imposed upon already existing pre-Columbian modes of governance in the so-called New World. These legal paradigms and cultures, regarded as the "other," were subsumed as though they did not exist.

Anishinaabe legal scholar John Borrows finds similar flaws in Canada's legal system. He argues that Canada's legal system is incomplete because Indigenous legalities are generally ignored, diminished, or denied as being authoritative sources of law. Therefore, he suggests, the legal system of Canada, a country that is made up of more than just European settlers, needs to be reconstructed around a broader framework, one that takes seriously Indigenous legalities embedded in larger lifeworlds.[11]

The colonialist ethos just outlined is present in other areas of the law, as well. For example, Steven Newcomb considers that "[i]nternational law serves as an excellent example of...'the linguistic colonization of the present by the past.' "[12] Western colonizers were portrayed as dominating "inferior" or "subordinate" people, and now these Western nations "...carry forward, from generation to generation, a reality of domination and dehumanization, especially in relation to nations and peoples termed 'Indigenous.' "[13] In other words, accepted international law supports the conquest claims of nations over other nations and peoples and then, additionally, the continuing right to control those conquered. Newcomb calls this "the domination of Indigenous peoples by states."[14]

Irene Watson, an Indigenous legal scholar from the Tanganekald, Meintangk Boandik First Nations Peoples of the Coorong in South Australia, calls the tension between Indigenous peoples and states "the story of the conflict between authority and power. Authority is in the hands of First Nations Peoples and is law, while power is held by states by way of a violent foundation."[15] Watson further argues that "[w]e already know and have known forever whom we are, *we were here first,* and we already know the land and each other. We have our own stories of whom we are and how we came to be, but now we are in a dialogue about our future and survival, about genocide."[16]

The purpose of the remainder of this chapter is to propose a solution so that Indigenous legalities may be practiced in plurilegal systems and, in doing so, transform the Western legal system, fostering the emergence of Earth law. As you will read, achieving this goal requires expanding notions of representation, agency, standing,

[11] John Borrows, Canada's Indigenous Constitution 23-24 (2010).

[12] Steven Newcomb, *Domination in Relation to Indigenous ("Dominated") Peoples in International Law,* Indigenous Peoples as Subjects of International Law 18, 20 (Irene Watson ed., 2017) (quoting email from Chet Bowers to Seven Newcomb (Feb. 27, 2016)).

[13] *Id.*

[14] *Id.* at 21.

[15] Irene Watson, *First Nations, Indigenous Peoples: Our Laws Have Always Been Here,* Indigenous Peoples As Subjects Of International Law 97 (Irene Watson ed., 2017).

[16] *Id.* at 101-102 (emphasis in original).

rights, and justice to include other-than-human beings within the legal system. It also requires understanding that Indigenous legalities address not only the normative aspects of legal systems but also their world-making and emancipatory (i.e., freedom-giving) capacities.

The next step in understanding how Indigenous legalities can transform Western legal systems is to understand how to discern Indigenous legalities from the myriad colonial, interrelated, and increasingly complex legal systems and sources in the world today.

III. RECOGNIZING INDIGENOUS LEGALITIES: FROM SACRED TO CUSTOMARY LAW

Indigenous peoples across the Americas hold different views on the character and practice of law, as well as different theories about what gives the law its binding force. The sources of Indigenous legalities are diverse and numerous and include "sacred teachings, naturalistic observations, positivistic proclamations, deliberative practices, and local and national customs," among others.[17] The study of these legalities, therefore, requires a particular epistemological approach through which human and nonhuman beings — including plants and animals, the supernatural, and even the inert — are all considered social agents.

We begin by exploring Borrows's justification for treating nonhumans as social agents in the North American context. Then, examples are given from Latin America to test these ideas. We also note the commonalities between the two continents.

A. Sacred Law: The Creator

Borrows writes that laws given in "creation stories or revered ancient teachings . . . are often given the highest respect," for they come from the Creator.[18] Creation stories, which refer to the formation of the world, are one source of such sacred law. They "contain rules and norms that give guidance about how to live with the world and overcome conflict. . . . They [also] contain instructions about how all beings should relate to specific territories."[19] The recognition, enforcement, and implementation of such "sacred laws" can be seen as foundational to the operation of other Indigenous laws.[20] Working with elders in Saskatchewan, Borrows learned that even treaties between Indigenous peoples and Canada are believed to flow from a sacred source because they "brought Canada into existence within their [ancestral] territories." Such treaties were also believed to be not only with the Crown but with the Creator, as well.[21] One reason

[17] Borrows, *supra* note 11, at 24.
[18] *Id.* at 33.
[19] *Id.* at 34.
[20] *Id.*
[21] *Id.* at 35.

Indigenous peoples did not abandon these treaties, despite generations of injustices, is because doing so would violate sacred law.[22]

STUDY QUESTIONS

(1) For the Indigenous Iku in northern Colombia, *Serankwa,* the creator, "left everything" — rivers, forests, the law:

> According to the spiritual teachings of our ancients, the rivers are our veins and arteries; the forests represent our hair and the hair of our bodies; the stones are our ancestors peacefully resting . . . we understand that everything was left by our father *Serankwa*— the creator of everything that exists and the Laws of Universal Order. . . . These laws are to keep the balance between humanity, nature and the cosmos.[23]

What are the challenges and possibilities of considering this creation story as a source of law? How does a sacred origin of the law challenge rationalist conceptions about the origin of the law? Does the idea of the "sacred" impose yet another dualism, in this case between a transcendental entity and the immanent powers of Earth itself?

(2) In the Andean context, the Constitution of Ecuador (2008) refers to a sacred entity as well:

Chapter 7: Rights for Nature

> **Art. 71.** Nature or Pachamama, where life is reproduced and exists, has the right to exist, persist, maintain and regenerate its vital cycles, structure, functions and its processes in evolution.[24]

Pachamama is a fertility goddess who presides over planting and harvesting, embodies the mountains, and causes natural disasters. Can you think of another example of state law (i.e., case law, statute, constitutional norms, etc.) with a specific reference to a sacred source or entity? What might happen if Western courtrooms invoked the Pachamama? What does this tell us about the transformation of constitutional law?

[22] *Id.*

[23] Translated from Gloria Amparo-Rodriguez & Kasokaku Mestre-Busintana, *Concepción y Aplicación de la Ley de Origen del Pueblo Iku (Arhuaco) in Somos Hijos del sol y la Tierra. Derecho Mayor de los Pueblos Indígenas de la Cuenca Amazónica* 58 (CONAI et al., eds., 2007).

[24] Ecuador Const. Tit. II, Ch. 7 (2008).

B. Natural Laws: Nature as Kinship

Natural laws refer to laws derived from observations of the natural world. These laws are based on how Earth maintains herself and help humans understand our role in the world. Natural laws also pertain to relationships, describing how all beings are connected to each other and must be respected for their roles. Indigenous practices draw from natural laws, as describe by Borrows:

> Indigenous peoples who practice this form of law might watch how a plant interacts with an insect, and draw legal principles from that experience. Others may study how an insect interrelates with a bird, and take legal guidance from that encounter. Some might examine how a certain bird relates to an animal or another bird and see standards for judgment in this relationship. There might also be analogies drawn from behaviors of watersheds, rivers, mountains, valleys, meadows or shorelines to guide legal actions. As such, these laws may be regarded as literally being written on the Earth. . . .
>
> For many Indigenous people, the casebook for learning natural law requires an intimate knowledge of how to read the world; understanding natural law from this point of view does not require an intimate knowledge of how to read legal philosophy.[25]

As decomposing foliage in the soil nurtures new life, humans too constantly experience the co-emergence and decay of human and nonhuman life. We experience how everything thrives in mutuality, serving its role in a functional interdependency of life. Under natural law, nonhuman beings, then, are not to be treated as discrete parts of an external reality, but instead must be recognized as "bundles of relations" that are constantly fluid—all of them being *subjects* rather than objects. In the context of legal personhood, the vision of Indigenous legalities contests deeply entrenched assumptions about what counts as a "person" in legal theory and practice. The following story from the Andean-Amazonian region is a case in point.

The Story of the Tapir

By the Inga Indigenous people of Colombia
Compilation by *Taita* Hernando Chindoy Chindoy

It was the time when plants and animals transmitted their powers and knowledge to men as they are hunting and dreaming. One day, *Taita Yacha Runa,* [a wise man], hunter, and *kuraka* [traditional healer] of the Inga people, left his home in search of the place of the tapir. He had walked for a long time together with his *alkusacha* [mountain dog], carrying with him his blowpipe and darts. He was so immersed in his thinking that he didn't realize he was in a place near the moor. Following a path among the *frailejones* [magnolias], he began to see the *rukusacha*

[25] Borrows, *supra* note 11, at 28-29 (footnote omitted).

[old mountain]—the thick and mysterious vegetation of the mountains of the moor. As the hunter and his faithful *alkusacha* went into the mountains, they began to feel a strange sensation in their bodies. Instantly, an incredible and beautiful place appeared before their eyes where different shapes and colors merged with the vegetation. There, *Taita Yacha Runa* began to look at diverse and varied types of plants. These plants with their pretty leaves formed a multicolored *chagra* [cultivated plot]. Having looked at this, he decided to cut some leaves from the *chagra* and immediately there was thunder and rain. Suddenly, he saw two different plants, one small and one large *shishaja* [sacred plants]. *It was mandatory for him to choose one of the two plants, and he thought of the smaller one.* It would be through this plant that he would be able to meet the good spirits. He rejected the large one because it showed the evil spirits. Right there he was able to see a lagoon, and the surrounding area. For the first time, he was able to see the place where the tapir sleeps. At that very moment and without even realizing it, he fell asleep. *In his sleep, he began to understand the value of each of the plants he had seen.* He learned that some of them were for good luck, and that the small *shishaja* was useful for avoiding evil spirits and as protection against enemies. In that same dream he was able to see the lagoon again, and then he saw two ducks swimming. One of them was white and other yellow. He chose the white duck. *Having the opportunity to take the yellow duck as well, he decided to leave it there.*

After a while, *Taita Yacha Runa* met an elderly *kuraka.* Believing it was convenient, he began to tell him what he had seen when he was awake and what he had observed in the dream as well. *He told him that he had taken all the knowledges that had been offered to him in the mountains near the moor,* but that he had left one knowledge in the place where he saw it. It was the yellow duck that he had left swimming in the lagoon. When *Taita Yacha Runa* stopped talking, the old *kuraka* replied: *Nuka kane dantakunapa suyumanda yaya* (I am the owner of the tapir, and of everything that you saw and heard). *You did well to choose what you wanted;* you should have taken the yellow duck when you looked at it; the white duck means money and the yellow duck, gold. Now you will never see the yellow one again, and he will never be yours. This is how *Taita Yacha Runa,* hunter and *kuraka,* discovered the knowledge that was in the place of the tapir. Since then the tapir is the augury of good times and the hooves of the tapir are used to cure diseases. Also, the dog is an animal with one of the most noble spirits. That is why the dog will continue to accompany humanity until the end of time. (Emphasis added.)

As illustrated in this excerpt, for some Indigenous communities, animals, plants, and other beings have human features, such as the ability to communicate and make decisions. For other Indigenous communities, it is the other way around: the human acquires the powers and personalities of nonhuman beings, for example, through ritual and dreams (the tapir brings good fortune).

A further dimension of the relationship between humans and nature in Indigenous legalities concerns what Australian Indigenous legal scholar Ambellin

Kwaymullina calls "relationship-based" citizenship. For her, all relationships ultimately trace back to the Ancestors and are expressed through kinship systems that go beyond the human. The kinship system reflects the networks of relationships; it is cyclical as it enfolds the present, past, and future. Then, "[t]o be an Aboriginal citizen of an Aboriginal Nation is to exist within these networks of relationship, the pattern—or story—of which was laid out by the . . . Ancestors and which is upheld through the law."[26] Kinship systems extend not only to humans but also to all forms of life. In Indigenous societies, to be a full human being is to be part of a larger ecological collective.

STUDY QUESTIONS

(1) How does a conception of life that is not centered on the human being impact the law?

(2) Can we think about the law beyond human modes of representation (that is, symbolic language)?

(3) How does one derive norms of conduct from the observation of—and participation in—the natural world?

(4) How does Borrows's notion of Indigenous natural law as law based on the observation of nature differ from the Western conception of natural law as a body of unchanging moral principles existing independently of human understanding and positive law yet discernible to humans? Appeals to Western natural law are often associated with human rights. For example, the Declaration of Independence states: "We hold these truths to be self-evident, that all men are created equal, that they are endowed by their Creator with certain unalienable Rights, that among these are Life, Liberty and the pursuit of Happiness."

C. Deliberative Law: The Community

Much Indigenous law is made through deliberation, discussion, and dialogue—which, following Borrows, can be called deliberative law. Because these legalities are developed through continual oral communications among people, the law maintains a dynamic and adaptive force. This fluid characteristic is also central to resisting colonial systems of domination:

> An especially broad source of Indigenous legal traditions is formed through processes of persuasion, deliberation, council, and discussion. While sacred and natural law might sometimes form the backdrop against which debate occurs, the proximate source of most Indigenous law is developed through people talking with one another. The human

[26] Ambellin Kwaymullina *Aboriginal Nations, The Australian Nation-State and Indigenous International Legal Traditions, in* Indigenous Peoples as Subjects of International Law 1, 14 (Irene Watson ed., 2018).

> dimension of these laws means that recognition, enforcement, and implementation make them subject to re-examination and revision through the generations. . . . When Indigenous people have to persuade one another within their traditions, they must also do so by reference to the entire body of knowledge to which they have access, which includes ancient and modern understandings of human rights, due process, gender equality, and economic considerations. . . . Since no Indigenous person or community is completely detached from the world, many influences will be brought to bear on Indigenous legal developments.[27]

Given its social participation, deliberative law is a process based on relationships that create strong legal ties. Collectivity and inclusion are important for laws to be established and enforced in Indigenous societies. Deliberative law is expressed, for example, in circles that invite you to participate in the development of legal standards. Circles are considered sacred and also represent the gathering of people in an atmosphere of equality. Everyone is allowed to speak. Circles are also meant to remind people of Mother Earth and her journey through life. Beyond the circle, gatherings and other large public assemblies may be held to encourage the discussion and resolution of issues.

STUDY QUESTION

Scholars Gloria Amparo Rodriguez and Kasokaku Mestre Busintana from the Iku Indigenous community of the Sierra Nevada de Santa Marta, northern Colombia, have written the following on the notion of deliberation:

> Within the principles of the Iku indigenous community [northern Colombia] we talk about the consultation or spiritual permission of nature. This means that if you are going to build a *maloca* [traditional hut], you must first agree with nature: with the trees, with the stones, with the vines, with the mud . . . with all the elements that are going to be used. You must pay the [spiritual] owners of these materials, otherwise, as indicated by tradition [the law], you are breaking the Law of Origin. You must perform the permission rituals with the guidance of the *Mamos* [spiritual leaders], otherwise there will be conflict between people and an imbalance of the natural order: droughts, heavy rains, landslides and other problems. These rites and ceremonies were established by father *Serankua* and the ancestors.[28]

The deliberative dimension of the law also includes the "consultation or spiritual permission of nature." How does this passage expand a human-centered vision of deliberation? How can a human-nonhuman theory of deliberation contribute to an expanded theory of democracy?

[27] Borrows, *supra* note 11, 44-45.

[28] Translated from Amparo-Rodriguez & Mestre-Busintana, *supra* note 23, 63.

D. Customary Law: Back to the Community

According to Borrows, customary law "can be defined as those practices developed through repetitive patterns of social interaction that are accepted as binding on those who participate in them."[29] It is also important to note that customary law is not specific to Indigenous communities. Western law also relies on custom as a source of normative authority. For example, in international law:

> Customary international law is one component of international law. Customary international law refers to international obligations arising from established international practices, as opposed to obligations arising from formal written conventions and treaties. Customary international law results from a general and consistent practice of states that they follow from a sense of legal obligation. Two examples of customary international laws are the doctrine of non-refoulement and the granting of immunity for visiting heads of state.[30]

Indigenous customary law in Canada has been most strongly recognized in the context of marriage and family relationships. However, while customary law has been a source of law in countries such as Canada, it should not be considered the only source of Indigenous legalities as sometimes occurs. In this chapter, we have already learned about three others: sacred law, natural law, and deliberative law. One more source of Indigenous legalities is discussed in the following subsection: positivistic law.

D. STUDY QUESTION

In *Casimel v. I.C.B.C.*, (1993) 30 BCAC 279 (CA), the British Columbia Court of Appeal held that a 77-year-old woman and a 99-year-old man had legally adopted their daughter's 30-year-old son according to Carrier[31] law and, thus, when he died, they were entitled to death benefits as dependent parents under the province's Insurance Act. This case rested on the finding that Carrier law allowed grandparents to be considered as full parents in their customary regime, and that natural parents were no longer considered to possess the rights or obligations of a parent under this system. Furthermore, the court held that neither Canadian common law, nor federal or provincial statute, nor constitutional law abrogated Carrier customary law.[32]

According to the broad definition of customary law ("repetitive patterns of social interaction"), both the law of Indigenous societies and the law of non-Indigenous societies are based on custom. How would one prove the existence of these customs in a family law case like the one just presented?

[29] BORROWS, *supra* note 11, 59-60.
[30] Legal Information Institute, *Customary International Law*, Cornell Law School, https://www.law.cornell.edu/wex/customary_international_law (last visited Feb. 10, 2020).
[31] The Carrier people are also known as Dakelh or Yinka Dene.
[32] Borrows, *supra* note11, 60-61. On the Carrier (Dakelh) community *see* Douglas Hudson & Michelle Filice, *Dakelh (Carrier)*, THE CANADIAN ENCYCLOPEDIA (Oct. 5, 2018), https://www.thecanadianencyclopedia.ca/en/article/carrier.

E. Positivistic Law: The Legislator

For Borrows, positivistic law refers to express rules that regulate social behavior. As such, "they do not necessarily depend on appeals to the Creator, the environment, or deliberative processes to possess their force." They are made by a person or group of people (a council) regarded as sufficiently authoritative in the community to establish the rules. Indigenous authorship of these binding norms is key. Expressions of positivistic law can be found in proclamations, regulations, codes, teachings, and even normative proposals to reform state law.[33] However, to remain faithful to the spirit of Indigenous legalities, these expressions of positive norms require some grounding in the other sources discussed above.[34]

IV. COLOMBIAN AND INTER-AMERICAN CASE LAW AND INDIGENOUS LEGALITIES

Up to this point, we have looked at how Indigenous legalities derive from sacred, ecological, participatory or deliberative, positivistic, and customary sources. In addition, these legalities should be considered as bodies of stories, naturalistic observations, deliberations, rules, procedures, and customs that change across time and space.

Indigenous legalities have influenced the construction of state law. The Colombian Constitutional Court, for example, has since 1991 widely cited Indigenous views and modes of government. There we find jurisprudence on Indigenous cultural identity, Indigenous special jurisdiction, and land rights, among other issues, where Indigenous ways of seeing the world have greatly impacted these legal constructions.

Below we present case law examples from the Colombian Constitutional Court and the Inter-American Commission of Human Rights (IACHR) to illustrate this point. As these cases reveal, different expressions of Indigenous knowledge and legal thought are being incorporated into regional and national legal systems, thus transforming legal concepts, practices, and paradigms of the Western legal canon.

[33] Borrows, *supra* note 11, 55.

[34] Borrows states:

> I must confess that positivistic law as a source of authority (without a broader justification for its use) prompts greater concern for me than the other sources we have been discussing. My concern about statutes and commands not only relates to Indigenous legal traditions; I see problems with the over-reliance on this source within common law and civil law traditions too. My worry is that if a prominent leader or group rules through this form of law for too long, without the restraining influences found in the other sources identified to this point, this could lead to great corruption.

Id. at 56-57.

A. The Colombian Constitutional Court

On several occasions, the Constitutional Court of Colombia has recognized the country's ethnic diversity and the ensuing need to protect Indigenous peoples, systems of knowledge, and fundamental rights. In what follows, we present examples of iconic constitutional cases that tackle different aspects of Indigenous legalities, namely the notion of "cultural identity," the concept of "traditional knowledge" and its relationship with life and territory, the idea of the Law of Mother Earth, and the right to prior and informed consent with Indigenous groups.

1. On cultural identity as a fundamental right of Indigenous groups

In Decision T-380/1993, the Constitutional Court gave the following opinion:

> The protection which the [Colombian Constitution] extends to the cultural diversity of the country comes from the recognition of different forms of cultural life—whose manifestations and permanent reproduction are attributable to these communities as autonomous collective subjects rather than aggregates of individual members. These members, precisely, come into being through the group and assimilate as theirs the unity of meaning that arises from the experience of being in a community. . . . When the community's interests are undermined, the defense of diversity can neither be reduced to a paternalistic attitude, nor to the will of individual members of the community. . . . It is impossible to speak of the protection of ethnic and cultural diversity and its recognition without first granting substantive constitutional *personality* to the indigenous community. Constitutional personality, then, is the only mechanism that gives indigenous communities a status to enjoy fundamental rights and to demand their protection every time these rights are violated (CP articles 1, 7 and 14). . . .
>
> The recognition of [the country's] ethnic and cultural diversity in the Constitution implies the acceptance of *otherness, which is linked to the acceptance of multiple forms of life and systems of understanding that are different from those of Western culture.* Several indigenous groups have retained their language, traditions, and belief systems. These systems do not conceive existence as something separate from the experience of the community as a whole. Thus, the sole recognition of fundamental rights of the individual . . . is contrary to the constitutional principles of democracy, pluralism, respect for ethnic and cultural diversity, as well as the protection of the cultural richness of the nation.[35]

As this case shows, the Constitutional Court considers that all the elements that make up an ethnic community, i.e., language, traditions, and knowledge systems, cannot be conceived separately. For this reason, the constitutional protection of Indigenous belief systems, languages, and traditions already implies the necessary protection of other elements that integrate the ethnic community, including Indigenous governance and justice systems.

[35] Corte Constitucional de Colombia (1993), Sentencia T-380/1993: Comunidad Indigena/Derechos Fundamentales/Derecho a la Vida/Derecho a la Subsistencia, https://www.corteconstitucional.gov.co/relatoria/1993/T-380-93.htm.

STUDY QUESTION

In T-380/1993, the court states: "[T]hese [knowledge] systems do not conceive [individual] existence as something separate from the experience of the community as a whole." If an Indigenous person has been removed from their community, how may this event affect their fundamental right to a cultural identity? Is the right to a cultural identity a collective right per se?

* * *

2. On Indigenous cultural identity and traditional knowledge

In Decision T-477/2012, Colombia's Constitutional Court addressed alleged rights violations of Indigenous cultural identity arising from the abusive use of Indigenous biological heritage, particularly the unauthorized use of sacred signs and symbols that allude to the sacred coca leaf. In its decision, the Constitutional Court continued to build important jurisprudence about traditional knowledge and its connections with cultural identity as a fundamental right of Indigenous groups. This decision refers to the notion of "intangible knowledge"—traditional knowledge that may be abstract or intangible and is exclusively held by Indigenous communities—and the relationship between knowledge and life. The ruling also addresses the fair distribution of benefits derived from the commercial use of genetic resources and associated traditional knowledge. Consider the following excerpt:

> Traditional knowledge is part of the cultural identity of ethnic communities, and it is the manifestation of an intangible cultural heritage as well. Traditional knowledge must be protected as a way to promote the cultural identity of a group, while avoiding the use and unduly appropriation of traditional knowledge by third parties. . . . *Traditional knowledge reflects indigenous communities' relationships with their land,* their ancestors, cosmogony, and history. *Traditional knowledge is an intellectual activity expressed in the social, cultural, environmental and political fields; it is the product of many generations and their relationship with the world around them,* and as such, this knowledge is consistent and valid. Various international norms . . . have recognized the need to protect the traditional knowledge of ethnic communities. . . .
>
> [T]he Convention on Biological Diversity (Rio de Janeiro, 1992) . . . established, among other obligations, that States must: a) respect, preserve and maintain traditional knowledge for the conservation and sustainable use of biological diversity; b) promote its application "with the approval and participation of those who possess that knowledge;" and c) encourage the benefits derived from that knowledge to be shared equally. In its turn, Andean Decision 391/1996 which established the "Common Regime on Access to Genetic Resources" recognizes the existence of traditional knowledge and the power of communities to make decisions about this knowledge. In the same vein, Statute 191/1995, "Through which provisions on Border Zones are dictated" establishes in article 8 the need to obtain prior and informed consent from indigenous communities when accessing traditional knowledge associated with genetic resources, as well as the duty to

> share fairly the benefits with indigenous peoples. Traditional knowledge is part of the fundamental right to a cultural identity of the indigenous community and therefore must be protected against any type of violation.[36]

In its ruling, the Constitutional Court also considered the use of Indigenous signs and symbols by others for products, finding as follows:

> The relationship between trademark law and the right of indigenous communities to cultural identity and the protection of their traditional knowledge only finds its expression in paragraph g) of article 136 of Andean Decision 486 (2000), which states that [people] cannot register as trademarks those signs whose use in trade unduly affects the right of a third party, in particular when [those signs] consist of the name of indigenous, Afro-American, or local communities, or of such denominations, words, letters, characters, or signs as are used to distinguish their products, services or methods of processing, or that constitute an expression of their culture or practice, unless the application is filed by the community itself or with its express consent. With the registration of a brand, it is intended to grant distinctiveness for the commercialization of a product and said distinctiveness also implies refraining from using generic or descriptive expressions, promoting acts of fair competition and not misleading the consumer, much less affecting the rights of third parties, such as that of indigenous communities through the use of expressions or denominations closely linked to their cultural identity, which consist of the name of the communities, or the denominations, words, letters or signs used to distinguish their products.[37]

As an extension of the theory of cultural appropriation, the Constitutional Court prohibited the use of an Indigenous sign on a coca-based product. In so doing, the court granted fundamental protection against economic abuse of Indigenous signs considered both as traditional knowledge and Indigenous cultural identity.

STUDY QUESTION

Article 136 of Andean Decision 486/2000 states that a person cannot register as trademarks those signs whose use in trade unduly affects the right of a third party, in particular when the use consists "of the name of indigenous, Afro-American, or local communities . . . unless the application is *filed by the community itself* or with its *express consent*." (Emphasis added.) A pharmaceutical company obtains the consent of members of an Amazonian community to use the name of this community on the label of a new product. However, several members of the community disagree with this. Can this consent be considered sufficient and/or legitimate for the purposes of using the Indigenous name on the product's label?

[36] Corte Constitucional de Colombia (2012), Sentencia T-477/12: Legitimacion por Activa de Organizacion Nacional Indigena para Interponer Accion de Tutela (emphasis added), https://www.corteconstitucional.gov.co/relatoria/2012/T-477-12.htm.
[37] *Id.*

3. On traditional knowledge and traditional Indigenous law

Decision SU-510/1998 of the Constitutional Court addresses the right of traditional authorities of the Ika people to uphold their cultural identity and integrity within their territory by prohibiting some activities of Christians in the community who challenged the material culture of the Ika. In its ruling affirming the rights of the Iku, the Constitutional Court wrote about the relationship between Indigenous law, cosmology, and material culture. When reading the following excerpt, consider the sources of Indigenous legalities that we have been previously discussed.

> For the Ika [an indigenous group from Northern Colombia], weaving is an activity that transcends the mere manufacture of cotton fabrics for the production of clothing. Thus, this is an activity of a profoundly moral nature with profound metaphysical consequences. The Ika consider that weaving a fabric is actually weaving "the fabric of one's life." The resulting fabric or tapestry represents a metaphorical activity where the cotton threads are considered *thoughts.* These thoughts slowly organize and intertwine the network of social relations where the weaver is also inserted. For the Ika, "weaving is thinking" and "thinking is living." This explains why "the person who does not think, does not live." Through weaving, thoughts are organized and embedded within a universal order. By weaving and thinking a balance between the opposites is achieved thus fulfilling the "Mother's Law."[38]

A headnote explaining the decision states:

> The Court has indicated that the limitations to which the principles of ethnic and cultural diversity and autonomy of indigenous communities are subject arise from the constitutional text itself, which determines, on the one hand, that Colombia is a unitary State with autonomy from its territorial entities and, on the other hand, that the political and legal autonomy of indigenous communities, that is, the ability to govern themselves and exercise jurisdictional functions within their territorial scope, can be exercised according to their uses and customs, as long as they are not contrary to the Constitution and the law. The foregoing determines that, in matters of indigenous communities, the Political Charter establishes a regime for the conservation of diversity in unity. According to the Court, "only with a high degree of autonomy is cultural survival possible," a statement that means ethnic and cultural diversity, as a general principle, can only be limited when its exercise ignores constitutional or legal norms of greater importance. According to jurisprudence, in principle, the effectiveness of the rights of indigenous peoples, determines that the limits that may be imposed on the normative and jurisdictional autonomy of such communities are only those that are referred "to what is truly intolerable because it attacks what is most precious to humanity."

[38] Corte Constitucional de Colombia (1998), Sentencia SU-510/98: En Nombre Del Pueblo y Por Mandato de la Constitucion, www. https://www.corteconstitucional.gov.co/relatoria/1998/SU510-98.htm.

STUDY QUESTIONS

(1) According to this constitutional decision, "fabric" and "thought" are expressions of the same action for the Iku community. Therefore, thinking is weaving, and weaving is thinking. What does Indigenous material culture have to do with the law?

(2) The materials for weaving come from nature, and the end product, a piece of clothing, is the representation of human thought. Insofar as the notion of traditional knowledge includes tangible and non-tangible elements, how does this idea transform our established concepts about the nature of legal meaning and practice? Is the law strictly reducible to the symbolic, that is, to language, i.e., what the law says on its face?

* * *

4. On informed consent by Indigenous communities and territorial and communal governance

Decision SU-039/97[39] of the Colombian Constitutional Court is a paradigmatic case on prior consultation with Indigenous communities. This piece of jurisprudence examined the scope of Indigenous peoples' right to participation in projects that affect their traditional lands. The Office of the United Nations High Commissioner for Human Rights summarized this case as follows:

> This case was taken to the Constitutional Court of Colombia by the Ombudsman on behalf of the U'wa people and against the Ministry of Environment and the private oil company Sociedad Occidental de Colombia, Inc. The case dealt with the right of indigenous peoples to *participate through consultations in decisions that may affect them*, in particular related to defense and preservation of indigenous land. . . . The legal question examined the scope of the right to participation of indigenous peoples in projects that affect their land. The Court considered Constitutional rights related to protection of ethnic integrity (Articles 7, 10 and 70) as well as the right to self-determination (Article 330) and the right to participation (Article 40). . . .
>
> The Constitutional Court found that the process used to secure an environmental license for oil exploration had not been adequate as it had ignored the U'wa community's fundamental right to be formally and substantially consulted. This decision was grounded on the principle that *participation through consultation is a fundamental right* because it is an essential way to preserve the ethnic, social, economic and cultural integrity of indigenous communities, which was necessary for their survival as a social group.[40]

[39] Corte Constitucional de Colombia (1997), Sentencia SU-039/97: Derechos Fundamentales de Comunidad Indigena [available at: https://www.corteconstitucional.gov.co/relatoria/1997/SU039-97.htm]
[40] Office of the United Nations High Commissioner for Human Rights, Land and Human Rights: Annotated Compilation of Case Law, 75 (2015). (Emphasis added.)

Similarly, in T-993/2012, which also addressed the fundamental right to prior consultation of Indigenous communities and ethnic groups, the Constitutional Court of Colombia said:

> For the Court, the right of indigenous peoples to have their own social, economic and cultural life, and to profess their own religion and practice their own language (article 27 of the International Covenant on Civil and Political Rights) is closely linked to the right to have their own territory... [T]he indigenous territory and resources, traditions, and knowledge systems together constitute a legacy that unites—as a whole—the present generation and the generations to follow.[41]

In its ruling, the Court highlighted the holistic nature of Indigenous worldviews as a cornerstone of the right to participation through prior consultation. Prior consultation is an expression of the principle of self-determination, which includes the power of self-government and the ability to guide behavior in accordance with a local system of norms, protocols, and procedures—which brings us to Indigenous law and governance systems. On this topic, the Court said:

> The right to the *protection* of ethnic cultural identity has been analyzed by this Body [the Court] from two different perspectives: a negative perspective... [referring to] how preventing public manifestations of religious practices outside of [indigenous] traditions is a way to avoid the disappearance of [a particular] culture; and a positive perspective expressed in the reproduction of [indigenous] cultural identity through ethnoeducation and other processes. In addition, based on the principle of self-determination.... *the Court has affirmed that ethnic communities have the power to determine their own institutions and government authorities; to determine and maintain their norms, customs, worldviews, development options, and life projects, and to adopt those internal or local decisions* that they deem most appropriate for the conservation, or protection of these purposes.
>
> As a manifestation of this principle, national and international law has established the obligation *to carry out a prior consultation with these communities before adopting legal or administrative measures* that may affect them directly.... [The Court has protected the right to prior consultation in cases of] environmental licenses, construction contracts linked to development projects that directly affect ethnic communities, as well as decisions that allow the exploitation of resources within indigenous territories, ...and issues related to ethnoeducation. It is thus a right in continuous construction whose protection depends on the impact that can be demonstrated in each specific case.[42]

STUDY QUESTION

Based on the constitutional principle of self-determination, Indigenous communities have the power to dictate their own systems of laws, justice, and government. Do you

[41] Corte Constitucional de Colombia (2012), Sentencia T-993/12: Derecho Fundamental a la Consulta Previa de Comunidades Indigenas Y Grupos Etnicos [available at: https://www.corteconstitucional.gov.co/relatoria/2012/T-993-12.htm].
[42] *Id.* (emphasis added).

think that the recognition of Indigenous governance systems based on a relational worldview could transform state notions of participation and consultation?

B. Inter-American Commission on Human Rights

1. On ancestral land, communal tenure, and Indigenous property rights

The collective tenure of land is a key component of Indigenous worldviews and ways of being. The Inter-American Commission on Human Rights (IACHR), a body created by the Organization of American States (OAS) that aims to promote and protect rights in the Americas, has referred to this issue in several cases. For the Commission, the communal property right to the lands that Indigenous peoples have traditionally used and occupied is a function of their customary patterns of land use and tenure. In addition, the Commission refers to the state's duty to take effective measures to recognize Indigenous peoples' communal property right to the lands that they have traditionally occupied and used and to delimit, demarcate, and title the territory on which their right exists.

In *Maya Indigenous Community of the Toledo District v. Belize*, Maya Indigenous communities argued that the State of Belize violated their rights over land traditionally used and occupied by the Maya people by granting logging and oil concessions and otherwise failing to protect those lands, amongst other claims. The IACHR ruled in favor of the Maya people:

> 95. [A] review of pertinent treaties, legislation and jurisprudence reveals the development over more than 80 years of particular human rights norms and principles applicable to the circumstances and treatment of indigenous peoples. Central to these norms and principles has been the recognition of the need for special measures by states to compensate for the exploitation and discrimination to which these societies have been subjected at the hands of the non-indigenous. . . .
>
> 98. In deciding upon the complaints in the present petition, therefore, the Commission will afford due consideration to the particular norms and principles of international human rights law governing the individual and collective interests of indigenous peoples, including consideration of any special measures that may be appropriate and necessary in giving proper effect to these rights and interests. . . .
>
> 151. In summary, based upon the foregoing analysis, the Commission concludes that the Maya people of southern Belize have a communal property right to the lands that they have traditionally used and occupied, and that the character of these rights is a function of Maya customary land use patterns and tenure. The Commission also considers that this right is embraced and affirmed by Article XXIII of the American Declaration.
>
> 152. The Commission further concludes that the State has violated the right to property enshrined in Article XXIII of the American Declaration to the detriment of the Maya people, by failing to take effective measures to recognize their communal property right to the lands that they have traditionally occupied and used, and to delimit, demarcate

and title or otherwise establish the legal mechanisms necessary to clarify and protect the territory on which their right exists.

153. In addition, the Commission concludes that the State, by granting logging and oil concessions to third parties to utilize the property and resources that could fall within the lands which must be delimited, demarcated and titled or otherwise clarified or protected, without effective consultations with and the informed consent of the Maya people and with resulting environmental damage, further violated the right to property enshrined in Article XXIII of the American Declaration to the detriment of the Maya people.

154. Finally, the Commission notes the Petitioners' contention that the failure of the State to engage in meaningful consultation with the Maya people in connection with the logging and oil concessions in the Toledo District, and the negative environmental effects arising from those concessions, constitute violations of several other rights under international human rights law, including the right to life under Article I of the American Declaration, the right to religious freedom and worship under Article III of the American Declaration, the right to a family and to protection thereof under Article VI of the American Declaration, the right to preservation of health and well-being under Article XI of the American Declaration, and the "right to consultation" implicit in Article 27 of the ICCPR, Article XX of the American Declaration, and the principle of self-determination.

155. In its analysis of this case, the Commission has emphasized the distinct nature of the right to property as it applies to indigenous peoples, whereby *the land traditionally used and occupied by these communities plays a central role in their physical, cultural and spiritual vitality*. As the Commission has previously recognized with respect of the right to property and the right to equality, "[f]or indigenous people, the free exercise of such rights is essential to the enjoyment and perpetuation of their culture." Similarly, the concept of family and religion within the context of indigenous communities, including the Maya people, is intimately connected with their traditional land, where ancestral burial grounds, places of religious significance and kinship patterns are linked with the occupation and use of their physical territories. Further, the Commission has specifically concluded in its analysis of this case that the duty to consult is a fundamental component of the State's obligations in giving effect to the communal property right of the Maya people in the lands that they have traditionally used and occupied.[43]

2. On the obligation to consult

In *Kichwa Indigenous People of Sarayaku v. Ecuador*, the IACHR considered the granting of a permit by the government to a private oil company in the ancestral territory of the Kichwa (alternatively, *Quechua*, or Quichua) people. The permit allowed oil exploration and exploitation and was issued without consultation with the Kichwa people. As with the *Maya* case, the IACHR ruled in favor of the Indigenous Kichwa people:

[43] *Maya Indigenous Community of the Toledo District v. Belize*, Report No. 78/00; Case 12.053 (2-20 October 2000) [available at: http://www.worldcourts.com/iacmhr/eng/decisions/2000.10.05_Maya_ Indigenous_ Communities_v_Belize.pdf].

Para. 149. In this case, the Court finds that there is no doubt regarding the Sarayaku Peoples' communal ownership of their territory, which is exercised in a time-honoured and ancestral manner. This was expressly recognized by the State through the adjudication made on May 12, 1992. Notwithstanding the foregoing, in addition to the points noted in the section on the facts of the case, the Court considers it pertinent to emphasize the deep cultural, non-pecuniary and spiritual ties that the community has with its territory, so as to fully understand the damages caused in this case. . . .

Para. 160. It is for all the aforementioned reasons that one of the fundamental guarantees for ensuring the participation of indigenous peoples and communities in decisions regarding measures that affect their rights and, in particular, their right to communal property, is precisely the recognition of their right to consultation, which is recognized in the ILO Convention No. 169, among other complementary international instruments. . . .

Para. 166. The obligation to consult indigenous and Tribal Communities and Peoples on any administrative or legal measure that may affect their rights, as recognized under domestic and international law, as well as the obligation to guarantee the rights of indigenous peoples to participate in decisions on matters that concern their interests, is directly related to the general obligation to guarantee the free and full exercise of the rights recognized in the Convention (Article 1(1). This implies the duty to adequately organize the entire governmental apparatus and, in general, all the organizations through which public power is exercised, so that these are capable of legally guaranteeing the free and full exercise of those rights. The foregoing means that States have the obligation to structure their standards and institutions in such a way that indigenous, native or tribal communities can be consulted effectively, in accordance with international standards in this matter. Thus, States must incorporate those standards within the prior consultation processes, so as to generate sustained, effective and reliable channels for dialogue with indigenous communities in processes of consultation and participation through their representative institutions. . . .

Para. 177. The Court has established that in order to ensure effective participation by members of an indigenous community or people in development or investment plans within their territory, the State has the duty to consult the community in an active and informed manner, and in accordance with its customs and traditions, in the context of a continuous communication between the parties.

Moreover, these consultations should be undertaken in good faith, through culturally appropriate procedures and must be aimed at reaching an agreement. Similarly, the indigenous people or community must be consulted in accordance with its own traditions, during the early stages of the development or investment plan, and not only when it is necessary to obtain the community's approval. Also, the State must ensure that members of the community are aware of the potential benefits and risks so they can decide whether or not to accept the proposed development or investment plan. Finally, the consultation must take into account the traditional decision-making practices of the people or community. Failure to comply with this obligation, or engaging in consultations without regard to their essential characteristics, compromises the State's international responsibility. . . .

> Para. 232. The State, by failing to consult the Sarayaku People on the execution of a project that would directly affect their territory, was in breach of its obligations, under the principles of international law and of its own domestic law, to adopt all necessary measures to guarantee the participation of the Sarayaku People, through their own institutions and mechanisms and in accordance with their values, traditions, customs and forms of organization, in the decisions made regarding matters and policies that affected or could affect their territory, their cultural and social life, their rights to communal property and to cultural identity. Consequently, the Court considers that the State is responsible for the violation of the right to communal property of the Sarayaku People, recognized in Article 21 of the Convention, in relation to the right to cultural identity, under the terms of Articles 1(1) and (2) thereof. [44]

V. *WUASIKAMAS*, THE LAW OF THE INDIGENOUS INGA OF APONTE IN COLOMBIA

This final section studies some aspects of one particular Indigenous legal system, the *Wuasikamas* of the Inga of Aponte, and how this system interacts with state law.

A. Introduction to the Inga of Aponte

The Inga people are part of the living culture of the Great Inca nation. By 1450, the Inca administered the territory they called *Tawaintinsuyu,* which included four regions—*Chinchaysuyu* (north), *Antisuyu* (east, the Amazon jungle), *Contisuyu* (west), and *Collasuyu* (south). The regions of Caquetá, Cauca, Putumayo, and Nariño of today's southern Colombia together made up what the Inca called *Chinchaisuyu.* In this territory of the Colombian Amazon, the Inga co-exist with other ancestral peoples, specifically the Cofán, Siona, Camentzá, Quillasinga, and Pasto. According to the Colombian census of 2018, the total population of the Inga was 19,561.

The ancestral territory of the Inga is part of the Colombian massif (part of the Andes mountains) eco-region in southwestern Colombia that covers an area of 4.8 million hectares. The central and eastern Andean mountain ranges originate here, and Andean, Amazonian, and Pacific ecosystems also converge. In addition, the five most important river tributaries in the country have their sources in the massif: the Magdalena, Cauca, Putumayo, Caquetá, and Patía rivers. The reservation is extraordinarily biodiverse, with more 471 species of birds, including parrots and the Andean condor, the spectacled bear, the tapir, deer, and cougars. There are also 28 lakes in this territory, as well as a great diversity of tree species.

[44] *Kichwa Indigenous People of Sarayaku v. Ecuador,* IACTHR Series C No. 245 (June 27, 2012) 62-63 (emphasis added, citations omitted), https://www.hr-dp.org/files/2013/10/22/Nkichwa_Community_v_Ecuador.pdf.

B. *Wuasikamas*: Guardianship of the Territory

Both the Inga language and culture have their origins in the Inca civilization that expanded through the Andean mountains in the current territories of Peru, Bolivia, Chile, Ecuador, Argentina, and Colombia between the thirteenth and sixteenth centuries. The *Wuasikamas* oral code originated in the department of Nariño, in the southwest of Colombia, and is maintained in the language of the Inga community.

Based on the testament of the *Taita de Taitas* ("Father of Fathers") Carlos Tamabioy, the Inga community of Aponte venerates Earth as mother and considers the rest of visible and invisible beings as part of a single family. This testament was dated March 1700 and was duly notarized before the Spanish Crown. Since 1750, the Inga community has continuously struggled to defend its ancestral territory.

Wuasikamas means "guardianship of the territory." This does not mean only physical defense of the territory as the English translation may connote. It means protection of *and* care for a way of being that is rooted in a particular ecosystem composed of infinite relations of people, culture, other living beings, and land. Consistent with the understanding that Indigenous legalities come from the Creator as understood through stories of origin, *Wuasikamas* begins with this story, which is in itself law.

Genesis of the Territorial Law of the Inga of Aponte

By the Inga People of Colombia
Compiled by *Taita* Hernando Chindoy

In the most painful moment of their history, the Spanish crown expropriated the lands of the Inga of Tawaintinsuyu—the Chinchaisuyu region. In a night of lightning, rain, and wind, *Taita Intí* [Father Sun] begat Carlos Tamabioy, a distinguished chieftain and spiritual leader of the Inga. Tamabioy was born in Aguarico, a sacred place in the pan-Amazonian territory, and seven mothers, before dying of hunger, had to breastfeed him. The child grew so fast and strong that by noon he was already an adult. By the afternoon, he had already toured the whole territory. At the end of the day, he gathered all the Inga and Camenzá peoples and said: "This is my land that I leave for you, my children and descendants, to take care of, protect, and benefit from as your own until the end of time. Nothing and nobody shall interfere. You must live in unity and not forget that you are never alone, for the rivers, forests, mountains, and everything that exists is part of our family. They will be your protectors." When he finished, he left with the last light of the sun. Since then, and for more than 300 years, all the Inga of today's Colombia each year celebrate the ritual of *Atún Puncha*—The Day of Forgiveness—a ceremony at the end of the year and the beginning of a new one. This is how the Inga commemorate the legacy and memory of Carlos Tamabioy, the *Taita* of *Taitas* [(Father of Fathers)]. In this ceremony, people ask

> the Earth and the spiritual beings for their forgiveness for all the damage humans have caused. And if there is enmity between neighbors, the *Atún Puncha* is the moment to embrace each other, to dance, and to enjoy *chicha* [(fermented beverage)] and food as a sign of kinship. The Inga also pray as acknowledgement of being alive. If somebody is no longer alive for the celebration, it means that their soul is calm because they have done their best in life.

Wuasikamas is found in the Inga language as one of the most important sources through which the ancestral knowledge of the community is revitalized; this knowledge holds the keys to understanding the Andean and Amazonian worlds, as expressed orally. *Wuasikamas* is recognized in daily life as the existence of the infinite network of relationships between human beings and nonhuman beings in their material and spiritual dimensions. Speaking from a perspective of "bioculturality" and a "political ecology of peace," *Wuasikamas* expresses the vital energy of the conductive threads of life and spirituality of the Inga people.

One of those principles of *Wuasikamas* is *Suma Kausai,* which, rooted in origin and history, is the foundation of the relationship between the Earth and the human. This relationship requires points or nodes of encounter and non-separation to "guard the territory"—what the West calls "property." For the Inga, however, the territory is *samai* or a point of joyful resting for living well. In other words, while the West defines property as an inert section of land, the Inga describe *samai* as a meeting and resting place of connection for the soul and the body which exists beyond this finite world to the infinite path of human and nonhuman existence beyond Earth, time, and space.

The methodology for recognizing and studying *Wuasikamas* is the return to ancestral knowledge from a decolonized perspective and through the people's own Inga language. This requires a journey of spiritual connection through sacred plants such as ayahuasca and yagé. This connection allows the Inga to understand and engage in dialogue with nonhuman beings throughout all time.

The *Wuasikamas* oral code is in constant dialogue with the constitutional law of the Colombian state, both of which need to be understood in order to maintain *Samai* or intercultural peace. There are clashes between these two kinds of law, and, strictly speaking, they do not *complement* each other but *support* each other. *Wuasikamas* exists in its own path. It is not only of human creation because there are other nonhuman forces involved. This conceptualization has traditionally been beyond Western-normative understanding. However, recent developments in human rights theories and Earth rights movements are the meeting point for strengthening these new dialogues.

C. Relationship with the State

Article 7 of the Colombian Constitution of 1991, as amended, provides: "The State recognizes and protects the ethnic and cultural diversity of the Colombian Nation." Under Articles 171 and 176, Indigenous people form a special constituency for the election of senators and representatives. Under Article 246, they exercise jurisdictional functions within their territory in accordance with their own rules and procedures, provided these are not contrary to the constitution or laws. They are governed by Indigenous councils according to their uses and customs in accordance with the constitution and the law under Article 330. Under Articles 63 and 329, their territories or reservations are collective property that may not be sold and are of a non-disposable, inalienable, imprescriptible, and unattachable nature. Under Article 13, paragraph 2, as groups that are discriminated against and marginalized, they deserve greater protection.

Since 1970, the Inga territory has been affected by indiscriminate deforestation and the presence of guerrilla groups, drug traffickers, and paramilitaries. Since 1991 poppy crops (*Papaver somniferum*) have been grown in the territory and eventually covered 2,500 hectares. From these crops, two or three tons of morphine or heroin were extracted and distributed weekly through international drug-trafficking networks. The indiscriminate logging and soil depletion caused by these plantations was further aggravated by the implementation of the *Plan Colombia*— a bilateral agreement between the governments of Colombia and the United States in 1999 to combat the guerrillas and drug trafficking in the country. This plan aimed to provide social programs for farmers so that they would abandon illicit crops. However, while attempting to protect farmers as the country's internal armed conflict intensified, the deadly herbicide glyphosate was sprayed on the illicit poppy crops, which had negative health effects on the Indigenous and peasant inhabitants of this area. Between 1986 and 2003, more than 150 people were killed and more than 1,000 were forcibly displaced from their lands. The life of the Inga people was being destroyed.

Courageous Inga women, facing the prospect of losing their children, led the Inga community in discerning how they would live as a people. During an intense community dialogue in 2003, the Inga rediscovered the traditional *Wuasikamas* oral code in the ancestral knowledge of the elderly based on the principles of nonviolence. Using this knowledge, the community developed a strategy to eliminate economic dependence on drug production and to confront the forces that were harming the community. This led to an unprecedented process of institutional strengthening and cultural identity.

In 2003, the Inga of Aponte achieved collective ownership over their territory through legal recognition of a reservation issued by the Colombian Institute for Agrarian Reform-INCORA, currently known as the National Land Agency-ANT. This title was created through Resolution 013 of July 22, 2003, which granted a collective title over 22,283 hectares, carefully delineated, and with the special protection by the state. The reservation is located in the municipalities of El Tablón de Gómez, Nariño, and Santa Rosa, Cauca, between 1,500 and 3,800 meters above the sea level. According to the 2015 census, the population of the reservation is 3,651 Indigenous inhabitants (951 families) and 620 non-Indigenous inhabitants (105 families).

In 2004, the Inga of Aponte agreed with the government of Colombia to develop the National Family Rangers Program designed to respect cultural and community values. A part of the program involved paying Indigenous peoples and peasants to stop growing illicit crops. The Inga of Aponte, with *Wuasikamas*, negotiated to receive the money through a communal fund created by themselves that would allow them to support the entire community and work together to strengthen their governance and free their territory from the presence of guerrillas, paramilitaries, and drug traffickers, as well as the army and the police. The payments were received from 2004 to 2006 and were used to create the pillars for the social, economic, cultural, spiritual, and environmental advancement of the Inga community. In 2007, the Inga stopped receiving money from the government and began to strengthen sustainable livelihoods, while being governed by the *Wuasikamas* oral code as part of the Integral Mandate of Life for the Survival of the Inga People in Aponte.

D. Intentions and Results of *Wuasikamas*

These are the intentions of *Wuasikamas*:

- Thriving as community in the infinity of time and space, while following the relational code between human and nonhuman beings. Also, by remembering the origin of this code in the sacred and ancestral territory of the central-eastern mountain range of the Andes. In this territory, the Inga people thrive to keep their own rules and procedures that have allowed them to survive as an autonomous community, with their own territory, customs, and language, as well as the spiritual and religious systems within the framework of principles that discourage theft, lies, and laziness, and affirm living with dignity, in a state of well-being, and in community with Mother Earth.
- Contributing to the unity of the Inga people, which is rooted in self-government, autonomy, legal standing, cosmology, and thinking that stems from ancestral knowledge.
- Decolonizing thinking under the principles of dignity, respect, and biocultural peace.
- Remembering is the thought and living memory of *Taita* of *Taitas* Carlos Tamabioy, as well as other guardian ancestors that are present in the wind, fire, water, earth, light, darkness, and peace.

In the midst of this long history of violence, and on the verge of physical and cultural extermination, the Inga of Aponte's re-encounter with *Wuasikamas* and its emphasis on knowledge of the ways of living well (*buen vivir*), has been the means to achieve peace and development. It is rooted in principles that discourage theft, lying, and laziness, and affirm living a dignified life.

Following the way of *Wuasikamas*, the Inga people are recovering their autonomy, sovereignty and spirituality, and the rights of Mother Earth. The Inga have been in *minga* (days of collective reflection) to revitalize and decolonize their governance systems. They adopted the Integral Mandate of Life for the Survival and Permanence of the Inga People of Aponte, which is the charter for the Inga of Aponte. Drawing on the political-administrative mechanisms of the *Major Cabildo* and the *Minor Cabildos* (similar to ministries) of health, education, communication, economy, public and community services, justice, women and family, children and youth, and Inga guardians, the Inga have established governing structures. The Inga High Council of Justice investigates and cures all kinds of what the Inga characterize as "diseases"—from the theft of a chicken to homicides, the creation of armed groups, drug trafficking, and harm of Mother Earth. For the Inga, there is no conception of "crime." Human beings commit what are called "crimes" because diseases have penetrated their bodies and taken over. Treatment with medicinal plants, advice, and isolation are ways of dealing with these diseases. In these ways, the Inga have brought into being and maintained a system of social cohesion that has also allowed them to face groups of guerrillas, paramilitaries, drug traffickers, state agencies, and public forces, among other actors that threatened their community.

The Inga have taken to sharing the *Wuasikamas* process with other peoples of the region in order to strengthen their communities and local governance. The Inga have created an Alliance of Indigenous Women of Nariño and a Court of Indigenous Peoples and Authorities of the Colombian Southwest, with the participation of seven ancestral peoples present in the regions of Caquetá, Cauca, Putumayo, and Nariño (the Awá, Cofán, Eperara Siapidaara, Inga, Nasa Uh, Quillasinga and Siona peoples). In the regional and global context, *Wuasikamas* is an organization that strives to lay its foundations in the form of cultural embassies in capital cities. The aim is to share the history and dignity of the Inga people, mutual understanding, and the life processes that are also kept in hearts beyond the human.[45]

The *Wuasikamas* oral code is a contribution to the dialogue around justice and public policies on Earth and nonhuman rights. The *Wuasikamas* oral code advances biocultural peace, that is, the harmonious co-existence achieved and maintained between human beings and all visible beings, from above and below, and from all places in time and space.

With *Wuasikamas*, the Inga people of Aponte have fostered dialogues and, sometimes, have received discouraging criticisms intended to break their ancestral spirit. However, the community has become stronger, and their legal cases in matters such as health, education, legal standing, and government have been a model for other Indigenous groups, people of African descent, and the peasants of Colombia. Globally, *Wuasikamas* is recognized by the United Nations Development Program as a global example of resilience and social, economic, and environmental progress. The Inga people were among 21 local and Indigenous initiatives recognized by the 2015 Equator Prize.

[45] *See Wuasikamas*, http://www.wuasikamas.org/about-us.

STUDY QUESTIONS

(1) Though the industrial revolution began in the middle of the eighteenth century, the West was still composed of largely agrarian societies until the twentieth century. In a sense, Western agrarian societies, not just Indigenous societies, were colonized by industrial civilization at this time. People tend to think of Indigenous societies as exceptions to Western development, ones that need protection but not ones to serve as guiding lights for future civilizational transitions.

Consider that colonizing industrial societies are not sustainable and the ways of agrarian societies have been sustainable and are in need of recovery. Using the Inga of Aponte and the recovery of their community through *Wuasikamas* as a guiding light, consider these questions:

a. What ancestral wisdom and knowledge might the modern West draw on for living well with Earth?
b. Where did this ancestral wisdom come from, what is its story of origin?
c. What do the Inga teach us about the meaning of property and guardianship of the territory?
d. What do the Inga tell us about the new commons and collective rights and responsibilities for territory?
e. How would the principle of non-separation, or being embedded in an infinity of relations change Western law?
f. What do the Inga tell us about the role of local communities in relation to states for purposes of Earth law? What are the similarities and differences between the Inga pursuit of local community rights and self-governance for the sake of sustainability and CELDF's approach to community rights (as discussed in Chapter 9, "The Rights of Nature Movement in the United States")?
g. What can bring a common mind and ethos, a *Wuasikamas*, to local communities in complex urban/globalized societies?
h. How can people in complex urban/globalized societies learn from nature so as to create laws in harmony with nonhuman beings?

VI. CONCLUSION

Earth systems are undergoing fundamental changes with increasing socioeconomic pressure on and demand for resources and ecosystem services. Most dominant Western environmental law and governance systems fail to prevent and remediate ecological degradation. Environmental law is primarily concerned with pollution management and control without considering ecological interdependencies; it takes the human as its exclusive subject and nature as its object, privileging, for the most part, neo-liberal conceptual practices within the sphere of governance. This ontology of separation — a vision of the real that separates humans and the rest of life —

reinforces the myth of human exceptionalism, namely the idea that humans operate above or outside Earth's ecological systems.

Indigenous legalities envision law and governance systems appropriate for the emergent conditions of a time period with mutually enhancing human-Earth relationships. Broadly speaking, they propose a fundamental transformation as a result of which social and legal institutions would foreground human-Earth interactions.

Drawing on and further contributing to the field of Earth law, Indigenous legalities incorporate the normative traditions and relational governance principles of Indigenous worlds as part and parcel of a new legal vision for times of transition. Such an approach aligns with Thomas Berry's notion of the "great law" based on the idea that the universe is a communion of subjects, not a collection of objects.[46]

In addition, and in conversation with scholars working with local communities in the Andean Amazonian region, Indigenous legalities are based on the principle of interdependence and mutual co-emergence of all beings. This principle orients "a vision of the world that echoes the autopoietic dynamics and creativity of the Earth and the indubitable fact that no living being exists independently of the Earth."[47] When it comes to the law, the principle of interdependence is at the root of both Indigenous legalities and Earth law.

Moreover, as extensively described in Amerindian cosmologies, animal studies, and plant science, among other fields of knowledge, nonhuman beings are capable of different forms of representation and communication. More than objects of cognition and control, nonhuman beings are agents of knowledge and even legal subjects today. Indigenous legalities across the Americas offer compelling elements for an expanded, multiple, and life-thriving legal paradigm beyond the individual and the state. Thus, Indigenous legalities contribute to the emergent Earth law concept that capacitates other-than-human selves as subjects of rights but also as legal agents in their own right.

From the Andean foothills to the Amazonian lowlands, the Inga's ancestral and highly strategic territories reach across the Southern departments of Nariño, Cauca, Caquetá, and Putumayo in Colombia. The environmental, cultural, and legal agendas of the Inga in the Andes-Amazon join long-standing efforts of Indigenous resurgence movements across Latin America, and beyond. Moreover, the work of the Inga is inspired by several interconnected normative principles which are part of the *Wuasikamas* oral code: (1) to defend life according to Indigenous legal and governance systems; (2) to care for the territory as the basis of environmental governance and decision-making models; (3) to foster epistemic autonomy—as opposed to epistemic dependence—in harmony with local ecologies and sociopolitical realities; and (4) to engage in intercultural dialogue with Western science and governance systems, among other principles.

[46] Thomas Berry, The Great Work: Our Way into The Future (1999).

[47] Arturo Escobar, *Sentipensar con la Tierra: Las Luchas Territoriales y la Dimensión Ontológica de las Epistemologías del Sur*, 11(1) Revista de Antropologia Iberoamericana 11, 14 (2016).

In this chapter, we have studied, among other things, how state law incorporates Indigenous legalities, and how legal practitioners may engage with their principles and methodologies. The increased recognition of Indigenous legalities is helping to bring into being the emerging paradigm of Earth law, thus becoming an important tool for the protection of Indigenous peoples and their territories. The wisdom of Indigenous legalities is becoming part of the legal system outside those territories transforming state law.

AFTERWORD[1]

BEYOND ANTHROPOCENTRIC LAW

The human and other members of the community we call "Earth" share an evolutionary history that scientists tell us goes back 13.8 billion years to the Big Bang. This incredibly beautiful and complex community of interrelated beings is held together and maintained by a complex network of interrelationships through which flow energy, nutrients, and more mysterious forces, such as creativity and love. Yet, most contemporary legal systems are almost completely blind to this reality. Instead of seeing what Thomas Berry referred to as a "communion of subjects," each with a contribution to make to the well-being of the whole, these legal systems see only discrete objects, most of which are classified as property susceptible of ownership by legal persons and available for consumption and commodification within the limits prescribed by environmental laws.[2]

For centuries many societies around the world have regulated themselves on the assumption that humans (or at least "civilized" humans) are separate from and superior to the community of life and are entitled to exploit Earth for personal gain. Today, as the dire consequences of degrading the biosphere become increasingly apparent, more and more people are realizing that humans and many other species have no future unless we self-regulate to ensure that we contribute to the health and integrity of the community of life, the "Earth community," instead of exploiting it. Consequently, the emergence of Earth law is part of a wider shift within global society—a shift from an unhealthy anthropocentrism toward a vision of humans as gifted members of a community of life who bear a special responsibility for healing the harm that they have caused. For lawyers, this shift in perspective opens up exciting new vistas as we contemplate what legal systems that govern people for Earth might look like.

[1] This afterword was authored by Cormac Cullinan, the director of the Wild Law Institute, and Cullinan & Associates Inc., in Cape Town, South Africa, and author of WILD LAW: A MANIFESTO FOR EARTH JUSTICE (2d ed., 2011).

[2] Thomas Berry's observation that "the universe is not a collection of objects but a communion of subjects" appears in many of his essays and works and books. For example: "[T]hat the universe is a communion of subjects rather than a collection of objects is the central commitment of the Ecozoic. Existence itself is derived from and sustained by this intimacy of each being with every other being of the universe." BRIAN SWIMME & THOMAS BERRY, THE UNIVERSE STORY 243 (1992).

DO EARTH LAWS HAVE A FUTURE?

The developing body of Earth law is based on the recognition that human legal systems arise within a preexisting natural system of order and should aim to guide human beings to seek fulfillment and well-being by contributing to the well-being of the Earth community rather than by severing and weakening the bonds that sustain it. However, the legal systems of most countries are based on a worldview that is fundamentally at odds with the reality that human beings exist as part of a community of life that is essential for their well-being.

For example, in the United States, many long-held legal principles, established both by legislation and common law precedent, deny that members of the Earth community (other than human beings) have legal personality, legal rights, or standing to litigate.

This means that humans who would nurture Earth law face very significant hurdles. First, most legislation and hundreds of years of legal precedent deny the validity of their fundamental propositions, such as that the law should recognize other-than-human-beings as legal persons with rights.

Second, the legal establishment, which includes legal academics, practitioners, and judges, have been trained to believe that the idea of nature having legally enforceable rights is absurd and even dangerous.

Third, the legal system privileges the interests of incorporeal, artificial legal entities, such as corporations, over corporeal, natural entities that have co-evolved with humanity within the Earth community. Through the law, these corporations restrict the legal liability of the humans who make the decisions for them. The interests attributed to these abstract, fictional beings, imagined by people to serve their ideological beliefs, take precedence over the interests of real beings who play a role in sustaining life. Corporations and their shareholders have vested interests in maintaining the status quo, and significant financial resources and political influence available to do so. The same can be said about nations and their political subdivisions which, through incorporeal, artificial constructs, are vested with legal personhood and legal power.

This raises several crucial questions: Is there is a long-term future for Earth law within a legal system that is hostile to the very worldview Earth law reflects? Can Earth law take root and flourish in legal systems that define all aspects of nature, other than human beings, as legal objects—property—without agency? Can Earth law co-exist with the legal fiction that abstract creations like corporations are legal persons endowed with scarcely fettered rights to take possession of and lay waste to other-than-human-beings and ecological communities?

If the answer to each of these questions is "no," then absent social upheaval that sweeps aside the legal system and replaces it with one that reflects Earth jurisprudence, Earth laws is doomed to wither and perish. However, as set out below, there is good reason to believe that Earth law will flourish and generate new legal systems.

LAWS OF NATURE TRUMP HUMAN LAWS

Despite these formidable obstacles, proponents of Earth law have even more powerful champions in their corner—Mother Earth and the laws of nature. By this I mean that no matter how human legal systems are constructed and function, they cannot protect human beings against the operation of the laws of nature. We are already beginning to suffer the consequences of acting with reckless disregard to the interests of the whole Earth community. As the negative impacts mount and more people become aware of the role of the legal system in legitimizing activities that are deeply anti-social from the perspective of the Earth community, the pressure for fundamental change will build. Some may advocate doubling down on the manipulation of Earth systems, for example by undertaking "geoengineering." Others will recognize that the only viable way forward is to reorient human laws so that they encourage humanity to relate in a responsible and respectful manner to nature and to restore ecological communities to health.

The laws or principles that govern how the universe functions, "the Great Jurisprudence," are non-negotiable and self-enforcing. They make it inevitable that if humanity increases the concentration of greenhouse gasses in the atmosphere beyond a certain point, the relatively stable climatic conditions that have prevailed throughout the Cenozoic era will be disrupted The global climate will then become chaotic (as we are already experiencing) until Earth's homeostatic capacity re-establishes a dynamic equilibrium—which may be at temperatures difficult for humans to tolerate. The fact that most of the human activities that are causing this disruption are currently lawful means that those responsible for these activities are immune from legal consequences. But this does not grant them immunity from the Great Jurisprudence, which will yield a judgment with the potentially fatal consequences of disrupting Earth's life systems.

As more people realize that current legal systems are maladaptive in that they hinder rather than aid our ability to adapt (in an evolutionary sense) to rapidly changing environmental condition, they will be more willing to accept fundamental changes.

CRISES AS CATALYSTS OF LEGAL TRANSFORMATION

Many of the consequences of failing to regulate human societies to ensure that harmful thresholds are not exceeded are readily foreseeable; scientists have warned of the dangers of doing so for many years. Other consequences, particularly those that arise from the interaction of several different phenomena, are less predictable. For example, increased emissions of greenhouse gasses, the wide-spread destruction of forests, the loss of fertile soils, and the use of inorganic fertilizers that decrease carbon-sequestration in agricultural land are interrelated phenomena with cumulative impacts which may result in irreversible, negative long-term changes. It is now clear that humans have destabilized the conditions within which the immense flourishing of life-forms during the Cenozoic era occurred. We must now cope with many different kinds of "natural disasters" that are occurring with increasing frequency and severity, all of which have the potential to cause cumulative effects of terrifying magnitude. These natural disasters will very possibly become a major driver of rapid, non-linear changes in legal systems and a proliferation of Earth law.

For example, as of June 15, 2020, the time of the writing of this Afterword, the novel coronavirus SARS-CoV-2 (commonly referred to as COVID-19) is spreading rapidly through the world, drastically interfering with supply chains and modes of transportation that have made human civilization a "global village." It is unknown whether humanity will find means to contain the spread of the virus and to cure those affected before millions or billions more are infected. The disease has had a profound impact on global society due to cancelation of events, restrictions on travel, quarantines, and the worst economic recession since the Great Depression of the 1930s.[3]

Scientists estimate that 75 percent of new or emerging infectious diseases in people are "zoonotic," meaning that the first patient contracted the disease directly from another species of animal.[4] In the case of COVID-19, it seems likely that the virus developed in bat populations and was transmitted to humans via body parts of pangolins or snakes that were bought at a market in Wuhan, China.[5]

The wet markets in China (and other countries) exemplify the brutally exploitative relationship between the vendors and consumers of wildlife products and those species. However, the sale and consumption of these products were legal until the health dangers posed by COVID-19 and its negative impacts on global human society became apparent and the Chinese government has sought to ban these markets. In many countries it is legal to sell parts of wild animals for human consumption, and there is also a thriving international trade in exotic pets. However, as people and governments around the world become aware of how much more important the health of the global community is than the right of a minority to trade and consume wildlife products, it is likely that the countries in which wet markets continue to operate will outlaw these vectors for the transmission of zoonotic diseases.

Increasing natural disasters and related emergencies may trigger changes at all levels of society. As discussed in this coursebook, in August 2014, a toxic algae bloom in Lake Erie rendered the lake water unsafe to drink for three days and catalyzed a campaign that resulted in the city of Toledo incorporating the Lake Erie Bill of Rights

[3] Szu Ping Chan, *Coronavirus: World Faces Worst Recession Since Great Depression* Apr. 14, 2020), https://www.bbc.com/news/business-52273988.

[4] A zoonotic viral disease occurs when the virus in the animal host develops a series of genetic mutations that allow it to infect and multiply inside humans; this is aided by some form of contact or interaction between the infected animal and humans, enabling the transmission of the virus. *See* Centers for Disease Control and Prevention, *Zoonotic Diseases,* https://www.cdc.gov/onehealth/basics/zoonotic-diseases.html (last visited Mar. 3, 2020).

[5] In China, so-called "wet markets" sell flesh from a wide range of wild animals for human consumption and bring human beings into close contact with a variety of live and dead animals. *See* Nsikan Akpan, *New Coronavirus Can Spread between Humans—But It Started in a Wildlife Market,* National Geographic (Jan. 21, 2020).

(LEBOR) into the city charter. The preamble to LEBOR makes explicit reference to the fact that existing laws have failed to protect the lake[6] and that an emergency situation now exists that merits the taking of extraordinary measures.[7] The decision by the U.S. District Court for the Northern of Ohio that LEBOR was invalid exemplifies the difficulty lawyers will face in advancing Earth law.[8]

It is very likely that future disasters will create a similar impetus for rapid legislative change that seeks to ensure that humans relate to Earth in ways that are more respectful of other members of the Earth community and prioritizes collective well-being. Despite the determination of some powerful world forces to deny the reality that we are now in the early stages of a climatically chaotic period, "natural" disasters such as cyclones, floods, droughts, and wildfires,[9] as the impacts mount, more people are likely to support emergency measures that would not have been contemplated in less extreme circumstances.

JUDICIAL INNOVATION

Most Earth law advocates around the world have tended to focus on educating people about the benefits and wisdom of recognizing the rights of nature and on promoting legislative reform as a means of implementing Earth law. However, during the last few years, many of the most significant advances have come from an unexpected

[6] "We the people of the City of Toledo find that laws ostensibly enacted to protect us, and to foster our health, prosperity, and fundamental rights do neither; and that the very air, land, and water—on which our lives and happiness depend—are threatened."

[7] The preamble to the LEBOR states that: "We the people of the City of Toledo . . . further declare that this ecosystem, which has suffered for more than a century under continuous assault and ruin due to industrialization, is in imminent danger of irreversible devastation due to continued abuse by people and corporations enabled by reckless government policies, permitting and licensing of activities that unremittingly create cumulative harm, and lack of protective intervention. Continued abuse consisting of direct dumping of industrial wastes, runoff of noxious substances from large-scale agricultural practices, including factory hog and chicken farms, combined with the effects of global climate change, constitute an immediate emergency. We the people of the City of Toledo find that this emergency requires shifting public governance from policies that urge voluntary action, or that merely regulate the amount of harm allowed by law over a given period of time, to adopting laws which prohibit activities that violate fundamental rights which, to date, have gone unprotected by government and suffered the indifference of state-chartered for-profit corporations."

[8] *Drewes Farms Partnership v. City of Toledo*, No. 3:19 CV 434 U.S. Dist. (N.D. Ill. Feb.27, 2020). Although this represents a setback for Earth law practitioners, it is instructive that the judge seemed to imply that such a measure could have been upheld if its application had been limited to the city's area of jurisdiction and if the rights had been articulated more precisely so that parties like the plaintiff could determine what conduct would infringe the rights in question.

[9] In 2019 there were major wildfires in Australia, California, the Amazon, Siberia, Indonesia, and Lebanon. For a ranking of the severity of fires in the USA *see* Insurance Institute Information, *Facts + statistic: Wildfires*, (March 8, 2020, 4,49 PM), https://www.iii.org/fact-statistic/facts-statistics-wildfires. For an overview of wildfires globally in 2019, *see 2019 Was the Year the World Burned*, HUFFINGTON POST (Mar. 8, 2020, 4:43 PM), https://www.huffpost.com/entry/wildfires-california-amazon-indonesia-climate-change_n_5dcd3f4ee4b0d43931d01baf.

quarter — the judiciary. Judges in many countries, including Colombia, Bangladesh, and India, have used their judicial powers to recognize rivers, glaciers, and forests as juridical persons that possess rights and to impose corresponding duties (particularly on public bodies) to take action to uphold those rights.[10] These judgments have occurred in both civil and common law legal systems. While the legal justifications have varied, in these and many other cases, the judges seem to have been motivated by a sense of frustration that the legal system has been ineffectual in protecting specific aspects of nature from degradation and by a determination to find a more effective means of doing so.

As more precedents from respected courts, such as the Colombian Constitutional Court,[11] accumulate, it will be easier for other judges to follow suit. Judicial innovation of this kind is particularly valuable because it can produce changes far quicker than is generally possible through legislative action.

A WILD IDEA

In his seminal 1972 article *Should Trees have Standing?*, Professor Christopher Stone referred to the importance of breaking through the intellectual framing that defined all of nature as objects incapable of having legal rights by "thinking the unthinkable."[12] The growth of rights of nature movement globally and the manner in which the ideas that inform Earth law have taken root in diverse places indicate that these ideas have a life of their own. What was once unthinkable has been thought, and once thought, it cannot be unthought. These ideas are now being rapidly transmitted from one mind to another, proliferating, mutating, and transforming legal systems. The ideas have gone viral.

THE CHALLENGE OF INNOVATION

"Necessity is the mother of invention" is a well-known maxim. Certainly adversity can spur humans to innovate and achieve things that they would not otherwise attempt. Surely now is the time for great innovations in law and governance — necessity demands it!

We can predict with a high level of confidence that crises and disasters will proliferate, but we cannot know precisely when they will occur and when their impact will

[10] *See, e.g.*, Corte Constitutional, Decision T-622 (Nov. 10, 2016) (Colombia), in which the Colombian Constitutional Court recognized the Atrato River as a legal person; *Mohd. Salim v. State of Uttarakhand & Others* (Mar. 20, 2017) Uttarakhand High Court (India) PIL 126/2014, in which an Indian court recognized the Ganges and Yamuna Rivers and their tributaries as having legal personality.
[11] *See supra* note 10; *see generally* Chapter 25, "Indigenous Legalities."
[12] Christopher Stone, *Should Trees Have Standing? Towards Legal Rights for Natural Objects*, 45 S. Cal. L. Rev. 450-501 (1972).

be sufficient to tip public opinion and public bodies in favor of enacting Earth laws. Consequently, it is now particularly important for Earth lawyers to conduct the research and development necessary to enable them to propose specific and practical legislation and other measures when that moment occurs. Where enabling legislation is unavailable, Earth lawyers need to be brave, bold, and creative as litigators and in rendering advice to their clients. Since we are facing unprecedented environmental conditions and have very little Earth law within modern contemporary societies, innovation and a high degree of creativity are essential.

CONCLUSION

It will not be possible to establish ecologically viable human societies without fundamentally changing legal systems so that they prohibit inflicting significant harm on the community we call Earth and prioritize contributing to the well-being of that community. We cannot know whether we will be able to transform our legal systems sufficiently, thoroughly, and swiftly to avert changes in ecosystem functioning that would be catastrophic for our species and others. However, the growing body of Earth law, some of which emerged unexpectedly and rapidly, holds the promise of further rapid, non-linear changes to legal systems. The task of every Earth lawyer is to imagine the legal systems that communities and societies will need to be viable in the foreseeable future and to innovate and collaborate with one another to bring them into being as the prevailing legal systems lose legitimacy as a consequence of their inability to address the most pressing challenges of the 21st century effectively.[13]

[13] The Earth Law Center, which brought this book into being, as well as the Global Alliance for the Rights of Nature and the Ecological Law and Governance Association are leaders among the increasing number of organizations and fora that provide a means to link up with others to promote Earth law.

TABLE OF CASES

Principal cases are indicated by italics.

INDEX